House of Commons

Law relating to local government and taxation of cities and towns

(Ireland)

House of Commons

Law relating to local government and taxation of cities and towns (Ireland)

ISBN/EAN: 9783741105234

Manufactured in Europe, USA, Canada, Australia, Japa

Cover: Foto ©ninafisch / pixelio.de

Manufactured and distributed by brebook publishing software
(www.brebook.com)

House of Commons

Law relating to local government and taxation of cities and towns

(Ireland)

REPORT

FROM THE

SELECT COMMITTEE

ON

LOCAL GOVERNMENT

AND

TAXATION OF TOWNS (IRELAND);

TOGETHER WITH THE

PROCEEDINGS OF THE COMMITTEE,

MINUTES OF EVIDENCE,

AND APPENDIX.

Ordered, by The House of Commons, *to be Printed,*
11 *July* 1876.

352.

Thursday, 16*th March* 1876.

Ordered, THAT a Select Committee be appointed to inquire into the Operation in Ireland of the following Statutes: 9 Geo. 4, c. 82; 3 & 4 Vict. c. 108; and 17 & 18 Vict. c. 103, and the Acts altering and amending the same; and to report whether any and what alterations are advisable in the Law relating to Local Government and Taxation of Cities and Towns in that part of the United Kingdom.

Friday, 31*st March* 1876.

Committee nominated of—

Mr. Kavanagh.
Mr. Butt.
Sir Arthur Guinness.
Mr. Brooks.
Mr. Mulholland.
Mr. Collins.
Mr. Assheton.
Mr. Rathbone.
Mr. Gibson.
Sir Joseph M'Kenna.
Mr. Bruen.
Mr. O'Shaughnessy.
Mr. Charles Lewis.
Dr. Ward.
Sir Michael Hicks Beach.

Ordered, THAT the Committee have power to send for Persons, Papers, and Records.

Ordered, THAT Five be the Quorum of the Committee.

Thursday, 6*th April* 1876.

Ordered, THAT the Committee do consist of Seventeen Members.

Ordered, THAT Mr. J. P. Corry and Mr. Murphy be added to the Committee.

REPORT.

THE SELECT COMMITTEE appointed to inquire into the operation in IRELAND of the following Statutes: 9 Geo. 4, c. 82, 3 & 4 Vict. c. 108, and 17 & 18 Vict. c. 103, and the Acts altering and amending the same; and to Report whether any and what alterations are advisable in the LAW relating to LOCAL GOVERNMENT and TAXATION of CITIES and TOWNS in that part of the UNITED KINGDOM;——HAVE considered the matters to them referred, and have agreed to the following REPORT:—

YOUR Committee have proceeded, to a certain extent, with the inquiries which they were directed by the Order appointing them to pursue.

Several witnesses have been examined; and in the progress they have made, your Committee have come to the conclusion that a material portion of their inquiry could be more advantageously and conveniently conducted by means of a local investigation into the circumstances of the several towns in which municipal bodies exist under any of the statutes mentioned in the Order of Reference, to ascertain the facts connected with the property and revenues of such municipal bodies, the rates levied by them for municipal and sanitary purposes, and the mode in which the property, revenues, and rates are administered and applied.

Believing that if the result of such local inquiry were laid before them it would materially facilitate them in completing the investigation entrusted to them by the House, they have come to the conclusion to report to the House the Evidence already taken, and to recommend the re-appointment of the Committee in the next Session.

11 *July* 1876.

PROCEEDINGS OF THE COMMITTEE.

Thursday, 6th April 1876.

MEMBERS PRESENT:

Dr. Ward.
Mr. O'Shaughnessy.
Mr. Collins.
Mr. Rathbone.
Mr. Butt.
Mr. Brooks.
Mr. Bruen.
Sir Joseph M'Kenna.
Sir Michael Hicks Beach.

Sir MICHAEL HICKS BEACH was called to the Chair.

The Committee deliberated.

[Adjourned till Friday, 28th April, at Twelve o'clock.

Friday, 28th April 1876.

MEMBERS PRESENT:

Sir MICHAEL HICKS BEACH in the Chair.

Mr. Rathbone.
Mr. O'Shaughnessy.
Mr. J. P. Corry.
Dr. Ward.
Mr. Kavanagh.
Mr. Brooks.
Mr. Collins.
Mr. Bruen.
Mr. Murphy.
Mr. Butt.
Mr. Mulholland.
Sir Joseph M'Kenna.
Sir Arthur Guinness.

Dr. *W. N. Hancock* was examined.

[Adjourned till Tuesday next, at Twelve o'clock.

Tuesday, 2nd May 1876.

MEMBERS PRESENT:

Sir MICHAEL HICKS BEACH in the Chair.

Mr. J. P. Corry.
Mr. Bruen.
Mr. Gibson.
Sir Joseph M'Kenna.
Mr. Murphy.
Mr. Kavanagh.
Mr. Butt.
Mr. Collins.
Sir Arthur Guinness.
Dr. Ward.
Mr. Brooks.
Mr. Charles Lewis.
Mr. Rathbone.

Dr. *W. N. Hancock* was further examined.

Mr. *Denis Moylan* and Mr. *R. P. Taaffe* were severally examined.

[Adjourned till Friday next, at Twelve o'clock.

Friday, 5*th May* 1876.

MEMBERS PRESENT:

Sir MICHAEL HICKS BEACH in the Chair.

Mr. Rathbone.
Sir Arthur Guinness.
Mr. Murphy.
Mr. J. P. Corry.
Mr. Bruen.
Mr. Kavanagh.
Sir Joseph M'Kenna.
Dr. Ward.
Mr. Brooks.
Mr. O'Shaughnessy.
Mr. Gibson.
Mr. Mulholland.
Mr. Butt.
Mr. Assheton.
Mr. Collins.
Mr. Charles Lewis.

Dr. *W. N. Hancock* was further examined.

[Adjourned till Tuesday next, at Twelve o'clock.

Tuesday, 9*th May* 1876.

MEMBERS PRESENT:

Sir MICHAEL HICKS BEACH in the Chair.

Mr. Collins.
Mr. Gibson.
Mr. Brooks.
Dr. Ward.
Mr. Butt.
Mr. Mulholland.
Mr. Bruen.
Mr. J. P. Corry.
Mr. O'Shaughnessy.
Mr. Murphy.
Mr. Charles Lewis.
Mr. Assheton.

Mr. *William Joseph Henry* was examined.

[Adjourned till Friday next, at Twelve o'clock.

Friday, 12*th May* 1876.

MEMBERS PRESENT:

Sir MICHAEL HICKS BEACH in the Chair.

Mr. Collins.
Mr. Brooks.
Sir Joseph M'Kenna.
Mr. Butt.
Mr. Bruen.
Mr. J. P. Corry.
Sir Arthur Guinness.
Mr. Mulholland.
Dr. Ward.
Mr. Gibson.
Mr. Assheton.
Mr. Murphy.

Mr. *John M'Evoy* was examined.

[Adjourned till Tuesday next, at Twelve o'clock.

Tuesday, 16*th May* 1876.

MEMBERS PRESENT:

Sir MICHAEL HICKS BEACH in the Chair.

Mr. Gibson.
Mr. Brooks.
Mr. J. P. Corry.
Mr. Kavanagh.
Mr. Bruen.
Mr. Butt.
Mr. Collins.
Dr. Ward.
Sir Arthur Guinness.
Mr. O'Shaughnessy.
Mr. Murphy.

Mr. *John Adye Curran* and Mr. *Joseph Pim* were severally examined.

[Adjourned till Friday next, at Twelve o'clock.

Friday, 19*th May* 1876.

MEMBERS PRESENT:

Sir MICHAEL HICKS BEACH in the Chair.

Mr. Brooks.
Mr. Collins.
Sir Joseph M'Kenna.
Mr. Butt.
Mr. Assheton.
Mr. Kavanagh.
Mr. Bruen.
Mr. J. P. Corry.
Mr. Gibson.
Mr. Rathbone.
Sir Arthur Guinness.
Mr. Murphy.
Mr. Mulholland.
Mr. O'Shaughnessy.

Mr. *Nugent Robinson* and Mr. *Thomas O'Donnell* were severally examined.

[Adjourned till Tuesday next, at Twelve o'clock.

Tuesday, 23*rd May* 1876.

MEMBERS PRESENT:

Sir MICHAEL HICKS BEACH in the Chair.

Mr. Gibson.
Mr. Brooks.
Sir Joseph M'Kenna.
Mr. Butt.
Mr. Kavanagh.
Mr. Bruen.
Sir Arthur Guinness.
Mr. Murphy.
Mr. Collins.
Mr. Mulholland.
Mr. Rathbone.
Mr. O'Shaughnessy.

Mr. *Frederick Stokes*, Mr. *Nugent Robinson*, and Mr. *Thomas O'Donnell*, were severally examined.

[Adjourned till Friday next, at Twelve o'clock.

Friday, 26th May 1876.

MEMBERS PRESENT:

Sir MICHAEL HICKS BEACH in the Chair.

Mr. Kavanagh.
Mr. Brooks.
Mr. Gibson.
Mr. Bruen.
Mr. Butt.
Mr. Rathbone.
Sir Arthur Guinness.
Mr. Assheton.
Mr. Murphy.
Mr. Collins.
Mr. Mulholland.
Dr. Ward.
Mr. O'Shaughnessy.

Mr. *Francis Morgan* was examined, and Mr. *Thomas O'Donnell* was further examined.

[Adjourned till Tuesday next, at Twelve o'clock.

Tuesday, 30th May 1876.

MEMBERS PRESENT:

Sir MICHAEL HICKS BEACH in the Chair.

Sir Arthur Guinness.
Mr. Gibson.
Mr. Butt.
Mr. Kavanagh.
Mr. Bruen.
Mr. Brooks.
Mr. Collins.
Mr. J. P. Corry.
Mr. Mulholland.
Mr. Murphy.
Dr. Ward.

Dr. *T. W. Grimshaw* was examined.

[Adjourned till Tuesday, 13th June, at Twelve o'clock.

Tuesday, 13th June 1876.

MEMBERS PRESENT:

Sir MICHAEL HICKS BEACH in the Chair.

Mr. Gibson.
Mr. O'Shaughnessy.
Mr. Brooks.
Mr. Bruen.
Mr. Assheton.
Mr. Collins.
Mr. Kavanagh.
Mr. J. P. Corry.
Dr. Ward.
Sir Joseph M'Kenna.

Mr. *George William Finlay* was examined.

[Adjourned till Friday next, at Twelve o'clock.

Friday, 16*th June* 1876.

MEMBERS PRESENT:

Sir MICHAEL HICKS BEACH in the Chair.

Mr. O'Shaughnessy.
Sir Joseph M'Kenna.
Mr. Brooks.
Mr. Gibson.
Mr. Kavanagh.
Mr. Bruen.
Mr. J. P. Corry.
Mr. Rathbone.
Mr. Assheton.
Sir Arthur Guinness.
Mr. Mulholland.
Dr. Ward.
Mr. Collins.

Mr. *Alexander M. Sullivan* (a Member of the House) was examined.

[Adjourned till Tuesday next, at Twelve o'clock.

Tuesday, 20*th June* 1876.

MEMBERS PRESENT:

Sir MICHAEL HICKS BEACH in the Chair.

Dr. Ward.
Sir Arthur Guinness.
Mr. Gibson.
Mr. Brooks.
Mr. Kavanagh.
Mr. Bruen.
Mr. Murphy.
Mr. Mulholland.
Mr. Collins.
Sir Joseph M'Kenna.

Mr. *James Boyle* was examined.

[Adjourned till Friday next, at Twelve o'clock.

Friday, 23*rd June* 1876.

MEMBERS PRESENT:

Sir MICHAEL HICKS BEACH in the Chair.

Dr. Ward.
Mr. Gibson.
Sir Joseph M'Kenna.
Mr. Brooks.
Mr. Murphy.
Mr. Bruen.
Mr. Kavanagh.
Mr. Collins.
Sir Arthur Guinness.
Mr. J. P. Corry.

Mr. *Parke Neville* examined.

[Adjourned till Tuesday next, at Twelve o'clock.

Tuesday, 27th June 1876.

MEMBERS PRESENT:

Sir MICHAEL HICKS BEACH in the Chair.

Mr. Collins.
Mr. O'Shaughnessy.
Dr. Ward.
Mr. Murphy.
Sir Joseph M'Kenna.
Mr. Brooks.
Mr. Gibson.
Sir Arthur Guinness.
Mr. Kavanagh.
Mr. Butt.
Mr. Bruen.
Mr. J. P. Corry.

Mr. *Parke Neville* was further examined; Mr. *John Norwood* was also examined.

[Adjourned till Friday next, at Twelve o'clock.

Friday, 30th June 1876.

MEMBERS PRESENT:

Sir MICHAEL HICKS BEACH in the Chair.

Mr. Brooks.
Mr. O'Shaughnessy.
Mr. J. P. Corry.
Sir Joseph M'Kenna.
Mr. Collins.
Sir Arthur Guinness.
Mr. Gibson.
Mr. Murphy.
Dr. Ward.
Mr. Assheton.

Mr. *John Norwood* was further examined.

[Adjourned till Tuesday next, at Twelve o'clock.

Tuesday, 4th July 1876.

MEMBERS PRESENT:

Sir MICHAEL HICKS BEACH in the Chair.

Mr. Butt.
Mr. Brooks.
Mr. Collins.
Mr. Kavanagh.
Mr. Bruen.
Mr. J. P. Corry.
Sir Joseph M'Kenna.
Mr. Mulholland.
Dr. Ward.

Mr. *Edmund Dwyer Gray* was examined.

The Committee deliberated.

Question, That Mr. J. Ball Greene be summoned to attend as a witness at the next meeting of the Committee—(Mr. *Butt*)—put, and *agreed to*.

[Adjourned till Friday next, at Twelve o'clock.

Friday, 7th July 1876.

MEMBERS PRESENT:

Sir MICHAEL HICKS BEACH in the Chair.

Mr. Brooks.
Sir Joseph M'Kenna.
Mr. Bruen.
Mr. Butt.
Mr. Kavanagh.
Mr. J. P. Corry.
Sir Arthur Guinness.
Mr. Charles Lewis.
Mr. O'Shaughnessy.
Mr. Assheton.
Mr. Mulholland.
Dr. Ward.

Mr. *J. Ball Greene* was examined.

[Adjourned till Tuesday next, at Twelve o'clock.

Tuesday, 11th July 1876.

MEMBERS PRESENT:

Sir MICHAEL HICKS BEACH in the Chair.

Mr. Brooks.
Mr. O'Shaughnessy.
Sir Joseph M'Kenna.
Mr. Rathbone.
Mr. Collins.
Mr. Butt.
Mr. Bruen.
Mr. Assheton.
Mr. Kavanagh.
Mr. J. P. Corry.
Sir Arthur Guinness.
Mr. Mulholland.
Mr. Charles Lewis.

DRAFT REPORT proposed by the *Chairman*, read the first time, as follows:

"1. Your Committee have proceeded to a certain extent with the inquiries which they were directed by the Order appointing them to pursue.

"2. Several witnesses have been examined; and in the progress they have made, your Committee have come to the conclusion that a material portion of their inquiry could be more advantageously and conveniently conducted by means of a local investigation into the circumstances of the several towns in which municipal bodies exist under any of the statutes mentioned in the Order of Reference, to ascertain the facts connected with the property and revenues of such municipal bodies, the rates levied by them for municipal purposes, and the mode in which the property, revenues, and rates are administered and applied.

"3. Believing that if the result of such local inquiry were laid before them it would materially facilitate them in completing the investigation entrusted to them by the House, they have come to the conclusion to report to the House the evidence already taken, and to recommend the re-appointment of the Committee in the next Session."

DRAFT REPORT proposed by the *Chairman*, read a second time, paragraph by paragraph.

Paragraph 1, *agreed to*.

Paragraph 2.—Amendment proposed, after the word "municipal," in line 6, to insert the words "and sanitary"—(*Mr. Bruen*).—Question put, That those words be there inserted.—The Committee divided:

Ayes, 8.
Mr. Kavanagh.
Sir Arthur Guinness.
Mr. Collins.
Mr. Rathbone.
Mr. Bruen.
Mr. O'Shaughnessy.
Mr. Charles Lewis.
Mr. J. P. Corry.

Noes, 5.
Mr. Butt.
Mr. Brooks.
Mr. Mulholland.
Mr. Assheton.
Sir Joseph M'Kenna.

Paragraph, as amended, *agreed to.*

Paragraph 3, *agreed to.*

Question, That this Report, as amended, be the Report of the Committee to the House,—put, and *agreed to.*

Ordered, To Report, together with the Minutes of Evidence and an Appendix.

EXPENSES OF WITNESSES.

NAME of WITNESS.	PROFESSION or CONDITION.	From whence Summoned.	Number of Days Absent from Home under Orders of Committee.	Allowance during Absence from Home.	Expenses of Journey to London and back.	TOTAL Expenses allowed to Witness.
				£. s. d.	£. s. d.	£. s. d.
Denis Moylan - -	Gentleman - - -	Dublin - -	4	4 4 –	5 15 –	9 19 –
R. P. Tuaffe - - -	- - - -	Ditto - -	4	4 4 –	5 15 –	9 19 –
W. Neilson Hancock -	Barrister - - -	Ditto - -	9	28 7 –	5 9 –	33 16 –
W. J. Henry - -	Gentleman - - -	Ditto - -	3	3 3 –	5 9 –	8 12 –
John M'Evoy - -	Ditto - -	Ditto - -	5	5 5 –	5 9 –	10 14 –
John Adye Curran -	Barrister - - -	Ditto - -	9	9 9 –	5 9 –	14 18 –
Joseph Pim - - -	Gentleman - - -	Ditto - -	3	3 3 –	5 9 –	8 12 –
Frederick Stokes - -	- - - -	Detained from Dublin.	5	5 5 –	- Nil -	5 5 –
Nugent Robinson - -	- - - -	Ditto - -	7	7 7 –	- Nil -	7 7 –
Francis Morgan - -	Solicitor to Corporation of Dublin.	Ditto - -	3	3 3 –	- Nil -	3 3 –
T. W. Grimshaw - -	Physician - - -	Dublin - -	9	9 9 –	5 9 –	14 18 –
George Finlay - -	Gentleman - - -	Kingstown -	3	3 3 –	5 6 –	8 9 –
James Boyle - -	Secretary to Corporation of Dublin.	Dublin - -	6	6 6 –	5 9 –	11 15 –
Parke Neville - -	Engineer to City of Dublin.	Ditto - -	6	6 6 –	5 9 –	11 15 –
John Norwood - -	Gentleman - - -	Ditto - -	5	5 5 –	5 9 –	10 14 –
Edmund Dwyer Gray -	Ditto - - -	Ditto - -	6	6 6 –	5 9 –	11 15 –
J. Ball Greene - -	Commissioner of Valuation (Ireland).	Ditto - -	3	3 3 –	5 9 –	8 12 –
					TOTAL - - - £.	190 8 –

LIST OF WITNESSES.

MINUTES OF EVIDENCE.

Friday, 28*th April* 1876.

MEMBERS PRESENT:

Sir Michael Hicks Beach.
Mr. Brooks.
Mr. Bruen.
Mr. Butt.
Mr. Collins.
Mr. J. P. Corry.
Sir Arthur Guinness.
Mr. Kavanagh.
Sir Joseph M'Kenna.
Mr. Mulholland.
Mr. Murphy.
Mr. O'Shaughnessy.
Mr. Rathbone.
Dr. Ward.

SIR MICHAEL HICKS BEACH, IN THE CHAIR.

Mr. WILLIAM NEILSON HANCOCK, LL.D., called in; and Examined.

Mr. *W. N. Hancock*, LL.D.

28 April 1876.

Chairman.

1. I BELIEVE you have studied the question which has been referred to this Committee of Local Government and Taxation of Towns in Ireland?—Yes; I was first employed in 1865 to report on a Bill for the Regulation and Audit of Municipal Taxation and Expenditure under Sir Robert Peel. In 1866 I was employed by Lord Carlingford to draw a Public Health Act for Ireland, and that eventuated in the 14 clauses by which the whole of the Public Health Law of England was extended to Ireland in 1866. I completed that under Lord Mayo. The Government was changed, but I went on with the work and completed it for him, and then I reported on the Public Health Legislation of 1866. I will hand in to the Committee these two Reports on Municipal Taxation and Public Health Legislation (*delivering in the same*). Then in 1866, in consequence of a recommendation of the Committee on Irish Taxation in 1865, that Returns of Irish Local Taxation should be collected, I was employed to organise them, and I organised the collection of Local Taxation Returns for the years from 1865 until 1872. In 1873, in consequence of an arrangement similar to what has been carried out in England, the collection and compilation of the Local Taxation Returns were transferred to the Irish Local Government Board. I reported upon the Returns for the several years from 1865 until the year 1872. In those Reports I went very fully into the question of the reform of local taxation and local government, and before I gave the Reports up I put an index to the whole series, and here is a collection with an index to the Reports and Returns. I present one copy with an index prefixed which shows all the matter in the Report and Returns for each year (*delivering in the same*). They are all Parliamentary Papers except the first. The Report on the Sanitary Laws was not presented to Parliament, but was printed for sale by direction of the Government. The Report on Municipal Taxation was sent to each town authority in Ireland; both can be got from Mr. Thom, the Queen's printer in Dublin. The Reports from 1865 to 1872 can be got from Hansard.

Chairman—continued.

2. I think that in the Public Health Act of 1874, there is a section which will pretty well give us a list of the different classes of towns into which it is our duty to inquire?—Yes, the Public Health Act of 1874 drew a division between the Irish town authorities. It said that certain town authorities should be the urban sanitary authorities and certain should not; and the line which it drew was that every town that had above 6,000 inhabitants, and was under a constituted government, should be the urban sanitary authority. Besides these, some few towns in which there were less than 6,000, but which had got local Acts of their own were, nevertheless, constituted sanitary authorities. In the classification of towns in the Local Taxation Returns for 1874, that distinction has not been regarded, but there is a very nice Table in the census for Ireland, which has classified the towns under the different governments. I will read from the Census Report, with one slight correction, what has happened since. The oldest form of existing town government in Ireland is that under the Act of 1828, the 9th Geo. 4. The towns with urban sanitary authorities under that Act are four: Tralee, Armagh, Bandon and Youghal. The next

Mr. W. N. Hancock, LL.D.

28 April 1876.

Chairman—continued.

next and most general form of government is that under the Towns Improvement Act, Ireland, 1854. The towns under that are Dundalk, Lurgan, Queenstown, Newtownards, Ballymena, Lisburn, Carlow, Carrick-on-Suir, Fermoy, New Ross, Portadown, Athlone, Dungarvan, Ennis, Kinsale, and Coleraine; that makes 16 in number. Then, the next class of towns are those under town councils, which I divide into two sections. There are five of those which have adopted either in whole, or in part, the Towns Improvement Act, 1854. Waterford has adopted it in part; then come Drogheda, Kilkenny, Wexford, and Clonmel, which have adopted the Act of 1854 entirely. Then the towns that are governed by town councils under Local Acts are Dublin, Belfast, Cork, Limerick, Londonderry, and Sligo. That makes 11 under town councils; five governed under the Act of 1854, and six governed under local Acts. Then the towns governed by commissioners under the local Acts are 11 in number, including in them the townships which are really a part of Dublin, viz., Pembroke, Rathmines (and Rathgar), New Kilmainham and Clontarf, with the towns of Kingstown, Galway, Newry, Blackrock, Bray, Enniskillen, and Dalkey. Five of those have a population of less than 6,000 inhabitants: Bray, Enniskillen, New Kilmainham, Clontarf, and Dalkey; but, nevertheless, they are sanitary authorities, because they are under special Acts.

3. You referred first to the Act of 1828; can you give us a brief sketch of the system of town authorities, which the authorities under that Act replaced?—That is very clearly indicated by the Acts which are repealed by it. The first clause repealed a number of Acts of Parliament, those of 1765, 1773, 1785, and 1796. Those were all temporary Acts of the Irish Parliament, and the British Parliament in 1807 renewed all of them for 21 years, and that renewal came to expire in the year 1828. It was then renewed for one year for that Session of Parliament to allow legislation to take place. Those Acts are all founded upon the vestry system of management of towns. Some of the large towns had by local Acts got lighting and other matters under vestries in the parishes, and all those Acts were founded upon the idea of extending the vestry system to the management of towns; but the vestries never made the way in Ireland which they did in England, because there was no poor law. The basis of vestries being so popular in England, being on account of the poor law administration. There was no poor law in Ireland until 1838, and the vestries had no real basis to rest on; and in 1828 they were in a most unpopular position, because the agitation which overthrew them in 1833 by the extinction of what is called parish cess, the same as the church rates in England, was just at its height. 1828 was within five years of the total extinction of Irish church rates, so that they had become quite unpopular and unmanageable bodies.

4. Did all the Acts to which you have referred, which were continued or expired in 1827 or 1828, relate to this vestry system?—Yes, all those Acts. But besides that there was an attempt by several of the corporations, where they could not work the vestry, to have local taxation through the corporation grand juries, and the leet grand juries. But the agitation that overthrew the corporations (1840) had begun at that time too, and the legality of the corporation grand juries was questioned, and the legality of the leet grand juries was questioned, so that those powers were found impossible to manage. All the corporation authorities in Ireland at that time (the old corporations) were in a state of complete decay. They are fully reported upon in the Report on Municipal Corporations in 1834. Out of 99 that were in existence at the time of the Union, 33 had become totally extinct, and eight had become partially extinct, so that there were only 61 corporations in existence, and of those 61 corporations no less than 38 were self-elective, irresponsible bodies, and of the remaining 23 there were only four from which Roman Catholics were not almost entirely excluded. The Report of the Commissioners on Municipal Corporations in Ireland of 1834, of which Mr. Justice Perrin was the Chairman, and which was presented in 1835, says at page 16: "The laws which for a series of years operated to exclude those professing the Roman Catholic religion from corporations were repealed in the year 1793 by the statute of the 33 Geo. 3, c. 21, but the Roman Catholics have hitherto derived little practical advantage from the change. In the close boroughs they are almost universally excluded from all corporate privileges" (the close boroughs are those 38 which I mentioned that were self-elective). "In the more considerable towns they have rarely been admitted even as freemen, and, with few exceptions, they are altogether excluded from the governing bodies In some, and among these is the most important corporation in Ireland, that of Dublin, their admission is still resisted on avowed principles of sectarian distinction. Even in those corporations where rights to freedom are acknowledged and conceded, the long operation of the penal code having prevented the acquisition of freedom by the immediate ancestors of the present Roman Catholic population, very few have been enabled since its repeal to establish the requisite titles. The admissions which have taken place whether upon a claim of right or by favour, have, for the most part, been either the result of personal influence with the members of the governing body or compliments to individuals of wealth or popularity. With the exceptions of Tuam, Galway, Wexford, and Waterford, the rule is exclusion." One of the great complaints in 1828, just before the passing of the Catholic Emancipation Act of 1829, was besides the total exclusion of Roman Catholics from corporate offices. The result of it all was that in 1840 those corporations were entirely abolished.

5. Of those old corporations that you have told us of, I think there were 61 in existence in 1834, 38 of which were self-elective?—Yes.

6. What was the basis of the franchise in the rest?—Freemen; and the Roman Catholics were practically excluded from the freemen, because they must come in by birth or by servitude; the old penal laws operated to throw very much difficulty in the way of their showing any servitude, or their being descended from freemen.

7. Then it was a corporation of freemen, not of householders?—It was originally the inhabitants, but the freemen had gradually displaced the inhabitants in effect, because freemen alone had the privileges of the inhabitants.

8. Were the freemen necessarily inhabitants?—No; they were not necessarily so, but the bulk of them in those large towns were really inhabitants.

9. Have

Mr. W. N. Hancock, LL.D.

28 April 1876.

Mr. Murphy.

9. Have not the corporations the power, and did not they exercise it, of creating honorary freeman?—Yes, that was one of the abuses.

10. In virtue of that power they created Roman Catholics honorary freemen on some occasions, did they not?—On some few occasions they did.

11. Those Roman Catholics had a right to take part, not in the governing body but as a portion of the freemen at large?—Yes.

Chairman.

12. Those old corporations were abolished, were they not, in 1840?—Yes.

13. What became of those 61 to which you have referred?—They were all abolished.

14. What was their future history?—Ten of them were replaced by municipal councils in 1840; the others were replaced by commissioners under the Act of 1828, or under local Acts. Some of them have had no government at all since; I do not recollect the exact figures.

15. Were not municipal commissioners created in some of them?—There were 19 bodies of municipal commissioners created by the Act of 1840; the object of those 19 municipal commissioners was to hold trust of the corporate property until commissioners were appointed under the Act of 1828. Of those 19 towns that came under the municipal commissioners, the vast majority either adopted the Act of 1828, or they adopted the Act of 1854, and most of them adopted both Acts; but there is one remnant of that system of government which still continues, namely Carrickfergus. That has lead to a great deal of confusion, because it was supposed in the Sanitary Act, 1874, that it was a sanitary authority, but the Local Government Board, after the Act passed, found that it was not, as, though the Parliamentary borough had a population of 9,000, the municipal borough had only 4,000. So that it is a great complication in the town law and the sanitary law of Ireland allowing this one body to remain as the municipal commissioners of Carrickfergus with a population of 4,000 inhabitants.

16. Carrickfergus then remains under a form of government which was intended by the Act of 1840 to be merely temporary?—Yes, it was the last of the 19 towns; all the other towns very promptly adopted one or the other of the Acts.

Dr. *Ward.*

17. What is the local authority of Carrickfergus?—The board of guardians is the local sanitary authority.

18. Is not that the case also in Galway?—I think not.

Chairman.

19. Did that Act of 1840 in any way recognise the existence of the Act of 1828?—Yes, in the Act of 1840 the Act of 1828 was recognised to this extent, that the town councils were allowed to adopt it for lighting purposes instead of their old vestry powers. It was also adopted in part for the mode of election, and in part for rating, and it was adopted in several other ways, and also all towns that chose to adopt it for town government got the corporate property. There were 10 created town councils, and all outside that number of towns that adopted the Act of 1828 got the corporate property.

20. Has any town in Ireland obtained a charter except the ten which did so immediately after the passing of the Act of 1840?—Yes; there is one town, Wexford; that is the only town, and that makes 11 town councils.

Chairman—continued.

21. Are you aware whether any other applications for charters have been made?—I was consulted some short time ago about applying for a charter to a town quite large enough to have one, but we found that it would lead to a great deal of complication because a number of the provisions of the Act of 1840 were quite inconsistent with the Act of 1854, and there would be considerable complication, and therefore I advised the town against its being applied for under that ground, because, owing to the two sets of provisions, there would be great embarrassment in working.

22. Did the town in that case remain under the Act of 1854?—Yes; it did.

23. What was that town?—Lurgan.

24. To what extent was the Act of 1828 adopted by the towns in Ireland?—By 66 towns.

25. How many are still under it?—There are only 12 still under it. There are the four sanitary authorities that I mentioned, and in addition to those there are eight: Tipperary, Mallow, Dungannon, Omagh, Monaghan, Downpatrick, Wicklow, and Fethard.

26. What led to this change in the popularity of the Act of 1828?—The first town, the most enterprising in Ireland, was Kingstown. It began to be developed by the making of the packet station there, and the commencement of the railroad. The inhabitants very soon found that the provisions in the Act of 1828 were very imperfect for a growing town, and they got an Act in 1834 repealing the Act for Kingstown, and getting all the most modern improvements that were adopted at that time. Then Belfast, the next that began to develope at that time, got a local Act in 1845, another in 1846, and another in 1847, adopting all the modern town legislation usual in England. Then, in 1847, the Towns Clauses Act and the Commissioners Clauses Act were passed for local Acts in England, and immediately the most enterprising suburb of Dublin, Rathmines, took advantage of it, and the inhabitants obtained, in 1847, a local Act adopting all those provisions. Then Dublin in 1849 got a local Act. After the Dublin corporation got their Act in 1849, it was felt that it was hard that so many towns should be under the machinery of local government which had been thus condemned, and at the same time the inhabitants could not afford the expense of local Acts; and that Act of 1854 was to enable towns to get the benefit of the Towns Clauses Act of 1847, and the Commissioners Clauses Act of 1847, without going to Parliament for a local Act.

27. Can you give the Committee such a statement of the provisions as to the powers of the town authorities in the Act of 1828 and in the Act of 1854, as will show to us the difference between them?—In the Act of 1828 powers were conferred for lighting, watching, cleansing, paving, wells, pumps, pipes, sewers and drains, fire engines, naming and numbering streets, removal of cellar stairs, compelling footways to be kept clean, prevention of nuisances, and providing against stray cattle. Those were all dealt with by the Act of 1854, and in many cases in a more complete manner. The Act of 1854 conferred new powers as to laying out new streets, dealing

Mr. *W. N. Hancock*, LL.D.

28 April 1876.

Chairman—continued.

dealing with ruinous buildings, the prevention of smoke nuisances, carrying party walls to roof, ventilation, regulation of lodging-houses and slaughter-houses, the sale of unwholesome meat, the sale of adulterated food, the sale of gunpowder, the prevention of obstruction in the streets during processions, bathing machines and bathing and hackney carriages; and then there are a whole lot of sewer provisions.

28. I should like to have something, if it were possible, which should show the Committee more clearly precisely what those two Acts were; a mere statement of the fact that one conferred the power of lighting, cleansing, and so on, and another added powers such as you have mentioned in your answer to this question, does not exactly show the Committee why the towns preferred the latter Act to the former one?—That is a mere enumeration; but taking a general view of the matter, it can be explained in an instant. In 1828 certain towns in England and Scotland were in the habit of getting certain powers of managing their affairs of paving, lighting, and cleansing, which appeared to them the most important subjects in those days. Then the Act of 1828 gave the Irish towns, without expense, exactly the same powers as a town in England or Scotland would have to pay for a local Act to get. The Act of 1854 simply gave Irish towns all the improved powers that a town would get in England or Scotland by a private Bill, and gave it to them without expense. I am now speaking merely of powers. The general idea is extremely simple. The Act of 1854 was to give Irish towns the sort of power that you would get in England at the expense of a local Act; the provisions were very like what would be in a local Act for a town in England.

29. In fact, the Act of 1854 represented the powers which were considered necessary in the higher state of civilisation at the time?—Yes; but not confined to Ireland. The one was the notion of what a town government should be in 1828, and the other was what was thought necessary for town government in 1854.

30. How many towns are now under the Act of 1854?—Seventy-six. I have mentioned 16, which are urban sanitary authorities; the rest are all set out in the Census Report; and I will read them in the order of the population:

Ballina.	Castlebar.	Dromore.
Nenagh.	Clonakilty.	Callan.
Banbridge.	Cookstown.	Roscommon.
Enniscorthy.	Templemore.	Balbriggan.
Killarney.	Cavan.	Bagenalstown.
Tullamore.	Boyle.	Killiney and Ballybrack.
Mullingar.	Mountmellick.	Trim.
Ballinasloe.	Larne.	Clones.
Thurles.	Newbridge.	Letterkenny.
Parsonstown.	Loughrea.	Antrim.
Cashel.	Ardee.	Carrickmacross.
Athy.	Ballyshannon.	Lismore.
Westport.	Kells.	Cootehill.
Longford.	Ballymoney.	Keady.
Tuam.	Newtown Limavady.	Castleblayney.
*Strabane.		
Navan.	Maryborough.	Belturbet.
Skibbereen.	Gilford.	Ballybay.
Naas.	Gorey.	Aughnacloy.
Middleton.	Bangor.	Tanderagee.
Holywood.	Rathkeale.	

* Strabane, changed from Act of 1828 to Act of 1854, after Census Report was printed, and is here introduced.

31. Some of those 76 are above the limit of 6,000 inhabitants which was adopted in the Public Health Act, 1874?—Yes, the 16 that I first read.

32. Can you quote any of them with a very small population?—Yes, the lowest population is Tanderagee, with 1,240; and the next lowest is Aughnacloy, with 1,465. They would not now get commissioners, because they would require 1,500 to have them; but they had 1,500 at the time they got them, and they do not lose them.

Mr. O'Shaughnessy.

33. Is it the Act of 1854 which limits commissioners to towns of 1,500?—Yes; the Act of 1828 had no limit.

Chairman.

34. Have any towns adopted the Act of 1854 only to a limited extent?—Yes, a very considerable number have adopted it only to a limited extent; of the 16 principal urban sanitary authorities I may mention that four have adopted it only to a limited extent, and the principal point that they limit it to is with regard to water, and that has become a nullity, because as an urban sanitary authority under the Sanitary Act they are compelled to have water.

35. They are compelled to have powers for supplying the town with water?—Yes, and they may be compelled to exercise them under the Sanitary Act.

36. You told the Committee that only four town councils have adopted the Act of 1854; have any done so to a limited extent?—Waterford alone.

37. What exception was made by Waterford?—They did not adopt it for anything that practically affected the rating; they adopted it for provisions relating to regulation of towns, obstructions and nuisances in the streets, suppression of vagrants, and as to hackney carriages.

38. You have told us of the powers conferred by the Acts of 1828 and 1854; what powers were conferred on town councils by the Municipal Corporation Act of 1840?—The principal powers of town councils under the Act of 1840 was with regard to the management of corporate property; it was not properly an Act for town government; it was simply an Act for the management of corporate property, and the chief additional power that they got was for lighting. They might adopt the Act of 1828 for that. And they also got power for making bye-laws. In the earlier legislation the notion was that a great number of nuisances and matters of that kind should be regulated by the town bye-laws, and not by direct legislation. Under that notion they got power to make bye-laws; but except the power of making bye-laws and the power of lighting, they got no other power. Most of those councils were, however, in towns where there were city grand juries which had charge of the roads. Several of them were under special Acts by which they had special powers.

39. Were there also powers of appointing officers?—Full power of managing property and appointing officers, but as to direct powers of town government it did not confer them further than I have stated.

40. Since the passing of the Act of 1854 have any towns preferred to come under local Acts to the adoption of that Act?—Yes; it is not so much that they preferred to come under the local Acts, a few townships in Dublin have, but very few even of them have not adopted it in part.

41. Why

Mr. W. N. Hancock, LL.D.

28 April 1876.

Chairman—continued.

41. Why has that been so; why has it been that any town has preferred to come under a local Act?—It is not that they preferred to come under a local Act, but local Acts have been found necessary, quite independent of the Act of 1854. There was one branch of the law which the Act of 1854 did not touch at all, and that was the divided authority over streets in towns. The principal cause of local Acts in Ireland both before and since 1854 has been to get authority over the streets.

42. By a divided authority you mean that the grand jury in a county, or a city, have the power of levying a rate, and repairing the streets in lieu of the town commissioners?—The town commissioners are bound to pave such streets as they choose, and then the grand jury are liable to repair such as go through the town; and then there is a doubt as to lanes which are thoroughfares, whether the grand jury are liable or not, but there is a divided authority over the streets, and that seems to be one of the principal causes of local Acts. The first town was Rathmines, which got separated from the county of Dublin in 1847; then Kingstown in 1861; Queenstown from Cork in 1862; Blackrock and Pembroke township, and Dungarvan followed Queenstown in 1863; Londonderry got separated from the county of Londonderry in 1864; then Belfast got separated from Antrim in 1865; Bray from Wicklow and Dublin in 1866; Dalkey in 1867; Belfast got separated from Down, and New Kilmainham from Dublin in 1868; Sligo in 1870; Enniskillen in 1870; and Newry in 1871. Then came the Local Government Act of 1871, rendering it unnecessary to go to Parliament for this purpose, but allowing the towns to be separated from the counties by a Provisional Order. One town was successful in getting a Provisional Order; that was Wexford; it is a town which I mentioned before that had a charter, and now it has a Provisional Order.

43. Do you know what the cost of that Provisional Order was?—£. 40.

44. Do you know whether any similar applications have been made to the Local Government Board under the Act of 1871?—Applications have been made in Belturbet, in Westport, in Ballina, and in Newtownards. In all those cases the grand jury imposed the veto that they had. In Ballina there were two grand juries. The grand jury of Mayo seems not to have interposed. The grand jury of Sligo had also a veto, because Ballina is in two counties, and in the grand jury of Sligo it was only 14 to nine; that is 14 were for exercising the veto, and nine were not; so that out of the two grand juries, or 46 in all, 14 in Sligo were successful in throwing out the proposal altogether.

45 That prevented the chance of their case being met by a Provisional Order, and left it to them to remedy it by a Local Act if they chose?—Yes, they went to Parliament for a Local Act, and then they were met by a point of law, that they wanted to repeal a general Act, because as the general Act gave the grand jury a veto they were trying to get round the general Act, and they were thrown out on Standing Orders after going to a considerable expense for a Local Act, and they were not able to get it done. It is recited in that Bill that application had been made to the grand juries for the counties of Mayo and Sligo respectively for their assent to the transfer of powers, but the assent of the Sligo grand jury was withheld, 14 members of that body voting against the proposition.

Mr. O'Shaughnessy.

46. What is the population of the town of Ballina where that veto was exercised?—Ballina stands at the head of the list of towns which are not urban sanitary authorities, with a population of 5,843. I should mention that the Local Government Board in their Report (1874, p. 34) say, "There is no likelihood, in the present state of the law, that any such application will again be made, and the question is asked why the consent of the grand jury was made a necessary preliminary, as it was most natural that the body which it was proposed to deprive of its jurisdiction and its power of taxation should object to the proposal, however beneficial it might be to the parties residing in the district which petitioned to be dis-annexed." I might explain why that veto was given, and why the Local Government Board complain of its existence at present. The Act of 1871 was passed before the Local Government Board was constituted. At that time the Chief Secretary alone had the power of instituting inquiries, and the Act of 1871 was merely permissive; it was not intended that the Chief Secretary should exercise any executive power in the matter, and therefore being merely permissive, the veto was not inconsistent with the constitution then. But in 1872, when the Local Government Board was constituted, giving them the whole charge, with a staff of inspectors and the whole machinery of the Government, then the veto became quite inconsistent with their present position. The Chief Secretary was merely to employ an occasional person, not a permanent officer, to make inquiries, and it was only *if* the parties agreed that they might have it all arranged; but in 1872 the Local Government Board was constituted, and therefore that power of veto was inconsistent with their present position.

47. When did this Ballina incident occur?—They applied for a Bill in 1874, and it was thrown out in the Session of 1875.

Chairman.

48. To what extent have town councils obtained undivided authority over the streets in their towns?—Dublin, in 1849, got the whole of the powers of the city grand jury transferred to them; Cork followed suit in 1852, and got the whole of the powers of the city grand jury transferred to them; and Limerick obtained it in 1853.

Mr. Brooks.

49. Were not there the wide street commissioners in Dublin?—Yes, but they were abolished in 1849; besides that, the grand jury had the power of building bridges, and the wide street commission was different. In Belfast they applied; as I mentioned, Belfast was under a town council, and it got separated from both county Antrim and county Down.

Chairman.

50. Do the town council of Belfast repair their own streets?—Yes, they do; they have the sole control over their streets. Waterford applied to

Mr. W. N. Hancock, LL.D.

28 April 1876.

Chairman—continued.

to have the same done, but they mixed up a distinct question which got their Bill overthrown; that is to say, they tried to extend the boundary of Waterford into the County of Waterford, besides transferring the powers of the city grand jury, and their Bill was thrown out in the Lords, although it had passed the House of Commons in 1875. It was a Bill to abolish the fiscal power of the city grand jury of Waterford, and to give it to the town council. They proposed to enlarge the borough so as to take in the whole of the poor law electoral division of Waterford, and so far as I recollect, it was the county opposition that overthrew their Bill.

51. But as to the other counties of cities, what is the state of things?—They still have a divided authority.

52. Can they obtain the sole authority by a Provisional Order?—No, Carrickfergus, for instance, could not. Waterford could not have done so by a Provisional Order, and so they went for a Bill. The Irish Local Government Act of 1871 is very narrowly worded, it is not worded so as to contemplate the idea of the county of a city; the wording applies to a county at large only. I should have mentioned before, the city of Derry has a town council, which has got separated from the county for road purposes.

53. In all those counties of cities it is the city grand jury that would have the divided authority?—Yes.

54. In those towns that are not counties of cities, it is the county grand jury?—Yes, for instance, in Clonmel it is the county grand jury.

55. Is the authority over the streets divided with the county grand juries in any other kind of urban sanitary authority?—In Carlow it is divided with two county authorities, a part of the town being in Carlow, and a part in Queen's County. In Carrick-on-Suir it is divided with Tipperary and Waterford. In Lisburn, with Antrim and Down. In New Ross, with Wexford and Kilkenny. In Athlone, with West Meath and Roscommon. In all the other urban sanitary authorities the authority is divided with one county only.

56. You have mentioned the control of the roads as the principal object for which local Acts have been obtained for towns since 1854; were there any other objects contemplated by those Acts?—One other object was water, another was markets, and another was borrowing powers. Those were the principal objects.

57. Have the town authorities generally the control over the markets and fairs?—They have the control over the markets only to a very limited extent. I think that there are only about 12 that have any substantial income from their interest in the markets.

58. Has that subject been at all inquired into with a view to legislation?—Yes, with regard to the question of the fairs and markets there was a Select Committee of the House of Commons in 1826, on that subject, and there was another in 1830; and legislation was attempted in 1830, but it failed, and the result of that was an insurrection over one half of Ireland, and the tolls were to a very large extent overthrown. That is described in the Report of the Fairs and Markets Commission of 1853, in which they represent the matter to be in a very unsatisfactory state. They say, "The agitation commenced in the counties of Meath, Dublin, King's and Queen's Counties, and soon spread to other parts of the country. If a straight line be drawn down the centre of Ireland from the city of Londonderry to the town of Youghal, it will be found that, with a few exceptions on the east side of the line, toll has been entirely abolished, while on the west side of the line, with also a few exceptional cases, toll is still exacted." In that overthrow of the markets the old system of toll was done up, and as regards the market authority, it was destroyed altogether. The object of modern legislation has been to restore the market authority within certain limits, but the matter is still in a very unsatisfactory state.

Chairman—continued.

59. With regard to borrowing powers, do you think that anything could be done to improve the present system of borrowing powers as exercised by town authorities?—Yes; the Sanitary Code of 1875 has been passed for England last Session, and has very simple borrowing powers, and the London Metropolitan Board have still better borrowing powers.

60. Will you tell the Committee what the existing system in Ireland is?—The existing system is very complicated. The towns are not satisfied with any of the borrowing powers under the general statutes, because where they can they always go for special provisions, and they would not do that if the existing general system was satisfactory.

61. What is the general system?—It limits the rating and creates a doubt as to the security. Then the borrowing is not in the first instance sanctioned by the Local Government Board; and then there is a certain amount of risk and doubt about the security. Then the object of all legislation is to get rid of that, and make the security perfect. In England they get the sanction of the Local Government Board in the first instance under the Act of 1875, to make the loan perfectly secure.

62. Under what Act do they borrow in Ireland generally?—Under each different Act, according to the objects of the loan. There is no satisfactory general provision in Ireland.

63. But in the case of a town under one of those general Acts to which you have referred, under which Act would the town borrow?—The Act of 1854 gives power to borrow, but that is by reference, under the Act of 1847. The borrowing powers in the Act of 1854 are under the mortgaging clauses of the Commissioners' Clauses Act of 1847.

Mr. *Butt.*

64. That is an English Act, is it not?—But it is incorporated in the Irish Act. The position of the whole law is this: instead of borrowing under the latest Act of 1875, or as the Metropolitan Board under their Act of 1869, we are still borrowing under the old Act of 1847, which has been superseded in England on account of not being the best way of doing the business.

Chairman.

65. Do you see any difficulty in extending such powers to Ireland?—No. I recommended that in my reports for 1871, p. 24, and for 1872, p. 15, and also in a paper which I read at the Dublin Statistical Society. I showed how the London Metropolitan Board's plan of borrowing might be extended to Ireland. It is on the idea of applying the system of debenture stock, which lately has been so successful in

Mr. W. N. Hancock, LL.D.

28 April 1876.

Chairman—continued.

ful in borrowing money, to town loans. The Metropolitan Board borrow now at 3¾ per cent., and I believe even lower than that. They have reduced their loans from 4½ to 3¾ per cent. by simply adopting the debenture stock system of borrowing. The London Metropolitan Board system is founded upon the debenture stock system, and that system is as good for town loans as for railways.

Sir *J. M'Kenna.*

66. The debenture stock gives a statutory power to the holder of it, which is what is desired by lenders?—Yes, and also it is divisible into the smallest amount to suit the lender. A fixed bond, which is only for a certain amount, merely suits a certain class of lenders; but the divisibility into any amount suits the smaller lenders. The simplest illustration that I can give of that will be to take the case of Newry. Newry is one of those towns which went for a local Act, which resulted in waterworks and various improvements; but I think it cost them 7,000 *l.* or 8,000 *l.* They got their Act, and then they had to borrow money; and they borrowed, I think, about 42,000 *l.*, and for that 42,000 *l.* they are paying either the Bank rate or 6 per cent. The Great Northern Railway runs past Newry, and their 4½ per cent. debenture stock is above par, and they are borrowing more, at 4 per cent.; so that it is simply legislative mis-management, or the town of Newry might have had 42,000 *l.* at 4 per cent., it being a prosperous and thriving town.

67. Is it not a question of security, I believe?—It is a perfectly safe security.

68. You told us that the cost of the Provisional Order which Wexford obtained, for the one purpose of securing control over its roads, was 40 *l.*; could you give us any figures which show the cost of local Acts which have had to be obtained by other towns for those and other purposes?—Yes. Pembroke township cost 1,200 *l.*; the cheapest of all was Rathmines and Rathgar, 469 *l.*; the Kingstown Act of 1869 cost nearly 6,000 *l.*; Blackrock 1,900 *l.*, Bray 1,900 *l.*, and Sligo 14,000 *l.*

69. Those cases were all before the Act of 1871, were they not?—Yes.

70. Do you think that you could go any further in relieving towns from the costs of local Acts?—Yes; for instance, in Cork they went for a Town and Harbour Act; and whenever harbour powers come in they are not allowed to get them by a Provisional Order; but I think that any arrangement between town authorities and harbour authorities ought to be done by a Provisional Order, just as well as between the town authorities and any local body, in the same way as in buying up gasworks, or local matters of that kind; any local matter at all, no matter what the authority is.

Mr. *Murphy.*

71. Did I understand you to say that there was an application on the part of Cork as between the corporation and the Cork Harbour Commissioners for a Provisional Order?—No. The Cork people within the last two years have had to go for a local Act.

72. What proportion of the Cork people?—I was looking up the local Acts, and I found that to be so with regard to Cork.

73. Who was it in Cork that went for this?—

Mr. *Murphy*—continued.

The town council were one party to it, and the Harbour Commissioners were another.

74. The Harbour Commissioners went for a local Act?—I merely mentioned it as I saw the town council mentioned in the Act; I do not know which party went for it. I thought that it might have been managed by a Provisional Order, and that they should not have been put to that expense.

75. The Cork Harbour Commissioners might have got a Provisional Order, but the Act for which the town council went, was for liberty to build a bridge?—They ought to have had that power by a Provisional Order. Since a Provisional Order has been adopted for all those town purposes, there should not be any occasions to go for a local Act.

Mr. *O'Shaughnessy.*

76. Are you aware that efforts have been made by some of the Scotch constituencies to substitute the system of Provisional Order, the Act giving their Commissioners general powers in gas matters for the purchase and erection of gasworks?—Yes.

77. You are aware that such a movement has been made by some of the Scotch constituencies?—Yes.

78. Are you acquainted at all with the details that have been brought in for the purpose?—No, I am not; but I am aware that the Scotch authorities have been put to an enormous expense for getting powers, each town getting one power after another that they ought all to have. I think they are behind us in that, because our Act of 1828 and our Act of 1854 puts Ireland in advance of the small towns in either England or Scotland.

79. Do you think that it would be possible or advisable to go even further than substituting a Provisional Order for a local Act, and to have a general Act enabling towns like those to do certain things?—Certainly. My idea about that is this: that it should be the duty of the Irish Local Government Board, where they find that any town has gone to the expense of getting powers sanctioned by Parliament, immediately to consider whether it ought not to be extended to all towns under town government, and that it should be the duty of the Local Government Board to bring in a general Act next Session, enabling every town to get it, because Parliament, having once sanctioned that for large towns, if the Local Government Board cannot see any objection to it, ought to bring in an Act next Session to give every town that is under town government that benefit at once.

Dr. *Ward.*

80. Subject, I suppose, to the veto of the Local Government Board?—By giving to them a power which they should not exercise without the consent of the Local Government Board under certain restrictions and precautions; but once the power is sanctioned by Parliament in the case of any large town it should be the duty of the Local Government Board to look after the small towns and see that they got it too.

81. Would you make it compulsory upon the towns to accept it?—No, not to accept the expense, but to accept the power; they need not exercise it, but they should have the power of exercising it.

Mr. *W. N. Hancock*, LL.D.

28 April 1878.

Chairman.

82. Would not that be rather substituting private legislation for general legislation?—In one sense it would be, but in the sense that I mean, it would not. For instance, the Towns Clauses and the Commissioners Clauses Acts were passed in 1847. Large towns, if they chose to go to the expense, got that benefit in 1847; but small towns did not get it till 1854. All I want is, that the seven years should not be lost. It was as clear in 1848 or 1849, when Dublin went for those powers, that every town ought to have them as it was in 1854: and I want to accelerate the local government, and that small towns should get it promptly. In the same way it was held in 1847 that it was a desirable thing to separate towns from counties, and to give the towns sole control over the roads. The Local Government Act did not give the power of getting that accomplished by provisional order to all towns in Ireland till 1871, but it might have been given at an earlier period. In the same way their borrowing powers ought to rest on legislation of 1875, and not on that of 1847.

83. Have you any suggestions to offer as to improving or simplifying the sanitary powers of those authorities?—Yes; the sanitary powers of the town authorities in Ireland, both urban and rural authorities, rest mainly on the extension of the English law to Ireland in 1866. It was the Sanitary Act of 1866 that extended to Ireland the provisions of the Public Health Act of 1848, the provisions of the Disease Prevention Act of 1855, the Nuisance Removal Act of 1855, the Local Government Act of 1858, the Nuisance Removal Act of 1860, the Local Government Act of 1861, the Sewage Utilisation Act of 1865, and the Nuisance Removal Act of 1866. The whole of that very complicated system of law was extended from England to Ireland by 14 clauses of the Sanitary Act of 1866. That was the only possible way of extending it at that time, but the inconvenience of that was remedied by a digest which was published of all those clauses that were so extended. It was the object of my report to Lord Mayo in 1866, to show how that could be done. A digest must always precede a code. The Public Health Acts had not been reduced to a code in England in 1866; in 1875 the whole of those Acts of Parliament I have referred to have been repealed, and in lieu of those Acts of Parliament there is one simple intelligible Sanitary Code for England in the year 1875, and that could be extended to Ireland in 10 clauses; but instead of that, we are now governed under half-a-dozen Acts of Parliament, dating from 1848 down to 1866, every one of which has been repealed in England. The simple proposal which I recommend is, that by 10 clauses this Code of 1875 should be extended to Ireland. There is an inconvenience in extending a code by reference clauses, but that could be simply remedied by the commissioners publishing a digest.

Mr. Butt.

84. Is the Public Health Act at present in Ireland and England the same?—No.

85. Would not it be better to follow the example of England, and bring in a consolidation of all the Irish Acts?—There were an immense number of clauses for a Public Health Act for Ireland separate from England, drawn in 1866; but I found it hopeless to have so long a Bill, and I recommended the course successfully adopted in 1866. The Act of 1875 might, as I say, be extended to Ireland in about 10 clauses, because it is much simpler than the earlier law. There is a certain convenience in extending these English Acts to Ireland, by reference with different clauses only, and then publishing a digest, because if you draw a separate Act the words get quite different, and then the decisions upon the English Act do not apply to Ireland; whereas if you copy the English Act verbatim with certain ascertained differences, you have the English text books and the English law books, and English cases, all applying to Ireland, subject to those differences.

Chairman.

86. Could you, in a similar way, simplify the powers of the town authorities, for other than sanitary purposes?—Yes. The great basis of town law in Ireland is the Act of 1854, because it governs a very large number of towns entirely. It has been adopted by a number of town councils, and it is adopted in nearly all the local Acts, more or less. All that you want is an amendment of the Act of 1854; and by a very slight amendment it would embrace all the powers that are in the local Acts. The local Acts might be repealed, and the towns placed under one general Act, an amendment of the Act of 1854.

87. What do you mean by a very slight amendment?—If you read over the local Acts which have been passed since 1854 you will find that one Act has a clause amending one defect in the Act of 1854, and another has a clause amending another defect in the Act of 1854. There are not more than about a dozen of these about borrowing powers, markets, and this question about roads, and a very few matters of that kind; and if you amended the Act of 1854 with respect to these, you might then repeal all the local Acts, except in the case of large towns, and even in the large towns their powers are really founded upon the same basis. For instance, the Dublin and the Belfast powers are founded upon the Commissioners Clauses Acts and the Towns Improvement Clauses Act. They are all derived from the same source, namely, the English Towns Improvement Clauses Act and the English Commissioners Clauses Act: therefore it would be quite easy to pass a general Act narrowing the local legislation to special matters.

88. What would you do with the Act of 1828?—That Act ought to be completely repealed; it is entirely out of date, and it is simply an embarrassment. There were 66 towns that adopted it, and there are only 12 that still remain under it, and they ought not to be allowed to remain under imperfect powers.

89. From what you have already said with regard to the municipal commissioners, I gather that you would in some way get rid of them altogether?—Yes; it is an absurdity to allow a town like Carrickfergus with 4,000 inhabitants to have a class to itself in every Act of Parliament. There is a schedule in every Act of Parliament, and that schedule sets out the class of towns under municipal commissioners; and under that whole class it all comes down to one town, and that town is not even large enough to be an urban sanitary district; and to allow one town of 4,000 inhabitants to have a separate class in every Act of Parliament only confuses the legislation. The reason that they did not

Mr. W. N. Hancock, LL.D.

28 April 1876.

Chairman—continued.

not adopt the Act of 1854 was because they had to go to a town meeting, and there was a doubt as to the effect of its adoption. There was a clause (Section 25) put in the Act of 1871 to remove the latter defect, but the inhabitants have not adopted the Act, though they have had the power free from legal doubt for five years, and I suggest that they ought to be compelled to do it. To show the complication from the Act of 1828, here is the latest Bill, Mr. Bruen's and Sir Arthur Guinness's Bill; and there is this class in the schedule: "Towns containing a population of 6,000 inhabitants having commissioners appointed by virtue of an Act made in the 9th year of the reign of George the Fourth, entitled 'An Act to make provision for the Lighting, Cleansing, and Watching of Cities and Towns corporate, and Market Towns in Ireland in certain cases.'" In every Act relating to Ireland for the last 10 years there has been a long elaborate schedule setting out this definition. All that might be got rid of by saying that those 12 townships should follow the rest of the 66, and adopt the Act of 1854.

90. You consider that the town law for Ireland might be limited to the Municipal Act of 1840, and to an amendment of the General Act of 1854, which might comprise nearly all the local Acts?—Yes.

Mr. *Corry*.

91. In fact it would be a Consolidation Act?—Yes, a consolidation like the Sanitary Code.

Chairman.

92. Referring to the powers of those different town authorities, there is one important point which we have not yet touched upon, and that is the power of taxation: can you inform the Committee what power of taxation the town authorities have under the different Acts?—In the first class of town authorities; the oldest is the commissioners under the Act of 1828. The main distinction between the town authorities is the limit of rating. Under the Act of 1828 houses between 5 *l.* and 10 *l.* a year can only be charged up to 6 *d.* in the pound (that is the ordinary limit of rating where there is not a special town meeting for an extraordinary rate); between 10 *l.* and 20 *l.*, the limit is 9 *d.*, and then above 20 *l.* a year the limit is 1 *s.*; houses under 5 *l.* are exempted altogether. Then when you come to the Act of 1854 the main limit there is 1 *s.* if water be not adopted; if water be adopted the limit was raised to 1 *s.* 6 *d.* Then, in the year 1874 that limit was raised to 2 *s.* if water be adopted, but it is 1 *s.* apart from water. Then there are certain classes of property, market gardens, railways, and canals, within the town boundary, and arable land and meadow and woodland, that is only charged at one-fourth of the limit; that is under the Act of 1854; originally it was 3 *d.* without water, and if water be adopted it is now 6 *d.*

Dr. *Ward*.

93. All houses under 5 *l.* were exempt?—Yes; but the 5 *l.* limit is done away with altogether when the Act of 1854 has been adopted instead of the Act of 1828.

Chairman.

94. How many towns are there under the Act of 1828 in which there is this varying limit of rating?—There are 12 still remaining under it; that is to say, it is still in force in those 12 towns.

95. How many towns were there under the Act of 1854?—Seventy six.

96. Can you tell us whether the limits fixed in those two Acts have generally been reached?—I have never calculated that.

97. You are not aware how far the different authorities tax the towns up to the legal limits?—No, I am not; but I could ascertain that for the Committee; at least I could make an approximation to it.

98. Have any limits of the kind been adopted in the local Acts?—Yes, there is a series of limits in all the local Acts. Take the class of towns where the obligations of the grand juries as to streets have been transferred; while the county cess is unlimited, the town authorities have been usually limited. In Rathmines (which is the first of them) in 1847 for all purposes, including charges on grand jury cess, it is 2 *s.* in the 1 *l.* and with the consent of two-thirds of the ratepayers it may be 2 *s.* 6 *d.* In Dungarvan in 1863, for roads alone without any other object of grand jury purpose, they have the same limit. In the Pembroke township in 1863, for all purposes except water, it is 2 *s.*, and with the consent of two-thirds of the ratepayers, 2 *s.* 6 *d.*; and then for water it is 1 *s.* In Dalkey in 1867 it is 1 *s.* for water, 1 *s.* for the pier, and for other purposes, 2 *s.*; and then with the consent of two-thirds of the ratepayers, a limit of 3 *s.*, making 5 *s.* in all. In Newry it is 3 *s.*, exclusive of county-at-large charges, which are levied by county cess, with an extra 1 *s.* for water. In Enniskillen in 1870 it is, inclusive of all county charges, 2 *s.* 6 *d.* for the improvement rate, and 1 *s.* 6 *d.* for water. In Blackrock the limits are for all purposes, except water, 2 *s.*, or, with consent, 2 *s.* 6 *d.*, and water 8 *d.* and 1 *s.* On meadow, pasture, market gardens, or railways, the limits are 1 *s.* 8 *d.* and 2 *s.*, and for water 6½ *d.* and 10 *d.* in the pound. In Belfast the Improvement Rate, under the Act of 1864, is subject to two limits; it is 1 *s.* 8 *d.* for premises of 20 *l.* and under, and 3 *s.* 4 *d.* for premises above 20 *l.* Arable and woodland and agricultural buildings were exempt. When the unlimited power of the grand jury cess of Antrim was transferred, a new General Purposes Rate was established, but it was limited to 2 *s.* within certain boundaries, and 1 *s.* 6 *d.* beyond these.

99. Have not town councils, under the Act of 1840, unlimited taxing power for any purpose?—No, they have not. By the Borough Rate Act, the 3 & 4 Vict. c. 109, s. 10, it is enacted, "The maximum rate of assessment of every borough rate to be made in any borough under the said recited Act, shall in no case in any borough exceed 1 *s.* in the 1 *l.* of the yearly value of the premises assessed thereto at which the same shall be estimated for the purpose of a rate for the relief of the destitute poor, and shall not in any borough in which an Act passed in the 9th year of the reign of King George the 4th, intituled, an Act to make provision for the lighting, cleansing, and watching, of cities, towns corporate, and market towns in Ireland in certain cases, or in which any local Act or Acts providing for the paving, lighting, and cleansing of such borough shall be in force, exceed 3 *d.* in the 1 *l.* of such yearly value of the premises so assessed

Mr. *W. N. Hancock*, LL.D.

28 April 1876.

Chairman—continued.

assessed to such borough rate as aforesaid: provided always, in any case in which the council of any borough shall be entitled, as to the whole or as to any part of such borough which shall not be within the provisions of any local Act for lighting the same, to levy rates for the purpose of lighting such borough or such part thereof; then the rate to be levied within such borough or within such part thereof, shall, in addition to the aforesaid rate of 3 *d*. in the 1 *l*., be of such an amount as will be sufficient to cover the expense of such lighting." That was a limit of 3 *d*., and it might be 1 *s*. if the Act of 1828 was not in force. Under the Sanitary Act, when sanitary charges are put upon the borough fund, if it is not sufficient, the limit of rating is departed from.

100. So that by adding another charge to the borough fund the limit is lost?—Yes, it is. In 1866 the limit was lost, because the charges under the Sanitary Act are put on the borough fund; but if it is insufficient, then the limit is to be departed from under section 58 of that Act.

101. Have all town councils taxing powers?—They all have borough rate powers; but, as I mentioned, the borough of Waterford did not adopt powers involving rating under the Act of 1854. They have a very large amount of property, and they did not adopt the Act of 1854 for a number of purposes, but only to a very limited extent.

102. Do they levy any rate at all?—They return no rates as levied.

103. Is any other town council in the same position?—No.

104. What is the limit in Dublin?—The limit of the improvement rate, under the Act of 1849, is a limit of 2 *s*.

105. Have the town council kept, to any large extent, within that limit?—No. Since 1866, it appears that they have levied the maximum amount every year, and, perhaps, further back, but the statistics I had at hand merely give the tables from 1866, and since 1866 they have been up to 2 *s*.

106. Is that rate applicable to the cleansing of streets?—It is.

107. Has that limit any effect upon that subject?—It has had a curious effect?—There has been a great deal of discussion about why there was not more spent on cleansing the streets of Dublin, but that effect has not been noticed in any complaint upon it. Once they got up to the limit of 1866, they could not increase the expenditure on the cleansing of the streets without disturbing some other objects to which the improvement fund is applied, the payment of debts and charges, and interest, and a number of charges on it. So that really they have not the power of increasing the expenditure. When once a fund of that kind gets allocated into a number of objects, and some of them first charges, the power of the town council is gone, because they cannot increase their expenditure on the cleansing of streets beyond what it was in 1866, without disturbing some other object. The reformed corporation are saddled with debts contracted by the unreformed corporation.

108. Amongst other objects which are charged upon this improvement rate, I believe, is the interest of the large debt which the corporation have inherited from their predecessors?—Yes, from the paving board a very large debt, and, as an improvement, I made that suggestion about borrowing powers. Some of the old debentures are most complicated securities, and if they could borrow under the improved borrowing powers which I have referred to, they might save the interest of money upon them, and so get money for cleansing.

109. The effect of having this limit on the improvement rate in Dublin, and other prior charges upon that rate, is that the corporation have but a small margin for the purpose of paving and cleansing the streets?—Yes, and they cannot increase it. Whatever they may have spent in 1866, the demand for the public now is greater than it was then.

Mr. Bruen.

110. Could you mention the amount of this large debt, the interest of which is charged upon this rate?—I have not the statistics.

Chairman.

111. Can you tell us what, in your opinion, is the value of those limits upon the rating powers as a protection to property?—I have formed a very strong opinion that they are unwise, although they were originally put in as a protection to property. For instance, they do not exist either in the grand jury presentment, where property is protected, nor do they exist under the poor law, where property is directly represented and protected. The poor law rate is only about 1 *s*. in the £. in Ireland, on an average; so that if you get a properly constituted body, I think it is most unwise to complicate them with limits. Then the limits involve the risk of litigation. For instance, the whole of the Belfast chancery suit arose out of ear-marking, such funds to be applied to one object, such to another, and such to another. Some of the funds happened to get out of being applied to the proper account, and it turned out that although they had been applied to proper objects, it was not to the technically right objects, and the whole result of the complication was expense. Then we have an endless question before the auditors. A great number of wealthy people are deterred from serving on town authorities in Ireland by the rigidity of the audit, because the administration of town funds is an extremely complicated matter. If anyone makes a mistake, they are liable to be surcharged by the auditor, and nine-tenths of the surcharges arise, not from any malversation, but simply from the complication of powers, and the complication of powers arises from the complicated limits. There is the improvement fund; then there is the borough fund; then there is the grand jury cess; then there is in Belfast the improvement rate and the general purposes rate. Then, in Dublin, you have the sewers, and so on. That causes an amount of complication which is wholly unnecessary. In the grand jury cess, the objects are all distinct, but the presentment is one.

112. I asked you whether you could give us any figures showing us how much in the £. the taxation levied by other town authorities was—can you give us any figures showing how much in the £. the taxation levied by town councils amounts to?—In my report for 1871 that matter was gone into to some extent, and it is classified in this way:—"Poundage on town valuation of rates and receipts of town authorities other than receipts

Mr. W. N. Hancock, LL.D.

28 April 1876.

Chairman—continued.

receipts from land and houses, money borrowed, or grand jury cess in 1871." Then I give the average of all Ireland, then the above average, below average, below half-average, and below fourth average.

113. Does that all come under the head of local taxation?—Yes; the average was 3*s.* 2*d.* for all Ireland. In Dublin it rose to 6*s.*

114. Let me ask you what "all Ireland" includes; does it include all the towns under town authorities of every kind?—Yes, town councils and every town authority. Then, in the City of Dublin it was 6*s.*; in Belfast it was 5*s.* 3*d.*; in Londonderry 4*s.* 6*d.*; in Cork 4*s.*; and in Sligo it was 3*s.* 7*d.* Then, taking all town authorities in the county of Dublin, it amounted to 3*s.*, in Fermanagh to 2*s.* 11*d.*; in Limerick City it was 2*s.* 10*d.*; in the county of Wicklow all the towns there came to 2*s.* 6*d.*; in the county of Tyrone to 2*s.* 5*d.*; in Westmeath to 2*s.*; in Kerry to 2*s.*; in Kilkenny to 1*s.* 10*d.*; in Roscommon to 1*s.* 7*d.*; and in Monaghan to 1*s.* 7*d.*; those are all below the average. Those below half-average, were Clare 1*s.* 4*d.*; towns in County Cork 1*s.* 3*d.*; in Tipperary 1*s.* 2*d.*; in Waterford 1*s.* 2*d.*; in Galway 1*s.* 1*d.*; in Longford 11*d.*; in Armagh 11*d.*, and in Louth 10*d.* Below fourth average, in Donegal 9*d.*, Kildare 9*d.*, King's County 8*d.*, Cavan 8*d.*, Carlow 7*d.*, Meath 7*d.*, Limerick County 7*d.*, Antrim 7*d.*, Mayo 7*d.*, Wexford 6*d.*, and Queen's County 5*d.*

115. The poundage that you have quoted includes, as I understand, rates levied by those urban authorities for sanitary purposes, but does not, of course, include the poor rate?—No, it does not include the poor rate. It is "poundage on town valuation of rates and receipts of town authorities other than receipts from land and houses, money borrowed, or grand jury cess."

116. Can you tell us whether there is any general system of audit of accounts of those different authorities?—Yes, the audit of the accounts was settled under a recent Act—the Local Government Act of 1871. That provided for auditors like the poor law auditors. They go to all towns in Ireland, with three exceptions: Cork, Kilkenny, and Waterford. Besides those the townships in the county of Dublin were to be excepted, unless they agreed to come under it. To what extent they have come under it I do not know; the Local Government Board could return it, but they were not bound to be audited unless they agreed to be audited. That system of audit is the Local Government audit, and it has one great advantage by being done in the locality by permanent officials. It is an admirable system of audit, but it is open to one objection. In the case of the grand jury, the grand jury can get the opinion of the judge as to any expenditure that they are going to incur. If the judge sanctions an expenditure, whether right or wrong, in point of law, once he decides it, the grand jury are exempt from all liability. If the Board of Guardians have any doubt of what they are going to do, if they write up to the Local Government Board, as formerly to the Poor Law Commissioners, the Board gives them an answer as to what their powers are, and if they act upon that they are free from all liability; but the town authorities have not the same advantage, they cannot get the opinion of a judge; the Local Government Board are not in the same absolute way bound to answer them; and the consequence is that they are left to a risk. There is not the same legislation as under the Poor Law. The sanction of the Local Government Board does not ratify the act of a town authority; and the consequence is that the towns have not the same protection; I think it very serious that they should not have the protection of either a judge on the one hand or of the Local Government Board on the other. They are left to act upon the opinion of counsel, but the opinion of counsel is no protection to them. It merely may protect them against being accused of fraud, but it does not protect them legally. That, of course, has a very bad effect, as in the case of the chancery litigation in Belfast, which has had the effect of deterring people of influence and wealth from serving on town councils because they do not like getting involved in litigation.

Mr. Bruen.

117. Have they to pay out of the rates for the opinion of counsel that they have to take?—I apprehend that they can pay for the opinion of counsel out of the rates; it is a proper charge to pay for; but then the opinion of counsel will not protect them.

Dr. Ward.

118. Have the auditors refused to allow the payment of counsel?—I am not aware of any case.

Chairman.

119. We will turn from the subject of the powers of town authorities to that of qualifications of persons acting as town councillors or commissioners, and of electors; first of all, with regard to the qualifications of commissioners under the first Act of 1828, what are those qualifications?—The qualification under the Act of 1828 is that a man must be rated to 20*l.* a year, must reside within the town boundary, and must have been residing there 12 months. Then in the Act of 1854 there was a new class introduced, namely, of immediate lessors of the value of 50*l.* a year residing within five miles; but they must reside for one year and nine and a half months before the election. Then householders rated to 12*l.* a year within the boundary were allowed to be elected. And then there is an excluding of ecclesiastics; but singularly enough the excluding of ecclesiastics is only for the householders; if they were immediate lessors, they were not excluded.

120. Did the qualification in the Act of 1828 in any way operate to prevent its working?—It operated very seriously, because the tendency in all towns is for people who make money to become villa holders, and live outside the town. The moment a man has made enough to be able to afford to live outside the town boundary he becomes disqualified if he does so. I should say that the 20*l.* was a very high qualification, and it was altered to 12*l.* in 1854; and on the change from one Act to the other in Lisburn, the number qualified was pretty nearly doubled by simply changing from the one qualification to the other.

121. The Act of 1854 attempted to remedy the defect in the Act of 1828 by allowing the lessors to be qualified, did it not?—It did; it introduced the principle of immediate lessors being qualified. Then it was subject to a defect again; for instance, they have got a five-mile limit; they must live within five miles. Take Newry,

Mr. W. N. Hancock, LL.D.

28 April 1876.

Chairman—continued.

Newry, one of the principal towns that were till recently under the Act; some of the wealthiest people lived down at Warren Point, more than five miles from Newry. The railroads have revolutionised the five-mile limit; and even in the Newry Local Act they have not remedied this: they have still the defect about the five-mile limit. In England the old five mile and seven mile limits have been enlarged to 15 miles; but we still have the seven and five miles in Ireland.

122. What are the qualifications of a town councillor and alderman under the Municipal Corporation Act of 1840?—There are 10 large towns that have got charters preserved under the Act of 1840. The qualification in them is first of all that the person must be a burgess, and that involves six months' residence within seven miles before the end of August. Then he should have 1,000 *l.* in either real or personal property above all his debts, or he might be qualified if in the occupation of a house of 20 *l.* rating if he had been in occupation of it for 12 months. In Wexford, and any other town that happened to get a charter, the qualification would be 500 *l.* or occupation of a house rated at from 15 *l.* to 20 *l.*; the exact limit between 15 *l.* and 20 *l.* was thought of so much importance at that time that the only authority who could determine it was Her Majesty in Council in England.

123. Under the Municipal Act of 1840 the qualification might be fixed, might it not, in the charter of each town that obtained a charter?—In each of the new towns it was to be in their new charter, and Her Majesty in Council in England was to fix it. That was a slip, no doubt, in the Act of Parliament. It is the 14th section of the Municipal Act, the 3 & 4 Vict. c. 108: "Be it enacted, that if a petition to grant a charter of incorporation under this Act to the inhabitants of any borough named in the schedule (B) to this Act annexed, or to the inhabitants of any other town in Ireland, in which the population according to the census or abstract then last laid before both Houses of Parliament as by law required, shall exceed the number of 3,000, signed by a majority of such of the inhabitants thereof as shall be rated to the relief of the destitute poor, under the Act for the relief of the destitute poor in Ireland, shall be presented to Her Majesty; and if the persons who shall have signed such petition shall include a majority also of such of the inhabitants of such borough as would be qualified (so far as such qualification can be ascertained from the assessment of the poor rate, made under the Act for the more effectual relief of the destitute poor in Ireland) to have been enrolled on the burgess roll of such town, if the same had been named in the said schedule (A), and such burgess roll had been made according to the provisions hereinafter contained, then and in every such case it shall be lawful for Her Majesty, by any such charter, if by the advice of Her Privy Council she shall think fit to grant the same, to extend to the inhabitants of any such borough or town within the district to be set forth in such charter, the powers and provisions in this Act contained; provided that notice of every such petition, and of the time when it shall please Her Majesty to order that the same be taken into consideration by Her Privy Council shall be published by Royal Proclamation in the "Dublin Gazette" one calender month at least before such petition shall be so considered," and it has been always considered by the English Privy Council.

Chairman—continued.

124. Has the same difficulty of the seven miles limit of residence been found with regard to town councillors and aldermen as has been found with regard to commissioners?—Yes, it is an absurd limit in Dublin, because a great many of the gentry and people of wealth live beyond seven miles from Dublin, at Killiney, for instance, which is one of the nicest parts of the suburbs now, and is beyond the seven miles limit.

125. I suppose the idea of requiring a qualification of that kind is that those elected should be persons of some position, but the effect of the limit is to exclude persons of the highest position?—The effect of the limit is simply to exclude the wealthiest people; it is perfectly accidental, if it does not; I think that that qualification of residence arose from another thing. One of the great abuses of the old corporations was appointing absentee freemen and other privileged officers in place of the natives, if I may so speak, who were excluded and crushed by the penal laws; and it was a feeling that one effect of that limit would be to enforce residence; but if we take care that the electors reside, it does not matter to limit the selection of councillors or commissioners; you might trust them to elect. But it was the panic against the abuse of non-resident freemen, and non-resident electors, in the old system that probably led to all these restrictions about residence.

126. Could you tell the Committee what the qualification of the governing bodies under the local Acts is?—Yes, in Pembroke if a man is resident it is 30 *l.* rating; if he is non-resident it is the receipt of 200 *l.* a-year out of rents in the township; in Rathmines it is the same; in Blackrock it is 20 *l.* rating if resident; then they introduced the 50 *l.* immediate lessor; then there is 100 *l.* a-year rent if non-resident. In New Kilmainham it is 12 *l.* rating, 50 *l.* immediate lessor, and 50 *l.* a-year rent.

127. Now will you turn to the qualifications of electors under those different Acts, referring first to the Act of 1828?—In the Act of 1828 they were 5 *l.* householders; in the Act of 1854 they changed that to occupiers of 4 *l.* rating; then they introduced immediate lessors at 4 *l.*, and if residing within five miles 50 *l.* a-year rental.

128. You have given us all the qualifications for municipal electors in those two Acts; can you state the qualification under the Act of 1840, and in what towns that qualification is still in force? Yes, in the case of the municipal electors, a municipal elector has to be an inhabitant householder. This applies in 10 out of 11 towns, that is in all, except Dublin. The qualification is first of all to be an inhabitant householder; next, to be resident within the borough or within seven miles of it for six months previous to the 31st of August. Then he must occupy a house, warehouse, counting-house, or shop, with or without land of the value of 10 *l.*, calculated as in the Act; then he must have been rated to the poor in respect of the premises; he must for 12 months previous to the 31st of August have occupied premises, or if he have changed his residence within 12 months, the premises of which he was previously in occupation must have been of the like nature and likewise rated to the poor, or if he has come into the occupation by descent he may

Mr W. N. Hancock, LL.D.

28 April 1876.

Chairman—continued.

may reckon the rating and occupation of his predecessor, as well as his own, provided that the predecessor had been enrolled as a burgess at the time of the devolution, and then he must have paid five rates, the improvement rate, the police rate, the borough rate, the grand jury cess, and the poor rate. I should mention, with regard to the Act of 1854, one thing which I omitted; that they originally required payment of three rates, the town rate, the grand jury cess, and the poor rate. The towns complained very much of that as a wholly unnecessary complication, and in 1871 they persuaded the Government to abolish it, and have only the town rate. They said they could know whether the town rate was paid or not by their own books, but it was a great complication to introduce the other two payments; and in 1871 they got it enacted that under the Act of 1854 the payment of one rate should do. Under the Act of 1828 there is no payment of rates required at all.

129. What is the qualification in Dublin?—In Dublin, in 1849, there was a change made, and the qualification was as follows: Every male person of full age who occupies a house, warehouse, counting house, or shop, having occupied the same for two years and eight months, or has been an inhabited householder within the borough of Dublin, or seven miles, and has during his occupation, the whole of that time, been rated to the relief of the poor, and who has paid the five taxes; the improvement rate, the police rate, the borough rate, the grand jury cess, and the poor rate. Under section 5, occupiers may claim to be rated; and under section 7, in the case of a title by descent, that is provided for.

130. What was the obligation as to the payment of rates in Dublin under the Act of 1840?—Under the Act of 1840 they had to pay about 12 rates. In addition to the police rate, the borough rate, the grand jury cess, and poor rate, they had to pay minister's money, the parish cess, the parish clerk's fees, the wide street tax, the watch tax, independent of paving, lighting, and cleansing, and for the watering of the streets; I think about 12 taxes altogether.

Mr. *BrWen*.

131. But that obligation does not subsist now?—They have five to pay now.

Sir *Arthur Guinness*.

132. Under what Act?—Under the Act of 1849, 12 & 13 Vict. c. 85, the Dublin Municipal Amendment Act, they have to pay five taxes.

133. Am I right in supposing that the Dublin occupation qualification is as follows. Every male person of full age who occupies a house, warehouse, counting-house, or shop of whatever value, for a certain period?—They must be rated to the relief of the poor, or they can demand to be rated. The theoretic qualification is occupation.

134. Is there any limit of value?—I do not apprehend that there is. But I may mention that whilst that is the theory of the thing, in practice it is not even a 4 *l.* rating, because in practice they do not enter a 4 *l.* man on the rate book.

135. Will you explain that?—As a matter of fact there is scarcely any one entered on the rate book below 8 *l.*, because the limit of rating in Dublin was 8 *l.*, and that is still the limit of rating in the Improvement Act. For instance, a landlord must pay all the local rates and taxes up to 8 *l.* I ascertained at the collector-general's office that there is scarcely anybody under 8 *l.* entered at this moment as entitled to the municipal franchise. The number of burgesses is quite different from what the Parliamentary electors are. In 1873 there were 5,584 burgesses, and 8,586 occupiers rated for the Parliamentary franchise. Theoretically, these ought to be the same.

136. Why?—I mean the rating would come in the same.

137. Have the burgesses a term of occupation?—They told me at the collector-general's that it was not so much the term that affected it as the practice of not putting people under 8 *l.* upon the rate book, and people had not claimed to be rated.

Chairman.

138. Do they collect the rates from premises below the value of 8 *l.*?—Not the municipal rates.

139. Do not the owners pay them?—The owners pay the municipal rates up to 8 *l.*; they must do it. I might mention I was struck with these figures, and I considered that they ought to be nearer, but when I inquired I found that the occupiers had not worked the municipal franchise to the full extent. The reason is, because in a very few wards there is any contest, but as a matter of fact the number of burgesses in Dublin is not what it might be.

140. If they cared to do so, they might claim to be rated, might they not?—Yes, but there is a vast number that do not claim it at all.

Sir *Arthur Guinness*.

141. There is no limit to the rating; they might be rated for 1 *d.*, might they not?—Yes, I should say so; it ought to be below the Parliamentary franchise, whereas it is within it.

Sir *J. M'Kenna*.

142. Does anyone pay in respect of property for which the occupier escapes?—Yes, the owner must pay it; it is only in the 12 towns under the 9th Geo. 4, that the owners escape altogether.

Mr. *Murphy*.

143. As a matter of fact, I suppose that in all cases the landlord or owner of premises that are rated at or below 8 *l.* pays the municipal rate?—Yes, he must pay it.

144. Is it open to the tenant to ask for himself to be put on the rate book, and to pay the rate which the owner pays?—He can claim to be put on the rate book and pay the poor rate; he would be qualified for the municipal franchise if he got upon the rate book at all.

145. But as a matter of fact he does not do so?—I was told at the collector-general's office that it was not worked; I was struck with it myself, and I just asked the question, and I found that they had not worked the thing. In a very great number of wards in Dublin there is no contest, and has not been for a great number of years.

Chairman.

146. Is the result of this that in the town of Dublin there is a considerable amount of property below 8 *l.* value on which the owners pay the municipal rates, but for which no one votes?—Yes, that is so.

147. Are

Mr. W. N. Hancock, LL.D.

28 April 1876.

Chairman—continued.

147. Are the owners legally liable for those rates?—Yes.

148. Under what Act?—Under the Dublin Rates Act, 1849.

149. Under that Act the owners of that property are rendered legally liable to pay the municipal rates upon it, but they have no right of voting?—No, the owner has no right of voting.

150. Is any deduction in the rate allowed to the owner upon the ground of his paying it?—There is in Belfast, Sligo, and Dublin.

151. Can you tell us how much it is?—Under Sligo Act, 1869, sect. 154, if owner be rated instead of occupier, he must be assessed at a reduced rate, not less than two-thirds nor more than four-fifths; if rate be made, whether occupied or not, they may be rated at one-half. Under sect. 353 of Belfast Local Act of 1845, a discount of 25 per cent. is allowed for payment of rates within one month. In Dublin, under 120 section of Act of 1849, the reduction is to be not less than two-thirds nor more than four-fifths.

152 To go on with this point, has it ever occurred to you whether it might be well to adopt the Poor Law system of liability, and divide the municipal rates between the owner and the occupier?—Yes, I was examined before a very important Committee that sat in 1870 on local taxation, and I gave very strong evidence before that Committee in favour of an equal division of rates between the owner and the occupier; in that year it was carried for the grand jury cess in Ireland as to all new contracts respecting holdings under the Land Act of 1870; that is, agricultural and pastoral holdings. But it was an English Committee and a very important Committee, of which Mr. Goschen was Chairman, and he wrote a very elaborate Report upon the whole subject. After I gave my evidence I was led to study the subject very carefully, seeing the importance that it had assumed from the Report of that Committee, and I adhere to the opinion very strongly that the solution of all satisfactory local government is the equal division of rates between owner and occupier. That applies now to all the Poor Law in Ireland, and to all future contracts with the grand jury cess for holdings under the Land Act (of course unless parties contract out of it), and it applies thus to the great bulk of local taxation in Ireland, and all that is wanted is to extend it to town taxation.

153. If you divide the rates between owner and occupier, how would you propose to represent the owner?—That question came up before that Committee too. I had not considered it then, but since that time I have studied it with great care, and I have come to the conclusion that the best plan would be to elect half the board by the owners of property, and half by the occupiers.

154. How would you carry that out?—In carrying it out, I would take first the occupiers; I would have one occupier's representative elected as at present, by each ward in a town, or by the whole town if not divided into wards, that is to say, by a simple majority; all the rest of the occupier's representatives I would elect for the whole town, on the cumulative principle which is applied so successfully to the English and Scotch boards.

155. I do not quite gather your reason for that proposal; that is a proposal simply with reference to the representation of occupiers?—Yes, that is one-half of the proposal.

Chairman—continued.

156. My question was rather with reference to the representation of owners; how do you provide for that?—With regard to owners, I would have one owner for each small town and one for each ward, to be the largest immediate lessor or interested in rental out of the town or ward, provided that he happened to be a magistrate. I put that in, just to secure that he has a personal qualification as well as property, and so fit to sit *ex officio*. All the rest of the owners of property I would elect upon the cumulative principle applied to the whole town, but I would give the voters multiple votes, that is to say, one vote for a certain sum, and instead of limiting the multiple votes to six I would give them without limit; for instance, take Trinity College, Dublin, with a valuation of 5,000 *l.*, giving them six votes, you might as well give them one as six. The Government also will have a great many thousand pounds of valuation in Dublin upon which they will pay rates; all the railway companies have very large valuations, and the large millowners and shopowners have very large valuations; they are generally the owners of their property, or they pay very small head rents, and I say that limiting them to six votes would give them a very small amount of influence, and therefore I would give them multiple votes without limit, but I would have the cumulative principle also in this case, as with the occupiers, to adjust the matter; that would work very fairly amongst the proprietors; it would protect the very large owners from being swamped by the very small ones, and it would equally protect the owners of very small property from being swamped by the large ones. In the religious question, also, it would just solve the religious difficulty, because in the north of Ireland it would allow such Roman Catholics as are buying property to get in some of their representatives amongst the owners of property. In the south it would operate in the same way as to acquiring property to allow Catholics that are buying property to gradually get adequate representation amongst the owners of property. On the other hand, the cumulative principle with the occupiers would first of all solve the religious difficulty in the north; that is to say, instead of having Roman Catholics excluded as absolutely now as they were before the Emancipation Act, in a great number of towns it would allow a certain number of Catholics to be elected by occupier votes; and in the south it would secure Protestants some representative amongst the occupiers, where they were in a sufficiently large minority. In the question of the future between capital and labour, it would allow you to reduce the franchise to the lowest basis you like, and admit the labouring class without any restriction; yet at the same time the cumulative principle would allow the wealthier people in a town, as occupiers, to return some employers of labour, and these, added to the owners of property, would secure a fair balance in the town, so as to secure the representation of all classes, and guard against the exclusion of any, or the overwhelming preponderance of any.

157. I think you have rather mixed up different questions in your answer. My point was rather the representation of owners; you propose, as I understand, that owners should be represented, not only by having votes on account of the property for which they would be rated, but by having votes rising in number according

to

Chairman—continued

to the value of that property, to an indefinite extent, and also by electing separate representatives of their own?—Yes; but they should only vote for their own representatives.

158. Supposing, instead of that, you gave the owners votes on account of the property, in common with the occupiers, why would not that be a sufficient representation?—The objection to that is the tendency that either the one or the other will carry the day, and whichever carries the day has the absolute government of the whole place; and then you run the risk of a sudden *bouleversement*. After one party has been governing the place for a number of years you may have a sudden revolution, and a total change the other way, and the advantage of their not voting together is that such a state of things would be rendered impossible.

159. Might not that be met, to some extent at any rate, by the adoption of the system of cumulative or minority voting?—I think that cumulative voting would work better if you divide them first. The cumulative voting could be equally introduced in each class, and it would work just as well in each class as in the whole.

160. Do you think there would be no disadvantage in having a separate representation of owners and occupiers?—That has existed under the poor law, practically, since the poor law was established, only not in so perfect a form, because the *ex officio* guardians are really the owners of property. I may mention a direct precedent for it, and a very important one, and that is the Scotch jury law. In Scotland they have settled the very difficult question about securing that there should be a representation of property and of numbers upon every jury; and they do it by having a fixed proportion of special jurors upon every jury; I think they are called landed men, and they have a fixed proportion of common jurors.

161. Are you acquainted with the working in Ireland of the owners' representation at boards of guardians?—I have never been on a board of guardians, but I know that on the whole the Poor-law system has been wonderfully successful, and I think the success is owing very largely to all classes being represented on the Board.

162. Are your aware whether the owners attend regularly or not?—I believe the owners do not attend as regularly as it is desirable they should do, and for that reason I would limit the *ex officio* element to one member of the council in the small towns, and one representative of each ward in the large towns. Then I would allow an *ex officio* owner to do as they do on the grand jury, that is, to allow him to return a member of his family to serve; for instance, a proprietor is allowed to return his son or his agent to serve on the grand jury as his representative. In that *ex officio* representation they would always attend or be represented. I think the *ex officio* representation is carried too far in the Poor-law, and if some of the representatives of property were elected they would attend. The Committee in England, in 1870, reported against the *ex officio* element, and I think they went too far; I think that the *ex officio* element ought to exist to a certain extent; it ought not to be the sole representation of property; but I think, on the other hand, the elective element ought not to be the sole representation.

163. Turning to the occupiers' franchise in considering such a scheme as that which you

Chairman—continued.

have put before the Committee, I gather that what you wish is to lower the present limit of the occupier franchise very considerably?—I think there is an irresistible tendency to lower. It is quite inevitable that the franchise will be lowered; and therefore I think it is desirable to meet it at once. On the other hand, I think that it would be very undesirable to hand over a town government altogether to a body elected solely by an extremely low franchise; I think that town government is not merely a matter of politics, but it is a matter of careful administration and management of money. I think, on the other hand, that the humblest occupier has a right to representation on the council, in order to see that his lane is as well kept as the best street in the town; he is interested in the town being kept clean and well paved, and well supplied with water; and therefore I do not see how it is possible to resist giving the humblest man a representation in it. On the other hand, I think that it is very undesirable to have the whole power in their hands. The French people find it necessary to have a second chamber; and in America a great number of people doubt whether having the whole Government elected on one basis is working satisfactorily there: it is not a question peculiar to Ireland. The Committee in England to which I have referred, had a very strong opinion about the representation of property, and I have endeavoured to look at it in that point of view. At the same time, I see that it is inevitable that there must be an extension of the franchise, and we had better meet it by an extension at once, with reasonable precautions in the representotion of property.

164. Your desire is to secure the representation of the owners of property on the boards of town commissioners or town councils, or whatever they may be, and also, as I understand it, to give votes to all occupiers whatever the value of their property?—Certainly, to every head of a family that has a house.

165. But you would abolish the present limits of exemption from rating altogether which now exists under the Act of George the Fourth?—I think that those limits of the qualifications of the Commissioners, the limit of rating, the qualification of the voter and all those things, were an indirect way of protecting property which has led to endless complication; I propose to substitute for that protection a real protection of property; and having given that real protection of property, I would then say to the inhabitants of a town: Let us go back to the old notion that the Municipal Corporation Commissioners had in 1835, when they said, "We do not hesitate to submit to your Majesty, as one great and pervading defect in the structure and constitution of these corporations, that they provide no means and contain no constituency by which the property, the interest, or the wishes, of the whole local community may be secured a fair representation in the corporate body." I take the terms of that Report. I think that property ought to be represented as property; and I think that the wishes of the whole local community, that is to say, every man that is the supporter of a family in it, the health and wealth of which family depend upon the town being well governed, should have a fair share of influence in it. I think that the neglect of our back streets arises from the poor inhabitants being excluded from any voice in the matter.

Mr. W. N. Hancock, LL.D.

28 April 1876.

Mr. W. N. Hancock, LL.D.

28 April 1876.

Chairman—continued.

matter. I think that the old notion of inhabitants, which lies at the root of all those corporations, ought to be preserved. I should mention about the religious question, that I was led to study it very much from being an Ulster man. I will give the case of the City of Armagh: In the City of Armagh the number of Roman Catholics is very nearly equal to the number of Protestants, and at one time they had 13 Commissioners out of 21. Then a panic seems to have got in that they were going to get the majority, and the result is that the Roman Catholics have not now for some years had a single Commissioner in the body. The whole of the 21 Commissioners in the Borough of Armagh are now Protestants.

166. Is not that merely a question of minority representation, quite apart from property?—It is quite apart from property. I merely mentioned that as in favour of the accumulative vote plan. If we come to Portadown there is not a single Roman Catholic Commissioner there; in Lurgan there is not a single one; in Lisburn there is not one: in Newtonards there is not one; in Ballymena there is not one; in Coleraine there are two; in Londonderry the Roman Catholics are an absolute majority of the population, and in a town council of 24 they have two; in Belfast they are one-third of the population, and at this moment they have two on the town council. That exclusiveness of the Belfast and Derry Corporations led to the overthrow of the Belfast local police and the Derry local police. That dissimilation between Ireland and England and Scotland as to the town government arose from the exclusive character of the Belfast and Derry Corporation. You cannot restore, supposing you desire to do so, the police of those towns, nor could you secure the government of those towns at this moment by such exclusive corporations as exist there. That I think ought to be remedied.

167. Is it the fact in those towns that the great majority of occupiers who are qualified to vote under the different Acts under which they are, are Protestants?—It arises from that.

168. Therefore, the constituency being Protestant, they elect Protestant representatives?—Certainly; but I think it is just a very important place to introduce the School Board principle of voting.

169. If you extended the constituency then the Roman Catholic population would obtain representation?—Yes, but I think that a sudden revolution the other way would be just as bad. For instance, in the borough of Armagh to have the whole of 21 Protestant Commissioners put out and 21 Roman Catholic put in would not of itself contribute to peace and the protection of property, but I think having the whole depending upon one vote, so to speak, one way or the other, or else to have a fair proportion of Catholics getting in by having a certain number of Protestants voting for them; compromises of that sort are hard to carry out in Ulster; and to get over a similar difficulty the cumulative vote principle has been applied in England and Scotland. They return Roman Catholics on the School Board in Glasgow, and I think a system which has secured that object in Scotland would work satisfactorily in those northern towns, and it would work equally well in the southern towns, because it would secure to the Protestant minority, where large enough, a certain amount of representation by the cumulative vote.

Chairman—continued.

170. I do not quite understand the system which you proposed, because the principle of the cumulative School Board vote is to give a number of votes to each elector varying with the number of candidates to be elected; but I gather that you do not propose that; you propose a graduated scale of voting, depending upon the value of the property, or house, which the voter occupies?—No, not the occupier. I do not propose any multiple voting amongst occupiers. Each occupier should have only a single vote, but he should have cumulative votes for the number of candidates. I will explain how it will work in detail. In Dublin there are 15 wards. There would be 15 occupiers' representatives elected for those wards, voting exactly as at present, only with a much larger constituency: there would be 15 *ex officio* immediate lessors in the wards. It would be the largest proprietor in the ward, or his son, or his agent, if he is a justice of the peace. Then, elected on the School Board principle, there would be 15 occupiers for all Dublin, each man having 15 votes, so that a minority of any amount above 1-16th could return their man.

171. So that, so far as the occupier goes, you would apply the English School Board principle?—Yes; I would allow one occupier's representative from each ward, and the rest to be elected by the whole town. Then, amongst the immediate lessors, 15 would sit *ex officio* in Dublin, and the other 15 would be elected by immediate lessors and owners with multiple votes and cumulative votes.

172. Will you give the Committee an example of how the Dublin system of multiple and cumulative voting would work?—The object of multiple voting is to secure the representation, say, of a government department, because they pay the rates now; it would give, say, to Trinity College, or the railway companies, or other large proprietors, votes in proportion to their value. Having got votes in proportion to their value, then you want to secure that they shall not thereby return the whole 15 owners' representatives; that they shall have some representation, but not the whole number. Again, you give all the small immediate lessors or owners of a certain value votes, but you do not want, where property is very much sub-divided, that the small proprietors should return the whole of the owners' representatives. In some towns there is only one large proprietor, and a vast number of small owners.

173. Supposing a large owner having property which would entitle him under your system to 50 votes, and supposing 15 town councillors to be elected, would that person have his number of 50 votes multiplied by 15?—Yes.

174. While a small owner would simply have 15 votes?—Yes; each small owner would only have 15, and that allows the representation to follow exactly the way in which the property is divided; if there is only one large proprietor, and a vast number of small ones, he could only return one or two members to the Board.

175. Do not you propose to apply the principle of multiple votes to occupiers as well as to owners?—I believe that the principle of multiple votes to occupiers was intended as a protection of property. If you give half the Board definitely to property, then you have not to give the multiple votes to occupation; I think the idea of

Mr. W. N. Hancock, LL.D.

28 April 1876.

Chairman—continued.

of the occupation is to represent the inhabitants; property represents a check on the expenditure of the money, and the inhabitants are represented to see that the duty is performed, and to see that the people are accommodated.

176. If the owner pays one-half of the rate and the occupier the other half, the occupier of a large building, a factory, a brewery, or what not, will pay a very much larger amount of rates than the occupier of a single small house; but you propose, as I understand, to give the occupier who pays this very much larger amount of rates only the same voting power as the occupier who pays a very small amount, while in the case of owners you recognise a difference?—Yes; because you are starting from the existing system, in which the occupiers have the whole of it. There is no multiple voting at present, and therefore you are starting without it; if you give cumulative voting on both sides the advantage is that you do not bring either part directly up against the other. If you had cumulative voting amongst the occupiers, the wealthier occupiers could, by combining, always return two or three members to the Board, and those two or three added to property would give property sufficient protection without a preponderance; what you want is to give property protection without absolute preponderance.

Mr. *J. P. Corry*.

177. Could you put in statistics that you have worked out for any towns, say Dublin or Belfast, of what the result of such a system as that which you propose would be; are there any statistics now whereby such a system as that could be wrought out?—I have formed a very clear conception in my own mind of what it would be; I could draw it up, and the results could be worked out for one or two places very clearly.

Mr. *Butt*.

178. Do I clearly understand you, as part of your plan, to propose that certain individuals, whom you call *ex officio* because they have large property, are to nominate men either to be themselves members, or to nominate members?—Just as the grand jury is at present.

179. The principle is this: a certain person from having been the largest ratepayer is to be, you say, *ex officio*; he is to be, by virtue of being the largest ratepayer, a member of the corporation?—Yes.

180. And if he does not choose to take his position he is to nominate anyone he likes?—No; I limit it to a member of his family or his agent.

181. By absolute nomination?—Yes; but that agent or member of his family must be a magistrate.

182. Do you consider that that is the present Grand Jury system of Ireland, that a man nominates one of his family or his agent?—Where they are very large proprietors, if he does not attend himself, some member of his family or his agent is called upon the jury.

183. Does he nominate them?—No, he does not actually nominate them, but he practically nominates them.

Mr. *Bruen*.

184. You propose to have an equal division of the governing body; one-half to be elected by the owners, and the other half by the occupiers?—Yes.

Mr. Bruen—continued.

185. So that, no matter how many votes you give to the owners, they cannot elect more than half the body?—Certainly.

186. It is only between themselves that a difference of voting power will exist?—Yes.

187. And among the occupiers it would be the same; no matter how you distributed the votes to individual occupiers, the occupiers will constitute one half of the body?—Yes. Dublin is at present divided into 15 wards, and there would be 15 *ex officio*; 15 elected by the wards as at present, 15 elected by the occupiers on the School Board plan, and 15 elected by the immediate lessors on the School Board plan. In Limerick there are five wards, therefore there would be five *ex officio*, five elected by ward voting, as at present, and there would be 15 occupiers elected on the School Board plan, and 15 immediate lessors. Then in Cork there would be seven *ex officio*, seven elected by wards, 21 occupiers elected on the School Board plan and 21 immediate lessors elected on the School Board plan. In Belfast and Waterford there are five wards, and there would be five *ex officios*; five elected by the occupiers of wards, and 15 elected in each of the other two classes on the School Board principle. In Londonderry, Drogheda, and Wexford there would be three *ex officios*; three elected by wards, nine occupiers elected on the School Board principle, and nine immediate lessors on the School Board principle. In Kilkenny, Clonmel, and Sligo there are only two wards. There they would have two *ex officios*, two elected by wards, and ten elected in each of the other ways. In the small towns, for instance in Carlow, supposing the present system of wards, which is an exceptional thing, under the Act of 1854, were done away with, there would be one *ex officio*, one elected by the occupiers of the town, and ten occupiers elected by cumulative voting, and 10 immediate lessors elected by cumulative voting. In Downpatrick there would be the same proportion. In Kinsale there would be one *ex officio*, one elected as at present; seven occupiers' representatives by cumulative voting and seven immediate lessors. In Galway there would be one occupier's representative on voting as at present, one immediate lessor *ex officio*, and there would be 11 occupiers elected on the cumulative voting, and 11 immediate lessors. In Youghal there would be one immediate lessor *ex officio*, one occupier elected for the whole town, and there would be 10 occupiers elected by cumulative voting, and 10 immediate lessors.

Chairman.

188. Do you wish to make any further observations on that subject?—No, I think I have stated all that I intended to do. I have considered very carefully the proposals in Mr. Butt's Bill, to reduce the franchise in the other towns to that of Dublin, and I have considered very carefully the provisions in Mr. Bruen's Bill, also the proposal which has been made on the subject in England, and as the result of extremely careful consideration of the matter for some years, I have come to the conclusion that a combination of all those elements would work out a full and satisfactory result. The great thing that is wanted in Ireland is to have a representation of all classes, and to create a body of electors from which no one would be excluded from voting, and that no one class, whether it is from religion or whether it is from property, should have an absolute

Mr. W. N. Hancock, LL.D.

28 April 1876.

Chairman—continued.

absolute preponderance, and it occurred to me that this would be a way of securing that object; that it would secure a body in Ireland that would manage the town affairs, so that no class would be excluded, and no class would have an absolute preponderance. Considering the way in which Ireland is divided, in races and in religions between class and class, that seemed to me to be the best way of solving the question.

189. I presume that in the scheme which you have sketched out to the Committee, you do not bind yourself to any particular proportions; you have simply suggested a basis upon which it might be framed?—As to the point which the honourable Member for Belfast was asking about, I do not bind myself to those numbers; I merely give the figures that would work. I really think that in large towns the ward system should not be altogether overthrown, because it has certain merits in it, and therefore it ought to be preserved; but how far it should be preserved is a matter which would have to be considered from the new point of view. In the same way, I think the *ex officio* element has some merit in it, although the Committee of 1870 condemned it altogether. I think they were wrong in that. I think it has some elements in it which are very important to maintain; just as with the grand jury, that part of the grand jury system works very well, through inducing the large proprietors to attend, that I propose to take out from the existing arrangements that which works well in England and Scotland, and combine it into a system which will include them all; but the exact proportions in which they would have to be combined would have to be considered.

190. Does any observation occur to you as to the term for which town authorities are elected?—I think that the notion of permanence is a very important one, and not to have them changed once every year. I think that the notion of three years' service is right. Of course *ex officio* men would sit perpetually, and it would be only when a vacancy occurred, by death or otherwise, that there would be a change; therefore there need not be a periodical election for *ex officios*, and as to the other elements, the election would be reduced to every three years. I would suggest the occupiers for wards to sit for three years and then retire. I would suggest that the immediate lessors by cumulative voting should sit for three years, and the occupiers in the same way.

191. What is the term for which the town council are now elected?—Three years.

192. And they retire by rotation, do they not?—Yes; and I would preserve that idea of three years. Then the whole board would not be changed, you would never have more than one of the four elements of the board changed at one election.

193. What is the term for which under the Acts of 1828 and 1854 are elected?—The Commissioners of 1828 are for three years, and the whole board go out for re-election every third year, which is a very bad plan. In the case of the Town Commissioners, under the Act of 1854, only one-third go out every year; but in the town council I think it is different; one-fourth go out one year, and one-fourth another year; and the year that aldermen are elected one-half go out.

194. What is the term for which an alderman is elected?—Three years. I would preserve that triennial idea by having only one-third of these elected.

195. Do you wish to make any other suggestion to the Committee?—No, I think that is all.

Mr. *Butt*.

196. Do I understand you to say that the aldermen go out every three years?—That is my impression.

197. Have you studied these Acts at all?—I have.

198. You are not aware that an alderman in Dublin holds office for six years?—I was not aware of that.

199. Will you just read the 62nd section of the Municipal Corporations Act of 1840?—"And be it enacted, that on the 25th day of October in every third year after the year in which this Act shall come into operation in any borough, except in Dublin, Kilkenny, and Clonmel, one of the aldermen of every ward shall go out of office, and the burgesses then enrolled in the burgess roll for that ward shall elect an alderman to supply the vacancy, and in the City of Dublin the burgesses of each of the nine southern wards and six northern wards alternately, shall separately elect in each third subsequent year the alderman of that ward, and in each of the boroughs of Kilkenny and Clonmel the burgesses of each ward alternately shall separately elect in each third subsequent year the aldermen of that ward."

200. Do you see now, that all the aldermen in Dublin continue in office for six years?—I do not quite see that.

201. Can you inform the Committee what is the qualification of a burgess in the City of Dublin at present?—Every male person of full age who occupies a house, warehouse, counting-house, or shop, having occupied during two years and eight months.

202. Where do you find two years and eight months?—It is two years, and the time elapsing from the beginning of the year to the 31st of August.

203. Will you tell the Committee the legal qualification?—It is that and the next two preceding years.

204. Is this the qualification: "Every male person of full age, who on the last day of August in any year shall have occupied any house, warehouse, counting-house, or shop, within such borough of Dublin during that year, and the whole of each of the two preceding years, and also during the time of such occupation shall have been an inhabited householder within the said borough, or within seven statute miles of the said borough of Dublin, shall, if duly enrolled in that year according to the provisions of the said recited Acts, be a burgess of such borough, and member of the body corporate of the mayor, aldermen, and burgesses of such borough. Provided always that no such person shall be enrolled in any year from and after the present year, unless he shall have been rated in respect of such premises so occupied by him within the said borough, to all rates made for the relief of the poor of the electoral division or union wherein such premises are situated during the time of his occupation as aforesaid"?—That is two years and eight months.

205. "And unless he shall have paid, on or before the last day of August as aforesaid, all such of the rates, cesses, and taxes specified in the schedules

Mr. *Butt*—continued.

schedules to this Act annexed, as shall have become payable by him (if any) in respect of the said premises, except such as shall become payable within six calendar months next before the said last day of August:" you say that a rating of any amount would qualify him?—Yes.

206. Can you inform the Committee where, in the city of Dublin, there are any restrictions upon the rating?—Under the Parliamentary Voters Act they are to be rated down to 4 *l.*

207. Is that the only restriction that is on the rating in the city of Dublin?—Under the Municipal Rates Act the lessor pays if he is rated below 8 *l.* Then there is also a restriction about houses let in tenements.

208. Is this the restriction as to rating, the 63rd section of the Collection of Rates in the City of Dublin Act, chapter 91, of 12 & 13 Vict? —Yes.

209. Will you be so good as to read it?—"The owners of all rateable property, of which the full net annual value does not exceed the sum of 8 *l.*, or which are let to weekly or monthly tenants, or in separate apartments, shall be rated to and pay the rates by this Act directed, to be made instead of the occupiers thereof."

210. Then in the case of a house that is let by the month, the occupier is not rated?—No, he is not.

Chairman.

211. Whatever the value?—No, "or which are let to weekly or monthly tenants, or in separate apartments, shall be rated to and pay the rates by this Act directed to be made."

Mr. *Butt.*

212. Were you not in error in supposing that the rating to the municipal rates was different from the rating to the poor law in Dublin, and can you inform the Committee whether in the city of Dublin there is a different rating for the municipal rates and for Parliamentary rates? —There is a different provision for the poor law.

213. For the rating of owners?—Yes.

214. Can a man be separately rated in Dublin to the poor rate and to the municipal rate?—Yes.

215. Under what statute or law?—Under the Representation of the People Act it only applies to the poor rate.

216. Does not the Collection of Rates Act apply to the poor rate too?—Yes, but the rating of property was not affected by the Representation of the People Act.

217. You think that the rating for municipal purposes was not altered?—So I was told by the department, that the Representation of the People Act only touched the poor rate; it did not touch the others.

218. You gave an answer before, that the difference between the number of burgesses and the number of occupiers entitled to the Parliamentary franchise was accounted for by the difference of rating?—No; it struck me as being very remarkable, and I went to the department, and I asked them to explain how it happened that the number of burgesses was so small, and what they called my attention to was that the Representation of the People Act had not dealt with this matter.

218*. If a person is rated to the poor to any amount he is entitled to the franchise?—As a matter of fact be is not.

219. Is he not entitled as a matter of fact under this Act to the municipal franchise, if he is rated to any amount?—I believe so, but he does not get it.

220. But do not you know that it is so?—He is entitled.

221. How could there be a person entitled to the Parliamentary franchise who would not also be entitled to the municipal franchise?—That is the construction that they have put upon it.

222. If a man has the Parliamentary franchise, must he not be rated?—Yes.

223. And must he not be rated to 4 *l.*?—Yes.

224. And if he is rated, and rated to 4 *l.*, is he not entitled to the municipal franchise?—They have not held it so.

225. If he has the Parliamentary franchise, is it not conclusive proof that he is rated to 4 *l.*?—Yes.

226. Is not every man who is rated to 4 *l.*, if he has occupied long enough, entitled to the municipal franchise?—That is what I thought; but when I went to the department I found that the Representation of the People Act had not dealt with it very clearly, and that the construction put upon it was that unless they claim they do not put any of those people on the rate book.

227. On which rate book?—On the municipal rate book.

228. Surely the municipal rate book has nothing to do with it?—Or even on the poor-rate book.

229. Do you mean to say that they do not put on this rate book anyone under 8 *l.*; or what exactly did they tell you at the Collector General's Office about it?—They did not go minutely into it. When I came to the conclusion of recommending a balance of property and no restriction upon the occupier, the exact qualification of Dublin ceased, from my point of view, to have any importance. I came to the conclusion that by giving property one-half of the representation, you might go down in the direction of occupiers as low as possible, and therefore the limit of Dublin came to be of no importance. If you were to balance the property in Dublin by any limit it would be of importance.

Mr. W. N. *Hancock*, LL.D.

24 April 1876.

Tuesday, 2nd May 1876.

MEMBERS PRESENT:

Sir Michael Hicks Beach.
Mr. Brooks.
Mr. Bruen.
Mr. Butt.
Mr. Collins.
Mr. J. P. Corry.
Mr. Gibson.
Sir Arthur Guinness.
Mr. Kavanagh.
Mr. Charles Lewis.
Sir Joseph M'Kenna.
Mr. Murphy.
Mr. Rathbone.
Dr. Ward.

SIR MICHAEL HICKS BEACH, IN THE CHAIR.

Mr. WILLIAM NEILSON HANCOCK, LL.D., called in; and further Examined.

Mr. *Hancock*, LL.D.

2 May 1876.

Chairman.

230. You have a Return, I believe, which you wish to hand into the Committee?—Yes, there was a Return which the honourable Member for Liverpool asked me for on the last day, which I made accordingly. It is a Return as to the towns showing the number of authorities that they are under (*delivering in the same*).

Mr. DENIS MOYLAN, called in; and Examined.

Mr. *Moylan.*

Chairman.

231. I BELIEVE you are the Collector General of Rates in Dublin?—Yes.

232. What is the Act under which you work?—It is the Rates Act of Dublin, the 12 & 13 Vict. c. 91, s. 63.

233. Can you describe to the Committee what your duties are under that Act?—The general superintendence of the office, the making of assessments on the 1st January in the different departments. The poor law unions, the corporation, and all of them send in their estimates.

234. Will you describe to the Committee the system of collection of rates in Dublin which you work?—There are 10 collectors; some of the wards have one collector and others two.

235. The Committee are informed that one of the senior clerks of your office is present, who might, perhaps, assist you in giving evidence, would you desire that he should be called with you and give evidence together with you; the Committee simply wish to arrive at a correct conclusion?—I think it would be better to examine me. Mr. Perry, being a mere writing clerk, could give no information.

Sir Joseph M'Kenna.

236. Would it not assist you in giving your evidence to the Committee, if he were beside you in order to supply you with detailed information when you would have occasion to refer to him?—You asked me about the duties. I have to see to the money collected by the different officers; all moneys collected in the office by the collectors must be lodged each day in the Bank of Ireland, and the bankers' receipts produced to me.

Chairman.

237. That is not quite the point which I wish to ascertain from you; I asked you first the name of the Act under which the rates are collected in the City of Dublin by your office; can you tell the Committee what system that Act supplanted; how many rates were levied in the City of Dublin?—Yes, I can tell that. The Act is the 12 & 13 Vict. c. 91. The rates collected are the poor rate for the North Union and for the South; the grand jury cess, the improvement rate, the water rates, the burial rate, which is a very small amount, and it is not struck annually; then there is a bridge tax, which was not struck last year, and there is a vestry cess which has nearly expired now; it is but a small amount. There is the police rate, which is 8 *d.* in the pound, and the main drainage rate, which is abandoned for the present as the corporation do not intend to go on with it. Those are all the rates.

238. Before the passing of the Act which you have quoted, by whom were those rates collected?—By different collectors; I cannot answer how many there were, but there was a grand jury collector, and several others. They were all consolidated when the office was appointed.

239. There was a poor rate collector, I suppose, a grand jury cess collector, and a town council collector?—There were several collectors; I have no personal knowledge of how many.

240. You have mentioned all the rates which you collect; can you tell us who the authorities are that levy those rates?—On the 10th of December I get estimates from the two Poor Law Unions and from the Police Commissioners; the

Mr. *Moylan*

8 May 1876.

Chairman—continued.

the improvement rate is always stationary of 2 *s.*

241. What body is authorised to levy the improvement rate; who is entrusted with the expenditure under the Improvement Act?—The corporation; there is a grand jury rate of the corporation also.

242. Is there any poundage limit fixed by Act of Parliament to the improvement rate?—It is limited to 2 *s.*

243. Is there any poundage limit fixed to the grand jury cess, as there is to the improvement rate?—No.

244. You have mentioned the water rate; who is authorised to levy that?—It is fixed at 3 *d.* in the pound and 1 *s.*; and there is a meter rate for manufacturers.

245. Is that levied by the corporation also?—Yes, by the waterworks department.

246. Do you mean that the domestic water rate is fixed at 1 *s.*, and the public water rate is fixed at 3 *d.*?—Yes.

247. You mentioned the burial rate; what is that?—That is a mere trifle of 1 *d.* or one halfpenny in the pound.

248. Who expends it?—The corporation.

249. Do you know under what Statute?—I do not; they send me the estimate.

250. How and where is it spent?—It is spent by the corporation.

251. What for?—For the burial of the poor.

Mr. M. P. V. Taaffe, called in; and Examined.

Mr. *Taaffe.*

Chairman.

252. What position do you hold?—Chief Clerk in the Collector General's office.

253. Can you tell us anything about the burial rate?—I believe it is expended by the Public Health Committee of the Corporation as the sanitary authority.

254. (To Mr. *Moylan.*) There is the bridge tax, who is that expended by?—The corporation; but there was no rate for that last year; there will, I am sure, next year, as they are engaged to re-construct Carlisle Bridge, and erect a new bridge near the Custom House; that goes to the credit of the Port and Docks Board. I allocate to the Port and Docks Board the amount of the collection.

255. (To Mr. *Taaffe.*) Is it levied for the maintenance of the bridges, do you know?—It was levied for re-building Essex Bridge.

Mr. *Brooks.*

256. I do not think that it is any part of the Collector General's duty to apply this money; he has simply to put the money in the bank to the credit of the grand jury, or whoever it is; in this case he does nothing but simply lodge it to the credit of this board?—Yes.

Chairman.

257. I understand that the corporation levy the bridge tax, and pay it over to the Port and Docks Board?—It is settled by presentment before one of the judges of the Queen's Bench.

258. Is it a part of the grand jury cess?—(Mr. *Moylan.*) It is to meet the assessment. (Mr. *Taaffe.*) No, I think not.

259. Is there any limit fixed by law to the amount of the bridge tax?—The rate for rebuilding Carlisle Bridge was limited to 6 *d.* in the pound, to be distributed over three years at 2 *d.* in the pound.

260. Was that by a special Act of Parliament?—The question was argued before, I think, Judge Fitzgerald, and settled by him.

Mr. *Dease.*

261. Was it done under the General Grand Jury Acts?—I cannot say. I know that there was a long discussion, and that the representatives of Rathmines and all the townships attended.

Mr. *Brooks.*

262. There was a Provisional Order, was there not?—Yes; Mr. Stokes attended, and several others, as representatives of the townships.

Chairman.

263. (To Mr. *Moylan.*) Who has the power to levy the vestry cess?—The corporation, by estimate; but it is very small.

264. Is there any limit fixed by law to that?—I believe not, for it is always a mere trifle, a penny or so. (Mr. *Taaffe.*) It is merely to pay off pensioners under the old vestry cess abolition rate; it is only 1 *d.* in the pound, and it is only levied probably once in five years. (Mr. *Moylan.*) They are temporary charges, and they are all dying out.

Chairman.

265. The main drainage rate is levied by the corporation, you say?—Yes.

266. Is there any limit fixed by law to that?—I believe not; I am not aware of any; but it was not collected last year.

267. Can you tell us what the total amount levied by you in the last year was for all those rates?—I think it was about 275,000 *l.* for several years; it varied between 270,000 *l.* and 300,000 *l.*; it is not always fixed; 270,000 *l.* would be, perhaps, a fair average. (Mr. *Taaffe.*) It ranged from 213,000 *l.* in 1870 up to 270,000 *l.*, one year; but has never been so high as that, except on one occasion.

Chairman.

268. Then from 213,000 *l.* to 270,000 *l.* is raised on the rates annually?—Yes. (Mr. *Moylan.*) I can give the exact amount collected in the years 1870 to 1874. In the year 1870 the amount was 213,000 *l.*; in 1871, 220,000 *l.*; in 1872, 220,000 *l.*; in 1873, 258,000 *l.*; in 1874, 276,000 *l.* I have not got it for 1875, but it must be rather under 1874.

269. What is the total valuation on which you levy those rates?—I have not got that with me.

270. Can you tell the Committee what the amount in the pound was, in the years you have quoted, for all those rates?—(Mr. *Taaffe.*) In the year 1870 the north poor rate was 2 *s.* 2 *d.* in the pound, and the south poor rate was 2 *s.* 6 *d.*; the grand jury cess was 1 *s.* 7 *d.*; the improvement rate, 2 *s.*; the police rate, 8 *d.*; the sewer rate,

Mr *Moylan* and Mr. *Taaffe*.

2 May 1876.

Chairman—continued.

rate, 4 *d.*; the domestic water rate, 1 *s.*; and the public water rate, 3 *d.* The last five rates, commencing with the improvement rate, were at their maximum.

Mr. *Murphy.*

271. Those five rates then are limited?—Yes, they are.

Chairman.

272. Each of the figures that you have given is the poundage figure, is it not?—Yes.

273. What is the total for that year of all the rates that you have named?—It is different on each side of the city. It was 8 *s.* on the north side, and 8 *s.* 4 *d.* on the south in 1870.

274. Now will you give us the same figures for the following year, 1871?—The sewer rate was 4 *d.* in the pound, the police tax, 8 *d.*; the grand jury cess, 1 *s.* 7 *d.*; the poor rate on the north side was 2 *s.* 2 *d.*, and on the south side 2 *s.* 8 *d.*; the improvement rate 2 *s.* on each side, the water rates were the same, and the total is the same.

Sir *J. M'Kenna.*

275. You appear to have collected in 1870, 213,000 *l.*, and in 1871, 220,000 *l.* although the poor rates in both years appear to have been the same?—There must have been some exceptional payments in the latter year, some case that was in dispute and unpaid in the year 1870.

276. Then those are not the levies which we took down from Mr. Moylan in the first instance, they are the sums collected?—Yes, they are the sums collected. (Mr. *Moylan.*) There was one year we recovered a large sum from the Port and Docks Board.

277. In this list that we have been preparing of 1870 and 1871, we have not got the port and docks levies?—No; I should not like to be taken as being perfectly accurate after such a lapse of time; but it is very easy to get the figures.

Chairman.

278. Do you collect for the Port and Docks Board?—No; those are the rates assessed on the property of the Port and Docks Board, and which were disputed. There were two actions, one against the Corporation for rates on the water mains, and the other against the Port and Docks Board.

Sir *J. M'Kenna.*

279. You will have to account for the difference in the sums raised by the difference between 596,000 *l.*, which is the total valuation of 1870, and the annual valuation to be put in for 1871, owing to having succeeded in making other property liable?—I should prefer, if the Committee would allow me, to write for the correct figures, and furnish them to you.

Mr. *Butt.*

280. What property have the Port and Docks Board that is rated?—They have got the Custom House, and various stores down on the North Wall, and the tolls and dues that were included in the assessment.

281. Always?—No; before the property came into the possession of the Port and Docks Board, they were regularly paid by Mr. Scovell; but now they are not paid.

Chairman.

282. Will you continue the figures for the following year, 1872?—Will you allow me to furnish the Committee with a Return, and thus get the correct figures?

Sir *Arthur Guinness.*

283. Up to when can you furnish them?—I can furnish them up to the end of last year, 1875.

284. The honourable Member for Youghal called your attention to the difference in the amount collected in two subsequent years, when the rate in the pound happened to be the same; what sort of proportion of the rate which is struck is generally uncollected?—It is always under 10 per cent.; that is, 10 per cent. is supposed to be allowed for non-occupancies, losses through bankruptcies, and such casualties; it has never reached 10 per cent.

Chairman.

285. Is there any particular class of property from which you find a difficulty in collecting?—Yes, two classes of property, one good and another bad. We find a serious difficulty in collecting rates in many places, on account of the bill of sale system which prevails very largely in Dublin. Bills of sale passed by the occupiers, and when warrants are out for rates they are presented, and they shut us out at once.

286. Will you explain how that prevents your levying the rates?—Under the Collection of Rates Act, as at present, the only goods that can be seized for rates in the City of Dublin are those belonging to, and the absolute property of the persons rated. The occupier is the person rated; but he gives a bill of sale on his furniture to a certain person, who does not reside on the premises, and consequently the property cannot be touched, and the rates remain uncollected. There are instances of that in some of the principal streets of Dublin, and it is one of the things which the Collector General suggested in that Amendment Bill, which he forwarded to the Irish Office, should be dealt with. (Mr. *Moylan.*) We believe that several of the bills of sale are fraudulent.

Mr. *Kavanagh.*

287. (To Mr. *Taaffe.*) Is the 213,000 in 1870 and the 276,000 in 1874 the net amount collected minus 10 per cent., or is it the gross sum?—It is the net amount collected; with reference to the difficulty of collection, there is another class of property, namely, tenement houses, on which there is an enormous quantity of rates lost.

Chairman.

288. How is that?—From the impossibility of collecting them from the occupiers. In fact the immediate lessors, who, under the existing state of the law are the persons liable, let those houses at rack rents to persons of no substance whatever and so escape their liability. There are men in Dublin some of them with as many as 20 houses who are quite able to pay themselves if they were liable, but they are not the immediate lessors, although they really have a beneficial interest in the property, but they never pay a farthing of rates.

Mr. *Bruen.*

289. Does that difficulty exist to a very large extent in Dublin more than in the rest of the country?—

Mr. *Moylan* and Mr. *Taaffe*.

3 May 1876.

Mr. *Bruen*—continued.

country?—Yes, there are a very great number of such cases.

Dr. *Ward*.

290. Who are liable for the rates on those houses?—The immediate lessors; the 63rd section of the 12th and 13th of Victoria, where houses are set to weekly or monthly tenants or in separate apartments, makes only the immediate lessor liable for the rates and not the tenant, unless the immediate lessor fails to pay; but virtually the occupier is not liable because he has nothing in the world to seize; at least he cannot be made amenable.

291. Then you cannot proceed against him?—Yes, we can proceed against him, we can collect the weekly rents when it is possible to get them. But persons occupying one room in a barrack-house have nothing on which to levy the rates, and if we get a warrant against them, and if they attempt to pay, the system is that the landlord immediately ejects them, and they find another place and he finds new tenants.

Chairman.

292. You stated that there were a good many cases of that kind in Dublin, can you tell the Committee at all what proportion they bear to the total number of ratings?—I cannot say that exactly, but they are a very large number in most of the poor portions of the city. (Mr. *Moylan*.) I cannot add the exact number, but I know it to be a vast loss to the ratepayers of Dublin through the action of those fraudulent house jobbers.

293. (To Mr. *Taaffe*.) Could you tell the Committee at all how much rate you consider is annually lost in that way?—I should say that the amount of rate lost is fully equal to that lost by bankruptcies and vacant houses; 10 per cent. is allowed for vacancies, and the loss by bankruptcy, and all that. It never reaches that; but if we say 5 per cent. of the rates are lost for those tenement houses and bills of sale, I think it is not at all an exaggeration.

294. I understood you to say that the total loss from all causes averaged about 10 per cent.?—That is what is allowed, but it has never reached that. (Mr. *Moylan*.) Perhaps 8 per cent. would be more correct.

295. (To Mr. *Taaffe*.) Of that 8 per cent., do you think about 4 per cent. would be due to the cause which you have just named?—I do, at least 4 per cent.

Mr. *Brooks*.

296. Do you mean 4 per cent. due to the destitution of the occupier, and 4 per cent. to the bill of sale?—No, 4 per cent. due to both.

297. I understood you to say that you failed to collect the rates, because the occupiers were destitute, and there was no property to seize?—Yes; but there is another cause of loss, vacant houses and bankruptcies.

Chairman.

298. I understood you to say that you attribute 4 per cent. of the 8 per cent. annual loss, to this system of tenement houses and bills of sale?—Yes, quite so.

299. Will you tell the Committee what persons in Dublin are liable to pay the rates which you collect?—The occupiers in all houses and

Chairman—continued.

premises valued over 8 *l.*, who are yearly tenants.

300. And in the case of premises valued below 8 *l.*, who is liable?—The owner, under the 63rd section of the Collection of Rates Act.

301. Will you read that section?—It is the Collection of Rates Act, the 12 & 13 Vict. c. 91, s. 63: "And be it enacted that the owners of all rateable property, of which the full net annual value does not exceed the sum of 8 *l.*, or which are let to weekly or monthly tenants, or in separate apartments, shall be rated to, and pay the rates by this Act directed to be made, instead of the occupiers thereof."

302. Of course you enter upon the rate-book the names of all occupiers of property above the value of 8 *l.*?—Yes, certainly, except in cases where the occupiers are weekly or monthly tenants; you see that that is part of the section.

303. Do you always enter the names of the owners of property below that value?—No.

304. What entries do you make with regard to property below the value of 8 *l.*?—We enter the name of the owner in every case?—In cases where the value is over 4 *l.* and not higher than 8 *l.*, and the occupiers are yearly tenants, we rate the occupier as well as the owner in a separate column of the rate-book.

305. You levy the rate from the owner?—We believe the owner to be the party still liable.

306. But you enter the name of the occupier?—We do. That is done under the advice of the present Judge Barry; I think he was Solicitor General at the time.

Mr. *J. P. Corry*.

307. Then do I understand that you have two columns in your rate-book?—Yes, we have.

Chairman.

308. Will you produce your rate-book?—Yes (*producing the same*).

309. Will you give me instances of what you have stated from the rate-book?—It is the rate-book for the last three years, 1873, 1874, and 1875; there is an instance of Patrick Coffey, the occupier, where the house was valued at 6 *l.*; we find the occupier is rated as well as the owner.

310. I see that in that same rate made on the 1st of January 1873, Patrick Coffey was the occupier, and he and the owner, James Kenny, were both of them rated; but in the rate made on the 1st of January 1874, I find Patrick Coffey's name is left out, he having then left, and James Kenny, as the owner, is rated alone; and in the following year's rate-book, on the 1st of January 1875, the house appears to be still vacant, James Kenny, the owner, being alone rated?—It is not necessarily vacant, but there is not a yearly tenant in it in occupation.

311. Immediately one tenant leaves, do not you substitute the name of the in-coming tenant for the one who has left?—Yes, if he be entitled, but the man who left was a yearly tenant, which his successor may not have been, and then he would not be entitled to be rated; possibly he has been succeeded by two or three.

Mr. *J. P. Corry*.

312. How do you find out how a tenant holds?—It is the duty of the collector to inquire.

Mr. *Moylan* and Mr. *Taaffe*.

9 May 1876.

Mr. *Gibson*.

313. Is that a statutable duty; is that pointed out by any Act of Parliament?—That I cannot say; it is a portion of his duty to keep a correct return on the rate-book of the names of all persons in his district.

Chairman.

314. Here I see a house occupied on the 1st of January 1873, by John Reilly, of the value of 6 *l*., but no owner appears to have been rated for that house either in 1873 or 1875; how do you explain that?—That John Reilly himself is the owner.

Sir *J. M'Kenna*.

315. Why is he not rated *qua* owner?—We never put the name of the same person in both columns.

Dr. *Ward*.

316. Why do you prefer putting them in as occupier instead of owner?—Because we should put them in as occupier to return them on the Parliamentary List.

Chairman.

317. That refers to tenements above or below 8 *l*. in value; but you have also told us that the owners of all rateable property let to weekly or monthly tenants, or in separate apartments, are rated instead of the occupier?—That is so.

318. Do you enter the names of the occupiers in the rate book in that case?—No.

319. Why not?—Because it would be absurd to rate weekly and monthly tenants to a yearly rate.

320. Does any question of franchise come in there?—I am not aware of it.

321. As any rate you do not consider yourself bound to enter their names?—We have acted upon the advice of the present Judge Barry in not doing so.

322. You told us that you experience great difficulty in obtaining the payment of rates from owners of that kind of property, but I suppose that there must be property of very considerable value in Dublin let to weekly or monthly tenants?—There is, but there is a very considerable part of it paid for.

323. Then it is entirely the low class of this kind of property in which you find a difficulty?—Yes.

Dr. *Ward*.

324. Because in the better class you could seize the property of the occupier?—Yes; but there are very many landlords of an excessively low class of property who pay the rates.

Chairman.

325. The 66th clause of your Act provides, "That the occupiers of any rateable property may demand to be assessed for the same, and to pay the rates in respect thereof made by the said bodies politic or corporate, boards, commissioners, or persons, and applotted, levied, and collected under the authority of this Act, and the Collector General shall assess every such occupier, so long as he duly pays the said rates, anything hereinbefore contained notwithstanding;" do any occupiers take advantage of that clause?—No; in my experience I have only met with two or three cases. It is availed of by agents who tender the poor rates for Parliamentary purposes. They hand in a list of claims to be rated, and they tender a portion of the poor rate, and that, I believe, is held by the revising barrister to be a sufficient qualification without their being rated at all, but we never get the money. If, when the time is approaching for the qualification for the Parliamentary franchise, the agent tenders a number of rating notices, and a sum of money is tendered for the poor rates, I believe that is held by the revising barrister to be sufficient to justify him in putting men on the list.

326. Does that happen in many cases?—I never counted the number of claims. Every year there are a number of them handed in, a great number of them not being *bonâ fide* claims at all.

327. What course do you follow in that case?—We have them all inquired into, and if we find that a man has a right to be rated, we rate him. As a general rule we get very little assistance in preparing the rate book by those claims.

Sir *Arthur Guinness*.

328. Is that for Parliamentary purposes, and not for municipal; have you found that done for municipal purposes?—Yes, both for Parliamentary and municipal; a number of claims are served by the agents on both sides.

329. Is that done to a considerable extent in the municipal matters?—Yes, there are a great number.

330. Is that every year or every three years, or in contemplation of an election?—Every year, but not every year in every ward, because it depends upon what is to come off in that particular ward, or how it is worked there, at all events.

331. Is it the agents of the landlord, or the agents of the registration associations that do this?—The agents of the registration associations. (Mr. *Moylan*.) There are two associations, one called Liberal and the other Conservative.

Mr. *Butt*.

332. (To Mr. *Taaffe*.) Does the rating of an 8 *l*. house depend upon the 63rd section of the Collection of Rates Act, which you have read?—Yes.

333. Are you aware that that section is repealed?—No.

334. Will you read the 19th section of the Representation of the People Act?—"From and after the passing of this Act, Section 116 of the said Act of the 13th and 14th years of Her present Majesty, chapter 69, and so far as regards poor rate in respect of lands, tenements and hereditaments of which the nett annual value shall be more than 4 *l*., the 63rd section of the Act of the 12th and 13th years of the reign of Her present Majesty, chapter 91, shall be and the same are hereby repealed; and whenever the nett annual value of the whole of the rateable hereditaments in any electoral division situate wholly or in part in any of the boroughs of Dublin, Cork, Limerick, Belfast, or Waterford, occupied by any person or persons having no greater estate or interest therein than a tenancy from year to year as holding under a lease or agreement, leases or agreements made after the 24th day of August 1843 shall not exceed 4 *l*., the poor rate in respect of such property shall, after the passing of this Act be made on the immediate lessor or lessors of such person or persons, and if at the time

Mr. *Moylan* and Mr. *Taaffe*.

2 May 1876.

Mr. *Butt*—continued.

time of making any such rate the name of the immediate lessor be not accurately known to the persons making the rate, it shall be sufficient to describe him therein as the immediate lessor."

335. Does not that section oblige you to rate to the poor rate every occupier who is rated over 4 *l.*?—Yes, where he is a yearly tenant, and we do do that.

336. Is not the section repealed as to the poor rate?—I will not attempt to form an opinion; all I can do is to act on the advice of counsel to whom the question was submitted, and we have done that.

337. What I want to know is, do you know that as a matter of practice they rate the occupier of property between 4 *l.* and 8 *l.* to the poor rates?—If he be a yearly tenant, and not otherwise.

338. But if he is not a yearly tenant you do not rate him?—We do not, and for the reason that I gave the Chief Secretary. I quoted the exact words of Judge Barry, that it would be an absurdity to rate a weekly or monthly tenant to a yearly rate. He advised that we should not do so, and we do not do so.

339. What proportion do you think, taking any one of these rate books, there are of persons rated above 4 *l.* who are weekly or monthly tenants, and so excluded from the rate?—I do not exactly understand your question; I say that there are no weekly or monthly tenants rated.

340. Have you a return which was made out for Dublin, specially showing how many were excluded from the rate?—Yes (*delivering a paper to the honourable Member*).

341. I see here is a return of "the number of tenements valued over 4 *l.* in respect of which at the time of transmitting the list," (from the Collector General to the town clerk, according to the Representation of the People Act,) "the owner was rated instead of the occupier in the books of the Collector General in accordance with the provisions of the 63rd section of the Act of 1849, providing for the collection of rates in the City of Dublin, specifying the numbers respectively in which the owner was so rated; on account of the value not exceeding 8 *l.*, nil; on account of their being let in separate apartments, 3,984; on account of their being let to weekly or monthly tenants, 1,316;" is that correct?—That is correct.

342. Then there were 1,316 persons left off the roll of Parliamentary electors, on account of their being let to weekly or monthly tenants?—There were that number of houses in which the occupier was not rated for that cause.

343. Could you tell me, does that occur in houses of high value generally?—No.

344. What class of houses does that generally occur in; could you give us any idea of what class of people they are that are over 4 *l.*?—I think that there are very few of them over 10 *l.* or 12 *l.* let to weekly or monthly tenants.

345. Are not some of them as high as 30 *l.* or 40 *l.* omitted from the rate on that account?—I think very few.

346. How do you ascertain whether they are let to weekly or monthly tenants?—The collector makes inquiry. We find in a great many cases where there are houses let to weekly or monthly tenants that the landlords of those houses have a lot of them, and they come in and pay for them

Mr. *Butt*—continued.

all together, and in that way we ascertain that the information obtained by the collector was correct.

347. Do you then assume that if the landlord pays the rate it is less than a yearly letting?—If he assert that it is so we can judge pretty well the class of house.

348. As a matter of fact, if a landlord pays the rates, is he not almost invariably rated?—No.

349. Are you sure of that?—I am.

350. Then it is the collector who ascertains whether it is let to a weekly or monthly tenant, or not?—It is his duty to do so.

351. And it depends upon the report which you get from him, whether you rate the person or not?—Certainly.

352. Who appoints the collectors?—The Lord Lieutenant.

353. And then it rests entirely with them whether a person is rated or not?—Yes, it does.

354. With regard to the collection of rates, what is the difficulty that you have in enforcing the rates from the immediate lessors?—The class of immediate lessors of whom I am speaking let their houses, and supposing that 50 *l.* a year would be got out of their weekly rents, instead of paying an agent 1 *l.* a week or 5 *s.* a week, or whatever the case might be, for collecting the rents, the landlord lets the house for a year or two or for three years at a rent which leaves him only the agent's fees, and that man has nothing himself on which to levy.

355. Whom do you rate then?—We must rate that man, he is the immediate lessor of the occupant.

356. Then the evil that you point out is that a landlord can evade, and does evade the payment of rates and taxes by substituting a middleman?—Yes, a sham immediate lessor; a middleman.

357. Who is a man of straw?—Yes, for the purpose of evading the rate.

358. Does that prevail to a large extent?—It does.

Sir *J. M'Kenna*.

359. As I understand it is a little more than that, because this middle-man is not liable, no matter whether he be a man of ability, or not?—Yes, he is liable.

360. I thought you said that only the immediate lessor is liable?—He is the immediate lessor of the occupier.

Mr. *Butt*.

361. The immediate lessor is the person who is immediately over the occupier, is he not?—Yes.

362. That man of straw is substituted between the real owner and the occupier, and he becomes the immediate lessor?—Yes, he does.

363. As a rule he is not liable?—No.

364. But the tenant is liable in that case?—Yes.

365. Why cannot you get at him?—For several reasons; first of all, instead of allowing us to take out a summons and to make an attempt to seize, if they pay their weekly rent over to the collector, the landlord immediately serves them with a notice to quit, in a great number of instances, so that it is quite impossible that we can enforce the payments. Of course they want to be on good terms with their landlord, and to help him to cheat us.

366. With

Mr. *Moylan* and Mr *Taaffe*.

8 May 1876.

Mr. *Butt*—continued.

366. With regard to the bill of sale; a bill of sale is, I suppose, according to law, an obstacle to a distress for rates?—It is; we cannot distrain on anything except the goods of the party rated.

367. You can distrain on them, can you not, wherever you find them?—Yes.

368. But you cannot distrain on any other person's goods that are on the premises?—No.

Dr. *Ward*.

369. That bill of sale must be dated previous to the assessment, must it not?—That I cannot tell; a bill of sale may last for several assessments.

Mr. *Murphy*.

370. Does any means strike you whereby, if this fagot or surreptitious immediate lessor exists, the real lessor can be got at?—A Draft Bill prepared by the law agent of the Collector General of Rates, and which has been forwarded to the Chief Secretary, suggested the only means that we can think of.

371. What were those means?—That the person in beneficial receipt of the rack rent should be liable; that the premises, in other words, should be in some way got at as they are in various townships. It is only in the city of Dublin that that state of things exists, so far as we can discover. This is the section which was proposed by the collector general: "In every case in which the immediate lessor of any property is rated under the provisions of the principal Act, and such immediate lessor is liable to pay a rack-rent in respect of the said premises, the person entitled to receive the said rack-rent shall, if the immediate lessor shall for 14 days after such notice in writing as is mentioned in the 53rd section of the principal Act, shall have been served personally on the immediate lessor, or left at his usual abode or last known place of residence, make default in paying said rates, the collector general may serve in the same manner a notice on the person entitled to receive the rack-rent a notice in writing stating that the immediate lessor has made such default as aforesaid in paying the said rates, and stating the particulars of the same, proceed to recover the said rates, or the part thereof remaining unpaid, from the person entitled to receive the same rack-rent."

372. You stated that at certain times of the year, in certain wards, there were frequent tenders made to the collector of a proportion of the poor-rate to which certain premises were liable for the purpose of enabling the occupier to get upon the municipal roll or the Parliamentary roll, as the case may be?—Yes.

373. I think you added that you very seldom got payment?—We never get payment.

374. If the agent tendered the amount, how is it that you do not get payment?—Because when there is an attempt made to receive the money they withdraw the tender at once; the money is merely handed to the agent to exhibit, and to make the tender a legal one.

375. Under those circumstances, do you say that the revising barrister feels himself justified in putting that man upon the rate-book?—I am informed that that is the practice.

Mr. *Butt*.

376. But if you said that you would take the money, has he refused to pay?—We frequently say we will take it. I have frequently tried it myself. It would take in some instances probably a week to calculate the amount up to the day on which the tender was made, and to fill in the receipts for all the persons who are claimants; and the agents know perfectly well that we cannot do that on the moment.

Mr. *Murphy*.

377. At all events, the machinery by which it is done is fruitless, so far as you are concerned, and it enables the party to get upon the roll?—Perfectly so; there is no intention of paying the money.

378. You stated that the police tax in Dublin is 8 *d.*, and that it is limited to that amount?—Yes, it extends beyond Dublin; it extends to the entire metropolitan police district, which is not Dublin proper.

379. Am I right in assuming that there is such a thing in Dublin as a hackney carriage tax?—Yes, I believe so; I have no doubt that it is so.

380. Do you know to what the payment of that tax is applied?—No, I do not know; we do not collect it at all.

381. You gave us a list of all the taxes that are imposed on the municipality of Dublin; is there any tax under Mr. Ewart's Act of 1 *d.* in the pound upon the valuation, for the purposes of science and art?—I am not aware of it.

382. Or for a free library and museum?—We collect no such rate.

383. You are aware that the ratepayers have the power to impose that rate, are you not?—I am.

Mr. *Butt*.

384. Did you not say before, or did I misunderstand you, that when there was a tender made of the rates, you inquired whether the man was entitled to be put on the rate or not?—Yes.

385. What inquiry do you make in that respect?—The collector takes up a bundle of notices, and in a great number of instances he finds that those notices have only been filled in in order to make a show to the agent's employer. A number of those persons are on the rate-book already, and others are not entitled, as we believe, on account of being weekly and monthly tenants.

386. Do you mean to say that if a weekly or monthly tenant claimed to be rated, and *bonâ fide* tendered the rate, you would refuse him?—Yes, certainly.

387. Even though he tendered it?—Yes, I think so; but the thing has never arisen, so far as I am aware.

388. Has it not arisen that in some cases you have inquired whether the person was entitled to be rated?—Yes; but we have never got the money, or a chance of receiving it.

389. What inquiries are made by you?—We send the collector to inquire at the premises as to how the occupier holds.

390. Then, I still am right in saying that you inquire whether he holds as a weekly or monthly tenant?—We do.

391. And if he was a weekly or monthly tenant you would refuse?—Yes.

392. Even although he *bonâ fide* tendered?—Yes, even although he *bonâ fide* tendered.

393. How

Mr. *Maylan* and Mr. *Taaffe*.

8 May 1876.

Chairman.

393. How do you reconcile that with the 66th section of the Act of the 12th and 13th of Victoria, c. 91?—I never tried to reconcile it. I took it for granted that the opinion of counsel was correct, and that in following him we were acting in a proper manner.

394. Does not that section clearly say that the occupier of any rateable property may demand to be assessed for the same, and in that case shall be assessable; is not a weekly or monthly tenant an occupier of rateable property?—I considered Mr. Barry to be much more competent to form an opinion than I was, and I did not attempt to question his opinion.

395. (To Mr. *Maylan.*) Is the opinion of Mr. Barry considered a confidential opinion, and do you object to produce it to the Committee?—I do not think it is confidential, and I think it can be produced; but until I return to Dublin it cannot be produced.

Mr. *Gibson*.

396. Mr. Barry was most likely the Attorney General when he gave that opinion?—He was either the Attorney or Solicitor General.

Mr. *Butt*.

397. At all events you have acted upon that opinion?—Yes; it was acted upon before my appointment, and has been continued since.

Mr. *J. P. Corry*.

398. When were you appointed?—In the year 1870.

Mr. *Murphy*.

399. I take it for granted that you got that opinion in your capacity of collector general?—Mr. Staunton, my predecessor, got it.

400. And he got it for the purposes of his office?—Yes.

401. (To Mr. *Taaffe.*) Could you let us have that opinion at a future date?—I think we shall be able to produce it during the course of the sitting of the Committee. I also think that a similar opinion was given by the present Judge Warren.

Dr. *Ward*.

402. Supposing that a man is rated over 8 *l.*, and assessed in your books, and there is an objection served by one of the political agents against him, is he obliged to appear in court to prove his right in the case of the Parliamentary franchise?—Yes, if he is rated and that objection is raised; if he appears on the Parliamentary List.

403. If he appears on your books?—The objection is not served on us, it is served on him, and that is a matter altogether for the Parliamentary Court. I believe, as a matter of fact, he is obliged to appear if it is for the first time.

404. Is he obliged by the municipal franchise?—I can speak with more authority, as I attend the municipal courts. He is obliged if he appears for the first time that he is objected to; he loses his vote if he does not appear, unless the objection be withdrawn.

405. Is not the entry of the name in the book sufficient evidence, without the appearance of the claimant?—No.

Mr. *Gibson*.

406. At no time since you have had anything to say to the collector general's office has there been any tenant of a weekly or monthly character ever rated?—There may have been, but not intentionally; such a thing may have crept into the books, but not knowingly.

407. So that it is not the fact of their being a limit of 8 *l.* that has interfered with their being rated?—No, certainly not.

408. You conceive that there is some principle which would prevent your putting on a weekly or monthly tenant, no matter of what value?—It was Mr. Barry's opinion that it would be an absurdity to rate a weekly or monthly tenant to a yearly rate; that was the ground.

409. You have told the Chief Secretary that the object of bringing in this Bill before me, was to enable you to get at the head lessor who may have sub-let to a middle man?—Yes, that was the object of that particular section.

410. But would not the section which you have read to the Committee enable you in every case to get at the head landlord no matter how *bonâ fide* might have been his sub-letting to a middleman; would not that enable you to reach every case whether of collusive or of perfectly *bonâ fide* sub-letting?—It certainly would.

411. Would not it enable you to enormously hamper and interfere with the house property in Dublin; for instance, if I spend 1,000 *l.* in *bonâ fide* buying up house property, and I *bonâ fide* sub-let it, if it turns out that by this Act of Parliament I am to be liable for the rates, would not it diminish the value of my property several hundred pounds to be worried by your collectors whenever they think that it is more convenient to come down upon a solvent man at once, who would make no bother about it, but give a check to be done with it?—I do not see that it would. (*Mr. Maylan.*) It is only the same power that they have in the surrounding townships of Rathmines and Pembroke. (*Mr. Taaffe.*) If you had any doubt of the tenant to whom you were subletting, you could very easily let your house at a rent, including taxes, to protect yourself.

Dr. *Ward*.

412. Is not that done?—Very frequently.

Mr. *Gibson*.

413. If a man is a *bonâ fide* man, and letting his house in order that he may receive a perfectly fair rent, and not be troubled about rates, is not it rather unreasonable to come down upon him with an Act of Parliament, and expose him in any contingency to a liability for rates?—That, of course, is a matter altogether for the House, whether the evil would counterbalance the good.

414. In the clause which you have read to the Committee, you say where the immediate lessee is liable to pay rack-rent; who is to be the judge whether it is rack-rent or not?—That is another matter of detail.

415. It is more than a matter of detail; it should have passed through some one's mind who is to decide it; is it to be the collector general of rates, or the person who goes to look for the rate?—It did not occur to me. I have never thought of the matter before.

416. Could you at all give the Committee any means of numerically deciding about how many lessors there were of this character in Dublin; what

Mr. *Moylan* and Mr. *Taaffe*.

2 May 1876.

Mr. *Gibson*—continued.

what I will call fraudulent immediate lessors, or collusive, or whatever word you choose to put in?—I should not like to undertake to do so. (Mr. *Moylan*.) They are very numerous, because they are cropping up every other day.

Dr. *Ward*.

417. Are they increasing?—They are not decreasing.

Mr. *Gibson*.

418. (To Mr. *Taaffe*.) When you say that they are very numerous, could you give the Committee a figure approximately within 100 of what you conceive to be accurate?—I could do it, but not off-hand. (Mr. *Moylan*.) We could not, without referring to the books of the establishment.

Dr. *Ward*.

419. (To Mr. *Taaffe*.) Several of those men have many houses, you say?—Several.

Mr. *Gibson*.

420. I ask what material you have in the collector general of rates' office of knowing what are the terms of letting between the head landlord and the immediate lessor?—The statement in a great number of cases of the immediate lessor.

421. That is, you want an Act of Parliament brought in against the head lessor on the statement of his tenant?—That statement should be substantiated before we could recover.

422. Up to this have you any material at all excepting hearsay for determining what are the relations between the head landlord and the immediate lessor?—We have no power of obtaining any such thing.

423. Am I right in saying that there are no materials whatever of a reliable character in the collector general's office, or within your knowledge, as to the actual pecuniary relations existing between any head lessor and what are called the immediate lessors in that Bill?—I consider the information on which the clause was based reliable.

424. Will you now state again to the Committee what that information is which you think reliable?—The statements made by the immediate lessors to the collectors and to myself on several occasions when I have endeavoured to force rates from them. I have discovered and seen in many instances leases produced to show that there was quite as much rent paid to the head landlord as would in all probability be got by the house, and I found that the immediate lessors were almost begging in many instances.

425. Were they trusted with the actual receipt of rent?—Yes, they were; the rent was received from them in weekly instalments; the immediate lessor merely collected it from the tenant, and handed it over to the landlord at the end of the week.

426. I would be glad if you could give in something of a return of the number of those cases?—I will try to do so.

427. Is there any memorandum made by your collectors of any communications of this kind that are made to them?—No, I cannot say that there is.

428. How many collectors are there altogether engaged in this work?—There are ten collectors employed in the City, and there is a warrant officer as well; we can form a very good opinion about them.

429. Are there any written instructions to your collectors telling them what their duties are?—No.

430. Do you know of any section in the Act of Parliament pointing out their duties?—I do not.

431. Except Section 8 in the Registration Act, you know of no other section?—I do not.

432. Do you know of any section of any Act of Parliament, or any printed system of rules that tells them that they are to make any inquiry whatever into tenancies?—I do not, but they receive verbal instructions.

Dr. *Ward*.

433. By this Bill, on which the honourable Member for the Dublin University has been examining you, you do not seek any powers beyond what already exist in the townships around Dublin?—I conceive that we do not; the section was drawn in order to assimilate the law in the City as nearly as possible to that in the surrounding townships.

434. (To Mr. *Moylan*.) Under this head is there much loss in the collection of rates in the townships around Dublin?—None; in Rathmines they are not 5 *l.* short at the end of the year. (Mr. *Taaffe*.) The property is liable, we conceive, first in any case, and the property in the City of Dublin quite as much so as in the townships.

Mr. *Gibson*.

435. Did you ever conceive that it was any kind of good getting into possession of the property and getting possession of the rents?—I do believe it is perfectly impossible. I do not believe that we should succeed in getting the rents; the landlord would eject the tenants immediately: they pay the first week's rent, and the landlord gives them notice to quit, and then they go into another place. But even supposing they did not serve them with notice to quit, if we were to take out warrants against those wretched people the entire contents of their rooms would not pay for their removal; and if they were removed we should not know what to do with them.

436. Is it not a fact that those places are let mostly to mechanics and tradesmen, and do not they generally pay the weekly and monthly rents with great regularity?—I believe so, but they pay it to the landlord.

437. Your point is that they pay it, not to the landlord, but to a go-between between the tenant and the landlord?—Yes.

438. You have never heard of any difficulty of collecting weekly and monthly rents?—Indeed I have.

439. Is it not a fact that they are paid fairly well?—In a great number of instances those lessors say that they do not get their rents. Whether that be true or not I have no means of judging; but I do know that in several cases where we have endeavoured to collect weekly rents we have found it to be an utter failure.

440. On what occasions have you tried to collect weekly rents?—On many occasions.

441. Under what power?—Under the section of the Collection of Rates Act.

442. What is that section?—The 75th and 76th section. The 75th says, "That when the owners of

Mr. *Moylan* and Mr. *Taaffe*.

8 May 1876.

Mr. *Gibson*—continued.

of any rateable property is rated in respect thereof under the authority of this Act, and the rate remains unpaid for three months, the collector general, or his collector, may demand the amount of such rate from the occupier for the time being of such rateable property, and on nonpayment thereof may recover the same by distress and sale of his goods and chattels."

443. As a rule, have you used any of these Sections 75, 76, and 77 in the Collection of Rates (Dublin) Act?—We have not used them to any large extent, because we find them to be a failure in every case.

444. How long have you been in the department?—More than 10 years.

445. When did you use them last?—Last year.

446. When did you use them before?—The year before, probably; there is scarcely a year when we do not try it.

447. Could you furnish the Committee with any papers showing the efforts made under those sections to go into possession of rents, the amount recovered, and the amount of valuation of property?—I could not.

448. Is there any record kept in your department?—No.

449. Is it a fact that your department might go into possession of property under the sections of the Act of Parliament, and not have any record of it?—Every farthing that is collected is posted in the ledgers of the department, but we keep no record of the amount that we do not get.

450. You have told us that as lately as last year your department has acted under those strong Sections 75, 76, and 77, going into direct possession of premises; is there any record whatever kept in your department of this Act of going into possession under those sections?—In every case where we receive money there is; but we have found it to be utterly useless to go in. I can give you an instance of last year, in which, after trying to serve his tenants with notices, we sought to make a man bankrupt, and even in that case we failed completely; he was before the Bankruptcy Court on three or four several occasions.

Mr. *Collins*.

451. I think I understood you to say that it is the collector who reports whether they are weekly or monthly tenants?—Yes, it is.

452. What means does he take to ascertain who are weekly tenants?—He calls at the premises and makes inquiries from the persons he finds there in some instances; in others he inquires from the landlord if he happens to know him; that often turns out to be a shorter way of doing it.

453. Then he depends upon the information which he gets personally from them; he does not investigate the nature of all the occupancies?—He does not.

454. You say that in many cases you yourself have seen the leases that have been granted between the lessors and the middle men?—Yes; I have seen such documents.

455. Does the collector general ask for those documents to be produced?—No; but when we have had proceedings against those men or obtained warrants against them, they have brought in those documents and showed them as a proof that they were utterly unable to pay, as an additional proof of their poverty and inability to pay; but we have not demanded such a thing.

Mr. *Collins*—continued.

456. At the same time, there is a general feeling or suspicion that the arrangements to a great extent between the lessors and the middle men are collusive?—That is so.

457. Under the effect of such an idea as that, do not you press the matter very much to investigate it?—We do.

458. What measures do you take for the investigation; do you take them before a tribunal of any kind?—We take them before the police magistrates in a great many cases.

459. Do you take the lessors or the middle men?—The middle men; we have no power to get at the lessor at all. The lessor ceases to be the immediate lessor the moment he puts in a middle man.

460. You take them before the police magistrate to establish the truth of what they state?—They very rarely defend a summons. A summons is taken out against them, and they know that a warrant can make no difference in their cases, as there is nothing to levy distress on.

461. However, does an investigation sometimes take place before the police magistrate?—Very seldom, because no investigation can take place when the defendant does not appear; he allows judgment to go by default, knowing that it can make no difference to him.

Sir *Arthur Guinness*.

462. What is the reason that you were unable to take the money which has been often tendered by various agents?—I did not say that we were unable to take it, but that the moment we showed a disposition to take it the offer was withdrawn.

463. Because you would not give a receipt for it?—We would give a receipt for it, but it would take a considerable time to calculate the amount of poor rate from the 1st of January up to a certain date, and to fill in receipts for it for 300 or 400 of them.

464. Then the practical difficulty was in the collector general's office, not being able to give proper receipts for this money which was tendered?—I do not say that. We could take it in some cases if there was any intention to pay it. I have myself frequently offered to fill the receipts, but as soon as I made the offer the tender was withdrawn.

465. Still you put them on the rate book, if their tender was made?—If we found that they were entitled, because they should be put on the rate book whether a tender was made or not.

466. What was the object of making the tender?—Because in the cases of weekly or monthly tenants, as I understand it, is a sufficient claim to be rated to tender the poor rate under the law.

467. What effect do you think this Bill of the collector general's would have upon the increase or diminution of those holding the franchise?—I do not think it would have any effect whatever; at least I think it would be inappreciable if there was any effect. So far as tenemented houses are concerned it would not make any difference.

468. On account of their being weekly tenants?—Because there are several persons in each of those houses, and if they are entitled at all they are entitled as lodgers.

469. Have

Mr. *Moylan* and Mr. *Taaffe*.

2 May 1876.

Mr. *J. P. Corry*.

469. Have you no power under the Act under which you collect rates to compound with the landlords for weekly or monthly tenants?—No, we have no power to compound.

470. In the case either of the Parliamentary or the municipal franchise, supposing any one comes forward and claims to be an elector, how do you deal with that person?—If he be a yearly tenant we rate him. The fact of his being rated, if he is a yearly tenant, is not sufficient to entitle him to the franchise; he must have also paid the rates to which he was liable.

471. Do I understand from you that people get upon the rate book without payment of rates at all?—Certainly. Men must be put on the rate book as a preliminary of their liability to pay the rates.

472. And that entitles them to the franchise?—If the rates are paid. That does not rest with the collector general's department at all.

473. Is the object of the landlord in creating this immediate lessor to avoid the payment of the rates?—Yes, certainly.

474. I presume that in Dublin you have registration agents for the different political associations?—I believe there is no doubt that that is so.

475. Are those registration agents not very active in getting their friends upon the rate book?—They take a good deal of trouble in doing so, but I cannot say that every claim of that sort to rate, is one that is necessary.

476. In the Revision Court, whether they are admitted or not admitted, have you to be present to give evidence in case they are objected to?—Yes. The department is represented there.

477. Do you think that the way in which the rates are collected in Dublin, operates materially against the parties being municipal electors?—No, I do not. I think it rather facilitates them.

Mr. *Bruen*.

478. As a matter of fact all the claims to be rated come to your office, do they?—They do.

479. Are there many such claims every year?—A great number; some of them served in duplicate, and some of them served in actually more than one rate book.

480. How do you mean in duplicate?—In some instances bundles of claims are handed in by the agent, and there are two or three claims by the same person for the purpose of making a large show of work.

481. Is each one of those claims investigated?—Each one of those claims is investigated by the collector.

482. And that from the rate book only?—That helps to form the rate book, but when the collector is serving his notices he is bound to ascertain the name of the occupier and owner of each house, and to insert them both in the claim to rate.

483. With regard to the taxes which you were examined upon at the beginning of your evidence, you spoke of the bridge tax; can you tell the Committee what year that tax was levied, and which was levied for three years, I think you said?—It was levied for three years consecutively; I think it was levied in 1872, 1873, and 1874.

484. And it was 2 *d.* in the pound for each of those three years?—Yes.

Mr. *Bruen*—continued.

485. Was there anything else; was no other levy made?—No, there was not.

486. Was that for the building of more than one bridge?—It was for the building of Grattan Bridge, as it is now called.

487. The main drainage rate was another rate that you spoke of, and which, I think you said, was suspended; has that in fact ever been levied?—Yes; it was levied for three or four years.

488. Can you give the Committee the poundage of those three or four years?—There were two years in which it was levied at 4 *d.* in the pound, and for another two years at 2 *d.* in the pound. I think that was all, but I cannot say positively without reference.

489. You cannot give the Committee any information as to how the money which it produced was expended?—No; the Collector General's duty ended when he lodged it in the Bank of Ireland to the main drainage account.

Mr. *J. P. Corry*.

490. In lodging the money in the bank, do you lodge it to the credit of the different accounts which you have specified?—It is in the first instance lodged to the Collector General's general account; those are the sums which are brought in daily from the collector's previous day's collection, and once a week it is allocated, and the various funds are transferred in the Bank of Ireland to their accounts.

Mr. *Bruen*.

491. You spoke of a great loss being sustained by a number of houses being let in tenements, for which the rates were not collected; could you, in the course of a day or two, give to the Committee the number of those houses for the last three or four years?—I could give something approaching it; at least, I should think so. I have said that I calculated the loss to be about 4 per cent. I cannot go nearer than that.

492. What I want is more in detail the number of houses, the rates for which were so lost, and the amount of rates which were lost?—I will endeavour to furnish that. (Mr. *Moylan*.) The Committee have asked about the amount of the bridge rate for 1872. I find that it was 6,015 *l.* for that one year.

493. (To Mr. *Taaffe*.) Probably as the poundage was the same for the other two years, the proceeds of the rate might be taken to be nearly the same?—Yes, for the other two years; but then you must recollect that that bridge tax is not collected from the city proper, it is collected from the entire metropolitan police district.

494. Do those figures which you have just given refer to what is collected from the city proper, or from the whole district?—From the entire district. (Mr. *Moylan*.) Dublin proper is a great contributor.

Mr. *Butt*.

495. (To Mr. *Taaffe*.) What distinction do you draw between Dublin proper and the entire district?—In the metropolitan police district we collect the entire metropolitan police tax; that extends outside the municipal boundary; it goes out to Dalkey, and we collect through the entire district.

496. Do

Dr. *Ward.*

496. Do you collect any other rates in that area?—No other, except the bridge tax.

Mr. *Butt.*

497. Under what Act do you collect the police rate?—I suppose it must be under the Police Act; we have got a special collector for the police tax outside the municipal district.

Dr. *Ward.*

498. How do you collect the bridge tax?—By the same machinery, there is a special collector appointed. (*Mr. Moylan.*) The bridge tax for 1874 was 6,306 *l.*, or very nearly the same as the preceding year.

Mr. *Bruen.*

499. The honourable Member for the University of Dublin examined you at some length with regard to the proposition which was made for the taxation of the owners of property; I think your proposition was, that where the tenant failed to pay, you could come down upon the owner and make him pay; was not that it, pure and simple?—Yes.

500. Do you give any corresponding power to the owner, supposing he had so paid, to recover the amount from the tenant?—Yes, he could recover from the tenant. (*Mr. Taaffe.*) The section provides that he should have power to recoup himself.

Mr. *Gibson.*

501. Will you read the proviso?—"Provided always that the person entitled to receive the said rack-rent, shall be entitled to recover the rates, or part thereof, so paid by him, from the immediate lessor, as if same were part of, and in addition to, the rent payable by the immediate lessor."

Mr. *Bruen.*

502. Did it ever strike you in treating that subject, to deal with it something in the same way as was recommended by the Report of the Local Taxation Committee in England, that is to say, that the lessee should have power, he paying the taxes first, to deduct from his rent a certain proportion of the taxes so paid by him, in the same way as the poor rate is now collected, as you are aware that the occupier being primarily liable for the poor rate, can deduct from his rent one-half of it?—Yes.

503. Did it ever strike you to extend that principle to those other rates and taxes with which you have to deal?—I find that in the cases where we seek to make it, even the poor rate is not paid.

504. And of course yours being a consolidated rate, failure to pay includes failure to pay the poor rate?—Yes, but we would accept payment of the qualifying poor rate from any person who tendered it, and we do so constantly, so that I find that it is not offered in these cases.

505. I suppose I may gather from your answer that the particular point to which I have just directed your attention had not been considered by you, that is to say, that particular change had not been considered?—But I have considered it now since you put it; it did not occur to me before, because I did not believe it was possible to recover any rate at all. I find that the poor rate is not paid, and consequently it did not occur to me to be possible to recover any of the others.

Mr. *Kavanagh.*

506. The amount of taxation that appears to have been raised in Dublin, you stated, was, in 1870, 213,000 *l.*, and in 1864 276,000 *l.*; that gives an average increase in four years of 68,000 *l.*; can you tell me whether that increase was scattered generally over the different items?—No, it was principally caused by the increase of the grand jury cess; the poor rate also was increased. There are four or five fixed rates, and as there could be no increase in the improvement rate, nor in the sewer rate, nor in the water rate, consequently it must have been in the grand jury cess and the poor rate.

507. You said that the poor rate which was 2 *s.*, the police rate which was 8 *d.*, the sewer rate which was 4 *d.*, the domestic water rate which was 1 *s.*, and the public water rate which was 3 *d.*, were all up to their maximum?—Yes.

508. And they could not be raised?—No, but the sewer rate has not been at its maximum ever since.

509. Have those five items all been at their maximum from the year 1870 until the present, except the sewer rate?—Yes, they have, and I think for much longer.

Sir *J. M'Kenna.*

510. In the year 1874 you collected 276,000 *l.*; can you tell the Committee what was the entire cost of collecting that sum?—The cost of collection is 2½ per cent.; it is limited to 2½ per cent.; it cannot cost more than 6 *d.* in the pound, and it never has reached that amount. There has always been a surplus to the office account, which has been returned to the various boards in proportion to the amounts that were collected for them. That surplus has varied within the last four or five years from 900 *l.* to 1,200 *l.* a year.

511. Who apportions the charge within that 2½ per cent.; who decides whether it shall be only 2 per cent. or 1½ per cent., or 2¼?—Two-and-a-half per cent. is deducted from the collection every week, and lodged to the account kept in the Bank of Ireland for the purpose. That sum is to be accounted for to the auditor, a Master in Chancery. Every item is vouched and the receipts produced, and the authority for the payment from his Excellency.

512. Can you tell me, 2½ per cent. being the maximum limit which the charge has reached, what is the actual charge?—I say that there has been a sum varying from 900 *l.* to 1,200 *l.* returned to the various boards each year for the past four or five years. (*Mr. Moylan.*) That saving was only effected within the last five or six years; up to that time, and previous, there was nothing returned to the boards.

513. (To Mr. *Taaffe.*) Have you any materials to tell the Committee what was the charge for collecting this amount of rates before the consolidation?—I have not.

514. (To Mr. *Moylan.*) It was much larger, as well as I remember, than 2½ per cent.?—Yes, very much larger.

515. I am asking the question simply with the view to the amount of economy reached by the mere consolidation; I think that the charge was much larger?—I think it was 5 per cent., and in

Mr. Moylan and Mr. Taaffe.

2 May 1876.

Sir *J. M'Kenna*—continued.

in some cases much more than that: but that was the lowest.

516. Have you at hand my items which will show the increase in the sums levied from 220,000 *l.* in 1871, to 258,000 *l.* in 1873, and to 276,000 *l.* in 1874?—I have not. One of those years we recovered a large sum from the corporation for water mains which they disputed, and another year we recovered a large sum from the Docks Board which they disputed, and went to the Court of Exchequer Chamber.

Dr. *Ward.*

517. Since that recovery do you get the annual sums?—No; we served a summons of plaint for a large amount.

518. And they contested it year by year?—Yes, but we are advised that it is a good case.

Sir *J. M'Kenna.*

519. Still you succeeded in bringing the revenue from 220,000 *l.* in 1872, to 276,000 *l.* in 1874?—(Mr. *Taaffe.*) That was caused by the increased poundage rate, an increase in the grand jury cess, and in the poor rates.

520. Have you any materials at hand that will enable us to see what was the precise increase in those years?—The Return that the Chief Secretary directed me to prepare, I think will show the poundage rate, and the amount collected for each of those five years.

Chairman.

521. On that point have you any means of knowing at your office how the different items of expenditure are allocated by the corporation to the different rates?—We allocate them.

522. The sewers' rate is limited to 4 *d.* in the £.; have you any means of knowing whether the corporation, having reached that maximum limit for a sewers' rate, place something on the grand jury cess which ought properly to go to the sewers' rate?—I should say that they do not, because Mr. Finlay, the auditor, would not allow it to pass.

523. Would you know anything about it?—No; that is a matter for the auditor. I have heard of his surcharging them with various amounts, so that I take it that he keeps a very accurate eye on the matter, and does not allow them to do anything of the kind. We divide the rates. For instance, for the year 1873 the amount lodged by the collector general to grand jury cess was 44,260 *l.*; to improvement rate, 52,440 *l.*; to the north sewer rate, 3,436 *l.*; to the south sewer rate, 5,063 *l.*; to the water rate, 45,367 *l.*; to the main drainage rate, 8,450 *l.*; and to the vestry rate, 1,970 *l.* Those were the amounts that the corporation had the disposal of.

524. Those were the amounts which the corporation called upon you to levy?—Yes; those were the actual returns made to them.

Dr. *Ward.*

525. Did you lodge those amounts in the bank to separate accounts?—They were lodged to separate accounts.

Chairman.

526. There is one point in your rate book of which I should like some explanation; I see in some cases no name entered at all as against the property, but I see the word "owner" entered; is that consistent with your Act?—It is. There is a section of the Collection of Rates Act which provides that where there is a doubt about the name of the owner, inserting the word "owner" is sufficient to make the rates leviable.

527. Then you afterwards discover who the owner is, and you levy on him accordingly?—Yes.

528. In one case I notice that record three times in three successive years?—It may be that there may be a difficulty in ascertaining the name of the owner. Our inserting his name as "owner" gives us the power at any time to put it on.

Mr. *Butt.*

529. You appear to think that your office, as I understand you, has nothing to do with the persons who are in arrear of rates; I mean as to making out a list of them for the purposes of either the Parliamentary or municipal franchise?—The returns are marked. In the first instance a return of the name of every occupier appearing on the rate book is made out. That return is checked immediately after the 1st of July, the last day for qualifying for the Parliamentary List, and the pen is drawn through the name of every person who owes arrears of rates on that day.

530. For the Parliamentary franchise you only strike out those in arrear of poor rates?—If a man has paid the poor rate to qualify, we leave him on, but if he owes all rates we strike him off.

531. For the municipal franchise what do you do?—The list is made out by the town clerk, and merely forwarded to the collector general to have filled in, into two columns that appear in it, the amount of the last payment made, and the date of it, or the amount that was due on the 1st of January preceding.

532. Does not that include all taxes?—It includes all taxes; but a quarter's rates paid before the 31st of August is considered to be the qualification.

533. When a person comes to you claiming to be rated, what tax does he pay to be rated, according to the practice of the office?—If he is entitled to be rated, it is not necessary that he should pay any taxes; we put him as a matter of course on the rate book.

534. Do you mean to say that a person can claim to be put on the rate book without his paying any rates or taxes?—Certainly, because without his name appearing on the rate book, he would not be liable, we could not recover from him. Probably I do not understand your question.

535. I will read to you section 66 of the Collection of Rates Act, and then you will see what I mean: "Be it enacted that the occupiers of any rateable property may demand to be assessed for the same, and to pay the rates in respect thereof, made by the said bodies politic or corporate, boards, commissioners, or persons, and applotted, levied, and collected under the authority of this Act, and the collector general shall assess every such occupier so long as he duly pays the said rates, anything hereinbefore contained notwithstanding;" suppose there were rates due on the premises when the man comes to claim to be rated, what would you do?—Are you dealing with a weekly or monthly tenant, because it makes all the difference to my answer?

536. I will

Mr. *Butt*—continued.

536. I will take first the question of a weekly or monthly tenant, what does he tender?—If he tenders all the poor rate that was due on the premises for the year, we would put him on.

537. Did not you say that you would not put on a weekly or monthly tenant?—If he pays the poor rate we would. The moment he pays it we would put him on; but we never have such a case; I do not think I have ever known a case of that kind to arise.

538. Did I understand you rightly to say that a man is put on without paying rates?—Not if he is a weekly or monthly tenant.

539. If he was rated under 4 *l.*, would you put him on?—If he was a yearly tenant we would, under 8 *l.*

540. Under 4 *l.*, I say?—No, not under 4 *l.*

541. You would not put him on at all?—No.

542. But you do not make the payment of rates any condition of rating, except in the case of weekly or monthly tenants?—No.

Mr. *Brooks.*

543. It being a tenement of that sort, should he tender the rate for the whole house of which he was occupier?—We would not rate him for the poor rate for the year preceding if he came in on this day and tendered the poor rate up to the day. If he tendered the poor rate for the present year, the amount that is due and payable, we would put him on.

544. Not without his holding a house?—Not unless he occupied the entire house, because he would then be a lodger.

545. Supposing a man paid 8 *l.* a year for two rooms, being part of a house let in tenements?—We would not rate him under any circumstances.

Sir *Arthur Guinness.*

546. Unless he claimed?—Not even if he claimed, because he is merely a lodger; he is not in the occupation of the entire rated premises.

547. If yearly tenants claimed to be rated, and you obliged the landlord or lessee by this Bill to pay, would not that entitle the tenants to the franchise before they had really paid the rent?—If the tenant was a yearly one and the valuation was over 8 *l.*, the tenant, and not the immediate lessor, would be the party liable.

548. Supposing it is under 8 *l.*, and you obliged the landlord or the immediate lessor to pay the rates, if those tenants then claimed to be rated, his paying would entitle them to the franchise, because you say that an agent tendering the payment of rates entitles those he tenders for to the franchise?—I believe that has been the practice.

549. Then this Bill of the Collector General of rates would tend to increase the franchise so far?—I do not see that it would. The object of the Collector General's Bill is to facilitate the collection of the rates entirely irrespective of the franchise.

550. This would be a collateral effect, would it not?—That may be so, but we did not consider it at all.

Mr. *Kavanagh.*

551. You said that in your experience there was a number of claims not *bonâ fide* made every year by different wards, according as elections

Mr. *Kavanagh*—continued.

Mr. *Moylan* and Mr *Taaffe*.

3 May 1876.

were coming on or not for the municipality, to be placed on the rate for the purpose of gaining the municipal franchise?—I do say so.

552. Do those claims for the municipal franchise go before the revising barrister?—Those claims, in the first instance, are handed to the collector of the district, and his duty is to go round and investigate in each separate case whether the claim be *bonâ fide* or not. If he finds that it is *bonâ fide*, his duty is to have the name inserted on the rate book; if he does not he takes no notice whatever of the claim.

553. Then the test of the revision court is not applied to the municipal franchise?—Yes, it is, certainly; because the municipal franchise claim is not served on the Collector General at all; it is served on the town clerk. A list of those claims is printed by the town clerk, and revised by the lord mayor and assessors, with the assistance of the Collector General's department.

Mr. *Bruen.*

554. You, in fact, act in the same way as the clerks of the poor law unions act with regard to other constituencies?—Exactly.

Mr. *Butt.*

555. Has your attention been called to the regulation about claiming to be rated both for municipal and Parliamentary purposes in the Municipal Corporations Act and the Representation of the People Act; will you take the Municipal Corporations Act (Ireland), the 3rd and 4th of Victoria, c. 108, and the 33rd section of that Act; do you see there that to make the claim effectual the person claiming must pay the rates that are then due?—Yes.

556. You do not consider that that applies to you?—I do, certainly; that is the reason that I say that if they had paid the rates for the year 1876, I would rate them at once.

557. If they do not pay, do not you say that you rate them?—If they are liable to be rated, we rate them whether they pay or not; and even if we do not consider them to be liable to be rated, if they do pay we rate them.

Mr. *Bruen.*

558. Just one question with regard to the sewer rate; you spoke of a north sewer rate and a south sewer rate, are they different?—Yes, they are.

559. Are they a different poundage?—Not as a rule; they are not a different poundage, but they might be; there is nothing to prevent them; they are in separate estimates.

Mr. *Brooks.*

560. You do not collect the borough rate, do you?—There has never been a borough rate in my recollection; the borough fund is made up of a number of rates which we do collect.

561. You do not collect their rents?—No, we do not collect their rents; those are a portion of the borough fund.

Mr. *Murphy.*

562. I presume, as a matter of fact, every tenement in Dublin is rated to the relief of the poor?—I believe so; of course there are some exemptions.

563. Do not you take any notice whatever of the occupiers of those premises unless their valuation

Mr. *Moylan* and Mr. *Taaffe*.

2 May 1876.

Mr. *Murphy*—continued.

valuation be above 4 *l.*?—We do if they are yearly tenants; we rate them as well as the owners.

564. No matter to what amount the premises are rated?—So that it is over 4 *l.*, but under 4 *l.* we take no notice of them whatever.

565. You take no notice whatever of the occupier of a tenement rated under 4 *l.*?—No; but I do not suppose there are a dozen occupiers rated under 4 *l.* who are yearly tenants.

Mr. *J. P. Corry.*

566. I presume that the reason that the amount collected in 1874 was much greater than that collected in 1870 arises somewhat from the increase of property in Dublin?—I should say not, to any appreciable extent; it is caused principally by the difference in the poundage rate of the grand jury cess and the poor rate.

567. Am I to understand that the rateable property is not extending?—The valuation in some districts is increasing very much, and in others it is depreciating in almost a corresponding degree.

Sir *Arthur Guinness.*

568. Is it revised every year?—Yes, it is revised every year.

Mr. *Butt.*

569. You were asked why you collected the police rate out of Dublin; has your attention been turned to the 29th section of the Collection of Rates Act, which says, "That the limits of this Act for the collection of the poor rates, borough rates, improvement rates, sewer rates, grand jury cess, and pipe water rates or rents, shall be the municipal district of Dublin, as defined by an Act passed in the third year of the reign of Her present Majesty, intituled, 'An Act for the Regulation of the Municipal Corporations in Ireland;' and the limits of this Act for the collection of the police rates shall be the district of Dublin metropolis"?—That is the section which I was looking for when the Chief Secretary said it was unnecessary.

Mr. *Murphy.*

570. How does the bridge rate come into this area?—By the special provisions of the Act under which the rate was levied. It met with considerable opposition from the surrounding townships.

Chairman.

571. (To Mr. *Moylan.*) Will you put in one of those statements: the Report of the Collector General of Rates in the City of Dublin for the Year ending the 31st of December 1874?—Yes (*delivering in the same*).

Mr. *Gibson.*

572. Who audits the accounts of the Collector General?—Master FitzGibbon.

Friday, 5th May 1876.

MEMBERS PRESENT:

Mr. Assheton.	Mr. Kavanagh.
Sir Michael Hicks Beach.	Mr. Charles Lewis.
Mr. Brooks.	Sir Joseph M'Kenna.
Mr. Bruen.	Mr. Mulholland.
Mr. Butt.	Mr. Murphy.
Mr. Collins.	Mr. O'Shaughnessy.
Mr. J. P. Corry.	Mr. Rathbone.
Mr. Gibson.	Dr. Ward.
Sir Arthur Guinness.	

SIR MICHAEL HICKS BEACH, IN THE CHAIR.

Mr. WILLIAM NEILSON HANCOCK, LL.D.; further Examined.

Mr. *Butt*.

Mr. W. N. Hancock, LL.D.

5 May 1876.

573. I BELIEVE you are aware of the Order of Reference under which this Committee is sitting?—Yes.

574. You see that there are three Acts of Parliament specially referred to us?—Yes, the 9th of Geo. 4, c. 82, that is the first mentioned; then the 3 & 4 Vict. c. 108, and the 17 & 18 Vict. c. 103.; and you have to report whether any and what alterations are advisable in the law relating to local government and taxation of cities and towns in Ireland.

575. Let me first take you to the second Statute mentioned, which is the most important one; was not that Statute the General Municipal Reform Act for Ireland?—It was.

576. Following a Statute that had been passed a few years before, for the reform of municipal corporations in England?—Yes.

577. Without troubling you with minute details, can you tell me, first, how many corporations existed in Ireland at the time of the passing of that Act, or were dealt with by it?—I think I mentioned that on the last day when I was examined; they are all in the schedule; the first Schedule A. contains 10 corporations; and the next, Schedule B., I think, contains the others.

578. Could you give us the numbers?—I took the numbers on the last day, not from the Act of Parliament, but from the Commissioners' Report of 1835. They report altogether 99 corporations in Ireland.

579. What I want to know is, how many of those were dealt with by the Act, and whether some of those have not become extinct?—The main dealing of the Act was by Schedule A. and Schedule B.; Schedule I. had also a large effect.

580. You may take them at 68?—That is the number I gave on the last day, 68, or more exactly 69.

581. If you have not gone into the question do not mind answering me so, but are you able to say generally how many of these corporations were entirely close corporations?—The only information that I had was contained in what I quoted from the General Report, and the numbers I gave, I think, were altogether 99; and of those, 30 became extinct; eight were almost extinct; and then there were 61 in actual existence.

Mr. *Butt*—continued.

582. Of the 69, can you tell me how many were close corporations?—Of the 61, 38 were self-elective irresponsible governing bodies, and the other 23 are returned as having, more or less, the power of election.

583. Can you tell me how did the Municipal Reform Act deal with the 69 corporations which it did affect, and into how many classes did it divide them?—I think that there were three main classes and divisions, and one of those was the towns that got new corporations without new charters; then those towns which had Municipal Commissioners, and then there was a class that had not.

584. In the first class there were 10 towns, were there not?—Yes.

585. When you say new corporations, is that strictly accurate?—They did not get new charters.

586. Is it not the fact that those 10 towns retained their corporate existence, and all their old chartered privileges and rights, except in so far as they were taken away by the Act?—Certainly; but whilst they did that technically and legally, as a matter of fact, the change was so great that it so revolutionised their powers, and the change was so great, that it amounted to a mere nominal retention of power. An indication of the total revolution is that, curiously enough, the freemen who were preserved, not only in those corporations, but in others, for Parliamentary purposes, had no vote preserved to them as freemen for municipal purposes in the reformed corporations.

587. Let us first take the 10 towns, what are what are they?—Belfast, Clonmel, Cork, Drogheda, Dublin, Kilkenny, Limerick, Londonderry, Sligo, and Waterford.

588. Can you tell me how many of those were close corporations before; I mean self-elected corporations, or nominated corporations?—This is what the General Report of the Commissioners

Mr. W. N. Hancock, LL.D.

5 May 1876.

Mr. *Butt*—continued.

sioners of 1835, says at page 8: "In reference to their constitutions and structure, the existing municipal corporations in Ireland may be divided into two classes, namely; first, those in which the commonalty or freemen have, directly or indirectly, a voice in, or control over, the election of the corporate officers, or the management of some of the corporate business; and, secondly, those in which no class of freemen is in practice recognised, or in which, if admitted, they are, from the defective constitution of the corporate body, or by usurpation practically excluded from all interference in the administration of the corporate affairs, and in the election of the municipal authorities. The greater number of the corporations belong to the latter class, and may be generally described as consisting of self-elected irresponsible governing bodies of 12 or more members, by whom the whole corporate powers are exercised. In many of this class the existence of freemen is unknown, and even where admitted, they are in most cases comparatively few in numbers, and have little, if any, power or influence. In Belfast there are but six freemen now known to be in existence." Then they go on: "the only municipal corporations which we find capable of being comprised in the former class." That is, the class where the freemen have directly or indirectly some voice in, or control over, and in that class I find Clonmel, Cork, Drogheda, Dublin, Limerick, and Wexford.

589. Are you able to tell me, by way of seeing what change was made by the Municipal Reform Act, what was the constitution of the Belfast Corporation before, what was the governing body of the Belfast Corporation, and how were they chosen before the Municipal Act?—The position of Belfast is thus described in the General Report of 1835: "In the town of Belfast the whole municipal corporation consists of the Sovereign, the lord of the castle, the constable, his appointee, 12 self-elected burgesses, and six freemen."

590. I believe the Marquis of Donegal was lord of the castle, was he not?—I believe he was lord of the castle, and the one sole proprietor of the place.

591. And of the corporation too?—Yes, and of the corporation.

592. And he nominated the Member of Parliament for Belfast?—Yes, practically; the Sovereign was his nominee; I believe all of them were his nominees.

593. Could you tell me how many counties of cities there are among those 10 corporations?—Amongst the 10 corporations there are six, the county of the city of Cork, the county of the town of Drogheda, the county of the city of Dublin, the county of the city of Kilkenny, the county of the city of Limerick, the county of the city of Waterford.

594. Were there any other counties of cities in Ireland except those six?—There was an anomalous county which was supposed to be a county of a city, but really was not; it was the county and city of Londonderry, and in that case the municipal corporation of Londonderry appointed the sheriffs for the whole jurisdiction, but it was really a county at large.

595. Thus the county at large was called the county of the city, and county of Londonderry?—Yes, the city and county; but really the whole county was one bailiwick; it was not made like the others; it had that peculiarity, that the municipal corporation appointed two sheriffs, who were both for the city and for the whole county.

Mr. *Butt*—continued.

596. There were two sheriffs appointed by one corporation?—Yes, in those days it had that peculiar jurisdiction; it was not really a county of a city, but it had the power till it was taken from them and the county made like other counties at large, and when that was taken away from them it was not made a county of a city, but a county at large.

597. There were also two other counties of cities; the county of the town of Carrickfergus, and the county of the town of Galway?—Yes, there were.

598. And they did not get corporations among those 10?—No; in the case of Galway, before the passing of the Corporation Reform Act, their in-gate and out-gate tolls were very severely reported on by the Municipal Commissioners, and they accordingly got a private Act of Parliament to protect their tolls. They had a Board of Commissioners working under that Act at the time that the Municipal Corporation Act passed, and they were dealt with specially. Then Carrickfergus was a small place; it was treated as similarly entitled to a municipal commission, and they can apply for a charter, only they have not the population that would entitle them to an urban sanitary authority.

599. When you say that Galway was specially dealt with, why was not Galway placed in Schedule B., as entitled to have municipal commissioners; I am speaking of the Municipal Corporation Act, the 3rd & 4th of Vict., the second towns, Schedule B. I want to know how was Galway dealt with by the Municipal Reform Act?—It is very peculiarly dealt with; if you look at Section 13 of the Municipal Reform Act, it says, "And be it enacted that from and immediately after the passing of this Act, the body or reputed body corporate named in the said Schedule B. to this Act annexed, in connection with the borough of Galway, shall be dissolved, and that on the 25th day of October 1840, in every borough named in the Schedules B. and I. respectively to this Act annexed, in which there shall have been then elected any commissioners under the Act of the ninth year of the reign of King George the Fourth hereinafter mentioned, and in every borough named in the Schedule H. to this Act annexed, were in any union in which such borough shall be situate, there shall be then guardians of the poor, and on the 25th day of October in the year 1841, in every other borough named in the Schedules B. and I. respectively to this Act annexed, the body or reputed body corporate named in each of the said Schedules B. and I. respectively in conjunction with that borough, shall be dissolved."

600. They stand in Schedule B., too, do they not?—They do; with the mayor, sheriffs, free burgesses, and commonalty of the town and county of the town. Galway had got commissioners, as far back as 1836, and I think they have been dealt with by special legislation, and ever since they have had a purely special code. The first Act is 1836; then there was an Act for the better paving of Galway in 1853; that was before the Towns Improvement Act; they anticipated that, and they got a Town Improvement Act of their

Mr. W. N. Hancock, LL.D.

5 May 1876.

Mr. *Butt*—continued.

their own. Then they had a special Act in 1863, and now again they have got Provisional Orders.

601. At all events, neither the county of the town of Galway, nor the county of the town of Carrickfergus got new corporations?—They did not.

602. What changes, generally speaking, did the Municipal Reform Act effect, first in the 10 towns in which the old charters were continued?—There is a very simple general view put in the General Report of the Commissioners of 1835.

603. That was before the Act, was it not?—Yes; but this will give you a view of the general result of it; it gives you the whole view of the principal corporations that it applies to. "We apprehend the term Municipal Corporation may, in reference to our present inquiry, and on a view of the several charters which have come under our notice be fairly considered to mean an incorporation of persons, inhabitants of, or connected with, a particular place or district, enabling them to conduct its local civil government; accordingly the regulation of the municipal district and its inhabitants," that is one object; "The preservation of the public peace within it by a magistracy chosen by and from the incorporated body," that is the second object. The third is, "The administration of justice to the community in domestic tribunals," that is the next object; those "are among the principal objects for which provision is made in the various charters of incorporation appearing to have been granted from time to time to the corporate cities and towns in Ireland. Another important object of many incorporations was the election of members to represent their respective cities and towns in Parliament." Then, again, "A further object, and one which appears to have engaged more attention on former times than at present, was the protection and regulation of the local trade by means of commercial societies or guilds." If you look into subsequent passages in the Report you will find a number of things, that their power under a charter was to make bye-laws, and instead of bye-laws, I apprehend that the power of making bye-laws under the Act of the 3 & 4 Vict., with the consent of the Lord Lieutenant, superseded the chartered power of making bye-laws; it was superseded and entirely taken away. Secondly, with regard to the Charter Justices, that is described at page 27, "The Corporate Charter Magistrates are usually those only who hold the temporary offices of mayor, provost, &c.; but in some cases the charters also confer magisterial authority on other officers as on the individuals belonging to a particular class of the corporation." "In the cities of Cork and Dublin all the aldermen are, by charter, justices of the peace for life." "In Dublin, the magisterial business is transacted at four divisional offices of police, to each of which an alderman, sheriff's peer, and barrister, selected for life, are attached with fixed salaries." "The ordinary duties of the justices of the peace are exercised by such officers of the corporation as are by charter invested with the authority of magistrates; in some instances, additional magistrates have been appointed under Acts of Parliament." The whole of that has been modified, that is to say, the magistrates are all apppointed by the Crown, and the police magistrates in Dublin are all public officers.

Mr. *Butt*—continued.

604. Then there was taken away from the old corporations, as taken away from the corporations of the towns, the power of appointing their own magistrates?—Whether by that particular Act, or whether by concurrent Acts, I will not say; I am only saying what the law was before, and what it is since; the change is part of one transaction.

605. Was it not expressly taken away by the Municipal Reform Act?—I cannot say.

606. Can you tell me is it a fact that, before the Municipal Corporation Act, a number of corporations in Ireland had the exclusive power of appointing charter justices within their jurisdiction?—Yes.

607. Can you tell me whether it was not just the same as in England, except in the case of London, to which the English Act did not apply, it being entirely taken away from the corporations?—I did not examine the Act upon that point, but it is substantially taken away either by that or by some concurrent legislation; whether it was that particular Act that did it or not, I cannot say.

608. Some of those have Admiralty jurisdictions, have they not?—Yes, there was a provision about that.

609. Are they not all taken away expressly by the Municipal Reform Act?—I believe so; let me turn, just to give their view of it, to page 15: "The preservation of the public peace within it by a magistracy chosen by and from the incorporated body, and the administration of justice to the community in domestic tribunals." Then, at page 22, it says, "In the corporate districts which are counties of cities and counties of towns, and in Londonderry, which is a county and city, two sheriffs are annually elected," and so on. That appointment of sheriffs was taken away from the corporate bodies of Ireland, and given to the Crown. The next is the recorder: "The office of recorder is in some cases expressly created by charter; in some we have found such an officer appointed without this authority; the appointment is in some cases, in form, annual. In Dublin, and some other corporations, it has been made permanent by Statute." The appointment of the recorder was taken away from them and given to the Crown, and then there was a limitation as to recorders, that they were only to exist in certain cases. Then the clerk of the peace was also a common officer of all the corporations, and in Limerick, he was clerk of the Crown. "A town clerk, who in counties of cities and towns is also usually the clerk of the peace, is a common officer in all the corporations. In Limerick, he is also clerk of the Crown." That patent was taken away from the corporations; all which is left to them, and which still exists, is the Lord Mayor's Court, in Dublin, and a few courts of conscience. Then about the election of Members of Parliament; that was taken away from them.

610. That is not a corporate privilege?—No; then about the regulation of local trade; the only remnant of that is, that they regulate the trade of pawnbroking.

611. Surely there is no guild of pawnbrokers?—But in analogy to a guild, the corporation of Dublin have special statutory powers over it which were not taken away, and the lord mayor is also the clerk of the markets.

612. In counties of cities, and in counties of towns,

Mr. W. N. Hancock, LL.D.

5 May 1876.

Mr. Butt—continued.

towns. the power of nominating sheriffs was taken away from the corporation, was it not, and transferred to the Crown?—Yes.

613. And so was the nomination of the clerk of the peace?—Yes.

614. In other corporations, the power of appointing charter magistrates was taken away?—Either by that or by concurrent legislation.

615. Was the power of regulating markets taken away from them?—No: wherever they had a charter clerk of the markets, I do not think that that was taken away; I do not think that that was touched, because the market question was a question, as I explained to the Committee before, which was not dealt with.

616. Are you aware that in a great many corporations they had a power by charter of holding markets?—Those were not touched.

617. A few had the power of collecting tolls, and those were not touched, were they, by the Municipal Corporation Act?—They were touched, so far as the privilege of freemen being exempt from tolls. It was very important still to particular traders to be exempt from tolls, and the privilege was preserved to these freemen only who were admitted before a certain date in 1835.

618. The power of levying tolls of any kind or description, that they could by charter levy before, they can levy still?—They made returns to me that they did levy tolls, and I believe that it is not touched.

619. Have you considered at all that some of them had the power of collecting toll traverse?—The only remnant of that that I found was in Galway, where they have got in-gate and out-gate tolls still. In Limerick and in Cork there was great litigation about it, but I believe that you will find it to be so.

620. The corporation finally failed, did they not, to establish their right to toll traverse?—I believe so.

621. I believe that a great many of those corporations in Ireland have rights of levying tolls in different ways?—They have rights of levying tolls, but then the legality of all those rights had begun to be questioned.

622. I mean that whatever rights they had before were in nine out of ten towns left untouched by the Municipal Reform Act?—I believe so.

623. You have heard of slippage and anchorage, I suppose, in Dublin; are you aware that there was a very litigated trial about that?—That was before my time.

624. Have you at all considered this; was there any difference between what was done in England by the English Reform Act and what was done by the Irish Reform Act?—I did not look at that point except for the franchise; that is the only point I looked at; but I believe that the appointment of sheriffs was not taken away; we had it up before the Select Committee of the House of Commons in 1870 on Municipal Privileges.

625. Charter magistrates were taken away in both countries?—Yes, I believe so. I do not know about magistrates in England.

626. Do you know what provisions the Municipal Reform Act made as to charities which were vested in the corporation?—The largest charity in Dublin was the Blue Coat Hospital. As I happen to be a governor of it, I know the way it was dealt with. The Lord Primate, the Archbishop of Dublin, the Bishop of Meath, and the Lord Chancellor are empowered by the Act of 1840 to nominate the new trustees, being Protestants; the old corporate trustees that were there at the time were allowed to remain.

627. Was it the fact that all charities, or with very few exceptions, that were administered by corporations, were taken away from them on the passing of the Reform Act and vested in trustees?—I believe so.

628. I believe that those were the principal things that were done at the time?—Yes, those are the principal things.

629. Do you know the franchise that was established by the Municipal Corporation Act?—Yes, I gave it in a general way on the last day. I have since made it out with exact precision, and I will read the effect of it: "Male inhabitant householder six months resident in borough, or within seven miles, occupying house, warehouse, counting house, or shop, which with land shall, at poor law valuation with landlord's repairs and insurance added, be equal to 10 *l.*, who has been rated for 12 months and must have paid poor rates, grand jury cess, municipal rates, and all rates and taxes except those within three months. The 10 *l.* valuation of rating, with a certain amount of landlord's repairs and landlord's insurance, is equivalent to about 8 *l.* 10 *s.* poor law rating." That is from a Return that was made on Mr. Bruen's motion by the corporation of Sligo, giving a definite figure as to their estimate of ratings; in Parliamentary Return for 1875, No. 455, page 15.

630. Is it not generally considered that that was very nearly equivalent to a 10 *l.* rating?—No, the 10 *l.* was made up of the poor law valuation with the landlord's repairs and insurance; but then they say that they come very nearly to an 8 *l.* 10 *s.* rating.

631. What I asked you was generally, that that comes much nearer to 10 *l.*?—I do not know. I give you the figure, because it happened to be returned in the Paper before the House.

632. Taking those 10 towns, confining yourself entirely to them, do you know whether any change has been made in the franchise of any of them?—In Dublin there was a change made in the franchise.

633. What was the change?—I will just give you what I believe to be the effect of it. It is regulated by the Municipal Corporations Act, Ireland; an Act to amend Municipal Corporations, Ireland, Act, so far as relates to the Borough of Dublin, passed in 1849, Section 3; "Every male person of full age who, on the last day of August in any year, shall have occupied any house, warehouse, counting-house, or shop, within such Borough of Dublin during that year, and the whole of the two preceding years, and also during the time of such occupation shall have been an inhabitant householder within the said borough, or within seven statute miles of the said Borough of Dublin shall, if duly enrolled in that year according to the provisions of the said recited Acts, be a burgess of such borough and member of the body corporate of the mayor, aldermen, and burgesses of such borough: provided always, that no such person shall be so enrolled in any year from and after the present year, unless he shall have been rated in respect of such premises, so occupied by him within the said borough to all rates made for the relief

Mr. *Butt*—continued.

relief of the poor of the electoral division or union wherein such premises are situated during the time of his occupation as aforesaid, and unless he shall have paid, on or before the last day of August as aforesaid, all such of the rates, cesses, and taxes specified in the schedule to this Act annexed, as shall be payable by him (if any), in respect of the said premises, except such as shall become payable within six calendar months next before the said last day of August: Provided also, that the premises in respect of the occupation of which any person shall have been so rated, need not be the same premises or in the same parish, but may be different premises in the same parish, or in different parishes."

634. Are you aware that that franchise then established in the city of Dublin was the same franchise as at that time existed in England?—It is substantially the same.

635. What is the difference?—Nothing material.

636. But is there any difference; are not those the very words of the English Act?—I believe so.

637. Do you know at all anything of the circumstances under which that change in Dublin was effected?—No, I do not.

638. Do you know anything of an inquiry made under the Act in two local inquiries that sat in the city of Dublin, presided over by Mr. Hayward?—I do not; I have not looked at that.

639. I suppose you do not know, do you, that that assimilation of the franchise of Dublin to the English franchise was assented to by all parties in Dublin?—I believe my recollection goes so far, that I believe that Act was the result of a settlement between all parties in Dublin. But it should be borne in mind that that Act was accompanied by another Act passed the same day, that is the Collection of Rates Act, and it appears from evidence which was given by the Collector General of rates and his chief clerk, and from the Returns which you have got, that it is under the Collection of Rates Act that the restriction of the franchise arises.

640. Independently of that, what I asked you was whether you are not aware that it was by a general agreement of all parties that the English franchise, as it then existed, was applied to the city of Dublin?—I only know that two Acts of Parliament were passed as the result of a general arrangement, but I was not taking any active interest in this at that time.

641. Have you not read the Parliamentary documents which discussed the history of that change in Dublin?—No, I have not.

642. Are you aware of this, that at the same time a very important change was made in the distribution of the wards?—I have only a mere recollection of that. My recollection was that the distribution of the wards was changed so as to give the representatives of property more weight than they had in the first distribution of the wards; the first was a distribution according to parishes, the next was a new distribution of wards, and I believe it was given with that view; but that is simply my recollection.

643 In fact you have not informed yourself upon the history of the changes in the municipal corporation franchise?—No, only from my recollection at the time; but I have not studied is since.

Mr. *Butt*—continued.

644. Are you able to tell me this: whether, taking the corporation of Dublin first, it had at the time of the passing of the Municipal Reform Act control over the local management of the city?—There was a paving board appointed by the Crown.

645. Had they control over the supply of water?—I have not had occasion to go into all this; but I will show you what will tell you in a better way what powers were given to the Corporation; there is this recital in the Dublin Improvement Act of 1849: "And whereas it is expedient that the said recited Acts, in so far as they relate to the paving, lighting, cleansing, widening, and improving of the streets and thoroughfares within the borough of Dublin, and to turnpike roads therein, should be repealed, and that other and enlarged powers and provisions should be made and granted for these purposes, and for the sanitary improvement of the said borough, and also that the public markets within the said borough should be better regulated, and that new markets should be established therein: And whereas it is expedient that the fiscal powers of the grand jury of the county of the city of Dublin, and the sessions grand jury of the city of Dublin, so far as they relate to matters required to be done within the borough of Dublin, should be transferred to the Corporation."

646. In those places which are counties of cities or counties of towns, I suppose you are able to say that they were entirely like counties at large in their several jurisdictions for every purpose?—In those very large towns there were modifying Acts of Parliament; there were local Acts; but in so far as they were not modified by local Acts they were so.

647 I do not ask what the jurisdiction was, but I believe the system is essentially distinct in the county of Cork and the county of Tipperary?—Yes, but their fiscal powers were modified in some cases by local Acts.

648. So might the fiscal powers of the county of Norfolk be modified, but I mean as a general principle, the county of the city of Limerick, or the county of the town of Drogheda, was a county in itself, just as distinct from all other counties as the county of Norfolk?—Certainly.

649. You of course know that there is a system of levying certain rates in Ireland by grand juries?—Yes.

650. Did the grand juries of those counties of cities and counties of towns exercise within their jurisdiction the same powers of levying rates as the grand juries in a county at large?—I believe so, and they do to this day with some slight modifications.

651. Are you not aware that by the Dublin Improvement Act, all the powers of the county of Dublin grand juries were transferred to the corporation?—Yes, all fiscal powers of the county of the city grand juries.

652. And that they exercise them now?—Yes.

653. Can you tell me whether that is the case in any other counties of towns or cities in Ireland?—Yes; the example of Dublin was followed by Cork and then it was followed by Limerick.

654. In both those cities of Cork and Limerick, the powers of the grand jury to levy rates have ceased,

Mr. W. N. Hancock, LL.D.

5 May 1876.

Mr. *W. N. Hancock*, LL.D.

5 May 1876.

Mr. *Butt*—continued.

ceased, and they are exercised by the corporation?—Yes.

655. Under special Acts relating to each of those towns?—Yes, and Waterford applied for it in the year 1875, and the House of Commons passed the Bill, but it was thrown out in the House of Lords on another point altogether; that is to say, they wanted to add a little bit of the county of Waterford, so as to extend the boundary, and I believe it was on that point that they lost the Bill, although the House of Commons passed the Bill with the extension of the boundary of Waterford.

656. So that I am right in saying that in the county of the city of Dublin, in the county of the city of Cork, and in the county of the city of Limerick, the corporation have got powers that the old corporations never had?—Certainly.

657. That is to say, they have got powers which were formerly vested in the grand jury?—Yes.

658. Are you aware that the city of Dublin retained the powers of managing the supply of water up to the time of the Municipal Reform Act?—It was under some local Act; I do not recollect how it was.

659. Do you know whether they had the power of paving and lighting?—I did not look at that; I looked at the legislation since; I did not go back to that date. The Act of 1849 says, "Whereas it is expedient that the said recited Acts in so far as they relate to the paving, lighting, and cleansing," and so on, of the city of Dublin, should be repealed.

660. You stated the other day, I think, that the freemen who were elected by the corporation of the city of Dublin took a part in the municipal government?—To some extent; they are returned in the General Report of 1835 that I have read as taking part to some extent, and therefore I took my information from that, that they had powers to some extent.

661. Do you know what the constitution of the corporation of Dublin was at the time of the passing of the Municipal Reform Act?—No, I do not.

662. Do you know that the corporation of the city of Dublin consisted, by charter and Act of Parliament, of a common council elected by the different guilds?—I did not know that. I think it right to mention that it is two years since I have been in charge of this subject at all. I am not in charge of the local taxation. When I got the summons I did the best that I could to refresh my recollection of it. I thought that what the Committee wanted chiefly was what passed since the Act of 1840 regulating these towns, and not the earlier part. I found the earlier history detail of the large towns too elaborate to go into in the time since I was summoned.

663. Are you able to tell me this, whether amongst those 69 corporate towns which were affected by the Municipal Reform Act, there were any of them bodies administering the local affairs of the town independently of the corporation?—In Dublin there were; there was a paving board appointed by the Government.

664. Were there not commissioners under the Act of Geo. 4?—There were in some of those cases.

665. Even though there was a corporation?—Yes.

Mr. *Butt*—continued.

666. As a matter of fact, the corporation retained its powers, whatever they were, and the commissioners, under the Act of the 9 Geo. 4, attended to whatever was intrusted to them?—There was a list published by Mr. Moore, in his Compendium of the Irish Poor Law, of all the towns under the Act of the 9 Geo. 4, and the only one of those corporate towns that I find mentioned that had commissioners under the Act of the 9 Geo. 4 is Clonmel.

667. I think you will find that almost all of them had corporations which existed up to the last. In Schedule B. you observe there was a corporation in Tuam?—But there were very few of them had Commissioners under the Act of 1828 before 1840. Most of those that are in the long list in the schedule were after the Act of 1840, because there was a technical defect in the Act of 1828; it was, that they could only adopt the Act where there had been a vestry cess levied. Then it was found that in a very large number of towns there was no vestry cess levied; then there was an Act of Parliament passed in 1843 to enable them to use the poor law valuation instead of the vestry cess, and I rather think that the bulk of those towns came in after 1843.

668. You say this, at Question 19 of your former evidence: "In the Act of 1840, the Act of 1828 was recognised to this extent, that the town councils were allowed to adopt it for lighting purposes instead of their old vestry powers," had, in point of fact, any power whatever inherent in them over the lighting of the city?—Some of them had under special Acts, but not inherent; they were all under special Acts.

669. Then, in fact, whatever powers the corporation had acquired to light the city must have been by some special Act?—Yes.

670. Which might as well have vested it in any other body as well as in the corporation?—It might.

671. Then in the Act of 9 Geo. 4, c. 82, s. 2, was there not this provision: "Be it further enacted, that from and after the passing of this Act, upon the application of 21 or more householders residing in any city, town corporate, borough, market town, or other town in Ireland, the lighting, watching, cleansing, or paving of which is not provided for by or under any Act of Parliament," and so on?—That exactly proves that whenever corporations had it, they had it under a private Act of Parliament.

672. Then whenever the paving, lighting and cleansing, were provided for by an Act of Parliament, those powers could not be got?—I believe not.

673. Is not that the meaning of the clause?—I believe so.

674. But whenever they were not so provided for, whether or not there was a corporation which could be elected, this body did pave, light, and cleanse?—Yes; if you look at the commencement of the Act of 1828, there is a recital of the Acts of the Irish Parliament that are repealed. I read those Acts over to see what the state of affairs was before that, and I have a recollection that where there is not a provision by a local Act, then the vestries were to have power to deal with it. In the large towns like Dublin and other places, there were local Acts. Then there was a provision in the Act of 1840, for substituting

Mr. *Butt*—continued.

tuting the powers of the corporation for those of the Commissioners on certain terms.

675. In towns corporate, and having corporations, might not there concurrently with the corporation exist Commissioners under the 9th Geo. 4?—Yes.

676. What I asked originally was. Are you able to tell me whether that, in point of fact, prevailed to any great extent?—I believe not to a great extent.

677. What was the qualification under the 9th Geo. 4?—The qualification under that Act was, occupation of a dwelling house of the value of 5 *l.* for 12 months.

678. Did the body so elected manage the paving, lighting, and cleansing of the town?—Yes; with a strict limit of rating.

679. Was not there a graduated scale of rating?—Yes.

680. And small houses were entirely exempt, were they not?—All below 5 *l.* were exempt.

681. And above 5 *l.* the rating increased as the house rose in value?—Yes.

682. That body of Commissioners so managing the lighting, paving, and cleansing of the town might co exist, at all events, with a corporation in that town?—Yes, they did co-exist with the corporation of Clonmel.

683. I believe that the Act of the 9th Geo. 4, is practically superseded?—There are 12 towns still under it.

684. Are they corporate towns?—No; that is to say, they are not municipal corporate towns.

685. Have they Municipal Commissioners?—No, they could not have; if they adopted the 9th of Geo. 4, the Municipal Commissioners immediately ceased.

686. Were they towns in Schedule B. of the Reform Act?—Some of them were. Armagh is the very first of them, and Bandon also.

687. Bandon had a corporation, had it not?—Yes; but Armagh is one of the first of them.

688. Then Armagh had a corporation?—Yes.

689. And Tralee had a corporation, and a close corporation?—Yes.

690. And Bandon and Youghal also?—Yes; these are the four principal towns of this class; there are eight other small ones still under the 9th Geo. 4; several of them are in this list in Schedule B.

691. How did the Corporation Act deal with the towns in Schedule B.?—Wherever they had commissioners under the 9th Geo. 4, the corporate property was transferred to those commissioners. Then there was an Act of Parliament immediately afterwards to facilitate their getting commissioners under the 9th Geo. 4; and that was allowing the poor rate valuation to be substituted for the vestry cess qualification; and I know that a very large number adopted it.

692. How did the Municipal Act deal with the towns in Schedule B. in the first instance?—That is the section which I was reading before, Section 13 of the 3 & 4 Vict. c. 108, "In every borough named in the Schedules (B.) and (I.) respectively to this Act annexed, in which there shall have been then elected any commissioners under the Act of the ninth year of the reign of King George the Fourth hereinafter mentioned, and in every borough named in the Schedule (H.) to this Act annexed, where in any union in which such borough shall be situate, there shall be then guardians of the poor," then the corporation shall be dissolved. Those corporations were all dissolved then.

Mr. *Butt*—continued.

693. What became of their property; was there any provision made for their government?—The property went in three ways. In certain boroughs it went to the Municipal Commissioners.

694. Will you take those in Schedule B?—I think they were re-classified in other Schedules afterwards dealing with them. The general view is very simple, and it was this: There were 19 towns, and as to those they were to have Municipal Commissioners; then those Municipal Commissioners that had transferred their property were to hold that property until the commissioners, under the 9th of Geo. 4 were elected, or until they got a charter. One of them, Wexford, got a charter. A certain number got commissioners under the 9th of Geo. 4; two did not get them under it, but got them under the Act of 1854, and the only one remaining of that body is Carrickfergus; they are the only surviving Municipal Commissioners which I mentioned in the former part of my evidence, and which I recommended to be abolished. Then the next class were those that had certain property, and if they had commissioners under the 9th of Geo. 4, they got that property; but wherever there were not commissioners in that way, it went to the poor law guardians.

695. Will you just look at the 15th section of the Municipal Corporation Act and tell us what is its effect?—That is just the effect that I say the real and personal estates of such corporations were to vest in the commissioners under the 9th of Geo. 4 until a charter was granted. In Galway there in the town commissioners under the Act of the 6th & 7th of William 4, c. 117, until a new charter was granted.

696. That was placing Galway in exactly the same position as if it was under the 9th of Geo. 4, because they had got a private Act for electing commissioners to pave and light before the 9th of Geo. 4 was passed?—No, it was in 1836, afterwards, but before the Corporation Act of 1840 was passed; the commissioners were treated as equal to the commissioners under the 9th of Geo. 4, and power was reserved to them to apply for a charter if they thought right.

697. That is reserved to all the corporations in Schedule B.?—Yes, but it is expressly reserved there.

698. Was not Galway treated exactly as all the other towns in Schedule B. were, with the exception that it was necessary to make a special provision recognising this special Act; that is the entire difference between Galway and the other towns?—Yes, it had commissioners under a local Act.

699. Where there were no commissioners under the 9th Geo. 4, what provision did this statute make?—Except as to the 19 towns which could have municipal commissioners, the corporate property went to the boards of guardians.

700. Not in Schedule B., in Schedule H. it went to the guardians; will you look at the 16th section?—Schedule G. is the class where they have Municipal Commissioners. Section 16 says that "In any borough named in the Schedule G. to this Act annexed, in which there shall not then have been elected any commissioners under the said Act of the 9th year of King George the 4th, there shall be constituted a board of commissioners for the disposition of such property according

Mr. *W. N. Hancock*, LL.D.

5 May 1876.

Mr. W. N. Hancock, LL.D.

5 May 1871.

Mr. *Butt*—continued.

according to the provisions hereinafter contained, to be called 'The Municipal Commissioners' of such borough, until such charter may at any time afterwards be granted, or until there shall be elected in such borough any commissioners under the said Act of the ninth year of King George the Fourth, and upon the grant of any such charter, and the election of a council under its provisions, or upon the election of any commissioners under the said Act of the 9th year of King George the 4th, such board of commissioners shall cease;" that is what I was explaining.

701. Were not their commissioners appointed in those towns mentioned in Schedule G. to administer their affairs?—There was power to elect commissioners.

702. They were obliged to elect them, were they not?—Yes, it says, "There shall be constituted a board of commissioners."

703. With one for every 500 inhabitants?—Yes.

704. Are there any towns in Ireland under that temporary provision of the Municipal Corporation Act?—Carrickfergus alone is.

705. Then there is no other town except Carrickfergus under that temporary provision?—I believe not.

706. And there are 12 towns under the 9th Geo. 4?—Yes.

707. In any other towns in Ireland in which there is anything like municipal government, what are they under?—The bulk of them are under the Act of 1854, the Towns Improvement Act, and there are many under special Acts.

708. Now as to the Towns Improvement Act of 1854, what are its provisions, franchise, and powers?—The first qualification under the Act of 1854, is the immediate lessor, whether a person or a corporation, of lands, &c., within the town boundary of the value of 50 *l.*, who resides within five miles of the town boundary, and then by the interpretation clause, "lands," includes all lands, springs, dwelling-houses, vaults, cellars, stables, breweries, manufactories, mills, and other house, buildings, and yards, and places. Then the second part of the section relates to the occupier's qualification, and that appears to let in occupiers irrespective of value. The restriction arises from the obligation to be rated to the poor law. By the Act of 1843, as to rating of lessors of small tenements, it is provided "That whenever the net annual value of the whole of the rateable hereditaments in any union occupied by any person or persons having no greater estate or interest therein than a tenancy from year to year, or holding under any lease or agreement, or leases or agreements made after the passing of this Act, shall not exceed 4 *l.*, the rate in respect of such property shall after the passing of this Act be made on the immediate lessor or lessors or person or persons."

709. What are the qualifications for an elector under the Towns Improvement Act?—The first is what I have mentioned; the immediate lessor, whether a person or corporation, of lands within the town boundary of the value of 50*l.* who resides within five miles of the town boundary. The second is a person or corporation occupying as owner or tenant, and rated for one year and nine months to the poor law at upwards of 4 *l.*, as an occupier, and having paid all rates under the Act, 1854, or any local Act except those imposed within six months. The provision in that statute as to the payment of poor rates and grand jury cess being necessary was repealed in 1871. Then the third qualification under the Act of 1854, is a person or corporation rated as immediate lessor to the poor law to the value of 4 *l.* or upwards, for one year nine and a half months, having paid all rates under the Act of 1854, or any local Act except those imposed within six months. Then the fourth qualification under the Act of 1854 is joint occupiers rated in respect of premises of the value of 4 *l.* or upwards for each occupier, and fulfilling the other conditions of occupier above mentioned under the second qualification.

Mr. *Butt*—continued.

710. Then the electors under this Towns Improvement Act are persons first of all occupiers rated at 4 *l.*?—Yes.

711. Then the immediate lessor rated at 4 *l.* or upwards?—Yes.

712. Then the immediate lessor of lands, tenements, and hereditaments of the value of 50 *l.* residing within five miles?—Yes; they need not occupy; the others are immediate lessors, and are rated as such, and immediate lessors of small tenements which they do not occupy.

713. Who are not rated?—Yes; that practically is the case.

714. The first qualification is the qualification merely as the landlord?—Yes.

715. The first landlord above the occupier, if he has premises of 50 *l.*, is entitled to vote?—Yes.

716. And that whether he is rated or not?—Yes; or if he makes up 50 *l.* from a number of premises

717. And that whether he is rated or not?—Yes.

718. It does not require rating?—No.

719. But any one who is rated as immediate lessor at the value of 4 *l.* would be entitled?—He would appear on the rate book, but he would not be rated to pay.

720. How would be appear on the rate book?—Because the immediate lessor's name appears if he is known.

721. Does it appear, no matter what the extent of holding?—If he is known it does; but he would not be liable to the rate unless the occupier failed to pay it.

722. Here is the qualification in section 22, "Every person of full age, who is the immediate lessor of lands, tenements, and hereditaments within such town, or within such boundaries of the same respectively, as aforesaid, of the value of 50 *l.* or upwards, according to the last poor law valuation, and who shall reside within five miles of the boundary of such town;" does not that include every person, whether his name appears on the rate book or not, who is the actual landlord of the premises rated to the value of 50 *l.*?—Yes, but his name would, as a matter of fact, appear in the rate book.

723. But his qualification does not depend upon that?—I could not say confidently whether it does or does not; I do not say that it does. I mean as a matter of business his name would appear on the rate book; I could not give an opinion off-hand as to the legal effect of it.

724. Then the immediate lessor who is rated at 4 *l.* has a vote?—Yes.

725. And the occupier who is rated at 4 *l.* has a vote?—Yes.

726. Except in the case of joint occupiers, that is the qualification?—Yes.

727. The

Mr. W. N. Hancock, LL.D.

5 May 1876.

Mr. *Butt*—continued.

727. The Towns Improvement Act is executed, is it not, by commissioners elected under it?—It is.

728. All these provisions need not be adopted by the town?—No.

729. Might not some of the provisions or all of the provisions of the Towns Improvement Act be adopted by the corporate authorities?—All except those about election.

730. But might not the power be adopted by the corporation?—No; there is an exception from that; the large towns are excepted from it. Section 100 says: "This Act shall extend only to Ireland, and nothing herein contained shall extend to or affect the cities of Dublin, Cork, Limerick, and Londonderry, and the town of Belfast." All the other town councils have, in fact, adopted it entirely, except Waterford, and Waterford has adopted it to a limited extent.

731. They might adopt it, and they have adopted it, without executing it by commissioners elected under it?—They might; there is a provision in it, that if there be a town council, the town council shall be commissioners; that is the way that they come in if they adopt it. There is an express provision to that effect in Section 16:—"Provided that in case of any borough or town corporate in Ireland, the town council of such borough or the Board of Municipal Commissioners elected under the provisions of the Act of the third and fourth years of her present Majesty, cap. 108, wherever the same shall be in force, shall be the commissioners for carrying this Act into execution therein."

732. Would the commissioners elected under that Act have a power of lighting?—Yes, if they adopt lighting; in Waterford they do not adopt lighting, but if they adopted lighting they would exercise those powers.

733. In a corporate town what is the tribunal which regulates the adoption of the Act; is it a meeting of householders?—It is a meeting of householders; it is the same as in other noncorporate towns, but if they adopted it it would not follow that two bodies should be incorporated.

734. Does the corporation get the powers of the Improvement Act by a resolution of the householders of the town?—Yes.

735. In any corporate town that might be done except the excepted ones?—Yes, and as a matter of fact in every corporate town that is done except the excepted ones.

736. But in towns which are not corporate, it must be an election under the Towns Improvement Act?—Yes, some of them have modified the election slightly by local Acts.

737. From your evidence on the last day, you appeared to be under the impression that all freemen elected in the city of Dublin had a vote in the corporation; just take the report in your hand relating to Dublin which I handed over to you?—I merely mentioned Dublin as one of a class; I did not mean to mention Dublin specially, but I mentioned that in the general Report, Dublin is returned as having the advantage under the peculiar arrangement of belonging to the class in which the freemen have some power; that is all I know about it, really.

Mr. *Gibson.*

738. The honourable and learned Member asked you as to the possession, by different corporations in Ireland, of certain powers before 1840, and he mentioned to you the power of appointing justices in some of them; was that power, so far as it existed, affected or taken away by the 171st section of the Act of 1840, of which the marginal note is, "Capital jurisdictions and all other criminal jurisdictions in boroughs, other than are specified in this Act, abolished." Is that the section which refers to the possession of those jurisdictions?—Yes, I apprehend so.

739. That is the section which deals with those charter justices?—Yes, that is the section.

740. You are aware that since the year 1840, 36 years ago, there has been no attempt to exercise any of those jurisdictions, nor claim to exercise them, on the part of any corporation in Ireland?—That I do not know; I only know that it has come under my official knowledge, that there are magistrates who are appointed in all those towns by the Crown, and that the police magistrates are appointed by the Crown, and all the corporate privileges are gone; I know that as a matter of fact, but exactly how it came about, I never had occasion to study.

741. Did you ever hear that the change in the appointment of those magistrates by the Crown has worked other than fairly and well?—No, there has been no complaint about it.

742. You were asked also whether in some of those old corporations they might not possibly be possessed of some Admiralty jurisdiction; I have been unable myself to find in the Act of 1840, the slightest reference to the word Admiralty in any section?—There is some reference to it.

743. Can you tell me which section deals with the Admiralty jurisdiction?—I am not sure which it is.

744. I know that in the report there is reference to the possibility of the possession of such power?—If you look at Section 174, it says, "And be it enacted, that from and after the passing of this Act, so much of all laws, statutes and usages, and so much of all royal and other charters, grants, and letters patent heretofore granted to any borough or any body corporate in any borough, whereby such borough or any place within the precincts or liberties of the same, or such body corporate, or the freemen or inhabitants of the same, claims or claim to be exempted and released from the jurisdiction and office of the Lord High Admiral of England, or of the High Court of the Admiral of England or Ireland, or whereby any such body corporate, or any mayor, bailiff, recorder, steward or other chartered or corporate officer of any borough, has, or claims anything belonging to the office of admiral, whether or not to be exercised by virtue of any commission to them or any of them to be directed, shall be, and the same is hereby repealed."

745. Are you aware whether at the date when that enactment was made to take away this old power, it was exercised, or had it fallen entirely into abeyance at that time?—I do not recollect.

746. Are you in a position at all to say what are the duties of the sheriff of the city of Dublin; for instance, do you know generally what his duties are; he is the person, is he not, who levies all writs of *fieri facias*?—He is.

747. Could you at all give the Committee the means of estimating of about how many thousands,

Mr. W. N. Hancock, LL.D.

5 May 1876.

Mr. *Gibson*—continued.

sands, or hundreds of thousands of pounds are levied by the sheriff of the metropolitan city of Ireland in the course of the year?—I have not that figure with me, but I could supply it.

748. Without referring to the accurate figure, could you give a tolerably close estimate?—I could not; but there is a return made of it. I am not sure of the amount, but the number of writs executed within the jurisdiction of Dublin is very large.

749. And that is all exercised by the sheriff of the city of Dublin?—Yes.

750. Are you aware what are the ingredients which go to make up the qualification for a sheriff; what is there to be found in the present state of the law to give you security about his position or status?—The high sheriff is responsible for the sub-sheriff, who actually does the work.

751. But is there anything regulating the position and status, or pecuniary circumstances of the high sheriff?—I think there is, but I have not it in my mind.

Mr. *Butt*.

752. At Question 10 you were asked by the honourable Member for Cork, "In virtue of that power they created Roman Catholics honorary freemen on some occasions, did they not;" and your answer was, "On some few occasions they did." Then he says, "Those Roman Catholics had a right to take part, not in the governing body, but as a portion of the freemen at large;" and you reply, "Yes;" do I understand this answer to suggest that my friend was asking you that those were mere honorary freemen, and do those answers suggest that being honorary freemen they have any power at all in Dublin in the corporation, or to vote in any way at all as honorary freemen in any borough?—I could not answer that question; I answered from recollection of the effect of reading the report of the Municipal Corporation Commissioners. It is at page 13 of the Appendix to the Report of the Municipal Corporation Commissioners (Dublin). "The common councilmen are those who have served the office of sheriff, called sheriffs' peers; and representatives elected triennially by the several guilds of the city. By the first section of the 33rd of Geo. 2, chap. 16, the number of sheriffs' peers is not to exceed 48, and in practice there are not so many. There were 35 on the 1st of January 1834, of whom four had become sheriffs' peers without serving the office on payment of a fine. The number of representatives of the guilds is 96 in the following proportions." Then they give the different guilds: Trinity Guild, or the Guild of Merchants, consisted of 31. Then there are a certain number of tailors, smiths, bakers, butchers, carpenters, saddlers, cooks, tanners, and so on. Then the goldsmiths are four; hosiers, two; brewers, four; barber surgeons, two; the whole number making up 96.

753. So far as you know, are you able to tell the Committee what powers were possessed by the honorary freemen?—No, I am not.

754. Are you in a position to show whether the honorary freemen in any case were by virtue of their appointment as honorary freemen, vested with the franchise in any place?—I am not.

Mr. *Brooks*.

755. Are there any honorary freemen now?—It is not the point whether there are now, but whether there were any before 1840. There are not any now.

Mr. *Gibson*.

756. The power of appointing the officers by the corporation is contained in the 93rd section?—Yes.

757. That section gives the council or board of commissioners acting in the execution of the Act, power to appoint "a fit person not being a member of the council or board, to be the town clerk of such borough, and in every year one other fit person, not being a member of the council or board, to be the treasurer of the borough, and the council of any borough may also appoint such other officers as have been usually appointed in such borough, or as they shall think necessary for enabling them to carry into execution the various powers and duties vested in them by virtue of this Act;" that is the power at present vested by that Act of Parliament in the corporation, is it not?—Yes.

758. Then the 94th section, which follows, places a little restriction upon that, "That no appointment of any officer, other than such as shall usually have been appointed in such borough, shall be made until a statement in writing shall have been submitted by the council to the Lord Lieutenant, describing the nature and proposed tenure of the office about to be created;" these are the restrictions, are they not, upon the appointment at present?—Yes.

759. Are you aware of the circumstances under which the revision of the burgess roll goes on in Dublin; are you aware of the tribunal and machinery created in all the boroughs under this Act of 1840, for the revision of the burgess roll in Section 70?—Yes, Section 70 is with reference to that.

760. Will you describe to the Committee how the assessors are appointed?—The peculiarity about their appointment is, the proviso that each burgess shall vote for only one, and the plain effect of that is that where parties are very nearly equally divided, they are both represented.

761. But the appointment is a popular election by the burgesses?—Yes; but unless one party has two-thirds or over two-thirds, it could not return more than one assessor. It is one way of working the minority clause. "Provided that, nevertheless, that in every such election of auditors or assessors of the borough, or assessors of the ward, no burgess shall vote for more than one person to be an auditor or assessor." If you follow the Act you cannot vote for two people, and the actual effect of that is, that if the majority are more than two-thirds they may elect both assessors; but in Dublin the parties are more equally divided than that; and it is so worked that each party always puts in one assessor.

762. The result is, that Mr. Curran is appointed on the Liberal side, and Mr. Hyndman by the Conservatives?—There is one avowedly appointed on the one side, and one avowedly on the other side.

763. It might be that if the majority was all one way the two would represent the same phase of politics?—Yes, or if the minority happened not to agree. On one occasion I recollect there were

Mr. W. N. Hancock, LL.D.

5 May 1876.

Mr. *Gibson*—continued.

were two candidates started on the minority, but, however, the bulk of the minority were wise enough to support only one.

764. The result is, that the court is constituted thus: the lord mayor sits along with the two assessors, and in all cases where the assessors differ, which occasionally happens, it is by the casting vote of the lord mayor that a decision is arrived at?—It is.

765. Have you any change to suggest in that: would you adopt the same system as is pursued in the revision of Parliamentary voters, or have you any other suggestion to make to the Committee upon that point?—It did not occur to me, but I can say that the system of Parliamentary revision has worked very satisfactorily.

766. Under that system two revising barristers are appointed by the Crown, at an adequate salary, and they sit at certain times of the year, and go through all the lists?—Yes.

767. Do you see any defect in the present system of municipal revision?—I am not familiar with it; it did not come under my notice. I think *primâ facie* it is an objectionable arrangement, but it did not come under my notice that there is anything very wrong in it.

768. You were mentioning something to th honourable and learned Member for Limerick on the subject of the pawnbroking jurisdiction of the corporation; will you develop what you were going to say to the Committee upon that subject; I believe you have prepared a report upon this question?—Yes; I was appointed a commissioner to investigate it.

769. What position is occupied in relation to the pawnbroking trade of the whole of Ireland by the corporation of Dublin?—The marshal of the corporation of Dublin is the registrar of pawnbrokers for the whole of Ireland; besides, the marshal of Dublin and the sword bearer of Dublin, are pawnbrokers' auctioneers. In connection with the whole system of law devised by the Irish Parliament, there are very exceptional taxes levied in Dublin. In the Report for the year 1869, of Returns of Local Taxation in Ireland, page 9, it is stated, "There are five taxes upon the trade of pawnbroking in Ireland all peculia. to this country, arising under Acts of the Irish Parliament still unrepealed. Only one of these taxes applies to all pawnbrokers, one is in virtual operation in only a few counties and towns; and three are by Statute limited to the municipal boundary of the city of Dublin. These taxes were noticed by the Commissioners, who, in 1835, inquired into municipal corporations in Ireland, and also by the Commissioners who at the same time inquired into the state of the poor in Ireland. They also came under the notice of the Select Committee of the House of Commons appointed in 1838, to inquire into the hours and regulations which affect the trade of pawnbroking in Ireland. They are also specially reported on in the Report on the Laws of Pawnbroking in Ireland of 1866." "Fees on pawnbrokers' returns. This is a small tax of 1 *s.* a month, or 12 *s.* a year, payable to the marshal of the city of Dublin by each pawnbroker in Ireland, who is also bound to make at the same time a monthly statistical return."

770. Have you any suggestion to make as to whether it is desirable to leave them jurisdiction with reference to the pawnbroking trade in Ireland, or otherwise?—The two officers I have

Mr. *Gibson*—continued.

mentioned have always discharged their duties as pawnbrokers' auctioneers by deputy. The marshal and sword bearer do not discharge the duty in person. The existence of those offices, and those privileges, and the whole system has prevented the Imperial law upon this point from being extended to Ireland; England was but a few years ago in the same state as Ireland, that is to say, governed by the laws of the last century. In the year 1870 or 1871, there was a Committee in the House of Commons, that investigated the matter, and recommended that the English law should be extended to Ireland. The existence of those sinecure offices and those special taxes stand in the way of that extension, and I believe it is a very great burden to the poor. The whole details are given in the Report on local taxation in 1869.

771. I believe that by the 15th section of the Town Improvement Act, 1854, town councils are empowered to adopt the provisions of that Act?—Yes.

772. Acting under that power, some corporate towns have done so?—There are five that have done so.

773. Are there any that have appointed Commissioners?—All except Dublin, Cork, Limerick, Londonderry, and Belfast, have adopted it.

774. I believe that in the present state of town law in Ireland, there are different franchises for electors under the Act of George Fourth; under the Act of 1854 in Dublin, and in the remaining corporate towns in Ireland, there are four separate franchises, are there not?—There are, and besides that, in some municipalities there are modifications. Under the General Act there are four distinct franchises.

775. Besides various special modifications under special Acts?—Yes.

776. Is it also a fact that there are a vast number of Statutes, many of them giving duplicate or cumulative provisions to corporations in the different towns?—Yes, the cumulative provisions arose from that.

777. Could you give the Committee an approximate figure showing the number of Acts of Parliament that confer on different towns in Ireland the various executory powers under which they work?—I could not.

778. Are they so numerous?—Yes, the Local Acts are very numerous.

779. I believe also there are very numerous general Acts, partially or wholly incorporated?—Yes, there are three distinct Acts. There are the Lighting and Cleansing Commissioners, the Town Council, and the Town Commissioners; they have three jurisdictions. Then as to the sewers, there is the Sewage Utilization Act, the Public Health Act, the Local Government Act, and the Sanitary Act. Then with regard to the water supply, besides the powers of the towns, there is the Sanitary Act of 1866, the Public Health Act of 1848, the Local Government Act of 1858, and the Local Government Act of 1861. With regard to the nuisance removal, besides the town power, there is the Sanitary Act of 1866, the Nuisance Removal Act of 1855 and 1860, the Sanitary Amendment Act, and the Nuisance Removal Amendment Act.

780. Will you hand in as a Paper a Table which will show the duplicate or cumulative provisions?—Yes. (*The same was delivered in.*)

781. I think

Mr. W. N. Hancock, LL.D.

5 May 1876.

Mr. Gibson—continued.

781. I think you are in favour, as you told the Committee, on the last day, of a codification or simplification of the Irish Town Law?—Yes; I should mention that the complication arose principally from the Sanitary Act of 1866; but in that I was under the orders and direction of the Committee of the House of Commons to follow the exact English law, and the English law is contained in Section 55 of the Sanitary Act of 1866, which applies to England as well as Ireland. "All powers given by this Act shall be deemed to be in addition to, and not in derogation of any of the powers conferred on any local authority by Act of Parliament, law or custom, and such authority may exercise such other powers in the same manner as if this Act had not passed." If it had not been for this instruction which was given me, I saw my way perfectly clear at that time, as I had cleared away the old Vestry Acts and old Boards of Health, under statutes peculiar to Ireland, to have dealt in the same way with duplicate powers. All those duplicate powers might have been swept away, but it was not the policy at the time, and I had to carry out my instructions.

782. What time was that?—1866.

783. You were asked by the honourable and learned Member for Limerick as to the legislation of 1840 upon existing charters; I believe that effect is indicated by the following passage in the 1st Section in that Act of Parliament: "That so much of all laws, statutes, and usages, and so much of all Royal and other charters, grants, and letters patent, rules, orders, and directions now in force relating to the several boroughs named in the Schedules (A), (B), and (I), to this Act annexed, or to the inhabitants thereof, or to the several bodies, or reputed or late bodies corporate, named in the said schedules, or any of them as is inconsistent with or contrary to the provisions of this Act, shall be repealed and annulled, from the time when this Act shall come into operation in each of such boroughs respectively." Is that the section to which you were referring?—Yes; that would appear to keep up a much larger amount of authority than it really did, because, as a matter of fact, all of the substantial powers were either existing under local Acts or were dealt with. For instance, in the case of Dublin, it is returned in the General Report of 1855 as having no governing charter.

784. You do not think that that would be met by the words, "as is inconsistent with or contrary to the provisions of this Act shall be repealed and annulled"?—That saving clause would appear to keep a good deal of power; but I believe, as a matter of fact, there was very little power reserved.

785. You were also asked, I think, about whether the Acts of 1849 were the result of a general arrangement?—I know that that was promoted by a meeting of the body of merchants, and I believe that Mr. Codd was the principal mover in it, the Secretary of the Chamber of Commerce. My recollection is that there was some understanding that the whole of that code, not the one Act, but the whole three Acts, the Collection of Rates Act, the Dublin Improvement Act, and the Municipal Corporation Amendment Act, were all part of one arrangement, and the Government took it up and carried it out.

Mr. Gibson—continued.

786. Is it your recollection or impression that that Act of 1849 gave to Dublin all that was then sought by any party?—The Act of 1849 and the Municipal Rates Act, because the Act of 1849 by itself would appear to confer a large franchise; but the restriction in the franchise is got, as appeared by the evidence of the Collector General and his chief clerk, by the Rates Act; and besides that there is the Dublin Improvement Act; those three Acts were all part of one arrangement to adjust the affairs in Dublin. My recollection was that it was accepted at that time by all parties as a settlement.

787. Have you any suggestion to offer to the Committee as to the number of houses that were returned as empty houses in towns in Ireland with regard to the adoption of any legislation on that subject?—There is the Return that Mr. Butt moved for, made last year; and in that I find a column of 2,209 tenements returned as empty. Besides that, there was evidence given on the last day of the sitting of the Committee about the state of a great number of houses, where the immediate lessors have a very wretched class of tenants. That is a subject which has been engaging the attention of the Charity Organization Committee of the Statistical Society of Dublin. We believe that both the empty houses, and a great deal of that unsatisfactory state of house property which was described on the last day, arises from a defect in the law. That is to say, there is no provision for repairing where there is a bad title, no safety in repairing houses. If there is a bad title, or if there is any defect or flaw in the title turned up, the temporary owner, if he happens to lay out his money, just makes it valuable for other parties to get possession of it, and then when they get possession of it they get the whole benefit of his improvements. That has been met by a law in Scotland, a very old law.

788. Is it still in existence and working, or has it fallen into disuetude?—My attention was called to it by Mr. McNeel Caird in his Cobden Club Essay, in the series on Local Government in 1875. He was good enough to send me the Scotch Act. It is a Scotch Act of Parliament of 1663. "Act anent ruinous houses in Royal Burghs: Our Sovereign Lord being informed that upon the high streets of several of His Majesties Burghs Royal, and in the vennels and other passages within the same, there be many houses in the public view of all people resorting thereto, very ruinous and not inhabited these divers years bygone, nor likely to be repaired by any, to the great opprobry of the said burghs, and common scandal of the Kingdome, as being altogether defective of that policy and good order which is, and ever hath been, so earnestly intended in the many wholesome and laudable laws already made, by his Majesty and his Royal Progenitors of most worthy memory. And finding the burroughs very desirous to have these many dangers and inconveniences prevented and remedied, which the inhabitants of these burghs, and the rest of the lieges frequenting the same, do continually fear from such ruinous buildings; doth therefore, with advice of and his estates of Parliament, ordain the provost and bailies of the burgh where such ruinous houses are, to cause, warn, and charge all persons that have or pretends right to the property of such lands and buildings or any annual rents forth thereof, to cause build and repair, in a decent way, within year and day such

Mr. *Gibson*—continued.

such houses and buildings as have been waste and not inhabited three years before the date of the present Act, or shall be waste and not inhabited hereafter by the foresaid space of three years, or else to sell the same to others, to be builded within the same space of year and day, and to charge all known persons, personally or at their dwelling places, and by open proclamation at the paroch kirk or Mercat Cross of the Burgh and all others by open proclamation at the said mercat cross and paroch kirk. And in case of their absence out of this realm at the Cross of Edinburgh and Peer and shoar of Leith upon three-score dayes; with certification to them if they failzie the said provost and bailies shall cause the said lands and tenements to be valued by certain persons to be chosen and sworn by them for that effect, and sell the same to any person that will buy them, and pay the price of the same to these owners, if they be known, and if they be not known, to consign the prices hereof in the hands of the provost, one of the bailies or dean of guild of the said burgh to be forthcoming to these who have interest thereto; and if no man will buy them, it shall be lawful to the said provost and bailies, after appraising thereof as said is, and payment or consignation of the prices of the same, to cast down the said ruinous houses and cause build the same of new. And His Majesty with advice foresaid declares that it shall not be lawful in time coming to any manner of person to pursue them nor their successors therefore, nor pretend any right or interest thereto, but that the said right shall be a perfect security to the builders thereof and their successors." Mr. Caird says, "In Scotland it applies to all Royal Burghs, 80 in number, some of them very small, and the burgh magistrates elected by its inhabitants and called the provost and bailies, are the parties empowered to sanction the proceedings and grant the necessary warrants. The power of a person having a limited or doubtful title to obtain authority from the Dean of Guild to execute improvements on houses in Royal Burghs and to charge the cost on the property, is not statutory, but has grown up by usage and effects an encumbrance equivalent to a mortgage." That is to say, if a man from fear of the powers against ruined houses being exercised, goes to the Dean of Guild, and says, "I will build, but I have not a good title," the Dean of Guild sends the city architect, and if he builds according to the approval of the city architect, he gets a charge before anybody else for the cost of the improvements; and if a person comes back from America, and claims the property before he can take the property, he has to pay the costs of the improvements that have been laid out under the sanction of the corporation. The Statistical Society sent a report on this to the town authorities, all the towns in Ireland which return Members of Parliament, and one of the most important towns has expressed their approval of it.

789. Which town?—The Improvement Committee of the Town Council of Belfast, who forwarded the following minute upon the subject. "A circular from the honorary secretary of the Statistical and Social Enquiry Society of Ireland, asking the council to co-operate in an extension of the Scotch Laws relating to ruined houses in towns to Ireland having been read, Resolved, That the secretary be informed the Members for the borough will be requested to co-operate in any proposition to extend such law to Ireland."

Mr. *W. N. Hancock*, LL.D.

5 May 1876.

790. Can you tell the Committee whether that old statute of Scotland which you have read to us is still acted upon and now in operation in Scotland?—My attention was called to it by Mr. McNeel Caird's Essay in the Cobden Club Series, 1875, and he called my attention to it as a most important provision, and which is still in operation. I was reading from Mr. Caird's letter, giving a description of how it worked at the present moment. He is an eminent man in Scotland, selected by the Cobden Club, to write upon the subject of Scotland.

791. Does the letter which you refer to show the extent of its operation?—No, it does not; he refers to it as an important provision.

792. Do you see from your own study of this question, and the correspondence which you have had upon the subject, any difficulty in passing a similar or analogous law for Ireland?—Not the slightest difficulty. We have in the city of Dublin in Sackville-street, next door but one to the Gresham Hotel, a house in very bad repair, and the probability is, that that house will not be rebuilt for 20 years, because I happen to know something of the complication of the title; I made some inquiries about it, and it is a very complicated title; in some other cases houses have fallen down and people have been injured.

Dr. *Ward*.

793. Was not that difficulty complained of just as much in Scotland as in Ireland?—They have remedied it there in 70 towns, but in Ireland it still exists.

Mr. *Gibson*.

794. The Act of Parliament which you have read was to deal with those houses?—Yes.

795. If you extended that Act to Ireland, would you extend it to all towns without restriction as to size?—Yes; I may mention that many years ago I had charge of a town in Ireland, acting in my brother's place, when he was ill, as agent for a large estate; the proprietor was granting new leases for improving the town; I thought to remedy a ruinous part of the old town of Lurgan, and I had an inquiry made as to all the ruinous houses there, and we traced them in every case to a defective title. We tried to remedy it by adopting the method, first, of getting tenants to consent to breaking the leases on terms of getting new leases; but then we found that the law intervened, that if we granted a new lease it would be what in law is called "a graft," upon the old. They were quite willing to be ejected and take a new lease on honour that they would be fairly treated, but if we ejected them and broke the lease by the ejectment and then granted a new lease, it came within the doctrine of graft, and all the defects of title settled on the new lease.

796. As to the question of auditing, do you see any reason why any town or governing body of a town in Ireland should be exempt from a full and complete Government audit?—No; once the principle is admitted there should be no exception.

797. Can you see any reason why those townships near Dublin which were exempted should remain exempt from the supervision of an adequate public audit?—I think probably they would

Mr. W. N. Hancock, LL.D.

5 May 1876.

Mr. *Gibson*—continued.

would like to have protection, as the grand jurors have, and the poor-law guardians have: but this forms the difficulty: at the time the audit was proposed, it did not give them protection: and I think that their opposition arose from that. If they were offered the protection of the grand jury, if they could go before a judge and take an opinion, they would be willing to adopt it. It is very absurd that the Town Council of Dublin, who administer a good deal of money as a grand jury, can, for every bit of money that they administer as a grand jury, go into the Court of Queen's Bench and get the opinion of a judge as to what they are to do. I will illustrate it in this way: There was a very serious question about the building of Essex Bridge, whether they could apportion the presentment or not; the lawyers were very much divided in opinion, and they applied to two eminent men, and they could not agree. Therefore they went to a judge of the Court of Queen's Bench, and he authorised them to divide it into three assessments; and once he decides it, it is conclusive, and they are safe in acting upon it. It is not fair that after a gentleman has acted upon a doubtful point like that, to be held liable afterwards.

798. You have told the Committee that they are perfectly safe so far as they act as a grand jury, but whenever they act simply as a corporation, they must have their accounts all audited by the local government auditor, Mr. Findley. I believe that the only means of setting them right is by a mandamus obtained at their own expense from the Court of Queen's Bench?—By *certiorari*; they have to take that audit in by *certiorari*; but it is very different having an appeal afterwards to doing it beforehand.

799. It has happened in some cases, has it not, that where they have done so the Court of Queen's Bench have allowed the costs of both sides out of the rates?—I am not aware; I am for the audit, but I am also for protecting gentlemen. I think that it is much nicer to have a case submitted to a judge before it is done, rather than have it fought out immediately afterwards who is to pay for it.

800. Are you aware that under the Local Government Amendment Act of 1871 there is the power of taking the opinion of the Local Government Board as to the surcharge of the auditor?—Yes; but I do not see that the Local Government Board are bound to give an opinion beforehand; that is an invidious thing, and I think that they ought to have power to go to the Court of Queen's Bench or to the Local Government Board beforehand, and then if the Local Government Board in their discretion put any interpretation upon the law, the local authority acting on that might be safe in carrying it out.

Dr. *Ward*.

801. I think you mentioned that Galway was under a special set of Acts?—Yes.

802. When were the mayor and town council abolished in Galway?—In 1840.

803. They had existed, had they not, under old charters?—Yes, they had.

804. Previous to the abolition of the mayor and town council, were there any other corporate bodies appointed in the town; were there not a body of Commissioners appointed by another Act?

Dr. *Ward*—continued.

—Yes, in 1836, the 6th and 7th of William the Fourth, c. 117, a local and personal Act.

805. And those Commissioners were put on the same level, were they not, with the Commissioners under the 9th of George the Fourth to the general Act?—Yes, in 1840 they had the corporate property handed over to them.

806. Under the Act of the 6th and 7th of William the Fourth, what position did those Commissioners occupy; did not they become quite similar to the commissioners under the 9th of George the Fourth?—Not quite similar; they were authorised to adopt the 9th of George the Fourth. The 25 commissioners under this Act were to be the commissioners under the 9th of George the Fourth, if they adopted it.

807. That is to say, it was similar in powers?—If the 9th of George the Fourth was adopted in the town by the householders, they were to be commissioners under that.

808. What was the qualification of an occupying elector then for voting for a commissioner under the Act of William the Fourth?—"A freehold estate of the clear yearly value of 10 *l.* at the least, or in respect of leasehold estate of the clear yearly value of 20 *l.* at the least, or in respect of the occupation or tenancy of a house or other property of the clear yearly value of 10 *l.* at the least."

809. Was not an elector under the 9th of George the Fourth qualified if he had an occupancy of 5 *l.*?—Yes, if the 9th of George the Fourth had been adopted that other qualification would not have been adopted.

810. Under the special Act for Galway you had a double amount for qualifying an occupier to vote under the Act of William the Fourth to what you have under the general Act?—Certainly.

811. Following that there was another local Act setting up those commissioners; why was this local Act brought about?—The Municipal Corporation Commissioners condemned the toll thorough in Galway; they condemned all those tolls in the Report which they made in 1835. The Galway people got a local and personal Act and changed the names of the tolls, of which there were a very large number, into in-gate and out-gate tolls, which took the place of their toll thorough and other tolls.

812. But they preserved their tolls under their next local Act?—Yes, they preserved their tolls.

813. And they came down to the next local Act for the town, did they not?—Yes, that was in 1853.

814. Immediately previous to the general Act of 1854?—Yes.

815. What Act was that?—That was the 16 & 17 Vict. c. 200.

816. There were commissioners appointed under that Act too, were there not?—Yes.

817. Was there any change in the qualification for electors?—Yes, the qualification was the annual sum of 8 *l.* or upwards; they were also to be on the register of voters in force for Members of Parliament for the borough of Galway.

818. In the general Act of 1854, for towns, we find, do we not, that an occupying elector was qualified at 4 *l.*?—Yes; that was passed the next year.

819. So that in Galway an elector was rated twice as high as in ordinary towns under the Act of 1854?—Yes, he was.

820. And

Mr. W. N. Hancock, LL.D.

5 May 1876.

Dr. *Ward*—continued.

820. And he has remained, so I believe?—Yes, the remaining Act is the Act of 1853, and that is not altered in it. At this moment it would appear that in Galway there is that rating qualification.

821. It is much higher; it is double the qualification, in fact, to be a voter for commissioners to what it is in any other town?—It is.

822. Were the tolls abolished by this last local Act?—No, the tolls were reserved, and they are still in force.

823. Was there any power of rating conferred?—Yes.

824. What was the power which did not exist previously?—The Act of 1853, was "an Act for better paving, draining, cleaning, lighting, watching, supplying with water, regulating in regard to markets, and other purposes." It was exactly running in the direction of what was done for all towns in 1854.

825. Is not the improvement rate in Galway just 1 *s.*?—Yes; there is one very peculiar thing in that rate, which is worth mentioning; it says, "That it shall be lawful for the commissioners to make an improvement rate "not exceeding in any one year 1 *s.* in the pound of the full nett annual value of the property included in such rate;" then it goes on to say, "To be apportioned as the poor law rate is apportioned between landlord and tenant;" so that there is an equal division of rating established; although Galway is behind other towns in the matter of tolls, it is in advance of the rest of Ireland in the equal division of rates between owner and occupier, as that principle was sanctioned by Parliament for Galway so far back as 1853.

826. So that there is no power of rating in the Commissioners under this Act except 1 *s.* in the pound?—No, they did not adapt either the Act of 1828 or the Act of 1854.

827. Their corporate funds came, did they not, from those tolls, and from this improvement rate of 1 *s.* in the pound?—Yes, if the improvement rate was levied.

828. Was the improvement rate levied as a matter of fact?—I find no rates levied by the municipal body; I am now referring to Mr. Bruen's Return, ordered the 13th of August 1875.

829. That is to say, in Galway?—It states no rates levied by municipal body.

830. Have they not power to levy those improvement rates?—Yes, they have the power to levy those improvement rates, but they appear not to have availed themselves of it; I found when I was looking into the matter in 1869, that at that time they levied no improvement rate either.

831. They trusted altogether then to the toll?—Yes; they applied for a Provisional Order to mortgage the tolls, and they have got the Provisional Order.

832. We find that under the Act of 1853, which you said they had not rated under, that they had power to provide water, and that they had to apply for a special Act, the 26th & 27th of Victoria, for a Water Bill, empowering them to levy a rate for water?—With regard to those powers, if they are not exercised in a certain time the power of taking land runs out.

833. What is the power of rating under the Act of the 26th & 27th of Victoria?—It is 3 *d.* for the general water rate, and 10 *d.* for the private water rate. I may mention another thing with regard to that toll thorough; the commissioners who inquired into the state of the fairs and markets in Ireland, in 1853, reported as to the tolls thorough: "This toll is exceedingly unpopular; it is, in fact, a tax levied upon the agricultural produce of the surrounding country, for the purpose of defraying expenses which should, in justice, be borne by local taxation."

834. Is that confined to Galway?—Yes.

835. Is that the only town in Ireland under that toll system?—Yes, under that peculiar toll system; it existed in all fortified towns in Ireland; they had it under an old charter from a very early period, and the only remnant of it is in Galway.

836. Are you aware of any disadvantages which their local Acts have placed them under with regard to subsequent legislation?—They were under great difficulties until the Provisional Order system came into operation; before that they could not meet any difficulties without a local Act.

837. When the fines for drunkenness were granted to corporations that became commissioners, were they not excluded by the nature of their Act from the use of those fines?—I do not know.

838. Are you aware that the Burial Act does not apply to them, because they are not regarded as a board of commissioners under the burial body?—That has never happened to come under my notice; the taxation came under my notice, but their burial powers did not come under my notice; they are not returned as a town burial board levying burial rates.

839. The board of guardians is the burial board, is it not?—Yes, but they do not appear to have spent anything in their return.

840. You spoke of Provisional Orders; what Provisional Orders were obtained by Galway?—The latest Provisional Orders were two that were got for Galway in 1875.

841. They came under the Act of the 38th & 39th of Victoria?—Yes; there was an Order dated the 27th of October 1874, authorising the Commissioners of Galway to levy a rate of 2 *s.* in the pound in addition to the rates already levied by them, to be called the paving and repairing rate of Galway. Also authorising the Town Commissioners to apply 4 *d.* of each shilling of the improvement rate, in providing and maintaining slaughter-houses, &c. Then there is an Order dated the 5th of February 1875, authorising the Town Commissioners to borrow money on the tolls, and to apply a portion of the same in paying off judgment debts due to the Galway Gas Light Company, and in enlarging and improving the slaughter-houses in the town of Galway, and in providing an office and watch-house. They borrowed their money not on their rates, but on their tolls.

842. The second Provisional Order was allowing them to borrow 3,000 *l.* on the tolls for paying off the gas debt?—Yes.

843. Is that power of levying a 2 *s.* rate additional to the power of levying the 1 *s.* rate?—Yes, it is.

844. You tell the Committee that they do not levy up to this date the 1 *s.* rate; why then did they get the power for the 2 *s.* rate?—The Order was granted in 1875, but the return would practically be for 1874, so that they may have levied it last year.

845. But

Mr. W. N. Hancock, LL.D.

5 May 1876.

Dr. *Ward*—continued.

845. But they got the Provisional Order in 1874?—But we have not exact information. except as to 1874.

846. Can you tell the Committee why they got this Provisional Order?—I am not aware.

847. Are you aware that that Provisional Order has created an anomaly in the area of the rating?—No, I am not.

848. What is the area of rating of the borough of Galway?—Really I cannot say.

849. The fact is, the old rating was four miles from the centre church, whereas under this Provisional Order they are confined to a two-mile circle?—They have an amount of anomalies there that is very peculiar.

850. You told the Committee, I think, that there were two sets of people dealing with the Borough of Galway: what are they?—The town Commissioners, on the one hand, and the grand jury of the county of the town on the other.

851. Does not that grand jury do the cleaning and paving of the roads to some extent?—Not the cleaning; they keep the roads in repair, I apprehend; as they only levied under the rates for paving they must do so; the grand jury do levy rates.

852. Are you aware that it is almost the same set of individuals on the town grand juries as they have on the town Commissioners?—I am not aware of that, but the grand jury levy 4,405 *l.* a year.

853. For what purpose?—£. 1,200 *l.* of that is for repairing the roads and bridges.

854. That is all the improvement, is it not, which you say could be done by the Commissioners under the 1 *s.* rate?—That comes under the head of paving and repairing streets

855. Is the area over which the grand jury exercise jurisdiction the same area as that of the jurisdiction of the Commissioners?—So far as I know, I believe not, the agricultural part of towns that had got grand jury powers transferred to the municipal power were separated from them and thrown into the county at large. In Cork and Limerick and the county of the town of Drogheda, to a certain extent the rural portion was transferred from the county of the town to the county at large, but that was not done in Galway or Carrickfergus.

856. Have you any suggestion to make with regard to a change of the law in Galway with reference to markets?—The only thing that came under my notice was the toll-thorough. I thought it my duty to report upon that as a peculiarly exceptional tax, which has been condemned by two Commissions before, one of 1835 and one of 1853, and therefore I thought it right to refer to that.

857. Are you quite sure that it was condemned by them?—1853 was the last Commission from which I read to you. The Commissioners who inquired into the fairs and markets in 1853, reported, "This toll is exceedingly unpopular. It is, in fact, a tax levied upon the agricultural produce of the surrounding country, for the purpose of defraying expenses which should in justice be borne by local taxation." If you go back to the Municipal Corporation Commission of 1835 they reported about the tolls generally, and they said with regard to toll-thorough, "The ancient public records show numerous grants of liberty to the corporate towns to take certain tolls for limited periods towards the building and repairs of the towns' walls. All the municipal corporations which claim tolls of this nature appear to have at various times obtained such temporary grants; and to a few, grants of such tolls were made in perpetuity, as in Galway, where very considerable tolls are collected under such title. They are, however, generally in practice, though we apprehend untruly, claimed as belonging by prescription, to the corporate bodies." Galway happened to get the toll in perpetuity, and the others only got it temporarily. The Commissioners go on to condemn it, and they say, "The considerations for which they were given have been almost everywhere neglected, some long unperformed, some imperfectly attended to; the ancient walls and fortifications are generally razed or fallen to decay. The occasional repairs of portions of the public streets, and, in some of one or more bridges are the only services of this character now performed by any of the municipal corporations; and in the great majority, a large share of the expense of such works is defrayed by grand jury presentments on the county at large, or on the corporate district of a county of itself;" then they go on to condemn it. "To the corporate bodies this source of income is uncertain in amount, and, especially in the small towns, expensive and wasteful in the collection. To the public at large it is obnoxious and unpopular as well from the nature of the impost, and the mode in which its payment is enforced, as from the exclusive character of the body in whose name it is demanded." I do not know the name of the body in which it is demanded.

Mr. *Bruen.*

858. Do those tolls still exist which were so denounced?—Yes.

Dr. *Ward.*

859. Is this with reference to tolls that were in the hands of the corporation, as well as in the hands of the Commissioners, because the Commissioners were not appointed in 1836?—They go on to say, "And for the purposes for which it is applied, which rarely include any beneficial expenditure for the accommodation of those whose property and industry contribute to the tax."

860. The Commissioners did not get them in that fashion, I presume?—The view taken in 1835, was corroborated in 1853 by the Fairs and Markets Commission.

861. That, surely, is not a condemnation of the tolls themselves; it is a condemnation of the way in which they were misapplied under the old corporation?—What they objected to was this; they say, "In the Schedules we often find charges on the petty articles of traffic of the poorer classes, and of which the tolls demanded form a serious portion of the intrinsic value," and so on. Then you will find in the Schedule to the Act that the very smallest things, such as rags and feathers, are still taxed.

862. Have you any suggestion to make for altering this system in Galway?—I think that is the only remnant of the old institutions which have been condemned by two Commissions, and that they ought to levy the money by rates.

863. You would then go in, I suppose, for lowering the qualification of the electors of those Commissioners, to the same point as in ordinary towns?—I think there ought to be no difference; they have not gone for a charter, and they have not got an Act of Incorporation.

864. Allusion

Mr. W. N. Hancock, LL.D.

5 May 1876.

Mr. *Brooks*.

864. Allusion was made by the honourable and learned Member for the University, to the sheriffs in the City of Dublin; can you inform the Committee from what body those gentlemen are appointed or selected?—It is the Crown that appoints the high sheriff, and the high sheriff appoints the deputy sheriff.

865. Who selects or nominates the sheriff?—The judges return three names to the Government, and out of those three names the Government select one for sheriff.

866. Can you say if anyone returns the names in the first instance to the judges?—That I do not know.

867. Are you aware that the proportion of Roman Catholics to Protestants, appointed to the office of sheriff, is very small?—I do not happen to know that; I never looked into the point, but my impression is, that it is not in proportion to the population; I have never made it out; I have merely a general impression.

868. Would you be surprised to hear that since the passing of the Act of the 3rd and 4th Victoria, chapter 108, there has been but six Roman Catholic to 29 Protestant sheriffs in the City of Dublin?—My impression is that it is an unequal proportion, but I never calculated the proportion.

869. Do you know, as a matter of fact, that there is much discontent amongst the Roman Catholic population of the City of Dublin at the disproportion?—That I do not know, with the exception of reports in the public papers.

Sir *Arthur Guinness*.

870. On the subject of what you said just now about the sheriffs in Dublin, do you not think that the proportion of the wealth and intelligence of the Dublin Roman Catholics is represented by 6 to 29?—I should think very likely it may be.

871. I mean amongst the merchants, as a general rule, do not you find that the leading merchants are not Roman Catholics in Dublin?—The great wealth of Dublin is certainly in the hands of Protestants.

872. Are you aware that there were two Roman Catholic sheriffs within the last three years?—I do not recollect.

873. As to the Octroi tax in Galway, do you think that it is a very unpopular tax?—Yes, it is reputed to be so by the last Commissioners who inquired locally and specially upon the subject.

874. You think that it is an undesirable tax?—Yes, we have abolished turnpikes, which is a parallel tax; we are in advance of the rest of the United Kingdom in that, and I think that the Galway tax is a most undesirable tax.

875. Do you think that that would be one of those privileges which were taken from the ancient corporations which ought to be restored to them?—I would certainly not restore it.

Mr. *J. P. Corry*.

876. Have you prepared the Returns which I asked you for as to what the effect of voting, such as you propose would be in Belfast or Dublin?—No; it was intimated to me that I should be asked specially about three Acts of Parliament, therefore I devoted my whole attention to that. I have some Returns which have been recently made upon the motion of the honourable and learned Member for Limerick, and very important Returns they are. The others I have not before me, but I will make out the figures carefully, and send them to the Committee.

Mr. *Bruen*.

877. I want to ask you a question with regard to some answers which you gave on the first day of your examination; first, with regard to the transfer of the powers of the grand juries to the urban authorities; I think you then expressed your opinion that it was desirable that the powers of the grand juries within the urban districts should be transferred to the urban authority?—Yes.

878. You instanced the case of Ballina, which is, I think, partly in the county of Mayo and partly in the county of Sligo, as a town which had applied and had been refused a transfer by one grand jury out of two?—Yes.

879. Does not this transfer of powers involve a very important question as regards the shifting of the burdens of taxation; for example, the mileage of the streets inside the borough boundary if compared with the mileage of the roads in the barony of course bears a very small proportion when the area of the borough is compared with the area of the barony?—Yes.

880. And in the same way in the valuation of property, the proportion between the amount of property inside the borough boundary and that outside the borough boundary, but in the barony the proportion of variation is the other way; let me put a case to you; take the borough of Carlow, with which I am acquainted; in the barony at Carlow at present the grand jury possess the power of taxing the whole of the property inside the barony of Carlow for the purpose of keeping up the roads; the valuation of the property in the barony of Carlow is 39,170 *l.*; in the borough of Carlow the valuation of the property is 10,940 *l.*; that is to say, in round numbers, the valuation of the property in the borough is one-fourth the valuation of the property in the barony; when you come to the charge upon that property you will find that the charge for maintaining the roads in the borough is very small compared with the charge for maintaining the roads in the barony, and, therefore, if you exclude the valuation of the property in the borough from the charge for maintaining those roads in the barony, and put it entirely upon the property in the barony, the poundage charge in the borough would be very small, and consequently the charge for maintaining the roads outside the borough in the barony would be proportionately increased; do you agree to that?—I assume that it is so in Carlow.

881. And in most other of those districts in which the boroughs are situated in baronies; I wish to put it to you whether the exercise of the powers of the grand jury in refusing their consent to this transfer of taxation may not be a very fair and just refusal, they being the guardians of the interest of the taxpayer?—Then, again, the towns under the poor law are very heavily taxed for want of union rating, and are hit very hard the other way. I rather think it is not so much a question of money as a question of dignity. The Town Commissioners do not like to have to go to the presentment sessions for the roads. For instance, Sir Richard Wallace's agent wanted to flag the footways of Lisburn. They are very nicely flagged in Lurgan, and the inhabitants of Lisburn insisted upon having the footways of Lisburn flagged, and they went to the county grand jury for leave to tax the barony in which the borough of Lisburn is situate, to flag the footways of Lisburn, which the cesspayers had passed,

Mr. *W. N. Hancock*, LL.D.

5 May 1876.

Mr. *Bruen*—continued.

passed, but the grand jury threw it out. The inhabitants of Lisburn did not like that. They are limited to their rating power for other purposes, and they may not wish to flag their streets out of the improvement rate, and when the inhabitants of the barony agreed to flag, they did not like the county at large to throw it out.

882. Did I understand you to say that the cesspayers in the barony agreed to the tax?—Yes.

883. And that in a county at large meeting the cesspayers threw it out?—No, it was the county grand jury threw it out.

884. Was it agreed at the county at large sessions?—It did not come before the county at large sessions; it was only a baronial charge; Lisburn wanted to have the same improvement as Lurgan had; the Lurgan footways were flagged, and they thought they would get theirs flagged, and the inhabitants of the barony using the town were quite willing to pay the expense; but although it is peculiarly a baronial matter, being all on the estate of one proprietor, Sir Richard Wallace, the grand jury of the county of Antrim said, "No, we will not allow you to spend your money in that way." The towns do not like this power of veto; I merely mention that case because it occurred at the last summer assizes.

885. That is one instance in support of your view?—I merely mention that as a late instance. I merely notice that towns one after another have endeavoured to get this done.

886. You merely retail to the Committee this complaint?—Yes, as far as my observation as an observer goes, there is a certain amount of justice in it. I may mention a very curious illustration of the effect of it. There is one road out of Dublin that was considered a most important road before the railway was made from Dublin to Kingstown and Bray. There was a special Act of Parliament passed about it before the townships there were formed; instead of handing each bit of road over to the township through which it went, the care of this road was divided between the grand jury of the county Dublin and the town council of Dublin, and the townships were to pay whatever the other bodies assessed upon them. At the last sitting of the grand jury of the county of Dublin in April last, the judge threatened to stop the county surveyor's salary on account of the disgraceful state that the road was in. Then the consequence was that the grand jury of the county of Dublin had to go to the town council of the city. The responsibility rests between them and the town council. The people that drive on the Rock-road, the wealthy people who drive into Dublin and do not use the railway, are the victims; the road is in a disgraceful state; such is the latest result of an exemption of the care of roads from the township authorities.

887. You will admit, I daresay, that where a transfer of power involves a considerable increase in taxation on the rural cesspayers, the grand jury may possibly be well founded in their refusal to grant those powers?—What I think is that that is a matter which the Local Government Board should be empowered to inquire into, and that they ought to be allowed to alter the town boundaries, or to refuse the application if it involved any injustice; but where it is a mere question between the inhabitants of a barony and the adjoining town the grand jury of the whole county ought not to be the tribunal to decide it.

Mr. *Bruen*—continued.

888. In other words, you would make the Local Government Board a court of appeal in which the power of the grand jury should be called in question, and, if necessary, controlled?—I think that the outside inhabitants, the agricultural inhabitants, might certainly be fairly heard before the inspector of the Local Government Board, and if the Local Government Board thought it a good case they should either alter the boundaries or come to some adjustment or refuse the application.

889. Do you mean to say that your idea is that the grand jury do not fairly hear the representations which are made to them?—I merely corroborate what you have in the Local Government Report, which I quoted on the first day I was examined. I mentioned in support of this what came under my notice on the north-east circuit at the last assizes in Belfast. It was a question simply between the inhabitants of the barony of Lower Massereene and the town of Lisburn; that when they had come to an agreement for flagging the streets, which was the fair thing to do, then the grand jury at large threw it out; therefore that is an illustration that towns do not like to have an accord between them and their neighbours in the same barony, or in the same estate, upset by a body that had no interest in it.

890. I should like to have from you an admission that the question of the disturbance of taxation involved?—Yes. Do not understand me as saying that the county cesspayers should not be heard; but when the Local Government Board had entertained the application, the grand jury absolutely refused, and the thing came to an end.

891. I think that one other recommendation that you mentioned in your evidence the first day was, that of extending this system of Provisional Orders for giving powers to towns, and to confer those powers upon all those towns by Act of Parliament without the necessity for a Provisional Order?—When once powers are sanctioned by Parliament for a large town by a general Act on any important question which has been well considered, I think that the Local Government Board should, in the next year, bring in an Act to extend it, if they think right. They should bring in a Bill next year to give other towns the benefit of it.

892. All other towns?—Yes; because sometimes they cannot afford to go for a local Act. The Act of 1828, the Act of 1854, and the Act of 1871, were all passed on the principle that small towns were not to be expected to go to Parliament for improved legislation. The effect of those three Acts is to cast on the Executive Government the duty of bringing in further Acts extending improvements in legislation. That duty is specially attached to the Local Government Board, and I think it would be very satisfactory to the towns if it were carried out.

893. It is for the purpose of granting additional powers to those town-governing bodies that you think this Act ought to be brought in?—Yes.

894. Cannot they get this power now by a Provisional Order?—No; a singular defect in the Local Government Act of 1871 is, that you can amend any local Act by a Provisional Order, but you cannot amend the Act of 1854. The Act of 1854 was the substitute in small towns for a local Act; but if there is any defect found in it you cannot amend it by a Provisional Order.

895. In

Mr. W. N. Hancock, LL.D.

5 May 1876.

Mr. *Bruen*—continued.

895. In those extended powers occasionally private rights are very seriously interfered with; is it not so?—Yes.

896. And the theory is, I believe, that where public rights and private rights come into collision in this way, there is an appeal to Parliament as the last court of appeal?—Yes.

897. Your proposal would be that by a general Act those powers which may interfere with private rights should be extended to all towns?—No; I put a qualification upon that, which perhaps you did not catch; it was that the Local Government Board should get power for the local authority to do it, with their sanction.

898. That is to say, you would make the Local Government Board the court of appeal instead of Parliament?—Exactly; because the towns are so small and the interests are so small that they cannot afford the expense of coming to Parliament.

899. As a matter of fact, this expense of which you complain of, only arises where the Act is opposed?—No one can embark in one of these Acts without wishing to carry it out; and if he once embarks, no one can tell him what the expense will be.

900. Because you do not know what opposition will arise?—The opposition may be very unfair.

901. But whether the opposition is fair or not, is the very point which is tried by the court of appeal?—If you pass an Act in 1854, putting all towns in the same position as if they got local Acts and charters, it is very unwise in 1871 to say: Now that glaring defects in the Act of 1854 have been pointed out by one or other of the local Acts that have passed, we will allow the people that have got local Acts to amend them by a Provisional Order, but we will not allow you to amend your Act of 1854 by a Provisional Order; that is very hard.

902. It is only then with regard to towns that are under the Act of 1854 that your proposal would come into play?—That is the part that would come into play, because those towns that are under local Acts can, by Provisional Order (which, as in the Wexford case, costs 40 *l.*,) amend their Acts. I do not object to a moderate expense, but when you get up to 14,000 *l.*, as in Sligo, or 7,000 *l.* or 8,000 *l.*, as in Newry, for a local Act, that is what I object to.

903. I want to know how you would under your system provide that individual rights should be fairly considered, and what court of appeal you would have for deciding as to those private rights which were interfered with?—Any privilege that a small town got, instead of going for a local Act, or going under a general Act, should be exercised only with the approval of the Local Government Board, and then every party having a private right should be heard before the action of the local body was confirmed.

904. Is not that in effect substituting the Local Government Board and its officers who might be appointed to hear cases for a Committee of Parliament?—Certainly; under the Burial Act there is a very similar jurisdiction. Questions about rights of burial are decided by the Local Government Board, after the inquiry of an inspector, and where private rights exist, they are determined by the Board.

905. I think you have detailed to the Committee in your evidence, that the local government of towns in Ireland varies very much, that there is no general uniform system of town Government subsisting in Ireland?—No, there is not.

906. Do you approve of the assimilation of the different systems of town government in Ireland, so that there should be one uniform, well understood, and simple plan?—Certainly.

907. How far would you carry that assimilation in a downward direction towards the small towns?—The old limit taken by the Act of 1854 is a very good one, 1,500 inhabitants. I would take the Act of 1854 as the basis.

908. You would go down to towns having 1,500 inhabitants; do you consider them to be communities of an urban character, which would be under urban government?—Yes, they have been so treated by Parliament for many years.

909. You are aware, of course, that the Public Health Act does not so regard them, that 6,000 inhabitants is the limit according to the Public Health Act, and that wherever the Sanitary Act comes into force it is only the urban authority of a town which has 6,000 inhabitants becomes the sanitary authority?—Yes.

910. But below 6,000 inhabitants the guardians of the poor are the sanitary authority?—Yes; I believe that that arose from the limit of rating and from the townships being so very heavily taxed under union rating. Under the limit of rating, the medical officers thought that there would be a difficulty in getting the payment for the proper sanitary officer, if the payment was to be made by too small an area; and that suggestion about limiting it came, I think, from the public health body, as looking after the medical officers. Another matter is that the want of union rating makes the rates in a small town very high, and makes the local authorities of towns very jealous of taxation. Therefore you have to take the whole system together.

911. With regard to the question of rating, you say that the rating in small towns is very high; do you consider Limerick a small town?—I am speaking of the common case of towns; I not know what it is in Limerick.

912. You told the Committee that you consider that the limits of rating were originally adopted as a protection to property?—I believe so.

913. Would you say that, if property was not fairly represented in town-governing bodies, it would be prudent to give up those limits of rating?—No; I am very strongly in favour of substituting for the limit of rating the representation of property.

914. You do not think that real representation of property exists at present?—Certainly not.

915. You have already told the Committee your opinion with regard to the proper form of town government. If you have got your printed evidence before you I want to refer you to Question 187; in that you speak of the distribution of the governing body into different classes, if I may so call it, and you say, "Dublin is at present divided into 15 wards and there would be 15 *ex officio*; 15 elected by the wards as at present; 15 elected by the occupiers on the School Board plan; and 15 elected by the immediate lessors on the School Board plan. In Limerick there are five wards, therefore there would be five *ex officio*, five elected by ward voting as at present, and there would be 15 occupiers elected on the School Board plan, and 15 immediate lessors." Then you go on to say: "Then in Cork there would

Mr. W. N. Hancock, LL.D.

5 May 1876.

Mr. *Bruen*—continued.

would be seven *ex officio*, seven elected by wards, 21 occupiers elected on the School Board plan, and 21 immediate lessors elected on the School Board plan." I want you to explain to me why you should give in the last two classes a proportion of three representatives to each ward, whereas in the Dublin case you only give the same number of representatives as there are wards?—There is the same number in both cases.

916. You say that in Dublin it is divided into 15 wards?—Yes.

917. Cork is divided into seven wards?—Yes.

918. In Dublin you give in the first two classes the same number of representatives as there are wards, and in the last two classes the same number of representatives as there are wards, whereas in Cork you give in the last two classes three times as many representatives as there are wards. I want to know what is the principle of the difference?—The ward system has got a certain hold in large towns; and in introducing any new plan you should not disturb existing arrangements of that kind more than is absolutely necessary. And I merely suggest that you should retain the ward system to a certain limited extent. Then the accidental way in which towns are divided into wards leads to that result. It is not that I approve of the ward system myself, but merely that it is an existing institution; and when an existing institution is there, it is very unwise if you are introducing a new system to disturb it more than is absolutely necessary.

919. I am not asking you to explain anything as against the preservation of wards, but why you treated it differently in Dublin and in Cork?—I simply say that I would only allow one representative for a ward or for a small town to be *ex officio*, and one elected by single votes, so as to allow the leading man now elected in each ward to retain his position, if the enlarged constituency were satisfied with him.

920. I suppose you consider Dublin and Cork to be towns very much in the same category of large and important towns?—Yes. It was simply not to disturb existing arrangements. My plan would give the most influential man in the ward his position. If there was any alderman that was in the habit of being always returned for his ward he would not be disturbed by my plan. It recognises the existing arrangements, and all the most popular men in their wards would hold their seats without disturbance. My own impression is not in favour of wards. Very likely the application of the School Board plan to the whole of the occupiers representatives will be the ultimate solution, but in recommending any new plan it is best to recognise any dignified vested interest like that.

921. As to the qualification for the persons who would elect, do you think that in all those towns to which you would extend this system the qualification for electors should be that which now exists in Dublin, or would you have a higher qualification?—What now exists in Dublin is practically a high qualification.

922. Theoretically, I should say?—I was not referring to a theoretical qualification. The returns that have been made down to 1 *l.* valuation, show all the real householders. Then for those cases where you have two or three families living in one house, I would select one of those to represent the house, generally taking the oldest inhabitant, that is the head of the family who had resided longest in the house. That would get rid of a great number of questions about migratory people. Then I would extend the limit of the poor law. At present, if a person is in receipt of relief within one year, he is not qualified; if you go down in the scale, I would extend the limit, and I would make the receipt of relief within seven years a disqualification. Also, I would go into the question of crime. If persons were convicted of felony at all, or if they were convicted repeatedly for minor offences, such as 10 times within seven years, I would exclude them in that way and get to all the respectable working classes that are earning their bread and maintaining themselves and their families.

Mr. *Bruen*—continued.

923. Then you would go below the limit of rating?—There are houses rated at 1 *l.*, and I would take every separate building that is a real dwelling house.

924. You would not make the rating to the poor law a qualification?—No. I think that all this rating was a plan of getting property in, to give property an indirect representation. Then, as to the inhabitants, I would collect their names through the Post Office; the letter carriers know the name of every person that is an inhabitant, and I would check that by the police. You would thereby get the real inhabitants and heads of families, and give them representation, if they had not received relief for seven years, or had never been convicted of felony, or had not been repeatedly convicted of minor offences.

925. I suppose that you are thoroughly conversant with the Report of the Select Committee on Local Taxation, in 1870, before which you were a witness?—Yes.

926. You remember that that Committee, in a part of its Report, said, "That in any reform in the existing system of local taxation it is expedient to adjust the system of rating in such a manner that both owners and occupiers may be brought to feel an immediate interest in the increase or decrease of local expenditure, and in the administration of local affairs; that it is expedient to make owners as well as occupiers directly liable for a certain proportion of the rates." Are you of that opinion?—Yes, very strongly of that opinion.

927. Would you make the qualification depend at all upon the payment of rates?—Not of the inhabitants; I would of the owner.

928. You are aware, I presume, of the provision which the Local Taxation Committee recommended for dividing the rates, so as not to interfere with existing contracts?—Yes.

929. Do you approve of that?—Yes, I do; I recommended it in my evidence before that Committee.

930. Have you got any examples in your mind of the working of the system of administration, where the administrators are elected somewhat on this plan which you would recommend, partly by owners, and partly by occupiers?—The poor law as an example.

931. You have mentioned the Ports and Docks Board in Dublin; that is something in the same way, is it not?—Yes. There is also the case of the Harbour Commissioners of Sligo, in which there is a representation of merchants, and the town council are represented on it also. On the Dublin Ports and Docks Board there is a representation of different interests, and it has worked remarkably well.

932. I was

Mr. *Bruen*—continued.

932. I was going to ask whether that has worked entirely to the satisfaction of the constituency who elected them and the public generally?—They are improving the Harbour of Dublin, and meeting the extending trade in a way to give extreme satisfaction.

933. You attribute the excellent working of that system to the very wide basis of representation by which it is elected?—The old body was self-elective like the old corporations, and then it was superseded by a *bonâ fide* representation of different interests, and that has worked with the greatest satisfaction.

Mr. *Kavanagh.*

934. How are the port and dock board elected?—I have not that made up; there is an Act of Parliament, a recent Act; I think it is mentioned in Mr. Pim's Pamphlet.

935. You gave your opinion to the Committee on several methods by which you would propose that property should be represented, and I gathered from you that you considered that Government property should have the power of voting in corporations?—Where they pay the rates.

936. Have you any precedent or authority for that, or is it merely an idea of your own?—I think there is some authority for it; Mr. Pim called my attention to it, but I do not recollect it at this moment.

937. Still you think that it would be an advisable system?—Perfectly; I think it would be very important to have it.

938. Do you know what proportion of property is held by corporate bodies, apart from the town government of Dublin?—I do not know; the railway companies are large ratepayers there.

939. As to your plan of conferring the franchise on owners as well as occupiers, have you any precedent for that?—The Poor Law is the nearest precedent for it; *ex officio* guardians under the Poor Law were first selected by election. Under the Act of 1838 they were to be elected by the *ex officios*. That was changed in 1847 or 1849, and now the highest rated *ex officio* guardian sits; it is not done by election. If the number of magistrates is large on the board then it is the highest rated one that sits; that is a precedent for it. The most direct precedent for a perfectly fixed division to represent property that I know of is the Scotch Jury Law, in which they provide that a certain proportion of all juries should be special jurors. That makes them certain of having a proportion of persons of wealth on every jury, and they solved that question in Scotland in that way.

940. I may have been wrong in using the word precedent, but you have an authority for the idea that has been recommended?—I am taking cases where it has been tried for a number of years, and not merely where it is recommended. As to this particular solution, I am not aware of its being applied. I may mention one very curious precedent that came to my knowledge since I came to London, that is, in the present Session of Parliament, on the 9th of February, there was a Bill introduced to amend the Law of the Election of Aldermen in Municipal Boroughs in England and Wales, that is, by the application of cumulative votes; aldermen in England are not elected as aldermen in Ireland are, by wards, but are elected out of the

Mr. *Kavanagh*—continued.

town council. That proposition was supported by the names of Mr. Heygate, Mr. Russell Gurney, Mr. Fawcett, Mr. Wheelhouse, and Mr. Morley.

941. That is a Bill which is in embryo, it is not an Act?—No, it is not an Act, but I merely mention that. I have not seen it before.

942. Is it not also recommended by the Report of the Royal Sanitary Commissioners of 1869?—When I was examined before the Commissioners, my recollection of that was that they went rather on a different plan. I am not quite certain but that the occupiers and owners of property were to vote together.

943. In conferring the franchise on owners as well as occupiers it is always contemplated, is it not, to divide the rates between them?—I think that is the basis.

944. Was not that recommended by Mr. Goschen in his Draft Report in 1870?—It is in his Draft Report, and also in the Report of the Committee.

945. Mr. Goschen is rather a high authority, is he not, on that subject?—Very high. And it was adopted in the Irish Land Act of the same year. The only limit in that case is to agricultural and pastoral holdings.

946. You made another suggestion as to plural votes; if I remember rightly plural votes were to be given to occupiers?—No, not to occupiers but to proprietors.

947. You meant votes on a sliding scale, in proportion to their property?—Yes, if a man had 50 *l.* he would have one vote; if he had 500 *l.* he would have 10 votes; and if he has 5,000 *l.* he would have 100 votes.

948. Have you any authority for that recommendation, I mean besides your own sense of what is right or wrong?—No, I have not. There are precedents for multiple voting up to six. There are plenty of precedents for multiple voting in some of the Local Boards of Health in England, and in the Poor Law in England and in Ireland, but they generally authorise some limit to both owners and occupiers; I thought that if we went into property at all we should have no objection to give it its full weight.

949. Was it always the case that they settled a limit?—Even in railway shares there is a limit, and I am not aware of any case where the right is unlimited.

950. Have you any knowledge of the Act which was proposed by Mr. Bourne, called the Select Vestries, in 1818?—No, I have not. What led me to think of unlimited voting was that in Dublin the complaint was that places like Trinity College, and the railways, and very large bodies, were not represented, and that is what attracted my attention to the limit, and six would not meet that case; then, the case of the Government coming in to pay the rates raises the question again.

951. Do you know what the amount of the valuation of Government property in Dublin is?—No, I do not.

952. In your Answer 107, with regard to cleansing the streets of Dublin, you say that, "When once a fund of that kind," that is, a fund for cleansing the streets, "gets allocated into a number of objects, and some of them first charges, the power of the town council is gone, because they cannot increase their expenditure on the cleansing of streets beyond what it was in 1866

Mr. *W. N. Hancock*, LL.D.

5 May 1870.

Mr. W. N. Hancock, LL.D.

5 May 1876.

Mr. *Kavanagh*—continued.

1866 without disturbing some other object." I want to know whether those funds that are appropriated to cleansing the streets in Dublin were saddled with any other extra liabilities than the interest on the debt of the old corporation?—I have not gone exactly into the whole object; a great number of objects are covered by the Improvement Act, and cleansing is only one of them.

953. I think you stated that some of the rates collected by those corporations were ear-marked for certain purposes?—Yes; but that is by the Act of 1849.

954. Can you state to the Committee whether they are saddled with any other liabilities than the old corporation?—I do not know whether they have not borrowed money.

955. Supposing they have not, were those debts the debts of the old corporation that existed before the Municipal Reform Act?—No, it is the debts of the paving board; the paving board was not transferred, and the wide streets board were not transferred until 1849. The old corporation was abolished in 1840, and upon the corporation starting in Dublin, they had a paving board appointed by the Government; the powers of that body were transferred in 1849, and it was their debts that I spoke of.

956. You say, in Answer 111, that "a great number of wealthy people are deterred from serving on town authorities in Ireland by the rigidity of the audit." I understand what you mean by that, that they have no appeal to a judge; they have nothing higher than the Local Government Board to protect them from the auditor; but how are the different corporation accounts in Ireland audited?—They are now, with three exceptions, audited by the Poor Law auditors, who are Local Government Board officers.

957. What are those three exceptions?—I think they are Cork, Kilkenny, and Waterford, which are excepted in the Act of 1871; and, besides that, all the townships in the county of Dublin are not audited unless the inhabitants vote for their being audited.

958. In these three exceptions, how are they audited, or are the accounts of those three corporations ever audited?—Originally they were to be audited by the Board of Audit, in London; but that system broke down. In 1871 the Poor Law Audit was passed. There was some opposition in Parliament to that being passed, and then there was a compromise; the Bill was passed provided certain exceptions were made in it.

959. That is to say, Kilkenny was excepted from it?—Yes, and Cork and Waterford.

960. How would the misapplication of the funds ever be detected, supposing such occurred?—A Chancery suit would bring it out. What first called my attention to that was, that the Belfast Corporation got into a Chancery suit. The prudent people of Derry wrote to the Government of Ireland that they were in a very awkward position, that they could not get an auditor to protect them. My first connection with local taxation was reporting upon the Derry Memorial. The Derry people are very prudent people, the most prudent in Ireland; and they complained of being left without an auditor, because the audit provided in 1840 broke down.

Mr. *Braen.*

961. Do you know who audits the accounts of the corporation of Kilkenny, or does anybody audit them?—I forget whether they have a private audit, but they have no public audit.

Sir *Joseph M'Kenna.*

962. You told us in respect to the allocation of the charges upon the towns, that you would keep them separate from the Grand Jury charges; and you were asked with respect to how it would work in a case such as Carlow. I want to make it clear upon the evidence before the Committee what it is that you mean, for I do not myself quite understand it. The honourable Member for Carlow was so good as to tell us that the valuation of the barony of Carlow was 39,170 *l.*, and of the borough it was 10,940 *l.*; taking it roughly, those outside the borough, in the barony of Carlow, would be in the proportion of three to one to those in the borough?—Yes.

963. Your recommendation is to this extent, that the barony would take charge of the expenses that were connected with the barony, the roads and such like, outside the borough, and the borough would take charge of its own expenses?—Yes.

964. Have you considered to what extent that would impair or affect the present incidence of taxation on the borough, or on the county?—That is a local question, each case depending upon the size of the barony.

965. Do you know of any case where it strikes you that there would be any practical injustice done by that?—I did not propose to go into that; the towns appear to be all anxious for it, and very likely they would get a benefit. They are rather hardly hit in other ways, which makes them rather more anxious.

Mr. *Rathbone.*

966. Will you name the number of towns in which there is a graduated system of rating?—Twelve towns.

967. Do you know whether in those towns this system does not, in practice, tend to prevent the improvement of houses, and to encourage the building of small and poor houses?—I have a very strong opinion against the system, but I have no practical knowledge of it.

968. With regard to the county burdens, such as lunatics, prisons, roads, police, &c., do the towns contribute to those county burdens?—Yes.

969. How are the towns represented, on the grand jury or the county authority?—Not necessarily at all.

970. How are their contributions, in fact, paid?—Take the ordinary case of a town in a county at large, all its value is part of the value of the county for grand jury purposes; what you call county rate in England, we call grand jury cess in Ireland, and that county rate covers not only what you have in England, but a road rate. We have no turnpikes; it is a road rate, and it is a county rate all in one. It includes prison expenses, keeping up court houses and every sort of county purpose; and the town pays to it in proportion to its valuation.

971. That is to say, the county rate is levied on the town, just as it is on the county?—Yes. Then towns suffer under a peculiar disadvantage, that their rating goes on increasing for every improvement in value, but the rating of agricultural holding does not increase under the terms and working of our Valuation Act.

972. Have

Mr. *Rathbone*—continued.

972. Have the towns anything to do with finding money, for instance, for the county roads?—Not necessarily; they may have, because some of the highest ratepayers in the county will live in the town.

973. And yet the towns do not have any representation on the grand jury?—No.

974. The county authority manages entirely the repair and maintenance of the roads?—Yes.

975. There is no representation from boroughs or towns in the county authority?—No

976. In this paper which you have handed in of towns containing a certain number of authorities within the town boundaries, for instance, take "towns with four authorities within the town boundary," does the authority, or the taxation, or the work of any of those town authorities go beyond the town boundary?—Take the case of Lisburn; the manor of Kiltultagh extends beyond the borough of Lisburn in county Antrim; Lisburn is only a very small town in the county of Antrim and the county of Down. The part of Lisburn that is in the county of Down is a very minute part.

977. Does the authority of the court-leet run within and beyond the town authority of Lisburn?—Yes, it runs within and beyond the boundary.

978. And the same with a great many other authorities?—Yes, the same with the board of guardians. In all cases of the first class the extra authority runs beyond the boundary.

979. Do you consider that it is a desirable thing to have different authorities with overlapping boundaries?—No. One of the most important that I will take first is Belfast. Belfast is one of the most enterprising and advancing towns, and they have put an end to that; they have got separated from the county of Antrim and the county of Down; they have got the whole within the town boundary into their hands, with one single exception, and that is the water commissioners.

980. Has it been found practically that this intercepting of the boundaries of over-lapping authorities has been inconvenient?—Certainly, and the towns are very anxious to get rid of them.

981. With regard to putting this right; there were several questions asked you as to the difficulty and as to the objections which were entertained by sometimes towns and sometimes county authorities to changing the boundaries; in your opinion does that difficulty arise a good deal from the mode of rating being by the area, and not in proportion to the benefits received?—No, it does not turn upon that.

982. What I want to ascertain is this: does the present incidence of taxation arising out of rating by area, instead of making the payment depend somewhat on the benefits received, throw a difficulty in the way of adjusting those areas, and making them conterminous?—It is the sole cause of the difficulty, because if the rating was exactly fairly distributed, there could be no objection.

983. If any plan could be devised by which that rating became fair, so that people should pay somewhat in proportion to the benefits received, that difficulty would disappear?—Certainly.

984. You gave the Committee a plan by which you wished to represent all parties concerned in the taxation which was to be expended by the authority which was to be elected; without expressing any opinion of my own upon that point, I want to ask you whether the object that you wish to attain could not be attained in a somewhat simpler manner. Supposing that the town of Dublin, for instance, were divided into wards so constituted that each ward had, as it were, five representatives, an alderman and four elected councillors, and that two of those councillors were elected by all those who paid rates as owners of property, under the plan of division of rates between owners and occupiers, as suggested by you, and those two represented the interests of the owners of property as taxpayers, and the two others were chosen by those rated as occupiers, and therefore presenting those paying taxes as occupiers, and that one was nominated by the lord lieutenant as a magistrate and alderman of the ward to represent the Government, who, I think, in Ireland even more than in England, are large contributors towards the local expenditure of the country; would some such plan as that meet the object which, as I understand from your cross examination, you have in view?—I think that any plan of mixing up officials with non-officials objectionable, except where the Government paid rates and had a member of their own on the board just to represent them, but to have one-fifth of the board Government officials would not work satisfactorily.

Mr. *W. N. Hancock*, LL.D.

5 May 1876.

985. Supposing that this local body had the management of all the local affairs of the town, police, education, and everything, would not the Government be a very large contributor towards the expenditure?—The Government contribute more largely towards the police than in England, and then they take the sole command. Their extra contribution to the police for Ireland was in consideration of their getting the sole command; but my object was to build up local authorities in Ireland that would be like the local authorities in England.

986. You have talked of the *ex officio* element; is not that exactly similar, in kind, to the representation of the *ex officio* element in England by the magistrates?—When the time has arrived that the police could be handed over to the towns, that question would then arise.

987. Do not you think that it would very much improve the local government of Ireland if you could have a local government which would have the confidence of all parts of the community and bring all sections of the community to work harmoniously together; do not you think you would have a very much better local government in Ireland then than even that which we have in England?—But the local authorities that I am talking of get no assistance from the State; they are expending entirely local rates. If the power of controlling the police were handed over, it would raise a new question for the future, which is a long way off yet.

988. Do not you believe that we could leave it to the magistrates to do any part of the magisterial duty in Ireland?—Yes, but not the power of taxing.

989. But they do a considerable part of the administration?—We have in Ireland stipendiary magistrates and local magistrates working very satisfactorily together in the administration of justice.

990. Do not you think that one great object that you have in view should be to bring all classes

Mr. W. N. Hancock, LL.D.

5 May 1876.

Mr. *Rathbone*—continued.

classes of the community to work together harmoniously and for some common object?—Yes.

991. Why should it not concur to this end if the magistrates sat with the other parties as they do in England in the administration of local affairs?—But our Government magistrates do not. Under the poor law we have *ex officio* magistrates, but the stipendiary magistrates do not sit upon the poor law.

992. I thought you said that the local government did not give any subsidy to lunatics, and so on, as they do in the case of the poor law?—That is only this last Session; it is a very small matter. The point which you make about the police is that the imperial taxpayer pays a large share as they do to the police, more than they do in England, would raise the question which you raise, but I do not consider the question of the police as at all an immediate question. My notion was to build up a local authority which in process of time would get the police, but not immediately.

993. Do not you think that you would give dignity and importance to the authority, if you confided to that local authority the whole local government of the district as one local authority instead of having a number of those authorities in one area?—We want to get one local authority in each area. But I should like to see them under way for some time before the police is handed over, but at present Ireland is not quite ready to pay for the police; when it is so the question will arise.

Mr. *Butt.*

994. I see you have put down in your return, "towns with four authorities within town boundary, towns with three authorities within town boundary, and towns with two authorities within town boundary;" take Lisburn, what power has the court-leet in Lisburn to control the manor of Kiltultagh?—To assess it.

995. What for; why do you call it an authority within the barony of Lisburn?—Because they impose leets.

996. What is the leet for?—The bye-laws show that. In my Report on local taxation, for 1869, I say, "It appears, however, that one court-leet is still in active operation, that of the town of Lisburn and manor of Kiltultagh, in the county of Antrim. Returns have accordingly been obtained of the leet levied, not only in the year 1869, but also in the years since 1865, to complete the information on the subject. From the bye-laws, it appears that the court-leet deals with town fountains and fire engines, which could be provided for by the Towns Improvement Act, 1854, if the town adopted that Act; it also deals, however, with fairs and markets." In 1872 I reported, "Court-leet Presentments bear some resemblance to Grand Jury Cess, in being made by a Court-leet Grand Jury and levied off land, and being partly applied to main roads."

997. That is a peculiar case. Take the next case, Ballina: the board of guardians are the local board of health, are they not?—The board of guardians are the sanitary authority for the town.

998. Do you think it would be possible to consolidate the corporation and the poor law guardians?—No; I beg your pardon; I was merely remarking the distinction that in other towns the poor law board of guardians are not the sanitary authority.

999. This only applies to sanitary authorities?

Mr. *Butt*—continued.

—To the ordinary town purposes; the return I have made applies to the powers that are ordinarily entrusted to town authorities.

1000. You say that there is great inconvenience in the overlapping of districts, in consequence of the taxes; do you mean to say that there is inconvenience in having the poor law union a totally different area from the town or the borough?—I was asked by the honourable Member for Liverpool for a return of the number of authorities within the same area, and I merely mentioned that in those small towns, like Ballina, the guardians are the sanitary authorities, and not the Town Commissioners. The result is, in the case of Nenagh, that a question has arisen about the cleaning of the streets. The local government board are reported in the newspapers to have decided that the cleaning of the streets is not a sanitary object, and the board of guardians are compelling the Town Commissioners to clean the streets.

1001. As to the inconvenience of the overlapping of areas, must not a poor law union be of necessity different from the boundaries of any town, or of any borough?—Certainly; but for sanitary purposes, I meant.

1002. That, of course, takes place in poor law unions; the poor law unions must be laid out separate from the boundaries of any town, as a general rule?—Yes.

1003. Are they in any other area but the area made for themselves?—Yes.

1004. You do not say that there is any inconvenience in the overlapping or the different area of the poor law union and of the town?—But there is often considerable inconvenience in the overlapping of the electoral division and the town. Take the City of Waterford; the City of Waterford applied to Parliament, saying that they wished to have their boundary extended to the electoral division of Waterford. Then the grand jury of the county of Waterford said, No, there is very much of the electoral division of Waterford in the county at large, and they threw out the Bill in the House of Lords upon that point, but the City of Waterford raised this point. They said, "We want to have the electoral division boundary and the town boundary the same."

1005. What is the inconvenience that results from their being different?—A great deal of complication in the Sanitary Acts.

1006. Is it purely in relation to sanitary matters?—Yes.

1007. That is the only inconvenience that you see?—But sanitary matters come into this whole legislation.

1008. Then it simply has to do with the sanitary arrangements for the whole of the poor law unions?—Yes.

1009. Now as to Ballina, you say that the Town Commissioners are one authority; are they not the only proper town authority amongst the four you have named?—If you take the definition of town authority to be the authority that is entrusted by Parliament with the power, in the City of Dublin, for instance, it is so.

1010. I am asking you about Ballina?—The town authority means the power exercising the town powers.

1011. In the case of Ballina, are the board of guardians the town authority in Ballina?—For sanitary purposes they are.

1012. That

Mr. *W. N. Hancock,* LL.D.

5 May 1876.

Mr. *Butt*—continued.

1012. That is to say, they exercise the sanitary authority in Ballina?—Yes, which is given in other towns to the town authority.

1013. Is the county of Mayo grand jury the town authority?—It exercises jurisdiction over the streets which in other places are entrusted to towns.

1014. Part of Ballina is in the county of Sligo, is it not?—Yes.

1015. As to this grand jury rate in towns, the grand jury levies its rate on the whole county?—No, there is a baronial rate.

1016. But it levies its rate on the whole county?—Yes.

1017. Part of that rate is levied on the county at large?—Yes.

1018. And a part of it is levied separately in each barony?—Yes.

1019. Do you consider as a matter of course that every small town is to separate itself from the county system and become a separate jurisdiction in itself?—A very large number of towns have done it.

1020. Would you think it desirable that any town that wished it should disassociate itself from the county at large and erect itself into a separate district?—All the most enterprising towns in Ireland have done it.

1021. Surely it would not be desirable to do it as a matter of course?—I think that there should be the power of doing it without going to Parliament.

1022. So there is the power of doing it without going to Parliament, is there not?—But there is an absolute veto in the case of every grand jury.

1023. The effect of that would be to exempt that town from, at all events, a part of the county rate that relates to roads?—Yes, it would.

1024. Formerly that could only be done by an Act of Parliament?—Yes.

1025. That now can be done by a Provisional Order?—Yes.

1026. But that Provisional Order (and this, I believe, is what you are complaining of), under the Act of 1871, cannot be given for that purpose without the consent of the grand jury of the county?—Yes, that is so.

1027. So that the grand jury of the county, who represent the ratepayers of the whole county, have over this Provisional Order at present a negative upon any town separating itself from the county?—Yes.

1028. That is the way in which the law stands at present?—Yes, and that has been condemned by the Local Government Board; they have reported against it.

1029. Belfast has done it by Act of Parliament?—Yes.

1030. Would you think it desirable that Ballina should be separated from the County of Mayo?—I would leave that to the Local Government Board.

1031. The only change that you propose in that is, that the Local Government Board should have the power to determine it?—On hearing both sides of the question without the veto of the grand jury. The grand jury should be heard as a party, but not have an absolute veto.

1032. You would take away the absolute veto of the grand jury?—Yes.

1033. If it was not for that veto, is not the provision of the Local Government Board perfectly sufficient?—Perfectly.

Mr. *Butt*—continued.

1034. Is not this the case, that the Local Government Board have power to substitute for an Act of Parliament a Provisional Order, which has to be subsequently confirmed by Parliament?—Yes.

1035. But they cannot exercise that power in this particular instance of separating the town from the county, without the consent of the grand jury of the county?—No.

1036. And you propose that they should exercise it without getting the consent of the grand jury?—I propose that the grand jury should appear as a party.

Mr. *Rathbone*.

1037. I understand you the first thing is that a town who wishes to become a local Government district, as we should term it in England, first applies to the grand jury for its consent?—No, it goes to the Local Government Board.

1038. The Local Government Board, if it approves, can go for a Provisional Order, as the Act provides, and the grand jury does not interfere?—Yes.

Chairman.

1039. Are you aware what happened in that Ballina case subsequent to the approval of the grand jury to allow the Provisional Order to pass?—Yes, they then went to Parliament to get an Act, and then they were turned round on Standing Orders, on the ground that they were going for the repeal of a general Act.

1040. Will you explain how that was?—They were told that Parliament decided that the grand jury veto was final, and that they were going to repeal a general Act.

1041. Are you aware whether that happened in the House of Lords or Commons?—In the House of Commons I think, but I am not certain; I am merely saying what I picked up from the Parliamentary Agent.

Mr. *O'Shaughnessy*.

1042. I believe the rates for municipal purposes are raised according to the same valuation as the rates for poor law purposes?—Yes.

1043. I presume you know the expression, "gross valuation"?—Yes.

1044. And you know the expression, "nett valuation"?—Yes.

1045. Will you explain to me the difference between gross valuation and the nett valuation, say in the city of Cork and the city of Limerick, as there happens to be a difference between the two?—I do not collect the exact point of the question.

1046. Is there any difference between the two?—As I understand, the gross valuation is the value before the taxes are taken off; there is a certain value put on the premises before the deduction for taxation; the nett valuation is the value when the tax is off.

1047. With regard to the auditors, are you not aware that before the Government auditors were appointed by the Act of 1871, under the provisions, I believe, of the Irish Corporation Act, auditors were appointed by the ratepayers every year, who gave a public audit to the accounts?—Yes, they were.

1048. Was it a public audit?—It was public, but not what I understand by an official audit.

1049. From your observation, since the Government audit has been established, have you any means of saying whether it has been considered

Mr. *W. N. Hancock*, LL.D.

3 May 1876.

Mr. *O'Shaughnessy*—continued.

sidered by the ratepayers more satisfactory than the old corporation audit?—I cannot say that.

1050. Do you know whether in Dublin and in other places the ratepayers are not in the habit of attending and inquiring into expenses, and appealing against certain payments?—I do not know that.

Mr. *Murphy*.

1051. Have you paid any particular attention to what the powers and duties of the auditors are under the Act of 1871?—Their powers are very stringent, and their duties are very obligatory; they are bound to look very strictly into all that is done.

1052. Do you think that their powers are very despotic?—They are not despotic, they are merely strict.

1053. Has it ever struck you that the powers given to auditors partake of the nature of the power of a judge as well as of a jury?—That is the nature of all audits.

1054. Taken, I say, the powers of a judge, they construe questions of law absolutely, and not mere fact?—That is necessary, if the audit is to be effectual; they must do that.

1055. You think that the auditor to be appointed under that Act, although as an unprofessional man he may not know anything about law, should have absolute power of doing matters of law as well as of fact; do you think that that is a proper condition of things?—I do not approve of the present system to this extent, that I think that there ought to be powers as under the Grand Jury Act, of taking an opinion of a judge beforehand; in doing that I think that the interpretation of a difficult point of law should not rest with the auditor, but with the Local Government Board or with a judge.

1056. Are you aware that under the provisions of the Act of 1871, if an appeal is made by a corporation, for instance, against an auditor, and that appeal is successful, the corporation are obliged to pay the costs of the appeal?—I do not know; I have not looked into that.

1057. Supposing an auditor makes a ruling, and then the corporation appeal from that ruling and go to the Court of Queen's Bench, and that Court decides, upon argument, that the appeal is right and that the auditor is wrong, do you think it a right and just thing, under those circumstances, that the corporation should be obliged to pay the costs; not alone their own costs, but the auditor's costs?—My suggested remedy for that is an indication of what I think.

1058. Do you think that a proper state of facts?—I think that the more satisfactory way would be to have the opinion of a judge taken beforehand. I would oblige them to do that.

1059. Do you or do you not think it is right and proper that an auditor in the first instance should be clothed with the power of giving a legal decision, he not being a legal man; and then, further, if the decision is appealed against the corporation should be bound to pay, not alone their own costs, but his costs, though they are

Mr. *Murphy*—continued.

successful; do you think that proper?—I have suggested a remedy for that.

Mr. *Bruen*.

1060. The auditor is a Government officer, is he not?—Yes.

1061. Government officers acting *bonâ fide* in an official capacity are not generally liable to costs, are they?—Not if they are acting *bonâ fide*; he is necessarily a *quasi* judicial officer. If the business is properly managed, costs would not be incurred.

Mr. *Brooks*.

1062. There are two questions arising out of the examination of the honourable Member for Carlow; will you inform the Committee what are the functions of the magistrates of the city of Dublin?—The city magistrates of Dublin are placed in a very peculiar position, because they do not exercise any criminal powers; they are qualified for boards of guardians, and they are qualified for signing affidavits, but they do not sit in the police court. In Belfast they do; in Belfast the town magistrates sit along with the stipendary magistrates.

Dr. *Ward*.

1063. Are there not other towns in Ireland in which they do the same?—They may in other towns except Dublin, but in Dublin they do not sit, nor do they exercise any criminal power.

Mr. *Brooks*.

1064. Can you inform the Committee why that power was accorded to the magistrates of Belfast, and not to those of the metropolitan city?—I think that the metropolitan city was treated in the way that London is, following the example of London, where the local magistrates have not jurisdiction. In fact, Dublin was placed for superiority above the other towns in Ireland, and treated like the metropolis.

Chairman.

1065. You are aware, I dare say, that the Middlesex magistrates do not sit in the metropolitan police courts?—That was the analogy in my mind.

Mr. *Murphy*.

1066. I presume that you are not aware that the corporation of Cork got a special Act in 1852, containing amongst other clauses the power of appointing auditors?—I was not aware of that.

1067. Nor of the provisions of that Act?—No; I did not happen to look into them. I apprehend that those auditors would not be independent official auditors, but were elected by the ratepayers.

1068. Are you aware that there was a special system of account, a special notice of account, and a special regulation that that account should remain open, and everybody come in and appeal to the Recorder of Cork specially, and that was the reason why Cork was not included in the Act?—I was not aware of that.

Tuesday, 9th May 1876.

MEMBERS PRESENT:

Mr. Assheton.	Mr. Gibson.
Sir Michael Hicks Beach.	Mr. Charles Lewis.
Mr. Brooks.	Mr. Mulholland.
Mr. Bruen.	Mr. Murphy.
Mr. Butt.	Mr. O'Shaughnessy.
Mr. Collins.	Dr. Ward.
Mr. J. P. Corry.	

SIR MICHAEL HICKS BEACH, BART., IN THE CHAIR.

Mr. WILLIAM JOSEPH HENRY, called in; and Examined.

Mr. *Henry.*

9 May 1876.

Mr. *Butt.*

1069. I BELIEVE you are the Town Clerk of the City of Dublin?—I am.

1070. When were you appointed town clerk?—Early in the year 1864.

1071. Who was your predecessor?—Mr. Farquhar?

1072. Before you were town-clerk, had you any experience in the revision either of the Burgess or Parliamentary Roll in the City of Dublin?—Yes; both.

1073. Is it your duty at present to make out the Burgess Roll?—Yes.

1074. Is it also your duty to make out the Parliamentary Roll?—Yes.

1075. First let me ask you, are you able to tell me at the time of the Municipal Corporation Act, 1841, how the local affairs of the City of Dublin were managed?—There was a corporation appointed by the guilds.

1076. I am rather asking you as to what part of the local affairs were in the corporation; they managed, did they not, the supply of pipe water to the city?—Yes, I think so; I cannot tell accurately.

1077. When the new corporation came into existence, I want to know the state of affairs from then until 1849, after the passing of the 3rd and 4th of Victoria; can you tell me how the paving, lighting, and cleansing of the city was managed?—There was a Paving Board.

1078. Who were the Paving Board?—I do not know how they were constituted.

1079. Were not three Commissioners appointed by the Lord Lieutenant?—I think they were, but I am not quite sure.

1080. Do you know whether there was a Wide Streets Board in the City of Dublin?—Yes.

1081. Not belonging to the corporation, I think?—No.

1082. And they managed the improvement of the streets by taking down buildings, did they not?—Yes.

1083. Do you know whether the police were under their control?—Yes, formerly.

1084. Have you there the Report of the Commission on Corporations, Ireland, on the City of Dublin?—Yes.

Mr. *Butt*—continued.

1085. Are you aware that in 1836 the police had been taken entirely away from the corporation?—Yes.

1086. And a new police instituted like there is in the metropolis at the west end?—Yes.

1087. And placed under the control of the Commissioners appointed by the Lord Lieutenant?—Quite so.

1088. Have you read the Report of the Municipal Corporation Inquiry, which sat in 1835, into the affairs of Dublin?—I have not.

1089. Do you recollect that, whatever was the management of local affairs between 1841 and 1849, in the year 1849 a very great change was made?—Yes.

1090. Can you tell me also what the nature of that change was; what additional powers the corporation got?—They got the fiscal powers of the grand jury, and they got the powers which the Paving Board had and the Wide Streets Commission had; that Act did not come into operation until the 1st of January 1851.

1091. At the same time there was a change made in the arrangement of the wards in the City of Dublin, was there not?—Yes, there was contemporaneously with it.

1092. There was also an assimilation of the franchise, was there not, to that which then existed in England?—Yes; it was mentioned in the Act that it was to be assimilated to England and Scotland.

1093. In fact, all the members of the existing corporation then went out of office, did they not?—Yes.

1094. In consequence of the change of the wards?—Yes, it was an entirely new election.

1095. And by a different constituency?—Yes; the wards were changed.

1096. Before that the constituency had been of persons rated to nearly 10 *l.*?—Yes, and a year in occupation.

1097. That was changed too, and raised, was it not?—Yes, to an occupancy of two years and eight months, and nominal rating.

1098. What

Mr. Henry.

9 May 1876.

Mr. *Brasn.*

1098. What do you mean by "nominal rating"?—I mean rated by name to any amount.

Mr. *Butt.*

1099. Are you able to tell me what was the alteration which was made in the distribution of the wards?—The direction of the Act of Parliament was, that the area should correspond with the population. It is not the Dublin Improvement Act, but it is an Act to amend an Act for the regulation of Municipal Corporations in Ireland, so far as relates to the Borough of Dublin, and that Act says, in Clause 9, "That, within three weeks from and after the passing of this Act, the Lord Lieutenant, or other chief governor or governors of Ireland, shall appoint two persons, one being a barrister-at law of not less than six years standing at the bar, for the purpose of dividing anew the said borough of Dublin into wards; and it shall be lawful for such persons so appointed, and they are hereby required on or before the first day of January in the year 1850, to divide anew the said borough of Dublin into 15 wards, and to determine and set out anew the extent, limits, and boundary lines of the said wards of the said borough, and what portions of the said borough shall be included therein respectively, and in making such division, and determining the extent and limits and boundaries of each such ward, the said persons so appointed shall have regard as well to the number of persons rated to the relief of the poor in such ward as to the aggregate amount of the sums at which all the said persons shall be so rated."

1100. Are you aware that before that there were very great inequalities in the wards?—I am.

1101. Do you know that complaint was made that St. George's Ward, for instance, had 1,831 inhabited houses, and was rated at 68,000 *l.*, and that Paul's Ward had only 938 inhabited houses, and was rated at 18,000 *l.*, and yet returned the same number of representatives?—Yes.

1102. It was to correct that that the distribution of wards took place?—Yes, that was the instruction.

1103. Are you aware that that clause is borrowed from the English Act?—I am not aware of that.

1104. Have the corporation, since that Act of 1849, acquired any additional duties or powers in relation to the local regulations of the city?—Yes, they have got the paving and lighting.

1105. They got by that Act the powers of paving and lighting?—Yes, and the powers of the grand jury.

1106. And the powers of the Wide Streets Commission?—Yes, and the powers to make sewers, and levy a sewer rate.

1107. But they were to make sewers in the Act of 1849?—Yes, I will just read it, if the Committee wish.

1108. Will you refer to the section that confers the powers to make sewers?—It is the 113th section of the Dublin Improvement Act, 12 & 13 Vict. c. 97: "Be it enacted that for the purpose of building and repairing sewers within each district into which the district comprised within the limits of this Act may be divided for the purposes of sewers, and for securing and paying off any monies which may be borrowed for such purposes, and the interest thereof, it shall be lawful for the council to make, assess and levy for each such district, such equal separate rate, to be called the 'district sewer rate,' as may be necessary for the purposes aforesaid, not exceeding in any one year 4 *d.* in the pound of the full nett annual value of the property included in such rate.

Mr. *Butt*—continued.

1109. Fourpence in the pound was then the limit of the sewer rate?—Yes.

1110. But in all those Acts, the lord mayor retained, did he not, his ancient right as clerk of the markets, having jurisdiction over them?—Yes, it is reserved to him here.

1111. And some new regulations were made?—Yes, it is recited here that he has it by charter, and it is continued to him.

1112. Have the corporation, since the Act of 1849, acquired any other duties or powers in relation to the management of the local affairs of the city?—Not that I am aware of, except what they have under this Act of 1849.

1113. Are not the sanitary arrangements thrown upon them since?—Yes.

1114. And the main drainage?—Yes, there was the main drainage, but that did not go on.

1115. They obtained an Act called a local Act?—Yes, and they obtained local Acts for the better supply of water.

1116. Could you tell me the different rates that are now levied by the corporation?—There is the improvement rate.

1117. Under what Act is the improvement rate?—Under the Act of 1849.

1118. What is the limit of the improvement rate?—Two shillings.

1119. How is that rate to be applied?—Section 118 says that it is to be applied, "Firstly, in defraying the charges and expenses which shall have been incurred or incident to the obtaining and passing of this Act; secondly, in paying the interest of all monies borrowed or expenses which shall have been incurred or shall be incident to the obtaining and passing this Act. Thirdly, in paying the amount of compensation awarded to any officer or person under the provisions of this Act. Fourthly, in setting apart the sum required to pay the debts hereinbefore mentioned, due by the Wide Street Commissioners to the Lords Commissioners of Her Majesty's Treasury, and to the National Insurance Company of Ireland. Fifthly, in setting apart and appropriating one-twentieth part thereof in payment off of the principal monies which shall have been borrowed or secured on the said improvement rate. Sixthly, in carrying all the purposes of this Act into execution except the building and repairing sewers; and lastly, in paying off the principal of all monies due on the credit of said improvement rate."

1120. What were the purposes to which that improvement rate was to be applied; was it the same purposes as the Wide Street Commissioners' powers?—Yes; the paving, cleansing, and lighting.

1121. Did the improvement rate also include the sums that were expended by the old Paving Board for paving, lighting, and cleansing the city?—Yes, and to pay off the debts which those two bodies had incurred.

1122. There is a clause in that Act, is there not, transferring to the corporation the powers of the Paving Board?—Yes.

1123. Is there any debt charged on the improvement

Mr. *Butt*—continued.

provement rate?—No, that was all paid off by the improvement rate.

1124. I am speaking now of 1849; at that time was there a debt due by the Paving Board?—There was, and the figures are given in this Act.

1125. Will you just read what the Act says?—It is Section 4 of the Act of 1849: "And whereas the said Commissioners for making wide and convenient ways, streets, and passages, in the City of Dublin, under the provisions of several Acts relating to the same hereby repealed, have borrowed from the Lords Commissioners of Her Majesty's Treasury, and from the National Insurance Company of Ireland, large sums of money, on the credit of the rates and assessments established and vested in them by virtue of the said Acts, and for securing the repayment of the said monies and the interest thereon, the said Commissioners of Wide Streets have granted mortgages on the said rates: And whereas the said Commissioners of Wide Streets have, from time to time, paid off certain portions of the sums so borrowed, together with the interest due thereon, leaving the sum of 21,263 *l.* 12 *s.* still due and owing to the said Lords Commissioners of Her Majesty's Treasury, and the sum of 18,500 *l.* still due and owing to the said National Insurance Company: And whereas it is expedient to provide for the payment of such debts by making the same a charge upon the rates to be levied under the provisions of this Act: Be it therefore enacted, that the said mortgages and securities for money which, before the commencement of this Act, were duly given and legally payable from and out of the rates which the said Commissioners of Wide Streets were under the provisions of the said recited Acts, hereby repealed, entitled to raise and levy, shall, together with all interest due and to accrue due thereon, be chargeable on, and paid by, the Lord Mayor, aldermen, and burgesses of Dublin, out of the rates authorised to be levied and collected under the provisions of this Act; and the said Lord Mayor, aldermen, and burgesses, shall discharge such portions of the principal monies so due as aforesaid, with all interest payable thereon, and also upon the principal monies remaining unpaid at such times and in such manner as has heretofore been lawfully done by the said Commissioners of Wide Streets, in compliance with the obligations contained in the mortgages and securities hereinbefore mentioned, and shall be recovered from the said Lord Mayor, aldermen, and burgesses, in like manner as the same might have been recovered from the said Commissioners of Wide Streets if this Act had not been passed."

1126. That refers to the debt of the Commissioners of Wide Streets?—Yes.

1127. Was there a debt due by the paving board, as they were called?—Yes, but I do not think that that is mentioned in this Act.

1128. Will you be so good as to read Section 63?—Section 63 says, "And be it enacted, that the council shall and may, subject to the provisions of this Act and of the Act and clauses of Acts incorporated herewith, cause to be paved, drained, lighted, cleansed, watered, and otherwise improved, the borough of Dublin, and do all necessary acts for promoting the health and convenience of the said borough, and for that purpose may exercise all the powers vested in them by this Act and the Acts incorporated herewith."

Mr. *Butt*—continued.

1129. Was not that the power that the Paving Board had previously?—Yes.

1130. Can you tell me whether the Paving Board had any debt?—I do not find any in this Act.

1131. There is no provision in this Act for paying it?—No, not that I can see.

1132. Then that 2 *s.* improvement rate was to fulfil all the improvement purposes of the Act of 1849?—Yes; and the payment of that debt.

1133. And that included the powers exercised by the Wide Streets Commissioners of paving, lighting, and cleansing the city, and any other things that were specified in that Act?—Yes.

1134. Do you happen to know whether in that Act any clauses of a general Act of Parliament were incorporated?—Yes.

1135. Clauses were taken, were they not, from the Towns Improvement Clauses Act, 1847?—Yes; I see in the section immediately before the one which I just read that the Towns Improvement Clauses Act, 1847, is incorporated.

1136. Do you know that the Act of 1847 was merely like the Lands Clauses Consolidation Act, a statement of clauses which were usually inserted in local Acts of Parliament?—Quite so.

1137. And which were all incorporated to save the trouble of repeating them?—Yes.

1138. But it did not in itself enact anything?—No.

1139. You say that that debt has been paid off out of the 2 *s.* improvement rate?—Yes.

1140. The sewerage has been paid for separately, I presume?—Quite separately; the sewer rate has its own liabilities. I can read the liabilities, if you will allow me; they are in Section 114, which says, "And be it enacted, that all monies which shall come to the hands of the council from the said rate" (that is, the district sewer rate, which I have read already), "or which shall be raised by any mortgage or security thereof granted by the council, shall be applied and disposed of as follows: firstly, in paying the interest of all monies borrowed, and which shall be from time to time due and owing on the credit of the said rate; secondly, in setting apart and appropriating one-twentieth part thereof in payment off of the principal monies which shall have been borrowed or secured on the said sewer rate; thirdly, in building and repairing sewers within the limits of this Act; and lastly, in paying off the principal of all monies due on the credit of the said rate."

1141. Is the grand jury rate unlimited?—It is.

1142. The purposes for which that is levied are provided by presentment, are they not?—Yes, by presentment.

1143. Exactly as they are by the grand jury in any county?—Yes.

1144. With the fiat of a judge of the Court of Queen's Bench?—Yes, they are fiated every Michaelmas term by a judge of the Court of Queen's Bench.

1145. Can you tell the Committee the purposes to which the grand jury rate is applied?—In paying off the debts to the Government in the first instance, for the buildings, for prisons, then for the maintenance of the prisons, the maintenance of the reformatory schools and the industrial schools, and the hospitals.

1146. Are those different rates paid in to separate accounts by the corporation?—They are not

Mr. *Henry*.

9 May 1876.

Mr. *Henry*.

9 May 1876.

Mr. *Butt*—continued.

not paid in by the corporation; they are paid in by the collector general who levies them.

1147. Are they paid in to separate accounts?—Yes.

1148. Is the grand jury account separate from the improvement rate?—Yes.

1149. And the improvement account separate from the sewerage?—No, the sewer and the improvement rate are one in the bank, but they are separately drawn for that rate; they are drawn by separate cheques.

1150. Have you got any additional powers as to bridges and quays?—No.

1151. What was the Act which has been passed under which the Essex bridge or the Grattan bridge has been rebuilt?—It is the 17th and 18th of Victoria, chapter 22.

1152. Is that a local and personal Act?—No, it is a public Act.

1153. What were its provisions?—They are recited in a Bill which is now pending in Parliament.

1154. Are you able to tell me generally what its provisions are?—I can tell you by reading the recital in this Bill, which says that by an Act intituled "An Act to enable the collector general of Dublin to levy money to repay a certain outlay by the corporation for preserving and improving the port of Dublin, in and about repairing the quay wall of the River Liffey, and for future repairs thereof, and for repairing and building bridges over the said river," it was among other things enacted, that when and so often as it should be necessary to expend any money for the purpose of repairing or rebuilding the several bridges between Carlisle bridge and Barrack bridge, including those two bridges, the amount required should be estimated by the corporation for preserving and improving the port of Dublin, and should be applotted, raised, and levied by the collector general of rates (hereinafter referred to as the collector general), in the same manner as the police rate, and that all the provisions contained in "An Act to provide for the Collection of Rates in the City of Dublin" (hereinafter referred to as the Act of 1849), for the applotting, assessing, raising, levying, lodging, accounting for, auditing and paying over the sums in the Act of 1849 mentioned, should extend and be applicable to the bridge tax by the Act of 1854 authorised, as fully as if the same had been specifically mentioned in the Act of 1849, and been declared to be one of the rates leviable thereunder."

1155. But there was an Act passed providing for the building of bridges and quays in Dublin. In what year was that Act passed?—That must be the 17 & 18 Vict. c. 22.

1156. Is any part of the municipal regulations of Dublin under the control of the Port and Docks Board?—The quay walls and the bridges are, and the bed of the river.

1157. Are you able to tell me, under that Act of the 17 & 18 Vict., by what process a bridge, for instance, is rebuilt in Dublin if it is wanted?—The Port and Docks Board send in a plan and estimate before a certain day in August to me. This is submitted to the council, and if the council approve of the plan they put the estimate in the schedule of presentments, and present it to the Court of Queen's Bench for fiat. If they do not approve of the plan they cannot compel the Port and Docks Board to alter or change that plan: and then the tax is levied by the collector general over the entire metropolitan district.

1158. In point of fact, then, the body that must initiate a proposal to rebuild or build a bridge in the city of Dublin is the Port and Docks Board?—Yes.

1159. And the corporation have the power of negativing it?—Yes.

1160. But they cannot originate, of their own authority, the building of a bridge?—No; nor need any of their suggestions, if they make suggestions, be accepted by the Port and Docks Board.

1161. Does the same thing apply to a quay wall?—Yes.

1162. Has the bridge which was formerly called Essex Bridge, but which was subsequently called Grattan Bridge, been built under the authority of that Act?—Yes.

1163. That is presented to the grand jury as a presentment by the corporation in the Court of Queen's Bench?—Yes.

1164. Over what area is the grand jury taxation levied?—Over the city area only; that is to say, the grand jury proper.

1165. Is there any other provision for the expense of a bridge presentment; over what area is that levied?—The entire metropolitan district; that is to say, the district over which the metropolitan police have control. It goes down very nearly to Bray, and I think it takes in a little of Bray.

1166. Does it not extend into a part of Kildare?—No.

1167. But it extends, does it not, a considerable distance from Dublin?—Yes; Bray is the greatest extent. It takes in Dalkey and Killiney.

1168. Is Cloudalkin within the police district?—No, not within the metropolitan district; nor Kilmainham, nor Clontarf.

1169. Are you sure of that?—Yes, I am quite certain.

1170. Over that metropolitan police district the taxation is levied for the bridges and the quay walls?—Yes.

1171. And also for the support of the metropolitan police; that is also levied over the same district?—Yes.

1172. The other taxes that we have been speaking of, I presume, are all levied only within the bounds of the municipality?—Yes.

Mr. *Bruen*.

1173. Can you tell the Committee whether the rate for those bridges is levied by an equal rate over the whole district, or whether the rate varies in proportion to the distance from the bridges?—It is an equal rate.

Mr. *Butt*.

1174. This is, I think, the provision about the bridges in future; in the 17 & 18 Vict. c. 22, s. 4; "From and after the passing of this Act, and when and so often as it shall be necessary to expend any such sum or sums of money for the purpose of preserving or repairing the said portion of the said quay-wall hereinbefore mentioned, and also for the purpose of repairing or re-building all the said bridges, the said corporation for preserving and improving the port of Dublin shall, on or before the first day of September in every year by their secretary or other public

Mr. *Butt*—continued.

public officer, estimate and ascertain, as nearly as may be, the amounts of the sums of money which they shall deem to be so necessary for preserving and repairing the said portion of the said quay-wall for 12 months next following the 1st day of January in each year, by the name of the quay-wall tax, and also for repairing or re-building the said bridges: and the said corporation for preserving and improving the port of Dublin shall, by their secretary or other public officer, sign and certify such estimate, and transmit the same, on or before the 1st day of September in every year, to the town clerk of the city of Dublin; and immediately after the day fixed by the council of the said borough of Dublin for receiving such applications, the said council shall proceed to investigate such estimate or application and decide upon them at an open meeting of the said council or of a committee thereof authorised in that behalf, in the same manner as the said council is authorised and empowered in respect of other presentments; and if the said estimate or application should be agreed to by the said council or committee thereof, then the said estimate or application shall be inserted by the town clerk of the said borough in the schedule of applications agreed to by the said town council, according to the provisions of the Dublin Improvement Act, 1849, to be made out; and every such estimate or application shall be subject to such consideration by the Court of Queen's Bench, or any judge thereof, and to such orders, allowance or disallowance by such court or judge respectively, and also to such traverses or objections as is provided with respect to applications or presentments in and by the said last-mentioned Act authorized to be made"?—That is what I referred to.

1175. Then the 5th section says, "In case any such estimate or application shall not be sanctioned by the said council, the parties making such application shall be at liberty (on giving six days' notice of his intention to do so) to bring the same before the court or judge respectively at the time of fiating presentments; and if it shall appear to the said court or judge respectively that such presentment or presentments should have been made, the same shall be added to the schedules sent by the town clerk, under the separate heading 'Quay-wall Tax' or 'Bridge Tax' respectively, as the case may be," so that the veto of the corporation upon the proceeding of the Port and Docks Board is controlled by a power in the Court of Queen's Bench to order them to make that presentment?—Yes; but that has never been done.

1176. And then the amount of that presentment, in the same manner as the police rate, is raised over the same district?—Yes.

1177. That is, over the whole district?—Yes, over the whole metropolitan district.

1178. In that respect the taxes for keeping the quay walls and the bridges in repair differ from all the other municipal taxes in the city of Dublin?—Yes.

1179. In this Act it speaks of the Act of the corporation for preserving and improving the port of Dublin; has any change been made since the passing of that Act in that body?—Yes, that body has been divided into two; there is what they call the Port and Docks Board and the Irish Lights Board. They were all originally included in the Ballast Board.

Mr. *Butt*—continued.

Mr. *Henry*.

9 May 1876.

1180. The proper name was, "The Corporation for preserving and improving the Port of Dublin"?—Yes; commonly called the Ballast Board.

1181. Do you know that an Act was passed in the year 1867, a local and personal Act, to alter the constitution of the corporation for preserving and improving the port of Dublin?—Yes.

1182. That is a local and personal Act of the 30th and 31st of the Queen, chapter 81?—Yes.

1183. The old constitution was that the lord mayor and sheriffs of the city of Dublin, together with 17 persons originally named in the Act, should be incorporated by the name of the corporation for preserving and improving the port of Dublin?—Yes.

1184. And it was to be constituted in this way: 17 members nominated by themselves, subject to the approval of the Lord Lieutenant and Privy Council of Ireland, three aldermen of the city of Dublin annually nominated by the municipal corporation, the lord mayor for the time being, and the high sheriff for the time being?—That was the constitution in the Act.

1185. Then the powers of attending to the lighthouses were taken away from them; they had before the control of the lighthouses round Ireland?—They had; it was one body at that time.

1186. Was this to be the constitution of the Port and Dock Board: the lord mayor for the city of Dublin for the time being, three citizens that were to be appointed by the municipal corporation, seven nominated members being persons from time to time nominated, subject and according to the provisions of this Act, by the Commissioners of Irish Lights from amongst themselves?—Yes.

1187. Fourteen elective members being elected in this way: seven by traders and manufacturers in the city of Dublin, and seven by owners of shipping registered in the Custom House books of the port of Dublin or trading to the port?—Yes; that is so.

1188. What are the qualifications prescribed for the electors in the 11th section:—"The qualification of electors of representatives of traders and manufacturers shall be regulated as follows, namely: (1.) Every person, partnership, or body corporate carrying on any business as a wholesale trader or wholesale traders within the city of Dublin shall be qualified to give one vote for each elective member to be elected as a representative of traders and manufacturers. (2.) Every person, partnership, or body corporate carrying on any business within the city of Dublin, and paying Customs duties at the port of Dublin to the amount of 500*l.* or upwards in the twelve months ending the 30th day of September in the year of election, shall also be qualified to give votes for each elective member to be elected as a representative of traders and manufacturers, according to the scale set forth in the schedule to this Act, Part I. (3.) Every person, partnership, or body corporate carrying on any business within the city of Dublin, and paying Excise duties in the city of Dublin to the amount of 500*l.* or upwards in the twelve months ending the 30th day of September in the year of election shall also be qualified to give votes for each elective member to be elected as a representative of traders and manufacturers, according to the scale set forth in the schedule to this Act, Part I."

Then

Mr. *Henry*.

9 May 1876.

Mr. Butt—continued.

Then Part I. of the schedule is as follows: "Scale of votes, according to amount of Customs or Excise duties paid. For duties paid to the amount of 500 *l.* and not exceeding 1,000 *l.*, one vote. Exceeding 1,000 *l.* and not exceeding 2,500 *l.*, two votes. Exceeding 2,500 *l.* and not exceeding 5,000 *l.*, three votes. Exceeding 5,000 *l.* and not exceeding 10,000 *l.*, four votes. Exceeding 10,000 *l.* and not exceeding 20,000 *l.*, five votes. Exceeding 20,000 *l.*, six votes. Six votes to be the maximum." Then, "(4.) Every person, partnership, or body corporate carrying on any trade or manufacture within the city of Dublin, and rated to the rate for the relief of the poor on an annual rateable value of 100 *l.* or upwards in respect of his or their property used for the purposes of such trade or manufacture, shall also be qualified to give votes for each elective member to be elected as a representative of traders and manufacturers, according to the scale set forth in the schedule to this Act, Part II." Then Part II. of the schedule is as follows: "Scale of votes according to assessment to poor rate. For assessment on annual rateable value of 100 *l.* and not exceeding 200 *l.*, one vote. Exceeding 200 *l.* and not exceeding 300 *l.*, two votes Exceeding 300 *l.* and not exceeding 400 *l.*, three votes. Exceeding 400 *l.* and not exceeding 500 *l.*, four votes. Exceeding 500 *l.* and not exceeding 600 *l.*, five votes. Exceeding 600 *l.*, six votes. Six votes to be the maximum."

1189. What is the qualification of shipowners in Section 17?—"The qualification of electors of representatives of shipowners shall be regulated as follows, namely: (1.) Shipowners respectively registered as owners of not less in the whole than 150 tons of shipping shall be qualified to give votes for each elective member to be elected as a representative of shipowners, according to the scale set forth in the schedule to this Act, Part III." Part III. is as follows: "Scale of votes for registered shipowners for 150 tons of registered shipping, and not exceeding 250 tons, one vote. Exceeding 250 tons, and not exceeding 500 tons, two votes. Exceeding 500 tons, and not exceeding 750 tons, three votes. Exceeding 750 tons, and not exceeding 1,000 tons, four votes. Exceeding 1,000 tons, and not exceeding 1,250 tons, five votes. Exceeding 1,250 tons, and not exceeding 1,500, six votes. Exceeding 1,500 tons, and not exceeding 1,750 tons, seven votes. Exceeding 1,750 tons, and not exceeding 2,000 tons, eight votes. Exceeding 2,000, and not exceeding 2,250 tons, nine votes. Exceeding 2,250 tons, 10 votes. Ten votes to be the maximum." (2.) Where a ship is registered in the name of one person or partnership, that person or partnership shall be deemed the owner. (3.) Where a ship is registered in distinct and several shares in the names of more owners than one, the tonnage shall be apportioned among the owners as nearly as may be in proportion to their respective shares, and each of such owners shall be deemed the owner of the tonnage so apportioned to him. (4.) Where a ship is registered jointly, without severance of interest in the names of more persons than one, not registered as constituting a partnership, the tonnage shall, if it is sufficient either alone or together with other tonnage (if any) owned by each joint owners to give a qualification to each of them be apportioned equally between them, and each of such joint owners shall be deemed to be the owner of the equal share so apportioned to him, but if it is not so sufficient, the whole of such tonnage shall be deemed to be owned by such one of the joint owners as is first named on the register; (5.) For the purposes of any apportionment under this section, any portion may be struck off so as to produce a divisible amount; (6.) The whole amount of tonnage so owned by each person, partnership, or body corporate, whether in ships or in shares of, or interests in ships, shall be added together, and if sufficient shall constitute his or their qualification; (7.) Shipowners not registered in the port of Dublin, but having an office and representative manager in Dublin, and paying harbour rates to the amount of 100 *l.* or upwards in the 12 months ending the 30th day of September in the year of election, shall be qualified to give one vote for each elective member to be elected as a representative of shipowners, and to give one additional vote for every additional complete amount of 100 *l.* so paid; but the maximum number of votes to which any person shall be so entitled shall be 10. Provided always, that shipowners registered in the port of Dublin, and paying harbour rates, shall, in lieu of qualifying as such registered owners, have the option of qualifying as payers of harbour rates in the same manner, and with the same qualification and number of votes as shipowners not registered in the port of Dublin, and the shipowners exercising such option shall not be inserted in the list of shipowners in respect of any qualification from the tonnage of vessels."

1190. That is now the constitution of the Port and Docks Board under that Act?—Yes.

Chairman.

1191. Are you acquainted with the working of the Port and Docks Board?—I am not.

1192. Do you know whether it gives satisfaction to the citizens?—I have never heard a complaint of them.

Mr. Butt.

1193. Is the improvement rate practically sufficient for the purposes for which it is wanted?—It is not.

1194. Was it sufficient in 1849, at the time it was imposed?—It was considered to be sufficient then, when they limited it to 2 *s.*

1195. Can you tell me any circumstances which will account for its having been considered to be sufficient then and being entirely insufficient now?—There are a great number of streets added to the city of Dublin since then, and labour and material have advanced enormously.

1196. How do you mean that streets have been added?—Streets have increased; new streets have been built.

1197. Within the municipal limits?—Yes.

1198. Would not the addition of those new streets supply an additional revenue at least equal to the additional expenditure?—I do not think it would be proportionate to the cost of the streets, because the streets that have been lately added to the streets of the city of Dublin have been for very inferior class of house indeed.

1199. There has been a great deal of building on the north side of the city, has there not?—Yes, but of very small, inferior houses.

1200. A new city, in fact?—Yes.

1201. Has not there also been considerable addition

Mr. *Henry.*

9 May 1876.

Mr. *Butt*—continued.

addition about Porto Bello?—Yes, of an equally inferior class of house.

1202. Do you think that those new streets have entailed additional expenditure, and that the additional revenue coming from taxation does not make up for it?—I do.

Chairman.

1203. How far do the municipal limits extend?—To the Circular Road.

1204. Do you mean that many new streets have been made within that boundary?—Certainly.

Mr. *J. P. Corry.*

1205. How are the streets made; do the corporation make the streets?—No, the owners of the property make the streets, and give them up to the corporation when they are made.

Mr. *Butt.*

1206. Have the corporation any control over the building of new streets?—As soon as they are taken up.

1207. Have they any control as to the way in which they are laid out, or is that done entirely at the option of the owners?—Quite at the option of the owners. They have no power to control the buildings.

1208. Has there been a very considerable increase in the cost of materials?—Very great.

1209. Could you form an idea what has been the proportion of the total increase?—No, but Mr. Nevill, our engineer, is here, and he could tell you.

1210. Have you, from your experience as town clerk, formed any opinion as to whether the area of the municipal limits is large enough?—I do not think it is.

1211. Can you give any reason for that opinion?—I think that the people living outside the boundary who use our streets ought to be taxed in the same way that they are for using the bridges.

1212. You would not extend that to the whole of the police district, would you?—No, I do not think you could go so far as that.

1213. Is there outside the municipal boundary any continuous town?—Yes, Rathmines.

1214. From the municipal boundary is there a continuous town in the case of Rathmines?—Yes, there is, most decidedly. I heard that spoken to by a member of the Port and Dock Board on the Committee of the House of Lords, about a month ago. It is as continuous as the streets inside.

1215. Rathmines is incorporated into a township, managing its own roads, is it not?—Yes.

1216. And its own municipal affairs?—Yes, they have a Board of Commissioners.

1217. In what respect should they be subject to the city taxation when they provide for their own affairs?—They use our roads.

1218. Do not you use theirs?—Not so much as they use ours.

1219. You think it would be a fairer thing if they were thrown into a common lot with the citizens of Dublin?—I think so.

1220. Are you able to tell me whether that would increase their taxation?—It would necessarily.

1221. Why necessarily?—If you add an additional tax to them, of course it would.

1222. What additional tax would that impose?—It would impose the 2 *s.* rate on them.

1223. In doing that, would you not exempt them from the maintenance of their own roads?—That would be a question of detail, I think.

1224. Do you think it would be fair to tax them more for your streets than for their own?—Yes.

Chairman.

1225. You mean, do you not, that if Rathmines were united to Dublin, the governing body of both should repair the roads of both?—Yes.

1226. And that the cost of doing so should be levied by a rate over the whole area?—Yes.

Mr. *Butt.*

1227. You mean, then, that the corporation should take the whole of the streets of Rathmines just as they do the streets of Dublin?—Yes; and equalise the rate.

1228. I will just bring you to another matter; in the year 1849, when that Act of Parliament was passed, there was a very great change, was there not, in the composition of the *personnel* of the corporation?—That I do not know. I was not acquainted with it at that time.

1229. Are you able to tell me whether there has been any change made, practically, in the election of lord mayors since 1849?—Yes.

1230. In what direction?—In alternate selection.

1231. How do you mean alternate?—Catholics and Protestants.

1232. Can you tell me whether, since 1849, the lord mayors have been selected from different classes, both of religion and politics?—Yes, I have a list of them here in my pocket.

1233. I believe the first lord mayor of Dublin was Sir Benjamin Guinness?—In 1851, Benjamin Lee Guinness was the lord mayor.

1234. In point of fact, have there been a number of lord mayors holding Conservative opinions elected since 1849?—Yes.

1235. Frequently?—Yes.

1236. The present lord mayor of Dublin is a Conservative, is he not?—He is.

1237. And the division between Protestantism and Roman Catholics has been equal, I believe?—Certainly.

1238. With one exception?—Yes, with one exception, when one gentleman, Sir William Carroll, was for two years elected.

1239. With regard to the elections in the wards, are there not some of the wards in which persons holding what are called Liberal opinions greatly predominate?—Yes.

1240. Are any of those wards represented by Conservatives?—There are.

1241. Can you give me an instance of that, in which you could positively say that it is so; which ward does Mr. John Jameson represent?—He represents Iron Quay Ward.

1242. In that ward, I believe, there would be a preponderance of political opinions opposed to those which he entertains?—Yes.

1243. Can you mention any other of the same class?—There is the Mansion House Ward; the present lord mayor is a councillor of it, and Mr. Fry, a Liberal and a Protestant, is a member of it.

1244. There is no exclusion on account of religion?—No.

1245. Which does Sir John Barrington represent?—The South Dock Ward.

Mr. *Henry*

9 May 1876.

Mr. *Butt*—continued.

1246. Is that a Liberal ward?—No.

1247. The qualification in Dublin for burgesses involves, does it not, a continued occupation for two years and eight months?—Yes.

1248. In your opinion, does that very much limit the constituency?—I should say so, very much.

1249. Has your attention been at all turned to the question of continuous occupation?—Yes.

1250. Will you tell me, on the question of continuous occupation, whether, in the case of a citizen changing from one premises to another, the occupation of different places is to be reckoned by law as of the same premises?—Yes.

1251. Does that prevent the loss of the franchise by change of residence?—It does in very many instances.

1252. Does it in all?—No, not in all. If an occupier changes directly from one house to another, he can keep up his occupation in as many houses as he likes, and the two years and eight months are reckoned as one occupancy; but if he for one week or for two days goes into a lodging, if the house is not prepared for him, and it is not occupied by his servant or himself, he loses the continuancy of his occupancy; he has to go back and begin again.

1253. So that if any person in any rank of life, giving up his house, did not instantly go into another house, he would lose the franchise?—Yes.

1254. And he must be three years in the new house before he acquires the franchise?—Yes.

1255. Can you tell me whether, in point of fact, that disqualifies any considerable number of persons?—I should say that it does.

1256. Do you say that from your experience at the registration court, the revision court, as town clerk?—Yes.

1257. Can you tell me what taxes are to be paid to qualify a man for the municipal franchise?—The 3rd section of the 12 & 13 Vict. c. 85, says: "That from and after the expiration of the present year in the borough of Dublin every male person of full age who, on the last day of August in any year, shall have occupied any house, warehouse, counting-house, or shop within such borough of Dublin during that year and the whole of each of the two preceding years, and also during the time of such occupation shall have been an inhabitant householder within the said borough, or within seven statute miles of the said borough of Dublin, shall, if duly enrolled in that year, according to the provisions of the said recited Acts, be a burgess of such borough and member of the body corporate of the mayor, aldermen, and burgesses of such borough: Provided always, that no such person shall be so enrolled in any year from and after the present year unless he shall have been rated in respect of such premises so occupied by him within the said borough to all rates made for the relief of the poor of the electoral division or union wherein such premises are situated during the time of his occupation as aforesaid, and unless he shall have paid, on or before the last day of August as aforesaid, all such of the rates, cesses, and taxes specified in the schedule to this Act annexed as shall have become payable by him (if any) in respect of the said premises, except such as shall become payable within six calendar months next before the said last day of August."

Mr. *Butt*—continued.

1258. Now will you look at the schedule, and tell me the taxes that he has to pay to qualify him; what they would be in the City of Dublin?—The tax for paving and lighting; for watering the streets; then the improvement tax, the grand jury tax, police tax, borough rate, and poor rates.

1259. Then, in point of fact, he has to pay, to qualify himself in Dublin, the improvement rate, the grand jury rate, and all the taxes?—Yes.

1260. Has he to pay a bridge tax?—That bridge tax is not a constantly levied tax. There is none in existence at present, and as it is not mentioned in the schedule, he would not have to pay it; but the taxes are improvement rate, sewers rate, grand jury cess, police tax, and poors rate.

1261. You are probably aware what the rate-paying provision is in England, in the 32 & 33 Vict. c. 55, s. 1, he is required to pay "On or before the 20th day of July in such year all such rates, including therein all borough rates, if any, directed to be paid under the provisions of the said Acts as shall have become payable by him in respect of the said premises up to the preceding 5th day of January;" are you able to tell me whether there is any difference in the rate-paying clauses of the Municipal Corporations Act of England and of Ireland?—I am not.

1262. Are you bound in the case of the Parliamentary representation to give a notice of the taxes being required to be paid?—Yes.

1263. What notice is that?—Two months' notice.

1264. In what manner do you give it?—I give it by posting it on the outer doors of the City Hall and posting it extensively all through the City. I do that under the Act.

1265. Do you give any corresponding notice of the necessity of paying the municipal taxes for a period to be qualified as a burgess?—No; there is no provision for that.

1266. Can you tell me the effect of the rate-paying clauses on the burgess roll?—Yes; many people have come into my office to complain that they were knocked off the burgess roll for non-payment of taxes, as they were not aware of the time to pay the taxes in, and they asked me why I do not publish a notice such as I do in the case of the Parliamentary Register.

1267. Is that of frequent occurrence?—It is very frequent for persons to come in and make complaints.

1268. Where the taxes are paid by the landlord, are you able to tell me whether it frequently occurs, or at all occurs, that he is put upon the rate and his name remains on the rate and not the tenant's?—Yes.

1269. You must have known of that from your experience at the revision court?—Yes; I have no other way of knowing it.

1270. From your experience, can you tell me whether it does happen, that where the landlord pays the taxes, his name is put upon the rate book instead of the tenant's?—Yes; the tenant not knowing how to go about getting himself rated.

1271. Is it not the duty of the collector to find out who the occupier is?—That I do not know. I have read Mr. Taaffe's evidence in which he said that it was his duty.

1272. I am speaking now of some time back; in your experience when you were attending the revision

Mr. *Butt*—continued.

revision court, do you think that the collectors did in point of fact ascertain the occupiers?—Some of them did, and some of them did not.

1273. Have you known any instances where the landlords have deferred paying the taxes until the day after the time which qualified the tenants to have the franchise?—I cannot say as to the day, but I have heard many complaints made that the landlords did not pay the tenants' taxes; but of my own knowledge, I do not know.

1274. Is there any other matter connected with the municipal arrangements of Dublin, which you think it necessary to bring before the Committee?—I have prepared a Return of the number of burgesses since the year 1843. I do not know whether the Committee would wish to have it. In the year 1843 there were 4,445 burgesses.

1275. How many were there in 1852?—In 1852 there were 5,267. The present burgess roll consists of 5,339; the variation has been very little.

1276. Has the substitution of what was then the English franchise for the former franchise had the effect of materially enlarging the burgess roll?—No.

1277. The corporation have, in addition to the taxes you have mentioned, the power of levying a borough rate?—They have that power.

1278. And that is limited to 3 *d.* in the pound in Dublin, is it not?—Yes.

1279. That is applied to the general purposes of the corporation, is it not?—Yes. The intention is to apply it in aid of the borough fund, the borough fund being the produce of the city rents.

1280. Has it ever been levied by the corporation of Dublin?—I think it was levied for two years, but not within my time of office.

1281. In your time there has been no borough rate?—Not within my time.

1282. The corporation of Dublin are possessed of considerable property in landed estates, are they not?—Yes.

1283. I think you told the Committee that it was your duty as town clerk to attend to the municipal and Parliamentary registers?—Yes.

1284. How do you form the registers?—In the municipal register I make copies of the collector general's rate books so far as the same relate to occupiers. Draft alphabetical ward lists are made of all male persons rated for two years and eight months, including all persons on the previous burgess roll who are rated for the same premises, no matter how long rated. Then the 31st of August is the last day for payment of taxes to entitle burgesses to be on the roll. After that there are fair copies of the ward lists sent to the collector general to have the taxes marked. This is one of them (*handing in the same*). We draw the pen across the names of those who have not paid the rates; and then a fair copy is made and sent to the printer, omitting those names.

1285. You take from the collector general, of course, the fact of payment or non-payment of taxes; do you take from him also the fact of occupation for the proper time?—I take that from his books. His books show the occupation by the date of the rating; any name I see rated for two years and eight months I put on that list; but I do not put any name that does not appear by his

Mr. *Butt*—continued.

Mr. *Henry*.

9 May 1876.

book in the column in which his name is rated to be two years and eight months in it. Then those burgess lists are printed and published. Then on the 1st of October, claims and objections are lodged; claims for names to be put on the list that do not appear, and objections to names that do appear, and those lists of claims and objections are all made out and published between the 1st and the 11th of October; then from the 20th of October to the 10th of November the court sits for the revision of those lists. After that the burgess roll is made and published, and on the 20th November is revised by the lord mayor and his two assessors.

1286. Does the name of any occupier below 8 *l.* appear upon that list?—Any name that is in the collector general's books appears on that list. I have no other guide to go by.

1287. Whatever the value of the occupation?—Yes.

1288. We heard, I think, from the collector general the other day that, for the purposes of the Parliamentary franchise, he inserted on his book the names of the yearly occupiers between 8 *l.* and 4 *l.*, although the owners of that property were actually rated; then do you take the names of occupiers between 8 *l.* and 4 *l.*?—I take every name that appears in the collector general's book; I have no other guide to go by; I must go by his book.

1289. Supposing the names of the occupiers of every kind of property, not only above 4 *l.* but below 4 *l.*, appear on his book, you take all of the names of the occupiers?—Yes.

1290. As to the loss of the municipal franchise from non-payment of taxes, the poor rate, in point of fact, and all the taxes that you have mentioned that qualify for the franchise are collected together, are they not?—Yes, by the collectors of the collector general's office; there are no other collectors.

1291. I thought you stated that complaints had been made to you by persons who found that their names were not on the municipal register; that you did not give the same notice of the necessary payment of taxes for municipal purposes as you gave for Parliamentary purposes?—They have not complained exactly in that way. They have complained to me that their names were left off, and that they were not aware of the time by which the taxes should be paid.

1292. I understood you to say that you did give notice for the purpose of forming the Parliamentary register of the necessity of payment of taxes?—Yes, certainly; I am obliged to do so under the Statute. There is a form of notice prescribed by the Statute.

1293. The Parliamentary register requires the payment of poor rate, does it not?—Yes, it does.

1294. But in Dublin the poor rate and all those other taxes are collected in one collection?—Yes.

1295. Therefore, if a man has paid the poor rate, he must have paid all the other taxes?—I do not think that the collector general would receive the poor rate by itself; but I cannot speak with any certainty about that.

1296. Do you see any difficulty in your giving formal notice as to the requisite payment of municipal taxes?—Certainly not, but there is no direction to do so.

1297. Would not the town council be competent to direct you to do so?—If they passed a resolution I should do so.

Mr. *Henry.*

9 May 1876.

Mr. *Butt*—continued.

1298. You spoke of a difficulty arising with regard to the municipal franchise if a person moving from one house to another occupied a temporary lodging, as it were, between the two houses; can you suggest any remedy for that?—There might be a limit, that he might be allowed to occupy a lodging for a month or so in order to have the house that he was going into prepared.

1299. Is the fact of his moving known, as it were, immediately to the collectors, do you suppose. Supposing a man moves from a house, we will say this week, is the collector likely to know that he has moved before the time arrives when it is necessary for him again to collect the rate?—If he occupies a lodging or any other place in the interval between going from one house to the other, he is disqualified through it. They do not hold it as continuous occupancy.

1300. How is that ascertained?—For both sides in Dublin, the Liberal and Conservative sides, there are agents who go about and ascertain all about those people; where they move, and how they move.

1301. Are you speaking of the municipal or Parliamentary register?—For both.

1302. You think that a person might be allowed to break the continuance for a few days, and yet not be disqualified?—Yes, I think so.

1303. You spoke of a kind of friendly arrangement which had existed in the town council as to the election of lord mayors, according to difference of political opinion; do you consider that politics have much to do with the municipal elections in Dublin?—Yes, they have.

1304. Has any similar arrangement been made, for instance, with regard to the election of aldermen?—No.

1305. Is that conducted upon purely political grounds?—That is entirely dependent upon the burgesses of the ward; the other is an arrangement with the council as members of the council.

1306. Are the aldermen and councillors elected mainly on political grounds?—There are Liberal wards in Dublin which have Conservative members. Rotunda Ward is a Liberal ward, and Alderman Purdon is the alderman of it, and he is a Conservative.

1307. When you give us some exceptions to the rule, do you consider that, as a rule, politics are the main cause?—Yes.

1308. In the exceptions which you have given us, have the burgesses been induced to waive their political opinions by the special knowledge or position of the candidate?—I think that is the reason.

1309. Has any idea occurred to you by which the prevalence of politics in elections could be obviated if it be evil?—I should not like to make any suggestion about it.

1310. You spoke of the division of the old corporation for preserving and improving the port of Dublin into the Port and Docks Board, and Irish Lights Board, and you have told us how the Port and Docks Board were elected; can you tell us how the Irish Lights Board were elected?—The 3rd section of the Dublin Port Act, 1867, says: "The constitution of the Commissioners of Irish Lights (to whom the expression, 'the Commissioners,' when used in this Act, refers,) shall remain and be as if this Act had not been passed." It was self-elective. Then they have the power of sending some of their members to represent them, namely, seven Commissioners of Irish Lights.

Mr. *Butt*—continued.

1311. You referred to the improvement rate of 2*s.* in the pound, and spoke of the charges on it. I gathered that the debts charged on that rate at first amounted to 21,000*l.* or thereabouts, and 18,000*l.* or thereabouts?—Yes, it is stated so in the Act.

1312. Is it your duty, or that of the city treasurer, to allocate the different heads of expenditure incurred by the town council under the different rates?—The treasurer does that, but there are estimates made out by the different committees having charge of the different funds, and after being approved by the town council on the 10th of December, they are forwarded to the collector general, with a precept directing him to levy the amount.

1313. Do you prepare the estimate?—No; the secretaries and the engineer prepare the estimates and send them to me for approval by the council.

1314. Who is considered responsible to the council for the estimates?—So far as the improvement rate is concerned, the city engineer; but as to that, it is always limited to 2*s.*, and he cannot go for more than is sufficient to make up that.

1315. Who is considered the responsible officer to see that each item of expense is put under its proper head?—The secretary of the committee and the city engineer; they all come up for the approval of the council from them. The committee who have charge of them receive the estimates from the secretary and the engineer and examine them; and then, having been approved by the committee, they come to me for approval by the council; and having been approved by the council the precepts are forwarded, under the city seal, to the collector general for collection.

1316. To what committee do you refer?—No. 1 is the principal committee.

1317. Is that the Finance Committee?—No. No. 1 Committee is the committee having charge of the lighting and paving, which is the principal expenditure under the Improvement Act, and the sewer rate.

1318. Will you explain how the Town Council of Dublin divides their business under those different committees?—No. 1 Committee have the charge of paving, lighting and cleansing, and the making of sewers. No. 2 Committee have charge of the markets; and No. 3 Committee have charge of the borough fund, and the grand jury fund.

1319. Are those all the committees?—Those are all the standing committees. Then there is the Public Health Committee, which is a new committee, but those are the three standing committees appointed under this Dublin Improvement Act. The Main Drainage Committee have ceased to act.

1320. Who does the work of the Old Pipe Water Committee, if there was one?—That is the Water Works Committee of the corporation, of which Mr. Lawler is the secretary.

1321. Is the management of these separate rates which you have told us of, divided among the several committees?—Yes; the sewage rate and the improvement rate are managed by No. 1 Committee; the grand jury fund and the city estates are managed by No. 3, and the revenue from the markets is managed by No. 2, and the revenue from the water is managed by the Water Works Committee.

1322. Does it rest with any single officer of the

Mr. *Henry.*

9 May 1876.

Mr. *Butt*—continued.

the corporation to supervise, as it were, the proceedings of all those committees, and to see that one committee does not propose some kind of expenditure, which properly should fall upon another committee, and be paid out of the rate managed by that other committee?—There is no officer whose duty it is to do that.

1323. Are the accounts of the corporation audited?—Yes, by a local government officer.

1324. Has any difficulty arisen in the audit as to the proper allocations of those items of expenditure?—No; there has been a difficulty about an expenditure of 6,700 *l.*, which the Main Drainage Committee made to the Port and Docks Board on account of the works that they got them to do when Grattan Bridge was being reconstructed, the officer imagines; he has made no ruling upon it as yet, but he imagines that that, instead of being paid out of the rates, ought to be paid out of the money borrowed, and the Main Drainage Committee borrowed no money.

1325. Had not the town council power to strike a main drainage rate?—Yes, and they did strike it.

1326. Why did not they pay this money out of it?—They did pay this money out of it. The officer said that they had no right to do it. He said that they could construct no new works except out of money borrowed.

1327. In fact, this was his opinion, was it not, that they must do the whole of the work, and borrow the whole of the sum that they were authorised to borrow by the Act, before they could charge anything upon the rate?—Yes.

1328. Has any other audit difficulty arisen within your knowledge as to the accounts of the corporation?—No; he suggests in some of his reports that the accounts ought to be kept separate, and acting upon that suggestion the improvement fund and the sewer rate have been divided, and are drawn on by separate cheques.

1329. Is not that the very point which I am asking you about, the proper separation of all those accounts?—Yes; that occurred.

1330. How were they kept before he made that suggestion?—They were kept all under the head of improvement fund, but the treasurer is here, who is more acquainted with that than I am.

1331. Do you refer us to the treasurer for evidence upon that point?—Yes.

1332. Can you speak as to the rateable value of the property within the municipal limits?—The valuation of the City of Dublin is 596,099 *l.*

1333. Is that the valuation for 1875?—That is the last valuation for 1875, and it includes the gas and water mains; the gas mains are valued at 8,130 *l.*, and the water mains are valued at 18,824 *l.*

1334. Does that include the Government property?—I do not think it does.

1335. Are you aware whether any or what payment was made in the year 1875 by the Government to the corporation on account of municipal rates on Government property?—I know there was a payment made, but I do not know the exact figure; I know that the fact is so, that there was a payment made.

1336. Are there any exemptions by law for any of the rates that you have made; for instance, does one kind of property, though it may pay the same as another kind to the poor rate, pay on a less sum for the improvement rate or the sewers rate?—I am not aware of that.

Mr. *Butt*—continued.

1337. Perhaps you will put in the different amounts of the valuation for each year from 1849 to 1875?—I will do so.

1338. Was not 1849 the year in which the 2*s.* improvement rate was first levied?—The Act was passed in 1849, but not to come into operation until the 1st of January 1851.

1339. Are you aware, generally, whether the rateable value of Dublin at the present time is much higher than it was in 1849?—I could not answer that.

1340. Do you think that the real value of property in Dublin has much increased since that time?—I do not think that it has so very much increased; I think building is more outside the city now than it had been.

1341. Do you think that the present valuation of Dublin represents the real value of the property?—I do not.

1342. What per-centage should you allow?—I am not prepared to go into details, but I think that the valuation does not represent the proper amount.

1343. Do you think as a total, speaking roughly, that it is 25 per cent. below it?—It would go very nearly that.

Mr. *Bruen.*

1344. When you say the real value, do you mean the rent?—Yes.

Mr. *Butt.*

1345. You think that the valuation of Dublin is under the letting value of the houses; is it equable all over the city, or are there some places where the valuation is more below than others?—There are.

1346. Do you know anything about the valuation of machinery in Dublin?—I do not.

1347. Do you know whether it is valued or not?—I do not think it is; but I am not certain of that.

Dr. *Ward.*

1348. You told the Committee that, in preparing the list for the municipal franchise, you took in the occupiers as returned to you by the collector general of rates?—All that appear on his book are put in a manuscript list, which I send to him to have the taxes revised.

1349. Even though they are below 8 *l.*?—Yes; any names, provided that they are rated for the specified sums.

1350. You mentioned, I think, that the number that got the franchise did not much exceed 5,000 a year?—Five thousand three hundred and thirty-nine.

1351. Are you able to account for the fact that the roll is so few, when you take in such a wide area?—I think a number of people lose their franchise by that two years and eight months' occupation; it is too long for them.

1352. It shuts them out, you think?—I think it shuts out a great many. I think that the burgess roll would be very nearly doubled if it was a one year occupation.

1353. Have you any reason to know whether there are many shut out by the landlords of many of those small holdings not paying the taxes at the proper time?—I know that there are such cases, but I could not give the number.

Chairman.

1354. This book, which I have placed in your hands

Mr. *Henry.*

9 May 1876.

Chairman—continued.

hands (*handing a book to the Witness*) purports to be a report of the city engineer, Mr. Neville, to the corporation, in 1869; are you acquainted with that report?—Yes.

1355. Will you turn to page 24, and read what Mr. Neville states with reference to the valuation?—He says: "In 1847 the valuation of the city was 663,068 *l.*, and it was on this sum that the Committee of the House of Parliament, in 1848, fixed 2 *s.* as the maximum improvement rate that could be levied for the repair and maintenance of the streets, and to carry out the other duties imposed upon the corporation by the Dublin Improvement Bill; and 4 *d.* was also in this Act fixed as the maximum sewer rate that could be levied. In 1851, when the corporation succeeded the late Paving Board and Wide Street Commissioners, the valuation of the city was found to be but 634,848 *l.*, which was still further reduced by the deduction of valuation on buildings exempted from taxation. This year (1851) a general revision of Griffith's valuation was made, and a reduction of about 100,000 *l.* on the valuation was the result, and consequently reducing the income of the corporation 10,000 *l.* per annum; and thus the funds placed at the disposal of No. 1 Committee each year since, for the repair and maintenance of the streets, has been quite insufficient to maintain them in that state of repair and cleanliness that they ought to be kept in; and owing to the trade created by the railways and other causes, the traffic through all the leading streets, the line of quays, &c. has been quadrupled since 1849; and this, of course, renders it more expensive to maintain those thoroughfares in repair and clean; and by Table No. 8 it will be perceived that the late Paving Board, for the last six years of its existence, actually had as much, if not more, money to expend on the limited district under their control than the No. 1 Committee had for years, although the latter had 21 miles more of streets under their charge, and the traffic over them annually increasing, and consequently the cost of maintaining and cleansing, increasing in proportion. The Table No. 8 shows the amount received and placed to the credit of the improvement rate during the years from 1851 to 1868, both inclusive, and the sum which remained after different deductions, applicable and at the disposal of No. 1 Committee for the lighting, cleansing, repair and maintenance of the streets, &c. For the last few years the amount collected as improvement rate has increased, and the expense of collection and bad debts, I believe, diminished; but the rise in the price of material, and that paid for labour, has more than used up this addition to the funds placed at the disposal of the committee. The Table No. 9 shows the charges to which the improvement rate is liable, independent of expenditure for repair and maintenance of the public works, and to which the funds of the last Paving Commissioners were not liable. Table No. 10 shows the expenditure by the last Paving Board Commissioners for the last six years of their term of office for the maintenance of the works in their charge, and paid out of the paving, lighting, and watering tax; as also the expenditure out of the improvement rate by the corporation on the public works of the city during the 18 years they have had charge of them. Table No. 11 shows the expenditure by the last Paving Board Commissioners on salaries, law costs, and other miscellaneous charges incurred in carrying on their establishment during the last six years of their existence, and the expenditure out of the improvement rate by committee No. 1 under the same head."

Chairman—continued.

1356. Will you be good enough to put in Table No. 8. (*The Witness delivered in the same.*)

1357. This statement of Mr. Neville's appears to show that the valuation of the city at the date of the Act of 1849 was considerably higher than it is at the present moment?—Yes, I am sure it was.

Mr. *Brooks.*

1358. Is it not the fact that many of our merchants and professional men, who formerly lived in Dublin, have now merely their offices in Dublin and live beyond the municipal boundary?—That is quite so.

1359. Is it the fact that there is a general opinion that many of these people do so on account of the inequality in the rates in the city, compared with the suburbs?—I could not say what their motive is. I can only speak as to the fact that it is so.

1360. Is it not the fact, that within the last few years, many extensive breweries, distilleries, and bakeries have been erected on the other side of the boundary which divides the suburban from the inter-mural district?—Yes, just outside the boundary.

1361. And they thereby avoid the taxation of the city, whilst they enjoy all the advantages of the paving, lighting, and cleansing?—Yes.

Mr. *Gibson.*

1362. What is the rental of the city estates at present?—I think it is 86,300 *l.*

1363. Are you aware whether the legislation of 1849, the three Acts that were passed in that year, were the result of a compromise, or an understanding between the several parties in the City of Dublin?—I have heard that there was something to that affect, but I cannot speak of my own knowledge.

1364. Are you aware that putting the qualification at two years and eight months was, to a certain extent, as a check upon the necessary operation of the throwing open the franchise to every rated occupier?—I do not know that; the Act says that it was to assimilate it to the franchise of England and Scotland.

1365. Did not the fact of putting a residential qualification of two years and eight months put a substantial check on having it a mere household suffrage?—It is a check to men getting on the burgess roll, I think.

1366. Having regard to the changes that have taken place about Dublin, railways being made, and various appliances for getting out of Dublin, do you think that seven miles is too small a limit now, and that it should be extended?—I think it almost is so.

1367. Is it not the fact that a great many of our leading merchants and shopkeepers have their family houses at Bray, and outside this seven-mile limit?—Yes.

1368. They come in and attend to their business in the day-time?—Certainly, it is so.

1369. Having regard to that, do you think it would be desirable to substantially extend the seven-mile limit?—I do not see the slightest objection to it.

1370. Would

Mr. *Henry*.

9 May 1876.

Mr. *Gibson*—continued.

1370. Would not that bring within the burgess qualification a great many people who at present are much interested in the city, but who now are excluded by it?—I do not think it would bring very many in, but it would bring in some.

1371. You were asked by the honourable and learned Member for Limerick as to whether it was not necessary to pay all those separate taxes that are mentioned in the schedule to the Act of 12 & 13 Vict. c. 85, and you stated that you thought so?—That was my reading of the Act.

1372. Are you not aware that they are collected together with one notice demanding the rate, and that it is practically one rate from every householder in Dublin?—Yes, I said so.

1373. So that it is all one payment, although, as a matter of pure theory, it is composed of seven? — Yes; I said so, in answer to the honourable Member for Limerick.

1374. Is not it also the fact that any occupier at present may, at any time he pleases, claim to be rated under the present law?—Yes.

1375. He has nothing to do but to claim to be rated, has he?—No, only that.

1376. And when he does claim to be rated he is entitled to be rated on the spot?—That I do not know.

1377. You know that he can claim to be rated?—I read Mr. Taaffe's evidence, and, on the contrary, I gathered that he refused to put some persons on when they claimed to be rated. It is with him that the rating rests, and not with me.

1378. You have not considered that point at all?—I have nothing to say to it; it is in the collector general's office.

1379. Do you know whether the corporation have made any arrangements at all for compounding with landlords for the payment of rates?—I am sure they have not.

1380. Are you aware whether they have any power to that effect?—There is a power.

1381. Do you know whether that is the power which is contained in the 120th section of the Dublin Improvement Act?—Yes.

1382. And do you know that that is not acted upon to any extent at all?—None; it never has been acted upon.

1383. With regard to the preparation of the burgess roll at present by you, does this occur; are you bound under the 2nd section of 6 & 7 Vict. c. 93, to do this: "On the completion of the entries so to be made in the said book, the said town clerk shall cause a notice thereof to be fixed on or near the outer door of the town hall or in some public and conspicuous place within the borough, and shall keep the said book in his said office to be perused by any person, without payment of any fee, at all reasonable hours, during the last 10 days of September (Sundays excepted), and shall deliver a copy thereof or any extract therefrom to any person requiring the same on payment of a reasonable price not exceeding one halfpenny for every name with the entries attached thereto, which may be included in such copy or extract so required; and that such copy or extract as aforesaid shall be delivered by the town clerk within four days from the date of the application"?—Yes, I am aware of that.

1384. You exercise your duty of preparing the burgess list, having due regard to the statement that I have read in that section?—Yes.

Mr. *Gibson*—continued.

1385. Is it also a fact that you are aware of that, under the 3rd section of 6 & 7 Vict. c. 93, any treasurer or collector failing to give that adequate information with regard to the due rating of all the burgesses and everything connected with their franchise, is liable to a penalty of 20 *l.*, to be recovered by anyone who sues?—Yes.

1386. Have you reason to think that you are given full and accurate information from the collector general's office as to every one who is rated and entitled to be a burgess?—I have no reason to think otherwise.

1387. You have never had any reason since you have been town clerk?—No.

1388. You always put up the notices in the way that is indicated by that clause?—Yes.

1389. The object is to enable any person whose name is omitted to come and make a claim?—That is the object.

1390. And the machinery pointed out in this Act of Parliament for a person making the claim is very inexpensive?—Yes; but if the taxes are not paid no claim will avail.

1391. If a man finds that his name is omitted from the list which you publish, and which you post in the town hall, that is an indication to him that there is some objection to his name, either for non-payment of taxes or otherwise?—Yes; for non-payment of taxes it is fatal, because the time for paying the taxes has passed.

1392. I suppose it is your experience, that if people have not paid their taxes there is no tremendous alacrity on their part to claim to pay them; you have not found any tremendous race to pay taxes?—I have nothing to do with the receipt of taxes at all.

1393. How many assistants have you in your office for this purpose?—Only two.

1394. Have you got their appointment, or is it in the corporation?—In the corporation. One of them I got the sanction of the Lord Lieutenant for; that is my first assistant, Mr. Martin; the other was an appointee of the council. I have the appointment of none of them.

1395. Can you tell me if, in the preparation of the list, it is the fact that the corporation in the period of eight years, from 1864 to 1872, spent 4,126 *l.* 14 *s.* 1 *d.* in promoting, and 14,073 *l.* 5 *s.* 1 *d.* in opposing Private Bills in Parliament?—I could not tell you the exact figures. I know that they have spent a large amount. I presume what you have stated is correct, but I could not say of my own knowledge.

1396. Is there any paper or return showing the names of all the officials in the Corporation, and their salaries?—No, I am not aware of any, except the treasurer's account books.

1397. Does your department have a list?—No.

1398. Have the Corporation any power of increasing the number of their officers?—No, not without the sanction of the Lord Lieutenant.

1399. What is the section which regulates that?—The 94th section of the 3rd and 4th Victoria, chapter 108.

1400. He is empowered under the 94th section to appoint all the old officers that they had been previously accustomed to appoint?—Yes.

1401. Under the 94th section, you are not allowed to appoint a new officer without the sanction

Mr. *Henry.*

9 May 1876.

Mr. *Gibson*—continued.

sanction of the Lord Lieutenant?—That is so; that was done in the case of my first assistant, Mr. Martin.

1402. The Lord Lieutenant must approve of the appointment of a new officer, and his salary must be submitted to the approval of the Lord Lieutenant?—Yes.

1403. But is there any check afterwards on the Corporation from increasing the salary of that officer?—Not that I am aware of.

1404. So that if the Corporation sent in a statement to the Lord Lieutenant that they wished to appoint two or three new officers, mentioning moderate salaries, when once they procure the sanction of the executive to the appointment, they may then increase the salaries at their discretion?—I know of nothing to prevent them.

1405. Is it a fact that the Corporation have from time to time, reasonably often, increased the salaries of their different officers?—They have increased the salaries from time to time.

1406. Can you recollect a single year that has passed since you were appointed, in which there have not been increases of salaries to their officers?—Very many years.

1407. Have they ever increased yours?—Very little indeed.

1408. When did they increase yours; have they done it more than once?—They have done it three times in 13 years.

1409. When was the first increase?—I think it would be in 1868.

1410. How long were you in office then?—Four years.

1411. How much did they give you then?—£. 100 a year increase.

1412. When did they give you the next increase?—I think it was in 1872 or 1873. I could not exactly tell the year.

1413. How much did they give you on that second increase?—£. 100 a year.

1414. When was the last increase?—The last increase, if I may call it an increase, was the other day. It was in substitution of the one that they gave me in 1870; the one that they gave me in 1870 was 100 *l.* a year, for the purpose of doing the duty of Secretary to the Main Drainage Committee. When the Main Drainage Committee ceased to work, the salaries were stopped, and then the Council added 100 *l.* a year to my salary in place of what had been taken away from it from the main drainage. So that I only really got two increases in those 13 years.

1415. What was your original salary?—£. 400 a year.

1416. Then they have given you an increase of half your salary over a period of 13 years?—Yes, exactly.

1417. I suppose you anticipate that you may have other increases in time?—I hope it will be a fruitful anticipation, but at present I have very shaky ideas about it.

1418. Can you tell me of any one of the City officers whose salary has not been increased by the Corporation?—I do not recollect.

1419. Have they not increased the Lord Mayor's?—They increased the Lord Mayor's salary by the sum of 200 guineas, I think, in order to supply him with a secretary, about three years ago.

1420. And they have only given you 200 guineas increase altogether?—Yes; I think that my salary as town clerk of Dublin contrasts very unfavourably with the salaries of the town clerks of the different towns in England.

1421. Do you know the salary of the town clerks in any of the large towns of England, say Liverpool?—The town clerk of Liverpool has 2,000 *l.* a year; and of Manchester, 2,500 *l.* a year; and the London town clerk has 2,000 *l.* a year; he has only been in office about two years, and he has got an increase during those two years of 500 *l.* a year in one vote.

1422. Who has the appointment of the secretaries of the different committees?—The council.

1423. The entire council, and not the committee?—Yes, the entire council.

1424. Those officers all hold their offices during good behaviour, do they not?—With the exception of the treasurer, who must be elected annually under the Statute, and some recent officers that have been elected for one year only, and are re-elected.

1425. I may take it that, with the exception of the treasurer, the marshal, the sword bearer, and Mr. Robinson, they are all during good behaviour?—Yes; the water bailiffs are elected annually.

1426. What is the salary of secretaries of committees?—It is limited to 400 *l.* a year, under the Dublin Improvement Act.

1427. Without any power of increase over the 400 *l.*?—Yes, without any power of increase over the 400 *l.*

1428. Have those gentlemen ever got any increase by giving them a cumulative office, or extra duties, or anything in that way?—I am talking now of the standing committees; the secretary of the standing committee No. 2 has had no increase since he came into office; he has been about five or six years there. The secretary of No 1 committee has only been about a year in office, and he has had no increase. Mr. Boyle, the secretary of the Public Health Committee, has had an increase on account, I suppose, of the extra duties.

1429. Although there is that absolute statutory limit that his salary should not be beyond 400 *l.*, he has got an increase of salary?—That does not apply to Mr. Boyle; the limit of the salaries of the secretaries applies only to the salaries of the secretaries of the standing committees, and Mr. Boyle is not a secretary of a standing committee.

1430. Have they given him a second office?—They have given him some office in relation to petroleum and gunpowder, I think.

1431. There is extra pay, I suppose, for that?—There is an increase of salary, 50 *l.* a year, upon the notice paper for him, but I do not think he has got it yet.

1432. With regard to the town clerks in England, is it a fact that they act as law agents and solicitors of the corporations?—It is not in any of the cases that I have named; Sir Joseph Heron, of Manchester, is not the solicitor for the Corporation of Manchester; the town clerk of London, also, is not the solicitor for the Corporation of London; neither is the town clerk of Liverpool.

1433. Is there any person whose business it is to supervise the officers of the corporation, and see that they do their duties?—The committees that have charge of them.

1434. Take first an office that is not under a particular committee, for instance, your own office, the

Mr. *Henry.*

0 May 1876.

Mr. *Gibson*—continued.

the treasurer's, and other principal officers of the corporation, is there anyone to look after the discharge of your duties?—Our own committees and the council.

1435. But, excepting in that general way, there is no special looking after, or supervision, of the officers?—I do not quite understand what you mean. Each officer is liable to the committee that he serves, and liable to the council.

1436. Has the Lord Mayor any special power of supervision or looking after the officers?—He can come in and look after us as often as he likes, but there is no direction to him to do so.

1437. With regard to the Dublin improvement rate, do you think that it would be absolutely necessary to increase that rate for the fair working of the city?—I think it would be, in some shape or another. It is in debt at this moment 15,000 *l.*

1438. And you think, then, that the corporation should have the same power in relation to the improvement rate that they have to the grand jury, or would you raise the limit?—I would raise the limit.

1439. Are you in favour of a limit?—Certainly.

1440. Why are you in favour of a limit; do you think that it is necessary to put a check on the taxation of the corporation?—I think when there was a limit put, as I have said before, originally it was fair not to increase it, and now it is very fair to put a limit to it for the future.

1441. Is it not the fact that in all those figures which are mentioned in the rates, they have got to the limit?—Yes.

1442. In every one of the taxes?—No, not in the sewers rate.

1443. What is the limit of that?—The limit is 4 *d.*

1444. I thought it was 4 *d.* now?—It was not last year, I know.

1445. In the notice for the collection of rates on the 1st of January 1876, I believe the sewer rate was 4 *d.*?—If so, they have resumed the limit this year; it was only 3 *d.* last year.

1446. So that all the taxes in Dublin at present are up to the full limit?—There is no doubt about that. The improvement rate is 2 *s.*, that is the limit; the sewers rate is 4 *d.*, that is the limit. The vestry abolition rate has no limit; the domestic water rate is 1 *s.*, that is the limit; and the public water rate is 3 *d.*, that is the limit.

1447. What would you say would be a fair limit to put upon the improvement rate?—I am not prepared to answer that question; I have not gone into the details sufficiently.

1448. Have the Corporation ever made any attempt to apply any of the Acts of Parliament enabling them to provide dwellings for the working classes, or for artizans amongst the great number of Acts winding up with the Act of last year?—Yes, they are doing it now.

1449. What do you mean by that; since when?—Very recently.

1450. Will you put a date on it?—Three or four weeks ago.

1451. What step was taken then?—A meeting of the Council was called, and several resolutions were passed.

1452. Was that the occasion when there was a count out in consequence of there being only seven members present?—No, there were two resolutions passed before that.

1453. Were the two resolutions passed on the occasion of the meeting which terminated by a count out?—Yes; but if you will allow me to explain, the two resolutions were passed, and there was a perfect understanding come to before they were passed, that the third resolution was not to be pressed on that day, and that was the reason that the members left.

1454. How many members were present when the two resolutions were passed?—I cannot tell you; there was more than a house, but I cannot tell you how many from memory.

1455. When the third resolution came on, is it the fact that they were counted out, only seven being present?—Yes; I say that there was a perfect understanding that the third resolution was not to be pressed.

1456. How long ago was this; was it within the last three weeks?—Less than that, I think.

1457. Has anything been done as a matter of fact?—I do not know what was done yesterday, but there was a meeting called for the purpose, yesterday.

1458. For the express purpose?—Yes.

1459. But until the meeting three weeks ago, and what may have been done yesterday, you know of nothing yourself that has been done with reference to the code of laws with regard to artizans' dwellings?—No.

1460. Has the power ever been exercised that is given in the City Act of erecting clocks by the Corporation in any convenient places in Dublin?—No.

1461. With regard to the powers that are given by the Public Health Act of 1874, of sending round, as in most English cities, and removing ashes and night soil from the different houses, has the slightest attempt ever been made to put them in force in Dublin?—I think they are in force.

1462. Could you tell me of any instance?—I cannot tell you where, I am not connected with that part of the duty, but I understand that it was.

1463. Have you any memorandum before you now to enable you to say positively that it is done?—No, I did not know that the question would be put to me, or I would have had it.

1464. You have not had occasion to look the matter up; it is not your department, is it?—No.

1465. What is the hour appointed for the meeting of the Council?—It varies, but generally the hour is one o'clock

1466. Could you prepare a statement for the last three years of the hours at which the Council was summoned, the hours at which the Council was actually able to go into business from a house being made; the occasions when there was no house from non-attendance, or from there not being a quorum; and the occasions when the proceedings had to terminate on a count out, and also a column indicating the occasions when officers were to be appointed, and the attendances that there were on those occasions?—Yes, I will do so. (*See* Appendix.)

1467. What is a quorum?—Twenty.

1468. Are you aware that there are fees paid by the Corporation of Dublin to the high sheriff?—Yes.

1469. That is for acquittals, is it not?—Yes, acquittals,

Mr. *Henry*.

9 May 1876.

Mr. *Gibson*—continued.

acquittals, committals, and convictions. They are levied by presentment on the returns furnished by the high sheriff, verified by affidavit.

1470. And as part of the grand jury cess, is it not?—Yes.

1471. Is this peculiar to Dublin, or does it extend over Ireland generally?—That I cannot tell you. The clerk of the Crown gets fees by presentment; then the session officers get fees by presentment, and the sheriff gets fees as well for committals, acquittals, and convictions at sessions; it is under the old Act of Geo. 4.

1472. Have you read those statements in the schedule of presentments that were made in the year 1874, and I suppose in every subsequent year. "Section, No. 2. Fees to officers. To Matthew P. D'Arcy, Esq., late high sheriff of the county of the city of Dublin, his fees on prisoners convicted at quarter sessions, from 4th October 1872 to 4th February 1873, 47 *l.* 13 *s.* 2 *d.*, pursuant to 49 Geo. 3, c. 101, 1 & 2 Geo. 4, c. 77; and account and affidavit. To same person a recompense for his fees on prisoners acquitted, or whose cases were postponed at quarter sessions, and the adjourned sittings thereof, held in said city, from 1st February 1872 to 31st January 1873, 30 *l.* 15 *s.* 4 *d.*, pursuant to 23 & 24 Geo. 3, c. 34; 49 Geo. 3, c. 101, and 1 & 2 Geo. 4, c. 77, and account and affidavit." Are you aware that these entries occur?—Yes.

Chairman.

1473. Are you aware whether those fees are paid to the high sheriff or to the sub-sheriff?—As a matter of fact the sub-sheriff gets them.

Mr. *Gibson.*

1474. I believe the sub-sheriff of Dublin gives a contribution, does he not, to the high sheriff?—I do not know that. I know as a matter of fact that it is the sub-sheriff who receives the money; I could not know if there was any private arrangement. On the contrary, I fancy now that the high sheriffs are paying the sub-sheriffs a salary. I know as a matter of fact that in the counties of Ireland the high sheriff is now paying the sub-sheriff a salary.

1475. Is it not the fact that in Dublin the clerk of the peace fees are all paid into the city treasury?—Yes.

1476. And he is paid a salary?—Yes.

1477. Do you chance to know what the fees of the clerk of the peace are in Dublin?—I think about 800 *l.* a year.

1478. That is what his salary is; his fees are more than that, are they not?—His salary and the fees are very nearly equal, but be has two assistants paid as well; he gets 1,100 *l.* a year altogether, and he has to pay out of this 100 *l.* to one assistant, and 75 *l.* to another, and 125 *l.* is allowed for stationery.

1479. Are you aware that the Marshal of Dublin is, under the present arrangement, paid a salary by the corporation?—Yes.

1480. The present marshal is only elected by the year, I believe?—Yes.

1481. Are you aware that there is litigation pending by the late city marshal as to his status and exact position?—Yes.

1482. Could you state about what are the fees that are received by the Marshal of Dublin as registrar of pawnbrokers; do not they amount to 1,200 *l.* or 1,300 *l.* a year?—No; the treasurer could tell you, for he receives them, but I could not.

1483. Is it over 1,000 *l.* a year?—I should say not.

1484. At all events, whatever fees there are received by the corporation, they pay the salary out of them?—Yes.

1485. Are you aware that the present constitution of the Port and Docks Board comprises the leading citizens of Dublin, without any distinction of creed or party?—I do not know that; I know that the leading merchants of Dublin are on it.

Mr. *Collins.*

1486. I think you stated that your salary was 600 *l.* a year; are you allowed to perform any other duties than those of town clerk?—No.

1487. You are limited strictly to these?—Yes.

1488. Will you kindly state what the nature of those duties may be?—I have to attend all the council meetings, to prepare the minutes of the council, to prepare the burgess rolls and the Parliamentary voters' lists, to attend the two revision courts, to attend No. 3 committee, to keep the minutes of that committee, to keep all the minutes of the council, to issue summonses, to conduct the correspondence of the corporation, and to prepare the schedule of presentments.

1489. Do those duties occupy your time altogether?—They do; I am obliged to devote my time to it.

1490. Are you a lawyer?—I was practising as a solicitor, and I had to give it up.

1491. You do nothing now in that special profession?—No.

1492. Then you relinquished your profession as a solicitor to accept this position of town clerk, and you are now restricted to 600 *l.* a year; that is, as I understand; the status?—It has reached 600 *l.* a year, but I hope I am not restricted to that.

1493. I think I understood you to say that you have very little hope of further increase?—That is a different thing; so I have, but I would not like to extinguish the last hope.

1494. With regard to the supervision of officers by the corporation you stated that there was no special supervisor or general superintendent to look after those officers?—No; they are answerable to their committees and to the council.

1495. They are directly under the control of the standing committees of the corporation?—Yes, and other committees, such as the Board of Health Committee and the Waterworks Committee; but the only standing committees are the three committees as settled by the Dublin Improvement Act.

1496. Do you think, generally speaking, that supervision on the part of the committees is quite sufficient?—I think it is.

1497. I think I understood you to say that the committees are, to a certain extent, responsible to the council?—Yes.

1498. Do they make their reports to the council?—Yes, they do monthly; and special reports oftener.

1499. Are you aware whether the council takes the trouble to investigate the reports sent in by the committees?—They take very great trouble.

1500. I think you stated that the number of burgesses

Mr. *Collins*—continued.

burgesses in 1875 was 5,339; I think those 5,339 burgesses, assuming your valuation in 1875 to be 596,096 *l.*, would represent about one burgess for every 110 *l.* of yearly valuation?—Yes, I daresay it would.

1501. Would you have any difficulty in replying to this question; has it ever come before you officially, that there is a complaint respecting the limitation of burgesses, compared with the extent of Dublin and its valuation?—Yes; I think that for a population of nearly 300,000, 5,000 and odd is a very small proportion.

1502. Does there come before you officially from time to time a complaint of that nature?—It never came in the shape of a written official communication, but it has reached me in several shapes; it is my own opinion, too, that a population of 300,000 ought to have a larger representation on the burgess roll than 5,000.

1503. Is it the subject of general comment that it is unduly restricted?—Yes, certainly.

1504. I think I understood you to say that if the period of occupation were reduced from two years and eight months to a year, it would have the effect certainly of about doubling the number of burgesses?—I would not say doubling, but it would go very near it.

1505. I understood you to say the fact of the extension of the residential occupation beyond the distance of seven miles would not very considerably affect the number of burgesses?—I do not think it would. The increase on the burgess roll of the inhabitants of Dublin who reside at a distance of 12 miles, that is five beyond the seven, would be but very small.

1506. Does any other mode of meeting the public complaints as to increasing the number of burgesses present itself to your mind?—I think if there were no obligation to pay the taxes beforehand, it would cause a very great increase indeed (a number lose their franchise by the non-payment of taxes) or, if the period for payment of taxes was extended to the time of voting.

1507. That would be a mode of meeting that point to some extent?—It would to a great extent.

1508. Would you limit the period to the day before the day of voting?—I would say the day before or a couple of days, so as to allow the collector general to have time to collect them.

1509. Do you think that the people, generally speaking, of Dublin are fairly represented on the municipal council?—I think so.

1510. And that it is a fair representation consistently with the present qualification?—I think so.

Mr. *Murphy*.

1511. You mentioned a fact with regard to a ruling made by the official auditor as to a sum of 6,700 *l.*?—It was not quite a ruling; it was in abeyance; he has not passed the order.

1512. He deferred giving an opinion as to this subject, at any rate until he had considered it?—Quite so.

1513. You have had, I presume, on more than one occasion to be before that officer when his rulings on matters of law, as well as matters of fact, have occurred?—Yes.

1514. Had he a professional gentleman to assist him?—No.

1515. He is not a lawyer himself, I believe?—No.

Mr. *Murphy*—continued.

Mr. *Henry*.

9 May 1876.

1516. Have you found occasions upon which he ruled matters of law absolutely by his own *ipse dixit*?—Yes.

1517. There is no appeal from that, except one to the Court of Queen's Bench, is there?—Yes, there are two appeals; there is one to the Local Government Board and one to the Court of Queen's Bench. You may take your choice, but if you go to the Local Government Board you cannot go afterwards to the Court of Queen's Bench.

1518. In a matter where questions of law necessarily must arise as to the legal applications of moneys, for instance, although they may be morally right, yet they may happen to be legally wrong; do you think that an unprofessional man, appointed as an auditor with a kind of despotic power to rule by his own *ipse dixit*, is a proper state of things to exist, and that he, an unprofessional person, should have that absolute power?—I would not think so.

1519. Have you turned your attention towards the clause in the Act of 1871, under which an appeal is given to the corporation; for instance, from a decision by the auditor on a question of mixed law and fact?—Yes.

1520. I believe, under that section, if an appeal is made by the corporation, we will say to the Court of Queen's Bench, upon a matter of law which has been adjudicated upon by the auditor, and if that is argued by counsel on either side, if the court decides in favour of the corporation upon that appeal, nevertheless the corporation are bound to pay the costs?—There is an option with the court to give costs or not, but they have given the costs although they overruled the auditor's decision, and the costs were paid out of the rate to the auditor.

1521. Do you think that that is a state of things which ought to exist?—I do not.

1522. Can you suggest any remedy for it?—I think that if an auditor is appointed, he ought to be appointed with sufficient experience to make good legal decisions; and that he should then be bound to abide by his decision, and on his decision being overruled, he should run the peril of costs.

1523. From your experience, which necessarily must be great more or less, do you think if a proper system or audit was created, we will say in a corporation by a special Act of Parliament, conferring powers upon the corporation, that two auditors, for instance, should be elected by the ratepayers at large, that they should go through their accounts publicly, that those accounts should lie open to the inspection of the public for three weeks or a month; and due notice given of them, and that an appeal then should lie from he decision of those auditors to the local judge, to the recorder, for instance; do you think that that would be a better system than merely appointing an auditor with full irresponsible power as he has now under the Act of 1871?—My idea is that the corporation would prefer to have a Government auditor than an elected auditor, because when we had elected auditors before the Local Government Board Act was passed, the corporation actually passed a resolution in Council to ask for a Government auditor to be appointed; but I think that they feel that the extreme power which the auditor possesses now is very oppressive; and I am almost certain that they would prefer having a Government auditor to an elected one.

1524. With

Mr. *Henry.*

9 May 1876.

Mr. *Murphy*—continued.

1524. With a modification of his powers, I presume?—Yes.

Mr. *J. P. Corry.*

1525. In answer to the honourable Member for the Dublin University, you gave us some information with reference to salaries, and you also gave us some comparisons with English corporations; but those corporations which you mentioned are very much larger than the Dublin Corporation, are they not?—Yes, I am aware of that.

1526. And consequently the duties and responsibilities of the officers are very much greater?—Yes, they are greater; but not in proportion to the salaries that are paid in Dublin and in those towns.

1527. Could you give us any towns about the same population as Dublin, or boroughs in England, where the salaries paid are higher?—No, I cannot.

1528. Has the corporation any power to give superannuation to their officers?—Yes.

1529. Does your office come under that?—Yes, it does. The power of giving compensations and superannuations to officers was taken away by the 3rd & 4th Vict. An Act was introduced by the late Sir John Gray, about six or seven years ago, or perhaps more, by which the corporation obtained the power to superannuate all their officers at a maximum of two-thirds of their existing salary.

Mr. *Murphy.*

1530. Does that refer to corporations generally, or to the Dublin Corporation alone?—I think it is confined to the Dublin Corporation; I am not quite certain, but I think so.

Mr. *J. P. Corry.*

1531. You stated that the improvement rate is limited to 2 *s.*, and that it is inadequate to discharge the different duties which are imposed upon it; but you have also told us that the corporation have the liberty of raising a borough rate?—Yes.

1532. And which they have not exercised?—Yes; but that borough rate would not at all aid the improvement rate; the borough rate could only go in aid of the borough fund; it could not be applied in aid of the improvement rate, even if they had one to-morrow.

1533. You have also told us that the increase in the number of streets has consequently increased the outlay for keeping the town properly cleansed. I asked you how those streets were made, and you told me by the owners of property; do the corporation lay down any rules for the making of those streets?—I do not think they do; but the corporation do not take up the streets until the engineer certifies that they are in a proper condition to do so.

1534. Of course, upon those streets, as a rule, property would be built?—Yes.

1535. And you get rates from that property?—Yes.

1536. Do not you think that the rates levied off that property far more than compensate for keeping the streets in order?—No. In my answer to the Right honourable Chairman, I said that I did not think that the rates levied from those houses were commensurate with the amount necessary to repair the streets.

1537. Will you kindly give the Committee an idea of the kind of property that is erected in those streets?—Small houses, some of them one storey and some of them two storeys high.

Mr. *Corry*—continued.

1538. They are valued at what?—A very small amount indeed; some 16 *l.* or 17 *l.* a year, perhaps.

1539. You propound a theory with reference to Rathmines, for instance, that they should be called upon to pay for the use of the streets of the city?—Yes.

1540. At present, do not they pay for the keeping up of their own streets?—Yes.

1541. Do the citizens of Dublin use the streets of Rathmines?—Not so much as the inhabitants of Rathmines use the city streets.

1542. That would rather go for an extension of the municipal boundary?—Yes.

1543. When was the municipal boundary last extended?—The municipal boundary was settled by this Act, 12 & 13 Vict. into the wards.

1544. And there has been no extension of municipal boundaries since that time?—No, nor was there an extension then; it was a mere revision of the wards, or a re-dividing of the wards.

1545. Then I am to understand that there has been no increase in the municipal boundary since 1849?—Certainly not; it was previous to that time.

1546. Are you aware whether there was a great deal at that time included in the city that was unbuilt on?—Yes.

1547. And that property has now been built upon?—Yes.

1548. In answer to the honourable Member for Dublin, you stated that breweries and other buildings of that kind were being erected outside the city boundary; what taxes do they escape?—They escape all the city taxes.

1549. Do they escape the grand jury rate?—Yes; the grand jury does not extend beyond the city boundaries, except for bridges and sea wall purposes.

1550. They would be subject to the county grand jury cess, I presume?—Yes, certainly.

1551. Does the gas and water go out beyond the Circular Road?—It does.

1552. They do not get gas and water free?—No, they have to pay for that, of course. They would pay for it if they were in the township: but they are not in the township, and they do not get either the one or the other except by agreement.

1553. Would it be a higher or a lower tax outside?—I forget what the townships pay now.

1554. I would like to have your opinion with reference to the corporation, and the Pier and Harbour Commission having pretty much the same power; you told us that the corporation receive from the Pier and Harbour Commissioners estimates and plans for building their walls and their bridges, and that the corporation might refuse, but have no power to alter or amend; do you not think that that work would be better done if it were transferred altogether to the Pier and Harbour Commissioners?—We have no such body; it is the Port and Docks Board, it is they who do the work; they prepare the plans and estimates, and submit them to the council; the council approve of it, and they levy a rate which rate is paid in by the collector general to the Port and Docks fund, and the Port and Docks Board enter into contracts to do the work.

Mr. *Henry.*

9 May 1876.

Mr. *Corry*—continued.

1555. Is not that rather a roundabout way of doing the work?—It is a very roundabout way of doing it.

1556. Do not you think it would be better that the Port and Docks Board should be altogether separate from the corporation?—I do not think it would be right to take away from the corporation the approval of the plans or estimates, and that they should be merely a taxing body. I think it is quite right that the corporation should have some veto upon their plans and estimates, and have the power of taxing.

1557. Do you tax the harbour property?—We tax all property that is taxable. Any property that they have that is taxable comes under tax; so does our own property come under tax.

1558. Do you levy the improvement rate off the quays?—I do not know what particular property there is taxable. I know that there is some dispute between the collector general and themselves about taxable property.

1559. You told us that, since 1849, the elections of the mayor were pretty equally divided between the different political parties, and also as to the wards, that sometimes in a ward where Liberals have predominated, Conservatives were elected, and *vice versâ*?—No, I did not say *vice versâ*. I said that Conservative wards never returned Liberals, but that Liberal wards do return Conservatives.

1560. Does that arise pretty much from the parties residing and being popular in the ward?—I think there is a great deal in that, and from a person's own local status.

1561. You told us what the secretaries to the different Committees were paid: are you aware whether that is a usual thing in corporations?—The Committees are appointed by the corporations.

1562. But are you aware whether it is a usual thing for corporations to pay their secretaries for their various duties?—They are officers of the Council, but merely appointed to do the duties of the Committee. I never knew an instance where a corporation would not pay their own officers.

1563. You spoke about the constitution of the Irish Lights Board; are you aware whether that Board has the supervision of all lights round Ireland, or not?—Yes.

1564. So that it is not confined to Dublin?—No.

1565. We were told by the collector general of rates, in his evidence, that parties came to him tendering rates, but that when he offered to take the money that tender was withdrawn; do you know anything at all about that?—No; for the first time I heard it, or knew it, when reading his evidence.

Mr. *Murphy.*

1566. I think you stated that the Port and Docks Board made plans and specifications for bridges and quays, that they presented those plans and estimates to the corporation, and the corporation approved of them, or otherwise, as they thought fit; do the Port and Docks Board build those quays?—They do build bridges and quays.

1567. Who keeps those quays in repair after they are built?—If anything should require repairing they come again for a presentment, with an estimate, in the same way.

1568. Do I understand you to say that the Port and Docks Board have any revenue of their own?—Yes, a very large revenue.

Mr. *Murphy*—continued.

1569. What does it arise from?—It arises from the shipping.

1570. Do they not apply any portion of the revenue which they derive from the shipping, which shipping use those quays, to repair the quays?—No.

1571. The bridges of course belong to the city proper, and the corporation have a right to pay for the bridges; but what do the Port and Docks Board apply their revenue to?—I could not say.

1572. Are they formed under a special Act of Parliament?—Yes, the honourable and learned Member for Limerick has already referred to that.

1573. I understand from you, that although the Port and Docks Board build the quays, and although the shipping from which the Port and Docks Board derive their revenue, use those quays yet the Corporation of Dublin pay for the building and repairing of those quays?—It is the quay walls.

1574. It is the wall facing the water and next which the ships lie; of course, the street at the back of it is kept in repair by the corporation, but I am talking of the face of the quays itself; supposing it is necessary to pile those quays would the corporation pay for that piling?—I do not know about piling.

1575. Supposing the foundation of the quay wall fails, do the corporation pay for that?—The Port and Docks Board pay for that. It is paid for out of the rates levied by the corporation.

Mr. *J. P. Corry.*

1576. Do I understand that, in the case of the present docks that are being built in Dublin, the money raised is from the taxes?—No, not for the docks. The quay walls and bridges are the only things.

Mr. *Bruen.*

1577. I want to ask you a question with regard to the representation of Liberal wards by Conservatives; do you say that those Conservatives are elected for those wards because they are eminently good business men, and on account of their conspicuous capacity for business?—I think so, and from their standing.

1578. At any rate they are so elected, not because they are Conservatives, but in spite of their being Conservatives?—I should say so.

1579. That arrangement which you mentioned of the alternate appointments of lord mayor from the two sides in politics, I think you said had been carried out generally for several years past?—Yes.

1580. And you said, I think, that in 1876, this year, the lord mayor is a Conservative?—Yes.

1581. Can you tell me who it was in 1875?—In 1875 it was Alderman M'Swiney, and he was a Liberal.

1582. I suppose in 1874 it was the turn of the Conservatives to have a good Conservative lord mayor?—In the year 1874, the honourable Member for Dublin was lord mayor.

1583. Then the turn is not always strictly observed?—I never meant to convey that it is Conservative and Liberal alternately; I meant to convey that it was Protestant and Catholic alternately.

1584. You said that before your appointment to the office which you at present hold you had had

Mr. *Henry.*

9 May 1876.

Mr. *Bruen*—continued.

had some experience in the formation of the list of voters for Parliamentary and municipal purposes?—Yes.

1585. What experience had you?—I was agent for the Liberal party in the city of Dublin, and as such I had to attend to the revision of the Parliamentary and municipal franchise.

1586. With regard to the division of Dublin into wards, the Act by which that division was revised, I think, was the 12 & 13 Vict. c. 85?—Yes.

1587. You cited a portion of a clause, telling the Committee that the persons appointed to revise the wards should have returns supplied of the number of persons rated to the relief of the poor in such ward, and as to the aggregate amount of the sums at which all such persons shall be so rated; I suppose that that was with the idea of having some sort of equality between the wards, having regard to the population and valuation?—No doubt.

1588. At present, do you think that the wards as they at present exist have any such division representing the equality of population and valuation?—I think they have.

1589. With regard to the valuation of property, I think, in the last year of which we have any record, which is stated in Thom's Directory, you will find that the valuation of property in North Dock Ward was 47,423 *l.*, and in Merchants' Quay Ward it was 25,422 *l.*; do you consider that a fair equality of property?—North Dock Ward has increased in value very considerably of late years, as you might see if you read some Irish papers. There is a compulsory purchase arbitration sitting now, and a judge of the Court of Queen's Bench revising those awards. The property has increased tremendously in that ward.

1590. Then, do you admit that, as regards those two wards, there is a very much larger amount of property in the North Dock Ward, represented by the same number in the council, as the smaller amount of property in Merchants' Quay Ward?—Yes.

1591. Going a little further, and comparing Merchants' Quay Ward, with its 25,422 *l.* valuation, with the South Quay Ward, there I find the valuation is 46,912 *l.*?—You are taking about the poorest ward in Dublin as a standard.

1592. I am comparing some of the different wards with each other, and I have a right, I suppose, to compare the highest and the lowest, in order to prove the inequality. I want to ask you whether you do not admit that there is very great inequality in the valuation of the wards at present existing?—I must do so.

1593. The wards being represented on the town council by equal numbers, it comes to this, does it not that, a very much smaller amount of property has the same power as a very large amount of property?—Yes, in that particular instance; but you will find that the other wards are pretty nearly equal.

1594. Take another ward. I find that Wood Quay Ward has 27,000 *l.* valuation, and compare it with the South Dock Ward, which has 45,000 *l.*?—Merchants' Quay Ward and Wood Quay Ward are two of the poorest wards in Dublin; they are exceptions to all the others.

1595. There is also a very considerable discrepancy between Arran Quay Ward, with its 32,000 *l.* valuation, and the South Dock Ward, with its 45,000 *l.* valuation?—The South Dock Ward is a very rich ward, and comprises Merrion-square and all the valuable property about there.

1596. You gave the Committee some evidence with regard to the debt which was charged upon the improvement rate. How long since has that debt been paid off?—I dare say that it is seven or eight years ago, or more perhaps, since the last of it was paid off.

1597. Ever since that time the improvement rate has therefore been relieved not only from interest on the debt, but also from the payment of instalments; is that so?—Yes.

1598. So that there has been a much larger amount since available to be spent upon improvements?—Yes, and they have gone into debt 15,000 *l.* since then. Their debt has been accumulating, and at present the debt is about 15,000 *l.*

1599. Do I understand you to say that since the old debt was paid off they have incurred a fresh debt?—Yes, they have been incurring fresh debts to the contractors to the gas company.

1600. So that not only the income derived from the rates has been spent, but also a considerable debt incurred?—Yes.

1601. Were any debts on the sewers rate paid off?—There are no debts on the sewers rate; they have none, I think.

1602. As to the grand jury cess debts; for what purposes were they incurred?—The payment of instalments to the Government for public buildings, prisons, and so on; for the maintenance of the two prisons, the maintenance of the industrial and reformatory schools, and the maintenance of hospitals.

1603. In 1849, when the corporation was invested with those powers of levying grand jury cess, were there any debts then affecting that cess which have since been paid off?—No, I do not think that there were any debts affecting it.

1604. So that all those debts on the grand jury cess have been incurred since?—There is no debt on the grand jury cess now; on the improvement fund, I said.

1605. My last question referred to the grand jury cess; I understand you to say that there were debts for prisons?—I mistook your question; what I thought you asked me was, what was the grand jury fund applied in payment of. There is no debt on that, but it is a yearly presentment for the maintenance of prisons and the payment of instalments to the Government, but they are decreasing every year.

Mr. *Butt.*

1606. Is there money advanced by the Government for prisons?—Yes, and we are paying it back to the Government by instalments without any interest, but it was an accumulated debt.

Mr. *Bruen.*

1607. I think you stated that about 86,000 *l.* a year in round numbers was the income available from corporate property?—Yes; the treasurer is here who will set me right, if I am not accurate.

1608. Is that income applicable in aid of the different rates; take the improvement rate for instance?—No; the application of the borough fund is thoroughly defined in the Act of the 3rd

Mr. *Henry.*

—.

9 May 1876.

Mr. Bruen—continued.

3rd & 4th Vict. c. 108, and it can be supplemented by a borough rate, but the fund itself can supplement no other fund, nor can the borough rate, if struck, supplement any fund but the borough rate.

1609. And the income from corporate property is a credit of the borough fund?—It is the borough fund.

1610. You stated that you should like to see the municipal area increased; have you formed in your own mind any opinion as to the extent of that increase?—I have not. I could not mention any.

1611. With regard to the questions put to you on the subject of continuous occupancy for two years and eight months being necessary for the franchise, you stated that an interruption of that occupancy in the case of a man who wanted to repair his house, or for some purpose to go out for a short time, broke his vote?—No, I did not mean to convey that. What I did mean to convey was this; that if a man left his house to move into another house, and pending the removal from one house into another he took a temporary residence or lodging, that would break the continuation and disfranchise him. They require to have an immediate removal from one house to the other.

1612. You stated that the sewers rate was not always up to the maximum; can you give the Committee a year when it was not up to the maximum?—I think the year before last; I think that there were two years, but I am certain of one.

Mr. *Mulholland.*

1613. Did I rightly understand you to say that there have been several complaints that occupiers have not been rated?—No.

1614. I thought you said that the immediate lessors' names have been down in the rate book, but not the occupiers' names?—No; I do not know whether it is the immediate lessor or not; I find it in the collector general's book, and I put it down upon the list.

1615. Have you never had any complaint that the names of occupiers have not been written in that book?—No.

Mr. *Butt.*

1616. As to the mode of appointment of secretaries to committees, would you just read the 12th and 13th sections of the Dublin Improvement Act (12 & 13 Vict. c. 97), to show how it enacts that this business shall be done in Dublin?—Clause 12 is: "And be it enacted, that the said council may appoint out of their own body from time to time such and so many committees not exceeding three, and consisting of such number of persons as they shall think fit, for all or any of the purposes of this Act, which in the discretion of such council would be better regulated and managed by means of such committees, and may fix the quorum of such committees: provided always, that the acts of every such committee shall be submitted to the council for their approval." And Clause 13 is: "And be it enacted, that the council shall appoint a proper person to act as a secretary to attend each committee, and may remove such person, and in like manner appoint another person in his place; and that no such secretary shall follow any other profession, occupation, or calling in addition to such office, but shall devote his entire time to the execution of those duties which he may by the said council be required from time to time to perform; and that each such secretary shall be paid by the said council out of the rates hereby authorised, such salary not exceeding, at the rate of 400 *l.* per annum, as they shall think fit, so long as he shall duly perform the duties of his office."

Mr. Butt—continued.

1617. Is it under those two sections that the business of the Dublin Corporation is managed?—It is.

1618. And have they appointed those three committees?—They have appointed those three committees.

1619. And have they appointed a secretary to each?—I act as secretary, without any additional salary, to No. 3 committee, but No. 1 and No. 2 have separate secretaries.

Chairman.

1620. At the full salaries named?—No; they are 300 *l.* a year each; they are recent appointments.

Mr. *Butt.*

1621. You were asked by the honourable Member for the University of Dublin as to the fees to the sheriff; will you just show what those are; just read the 1 & 2 Geo. 4, c. 77, ss. 2 and 4?—Section 2 is: "And whereas prisoners have been frequently detained in custody for fees due to the clerks of the Crown, clerks of the peace, and other officers, and were during such detention supported at the public expense, and great inconvenience has arisen thereby from the crowded state of the gaols and bridewells in Ireland: Be it therefore enacted for remedy hereof, that from and after the expiration of 14 days next after the passing of this Act, no prisoner shall be detained for his fees only, and that no fee whatsoever shall be taken or demanded from any prisoner by any clerk of the Crown or his deputy, clerk of the peace or his deputy, sheriff, under sheriff, jailor, turnkey, crier, or other officer, anything in an Act made in the 49th year of his said late Majesty's reign for regulating the fees payable by persons charged with treason, felony, and other offences at assizes and quarter sessions in Ireland, or any other Act or Acts, or any usage or custom to the contrary notwithstanding." Section 4 is: "And be it further enacted, that it shall and may be lawful to, and for the several grand juries of the several counties, counties of cities, and counties of towns in Ireland, in addition to the sums which they are at present authorised to present off the several counties, counties of cities, and counties of towns respectively, to present for the several clerks of the Crown, clerks of the peace, and other officers and their deputies, sheriffs, under sheriffs, jailors, turnkeys, and criers, such a compensation to the said officer for the fees of prisoners discharged without payment of fees pursuant to the provisions of this present Act, as would have been payable by such prisoners themselves if this Act had never passed."

1622. That is a general Act applying to all counties, is it not?—Yes.

1623. And it requires grand juries to present in lieu of the fees formerly exacted from persons acquitted?—Yes, and it is under that Act that we act.

1624. You were asked as to the sum of 6,000 *l.* or 7,000 *l.* that the auditor refused to pass; will you

Mr. *Henry*.

9 May 1876.

Mr. *Butt*—continued.

you explain to the Committee what that sum is? —The sum is 6,700 *l.*, which, under advice, the city engineer contracted with the Port and Docks Board for building two culverts under the Essex bridge when it was undergoing repair, the engineer having reported that they could do it very much cheaper then, the work being open, than if they allowed the work to go on and opened it again and built a new sewer. They had borrowed no money. They contracted with the Port and Docks Board to pay it out of the rates.

1625. Was that an expenditure of money which was clearly for the interest of the city?—Clearly.

1626. And the objection that was made was, that it was paid out of rates, and not out of money borrowed?—Yes.

1627. Arran Quay Ward is one of the small wards, is it not?—No, it is rather a large ward; it is a poor ward, and Wood Quay is a very poor ward.

1628. Do you know what the valuation of Arran Quay is?—No, not without book.

1629. Are you aware that when the officers appointed by the corporation in 1849 set out the wards with a view to make them equal as far as they could in population and in taxation, that there was an appeal to the Privy Council against that distribution of wards?—I am not aware of that.

1630. Of course there is a record of that if it be so?—Yes.

1631. You were asked as to Conservative and Liberal lord mayors alternately, but you say that the arrangement was to have them alternately, Protestant and Roman Catholic?—Yes, that is what I have heard.

1632. The first lord mayor after 1849 was Benjamin Lee Guinness, in 1851. There is no doubt what his politics were?—No.

1633. Robert Henry Kinahan; was there any doubt about his politics?—No.

1634. Joseph Boyce?—No doubt about him whatever.

1635. He was a very eminent merchant, of course, and of very strong Conservative opinions, was he not?—Yes.

1636. Was there any doubt about the late Richard Atkinson?—None.

1637. Or James Lambert?—None.

1638. Then Richard Atkinson a second time; then the Honourable J. P. Vereker; I think there is no doubt about his politics?—None whatever.

1639. John Barrington; have you any doubt about him?—I have not.

1640. Edward Purdon; I believe he is a Conservative?—Yes.

Mr. *Butt*—continued.

1641. Robert S. Durdin?—He is a Conservative.

1642. Then, with Maurice Brooks, M.P., the present lord mayor, out of 26 lord mayors since 1850, there have been 12 Conservatives?—Those names that you have read have been so.

Dr. *Ward*.

1643. With regard to auditing, have there not been appeals made against the rulings of the auditor in the case of Dublin?—Yes.

1644. Were they not decided by the Court of Queen's Bench in his favour always?—No; decided against him.

Mr. *Brooks*.

1645. Is it not the practice of the various members of the corporation to visit, almost daily, the City Hall and the committee rooms, and to exercise a watchful supervision day by day?—Yes, a great many of them do so every day; I never recollect a day pass when more or less of them have not been in.

1646. As to the failure always to make a quorum, and as to what has been said about counts out, do you know whether such occurrences have ever taken place at the Port and Docks Board for the want of a quorum or through a count out?—I am not aware.

1647. You are aware that the Port and Docks Board sit with closed doors?—The Port and Docks Board proceedings are not reported; they sit with closed doors.

Mr. *Mulholland*.

1648. Am I right in supposing that you now say that there has been no complaint of occupiers ever having been omitted from the rate book?—Not to me.

1649. Under the present system you believe, therefore, that occupiers are entitled to compel that their names should appear upon the rate book?—I should say so; but I have no control over the rate book and nothing to do with it.

1650. But you have had great experience at the Revision Courts, have you not?—I had a great many years ago; 13 or 14 years ago.

1651. I daresay you know that the occupiers' names are not omitted?—I could not answer that question.

Mr. *Butt*.

1652. I think you say that on the present rate book all the occupiers between 8 *l.* and 4 *l.* are placed on the rate?—I could not say anything at all about that.

Friday, 12th May 1876.

MEMBERS PRESENT:

Mr. Assheton.	Mr Gibson.
Sir Michael Hicks Beach.	Sir Arthur Guinness.
Mr. Brooks.	Sir Joseph M'Kenna.
Mr. Breen.	Mr. Mulholland.
Mr. Butt.	Mr. Murphy.
Mr. Collins.	Dr. Ward.
Mr. J. P. Corry.	

SIR MICHAEL HICKS BEACH, IN THE CHAIR.

Mr. JOHN M'EVOY, called in; and Examined.

Mr. M'Evoy

12 May 1876.

Mr. *Bruen.*

1653. I BELIEVE you are a Merchant in the City of Dublin?—Yes.

1654. And you have carried on business there for a long time, and have resided there for a long time?—Yes.

1655. I believe that you have taken a very considerable interest in the affairs of municipal government?—In Dublin and Kingstown I have.

1656. Have you ever been officially connected with municipal government in Dublin or in Kingstown?—Yes, I have been auditor for some time of the township accounts in Kingstown, and I have been chief promoter of a Bill for the reform of the Commissioners there, and subsequently became Chairman of their Board.

1657. Are you of opinion that the present condition of municipal government is unsatisfactory?—I am.

1658. You would be glad to see some reform of the government and of the powers which are entrusted to the government of towns?—Yes, beginning with the central authority and going on to the local authorities; I think if they are to be efficient for carrying out sanitary improvements they should be strengthened and reformed.

1659. Are you of opinion that the basis upon which municipal government rests should be a very broad and comprehensive one?—Yes, I think it should embrace all classes; the great defect which I see in the present system is that it vests the local government practically in one class, excluding the upper and the lower classes from their fair share, as I think, in the government.

1660. In order to remedy these defects you would like to see some reform in the method of electing the governing body, and in the qualifications for the franchise?—Yes.

1661. In general terms are you prepared to tell the Committee what you think would be a good method of reform in this particular point?—I think that in the case of large towns and cities it would be best to proceed on the old lines of occupancy and rating, and having first ascertained who really pay the rates, beginning with the large rated proprietors and going down to the smaller ones, I would give them all their fair share in the management of the funds that they contribute; if you take the returns recently published of the valuation of house property rated for municipal purposes in the various cities and towns in Ireland, you will find that in Dublin 220,000 *l.*, out of a total valuation of 660,000 *l.*, which includes ecclesiastical property which is not contributary, inasmuch as this return covers that kind of property practically unrepresented. In Belfast there is no less than about 200,000 *l.* of that kind of property; Cork has 42,000 *l.* of this kind of property, and I think it is a serious defect in the existing system that that property is practically unrepresented. To begin with the case of the Government, which has recently allowed its property to be rated, and to contribute to the rates, I find that the Royal Sanitary Commission of 1869 in recommending that the Government should pay rates on property held by it, recommended also that it should be represented directly in the local bodies dealing with their funds. That recommendation has been made also by the Select Committee of the House of Commons with regard to London taxation in the year 1871, and in the recent discussion with reference to the main drainage of Dublin, the principle was admitted by the Dublin corporation as a sound one, that the Government contributing so largely to the rates should be directly represented. The amount of the valuation of Government property in Dublin is 30,000 *l.*, and that is too large an amount of property to be unrepresented. If I go on I find Trinity College rated at 5,000 *l.*, and the various banks and other large institutions rated at a very large amount, beginning with the Bank of Ireland at 1,000 *l.*, and the railway companies who also pay very large rates on their property. Then we have those large breweries and distilleries, all of whom are practically unrepresented in the town council. I find on the burgess roll for Trinity Ward, in which Trinity College stands, that not one single burgess, not even the provost, is on the burgess roll for that ward. In the case of the South City Ward, where those large banking institutions and large buildings are,

Mr. M'Evoy.

18 May 1876.

Mr. *Bruen*—continued.

are, I find the same state of things; no person whatever to represent the large amount of money that they contribute to the rates. I think that that evil should be cured by a system of direct representation; that instead of being mixed up with the ward system in Dublin (and the same rule would apply to every other place), they should in some way, which no doubt can be found out, whether under the *ex officio* system or under the electoral system, send their representatives into the town council; in the case of Dublin, certainly fifteen or one-fourth of the town council should be the representatives of the Government, the manufacturing, and the great commercial interests of the city directly, and independently of the ward constituency.

1662. I gather from your answer that you think that property should not only be represented in a direct way, but also that it should be proportionately represented, in proportion to the value of the contributions which it makes to the taxation of the city?—Yes, I confine my answer at present to the class of property just referred to; when I come to residential house property, I must view the matter in another light; when you come to residential house property, you have to consider the rights of the householder as a human being, as a man entitled to have a municipal body to care for his health and for his convenience; and I do not think that the doctrine could be laid down that in that branch of the subject the mere ownership of property should be allowed to militate against those rights of mankind as individuals, to have their health and their convenience or anything else attended to; I would therefore, in the case of residential house property, adopt a different mode of dealing with it; and what I would suggest would be this: that after you have taken out the public and large ratepaying property, the sort of property which I am speaking of, which in Dublin is now unrepresented, you have at least 170,000 *l.* taken out of the valuation of the City of Dublin, and taking that from the 600,000 *l.* you come down to 430,000 *l.*; I think that that property should be arranged in wards of an equal value; that the present small wards should be abolished, and the city arranged in large substantial wards of a valuation of at least from 40,000 *l.* up to 50,000 *l.*; I find in support of that view, that in the discussions in 1848 about the re-arrangement of wards in Dublin, it was an admitted principle that the wards should be between 40,000 *l.* and 50,000 *l.* valuation; everybody seemed to see the evil of having too small wards; say that there were 10 wards, with from 40,000 *l.* to 50,000 *l.* each, divided in the way I mention, property would under that system come to have its due weight; you would have wards where the property was of large rateable value, although they might be small in the number of inhabitants and of rated occupiers to counterbalance the large population in the wards of smaller rateable valuation, and in that way property would have its weight; that being done, I think that in settling the franchise for those wards, you should give the widest possible extension to the franchise; you should give a vote to every man who occupied a house, and when I use the term house, I mean a dwelling fit for human habitation; I do not think that it would be wise policy to give a vote to a man who lived in a place that was actually condemned by our sanitary system as unfit for human habitation; I have given myself some trouble to inquire into what happens in Dublin itself with regard to such property, and from the report of the Collector General of 1861, I find that such property contributes scarcely anything to the rates; there are a number of places mentioned in this report, and I take one, Cole-alley, which is 208 *l.* annual value, and all the rates got out of it in that year was 9 *l.* 6 *s.*

1663. Could you say how much ought to have been got out of it?—There should have been got 62 *l.* 8 *s.* But what happens with that class of property is this: they are unable to collect the rates in the same proportion as elsewhere; in those poorer wards they have never been able to collect much more than 80 per cent., whilst in the better wards they collect up to 98 per cent. of the actual assessment.

Chairman.

1664. How many tenements are there in that place to which you are referring?—In Cole-alley there are 33 houses; 171 rooms, and 915 persons.

1665. Do you mean that 33 houses are only valued at 208 *l.*?—Yes, that is all; although 915 persons live in them. It is now contended that the proper principle of paying for water should be by meter; that it is, in fact, levying taxation on the rich for the benefit of the poor to have a rating system, and we shall probably hear more of that discussion, but if at 2 *d.* per 1,000 gallons that population was supplied with water it would cost the City 27 *l.*; that would be the value of the water at 2 *d.* per 1,000 gallons, a ridiculously low value to set upon water supply.

1666. Where is this Cole-alley?—It is off Meath-street, in Merchant's Quay Ward, near Cork-street.

Mr. *Corry.*

1667. Is that an official document to which you are referring?—Yes, this is the Report of the Collector General for the year 1871. Pimlico, Elbow-lane, and Engine-alley are also given as specimens.

Mr. *Bruen.*

1668. Is that year rather an exceptional year, or have you reason to believe that the same state of things have existed from year to year?—I can say that I have no doubt whatever that it does exist; I wish also to add, that there is another wrong put upon the city by the expense which is thrown upon it for the sanitary inspection of such places. I have inquired at the office of the Public Health Committee in Dublin as to what would be the probable expense of inspecting such localities, and I am informed by the secretary that it is necessary to have a sanitary sergeant to visit such property, every house three or four times in the week; and then they have to serve notices, and continually supervise that property, otherwise it would become dangerous to the public health, not only of the people in it but of the whole city, and that the cost of that supervision exceeds the rates received from that property.

1669. A case of that sort would probably be met by the application of the Artizans' and Labourers' Dwellings Act?—Yes, it is just a case for that Act.

1670. Has that Act been adopted by the corporation?—That Act has not been adopted by the corporation; but now that you remind me

Mr. M'Evoy.

12 May 1876.

Mr. Bruen—continued.

the subject, I wish, before I leave that point of valuation, to ask the attention of the Committee to what has happened elsewhere, where the Act, or something like it, has been put in force. In Edinburgh, the corporation have been at work on that class of property, and they say that after they have taken down the old unsanitary houses, and have erected dwellings fit for human beings to live in, the average rent of even rooms in such buildings is from 6 *l.* 10 *s.* to 7 *l.* per annum, and they cannot be provided for less. In Glasgow the same state of things exists, and according to a Return furnished to the Government by the corporation I find the same thing, that where they had removed houses of that bad character and replaced them by good ones, the lowest rent to enable them to pay for the improvement was 8 *s.* per month for a single room, 11 *s.* 6 *d.* per month where there were two rooms, and 18 *s.* a month for three rooms. In Liverpool I observe the same thing. I have also read in the speech of the mayor of Birmingham at the recent investigation preliminary to the adoption of the Artizans Dwellings Act in that city that his estimate for a single room in the improved houses that are proposed to be erected there is 2 *s.* per week. And that brings it out in this way, that to allow only a single room in those houses to one individual, or two, if two be not too much, for one room, you cannot provide it under 2 *s.* per week, or 5 *l.* per year, and a rateable valuation of 4 *l.*; and on that ground I say that the rateable valuation should not be fixed for a house at a lower rate than 4 *l.*, on the ground that it is not possible to provide even a single room fit for human habitation furnished with all necessary sanitary appliances and conveniences for less than 2 *s.* a week.

Chairman.

1671. Surely you must fix the rateable value of a house by what its value is; you cannot say that no house shall be rated at less than 4 *l.*, if the house actually is not worth 4 *l.*?—I am speaking now of the franchise; that the franchise should not be lower. When I speak of household suffrage, I mean a house of 4 *l.* value, or a house fit for human habitation, whichever term is thought best to adopt.

1672. Then as regards houses below that value; you would leave the occupiers outside?—I would leave them outside.

1673. On the ground that the houses are not fit for human habitation?—And that the owners or occupiers of such houses contribute nothing to the rates of the city, to the cost of inspecting their property, and the cost of supplying them with water. Over and above what they are entitled to as contributors to the common fund, they absorb, and more than absorb, all the rates received from them.

1674. If a house is not fit for human habitation, there are certain sanitary powers, are there not, in the hands of the sanitary authorities, which it is their business to exercise with reference to that house?—Yes, certainly; and I would contemplate under an improved system of administration that in a very short time every house in a city in Ireland would be raised to that class, and that this 4 *l.* limit might be removed altogether, and we might speak of household suffrage in Ireland as we do in England and Scotland. I look forward to that state of things occurring under a reformed local administration.

Mr. Bruen.

1675. I think you spoke a little while ago of the franchise, and your own opinion is that it ought to be dependent upon occupancy and payment of rates?—Yes.

1676. Let me ask you whether in the case of owners who are not now primarily liable for the payment of rates, the rates do not in fact fall upon their property, whether they pay them or not directly?—That is an exceedingly difficult question to answer. People who have given the subject a great deal of consideration are very much divided on that point, whether as a matter of actual fact it is the occupier or the owner in a general case, where the owner is not directly rated, pays the rates. It is a very difficult question to answer.

1677. Probably you do not wish to answer it?—I am unable to answer that question; but there is a right to a property franchise in Dublin, founded upon actual payment by the owner himself. We have in Dublin a public water rate of 3 *d.* in the 1 *l.*, which is a tax altogether on the owner; it is the owner alone pays it. We have also the fact that the owner's property is under all these new borrowing arrangements mortgaged, in fact, year after year by the local body; for 40 or 50 years his property is actually mortgaged for various purposes, sewage purposes, water purposes, and so on: and I think it is only just that he should have a vote founded upon that contribution, and upon the charge that these local bodies have the power of putting upon his property. I would take what I find in the Towns Improvement Act as a basis for a property franchise. Under the Towns Improvement Act every immediate lessor of 50 *l.* and upwards value is entitled to a vote; but that immediate lessor franchise is not the best sort of franchise, for the immediate lessor may actually have none, or very little interest, whatever in the property. I have known instances in Kingstown, from attending there at the Revision Court for two or three years; I have had opportunities of observing the working of the franchise, and I know that persons who have had none, or scarcely any, interest whatever in the houses happen to be in the position of immediate lessors and get a vote, whilst persons above them in title, and who are the persons who are really beneficially interested in the property, have no vote at all. I would suggest that instead of being the immediate lessor it should be the person beneficially interested (such as under the poor law system); any man possessing a beneficial interest, of say 50 *l.* and upwards, in house property, should have a vote. The third franchise which I think is necessary is a non-residential occupancy franchise to meet the case of occupiers of houses, shops, offices, and so on, who do not live in the city; and I would fix that at say 10 *l.* That, I think, would meet the case of persons who are contributors to the rates, more or less, but who have no vote, from the fact of their living outside of the city, or from a great many other causes, that under our very complicated burgess arrangements at present disqualify him. I may mention cases within my own knowledge. Where a man who is rated at 100 *l.* for his shop and the premises adjoining to that shop, but because he happens to live with his father, and there was no arrangement entered into between his father and himself that they should be joint contributors in the house that they occupied to the rent and taxes that man was disqualified.

Mr. M'Evoy.

12 May 1876.

Mr. *Bruen*—continued.

disqualified. If they had been made joint occupiers of the dwelling-house in which this man lived with his father, the individual would be qualified, but because he had no such arrangement, and he paid a lump sum to his father for his board, he was disqualified. I think it would be much better to have a simpler franchise founded altogether upon occupancy. I would make that qualification higher, because, as I before observed, I see certain rights that a man residing in a city has as a man to be represented, and to have those interests as a human being looked after, and therefore I fix the occupancy much higher than the residential franchise, and I think that 10 *l.* would meet the case.

1678. Have you any further suggestion to make with reference to the reform of the franchise for municipal government?—There are some points incidental to this subject. I think that I cannot do better to show the working of the present franchise than to hand in a burgess roll of the Royal Exchange Ward, the central ward of Dublin.

1679. What does that show?—It shows the present system, and it shows, in my opinion, that the persons who contribute largely to the rates are not represented at all, and that other persons who do not contribute largely, and who have interests certainly not in accordance with sanitary improvement, are very largely represented. This burgess roll shows that 354 persons are on the roll, 22 of them vote out of a single house valued at 50 *l.*, and 84 vote out of tenements and lodging houses in second and third-class streets and lanes. That is an interest which is certainly not friendly to sanitary improvement. The burgess in those cases occupies only a room. I have known instances where he has only a yard and he lets the remainder to tradesmen; but he only is rated, and is the only person enrolled, and his interest is not with sanitary improvement. He is not in favour of the Public Health Acts being carried out rigidly, because they militate against himself. There are no less than 84 such burgesses in Royal Exchange Ward.

Mr. *Butt.*

1680. How was that?—I do not understand it. I suppose that they were treated as the legal occupiers.

Mr. *Bruen.*

1681. What was the valuation of the premises occupied by the 84 burgesses that you have mentioned?—They are different valuations, but they are low valuations, for they are inferior streets. There are 42 other burgesses out of houses in the better streets, such as Grafton-street, Dame-street, and Nassau-street where the burgess occupies only a shop, and has the whole of the rest of the house let to professional gentlemen and others. I find one gentleman votes out of a house in ruins, and three vote out of houses, which, according to Thom's Street Directory, are in the occupation of females. And on that point, in which the female franchise may be to some extent concerned, I would like to make this observation, that I find that there is a very large amount of valuable property in the occupation of females. The recent returns show that in the city of Dublin we have only 55 out of 2,200 female occupiers rated at 4 *l.* and under; whilst we have 234 rated at over 50 *l.*; and we have 544 rated between 25 *l.* and 50 *l.* I estimate that the total valuation of that property is certainly 50,000 *l.*, and therefore very nearly one-tenth of the city is wholly unrepresented. In the townships the proportion is even larger. In Kingstown, Rathmines, and Black Rock the female ratepayers contribute a still larger proportion to the rates. In Kingstown I find that there are no less than 729 female rated occupiers out of a total of about 3,000, or nearly one-fourth of the total; and then, if you come to the valuation of the property, there are only 60 under 4 *l.*, but between 10 *l.* and 50 *l.* there are no less than 510. The operation of the jury laws tends very much against the enfranchisement of property of that class. I have examined the squares in "Thom's Directory," both Merrion and Fitzwilliam Squares, and I find that there are a great many female occupiers there, but when I go to the burgess roll of the wards I find not a single person qualified out of those houses. But when I come to a lower class of street, and when I came to Royal Exchange Ward, and come to York-street, I find that somehow or other there are male burgesses found for what appear to be female occupiers; that is to say, according to "Thom's Directory" you find females in occupation, but you find on the burgess roll some gentlemen who are qualified to represent that property. I trace that to the operation of the jury laws; in the case of the lower class of property there is no reason for any man attempting to escape his obligation to serve as a juror by keeping off the burgess or rating list, but in the case of a higher class of property he has an interest. By having his mother, or his sister, or somebody else rated for the premises, when the property is of a higher value, and of the value that is fixed by the Jury Acts, he may escape discharging his duty as a juror; and that operates with, I daresay, other circumstances in this direction, that when you do not extend the franchise to females the higher the valuation of the property the less chance there is of its being represented. I think that the law ought to be assimilated to England, and that female occupiers should, like male occupiers, vote for the members of the town council.

1682. As we have probably finished your opinion, as regards the qualification for the franchise, will you be good enough to give the Committee your opinion with reference to the qualification of the persons elected?—I think that the qualification of the persons elected should be higher than it is at present, and that the disqualification provisions of the Act should be amended. I think that the special juror qualification is not too high to fix for a member of the local body. He has just as important duties to discharge as a special juror, and I think the qualification ought to be the same. I think that the property qualification should be out of property that was in his own exclusive possession. In the case of hotel proprietors and tavern keepers, they are not, and cannot be said to be, in the exclusive occupation of their premises, and I think the law should not permit persons qualifying out of property that was not in their own occupation, and you would thereby have a superior class of persons to sit on those Local Boards. The bankruptcy disqualification is at present in a very unsatisfactory state. The question, I believe, was raised in the Court of Queen's Bench about the year 1871, and the judges were unable to solve

Mr. *Bruen*—continued.

solve it; they were two and two on the point, two members of the court thinking it a hardship that a man should be perpetually disqualified by being a bankrupt, or an arranging trader, and they were not in favour of the party who sought to have a *quo warranto* issued. The present system does appear a hardship, and I think it would be advisable to fix a limit of time. If any person who was unable to pay his debts was obliged to retire into private life, for, say, seven years, I do not think that the public, or that the gentleman himself, would be anything the worse for it. There is another evil I observe, that persons not satisfied with sitting upon one of these boards will insist upon sitting upon a great number of them. We have in Dublin one gentleman who is at present vice chairman of the North Dublin Union; he is a guardian of the South Dublin Union; he is an alderman of the corporation of the city of Dublin; he is town commissioner of Kingstown; and he is a town commissioner of Dalkey. I think it is wholly impossible or, very unlikely, that that gentleman can discharge all those duties, and I think it would be a wise provision that a gentleman should make his election and serve only on one of those bodies. They have very often conflicting interests which would cross each other. The view which he should take as town commissioner of one of the townships might be wholly opposed to the view which he would take as member of the town council. I think that it would be no harm, and it would bring a greater number of people into the public service if gentlemen were required to make their election. I would also observe that the working of the valuation system in the two countries, England and Ireland, is, I think, very important in connection with the franchise. In Ireland we have a system of Government valuation; in England the local authorities are the valuators, and it will be readily understood that if the officers in both countries are equally anxious to please their employers, the results will work out differently. In England the valuators, the overseers, have to please their employers by making the most of the property; they therefore value it as high as they possible can, and they subdivide the property in the case of houses let, such as the Westminster Chambers. I have been looking at the parish books and papers since I came to London, and I find that all those offices are separately rated. Instead of rating the whole building as one, and rating the landlord, every occupier is rated, and that principle is generally applied. But we have not that in Dublin. Take the case of Commercial Buildings in Dame-street; that is rated as one building, with the result, that there is but one ratepayer and one burgess instead of something like 40 gentlemen who occupy offices in that building, all of whom, on the English system, would come to be rated.

Chairman.

1683. Does that come under the Section of the Dublin Act which provides that houses let in separate apartments should be rated to the owner?—No, that is a different thing altogether; that is as to the smaller ratings, under 8 *l.*, I think it is in Dublin.

1684. To whom are those Commercial Buildings rated, to the owner or occupier?—It is rated to the person who is supposed to be the landlord of the whole.

Chairman—continued.

1685. To the immediate lessor?—Yes, to the immediate lessor over all those sub-tenants as you might say; suppose a person takes a house, and lets it off into offices, he keeps his shop to himself; but there is a solicitor perhaps who occupies the apartments over-head; in Dublin the shopkeeper would be the only person rated, unless the other person made a claim to be rated; in England the overseer does not wait in such a case as that for a claim to be rated to be served upon him, but finding the buildings laid out like these Westminster Chambers with a common entrance and a common passage to all the offices, he values all those offices and puts them on his rate book without the parties making any claim whatever; that is not done in Ireland; they wait until there is a claim to be rated served upon them; and this claim to be rated will not be served very generally for this reason, that the last valuation of property in Dublin, and generally throughout Ireland, was in the year 1863; and since then property has considerably increased in value; if a man now serves a claim to be rated, and I know two instances in Dawson-street where that has been done, what is the result? The value of the whole property is increased to bring it up to what they believe to be the value of the property at the present day; any man knowing that that will certainly happen, will leave things as they are, and not serve this claim to be separately rated.

1686. Do you know under what provision of the law that custom which you have mentioned in Dublin arises?—I think it is simply in the Valuation Office itself; they thought in carrying out the Act that they were not bound to make any inquiries with reference to sub-letting; I do not think you will find it in any Act of Parliament. In the large English towns, in Manchester for instance, they have a re-valuation every year; they go over the whole of the property *de novo*, and re-value it. In London, it is every five years, and the result is, that all those changes in the arrangement of houses are taken notice of; a house 20 years ago was one house without any sub-divisions, but since that time it has been split into those separate occupancies, and under the system of periodical re-valuation all that would be gone over; and as the law allows the franchise to persons found in occupancy of premises that are distinct with separate entrances, and separate modes of egress to the particular apartment or office, all those are rated. I have made out a return which I think will illustrate the state of things. In Thom's Street Directory you will find in every street the names of the persons occupying houses, offices, and shops; I will take it for Dame-street; this is from the last year's directory, 1875, and I find that there were 251 male occupiers of houses, offices and shops, who, presumably, are entitled to the franchise; the valuation of that property is 7,000 *l.*, but the number of burgesses enrolled in that street is only 51, so that there are 200 persons that presumably would be entitled to the franchise, not enrolled. In Upper and Lower Sackville-street, there are 259 occupiers of houses, offices, and shops in Thom's Directory, and the valuation of that property amounts to 13,100 *l.*, and the number of burgesses enrolled is but 79; comparing that with some of the poorer streets, I find that in Aungier-street and Exchequer-street, where there are 108 occupiers of houses, offices, and shops

Mr. M'Evoy.

12 May 1876.

Mr. M'Evoy.

12 May 1876.

Chairman—continued.

shops given in Thom's Directory, with a valuation of 2,510 *l.*, there are nevertheless 61 burgesses; those are, a great number of them, owners of tenement property who put out the houses to others and who only occupy a very inconsiderable portion of them themselves.

Mr. *Butt.*

1687. Are you quite sure that they are not immediate lessors?—Immediate lessors have no right in Dublin to be burgesses.

1688. They are rated, are they not?—Only where the valuation of the property is 8 *l.*, they are not rated otherwise; I am speaking of those on the burgess roll as occupiers who are rated for the house because they occupy a portion of a house. If a man has only a yard in the house and he lets the whole of the rest to tenants he is nevertheless rated for that house without having any substantial interest in it; and he is not the man who really pays the rates, in my opinion.

Mr. *Bruen.*

1689. I think you stated that you had a paper drawn out to show the effect of those provisions which you have been reciting to the Committee?—That is the way that I worked it out; that there is apparently a large number of persons who ought to be on the burgess roll, and who would, if they were in England, be on the burgess roll. There are no less than 70 rated out of the Westminster Chambers.

1690. Does the working of this system operate principally against one class of the community?—It operates against all classes, and, in my opinion, chiefly against the parties who really pay the rates.

1691. The general effect of all these defects in the present system, the electing and governing body in Dublin especially, appears to be that the class who ought to be represented are not represented?—They are not represented at all.

1692. And those classes who are not represented are, perhaps, those who, from intelligence and from the proportion of the burthen of the rates which they bear, ought to be represented?—It operates to the exclusion of the great ratepayers, the merchants, the manufacturers, and the persons who contribute so largely to the rates on the one side, and it operates to the exclusion of the representation of what I would call the intelligent working-class interest on the other, which, I think, ought to be represented in a town council, and which is not at present.

1693. Do you say, from your experience of the general feeling in Dublin, that there is dissatisfaction amongst the citizens with the results of this system?—The state of things in Dublin amounts to this: that there is no confidence in the present corporation, and I believe it is powerless alike for good or evil. To illustrate its position I may state that in this present Session of Parliament there is being promoted a Markets' Bill. In no town in England or Scotland would private persons be allowed by the corporation to promote a Bill for establishing a public market and carrying out the duties of the corporation; but it is allowed in Dublin because the corporation is so weak and so discredited as I am driven to the conclusion; the market is wanted, the improvement is wanted; we have not a corporation to do it; not a corporation that can be trusted to do it. It must be done by somebody, and it is well to have it done, but it is not a state of things which should exist.

Mr. *Bruen*—continued.

1694. Who is the promoter of that Bill?—A number of leading gentlemen. I believe I am correct in saying that the honourable Member for Dublin, Mr. Brooks, the late Lord Mayor, and one of the corporation are the leading and active promoters of the Bill, and I wish them success. But at the same time I say that if we had a better state of things it should not be allowed for one instant, that private individuals should establish a public market and carry out street improvements in the city.

1695. You speak of this Market Bill as an instance of the shortcomings of the present system of Government; with regard to another point, have the citizens of Dublin ever complained of the system of auditing the accounts?—That is an old system. Previous to 1871 the accounts were audited strictly according to the English system; the ratepayers or burgesses elected two auditors, and that system continues in England to the present day. The Government last year attempted to meddle with it, but the English corporations let the Government know that they would not allow their interference. I have with me the accounts of Manchester and of Birmingham; full detailed accounts of their receipts and expenditure, and if I were a citizen of either of those places, I would join the corporation in opposing any interference by the Government. But the state of things in Dublin is so bad that we are reluctantly obliged to allow the Government to interfere and audit the City accounts, and since the introduction of the Government audit of accounts, there has been a considerable improvement in various matters connected with the expenditure. I have here a Parliamentary Paper, showing the Private Bill costs of the Dublin Corporation. That is but one return; it is of continuation of former Parliamentary Returns, and it is Number 133 of the year 1872. The previous returns of the year 1864 or 1865, showed an expenditure of about 30,000 *l.* in promoting and opposing Bills in Parliament; this adds 18,000 *l.* to it, and any one looking at it, will see the absolute necessity of introducing a system of Government audit of accounts. There was 65 *l.*, for example, paid for opposing the Bray and Enniskerry Railway Bill. Any one acquainted with Dublin will see, and I think will say, that the making of a railway between Bray and Enniskerry had nothing whatever to do with the City of Dublin.

Mr. *Butt.*

1696. Was that expenditure allowed?—It was allowed under the old system amongst other things. I have no political feeling in mentioning it, but they voted 500 *l.* out of the city funds for the French during the time of the war. I would oppose a vote for the Germans just the same; but that passed under the old system. Then on the education question the corporation thought fit to act, and they sent over a deputation, and that expense was allowed. All those things are now absolutely stopped; there is no member of the corporation would venture to propose such expenditure.

1697. What

Mr. M'Evoy. 12 May 1876

Mr. Collins.

1697. What Return is that which you are reading?—It is headed "Private Bill Costs of the Corporation of Dublin. Return to Order of the House, dated 9th August 1872." This is a continuation of previous Parliamentary Returns.

Chairman.

1698. With regard to the expenditure in opposing the Bray and Enniskerry Railway, had that scheme any connection with the Vartry Water Works?—I do not know that.

Mr. Butt.

1699. Did it interfere with them?—I think that there is a pipe from the Vartry passes along the road, but I do not know whether it is so.

Chairman.

1700. Do you know what the reason given by the corporation for opposing it was?—I am not aware of the reason; I merely see it in this return.

Mr. Butt.

1701. Do you know whether they appeared before the Parliamentary Committee?—I know nothing only this, that they paid John Smith, their law agent, 65 *l.*

1702. Do not you know that no party would be allowed to oppose a private Bill unless he had what is called a *locus standi?*—He may have a *locus standi*; that is to say, the corporation may have a *locus standi*, and yet the members be obliged to pay out of their own pockets for the opposition.

1703. Are you aware that neither a corporation nor a private individual can appear to oppose a private Bill in which they have no interest?—I know that.

1704. Therefore, although you are not able to tell me what it was, the corporation of Dublin must have had an interest in that Bray and Enniskerry Railway scheme?—Perhaps they were not allowed a *locus standi*; I do not know how that was.

1705. Have you informed yourself upon that subject?—I am not aware.

1706. Have you any facts which would enable the Committee to determine whether that was not a very proper expenditure of public money?—I have my suspicions.

1707. Can you tell me of any facts so as to enable the Committee to judge whether it was not a most prudent step of the corporation to oppose that Bill?—I could not say that.

1708. In fact, you know nothing about it; you see 65 *l.* down there, and therefore you assume that the corporation improperly spent it, or you suspect it?—I suspect it. Then I find further an expenditure of several hundred pounds in opposing the Stephens Green Bill, and there are all sorts of other Bills that they opposed. Of course they had a *locus standi* in the case of the Stephens Green Bill, but I think that it would have been much better if they had supported that Bill, or brought in a Bill of their own for that purpose. But I can state positively that the appearance of the auditor in the city hall has checked very considerably this particular item in the city accounts. We no longer have to pay the large sums for promoting and opposing Bills that we formerly had to pay.

Chairman.

1709. Are you acquainted with the provisions of the Municipal Corporation Borough Funds Act; an Act which was passed three or four years ago, and which I believe applies to Ireland as well as to England; by which it is provided that before promoting or opposing a Bill in Parliament, the governing body of a town must obtain the assent of a meeting of ratepayers?—That Act applies only to England. What we have in Ireland is certain clauses of the Towns Improvement Act of 1847; a different system altogether, and which is only applicable to promoting Bills. It does not deal at all with the question of opposing Bills.

Mr. Bruen.

1710. Have you any further observations to offer with regard to the auditing of the corporation accounts?—The present system of appeal from the auditor's decision I do not think is the best one. A party who is aggrieved has his option to appeal to the Local Government Board or to the Court of Queen's Bench; I think that there should be but one place to appeal to, and that that should be a court of law. I do not think it is at all desirable that the Local Government Board, sitting privately, should decide this question. It should be decided, I think, openly in a Court of Justice only.

1711. It was given in evidence before the Committee by Doctor Hancock, that the municipal governing bodies in Ireland had no opportunity of ascertaining authoritatively difficult points of law with regard to expenditure such as were afforded to grand juries and to boards of guardians; is it your opinion that it would be an improvement of the law, if the governing bodies could obtain some such assistance in their administration of money?—I think that the Local Government Board strengthened and made like the English, or placed under a department of the English Local Government Board, should have officers in Dublin to instruct and advise the local authorities generally on the administration of affairs, to whom they should carry any very difficult question, which it is absurd to suppose that men of ordinary occupations are to solve. It is the duty, I think, of the Government to provide advice for them; and, among other things, they should be able to advise them as to whether this or that expenditure was legal or illegal before they incurred it.

1712. And that such advice should be a protection to the governing body if they *bonâ fide* carried out that advice?—I would not say that. I think that the ratepayers should have an opportunity of bringing the matter to an issue in a court of law; that is to say, if the Local Government Board happened to be wrong, that they should not be set up as a legislative or legal or judicial tribunal. They should give an opinion to the best of their judgment, but if it was wrong, of course there would be very few cases in which such a thing would happen, I think that the ratepayers should always have a right of appeal.

Mr. Gibson.

1713. What protection then would the action of the Local Government Board be to the municipal authority?—It would reduce to a very small compass indeed any difficulty whatever. It is well known to everybody who has given the subject anything like a reasonable amount of consideration what are properly chargeable

Mr. M'Evoy.

12 May 1876.

Mr. *Gibson*—continued.

able to the local rates, and what are not. But I would preserve the principle of the right to appeal to a court of law. I think it would act very usefully with both the Local Government Board and the corporation.

Mr. *Bruen*.

1714. To pass to the audit of the Collector General's accounts, is not the auditor altogether a different authority from the one who audits the accounts of the corporation?—Yes.

1715. Who is the auditor of the Collector General's accounts?—The auditor of the Collector General's accounts is Master Fitzgibbon.

1716. Has there appeared in the public papers any complaints by Master Fitzgibbon with regard to the powers which he has in auditing the Collector General's accounts?—Yes. I remember last September I called public attention through "Saunders' News Letter" to the extraordinary Report of the Collector General of Rates, and the extraordinary figures which he gave to the public. In that report he tells us that we have a burial rate of 10½ *d.* in the pound instead of a halfpenny, a bridge tax of 12 *d.* in the pound, and so on. Then he gives the Public Water Rate at 3 *d.* in the pound, and the Domestic Water Rate at 12 *d.*, and yet the Public Water Rate at 3 *d.* and the Domestic Water Rate at 12 *d.* I see produces the same amount in one case.

Chairman.

1717. What are you quoting from?—The last report of the Collector General. My letter brought out a letter from Master Fitzgibbon, and in this letter Master Fitzgibbon stated that there was no proper audit of the accounts of the Collector General; that he attempted to establish a proper audit, and for one year he did carry out something that he thought was a proper audit.

Mr *Gibson*.

1718. Have you got the letter of Master Fitzgibbon?—Yes.

Mr. *Bruen*.

1719. The complaint, I think, that you made was that the audit of the Collector General's accounts not being an effectual audit, the ratepayers suffered some loss in consequence of the laxity with which those duties were performed?—Yes.

1720. Was the laxity to which you referred principally in allowing a large amount of taxes to be lost by non-collection?—Yes, that is so.

1721. And in the letter which was elicited from Master Fitzgibbon, in answer to your comments, there is a statement given of the total amount which was lost to the ratepayers of Dublin by reason of the non-collection of rates?—Yes.

1722. Is that total amount stated in the letter?—It is; first from 1860 down to 1870, and then from 1870 down to 1873, which is the latest date of his audit, I believe.

1723. Have you made any calculations yourself with regard to the collection of those arrears what amounts really were lost unavoidably, and have you any idea whether any portions of the arrears could be collected?—I have nothing beyond this letter and the Reports of the Collector General. I know nothing personally on the subject.

Mr. *Bruen*—continued.

1724. Will you produce that letter? (*The Witness delivered in the same*).

1725. The result is that there appears to be an ineffectual system of audit?—Yes, and that the people who pay the rates have not only their own rates to pay, but those of their neighbours, in the poorer localities especially.

1726. That is on the assumption that some rates are not collected which could be collected?—Yes.

1727. Is there a general dissatisfaction in Dublin with regard to the large amount of arrears?—Yes, there is.

1728. Do you think that the arrears are larger now than they were a few years ago?—According to Master Fitzgibbon they are.

1729. Can you give the Committee any reason in your own mind for that?—He says in this letter that he adopted in the year 1861 a system that he thought proper for auditing the accounts, and the result was an immediate reduction in the amount of uncollected rates to the extent of 4,000 *l.*, which means saving 2 *d.* in the pound to the ratepayers of Dublin; but the Privy Council interfered on the motion of the Collector General, and forced him to adopt another mode of auditing those accounts, which he considers ineffective and informal, and not proper for the purpose, and the result has been that the amount of uncollected rates has considerably increased. What I think ought to be done is the adoption of the sound English principle of having the municipal bodies, or the poor law bodies, to superintend the collection of their own rates, that the Poor Law guardians ought to superintend the collection of their rates, and the Corporation ought to superintend the collection of their rates, that the office should be merged into the corporation and the Poor Law system, and then the accounts would be audited by the Local Government Board's auditor when he audited the Poor Law accounts and the corporation accounts. Where you have a local authority, supposing that it is doing its duty, it will best superintend and see that the rates are collected; you may reasonably suppose that they will try to get in all the money that they possibly can, whereas the Collector General, who has no interest in the matter at all, may not be so very zealous and efficient.

1730. You have in Kingstown, I think, a Local Government Board audit of accounts, have you not?—Yes.

1731. Is that satisfactory?—It has worked satisfactorily.

Dr. *Ward*.

1732. Are you not aware that previous to the appointment of the Collector General there was very much more loss in the collection of rates?—I am quite aware that they had a very bad system before that.

1733. What was the system?—At that time in Dublin there were a number of boards. There was the wide street commission, the paving board, and so on, all of them collecting their several rates, and it will be very obvious that that was a very bad system. The Acts of 1849 abolished that, and consolidated the business into the hands of the corporation.

1734. Was not each of those boards in that position of direct interest which you now say would be so beneficial in the collecting of the rates?—Yes, they had a direct interest, but they had

Mr. M'Evoy.

12 May 1876.

Dr. *Ward*—continued.

had that defect that they were not representative bodies; and my observation is, that where you have representative bodies who are responsible to the ratepayers for their conduct, and who superintend the collection of the rates, they will do it better and will look after the collection much better than any others. I find, with regard to the Collector General's office, that whilst it has been so inefficient, its expense has considerably increased. It has grown from costing the city 3,500 *l.*, to be an institution costing 7,000 *l.*; about one-half of that money is paid to the Collector General and his clerks, while the other half goes to the real working men, the collectors. It seems to me a wrong state of things that the parties who are simply to superintend should get nearly as much as the persons who do the work.

Mr. *Bruen.*

1735. Have you any suggestions to make to the Committee with regard to the revision of the list of voters for the burgess roll?—I think that the recommendations of the Parliamentary Committee last year for England might be very well acted on in Ireland; that is to say, the list should be subjected to the revision of the revising barrister for Parliamentary purposes, and for that purpose, as well as for other reasons, the qualifying period should be the same as for Parliamentary purposes, that is, one twelvemonth instead of two years and eight months at present in Dublin, and other periods in the other boroughs. I think that the qualifying period being the same and the revision held at the same time, there would be a great deal of expense saved, and the judge would be perfectly neutral and impartial. It may come to pass that the Lord Mayor presiding at the revision court is objected to himself as to his right to be on the burgess roll; that has actually happened in the case of the Mayor of Cork, who a few years ago was objected to as a burgess, and he had to sit and had to decide his own case. And besides that, the Lord Mayor is usually of one party or another; he may be going out, or may be a candidate for re-election at the very time of the revision. I have known instances of that where the Lord Mayor was an outgoing town councillor in his ward. He was opposed, and he was deciding in the revision court on who should vote for him, or who should vote for his opponents. I think that it would be far better to have a perfectly neutral and impartial authority, and that would be the revising barrister for the cities and the chairman of quarter sessions for the towns in the counties.

1736. Have you any other suggestion to make?—I have some suggestion to make about the appointment of the officers of municipal bodies; there appears to me to be a very serious evil, and only those who are acquainted with the actual working of municipal matters know it to the full extent, that it exists in the system of appointment, of increasing salaries, of dismissal, and of dealing with the misconduct of municipal officers. I think that if the principle of the Civil Service were introduced, and the clerkships and surveyorships were the result of a competitive examination, it would be a great improvement. I think that the salary should be fixed at a certain sum, increasing by yearly increments; that inquiry into the conduct of officers should be conducted by the Local Government Board; and that that

Mr. *Bruen*—continued.

board should possess the same powers with regard to municipal officers that they do with regard to Poor Law officers; if that were carried out it would lead to very considerable improvement in the local administration of affairs.

1737. Is there now no qualifying examination?—No qualifying examination whatever, and the result is that in Dublin we have a great number of gentlemen appointed, most respectable gentlemen no doubt, but who owe their appointment either to their connection with some political party or to their relationship to the lord mayors or aldermen, or town councillors. They may be competent or they may not, but they clearly do not owe their election to the fact of their being competent.

1738. And your point is that there is no examination which would test their competency?—There is no examination whatever. It seems strange that the principle has been applied to the case of the county surveyors; there is an examination for a county surveyorship.

1739. Then would you rather desire that the examination to which these gentlemen should be subjected by the Civil Service Commissioners would be a qualifying examination rather than an open competitive examination?—Yes. Anything that would prove their fitness for the office. There can be no reasonable doubt that in cases of misconduct the elective body is not the proper body to deal with it. The members of an elective body are not likely to take that stern view of public interests and public duty that they will sacrifice private feeling, and say to an officer, "You must go; no matter what your family or what your claims upon our generosity are, or anything of that sort; the public interests require you to go, and we must dismiss you." It would be better to put into the hands of something like a judicial tribunal the exercise of such powers as that. I have heard from a great many people who are acquainted with the working of the poor-law system in Ireland, that but for that power which the Poor Law Commissioners have of dismissing by sealed order, the poor-law system in Ireland would have broken down years ago; it is the great preservative of it.

Mr. *Butt.*

1740. Do I understand you to say that you think that the corporation should not have the power of dismissing their officers?—I would not say that they should not have the power of dismissing them, but I would say that the Local Government Board should, upon a complaint either from the corporation or from the ratepayers, hold an inquiry into the conduct of the officers, and that then they should give their decision as they do in the case of poor-law guardians; and if the corporation refused or neglected to do their duty the Local Government Board should have the power of dismissing by sealed order.

1741. In fact, you would place the Corporation of Ireland under the same control as the poor-law guardians are now?—In that particular.

1742. Speaking of Dublin particularly, have you heard of any instances of unjust dismissals of officers on the part of the Corporation of Dublin?—I have heard of no unjust dismissals, but I have heard of instances where they should have dismissed, but did not dismiss.

1743. Would

Mr. M'Evoy.

12 May 1876.

Mr. *Ashton.*

1743. Would the examination which you have just now recommended for the officers of the corporation be a test examination or a competitive one?—I prefer a competitive one, but the next best thing would be a qualifying examination.

1744. I think you said that you thought that the system of the poor law worked well as regards the circumstance of their having some control over officers from head quarters?—Yes, I think it does work well; what I referred to was the power of the Local Government Board for holding an inquiry into the conduct of the officers and dismissing them.

1745. Not as to their appointment?—No.

1746. Is there in Ireland any examination for poor law officers?—No, there is not, but I think that there ought to be.

Mr. *Butt.*

1747. You spoke about the examination for county surveyors; are you aware that that is not a competitive examination, but a qualifying examination?—I am not aware that it is competitive.

1748. Is not this the way in which it is conducted, that any person who thinks he is fit for a county surveyor may at any time be examined by a Board of Examiners, and when there is a vacancy for one he is put upon the list of qualified candidates?—I am not aware of that; I may say that I have seen from time to time advertisements in the papers that the examination would be held at such and such a place for county surveyorships.

1749. Take Commercial Buildings, in Dame-street; those are all, in fact, separate tenements and separate offices, are they not?—Yes, they are.

1750. And the occupiers of them are not now rated?—They are not rated.

1751. Of course, by not being rated, virtually those offices neither get the Parliamentary nor the municipal franchise?—I have only looked into the burgess roll.

1752. They could not get it except they were rated?—No.

1753. You think it would be an improvement if offices of that kind were separately rated?—Yes; I think they ought to be.

1754. Your impression is, that that could be done by the General Valuation Office without any change in the law?—I think it would be necessary to have a re-valuation of the City and of the whole of the country.

1755. Is there not, under the existing law, a re-valuation every year?—There is a revision; but the way it would work against Commercial Buildings, taking that case, would be this: if an application was made to re-value them for the purposes of separate rating, it would work out to a much larger aggregate valuation than was fixed 12 or 13 years ago, at the time when the valuation was made; and consequently the people who are interested will not make any complaint.

1756. But you say that the other ratepayers would be benefited by it?—They would be benefited; but it is an evil not to have a re-valuation, because it discourages improvements. If a man is thinking about building a new house in Dublin he knows that that house will be valued at a higher standard of value than what existed 12 or 13 years ago, and the knowledge of that fact would discourage him from building.

Sir *Arthur Guinness.*

1757. On altering a house?—Yes, or altering a house; it has the same effect in both cases.

Mr. *Butt.*

1758. I understand your opinion to be, that the standard value of property has risen in Dublin within the last 12 or 13 years?—In parts of Dublin; in fact, I may say in the greater part of Dublin.

1759. And that the present valuation does not fairly represent the value of the houses?—I do say that.

1760. As a whole, would you say that they are valued too high, or too low?—The whole city I would say, judging by the English standard, is too low.

1761. Do you think it is an equal valuation over the city?—No, I think not; I think that the effect of a re-valuation now would be to increase the valuation disproportionately in the better parts, the improving parts of the city, perhaps leaving the poorer parts just as they were; something like that would be the effect of it.

1762. With regard to Cole-alley, what did you say was the aggregate value of Cole-alley?—The Collector General says in his report that the total annual value of Cole-alley is 208*l.*

1763. I believe it runs from Meath-street to Tripoli; do you know where Tripoli is?—Yes, I think so.

1764. How many houses are there in Cole-alley?—Thirty-three houses.

1765. And the rates are not collected there?—So this report says.

1766. How much was collected?—£. 0 6 *s.*

1767. Will you look at "Thom" and see how the houses are rated in Cole-alley; there are only two houses rated there; James Wheeley, coachmaker, is rated at 14*l.*?—This is a report for the year 1861. There may have been alterations since then. In Cole-alley there are only six houses given in "Thom;" they are, I suppose, the chief houses in it; the rest are small ones, but you will find that the last is given as No. 31, showing that there are other houses.

1768. You gave reasons that a house if rated at 4*l.* is not fit for human habitation?—I presume so.

1769. Therefore you would, in fact, divide the inhabitants of Dublin into human beings living in houses fit for human habitation, and into persons living in houses unfit?—I would not do any such thing; I would rather have them all living in houses fit for human habitation.

1770. For the purposes of the franchise you would divide them in that way?—For the reason which I have already stated, I would look forward at a not very distant date under a reformed corporation to their being all fit, and then we could have the English franchise without any difficulty.

1771. We are dealing with all the corporate towns of Ireland; would you apply that to all municipal towns?—Yes, certainly.

1772. Do you mean to say that in the town of Belturbet there is no human being living in a house rated under 4*l.*?—I should have stated that according to my view of the matter the civic districts ought to be large towns. If you have a very little town, with a separate sanitary and highway authority, it would not have the funds unless it unduly taxes the ratepayers to provide the

Mr. *Butt*—continued.

the necessary officers to carry on the business, so that Belturbet would not be in my view at all.

1773. Are you aware that there are a large number of towns at present not having corporations, but town commissioners?—Yes, I know that.

1774. And not divided into sanitary districts, but still having town commissioners for their own purposes?—I think it is a bad system to have them; I think that they should be put under the county boards if we had county boards.

1775. I do not know whether you know the town of Belturbet?—I do not know it; I know that it is a small town.

1776. Take any small town that you do know, do you think it a bad system to allow it to light, pave, and provide for its own improvement?—I think it should be allowed to pave and light, but it should not be a highway or sanitary authority.

1777. Do not you know that there is no case of a small town in which it is a highway authority?—There are some.

1778. What small town is separate from the county?—There is Kilmainham township and Dalkey township; they have got grand jury powers to their very serious injury.

1779. Do you know what is the population of Dalkey township?—I do.

1780. What is it?—It is about 2,500.

1781. Will you look at "Thom," and tell me what the population of Dalkey township is?—Two thousand five hundred and eighty-four, and its rateable valuation is 11,736 *l.* I have been told by the secretary of the grand jury that it is with the greatest difficulty that they can get the grand jury warrant paid in those small townships.

1782. Is Dalkey a separate township, exempt from the grand jury taxation of the county of Dublin?—It is under a local Act exempt.

1783. Although you think that an improvement, you would not think it an improvement that Dalkey should provide for its own lighting and paving?—It should provide for its own lighting and paving, but it should not be a highway or a sanitary authority. It works very badly; I am speaking merely as to its effect in an administrative point of view. They cannot have proper officers, and they cannot incur the necessary expenditure for carrying on the business properly.

1784. Supposing that you were to allow small towns to have their municipal commissioners under the Towns Improvement Act; you would see no objection to that?—No; I would have them to carry on their own paving and lighting.

1785. You would leave those towns under the Act of the 9th of George the Fourth?—Yes, I would confine them within the limits of that Act.

1786. In many of those comparatively small towns in the country that have municipal commissioners of their own, do you think that there are no comfortable houses not rated at 4 *l.*?—In any town that I know, with a population of 10,000 and upwards, there would be instances, no doubt, but they would be rare.

1787. How many towns in Ireland have a population of 10,000?—I should think about 20.

1788. Are there not a great many towns under 10,000 that have those separate town commissioners?—Yes, certainly.

1789. I ask you again whether, to the great majority of those towns, you would apply the 4 *l.* limit as the test of fitness for human habitation?—I think it would be in the long run a judicious arrangement.

Mr. *Butt*—continued.

1790. Whether in small towns or in large cities?—Or in large cities. I would leave the Towns Improvement Act with its machinery at present in those towns.

1791. When you speak of a great many persons having offices, for instance, in Dame-street, without being rated, do not you include in that persons who merely keep one office in the upper part of the house?—I do.

1792. Such as an attorney's office?—Yes, an attorney's office, who has access at all times that he pleases; he is not a lodger in any sense, and he should be separately rated.

1793. Wherever that takes place you would apply the same principle to that in the same way as to Commercial-buildings?—Yes, I would.

1794. Then the difference between a number of persons rated in Auinger-street, and rated in Dame-street, is that Dame-street is a good place for persons that have offices, to let offices of that kind?—Yes.

1795. And Auinger-street is not?—No.

1796. And therefore offices do not let?—No.

1797. I presume the same thing would apply to Merrion-square?—Of course it would.

1798. You would find in Merrion-square as well as in Auinger-street, a much larger proportion of persons entered in "Thom's Directory" registered as burgesses than you would in Dame-street?—Yes.

1799. And the same thing, of course, would apply to all the other streets of the city?—To meet the case of Merrion-square you must go for plurality of votes; that is the only way it could be met.

1800. Then it is not because Auinger-street is to some extent an inferior street that the burgesses bear a larger proportion to the houses than they do in Dame-street?—It is the circumstance that I mentioned, that if the houses in Auinger-street were sub-let they would be sub-let in tenements, and are sub-let in tenements to persons in a lower class, whereas in the case of Dame-street you have a different class of persons altogether. You have intelligent independent persons who take an interest in affairs.

1801. You think it would be an advantage that persons occupying offices should be separately rated, and so acquire the franchise?—Yes, I think it would be so.

1802. And is there any difference in that respect between the municipal franchise in England and Ireland, do you know?—There is nothing in the Acts that I can see; I think it is in the valuation system that the difference is.

1803. You were asked as to the wards; was not there in the year 1848 or 1849, before 1851, a re-distribution of the wards?—There was; I have taken a good deal of notes about what took place then; it was the result of a long controversy. There was a Mr. Jackson, a solicitor in Dublin, promoting Bills on the one side, and the corporation were promoting Bills on the other. They were at it for three years in succession, and those Bills fell through, and at last the Government interfered to settle the matter in 1849. In 1848 they were very near settling the matter on the Dublin Corporation Improvement Bill. The Chamber of Commerce and the citizens represented before the Committee had agreed to accept the

Mr. M'Evoy.

18 May 1876.

Mr. M'Evoy.

11 May 1876.

Mr. Butt—continued.

the Corporation Bill subject to some modifications, and the matter would then have been settled but for the Wide Street Commissioners, who were also opponents of the Bill. They pressed Standing Orders' objections, that no notice had been given for them; in that way the Bill fell through.

1804. Do you happen to know who first suggested that compromise as to the change in the wards?—I cannot say that I do.

1805. Do you know that after the barristers had re-divided the wards there was an appeal to the Privy Council against the division?—Yes, there was.

1806. And it ended in the Privy Council confirming the division?—Yes, I think that that was so.

1807. Was not the division made upon the principle of the English division of wards?—Yes, it was.

1808. I will read to you what the principle in England is. In England the wards as originally framed might have been different, but the number of councillors was assigned to them in this way. The barrister or barristers were to assign a number of councillors to each ward, "and, in assigning the number of councillors to each ward the said barrister or barristers shall, as far as in his or their judgment, he or they may deem it to be practicable, have regard as well to the number of persons rated to the relief of the poor in such ward as to the aggregate amount of the sums at which all the said persons shall be so rated;" has your attention ever been called to that provision of the English Act?—I know that; but the parties before the Committee in 1848 agreed upon the principle of equal property valuation. You will find that that was so. The City was to be divided into wards of not less than 40,000 *l.*, and not more than 50,000 *l.* valuation. I quote from "Saunders" of June 1848, and it gives the Bill as agreed upon between the parties when before the Parliamentary Committee.

1809. What were the provisions of the Act of 1849 as to the re-distribution of the wards?—They were quite different: when the Government interfered the next year they took the English principles altogether.

1810. And will you undertake to say that the agreement between the parties was not that the wards were to be re-valued and re-distributed, according to the English system?—It was not; they struck out the consideration of proportion altogether; they handed in a Bill with all the clauses in it to the Committee, and it was agreed upon between the parties.

1811. It was to divide them merely upon the old valuation?—Yes.

1812. But the Act which was, in fact, passed, adopted the English principle?—It did; I may mention how it was passed, as I have read. Both parties opposed the Government Bill in 1849; the corporation and Mr. Jackson's friends both opposed it; they were in this position, that they could have thrown out the Government Bill as it was introduced so very late in the Session, but they had to look for a costs clause; the corporation had been obliged by a decision of the Court of Queen's Bench to repay into the Borough Fund some money that they had advanced for promoting some Bills the previous year; and, of course, the others had no fund whatever to get theirs from; they both applied to the Government to give them a costs clause as a consideration for withdrawing their opposition. The Government refused, and said, "Apply to the Committee, and if the Committee passes your costs clauses, well and good; we will have no objection to it." They applied to the Committee, and the Committee turned round and said, "We will not pass it unless the Government on its own responsibility asks for it." The Government at last apparently very reluctantly consented, and it was to get their costs that both sides consented to the Government arrangement of 1849. You will find that that costs clause is a most extraordinary clause; it gives the costs for three years of both parties against the ratepayers of Dublin.

Chairman.

1813. Do you know what was the amount?—The amount was something like 11,000 *l.* for three Bills.

Mr. *Butt.*

1814. I do not quite understand the occupation franchise which you suggest; can you tell me what that is?—It is to meet the case of those occupiers of offices who do not live in the house. They are under different circumstances altogether to persons resident.

1815. If they are either occupants or joint occupants, are they not at present entitled if they live within seven miles?—They are if they are rated, if they live within seven miles.

1816. What I did not exactly understand was, whether the fact of their not voting was that they were not rated, or that they were resident beyond the seven miles?—They are disqualified, not only by not living beyond seven miles, but also if they are not resident householders within that limit. They may live, but they may not have a house of their own.

1817. Are the persons of whom you were speaking as excluded, rated occupiers?—They are rated occupiers; I may mention one case that I happen to know. One of the Pims is in that position. He lives with his father outside the city within the limit, but because he has not a house of his own he is on the burgess roll, but it is by sufferance, I believe; if either party liked to object to him they could do so.

1818. One change to remedy that evil would be not to require a man to be a householder, but if he was rated in the city taking residence as sufficient, whether he was a householder or not?—Yes, I would take occupancy, whether he was a householder or not.

1819. Occupancy in the city, and residence outside?—I would not care where he lived; if he was a rated occupier of 10 *l.*, I would put him on.

1820. Then you would admit non-resident occupiers?—Yes, but I would fix the qualification for those non-resident occupiers much higher than for resident occupiers.

1821. Without adopting this new principle, do you think that it would be an advantage to extend the limit of residence to 15 miles instead of seven miles?—Yes, if you continued the residential franchise. Practically, 15 miles means now, in Dublin, the same as seven miles at the time of the passing of the Act, 40 years ago.

1822. Do you think it would also be an advantage to use the word "resident," without requiring him to be a householder; so that if a person were

Mr. *M'Evoy.*

12 May 1876.

Mr *Butt*—continued.

were in lodgings at Bray, or stopped at the Bray hotel, he might still have the franchise?—Yes; I think it is a frivolous distinction.

1823. You are proposing, are you not, a new qualification for the members of the council?—Yes.

1824. What qualification do you propose?—I suggest the special juror's qualification, which varies; it is 50 *l.* in the city of Dublin, but in the small towns they have a lower qualification.

1825. Might not that 50 *l.* qualification exclude a great many of the best persons, the very persons who are resident outside the limits, and are not rated at 50 *l.*?—I think not; of course, there would be some, but I think there are very few who would be excluded.

1826. Do you think that there are very few persons in that station which you consider so desirable for councillors, who live in houses under 50 *l.*?—I would meet that evil by allowing persons, if they had houses within the 15-mile limit, rated at 50 *l.*, to be on the list.

1827. Do you not think that there are a great many people who are perfectly fit to be councillors whose houses are not rated at 50 *l.*?—There are some, but not many.

1828. Are there not some very respectable streets in Dublin in which the houses, as a rule, are rated under 50 *l.* in the present valuation?—The persons occupying those houses usually have other property elsewhere, which would have to make up their valuation.

1829. But they might not be rated for that property?—I mean property that they are rated for.

1830. Do not you know that there are several persons possessed of very considerable property in the city of Dublin who do not live in houses rated at 50 *l.*?—I know there are.

1831. Then your qualification of 50 *l.* rating would exclude all those?—There are not many who could not make up that qualification by other property besides what they live in.

1832. But they must be rated upon that other property?—Yes, they would be rated to that other property.

1833. In what respect are those persons rated?—Say that a man has a place of business, he has usually a warehouse, he has his stables, and he has his house of residence.

1834. Supposing that he is a person of property, say outside the city of Dublin, and lives in a house rated under 50 *l.*, a house rated at 40 *l.*, would you say that he ought to be excluded from being a councillor if his fellow-citizens choose to elect him?—I look upon it as necessary for the public good to fix a qualification of that sort, and I think it would work well.

1835. Do not you think that you might safely trust the citizens to elect the person who will best discharge the duties?—It is unfortunately the case that the citizens are not usually left to themselves in this matter. At a contested election it is the men that are the most pushing, and the most importuning that force themselves into the town council, whilst very superior men who will refuse to do that sort of thing will be left out.

1836. Would not that evil still prevail, whether you fix the qualification above 50 *l.* or below it?—If you fix it at a high qualification, you get rid of those very pushing people that want to

Mr. *Butt*—continued.

make something out of being members of the town council.

1837. You think that the fact of a man living in a house of 50 *l.* a year value gives a security that he is fit to be a town councillor, while a man living in a 40 *l.* house would not be?—In the general sense, of course there are exceptions, but as a rule, in the general sense, the possession of property marks him out as a man that would be above petty jobbing, and that of forcing himself into the town council for perhaps objects of his own; I think that if the public good were consulted it would be well to fix that limit.

1838. You think that that would never apply amongst people living in houses rated far above 50 *l.*?—Decidedly I do; there are plenty of people living in houses above 50 *l.* who would be just as dishonest as people living in houses under that amount; I speak on general principles.

1839. With regard to the audit of the Collector General's accounts, have you looked into the controversy between Master Fitzgibbon and the Collector General?—I have.

1840. You are aware, I suppose, that Master Fitzgibbon is the Receiver Master in Chancery?—Yes.

1841. And that he passes the Receiver's accounts?—Yes.

1842. Have you ever had the misfortune to be in any way engaged in passing a Receiver's account in Chancery?—Never.

1843. Was not this the controversy between Master Fitzgibbon and the Collector General, that the Collector General thought that in auditing his accounts the duty of the auditor was to see that he paid over all the money that came into his hands?—Yes; that is what the Collector General contended.

1844. And that there the duty of the auditor ceased?—Yes.

1845. The Master's opinion was that he had a right to call him to account for not exercising due diligence in the collection of his accounts?—Yes, that is the whole point.

1846. And the highest authority, the Privy Council, decided that the audit did not embrace that?—Yes; I believe that is just the whole thing.

1847. I do not know whether you are aware, from general knowledge, that in passing a Receiver's accounts in the Court of Chancery, the Receiver is, in the first instance, charged with the whole rent of the estate, and then obliged to discharge himself of it by showing that he used due diligence in collecting the rents?—I know that that is so.

1848. And, in fact, Master Fitzgibbon wanted to apply to the audit of the Collector General the same principle?—Yes; but it would appear to me that the Master's audit would have been very advantageous to the ratepayers of Dublin if it had been carried out.

1849. And we may take it from that letter that, as a fact, while he put that screw, or was supposed to have the power of putting that screw on the Collector General, the rates were better collected than they were before?—Yes.

1850. Is there anybody now that has the power of calling the Collector General to account for neglect; is there any power of removal, or of supervision of his office?—Yes, the Lord Lieutenant, I daresay, could dismiss him.

1851. Could

Mr. M'Evoy.

12 May 1876.

Mr. *Butt*—continued.

1851. Could he call him to account?—I think so.

1852. Has any complaint ever been made to the authorities, praying to have the law revised upon this subject?—There have been several complaints made by the guardians, and I think by the Corporation themselves.

1853. To whom?—Resolutions have been passed by them at their meetings, but I do not know whether they ever formally appealed.

1854. The Collector General is now appointed by the Government, is he not?—Yes.

1855. And he is totally independent of all the local bodies?—He is.

1856. With regard to the old law, when auditors were elected by the burgesses, as they are in England, could you tell me whether those auditors had any power to inquire into the legality of payments?—Yes, they had; they could have taken proceedings in Chancery, I think.

1857. That is another matter, but supposing there was an order of the corporation properly made for the payment of a certain sum, had auditors, under the old system, any power to go behind that?—I do not think they had.

1858. They had simply to check the accounts like the auditors of a railway company?—Just so.

1859. Do you know what the remedy was if the corporation made an illegal order for the payment of any money?—A reference to the Court of Queen's Bench.

1860. It was open to any ratepayer upon the order being made to question it by appeal to the Court of Queen's Bench?—Yes.

1861. If it was not so questioned it remained?—Yes.

1862. And the auditor did not inquire into its legality?—No; but he used to mark on the face of the city accounts their disapproval of certain payments; I have seen that done.

1863. And if they were not satisfied, could they bring it to the Court of Queen's Bench and quash it?—Yes, if they thought it worth while.

1864. And that power remains still, does it not?—I think so.

1865. But in addition to that now the auditor of the Local Government Board decides upon the legality of the payments?—He does.

1866. And he disallows them if he thinks them illegal?—Yes, he does.

1867. Do you know whether there is anything like that which exists in England?—Not in the case of the municipal boroughs; in local boards it does.

1868. The auditor of the Local Government Board is not a professional man in Ireland, I believe?—He is not a legal man.

1869. And yet he has to decide very important questions as to the legality of payments?—It appears so; but the fact is that his decisions are narrowed down to within really a very narrow compass; no question can possibly arise requiring any very abstruse knowledge of the law.

1870. What do you say as to the question which is now before him about the 7,000 *l.* for the culvert under Essex Bridge?—I was the objector in that case; the Act of Parliament is very plain; the Act of Parliament of 1871 prescribes that the corporation are not to levy a main drainage rate, unless for the purpose of paying the interest and providing a sinking fund for the cost and maintenance of the works authorised by that Act to the extent of 350,000 *l.*

Mr. *Butt*—continued.

1871. They thought it prudent to raise a small sum for the partial execution of those works?—The expenditure was made on what might have been useful or might have been part of the main drainage system, or might not, as it might turn out.

1872. You thought it was an imprudent expenditure?—I thought it an improper expenditure, an illegal one.

1873. That question would be decided in the first instance by the auditor?—It has been decided against the corporation by the auditor; an appeal to the Local Government Board, or to the Court of Queen's Bench, however lies.

1874. You instanced as an improper expenditure by the Corporation of Dublin a grant of 500 *l.* to the sufferers from the French War?—I did.

1875. Are you aware that the Corporation of London have made very munificent grants to sufferers in different foreign countries?—Yes; but that is a corporation under different rules to all other corporations in the United Kingdom; I know they have done it; they have very large property at their disposal; it is an unreformed corporation; they are allowed to do those things.

1876. They are going to some expense now for an entertainment in honour of the return of the Prince of Wales; there is no auditor to decide that that is an illegal expenditure, and to compel the alderman who signs the cheque to pay it out of his own pocket?—No; they are just like the Dublin Corporation 40 or 50 years ago, they can practically do what they like.

1877. Have not the Corporation of Dublin considerable property of their own?—Yes, they have.

1878. Then if they expend money on anything of the kind, is it not out of their own property that they must pay it, and not out of the rates. Could the Corporation of Dublin pay a penny of any rate to any expenditure of that kind?—The Municipal Corporation Act, I think, would be against their doing anything of the kind.

1879. When they have done it, it has been out of their estates, the corporate property just the same as the Corporation of London does?—That particular 500 *l.* was charged to the borough fund, but they would not pay it now I say, because the auditor would not allow it; I merely instanced that as a proof of the value and the necessity of an audit.

1880. You would probably have the Corporation of Dublin never apply money in that way?—Speaking as a private individual, if we had a corporation in Dublin, such as they have in Birmingham, or in Manchester (I take those two corporations as examples), I for one would never object to their expending 500 *l.* on any public purpose that they thought fit, as those corporations are entitled to public confidence by their services.

1881. Those Corporations are elected, are they not, by household suffrage?—They are; but I may mention to you that an alderman of the Birmingham Corporation, Mr. Avery, recently told me that they were able to do what they were doing, not in consequence of the household suffrage, but in spite of it.

1882. Suppose we tried to do that in spite of the people of Dublin, too, do you think it possible

Mr. *M'Evoy.*

12 May 1876.

Mr. *Butt*—continued.

sible that the result might be the same?—The Royal Sanitary Commission have been investigating the question of the influence of the poorer classes upon municipal government and towns improvement, and after having examined a number of witnesses (and another Committee in England has been doing the same thing), the opinion of both Commission and Committee are that the poorer classes do not support measures of improvement; the same thing happens in Ireland; we are not worse than the English in that respect.

1883. In fact, you would like not to exclude them from the franchise, but to have the other elements in?—I think that matters should be so balanced that no class should control the other.

1884. Have not the corporation given water to Dublin?—They have.

1885. Do you approve of that?—I supported the Vartry project.

1886. Has not that been a most beneficial thing for Dublin?—It has.

1887. Do you recollect when that Vartry scheme was pending?—I do.

1888. Do you recollect that the people that you call the intelligent and respectable classes of Dublin denounced that as a job?—No.

1889. Not the great majority of them?—No. The facts are these: an improved water supply for Dublin originated with the corporation that was established through the exertions of Mr. Codd in 1851; I speak of the corporation established then, all of them leading men. There was a disposition to bury the hatchet of party at the time, and they all went to together to put into the corporation the leading merchants of Dublin, and it was that corporation that commenced taking in hand the reform of the water supply of Dublin. They appointed a committee, presided over by Mr. Sweetman, the eminent brewer, and having on it the late Aldermen Roe, Kinahan, George Woods, Mansell, and Darcey, I think; they were all men of position and large ratepaying merchants in Dublin, who took the first part in the matter before Sir John Grey joined the corporation. He became a member of the body in 1855, I think, and he was backed up most earnestly by Mr. Kinahan, by Mr. Roe, and by Mr. Codd; I have heard him myself say that he never would have carried the Water Bill but for the support of the men that I have referred to.

1890. Is it not the fact, as shown by the very paper that you have been quoting to us, that scheme was vehemently and violently opposed?—It was chiefly by the canal interest.

1891. I mean by the upper classes of Dublin, was not that scheme most vehemently and violently opposed?—I do not think that the upper classes, as a class, opposed it; the canal people of course opposed it.

1892. Were not there in that corporation some whom you have described as the upper classes of the City of Dublin, and were not they just as vehement in denouncing the scheme of the Vartry Waterworks as you now are in your complaints of the corporation?—Such of them as were connected with the Grand Canal and the Royal Canal Company.

1893. Was Master Fitzgibbon connected with the Grand Canal?—I do not know. One should have a list of the shareholders; but you can easily fancy that they bought for their own interests.

Mr. *Butt*—continued.

1894. From your knowledge of the City of Dublin, do you not know, and do you not believe, that there was a most general and determined opposition to that Vartry scheme on the part of those whom you call the upper classes of Dublin?—No, I think the contrary. I think that the intelligence and wealth of the city was always in favour of an improved water supply, with the exception of those who were personally interested in opposition to it.

Mr. *Brooks.*

1895. You were Chairman of the Commissioners of Kingston, were you not?—I was.

1896. And you resigned that position?—No, I was put out.

1897. You declined to accept a seat, I think, for any ward in Kingstown amongst the many wards there. I mean after you had occupied the chair?—I have a seat at present.

1898. I mean in the election that immediately followed your chairmanship?—No, I never refused. I said if they chose to elect me, I was there to take the place, but I would not give myself any trouble about it.

1899. There was a Bill, I think, attempted to be carried through Parliament, for the improvement of Kingstown under your auspices?—Yes.

1900. As you were a member of that Committee, can you tell me what were the Parliamentary costs of that Bill?—The costs fell altogether on the promoters. The Bill fell through, and they had to pay their costs.

1901. What were the costs?—About 1,100 *l.*, which we paid, unlike the Dublin Corporation, who have not paid the costs of the Gas Bill of the same Session.

Mr. *Butt.*

1902. Were they not bound to pay them?—They have attempted to put them on the rates, but they have not succeeded.

Mr. *Brooks.*

1903. Speaking of the constitution of the corporation of the City of Dublin, I think you say that it is now composed of men of an inferior grade?—I did not say any such thing. Taking its constitution, whatever it may be, I said that it was powerless for good or evil; I did not make any personal reflections on the constitution of the corporation.

1904. Is that due in any degree to the opposition which is given by any section of the citizens to this reformed council, do you think?—No, I think not; I think that if they were doing their duty in carrying out civic improvements they would have the intelligent classes that are now opposed to them entirely with them.

1905. Can you say how many justices of the peace are in the corporation of the city?—A great number, I should think.

1906. And how many of the first merchants and manufacturers are represented?—I would not say by those justices that are in the corporation.

1907. As a matter of fact, how many are there?—There are very few of the leading merchants of Dublin in the corporation.

1908. Do you call Mr. John Jefferson a leading merchant?—He is one, and he is a very large ratepayer.

1909. Is Sir John Barrington an eminent manufacturer?—

Mr. M'Evoy.

12 May 1876.

Mr. *Brooks*—continued.

manufacturer?—He is; but those are not leaders of the corporation; they are not the gentlemen who dictate its policy.

1910. Who dictates its policy?—I do not like personalities; but anyone reading the newspapers knows that those two gentlemen do not take a very leading or active part in municipal affairs in Dublin.

1911. With regard to the officers, you say that the officers have been chiefly elected on account of their being relations of lord mayors?—I did not confine myself to lord mayors, but to aldermen and town councillors, and to those useful to them often in their elections.

1912. Will you give me the name of any one single person who has been so appointed?—A relative of a mayor; take the City Marshal; the late City Marshal was a brother-in-law of Lord Mayor M'Sweeny.

1913. He was dismissed, I think?—Yes, he was dismissed.

1914. By the corporation?—I do not know whether he was dismissed by the corporation, but he gave up his position; then to succeed him came a son of Sir William Carroll, who was Lord Mayor.

1915. That is the present marshal?—Yes.

1916 Is it not the general opinion that the duties of marshal in the City of Dublin are now performed in an efficient manner?—Judging by the receipts, and comparing them with former years, I find that the receipts in the marshal's office have fallen off from 741 *l.* in 1863 to 447 *l.* in 1874.

1917. To what is that due?—I do not know what is the cause of it; I am unable to assign any reason.

1918. Do you think that the duties are performed in an inefficient manner by the city marshal?—I do not charge any gentleman with neglect of duty without knowing the fact.

1919. Do not you think it likely that the Committee might infer, in the absence of any explanation from you, that the duties were inefficiently performed?—If it can be explained, I suppose it will be.

1920. Can you name any other officers who have been relations of lord mayors or town councillors?—I think you have the secretary of the Waterworks Committee; he is a brother of one who was a town councillor.

1921. Do you wish that officer to be taken as an example?—I do; he is a brother of town councillor Lawler now dead; he was a town councillor formerly.

1922. You mean that the present secretary of the Waterworks Committee had formerly a brother in the corporation?—Yes.

1923. Do you know whether that gentleman was deceased before the appointment of the present secretary?—That I do not know.

1924. Do you know whether the present secretary of the Waterworks Committee was not himself an eminent merchant in Dublin?—He was.

1925. And of standing and attainments and position?—He is a most respectable man; I have not a word to say against him.

1926. Except that he is the brother-in-law of a councillor?—I do not regard that as any objection to him; but it only shows that those appointments are not the result of inquiry, as it were, into the relative merits or demerits of particular gentlemen.

1927. But you charge it upon the corporation that those officers were appointed on account of their connection with certain members of the corporation?—I think it operated in their favour.

Mr. *Butt.*

1928. Do you seriously say that you believe that Mr. Lawler was elected secretary of the Waterworks Committee, because he had a brother who had once been a town councillor, and who was dead?—I do not think he would have been elected to the office at all, if it were thrown open to public competition.

1929. Would you say to this Committee that you seriously believe that the corporation were influenced in electing him, not by his being fit for the office, but by the fact that at some time or other a brother of his was a town councillor, who was dead?—I think that friendship created by relationship operates upon the minds of the corporation, not corruptly, or anything of that sort.

Mr. *Brooks.*

1930. As to the fitness of that gentleman, I think you have already said that he was an eminent merchant, and a man of education, attainments, and position?—Yes; but if you ask me the question, I must tell you that yesterday a member of the corporation told me that he was not a very fit officer.

1931. Will you favour the Committee with the name of any other officer?—Yes; you have the macebearer, a son of town councillor Barlow, that was.

1932. How long is it since Mr. Barlow was in the corporation?—I am not able to say.

1933. Is it not 20 years since he was in the corporation?—It is certainly some time ago. I think he is dead.

1934. Twenty years ago?—I do not know when he died.

1935. Can you mention any other?—Mr. John Byrne has a brother, a storekeeper.

Mr. *Butt.*

1936. He is one of the Conservative town councillors, is he not?—I do not know his politics. I wish to keep clear from political considerations.

Mr. *Brooks.*

1937. You will remember that it is your own suggestion that those persons have been appointed from political motives?—No; I say on account of their relationships.

1938. He is a storekeeper, you say?—Yes.

1939. Any other?—Your water bailiff is a son of another town councillor, Mr. Murphy.

1940. Are you sure about that?—I think so.

1941. That is not so; can you say if the town clerk has any relatives in the corporation?—The present town clerk has told you himself that he was the agent of the Liberal Registration Society before he was appointed. He was succeeded in the office of Liberal Registration Agent by an accomplished gentleman, Mr. McSheehy, and that gentleman has now succeeded to the place of law agent to the corporation. There are two in succession taken from that office.

1942. Had they any kinsfolk of position in the corporation?—Not that I know of.

1943. Then

Mr. M'Evoy.

12 May 1876.

Mr. *Brooks*—continued.

1943. Then they have not been elected on account of any kinship?—No; not on account of any kinship.

1944. Mr. Boyle, the Secretary of the Public Health Committee, do you know if he has any connection in the corporation?—He is a gentleman I think a good deal about; he is an efficient officer, and perfectly competent.

1945. The city treasurer?—The city treasurer is a very respectable gentleman too.

1946. Has he any kinsfolk in the corporation?—Not that I know of.

1947. Mr. Grice, the deputy town clerk?—No, I do not think he has.

1948. Mr. Andrews, the engineer, do you know if he has any relative in the corporation?—There is another engineer of the name of McCan, who is the son of an alderman.

1949. I am talking of gentlemen who hold the responsible offices of the corporation. Mr. Neville, the city engineer, do you know if he has any relation in the corporation?—No, I do not think that he is related to any of the body; I have not one word to say against any of those gentlemen. I think I myself, if I were a member of the Town Council, and I was asked by a brother town councillor to vote for a relative of his, I would feel myself in a very awkward position to refuse him, and I would rather have it that the appointment was outside of my body altogether, and let the best man get it, than be obliged to say "No" to a brother town councillor.

1950. The most recent appointment has been that of secretary to No. 1 Committee, which you will undertake to say, probably, is an office hardly second to any in the Corporation?—Yes, that is an important office.

1951. Do you know whether that appointment was made with or without reference to political opinions, or to considerations of private friendship?—If it is Mr. Beveridge that you allude to, I saw a letter in the "Freeman's Journal" a day or two after his appointment, in which one of the candidates, Mr. Dwyer, stated that he, Mr. Beveridge, was a relative of Lord O'Hagan's, and that it was the interference in some way of ecclesiastical authority that defeated Mr. Dwyer, and appointed Mr. Beveridge, or something to that effect.

1952. Will you favour the Committee with an answer as to your own knowledge or your own belief?—I would not be at all surprised if some clergyman or other thought fit to ask the members of the corporation as a personal favour to vote for a relative of Lord O'Hagan, and I think they would hardly like to refuse him.

1953. What do you say as to the personal fitness of Mr. Beveridge?—I have heard that he is a very efficient officer.

1954. With regard to Cole-alley, Cole-alley, I think, is at the west end of the town, near to Coombe?—Yes.

1955. The inhabitants of the City of Dublin are moving, are they not, from the west end to the neighbourhood of Fitzwilliam-square, and the other part of the town?—Yes, the tendency is towards Rathmines and Kingstown, and that way.

1956. Many of the houses in which these poor people live were formerly the mansions of manufacturers?—Yes, they were.

1957. And the owners of the houses in that district, I suppose, would get higher rents if they could?—Of course they would get the highest rents that they could.

1958. I think you said they were inhabited by a very poor population, and that the houses were of so little value that it was hardly possible to collect the rates?—That is not my statement; it is a statement of the Collector General in his report.

1959. You think it is true, do you?—I am quite sure it is true.

1960. The factories which formerly existed there, the woollen and cabinet manufactories of that district, have ceased to work, have they not?—Yes; it is the declining part of the city.

1961. And a large number of the houses are not only unoccupied but are dismantled and are being removed from the ground?—Yes, they are.

1962. Do you know if any officers of the Corporation take any part in politics?—I think not; I never heard that they did.

1963. Neither in securing the election of candidates or otherwise?—There was some rumour of interference at the last election by the town clerk. I saw something in the "Freeman's Journal," I think, about his interfering, but I do not know whether it is true or not.

1964. Was that signed by any person or not?—I do not know.

Mr. *Butt*.

1965. Do you believe everything that you see in the "Freeman's Journal"?—I do not; I believe very little of it.

Mr. *Brooks*.

1966. Are you aware that there is in Dublin a company called the Industrial Dwellings Company?—Yes.

1967. And that they have, at considerable expense, erected dwellings for the poor in the neighbourhood of Cole-alley?—No; I think that their operations are rather limited; they have only dealt with very few houses, I believe.

1968. However, there is such a company who have erected such dwellings?—Yes.

1969. Do you know whether their efforts have been of so successful a kind as to prompt them to engage in further undertakings?—I think their last report shows that they have not been very successful financially.

1970. Do you know whether they have paid any dividends?—I only looked at the report some time ago, but if my memory is correct they were not able to pay a dividend last time, or a very small one, if any.

1971. Then success in that direction has not followed the efforts of the company?—There are many reasons for that; we should not take an isolated case of that kind; according to English experiences you must open up a large district and take a whole locality into a general scheme for improvement; for instance, the Mayor of Birmingham stated, the other day, that unless the Local Government Board allowed them in Birmingham to take down a district which was not strictly within the operation of the Act, it would be unprofitable to carry out the Act: that is, unless they were allowed to take in some houses that were not strictly within the operation of the Act; the operation could not be carried to a large district.

1972. With regard to the efforts hitherto made in

Mr. M'Evoy.

12 May 1876.

Mr. *Brooks*—continued.

in Dublin, I understand you to say that they have not been remunerative or successful?—In that particular instance they have not: but I would not be taken to say that that conveys anything against the carrying out in an efficient and thorough way of the Artizans Dwellings Act.

1973. With regard to the Markets Bill, can you inform the Committee whether the corporation have made any efforts to have the markets scheme transferred to the corporation?—I do not know anything about their efforts.

1974. Do you know, as a matter of fact, that they have come before the Committee of the House of Lords, and have obtained the power?—They opposed the Bill, I believe.

1975. Do you know as a fact that they have come before the Committee of the House of Lords, and that they have obtained power to take over the markets?—No, I do not think that they could do such a thing as that.

1976. As a matter of fact they have done so, but is there any want of market shops or market districts in Dublin?—There is a great want of public markets in Dublin.

1977. I mean of market shops, such as we have in London?—Yes, a very great want.

1978. Are you aware that there are no public markets in London?—I know that they exist in large towns in England to the great public advantage, and that they are much wanted in Dublin.

1979. Is there not a system in Dublin of buying in district markets, butchers, greengrocers, confectioners, chandlers, and so forth, being centred round one spot, like, say, Merrion-street or Baggot-street, or Moore-street, the same as it is in London?—There is no retail public market in London that I am aware of. I think it would be very well if they had one.

1980. Is not the system in Dublin exactly the same as that in London?—I have never seen the whole of London or anything like it, but I do not know any places in London where meat is sold so horribly bad as Bull-alley, and that part where so much evil could be inflicted upon the poorer classes in selling diseased meat and so on, as in such places as that, Bull-alley and those places are really very bad. I do not know of anything in London like it.

1981. With regard to the auditor of the corporation, can you inform the Committee if that auditor was appointed on the application of the corporation?—No; there were a number of people, I was one of them myself, who pressed the application of the principle on the Government, and we succeeded, and then the corporation said that they did not object to it.

1982. Did the corporation apply to the Government?—They did, after the Act passed; they did not apply for the passage of the Act, but when the Act passed they succeeded in getting Lord Hartington to postpone putting the Act into operation.

1983. Was there any use in applying for an auditor before the Act was passed?—I mean that they did not ask the Government to pass such an Act to provide for an auditor, and when the Act did pass they succeeded with Lord Hartington in getting the operation of the Act suspended for a year; I myself had to get a Member in the House to put a question to Lord Hartington why was the Act not put into operation in the City of Dublin.

Mr. *Brooks*—continued.

1984. It was your belief that Lord Hartington assented to its being deferred whilst he was Chief Secretary?—Yes, it was.

1985. At whose request?—It was at the request of the corporation.

1986. It was with the consent of Lord Hartington, was it not?—Yes, it could not have been done without. The Local Government Board had appointed an auditor; the corporation intervened, and I believe a deputation went to Lord Hartington, and succeeded in getting the auditor withdrawn for a year.

1987. Did the corporation afterwards apply for the appointment of an auditor?—I never heard that they did. I know what I had to do myself. I had to get a Member to put the question to Lord Hartington, why the Act was not put in force in the City of Dublin, and Lord Hartington stated in reply that it would be put in force next year, or the next time that the accounts were to be audited.

1988. Then you do not know whether or no the appointment of the auditor was on the application of the corporation?—I should think not. I think that they appeared rather unwilling to be put under the operation of the Act.

1989. I think I understood you to say that many merchants and professional men who rent offices in commercial buildings, and I suppose also in Leinster Chambers, claim to be excluded from the list of the Collector General in order to avoid the duties of jurors?—Of course it might operate in that way, and that would be a reason for their not liking to claim to be rated; but there was the other reason that I mentioned, that they would be pretty sure to have their valuation increased.

1990. Did not I understand you to say that it operated in that direction?—It did, along with the other; but I suggested that whether they liked it or not they should be rated and put upon the register.

1991. With regard to the French donation; that was given, I think, at the time of the famine and great distress in Paris; do you remember what was the occasion of that donation?—I think it was for the relief of the French wounded after the war or during the war. I think there were subscriptions got up.

1992. Do you know whether the corporations of English towns, including London, subscribed?—You cannot go beyond London; London can do what it likes, being an unreformed corporation.

1993. Do you know whether there were subscriptions got up in the English and Scotch towns?—No public funds were used; no rates were used in any town, but merchants and others did subscribe most liberally out of their own private pockets.

1994. Do you recollect the amount of the sum which was contributed by the City of Paris to the poor of Dublin at the time of the famine?—I have no recollection; I subscribed myself to the French fund, and to the principle of subscribing to it I have not the slightest objection, but I contend that the rates collected for lighting, cleansing, and so on, should be strictly kept to the one purpose for which they were collected, and no other.

1995. Will you inform the Committee whether we did in Dublin accept from the Municipality of

Mr. M'Evoy.

12 May 1876.

Mr. *Brooks*—continued.

of Paris a contribution at the time when our people were at their sorest need?—Very likely you did; I do not know anything about the fact; of course if they offered a subscription you would be very glad to get it from them.

1996. Do you remember the debates in the corporation when this suggestion for sending a sum of money to the poor in Paris was mooted?—I do not recollect anything about their discussions; I remember the fact that money was voted, and that it was never disallowed, and that if such a thing was done at the present time it would be disallowed, and in consequence nobody thinks of doing such a thing.

1997. Do you know, of your own knowledge, that the reasons given by the members of the corporation for sending the money to Paris was that it was a slight recognition of the large sum that was contributed by the French people and the Paris people to our people at the time when they were in distress?—I do not know; I do not object at all to the principle; it is a very proper thing, and I subscribed to it myself.

1998. You mentioned the Bray and Enniskerry Railway; do you remember the state of alarm in which the people of that district were when a little leak was discovered in the reservoir?—I do.

1999. Can you tell how much it cost to repair that leak?—It cost a large sum; I forget the precise amount.

2000. Could you inform the Committee if the opposition of the corporation to the carrying of that railway along the line of the main from the reservoir at Vartry to Dublin was the reason for their objecting to that railway scheme?—If there was anything objectionable, this main, I suppose, was laid in the road, and the railway bridge, I suppose, was to pass over it; I cannot see why, if the corporation had anything to object to in the plans, or anything of that sort, a simple letter from the law agent of the corporation to the promoters of the Bill would not have set matters to rights. I believe the promoters of the Railway Bill would not have been such fools as to have the corporation of Dublin come in to oppose their Bill if they were told we want some little protection there about that pipe. They would have gladly put in anything that would have efficiently protected that pipe if they had been only asked, but the system at that time was to lodge petitions against every Bill, without giving the promoters the slightest chance or opportunity of removing anything that might be objectionable in the Bill. The resolution was to oppose all the Bills that would be introduced for Dublin in any Session. I have seen such resolutions; I do know well that in the case of some Bills, without reading them, or apparently knowing anything about them, the corporation would pass such sweeping resolutions as that to oppose all Bills relating to Dublin.

2001. Can you inform the Committee of the object of the last Bill which was promoted by the corporation in Parliament?—If you will tell me what it was; there are so many Bills that I cannot recollect.

2002. How many Bills have they promoted in the last three years?—I think that the Main Drainage Bill was their last. They had another Bill last year.

2003. The last Bill promoted by the corporation was for bringing the adjacent townships under rating for their extra supply of water?—Yes, I know it well.

2004. Was that Bill not indispensable for the citizens of Dublin?—It is a useful Bill, no doubt, but I believe that it has never been carried out. They have got their Bill, but they have never got a shilling, I think, from any of those townships for extra water.

2005. Would you be surprised to hear that we are in receipt of a sum exceeding 2,000 *l.*?—It is certainly not in the last account that I have seen; I have not seen your last account, and my impression is that none of the township people have paid anything for water in excess; my impression is that the Bill has been passed, but you have got nothing under it as yet.

2006. Are the board of guardians also dissatisfied with the mode of collection by the Collector General?—I have seen resolutions passed by them.

2007. In the newspaper, do you mean?—Yes.

2008. Could you give any information to the Committee upon that subject, excepting what you have seen in the newspapers?—I cannot add anything to what I have already stated.

2009. Why is it that ratepayers like yourself, whom I am sure we would be very glad to see in the corporation, and the gentlemen of standing that you desiderate, do not approach the corporation?—There are many reasons; one of them is that people engaged very largely in business have not time to devote to municipal affairs, and they do not seek the office very much. Then there is the other reason, that if they got into the corporation they might find themselves turned out again on some political issue; that would place them in this humiliating position that they should either profess views that they did not believe in, or that they should speak what they believe, and be turned out at the next election, and it is not surprising that gentlemen of high standing should rather decline to be placed in that equivocal and disagreeable position.

2010. Do you think that it is the duty of the citizens of Dublin to take an interest in municipal affairs?—I do think it is the duty of men of wealth to take an interest in the local affairs. I do not at all defend the general apathy that is displayed by that class.

Dr. *Ward*.

2011. Do I understand you to say that you ascribe the loss in the collection of rates partly to the inefficiency of the Collector General's department?—I simply give you the facts, and I rather leave the Committee to draw their own conclusions. I do not like to say anything about inefficiency when I do not know it from my own personal knowledge.

2012. If I understand you, you found that statement upon the Report of the Collector General's office printed last year?—Yes, I say at once, this is a disgraceful Report to issue from any public department.

2013. You recollect pointing out errors in it, in a communication to "Saunders' News-Letter"?—Yes.

2014. Immediately after you wrote, or the next day, did not a letter appear from the printer, stating that those errors were printer's errors, and did he not immediately publish a corrected report?—Yes, as an advertisement.

2015. Did they pay for it?—I do not know who

Mr. M'Evoy.

18 May 1876.

Dr. Ward—continued.

who paid for it. I do not think that the Collector General, or his officer should have issued such a document as that without reading and correcting the proofs. They should not have left it to the printer to send out.

2016. The printer states distinctly that the errors were not the Collector General's, but were accidental errors of the printer?—I say, that before it was issued it should have been corrected by somebody in the office.

2017. You spoke, did you not, of the increase of the cost of the office?—Yes, it has increased very much.

2018. Are you aware that no increase can take place without the approbation of the Lord Lieutenant?—Yes, I am aware of that with regard to salaries, and I think that it is a very objectionable state of things.

2019. Can the salaries be increased without the approbation of the Lord Lieutenant?—They cannot; and I say that it is an objectionable state of things, that the Lord Lieutenant instead of the people who represent the ratepayers, should have anything to say to those increased salaries that are paid by the ratepayers of Dublin.

2020. Are you aware that the cost of collection at present does not exceed what the Legislature thought a fair sum for collection?—The words of the Act are, that it shall not exceed 6 *d.* in the pound, but it does not enact that he must expend 6 *d.*; that was the outside limit assigned to him.

2021. But they put that as a fair sum, did they not? I may mention my experience in Kingstown. We have a small rate of only 3 *s.* in the pound to collect, and we get it collected for 4 *d.* in the pound, and here is a large rate of 8 *s.* collected at 6 *d.* There is as much trouble in collecting a 3 *s.* rate as an 8 *s.* rate, and we get the 3 *s.* rate collected for 4 *d.* I think 6 *d.* is too much for collecting an 8 *s.* rate.

2022. In the case of Kingstown, are not the 3 *s.* ratepayers persons that can be more easily got at for the payment of the rate than in the case of the ratepayers of Dublin; there are not such purlieus there as there are in Dublin?—There is a good deal of lower class property in Kingstown; but you will notice the great difference in the amount of collection, 3 *s.* and 8 *s.*; there is a very wide difference, and it ought to be easier to collect their 8 *s.* rate at 4 *d.* commission than to collect our 3 *s.* rate at 4 *d.*

2023. Whilst you object to this cost, you would revive two sets of collectors and officers?—No, I would not revive them; that would not be at all necessary. If you broke up the office you might transfer some of the officers to the Poor-law guardians, and some of them to the Corporation, without any necessity whatever for increasing their number.

2024. With regard to Commercial-buildings, is it not the case that some time ago most of the persons rated there, having offices in the place, were on the burgess roll?—I do not know that; I only speak for the last burgess roll that I have seen.

2025. Are you aware that they themselves applied to be taken off?—I did not know that.

Mr. *Gibson.*

2026. Are you quite sure that you are not in error in saying that the assent of the Lord Lieutenant is necessary to any increase in the salaries of the officers of the corporation?—I have not the Act before me, and therefore I cannot say.

Mr *Gibson*—continued.

2027. I will read you this passage, and then you will see whether you adhere to that opinion. It is the 94th section of the Municipal Corporation Act, the 3 & 4 Vict. c. 108, which states, "That no appointment of any office, other than such as shall usually have been appointed in such borough, shall be made until a statement in writing shall have been submitted by the council to the Lord Lieutenant describing the nature and proposed tenure of the office about to be created and the reasons for creating it, and also the salary proposed to be paid to the officer when appointed." Does not that indicate that the consent is only necessary to the original salary, leaving the corporation unfettered as to their discretion about increasing it afterwards, as was also stated by the town clerk in his evidence?—That, perhaps, is correct. I was under the impression that the Lord Lieutenant had full control over the salaries of the officers.

Dr. *Ward.*

2028. With regard to the collection of rates, are you aware that the South Dublin Union passed a resolution asking the Lord Lieutenant to hold an investigation; that an investigation was held, and that as the result of that investigation it was stated that there were no grounds for complaint?—I do not know that.

Mr. *Gibson.*

2029. Have you already expressed to any honourable Member your views about giving the cumulative vote to electors?—No, I have not.

2030. Have you considered that question?—I have considered that point, and I think it would be very desirable, in the existing state of things in Ireland, to give the cumulative vote. It would give all classes and religious denominations their share in the representation; and it would do more than that, if a really good man consented to stand for a seat in the town council anywhere, such a man would be sure to have cumulated on him a large number of votes of moderate men, who would look upon him quite apart from political motives.

Mr. *Collins.*

2031. I think you stated that, in your opinion, houses in Ireland valued under 4 *l.* a year were not fit for human habitation?—I would not go to that length. I merely quoted what I found in these official returns, that it is thought in carrying out the Artisans Dwellings Act, that the improved dwellings that would be established, provided with all the necessary sanitary requirements, could not be let to tenants at less than 2 *s.* a week per single room; and from that I reasoned that it is a fair limit to fix about 4 *l.* for the franchise.

2032. I think you will like to correct a statement that you made when you were being examined by one of the members of the Committee, in which you gave it as your opinion that houses valued under 4 *l.* a year were not fit for human habitation; and in answer to a question from the honourable Member for Limerick, you said that you applied that observation to all the towns in Ireland, which struck me as being a very strong expression of opinion?—I confined it to the large towns

Mr. *M'Evoy.*

19 May 1876.

Mr. *Collins*—continued.

towns that I proposed that franchise for. I am speaking altogether now of towns of 10,000 population and upwards, to whom it might be desirable to entrust full sanitary and highway powers: that in those towns, I think, the instances would be very rare of houses alone, without any garden or anything else attached to them, but taken as houses that would be only 4 *l.* valuation if they were in that proper sanitary condition which now-a-days is thought desirable that houses should be in.

2033. You would correct your evidence, would you not, by saying that you would like to apply that observation to towns having 10,000 inhabitants?—Yes. I thought I had sufficiently conveyed that impression.

2034. Do you know about what are the average earnings of artisans and working men throughout Ireland?—I do not quite understand whether the honourable Member's question applies to skilled or unskilled artisans, because they vary very much.

2035. Say the artisan class; the carpenters and stonemasons, and so on?—They range from 30 *s.* up to 40 *s.* a week.

2036. Do you think that it would be as much as that throughout the country?—Perhaps 40 *s.* would be rather high; it would be about 30 *s.*, I should say. In Dublin and Belfast it would be a higher rate of wages than in the small country towns.

2037. You think that in Dublin the rate of wages would be about 30 *s.*?—Yes, about 30 *s.* and upwards.

2038. Throughout the rest of Ireland, generally speaking, do you happen to have such information as would enable you to give an opinion upon that subject?—No, I have not; but I would imagine that wages would be something less than in Dublin and Belfast.

2039. Would they be 20 *s.* a week, do you suppose, throughout the year?—I think that a good carpenter would hardly work for 20 *s.* a week anywhere. I think he would leave the district.

2040. That would be 3 *s.* 4 *d.* a day?—Yes; and I think that a good carpenter would not stop in the country at 20 *s.* a week.

2041. With regard to the working classes that you have referred to; the labouring classes in towns; what would be about their average earnings per week?—The labouring classes, I would say, would earn about 15 *s.* a week.

2042. Would that be throughout the whole country?—No, I believe it would be too high; I believe that 12 *s.* in some places is all that they get in the small towns.

2043. In the case of a man earning wages of about 12 *s.* a week, do you think that 2 *s.* a week would be a fair standard house rent for a man of that kind to pay; would it be too much or too little?—That would depend upon his circumstances; if he had a family I would say that it would be too much.

2044. Generally speaking, do you suppose that the working classes in Ireland on an average in the small towns pay 2 *s.* a week for house rent?—I think not in the small towns.

2045. How much less than 2 *s.* do they pay?—I should think about 1 *s.* 6 *d.* would be about the rent.

2046. Then it would be under the standard that you would take for house rent for a working man to whom you suggest the franchise ought to be given?—The class I speak of would be in the small towns; I would not meddle with small towns at all; I would leave them as they are now under the Towns Improvement Act, where you would have wages so low as 12 *s.* a week, and rents so low. I do not think that there would be any public interest served in giving that class the franchise; they are not a very intelligent class, and I do not think there would be any great advantage to the public.

Mr. *Collins*—continued.

2047. Then, according to your opinion, the men of that class, the working class in small towns in Ireland, ought to be deprived of the franchise which they enjoy at present?—No, they do not enjoy it; I do not meddle with their present franchise. Their present franchise is 4 *l.* Under the Towns Improvement Act any man occupying a house of 4 *l.* has a vote; I would not meddle with them, I would deprive them of nothing. But if you lower the franchise down to every house, even if it were only 5 *s.* or 1 *l.* valuation, I think you would find in many of those towns that the agricultural labourers just fringing the town would control the real town. The people in the centre of the town, the real town, would be outvoted, and controlled by people who were not, properly speaking, townspeople at all.

2048. In your opinion, a person ought to be limited to serve on one corporate board only?—Yes, within the same municipality.

2049. Would that, generally speaking, work well, do you think?—There might be cases where it would be very desirable to have a very active man on two boards, but I think, as a general rule, by bringing in a larger number of people in the locality to be acting on those boards, and not having a few men taking on themselves all the places, would be for the public good.

2050. Does not it happen at times that the experience which a man acquires from sitting on one board may aid him very considerably in bringing greater efficiency to another board, to enable him to perform the duties of it?—I think those are exceptions; I mean those very clever men who give themselves up altogether to the discharge of those duties. But the majority are men of very medium acquirements, and I do not think their being on several boards is the slightest advantage to the public, whilst it keeps out others that would be as good, and perhaps might be better.

2051. Your own experience leads you to believe that they should be limited?—Yes, they should be limited, certainly; I believe there is a little vanity in being a member of a number of boards.

Sir *Arthur Guinness.*

2052. You were asked some questions on the subject of the opposition to the Vartry scheme; what do you think were the principal causes of the opposition to that scheme; was not this one, that the canal scheme was the cheapest, and considered by many to be equally effective?—The opposition to the Corporation Bill of 1860, who brought in a Bill the year before for taking in water from a place called Coyford, on the River Liffey, now that I recollect it, led to the appointment of a Royal Commission, and to the adoption of the Vartry scheme, so that that opposition at all events was useful.

2053. What was the estimated cost of that Vartry

Mr. M'Evoy.

12 May 1876.

Sir *Arthur Guinness*—continued.

Vartry scheme? — The estimated cost was 300,000 *l.*

2054. Are you aware what it really did cost? —I think that it cost something like 600,000 *l.* in round numbers.

2055. Would you approve of a very strict audit of the Collector General's accounts?—Yes, I think that they should be audited.

2056. Can you give any reason for the great increase of arrears of late years since 1861?—According to Master Fitzgibbon's letter it is that he was not allowed to make the collector's account, for why they struck off this or that person in the returns of rates uncollected on any given property; he was not allowed to do that; and he ascribes to that the falling off in vigilance and efficiency of the collectors in collecting the rates.

2057. Was he allowed to do that in former years?—He did it in one year in 1861, as he states in this letter; and he says that the consequence was that the collection that year was 4,000 *l.* over the average of the ten years before.

2058. Do you know anything about the management of the borough estates?—Yes; I have got some figures here on the subject. It has often been said that the present corporation's embarrassments arose from the load of debt put upon them by their predecessors; that is not, I think, in accordance with the fact; I have here the report of the Corporation itself on their own finances, and according to this I find that the old corporation in 1841 had a debenture debt and a pipe water debt amounting altogether to 292,723 *l.*; the account of 1874 shows that these items now are 286,200 *l.*, showing that in the space of 33 years 6,500 *l.* only was paid off; they also paid off, or continued the payments under a tontine created by the old corporation, which was extinguished shortly after the new corporation came into office; then I find that at that time there was handed over to them by the old corporation a rental of 15,016 *l.*, according to the return of Sir J. R. James; that was the property which they got from the old corporation, and they have had several leases falling in since then, and yet the rental of last year was only 17,800 *l.*

2059. Is that the gross or the net rental?—That is the gross rental; you have to take off that the interest and other charges. Then I find in connection with the borough fund slippage and anchorage dues; in 1863 those dues were 200 *l.* more than they are at the present time, although everybody knows that the trade at the port of Dublin has considerably increased in that interval.

2060. Do you know how leases and lettings are made and valued?—I do not know how that is done.

2061. Is there any Government officer in connection with that?—Yes; they must obtain the sanction of the Treasury to the disposal of any of the property.

2062. Have you ever heard it proposed to pay off the debenture debt by selling some of the estates, and thus save the cost of management?—Yes, I believe that that has been proposed by their own law agent, Mr. Morgan.

2063. What do you think of that?—I think it commends itself to common sense.

2064. What is the feeling in Dublin, mistaken or otherwise, as to the action of the corporation as the sanitary authority?—The feeling is very general that it has neglected its duties. Some time ago an application was made to them to carry out a system of nuisance removal. If you look at the accounts for Manchester and Birmingham you will see considerable sums expended in both those corporations in carrying out a system of removing the house refuse and ashes from the population, a sanitary improvement of the very highest character. The Dublin Corporation have refused to carry that out. They have instituted a system that works very indifferently, if I may judge by an instance related to me by a gentleman not very long ago, Mr. Webb, a well-known gentleman in Dublin politics. He applied to have his ash-pits and matters removed by the corporation, and they sent persons to do it; he says that he had to watch them at the work; that he had to go to the city hall first to make a deposit before they would come to him; and, then, when the work was done, he had to go there again to get whatever was due to him, and that he had to pay three or four visits to the corporation before the matter was adjusted.

2065. Is that a case which was stated in the papers?—Yes, he published a letter in the newspaper. In Birmingham and Manchester and those great towns, all that is done by the corporation, and in London too. They had powers under the Artizans Dwellings Act of 1868 to have dealt very largely with the poorer class of property in Dublin, and they have not used those powers.

2066. Do not you think that they have had sufficient reason for not using those powers up to the present?—Of course I am subject to correction, but I think they could have done a good deal under that Act, not in clearing away districts, but in having houses put in repair, and taking houses down in some instances. I think that the Act gives them power to do a good deal of useful work.

2067. Are you aware what is the present state of the Improvement Rate Fund?—It appears to be very much in debt; they are unable to meet the charges upon it.

2068. To whom is it in debt?—It is in debt to various creditors; for instance, the gas company; I find that they are not able to pay them every quarter, and their contractors are not getting their money. One gentleman told me that he had been two years looking after his debt before the corporation could be got to pay him.

Mr. *Butt.*

2069. What is the name of that person?—Mr. Boyd, of Mary-street.

Sir *Arthur Guinness.*

2070. Are you aware whether there is any system of paying one account from another; that is to say, if there is a surplus in one paying it to another?—Yes; they were doing that until they were checked by the auditor; the auditor has now checked it to a very considerable extent.

2071. In the case of accounts in which there was a surplus, has he obliged that surplus to be refunded to the credit of those accounts again?—Yes, I think in some instances he has been able to do that. By the way in which it was conducted formerly, there was no money in the improvement fund, to pay back the sums drawn from another account.

2072. Do

Mr. M'Evoy.

12 May 1876.

Sir *Arthur Guinness*—continued.

2072. Do you think that that is a proper and desirable way of managing those accounts?—Of course, they should keep their accounts better, and pay only out of particular rates, what is chargeable to those rates.

2073. In what way would you propose that the corporation should obtain a sufficient income for keeping the streets in better repair?—I think that they could effect a good many reforms; they have too large a staff of officers for one thing. I find that in the years between 1863 and 1875, the amount of salaries had grown from 10,000 *l.* to 15,000 *l.* in round numbers, and there is a very general feeling that there is not sufficient superintendence over the workmen; in fact, if there had been a more efficient superintendence over the workmen they could get more work from them in street-cleaning, paving, and so on, and it would be better if a number of things that they now spend money on were stopped. I find that in 1848 the total taxation for improvement purposes under one of those old boards of sewage was only 1 *s.* 7 *d.* The corporation got a 2 *s.* improvement rate, and a sewage rate of 4 *d.*; that gave them 9 *d.* beyond the old system. Then instead of making use of the old officers, they dismissed them all and got in a new staff, putting at once upon the citizens a pension list of about 6,000 *l.*; a most extraordinary pension list.

Mr. *Gibson.*

2074. Are many of those pensions still payable?—About 3,000 *l.* odd are still payable.

Mr. *Collins.*

2075. In what year was that done?—Part was done in 1842. They got rid of all their old officers, and pensioned them off, and then when another reform took place in 1849, they got rid of another lot of officers, and by the result of that they put 6,000 *l.*, amounting to 3 *d.* in the pound, upon the citizens.

Mr. *Bruen.*

2076. Do you mean to say that all the officers in 1849 were superannuated?—All superannuated; here is a list in this return.

2077. Do you mean that they were superannuated in 1849, having been appointed anew in 1842?—No. What I wished to say was this: the old corporation officers of 1841 were all got rid of, and a new lot of persons came in; but at that time the corporation had nothing to do with the paving and lighting; there were boards for those purposes. They got all those powers transferred to them in 1849, and they did the same thing again in 1849 with the officers of those old boards; they pensioned them off, and with the result that the two pension lists came to 5,500 *l.* I do not think that there is a parallel in England, Ireland, or Scotland, for such a list of pensions as that.

Sir *Arthur Guinness.*

2078. Did the Wide Street Commissioners effect very great improvements in Dublin?—They did.

2079. Are you aware that their powers have been vested in their corporation?—They have been all vested in them.

2780. Have they done anything with those powers?—They have done nothing since this Wide Street Commission ceased to exist in the way of widening the streets.

Mr. *J. P. Corry.*

2781. Am I to understand that the markets in Dublin are not in the hands of the corporation?—They have the cattle markets, but the retail markets are not.

2082. And that a private Bill is being promoted just now for increasing the market accommodation in Dublin?—For establishing a new market in Dublin.

Mr. *Gibson.*

2083. Are not the hay and straw markets also under the corporation?—Yes; they have the hay and straw markets; but as to a general retail market there is no such thing in Dublin; but it is proposed now to establish one, and it is a private company that is doing it.

Mr. *J. P. Corry.*

2084. And of course that will be upon private property, not upon corporation property?—It will, of course; it is a private enterprise.

2085. Have the corporation property on which markets could be established in the city?—I do not think they have.

2086. Could you give the Committee any reason why the corporation wished the public auditors deferred for a year?—I think that the French item was in the accounts of that year; that is my recollection.

2087. Do you say that joint occupiers are not rated?—Yes; joint occupiers are rated; but I spoke of houses sub-let, and cut up into sub-tenements.

2088. You are of opinion that the valuation of property in Dublin at present is not in a very desirable state?—Yes; I think that it would be very desirable that it should be received as a part of the general revision of the country. We should not have the benefit of it in Dublin alone, because we should then have our contribution to the income tax increased, whilst our neighbours in the country would not have theirs, and I think it certainly should include all.

Mr. *Bruen.*

2089. With regard to the corporate estate, you said that in 1842 the rental of it was 15,016 *l.*, and that now it is 17,800 *l.*; is it your opinion that if the most had been made of that property it ought to be more than that?—I think it should be. I think that when they had got that Baldoyle property out of lease, they might have made more of it.

2090. When did that Baldoyle property fall out of lease?—I think it fell in hand in the year 1867, and I think that they might have made more of that and some other property too.

2091. In 1867 was that provision in force that leases or lettings of the corporate estate must obtain the sanction of the Treasury?—Yes, but they get a Private Bill passed giving them some additional powers for letting land. In the Baldoyle case there was an Act passed at their instance, which I do not think was for the benefit of the citizens.

2092. Are you aware whether this sanction of the Treasury extends not only to the amount of rent inserted in the new letting, but also to the persons to whom the property is let?—I do not know exactly the working of it. I know that they are generally under the control of the Treasury.

2093. Is there a prospect of a large increase being made to the corporate estate within a short time?—

Mr. M'Evoy.

12 May 1876.

Mr. *Bruen*—continued.

time?—Yes, there is. Some property will be out of lease in a very short time, in the best part of Dublin, in the neighbourhood of Grafton-street and thereabouts.

2094. Do you know whether the corporation in letting those estates adopt a system of offering them to the highest bidder?—Certainly they did not in the Baldoyle case. I think they thought that they should not do it, and I believe that they got powers not to do it.

Mr. *Butt.*

2095. You spoke about a burthen being put upon the citizens by the superannuation of officers: can you tell me whether the first time that the reformed corporation came into power was in 1841?—Yes, I believe it was.

2096. It would be in 1841 that the pensions were given to the officers who were dismissed or removed?—Yes.

2097. I find from the corporation that in 1842 from the pipe water, there was granted about 1,700 *l.*?—I should think there was more; it was on the borough fund, I think.

2098. And the pipe water too?—Yes. In 1842 it was 913 *l.* and 1,500 *l.*

Mr. *Butt*—continued.

2099. It was something over 2,400 *l.* in 1842?—Yes.

2100. In 1831 or 1852, what was it?—In 1852 they added 1,042 *l.* to the borough fund, 242 *l.* to the pipe water, to the improvement fund 3,426 *l.*, and to the grand jury fund 922 *l.*

2101. That was of course done by the council, which you said had been formed by Mr. Codd, of the most eminent merchants of the city?—Yes, it was done by that corporation.

2102. So that, I suppose, we may say that the superannuations made in 1852 were done with the consent of such men as the late Sir Benjamin Guinness, Mr. Codd, and other gentlemen who then took the management of the corporation? Yes, and they amounted to 6,872 *l.*

2103. Do you not think that they probably exercised their discretion in changing their officers, without reference to political feelings?—I think they got the idea in their heads that it would be desirable to drive away the whole lot and get an entirely new set.

2104. At all events, it was done by a body who enjoyed the confidence of all classes?—Yes.

Tuesday, 16th May 1876.

MEMBERS PRESENT:

Sir Michael Hicks Beach.	Mr. Gibson.
Mr. Brooks.	Sir Arthur Guinness.
Mr. Bruen.	Mr. Kavanagh.
Mr. Butt.	Mr. Murphy.
Mr. Collins.	Mr. O'Shaughnessy.
Mr. J. P. Corry.	Dr. Ward.

SIR MICHAEL HICKS BEACH, BART., IN THE CHAIR.

Mr. JOHN ADYE CURRAN, called in; and Examined.

Mr. *Curran.*

16 May 1876.

Mr. Butt.

2105. I BELIEVE you hold the office of one of the Assessors to the Lord Mayor at the revision of the burgess roll?—I do.

2106. Who is your brother assessor?—Mr. James M. Hyndman.

2107. We know that one assessor is selected by each party in the city?—Yes, the burgesses can only vote for one, and the result of that is, that one representing each party is elected.

2108. How long have you been assessor?—I was elected in the year 1869, but I revised the list for 1868 in consequence of my father's illness at the time.

2109. Was your father assessor before you?—He was.

2110. Have you as assessor had any opportunity of judging of the state of the franchise?—I have had considerable opportunity.

2111. In the first place, let me ask you as to the objections; are you able to form an opinion whether any or many qualified persons are struck off the roll by objections?—My experience has been that a considerable number of burgesses who ought to be on the list are annually struck off, in consequence of the service of objections, and of their not coming up to prove their claim.

2112. Is it the rule that everyone must appear upon an objection being served?—The rule, or rather the law is, that a party who is on the burgess roll of the last year and objected to this year, has what is called a *primâ facie* case, and the objector must prove his case against him; but a party who appears for the first time this year, or who was not on the roll last year, notwithstanding the fact that he appears on the list, must prove his claim or his case if he is objected to.

2113. That is the same as the law with regard to Parliamentary voters?—Yes.

2114. Could you form anything like an estimate of how many persons you think have been struck off the roll, the municipal burgess roll, who, you had any reason to think, were qualified?—I looked over my book for the last year, and I found that there were 1,979 objections served on both sides, and of those, about 520 came up and proved their cases, that about 50 came up and did not prove their cases, and were struck off on their own evidence, and that there was a balance of about 1,400 names, and about 400 of those at the outside would be parties objected to in consequence of death and double entries. The result would leave about 1,000 names who went off the list last year in consequence of the service of objections.

Mr. Butt—continued.

2115. Altogether last year, that was the number on the list to whom objections could be served?—I am allowing for double entries, and I say that about 1,000 were struck off in consequence of objections. As a rule the objectors do not object to a party who may be on the roll of last year, and under the Act of Parliament we are bound to strike out all double entries, whether objected to or not.

Chairman.

2116. You have no supplemental list?—No.

2117. What was the total number on the burgess roll to whom those 1,799 objections were made?—There is a burgess list and a burgess roll; the burgess list is larger than the roll; the burgess list is made up of all the burgesses' names returned by the town clerk; the burgess roll is that list after it has been revised by us; at present I cannot say the number on the burgess list of the names returned by the town clerk, but the number of parties objected to was 1,979. That number of objections were served; I may say that in a great number of those cases where parties came up to prove their claim, the moment they appeared in court the objector on either side withdrew the objection, merely waiting for the purpose of seeing whether or not the party would turn up to prove his claim.

2118. Have

Mr. *Curran*.

16 May 1876.

Mr. Butt.

2118. Have you in the course of the revision any opportunity of judging as to the rating, whether any parties are excluded from the franchise by the law of rating in Dublin?—Up to about the year 1874 all parties who were rated at 8 *l.* and under were excluded.

2119. When you say that up to 1874 all persons rated under 8 *l.* a year were excluded, would you just explain to the Committee what you mean by that?—The Municipal Corporations Act, Ireland, the 12th and 13th of Victoria, chapter 85, makes it necessary that all parties claiming the franchise should be rated; but a section of that Act says, that if the party be liable to be rated it is the same as if he were rated, and that he is entitled to be on the burgess roll if he be liable to be rated, and has paid all the rates. The 3rd section of that Act, dealing with the qualification of a burgess, says, "And be it enacted, That every male person of full age who on the last day of August in any year, shall have occupied any house, warehouse, counting-house, or shop within such borough of Dublin during that year, and the whole of each of the two preceding years, and also during the time of such occupation shall have been an inhabitant householder within the said borough, or within seven statute miles of the said borough of Dublin, shall, if duly enrolled in that year according to the provisions of the said recited Acts, be a burgess of such borough, and member of the body corporate of the mayor, aldermen, and burgesses of such borough: Provided always, that no such person shall be so enrolled in any year from and after the present year, unless he shall have been rated in respect of such premises." Then the 6th section says, "And in order to provide against any person being prevented from being enrolled as a burgess by reason of any misnomer, or inaccurate, or insufficient description in a rate of the person occupying any such premises as hereinbefore mentioned, or by reason of any inaccurate description of the premises so occupied, be it therefore declared and enacted, That where any person shall have occupied such premises as in this Act are mentioned for the time hereinbefore mentioned next previous to the last day of August in any year, being the person liable to be rated for such premises, shall have been *bonâ fide* called upon in respect to such premises to pay, and shall have *bonâ fide* paid on or before the last day of August in such year, all rates for the relief of the poor made in respect of such premises which he would be required to pay in order to be enrolled as a burgess for the borough of Dublin, if he had been named in each rate as the occupier of such premises, such person shall be considered as having been rated to the relief of the poor, and paid all such rates in respect of such premises within the meaning of the said recited Act and this Act." Having regard to that section in Dublin one would imagine that every householder would be entitled to be rated, but the Collection of Rates Act makes the immediate lessor liable in cases of rating at or under 8 *l.*, and takes away the liability from an occupier of premises rated at or under 8 *l.* Strange to say, an occupier under 8 *l.* would not have been, in the words of this section, the person liable to be rated. All occupiers, therefore, at or under 8 *l.* were struck off the rate book, and we were obliged to strike them off the roll.

Mr. Butt—continued.

2120. I presume you are speaking of a person not rated coming up to claim?—Yes, a person not rated coming up to claim without having been put on the rate.

2121. Up to 1874, as I understand, the rule of leaving out was not to admit such person under the 6th section if he was under 8 *l.*, because he was not liable to be rated?—Yes, that was the rule.

2122. Would the same thing apply to weekly or monthly tenants?—Yes, certainly.

2123. As a rule, the 6th clause, in fact, had no effect as to persons under 8 *l.* and as to weekly and monthly tenants?—Precisely so.

2124. From your experience, can you tell the Committee whether in Dublin many persons who occupy houses as tenants for two or three months continue to occupy the same for any length of time?—I have found a very considerable number coming up before me as assessor year after year. In fact, as a rule, the first question that is put to all small men coming up, by the one side or the other, is, "How do you hold?"

2125. I understand you to say that a great many persons who hold their houses for three months, or as weekly or monthly tenants, continue to live in them for years without leaving?—Yes, certainly.

2126. And who would therefore be entitled to the municipal franchise?—Yes, except for the Collection of Rates Act.

2127. You were going to say that a change was made in 1874; what was that change?—The Representation of the People Act was passed in 1868, but no change was made in the course pursued at the revision court until the year 1874, when my attention was called to the 19th section of the 31 & 32 Vict. c. 49, the Act of 1868.

2128. Will you read that section?—"From and after the passing of this Act, section 116 of the said Act of the 13th and 14th years of the reign of Her present Majesty, chapter 69, and so far as regards poor rate in respect of lands, tenements, and hereditaments of which the net annual value shall be more than 4 *l.*, the 63rd section of the Act of the 12th and 13th years of the reign of Her present Majesty, chapter 91, shall be, and the same are hereby repealed." That is the only portion to which I need refer now. I came to the conclusion that as there was only one rating for municipal and Parliamentary purposes, viz., the poor-law rating, the municipal taxes being struck at so much in the pound upon the poor-law valuation, the moment a man becomes rated to the poor-law he becomes thereupon liable for the taxes, because you will see that that makes the party liable to pay the whole rate.

2129. Being the person liable to be rated?—Yes; there is only one rate, and that is the poor-law rating. Then I held, contrary to the opinion of my brother assessor, that that repealed the 63rd section of the Collection of Rates Act; and I, from that time forward, always admitted parties who were liable to be rated between 4 *l.* and 8 *l.*, and who came up and claimed the franchise. I told the collector-general to rate them, and I think he did rate them after that.

2130. Would you say that you admitted the claims of a considerable number of persons?—Yes.

2131. Did

Mr. *Butt*—continued.

2131. Did your brother assessor agree with you?—No, there was a difference between us.

2132. Did the Lord Mayor decide the point?—Yes; the Lord Mayor decided with me.

2133. That was in 1874; did the same thing occur in the last revision, in 1875?—In the last revision we went further still, because not only did we admit (I mean the majority of the court, because Mr. Hyndman, all through, was opposed to my view of the matter), but we not only admitted all who were rated between 4 *l.* and 8 *l.*, but we also admitted all who claimed, notwithstanding the fact that they were admitted to be weekly or monthly tenants; because I came to the conclusion that this 63rd section, so far as the poor-rate was concerned, repealed *in toto* the 63rd section of the Collection of Rates Act. I admit, and did admit last year, all the weekly and monthly tenants; but the Collector General will not rate them for me.

2134. Did the Lord Mayor, in 1875, as well as the Lord Mayor in 1874, agree with you in that?—He did.

2135. So that there are two years' decisions of the court?—Yes.

2136. There is an opportunity, is there not, of questioning the opinion of the court by an appeal to the Court of Queen's Bench?—There is, and they threatened that, but they never did so.

2137. Has an appeal ever been taken against that decision of yours?—No. I may say that the present Judge Barry's opinion was produced, to show that we could not rate weekly and monthly tenants; but I did not act upon that, and I think Judge Warren's opinion was the same as Judge Barry's. Judge Barry grounded his decision upon the fact that it would be folly to rate weekly and monthly tenants to a yearly rate. Now, I say that it is not folly to rate a weekly or monthly tenant where it is a rate made once a year. The Act of Parliament obliges the Collector General to rate three-monthly tenants and half-yearly tenants, and it would be just as much folly to rate half-yearly tenants to a yearly rate, as to rate monthly tenants to a yearly rate.

2138. Are you practically aware that the Collector General does not rate weekly or monthly tenants, or persons under 8 *l.*?—I am practically aware of that, because he refused me when I asked him. He does not rate weekly or monthly tenants. I think under Judge Barry's direction he has made two columns for ratings under 8 *l.*, and rated them merely for Poor Law purposes. I think that Judge Barry gives those directions, but the reason that I did not agree with him was that there is no such thing as double rating; you cannot rate a man for any municipal purposes without rating him *in toto*, and you cannot rate a man for Parliamentary purposes without rating him *in toto*, and making him thereby liable to municipal taxes.

2139. Is this then the state of things: if a weekly or a monthly tenant claiming to be rated paid his rates, is he not put upon the rate then?—No.

2140. Then a weekly or a monthly tenant cannot by any means get on the rates?—No.

2141. Are you sure of that?—I am; the Collector General has always stated so; he refuses, even though they tender the rates, to rate weekly or monthly tenants under 8 *l.*

2142. Can you tell me, from what you have seen of the Revision Court, whether a weekly or monthly tenant claiming to be rated, and tendering all the rates due, could get upon the rate?—No; I am able to say that he cannot, and why I know it is this: outside altogether what I know to be the Collector General's course of procedure, I know it. Supposing one year a man gets on the burgess roll as a weekly tenant, the next year he would not appear on the burgess roll because he had not been rated, but he would have to claim again. In 1874 one or two weekly tenants were admitted. I recollect that the next year, 1875, in the place of appearing on the burgess roll, which they would have done had they been rated, they had to claim a second time to be put on the burgess roll, and they were put on.

Mr. *Curran*

16 May 1876.

Chairman.

2143. How do you reconcile that with the section of the Collection of Rates Act which enables any person to claim to be rated, and then provides that he shall be rated; I think that it is Section 66; will you be good enough to read it?—"And be it enacted that the occupiers of any rateable property may demand to be assessed for the same, and to pay the rates in respect thereof made by the said bodies politic or corporate, boards, commissioners, or persons, and applotted, levied, and collected under the authority of this Act; and the Collector General shall assess every such occupier, so long as he duly pays the said rates, anything hereinbefore contained notwithstanding." I have nothing to do with this Act, but the view which the Collector General takes of it is, that those are parties who would be liable to be rated. If you are left off you may claim to be rated. Supposing that you go into premises, and another party was rated before you, or the landlord was rated, if they were premises for which you would be liable to be rated you may claim by sending in your name, and would be put upon the burgess roll, but that does not apply to parties who are not liable at all to be rated.

Mr. *Butt.*

2144. Do you mean to say that in point of fact that section of the Act is not applied in Dublin to weekly or monthly tenants?—Certainly it is not.

2145. Are you able to form any opinion of what proportion of houses in Dublin are held by persons as weekly or monthly tenants?—The Collector General furnished, I think, that report here; I could not say of my own knowledge.

2146. As to rating for three years, you are aware, of course, that under the Act the rating must be continuous?—Yes.

2147. How is that continuous rating interpreted?—It is interpreted in this way: if a party comes before us between the 20th of October and the 10th of November, he must have been in occupation of the rated premises, or of other premises, if it is a removal claim, for two years and eight months previous to the 31st of August of that year. I may say that Dublin is the only city in the United Empire at the present moment that requires an occupation of two years and eight months for the franchise. At the time that the 3 & 4 Vict. was passed for Ireland one year was sufficient for Dublin, but at that time the English Municipal Corporations Act required in England

Mr. *Curran.*

18 May 1876.

Mr. *Butt*—continued.

England two years and eight months, and then the 12 & 13 Vict. was passed assimilating the law for Dublin to that in England, and subsequently by the 32 & 33 Vict. c. 55, the English time was reduced from two years and eight months to one year, leaving Dublin the only city in the empire requiring an occupation franchise of two years and eight months.

2148. In your opinion are there any persons excluded from the franchise who have been substantially occupiers of premises in Dublin for three years by some little break in their occupation?—There are.

2149. Will you explain that to the Committee?—Parties frequently in two years and eight months move from one set of premises to another, and during the time of their removal they may be out of possession for say a week or so, and according to the strict letter of the law that break knocks them off the burgess roll.

2150. So that, according to the strict letter of the law, a person leaving a house, and within a week, say, going into another house, would lose his franchise by the fact that there was an interval of a week?—Yes, he would; that is the strict letter of the law.

2151. When you say the strict letter of the law, is that carried out?—So far as I am concerned, I never did strike off a party who only went out of occupation for a week. There was one case in which that very matter was tried in the Court of Queen's Bench. Mr. Fry was objected to on the ground that he left his possession for a few days. I refused to strike him off, and the case was brought to the Court of Queen's Bench.

2152. Did the majority of the Court admit him?—Yes, the Lord Mayor decided with me.

2153. Who was Lord Mayor?—Lord Mayor Purdon.

2154. We know him to be on what is called the Conservative side in politics?—Yes; he had some common sense, and he decided with me. It was brought to the Court of Queen's Bench, and the Queen's Bench upheld our decision.

Mr. *Gibson.*

2155. I believe his seat in the town council depended upon it?—Yes, but that did not alter the law.

Mr. *Butt.*

2156. Mr. Fry is one of our first mercantile men in Dublin, is he not?—Yes.

2157. If the Lord Mayor had decided it in the same way as your brother assessor, Mr. Fry would have lost his place in the council?—He would.

2158. You, I suppose, considered that you were at liberty to act upon the maxim *de minimis non curat lex*, and you held that it was continuous occupation technically, and that you might overlook a slight break?—I have always acted upon that principle.

2159. How was that decided in the Queen's Bench?—It was there twice; they first brought it into the Queen's Bench immediately after the burgess roll had been signed, and they applied too soon, because they brought the burgess roll of the preceding year to have his name struck out; they were defeated there. It was decided that I was right.

Mr. *Butt*—continued.

2160. How many days was Mr. Fry out of possession?—I think some three or four.

2161. Is that case reported in the Irish books?—No.

2162. But you know of your own knowledge that the decision of the Revision Court, such as you describe, was upheld?—Yes.

2163. Have you heard it suggested that 50 *l.* rating should be the qualification for a member of the town council?—I have.

2164. What effect, in your opinion, would fixing the qualification at 50 *l.* have?—I think it is much too high. If the matter were ascertained now you would find that the majority of the town council, or the corporation, have premises rated at over 50 *l.*, but it would exclude practically a considerable number of very respectable parties in Dublin from the corporation. A great number of houses in Dublin are rated at from 30 *l.* and 40 *l.* up to 50 *l.* Mr. McEvoy's own shop in Baggot-street is only rated at 40 *l.*, and his stores are rated at 6 *l.*, so that a 50 *l.* qualification would exclude him.

2165. He has been chairman of the commissioners, has he not?—I am speaking of rateable property in his possession in the city.

2166. That would disqualify him from being a member of the town council?—Yes.

2167. Speaking of those which have been called the better streets in Dublin, where persons of our own class live, should you say that there were many houses in which very respectable persons live that are rated under 50 *l.*?—There are a great many in the private streets of Dublin; my house is rated, I think, at 50 *l.*, that is in Gardiner's-place.

2168. Gardiner's place is considered a very good street, is it not?—It is.

2169. Do you know Mr. Norwood, who is a town councillor?—I do.

2170. And a very active and useful one, I believe?—Yes.

2171. He has considerable property in Dublin, has he not?—He has.

2172. Do you happen to know what he is rated?—He lives in Nelson-street, and the Directory will tell you in a moment his rating; the rating of Mr. Norwood's house is 42 *l.*, so that that would exclude Mr. Norwood.

2173. That would be a great loss to the corporation?—That is according to the way that you look at it.

Chairman.

2174. Are you aware whether the law as to continuity of occupation is the same in England as in Ireland?—It is.

2175. Are you aware whether it is strictly construed in revising the burgess lists in England?—I should not have the slightest objection in construing it very strictly if it were only as a lawyer.

2176. Are you aware whether it is strictly construed in revising the burgess lists in England?—I am not; but if it is not it ought to be.

Dr. *Ward.*

2177. You have large experience with regard to the number on the roll; do you think that the number is at all adequate to the population and the rating of Dublin?—I am sure it is not; the number

Dr. *Ward*—continued.

number on the burgess roll this year is something over 5,000.

2178. Looking at other cities as you see them in England, what would be a fair proportion in Dublin?—If we had the time limited as it is in England now to a year, and other fair amendments brought in, the burgess roll would, I am satisfied, go very nearly to 15,000.

2179. To what do you ascribe the difference, is it to the three years' clause?—I ascribe it to many reasons, first of all to the three years' clause, and then I ascribe it to the wholesale service of those objections. Then there are many amendments in the Act which have been incorporated in the English Act, but which are required to be, but have not been, incorporated in the Irish ones.

2180. Are you aware that there are many cases where both parties, the Conservatives and the Liberals, object to a man being placed on the burgess roll?—I am.

2181. When they do not know the political views of the person objected to?—Yes, exactly. I know several instances of that.

2182. Are there several people of position who will not bother themselves to go into the court on that account?—Parties object; for instance, merchants, in Dublin, who would not claim because as partners they object to go up there and undergo cross-examination as to the nature of their partnership dealings, and as to whether they are partners or not. They will not go up. I have known several very large merchants refuse to go up to prove their case in consequence of having to give evidence as to their private dealing between themselves and their partners.

Mr. *Gibson*.

2183. At present I believe the assessors are elected by popular election?—They are.

2184. Of course that might occur, after a contest, and after canvassing with other popular arrangements?—I was elected after a contest.

2185. But you have never been subjected yourself to a contest since, I believe?—No.

2186. There is to be, in theory, an election every year, is there not?—There is an election every year.

2187. There has been, you are aware, a contest; Mr. Hyndman has had to undergo a contest, I believe, in the last few years?—No, that is the contest I speak of. If one seat is contested both are contested. That was in the year 1870, the year after I was first appointed.

2188. Do you think it satisfactory that a man discharging judicial functions should be elected by popular suffrage?—Under some circumstances no, but I would not take a privilege from the people unless it had been found that they had abused that right. In this instance, up to my appointment, I will not say anything about my own, but up to my appointment all the appointments by the people to that office have been unexceptional. You had Judge Hayes, you had Mr. Coffey, the Queen's Counsel, and my father, and Mr. Mullins, and Mr. Hyndman, and in all those cases they elected very competent men, and unless the people have abused that right I do not see why it should be taken from them.

2189. On account of their not having abused the right you do not see any objection in it?—I

Mr. *Gibson*—continued.

Mr. *Curran*

16 May 1876.

certainly should object to having an annual election, because an annual election leaves parties open to be threatened with opposition if you do not decide one way or the other. That I think is the fault of the system of having an annual election, and, therefore, I would extend it to three years.

2190. You are aware, of course, that as a rule the Lord Mayor of Dublin is a leading merchant?—Yes.

2191. Apart from the question of his having any acquaintance with law, do you think it is an unsound principle that would allow a casting vote in a legal question to the Lord Mayor?—As a rule, the Lord Mayors act upon one principle, and that is to decide whichever way the franchise leads, that is if one of the assessors is in favour of letting on a burgess the Lord Mayor decides with him. But I certainly think myself it is a faulty system that the Lord Mayor, who is not a legal man, should be allowed to have the casting vote as between two barristers; but at the same time it must be remembered that there is another fault in the system, and that is, that the two assessors need not be barristers; they may be grocers under the law as at present. I think the law requires some change in that respect; I should have, say, one man appointed, as is appointed now, by the burgesses generally, and that man to be a barrister, say, of over 10 years' standing, and if it was thought well to let that appointment be subject to the veto of the Lord Lieutenant.

2192. You would have some such court as that which is for the revision of Parliamentary voters, and have two revising barristers appointed?—Two or one.

2193. I believe that the pay of the revising barrister for the municipal franchise is not very high?—It is 10 guineas the first day and five guineas every other day, as far as that is concerned; it is about 100 guineas a year.

2194. How many days does it take for the revision?—It takes from the 20th of October to the 10th of November, and we frequently sit at night as the time is too short to revise the list; and if the burgess franchise is extended that time will have to be extended, because even with the small burgess roll that we have now, we have frequently to sit at night for the purpose of finishing.

2195. Is there a statutory limit for the days of your sitting?—Yes, from the 20th of October to the 10th of November inclusive.

2196. Is there no power of extending the time, no matter what the exigencies may be?—No, we have to sit at night.

2197. At present if a man has got on the list he remains there, and the *primâ facie* presumption is that he is entitled to be there?—Yes, if he were on the burgess roll of the preceding year.

2198. If a person objects to him, the service of objection avails nothing, he must give proof?—Quite so.

2199. Is it not also a fact, that on the first appearance of a person's name upon the burgess roll, which corresponds to the appearance of the name on the supplemental list for Parliamentary purposes, the mere service of objection will not avail, and that the person who objects must also appear?—The service of objection takes place first; then the party comes forward to prove the service

Mr. Curran.

16 May 1876.

Mr. *Gibson*—continued.

service of objection; the proof of that is his appearing. If you take that in connection with the subsequent portion of the section you will find that a party who was on the burgess roll last year has a *primâ facie* case to keep his name on the list, but the mere proof of service of objection by the party is his appearing in court; that is the only proof required for the purpose of sustaining the objection, because if proving the objection really threw upon him the onus of proving the facts of the objection there would be no necessity then for declaring the other party's *primâ facie* case.

2200. I believe both parties attend pretty closely to the municipal revision in Dublin?—They do.

2201. I suppose they give you a great deal of assistance in sustaining the parties' claims?—They give me very great assistance in striking off names on both sides, but very little in putting them on.

2202. Do I understand you to say, that your opinion about the law as at present is, that any person who wants to pay the rates is entitled to be rated, and you would put him on the burgess roll?—Yes.

2203. That is your opinion of the law?—Yes.

2204. That has been acted on for the last two years?—Yes.

2205. That has enabled you to put on all people who are rated between 4 *l.* and 8 *l.*?—Yes.

2206. Also I believe you now put on all who are rated between 4 *l.* and 8 *l.*, even occupiers within the words of the 63rd section of the Rating Act, people who occupy in monthly and weekly tenancies?—Yes, but they must keep up the claim every year; I do not know what the man who succeeds me may do if there be an assessor after me.

2207. But at present you have put on monthly and weekly tenants?—I have, to the horror of Mr. Hyndman, who is my colleague.

2208. At all events they claim to be on the list, and that has been affirmed for two years?—Yes.

2209. Had you given that opinion to the Collector General at the time?—Yes, but the Collector General will not act upon my opinion, because he says (I think it is quite right) that he will take Judge Barry's opinion in preference to mine.

2210. What break in the occupation do you think would interrupt the continuity as a legal proposition?—As a legal proposition, a single hour would do it.

2211. Where would you draw the line if you once admit that discretion; you would hardly do it for a year; would a fortnight be enough?—If the terms were so framed that all parties who came forward to claim should have been in occupation for 12 months only, they ought to prove one continuous occupation; but when you are dealing with an occupation of two years and eight months during which interval a party may be moving from one to two or three premises, it is very hard that a gentleman should lose his franchise because he is without occupation for one day.

2212. Mr. Fry's case was an extremely hard one, was it not, because he was only a few days out, and he remained rated all the time at a very high rate to the city of Dublin?—Yes. With respect to that matter of continuous occupation, I should not for a moment think of allowing a party to remain on the burgess roll unless I was perfectly assured from evidence before me that he had the intention of moving directly from one house to another, but that from some unforeseen circumstance in the case he was unable to do so directly. For instance, in Mr. Fry's case, the premises were being re-built, or something in that way, and he intended to move from the one to the other, but from some unforeseen circumstances he was out of them a few days. Under those circumstances I think if a party went direct from his house to lodgings for a week, and then went from his lodgings to another house, I certainly would strike him off.

2213. You consider that practically equitable, and taking a broad view, you think that the occupation of Mr. Fry was continuous?—Yes. If the thing is viewed strictly legally, I quite agree that the occupation should be continuous; I think it would be a very faulty system the other way.

Mr. *Brooks*.

2214. I think in Mr. Fry's case there was an attempt to strike Mr. Fry off the rate-book, and there was no ruling in the matter?—There was.

2215. There was no ruling in the matter; they did not strike him off?—They did not strike him off; I think the Court of Queen's Bench were satisfied upon the point that he was equitably there in continuous occupation, but from some unforeseen circumstance, his house being under repair, he was out for a few days.

Mr. *Gibson*.

2216. Mr. Fry held to the argument that it was practically continuous?—Yes.

2217. I believe you have also considered the effect in Ireland of the Towns Improvement Act, 1854, and also the effect on the small towns that are under local Acts?—I have.

2218. Are you aware that in the case of towns which have local Acts there is a power vested in the Local Government Board of making variations in the provisions of those Acts to suit the varying exigencies of the towns?—I am. By the Local Government Act, 34 & 35 Vict. c. 109, s. 5, the Act of 1871, by the Public Health Act, 1874, the 37 & 38 Vict. c. 93, s. 76, power is given to the Local Government Board to make Provisional Orders in the case of towns having local Acts, that is as to changing the hours of holding elections, or making other similar changes.

2219. Are you aware also that the great majority of the towns in Ireland are under the Act of 1854?—Yes.

2220. Many of them are very small towns, are they not, that could not go to the expense of getting private Acts without great inconvenience?—Quite so.

2221. Are you aware that in some of those towns under the Act of 1854, there is no power vested in the Local Government Board to make any changes whatever in any of the provisions of that Act?—Precisely so; it is a General Act.

2222. Have you any change to suggest in that subject?—The only suggestion that occurs to me is

Mr. *Gibson*—continued.

Mr. *Curran*.

16 May 1876.

is that as to the towns under the Act of 1854, that the Act shall be deemed to be a local Act for the purpose of the provisions of the 34 & 35 Vict., and of the 37 & 38 Vict.

2223. For instance, take Kingstown; Kingstown is now under a local Act, is it not?—Yes, they have the power to change, for instance, the day of voting there.

2224. Then the Local Government Board on an application from Kingstown can change the day of voting?—Yes; our small towns under the provisions of the Act of 1854 have no such power.

2225. I believe you have been professionally engaged in the controversy which has been going on in the two Courts in Dublin, the Court of Queen's Bench and the Court of Common Pleas, as to the power of the police to prosecute for drunkenness in towns that are under the Act of 1854. Will you state to the Committee what change in the law you think would be desirable upon that subject?—The question arose under the Towns Improvement Act, 17 & 18 Vict. c. 103, sections 72 and 92. The point occupied the Court of Queen's Bench some time last year, and the Court of Common Pleas the last two or three days.

2226. Without going through all the sections, are you aware that at present there is a difference of opinion among the judges as to whether the police have of themselves the power of prosecuting a drunken person under the Towns Improvement Act, 1854?—I am. Under the Towns Improvement Act to which I have referred, the commissioners were directed, in the name of their clerk, to sue for the recovery of all the penalties. Under that Act, in some of the townships the town clerk sued in his own name, or summoned the parties who were found drunk in the streets. Being the prosecutor under the section, he was entitled then to the entire of the fine. The Licensing Act of 1872 was then passed, and by Section 57 of the Act of 1872 that power was taken away from the towns commissioners, and the prosecutions were directed to be carried on, and the fines and penalties applied as under the Petty Sessions Act and the Fines Act, Ireland. In consequence of that the police have, in the large townships, summoned parties for being drunk, and the fines then went, one-third to the prosecutor, and the rest to the Crown. There was a debate in Parliament then as to this power having been taken away from the towns commissioners, and I think the Chairman took part in it. I remember reading "Hansard," and the result of all this was that the Licensing Act of 1874 was passed, and the 30th section of that Act says: "Wherever the 'Towns Improvement (Ireland) Act, 1854,' or any local Act incorporating the said Act in whole or in part, is in force in any town or place, any person empowered for the purposes of the said Act or of such local Act, to act as a justice of the peace within the boundaries of such town or place shall, notwithstanding anything in the principal Act to the contrary, have all and the same jurisdiction, power, and authority to hear and determine charges for offences committed within the boundaries of such town or place against section 12 of the principal Act" (that is for drunkenness), "as any justice of the peace having jurisdiction in that behalf, and may, for such purpose, sit alone or in his own court together with any justice or justices of the peace, according as the offence against the said section may be tried by one or by two or more justices, or any justice or justices in petty session of the peace. The penalty imposed by such justice or justices, or by the justices in petty sessions in every such town or place as aforesaid, and in every town in which the Act of the Session of the 9th year of the reign of King George the 4th, chapter 82, is in force for any such offence committed within the boundaries of such town or place, shall be enforced as penalties are by the Towns Improvement (Ireland) Act, 1854, or such local Act, or such Act of the 9th year of King George the 4th, chapter 82, respectively directed to be enforced, and shall be applied in manner prescribed by the Towns Improvement (Ireland) Act, 1854." The result of that was that it gave back to the towns commissioners the fines, or at least half the fines, but then a doubt arose as to whether or not they could, as they have been doing in some instances prior to the Act of 1872, summon in their own name, or whether it was the police who should summon in their name under the Petty Sessions Act, as directed by the Act of 1872. The matter came upon a case stated before the Court of Queen's Bench some time last term at the end of last year, and the Court of Queen's Bench decided that the police had no power whatever to interfere; it was the town clerk who should sue for all those penalties in his name as representing the town commissioners, under the Act of 1854. A case was then taken to the Court of Common Pleas, and the Court of Common Pleas decided the very opposite. Last week they decided that it was the police who should summon, and that they had the power to summon, and that one-half of the penalty should go to the commissioners and one-half to the prosecutors, that is the police, to be applied by them as the Fines Act (Ireland) directed.

2227. Assuming that there is any doubt as to the law, do you think that it would be a matter of public convenience to adopt the Common Pleas decision?—I think it would; I think that if the fines went one half to the commissioners, they ought to be very willing and satisfied to allow the police to prosecute, who are much better adapted for that sort of proceeding than the town clerk of the corporation, who has other duties to attend to.

2228. Were the Court of Queen's Bench unanimous?—No; Mr. Justice Fitzgerald decided according to the decision of the Court of Common Pleas.

2229. Were the Court of Common Pleas unanimous?—They were.

Mr. *Bruen*.

2230. Would you state how long a break in the occupation you would admit as being material in the continuousness of the occupancy?—I would not admit of any break unless I was satisfied that it was equitably a continuous occupation, and that it was by reason of some unforeseen occurrence at the time that the break took place; I should say that for a matter of two or three days I would not disfranchise a man who had been in continuous occupation for three years because an unforeseen circumstance happened

Mr. Curran.

16 May 1876.

Mr. *Bruen*—continued.

pened which made him leave his house for that time.

2231. Admitting all those conditions that you have mentioned, would you go beyond three days; would not you say a week?—I should not like to go beyond three days, because that would show that it was not equitably the same occupation.

2232. I think you said, in answer to the honourable and learned Member for Limerick, that the Collector General of Rates did not put on his list which he sends to you the weekly and monthly tenants, even if they claim and have paid their rates?—Yes, I say so.

2233. Have you read the evidence of the collector general for rates?—I have.

2234. Will you allow me to refer you to Question 335, in which the honourable and learned Member for Limerick is examining the collector general, and where he says "I will read to you Section 66 of the Collection of Rates Act, and then you will see what I mean." Then follows the cital of the section, and the Question is, "Suppose there were rates due on the premises when the man comes to claim to be rated, what would you do?" and the collector general's answer is, "Are you dealing with a weekly or monthly tenant, because it makes all the difference to my answer." Then the honourable Member asks, "I will take first the question of a weekly or monthly tenant, what does he tender?" and the answer is, "If he tenders all the poor rate that was due on the premises for the year, we would put him on." Is not that quite at variance with your understanding of what he does?—I think that must be a mistake of the collector general's, because I think earlier in his evidence you will find that he positively states that he would not rate a weekly or monthly tenant.

2235. Allow me to refer you to the very next Question and answer which the honourable and learned Member for Limerick asked him: "Did not you say that you would not put on a weekly or monthly tenant"? to which he replied, "If he pays the poor rate we would. The moment he pays it we would put him on; but we never have such a case; I do not think I have ever known a case of that kind to arise"?—I think you will find in his evidence that he corroborates me. He may have made that statement, but you will find that in the earlier portion he says what I say; that in no case would he rate a weekly or monthly tenant, because he acts upon the decision of Judge Barry, who tells him that he could not do it, because he would be rating him to a yearly rate; and that, acting upon the opinion of the present Judge Barry, he refuses to rate him.

2236. I will direct your attention to a Question still further on, No. 557, in which he was asked, "If they do not pay, do not you say that you rate them?" and his answer was, "If they are liable to be rated we rate them whether they pay or not, and even if we do not consider them to be liable to be rated, if they do pay we rate them." Considering that those answers were given to questions at the end of the collector general's examination, and that his attention was drawn to his previous answers, do you suppose that he would deliberately have made a misstatement?—I do not think that the collector general would deliberately make any misstatement, but what I do say is, that he may have laboured under a misapprehension. The reason that I am positive about this is, so far as my recollection can be positive, that when this matter of the weekly and monthly tenants came before us, I directed the collector general to rate them, and he produced then and there Judge Barry's opinion, and said "No; Judge Barry says that I am not to rate them, and I will not." I think you will find, if you will allow me to look at his evidence, that at Question 317, he was asked by the Chairman, "That refers to tenements above or below 8 *l.* in value; but you have also told us that the owners of all rateable property let to weekly or monthly tenants, or in separate apartments, are rated instead of the occupier? (*A.*) That is so. (*Q.*) Do you enter the names of the occupiers in the rate book in that case? (*A.*) No. (*Q.*) Why not? (*A.*) Because it would be absurd to rate weekly or monthly tenants to a yearly rate. (*Q.*) Does any question of franchise come in there? (*A.*) I am not aware of it. (*Q.*) At any rate, you do not consider yourself bound to enter their names? (*A.*) We have acted upon the advice of the present Judge Barry in not doing so. (*Q.*) You told us that you experienced great difficulty in obtaining the payment of rates from owners of that kind of property, but, I suppose, that there must be property of very considerable value in Dublin let to weekly or monthly tenants? (*A.*) There is, but there is a very considerable part of it paid for." That is what he says.

2237. Does not this appear to be the case, that the collector general does not put the names on the rate book until they pay or tender the rates, but if they do pay or tender the rates he does put them on?—I am not aware how that is; but I know as a fact, that there are no weekly tenants on the rate book. Then further on, in Question 338, he is asked, "But if he is not a yearly tenant, you do not rate him?" and he says, "We do not, and for the reason I gave the chief secretary. I quoted the exact words of Judge Barry, that it would be an absurdity to rate a weekly or monthly tenant to a yearly rate. He advised that we should not do so, and we do not do so, and see Question 386."

2238. Is not that quite consistent with the collector general's subsequent answers, that in making out the original list he does not put them on, but that if they claim to be rated, and tender the rates, he does, even though they may be weekly or monthly tenants?—I admit that it is perfectly consistent as a matter of fact; I am not so conversant, of course, with the duties of his office as I am with my own, but I am only acting upon information supplied to me by him in the Revision Court, because when parties who come up there and claim as weekly tenants, he refuses to rate them at all, although they might have paid taxes to qualify them. I am speaking of certain parties who come up, and are rejected because they are weekly tenants, and must be weekly tenants for whom rates have been paid, or who have paid them themselves.

2239. I think you stated that you had yourself made no change in respect of those weekly or monthly tenants until the year 1874?—Yes, not until 1874 or 1875.

2240. And then you made a change in consequence of a section in an Act of Parliament which was passed in 1868?—Yes.

2241. How

Mr. *Curran*.

16 May 1876.

Mr. *Brsen*—continued.

2241. How came it that in all those years, from 1868 to 1874, no change was made although the Act was in operation?—When I was elected first I found that the assessors had been acting as it were in a sort of groove for years past. There were a great many changes that I made in the law. When I say "I," I mean that the Lord Mayor decided with me. I did not bring them all into being at once. I did a little one year and a little another. I did not act upon the weekly or monthly tenants until the year after I acted upon the difficulty between 4 *l.* and 8 *l.*; I went for a decided change according to what I thought the law was. Another reason was this, that at the time I was first elected, I was a good deal younger than I am now, and I did not like, as a young man, to take upon myself to change the law that had been acted upon by others, and I also had regard to the opinion of Mr. Hyndman, who had been there for many years, and who of course was thoroughly conversant with the law. I did not like to take it upon myself. However, the more I thought upon the subject, the more I thought I was right, and then I went on from one matter to another.

2242. In acting as assessor, although you were aware of the change of the law in 1868, you did not propose any variation in the practice which was against the law until 1874?—So far as publicly doing it, I did not, but over and over again I suggested to my colleague, Mr. Hyndman, that I thought we were not carrying out the law, as the law intended that it should be carried out. But as he was opposed to it, I did not like to act. I could not look upon myself as infallible, and I could not but defer somewhat to the experience of a gentleman like Mr. Hyndman, who had been for so many years in the office. But there are a great many other amendments in that place which I should like to see carried out, besides what I have suggested.

2243. With regard to the 50 *l.* qualification I think you said the operation of the 50 *l.* qualification would be to disqualify a gentleman whose name was mentioned, Mr. M'Evoy?—Yes, taking the rating as I find it in the Directory.

2244. Will you take the Directory for 1876, page 1329, and look for 137 Baggot-street; what is the valuation of that house?—"John M'Evoy (this is the entry that I looked at), soap boiler, tallow chandler, and importer of composite candles, and 72, George-street, Lower Kingstown—factory 37 and 38, Boyne-street, 40 *l.*"

2245. Forty pound is the valuation of the house in Baggot-street; will you look at 38, Boyne-street?—In the Directory I looked at (that valuation has been increased since last year) it was 6 *l.* last year; it is 15 *l.* this year.

2246. You take your information altogether from the Directory?—Yes.

2247. You are therefore not aware, because it is not in the Directory, that within the municipality of Dublin Mr. M'Evoy holds other premises in Phinn's-lane, which are rated at 15 *l.*?—No; I only instanced that for the purpose of showing that Mr. M'Evoy would be qualified, so far as you could judge of him here, to be a town councillor, but still putting it on the value of his rating he would not be qualified.

2248. But, as a matter of fact, he would be qualified?—He is qualified this year; he was not qualified last year.

Mr. *Brsen*—continued.

2249. That is to say, supposing there were only two houses that be was rated to, he, in fact, being rated to three?—But I am not aware whether he holds the house in Phinn's-lane as occupier.

2250. Yes, as occupier?—I stated that the parties should be in occupation of the premises. I only took it from the Directory, and I found there that he was rated at 46 *l.* I did not know whether, in any part, he was qualified to be a corporator; but still he was under the value for those premises which I referred to.

Mr. *Kavanagh*.

2251. I think I understood you to say that the collector-general is supported in his action by Judge Barry's opinion?—Yes.

2252. And that you thought that you were supported in your action by the opinion which Judge Warren gave?—No; pardon me, he was supported by Judge Barry, and also by the opinion of Judge Warren; I was alone, so far as that goes; but I gave the matter the best consideration that I could, and that is the conclusion to which I came, that the repeal of the section was complete, so far as poor law purposes were concerned.

2253. You said that the burgess roll, which is now 5,000, would, if matters were as you thought right, be 15,000?—I am sure it would come very close to that, having regard to the very large population in Dublin, and having regard to the numbers whom I see disenfranchised every year, even taken the burgess roll as it is formed at present.

2254. I suppose you consider that a great increase in the burgess roll would have a considerable effect on the management of affairs?—I am only thinking now of the parties who ought to be entitled to have the franchise; what you mention is another matter; I do not think that it would make any material change with respect to the politics of the parties represented; I think that in the Conservative wards it would give an increased number of Conservatives, and in the Liberal wards, if I may so call them, it would give an increased number of Liberals.

2255. I was not thinking of politics at all, but in the general way in which affairs are managed by the Corporation of Dublin, would it produce any change in that?—I do not know, because it all depends upon what a person thinks of the present management of the Corporation of Dublin; a great many people in Dublin think that the management by the Corporation at the present moment is as well as it possibly could be, considering the money that they have at their command, and some people think that they could do better if they got in themselves.

2256. Of course you must found your opinion upon something, either that it is wrong to keep those 15,000 off, or that their being on would do some good?—My view of the matter is this, that I find Dublin an exception in the United Kingdom; that in other towns in the United Kingdom parties are required only to be in occupation, say for one year, whereas in Dublin they are required to be in occupation for two years and eight months; that must necessarily keep off the burgess roll a great many parties who are in occupation, say for 12 months, or for 18 months; and I say that those parties in Dublin

Mr. *Curran.*

16 May 1876.

Mr. *Kavanagh*—continued.

Dublin ought to have the franchise, and they have just as much a right to it as parties in Belfast, or in any large towns in Ireland, or Manchester or Liverpool in England, and others, and in that way it injuriously affects those parties who, I say, ought to be entitled to the franchise.

Mr. *J. P. Corry.*

2257. Do you know how many are on the burgess roll in Belfast?—I do not, but I have heard that it is larger than Dublin.

2258. Is the qualification higher in Belfast?—Belfast I know is under the 3rd and 4th of Victoria; the qualification in Belfast is residence of only one year and 10 *l.*, and, I may say, in the townships around Dublin, Pembroke, Blackrock, and Clontarf, the residence required there is only three months.

Mr. *Murphy.*

2259. As to the principle upon which the break of continuity was decided, you said that if a person left one house and there were only two or three days intervening before his going into another, you do not consider that such a break of continuity as that would disfranchise him?—Not if at the time he left one house he had a *bonâ fide* intention of at once removing or going into another; but if, from some unforeseen circumstances, he was unable to carry out that intention, I would not put the man off the burgess roll on that account.

2260. Your idea is this, that he must have made an inchoate contract for going into another house before he left the previous one?—Certainly.

2261. Although he may not be able to perform that contract for two or three days or a month for instance, it is the same thing, because the principle is easily reconcilable; if he has made a contract to go into the new house before he has left the old house any break that occurs in that would not be considered by you to invalidate his vote?—Not by me; I will give an instance which occurred recently. A gentleman was to leave a house on the 31st of August; he had made arrangements to go into the next house on the 1st of September, and he had made all arrangements with the two landlords to leave the one house, and to move his furniture to the other house. The landlord asked him to go out two or three days earlier, and he left at his request, leaving a few things in the house in order to keep up his qualification. But after he had left the one house the former tenant could not be got to leave the other house for three or four days after the 1st of September; and the result was that he was out of practical occupation, but I refused to strike that man off.

2262. You decided it to be a kind of constructive occupation?—Yes; it is only upon that principle that I would do so.

2263. Supposing a man *bonâ fide* leaves his house on the 31st of August, and supposing he has made no contract whatever to go into another house, but on the 2nd of September he has contracted, and has gone into another house, and only one day elapsed between his actual passing out of the previous premises, and his actual occupation of the new premises, would you consider that to be a break?—As a lawyer, sitting there, I should at once be obliged to strike him off; there is no doubt about that.

Mr. *Murphy*—continued.

2264. Do you think under those circumstances any remedial measures should be brought in to provide for such a case as that where there was an absolute break of but one or two days?—It would be very difficult to draw the line. I think if the qualification were one year, no one could complain of being required to be in continuous occupation during those 12 months; you should draw the line somewhere, but it would be very difficult to draw it in an Act of Parliament.

2265. Would it be, do you think, a proper thing to introduce, if necessary, a clause that a break not exceeding one month should not invalidate the qualification to vote, provided the party within the month had gone into a house of the same adequate value as the one he left?—I think it is better to leave it to the common sense of the man who has to try the matter, if he finds that there is that break, but there is a *bonâ fide* intention to go from one house to the other, interrupted by some unforeseen circumstances. It was not only according to the law that I retained those names on, but also according to what I thought the principle of common sense.

Mr. *Bruen.*

2266. So that you have attempted to remedy what you consider to be a defective law, by interpreting it according to what you consider common sense?—No, I beg your pardon. What I mean was this, that I came to the conclusion that I was acting up to the law by using a little common sense in deciding the matter.

2267. Still it was not the law?—It was the law. It was because I thought it was an equitable continuance that I left the parties on. In the case put by the honourable gentleman of the party leaving one day without any *bonâ fide* intention of going into a new house, and perhaps going in two days afterwards, I should find myself constrained as a lawyer to strike that man off.

Mr. *Gibson.*

2268. I suppose you considered Mr. Fry's intention and state of mind in making that small break?—Yes, I considered the fact that an unforeseen circumstance arose which prevented Mr. Fry acting upon what he intended, that is, having a continuous occupation, as in the case of that gentleman who was prevented by the former tenant refusing to leave the house, so that he could go into it.

Mr. *Butt.*

2269. With regard to the rating, are you aware that there are two provisions in force in the City of Dublin under which a person omitted from the rate may claim to be rated?—Yes.

2270. One of which is the 66th section of the Collection of Rates Act?—Yes.

2271. And that is this, "and be it enacted that the occupiers of any ratable property may demand to be assessed for the same, and to pay the rates in respect thereof, by the said bodies politic or corporate, Boards Commissioners, or persons, and applotted, levied and collected under the authority of this Act, and the collector general shall assess every such occupier so long as

Mr. *Curran.*

16 May 1876.

Mr. *Butt*—continued.

as he duly pays the said rates anything herein before contained notwithstanding"; you observe that that clause does not require a tender o rates?—I do.

2272. Therefore if that clause was put in force any person omitted from the rate claiming to be rated in the city of Dublin can do so without paying the rates?—Yes.

2273. Is it not to that clause that the collector general has applied the principle that he must be liable to be rated?—No, I think that there is a clause in the 12th & 13th of Victoria, under which he does that.

2274. I was going to call your attention to that clause later, but are you aware that to that clause which enables the occupier to claim to be rated without paying the rates, the collector general does apply the principle that he must be liable to be rated, and therefore he excludes from that clause weekly and monthly tenants?—Yes, that is my view of the way in which he acts.

2275. There is another clause in the Act for the reform of the Dublin Corporation which also occurs in all the Parliamentary Acts, Section 5 of the 12th & 13th of Victoria, chapter 85, which says, "It shall be lawful for any person occupying any house, warehouse, counting-house or shop, to claim to be rated to the relief of the poor in respect of such premises, whether the landlord shall or shall not be liable to be rated to the relief of the poor in respect thereof;" those words are not in the other Act?—No.

2276. "And upon such occupier so claiming and actually paying or tendering to the collector thereof, or to the person or persons entitled to receive the same, the full amount of the last made rate then payable in respect of such premises the guardians or other such persons charged with making any rate for the relief of the destitute poor which shall or ought to include such premises are hereby required to put the name of such occupier upon the rate for the time being, and in case any such guardians or other persons shall neglect or refuse so to do, such occupier shall, nevertheless for the purposes of the said recited Acts and this Act, be deemed to have been rated to the relief of the poor;" do you observe that in that Act the provision requires a tender of the rates?—Yes.

2277. And also that the claim, even if the party is refused to be rated, makes it equivalent to his being rated for the purposes of any franchise?—Yes.

2278. The latter provision is not in the first clause which I read to you?—It is not.

2279. Are you sure of the fact, that what is done in the collector general's office is to refuse to admit those persons under the 66th Section, and not that he said that he would not admit them under the other section if they tendered the rates?—I am not at all conversant with the duties of the collector general, or what he does in his office. I am only acting upon what the collector general told me; I do not know what the course of proceeding in his office is, or what his opinions upon such matters are; I have never consulted with him.

2280. Have you ever had a case before you in which a man had tendered his rates and had been refused to be rated?—No, because, as a matter of fact, very few of those claims for rating come before me at all; it is mainly the Parliamentary ones, and I very seldom have those before me at all.

2281. Did you ever hear of a case in which a man had tendered his rates and been refused to be rated?—No; I cannot give you any information of what the collector general thinks or does in his office except what he tells me himself.

Mr. *Brooks.*

2282. You said, as I understood you, that when you and your colleague do not concur with regard to the qualification of a claimant the Lord Mayor invariably rules with the assessor, whose politics are like his own?—No, I never said that; on the contrary, as a fact, I may say this much of different Lord Mayors, that very frequently a Conservative Lord Mayor has decided with me and the Liberal against me, according to the view that he might take of the matter.

2283. In Mr. Fry's case, the Lord Mayor and Mr. Fry do not sit on the same side in politics, I believe?—No; but do not take me as having said that. What I said was that they usually decided in favour of the franchise. Frequently it is a Conservative whom I am anxious to put on. Probably Mr. Hyndman may be against the claim, and the Lord Mayor, if he be a Liberal, decides for the Conservative, and *vice versâ* sometimes. I know the case of one Lord Mayor (it was Mr. Campbell), who frequently got himself the opinion of a learned gentleman, outside the assessors altogether, as to what he should do under the circumstances, and in several instances he acted upon his own opinion in the matter.

Mr. *Bruen.*

2284. Have you any suggestions to make to the Committee with regard to any amendment of the Act?—I just want to make one or two small amendments in the Act with respect to the qualification for the burgess roll. In the first place, I would beg to suggest that the residential clause is too confined, that is to say, with regard to the distance of seven miles, which was the original limit for residence in Dublin. At that time Kingstown was the principal suburban residence of the inhabitants; but now a great number of the inhabitants live between Kingstown and Bray, at Ballybrack, Killiney, and Dalkey, and all those places. I am sorry to say that I am obliged to strike off a vast number of merchants of the city of Dublin year after year, because they live outside the limit of seven miles. I think, having regard to the fact that so many Dublin people live out there, say within a distance of 12 miles, that the area of residence ought to be extended to such a distance as would include Bray; I think that would include Howth and Malahide, and all those towns about Dublin.

2285. Why should you confine it to that particular district; supposing a merchant were to live some 20 miles out of Dublin, and were to come in every day to his business, as we know many merchants do, should you say that that person should be disqualified from having the municipal franchise?—I say that in England he would be disqualified.

2286. I ask you whether you think such a man should be disqualified?—Yes, I do; because we must

Mr. *Curran*.

16 May 1876.

Mr. *Bruen*—continued.

must draw the line somewhere, and the question as to residence has always been insisted upon. In the report of the Commissioners in the year 1835, they reported against non-residence of burgesses in certain cities, and that was one of the charges that they made They say, "As to the structure and operation of these bodies, with reference to their component members, particular defects in the constitutions are noticed in the separate reports as they came under our observation; those which appear to us to prevail generally, and to influence most injuriously the condition of the corporations, are, first, the power of self-election in the governing bodies; secondly, the absolute control vested in these bodies over admission to the corporate franchise; thirdly, the dispensation with residence as a qualification in their members and officers." Therefore I would put some residential restriction on parties, because it may probably be in one instance that a man lives 20 miles, but very few merchants or traders of Dublin live 20 miles away. A great many do live at Bray, 12 miles away; but parties living 20 miles away would never come near the city of Dublin perhaps once in a month. I would make a man have some interest in the city in the way of residence, if he sought either to be a burgess, or to be a member of the corporate body.

Mr. *Collins*.

2287. Would you object to extending the distance to 15 miles?—There are two distances in England; there is one distance of 15 miles for corporators, and there is a separate distance for those entitled to be on the burgess roll; I think that the corporators have a 15-miles limit; but for parties who are to be burgesses. I think that the limit is smaller; you will find that in the Act.

Chairman.

2288. Is there any other point which you wish to mention?—Yes, with respect to succession; the 7th Section of 12 & 13 Vict., gives the court the power of putting on the burgess roll parties who claim by descent or marriage. That was copied from the English Municipal Act of 5 & 6 Will. 4, c. 76, but that section of the English Act was found to be inoperative in consequence of the concluding words of the section itself. I will just read the section: "Be it enacted, that where any house, warehouse, counting house or shop in the said borough, shall come to any person by descent, marriage, marriage settlement, devise, or promotion to any benefice or office, such person shall be entitled to reckon the occupancy and rating in respect of the occupancy thereof by the person from or by whom such house, warehouse, counting house or shop, shall have so come to him as his own occupancy, and rating conjointly with the time during which he shall have since occupied and been rated for the same, and shall be entitled to be enrolled a burgess in respect of such successive occupancy and rating, provided he shall be otherwise qualified as herein provided." The view which the courts took in England with respect to 5 & 6 Will. 4, which is exactly similar in words to our Act, was that those concluding words nullified the section, because "provided he shall be otherwise qualified," would require him to be

Chairman—continued.

an inhabitant householder, and the result was that they had to pass an Act in England, the 7th of Will. 4, and the 1st of Vict. c. 78, s. 6, to amend that section, which dispensed with the necessity in a case like that of proving household inhabitancy for the required period. But in passing the Act for Dublin, in copying the English 5 & 6 Will. 4, assimilating the law in Dublin to that which then existed in England, they gave us the section, without giving us the correction, so that the law in Dublin now is the same as it was in England before the amending Act of the 1st of Victoria.

Mr. *Murphy*.

2289. Then they left in the proviso?—Yes, they left in the proviso in that way. So far as I am concerned, I have always acted upon the opinion that these words should be otherwise limited, and refer to a male party not being an alien; but Mr. Hyndman, the other revising barrister, had held the opposite view, and if any improvement be made in the law I would suggest that the 1st of Vict. c. 78, should be incorporated in the new Act. Then there is just one other matter which I would mention with respect to the service of notice of objection. The service of notice of objection is under the 43rd section of the 3 & 4 Vict. c. 108. It directs the notices to be served upon the party or on the premises in respect of which he is rated. In many instances in Dublin I have found notices served, say, upon a person on the premises, and that leaves the door open to fraud, because you may serve a notice upon a party on the premises without knowing whether he knows or is part of the family of the party objected to, and the party objected to may never receive the notice. In many instances it is impossible to serve on the premises. In the case of non-personal service, it must be on the rated premises, and in many instances I have found that the party serving the objection had found it impossible to serve rated premises, such as stores which are constantly shut up, and matters of that description; and what I would suggest would be that the mode of serving should be assimilated to that of Parliamentary voters; that is to say, by post at the residence. Then with respect to the taxes, our Act requires that you should pay all the taxes which become due within six months of the 31st of August in the year before the 31st of August. In many instances the taxes are paid in Dublin by the landlords, and the landlords in some instances make it a rule, and in other cases they do it probably from habit; but they do not pay the taxes until some day subsequent to the 31st of August. In many cases the collectors do not call for the taxes until after the 31st of August. I would suggest that the party claiming should have a right when he served his claim, on the 1st of October, to be on the burgess roll, provided he has paid a certain proportion of the taxes previous to the 1st of October; and that a claimant who has found himself off the burgess list in consequence of any such mistake of the landlord, or of the collector, or of himself, should be able to be reinstated. Many instances of hardship occur where respectable merchants and traders have found, in consequence of the non-payment of taxes by the landlord, that they have been struck off, which they would have paid, because

Mr. *Curran.*

16 May 1876.

Mr. *Murphy*—continued.

cause they valued the municipal franchise. There is no notice similar to that given in the case of the Parliamentary franchise, and parties are not aware at what time they should pay their taxes. I think you must pay a quarter's taxes before the 31st of August, and if the party claiming paid half a year's taxes before the 1st of October as a sort of penalty on him, that would be the means of putting on a great number who are struck off the burgess roll year after year for non-payment of taxes. That would also be the means of collecting in a good deal of taxes, because parties would pay half a year's taxes where they found that they had been struck off the list in consequence of not having paid before the 31st of August.

Chairman.

2290. Would not that be met a good deal by some provision that notice should be given as in the case of the Parliamentary franchise?—That would in some respects meet it, but not altogether. It would be a very great improvement of the law, because for Parliamentary purposes the rate collector, if you go to the office and pay the poor rate, will take the poor rate from you without the other taxes; but there is no notice to the parties in Dublin to pay the rates before the 31st of August, excepting the agents on either side do it. The Liberal agent would be afraid to do it, because he might give notice to the Conservative if he gave public notice to come in and pay the taxes; and the Conservatives would not do it because they might be giving notice to the Liberals, and between the two the burgesses come to the ground.

Chairman—continued.

2291. Could not the town council under their present legal powers give notice?—I do not know; it would be better to make it their duty; I would not leave it within the discretion of any one, but would make it compulsory.

Mr. *Collins.*

2292. You stated that the person so applying should pay some portion of the rates?—Yes, the party is now put on the burgess roll if before the 31st of August he has paid a quarter's taxes, and I would let a party prove the claim and be entitled, if he paid before the 1st of October a half-year's taxes so as to be some penalty on him; and that will bring in a large amount of taxes.

Mr. *Butt.*

2293. Would not your suggestion be practically carried out if the test of payment of taxes was made to apply to the time of revision and not to any previous time?—It would. In some of the townships round Dublin, if you pay your taxes at the very time that you are voting, it is sufficient under the Act.

Mr. *Kavanagh.*

2294. Do you mean that in the polling booth you have a receipt of customs?—I was assessor at the election for the Pembroke Township Commissioners the last election, and in the polling booth, when the parties came in there was a table at which two tax collectors were sitting, and they received a considerable sum of money during the day for taxes.

Mr. Joseph T. Pim, called in; and Examined.

Mr. *Pim.*

Mr. *Bruen.*

2295. I think you are a member of a firm of merchants in Dublin under the title of Pim Brothers & Co., carrying on a very extensive business?—Yes.

2296. You have given a great deal of attention to the management of municipal affairs in Dublin, and also to the general question of municipal arrangements throughout the country?—Yes, rather to the question of municipal arrangements, than as to the precise mode in which things are now managed internally, within the corporations themselves.

2297. Taking the present condition of the municipal government in Ireland, apart from Dublin; just at the first, generally speaking, do you consider that that condition is unsatisfactory?—Yes, I think so.

2298. And in Dublin do you think it unsatisfactory?—Yes; I think, perhaps, it is more unsatisfactory in Dublin than in other places.

2299. Perhaps you will tell the Committee in what respects you consider that the state is unsatisfactory at present?—I think that chiefly owing to the present condition of the franchise; the character of the town council has been deteriorating since the last reform; that it has consequently been losing public confidence, and that it is felt by very many of those who are the largest ratepayers in the city that it does not satisfactorily perform its functions; and they are very desirous that there should be some change.

Mr. *Bruen*—continued.

2300. Can you specify some of its functions which you believe to be performed in an unsatisfactory manner?—It is generally felt that the streets are very badly paved, scavanged, and watered, and what I think is worse even than the large streets, is that the back streets, where the poorer classes live, are especially neglected; and I think that insufficient care is given to sanitary matters; I believe that there are in Dublin a considerable number of houses used as dwellings that are not fit for people to live in, and that there is not sufficient care and oversight exercised by the corporation of the dwellings in which the poorer classes live, and within the last year there have been three cases in which houses have fallen in Dublin. One of those was certainly not a house in one of the poorer streets, and not in itself a poor house; I believe that its fall was chiefly due to structural defects, owing to its having been altered some years ago, it was in Sackville-street. There were two houses that fell in George's-street, and one child was killed, and there was also a house that fell in one of the small streets of Dublin, a back lane. Then it is believed by a great many people that the financial affairs of the corporation are not

Mr. *Pim.*

16 May 1876.

Mr. *Bruen*—continued.

so well managed as they ought to be; people very often talk of jobbery, and there is a good deal of feeling of suspicion as to the way in which things are managed; I am not at all meaning to say that I am aware that there is real ground for that feeling of suspicion, I am only stating that the feeling of suspicion does exist. I believe that there are many members of the corporation who are very well fitted for their positions, and who are very anxious to do their duty thoroughly well in the position that they are in, but I am quite aware that there is also a very strong feeling that there are a number of men in the corporation who are not as well fitted for their position as members of the town council as they ought to be. There is a great feeling of want of confidence in the minds of those who are most heavily taxed in seeing the city funds in the hands of the present corporation. And the consequence of this want of confidence is, that whether rightly or wrongly almost every movement of the corporation involving much expenditure of money is vehemently opposed. The consequence of that is that at one end the corporation often neglect their duties and at the other end when they attempt to obtain fresh powers to improve matters they are opposed by the large ratepayers, and they are unable to obtain those increased powers because the ratepayers have not sufficient confidence in the corporation. The attendance of the members at the meetings of the town council is very irregular, and a quorum is, I believe I am correct in saying, very seldom obtained till from half an hour to three quarters of an hour after the appointed time; and it not unfrequently happens during the year that no quorum is obtained, and the business is deferred to another day. Then a great deal of the time of the town council is spent in discussions of political questions, and those questions are very often too of a strong party character.

2301. You say that the character of the town council has been steadily deteriorating, how do you account for that?—The men who would make more suitable members of the corporation cannot be induced to come forward and to enter it, and abstention from participation in municipal affairs is now in fact just as much the rule in Dublin amongst the more extensive mercantile men as it is in the United States.

2302. Why is that?—There are two reasons for it. One is, that under the existing franchise, where there is no rating qualification, and where the owners of property, as such, do not enjoy the franchise, the control of the elections is in the hands of the small ratepayers who, either from want of real interest in the matter, or from ignorance, do not take as much care and interest about the proper business of the corporation as they ought to do; and they think a great deal too much of the political opinions of the candidates. I believe that no man who is not a political partisan, has much chance of being elected, and if elected once, unless his conduct on political questions when they arise in the meetings of the corporation, should be satisfactory to the majority of the electors, he would have little or no chance of re-election. Then the loss of time involved by the delay in forming a quorum at the meetings of the corporation, and in these political discussions, deter men who value their time from entering the corporation. The men who are

Mr. *Bruen*—continued.

best fitted, by position, character, and abilities, for the performance of the functions of town councillors, and who would willingly devote their time and energies to the practical business of the government of the city, and who do willingly devote their time and energies to the government of other public matters, will not come forward in the character of political partisans; will not join in these political discussions, and cannot afford the enormous waste of time involved; and despairing of being able to accomplish any good, they will not subject themselves to the general discomfort of having to take part in discussions carried on in the style which is very frequently the case in the Corporation of Dublin. I do not believe that there is any hope of improvement in the condition of affairs, unless some change in the franchise is made by which the representation will be adjusted with more fairness in proportion to the incidence of taxation. I believe that the error which is at the root of the whole matter is due to the idea that our municipal governments are, and ought to be, semi-political representative assemblies; and I believe that it is this idea which has done more to produce the present low condition of the corporation of Dublin than anything else, and to keep out of it the men who ought to be in it, and to put into it the men who ought not to be in it.

2303. Should you say that at no time have corporations done good by taking cognizance of passing political questions?—In past times I think they have, but I do not think that they have in recent years; I think that in recent years the evil which has resulted from their taking part in political matters has counterbalanced the good. It appears to me that there is no reason for their doing so now, seeing that by the reduction of the parliamentary franchise all classes can obtain representation in Parliament; and that the freedom of the Press and the right of public meeting affords the fullest and freest opportunity for giving expression to local public opinion upon all questions of the day.

2304. Have you considered the proposal which has been made for assimilating the Irish to the English municipal franchise?—Yes. The great argument in favour of it is that it would give a nominal identity between Irish and English institutions, and would consequently appear fair and just to Ireland. But I think that a little consideration shows that the argument is a bad one unless it can first be shown that the English institutions give satisfaction in England, and are the best that can be devised; and also that an identity of the franchise would produce identical results in the two countries. I do not believe that the system gives satisfaction in England or is the best that can be devised; and, as an Irishman, I object to a bad system being imposed upon Ireland simply because it exists in England. I do not believe, moreover, that it would produce identical results; because, whereas in Ireland the number of ratings at 8 *l.* and under is two and a half times greater than the number over 8 *l.* in England the relative proportions are the other way.

2305. Do you, or do you not, think that the assimilation of the Irish to the English municipal franchise would be for the benefit of Ireland?—I think that the simple reduction of the franchise, without any compensating arrangements, would intensify

Mr. *Bruen*—continued.

intensify the evils that now exist. It would place three-fourths of the voting power in the hands of those who pay only one-fourth of the taxation; and three-fourths of the voting power means, practically, the entire representation; and besides, what I consider would be the social injustice and danger of placing the control of the local expenditure in the hands of those who contribute but a minor portion of the taxes, there would in Ireland be the political danger that such a fresh recognition of the claim to a personal equality of electoral power, without regard to the extent of individual contribution to the town exchequer, would be considered as an express approval of an idea which I hold to be erroneous, as I have already stated, and to be at the root of the matter, viz., that town councils are and ought to be semi-political representative assemblies. I believe that if this proposal for a reduction of the franchise were carried out, town councils would devote still more of their time than at present to political debates, and that the abstention of common sense business men from taking any part in municipal government would become more marked than at present.

2306. You said, at the beginning of your evidence, that by the assimilation of the Irish to the English franchise the payers of only one-fourth of the taxation would have given to them three-fourths of the voting power, can you give any figures in support of this statement?—Yes, I find in Parliamentary Return, No. 422 of 1872, figures that would prove that. In Dublin there is at present, theoretically, no limit of qualification. Every one whose name appears on the rate book is entitled to the franchise. But, practically, it appears that no one in fact, so far as I can learn, who is rated under the 4 *l.* valuation is put on to the rate book, and a great many under 8 *l.* are not put on. I do not know what proportion of persons who are rated at 8 *l.* and under get on to the burgess roll. I think it would be interesting to find that out, and I suppose that the collector general could give the information. I find from the Parliamentary Return which I have just mentioned, that in Dublin the number of separate ratings at and under 8 *l.* is 10,598 or 40·6 per cent of the entire number of separate ratings, and their total valuation is 45,961 *l.* or 8·3 per cent. of the gross total valuation of Dublin; while the number of separate ratings over 8 *l.* is 15,519 or 59·4 per cent. of the whole, and their total valuation is 508,147 *l.* or 91·7 per cent. of the whole. So that in Dublin the payers of only 8·3 per cent. of the taxation might, under existing circumstances, if they got on to the roll, possess 40 per cent. of the votes. In the other 10 municipal boroughs the number of separate ratings at and under 8 *l.* is 52,470 or 72 per cent. of the whole, and their total valuation 183,003 *l.* or 22 per cent. of the whole; while the number of ratings over 8 *l.* is 20,063 or 28 per cent. of the whole, and their total valuation 639,843 *l.* or 78 per cent. of the whole valuation. So that in these 10 boroughs the payers of only 22 per cent. of the taxation might have 72 per cent. of the votes. The same return shows that the number of ratings not exceeding 4 *l.* in Dublin is 21·8 per cent. of the whole number, and they pay only 2·7 per cent. of the total taxation. In Belfast 28·9 per cent. of the whole number of ratings do not exceed 4 *l.* in value, and they pay only 6 per cent. of the taxation. In Londonderry 36·5 per cent. of the whole number of ratings do not exceed 4 *l.* in value, and they pay only 4·6 per cent. of the taxation. And in the other eight municipal boroughs the number of ratings not exceeding 4 *l.* varies from 50 per cent. in Clonmel and Cork to 75 per cent. in Limerick, represented by a percentage of valuation varying from 10 per cent. in Cork to 27·6 per cent. in Kilkenny. Taking the figures for the whole 11 boroughs, the separate ratings not exceeding 4 *l.* in valuation are 39·3 per cent. of the entire number of separate ratings, and their total value is 6·5 per cent. of the gross total valuation of the 11 boroughs. The separate ratings exceeding 4 *l.* and not exceeding 8 *l.* are 24·6 per cent. of the whole number of ratings, and their total valuation is 10·1 per cent. of the gross total valuation; and the separate ratings exceeding 8 *l.* are 36·1 per cent. of the total number of separate ratings, and they are valued at 83·4 per cent. of the total valuation. So that the payers of 6·5 per cent. of the taxation might have 39·3 per cent. of the votes; the payers of 10·1 per cent. of the taxation 24·6 per cent. of the votes, and the payers of 83·4 per cent. of the taxation only 36·1 per cent. of the votes.

Mr. *Pim.*

16 May 1876.

2307. What inference do you draw from those figures?—It appears to me from these figures that under a system of taxation in direct proportion to valuation, the simple abolition of any limit as to qualification would in Ireland be grossly unjust, and would place the control of the representation in the hands of those who are least fit for the exercise of electoral power, and the control of the expenditure in the hands of those who are most exposed to the temptation of directing its current to their own personal advantage.

2308. That last answer brings us at once to the suggestion of cumulative voting, what opinion have you formed of the effect of cumulative voting, which has been tried in England, I think, in School Board elections?—I think that it suits very well for School Board elections, but I do not think that as a means for correcting the effects of an unlimited franchise for municipal purposes in Ireland it would suit.

2309. What reason do you give for this opinion; why do you suppose that it would not suit?—The cumulative system of voting appears to me an admirable device for protecting minorities in matters of opinion, and for this reason, it is exactly suited to the circumstances of School Board elections, and has worked most successfully in their case, because the essential connection between religion and education has made it desirable to secure on School Boards a proportionate representation of the chief religious bodies in the community. So that no considerable sect should feel that the religious principles of the children belonging to its fold were endangered for want of representatives of its tenets to guard their interests on the School Boards. Similarly the cumulative system of voting is very suitable where you want to obtain the proportionate representation of political parties, and for this reason I think it would have a most beneficial effect if applied to the Parliamentary elections in Ireland whenever the long-talked-of Redistribution of Seats Bill is brought in. But it appears to me that the very reason which makes

Mr. *Pim.*

16 May 1876.

Mr. *Bruen*—continued.

makes the cumulative system of voting suitable for School Board and Parliamentary elections, viz., that it is certain to bring out representatives of religious and political parties, is the very reason why it is not suited to the elections of members of local boards, especially in Ireland, where the bane of all local governing bodies is the unceasing conflict between political parties and religious sects. This conflict would, as it appears to me, be intensified by the adoption of cumulative voting, because religion and politics would necessarily become the test of fitness; and it appears to me that it would be the representatives of the extreme opinions on each side, and not the representatives of moderate opinions that would be elected in almost all cases. In municipal elections the minority whose representation we want to protect from being extinguished by the majority is not a minority of religious or political opinion, but a minority of social position, a minority whose contribution to the municipal exchequer is much greater than the contribution of the majority. In Ireland the real question between one candidate and another almost always resolves itself into the difference between Protestant and Catholic, for almost all Protestants vote on the so-called Conservative side, and almost all Roman Catholics on the so-called Liberal side. For this reason the cumulative system of voting will not, as it appears to me, be any protection to the minority of larger ratepayers, for as that minority is composed of both Roman Catholics and Protestants, they can never be expected to accumulate their votes on particular candidates whose position and character might make them especially suitable as representatives. On the contrary, as I have already said, the accumulation of votes will take place amongst the Protestants on one side, and amongst the Roman Catholics on the other side, to elect representatives of their own way of thinking in religious matters. Under such circumstances it is almost certain that it is men of extreme opinion who will be chosen; and they will be chosen because of their religious opinions, and not because of their fitness for the positions to which they will be elected.

2310. Do you think that that would be a great evil?—I think it would be a great evil, and instead of the tendency, in the process of time, being towards the obliteration of this hard line of social demarcation between the one religious body and the other, it appears to me that the effect of the cumulative system of voting will be to stereotype it.

2311. If you object to the cumulative system of voting, what substitute can you suggest?—I think that the system of plural voting under which within certain limits each elector would be entitled to give a number of votes in proportion to the amount of rates for which he was liable, would be not only more just than the cumulative system of voting, but much better calculated to secure the election of suitable representatives on local boards; and, in my opinion, its tendency would be to soften the conflict between religious parties, and to lead to the election of men of moderate, rather than of extreme, opinions.

2312. Will you give the Committee a reason why you think that?—Because by the plural system of voting an increased share of power

Mr. *Bruen*—continued.

would be conferred on those who are most heavily rated, and the large ratepayers are generally persons who are extensively engaged in business. The possession of an extensive business is generally the result of greater energy and capacity; and seeing that in proportion to the interests which he has at stake is the strength of a man's motive to make a wise choice of a representative, it may be considered certain that the tendency of plural voting will be towards the election of better representatives. The man who has to pay a large amount of taxation will be particular as to the sort of man whom he selects to control the expenditure of the city funds. He will think much more of his business qualifications than of his political opinions. It is not merely the amount of money that is taken out of his pocket in the form of taxes that he will think of, but the manner in which those taxes are applied, and the effect produced. To a man extensively engaged in business, it is of great importance that the streets should be well paved, scavenged, and watered; that the water supply should be abundant and good; that the fire brigade should be well disciplined and equipped; that the streets should be well lit; that dilapidated houses should not be allowed to exist; and that the dwellings of his workpeople should be looked after, and everything done to improve their sanitary condition. Accustomed in his own business to take a wide view of things, and at the same time to be careful about details, to look forward, and to be willing to incur an outlay of capital where he sees that by making some improvement he can add to his business, he will look for similar conduct on the part of his representative, and will be careful to select a candidate who will reflect his own views. For these reasons I think that every thing will conspire to induce the large ratepayer to make a good choice of a representative.

2313. I would ask you to give a reason why you think that this plan of plural voting would tend to soften down those asperities of feeling which exist between religious and political bodies? —A large proportion of those who would gain in voting power by the institution of plural voting are Roman Catholics. And the remarks which I have just made with respect to the conduct and feelings of the larger ratepayers, of course apply to them equally as well as to the large Protestant ratepayers. In my opinion, they would give their preference to practical men of moderate opinions. And I think there would be more probability under the system of plural voting of the large ratepayers on both political sides combining to elect good business men than under the cumulative system.

2314. With reference to your remark about the gain to Roman Catholics by this system, it is your opinion, I believe, that there has been a very considerable accumulation of money and an increased business amongst Roman Catholic traders of late years?—I think so, decidedly, out of Ulster, at least, and I think that the tendency is in that direction, and that consequently, under a system of plural voting, the Roman Catholics would gain gradually in voting power, and that you would be giving the voting power to the very class amongst them who take the most moderate opinions and who are the most practical business men.

2315. Did I rightly understand you to say that

Mr. *Pim.*

16 May 1876.

Mr. *Bruen*—continued.

that if the system of plural voting was applied to municipal elections, and the franchise reduced at the same time, all the requirements of the case would be satisfied, in your opinion?—No, I think not, because the owners of property at present are excluded from the franchise; and I think that that is the most important point of all. And I think that, in considering the distribution of voting power with regard to the enfranchisement of owners, the question of the incidence of taxation must also be considered.

2316. On that point what is your view?—I am in favour of the equal division of the taxation and the representation between the owners and the occupiers. In the provisions of the Scotch municipal franchise we have a precedent for giving votes to the owners in municipal elections. In Scotland the municipal and Parliamentary franchises, if the information which I have obtained be accurate, are identical, and owners of property, as such, have votes for municipal elections, just as for Parliamentary elections. Then in England there are over 500 towns, some of them of considerable importance, in which the owners of property, as such, have votes for the local boards of the towns under the provisions of the Public Health Act of 1848, and the Local Government Act of 1858, and in Ireland in the towns which elect their local boards under the provisions of the Towns Improvement Act 1854, the owners, as such, enjoy the franchise. According to the Parliamentary Return, No. 381 of 1874, there were in Dublin in the year 1873, 1,728 Parliamentary electors on the register as owners, all of whom, although permanently interested in the city government, are debarred from voting for members of the town council unless they happen to come in under the occupiers' franchise. Under the English Public Health Act owners who are also occupiers are allowed to vote for members of local boards in both capacities; and as plurality of voting, as far as six votes, is allowed under the same Act, a man who is both owner and occupier of premises may have as many as 12 votes if the valuation of his premises is high enough, namely, 250 *l.* or over.

Chairman.

2317. What Acts do you refer to?—The Public Health Act of 1848, and the Local Government Act of 1858. In both England and Ireland owners, as such, are entitled to vote in the election of poor-law guardians, and a man who is both owner and occupier may vote in both capacities, and as plurality of voting, as far as six votes, is allowed, a man may have as many as 12 votes if his valuation be sufficiently high. I am not able to see that there is any such inherent difference between the functions of poor-law guardians, members of local boards in England, and town councillors in Scotland, and the functions of town councillors in Ireland, as should warrant the enfranchisement of owners in the first three cases, and their disfranchisement in the last case. In fact, I consider it a positive injustice to owners of property in Irish municipal boroughs that they should be debarred from voting, and the results of their exclusion from the franchise I believe to be very injurious to the interests of the towns.

Mr. *Bruen.*

2318. The municipal taxes are paid, I believe, by the occupier, and in that case why do you think it unjust to exclude the owners from the franchise?—Owners are liable for taxes on all premises not exceeding 4 *l.* in value. In Dublin the public water rate is chargeable against the owner; but whether owners pay taxes directly or not, the burden of the rates must ultimately be borne by owners; if not wholly, at least in part, and the share of the burden ultimately borne by owners will depend on the circumstances of the locality and of the times, and will be governed by the laws of supply and demand.

2319. Why do you say that?—I think that heavy rates tend to depress rents, and consequently to reduce the value of house property. If two houses, otherwise equal in value, are subjected to different rates of taxation, the house which is more heavily taxed will bring the lower rent, and the house which is less heavily taxed will bring the higher rent. And if you carry the argument to two streets or two districts of a town, it will be found, I believe, to be equally true. The rents will be higher where the taxation is lower, and rents will be lower where the taxation is higher. The tendency is to the equalisation of the rent plus the taxes, in the two houses, two streets, or two districts. The City of Dublin appears to me a strong case in point. The area of the city is circumscribed, practically, by the two canals. There are large vacant spaces within that area; but for the past 20 or 25 years there have been very few new houses built; the population has actually diminished; and there has been very little increase in the total valuation. This is not due to want of prosperity; Dublin has been very prosperous during that period. There has been a great expansion of commerce, and the total tonnage of the shipping entering and leaving the port has doubled in less than 25 years. This state of things is due, I believe, chiefly to the fact that the rate of taxation within the city is more than double what it is outside the city. This has influenced tenants in the choice of a residence, and driven them away from the city, to the injury of houseowners in the city; and in its turn the set of the current of building speculation has been diverted from the city to the injury of landowners in the city. Yet neither the houseowner nor the landowner has had any direct control over the expenditure of the taxation, the burden of which he has had to bear. It is an evil which does not tend to work its own cure; but, on the contrary, I think that its tendency is to grow greater. The check given to the outlay of capital prevents the total valuation of the city from rising, while at the same time there is a natural tendency for the taxation to rise, because of the increasing demands on the city funds for various purposes; while the favourable set of the current of building speculation towards the suburbs tends to increase the total valuation of the suburbs more rapidly than the demands on their corporate funds; and consequently the tendency is to make the comparison of the rate of taxation within and without the city more and more unfavourable to the city. This tells not merely on dwellinghouses. It tells still more severely on commercial enterprise than on dwellinghouses. The inordinately heavy taxation

Mr. Pim.

16 May 1876.

Mr. *Bruen*—continued.

ation in Dublin is a penal tax on all manufacturing or mercantile enterprises for which extensive premises are necessary; and I know, as a matter of fact, that it prevents capital from being invested in manufacturing industries in Dublin. This is detrimental to the interests of the owners of lands or houses, which might be occupied as premises on which to carry on such industries. Yet these owners have no control, as I have already said, over the taxation; and the capitalist who invests his money, or carries on his business in extensive premises bearing a heavy burden of taxation, has no control beyond one vote over the taxation, and not even one vote if he happens, as is very often the case, to live more than seven miles from the city. That the owners of property in a town should have no direct control over the expenditure of the municipal funds is, in my opinion, radically unjust and impolitic.

2320. Do you think the only interest that the owners, as a class, have is in keeping down the expenditure?—No, certainly not; I think the owners, as a class, have a permanent interest in the well-being of the town, whereas the occupiers have only a temporary interest just so long as they choose to reside in it. The owners' interest is really greater than the occupiers' interest, especially in all matters involving outlay on permanent improvements. It will often be his interest that such an outlay shall be incurred when the occupier might feel no interest in the matter, because of his not intending to continue to reside in the city. The real interest of the owner is not in keeping down the expenditure to the lowest point, but in seeing that it is devoted to proper purposes, and that the best value is obtained for it. At present the feeling amongst the owners of property in Dublin, as well as amongst the occupiers whose premises are extensive, is almost universal, that very bad value is received in return for the heavy taxation. Having no power of control, want of confidence in the corporation is engendered, and they suspect jobbery where, very likely, there may be no grounds for their suspicions. If they have no power of control in Dublin, they can at least oppose the corporation before Private Bill Committees when fresh powers are sought. For, although owners neither pay taxes nor vote, they have a *locus standi* in the Committee-room. Every project of the corporation is certain to be vehemently opposed, water, gas, drainage, or anything, because the opposing parties having no power in the municipal council, have no confidence in its proceedings, no respect for its authority, and a good deal of suspicion as to its honesty. In fact, when such Parliamentary contests arise the motives of the leaders of the corporation are called in question, and talk of jobbery and corruption is freely indulged in. The prevalence of this unfortunate feeling of want of respect for the corporation keeps good men out of it, and discourages those who are in it, and I think it is a scandal and a danger to the city; my own opinion is, that this evil will never be cured until those who really bear the burthen of the expenditure are given a corresponding share in the administration.

2321. You stated, as your opinion, that although the taxes are collected from the occupier, a considerable share of the burden falls on the owner. If that is the case, why should not the franchise be conferred on owners, and the tax still continue to be collected as it is now?—Because, I think, that the law ought to be consistent with equity, instead of leaving it to the working of supply and demand to counteract the inequality of the law. Besides, there are many cases in which the working of supply and demand cannot counteract the inequality of the law. A tenant contracts to rent a house for a term of years, at a fixed rent, and agrees also to pay all taxes; subsequently some permanent work is carried out by the corporation, such as water works or drainage works. The cost of these works is to be repaid by a sinking fund for a term of years in addition to the interest. The tenant pays his share of the sinking fund for the whole of his term, and at the end of it the landlord gets back his house, increased in value by the works for which he has not had to pay anything. If the burthen of the taxation is allowed to reach the landlord indirectly only, he loses sight of his real interest, and is apathetic where he ought to be active.

Chairman.

2322. The tenant receives the benefit, does he not, while his holding lasts?—Yes; but he pays, and is quite prepared to pay, his share of the interest on the improvements; but I think that he should not be made to pay for buying back the capital sum by a sinking fund; for when he leaves his house he has no interest in the capital sum.

Mr. *Bruen.*

2323. Conferring the franchise on owners, without making them directly liable for the rates, will have the appearance of injustice to the occupiers, and will, in reality, be unjust in many cases, will it not?—Yes, I think so.

2324. What precedents have you for your proposal for converting the indirect interest of owners of property in the local taxation into a direct one?—That proposal is in accordance with the recommendation of the Select Committee of 1870 on local taxation, and that opinion, I believe, was arrived at unanimously by that Committee. Then we have in Ireland a precedent already for the division of the rates between owner and occupier in the case of the poor's rates since 1838, and the grand jury cess on agricultural holdings since 1870. In Scotland the poor rate is divided equally between owner and occupier, and also the county rate for the construction and maintenance of roads, bridges, &c., and in Scotch towns, where owners, as such, enjoy the municipal franchise, about one-seventh of the municipal taxation is paid by the owners.

2325. Then your proposal is, that the municipal taxes should be paid, half by the owner and half by the occupier, and that the governing body should be a mixed board, half elected by the owners and half by the occupiers; do you know of any governing body in existence which is constituted on this principle?—Yes, the Boards of Guardians in Ireland, and the Scotch county boards, that I have just spoken of, are constituted very much on this principle, though not exactly in the way I proposed for municipal boards. The Irish boards of guardians are mixed boards composed

Mr. *Pim*.

16 May 1876.

Mr. *Brien*—continued.

posed half of *ex officio* members, magistrates, and half of elected members; I think the *ex officio* members may be looked upon as a direct representation of property; the elected members represent both owners and occupiers. The plan proposed for municipal councils is more favourable to the occupiers than the Poor Law system, because the occupiers by themselves would elect one-half.

2326. As to the Scotch County Boards, what information can you give the Committee about their management?—The taxation is divided equally between landlord and tenant, and the Boards are mixed Boards, composed of all owners whose annual rental exceeds a certain sum, and of a certain number of representatives elected by the ratepayers of each parish. From all that I have been able to learn upon the subject, I believe that the system works very satisfactorily. It will be found in the evidence given before the Select Committee on Local Taxation in 1870, that Mr. James Caird gave interesting evidence on the working of the Scotch system of joint Boards before that Committee. There is just one short sentence from his evidence which perhaps I might be allowed to read. He says, in answer to Question 4189, "In Scotland we have found "that the owner, from being directly called upon "to pay a large proportion of the rates, takes a "very active interest in the administration, and I "think that has led to much economy, and also "probably to a more liberal and far-seeing view "of the position of affairs in the district than "would be the case when it falls entirely on the "occupying tenant."

2327. It has been said that *ex officio* guardians of the poor in Ireland are less regular in their attendance than the elected guardians; what proof have you that *ex officio* guardians attend badly?—I find in the Report of the Select Committee of 1871, on the Law of Rating in Ireland, that although the number of *ex officio* and of elected guardians is almost equal throughout Ireland, the average attendance in the whole of Ireland was, in 1870–71, *ex officio* guardians, 2·03, and elected guardians, 6·75; and in the North and South Dublin unions the figures were, *ex officio* guardians, 4·75, and elected guardians, 17·5.

2328. Do you consider that the double system of election and mixed board would be complicated in its working?—No, I do not think it would; I believe the system would work quite smoothly, and it is not at all so complicated as it looks when expressed on paper. The system, it appears to me, is simply analogous to the Parliamentary system, in which you have county and borough members elected by different constituencies and under a different franchise. The system which I have just proposed for town government is much simpler than the system under which boards of guardians are constituted.

2329. Do you think that there would be a risk of a conflict of opinion upon the board or the governing body between the two classes of representatives?—No, I see no reason for thinking that it would. I do not think it arises in the House of Commons between county and borough members, and so far as I can learn I believe that it does not occur in the Scotch county boards.

Mr. *Brien*—continued.

2330. Not even in a case of conflict of interest between the two classes represented?—*If* such a case should arise in which there would be a conflict of interest between owners and occupiers, it appears to me that it would be a very strong argument in favour of the mixed board, because it is clear that if the board were not mixed, and solely represented one or other class, injustice would be done to the class unrepresented by some measure being carried out inimical to its interests, in consequence of their having no power of control by reason of being unrepresented. It would be much better, I think, that a deadlock should arise than that injustice should be done. But when a difference of opinion of that kind arises, it is very generally settled by some compromise; but I think that it would be found in practical working that those difficulties would prove only imaginary. We have a mixed board in Dublin at the present moment which is of quite a complicated character, and there those difficulties are not realised; it works extremely smoothly.

2331. What is the Board which you are speaking of?—The Port and Docks Board. It appears to me that the complicated constitution leads to the representation of every variety of interest and opinion, and when all interests and opinions are fairly represented by men of ability and good sense, things are pretty sure to work smoothly. The Port and Docks Boards is composed of four classes of representatives elected by four different constituencies in four different ways, and they are all first-rate men.

2332. How is that composed?—It is composed of 25 members; seven of those are nominated by the Commissioners of Irish Lights, and serve for three years. Seven are elected by the traders, merchants, and manufacturers of Dublin, and serve for six years. Seven are elected by the shipowners of Dublin, and serve for six years; and three members are nominated by the municipal corporation of Dublin, and serve for three years; and the Lord Mayor is an *ex officio* member. Outgoing members of all four classes are eligible for re-election.

2333. As to the bodies by whom these members are chosen, can you tell the Committee what they are?—The Board of Commissioners of Irish Lights, by whom seven members are elected, is composed of 17 members nominated by the members for the time being of the Board, subject to the approval of the Lord Lieutenant and Privy Council of Ireland, and they hold office for life. Then there are three aldermen of the city of Dublin annually nominated by the municipal corporation of Dublin; and also the Lord Mayor for the city of Dublin for the time being, and the High Sheriff of the city of Dublin for the time being, making 22 commissioners in all.

2334. At all events, the Port and Docks Boards, such as you have described, and as has been described to the Committee, is a very complicated machinery?—Yes.

2335. But it is found to work well and smoothly?—Yes; I think that there is great confidence felt by the traders and shipowners of Dublin in the way in which it conducts its business.

2336. Has it been successful in its undertakings?—Yes.

2337. In one of your former answers you spoke of

Mr. *Pim.*

16 May 1876.

Mr. *Bruen*—continued.

of the reduction of the franchise; to what extent do you think that it would be advisable to reduce the franchise?—With the other arrangements which I have suggested, I think that the franchise should be reduced to household suffrage.

2338. The question arose as to what a "house" was, which Mr. McEvoy, a witness before the Committee, gave his views about; will you say what you consider to be a house of a description that ought to qualify a voter?—In Dublin the artisan class very largely lives in tenement houses, and that makes a very great difficulty in the arrangement of the franchise, because those people living in tenement houses simply pay for a room, or whatever number of rooms they occupy, so much per week. Then they are not bound to that house for any length of time, and there is a difficulty in arranging for the placing of the occupiers of tenement houses upon the franchise which I am not able to see my way out of; but I think where a man lives in a separate house, no matter what the value of the house may be, I would give him a vote.

2339. Are you aware that in the Parliamentary representation that difficulty has been somewhat met by giving votes to lodgers who pay rather a high qualifying rent; do you think that anything of that sort could be done with the view of getting rid of the difficulty of those tenement lodgers?—I do not think that those tenement lodgers would come in under the Parliamentary qualification for lodgers; the qualification being above the rent usually paid for rooms in these tenement houses.

2340. Do you think that it would be safe to reduce it for municipal purposes?—I doubt its being wise to do it.

2341. As to the scheme for plurality of votes, what is your opinion upon that?—My idea is to make that the same as the Poor-law system, simply because the precedent is there already, and it is better to work to a precedent than to start a new arrangement.

2342. If you had a governing body elected under this proposed plan, do you think that it would be advisable to do away with the limitation upon the taxing power of the corporation?—Decidedly. I look upon the limitation of the taxing power as an expression on the part of the Legislature that the local governing body is not worthy of the confidence which ought to be reposed in it; that they are afraid to allow people who are the nominal representatives of the citizens, to levy taxes on the citizens, even though it may be requisite. I know that as things are in Dublin, the usual answer made by the members of the corporation, when complaints are made that they do not do this or do not do that, is that they have not got the money; and they have no power of getting more money except in two ways, the one by increasing the rate of taxation, and the other by raising the valuation. I think, constituted as the corporation now is, I should not like to see the limitation removed; but if you had a body constituted in such a way as to give a fair representation to the classes who really have to pay the taxes, I would remove the limitation.

2343. Then as to the term of residence necessary for qualifying, what have you to say?—I think that the term in Dublin is too long; it is the same term as was fixed in the English Municipal Reform Act until the last reform after the Parliamentary Reform Bill was carried; but I think it is too long, and I would reduce it to the same as the present limit in England.

Mr. *Bruen*—continued.

2344. What do you say with regard to the distance of residence?—I do not see any necessity for any limitation of distance, because if a man pays taxes in the city, and will take the trouble of coming to vote, I do not think it makes any difference where he lives. But the present limitation in Dublin is particularly unjust, for this reason, that the municipal area is exceedingly small; the city of Dublin is confined by the two canals, and then when you get seven miles from the two canals you do not include anything like all the really out-lying districts of the city; that is to say, districts in which people live who pay taxes in the city; and if it be considered unwise to do away with the restriction altogether as to the limit of residence, I would certainly extend it to say twenty miles.

2345. With regard to the revising of the burgess list, do you consider the present system a satisfactory one?—No, I think it would be better conducted in the same way as the Parliamentary revision. I think the plan of having two assessors, one elected by each party, and the Lord Mayor as umpire is a bad one, and leads to uncertainty in the decisions. If there is a difference of opinion between the two assessors it must depend upon the idea of the Lord Mayor for the time being as to what decision is given.

2346. Do you consider the present system of valuation of property in Dublin a satisfactory one?—No; I think that it is unequal, and that it requires revision.

2347. In what respect do you consider it unequal?—If I understand correctly what takes place, so long as an occupier makes no change in his residence, or his warehouse or shop, or whatever it may be, no change is made in his valuation. Although the general value of houses in the city of Dublin has risen during the last 20 years, or since the last general valuation was made, there has been no general increase made to the valuation of houses. But a man who improves his house, or his warehouse or his shop, is immediately valued up to the present level of value; and therefore, if I understand correctly what takes place, the present system of valuation amounts to a penal rate on enterprise. I think there ought to be a periodic revision of all the property in the city, and the value to be put down in the rate book ought to be some definite percentage upon the real letting value, which is, I believe, the principle adopted in London. If that were done, I believe the total valuation of Dublin would be considerably increased, and it would give the corporation more money to expend.

Mr. *Brooks.*

2348. Do I understand you to say that you desire to have the valuation revised?—Yes, I should be in favour of re-valuation, excepting for this, that as that valuation is made the foundation for the income tax, as well as for the local taxes, I think that the whole of Ireland should be revised at the same time, or otherwise Dublin would come under a heavier income tax than elsewhere.

2349. The valuations in Dublin and in the provinces

Mr. *Brooks*—continued.

vinces are on the same basis, are they not, by Sir Richard Griffith's valuation?—I cannot say exactly what the valuation is based upon, but it is a valuation which was made a good many years ago.

2350. If there was a re-valuation, would not it give to the corporation increased funds?—That is exactly what I said.

2351. Do I understand you to advocate the augmentation of the funds of the corporation?—If the result of the re-valuation of the city of Dublin should be to make the total valuation of Dublin higher than it is now, it would, of course, increase the amount that the corporation would receive under its present taxing power; at least, I presume that the corporation would not reduce any of the rates from their maximum, for they do not generally show any disposition to do so.

2352. I think I understood you to say that the social position of the corporation was more to be complained of than the religious inequalities, or the want of property on the part of the members?—I do not think I used the words "social position," as respects the members of the corporation, nor do I wish to do so, in speaking of the members of the corporation; it is not the actual wealth that any member of the corporation is possessed of that I speak of; what I am objecting to relates to the constituents of the members of the corporation; what I object to is that those who pay the heaviest amount of taxation have not a corresponding voting power, and that consequently the men who are now members of the corporation, are the representatives of those who pay but a very small proportion of the taxation; I am not saying that the members of the corporation themselves pay a small amount of taxation, although I believe that to be true, but that they are elected by men who pay but a small amount of taxation.

2353. Do you see any reason to be dissatisfied with the social or property qualification of the members of the corporation?—I do not wish to make any remark about their social position, but this I will say, that, looking at the members of the corporation, they do not occupy the same high mercantile position at present that they did in the year 1851 or 1852, after the Reform Bill was carried, under which the Corporation of Dublin is now constituted.

2354. Was not it at that time that the limitation of the rating power was fixed by the Legislature?—You mean by that, the limit as to the taxation which individual members of the corporation pay?

2355. No; the limitation which the Legislature placed as to the amount of the improvement fund; you said just now that the Legislature very wisely limited the taxing powers of the corporation in consequence of the position of the corporation?—Excuse me; I did not say that the Legislature had done that very wisely, but I said that for them to undo that now which they had done then would be unwise. I believe it is correct that the present limitations were fixed at the time that the last Reform Bill for Dublin was carried; but the limitation was fixed before the members of the town council were elected; therefore it had nothing to do with the individuals who were then members of the corporation.

2356. Then you do not complain of the social

Mr. *Brooks*—continued.

Mr. *Pim*.

16 May 1876.

position of the members of the corporation?—No; I have not made any remark about their social position.

2357. May I ask you if the corporation does not comprise many men of the very highest position in Dublin?—I do not know exactly what the very highest position in Dublin may mean. There are members of the corporation, I am perfectly aware, who do occupy a high position in Dublin.

2358. The very highest position?—The very highest means whoever is at the very top, and I think we need not go into the question as to who is at the highest point; but I am of opinion that there are members of the corporation who occupy a very high position in Dublin.

2359. The Chairman of the Waterworks Committee, for instance?—Yes, Mr. Jameson has been a member of the corporation since 1851.

2360. And he occupies the very highest position, and is a man of the highest rank?—Yes, of the very highest rank of mercantile men in Dublin.

2361. Would you kindly give the Committee the names of the members of the corporation?—I can hand in to the Committee a list of the members of the corporation at the present moment, and of the members of the corporation in the year 1851, if it is of any interest to the Committee. I have also a list of the Directors of the Bank of Ireland, of the Royal Bank, of the Hibernian Bank, of the Great Southern and Western Railway Company, of the Midland and Great Western Railway Company, of the Dublin and Kingstown Railway Company, and of the Dublin and Drogheda Railway Company; of the members of the Council of the Chamber of Commerce, and of the members of the Ousel Galley Society, in Dublin, in 1851, and in 1876. Now I find that of the members of the corporation in the year 1851, there were 14 who were on one or other of those boards, and that at the present moment there are only two who are members of any one of those Boards, and that the two who are now members of the corporation, and who are at the same time members of any one of those boards, were members of the corporation in the year 1851, and the two gentlemen are Alderman Campbell and Mr. Jameson.

2362. Will you explain to the Committee why it is that those gentlemen do not now come into the Corporation?—I endeavoured to explain it. Of course I cannot tell what prevents individuals from going in, but I can only tell what is my general opinion. I believe that what prevents their going into the corporation, is this: that in order to get into the corporation it is almost necessary that a man should profess the opinions of a political partisan, and that, after he has become a member of the corporation, he must conduct himself within the corporation as a political partisan.

2363. That happens in the House of Commons, does it not?—But that is the business of the House of Commons, and not the business of the corporation, and that is exactly what makes the difference, in my opinion, between the two institutions.

2364. Are you aware of the constitution of the Board of the Bank of Ireland is that a political body?—I should think that the Board of the Bank of

Mr. Pim.

16 May 1876.

Mr. *Brooks*—continued.

of Ireland was very careful to have no political opinions.

2365. What are the political opinions of the Board of the Bank of Ireland?—I should say that the board as a board, has no political opinions.

2366. But you say that the corporation has, because individuals happen to hold political opinions?—I do not say that the corporation as a corporation has political opinions, but I say that the corporation is divided into two political parties. I do not think that on the Board of the Bank of Ireland, or on any board governing a mercantile institution in Dublin, there is such a thing existing as having two political parties on that board. I should say that the shares of the institution would rapidly decline if such a thing existed, and indeed what has taken place in the city of Dublin, is that the shareholders in the city of Dublin, that is the ratepayers, have lost confidence in the governing board, that is the corporation, because of the existence of this strong party feeling between the two sides who spend so much time over these party matters, and so little over the real business of the corporation.

2367. You say that no complaint is to be made of the social position of the members of the corporation?—I do not wish to make any complaint of the social position of any member of the corporation.

2368. Can you say that any member of the corporation of whose social position you do not complain has ever raised his voice in public against the internal management of the corporation?—It is not the usual thing for men to do when they belong to such a body as that, to throw dirt at the body that they are members of. I think, when a man has got a strong feeling on the subject he retires, and I think that a good many of those who have retired from the corporation have retired, to a large extent, from that feeling.

2369. Has anyone ever raised his voice in public against the management of the corporation?—I think that one of the misfortunes of Dublin is, that persons outside the corporation are very frequently raising their voices, and pretty loudly too, in complaint of the way in which things are going on inside and expressing their want of confidence in the whole institution.

2370. Do they complain of any particular mismanagement?—They complain that the streets are very badly cleansed; they complain that sanitary matters are not sufficiently attended to; that the back streets of Dublin are not cleansed as they ought to be, that the artisan class are allowed to live in dwellings that are not at all fit for them; and that there is not sufficient care exercised about that class.

2371. Is that in any part due to insufficient funds?—I cannot say how far it is due to insufficient funds.

2372. Have you not said that the Legislature have limited the means at the disposal of the corporation?—I can believe that it is due to insufficient funds.

2373. And not to mismanagement?—I think that the funds which they have got are not so economically managed in other respects as they ought to be, and that, consequently, there is not sufficient left for attending to matters that are of more importance than the matters that are attended to.

Mr. *Brooks*—continued.

2374. Can you inform us of any particulars of mismanagement of the funds?—No, I cannot.

2375. You say that the complaints are general in Dublin about the management of the corporation?—Yes.

2376. But do you know any of the particulars that have been advanced?—No, I did not say that I charged them with any particulars; I said I was not prepared to advance any particulars as to malversation of the funds. I have no reason to suppose that such a thing exists; but I do believe, speaking generally, that there is not due care taken as regards economy, and I am further of opinion that there are a great many things which the corporation ought to do that they entirely neglect doing. Whether that is due to want of funds or want of legal powers, I am not able to say. I am aware that members of the corporation have frequently told me that they have not got the money and have not got the power; but if they feel that a thing ought to be done, and that it is badly wanted to be done, they ought to apply to Parliament for legal powers or for increased taxing powers.

2377. Can you say how many members, or whether any members that are on the corporation, have been opposed by the larger or smaller ratepayers at the annual elections?—I think there is, unfortunately, in Dublin, very little interest taken in the whole matter, and, as I have said, abstention from interference in municipal affairs is very much the rule in Dublin amongst the mercantile classes.

2378. Does not that rather argue that the ratepayers of Dublin are not dissatisfied with their representatives?—I am quite willing to admit that the present corporation is a fair representative of those by whom they are elected; but I say that those by whom the corporation are elected are not the classes who ought to have the power of electing the corporation. There are only between 5,000 and 6,000 persons in Dublin on the burgess roll, and those 5,000 or 6,000 persons on the burgess roll are, in my opinion, not those who are best fitted for the exercise of the electoral power.

2379. But do not the ratepayers themselves, those who are chiefly interested, seek to get gentlemen of the higher classes, as a matter of fact, to stand at elections?—No; because they feel that they would be incapable of succeeding at a contested election in getting the class of men returned that they would wish to have returned. There is a very considerable number of the mercantile classes of Dublin, as has been already explained before this Committee, who have no voting power from various circumstances, one of which is their not residing within the necessary limit.

2380. Do you know of any unsuccessful efforts on the part of large ratepayers to be placed upon the burgess roll?—No, I do not know that I do; the reason why they are not on the roll is, in many cases, because they do not themselves pay the rates; they are paid by the landlord, as was explained with reference to persons who occupy premises in the Commercial Buildings. There are several houses adjoining the Royal Bank, owned by the Royal Bank, and the Royal Bank pays the taxes on them, and the occupants of those houses are not on the burgess roll.

2381. Do

Mr. *Brooks*—continued.

2381. Do they care to go upon the burgess roll?—I believe they do not; I believe they make no efforts in that direction.

2382. Are they all ratepayers who are duly qualified?—No, it is because they are not ratepayers at all that they are not on the burgess roll; if they were ratepayers they would be on the burgess roll, provided they lived within the necessary limit.

2383. You say, do you not, that the more respectable and more intelligent classes in Dublin avoid the corporation because of the social position of the members in fact?—No, I made no remark of that kind; I do not think that they avoid it because of the social position of the members, but on account of the fact that politics are largely discussed, and that the time of the meetings of the corporation is very much wasted, which men whose time is of value cannot afford; further, that the members of the corporation are very irregular in the hour of meeting. Often three-quarters of an hour or an hour of a man's time is wasted in waiting for a house, and people whose time is of value do not care to go into the corporation on that account.

2384. May I ask you if you think it would not be wiser and better if those gentlemen who are qualified by property and intelligence to act as members of the corporation would endeavour, like many of us do, to go in and mitigate those evils of which you complain?—It is quite possible that it might, but people do not always do the wisest thing. My own impression is, that they would not be in long, that they either would not be returned at the next election, or they would retire from the body themselves.

2385. Then I must do what I am loath to do; I must refer to gentlemen who are members of the corporation, Sir John Barrington, for instance?—I have made no charge whatever against any individual member of the corporation as to his social position, nor as to his individual conduct. I do not wish to make any personal remark whatever about any member of the corporation; I have spoken of it as a body, and as to how it conducts itself at its meetings.

2386. You say that the corporation do not meet within half-an-hour or three quarters of an hour of the advertised time?—Yes, I say so.

2387. Are you aware that there is a rule which prevails not only in the Corporation of the City of Dublin, but in most public bodies, that they have a nominal time set down for actual work, that in the Corporation of the City of Dublin although the time is set down for one o'clock, they well understood the law upon that matter is one for half-past one?—I never was aware of that before, and I think that it is a very bad law. I can give you an instance of the way the thing works. Some time ago there was a deputation of the leading mercantile men in Dublin to the corporation, on the subject of the bridge that was to be built at Beresford-place. The hour appointed for the deputation to attend was one o'clock. There were over 20 of the leading mercantile men of Dublin at the City Hall at one o'clock, or a little before, ready to meet the corporation. There was the governor of the Bank of Ireland, there was the high sheriff, and there was the chairman of the Great Northern Railway Company, and other mercantile men whose time is of the greatest possible value. They were all there at one o'clock to meet the corporation, and I happened to be one of the number; I think we waited about 20 minutes before anything whatever was done. There was then not a quorum, and if I understood what took place, although there was not a quorum to constitute a house, they voted themselves into a committee of the whole house in order that they might hear us; and before there was a house made the memorial from the deputation was read; a discussion took place upon it, and at about a quarter to two o'clock a quorum arrived, and the house went back from the state of committee to the state of a house; and then our interview lasted about five minutes more and we came away, but we waited fully 20 minutes before anything took place. There was a good deal of remark made amongst the gentlemen there, as to the way in which things were conducted in the City Hall, and, I think, the general opinion of the gentlemen who were on that deputation was that they could not afford to waste their time in such a way; if the real hour for meeting had been half-past one instead of one, I certainly think we ought to have been informed of the fact.

Mr. *Brooks*—continued.

Mr. *Pim*.

16 May 1876.

2388. Are you aware whether that is the common practice in other public bodies?—No, I am not. I am aware of what is the practice at the Port and Docks Board. They have 25 members, and the nominal quorum is 5. I put the question in writing to the secretary, and I have his answer. "Have you ever known a public meeting put off for want of a quorum?" his reply is, "Never." "Have you ever to wait more than five minutes for a quorum?" his reply to that is, "The attendance is so exceedingly regular, I have never known, with one or two exceptions (caused by special circumstances), the Board having to wait for a quorum." I asked him then, "Can you state the average attendance at Board meetings?" and he stated "About 18 out of the 25 members."

2389. Do you know that the Port and Docks Board immediately before business always have a hot luncheon provided for the members?—I am quite aware that they have luncheon, and I say, if providing luncheon for the members of the corporation would induce them to come to their meetings in due time, I would not as a citizen object to the expenditure for providing them with that luncheon.

2390. Can you inform the Committee whether before the business of the Port and Docks Board and of the Commissioners of Irish Lights, a hot luncheon is provided?—I do not know whether it is hot or cold, but there is a luncheon provided.

2391. Can you say with regard to the corporation, whether any luncheon is provided?—I do not know. I do not think it appears in the accounts of the city treasurer, if any luncheon is provided.

2392. You are not aware that the corporation do as the Port and Docks Board do?—I am not at all aware of that.

2393. You spoke also of the Fire Brigade, did you not?—I mentioned the subject of the Fire Brigade.

Mr. *Pim*

16 May 1876.

Mr. *Brooks*—continued.

2394. You said that the efficient management of the Fire Brigade should be one of the duties of the corporation?—Yes.

2395. May I ask you to inform the Committee, is there an efficient management of the Dublin Fire Brigade?—I believe that it is very efficient. I never heard any complaint made of it.

2396. I think you said also that gentlemen who confined themselves to their own business, and who did not engage in politics, would probably be better members of the corporation?—No, I did not say that. A man need not avoid politics in order to fit himself for becoming a member of the corporation, but I think that once he enters the city hall he ought to leave politics behind him. I do not think that the fact of a man being a politician makes him a bad citizen; but I think that politics and the business of the corporation do not go well together.

2397. If you had wealthier members of the corporation, and large owners of property, would the taxation, do you think, be less?—I have not suggested making wealthy men members of the corporation; what I am in favour of is to have the members elected by those who pay a heavy amount in taxes. Those who pay a heavy amount of taxation are not always particularly wealthy. A man may be engaged in a business which necessitates his having large premises in order to carry on that business, but he is not necessarily a bit wealthier than the man who is in the house next door to him, who perhaps only occupies a small house; but the taxation that he pays on the premises that he occupies for his business is a tax upon his business, and in competing with men in the same business in another town where the taxation is not so high, he is uncomfortably weighted in the competition; that is what I am objecting to in the case of Dublin, that the taxation in Dublin is higher, I believe, than the taxation in any other town in Ireland, or probably than in any town in England.

2398. With regard to the improvement rate, could you by any possibility make it lower?—No, I do not think you could do the work for less than 2*s.* on the present valuation of Dublin.

2399. I think that you are one of the advocates of a system of main drainage?—I have been spending the last two years in opposing the system of main drainage.

2400. You do not advocate the main drainage of the City of Dublin?—If I had my own way in Dublin, I would try whether something could be done to improve the condition of the river itself by much cheaper means, and test that before going in for any system of main drainage; but I certainly would not like a system of main drainage for Dublin that was to cost something like three quarters of a million, as I believe the system which the corporation was proposing would be likely to cost.

2401. If members of the corporation were to be elected now on the cumulative vote system, you do not expect that the merchants in Dublin would even then be placed upon better terms relatively than their competitors in provincial towns?—I presume you mean the plural system of voting. I do not advocate cumulative voting. With plural voting I think that they would probably get better value for their money, which is an important point. I rather doubt the fact of taxation being reduced in Dublin by getting in a new body; it is quite possible that we should have it increased, because a new corporation would wish to do many things which in their opinion ought to be done, and we should be willing to pay the money to have done, which the present corporation is not willing to do.

Mr. *Brooks*—continued.

2402. Then they would not be less heavily weighted?—No. I have not advocated the change in order that they should be less heavily weighted, but that they should have a control over the taxation, and that the people who pay it should feel that they were getting value for it.

2403. You said something about their competitors in provincial towns, that they were now more heavily weighted in comparison with them by the local taxation of the City of Dublin?—So they are; and for that reason we should be very careful about increasing taxation any further.

2404. The member elected to the corporation by the cumulative vote would not relieve them of any weight that they now suffer from?—I think it is scarcely likely that they would.

2405. You do not charge the corporation with any misapplication of the funds?—No, I do not.

2406. Can you inform the Committee what proportion of the members of the corporation now elected is under the rating which is proposed, that is to say, a 50*l.* rating?—I have no idea; I place very little value upon the qualification for members of the corporation; what I place importance upon is the qualification of the electors, and not of the men that are elected. I think in very many cases a man who might not be rated at 50*l.* a year might be a very much better representative than a man who is rated at more than 50*l.* I would not place any restriction upon the rating qualification for members of the town council, provided that you get a satisfactory electoral body, but the electoral body is the important thing. That is where we start from.

2407. With regard to the houses that have fallen in the City of Dublin, is it the duty of the members of the corporation, or of the police, to look after the dangerous condition of houses?—I think that it is the duty of the officer of the corporation.

2408. What officers would you say?—I should say the city engineer was the officer who had the oversight of the matter.

2409. The city engineer has not so large an eye as the commissioner of police?—I really do not know the relative sizes of their eyes.

2410. Are you aware that the Commissioner of Police has a thousand men continually patrolling the town, and that it is the duty of the police to inform the city engineer when the houses are in that dangerous condition?—I do not think myself that there are many policemen that know anything about architecture or building. What we want in Dublin is a Building Act. I believe the corporation is at present deficient in the necessary powers, but I believe the power which it has got it does not adequately exercise with regard to dilapidated buildings, or buildings that are unfit for human habitation from being in a bad sanitary condition.

Mr. *Pim.*

16 May 1876.

Mr. *Brooks*—continued.

2411. Can you favour the Committee with any instance of want of supervision or any mismanagement with regard to dilapidated houses?—There are the two houses, which I instanced, which fell in Georges-street recently.

2412. That was nearly opposite your own premises?—Yes, nearly opposite them. There was one child killed by the fall of one of the houses.

2413. Do you think that the corporation are to blame for that?—I think that those houses ought to have been repaired, or something should have been done about them long ago. They had been in a very bad condition for years.

2414. Did you call the attention of the police or the corporation to them?—Several years ago a gentleman asked Mr. Neville to come there; unfortunately he is no longer living, and therefore I cannot produce his evidence; but I was informed the other day that Mr. Neville had been asked, several years ago, by him, to come into our place and get up to a height, from which he could look down on the roofs of those houses opposite, to see the state they were in; that may be six or eight years ago, I dare say.

2145. Can you give the Committee any instances of any jobbery committed by the corporation?—No, I have not made myself up upon that point; I know nothing whatever about it.

2416. I think you said that in Dublin the electors were in some sense similar to the electors of the United States?—No, what I mentioned was, that the people who are in the higher mercantile classes with us in Dublin abstain from interfering in municipal affairs very much in the way in which I know that people in similar circumstances in the United States regularly abstain from interfering in municipal or Parliamentary affairs.

2417. Is it not said of them that they object to rubbing their skirts with their poorer neighbours?—I really do not know; I never heard it said myself.

2418. Is not that the common opinion with regard to the abstention of the higher class of merchants in the United States?—I never heard anyone say that. I really do not know; my own belief as to the reason why they do not take any interest in it is, that they are completely outvoted; that having tried the thing once, and finding that they have no power, they wash their hands of the whole transaction, and say, "we will have nothing to do with it, we cannot help it."

2419. Can you favour the Committee with the number of members necessary to form a quorum of the corporation?—Twenty.

2420. How many in the Port and Docks Board?—Five.

2421. And the Poor Law Board?—I cannot tell you.

Sir *Arthur Guinness.*

2422. It is a fact, is it not, that there is very frequent oppositions by the citizens committee to different schemes of the corporation?—Yes, almost always.

2423. I suppose the citizens are obliged to subscribe to support those oppositions?—Yes. they are always conducted at the expense of the opponents.

Sir *Arthur Guinness*—continued.

2424. In the recent opposition to the main drainage scheme, are you aware what it cost the citizens who took up that opposition?—I do not know the figures precisely, but I should think from about 600 *l.* to 800 *l.*

2425. Do you think that this frequent opposition is caused by any tinge of political bias against the corporation, or simply for the purpose of the good of the city?—I do not think that politics has anything whatever to do with it.

2426. You are aware that there are people of different political views on those committees?—Almost always; in fact, I may say always. These opposition committees are composed of persons of various political opinions.

2427. Both in the case of the committee which opposed the main drainage scheme, and in the case of the committee which opposed the purchase of the gas scheme which were proposed by the corporation?—Yes, in both cases.

2428. Do you know that the great majority of the well-to-do and educated citizens of Dublin and ratepayers opposed those schemes, simply from a fear of their being injurious to the city?—That has been their reason; that they did not feel that they would be useful; and also it is due to the fact that there is a great feeling of want of confidence in the corporation on the part of those who pay the largest amount of taxation, because they feel that they have no real power in controlling the elections or the conduct of the corporation.

Mr. *J. P. Corry.*

2429. Are you aware what proportion of the burgesses on the roll vote at municipal elections?—No, I am not aware, but it is not a large number.

2430. Even of those who are on the burgess roll?—No, even of those who are on the burgess roll. When there is a contest in Dublin there is usually comparatively little interest felt in it; and there are a great many burgesses left unpolled very frequently.

2431. You said that the limit of the municipal borough is small; would you be in favour of the extension of your borough boundary?—I think it a great pity that the outlying townships have been allowed to come into existence as separate governments, but I see great difficulty in extending the borough boundary now, because of the very great difference in the rate of taxation inside and outside the city limits. The people, I think, who live outside have acquired a vested interest in a low rate of taxation which you cannot fairly interfere with now.

2432. Are you aware of the Act which was passed last Session with regard to giving corporations the power to take steps to improve the town by the Artisans Dwellings Act?—Yes, I am aware of an Act having been passed.

2433. Has any attempt been made in Dublin to clear away that property which you complain of, under the provisions of that Act?—No attempt has yet been made, but two or three resolutions have been carried in the corporation within the past fortnight in favour of taking some steps, but there is a great objection felt by a large proportion of the members of the corporation to expending any money or anything beyond a very small

Mr. *Pim.*

16 May 1876.

Mr. *J. P. Corry*—continued.

small amount; a halfpenny or a penny in the pound is what has been spoken of for the purpose.

Mr. *Kavanagh.*

2434. The honourable Member for Dublin asked you whether you could specify any instance of, I will not say malversation of funds, but of what you call not very wise management on the part of the Dublin Corporation; is is not the fact that some time ago they voted 500 *l.* to the French?—Yes, I am aware that that took place. My feeling about that is that it was done from the political feeling of the majority of the corporation towards the French. I think it was a thing which would have been a great deal better not done. The persons to whom that money was devoted were no doubt very badly in want of the funds, and it may have done a great deal of good, but I think it would have been better if it had been left undone.

2435. The point of my question is not whether it was voted to the French or to the Germans; I mean irrespective of political feeling altogether, do not you think that it would have been much better devoted to the purposes of the corporation, such as cleaning the streets and sanitary arrangements?—Yes, I think so; the sanitary arrangements of Dublin, in my opinion, are very much neglected by the corporation, and the reason which they give for that neglect is that they have not got funds to spend upon them. I think that that 500 *l.* would probably have saved a good many more lives if it had been devoted, within three minutes' walk of the City Hall, to sanitary purposes in the city of Dublin, than it did by being sent over to France; and I do not think that the corporation really had any right to make use of their funds in that way. Certainly not, unless they had a surplus, and they always say that they have not got a surplus, in fact, they have extreme difficulty in paying their way from month to month.

2436. I presume you cannot call to your mind any other expenditure of a like kind?—No, I do not recollect anything in particular.

2437. The honourable Member pressed you rather hard upon that point; is it not the fact that the duties thrown upon the towns commissioners and corporations since the Act of 1849 was passed, have very greatly increased?—Very much increased, and especially in the direction of sanitary arrangements, and I think that there is no part of the business of the Corporation of Dublin which is less effectively done than the attention to sanitary matters.

2438. Do you think that the sanitary matters would be more effectively carried out if the burgess roll was increased, as Mr. Curran suggested, from 5,000 to 15,000?—I think it is just possible that in Dublin, if the artisan class who live in tenement houses had votes, they would use their influence towards getting more attention paid to sanitary matters. I say I think it possible, but at the same time they would be spending money which they did not themselves contribute, and even if their opinion were in favour of the expenditure of money in sanitary matters, I do not think it would be just that they should be given the controlling power, as they would be by the increase from 5,000 to 15,000

Mr. *Kavanagh*—continued.

electors over the expenditure of money which they did not themselves contribute.

2439. You do not agree with the Report of the Royal Sanitary Commission, in which they say that the working classes are found to be more inimical than any other class to the carrying out of sanitary arrangements?—I think that from being ignorant of the value of the improvements that are to be carried out, they do not support them, and they do not know what to approve of. If you want to get sanitary matters properly attended to, you must obtain constituents that will elect men of considerable knowledge in that particular branch. But in Dublin the franchise, in my opinion, at present rests, that is to say, the controlling power rests, in the hands of the very small traders, and I think that they are even less disposed than the artisans themselves to improvements of that kind; they feel the taxation rather more, and they have less faith in the improvement of the artisans' class than the classes who are above them have.

Mr. *Brooks.*

2440. With regard to the French donation, your honoured father distributed, did he not, in the time of great distress in Dublin, large sums of money which were contributed from other sources than Irish?—Yes, that is quite true.

2441. Can you say whether we received any donation from the municipality of Paris in the time of our need?—I cannot say whether we did or not.

2442. Do not you know as a general fact, that almost every Christian country on the globe contributed to us at that time?—I am quite aware of that.

4443. You are aware that at the time when the municipality of Dublin contributed 500 *l.* to the poor of Paris, larger sums were contributed also by the municipalities of London and Edinburgh?—I heard in this Committee-room the other day that the municipality of London had contributed, but the municipality of London is in a very different position from the municipality of Dublin; they are extremely wealthy, and they stand on a different foundation altogether.

2444. There were also poorer municipalities in France than that of Paris that contributed to the Irish distress, were there not?—I am not aware whether they did or not, that is to say, whether the municipal governments did it or not; I know nothing about it.

2445. In London you know they did?—Yes, I believe the Corporation of London usually joins in public subscriptions of the kind.

2446. Did you not, in the Statistical Society, at the same time discuss the condition of artisans' dwellings in London?—I am not aware that we had any paper on the subject recently.

2447. Do you know that complaints have been made of the sanitary condition of artisans' dwellings in London?—Yes; and I am aware that very large measures are being taken at present under the Artisans Dwellings Act to improve the sanitary condition of that class.

2448. Can you tell us in what year that Bill was enacted?—It was enacted last year, I think.

2449. Do you know whether it has been applied in London?—My impression is that the Metropolitan

Mr. *Brooks*—continued.

litan Board of Works have several schemes on foot at the present moment applying it.

2450. In Dublin are any steps being taken?—Steps are being taken by some independent citizens outside the corporation, an independent association, for the purpose of improving the dwellings of the artisan classes, but whether they will make use of the Artisans Dwellings Act or not I cannot tell.

2451. With regard to the opening of St. Stephen's Green, which was referred to by the honourable Member for Carlow, you know that my honourable friend the Member for Dublin has offered the municipality a sum of money for the purpose of opening St. Stephen's Green?—He has, and the other day the corporation had a meeting upon the subject, and that just shows how little interest they felt in the matter; there were only 23 members of the corporation, including the Lord Mayor, present to discuss that question, and they were equally divided, and the Lord Mayor gave the casting vote in favour of the adoption of the proposal for opening the Green. I think that is an instance of the way in which things are done by the corporation of Dublin. As St. Stephen's Green has been mentioned, I may as well say that things had reached 10 years ago, as regards the opening of St. Stephen's Green, almost the precise position which they have now reached, with this difference, that no one then came forward in the way in which Sir Arthur Guinness has done to offer 5,000 *l.* towards the expense. A private Bill was promoted in Parliament by several citizens of Dublin with, I think, the Duke of Leinster at their head, and they carried the thing on to a point at which the Government were willing to have undertaken the management of the Green, as I understand they are doing in the present case: and all that was wanted was that the corporation should be willing to surrender the rent of about 300 *l.* a year, which they get out of the Green. But the corporation refused to do that and the Bill fell through in consequence, and therefore the Green has not been opened.

2452. Do you know what outlay it would entail upon the corporation, or upon citizens, if the offer of the honourable Member for Dublin was accepted?—I saw an estimate by a member of the corporation that it would require an outlay of 26,000 *l.*; that is to say, I presume, the annual charge would be equal to the interest upon an outlay of 26,000 *l.*

2453. Do you think that it is a fair subject for consideration with the corporation, whether they should expend 1,000 *l.* upon the maintenance of St. Stephen's Green, or upon the streets?—I think it is a fair subject for the consideration of the corporation.

2454. May I ask, would you prefer that it should be spent upon St. Stephen's Green or upon cleansing Cork Hill?—When they are thinking the matter over they might think it necessary to do both.

2455. Do not you think the corporation are wise to take time to think it over?—If I thought that they were taking time to devote 1,000 *l.* to some better purpose I might think that they were doing very wisely, but I think that when they have got a chance of opening St. Stephen's Green which may never occur again, when Cork Hill may remain and be attacked at another time, they ought to close with the offer of opening St. Stephen's Green.

Mr. *Brooks*—continued.

Mr. *Pim.*

16 May 1876.

2456. And spend 1,000 *l.* a year upon it?—Yes, and spend 1,000 *l.* a year upon it. I should be very happy to contribute my quota to that 1,000 *l.* a year.

2457. Can you say whether the corporation have funds for carrying out the purposes of the Sanitary Act?—I cannot say of my own knowledge, but I have been told by members of the corporation that they have not, and that that is one of their difficulties; but I do not know why they have no funds.

2458. Where could the funds come from?—From the taxation which they now raise from the citizens, and they could spare a portion of that for the purpose of improving the sanitary condition of Dublin. Besides, I am not quite sure whether they have not power under the last Sanitary Act of levying a special rate for sanitary purposes. There is nothing so bad in Dublin at the present moment, I think, as the condition of the slaughter-houses. It is a frightful condition of things, having slaughter-houses scattered through the city, and usually in places where they are surrounded by the dwellings of the poorer classes. Between William-street and George's-street, Castle Market is situated, and there are people there actually living in rooms over the places where the beasts are slaughtered, and in the same neighbourhood pigs are kept, and fowl are kept in large numbers in confined and filthy places. These are things which ought not to be allowed to exist; the corporation ought long ago to have established abattoirs, and done away with those private slaughter-houses. They actually introduced a Bill for that purpose, and the Bill was not opposed by the citizens of Dublin, so far as I remember; but the corporation's own report states that it was withdrawn.

2459. Did not you say, that the Legislature has restricted the funds at the disposal of the corporation?—Yes, but the question is, why they do not go to work at once to get power to construct abattoirs. They could get power to levy a rate for that purpose.

2460. Do you know why they did not get that power?—As I understand from the report of the city engineer the reason was, that they withdrew the Bill.

2461. Do you know their reason for not proceeding?—No, I do not know. My own recollection about it is that the owners of the present slaughter-houses and their friends brought pressure to bear upon the members of the corporation, and they did not wish to annoy the people who were at present in the trade; if I do not mistake, I was told so by a member of the corporation.

2462. Are you in a position to say whether the Bill for constructing abattoirs in the City of Dublin was opposed by the citizens' committee?—I have no recollection, but in the same Bill in which powers were sought for abattoirs powers were sought to do a great variety of other things, and it is quite possible that between the multifarious objects of the Bill that it may have been opposed or that the corporation feared opposition, and therefore withdrew the Bill; but I have no recollection

Mr. *Pim.*

16 May 1876.

Mr. *Brooks*—continued.

recollection of there having been any opposition. There is no statement given in the report of the City Engineer which I have here, that there was opposition. If there had been opposition I think he would have said so.

Mr. *J. P. Corry.*

2463. Are you aware whether the Corporation of Dublin have any powers as other corporations in Ireland have of applying to the Local Government Board for Provisional Orders for doing any works?—I believe they have the same powers as other bodies.

2464. Have they exercised any of those powers?—I do not think that they have ever applied for those powers.

Mr. *Murphy.*

2465. Do you know whether the Corporation of Dublin have applied their attention towards the regulations as to shipping cattle from Dublin on board steamers to England, or have interfered in any way, or laid down any regulations as to the laying of cattle before their shipment, or the examination of them, irrespective of the orders of the Privy Council?—I am not aware whether they have or not. They constructed, some years ago, a very good cattle market.

2466. Is that near the waterside?—No, it is some distance away from the waterside, but it is pretty close to the railways, and it will be nearer when the new line has been made round Dublin.

Friday, 19th May 1876.

MEMBERS PRESENT:

Mr. Assheton.	Sir Arthur Guinness.
Sir Michael Hicks Beach.	Mr. Kavanagh.
Mr. Brooks.	Sir Joseph M'Kenna.
Mr. Bruen.	Mr. Mulholland.
Mr. Butt.	Mr. Murphy.
Mr. Collins.	Mr. O'Shaughnessy.
Mr. J. P. Corry.	Mr. Rathbone.
Mr. Gibson.	

SIR MICHAEL HICKS BEACH, IN THE CHAIR.

Mr. WILLIAM J. HENRY, called in; and further Examined.

Mr. *Henry.*

19 May 1876.

Chairman.

2467. I THINK you have a statement to make in addition to you former evidence?—I was asked the number of names upon the burgess list. I was not able to give it at the time, but I have written to Dublin, and I am able now to state that there are 7,851 names on the burgess list, which forms the present burgess roll.

Mr. Kavanagh.

2468. Then the 7,000 that you referred to does not mean those who have the franchise?—Everyone who appears on the rate books is put on the list, then they are reduced by the revising barrister, or reduced previously by non-payment of taxes.

Mr. NUGENT ROBINSON, called in; and Examined.

Mr. *Robinson.*

Chairman.

2469. I BELIEVE you are the City Treasurer of Dublin, are you not?—I am.

2470. The Committee are anxious to ascertain from you the financial position of the Dublin Corporation. In the first place, can you tell us what amount of property is held by the corporation?—I can; I assume that you mean by that the city estates; we have city estates, the rental of which produces 19,200 *l.* on an average. The number of tenants on the rent roll is 550; the number of houses is very large. The gross rental in 1850-51 was 15,800 *l.*; in 1860-61 it was 17,600 *l.*, showing an increase in 10 years of 1,800 *l.*; in 1870-71 the gross rental was 18,750 *l.*; the increase in these 10 years was 1,150 *l.*; in 1874-75 the gross rental was 18,700 *l.*; showing that the gross increase in the city rental in 25 years was 3,450 *l.* But a property of 540 *l.* a year was sold to the Hibernian Bank, which causes the difference. The net city rental now is 18,700 *l.*

2471. Then there is a margin between that and 19,200 *l.*?—Yes; the reason of that is that since I had the honour of coming into that office, which is only three years, the collection has been much better. In the year 1873 it was remarked here by Mr. M'Evoy, that the collection was very low, being only 17,000 *l.*, but that was an exceptional year. It was in the time of my predecessor in office, who was a very old man, and matters got rather into arrear.

Chairman—continued.

2472. Nineteen thousand two hundred pounds, as you mentioned, is the gross rental?—Yes.

2473. And 18,700 *l.* the rental actually received?—Yes; the gross rental is 18,700 *l.* a year, and last year I collected 19,200 *l.*, but that included arrears.

2474. Where is this property situate?—It is situated in various portions of the city.

2475. Is it all house property?—Principally house property and ground rents. We have also the Baldoyle rents.

2476. When you speak of the Baldoyle rents, where is Baldoyle?—That is an estate on the seashore near the district called Howth and Baldoyle.

2477. Is it reclaimed land?—No, it is a sandhill; I am not aware that it is reclaimed.

2478. What is the annual value of the Baldoyle property?—It is about 1,200 *l.* a year.

Mr. Bruen.

2479. Is that rental or valuation?—The rental.

Chairman.

2480. Do the corporation hold any other property outside the municipal limits?—They have some property in the neighbourhood of Coolock.

2481. What is the rental of it?—About 500 *l.* a year.

2482. And any other?—No, I think those are the

Mr. Robinson.

10 May 1876.

Chairman—continued.

the principal sources of revenue from the rental.

2483. Taking the outside property first, how is the Baldoyle property let?—It is a yearly tenancy; it has been let on lease for 31 years, and we have yearly tenants.

2484. Do I understand that the lease has expired, and that now it is let by the corporation on yearly tenancies?—No, it was let upon lease, and the tenants pay yearly or half yearly.

2485. Is it let at a rack rent?—No; as regards Baldoyle, the rents commence from the year 1857. In 1855 the Baldoyle estate fell in, and the rents commenced in 1857.

2486. Previous to 1855 on what terms had it been let?—I must inquire into that, I do not remember at the moment.

2487. You told us that the rent of the Baldoyle property is 1,200 *l.* a year. Can you inform the Committee how those estates are let, whether the rent received by the corporation is a rack rent, or whether the estates are let on the old system of low rents and fines?—The estates were let upon a lease of 31 years.

2488. Was any fine taken?—No, not that I am aware of.

2489. Can you institute a comparison between the rental and the valuation, in the case of the Baldoyle estate?—No, I cannot answer that question from memory; I would be able to show it from my rental at once.

2490. Is it all let to one tenant?—No, there are several tenants.

2491. Are they agricultural tenants living on the spot?—Yes, agricultural tenants on the spot, principally farmers; there are a lot of small holdings from which the collector collects, and lodges the rents with me monthly.

2492. Are the tenants on the Baldoyle estate in any way connected with the corporation except as tenants?—No, not in any way.

2493. As to Coolock, how is that let?—It was an old lease, and the lease is about falling in now.

2494. When did it commence?—It is long anterior to my coming into the appointment.

2495. I think you stated that the rent of Coolock is 500 *l.* a year; how does that correspond with the valuation?—I cannot answer that question; I have not my rental with me.

2496. When will that lease expire?—It is about expiring now, and about to be re-let.

2497. Do you anticipate an increase of rent?—Decidedly.

2498. To what extent?—I have not considered that question.

Mr. Brooks.

2499. Is it your department to attend to the rental; is not it the law agent's department?—It is the law and land agent's department; my department has nothing whatever to say to it.

Chairman.

2500. Have you not, as the City Treasurer, some idea of the value of the corporation property?—Yes, of the value of it I have.

2501. Referring now to the corporation property outside the city limits; you have stated that this property at Coolock is let on a lease which is just expiring, at a rental of 500 *l.* a year, and you anticipate an increase; can you tell me, speaking quite roughly, whether you think that 500 *l.* a year will be doubled?—I do not think it will.

Chairman—continued.

2502. What is the acreage of the property?—I do not know.

2503. In fact, you cannot give the Committee any particulars about either the Baldoyle or the Coolock property?—That is in the department of the land and law agent. I can only tell you what I know myself.

2504. When the leases of these properties expire, and they are to be re-let, are they put up to be let by auction?—They are, by a clause in the bye-laws. There is a new bye-law upon that subject, No. 55, "That no property of the corporation shall be disposed of (save as hereinafter mentioned) except by auction, after public advertisement, subject, however, to confirmation by the council: provided that if, after being thus set up to public competition on two occasions without a sale or letting being effected, the council, upon a special report thereof, shall have the power to dispose of such property in the manner by them considered most judicious. The exception to the foregoing being in the case of a tenant who is in actual occupation, and where the lease is within a period of five years' expiration, who shall, by memorial to the council, ask for a renewal of said lease; that then, and in such case, the council may, with the consent of the Lords of the Treasury, grant a renewal of said lease without offering the premises to public competition for a term not exceeding 31 years; or, in the event of the tenant proposing to rebuild the premises for a term not exceeding 75 years, at a yearly rent to be calculated by a sworn and competent valuator to be appointed by the Lords of the Treasury, as the yearly value of the premises at the time, and upon the express condition of the tenant before the execution of such new lease expending such sum of money upon the premises as the city architect for the time being, upon his oath, may declare as necessary."

2505. Is this Coolock property let to one tenant or to several?—To one tenant.

2506. Is he a farmer, living on the spot?—I think that he is a resident gentleman.

2507. Is he in any way connected with the Corporation except as a tenant?—No, not in any way.

2508. As to the property within the city limits, I understood you to say that it consists of houses; what is the net rental of the property within the city limits?—The property within the city limits is about 17,500 *l.*

2509. You gave us, did you not, 18,700 *l.* as the net rental?—£. 18,700 is the gross rental.

2510. What, in your mind, is the difference between the net and the gross rental?—The gross rental is the sum of the rent without deductions for taxes.

2511. What is the net rental?—The net is the sum that you receive after deducting taxes.

2512. Then 18,700 *l.* is the net rental, is it not?—No, the gross rental.

2513. You told us that you had actually collected that, I understood you?—I collected 19,200 *l.*; but that included arrears.

2514. Putting arrears out of the question, what was the net rent that you collected?—The actual sum that I collected was 19,139 *l.* 15 *s.* 3 *d.* last year.

2515. That was what you received, including arrears. What I want to ascertain is, what you received, excluding arrears; what was the net rental?

Mr. *Robinson.*

19 May 1876.

Chairman—continued.

rental?—If I had my rental I could tell you in one second, but I have not made it out.

2516. Can you tell us how much arrears you collected last year?—Without my rental I cannot answer that question.

Mr. *Butt.*

2517. Have a copy of last year's accounts?—I have for August 1874, but not for 1875.

Chairman.

2518. Taking the year ending the 31st of August, 1874, I see this: "Account of the receipts and expenditure of the Corporation of the City of Dublin, per the Treasurer of the City of Dublin" (that is yourself, and signed by yourself), contains a statement of cash balances and other particulars; and on page 6 I see, "City Rental Account, rents and arrears of rents, per standard rental, half-year to February 1874, 10,509 *l.*"; is not that the gross rental for the half-year?—Yes, that is the gross rental.

2519. From that you deduct poor's rate, public water rate, income tax, and Pell's poundage; what is Pell's poundage?—It is an old tax; I might use the term an obsolete tax, called Pell's poundage, and it is deducted only on the grant of the city, which is paid to the Government.

2520. But whom is it paid to?—It is allowed to the Government; there is a Government grant, by charter.

2521. Is it paid to the Government?—Yes.

2522. All those deductions amount to 661 *l.* 1 *s.* 8 *d.*, and leave a net half-yearly rental of 9,847 *l.* 18 *s.* 4 *d.*?—Yes.

2523. But then, in addition to that, I find, "Quarterly rents, Baldoyle town, half-year February 1874, 102 *l.* 9 *s.* 1 *d.*," and, deducting the poor rate from that, it leaves 100 *l.* 15 *s.* 10 *d.* Then there is, "Weekly rents, Baldoyle town, half-year February 1874, 127 *l.* 15 *s.* 8 *d.*," making a total net rental for the half year of 10,076 *l.* 9 *s.* 10 *d.*; how do you reconcile that with your statement that the net rental for the whole year, including arrears, was 18,700 *l.*?—I think you will find there that 47,831 *l.* is the net cash collected in the second half-year.

2524. Then a considerable portion of that first half-year was arrears?—Yes.

2525. Then for the next half-year, the 31st of August 1874, taking the gross rental and allowing for deductions, as before, I find a net rental received for that half-year amounting to 7,747 *l.* 2 *s.* 10 *d.*, so that the total net cash for the whole year was 17,831 *l.* 4 *s.*?—Yes, that is so; in the year ending the 31st of August 1875 the total cash was 19,139 *l.* 15 *s.* 3 *d.*

2526. Are your arrears large?—At the present moment there is only 2,600 *l.* due on the September rent.

2527. Will you look at page 2, at the "Recapitulation of rental"; in the first column I find the total arrears, under various heads, amounting to 7,950 *l.* 18 *s.* 1 *d.* in September 1873; how do you explain that?—That the arrears at the end of any half-year will be nearly the same as at the end of the whole year, the financial year being divided into two half-years, ending the 28th of February and the 31st of August. The arrears due the 1st of September 1873 were 7,950 *l.* 18 *s.* 1 *d.*; half-year's rent, due 29th of September 1873, 9,202 *l.* 4 *s.* 6 *d.*; and half-year's rent, due 25th March 1874, 9,218 *l.* 2 *s.* Then, on the other side, we have, "Received, half-year ended 28th February 1874, 10,503 *l.* 5 *s.* 10 *d.*; received, half-year ended 31st August 1874, 7,867 *l.* 3 *s.* 3 *d.*; arrears due 1st September 1874, 8,000 *l.* 15 *s.* 6 *d.*"

Chairman—continued.

2528. Do those represent old arrears, or do they represent hanging gale?—They represent hanging gale; all the tenants pay hanging gale.

2529. Before we go on to the City property, you read to us a bye-law providing that in re-letting the property such re-letting or sale should be by auction, and I understand that the property has been so re-let?—Yes.

2530 Has any instance ever happened in which City property has been re-let by auction, and the rents agreed by biddings at the auction have afterwards been reduced?—I am not aware of any instance.

2531. Are you aware whether anything of the sort happened with reference to the Baldoyle property?—Except in that case of the Baldoyle estate.

2532. Will you tell the Committee how that happened?—That was before my time, and I cannot tell. I have been treasurer only since 1873. As regards Baldoyle, and the arrangements anterior as regards reductions, or otherwise, I have not studied the subject.

2533. You can tell the Committee, I suppose, whether the compulsory bye law for re-letting in that way was in force at the time that this was done?—Yes, I should say that it was.

Mr. *Bruen.*

2534. When was that bye-law passed?—This has been passed quite recently, and there has been an additional bye-law; this bye-law has been added to it.

Chairman.

2535. What was the date of the bye-law that you read to us?—These are dated 1876; it is the new print, but as regards these bye-laws, the town clerk can answer, though I cannot.

2536. (To Mr. *Henry.*) Can you tell the Committee when that bye-law was made with respect to letting by auction the lands of the Corporation?—That bye-law was made in 1851, after the passing of the Dublin Improvement Act.

Mr. *Brooks.*

2537. And the alteration of that bye-law was made with the sanction of the Lord Lieutenant in this year?—Yes.

2538. What was that alteration?—That alteration was, that in the event of the tenant in occupation wishing to have his lease extended, and memorialising the Corporation to that effect, they could, without setting the premises up to public auction, let them, with the consent of the Lords of the Treasury, at a rent to be appraised by a sworn valuator appointed by the Lords of the Treasury.

Mr. *Butt.*

2539. That was added to the bye-law this year?—Yes.

2540. The rest of the bye-law, as I understand you, has been in force since 1851?—Yes, since 1851, after the passing of the Dublin Improvement Act, no rents have ever been reduced, except in the case of the Baldoyle tenancy, and a special Act was passed, called the Dublin Improvement

Mr. Robinson.

19 May 1876.

Mr. *Butt*—continued.

provement Amendment Act in 1864, giving certain tenants upon the Baldoyle estate, a reduction of rent, and the names of those tenants and the reduction of the rent are all scheduled to the Act.

Chairman.

2541. Can you tell the Committee why those rents were reduced?—Because they considered that they were too high. It was set at public auction, and the competition was so great that the tenants were induced to give higher rent than was afterwards considered to be fair, and the Corporation, upon the passing of that Dublin Improvement Act, 1864, asked permission to reduce the rent. That sanction was given, and to the Act of 1864 they scheduled the names of the tenants, with their original rents and the reduction.

2542. Was that considered to be a complete carrying out of the bye-law?—No, they had to go to Parliament to do it.

2543. Did the Corporation consider that they had carried out that bye-law by going to Parliament to reduce the rents which had been agreed upon by auction held under the bye-law?—The Corporation thought that the tenants had given too much. The tenants had all memorialised for a reduction, and then they asked Parliament to give them power to do so, but in no other instances has a reduction been made.

Mr. *Butt.*

2544. The Act to which you refer is a public Act, and it says in Clause 27: "And whereas the several persons named in Schedule A. to this Act annexed, had heretofore become tenants to the corporation by leases or agreement for leases to other portions of the said lands called the Grange of Baldoyle, and the lands of Baldoyle, for the term of 31 years, at the yearly bulk or rack rents as specified in the said Schedule A.: And whereas it afterwards appeared upon comparison of the said reserved rents with the public valuation of the said lands for assessment to the relief of the destitute poor, and with other special valuations of the said lands made by competent persons, that having regard to a proper system of husbandry, the said tenants were totally unable by the produce of the said lands to pay the said rents reserved in the said leases as agreements for leases: And whereas the corporation by resolution of council, resolved to make abatements from the said reserved bulk or rack rents to the several reduced rents as specified in the said Schedule A., from the 25th day of March 1859: And whereas doubts have arisen whether such abatements, although *bonâ fide* made without fine or foregift were not in excess of the legal powers of the corporation, and whether such abatements can be legally continued without the sanction of Parliament; therefore the said several abatements specified in the said Schedule A. are hereby sanctioned, allowed and confirmed, and such abatements shall take effect from the said 25th day of March 1859, and shall continue during the tenancies in respect of which the same respectively were made;" then there are the names of 13 tenants in the schedule, and they are reduced from 1,506 *l.* 9 *s.* 4 *d.* to 1,108 *l.*?—Yes, that is so.

Chairman.

2545. I see the names in the schedule are James Doyle, Gerald Rice, John Gill, Luke White, Luke White, Patrick Butterly, John Font, James O'Reilly, James O'Reilly, Richard Carpenter, Patrick Weldon, John Fitzsimons, and Henry Darley; had any of those persons any connection with the town council except as tenants?—Not one.

2546. Have the corporation expended any money in draining or improving the land?—No, not a shilling.

Mr. *Butt.*

2547. At all events it was done by Act of Parliament?—Yes.

Chairman.

2548. (To Mr. *Robinson.*) With regard to the property within the municipal limits of Dublin, it consists, as I understand you to say, of ground rents and of house rents?—Yes, of house rents, and we get rents from the Stephen's Green Commissioners, and in addition to that there are two old grants from the Government granted in the time of Charles the Second, of about 800 *l.* a year, which we include in the city rental.

2549. Is that by way of ground rent for Government buildings?—No; it was originally granted to the Lord Mayor to keep him a troop of horse; it was also a further grant in the shape of goodwill towards the Corporation of Dublin from Charles the Second, and we include it in our city rental.

2550. Is it included in your rental account?—Yes, because we give a receipt, we are obliged to call it rent; we do not know exactly what to call it except rent.

2551. What kind of proportion of your rental within the municipal limits consists of ground rents, and what of house rents?—I am not the land and law agent; I have only to take the money. I only receive the rents as they are paid in; that is the land and law agent's department.

2552. I understood that you could inform the Committee as to the city property?—I can merely inform you as to the money which I receive and expend.

Mr. *Butt.*

2553. You do not collect the rents, do you?—No, they are paid in by counter.

2554. Are they paid in by the tenants to you?—They are paid in by the tenants to me, and a receipt is issued from my office for the amount.

2555. Then you really collect rents in that case?—Yes, I am the agent for the rents.

Chairman.

2556. Surely, if you collect the rents, you know who pays them?—The whole charge of the city rental, as regards that department, is in the hands of my chief assistant, Mr. Curtin, a most able official, who has been in the office for 13 years. I take up the rest of the departments of the office.

Mr. *Butt.*

2557. Is the accountant here?—Yes.

2558. Does he know?—I cannot answer for him. I do not suppose he does.

Sir *Arthur Guinness.*

2559. Do you include in the estates the lease what

Mr. *Robinson.*

19 May 1876.

Sir *Arthur Guinness*—continued.

what Lord Charlemont holds for his property, which is outside the city boundary?—No; that is outside the city boundary.

Chairman.

2560. Do you know the value of the property which Lord Charlemont holds at Marino?—He pays about 420 *l.* a year.

Mr. *Butt.*

2561. Have you any document that will show that?—The rental will show everything.

2562. Have you there the account, signed by yourself, for 1874?—Yes.

2563. I find here that the rental of the Corporation is divided into four denominations: Ancient Revenue, All Hallows' Rents (which, I suppose, is for Trinity College), St. Mary's Abbey Rents, and St. George's Rents; under which of those heads does Marino come?—That is outside the city boundary.

2564. Does not this profess to be a recapitulation of the whole rental of the city?—It does.

2565. Under which of them does Marino come?—Whether it is under Ancient Revenue, All Hallow's, St. Mary's Abbey, or St. George's, I cannot tell without the rental.

2566. And of course you cannot tell whether Baldoyle is there?—Baldoyle is included in All Hallow's.

Chairman.

2567. You stated, as I understand, that the only Corporation property outside the city limits was at Baldoyle and Coolock; now we have discovered another?—I omitted Lord Charlemont; I forgot him.

2568. Have you omitted any others?—I cannot call to mind at the present moment any others.

2569. You are the City Treasurer, and cannot tell us where the Dublin City property is?—I can tell you.

2570. Will you please tell us then?—I cannot without my rental being here; I can tell you where it is situated, but nothing more.

2571. Have the Dublin Corporation any property besides Baldoyle, Coolock, and Marino, outside the city limits, and if they have, where is it?—They have property at Clontarf.

2572. Where is that?—That is the north-western side of Dublin.

2573. What is the extent and rental of that property?—From memory I cannot trust myself to tell you.

Mr. *Butt.*

2574. Have they not some property near Drumcondra where they have the presentation to a church?—Yes, at Clonliffe.

2575. Have they any at Dolphin's Barn?—Nothing that I know of.

Chairman.

2576. I understood you to say, in answer to one of my questions, that the details of the city rental were attended to rather by a clerk who had been a long time in your office, rather than by yourself?—They are completely attended to by him.

2577. Taking the Account for 1875, there are a good many other items of receipts besides the city rental account; can you explain any of them to the Committee?—Yes.

2578. I see on page 10 an item of "slippage and anchorage," of which there are four quarters, ending with the 24th of June 1874, and the net receipts under that head, deducting the commission of 6 per cent., amounted to 2,306 *l.* 14 *s.* 10*d.* in that year; can you tell us what that is?—Slippage and anchorage are the dues payable upon ships coming into the harbour. The anchorage dues are 3 *s.* 1 *d.* on each ship that enters the harbour; the slippage is 11 *d.* on each ship as it enters the harbour. Then there is 2 *s.* 3¾ *d.* paid to the Lord Mayor once a year by each ship, 5 *s.* 6 *d.* for scales and beams for coal vessels only, and 1 *s.* 6 *d.* chapter and guild fee once a year only.

2579. Are those charges in addition to the amount paid to the Port and Docks Board?—Yes, those are all city dues. I am not aware of the charges of the Port and Docks Board.

2580. Does the Corporation perform any duties with reference to the port of Dublin in return for those payments?—They do; they give tubs and beams and scales to the colliers when they come into the harbour.

2581. Can you tell the Committee what the origin of those payments was?—It is from time immemorial.

Mr. *Butt.*

2582. Is chapter and guild the same as slippage and anchorage?—Yes, slippage and anchorage is the general title, and one of the items of slippage and anchorage is called chapter and guild.

Chairman.

2583. Have the receipts from this source increased or decreased of late years?—They have decreased.

2584. To what extent have they decreased?—I suppose that they have decreased between 200 *l.* and 300 *l.* a year within the last 10 years; the cause of decrease arises from the fact that now one large iron steamer will take such a quantity of coal in it that it decreases the number of colliers coming up the river, and consequently, as the charge is per ship, the slippage and anchorage fees are reduced by that sum.

2585. The charge is levied, is it not, on all vessels, and not on colliers only?—Yes, on all vessels. I might mention that the Government Auditor looked into the question of the decrease of the receipts. The slippage and anchorage dues are now collected by the Custom House officers, but the decrease arises from the fact that I have mentioned.

2586. Do you pay a commission of 6 per cent. to the Custom House officers?—It is paid to Mr. Palgrave, who sets it out in his account. He is the collector appointed, but by the advice of the auditor and his own desire, the Custom House officers collect it.

Mr. *Kavanagh.*

2587. What is the total amount per ship of slippage and anchorage?—Six shillings and threepence three farthings for the slippage and anchorage and Lord Mayor's duty; then in addition to that there is 5 *s.* 6 *d.* water bailiff's fee for scales and beams.

2588. Therefore

Mr. *Robinson.*

19 May 1876.

Mr. *Kavanagh*—continued.

2588. Therefore colliers would pay 11 *s.* $0\frac{3}{4}$ *d.*, and all other ships would pay 6 *s.* $3\frac{3}{4}$ *d.*?—Yes.

2589. What is the amount of those dues in the year?—About 2,200 *l.* or 2,300 *l.*

Chairman.

2590. There are some other items in the receipts; I see there is an item of 260 *l.* for the same year ending July 1874: "Cash lodged by swordbearer, being rent of Sales Room;" and in the city marshals account there is another large item for "Rent of Sales Room and fees of office," amounting to a net lodgment for that year of 447 *l.*; can you explain what that is paid for?—It is on pawnbrokers' licenses.

2591. Is it a tax paid by pawnbrokers on their licenses?—Yes; paid on their licenses and the amount in deposit.

2592. Are the fees paid by the pawnbrokers to this officer?—They are fees paid on pawnbrokers' licenses through the City Marshal and fees on notices.

Mr. *Butt.*

2593. Are you not aware that formerly the city marshal and the swordbearer received those fees themselves as perquisites of their office?—Yes.

2594. An arrangement was then made by which they were put upon salaries, and the fees were received by the corporation?—Yes.

2595. And it is those which are in the accounts?—Yes.

Chairman.

2596. When was the alteration made?—That is of very long standing, and it has been a very vexed question.

2597. Has there been a falling off in those receipts?—Yes, there has.

2598. To what extent in the last ten years?—Between 400 *l.* and 500 *l.* altogether within ten years.

Mr. *Gibson.*

2599. I believe that the Marshal of Dublin receives those fees from all the pawnbrokers in the whole of Ireland, and it is not limited to Dublin?—No, it is not limited to Dublin.

Chairman.

2600. Then that falling off of 400 *l.* or 500 *l.* is a falling off of 100 per cent., is it not?—It was formerly much higher; now it is only 420 *l.* a year.

2601. What is the reason of the decrease?—As I have been informed by the marshal, the reason for the decrease is the reduction in the number of pledges. In 1874 there were 3,128,684 pledges, and in 1875 there were 2,715,555, being a deficit of 413,129, and in the amount lent there was a falling off of 54,108 *l.*

2602. What is the salary paid to the City Marshal?—300 *l.* a year.

2603. And what to the swordbearer?—250 *l.* a year.

2604. So that the receipts from the fees still are larger than the salaries paid to those officers?—Yes.

2605 How are those fees from pawnbrokers collected?—The city marshal collects them; he sends me in a weekly lodgment; he sends me in a docket with the amount, and I lodge it to the credit of the borough fund.

Chairman—continued.

2606. How is it paid by the pawnbrokers?—I do not know that.

Sir *Joseph M'Kenna.*

2607. Are they not fees which are paid on the sales at the divisional sales room as a poundage on the sales?—Yes, I believe they are.

Mr. *Butt.*

2608. Are you aware that under the Statutes regulating the trade of pawnbroking in Ireland, the Marshal of the City of Dublin is registrar of pawnbrokers all over Ireland?—I have heard so; I do not know it.

2609. Of course wherever he gets the fees you get them, that is all you know?—Yes, and that is all I care about.

Chairman.

2610. Can you tell us anything about the city debt?—I can.

2611. In the Act of 1849 there were two sums, one of 21,263 *l.* 12 *s.*, and the other 18,500 *l.*, debts due by the Commissioners of Wide Streets to the Lords of the Treasury; those debts were to be paid off according to the Act by the Lord Mayor and Corporation of Dublin, to whom the Act transferred the powers of the Commissioners of Wide Streets; can you tell us whether at the time of the passing of the Act of 1849 there was any other debt upon the Corporation of Dublin besides that?—Yes, at that particular time there were judgment debts of 2,800 *l* for which a receiver was put over the City estates.

2612. What were those for?—I cannot tell the items, but it was for expenditure by the outgoing corporation.

2613. Was it for work done for the corporation?—Yes; and there were law costs, 1,729 *l.*, in addition.

2614. How were those incurred?—I cannot tell; all those debts were transmitted to the incoming corporation.

Mr. *Butt.*

2615. What do you mean by the in-coming corporation?—I mean that the out-going corporation left those debts to those who succeeded them.

2616. When you speak of the out-going and in-coming corporation, do you mean the change that was effected in 1851?—Yes.

2617. Is not this the fact, that the corporation at that time, somehow or other, got into debt from their current expenditure amounting to between 2,000 *l.* and 3,000 *l.*?—Yes.

2618. Are you aware that they were unable to pay it, and an execution was put into the Mansion House?—So I have heard.

2619. And a receiver was applied for over the corporate estates?—Yes.

2620. In what year was that?—In the year 1850, I should say.

Chairman.

2621. Do you know how that small debt was paid, and when?—There was a guarantee formed by members of the corporation.

2622. Was it paid by the members of the corporation personally?—I do not know how it was paid.

2623. Are you able to inform the Committee whether there were any permanent debts, so to speak, charged on the corporation at the time of the

Mr. *Robinson.*

19 May 1876.

Chairman—continued.

the passing of the Act of 1849, besides the two debts of the Commissioners of Wide Streets, which I have quoted?—Not unless you mean the debenture debt.

2624. What was the debt of the corporation?—It was 292,723 *l.*

2625 Was that Irish currency or English currency?—It was Irish currency.

Mr. *Murphy.*

2626. In what year was that?—In 1850.

2627. Will you just look at the accounts of 1874; you see on page 119 there is a "Schedule showing amount of debt charged on city estates and upon municipal rates, the amounts raised or borrowed under the authority of various Acts of Parliament, and also the amount of debt secured by bonds of indebtedness, &c., on the 31st August 1874," and the first heading I see is, "City Estate Liabilities, Debenture Debt of 203,000 *l.* late Irish currency, equivalent in British currency to the sum of 187,384 *l.* 12 *s.* 3 *d.*"; was that debt due by the corporation in the year 1849?—Yes, that was a portion of the debenture debt that was due; we pay 500 *l.* a year off the debenture debt

Sir *Arthur Guinness.*

2628. Do you mean in reduction of the debt?—Yes, we take up five debentures at par.

Chairman.

2629. In addition to that, I see that there is a debenture debt of 26,000 *l.* British currency; was that also a debt of the corporation at that time?—Yes.

2630. What is the annual charge on the city for the interest of those debts?—The annual charge, at 4 per cent., is 8,404 *l.* 6 *s.* 10 *d.*

Mr. *Collins.*

2631. Does not that 4 per cent. extend to the entire debt?—No; we pay as high as 5 per cent. upon the Waterworks Loan.

Chairman.

2632. That debenture debt, as I understand it, has remained precisely the same since the date of the Act of 1849?—We have been paying 500 *l.* a year to reduce the debt; as I say, we take up five British debentures every year from the Hibernian Bank.

2633. Then it is not the same amount now that it was in 1849?—It is reduced by the 500 *l.* a year.

2634. Do you mean 500 *l.* a year for 27 years?—Yes.

2635. Then those figures which stand in this account as the city estates liabilities on the 31st August 1874 were not the city estates liabilities in 1849?—It is the same debt; there is a difference in the amount which I cannot at present account for.

2636. You do not know whether it is the same amount or not?—I do not.

2637. The next heading is, "Improvement Fund Liabilities"; have those been incurred under the provisions of the Act of 1849?—Yes, they have.

2638. The first is "Cattle Market Bonds issued to subscribers to cattle market: Interest at 6 per cent. per annum, payable out of profits of market, 17,000 *l.*; bonds issued to Michael Meade at 5 per cent. per annum, 550 *l.*; mortgage to Alderman Tarpey, interest at 4½ per cent. per annum, 3,500 *l.*; total debt on account cattle market, 21,050 *l.*?"—Since then there has been an increase in that debt; in the year since that account was published the corporation have borrowed 20,000 *l.* for the purpose of improving the streets under the provisions of the Act of 1849. They have also borrowed 3,500 *l.* to increase the cattle market, and to extend it.

Chairman—continued.

2639. Where do those items appear?—They appear in the account of 1875, which is not printed yet; the audit is not complete.

2640. Where do the receipts from the cattle market appear in these accounts?—At pages 80 and 81.

2641. I see on page 81 the sum of 2,346 *l.* 6 *s.* 1 *d.*; does that represent the income from the cattle market within that year?—It does.

2642. And the expenditure is 1,822 *l.* 6 *s.* inclusive of interest on the cattle market bonds and mortgages?—Yes

2643. I see that this debt was borrowed under sect. 24 of the 12 & 13 Vict. c. 49; what has been the total sum borrowed from time to time by the corporation for the cattle market purposes only?—£. 24,450.

2644. Has any of that been paid off?—No, none.

2645. I see in the income account for the year ending the 31st of August 1874, there is a balance to credit of 3,901 *l.* 5 *s.* 3 *d.*; did not the corporation devote any of the profits of the cattle market towards paying off the debt incurred in making it?—They have not done so yet.

2646. To what purposes are the profits devoted?—The profits are devoted to repairs and maintenance; the surplus is very small, after the repairs and maintenance.

2647. From the figures which I quoted to you from this account, there appears to have been a surplus in that year of 500 *l.*, speaking roughly. Is that 500 *l.* the surplus after deducting all those payments?—Yes, that surplus has not been applied in any way towards the liquidation of the debt; I should also say that there is a quantity of ironwork, the repairs of which are very expensive as a rule.

2648. To what purposes is the surplus devoted?—It remains as a surplus to credit, in case it should be called upon or required.

2649. But there is a balance to credit from these repeated surpluses, amounting in the total to 3,901 *l.*; is that placed out at interest?—It is not.

2650. Can you show me any place in the general account of the corporation where the profits from this cattle market appear?—No, there is no place in the accounts.

Sir *Joseph M'Kenna.*

2651. Is there a separate account at the Bank of Ireland for this surplus; is the surplus put apart in any way in an account by itself in the Bank of Ireland, or anywhere?—No; there is no surplus account.

2652. Therefore, any surplus that may have accrued from this special source has gone into your general cash account?—Yes.

Mr. *Butt.*

2653. Are not there separate accounts kept in the Bank of Ireland of the receipt and expenditure of the different departments of the corporation?—Yes.

2654. Is

Mr. Robinson.

19 May 1876.

Mr. *Butt*—continued.

2654. Is not the pipe water account kept separate?—Yes.

2655. Is not the improvement account kept separate?—Yes.

2656. And, latterly, the sewer rate is also kept separate, having been severed from the improvement account, with which it had been previously mixed?—Yes.

2657. Is there now a separate account kept in the same way for the cattle market?—Yes.

2658. If there was a surplus of 3,000 *l.* or 4,000 *l.*, at the end of the year standing to credit in the account of the cattle market, would not it so stand to the separate credit of the cattle market?—It would.

2659. Must you not, therefore, correct your previous answer, that the surplus of the cattle market went into the general account of the corporation?—Yes; I would correct it in that way.

2660. It stands by itself, totally distinct, to the credit of the cattle market, and could only be drawn out by a cheque drawn on the cattle market account?—Precisely so.

2661. Have you any general account for the corporation at all?—Nothing, but my personal account at the Bank of Ireland; as a matter of fact, there is no general account.

2662. The whole of the accounts of the corporation are divided, are they not, into several accounts, and separate cheques drawn against each account?—Yes.

Chairman.

2663. So that that 3,000 *l.* is not only balanced to the credit of the account, but there is 3,000 *l.* more in the bank on account of the cattle market?—No, that is a matter of account; it is due by capital account; you will find the particulars of the balance due by capital account 2,445 *l.* 12 *s.* 2 *d.*, and cash 1,455 *l.* 13 *s.* 1 *d.*, making a total of 3,901 *l.* 5 *s.* 3 *d.*

Mr. *Butt.*

2664. Under the former system, unless it has been changed since, any person entitled to draw cheques on the cattle market could draw them?—Yes.

2665. And no one else could?—No. The cheque might be separately drawn by the No. 2 committee, who have charge of the cattle market affairs.

2666. They could draw a cheque on the Bank of Ireland; is that the same now?—Yes, they could draw a cheque for any balance that was in the bank.

2667. What has become of that balance?—This sum of 2,445 *l.* 12 *s.* 2 *d.* is the sum due by capital account; that was the sum expended.

2668. Will you look at the income account, and tell me if there is not a balance there?—Yes.

2669. Is that balance in the Bank of Ireland, or what has become of it?—The cash in the bank on that day was 1,455 *l.* 13 *s.* 1 *d.*, to the credit of the market account.

2670. To be drawn against in the usual way?—Yes.

Sir *Joseph M'Kenna.*

2671. At page 90 of the Treasurer's Account of 1874, there is a statement of cash balances on the 31st of August 1873, and there is a statement of balances debtor and balances creditor, and there are certain accounts there to which there are credit balances charged, and there are other accounts, for instance, the Improvement Fund Account, to which there is a debtor balance?—Yes.

2672. What account appears first in that statement with a creditor balance?—The borough fund, which has a creditor balance of 728 *l.* 6 *s.* 8 *d.*

2673. Which fund has a debtor's balance?—The improvement fund, 4,032 *l.* 19 *s.* 4 *d.*

2674. You see that there are a number of credit balances that are put on one side and a number of debtor balances on the other, and you find there is a debtor balance to the improvement fund; where did the money come from in order to be able to pay the monies for which that debit arises there?—At that time the council drew from a general account. You will find further down there is a large credit on the north and south sewer fund.

2675. Am I right in saying that, at that date, at any rate, the general account was kept in this manner: that those funds which you had to the credit of one set of accounts were capable of being used for the purposes of others?—Quite so.

2676. That took place in 1873?—Yes.

2677. Am I right, then, in saying that the creditor balances to whatever accounts they existed, at the time that that account was made up, were swamped or absorbed so far as the debtor balances would tot up to, by the debtor balances?—Yes, so far as they would tot up.

2678. That has been corrected since, has it not?—Yes, that has been corrected since.

2679. Then you see at the foot of it there is a balance of balances? Yes.

2680. May I ask you whether at the date at which that account was made up for the Bank of Ireland there were separate sums to the credit of each of those accounts at the Bank of Ireland to the figures that are there represented?—Yes; there were at the Bank of Ireland.

2681. There was the debtor balance, was that due to the Bank of Ireland also?—If you will allow me to explain, at that time they were not drawing upon the north and south sewers; the north and south sewers and the improvement fund were kept in the one account, and there was 2,836 *l.* 6 *s.* to the credit of the south sewers, and 736 *l.* 18 *s.* 3 *d.* to the credit of the north sewers, and that went as against any debtor balance.

Mr. *Collins.*

2682. As I understand you, the balance as appearing on the accounts amounted to the credit of the cattle market account with the Bank of Ireland, to about 3,900 *l.*?—Yes.

2683. And that was the accumulation of balances accruing over a period of time?—Yes.

2684 You stated further that the present amount to credit at the Bank of Ireland would be 1,400 *l.*?—Yes.

2685. I think I understood you to say that the difference between 1,400 *l.* and 3,900 *l.* could be accounted for in this way: that although it did not stand to the credit of the cattle market account with the Bank of Ireland, it was expended under the head of capital debt account?—Yes.

2686. Then the balance which is not standing at present to the credit of the cattle market account at the Bank of Ireland, that is to say, the difference between 1,400 *l.* and 3,900 *l.*, was expended

Mr. *Robinson.*

19 May 1876.

Mr. *Collins*—continued.

expended on the cattle market, and carried to the capital account?—Yes, it was.

Chairman.

2687. Turning to the next account in 1874, I see "Waterworks Fund Liabilities," and they seem to consist of a sum of 363,368 *l.* 13 *s.* remaining due on account of a loan, which originally amounted to 382,000 *l.*, from the Public Works Loans Commissioners?—Yes.

2688. Is that in process of repayment by instalments?—It is. We have repaid of that loan in capital 25,127 *l.*; it is payable by two half-yearly instalments.

2689. You are speaking of up to the present date; but up to the date of this account 18,631 *l.* appears to have been paid off?—Yes, precisely so.

2690. Then, in addition to this amount which is still due to the Public Works Loan Commissioners on this account, I see that there are several other loans due to the Bank of Ireland, to two assurance companies, to Dr. Kane, to Mr. John Jameson, and amounts due on debentures, making a total remaining due on account of the sum of 509,000 *l.*, borrowed under the powers of the Dublin Corporation Water Works Act 490,368 *l.* 13 *s.*; has any portion of the loans borrowed under the powers of that Act been repaid, besides the part that has been repaid to the Public Works Loan Commissioners?—No, it has not. We took up mortgages, but we re-issued them.

Mr. *J. P. Curry.*

2691. At a lower rate of interest, or at the same rate of interest?—In some cases at a lower rate, 4½ per cent.

Chairman.

2692. I see Mr. Jameson holds a mortgage on this account of 2,000 *l.*, at 5 per cent.; is that an old mortgage?—That is an old mortgage; it is a mortgage which is about expiring, and we are going to re-issue it at 4½; we will not give more.

2693. Then, in addition to that, there is an old pipe water debenture debt of 72,015 *l.* 7 *s.* 8 *d.*; what was that?—That was for the formation of the original pipe water works.

2694. By whom was that liability incurred?—By a corporation of a bygone period.

2695. Do you know how much that debt originally amounted to?—I do not know that it ever was printed.

2696. Do you know whether any of it was ever paid off?—None of it was ever paid off to my knowledge.

2697. Was there ever a sinking fund?—No, there has been no sinking fund.

2698. In addition to what I have already quoted, there is another head, "Bonds of Indebtedness," under which I see "Amount due on Lloyd's bonds issued to contractors, &c., 11,216 *l.* 6 *s.* 1 *d.*"; what is that for?—Those were for the construction of the Vartry Waterworks, and they have all been paid off.

2699. Would not the heading "Waterworks Fund Liabilities" embrace the construction of the Vartry Waterworks?—Yes; but under our borrowing powers we could only go to a certain sum; but since this account which you are reading now was furnished we got an Act of Parliament, by which we could borrow 50,000 *l.*, and

Chairman—continued.

one of the items in the schedule of that Act set forth the debts due on those Lloyd's bonds, and we discharged them out of the moneys which the Board of Works have lent us to do it with under the powers of that Act of 1874.

2700. Was that a private Act?—It was a Provisional Order.

2701. What were the purposes for which you were allowed to borrow under that Act?—We were allowed it for the purpose of constructing new filter beds at Roundwood, and a larger storage reservoir at Stillorgan, and for the purpose of paying off those debts, those debts having been incurred for the construction of the works.

2702. Then are we to understand that the borrowing powers under that Act were solely on account of the waterworks?—Solely on account of the waterworks.

2703. And this item here, the amount due on Lloyd's bonds that I quoted, was solely on account of the waterworks?—Solely.

2704. And that, you say, has been paid off since under the powers of that Act?—Yes, under the powers of that Act, from money borrowed from the Board of Works.

2705. On what terms were those moneys borrowed; was it arranged to be repaid by instalments?—Yes, by yearly instalments. We have repaid over 1,100 *l.* of the principal.

2706. Have you borrowed the whole 50,000 *l.*?—No, we have borrowed 35,400 *l.* We have still a sum of 15,600 *l.* to borrow for the construction of a large reservoir at Stillorgan.

2707. There are two other items of 3,327 *l.* 5*s.* and 2,700 *l.*, also under the heading of "Bonds of Indebtedness," in this account; these, I presume, were also incurred for the waterworks?—Yes, both.

2708. And they have been paid off by the powers of the Act of 1874?—They have.

2709. It appears from this account that the total debt of the Corporation on the 31st of August 1874, was 820,262 *l.* 4 *s.*; is that correct?—We have increased it since by that borrowing, so that the total debt at the present moment is 834,329 *l.*

2710. Can you tell the Committee what happened to those two items of 21,263 *l.* 12 *s.* and 18,500 *l.* which were due by the old Commissioners of Wide-street?—They were to be paid off out of the improvement fund from time to time by instalments.

2711. Have they been paid off?—They have.

2712. The only improvement fund liabilities that appear on this account are the cattle market debt and the balance due on account of advance of 2,000 *l.* for the improvement of the College railings and College-green?—There is a further liability since that account of 20,000 *l.*, and that is part and parcel of a loan of 50,000 *l.* which the Corporation applied for and obtained from the Law Life Assurance Society, at 4½ per cent., under the Improvement Act of 1849, for the purpose of improving and paving the streets.

2713. Has that got to be added to the debt of which you have told us?—£. 20,000 of it has; we have only taken up 20,000 *l.* of it as yet.

2714. You are in process of taking up the rest, are you?—Yes; in that sum of 834,329 *l.* that 20,000 *l.* is included, because we have taken it up.

2715. Have you any of your borrowing powers in process of exercise that have not yet been exercised?—Our only borrowing powers unexercised are

Mr. Robinson.

19 May 1876.

Chairman—continued.

are about 25,000 *l.* under the Act of 1849, and 15,600 *l.* under the Waterworks Provisional Order Act, 1874. We sold two houses, a portion of the estate in College Green, and we got 13,600 *l.* for them, and we were able to buy in our debentures from 85 up to 88.

Mr. *Brooks*.

2716. Did you apply the whole of that 13,600 *l.* to the extinction of debentures?—Yes.

2717. At what price?—From 85 to 88.

Mr. *Bruen*.

2718. How much cash did you get for each 100 *l.* debenture when you issued them originally?—That is so very long ago that I cannot remember.

Sir *Joseph M'Kenna*.

2719. Some of them were issued in settlement of claims, I suppose?—Yes.

Mr. *Collins*.

2720. What rate of interest do those bonds bear which you bought at 85 to 88?—Four per cent.

Chairman.

2721. Your improvement rate is limited to 2 *s.* in the 1 *l.*, is it not?—Yes.

2722. Can you tell us what annual charge that rate has to bear for payment of interest or repayment of debt?—Under the recent law we are obliged to repay it at the rate of 2,000 *l.* a year.

2723. What did you receive last year from the improvement rate?—We received 52,009 *l.* for the year ending the 31st of August 1875.

2724. How much of that went to repayment of debt, or payment of interest?—We have only paid to the Bank of Ireland a portion of the sum borrowed to widen College Green, and for the railings.

2725. I want to know how that 52,000 *l.* was expended, and how much of it went in repayment of debt, or in payment of interest?—I find these items: General works, viz., paving, 9,069 *l.*; macadamising, 13,143 *l.*; scavenging and watering, 6,099 *l.*; flagging and asphalting, 4,584 *l.*; construction of house drains, 713 *l.*; stores, White Horse Yard, 408 *l.*; miscellaneous small items, 1,491 *l.*; carters' wages, 2,786 *l.* Then the horse account is: Purchase of horses, 599 *l.*; forage, 4,051; veterinary expenses, 252 *l.*; harness and repairs, 72 *l.*; miscellaneous, 123 *l.*; stable expenses, 513 *l.*; weekly wages, 530 *l.*; salaries, 2,266 *l.*; compensations, 1,369 *l.*; law and Parliamentary, 244 *l.*; Smithfield Market, 597 *l.*; City weigh-houses, Burgh Quay and City Quay, 348 *l.*; public lighting account, 6,970 *l.*; domestic scavenging 346 *l.*; expenses of maintenance of City Hall, 524 *l.*; proportion of audit fee to Local Government Board auditor, 32 *l.*; wide street rents, 182 *l.*; circular road turnpike trust, 2 *l.* 6 *s.* 8 *d.*; repayment on account of deposits for licenses, 1,144 *l.*; widening and improving streets, &c., 673 *l.* That gives a total in round figures of 61,000 *l.*

2726. I thought you told me that the total receipts were 52,000 *l.*?—I thought you meant the total received from the 2 *s.* rate; that is 52,909 *l.* The total received from all sources is 63,828 *l.* 15 *s.*

Mr. *Kavanagh*.

2727. Does that include the estate rental?—No, that is another fund; this is the improvement fund, and these are the details of the receipts: Law expenses account, sundries, 11 *l.*; Smithfield Market and weigh-houses, 350 *l.*; City weigh-houses, 2 *l.* 12 *s.* 6 *d.*; domestic scavenging, 300 *l.*; coal duty, 440 *l.*; circular road turnpike trust, 33 *l.*; deposits for licenses, 3,078 *l.*; widening and improving streets account, 2,300 *l.*; Alliance Gas Company, street openings account, 1,450 *l.*; Collector General of Rates' lodgments, 52,909 *l.* The north and south sewers rate are in this 52,909 *l.* The whole receipts from the Collector General were 52,909 *l.* 5 *s.* 5 *d.*

2728. How much of the 52,909 *l.* represents the 2 *s.* improvement rate?—I have only an abstract of the account. I cannot tell you that, but that is the total collected.

Mr. *Butt*.

2729. You cannot distinguish the sewer rate and the improvement rate?—Not from this abstract.

Mr. *Kavanagh*.

2730. Does it not include other items?—No.

Chairman.

2731. What year do those figures refer to?—The year ending the 31st of August 1875. Then the account goes on: Dividends on purchase money, 100 *l.*; Dublin Tramways Company, 49 *l.*; proceeds of old iron, 100 *l.*; recoupment of account charged last year, but not drawn out of bank, 25 *l.*; and amount from north and south sewers transferred by order of Committee No. 1, 2,482 *l.* 12 *s.* 8 *d.*

2732. Then that is not included in the 52,909 *l.*?—No, this is not; this is a transfer; but the collection of the north and south sewers rate is in that 52,909 *l.*

Mr. *Collins*.

2733. What do you mean by a transfer?—Formerly the corporation used to draw against the north and south sewers rate and the improvement rate, which were treated as one fund, and if there was a credit balance to the north and south sewers rate, the improvement rate levied upon it.

2734. It was a transfer to adjust the sewers fund?—Yes. We have now separate accounts in the Bank of Ireland for the north and south sewers fund.

2735. Practically, that would not affect the balance either of revenue or of expenditure; it was a mere transfer for the purpose of adjusting the account?—Yes.

Mr. *Bruen*.

2736. What was it transferred from?—From the improvement fund to the sewers rate.

2737. In fact, it is a record of opening a new account?—Yes, it is opening a new account and a new audit; I have looked into it closer, and I see that it is a receipt from the sewers rate account from the north and south sewers.

Mr. *Kavanagh*.

2738. Then it is not included in the 52,909 *l.*?—No.

Mr. *Butt*.

2739. This is taken here amongst the receipts, is it not?—Yes, I did not make it out; the city accountant is here who made it out.

Mr. THOMAS O'DONNELL, called in; and Examined.

Mr. O'Donnell and Mr. Robinson.

19 May 1876.

Chairman.

2740. You are the City Accountant, are you not?—I am.

2741. Will you explain this item: "Amount from north and south sewers transferred by order of Committee No. 1, 2,482 *l.* 12 *s.* 8 *d.*"?—This item which is transferred to the credit of the improvement fund, consists of charges which had been formerly made against the improvement fund, charges which should have been borne by the sewers fund, and by the order of Committee No. 1, I transferred this sum to the credit of the improvement fund as it stands, and consequently it increases the revenue of the improvement fund for the year ending the 31st of August 1875, and it diminishes the revenue of the sewers; it is debited to the sewers, and credited to the improvement. This matter has been before the auditor, and he has approved of it.

Mr. Butt.

2742. It is simply the amount of the 2 *s.* rate for improvement purposes, which you separate from the account for the sewers?—Yes.

2743. That account that you hold in your hand was strictly framed, according to the view of the auditor of the Government, showing nothing but the receipts and expenditure on account of the improvement fund?—Precisely.

2744. But there having been money taken out of the improvement fund to apply to sewerage purposes before, it was refunded from the sewerage fund?—Yes.

2745. And so increased the improvement fund for that year?—Yes, there are three years' charges included in that sum; money that was charged during three years against the improvement fund, which should have been charged against the sewers, because during those three years there was only one account in the Bank of Ireland for improvement rate, sewers rate, and grand jury rate, all kept under the account called "improvement fund."

2746. Is it correct to say that that was a recoupment of the improvement fund of money previously applied out of it for sewage purposes, which ought not to have been taken from that fund?—Certainly; a recoupment to that extent.

Mr. Kavanagh.

2747. The sum put down as 52,909 *l.*, is derived, is it not, from the 2 *s.* rate?—Altogether.

2748. And the sum brought back from the other rate is in addition to that?—Yes, quite so.

Chairman.

2749. (To Mr. *Robinson*). You have given us the total of the different items of expenditure; what is the total of the different items of receipt?—£ 63,828. 15 *s.*

2750. My original question to you was, how much of that 2 *s.* improvement rate was expended in the repayment of debt or in payment of interest, and you have given us the items for the year last past of the expenditure of the improvement rate; but I do not find any such item under the heads that you have given us?—Except under the head, Widening Streets, 673 *l.* 17 *s.* 1 *d.* That is part and parcel of the repayment to the Bank of Ireland of the sum borrowed for widening College Green.

Chairman—continued.

2751. Is that in the payment of interest and the repayment of debt?—A portion of both.

2752. How much?—I cannot tell you how much; I have not the details.

2753. The total amount advanced from the Bank of Ireland for widening College Green was only 2,000 *l.*, was it?—£. 3,000 *l.*

2754. I will take some of the larger items that you have given us in that account; you stated that 9,000 *l.* was spent for paving; how is that made up; is any of that repayment of debt?—No, not a farthing; that is merely labour and work.

2755. Is the next sum of 13,000 *l.* for macadamising the streets entirely labour and work?—Entirely.

2756. Are you quite sure of that?—I am; these are the weekly bills for labour and work which I hold in my hand, and they will show.

Mr. Butt.

2757. Does this show that any portion of the improvement rate has been applied to paying off debt?—No, nothing but that item of 673,000 *l.*

2758. That was not debt; that was an overdrawn account. Was it anything more than an overdrawn account at the Bank of Ireland?—It was the sum borrowed under the Act of 1849.

2759. I will ask your attention to a provision in the Act of 1849. Under that Act are you aware that, by the 116th section of the Dublin Improvement Act, the fifth application of the improvement rate was in setting apart and appropriating 1-70th part thereof in payment off of the principal moneys which shall have been borrowed or secured on the said improvement rate?—I am aware of that.

2760. And lastly, in paying off the principal of all moneys due on the credit of the said improvement rate; that is, if they have a surplus; but now tell me is there any money due that has been borrowed on the improvement rate?—Yes, those are the loans that I have already gone through.

2761. To what amount?—There is 25,000 *l.* for the Cattle Market.

2762. Is the Cattle Market on the improvement rate?—It is the money borrowed under that section.

2763. Are you now applying one-twentieth of the rate in paying off the debt?—It has not been done.

Chairman.

2764. Then it is, as I understand it, taking the several items that you have given us, paving, macadamising, scavenging and watering, flagging and asphalting, house drains and stores, miscellaneous, and carters' wages, making a total of 40,299 *l.*, out of the improvement rate; all that is spent in work in the year?—It is.

2765. And in the same way that, taking the various items which you have given us on the horse account, amounting altogether to 6,143 *l.*, that is spent in work in the year?—Yes.

2766. How many horses do the corporation keep?—Eighty.

2767. Does not that seem rather a large expense per horse. I see that there is an item of 599 *l.* 6 *s.*

Mr. O'Donnell and Mr. Robinson.

19 May 1876.

Chairman—continued.

599 *l.* 6 *s.* for the purchase of horses; but how is it that the 80 horses consume 4,051 *l.* worth of forage?—I did not expect to be asked the question, and I cannot explain it.

2768. You cannot understand it?—I cannot.

Mr. *Butt.*

2769. What officer of the Corporation checks the expenditure on horses?—The secretary of No. 1 Committee.

Chairman.

2770. Can you explain at all how 40,000 *l.* is spent on general works; how many labourers do the Corporation employ?—The number varies from 500 to 700.

2771. Taking 700 as the maximum, 40,000 *l.* a year is spent on their wages?—Yes, it is; their wages are about 530 *l.* a week on the average.

2772. Will you inform us, as you cannot explain these items yourself, what officer of the Corporation can explain them?—The secretary of No. 1 Committee is the officer who prepares those items, and to whom the accounts are submitted; perhaps the City Accountant can do so, but in the absence of the details I cannot explain them.

2773. Is the general works account under No. 1 Committee?—Yes; No. 1 Committee have the sole control and disposal of that rate.

2774. Is the horse account under No. 1 Committee?—Yes.

2775. Do they regulate the expenditure, and are they responsible for it?—They do, and they are responsible for it.

2776. The next one is, salaries, 1,931 *l.*; ditto, general account proportions, 335 *l.*; making a total of 2,266 *l.*; can you explain that?—I could tell you the amount of the salaries of each officer.

2777. What officers are included in that No. 1 Committee?—There is the secretary and his staff: Mr. Beveridge gets a salary of 300 *l.* a year; the inspector of gas meters, Mr. Conolly, 300 *l.*; Mr. Clarke, the first clerk in the office, 150 *l.*; Mr. Kerrison, the bookkeeper, 100 *l.*; and Mr. Rosborough, 125 *l.* In addition to that, as attached to No. 1 Committee, there is the inspector of streets, Mr. Newman, 200 *l.*; Mr. Morrison, 130 *l.*; Mr. Patrick Kenny, 160 *l.*; Mr. Patrick K——, 111 *l.*; Mr. Moore, 117 *l.*; Mr. Duffy, 104 *l.*; those are the street inspectors.

2778. Are those all the officers of No. 1 committee?—Yes, whose salaries are paid by that committee out of that particular fund.

2779. And that item for salaries includes everything, but the wages of the ordinary day labourers?—Yes.

2780. What is this item for compensation, 1,369 *l.*?—I am obliged to quote from the published accounts of last year, as I have not the details of that abstract with me, but those details will suit your purpose equally well, I imagine. Thomas Reilly, the late paving clerk, 59 *l.*; Richard Travis, 31 *l.*; William Clarke, the late overseer of flagging, 39 *l.*; C. Palmer, paving tax collector (he is dead), 102 *l.*; G. Hasler is alive, 88 *l.*

2781. Were they compensated on the abolition of office, or what?—Reilly was compensated on abolition of office, and so was Richard Travis, and William Clarke, the late overseer of flagging. Palmer was compensated in the same way, and so was Hasler, the late paving tax collector under the old Wide-street Commissioners. There is another, Eades, 17 *l.* 6 *s.* 8 *d.*, but he is dead.

Mr. *Butt.*

2781*. When the powers of the Wide-street Commissioners and the Paving Commissioners where transferred to the corporation in 1851, was not there a general retirement of the old officers?—There were some exceptions, but it was very generally done.

2782. And under the Act of Parliament which transferred the powers, they received compensation for their offices?—Yes.

2783. Are those the compensations that you are reading?—Yes, those are the compensations.

2784. Are there any compensations created by the corporation, since they acquired the powers of the Paving Board and the Wide-street Commissioners?—Yes, I have two items, Denis Costigin, ex-city treasurer, 121 *l.* 9 *s.* 10 *d.*, and John Conolly, ex-city accountant, 61 *l.* 16 *s.* 2 *d.*; those are the proportional charges against the general fund on their retiring or superannuation on account of extreme age. Mr. Costigin, who was city treasurer, is 84 years of age.

2785. And you succeeded him?—Yes.

Mr. *Brooks.*

2786. What age was he when he was retired?—He was 82.

Chairman.

2787. I do not think that you have told us what your salary is as city treasurer?—£. 400 a year.

Mr. *Bryan.*

2788. I suppose this, in fact, ought to be called a pension list?—Yes, a pension list would be a better term. Those compensations at the foot of this account amount to 1,529 *l.* They are getting less. The compensation list all round now, is only 2,180 *l.* for the whole corporation.

Sir *Arthur Guinness.*

2789. May I ask in what year Mr. Costigan's pension commenced?—In 1873.

Chairman.

2790. Passing over several smaller items, I find one of 6,970 *l.* for public lighting account; is that paid to the gas company?—Paid to the Alliance Gas Company.

2791. Does that include the payment of any officers?—It includes the payment of the lamplighter's wages, which are 22 *l.* 4 *s.*; it includes also the salary of the inspector of gas meters, Mr. W. F. Conolly, 300 *l.* a year.

2792. All the rest is paid for gas?—Yes.

2793. Does that include maintenance of lamps also?—Yes.

2794. What is this item of 1,144 *l.* for repayment on account of deposit for licenses?—When street-work is required to be done, such as street-opening, there is a certain amount handed in by the party that wants it done, and the expenses are deducted, and repayment is made to the party.

Mr. *Butt.*

2795. Of course those deposits were credited in some previous account?—Yes, you will find the

Mr. *O'Donnell* and Mr. *Robinson.*

19 May 1876.

Mr. *Butt*—continued.

the credit on the other side, and it shows a large profit.

Chairman.

2796. With regard to some of these receipts, for instance, "widening and improving streets account, 2,810 *l.* 15 *s.*;" what is that; from whom was that received?—That is the amount of a presentment for repairing and paving the roadway of north wall and the city quays, and that was received from the grand jury account.

Mr. *Butt.*

2797. For work which had been wanted by the corporation?—Yes, for work executed by the corporation.

Chairman.

2798. How do you divide the cost of widening and improving streets between the improvement fund and the grand jury account?—There is a scale of proportions, a graduated scale to which the different items are allocated.

2799. Upon what principle, or is the principle laid down in any Act of Parliament?—I really am not aware; I cannot answer that question; my impression is that it is

2800. (To Mr. *O'Donnell.*) On what principle is the cost of widening and improving streets divided between the grand jury account and the improvement fund?—I do not know exactly the principle, but I know that there is a presentment made by the grand jury for this particular work at the north and south quays. It comes under Section 15 of the grand jury account, the repair of roads. I think you will find it is in the exercise of powers under the Dublin Port and Docks Act, 1869, 32 & 33 Vict. c. 100, sect. 244, the presentment is made.

2801. Is this work on the quays done out of the improvement fund?—Yes, certainly; the money is passed to the credit of the improvement fund, but the corporation sitting as a grand jury having presented for the work that is done on the roads, that work is done by No. 1 Committee.

2802. Is it the repairs of the quays, or the repairs of the roads?—It is repairing the roadways down at north wall and at the south quay wall, not for the quays, it is for paving purposes.

2803. Is it, roughly speaking, an annual repayment of the grand jury fund to the improvement account?—For the last three or four years those presentments have been made for those purposes.

2804. I think, although the improvement fund is limited, there is no limit on the grand jury cess?—No, it is unlimited; at present the grand jury cess is 1 *s.* 10 *d.* in the pound.

Mr. *Brooks.*

2805. Can you say whether the liability of the grand jury for the quays is under the Old Port and Docks Act?—It is under the powers of the Dublin Port and Docks Act, 1869.

Mr. *Bruen.*

2806. How is it then that in this charge of 18,000 *l.* on the improvement rate, for macadamming, and so on, there is no corresponding credit given by the grand jury, is not that macadamising of the streets a part of the duty of the grand jury, and ought there not to be a credit paid out of the grand jury cess?—It is the duty of No. 1 committee. You will find the payment of the sum presented for duly credited to the grand jury having been passed to the debit of the improvement rate.

2807. But we have got it here to the debit of the improvement fund?—Yes, the improvement fund is debited with that sum, and of course the grand jury, account would be credited with the payment of it; we can show that as a credit to the grand jury.

Chairman.

2808. Will you read the presentment in the city's accounts of 1872?—"Section No. 15, repair of roads. To the treasurer of the borough of Dublin for paving and repairing 5,413 superficial yards of the road upon the south wall or quay bounding the river Liffey, known as the city quay, from a point at the west end of the Diamond of Moss-street, running in an easterly direction and terminating at the east side of the Diamond at Creighton-street at No. 1, Sir John Rogerson's quay pursuant to the specification and estimate of the city engineer and the powers and provisions of the Dublin Port and Docks Act, 1869, 32 & 33 Vict. c. 100, s. 244: Estimated expense 2,706 *l.* 10 *s.*, contingencies 5 per cent., 135 *l.* 6 *s.* 6 *d.*, making a total of 2,481 *l.* 16 *s.* 6 *d.*

2809. Are you aware, now, that you see that reference to the Port and Docks Act, whether they have the power of sending presentments in the corporation in the capacity of a grand jury for repairing certain places near the docks and quays?—Yes, it would appear so.

2810. Do not you know so yourself?—I do not; it is a matter which I have never given any particular attention to.

2811. (To Mr. *Robinson.*) Do you know anything about that?—No, I do not.

Mr. *Murphy.*

2812. (To Mr. *O'Donnell.*) Are you aware upon what ground the grand jury find a presentment outside what is called the jurisdiction proper of the corporation of Dublin; that is to say, outside the Circular road?—I believe it is within the municipal boundary.

Chairman.

2813. (To Mr. *Robinson.*) You have stated what the indebtedness of the corporation on the waterworks account was; can you mention what are the profits which the corporation have obtained from that source?—I believe that the revenue which the waterworks department derives from places beyond the municipal districts is probably 4,800 *l.*; when I say probably, I mean it in this sense, that under the Act of the 37 & 38 Vict. we got power to charge the township for excess of water consumed over the statutory allowance, which is estimated at 2,000 *l.* a year. I estimate the whole revenue from the extra municipal districts is 6,800 *l.* We have not begun to derive profit from that, we have only received some few hundred pounds.

2814. Do you pay from that revenue the interest and the instalments of the debt?—We do from our general resources.

2815. Is that kept as a separate account for that purpose?—No, it is not kept as a separate account; the next item is city contract water to

Mr. O'Donnell and Mr. Robinson.

19 May 1876.

Chairman—continued.

to brewers and manufacturers, 15,000 *l.*; domestic water rate at 1 *s.* in the pound, 24,500 *l.*; public water rate at 3 *d.* in the pound, 6,900 *l.*; making a total to the collector general for these rates of 31,400 *l.* Public water rate on Government buildings, 381 *l.* 8 *s.* 9 *d.*; supply to shipping, 150 *l.* Extra receipts: water supply to private parties' works, sale of old iron and miscellaneous, 600 *l.*; pipe water rents, 114 *l.*; fire department receipts, moiety of expenses of fires under the Act of 1872, 237 *l.*; making a total of 54,682 *l.* 8 *s.* 9 *d.*

2816. Is it an increasing revenue?—It is.

2817. To what extent?—My estimate for the year ending 31st August 1874, was 47,609 *l.*; for 1876, it is 54,682 *l.* Of course that includes that exceptional payment of 4,000 *l.*, which will only come in force now, which is the cause of the very great rise; it has been a rapidly increasing income.

2818. What is the annual expenditure under the water works for maintenance and other matters?—£. 47,633. 12 *s.* 6 *d.*

2819. Does that include interest on debt?—Yes; it includes interest on the debt to the old pipe water board and all.

2820. How much is the interest on the old pipe water debt?—The interest on the old pipe water debt is 2,880 *l.*

2821. And the interest on the general debt is how much?—£. 25,100 *l.* in round figures; that includes the Government debt.

2822. What is the total interest including the Government debt, the debt to private creditors, and the pipe water debt?—£. 27,980.

Mr. *Butt.*

2823. Does that include the sinking fund?—Yes, it does; it includes a terminable annuity of 19,100 *l.* a year.

Chairman.

2824. What is the amount expended in maintenance and salaries?—Salaries 1,564 *l.*; rent and taxes and stationery, &c., 1,800 *l.*; law agents, 300 *l.*; balance of law agents' costs, 250 *l.*; sustaining and repairing present works, incidental expenses, staff, &c., 5,500 *l.* (that is along the line of works up to Roundwood); fire brigade, 3,000 *l.* The contingencies I have put down at 1,000 *l.*, they generally come to that. Miscellaneous water pipes, meters, renewal of mains in city, &c., this year, I have been obliged to put down at 6,000 *l.*, because we owe a debt of 4,000 *l.* for pipes. I estimate the total expenditure, including the 2,880 *l.*, at 50,513 *l.* 12 *s.* 6 *d.*, and the balance to the credit of excess of income over expenditure for the year ending 31st August 1876, 4,168 *l.* 16 *s.* 3 *d.*

2825. Do the Corporation contemplate any increase in the charges for the water?—No, not that I have heard; it is fixed by scale.

2826. There was a small point mentioned here the other day, the charge for the cost of opposition in Parliament of the Bray and Enniskerry Railway Bill; can you give us an explanation of that?—That was in order to obtain a *locus standi*; we were obliged to petition to obtain a *locus standi* for the purpose of preventing the water mains being interfered with.

2827. Did you obtain a *locus standi*?—Yes, we did.

2828. The corporation has to bear the general charges of the public health, has it not?—It has.

Chairman—continued.

2829. Out of what fund are they defrayed?—The borough fund portion of the city estate.

2830. What has been the annual expense on that account?—That is a gradually increasing expenditure; it has become rather alarming; it has gone up in six years from 1,400 *l.* a year up to 4,000 *l.* There was an exceptional expenditure last year for the Floating Hospital (it is only right that I should mention that), of 1,140 *l.*

2831. What was the expenditure for the last year of which you have an account?—£. 4,000.

2832. Of which about 3,000 *l.* has been paid in salaries to the officers, has it not?—No, not so much in salaries; the chief officers' salaries amounted to 900 *l.*; the police cost 1,100 *l.* for the sanitary serjeant and sanitary staff.

2833. What would the expenditure comprise besides this 900 *l.* and 1,100 *l.*?—There are extra services, small sums to the police in the matter of the detection of diseased meat, varying from 3 *l.* to 5 *l.*; cleansing the Liffey last year cost 157 *l.* 2 *s.* 1 *d.*; flushing sewers 18 *l.* 11 *s.* 4 *d.*; the laboratory expenses of the public analyst come to about 50 *l.* a year; the expenses of the Morgue 126 *l.* 1 *s.* 6 *d.*, disinfecting chamber 85 *l.*, graves and interments for destitutes 54 *l.* 16 *s.*; the law costs for the year ending 1874 were 162 *l.*, stationery and printing 131 *l.*

2834. When was this department originated?—In 1866.

2835. In what condition was the borough fund on which the charge for that was imposed at that time?—The borough fund was only a self-supporting institution at that time. I can give the receipts and expenditure for five years anterior to 1866, to show its condition.

2836. How do you mean that it was a self-supporting institution?—I mean it was only living. In 1861 the receipts were 20,300 *l.*, expenditure 20,100 *l.* in round figures. In 1862 the receipts were 22,390 *l.*, and the expenditure 22,480 *l.* In 1863 the receipts were 22,000 *l.*, and the expenditure 23,000 *l.* In 1864 the receipts were 22,500 *l.*, and the expenditure 22,400 *l.* In 1865 the receipts were 22,032 *l.*, and the expenditure 22,850 *l.*

2837. Can you give the receipts and expenditure of the borough fund for the last year?—Yes; it began with a credit balance of 237 *l.* 2 *s.* 7 *d.*; rents, as per city rental account, 19,139 *l.* 15 *s.* 3 *d.*; purchase-money, property sold to Hibernian Bank, 13,436 *l.* 19 *s.* 7 *d.*; rent of divisional sales room, per sword bearer, 240 *l.*; proceeds of confiscated hay and straw lodged in error to credit of borough fund, 3 *l.* 19 *s.* 3 *d.*; fees, &c., lodged by the City Marshal, 429 *l.* 16 *s.*; law expenses account, 9 *l.* 2 *s.* 8 *d.*; rents in advance for last year of lease, 55 *l.*; surplus dog tax, 275 *l.* 1 *s.*; stationery account, 5 *s.*; municipal expenses account, fees, &c., from clerk of the peace, assistant to town-clerk, &c., 865 *l.* 15 *s.* 5 *d.*; fees from Lord Mayor's Court, 130 *l.* 16 *s.* 3 *d.*; police fines, &c., sanitary account, 399 *l.* 2 *s.* 9 *d.*; slippage and anchorage, city dues, &c., 2,153 *l.* 19 *s.* 4 *d.*; city weigh-house tolls, &c., 105 *l.* 8 *s.* 3 *d.*; burial rate recoupments, 86 *l.* 18 *s.*; recoupments from improvement fund and waterworks fund account, general compensations, 68 *l.* 1 *s.* 3 *d.*; city treasurer, lodgments in excess of rents received, 11 *l.* 18 *s.* 9 *d.* The total receipts were 37,411 *l.* 11 *s.* 8 *d.*

2838. What was the expenditure?—Reduction of

Mr. *O'Donnell* and Mr. *Robinson*.

19 May 1876.

Chairman—continued.

of debt, five City Debentures, Hibernian Bank, 500 *l.*; purchase of 161 *l.* City Debentures, Irish currency, by application of proceeds of property sold to Hibernian Bank, together with interest, &c., 13,467 *l.* 10 *s.* 9 *d.* (I have explained that already): compensation, 160 *l.* 5 *s.* 10 *d.*; salaries, 6,345 *l.* 6 *s.* 4 *d.*; dividends on debentures, 8,403 *l.* 9 *s.* 10 *d.*; interest on Powell's legacy, 38 *l.* 18 *s.* 6 *d.* (that was a man who died, leaving a certain sum to be distributed to the poor debtors confined in the City Marshalsea at Christmas and Easter); stationery, printing, scrivenery, &c., 346 *l.* 10 *s.* 2 *d.*; proportion of City Hall expenses, 142 *l.* 3 *s.*; charges account, sundries, 416 *l.* 4 *s.* 5 *d.*; Mansion House expenses, 1,791 *l.* 2 *s.* 7 *d.*; Baldoyle estate expenses, 373 *l.* 7 *s.* 8 *d.* (that 373 *l.* for Baldoyle was for the construction of a main sewer through it last year); municipal expenses account, 483 *l.* 11 *s.* 5 *d.*; law expenses, 103 *l.* 3 *s.* 5 *d.*; expenses, City Marshal's department, 104 *l.* 7 *s.* 11 *d.*; Local Government Board, Ireland, proportion of auditor's fee, 14 *l.* – *s.* 9 *d.*; head rents and taxes, 590 *l.* 12 *s.* 8 *d.*; City weigh licence expenses, 451 *l.* 6 *s.* 2 *d.*; slippage and anchorage, &c., water bailiffs, &c., 960 *l.* 4 *s.* 9 *d.*

Sir *Arthur Guinness*.

2839. Is that on the increase?—No, that is on the decrease.

Chairman.

2840. What do the water bailiffs do?—They supply ships with plant, beams, and scales, and see that proper hoardings are constructed on board, and they board all ships that come into the river.

Mr. *Butt*.

2841. Do they execute any writs on board?—I have never heard of their doing so. Then the next item is River Liffey, payments to engineers, 150 *l.*; Sanitary Account, Public Health Committee expenditure, is 4,073 *l.* 6 *s.* 3 *d.*; repayment to sewers fund amount obtained as temporary loan in 26th September 1872, 1,000 *l.*; total, 39,962 *l.* 12 *s.* 7 *d.*

2842. Then the expenditure was greater than the receipts?—Yes, the expenditure was greater than the receipts by 2,313 *l.* 18 *s.* 4 *d.*

Chairman.

2843. Have you power to levy a rate in aid of that fund?—We have.

2844. Is it levied?—No.

2845. You have stated that 6,345 *l.* was given in salaries; whose salaries are they?—They are all payable out of the borough fund. There is Mr. Lalor, the secretary to the Waterworks, No. 2 committee, 200 *l.*; and he gets 100 *l.* from the borough fund, that is, the City Estate. There is E. J. Murphy, the water bailiff, 200 *l.*

2846. Are the water bailiffs the same as those who are paid under slippage and anchorage?—Yes, those are the slippage and anchorage bailiffs.

Chairman—continued.

2847. Did not you give us a separate head of expenditure for the slippage and anchorage bailiffs?—Yes, I did. The salaries of the water bailiff are included in that 960 *l.* (*Mr. O'Donnell.*) The salaries of the water bailiffs are included in the figures 960 *l.* 4 *s.* 9 *d.* under the head of Slippage and Anchorage. It is not charged against the salaries account as set out in those figures, 6,345 *l.* 6 *s.* When this account for the year which is under audit is printed, it will be set forth in the same way as it is set forth in the printed account for 1874.

2848. Can you tell us now the salaries?—I can give an approximate idea. The Lord Mayor has 2,000 *l.*, and an increase of 250 *l.* for his secretary, in lieu of fees received in the Lord Mayor's court, which fees are passed to the credit of the borough fund. Then there is the Right Hon. the Recorder; he is paid a portion of his salary out of the borough fund, 369 *l.* 4 . 8 *d.* The swordbearer's salary is 250 *l.*; the city marshal's salary, 300 *l.*; the high constable, 100 *l.*; the macebearer, 206 *l.* 3 *s.* 9 *d.*; secretary to No. 2 committee, 100 *l.*; the assistant to the city accountant, 100 *l.*: the town clerk's assistant has about 230 *l.* in round numbers; the treasurer's assistant, 300 *l.*; and the proportion of my own salary charged against the borough fund would be about 78 *l.* a year altogether, making close on the figure which was mentioned before. I have not got an exact analysis of that figure at band, but I am giving an idea of the salaries that are paid from the account in former years.

2849. What is the total for that year?—It is 5,241 *l.* 16 *s.* 9 *d.*

2850. That is 1,100 *l.* less than the year we are dealing with now?—I may have included in this figure some additional salary which is not charged here, but in the absence of an analysis of the figures I cannot exactly tell what it is.

2851. What year is it that you are quoting from?—This is 1874.

2852. Are we to understand that the difference between the year 1874 and the year ending March 1875 is this, that there is 1,000 *l.* more charged by way of salaries in the latter year than in the former year?—I forgot to mention that there is included in this figure a proportion of the treasurer's salary, a proportion of the city engineer's salary, and a proportion of my own, transferred from the general account of salaries; that is from the account which you will find at page 113 in the accounts of the year ending 1874, at which page you will see what are the amounts that are charged against the borough fund; the town clerk's salary is also included in this figure of 6,345 *l.* 6 *s.* 4 *d.* The analysis would account for the difference, if I had it at hand.

Mr. *Brooks*.

2853. (To Mr. *Robinson*.) Is it any part of your duty to acquaint yourself with the mode of letting, or the duration of leases?—No, it is not. I receive the money and account for it.

2854. If the Committee want information upon that point, who is the proper person to give it us?—The land and law agent.

Tuesday, 23rd May 1876.

MEMBERS PRESENT:

Sir Michael Hicks Beach.
Mr. Brooks.
Mr. Bruen.
Mr. Butt.
Mr. Collins.
Mr. Gibson.
Sir Arthur Guinness.
Mr. Kavanagh.
Sir Joseph M'Kenna.
Mr. Mulholland.
Mr. Murphy.
Mr. O'Shaughnessy.
Mr. Rathbone.

SIR MICHAEL HICKS BEACH, BART., IN THE CHAIR.

Mr. FREDERICK STOKES, called in; and Examined.

Mr. *Stokes.*

23 May 1876.

Chairman.

2855. I BELIEVE you are Chairman of the Township Commissioners of Rathmines and Rathgar?—Yes, I was one of the founders of the township in 1847. I was the first chairman, and have been for 16 years past their chairman.

2856. Does that township border upon the municipal limits of Dublin?—Yes.

2857. What is the area and population of it?—The area is about 1,300 or 1,400 acres, and the population about 22,000.

2858. What is the annual valuation of it?—The annual valuation is about 92,000 *l.*

2859. Are the township commissioners constituted under the local Act of the 10 & 11 Vict. c. 253?—They are constituted under a special Act of 1847, incorporating the Towns Improvement Act passed the same year.

2860. How many commissioners are there?—Twenty-one.

2861. What is their qualification?—Their qualifications are, a rating for residents of 30 *l.*, or if non-residents the possession of property to the value of 200 *l.* a year or upwards. I myself qualify as a non-resident.

2862. What is the qualification of the electors?—Ten pound householders only; there is no owners' qualification. I may state that I did not come to London to give evidence upon this Committee; indeed I had refused to do so; but in consequence of the attack made by the corporation on my township I wished to give evidence, and therefore I have not come provided with any papers.

2863. What are your rating powers?—Our rating powers are 2 *s.*, with power to raise it to 2 *s.* 6 *d.*, with the consent of a meeting of the inhabitants, which has never been done. Our rates have been occasionally below 2 *s.*, but never above.

2864. What is the present rate which you raise?—Two shillings.

2865. What does that cover?—It covers grand jury, water, sewerage, sanitary, and improvement.

2866. How much of it is due to the grand jury cess?—About 6 *d.*; sometimes a fraction more and sometimes a fraction less, but one year with another nearly or quite 6 *d.*

Chairman—continued.

2867. Have you a separate water supply, or do you share in the Vartry water?—We have an independent water supply.

2868. What is your water rate?—I should have mentioned that that is also included in the 2 *s.*

2869. How much is the water rate out of the 2 *s.*?—The cost of the water for the first 10 years was about 2 *d.* in the pound; but for the last two or three years, in consequence of our erecting new works, it is about 4 *d.*

2870. What did your waterworks cost you?—The original waterworks cost 17,700 *l.*; the increased waterworks cost about 11,000 *l.*

2871. Have you repaid the original cost?—We owe 22,000 *l.* out of 28,000 *l.* or 29,000 *l.*; we have repaid a sum of 6,000 or 7,000 *l.*

2872. What rate of interest does that money bear?—Four and a quarter per cent., with the exception of a small sum borrowed from the Board of Works lately, which we only pay 3½ per cent. for; money borrowed from private individuals we pay 4¼ per cent. for.

2873. That is less than the rate paid by the Corporation of Dublin, is it not?—Yes, we are in better credit.

2874. Have you the power of repairing your own roads?—Yes, the town commissioners have the powers of the grand jury in that respect for repairing and making roads, and lanes and streets, and everything of that kind, with the single exception of bridges.

2875. Then the rate which you raise by way of grand jury cess is expended by yourselves?—It is called an improvement rate, out of which we pay to the grand jury our proportion for the gaols and lunatic asylums, and other county-at-large charges, much the same as the city grand jury cess for the same purposes; those are the two leading items, lunatics and prisons.

2876. Do you pay anything for bridges?—As commissioners we do not, but unfortunately as ratepayers we have been drawn into the police area, and have to pay our contribution towards the bridges and the quay wall in the city.

2877. You pay it to the town council of Dublin?—We pay it to the collector general.

2878. How much of the 2 *s.* rate goes to paying

Chairman—continued.

paving and lighting?—You may put it down at about a 1 *s.*; I should divide the 2 *s.* thus: 1 *s.* for paving and lighting, 6 *d.* for grand jury, 4 *d.* for water, and 2 *d.* for sewerage and sanitary purposes; the present year's account contains all the details

2879. Have you any debt for paving and lighting?—None at all; our debt is solely for waterworks

2880. Have you made any system of sewers?—Yes; we consider our system of sewers perfect, or very nearly so; when we first were incorporated we had a general system for the whole district made out, and we have done it piece by piece, according as our funds would permit without borrowing; we consider it now to be complete with some very trifling exceptions.

2881. Where do you discharge into?—We discharge into the Swan river in the Pembroke township, which flows into the Dodder, and from the Dodder into the mouth of the Liffey.

2882. Can you tell the Committee what is the poundage in the city of Dublin for the different rates which in Rathmines you find you can meet by a levy of 2 *s.*?—I issued last year a printed statement which will give the Committee all those particulars (*delivering a paper to the Committee*); in point of fact in Dublin it is about 5 *s.* 7 *d.*, as against 2 *s.* in Rathmines.

2883. Do you pay any police tax?—Yes, the same as in the city, 8 *d.*, which you will also find in this paper.

2884. How does your poor rate stand, as compared with that paid in the city?—Our poor rate last year was 1 *s.*, against 1 *s.* 10 *d.* in the city; this year it is 1 *s.* 2 *d.*, against 1 *s.* 10 *d.*

2885. How do you account for that difference?—We have scarcely any paupers at all; we merely have to pay our share of the union paupers, but that is a charge which increases year by year in consequence of the operation of the last Act which was passed upon the subject, by which they are all charged to the union except where there is an electoral division residence in 30 months out of 36.

2886. Does not that point to a considerable difference in the kind of property in Rathmines and in the City of Dublin?—The property in Rathmines may be represented by the middle class; it is neither very valuable, nor very poor. In the city it is better and worse than others; ours is all newly erected, or nearly all, since I have presided over that district. Two-thirds has been erected since it became a township.

2887. Are you acquainted with the condition of the Dublin Corporation; that is to say, do you consider that it is a fair representation of its constituents?—Certainly it is not.

2888. Why not?—Because the lower class of voters so completely outnumbers the better class, that there is no chance for the wealthy inhabitants to be represented.

2889. Do you trace any effect of that upon the composition of the corporation itself?—The corporation, I consider, has gradually deteriorated from the time that it was reformed in 1850. I think that every change pretty well has been for the worse. It was a very first-rate body of men as a whole when reformed in 1850.

2890. Do you think that the publican interest has anything to do with the corporation representation?—There is a very undue proportion of publicans in the corporation, no doubt. I would not trace any particular connection.

Chairman—continued.

Mr. Stokes.

23 May 1876.

2891. What do you mean by undue proportion; what is the proportion now?—I should say one-fourth. I am told that there are more; Mr. McEvoy says there are 17, but I should say that there are 15 at any rate; one individual instance I may mention which struck me very much. One of the most independent and able members of the corporation was expelled by the interest of the publicans, because he took the view contrary to them on the temperance question, and that was Mr Sullivan. In that instance it was due to the direct influence of the publicans.

2892. Do you consider that political influences have great weight in the elections for the corporation?—They do not think of anything else as a rule.

2893. Do you think there are any exceptions to that?—Of course there are, but they are very few; every election is conducted with reference to political reasons with a very odd exception, and the more extreme the politics are on either side, the better.

2894. Have particular influences any weight in the elections for the commissioners of your township?—None whatever; we never allow politics to be introduced in any shape. Our district is overwhelmingly Conservative; the majority of the representatives are Conservative, but politics never enter into it.

2895. Are some of the members of your body known to be opposed to Conservative politics?—Yes; when we have an opportunity for electing a respectable Roman Catholic, we do so. The election is in our own hands whenever a vacancy occurs.

2896. In what way do you mean that it is in your own hands?—The board can fill up vacancies.

2897. For how long?—For the same time that the retiring member held his seat.

2898. Then the newly elected person, though co-opted, has to appeal to the constituents to be re-elected?—Yes; he comes in in the regular list. We never take any one on either side of strong political opinions, if we can help it at all.

2899. Recurring to the difference in the poundage-rates between the city and Rathmines, are there any reasons to which you would attribute that difference; first of all, as to the purchase of materials for work done?—In the purchase of materials for work done they pay much higher than we do.

2900. Can you give the Committee any instances of that?—Not a late instance; but I remember that when we were paying 2 *s.* 7 *d.* for broken stone, they were paying 3 *s.* 6 *d.*, but we pay cash, and they do not. In one particular instance in which I was myself concerned, they were paying 11 *d.* a foot for 12-inch granite kerbing, and we were getting 14-inch for 9 *d.* Upon that occasion I took a contract for some new streets which I was erecting myself, at 25 per cent. under the corporation estimate, and that about balanced the cost.

2901. Do you think that your work was as well done as that which was done for the corporation?—That was in the city of Dublin; I am speaking of new streets which I made in the city.

2902. Do you think that the work and materials that you obtained at a cheaper rate than the corporation

Mr. *Stokes.*

23 May 1876.

Chairman—continued.

corporation are equal to what they had?—Just the same; they were the same contractors. Mr. Neville states in one of his reports that they cannot buy at the same price, because they have to pay credit prices instead of cash. I think it was in his report of 1871. I have not the report here to refer to, but it is notorious, at any rate.

2903. Do you think that the difference has amounted to as much as 30 per cent.?—Not all round, but in every instance, more or less.

2904. How do you compare the labourers in your employ with those employed by the corporation?—I think we have better labourers than they have. I think that the system of patronage has operated to such an extent in the corporation that their officers are probably obliged to take men that they would not otherwise take, because they are recommended by members of the Town Council. I do not know that it is a fact, but it is general repute. Our people call them St. Vincent de Paul's men, which is the name of a charitable society which takes an interest in labourers; but I have no doubt that we can get the pick of the labourers, but there is not much of importance upon that head.

2905. I suppose that that might lead to this; that a great deal of waste might be occasioned in wages paid to men who do not do the work properly?—They have not the best men; that I can see with my own eyes, and probably the officers would say the same.

2906. Perhaps there are other points, besides matters such as those under the control of the corporation, that might account for the difference in the poundage of the rates of which you have spoken; and first, as to the valuation of Dublin, what have you to say?—There are some points which are beyond their control, except that they might have stirred in them, but they have not. The valuation is shamefully low as compared with my district, and the rates are badly collected. I mean that the law is imperfect.

2907. Of course if the valuation be low, the poundage rate necessarily rises?—Yes, of course; the valuation in many cases is not one-half, and in some cases not one-third what it ought to be; there is not one of our principal streets in Dublin which I could name, which is valued at much more than half of its real value.

2908. As to the collection, in what way does it fail?—The powers of collection are very imperfect, and that of course is beyond the control of the corporation, but the loss I think from that cause in the city is from 12½ to 15 per cent.; I am not quite sure whether that includes the collector's poundage or not, but at any rate about one-eighth is totally lost.

2909. Has your attention been called to the evidence that has been given before us by the collector general and Mr. Taaffe upon that subject?—It has not; I have not taken any interest in this matter at all, except as regards defending my own township against the corporation. I can give you the figures of our own township.

2910. What is the system of collection in your township?—We have two collectors; there are no exemptions for unoccupied houses; an exemption which I think most unjust, because it is the most improvident class of landlords who escape; we have the power of distress; we have the power of suing the owner; in fact we have made it as complete as we could. According as we have found holes in our law we have mended them, and the result has been that out of 161,354 *l.* altogether struck, there is only 41 *l.* now outstanding, and 317 *l.* was written off. Our total losses for 20 years have been under 4 *s.* per cent., in place of 12 *l.* 10 *s.* per cent. in Dublin.

2911. In your township what is the limit after which the owner becomes liable to the payment of rates?—If there is no distress we can sue the owner.

2912. Is there any limit of value after which the owner becomes liable in place of the occupier?—Yes, all houses under 10 *l.* can be rated to the owner; the owners of furnished houses are liable, no matter what the value is, and the owners of all houses under 10 *l.* are liable, and the owner of a house of any amount is liable if we cannot get it off the premises.

2913. Is the owner of a house let in separate apartments liable?—Certainly; he would be the occupier in that case.

2914. And the owner of houses let to weekly or monthly tenants?—Yes, we merely rate the owners then. My attention was called to that in a case where the collector general had taken 5 *s.* in the 1 *l.* from a man, and we got the full amount, for he was perfectly well able to pay.

2915. Do you find any difficulty, such as I think the collector general spoke of, owing to the immediate lessor fraudulently escaping his liability?—No, that is not the man that we put down, we would look to the owner. We have another clause; we say that the receiver of rent shall be deemed the owner, no matter who he is. In point of fact I may say that our rates were 9,000 *l.* last year, and there is only 15 *l.* now outstanding, and we never summoned any one.

2916. I understood from your previous answer that although the owners of the different classes of property that you have named are liable to pay all the rates, yet they have no voice in the election of the commissioners?—None whatever.

2917. Nor have the occupiers of the property?—The occupier, if rated, would have a vote, no matter who he was.

2918. But the occupier is not rated in your township, is he, if the owner is liable?—Yes, the owner may be liable, but the occupier is rated. We are not bound to look to the occupier, as for a personal debt; we look to the house, no matter who is in it.

2919. Do you rate the occupiers below 10 *l.*?—I think we do, but I am not sure. I may say, that inasmuch as no one has a vote below 10 *l.*, the question does not arise.

2920. Do you rate the occupiers of furnished houses above 10 *l.*?—Yes, we rate them.

2921. And the houses above that value that are let to weekly or monthly tenants?—They would be rated, most probably, to the owner.

2922. And the occupier would not be rated?—No, but there are very few of them; we have very few tenement houses in Rathmines. The 44th Section is the section I refer to: "And be it enacted, that every person who shall let his house in separate apartments or ready furnished, shall be rated as the occupier thereof," not as the owner but as the occupier.

2923. Then the occupier's name would appear on the rate book?—The real occupier would not. We are very peculiarly circumstanced as to this Act. The Towns Improvement Act, 1847, was passing

Mr. *Stokes.*

23 May 1876.

Chairman—continued.

passing through the House *pari passu* with this, and we got the general Act amended, and we got our own at the same time. By Section 40 the owners are rated; it says, "And be it enacted, that the owner of all rateable property within the limits of this Act, the yearly rent or value whereof respectively shall not amount to the sum of 10 *l.*, shall be rated to, and pay the rates by this Act directed to be made, instead of the occupiers thereof." The next section is, that whenever we do not know the name of the owner, it is sufficient to put "the owner." In point of fact, we have caught everyone, so far.

2924. Has any proposal ever been made by or on behalf of the corporation to annex your district to the city?—Often; like the sword of Damocles it is constantly hanging over our heads. It has been threatened, but they have never made any real attempt.

2925. What would be your view of such a proposal?—That the real idea is annexing a municipality which is distinguished for success, to a municipality which is distinguished for want of success, as is pretty well obvious.

2926. Might it not be also that a great proportion of your residents are city tradesmen, and therefore are interested or mixed up with the city, and that therefore they should bear their part of the weight of the city rates?—No; it is not the fact in the first instance, and even if it was we should argue that they could not have any claim upon us. We keep the principal avenues to the city, without expense to the city, whereas, in the case of Rock-road, they have to pay a part of the expense themselves. Besides, a very large proportion of our inhabitants are females; there are as many as 800, I think, out of 3,000 rated occupiers who are females, and a very large proportion of the remainder are country people who come in there for cheap taxes, and for comfortable middle-class houses. I think it is not by any means the fact that the majority of our inhabitants are traders in the city; on the contrary, I think in Kingstown it is much more the case. But we say we keep the four principal roads on the south side in order, and if there is any question of contribution, it is the other way.

2927. Has the valuations of Rathmines increased largely since you have been a commissioner?—Very largely; it was 33,000 *l.* about 1850, and it is now 92,000 *l.*, and it is increasing every year.

Sir *Arthur Guinness.*

2928. How many are rated in the township?—There are 3,570 rated, of which there are 270 duplicates, so that it would be 3,300 rated, and 788 are females.

Chairman.

2929. Do females vote at the elections?—They do not; but we very rarely have a contest.

Mr. *Murphy.*

2930. Are they excluded by the special Act from voting?—Yes, they are.

Chairman.

2931. Are you acquainted with any instance in which an outlying district has been annexed to Dublin?—Yes; you asked me a question some time ago as to what was the cause of the embarrassments of the corporation, and that was one of them; they took in a large district between the Circular-road and the canal, which was a most disastrous annexation for them, and never at any time has it paid the cost which it involved; they extended the municipal boundary in 1850 from the Circular-road to the canal, taking in a very unremunerative district, Mud Island, for instance.

2932. I presume that whether it answered or not to annex would depend upon the valuation of the district, and the character of the property in it, would it not?—Of course it would; they took a bad piece very unwisely; it was a kind of *terra incognita* that belonged to nobody and wanted everything, Mud Island on the one side and Dolphin's Barn on the other side.

Mr. *Butt.*

2933. Was not there a king of Mud Island?—Yes, Mr. French; the same result would follow if they took in Rathmines, and it would be a loss to the commissioners' property, because people would go further out.

Chairman.

2934. Can you remember the work which was done by the old paving board before the present system of repairing the streets in Dublin was adopted?—Perfectly.

2935. Do you remember what the rate levied by the paving board was?—One shilling and twopence, and there was a voluntary rate for water which might be called another 1 *d.*

2936. That is considerably less than the 2 *s.* improvement rate now levied by the corporation?—Of course it was; and it is now 2 *s.* 4 *d.*, because there is 4 *d.* for sewerage.

2937. How was the work done by the old paving board as compared with the work done by the corporation?—I think it was quite as good and, I think that the general opinion is that it was better.

2938. Have you ever taken any part in municipal affairs in Dublin?—Never, except to fight them.

Sir *Joseph M'Kenna.*

2939. Do not you call that taking part?—It is, perhaps; I have been in every fight pretty well for the last 30 years.

Chairman.

2940. Should you be qualified for election as town councillor?—Certainly.

2941. Did you ever think of endeavouring to amend the corporation by entering it?—Nothing would induce me to go into it.

2942. For what reason?—In the first place, I would rather be first in a village than second at Rome; and in the next place, as a single individual, I would be helpless. Both parties have asked me to go in, and both parties have been kind enough to say that they will make me lord mayor if I will go in; but one person could do nothing. I have always met, both from the corporation and from its members, with every kind of courtesy, and personally I have nothing in the world to say in that respect. Upon a recent occasion one of my friends wished to leave the corporation, but I could not get any one to take his place; I asked everybody that I could think of, and he was obliged to stay where he was, because I could not get any substitute for him, and that was an uncontested ward.

2943. Are you anxious to see a new system of voting

Mr. Stokes.

23 May 1876.

Chairman—continued.

voting adopted in the municipal elections of Dublin?—I am not particularly anxious in any way about the municipal affairs of Dublin. I think it is enough to mind our own; but it is quite obvious that in any system pretending to be fair play, there should be a better representation of the people who pay the rates. At present, persons who do not pay the rates, or who pay very little, are the persons represented.

Mr. *Butt.*

2944. Then your objection of course is to extending the franchise?—Quite so.

2945. And you think that any franchise would be objectionable which gave the majority to persons of a comparatively poor class?—Certainly; where other people pay the majority of the rates. It is a pure fiscal affair. Perhaps I might be allowed to say that I am not in any degree favourable to the representation of owners; nor do I think that people who do not pay rates have any right to be represented.

2946. You do not think that it would be an advantage to the corporation to adopt the principle of the Towns Improvement Act, and allow persons of enlarged property in the city, but not rated themselves, to be voters?—It would be an improvement, because anything would be an improvement, but it would not be fair. I see no reason why a person who pays no taxes should have any representation. Certainly in the poor law we have representation, but then we pay our rates. I think that the taxpayer who does pay them should be entitled to vote according to the amount which he pays. I would adopt the poor law system in that respect.

2947. That would be what is called the multiple vote?—Yes, the plural vote.

2948. I believe that in your Act of Rathmines, the first commissioners were named?—They were.

2949. You say that you have different parties represented?—Yes.

2950. Do you yourselves, when you co-opt a person, ever think of his politics or his religion?—Except in the case of a Roman Catholic; when a Roman Catholic goes out we make a point of putting a Roman Catholic in his place. The vast majority of our ratepayers are Conservatives.

2951. I think you said that you were influenced so far as this, that you wished to have a certain proportion of Roman Catholics represented on the Commission?—Certainly; but we find great difficulty in getting eligible persons; there are so few of them.

2952. Can you tell us, out of the 21, how many Liberals you have?—Usually we have three. There were originally six; but whenever there was a contest, which is very rarely, the Roman Catholics always went to the wall, and we replaced them according as we had the opportunity ourselves.

2953. Whenever you have had a contest, the Roman Catholic or Liberals have generally been excluded?—Very often; sometimes they were successful, because they were always supported by the board. If it was left to the ratepayers, they would send them everyone out. The Conservatives, I should say, are six to one, at any rate.

2954. And the result is, that you have about three Liberals out of 21 Commissioners?—Yes; the property of the township is tolerably well represented, because upon the poor rates, when the votes are calculated, they will count about six to one. Whenever there has been a contest, we have been about six to one.

Mr. *Butt*—continued.

2955. Are you a guardian of the South Dublin Union?—I am *ex officio* guardian; I have been a magistrate for 21 years, and all that time a guardian, of course.

2956. Have you found the mode of election in the South Dublin Union very effective in excluding religious and political considerations?—No, I do not think it has.

2957. Have you a single Roman Catholic that you employed in the South Dublin Union in any official position?—Yes, I am sure there are.

2958. Who are they?—The matron is a Roman Catholic.

2959. Anyone else?—I could not tell.

2960. I suppose you have a chaplain; is he a Roman Catholic?—If you ask me, I may answer in general terms that one party is just as bad as the other. There is not a pin to choose between them.

2961. But, in fact, in the South Dublin Union do not you think that the officers in the workhouse are to far too great an extent exclusively given to one religion?—I do; but I may add to that that the South Dublin Union is, or has been till lately, in the hands, and almost entirely governed by a clique of the corporation.

2962. It being all Conservative?—Mostly Conservative.

2963. Is it a Conservative clique that governs it?—They all stick together there, but the majority are Conservatives.

2964. Have you been quite clear of all kinds of mismanagement in the South Dublin Union, where you have what you consider your model franchise?—I have been stirring up myself one or two things.

2965. Have you succeeded in rooting out any mismanagement?—Yes.

2966. I believe some very gross cases?—There was a case where a gentleman, a member of the Board, bought some sheds that we had property in for 1,100 *l.* to sell to us at 2,500 *l.* We rooted that out.

2967. Have you not had some gross cases of misapplication by officers?—There has been some great deficiency not accounted for. I stirred up that too.

2968. I suppose you would not consider the management of the South Dublin Union quite perfect?—It is very fair.

2969. Notwithstanding those things which you have rooted out?—It is an immense concern.

2970. I think you say that you have a rating of 92,000 *l.* to a population of 22,000?—About 22,000.

2971. Of course, in your Rathmines district you have a great deal of property without houses on it?—Not a great deal. We are filling up very fast; there is some.

2972. I suppose you have not by any means, in proportion to your area, the same quantity of gaslight as the streets in the City of Dublin would have?—No.

2973. Nor the same quantity of water pipes?—Yes, we have. Of course there must be a pipe in every road, so that there is the same quantity. We rather have a disadvantage, so far as the City of Dublin is concerned, as to this, because we put

Mr. Stokes.

23 May 1876.

Mr. *Butt*—continued.

put them where there are no houses. We have 300 gaslights.

2974. Is Rathmines fairly valued?—The valuation of Rathmines is low, but not by any means compared to the city.

2975. You used rather a strong expression when you said that the valuation of the city was scandalously low?—Yes; I was speaking of the best part of the city; the poor districts of the city are over-valued. Every new valuation in the city is valued up to the new scale: but all the old premises are valued up to the old scale.

2976. And the old scale is deficient?—Very deficient; there are two houses which may be known to any man who knows Dublin at each corner of Sackville-street; one on the east side, and the other on the west. Kelly's, the gunpowder shop on the one side, and Hopkins' on the other; the latter was originally two houses thrown into one, and when it was divided it was re-valued; of those two houses which are in every respect identical, one is valued at 66 *l.* and the other at 110 *l.* Anyone, I should say, would give 200 *l.* a year for either of them.

2977. Which side is valued the highest?—The east side is valued the highest; the Eden Quay side, where the corner house is, 110 *l.*, and Kelly's, the other side, is 66 *l.*

2978. Do you think that the valuation of Dublin, from your knowledge of it, is unequal?—Very unequal; I will give you an instance which is patent to everybody. There is the Munster Bank in Dame-street, which you know is just erected, that is valued at 650 *l.*; the Hibernian Bank, in a much better position and twice the size, is only valued at 620 *l.*

Mr. *Murphy.*

2979. Is that the value of the new building of the Hibernian Bank?—I presume so; it is the last valuation in November last, and I presume it was made after the new building. Then again, for instance, the Ulster Bank, one of the finest buildings on College Green, although not a very large one, is valued at 125 *l.*; and Atkinson's poplin shop at 95 *l.*, which is worth 250 *l.* or 300 *l.*

Mr. *Butt.*

2980. Do not you think Atkinson's house a better house, and of greater value, than the Ulster Bank?—I daresay it is.

2981. And yet it is valued much lower?—£. 30 less.

2982. I do not know whether you could form an opinion as to how much the whole City of Dublin is undervalued?—I should say that the 596,000 *l.* might be raised to 800,000 *l.* and still be low, because the chief of the low valuations are in the great streets, and the over-valuations in the small streets. The rectification of one or two of those houses in Dame-street would give justice to 50 houses in some of the poorer streets.

2983. Are you yourself a burgess of the City of Dublin?—I am.

2984. I believe you are the only one out of Commercial Buildings?—The only one; they hunted all the rest off.

2985. How were they hunted off?—They were continually objected to, and I would have been hunted off too, only I stuck to it every time they objected.

2986. Do you know whether any persons got themselves put off, in order to avoid being on juries?—When I found I could not get them on, I struck them all off the rate, so that they should not be called upon to serve on juries; I was accountable for that.

2987. Was it you that disfranchised all of them?—I did not disfranchise all of them, because they were struck off the burgess-roll first; of course, I would not leave them on the rate.

2988. You got them off the rate?—Yes.

2989. Did you try to get yourself off the rate?—No, I kept myself on to vex them.

2990. You disfranchised your brother tenants?—But the company pay taxes.

2991. Are you the owner of the house?—I am one of the principal owners, but the company pay the taxes.

2992. With regard to the poor-rate, of course, neither the corporation nor the commissioners have anything to do with that?—I do not agree with you there.

2993. Why?—Because the corporation, through their members, exercise a very important influence over the poor-rates.

2994. Do the corporation as a body exercise any control whatever over the poor-rates?—No, none whatever.

2995. The different taxes which are payable by the occupier are the improvement rate of 2 *s.* in the £., the paving, lighting, and watering, the grand jury cess, and the pipe water?—Yes, certainly; there is the sanitary rate besides, which is not very important, and which goes to the borough fund.

2996. I believe you pay out of your own rate, if I understand rightly, your proportion of the grand jury cess for county purposes?—Yes.

2997. The grand jury levy nothing within your district?—Nothing.

Sir *Arthur Guinness.*

2998. Are the corporation in favour of a re-valuation of the city?—You had better ask them; I have put it before them a good many times, but I could not get their attention; they were afraid that it would kick up such a row that it would make them very unpopular; that is the answer that I have got; I have brought it under their notice again and again individually.

2999. Do not you think that it is a great discouragement to improvement as the rate stands at present, because if there is any alteration made the rates are raised?—Yes; in your own case they were raised from 880 *l.* to 2,200 *l.* within the last few years.

Mr. *Butt.*

3000. If a person improves his house it is re-valued, is it not?—Yes; if you were to put a new water-closet in your house they would not add the value of the water-closet, but they would re-value the whole house.

3001. So that it would be valued under a far higher scale than before?—Yes.

3002. Therefore, a person making any improvement to his house subjects himself to re-valuation, and to a higher rate?—Yes, certainly; not merely for the improvement, but for the whole house.

3003. I need scarcely ask you, do you consider that a desirable state of things in the City of Dublin?—I think that is one of the great difficulties that the corporation have had to struggle with. They have had to do with an increasing expenditure,

Mr. *Stokes*.

23 May 1876.

Mr. *Butt*—continued.

expenditure, with a rate which does not increase, but which ought to increase, because the value of property has increased. The value of property in the best parts of the City of Dublin has actually increased 50 per cent. within the last 20 years. If any Member of the Committee who knows Dublin will take up College Green or Sackville-street, or Dame-street, or any other first-class street, there is not a house in them that is valued at half its value.

3004. By that means not only the city loses the rate, but the Exchequer loses the income tax?—Now that you remind me of it, that was one of the absurd arguments that I have heard applied, that it would raise the income tax, a 2 *d.* or 3 *d.* affair, and would bring down the Government upon them.

3005. Although it would increase the Imperial funds by increasing the income tax, would that be a very formidable thing?—I think not, especially as the owners pay it. If the corporation had 20,000 *l.* a year more, I need not tell you that they could do a great many things which they are charged now with not doing.

Chairman.

3006. Are you aware whether it is not the fact that the corporation having grand jury powers, might, if they chose, apply to the Government for a re-valuation?—Where there is a will there is a way, but there is no will.

3007. As it stands, the law gives them power to obtain a re-valuation if they desire it?—I know that if it was our case we should not have rested until we had got a re-valuation allowed, and had made it.

Mr. Butt.

3008. I was asking you as to some of the deficiencies and difficulties which you have pointed out in the corporation, and I understood you to say that in your opinion they proceed from their limited revenues?—Of course. Solomon was a wise man, but he could not do anything without money. They are always, in fact every branch in the corporation has been in distress for money as long as I can remember.

3009. With regard to prices, you say that the corporation have to pay higher prices for materials, &c., from not being in good credit?—Yes.

3010. Is there any difference relatively in the instance of cartage of the block stone and Dodder sand that they get, and that you get; have they to be brought further to them than to you?—A little further; there would be a little difference in that respect, but not much.

3011. Still it would make some difference?—Yes.

3012. Is it the same material that you use as they use?—In the case that I have put, it was the same article exactly. One of the carts went to us, and another to the corporation. In fact, we could get them when the corporation could not get them, because they wanted the money down.

3013. That is on account of your having the cash to pay instantly, and they not?—Yes, we pay instantly. The remedy for that would have been to borrow a respectable sum of money and pay cash for everything. In the case of the Main Drainage Committee, I was urgent for that, and they borrowed a lot of money, and paid everybody off, and you would be astonished at the discount that they got.

Mr. *Butt*—continued.

3014. Did you yourself borrow money to meet current expenses at Rathmines?—We did not.

3015. Do you think that was a prudent system of public finance?—There was no power of striking a rate, and we could not hold out until the rate was struck. We overdrew the bank 6,000 *l.*, and paid everybody.

3016. Still your annual income was quite sufficient, was it not, to meet your annual expenditure?—Yes, but this was the inception of the Act.

3017. Suppose that there was not income sufficient fairly to meet it, the annual expenditure, you would not advocate borrowing money to meet the additional expenditure, would you?—Yes, I would, because the expenditure might exceed the income, but still I would borrow the money, because it would save 5,000 *l.* or 10,000 *l.* a year in the expenditure. I have no doubt that if the corporation when they first began to be in embarrassed circumstances, had borrowed 25,000 *l.*, they could have saved 5,000 *l.* a year.

3018. But would you really recommend borrowing money to meet current expenditure?—Certainly.

3019. I do not know whether you spoke from knowledge when you spoke about the number of publicans in the corporation. I think you said that there were 15?—I counted them when reading over the list; there are about 15, I should say.

3020. Will you look at the list and tell me how many there are?—I am not very intimate with them. There is Hugh Tarpey, he is a licensed hotel keeper.

3021. Did you count him amongst the publicans?—No, I think that there are 15 beside him. There is Philip Redmond, one of the best members that the corporation have got.

3022. And a man in a very high position, is he not?—He is the most independent and upright man that they have got with them.

3023. Is he one of the 15?—Certainly; I only guessed at 15. There a number of names that I have marked on a list that I have there; I do not know whether they are all publicans. There is William Dempsey; he is undoubtedly a publican.

Mr. Brooks.

3024. Mr. Dempsey is wholesale and retail, is he not?—He is both.

3025. Then there is Mr. Findlater?—Mr. Findlater is just as much a retail publican as anybody else holding a retail license. I have no other means of distinguishing them.

Mr. Butt.

3026. Is Mr. John Jameson a publican?—He is a wholesale distiller; you could not call him a publican.

3027. You would not put him amongst the 15?—Certainly not. If you take the drinking interest I think you will have many more than 15.

3028. Among the publicans I presume that you would include Alderman Campbell of Sackville-street?—No, he has both a wholesale and retail license, but he is not a publican. He is a wine and spirit merchant having a retail license merely for the convenience of his trade.

3029. Is he not a spirit grocer?—No, he is a wine

Mr. *Stokes.*

23 May 1876.

Mr. *Butt*—continued.

wine and spirit merchant, and he has as well a retail license, I believe, but I do not know.

3030. At all events you did not count them amongst the 15?—I did not count them.

3031. Who are the others?—There is Mr. M'Cann, he is undoubtedly a publican. It is very invidious picking out people in this way. As you know very well, trade in Dublin is carried on in such a peculiar style that it is very hard to draw the line where the grocer finishes and the publican begins, because they are so closely connected. Mr. Gunn has a retail license; he is the proprietor of the theatre.

3032. Would you include him as a publican?—Yes, I would; you can buy a glass of whiskey in his place. Then there is Richard Bolger; he is undoubtedly a publican.

3033. He is a very high-class man; he has a great many houses in Dublin, has he not?—Yes, a good deal too many. He is a man of great wealth.

3034. Do you call our friend Cornelius Dennehy one of them?—I would not.

3035. He is a rectifying distiller, is he not?—That is, perhaps, worse than a publican.

3036. You include in these 15 publicans a dozen such men as Mr. Tarpey, who keeps a very respectable house?—I would not include him; I would not count him particularly. There are about 20 names; I should say that there are 15 of them who are sheer publicans, that is, they keep a place where anybody that has got 1 *d.* or 2 *d.* can get a glass of whiskey. I would not include Mr. Tarpey and Mr. Campbell, but I would include Mr. Dempsey or Mr. Gunn.

3037. Mr. Gunn is the lessee of the Theatre Royal and of the Gaiety, too, is he not?—I believe so.

3038. And there is a refreshment room there? I never was there, so I cannot say; I presume there is.

3039. And it is on that ground that you class him as a publican?—Yes. There is Mr. Dolan, a highly respectable man; he is a retail man.

Mr. *Brooks.*

3040. Among the people that you class as publicans are some of the most respectable men in Dublin, are they not?—I am not saying that any of them are not respectable; I know nothing against any one of them.

Mr. *Butt.*

3041. Mr. Dolan was the last you mentioned; are there any others?—There are others.

Sir *Joseph M'Kenna.*

3042. With respect to the card, which has been put into the hands of the Committee, I see that the progress of taxation in Dublin between 1850 and 1875 has been from 4 *s.* 7 *d.* to 8 *s.* 1 *d.*, and in Rathmines it has been from 3 *s.* 6½ *d.* to 3 *s.* 8 *d.*?—Yes; the 8 *s.* 1 *d.* was 9 *s.* 5 *d.* the year before.

3043. You know that includes the poor rate. You say, do you not, that the valuation of Rathmines is a fair valuation?—I have not said that; I said it is a fairer valuation than in the City of Dublin; it is a low valuation.

3044. I think you said that the city valuation was frequently less than one-half of the actual rental value?—Yes, very frequently so.

3045. Then might we assume the city to be valued upon a scale twice as low as that of Rathmines?—No, I would not say that; Rathmines is considerably below the real value.

Sir *Joseph M'Kenna*—continued.

3046. What proportion below the real value would you say?—Perhaps a third.

3047. What proportion would you say that the city of Dublin was below the real value?—One-half.

3048. Then there is only a difference of one-sixth between the two; the one is two-sixths below its proper valuation, and the other three-sixths?—Yes, upon that scale; and it is upon that assumption that I make it 800,000 *l.*: that is to say, two-sixths added to the present valuation would raise the city rate from 600,000 *l.* to 800,000 *l.*

3049. You would require, I think, to add one-third to do that?—Yes, it would be 200,000 *l.*; I believe that the proper valuation of the city of Dublin, equalising it with Rathmines, would raise the city to 800,000 *l.* for its full valuation.

3050. Then that would immediately bring down the 8 *s.* to 6 *s.*?—Yes, the difference is more apparent than real.

3051. Then the pressure of the rate would be as 6 *s.* in the 1 *l.* in Dublin is to 3 *s.* 8 *d.* in the 1 *l.* in Rathmines?—That is not all, because of the 6 *s.* all that you get in Dublin is 5 *s.* 3 *d.*, in consequence of insolvents and arrears.

3052. That is in addition to the poor-rate?—But where we have 2 *s.* we get 2 *s.*, and where they have 2 *s.* they can only get 1 *s.* 9 *d.*

3053. I am now coming to the fact of the amount raised in proportion to the actual value being not so much greater in Dublin than it is in Rathmines?—Certainly not.

3054. Supposing the service to be equally well administered in Dublin as in Rathmines, which I do not say is so, but, assuming that to be the case, the pressure of the rates would not be very much increased on the Dublin population in comparison to your well-managed townships of Rathmines?—It would only be about double instead of treble.

3055. Then there is 1 *s.* 10 *d.* comes off for poor rates?—Quite so.

3056. That is 1 *s.* 10 *d.* would come off the 6 *s.* to bring it down to the actual pressure?—No; that is not the case, as it stands at present.

3057. Do you mean it to be inferred that the ratepayers of Dublin have to pay 1 *s.* 10 *d.* for the poor, and you have only to pay 1 *s.* for your poor?—Yes.

3058. If you carry that proportion all through you will find that, assuming the valuation in excess in Rathmines as compared with Dublin (I do not say that they are in excess, but only Dublin being too low), the proportion of charges over which the Dublin Corporation have power, is not greater than the rate over which the Dublin Corporation have no power, that is the poor-rate?—There is this difference between the two rates in question; the poor-rate is a definite sum that has to be provided, no matter what the rate is, whereas in the other case there is a definite rate, no matter what the sum is; the one is a limited rate, the other is an unlimited one. If the expenditure was the same, of course it would be as you say.

3059. The same proportion would be carried through with regard to the other rates as in the case of the poor rate?—The result of the question

Mr. *Stokes*.

23 May 1876.

Sir *Joseph M'Kenna*—continued.

time that is asked me would be this; that if the paving, lighting, watering, and grand jury cess were properly under the control of the corporation, for what now you pay 5 *s.* 7 *d.*, 4 *s.* would suffice against 2 *s.* in Rathmines, and if they managed to get the rates better paid, of course it would be still less.

Mr. Brooks.

3060. I think you have no old debts at Rathmines?—None.

3061. You came in quite unembarrassed and unincumbered?—Quite so.

3062. Is it the case that many persons who would otherwise live in Dublin live at Rathmines, on account of the lesser taxation?—That is obvious, I think; at the same time the convenience of the city is so very great, that in certain cases the taxation would not have that effect; you may depend upon it there would have been several hundred houses built in the municipal district if it were not for the taxation within the city.

3063. Therefore you think that to escape the poor rate and the city rates would be an inducement to live beyond the Circular-road?—Of course it would be; but, as I have already mentioned, the poor rate is gradually approximating, and in a few years I do not expect that there will very much difference in the poor rate. It could not make very much difference to us now when it is coming as a charge upon the union. The union rate gets more and more instead of less and less every year. The city rate was 2 *s.* 6 *d.*, and it has fallen to 2 *s.* 2 *d.* and 2 *s.*, and now it is 1 *s.* 10 *d.*, and our union rate has risen in the same way.

3064. At present there is an inducement to leave the precincts of the city and to live in the neighbourhood over which you preside?—Yes, and of course we make it as strong as we can. We give them the best value that our means admit of.

3065. Apart from any virtue of yours, the nature of things would account for that?—That goes without telling.

3066. Are any complaints made by any persons who reside at Rathmines; have you any quarrels or complaints that the paving or lighting are insufficient?—I could count them all on my fingers. I hardly think there is one. Occasionally, of course, they may grumble, but it is so rare that I can scarcely remember an instance. We are all largely interested in the district, and we give a good deal of time to it, and if there was a grievance we would try to remedy it, and that the citizens are well content is obvious from the fact of the Board being returned year after year without opposition; there were 10 years and not a contest.

3067. Being myself a member of the corporation, I will ask you if you will be kind enough to go through the names of the persons which I think you said you had jotted down who are in the publican interest?—I could not unless I had the Directory. I have only ticked them off since I have been here upon guess. I have no information which would enable me to answer you with accuracy, but it is a matter that could be got at; I could only get at it from the Directory. Some of the names I know and some I do not.

3068. Am I to understand, when you say there are 15 out of 17 persons who are publicans that it is a guess, and you do not vouch for its accuracy?—I do not; I believe there are at least 15, but I could not say with certainty.

Mr. *Brooks*—continued.

3069. Will you kindly give me the names?—There is one retail spirit dealer, Alderman Redmond, and Alderman Dempsey also; Alderman O'Rourke I do not consider is a spirit dealer; he is an hotel keeper; Alderman M'Cann is one, I believe; I will omit Alderman Tarpey; I do not think he comes under that category. Councillor Finegan I do not know, but I see his name stated on the list before me, and you may put down Mr. Finegan. I presume it is correct. Then there are Councillors Carey, Gunn, Dolan, Reilly, and Franklin.

3070. Franklin is an hotel keeper; would you call him one of the publicans?—Yes, I would; his is a place where you can get a glass of spirits; then Councillors Bolger, Gavan, McDermott, Keating, and Meagher; I am only speaking from belief, but I believe those are all retail spirit dealers.

3071. I have 13 down here; are there any others that you know of?—I really do not know; I think that the number in the list before me is probably exaggerated; there are 20 here.

3072. But those 13 are the only persons that you will vouch for?—Yes, I think so; Alderman Campbell is not a retail spirit dealer, nor Mr. Jameson, nor Mr. Donnohy; I do not think anything turns upon that, because a publican may be just as good an administrator as anybody else, but there are too many of them.

3073. I understood you to say that your objection to the constitution of the corporation was in consequence of the number of publicans?—I did not say so.

3074. May I ask what is your objection?—That it does not represent the wealth and intelligence of the city, to put it in a short phrase, and that those who pay the taxes are shut out from a voice in it and that those who are in generally are not a fair representation of the city.

3075. Was it not you who introduced the question of the publican interest?—Somebody asked me a question on the subject, but I certainly do not recollect introducing it.

3076. Then you would not disavow it?—I do not; if I said so I will stick to it. It is one of the crying grievances of the citizens that there are so many publicans in the corporation; there is no doubt about that. It is one of the first things that any man would ask: what is the matter with the corporation, there are so many publicans in it.

3077. Having regard to the high character that you have given of Alderman Redmond, who is one of the 13, and recollecting that there are 60 members of the corporation, and having in view the large number of our shopkeepers, who are publicans in Dublin, do you think that they are unduly represented?—I do, most unquestionably; there are only 800 publicans in Dublin of all descriptions, and I say that 15, or 13, or 10 is too great a representation of them when you remember that there are 30,000 houses in Dublin.

3078. Would you have publicans altogether disqualified?—Certainly not; if they were all timber-merchants, it would be just the same. I do not see why any particular interest should overshadow the rest.

3079. With regard to the merchants; if there were more merchants than publicans, would you exclude

Mr. *Brooks*—continued.

exclude the merchants?—They are pretty well excluded; there are very few merchants in the corporation.

3080. What do say with regard to Sir James Mackey?—Sir James Mackey is one of the most independent members of the corporation, and he has found it very hard to retain his seat in consequence; he does not please his own party.

3081. Alderman Manning; what do you say with regard to him?—He is a most respectable shopkeeper; I would not call him a merchant; but it is an ungracious thing to deal with individuals; I have always found the members of the corporation very friendly with me, and I have no complaint to make individually against the corporation; most of them are my personal friends; I am only speaking of them as a body.

3082. I think you said that you object to the introduction of politics into the corporation?—Yes, decidedly.

3083. Can you say that the Commissioners of Rathmines take any part in the Parliamentary elections?—I presume they do, but, as commissioners, they never take any part in politics.

3084. Not in your town hall?—No, never.

3085. Is the town hall not lent for election purposes?—Certainly; it would be lent to you if you wanted it and were a candidate for the county or city; we would lend it to anybody.

3086. Do you lend it sometimes for religious purposes?—Never; that was one of the rules we made, that it should never be used, under any conditions, for religious purposes, and we stick to it. For election purposes we charge 5 *l.* every time it is used; we have had 20 *l.* one day for the use of it by two Radicals in the morning and two Conservatives in the evening.

3087. I think you said that you retain your name upon the burgess list in order to vex somebody?—I like to have my status; that was only a slip of the tongue; I did not mean it literally.

3088. May I ask you whom you desire to vex?—I like to retain my power as a burgess. The corporation and the Rathmines Commissioners are pretty often in disagreement, and it is convenient to have all the power you can.

3089. Does that mean power to obstruct?—No; except to obstruct them, certainly, if they come poaching upon our preserves. We make it a point never to attack the corporation and never to interfere with them, either individually or collectively, unless they attack us, and then we hit as hard as ever we can, as I am doing now.

Mr. *Murphy.*

3090. Since 1850 has the valuation of Rathmines township been changed, or rather, has the principle of the valuation been changed?—It has not, but of course new houses have been newly valued; there has been no revaluation.

3091. Are those valued upon the same principle as houses that stood in 1850?—No, quite the reverse. They have been valued progressively higher. That is what I complain of.

3092. Has the standard of valuation been changed?—The standard has been changed.

3093. And the same has taken place in Dublin, has it not?—Yes, but inasmuch as ours are nearly all new houses, and there are no new houses in Dublin, or very few, the disproportion becomes greater.

3094. Can you state generally from memory with regard to Dublin, whether or not the standard of valuation that existed in 1850 was higher than the standard of valuation that exists now?—No, it was lower. The present standard of valuation is considerably higher. As I have already shown you, two houses of the same quality are put, one at 66 *l.* and another at 110 *l.*

Mr. *Murphy*—continued.

3095. But if the same class of house that stood in 1850 was to be valued now in 1876, would the standard or principle of valuation that was applied in 1850 be higher than it is now?—The present standard is higher; if you take four houses that were built in 1850, and build four more in the same row, you would have to pay half as much more rates for the new houses.

3096. I may take for granted that the valuation existing in Dublin in 1850 was a good deal lower than what it would be now if a revaluation took place?—Yes, if it was revalued, even according to the present standard, it would be enormously increased, or greatly increased at all events.

3097. I am talking of the valuation that was in existence before Griffiths' valuation?—They are both Griffiths' valuations.

3098. Were not the valuations by the Poor Law Board valuators, made before Griffiths' valuation came in?—No, Griffiths' valuation was made about 1847 or 1848.

3099. Prior to that, was not there the poor law valuation by private valuators?—Anybody could value then; we did it ourselves.

3100. Did not the poor law get their valuation made by Griffiths?—Yes.

3101. Can you take upon yourself to say whether the standard which those poor law valuators took upon themselves to use prior to Griffiths' valuation was higher than Griffiths' valuation?—I think it was rather higher.

3102. Therefore, I take it for granted that the total valuation of the City of Dublin prior to the existence of Griffiths' valuation was higher than what it subsequently became?—I cannot answer that question, but I think it was much about the same. Griffiths made the new valuation much higher than the old one, and then he dropped it afterwards considerably. Between 1848 and 1850 it was dropped, I think, as much as 100,000 *l.* I think the old valuation was much about the same as the valuation of 1850. In the first instance Griffiths raised it very high, and then he dropped it again.

3103. Did he raise it higher than the poor law valuation?—Yes, very much higher. In our own case we were raised to 42,000 *l.*, and then dropped to 33,000 *l.*

3104. Are you aware that the valuation of the city of Cork is very nearly one-half what it was 30 years ago?—If I were to offer an opinion I might say that the valuation of 1850 was lower than it was prior to 1850. I have heard the corporation say so very often, and I presume they say so with good grounds. There was a substantial drop in the valuation.

Mr. *Gibson.*

3105. What system of audit have you at Rathmines?—We have two ratepayers auditors.

3106. How are they elected?—They are appointed at a public meeting of the ratepayers.

3107. Is there a qualification by your Act?—The same qualification as for a Commissioner.

3108. Is

Mr. *Stokes.*

23 May 1876.

Mr. *Gibson*—continued.

3108. Is that purely a ratepaying qualification?—Yes, rate or property.

3109. They are not required to be qualified to discharge the duty?—No.

3110. So that you might elect two people who knew nothing about figures if you pleased?—We might.

3111. Has there been any contest for the office of auditor?—Only on one occasion.

3112. Is there any payment attached to it?—Two guineas.

3113. There has been no change, I suppose?—No; in fact, we, the Commissioners, generally select the auditors ourselves; we generally select two persons of high standing; the accountant of the Bank of Ireland, or some one in that capacity; in fact, except on one occasion, the two persons that we named were always elected.

3114. You are aware, of course, that in the case of the city of Dublin, and with, I believe, three exceptions in all the other cities in Ireland, the audit is now of a public character?—Yes, in the City of Dublin it is.

3115. But it is excluded, I believe, from Rathmines?—Yes.

3116. Can you give any reason why that should be kept up?—I think a public audit would, we consider, add very much to the expense, and hamper us in our operations very much, and we object to it on that account.

3117. How would it hamper you?—Things must be done precisely according to rule and form.

3118. That is to say that the audit would be more rigorous?—Yes.

3119. You prefer it to be done by an auditor appointed by yourselves, who would apply the principle of give and take?—Yes.

3120. Have you any other reason to suggest than that why the difference should be kept up?—None in the world.

3121. Do not you think that, as a rule, it is better that an independent public officer should intervene and audit the accounts of a corporation?—Quite so.

3122. You approve of the principal generally?—Yes; we possess the confidence of the ratepayers, so that if there was no audit at all, it would make no difference.

3123. Do you think it would be an improvement for the city of Dublin and other cities to have a public auditor?—I do not know that he has done much good in the city of Dublin. He has found out plenty of holes, I believe. The auditor has made a good many objections, but I do not think they seem to have come to anything in the city. I do not see any practical result, unless it keeps them in check.

3124. You do not think that the feeling that the accounts will all be examined and scrutinised has of itself a healthy action upon the corporation, and induces them to act so that nothing may be discovered on scrutiny?—I would not like to say that; the accounts are very well kept.

3125. Do you not think that the feeling that the accounts will be subjected to audit always exercises a healthy influence upon the keeping of accounts?—I am scarcely a fair judge upon that, because you have to do with rather illegal things in public matters, and if you want to get them done it is very inconvenient to have those illegal things picked to pieces by an auditor. You must break through the law constantly. I will give you a case in point. There is a bridge between us and the corporation, called the "Portobello Bridge," entirely in the city; a very bad bridge and very narrow. We were very anxious to have it improved. The corporation met us very kindly, and with the aid of the tramway company we widened this bridge 14 feet, at a cost of about 350 *l.* The corporation paid one-third, the tramway company paid one-third, and we paid one-third. If that had been audited it would have been disallowed, because it was perfectly illegal. But having no auditor except a friendly one, we took the risk, and the result was that by an expense of 116 *l.* we got a very large addition to the comfort of our ratepayers. I must say that on that occasion the corporation met us with great promptitude and liberality.

Mr. *Gibson*—continued.

3126. That saved the necessity of all sides going to Parliament, and going to a great deal of expense?—Yes; I could give you plenty of others. But we have constantly to break the law in that way.

3127. Do you think it would be convenient in the administration of the public audit to vest the power in the Local Government Board, or some public department, to legalize such a transaction as that you have mentioned?—I think they do take it. I think they have it, if they do not take it.

3128. Do you not think, assuming that they have not the power at present, it would be desirable to vest the power of legalizing such a transaction as you have stated?—Certainly. I know a case where the thing was done. We borrowed 6,000 *l.* for the main drainage committee, from the Hibernian Bank, at six per cent. That was perfectly illegal. We had no power to borrow, and no power to pay interest; and the auditor disallowed the interest, although it had saved us hundreds of pounds in paying accounts. I went and explained it to the auditor, and it was all right, and he passed it on.

3129. When was that?—That was in 1871; it was sanctioned by the ratepayers of the city of Dublin, and saved hundreds of pounds.

3130. And it was never sought to be questioned?—Yes, the auditor questioned it.

3131. But no ratepayer sought to bring it in question?—No.

3132. With regard to the meetings of your council, what forms a quorum?—Five.

3133. Do you find that at the hour appointed you generally have a quorum?—In 29 years we never have failed, or had a break down.

3134. That is to say, you never had a count out?—No.

3135. You never failed to make a house?—Never; I never had to adjourn my meetings for the want of a quorum for 25 years.

3136. Do you find that the commissioners usually meet with reasonable punctuality?—We are never five minutes late.

3137. Your quorum, as I understand, is five out of 21?—Yes.

3138. Are you aware that in the corporation of the city of Dublin the quorum is as high as 20?—Yes.

3139. Do you think that that is too high for a corporation of 60, taking men away from their business at the busy time?—It is proved to be so, because their meetings are never punctual.

3140. Would you suggest that it would be desirable

Mr *Stokes*.

23 May 1876.

Mr. *Gibson*—continued.

desirable to reduce the size of the quorum in such a city as Dublin?—I should say that seven would be plenty.

3141. At all events, you are in favour of the principle of reduction?—Yes; they would have a better attendance with a small quorum, because the knowledge that four or five or 10 men would do all the work would make them rush in, and there would always be a good attendance.

3142. You are in favour of reducing the quorum?—Yes. In the case of the Main Drainage Committee there was six members of the townships, three members representing my township and three representing the other townships, and 12 from the corporation; and from a fear that all six members might meet and do something that they did not like, they fixed the quorum at seven, and the fact of it is that there never was a quorum without some of the township members, or rarely ever.

3143. One member came to watch the others to see that there was no start?—Yes.

3144. You said something about your commissioners being free from any political bias in the performance of your duties; have you ever had political discussions at your board?—Never.

3145. Do you think that that facilitates the dispatch of business?—Of course it does; our time of meeting is nine o'clock sharp, and we are never unpunctual; no business can be brought on after 10 o'clock; I need not tell you that people who have only one hour to do their business in must look sharp; there is no speechifying and no waste of time, because at 10 o'clock any gentleman can go who likes, with the certainty that no business will be originated after he has gone.

3146. They would only conclude what business was in hand, I suppose?—Yes, and routine matters.

3147. You think that business men are more likely to attend if they know that they will be kept wholly to fiscal business without anything of the character of a political discussion?—We have some of the first citizens of Dublin on our board who could not come if they were not allowed to go to their business at 10 o'clock or shortly after.

3148. I gather from your evidence that you consider the principal duties of a corporation or commissioners to be fiscal; that is to say, the administration of the rates that they collect?—That, of course.

3149. You suggested also that in consequence of that you would regard a corporation elected by those who paid a very small quantity of rates as not being adequately representative?—Precisely so.

3150. I think you stated, also, that you would remedy that by giving a better representation to those who paid a large sum; have you any remedy to suggest, except the system of plural voting?—I would introduce the qualification for the members of the corporation that we have, and that is a property qualification of 200 *l.* a year, because there might be many persons not rated to the city at all who would be valuable members of the corporation. For instance, I have been chairman of the Rathmines Board for the last 16 years, and for seven or eight years past I have lived out of Rathmines, and they would lose me, if that was a loss, but for that qualification.

3151. You would allow no lesser figure than 200 *l.*?—No. The words of the Act are "in the enjoyment of rents and profits to the extent of 200 *l.*"

3152. Would you put it as high as 200 *l.* a year?—No, it need not be.

3153. Do you think that you could take a lesser figure, such as 30 *l.*?—No, 50 *l.* would be too small.

3154. You stated that you were against the principle of allowing the owner, as owner, any right to vote?—Certainly.

3155. Is the reason because they do not pay rates?—Certainly; I think that the persons who govern the rates should be the persons who pay the rates.

3156. Is it not the fact that at present in Dublin the owners are directly rated, at all events, to the water rate?—Very slightly; it is not worth speaking of much.

3157. Wherever the tenant pays rack rent, is not the owner directly rated?—That is very rarely the case.

3158. That would be a direct way of paying the rates, but is there not also an indirect way, which is this, that now the taxation is so high in Dublin the people will pay less rents to the landlords; and does not that indirectly compel the landlords to pay the rates?—Indirectly it does.

3159. If any person had to pay 50 *l.* a year taxes, would not that leave him less to pay for rent?—It is very slender, because when once a man has got a lease the interest of the occupier is to reduce the rates, the owner does not care twopence about the matter, except with regard to the poor rate.

3160. In the first take by a tenant from year to year, would not a man give less rent, according to the amount of his taxation?—Yes.

3161. And in that way the landlord indirectly pays the taxes?—Yes, but that does not seem to me to be practical.

Sir *Arthur Guinness*.

3162. What is the annual rate of mortality per 1,000 of the population of Rathmines?—A fraction over 19.

3163. Do you know what it is in Dublin?—About 26, I think.

3164. With regard to epidemics, small-pox and cholera, how do they affect Rathmines, as compared with Dublin?—The deaths from cholera were, in the city of Dublin, 1 in 280; in Kingstown, 1 in 142; and in Rathmines, 1 in 685.

3165. You are the largest ratepayer on your board, are you not?—I am not; there are four or five larger than I am; I am not a ratepayer in Rathmines at all.

3166. How much does the largest ratepayer pay?—The largest ratepayer in Rathmines pays 193 *l.*

3167. Have you any idea what the lowest ratepayer of the Commissioners is?—The lowest Commissioner would be 30 *l.*; I am speaking now of Rathmines rates only. Their city ratings are much higher; they are mostly large ratepayers in the city.

3168. Do you know how many members of the corporation of Dublin are rated under 100 *l.*?—Forty-five, I think.

3169. Do you know how many under 50 *l.*?—Twenty-three.

3170. Are there many members of the new corporation, that is the corporation of 1850, who have

Mr. *Stokes.*

23 May 1876.

Sir *Arthur Guinness*—continued.

have seats in the present council?—There are two; Alderman Jameson and Alderman Campbell.

3171. Had you any dealings with the corporation yourself as to the main drainage?—I represented the township of Rathmines upon that committee; we had a contract with them.

3172. Had you any experience of the business capacity of the members of that committee in financial matters?—We got on very well together; I generally managed the finance myself, so I am hardly qualified to give an answer. They were very ready to adopt any suggestion that I made, and we got on perfectly harmoniously.

3173. Have you heard it stated that the deficiency in the city improvement rate to meet the charges on it were due to the addition of new streets; what is your opinion of that?—I saw it in Mr. Henry's evidence, and I dissent from it altogether. I have made as many new streets as most people; I made them all at my own expense, and so far from their costing them anything, they are bringing them in a very large revenue every year.

3174. You mean that the new streets would increase the revenue?—Yes; but in a portion of that district which they took in, which was a very disastrous affair, there were not any new streets.

3175. But that was only a portion?—Yes.

3176. You have heard of the Sanitary Committee of Dublin, I suppose?—Yes; that is to say, an amateur sanitary committee.

3177. Have they much to do with Rathmines; do they make many complaints to you?—I have not heard of any. We gave them our Town Hall for a lecture, and for experiments.

3178. Have they made no complaints to the commissioners on sanitary matters?—Once they wrote to us; that is all.

3179. I think you have already said that you do not think that the corporation adequately represents the wealth and intelligence of Dublin; what remedy would you propose for that?—As I have already mentioned, I would give the plural vote, and give a property qualification.

3180. Will you tell us if you have had any experience of the financial operations of the corporation; what I particularly refer to is the rate of interest at which they borrow money?—I have made money of them myself.

3181. Why do you think they are not able to obtain money on as good terms as you?—That I cannot tell you. I lent them 35,000 *l.*, and got five per cent. interest and two per cent. commission; one of the best transactions I ever had.

3182. For how long did you lend them that money; have they paid it yet?—I got bonds for the money, and sold them directly at a premium.

3183. Do any members of the corporation lend money to the corporation for similar purposes?—Yes, I think they do. Mr. Jameson very frequently lends them money, I believe; but I am not aware of it personally. I can see by the accounts that whenever they want money they go to him. I think that is for the waterworks.

3184. There was a sum of money lent by the treasurer, Mr. Costigin, was there not?—Mr. Costigin was appointed a long time ago. The corporation, that is the old corporation, the O'Connell corporation, were in great embarrassment, and it was part of the conditions of his office that he should lend them 5,000 *l.* at five per cent. If I do not mistake, there was an execution in the Mansion House, or something of that kind; but, at any rate, they were in urgent need of the money.

Sir *Arthur Guinness*—continued.

3185. Do you believe that the corporate elections are mainly due to political considerations?—There is no doubt about it; no one has any chance who has not strong politics.

3186. Can you give any instances of that kind?—It is the case in nearly every election. There was a very noteworthy case, that of Mr. Casson, one of the most respectable and moderate members of the board, and he was turned out recently, simply from political reasons. He was the last of the moderate men.

3187. He was a merchant, was he not?—Yes, a very wealthy merchant.

3188. Will you tell us what you think of the presentments made by the grand jury of Dublin; with respect to North Wall, is it a fact that the North Wall is outside the city boundary as stated by some of the corporation witnesses?—That was a mistake, it is not outside, it is inside.

3189. I think that a financial transaction about it was spoken of here the other day; will you explain what it was?—The transaction was this: the corporation got a clause, as the Chief Justice said, smuggled into the Port and Docks Act of 1867, which enabled them to levy out of the grand jury rate whatever sum was required to repair the North Wall. It was, in fact, stretching the improvement rate to that extent. They made the presentment in an indirect way, increasing the rate 5,460 *l.*; it was opposed by an active corporator of the name of French; and the corporation were defeated for this reason, that the provision in the Act was, that they should only have this power when there was a deficiency in the improvement rate. Mr. French proved that they had lent 2,000 *l.* to some other rate, the sewers rate from the improvement rate, and therefore there was not a deficiency, and the presentment was quashed.

3190. What remark did the judge make on the transaction?—The Chief Justice said: "After dealing with docks, ballast stores, wharfs, &c., there suddenly appeared a section, the 244th, which enacted that the municipal council should from time to time cause to be presented and raised upon the county of the city at large in the manner prescribed by law, for the time being, the sums of money sufficient for repairing the roads upon the north, south, and east walls, bounding or near the River Liffey. That was a taxing section, and he must say it appeared to him to have been smuggled into an Act where no person expected to find it, in order to accommodate the municipal body, and enable that body to effect indirectly what very possibly it was afraid that the Legislature would not grant if asked openly." Then he goes on to say that "a portion of the improvement rate alleged to be insufficient for its proper purposes was lent to a committee for sewer purposes. Now, that was a clear violation of duty." He said he "could not say that the 244th section of the Port and Docks Act was to be resorted to for raising money for the very object that the improvement rate should have been applied to, but was not, and he therefore thought that Mr. French, who had brought the matter

Mr. *Stokes.*

23 May 1876.

Sir *Arthur Guinness*—continued.

matter before the court, had acted very properly. They were unanimously of opinion that the presentment in question should not be fiated." Mr. Justice O'Brien said: "It was a very irregular proceeding to lend the improvement fund for sewer purposes." Mr. Justice Fitzgerald said that the "fund clearly was not exhausted, for portions of it had been lent. The court, exercising a proper judicial discretion, could not sanction the presentment." The next year it was brought in and carried.

Mr. *Butt.*

3191. I suppose that was because there was then a deficiency in the improvement fund?—Yes.

Sir *Arthur Guinness.*

3192. Do you know of any other transaction of that kind in connection with the sewer rate and the improvement fund?—I heard what was discussed the last day about the transfer from the sewer rate to the improvement fund; there was a large balance in hand of the sewer rate, and it was transferred to the improvement rate, to repay, as was stated then, an expenditure on the surface of the streets which had been either neglected or overlooked, but still covering the same debt. It was 2,800 *l.* that was lent.

3193. Do you not think that that was an indirect way of increasing the improvement rate?—Of course it was. It entirely depends upon the justice or injustice of the charge, but inasmuch as it extended over several years, it was stated by some member of the Corporation to have been made on purpose to swallow up this surplus of 2,800 *l.*

3194. Do you know of any instance in which the Council has delayed or neglected to act upon the report of their committees?—I think they always do; the reports always lie over a very long time. I think in one case the Main Drainage report lay over for a year and a half; but several months is not at all uncommon.

3195. What was the original estimate for the waterworks?—£. 300,000, in round numbers.

3196. What did they cost?—Between 600,000 *l.* and 700,000 *l.*

3197. You took a part in the opposition to that scheme, did you not?—I did; I fought hard, and was beaten.

3198. You still think that the other scheme might have been carried out for less, and have been equally advantageous?—The Vartry supply has turned out very good in quality and sufficient in quantity, but it was not, as was represented, perfectly white; it was yellow, and required filtering, which it was stated it would not. I believe that the Coy Ford or Ballysmuttan scheme could have been carried out for half the money.

3199. They are obliged now, are they not, to filter the Vartry water, which was not anticipated?—It was not anticipated. It is splendid water, there is no doubt.

3200. Do you know anything of the issue and purchase of City Debentures?—There was a large sum of debentures taken up many years ago by the Hibernian Bank at par. I think they pay off 500 *l.* a year of them every year. It was a transaction very advantageous for the Corporation, and disadvantageous to the Bank.

3201. Were they as low as 88 at any time?—I never knew them to be so high. There was a rush came a few months ago for debentures, and they ran up, I think, to 82 or 83; I sold some myself at 79, which I bought at 75.

3202. Do you know much of the working of the Port and Docks Board in Dublin?—Not much; they are very respectable men; they are rather lofty in their ideas, and too squeezable by the Corporation.

3203. Do you think that they enjoy public confidence as a board?—I think as a board they stand first of any board in Dublin; they seem to have the confidence of everybody.

Mr. *Collins.*

3204. I think you said that you lent the Corporation some time ago 35,000 *l.*?—Yes.

3205. And they paid you for it interest at 5 per cent., with a commission of 2 per cent.?—Yes.

3206. You took bonds at 98?—Yes.

3207. You sold them very soon afterwards?—Directly.

3208. Is it an unfair inquiry to put to you, at what price did you sell those bonds?—Those that I owned myself I sold at 102 the same week.

3209. You sold bonds which you got at 98 immediately, at a profit of 4 per cent.?—Yes.

3210. The Corporation lost 4 per cent. by the bonds that they issued to you?—I do not agree with you. They got the stamp of my name at 4 per cent., which they would not have got otherwise; they had tried everyone else before they offered them to me; I did not offer to take them. I happened to meet Mr. Smith, the law agent of the Corporation. He had, he said, very great difficulty in getting 35,000 *l.*; they had tried London and they had tried Dublin. I said, "What will you give?" he said, "5 per cent." I said, "If you will give me 2 per cent. commission I will take them."

3211. What did you mean by the stamp of your name?—Being well known, people took them, on the faith of my having taken them.

3212. It was simply to follow your example?—Yes; they bought them from me; they would not buy them from the Corporation.

3213. You did not endorse them, did you?—Yes, they were all endorsed to me. There was no liability; I pocketed the 4 per cent. and had done with it. The only expense that I had, was that I employed a solicitor and counsel. I prepared the bonds for them, or my counsel did.

3214. What might have been the cost of preparing those bonds?—£. 10 altogether.

3215. That would be 3 *s.* per cent.?—A mere nothing.

3216. Practically you made by the transaction 6 per cent.?—Ninety-eight was for cash, 2 per cent. was for commission, or discount, making the bonds stand at 96.

3217. Does the Corporation issue bonds very largely on or about those terms?—I think that was the only transaction on those terms; they were able to do it afterwards at 4½ per cent.

3218. They would not be willing to repeat a transaction of that kind?—No; it was the first transaction of the kind they had had. In fact I showed them how to do it (they had never heard of a coupon, I think, before), and their bonds and coupons were payable at the Bank of Ireland, and therefore marketable.

3219. I think I understood you to say that some of the difficulties which you allege in reference

Mr. *Stokes.*

23 May 1876.

Mr. *Collins*—continued.

ference to municipal matters are, first of all, the system of valuation?—Those are the disabilities under which the Corporation labour, with the valuation and the insolvency.

3220. Have you formed any opinion as to the best means to be introduced for re-valuing the property of the municipality?—It must be done by Imperial legislation, of course.

3221. Have you formed any opinion yourself upon the subject, so as to be able to give advice?—The valuation ought to be made equal. Of course the machinery is in existence, and only wants to be put in motion.

3222. Would you recommend any compulsory means to be adopted, say by the Government, to compel re-valuation?—Yes, certainly, that is the proper way of doing it.

3223. I think the next difficulty was the want of available funds or ready money, which you said necessitated paying so largely for work to be done?—Yes.

3224. You said in some cases as much as between 20 and 30 per cent.?—Quite that. In the case of the main drainage a number of accounts were sent in for payment, and we should have had to pay them in full if we had taken credit. There was one account of 370 *l.*; we offered 250 *l.* and he took it; that was one of our Parliamentary Accounts. There were accounts of some 400 *l.* or 500 *l.*, or several hundreds with the newspapers, and we offered them half the money, and they took it, and so on.

3225. You stated that they could get work done at a considerably lower price if they paid ready money for it; I should like to ask you whether you think it less objectionable to incur further debt, than to go on paying excessively for work and materials, as at present?—Less objectionable to incur further debt, certainly.

3226. By the issue of additional debentures?—In any way that they could get it.

3227. That you would consider perfectly unobjectionable?—Yes, if you are paying 25 per cent. for the money that you want, it is clearly better to borrow than to go on paying at that rate. They owe many large sums to contractors.

3228. Do you think that a largely increased additional amount could be raised by loans, without paying an excessive rate of interest?—Yes, the security is first-rate; there is no better security in the world.

3229. Do you think that there would be sufficient available funds raised by debentures at such a rate of interest as about 4½ per cent., as would make the Corporation independent?—Perfectly easy; I should be very happy to take them myself at 4½ per cent.

Mr. *Bruen.*

3230. With regard to those bonds and debentures, have you ever dealt with them in the open market; have you bought and sold them?—Yes.

3231. Besides those ones that you got from the Corporation?—Yes; I have got a lot of them now.

3232. Can you tell the Committee about what would be the rate in the open market for debentures which bear 4½ per cent. interest?—About par; but you can buy a quantity of pipe water debentures, 4 per cent. debentures, at about 80, which are prior to the Government loan, and perfectly undoubted securities; I have held them myself, and frequently bought them at 80, paying

Mr. *Bruen*—continued.

5 per cent., with a security ranking before the Government loan.

3233. What reason could you give for this depreciation?—The bad odour that the Corporation are in.

3234. Is not the security in both cases derived from the same source?—Yes, in both cases.

3235. How can the bad odour of the Corporation affect the one class of securities without affecting the other?—They are not the same class of securities; the one are non-redeemable debentures; whereas the other are redeemable in 21 years. The 5 per cent ones that I spoke of just now were redeemable in 21 years; but the pipe water debentures of which I spoke are irredeemable, that is to say, the Corporation cannot be called upon to pay them off. Perhaps I flatter myself that this loan brought a good price, because it was known that it had passed through my hands, and that it was sure to be all right.

3236. As regards the price in the open market for those debentures bearing interest at 4½ per cent., have they been as high as par for any number of years?—There are no debentures at 4½ per cent.; those are bonds. The debentures are all 4 per cent. The bonds such as I took for them were 5 per cent. and 4½ per cent.; the 4½ per cent. are usually sold at a slight premium; those at 5 per cent. that I bought at 2 per cent. discount are worth about 5 *l.* premium. The 4 per cent. debentures are about 80. The City debentures are somewhat better. The City debentures bear a better price, because occasionally they are bought up for the purpose of redeeming ground rents and things of that kind; and whenever there is a demand for that purpose, up they go.

3237. Can you tell the Committee whether these prices were speculative, or had they borne those prices in the market for any number of years?—About the same. I think they are rather better now; their credit is improving, and the position of their bonds is improving.

3238. Then that transaction which was mentioned to the Committee by the City Treasurer of employing the proceeds of the sale of a house, 13,000 *l.*, I think he said, in buying up debentures which were bought for 85 and 88, was quite an exceptional transaction?—If they paid 85 or 88, it must have been very improvident, because that is far above the normal value of them; I sold some of them at the same time that the transaction was going on at 79. Of course the transaction would raise them in the market inevitably.

3239. What was the date of that transaction?—About two years ago, I should think.

3240. At the same time, at all events at which they were buying them in the open market for 85 and 88?—I do not know whether they were buying them in the open market at all; I have no knowledge of that.

3241. There has been some evidence given before the Committee a few days ago that the addition of the new streets which have been made within the city bounds has not brought any increase of revenue corresponding to the increase of expense. I think that you yourself have built some new streets, and you could give us evidence upon that point?—I have laid out many streets, but I have not built them myself; but upon my land there have been several hundreds of houses built, all of which bring in a large revenue, of course.

3242. Is

Mr. *Stokes.*

13 May 1876.

Mr. *Bruen*—continued.

3242. Is it your opinion that the revenue which they will bring in, more than balances the extra expenditure that is involved by them?—Yes, very much more; because they were formed and sewered by myself; the kerbs and everything of the kind.

3243. With regard to the valuation of houses, could you tell the Committee from memory, about what the valuation of the houses in those streets might be?—They are small houses, I should say, of not more than 20 *l.* a year.

3244. In point of fact, although they are small houses, you do not think that the expense incurred by the Corporation swallows up the increased revenue derived from them?—There is no expense at all, except lighting and watering; if road is well made it stands to reason. The pipe water rate, for example, was all profit on those houses; there was no additional expense for water, and the whole of the grand jury rate was profit. There is merely whatever proportion of the improvement rate has to be set against the cost of keeping them in repair.

3245. You are a member of the Main Drainage Committee, are you not?—I am, and have been from its formation.

3246. Has the main drainage plan been abandoned?—Practically, I take it that it has; it was thoroughly impracticable from the very first.

3247. With regard to some of the levels of the sewers which were contemplated in the main drainage scheme, was there any remarkable error?—In the case of Pembroke township the corporation abandoned about one-half, because as I am informed, the levels were not suitable; there had been an error in taking the levels; they could not, in fact, drain a portion of the district, and at any rate they abandoned it; I believe there is no doubt that it was below the leve at which the corporation could drain.

3248. Has that anything to do with the breaking down of the original scheme?—Nothing whatever.

3249. What was the cause why any of this scheme was abandoned?—They wanted to get a scheme that could not be done for the money; the scheme was too extravagant, and the estimate entirely fallacious; the estimate was something like 250,000 *l.*, and we could not get it done much under a million. £. 350,000 *l.* was the original powers of the Committee, and the tenders averaged about 900,000 *l.*; indeed some of them were close upon a million.

3250. With regard to the municipal franchise, you told the Committee that you thought the franchise should not be conferred upon owners who did not pay rates?—I think not; I do not see the justice of it.

3251. Supposing they did pay the rates, what then?—Then they should be allowed to substitute their own names as occupiers.

3252. If the rates were divided as they are in the poor law organisation, I suppose in that case you would allow votes both to owners and occupiers on the same premises?—Of course but that would be a dreadful infliction.

3253. In what way?—Owing to the difficulty of completely adjusting it. You could not make the holder of a lease pay a portion of the rates; he would require to have some contrivance for that; it would be thoroughly impracticable. It is not impossible, of course, but speaking as an owner myself, I feel that it would be very objectionable.

Mr. *Bruen*—continued.

3254. In a case where the rate has existed for a very long time affecting the property, perhaps before the beginning of the lease, are you not aware that you pay that rate yourself, although the occupier's name may be entered in the rate book as paying it?—I pay it myself in some cases.

3255. But is it not the fact that those rates and taxes of any old standing do in reality come out of the fee?—They do, of course.

3256. And therefore the owner pays them in so far as his rent is reduced thereby?—Yes.

Mr. *Rathbone.*

3257. I think I understood you to object to the representation of the owner on your board, because, as he did not pay the rate directly, he did not feel the rate at all?—That was one reason. I do not object to the representation of owners, because I may say that my board is almost entirely composed of owners; those who are mere occupiers are only two or three; the great bulk of the Commissioners are owners of property.

3258. As I understand, you do not wish owners to vote as such, because they do not directly pay rates, and do not feel a sufficient interest in their expenditure?—Quite so.

3259. You are aware, I presume, that in Scotland the owners pay half the rates and the occupiers the other half?—I know nothing about Scotland; I never was there.

3260. Supposing that such a plan was introduced reserving the right during the present tenancies do you not think that the direct representation of owners might be a good thing?—I think if we had occupiers who were largely interested in the rates, that would answer the same purpose; that is one objection to the Corporation of Dublin at present, that the owners are not interested in the rates.

3261. But would not an owner have a more permanent interest in the rates if he had an equally direct one with the occupier?—Yes, of course. I would rather have owners.

3262. Would he not be likely to look with greater vigilance against borrowing money which had subsequently to be repaid?—Certainly; no doubt the value of having owners on the Board would be very great, but the price that you would call upon them to pay for it would be very great.

3263. What would be the price that you would call upon them to pay?—To pay half the rates.

3264. Do not you think that if this large expenditure which is borrowed comes ultimately upon them, it would be to their interest that their attention should be called to the expenditure while it was yet time to keep it in order?—Yes, it would; but the complication would be very great in dividing the rate between the owner and the occupier. I speak feelingly upon that point, for I have several hundred tenants, and I should have a nice little job with every one.

3265. Might they not pay it, and deduct it from their rent?—That is what they would do, of course. I should have poor rate, income tax, and improvement rate to divide. I find it quite complex enough as it is.

3266. Would it not be possible, if the system was a good one, to levy the whole of the rates in one consolidated rate, distinguishing the purposes for

Mr. *Stokes*.

23 May 1876.

Mr. *Rathbone*—continued.

for which they were intended?—That is the way in which it is done in Dublin at present.

3267. Then it would be only one deduction?—Yes, in that case; it might be incorporated with the poor rate, and in that way you might get it; but you must recollect that the immediate owner might be a person who had a very small interest in his holding; he might get 100 *l.* a year, and pay 95 *l.* of it. You would have to go climbing up through all the owners. I have a case in point; my son-in-law has a house in Kingstown which he gets 6 *l.* a year from, although it is rated at 50 *l.*, and he votes the same as if he owned the whole 50 *l.* and paid nothing out of it.

3268. He might deduct that?—As he does, of course, but he is not in any degree the owner.

3269. I suppose that he would deduct on 45 *l.*, and pay tax upon the other?—Yes.

3270. You do it in the case of income tax without much difficulty, do you not?—But still you would not give the franchise to every one who had the deduction made who paid 35 *l.* out of 40 *l.*, or whatever it was.

3271. Would there be any objection to the owners of property having votes?—Then you might have twenty votes in one house.

3272. If they were all owners of property, do not you think that they would be very good voters?—I should rather that you would undertake the task than I.

3273. Are there many cases in which there are twenty owners in one house?—In Ireland, it is so; possibly not twenty, but there are very few cases in my township where there are not several persons interested.

3274. The more people that you can interest in good government the better, is it not?—Yes, the more you can interest the owners in the government undoubtedly the better.

3275. If, as it is suggested, the property is so split up, that would give to the owners a very large property interest?—Yes, very large. The thing is done at present in the poor law, and could be done here. In the poor law every fragment of an owner is represented, no matter how many there are, every one of those owners can act as a poor law guardian.

3276. If you had a consolidated rate there would be probably a great deal more interest on the part of owners if they had to pay their part of it, as in the case of the poor rate?—Yes, but you would have to deal with existing interests. It could be done no doubt, and it would be of course perfectly fair.

3277. And probably a very advantageous thing for the government of the country?—It would.

Chairman.

3278. You gave us a general opinion as to the cost of labour to the Corporation of Dublin. I think that you were present when Mr. Robinson was giving his evidence the other day?—Yes.

3279 Did you hear the items that he stated to the Committee of the cost of labour, and work, and expenditure on horses, by the No. 1 Committee of the Corporation?—Yes, I recollect his evidence upon that subject.

3280. He stated that something like 40,299 *l.* were paid out of the improvement rate for labour and work in macadamising and repairing streets, and so on, the maximum number of labourers being 700; and 6,143 *l.* for the keep of eighty horses; what is your opinion as to those items?—£. 6,000 would be an outrageous cost for eighty horses; it is impossible almost, because if I remember rightly, the carters were charged separately.

Chairman—continued.

3281. The carters were charged for in the 40,299 *l.*?—Yes; so that it is only forage.

3282. The 6,143 *l.* included an item of 599 *l.* for the purchase of horses; but, deducting that, there was an item of 4,051 *l.* for forage, 252 *l.* for veterinary expenses, 72 *l.* for harness repairs, 123 *l.* miscellaneous, 513 *l.* stable expenses, and 530 *l.* weekly wages?—I think 16 *s.* a week would be sufficient to cover all those expenses per horse; I think that is what it costs us, about 15 *s.* a week per horse.

3283. Must not the corporation pay ready money for all those expenses?—Labour, of course, must be paid ready money for; I do not know whether they pay cash for forage or not.

3284. But so far as labour is concerned, the excuse which you gave on their behalf, that the extra charge incurred by the corporation was due to their being unable to pay ready money, would not hold?—No; it must be obvious to any man who ever had a horse that it should not cost more than a pound a week for a cart-horse.

3285. As a practical man, having yourself experience in these matters in Rathmines, would you give the Committee your opinion as to these figures?—If you keep 80 horses it is manifest to everybody, of experience or no experience, that it is excessive. As well as I recollect, it stands us about 15 *s.* or 16 *s.* a week, certainly not 1 *l.*; and there is 1 *l.* here for forage only.

3286. Turning to the figures, 42,990 *l.* for labour, what do you think of that. It did not clearly appear from Mr. Robinson's evidence how many the exact average number of labourers was, but he said that the maximum was 700?—But it is not labour, it is everything; it does not show what it is at all.

3287. Do you think that the materials are included?—Certainly they are.

3288. Mr. Robinson distinctly stated that they are not?—But you can see yourself that it is so. When you have such items as paving, 9,000 *l.*; macadamising, 13,000 *l.*; scavenging and watering, 8,000 *l.*; flagging and asphalting, 4,000 *l.*; and so on, one must see that the labour is not separate at all. It is obvious that 40,000 *l.* for labour could not have been paid; all the stones, all the pavement, all the watering carts, and everything else is included in this; it does not in any way explain the matter.

Mr. *Butt*.

3289. Forage here is put down at 4,051 *l.* 16 *s.* 5 *d.*, and that, for 80 horses, would be just about 1 *l.* a week?—A little short of 1 *l.* a week.

3290. And you think that too high?—That is merely for forage, without labour, or shoeing, or anything else; you can calculate it yourself.

3291. With regard to the case in the Court of Queen's Bench, which you referred to, will you just read for the Committee the 244th section of the Port and Docks Act of 1869?—"The municipal corporation shall, from time to time, cause to be presented and raised upon the county of the city of Dublin at large, in the manner prescribed by the laws for the time being in force for raising money by presentment, for repairing roads in counties or counties of cities, a sum of money

Mr. *Stokes.*

13 May 1876.

Mr. *Butt*—continued.

money sufficient for repairing the roads upon the north, south, and east walls bounding or near the River Liffey." That appears to be the whole clause.

3292. Do you observe that in that clause there is no provision that the improvement rate was to be deficient before the money could be raised in that way?—I observe that.

3293. But when the presentment came before the Court of Queen's Bench, I believe the Court of Queen's Bench held that the true construction of it was that it was not to be used until the improvement rate was deficient?—They held so, but there seems to be no foundation for it.

3294. We must not say that of the judges; however, they did hold that?—Yes, I heard the argument.

3295. The Court of Queen's Bench, I think, decided unanimously?—Yes.

3296. Did they argue that the primary fund to meet that expense was the improvement fund, and that the extraordinary power was only to be resorted to when the improvement fund had been deficient?—That was what they decided at any rate, right or wrong.

3297. And, thereupon, they disallowed the presentment?—Yes.

3298. Was not this the reason why they said that the improvement rate was not deficient, that a sum of money had been lent to the sewerage?—Yes.

3299. Do you remember Mr. Justice O'Brien saying this, I am reading from the Report: "Mr. Justice O'Brien remarked that he rested his judgment mainly on the ground that it was not shown that the improvement rate was insufficient for its proper purposes. He had no doubt that the Corporation were wholly free from any charge of misappropriation. That body seemed to him to act with economy, and with due regard to the interest of the citizens, but it was a very irregular proceeding to lend the improvement fund for sewer purposes, which, he supposed, must have been done in ignorance of the law?"—In the course of the decision that took place no imputation was cast upon the Corporation of misconduct; it was only stated that they were stretching the improvement rate.

3300. Let me read to you what Mr. Justice Fitzgerald said: "The Court, having the 244th section before it, had to deal with it just as with any other section; he believed it was to avoid the expense of borrowing money that the portions of the improvement fund were lent for seven years; but the act was an illegal appropriation, and he founded his judgment on the fact that until the primary fund, the Dublin improvement, was exhausted, the 244th section of the 32 & 33 Vict. c. 100, could not be resorted to; that fund clearly was not exhausted, for portions of it had been lent. The matter appeared to have never been investigated in the town council, the proper place for considering it. The Court exercising a proper judicial discretion, could not sanction the presentment." I believe that is a correct statement of the decision of the Court?—Yes, that is a very good report.

Mr. *Brooks.*

3301. I think you said that the status of the Commissioners of Rathmines was satisfactory?—Certainly.

3302. And the highest rating to which they were rated was, how much?—I fear that when I answered Sir Arthur Guinness's question I must have conveyed a wrong impression if you measured their status by that, because their rating in the city is infinitely greater than it is at Rathmines.

Mr. *Brooks*—continued.

3303. You stated, I think, that the highest rating in the township was 193 *l.*?—Yes.

3304. And that they ran down to 30 *l.*?—Yes.

3305. And that the rating of members of the corporation was not so high?—There are 58 members of the corporation rated below my rating in the city.

3306. May I ask you to take that paper in your hands and read the names as they appear in the corporation (*handing a document to the Witness*). This is a list of the corporation with the rating; and it is the order in which they stand on the rota; will you kindly read them?—"Alderman Harris 110 *l.*" The return that you have given me is totally different from the return which I have received myself from my own secretary, in almost every degree; I do not believe that this is correct. I am satisfied that it is not correct.

3307. I am quite satisfied that it is correct; will you kindly read the first dozen names?—"Alderman Harris, 110 *l.*; Sir J. W. Mackey, 263 *l.*; Alderman Manning, 220 *l.*"

3308. Are not those all correct?—They are all different from the return that I have. You have Mr. Alderman Harris, 110 *l.*; I have him only 68 *l.* Sir James W. Mackey, 263 *l.*, and my return gives 95 *l.* only.

3309. I think you have only a return of his house in Westmoreland-street, whereas he lives in Mountjoy-square. The next is: Alderman Tarpey, 378 *l.*?—I have it 236 *l.*

3310. "Alderman Redmond, 38 *l.*"?—I have it 80 *l.*

3311. This says 38 *l.* If Alderman Redmond be rated at 38 *l.*, would you not by the system which you recommend of raising the rating status of members of the corporation exclude Alderman Redmond?—Certainly not.

3312. I think you said that they should either have a property or a rating qualification?—I do not propose to raise the rating qualification in any way.

3313. Did you not say that it was too low?—No; I was not asked the question.

3314. Then you do not think the rating qualification too low?—I would not alter the rating qualification. I have said so. I would merely add a property qualification.

3315. "Alderman Draper, 154 *l.*"?—He is only rated at 30 *l.* according to my list.

3316. He has house property in the city, has he not?—Yes. If he has house property and he is not rated for it, it might be made on some extra basis that I do not know. It must include property which he does not occupy. I know Alderman Draper's house very well, and I am quite certain that he is not rated at any such sum as that. Alderman O'Rorke's valuation is only 122 *l.*, and he is put down at 559 *l.* If you have added the new valuation of the property that is evidently what has been done. Now "Alderman Jameson, 971 *l.*" That is correct.

3317. "Alderman McSwiney, 755 *l.*"?—That is right; but he is only chairman of a joint stock company, and therefore that is not his own

Mr. *Stokes.*

23 May 1876.

Mr. *Brooks*—continued.

own rating. He is rated there as chairman of McSwiney and Company, Limited.

3318. "Councillor Gunn, 631 *l.*"?—He only appears to be rated at 20 *l.*

3319. But surely you know that that must be inaccurate?—The theatre is probably taken into account there; that must be an error.

3320. "Alderman Gregg, 337 *l.*"?—£. 130 that should be; at least, I have it 130 *l.*

3321. The return which I have in my hand, and which is made by members of the corporation, and which I believe to be true, gives a total of 10,029 *l.*, or an average rating of 167 *l.* for every member of the corporation?—If that were true it would be a very good rating, but I am quite satisfied that it is not true; I have sufficient knowledge of the city to know that. Some of my figures are evidently wrong; but to say that that is substantially correct, I am quite satisfied it is not.

3322. Could you point to one that is not correct?—There is Alderman O'Rorke, who is put down here at 559 *l.*, and the amount, according to my list, is only 129 *l.*

Mr. *Butt.*

3323. With regard to Alderman O'Rorke, if you will be good enough to look in the Almanack, at No. 9, New Row, West, you will see "O'Rorke, Hugh & Co., Ironmongery, Hardware, Trimming, and Paper Merchants, and 27, 28, and 29, 30 *l.*"; then lower down, for 27, 28, and 29 you observe he is rated at 77 *l.*, and his stores at No. 8, John-street, are rated at 22 *l.*, and adding those together you will find that 129 *l.* is his rating in all?—That appears to be the rating there.

3324. Then your attention was not called to this: that at Nos. 8, 9, 10, 11, and 12, King's Inn Quay, Hugh O'Rorke, proprietor of the Angel Hotel, is rated at 348 *l.*; and 348 *l.* and 122 *l.* would make up between them, 470 *l.*?—That is perfectly satisfactory.

3325. That accounts for the mistake in your rating, does it not?—Quite so.

3326. Then, plainly, the return was a mistake as to Alderman O'Rorke?—Yes; the Angel Hotel was not taken in.

3327. With regard to Alderman Sir James Mackey, what is he rated at according to you?—£. 95. I presume that is the Westmoreland-street house only.

3328. Sir James William Mackey is rated in the Westmoreland house at 95 *l.*, but his residence is given at 69, Mountjoy-square, and in the same almanack which supplies that information, upon looking at 69, Mountjoy-square, you will find that he is rated there for 95 *l.*?—But that would not make up what is set down here.

3329. However, he is rated in those two places at 190 *l.*?—I do not know.

3330. Then again, your return as to the valuation of Alderman Sir James Mackey is wrong, is not that so?—Evidently.

3331. And that by the same reason, only looking at the one valuation?—I did not prepare this return myself; I wrote for it to Dublin since I came to London.

3332. It is quite plain that whoever prepared the return has prepared it very inaccurately?—Yes, it is done carelessly, I think.

3333. I may say, may I not, that I have shown you mistakes enough in your return to show that it cannot be relied upon?—It is evident that it is not reliable.

Mr. *Brooks.*

3334. You referred also to Mr. Casson, if I heard you aright, and you said that he lost his seat on account of his politics?—Yes.

3335. You also, if I heard you aright, said that he was the last of the moderate men?—That came in with Codd's Corporation, as I called them; the last of those. They were a number of gentlemen put in by the Chamber of Commerce in 1850.

3336. Do you mean the last who survived them?—Some of them are surviving, but a great many of them are dead, of course. I mentioned Alderman Jameson and Alderman Campbell; they are the only two men remaining except Mr. Casson; he was the last of that set who came in in 1850.

3337. Are you aware that the gentleman who replaced Mr. Casson is, as you have seen, one of the largest ratepayers in Dublin?—He is the proprietor of the theatre.

3338. He is one of the largest ratepayers in Dublin and the proprietor of the theatre, and therefore, of course, he is a man with an exceedingly great interest in the rates?—I have not said for a single moment that Mr. Gunn was not a good representative; I do not know.

3339. But you said he was elected on account of his politics?—Clearly.

3340. May it not be that those who elected him may have supposed that he had a greater interest in the rates than Mr. Casson?—I do not believe it; I cannot tell the motives of the voters, but it is perfectly patent that if Mr. Casson had not been a Conservative he would not have been evicted; it was not pretended, so far as I remember, that it was anything else but that they thought that a Liberal was better than a Conservative.

3341. Do you remember the advertisements which were inserted in the newspapers by Mr. Gunn, in his address to the electors, in which he stated the number of attendances on committees or in council at which Mr. Casson was present?—I just saw them in the paper.

3342. Do you remember that he showed that Mr. Casson attended but twice a year in the corporation, and that that was the reason why he, Mr. Gunn, recommended himself to their votes?—I read that.

3343. Was not that publicly advertised in every newspaper in Dublin as the ostensible reason?—That was the ostensible reason. That is what Mr. Gunn gave as the reason.

3344. Was it ever denied?—Yes; Mr. Casson emphatically denied it. To satisfy myself, I referred to the attendances, and I found that it was correct in some instances, though it was not correct in the whole, for Mr. Casson had given a very large number of attendances in one of the committees.

Mr. *Gibson.*

3345. I believe Mr. Casson's point was that he had attended meetings of the committee, although he may not have attended many meetings in the house?—I think so.

Mr. *Brooks.*

3346. Or that he had attended the meetings of the Port and Docks Board?—I think not.

3347. You

Mr. *Stokes*.

23 May 1876.

Mr. *Brooks*—continued.

3347. You said that the cost of the Vartry Waterworks was very much greater than would have been the cost of bringing the water from Coy Ford?—I believe so; I believe that both Coy Ford and Ballysmuttan could have been done for the original estimate of the Vartry; about 300,000 *l.*

3348. Can you tell me the names of the townships the whole way from the reservoir through which the Vartry mains pass, and the townships which in its passage to the city of Dublin it now supplies with water?—It passes through them all, and supplies them all: Bray, Dalkey, Killiney, Kingstown, Blackrock, and Pembroke, on the south side, except Rathmines; and Clontarf, on the north side.

3349. The Coy Ford scheme could not have supplied those on the east, could it?—I am not able to answer that; but obviously the supply is a supply to the city of Dublin, and they could have supplied all the townships that might want it, in the same way.

3350. If you had adopted the Coy Ford scheme, how could you have taken a supply of water from Dublin to the townships, and not through the townships? — I see no difference; the one is quite as good as the other. The city of Dublin is at a disadvantage in that respect, because the townships have a preferential supply of water before anybody in Dublin is served.

3351. But there is an ample supply, is there not, for all?—Yes, I think there is; I would not call it ample, but there is sufficient.

3352. May I ask you if it is not the fact that the sums contributed by the townships through which the Vartry water passes much more than compensate for the increased cost, leaving out of consideration the great convenience to the inhabitants who do not get the water for nothing, but who contribute towards the cost rateably to the city for the supply of water?—The Blackrock and Pembroke townships receive for 3½ *d.* what the citizens of Dublin pay 1 *s.* 3 *d.* for; and they do not pay, in my opinion, on the first cost of the water.

3353. If we had brought the water from Coy Ford, it would not have done anything for Blackrock or Kingstown?—I do not see that at all; you could have supplied it from Coy Ford just as well as the other; it would not have gone the same route; it does not matter at all where it came from; the same quantity of water would supply the townships whether it came from above or below.

3354. You surely do not say that you think that you could have supplied Kingstown from Coy Ford, when you had the Vartry coming down that way?—No, but your bargains with the townships are very unprofitable to the citizens, in my opinion.

3355. Do you mean in that, we charge them too low for the water?—Yes.

3356. Could we have obtained a higher sum, or was there not a Parliamentary opposition upon that point?—I will tell you; you could have got 6 *d.*, because Pembroke could not have insisted upon having water. I offered it to Pembroke at 4 *d.*, and Sir John Gray immediately said, I will give it you at 3½ *d.*

3357. How could we have got 6 *d.*, if you supplied it at 4 *d.*?—I happened to have the chance of offering it.

3358. How do you reconcile that with the fact that you offered it at 4 *d.*?—As soon as I heard that the corporation offered 6 *d.*, I tried to cut them out; we were at war at the time, and I would have given it for 2 *d.* sooner than the corporation should have had it. As it turned out we have not water to give away, so that it is very lucky that we did not.

3359. So that you offered that which really you had not?—We had not.

3360. With regard to the extensions of streets, the honourable Member for Carlow asked you, if the extension of streets did not often bring an extension of rating power?—I understood new streets. I said new streets were a source of revenue to the corporation, but I think when you say extension, extension was a source of loss, not of profit.

3361. Did I understand you to say that Mud Island and Dolphin's Barn, which are extensions, were rather a source of loss than gain?—Certainly. You paid 6 *l.* 10 *s.* for lamps in Mud Island; you can get them in the city for 3 *l.* 1 *s.* 8 *d.*

3362. The increased cost of lighting, paving, and cleansing, was not compensated for?—It was not, I should say.

3363. Does not that conflict with your answer to the honourable Member?—No; the question put me with regard to new streets; these were not new streets, but they were old streets which were annexed to the corporation, it was a most disastrous annexation, and was the first beginning of their troubles, taking in a bad poor district requiring everything; but when you talk about new streets, I say that every new street brought in more than the revenue. It is the space between the Circular Road and the Canal, a fringe all round that district of a very poor description; Upper Clanbrassil-street, Dolphin's Barn, Mud Island, and all those low streets about the Canal; Quebec street, Seville-place, and all that very poor district, distant from the centre of government and expensive to keep in order. I attribute the first misfortunes of the corporation to what they want to do now, extending their area.

Mr. *Butt.*

3364. That was done by the Act of 1850, which appears to have won universal approbation?—It was the greatest misfortune that ever befal the citizens of Dublin.

3365. It was the Codd Corporation that did it, was it not?—Yes, and we gave them a testimonial; I wish we had it back again.

Mr. *Brooks.*

3366. If we extended our area so as to include Rathmines, do you think that that would benefit the citizens?—I do not, and I will tell you why. It would not alter the grand jury cess, because you could not oust the jurisdiction of the county grand jury. It would not alter the poor rate, because that would follow the general law of the kingdom; so that it comes after all to the improvement rate, and the result upon the improvement rate would be that you would get a certain amount of revenue, but you would have to do a great deal more for it; it would ruin us, because property would fall out of occupation directly; people would go further out beyond your grasp, and property would gradually fall, and the event would be, that you would gain nothing upon it; the only thing that you would gain would be, that you would increase your opponents, and people would

Mr. Stokes.

23 May 1876.

Mr. *Brooks*—continued.

would then stick together; you would perhaps do some good in that way.

3367. With regard to the enormous estimates that were made as to the cost of the main drainage scheme, I think you said that we proposed to the citizens that it should be done at an expense of 350,000 *l.*, and that afterwards the tenders amounted to nearly a million?—£. 900,000.

3368. May I ask you who prepared those estimates?—Mr. Bazalgette and Mr. Neville.

3369. Then the estimates were obtained by the corporation from the very first authorities to whom they could apply?—Yes.

3370. And those estimates were not the work of the corporation?—Not in any degree; I do not blame the corporation in any way for that.

3371. Those estimates were, in fact, the work of an official employed by the Government?—I do not know whether he is employed by the Government, he is a first-rate engineer; I do not conceive that the corporation were in any degree to blame for that insufficient estimate; they went to the best shop.

3372. They took every care that they could in the matter?—Yes.

3373. With respect to this 35,000 *l.* which you lent the corporation, upon what fund was it lent?—It was a very curious transaction, and if you wish me to explain it I will do so: by the Water Works Act there was a sum of 75,000 *l.* authorised to be borrowed for the purpose of laying pipes in the external townships and districts; in point of fact, those pipes, except to some very small extent, were laid by the townships themselves, and no portion of the 75,000 *l.* was expended, and it was a very fortunate thing. The corporation, having exhausted their own borrowing powers, borrowed 40,000 *l.* of this money from an insurance company in London, upon the security of the rates in the extra-municipal district; subsequently they obtained a clause in an Act of Parliament empowering them to divert this 75,000 *l.* to general purposes; then the 35,000 *l.* became available, and that was charged upon the general water rates. But in the Waterworks Act there is an unlimited power of taxation for the purpose of paying the interest; therefore the security is perfectly undoubted.

3374. Does not that unlimited power of taxation extend over the entire city, I mean upon those who receive the water?—The whole city; the water rate is a compulsory rate over the entire city.

3375. Is there any limitation as to the amount?—One shilling and threepence is the limit, except for the purpose of paying interest, and they can get a receiver in Chancery for their interest.

3376. Do I understand you that the waterworks rate is limited to 1 *s.* 3 *d.* for the supply; and independently of that they have power to tax the city to pay the interest of the money that they borrowed?—Yes, they have by the process that I have referred to; if a mortgagee cannot get paid his interest he can apply for a receiver, and the receiver can strike any rate that he thinks fit.

3377. Now as to the issue of bonds to you at 96, that gave you a chance to make money or lose according as the turn of the market came?—Yes, exactly.

3378. What is the general rate at which those bonds are selling now?—About 105, I think.

3379. What are the water works bonds, upon which they borrowed money at 4½ per cent., selling at now?—Rather above par; generally they issued them at a slight discount; of course, the parties who take them must have something.

3380. Are the bonds which the corporation issued for various causes, such as the improvement fund liabilities, including the 6 per cent. preference, which was raised upon the cattle market, and the bonds for the water works fund liabilities, negotiable?—Yes, the cattle market bonds are at a premium, but they are all in the hands of a very few persons.

Mr. *Brooks.*

3381. Whatever the increased cost of the Vartry Water Works has been, the water rate has never been exceeded?—That is so, owing to the revenue from the contract water.

3382. Do you mean in going through those townships?—No, not at all; but from brewers and distillers.

3383. The estimated rate when they were before Parliament has never been exceeded?—There was a transaction with respect to that which goes against the observation which you have made. There was a deficiency of something like 19,000 *l.* in the early years, and they managed to get a clause in the Bill enabling them to consolidate their water rates, by which, by a scrape of the pen, in one of those books, you will see that 19,000 *l.*, the deficient rate, was taken off out of the money borrowed for increasing the works; the one was balanced against the other, and in that way they expended their capital.

3384. It has been paid out of the rates since, has it not?—No, it has been paid out of borrowed money.

Mr. *Murphy.*

3385. Is 18,631 *l.* 7 *s.* the amount of the sinking fund?—At the close of the account of 1870–71 the sum to the debit of rates' account was 18,399 *l.* 3 *s.* 10 *d.*; at the same time there was a balance to the Water Works Loan Fund of borrowed money, nearly about the same amount, 18,695 *l.* 8 *s.* 5 *d.*; and they took the one from the other, and extinguished them.

Sir *Joseph M'Kenna.*

3386. Was the deficiency of the revenue each year capitalised?—Quite so; but since that, I believe, there has always been sufficient to cover the expenditure. I am not aware that any similar transaction has occurred since.

Mr. NUGENT ROBINSON and Mr. THOMAS O'DONNELL, called in; and further Examined.

Mr. Robinson and Mr. O'Donnell.

Chairman.

3387. (To Mr. *Robinson*). WHEN the Committee concluded on Friday, I think that we were going into the details of the expenditure of the borough fund, and I then asked you to account for the item of 6,345 *l.* under the head of salaries; could you give us the exact figures of which

Chairman—continued.

which that item is composed?—The Right honourable the Lord Mayor, 12 months' salary, 2,000 *l.*, less income tax 16 *l.* 13 *s.* 4 *d.*; 1,983 *l.* 6 *s.* 8 *d.*; the Right honourable the Lord Mayor's increase of salary, four quarters, 260 *l.* 6 *s.* 1 *d.*, that was an increase of salary for his secretary, in lieu of fees in the Lord Mayor's Court; the Right honourable the Recorder, 366 *l.* 3 *s.*; Thomas Atkins, sword bearer, 247 *l.* 19 *s.*; J. S. Carroll, city marshal, 297 *l.* 10*s.*; Francis Dowling, high constable, 99 *l.* 3 *s.* 4 *d.*; John Barlow, mace bearer, 198 *l.* 7 *s.*; J. J. Lalor, secretary to committee No. 2, 99 *l.* 3 *s.*; Francis Lees, assistant to the city accountant, 117 *l.* 14 *s.* 3 *d.*; J. R. Price, town clerk's assistant, 123 *l.* 19 *s.*; John Curtin, chief assistant to treasurer, 292 *l.* 6 *s.*; John McSheehy, law agent, salary and allowances for clerk, 785 *l.* 1 *s.* 7 *d.*; John Glynn, 12 months' salary, 100 *l.* 16 *s.*; proportions transferred from general account, 1,273 *l.* 11 *s.* 2 *d.* That is a total of 6,345 *l.* 6 *s.* 4 *d.*

3388. What is that 1,273 *l.* proportions transferred from general account?—The proportions of that 1,273 *l.* are made up in this way: Nugent Robinson, city treasurer, 184 *l.* 18 *s.*; Thomas O'Donnell, city accountant, including increase to the rate of 50 *l.* per annum, from 16th of January 1876, 44 *l.* 9 *s.* 10 *d.*; Francis Morgan, law agent, 347 *l.* 1 *s.* 8 *d.*; William J. Henry, town clerk, 424 *l.* 7 *s.*; P. Neville, city engineer, 49 *l.* 11 *s.* 8 *d.*; J. Martin, assistant to the town clerk, 223 *l.* 3 *s.*, making a total of 1,273 *l.* 11 *s.* 2 *d.*

3389. That does not include any of the officers whose separate salaries are charged on this fund; can you give the Committee a list of a certain number of officers who, as I understand, are entirely paid from the borough fund?—Yes.

3390. In addition to those proportions of the salaries of the officers which are comprised in that 1,273 *l.*, are there other proportions of their salaries charged upon other funds?—Yes, there are; I can give the proportions right across on the different funds; my own salary on the borough fund is 184 *l.* 18 *s.*; on the water rate, 78 *l.* 14 *s.*; on the improvement fund, 182 *l.* 13 *s.*; on the grand jury, 148 *l.* 15 *s.*, making a total of 595 *l.*; that is 600 *l.* a year, less income tax. The salary of the city accountant on the borough fund is 44 *l.* 9 *s.* 10 *d.*; on the water rate, 44 *l.* 9 *s.* 10 *d.*; on the improvement fund, 119 *l.* 18 *s.* 6 *d.*; on the grand jury, 74 *l.* 7 *s.* 9 *d.*; and on sewers, 44 *l.* 9 *s.* 9 *d.*; making a total of 327 *l.* 15 *s.* 8 *d.* The salary of Francis Morgan, law agent, on the borough fund is 347 *l.* 1 *s.* 8 *d.*, on the water rate there is no charge, nor on the improvement fund, as he does not contribute any services to either of those funds; on the grand jury it is 49 *l.* 11 *s.* 8 *d.*; making a total of 396 *l.* 13 *s.* 4 *d.* The salary of William J. Henry, the town clerk, on the borough fund is 424 *l.* 7 *s.*; and on the water rate, 71 *l.* 10 *s.* 3 *d.*; making a total of 495 *l.* 17 *s.* 3 *d.*

3391. I think the Committee understood from Mr. Henry that he received 600 *l.* a year?—This is on the 31st of August 1875; the town clerk had an increase of 100 *l.* a year to his salary the other day in lieu of 100 *l.* a-year that was paid to him by the main drainage committee as secretary; when the main drainage project ceased for the time being, they gave him 100 *l.* a-year upon the borough fund. The salary of Mr. Parker Neville, the city engineer, on the borough fund, is 49 *l.* 11 *s.* 8 *d.*, on the water rate, 314 *l.* 0 *s.* 8 *d.*, on the improvement fund, 31 *l.* 1 *s.*, on the grand jury, 99 *l.* 3 *s.* 4 *d.*, and on the sewers, 99 *l.* 3 *s.* 4 *d.*; making a total of 595 *l.* The salary of J. Martin, assistant to the town clerk, on the borough fund, is 223 *l.* 3 *s.*, and on the grand jury, 123 *l.* 19 *s.*; making a total of 347 *l.* 2 *s.*

Mr. *Robinson* and Mr. *O'Donnell.*

13 May 1876.

3392. That accounts for the item of salaries; there is an item, I see, of 1,791 *l.* for Mansion House expenses, is that for entertainments on the part of the Lord Mayor?—No; the Lord Mayor's entertainments he pays for himself; the corporation only provide certain fixtures for the occasion. As regards that 1,791 *l.*, the principal outlay in that year was for taking down some very old ruinous buildings, coach-houses, and an old kitchen, which was a great disfigurement to Dawson-street; the removal of that, and the building of a kitchen on the other side of the Mansion House, affords a much more pleasing prospect from the street than heretofore.

3393. Then, in fact, I suppose that item is not limited in any way; it is charged each year, according to the requirements?—Yes.

3394. And it is charged for maintaining the Mansion House in repair, and providing proper furniture for the Lord Mayor?—Precisely so.

3395. Then there is a charge of 483 *l.* or municipal expenses; what is that?—We have it for 874 *l.*, and they are similar charges almost each year, generally speaking. There are the salaries of the borough assessors who get 210 *l.* for their expenses during the revision; there is the preparation of the burgess roll; the assistant to the town clerk's attendance at the revision of Parliamentary voters' lists, 37 *l.* 7 *s.*; printing the burgess roll, 38 *l.* 5 *s.* 3 *d.*; expenses of accommodation for ward elections, 20 *l.*; poll clerks at elections, 6 *l.* 5 *s.*, and so on; it is the same class of charge exactly.

3396. Those figures to which you have been referring were for the year ending March 1875?—The figures that are taken up, 483 *l.* 11 *s.* 5 *d.*, are for the 31st of August 1875, but I am obliged to quote from 1874 because the details are not printed yet.

3397. I am quoting from your answer to Question 2841. The last item under this head was a charge of 1,000 *l.* for repayment to the Sewers Fund, amount obtained as temporary loan on 26th September 1872; will you explain that?—There was a flooding on the north wall, and there was an action against the corporation for damages; I forget the exact figure, but in order to aid the borough fund to discharge the claim they borrowed a certain sum from the sewer rate, and they had a balance to credit; that is the repayment on account of that sum which was borrowed.

3398. Are those kind of loans and repayments frequent from one fund to another?—No, they are not frequent; in this case there is rather a disputed opinion still as to whether the sewer fund, or the borough fund, is liable.

3399. You gave as another instance that the account of the improvement rate, I think, for some years was charged with a repayment you received in the same year to the credit of the improvement rate a repayment from the sewers rate of between 2,000 *l.* and 3,000 *l.*?—That was a transfer; it was an adjustment of account.

3400. (To Mr. *O'Donnell.*) Was not an adjustment

Mr. Robinson and Mr. O'Donnell.

23 May 1876.

Chairman—continued.

justment of account required for precisely the same reason, that one fund had borrowed from the other?—It was not a sum that was borrowed from the improvement rate; it was outlay incurred and charged against the improvement fund instead of having been charged against the sewers. Then when we came to adjust the accounts, previous to opening separate accounts with the Bank of Ireland for each of these funds, we passed the amount by order of No. 1 committee to the debit of the improvement fund. (Mr. *Robinson*.) As a rule, I might remark, that one committee is very anxious to accommodate another committee if there is an exigency with a loan in order to avoid paying any extra interest for money.

3401. I think perhaps that there may be a little over anxiety of that kind?—I do not think there is; at least in my experience there has not been any over anxiety.

Mr. *Kavanagh*.

3402. Is not that illegal, strictly speaking?—It is practised; I do not know about the legality of it. As a matter of fact whenever a sum is repaid during the financial year to the committee from which it is borrowed, the Government auditor allows it. That is a good test as to its legality, I suppose.

3403. But this might lead on from one year to another?—It arose before the auditor was appointed.

3404. Have you an account for this last year, ending August 1875, of the grand jury cess?—Yes (*delivering in the same*).

3405. I see you levied by way of grand jury cess, 55,781 *l*. 10 *s*. 4 *d*. during the year ending 31st August 1875?—(Mr. *O'Donnell*.) That is the amount which was lodged by the Collector General for grand jury purposes, the proceeds of the grand jury rate.

3406. That amount included the whole expenditure of the town council on matters properly borne on the grand jury account, such as prisons and lunatic asylums?—Yes, it was practically collected for those purposes. One side of the page will show you the expenditure on account of the rate collected.

3407. I have a card here which was handed in by Mr. Stokes, which states that the grand jury cess in 1850 amounted to 10½ *d*. in the pound, and in 1875 it was 2 *s*. 2 *d*.; how do explain the reason for that increase?—I can partly do so. I have been but six years connected with the corporation of Dublin. I have not gone back to the year that you allude to, but I think that I can explain the increase by stating that there has been additional expense in reformatory schools and likewise in industrial schools. There are large payments made on account of both of them.

3408. I see that in this year you paid 3,369 *l*. 6 *s*. 4 *d*. to reformatory schools, and 5,582 *l*. 7 *s*. 10 *d*. to industrial schools; both of those are fresh charges since the year 1850, are they not?—Yes, they are.

3409. Can you mention any other head under which there has been an increase?—There has been a large increase, I think, in the expense of lunatic asylums and prisons since that year; there are sums headed "Instalments to Government on account of Advances from the Lords Commissioners of Her Majesty's Treasury for the Building of Prisons and Lunatic Asylums;" and

Mr. *Kavanagh*—continued.

then there are large items voted for the support of those lunatic asylums and prisons as well, and charged in our accounts, and I think that there has been an increase in those expenses, so that they have helped to swell the amount.

3410. I find in this account that you paid, during the year, 16,633 *l*. 18 *s*. 8 *d*. for prisons?—Yes.

3411. And 18,230 *l*. 14 *s*. 11 *d*. for lunatic asylums?—Yes.

3412. And you received an order from the Government on account of prisoners?—Yes, that goes to the credit of the board of superintendence account.

3413. Where is it shown in your accounts?—It will be shown in the grand jury account; it will be shown in the printed book, I fancy; I can show it in the last year's account, and the way that we dealt with it.

3414. Ought it not to be shown here; is not this an account of your receipts on account of the grand jury fund, and payments from it?—That is a general statement of the account which has to be analysed yet before it will be printed; it is the general abstract which we submit to the auditor before he closes his audit, and he uses it according as he thinks fit.

3415. Will you tell the Committee how much you received for prisons during the year ending the 31st of August 1874?—It will be to the 31st of October 1874, because we are obliged to make up that account from the 1st of November in one year to the 31st of October in the next year, I am dealing with the account ending the 31st of October 1874, the account which is sent to the judges to be fiated, and which has to be sworn to by the city treasurer; you will find "To cash lodged by the Paymaster for maintenance of prisoners tried by juries being repayments, 1,579 *l*. 10 *s*. 10 *d*.;" that is the amount that we received during the year ending the 31st October 1874.

Mr. *Bruen*.

3416. You do not generally receive this every year, do you?—There may be arrears; this account is brought up to 1874; the first payment in it on account of these prisoners was to the 31st of December 1872, and received on the 30th of November 1873.

Chairman.

3417. In this manuscript there appears a sum of 1,725 *l*. 17 *s*. received from the Paymaster General on account of maintenance of prisoners during the year?—Yes.

3418. Going on to lunatic asylums, was anything received from the Government during the year ending the 31st August 1875 for the maintenance of lunatics?—The corporation of Dublin received no money, but I think there was a sum of money paid which went to lower the presentment. That would be treated in the schedule of the presentment; but the corporation of Dublin did not receive that money.

3419. But the presentment for the year previous to this in your printed account for the maintenance of lunatics was 14,473 *l*.?—Yes, that is in the account ending the 31st of October 1875.

3420. In this manuscript account it is 18,230 *l*., and therefore there is a large increase in that; so that I think that the payment by the Government could hardly have been deducted from the 18,230 *l*.

Mr. *Robinson* and Mr. *O'Donnell.*

23 May 1876.

Chairman—continued.

18,230 *l.* before it was entered?—That sum is made up of amounts presented by the corporation of Dublin, sitting as a grand jury, without the amount which the Government allowed to assist in the support of lunatic asylums.

[*The following Statement was handed in*:—]

	£.	s.	d.
1874:			
13 September.—Account, second moiety of presentment, 1873 - - - - -	4,007	6	1
24 October.—Balance of same presentment, 1873 - - - - - -	1,370	8	11
28 November.—Account presentment, Michaelmas, 1873 - - - - - -	5,000	-	-
19 December.—Account - like - like -	3,702	10	1
1875:			
8 May.—Account - - - like - like -	4,000	-	-
£.	18,230	14	1

3421. This 18,230 *l.* is the sum presented by the grand jury, according to this account?—This is the amount which the corporation paid, the actual money which they paid to the Paymaster General for the support of lunatic asylums. We paid it to the Paymaster General. We call it a payment under Section 2; it is instalments to the Government on account of presentments for the support of lunatic asylums.

3422. What I want to know is where the payment from the Government for lunatics appears in your accounts?—We take no cognisance of it. It does not come through our books. We deal with the sums that are presented for payment to the Government for those purposes, and when we pay any money on account of those presentments we charge it against the account as it is charged there.

3423. How do you account for the great increase of 4,000 *l.* the next year on the charge for lunatics?—You are not to take that as representing a year's charge; they are payments on account of more than one presentment, and when the account is analysed for publication that would be set forth. They are not always able to pay the instalments to the Government on account of the presentments, perhaps the rate not having been collected and lodged, and then you have to wait until they get the rates, and pay according to convenience.

3424. So that the amount of the presentment for this purpose in each year is not necessarily the expenditure of the previous year, and you cannot argue from the difference between two presentments in two successive years that the expenditure of the year has been greater or less than the other?—No; you must argue by the amount that is actually paid.

3425. And that you do not know?—No, not having analysed those figures here; but I could easily send in a return of it. When the account is made out, it sets forth what the presentment was, what the particular sum which is charged there is for, whether it is for a presentment made in 1873, or for a presentment made in 1874. If you look at the account for the year ending October 1874, you will see how we deal with those things: it commences, "Michaelmas Term, 1872; Instalments to Government," and we set forth the different matters for which the instalments have been made. Then at page 93 you will see Section 2, and the same term, that is, Michaelmas Term, 1872, payment on account of presentment, 16,875 *l.* 10 *s.* "By cash paid the Lords Commissioners of Her Majesty's Treasury for the support of the Richmond Lunatic Asylum from 25th May to 24th December 1871, 10,094 *l.* 7 *s.* 11 *d.* By cash paid same for the support of same asylum from the 25th December 1871 to 24th May 1872, 6,781 *l.* 2 *s.* 1 *d.*" If you turn to the next term that is charged in this account you come to "Michaelmas Term, 1873, Section 1; Instalments to Government, nil. Section 2; Lunatic Asylums, nil." That is to say, we had paid no money at all on account of the presentments for those purposes made Michaelmas 1873.

3426. As to the asylum money, that is not under the control of the corporation at all?—No, we have to pay the money over to the Lords Commissioners of the Treasury.

3427. There is an item here, repair of roads, Section 15, 2,310 *l.* 15 *s.*; what is that for?—That is money that is presented, as I explained the other day, or as I should have explained, under the powers of the Dublin Port and Docks Act. The corporation, sitting as a grand jury, presents for the purpose of getting money to repair those roads. I stated that I thought that those roads were outside the municipal boundary, but now I am informed that they are within the municipal boundary. But the corporation, availing themselves of the power under that Act, 7 & 8 Vict. c. 106, s. 117, have presented for those sums, and got the money to lay out on the repairs and the paving of those roads.

3428. Those roads being on the Quays?—Along the Quays, as set forth in the schedule of presentments, which I read to the Committee the other day.

3429. Then there is the quarter sessions account; what is that?—That is in connection with the recorder's court, and the sessions court, in Green-street. We call them the October sessions, and we charge in the same way as in that presentment, every October, the different expenses that are incurred in the maintenance of this court, and in paying the salaries of the officers in connection with this court. The clerk of the peace's salary is presented for, and comes under that section. You will find, for instance, at page 89 in the printed account, salaries on account of sessions, October 1872. This will give you an idea what the nature of the expenditure is which the money has been presented for: "By cash paid Charles Karnan, Esq., clerk of the peace," and so on; "tradesmens' accounts," that is accounts in connection with keeping up the court-house and the sessions-house.

3430. A considerable portion of that charge, and also of some one or more of the other charges, is salaries and wages to officers, and other persons employed?—Yes, but they are not corporate officers at all.

3431. Can you tell me whether the charges for those persons have considerably increased, or not?—I believe not very much, because I think that the salaries were nearly all fixed by Act of Parliament, the salary of the clerk of the peace and the salaries of his assistants. There has not been a very great increase since the corporation got power to make those presentments for those purposes.

3432. Do you know at all what the increase has been?—No, I have never made a comparison between the payments of one year and the payments

Mr. Robinson and Mr. O'Donnell.

23 May 1876.

Chairman—continued.

ments of another; I have never been asked to make it.

3433. And in the same way a considerable portion of the charge for prisons is composed of salaries and wages?—Certainly, over which the Corporation of Dublin, as a corporation, have no control. As a board of superintendence they may have, but those are not corporate officers at all; they are more or less Government officers.

3434. The board of superintendence is composed of the members of the corporation, is it not?—Yes, they have the supervision of the prisons, and the regulating of the expenses, and so forth, but I do not think that the appointment of the officers altogether rests with the board of superintendence; I think they must be all sanctioned by the inspectors of prisons, and by the Lord Lieutenant, if they are appointed.

3435. Who fixes their salaries?—I should say that the salaries would be fixed by the Lord Lieutenant too; the salaries being submitted to him by the board of superintendence, and I think his sanction is required.

3436. Is there any sum spent from the grand jury cess in the repairs or in the improvement of the streets, except on the quays?—None that I am aware of; and those presentments are the only presentments that have been made within my knowledge. There is a road called the Rock-road, and there is a presentment made for that, a presentment of about 284 *l.* a year. It is a road outside the city.

3437. That is the road leading to Kingston, is it not?—Yes.

3438. Is it ever repaired?—It used to be, but it is not now in good repair now. The grand jury of the county of Dublin try to cast the blame upon the Corporation of Dublin, but I think they do it very unjustly. It is the fault of the grand jury of the county of Dublin not looking after those things, and seeing that the road is properly kept in order.

3439. How is that charge spent, if it is not laid out upon the road?—It is paid to the secretary of the grand jury of the county of Dublin; they have the outlay in their own hands.

3440. (To Mr. *Robinson*.) I think we have had it in evidence already that the accounts of the corporation are audited by a Government auditor; can you tell me when he was appointed to audit the accounts?—The first account that he audited was the account ending 31st of August 1872.

3441. At whose instance was he appointed?—He was appointed at the instance of the corporation; there was a resolution passed in the town council, a copy of which I have here: "At a meeting of a committee of the whole house, held upon 17th February 1871, it was moved by Sir John Gray, seconded by Alderman Campbell, and unanimously resolved, That the committee of the whole house are strongly of opinion that it would be an advantage to the public and the corporation if a public auditor were appointed, with the consent and approval of the Executive Government, or some competent legal authority, to audit half yearly the accounts of the corporation. and that this resolution be recommended for adoption by the council, with our further recommendation that steps be taken at once to bring the matter under the notice of the Executive." There was a further resolution, which is as follows: "At a meeting of the municipal council of the city of Dublin, held upon the 24th February 1871, resolution of committee of whole house of 17th February 1871, read; moved by Councillor Sir John Gray, seconded by Councillor Dennely, That this council do hereby adopt the resolution of the committee of the whole house. Question put and carried. Moved by Councillor Sir John Gray, seconded by Councillor Dennehy, That the Lord Mayor, Sir John Gray, Councillor Purdon, Alderman Plunkett, and Councillor Dennehy be appointed as a deputation to wait upon the Irish Executive Government in reference to this matter."

3442. How long does the audit last in each year?—It lasts, we may say, three months.

3443. Has the auditor made any disallowances and surcharges?—He has, from time to time.

3444. Take the year 1872, I think that was the year in which I began; will you state the nature of the disallowances that he made then?—The amount in the aggregate in 1872 was 2,125 *l.* 6 *s.* 1 *d.* "The payments referred to may be thus classified: interest on promissory note for 8,000 *l.*, and bill of exchange for 15,000 *l.* issued by the Water Works committee, and on temporary advances by the Hibernian Bank, 1,896 *l.* 17 *s.* 1 *d.*; interest on overdue mortgages, and overdue instalments of terminable annuity to Public Works Loan Commissioners, 85 *l.* 14 *s.* 6 *d.*; interest to the widow of a late engineer in the employment of the corporation, on the sum of 667 *l.* 10 *s.* due to her late husband, as salary at the time of his death, 32 *l.* 17 *s.* 6 *d.*; printing copies in pamphlet form of the report of the debate in the council on the education question, and hire of rooms in London for deputation from the council to meet the national deputation on the same question, 21 *l.* 3 *s.*; expenditure in connection with the reception by the corporation of a deputation on the question of Home Rule, 7 *l.* 9 *s.*; scarfs provided for the aldermen and town councillors on the occasion of the funeral of the late Alderman Bulfin, who died while serving as Lord Mayor, 14 *l.* 5 *s.*; amount handed to Mr. James Boyle, secretary to the Public Heath Committee, for payments alleged to have been made by him for scrivenery work executed for the committee, but for which there were no receipts forthcoming, 34 *l.* 2 *s.*; payment to board of guardians, north and south Dublin unions, and to undertakers, for interment of the remains of poor persons, 23 *l.* 17 *s.* 6 *d.*; car-hire to Mr. Morgan, one of the law agents of the corporation attending the weekly meetings of committee No. 2, owing to physical disability and overcharge by him for scrivenery, 3 *l.* 8 *s.* 8 *d.*; payments made by the treasurer in respect of annuities for periods subsequent to the deaths of the annuitants, 5 *l.* 11 *s.* 10 *d.*"

3445. Were all the auditors' surcharges that year sustained?—Not at all. The large one of 1,896 *l.* 17 *s.* 1 *d.* was not sustained. A deputation of the Water Works Committee waited upon the Local Government Board, and they stated the nature of the case; the *bona fides*, and the exigency; and the Local Government Board, taking those circumstances in consideration, did not sustain the surcharge of the auditor. The surcharge of 32 *l.* 17 *s.* 6 *d.* on the same committee, the members of the Water Works Committee paid out of their own pockets.

3446. Were there any surcharges and disallowances made in 1873?—Yes, 115 *l.* 19 *s.* 9 *d.* The first item is "Interest to Mrs. Margaret Duncan,

Chairman—continued.

Duncan, on debt due by the corporation to her late husband, 16 *l.* 8 *s.* 9 *d.*" That was the same class of surcharge as in the previous year. The committee had signed the warrant, and the money had been paid. "Payment to the North Dublin Board of Guardians for graves, 9 *l.* 17 *s.*; like to undertakers for interment of small-pox patients and 'destitutes,' 22 *l.* 6 *s.*; paid to the city engineer, to recoup him amount expended on dinners, &c. at Roundwood, 1 *l.* 11 *s.* 10 *d.*; paid for printing estimate of income and expenditure of Alliance Gas Company, 12 *l.*; for Acts of Parliament relating to the gas supply of certain towns, 1 *l.* 18 *s.* 1 *d.*; for printing circular in relation to the Gas Bill of Session of 1873, 8 *s.* 6 *d.*; payments to Mr. Boyle, secretary to the Public Health Committee, to recoup him amounts alleged to have been paid for scrivenery work, in support of which there were no receipts forthcoming, 1 *l.* 9 *s.*; paid to the town clerk during the year as salary, in excess of the amount due to him, 50 *l.*"

3447. Was there any charge of misappropriation?—In the first year there was, with regard to Mr. M'Cauor, the collector of the cattle market. He had been misappropriating the funds for four or five years, and had been falsifying his accounts.

3448. Was he discharged?—He discharged himself.

3449. Was he prosecuted?—We could not prosecute him, but they got as much as they could from the relatives.

Mr. *Brooks*.

3450. He absconded, did he?—Yes.

Chairman.

3451. Were there any surcharges or disallowances in 1874?—The auditor states the only payment I felt it my duty to disallow, was one of 3 *l.* 8 *s.*, the cost of printing and publishing certain notices in relation to the abortive Bill promoted by the corporation in Parliament last year, to enable them to purchase the works and property of the Alliance Gas Company.

3452. As to the surcharges and disallowances which were sustained; on whom did the payment of those expenses fall?—On the individual members who signed the cheques, principally. A cheque is signed by three members of the committee.

3453. Did they pay them?—They did; you will find the records in the annual accounts.

3454. With the exception of the case of the collector of the cattle market to which you have alluded, has there been any charge of malversation or misappropriation?—Michael Angelo Hayes, the late city marshal of Dublin; but that is a disputed case. He was charged with the appropriation of fees in the marshal's office. It is a question for litigation still. The corporation are prosecuting him for retaining the fees which he did not lodge.

3455. And there is another case also, is there not?—No, there is no other case. There was a case, but that was the marshal anterior to Hayes. "Fees to the amount of upwards of 300 *l.* received during Mr. Thomas Reynolds's last illness, and which passed into the hands of his executor as a portion of his personal assets, have never been received by the corporation, nor have any legal steps been ever taken to recover them; and a sum of 100 *l.* received as fees by Mr. Reynolds's successor, Mr. Martin Crean, was at the time of the death of the latter in his hands; 46 *l.* only of this sum was received from his widow. In the two latter cases the officers had not given security for the lodgment of the fees received by them, and the money has been lost to the corporation. In the case, however, of Mr. Hayes, the corporation hold a bond with ample security for the amount of his defalcation, but although considerably more than a year has elapsed since his removal from office, no legal steps have been taken to obtain payment of the amount."

Mr Robinson and Mr. *O'Donnell*.

23 May 1876.

3456. Why have no legal steps been taken to obtain payment of the amount?—It was considered that it has been a vexed question between the city marshals for a very considerable period as to the power of the marshals to retain those fees or not. There have been opinions of eminent counsel time after time, but the corporation have proceeded now; and, as I have already had the honour of stating, there is an action pending, and they are waiting for the decision of the Court.

Mr. *Gibson*.

3457. The case was argued before the Court of Common Pleas the last time, and they reserved their judgment, and it will not be given until next term?—Yes, that is so.

Chairman.

3458. Do you, as treasurer of the corporation, consider that the present system of audit is satisfactory?—Yes, I do, very satisfactory, and I consider that Mr. Finlay is a most able, painstaking, and careful official.

Mr. *Gibson*.

3459. Have you got any books to show the allowances and payments that were made to Mr. Samuel Crampton under the 26th section of the 27 & 28 Vict. c. 305, on account of the Baldoyle Estate?—Yes, the land and law agent will be prepared to speak to that.

3460. I suppose Mr. Morgan, the land and law agent, will be able to produce a document showing, according to the statement in the 27th section of the Act of Parliament that I have referred to, that there was a calculation made in respect of the rents, and special valuations of the land made by competent persons?—I presume so.

3461. I suppose he will also have the memorials, if any, that were furnished by the tenants for those reductions?—It is not in our department.

3462. I presume that you cannot explain how it is that in the column in the account the Baldoyle Estate is the only one city estate in which there is an entire blank in the column for poor law valuations and holdings where the rent was reduced?—I am not able to explain.

Sir *Arthur Guinness*.

3463. I think you omitted to read this about Mr. M'Cann's appointment; perhaps you will have no objection to reading this paragraph?—"The loss thus sustained must be attributed to the remissness on the part of some officer or officers of the corporation, for, on Mr. M'Cann's appointment, he was required to give security to the amount of 500 *l.* which was subsequently reduced to 100 *l.*, on the ground that the largest amount likely to be at any one time in his hands would be

Mr. Robinson and Mr. O'Donnell.

23 May 1876.

Sir *Arthur Guinness*—continued.

be under 60 *l.*, and that arrangements had been made by the city accountant, whereby all monies received each market day would be lodged on the following Friday with the city treasurer, and accounted for to the city accountant on the same day. It was further directed by the market committee that Mr. M'Cann should deposit with their secretary on each Friday his account and vouchers to be laid before the committee that day. These directions, it would appear, were never carried out as regards either the vouchers or the bond. Had a bond with securities for the original sum contemplated (500 *l.*) been entered into, or had the duty of obtaining the superintendent's vouchers, with a view, it is presumed, to their being compared with the account sent in by him weekly, been performed, this loss could not have occurred; for while the weekly account appeared to be correct in the face of it (and that was all that was ascertained), a reference to, and examination of, the basis of the account would have at once revealed the fraud, which could only have been attempted in the full assurance that such a test would not be applied. That there was no bond whatever entered into by Mr. M'Cann is a matter of serious moment, and was a grave omission on the part of the officer responsible for seeing to the execution of bonds from officers to the corporation, and the latter would do well to ascertain from time to time whether all their officers entrusted with the receipt or disbursement of the monies of the corporation have entered into the necessary bonds with sureties, and whether the bonds are forthcoming, and the sureties living, and solvent."

Mr. Brun.

3464. I see on page 74, in the account for the year ending the 31st August 1874, an entry "By amount of loan advanced to William Cotton in April 1873, and now repaid by him, 250 *l.*;" will you explain that?—Mr. Cotton at that time was gas inspector for the corporation of Dublin; he applied for that loan on account of his salary, and got it.

3465. When was it paid to him?—In April 1873.

3466. When was it repaid?—It was repaid just at the close of August 1874, within the year of audit.

3467. Then that money was a loan, and he had the loan for rather more than a year?—Yes.

3468. What is the amount of his salary?—He is not with us now; it was 600 *l.* a year; he is now secretary to the Alliance Gas Company.

3469. And this loan was advanced to him out of the rates?—It was advanced to him out of the improvement fund on account of his salary.

3470. Is it the habit of the corporation to make loans to their employés?—It is not the habit, but it is done occasionally, and the Government auditor allows it when the sum so borrowed is repaid within the year under audit.

3471. But that was not the case in this instance?—No, it was not so in this case. It was borrowed in April 1873, and it was not paid until the following August. I think the auditor has alluded to it in his report.

3472. (To Mr. *O'Donnell.*) In page 95 of the same account, with reference to the cash paid for the expenses of maintaining boys in the reformatory and industrial schools, is there any account

Mr. *Brun*—continued.

given of the number of boys so maintained?—There are returns sent in from each school to the inspector of industrial schools and reformatory schools, who has an office in the Castle in Dublin. He certifies the account, and sends it on to the town clerk, and the town clerk sends it to me, and I check the calculations as to time, and the calculations as to money, and I certify it if I find the time calculations are right and the money calculations are right, and pass it on to the committee.

3473. But are there any means for letting the ratepayers know the number of boys who are so maintained?—Yes, from the returns that are made from each school; you get the number in each of those schools in the returns that are forwarded by the managers.

3474. They can be seen; but as a matter of fact, are they published in any form in which the ratepayers can see them?—We do not publish them; but inasmuch as the accounts are always certified by the Government officer, the inspector of those industrial schools and reformatory schools, we simply confine ourselves to checking the time calculations and the money calculations, and pay the amount. (Mr. *Robinson.*) They are published in the Government Blue Book, and presented to Parliament.

3475. In your evidence, which you gave on the last day to the Committee, at Question 2661, you were asked, "Have you any general account for the corporation at all"?—If the Committee will allow me, I meant to convey that we have an account for every fund in the bank; as a matter of fact we have not; we have only accounts for seven funds. I have not had time to look over this, but I just happened to catch it, and I wish at once to state that I intended to convey that we have only an account for seven funds in the Bank of Ireland. The Borough Fund, the Improvement Fund, the North Sewer, the South Sewer, the Vestry Cess Rate, the Burial Rate, and the Cattle Market.

3476. Have you anything to explain with regard to your answer to that question, "Have you any general account for the corporation at all," as to which you say, "Nothing, but my personal account at the Bank of Ireland?"—There is no general account.

3477. That answer would rather raise the idea in minds of persons who are not acquainted with the matter that some of those funds went through your own personal account at the Bank of Ireland?—I am very glad that you asked the question, so as to disabuse the minds of the Committee upon that subject. What I meant by my personal account, is not Nugent Robinson's account; it is an account of the City Treasurer; for instance, repayments by the Government for sums paid to prosecutors, witnesses at commissions and sessions; the Government send me a notice that they have lodged so much to my personal account, as it is called, in the Bank of Ireland; I immediately transfer it to the credit of the grand jury fund, so that there must be some account over which I have just that control.

3478. Can you tell the Committee what payments go to the credit of that personal account, generally speaking, in the year?—I suppose about 2,000 *l.* a year in round figures.

3479. From whom are those payments derived, from what sources?—I pay all prosecutors and witnesses at commissions and at the sessions through

Mr. *Robinson* and Mr. *O'Donnell*.

23 May 1876.

Mr. *Bruen*—continued.

through my office, and those sums are repaid to me when I send the account with the vouchers into the chief secretary's department of the Government, and I get a letter to state that the amount of the account, as sent in by you on such a date, check to be lodged to your personal account in the Bank of Ireland; I immediately report that to committee No. 3, and transfer it to the grand jury fund account.

3480. This is, in fact, confined entirely to those payments that you get from the Government on behalf of the prosecution of prisoners?—There is another item, the saving on prison labour, which is also lodged in the same way; I get notice and transfer it in the same way, and also there is the account for the maintenance of prisoners.

3481. When you speak of saving on prison labour, that is, I presume, the amount made by the labour of the prisoners in the prisons?—It is the mainteuance of prisons. (Mr. *O'Donnell*). The money which we passed to the credit of the Board of Superintendence Grand Jury Account, which the honourable Chairman asked about for the support of prisoners, is lodged in the first instance by the Paymaster General to the credit of the personal account which the treasurer has been mentioning. Then he, the treasurer, transfers it from that account by cheque to the credit of the grand jury fund (Board of Superintendence Account), that is to say, he debits the grand jury fund with it, and he places it to the credit of the fund in the bank.

3482. (To Mr. *Robinson*.) Is it the fact that the whole of the personal account in the bank is 2,000 *l.*?—That is all the personal account; when they pay interest on debentures, the committee give me the cheques to pay the interest on debentures on what is called the No. 1 Account in the National Bank of Ireland, which I draw against, and pay parties across the counter as they come in.

Mr. *Bruen*—continued.

3483. Are those accounts published?—They are audited.

3484. They do not come into this account?—The interest on debentures comes into this account.

3485. But not in any other form?—No.

3486. There was a paper handed in by Mr. Henry, the town clerk, which had something to do with the city funds. I will just ask whether you can explain the omission in the years 1860, 1861, 1862, 1863, 1864, 1865, 1866, and 1867, of any credits on account of the items, "scavenging and sewerage"; that whereas in other years in this return there is a credit from that source, in those years there is none?—I cannot explain it; I have not looked at this table; I have not seen it before.

3487. I think that there is a limit fixed, is there not, in the Act; is the price which is charged for the water up to its maximum?—There is a limit to the rate; it is at its maximum, 1 *s.* 2 *d.* the domestic, and 3 *d.* the public water rate.

3488. It is at the maximum which the Act allows them to charge?—Yes.

3489. Can these accounts be placed in the hands of the ratepayers; are they purchasable?—They are by payment of 1 *s.*

Mr. *Murphy*.

3490. You stated that you paid, amongst your payments out of the borough fund, 369 *l.* 4 *s.* 7 *d.* to the Recorder of Dublin; are there any other payments made by you to the Recorder of Dublin besides that?—No, none whatever.

3491. Is that all the amount of salary that he has?—That is all that the corporation pay; it is one of the charges on the borough fund set forth in the Act.

3492. Is he not paid other sums by the city?—Not by the corporation.

3493. Not out of the funds that you have any control over?—We have no control over them.

Friday, 26*th May* 1876.

MEMBERS PRESENT:

Mr. Assheton.
Sir Michael Hicks Beach.
Mr. Brooks.
Mr. Bruen.
Mr. Butt.
Mr. Collins.
Mr. Gibson.
Sir Arthur Guinness.
Mr. Kavanagh.
Mr. Mulholland.
Mr. Murphy.
Mr. O'Shaughnessy.
Mr. Rathbone.
Dr. Ward.

SIR MICHAEL HICKS BEACH, BART., IN THE CHAIR.

Mr. FRANCIS MORGAN, called in; and Examined.

Mr. *Morgan.*

26 May 1876.

Chairman.

3494. YOU are the Law and Land Agent to the Corporation of Dublin?—Yes, I have had that honour for some years.

3495. How long have you held that office?—Thirty-three years.

3496. I presume that you are well acquainted with the corporation property?—I think that I have a good knowledge of it. I am beginning to scatter now.

3497. Can you tell us where it is situated?—Yes; I will begin at the north side of Dublin. On the north side of Dublin we have one property called Ballycoolane; then the next in that direction is Clonturk; Donnycarney is next to Clonturk, and then come Grange and Baldoyle

3498. All those are outside the municipal limits, are they not?—Yes, they are outside; they were part of the lands of the suppressed monastery of All Hallows.

3499. When did it come into the possession of the corporation?—By grant from Henry the Eighth.

3500. Has the corporation any other property outside the municipal limits?—Yes, there is Colganstown and Kingwood, or Ringwood, as it is now called, on the south side, about nine miles from Dublin, near Hazelhatch.

3501. Where else have they any property?—There is Baggotrath, a very valuable district. The occupiers pay rent for it, but it is undecided whether it may be a terminable tenancy or not. Baggotrath is in the possession at present of the Earl of Pembroke's representatives.

3502. Baggotrath is partly within and partly without the municipal limits, is it not?—Yes.

3503. Are there any other outlying properties besides those you have mentioned?—That is all. At page ix. in the preface to the rental you will find a synopsis of the rents and annual income of the city estates. There is a large denomination of the estate called "Antient Revenue." That is the most ancient of them derived by Royal Charter, giving authority to the corporation to be established in Henry the Second's time to inclose all void spaces that were not already in the possession of other owners.

Chairman—continued.

3504. Will you state to the Committee what is mentioned in that synopsis?—The ancient revenue which was acquired, as I have mentioned, by Royal Charter, under which the corporation were allowed to inclose void spaces, and it comprises 311 holdings producing 11,495 *l.* 4 *s.* 10 *d.* a year. St. George's, which were derived under the grant of Henry the Eighth's seven holdings, producing 168 *l.* 0 *s.* 10 *d.*; All Hallows, which includes those townlands which I mentioned of Ballycoolane, and so on; 137 holdings producing 6,224 *l.* 3 *s.* 4 *d.*; St. Mary's Abbey, 67 holdings, producing 1,392 *l.* 11 *s.* 2 *d.*; Royal Gifts, three holdings, producing 1,047 *l.* 13 *s.* 9 *d.* Those latter comprise two annuities which were given to the corporation formerly to sustain their dignity. The lord mayor formerly had the pay of a captain in the army, and 300 *l.* Irish and 500 *l.* Irish were assigned by King Charles the Second as a Royal allowance to the corporation to sustain their dignity.

3505. Those are not estates?—No; they are not lands; the amount is paid at the Castle to our treasurer annually. But there is another Royal gift, the ferries over the River Liffey, from which we derive 309 *l.* 4 *s.* 6 *d.* a year; the three holdings together producing an annual revenue, as I have said before, of 1,047 *l.* 13 *s.* 9 *d.*

3506. With regard to the landed estates, the total gross rents from all those sources I see is entered here as 20,327 *l.* 13 *s.* 11 *d.*?—Yes. Then the head rents are deducted; we pay Crown rent, quit rent, and some head rents. I should mention that the shippage and anchorage dues, which average about 1,250 *l.* a year, are included in that.

3507. Is that included in the ancient revenue?—Yes, it is classed under ancient revenue.

3508. You deduct these Crown quit and chief rents, which amount to 426 *l.* 13 *s.* 4 *d.*, and there is a net revenue entered here of 19,901 *l.*?—Yes, it is rather more than that now. This rental was drawn up in 1867, and every holding almost, which has since fallen out of lease, has produced an increase.

3509. After deducting the Royal gifts, and the shipping

Mr. *Morgan.*

26 May 1876.

Chairman—continued.

shipping and anchorage dues, can you tell the Committee what remains as the net revenue from the landed estates?—£. 17,713 would be a little under the exact amount.

3510. Will you put in a similar total for the present year?—Last year and this year were nearly alike. We have had a rise progressively now for three or four years, and expect a large rise within five years.

3511. Are the figures which you have given the Committee, of 17,713 *l*, the net rent actually received by the corporation?—That would be the net rental, or rather under, as I have said.

3512. From that has to be deducted the poor's rate, has it not?—Yes, a proportion of the poor's rate is allowed to each tenant.

3513. Is this 17,713 *l*. what the corporation actually receives, or is it the net rental before any deduction?—It would be the rental without the allowance for poor rate. You may take 18,000 *l*. as the income without allowance for the poor rate, and you may take that at 1 *s*. in the pound.

3514. Then you have to deduct from that the poor rate and the income tax?—Yes.

3515. Is there anything else to be deducted?—That is all that I am aware of.

3516. I think that the city treasurer stated the other day that Pell's poundage was also deducted; will you explain what that is?—That must be some small obsolete matter that I do not know of. If you look at page 47 of my rental, there is a list of all the head rents. I do not know of Pell's poundage.

Mr. *Kavanagh.*

3517. Pell's poundage is paid to the Government, is it not?—We pay some ground rents, but I know most of them.

Chairman.

3518. Do you think Pell's poundage is a chief rent?—There was Powell's legacy, and Pell's poundage may be something that is directed under a will, but it is nothing at all connected with the estate. It is not a charge on any part of the property. I have heard the word before, but it must be something very remote when I am not quite aware of it, for I have turned these things over and over; it must be something that has changed into another direction or denomination.

3519. Mr. Nugent Robinson gave us a statement of the gross rental taken from the accounts for the half-year ending February 1874, and he told us that Pell's poundage, poor's rate, public water rate, and income tax, were to be deducted from it, and that Pell's poundage was paid to the Government?—We pay a Crown rent for our ancient revenue under the Royal charter; reduced to 20 *l*. Irish; that is reduced Crown rent. It was 200 marks a year under the charter of John, and it was reduced by the other kings, until King Charles reduced them, in one lump, to 20 *l*. Irish, which is the sum payable now.

3520. Turning from that, let me ask you some questions about the estates separately, taking Ballycoolane first; can you tell us the area and the rateable value of that?—It is at present held by four tenants on very old leases. In my opinion the value might, perhaps, be higher than the tenants would expect. It is held in four tenures; three of them on leases that will expire

Chairman—continued.

in the year 1880, and there are two lives living in the case of the last.

3521. What is the area of Ballycoolane?—Seven hundred and fourteen statute acres.

3522. What is the poor law valuation of it?—The poor law valuation of it is 1,026 *l*. a year.

3523. Do you think that represents the real value?—No, it is far below the real value; property has been looking up of late, I think, very much; particularly near cities.

3524. That is about five miles from Dublin, is it not?—It is not more than five miles from Dublin.

3525. Should you put on 25 per cent. to represent the real value?—Indeed you may. I would say perhaps more, but you may safely put on 25 per cent.

3526. Would you say perhaps 50 per cent.?—Fifty per cent. is a large item; it lies very advantageously, and I have advised the corporation to have it surveyed and sold in small lots of 10 acres and sold in perpetuity; it would bring a very large price, according to my view, because there are so many persons in Dublin that would like to be owners of a small piece of land.

3527. A portion of that, I see, is let on long leases of 99 years, expiring in the year 1880?—Yes.

3528. The rents, of course, payable under those leases are very small as compared with the real value?—Yes, the leases are nearly 100 years old, and there has been a very great change in the value of land since then.

3529. Have the corporation taken any steps since the publication of this volume in 1867 as to the renewal of the terms of those leases?—No, they have not authority to renew those leases, and until the other day the rule was to let everything by auction when a holding fell out of lease. The Treasury have lately consented that they may set them at rents to be fixed by a valuator to be appointed by the Treasury, or approved by the Treasury.

3530. Then the leases will be allowed to run out and the property will fall into the hands of the corporation in 1880?—Yes, in March 1880; that is to say, three of the principal denominations of them, and there is one that is held for two lives.

3531. There is one part 116½ acres; that was let on a 70 years' lease?—It is a lease renewable within 70 years, and that term has expired and there can be no further renewal of that lease; it was renewed last in 1851, just on the expiry of 70 years, and there are two lives on it, the Prince of Wales and a Mr. Thompson, a brother of a gentleman who is in the possession of the property, and who is in Australia; they are both about the same age.

Mr. *Kavanagh.*

3532. Do not the letters "L. R." mean lives renewable?—Yes, lives renewable for 70 years. There were a class of leases made in that way that were granted for three lives renewable during 70 years.

Chairman.

3533. You stated that that was renewed in 1851. I see that the rent payable for that property of 116 acres is 67 *l*. 9 *s*. 4 *d*. whereas the poor law valuation, which you have told us is very low, is 152 *l*. 15 *s*.?—Yes, that is so.

3534. Did

Mr. *Morgan.*

26 May 1876.

Chairman—continued.

3534. Did the corporation receive any fine on renewal?—No, the party was entitled to renewal at the old rent.

3535. Are these properties sublet by the lessees?—That one was not. That is all held by Mr. Thompson almost entirely in his own occupation. The other holdings which you see are held by a gentleman who is known to this House; Mr. Hamilton, the honourable Member for the county of Dublin, holds that lease of All Hallowes, No. 73, and he holds a portion of another holding.

3536. Turning from that property to the next one, Clonturk, what is the total area of that property?—The total area is 356 acres 2 roods and 2 perches. It is an entire parish.

3537. What is the Poor Law valuation?——

3538. I see in this account of the property the Poor Law valuation is only set opposite to some of the holdings. There are 20 holdings in all, let to 20 separate lessees?—There was a very intelligent gentleman, Mr. Charlesworth, who assisted me in the preparation of this rental. He took those valuations from Thom's "Directory," which is generally very correct. As regards these county holdings, I have extracted them from Griffiths' Valuation, which is perfectly reliable, and distinguishes each holding very well. I used it in the compilation of this book, and I can hand it in to the Committee.

Mr. Bruen.

3539. As regards this holding at Clonturk, have you not the same materials?—I have Griffiths' Valuation for all the county holdings; the city holdings were taken from Thom's "Directory," as it was quicker; one had nothing to do but to turn to each street.

3540. Was the valuation which was followed in Clonturk taken from Thom's "Directory" or from Griffiths' Valuation?—All the county holdings are taken from Griffiths' Valuation. This is an office copy that I procured.

3541. Can you supply from that Griffiths' Valuation the omissions which are here made as to some five holdings in Clonturk?—I can very well.

Chairman.

3542. I see that, in this valuation, as in the case of Ballycoolane, the poor-law valuation is considerably higher than the rental?—Yes; because the leases are nearly 100 years old.

3543. Do you consider that in this case, also, the Poor Law valuation is lower than the real value?—I think that they would produce much more now, if vacant and to be let.

Mr. Kavanagh.

3544. Your observation that the Poor Law valuation was 25 per cent. higher does not apply to those?—It applies to the lands of Ballycoolane. If you recollect, they are held under a lease 100 years old, which is just now about expiring.

Chairman.

3545. This property is held on leases expiring at a great many different dates?—Yes, Clonturk is so held.

3546. A considerable portion of it, nearly 39 acres, is held on 1,000 years' lease, I see?—Yes. All Hallowes is a denomination that comprises a great many holdings.

Chairman—continued.

3547. In the case of Nos. 14 and 15, the lessees are the executors of the Rev. J. Hand, and the occupiers of All Hallowes College?—Yes; that is a lease made within my time, at 10 *l.* Irish an acre. There was a large old house on it that was the residence of the Beresfords, and afterwards proposed for as a lunatic asylum; it was Sir Guy Campbell who occupied it just before I came into the service of the Corporation; it is too large for a private residence. They added very large buildings to it, and the Treasury sanctioned a lease for 1,000 years in consideration of an outlay of 10,000 *l.*

3548. That is let at a rental of 237 *l.* 11 *s.*?—Yes, that is a rent of 10 *l.* Irish an acre. There are 24 Irish acres in it.

3549. That is less than the Poor Law valuation, is it not?—Yes, the Poor Law valuation on it now would be something very large; a college has been built on it. The college is included in the valuation, and they have built a church on it, at a very large outlay indeed.

3550. Could you tell the Committee what the poor law valuation was when the lease of that property was made?—Not off the books, but I will let the Committee know.

3551. It is a Roman Catholic college, is it not?—It is a Roman Catholic college.

Mr. Bruen.

3552. May I ask you whether the college was built before the year 1852?—The college was first established by the Rev. J. Hand in 1843, in a large old mansion house; it was the mansion house of the Beresfords. He died in 1849 or 1850. His executors proposed to the corporation to make a large outlay in building, in consideration of extension of the lease from 75 to 1,000 years. The corporation memorialled and got the consent of the Treasury to a long lease, in consideration of an outlay of 10,000 *l.*, and it was about the year 1852 that a new lease was made for a term of 1,000 years, I think, with the consent of the Treasury.

Chairman.

3553. They were already in possession under a 75 years' lease, and then they wished to fortify themselves with a longer lease in order to make a large outlay on the land?—Yes.

Mr. Kavanagh.

3554. Was any alteration made in the rent?—No, the rent was the same; it was 10 *l.* Irish an acre.

Sir Arthur Guinness.

3555. They got 1,000 years' lease without a change of rent?—They got 1,000 years' lease in consideration of their undertaking to secure the rent by an outlay of 10,000 *l.*

Mr. Bruen.

3556. Was not the rent secure before; was not it below the valuation?—It was not so secure as when the college was built on it. There were only clergymen there, and no person liable for it, but now there is a very large amount of money spent upon it, and its value was very greatly increased to the citizens. It was under eviction, when I knew it first, for non-payment of rent.

3557. If the corporation had tried to get possession of it could they have got more rent?—We did let it to the Rev. Mr. Hand. I think it

Mr. *Brown*—continued.

it was advertised for nearly a year, and proposals were made for it; we had proposals for it for a lunatic asylum, and from other persons that were not considered able to pay the rent of a place like that.

3558. Did they offer more than 10 *l.* per acre a year?—Mr. Hand offered 10 *l.*, and as that was considered about the best offer, he got a lease for 75 years. Then he induced those with whom he was in communication, the authorities of the Roman Catholic Church, to adopt this tenancy.

3559. Was Mr. Hand's offer the highest?—I think it was; my recollection is that it was the highest.

3560. At all events in that particular demise the rule of letting by open competition was not adopted?—It had not commenced at that time.

Chairman.

3561. In this rental for Clontark, I see that there is a lease, No. 6, to Thomas Dooley, of 14 acres, dated September 1854, for 66 years; at a rent of 70 *l.*?—That lease was made with the consent of the Treasury; he held a lease under which he was wasting the land; he had begun to sell gravel off the surface and he was beginning to do things which the corporation considered improper. We applied for an injunction, and then he agreed to surrender the lease that he had. There were four leases adjoining each other, and they were all different tenures. One party lived on it who had a little bit not larger than this room, and if we wanted to serve an ejectment, or enforce the payment of the rent, or re-survey the property, it was a very embarrassing tenure, and we got the leave of the Treasury to consolidate it into one. It had been under lease to Mr. Duval and not under lease to Mr. Dooley: he threatened to build mud cabins upon it, and things of that kind.

3562. What was the term he had it for?—It was the residue of 99 years; he has it exactly on the same terms with the consent of the Treasury; the present lease is the residue of 99 years.

Mr. *Butt.*

3563. Was that Mr. Thomas Dooley, the attorney?—Yes.

3564. Was not he a very active member of the old unreformed corporation?—He was a prominent member; I believe he was considered very litigious, and the corporation wished to give him a lease in such a way that he would probably dispose of it to some other person, for he was very troublesome; we generally had to bring ejectments against him for non-payment of rent.

3565. Was not he very violent in expressing his opinion upon the corporation with regard to the politics that they adopted?—As a matter of history I believe he had, but he never showed any particular opposition during my time.

3566. What do you think is the annual value of that property?—His rental here is 70 *l.* a year; its area is 13 acres 3 roods and 1 perch, but this is statute measure. The garden was on a different tenure, and the gate lodge was on a different tenure; it was altogether in a very unpleasant position. However his interest has been lately sold in the Landed Estates Court, and purchased by a gentleman who will improve it if he gets leave to buy the perpetuity.

Mr. *Butt*—continued.

3567. Do you know what his interest fetched?—He gave 3,000 *l.* for such interest in the four denominations as Mr. Dooley held.

Mr. *Brown.*

3568. Are these four denominations mentioned here?—Yes. The holdings that have been held by Mr. Dooley (in page 39) were No. 2, All Hallowes, 92, Andrew Coffey, tenant; measurement, 5 acres 4 perches. The next was No. 6, All Hallowes, 190, Thomas Dooley, lessee, for 70 *l.* a year, and it contained 13 acres 3 roods 1 perch. Then there was Curtis. No. 7, All Hallowes, 101. Mr. Dooley himself got a lease of a small bit for 10 *l.* 15 *s.* a year. No. 8, All Hallowes, 146.

3569. And you say that Dooley's interest in those four holdings just now fetched 3,000 *l.* when sold in the Landed Estates Court?—Yes; there was a house, constabulary station, gate, lodge, and some decayed offices on them.

Mr. *Butt.*

3570. What interest had he when he got a new lease?—He valued his interest always extravagantly high; it was a disagreeably situated property.

3571. What was the term?—He got an unexpired term of 66 years; it was an unexpired term under an old lease.

3572. He surrendered, did he?—Yes.

3573. What was the new term which you gave him?—The residue to which he was entitled.

3574. Was the rent increased?—No, the rent was not increased, but it was not very much diminished either.

Chairman.

3575. It was diminished, was it?—There was a little difference; they squared it to even pounds.

Mr. *Butt.*

3576. How much would the reduction have been; was it 1 *l.*?—There might have been 2 *l.* or 3 *l.* more in the old lease.

Mr. *Kavanagh.*

3577. But he paid no fine for the change?—No, he did not.

Mr. *Butt.*

3578. Was the change merely consolidating into one lease what was held previously by several leases?—It was to put him under terms that he could not build cabins and disfigure the rest of the properties, which he threatened to do, and he was selling gravel off it.

Chairman.

3579. Are we to understand that the case, which was renewed in 1854, only applies to one of his holdings?—Yes, that was the one that was called Duval's holding previously.

3580. He held the others, and still holds them, under other leases?—The same tenure that he held before as holder of No. 92. There was an interest in that, because there was a police station on it, and that was the best interest in it; the dwelling was a decayed house. There is a constabulary station and the court of the petty sessions in it.

Mr. *Morgan.*

2d May 1876.

3581. Have

Mr. *Morgan.*

26 May 1876.

Mr. *Brun.*

3581. Have you any idea what the occupying tenants of property No. 2 pay to Mr. Dooley's representatives?—I do not know what the Government pay for the court house; a portion of it is the police station. There is a police station on it that holds about four men, I think, and a sergeant, and there is a petty sessions court, and that is all; the rest, 5 acres and 4 perches, he used to let to his tenants. It is in great demand for grass for cows, being very close to Dublin.

Chairman.

3582. Now with regard to No. 17; that, I see, is another lease, renewed in 1852?—Yes, Blaney Mitchell is the lessee.

3583. Will you tell me the circumstances of that lease?—It is for 31 years from 1852. The previous lease had been held by a gentleman named Kirwan; he had been the previous tenant, and he surrendered it. It was a very rotten old house, and he ceased to reside there, and a man of the name of Mitchell became the tenant of it.

3584. And he got a 31 years' lease?—Yes, that is our leasing power under the 3 & 4 Vict. c. 108.

3585. He got a 31 years' lease, to expire at Michaelmas 1883, at a rental of 40 *l.* 16 *s.* 6 *d.*; that amount is not equivalent, is it, to the Poor Law valuation?—You will observe that the Poor Law valuation is applied to two other holdings at the same time, and it comprises the executors of the Rev. Mr. Hand and John Holmes. The executors of Mr. Hand purchased the interest in John Holmes's lease and in Mr. Mitchell's, and they hold all three, and they have purchased another since.

3586. All Hallowes College occupies the whole of it, does it not?—Yes.

3587. Did they purchase Holmes's and Mitchell's interest?—Yes, they purchased their interest.

3588. Does that 40 *l.* 16 *s.* 6 *d.* represent the Poor Law valuation of that property?—I would say that the Poor Law valuation was not more, from my knowledge of the holding; it is on the road side.

3589. But it is 10 acres very near Dublin at 40 *l.* a year rental?—Yes; Mr. Mitchell took it as a residence, Mr. Kirwan having surrendered it. But it is very undesirable as a residence; it is a cartmaker that has it now.

3590. Did Mr. Mitchell pay any fine?—One year's rent, the last year in advance; that is what he paid on getting his lease. Every tenant does the same.

3591. How does his rent of 40 *l.* compare with the rent paid by the former lessee?—I have not the rental of that time here, but I think that there is no great deal of difference.

3592. Which was most?—I can let you know.

Mr. *Brun.*

3593. I suppose that you can also let us know what the Poor Law valuation of that particular holding is?—Yes, I can tell you that now. It is valued in the name of the previous occupant, namely, Michael Lynch. Michael Lynch is the occupant, and the Corporation of Dublin the owners of offices and lands, 6 acres 7 perches, rent 15 *l.*, buildings 3 *l.* 10 *s.*; and I am told that it was a very rotten, decayed, old house at 15 *l.* That makes it 18 *l.* 10 *s.* for the valuation for the whole of that holding.

Mr. *Brun*—continued.

3594. Are those statute acres in Griffiths' Valuation?—Yes; they are all in statute acres.

Chairman.

3595. Then that cannot be the same holding as this, because this is 10 acres 7 perches?—The next holding to that in Griffiths' is 10 acres 1 rood 10 perches, but I do not remember the name of Fortune as the occupant; 26 *l.* 10 *s.* is the value of those 10 acres. Well Park House is the name of the place, but there is the name "William Fortune," which I do not recognise because he was not a tenant of the corporation, but Michael Lynch was in occupation according to my recollection, and paid rent to the corporation.

3596. For what year is that copy of Griffiths' Valuation which you hold in your hand?—The date of the certificate is the 13th of December 1866, but the valuation was before then. I think that some of the valuations were very much earlier than that, but that is the date of this certificate.

3597. Then I am afraid that it does not give you any very distinct means of identifying the holdings mentioned there with the holdings mentioned in your rental?—I think they have been examined. There was a gentleman who was much more competent than I, Mr Charlesworth, who was the conductor of that department at Hodges and Smith's, who assisted me in the preparation of those particular rents, and he was very anxious to get the valuation correct, and I think that he has extracted them all correctly.

Mr. *Brooks.*

3598. Have you the holding there of Blaney Mitchell, described as containing 6 acres and 7 perches?—Yes; I have it in my rental as 10 acres 7 perches.

Chairman.

3599. If you turn to page 40 of the rental, you will find Blaney Mitchell, lessee; occupier, Michael Lynch, 6 acres 2 roods 32 perches?—Yes; Blaney Mitchell occurs in two places.

3600. You have been telling us what is the valuation of one holding, but we have been asking you about the other?—I have them both now separately. I did not remember that Blaney Mitchell's was one of the two holdings. He has one holding of 6 acres 2 roods 32 perches, number 21, on page 40, and Michael Lynch succeeded him in that occupation. I recollect those two holdings; they were on different sides of the road, and quite separate holdings. Blaney Mitchell had a lease, and he sold his interest to the college of All Hallowes, and the other lease that Blaney Mitchell held he let to Michael Lynch.

Mr. *Brun.*

3601. Can you give the valuation of the holding which he sold to All Hallowes College?—No; the portion that is held by All Hallowes College is not separate.

3602. Can you give it by reference to Griffiths' Valuation?——

Chairman.

3603. I see at page 41 that Lord Charlemont holds Donnycarney in two holdings, one of which is 49 acres; that is, Marino, is it not?—Yes, that is Marino, and there is a portion of that which is

Mr. *Morgan.*

26 May 1876.

Chairman—continued.

is held for ever. He took a grant in perpetuity.

3604. The rent there, I see, is put down at 743 *l.* 13 *s.* 2 *d.* and 113 *l.* 19 *s.*?—Yes; the 113 *l.* has been increased the other day, I think, to 118 *l.* or 119 *l.* He took a grant in perpetuity to sink all the lower charges.

3605. And a large portion is held on a lease for 99 years, from November 1822?—Yes, and that surrounds his perpetuity; he has the kernel of it, the interior, for ever. The outer portion is all on a terminable lease of about 44 years, I think.

3606. Can you tell us what is the poor law valuation of the whole of that?—The poor law valuation of the larger portion is 554 *l.*, and the perpetuity, where the temple is, appears to be only valued at 16 *l.* 15 *s.* a year, according to this valuation, but I think it must be a great mistake of theirs. There are 30 Irish acres in the interior portion, and a very expensive building which the first Earl of Charlemont erected on it, a great curiosity in its way, but more curious than useful. The other day there was 5,000 *l.* offered in the Landed Estates Court for all his lordship's interest; he pays so high a head-rent to the corporation.

3607. There is another property called North Liffey Strand, wet lots, which appears to be in hand?—Yes, they were never in charge in my time; I have endeavoured to get the corporation to recover them. They were sold in the year 1717, with liberty to inclose them. Those are wet lots that are outside Lord Charlemont. There were dry lots and wet lots sold; the dry lots were on the river side, and have become most valuable, and those who purchased them have abandoned the wet lots and retained the dry lots; the corporation did not follow the parties to make them inclose the wet lots and keep the tide from flowing over them, and they have remained derelict for more than 100 years.

Sir *Arthur Guinness.*

3608. But they were sold with some of the dry lots, were they not?—Yes; there is a map which is now to be had in the Port and Docks Board office which shows exactly how those allotments were. The parties who had got the dry lots which were close by the river border used them and abandoned the wet lots.

Chairman.

3609. Then the corporation have parted with their interest in them?—I think the corporation would get leave through the Lands Clauses Act to re-purchase their interest in them. I have advised them to try to get an Estates Act to get them back again, for they will be very valuable by-and-bye.

3610. There is an area of 55 acres, is there not?—Yes, the 55 acres is open now between the demesne of Lord Charlemont and the railway. There was a great deal more than 55 acres there which the Corporation might have laid claim to; and with that portion they could make a very useful and very valuable property, if they could recover it.

3611. That still is in their power, you think?—I think it is. I do not think that Parliament would refuse that to them.

Mr. *Kavanagh.*

3612. It is absolutely sold, is it not?—It was sold, but the purchasers did not comply with the conditions by inclosing and keeping the tide off it.

Mr. *Murphy.*

3613. They are in this condition, are they not, that the original grantees, the parties who got the dry lots, also got powers to reclaim the wet lots, and they were bound to reclaim the wet lots in consideration of their getting a grant of the dry lots?—Yes.

3614. They took advantage of a portion of their grant and retained the dry lots, but they did not comply with the condition of reclaiming the wet lots?—Precisely so.

3615. Then whatever interest they had was sold, and whoever purchased it purchased all their rights; and, is it not your case, that they also purchased all the liabilities; one of the liabilities being to reclaim the wet lots?—The liabilities are to reclaim the wet lots; that is the reason that I think that if the Corporation now sought for leave to repurchase or to apply the Lands Clauses Act they would be obliged to pay but a very small amount to those owners who had abandoned the property for 150 years.

Mr. *Butt.*

3616. Is there any one at this moment exercising any right of ownership over it?—No one whatever, except so far that the Port and Docks Board have two boards up desiring parties not to dig sand or commit a nuisance there; but I do not know of any act of ownership being exercised over it. That is one of the mouths of the River Tolka; the river discharges in an irregular line across it.

3617. Is not it clearly within the grant made to the corporation of that land?—It was a portion of the north bank of the Liffey which passed to them under one of the Royal Charters.

3618. What is there to prevent the corporation taking possession of it?—Because they have sold the fee of it in 1717.

3619. Why could they not claim it if there has been no possession for 30 years?—I have taken very great trouble in looking it up in order to induce the corporation, and I think they ought to bring in a Bill to take it, for it would be very valuable land worth 20 *l.* an acre for market gardens. They would have the means of laying out their street sweepings there and raising the surface, and it would be a very important place.

3620. Supposing that the corporation were to take possession of it now under their own grant, who could disturb them?—They ought, and I think they will take possession of it when they get a more efficient and younger man than I to fight their battle. If they took possession of it and retained it for 20 years I think they would have a very good title.

Chairman.

3621. Now let us go on to Baldoyle; is the acreage of that property 621 acres?—Yes, the lands were let to 16 tenants by lease in the year 1855, when they fell out of lease.

3622. Were they all re-let?—Yes, excepting the first lot; that was the old take that Master King had for 99 years which will not expire till 1914; the rest were all re-let for 31 years from the 17th of September 1855 to the 17th of September 1886.

3623. How

Mr. Morgan.

26 May 1870.

Chairman—continued.

3623. How do the rents at which they were then let compare with the rents which were given before?—The rents under which they were previously held were very low indeed; seven leases for 99 years expired in 1854, and one gentleman purchased up the entire of them, including the town of Baldoyle. He was supposed to be worth 900 *l.* or a 1,000 *l.* a year, and a very respectable gentleman. When his time was up he handed the town rents over to his steward, and when the lands came into the hands of the corporation they put them up to auction.

3624. Do you know what difference there was between the old rent and the new rent?—About 30 *s.* an acre; there were some very old houses; the town of Baldoyle is a miserable decayed fishing village.

3625. Was any fine paid on the renewal of those leases?—They were not renewed; I took possession of them all, and they were set up to be let by auction, and some members of the corporation who were not accustomed at the time to deal with land thought it necessary that the boundaries of the fields should be nearly all altered, and it was scored out almost like a chess-board; that alarmed the occupants very much, and some of them bid wildly, not knowing what would remain to them, or how much they might get, and it created a good deal of ill-will and wild bidding for them. I think that letting by auction of country lands in that way is not desirable; some of them went very much beyond the value.

3626. How many of the old lessees became the new lessees?—Some of them were the descendants of the old occupants, upon leases for 99 years that then expired; many of them had disappeared.

3627. Can you tell us what the Poor Law valuation of this property is?—Yes; will you permit me to hand in Griffiths' Valuation (*delivering in the same*).

3628. What I wanted to know was how those rentals compare with the valuation in each case?—Griffiths' Valuation is much more modern. The new letting that was made in 1855 was a high letting, and it had to be reduced by leave of Parliament.

3629. I am speaking now of the rental that appears in this column on page 42 against the names of those occupiers. How does that rental compare with the poor law valuation, because you have not entered the Poor Law valuation for this property at all?—No; my attention was called to that since I came here. Mr. Charlesworth, I suppose, omitted to do it. The corporation pay all the poor rate on the small holdings, and the tenants pay a fixed rental weekly and quarterly. I did not know that it was deficient in that respect till I came here, but I can supply it.

3630. Take the first; A. H., No. 153, Samuel Crampton; do you know that?—I know that holding very well.

3631. The rental of that is is 107 *l.* 1 *s.* 2 *d.*; and that is a rental, as I understand, which has not been reduced. What is the Poor Law valuation of that?——

3632. Can you tell us generally whether this rental is equal to the Poor Law valuation?—I consider that it is over the Poor Law valuation; it will be found so.

3633. Does the Poor Law valuation, in the case of Baldoyle, represent anything like the real value of the lands?—I should like to collate them and examine them; but I believe, generally speaking, so far as my experience goes, the poor law valuation does not amount to the letting value at a rack rent.

Chairman—continued.

3634. Are any of those lands sublet by the lessees to other tenants?—Not one of those Baldoyle holdings to my recollection. One of the tenants died, and Carpenter's holding has passed into the hands of another person. I do not remember any other. James Doyle has died, and as the daughter was married of course her husband had it. You may say that they are the same persons; they are very tenacious of their holdings.

3635. Are the persons whose names are down in this column as lessees the actual farming occupiers of the lands?—They are or their representatives. Mr. Crampton is dead. He built a very nice villa residence, and his sisters reside in it now. They are very old ladies, but it is still in the family. Henry Darley parted with his land to a Mr. Van den Eynde, a very respectable Belgian horse dealer, with the consent of the corporation.

3636. Can you tell us whether any of those persons sub-let their lands at a profit rent; here is one A. H., No. 158, No. 6 on page 42, Luke White; and No. 7, ditto; Luke White has two holdings, one of 59 acres 3 perches, and the other 47 acres 3 roods 23 perches; does he farm that land?—No. At the time that Mr. Luke White, now Lord Annaly, became a tenant to the corporation he did farm those two lots. He came with an agent and bid for that land at the auction. He was very anxious afterwards to get about of it, but he could not.

3637. He got a share of the reduction; he bid at the auction for that land 192 *l.* and 191 *l.* a year for the two lots?—Yes.

3638. That was subsequently reduced by Act of Parliament to 152 *l.* 15 *s.* and 124 *l.* 2 *s.*—Yes. He gave it between two farmers, Gill and Rice, and his agent, Mr. Joynt, held the remainder of it. I do not think he has made any profit rent out of it. I rather think it is the other way.

3639. Those two lots are sub-let by Lord Annaly to Mr. Joynt and the two farmers, are they?—To Mr. Joynt, to Gill, and to Rice; they all hold a part of it.

3640. Do you know what rent Mr. Joynt, and Rice, and Gill, pay for that land?—I had heard that he gave Mr. Rice his land at a little less than he had it for himself, and I believe it is the same as to Mr. Gill. They are both industrious farmers. Mr. Joynt is or was agent to Lord Annaly; I think that he agreed to take it off Lord Annaly's hands, who built a large range of stables and offices, and had laid out a great deal of money on it.

3641. Does he live there?—No; he was living in it, but he has not lived there for many years. Mr. Joynt lives there.

3642. How long has he been living there?—He was there in 1863, to my recollection.

3643. Was he living there in 1855?—No, not in 1855. Colonel White, who is now Lord Annaly, lived in it. I think he held it for about five years, and he lived there with his wife and children.

3644. Was Mr. Joynt his agent in 1855?—I think he became his agent then, or very soon after. He came to me with Colonel White, now Lord Annaly, as agent and solicitor.

3645. This

Chairman—continued.

3645. This was in 1855?—Between 1855 and 1860, or some time after 1855, while he held it himself.

3646. Did he come to you at the time when the arrangement was made by which the rents were reduced?—He applied for a share of that reduction; there was a very strong effort made to reduce the rents. It was debated several times, and his holding was the dearest of all, with one exception. There was a large, old mansion on it, and he first applied for leave to pull it down and build farm offices with the materials.

3647. You told us of one case where the land is sub-let, but, as far as you know, you think it is not sub-let at a profit rent?—Colonel White certainly had no profit out of it at the price he was paying, and in order to be shut of it he gave it over to those farmers, who are very proper persons.

3648. Is there any other instance amongst those holdings where the land is farmed by sub-tenants?—Mr. Darley's land was sold with the consent of the corporation to Mr. Van den Eynde, a Belgian horse dealer, who buys horses for the Belgian Government, a very respectable man. He had other land in connection with it that was not on the corporation estate.

3649. You mean that he bought up Mr. Darley's interest?—Yes.

3650. Then he is not a sub-tenant?—He pays us rent now.

3651. He is your lessee?—Yes, he stands in the place of Mr. Darley.

3652. Does Mr. Butterly farm his own land?—Mr. Butterly farms his own, Gerald Rice farms his own, and Mr. Gill also, and Mr. Joynt farms and owns one of those holdings on lot No. 7, All Hallowes, No. 159. He lives in that house; Colonel White built very large stables and offices there and intended to be a grazier.

3653. Do you mean that so far as you know none of those lessees make a profit out of their lease by sub-letting their lands?—Indeed I did not say so; but I may safely say so. They were all at first quite anxious to get shut of them; but we were advised by most eminent counsel that we could not release them in any way except by applying to Parliament for leave to alter those rents.

3654. In what year was the alteration in the rents made; how many years did they pay the high rents?—The alteration was made in 1863 according to my recollection. It was referred from the House of Lords to Judge Monaghan, Chief Justice of the Court of Common Pleas.

3655. Is there a covenant in the leases against sub-letting?—There is a covenant that they are not to be sub-let without the consent of the corporation, nor assigned, nor mortgaged.

3656. What are those other lots from No. 22 to No. 42, "16 lots of land containing 97 acres 3 roods 14 perches, producing 201 *l.* 18 *s.* 5 *d.* next to the town of Baldoyle," and which are held quarterly by 12 tenants?—They are town parks that lie immediately between those lands of Baldoyle and the town. The inhabitants are some of them occupied with fishing, and some with farming, and those lots were reserved as town parks and are paid for quarterly.

3657. What is the term of occupation on which those town parks are held?—They are only held quarterly.

3658. Are they let by auction every year, or do you continue them in the same occupation?—The letting was considered a fair letting, and it has not been changed. There was another tenant of one of those town park lots, who sub-let a small portion for the racecourse.

Mr. *Morgan.*

18 May 1876.

3659. What have you to state with regard to the property of Colganstown and Ringwood, which you have mentioned?—That will be out of lease next March. It is now being measured with a view to its either being re-let, or, as I would wish, sold.

3660. What is the acreage of that?—You may say 200 statute acres in Colganston, with a very good house which was built for a gentleman of fortune. It was a very good house, but it has gone a little out of repair, especially the offices, but it is fit for a man with a couple of thousands a year. The other at Ringwood, is a very fine farm as a grazing farm; it has been highly manured and treated in the best manner; it has very good stabling and offices. It is held by Mr. Gerty, who represents Mr. Sherlock the tenant who is named there, and certainly it is in splendid order; but Colganstown is a colder land and that has not been so well treated.

3661. On this map I see that your property is divided into three descriptions: first (green), leases in perpetuity; second (red), terminable; third (yellow), alienated and unproductive; we have been dealing so far with the red entirely, property let on terminable leases; there seems to be a very large lot coloured red?—I have coloured it red because the corporation, I consider, could make good their claim to get a larger rent out of it; but after two trials (there was a severe battle fought), and we established our right as landlords, which never had been asserted before, it was considered too heavy a thing to re-open, but it is in a better position now than it ever could have been tried in. There was a debate upon it, after getting a verdict, whether we would go on with our case. Mr. Vernon, a very intelligent gentleman who was agent to the late Lord Herbert, and is now agent to Earl Pembroke, has great influence. There was a division in the corporation, and even it went to a vote whether they would secure the verdict that they had got. I felt, after I had worked so hard for it, that they abandoned it too easily. I hope it is not abandoned finally.

3662. That is very valuable property?—Most valuable. There has been an enormous outlay upon it. The nominal rent is 10 *l.* a year Irish, and it would be a great deal more than 10,000 *l.* a year, if it was let according to the ordinary course of the present day.

3663. It is held by Lord Pembroke, is it not?—Yes, it is held by Lord Pembroke at present.

3664. It comprises far the best part of Dublin?—Yes, it is highly improved, and the best part of Dublin.

3665. Then there are some other properties of the same sort in Dublin, also on terminable leases; for instance, the Custom House, and along the quays?—The Custom House is on a lease that has nearly 100 years to run, Amory's lease. There is this lease, A. R. No. 4, Oxmantown, which is about to expire in four or five years, of a very valuable property which was held by Wm. Ellis, an ancestor of Viscount Clifden, a minor, for 199 years.

3666. What is the property called Oxmantown?

0.105.

Mr. *Morgan.*

26 May 1876.

Chairman—continued.

town?—That is it. Oxmantown was held by Mr. Ellis under a lease, which is now within four years of expiration. Lessee was under covenant to build a bridge. He straightened the banks of the river, and improved the property very much.

3667. That lies all about the Royal Barracks, does it not?—Yes, the Royal Barracks was originally corporation property. It was granted some time in the reign of King Charles to the Duke of Ormond for a pair of gloves yearly rent.

3668. That property appears in your rental as producing 36*l.* 4*s.* 7*d.* a year, but valued for the poor law valuation at 3,486*l.*?—A. R. No. 4, is fully worth that, perhaps more; it may go to 4,000*l.* a year.

3669. This book which you have handed in is dated 1867, is it not?—That is the time that I was able to finish the arrangements. There have been a good many changes since; some increase in the rental and some other leases granted.

3670. A good many new leases have been granted or renewed, have they not?—A good many of the old leases have fallen in, and we have re-let the holdings, and they have produced higher rents in most cases.

3671. Could you tell me in gross what the increase in your rental has been since 1867?—I should say 1,000*l.* a year on the whole rental. The Baldoyle land at that time appears about a guinea an acre. That was the original rent in the leases which ended in 1855; and that is by the Irish acre, too, which makes a very great difference.

3672. Your practice now, as I understand, when a lease falls in, is to put it up to auction?—That has been the practice; but the corporation have, within the present year, asked the Treasury to appoint a valuator; they have not yet done so. There are several very valuable holdings just now on the verge of being out of lease, and the parties who are the occupants are for the most part, or nearly all, persons who have made establishments by their close attention to business, and they all say they would pay as much or more than the place is worth if they are allowed to have it without disturbance. The corporation have memorialised the Treasury, and got their concurrence to abandon the system of letting by auction, and the assent of the Government to appoint a valuator to fix the value.

3673. Is that value adhered to by the corporation?—It has not come yet into operation, unless the Treasury have since I have arrived in London, named a valuator that I am not aware of. We are just now waiting for his appointment. There are several very valuable holdings indeed in the neighbourhood of Grafton-street and in that direction. The tenants are all most anxious to get new leases in reversion at full present value.

3674. What is your rule as to the terms at which you let?—Thirty-one years for a tenement, or 75 years for rebuilding; 75 years is not quite enough to rebuild a good house, but that is the restriction in the Act of the 3 & 4 Vict. c. 108.

3675. Have the corporation sold any property since you have been law agent to the corporation?—Yes, with the leave of the Treasury. We must get the leave of the Treasury to sell anything, and we must apply the proceeds in the discharge of the debenture debt. We have got leave recently to sell for 13,000*l.* the site for the Royal Hibernian Bank in College Green, and that was applied in the purchase of debentures which were originally issued at 92, and we were able to buy the debentures at 82, so that we made a profit of paying our debts.

Chairman—continued.

3676. Have you sold any other property?—Yes; there was a small piece of Baldoyle sold the other day as a police station; the conveyances are not perfected, but there is an application for it; and there are two or three small things more that I could mention if you desire the particulars of them.

3677. Could you tell me roughly what the value of the property sold beyond the Hibernian Bank is?—We got leave to sell a small piece of ground, the site of an old house in High-street, to add to a place of worship; they did not seem inclined to grant it except for public purposes.

3678. So far as you can, will you give us the total?—We got a large price and, as I say, we were able to purchase the debentures at that price; in fact, we made income by the sale. There is 80*l.* a year realised, the difference between the interest on the debentures that are bought up and the rents that we sold; that is the only large case that we have had.

3679. Have you sold 5,000*l.* worth of property besides that?—Yes; the Government wanted some enlargement near the Four Courts some years ago, and then there was an inquiry, and they passed a short Act for the purpose, and we got a very liberal rate of purchase for it. I cannot exactly recollect what it was, but there was a jury under the Lands Clauses Act empanelled to value the property.

3680. Do you remember how much they gave you?—I know that we got more than the value of it; they were very rotten old houses, and they purchased them on the rack rent.

3681. When did it happen?—It was about the year 1852.

3682. What was done with the money which the corporation obtained for it?—It was applied to pay off the City Debenture debt. The general rule was that if it reached within 40*l.* of what would buy a debenture, any odd money we were obliged to make up, and buy another debenture; the Treasury always required that, and we have always done it.

Mr. Butt.

3683. At present the Bagotrath property is held by the representatives of Lord Fitzwilliam, is it not?—Viscount Fitzwilliam was the holder when he died, about 1817, I think.

3684. And he left it to the Pembroke family, did he not?—It fell to the Honourable Sydney Herbert; he held it at the time that I first came to the office.

3685. Do you know how Lord Fitzwilliam originally acquired it?—I have stated it in print in the Appendix to the Rental, that it was by usurpation, and by an act of violence. The chief baron was captured and murdered in the castle of Bagotrath by an ancestor of Lord Fitzwilliam.

3686. Do you know what was the date of the lease from the corporation?—There is no lease, at least none that I can find.

3687. You established against Lord Fitzwilliam a Parliamentary tenancy and payment of rent?—Yes.

3688. But it is still undetermined whether the tenancy is a yearly tenancy or is under some document that will entitle him to hold it?—Lord Pembroke's advisers say that they have been so long in

Mr. *Morgan.*

26 May 1876.

Mr. *Butt*—continued.

in possession that the length of the possession has consecrated their title, although it is clearly proved that it was founded upon an act of usurpation.

3689. What is established is, that he is a tenant of the corporation?—Yes.

3690. And that he is liable to pay rent?—Yes, and he does pay 10 *l.* a year Irish.

3691. But whether that is a yearly tenant or under some tenure that is permanent, is not determined?—No, I think not.

3692. With regard to the Baldoyle rents, a Bill was passed through Parliament in 1864; will you take the Journal of the House of Lords in your hand, and refer to a thing which I will ask your attention to (*handing a book to the Witness*); in the year 1864 had you anything to do with soliciting a Bill in Parliament?—Yes; I attended the House of Lords when it was referred.

3693. Is that the Journal of the House of Lords of 1864 which you have in your hand?—Yes.

3694. Now, will you turn to the entry on page 396 of the 17th of June; do you find there an Order referring the Dublin Improvement Bill to the judges?—Yes.

3695. Will you read that order to the Committee?—"Ordered that a printed copy of the Dublin Improvement Bill attested by the clerk of the Parliaments be and the same is hereby referred to the Lord Chief Justice of the Court of Common Pleas in Ireland, and Mr. Justice Fitzgerald in Ireland, who are to consider Clauses 27 and 28 in the said Bill, and the facts stated in the Preambles to both of the said Clauses, and to take evidence thereon, and such other evidence as they may think necessary and proper in reference to the enactments therein; and they are forthwith to summon the Corporation of the City of Dublin before them, and to take their consent to the said Clauses; and they are to report to the House under their hands the evidence so taken, and to state their opinion whether it is fit and proper that the Clauses should pass into a law, and what amendments, if any, are necessary in the same; and whether the Corporation of the City of Dublin have consented to the said Clauses, and the said judges are to sign the said printed copy of the said Bill."

3696. Clauses 27 and 28 in the printed Bill were the clauses relating to the reduction of rent, were they not?—Yes.

3697. They appear as Clauses 26 and 27 in the Act, as it ultimately passed; are you aware whether that reference was in point of fact carried out?—Yes, I was present at it.

3698. Can you produce to the Committee a copy of the judges' report?—I am not provided with it, but it is possible to get it.

3699. Now will you turn in the same Journal to page 557, July the 12th; on July the 12th, is there any entry about the Dublin Improvement Bill?—Yes. "Resolved that the following Lords be proposed to the House to form the Select Committee for the consideration of Pier and Harbour Orders Confirmation Bill, of the Dublin Improvement Bill, of the Sheffield Waterworks (Bradfield and Inundation) Bill, of the Local Government, Supplemental (No. 2) Bill, and of the Thames Conservancy Bill."

3700. Who were the Lords?—The Duke of Buckingham and Chandos, the Earl of Malmesbury, the Earl of Harrowby, the Viscount Falmouth, and the Lord Saye and Sele, of whom the Duke of Buckingham and Chandos shall be the Chairman; which report being read by the Clerk, was agreed to by the House. Ordered, That their Lordships do meet to consider the said Bills, on Tuesday next at 11 o'clock in the forenoon, in the Prince's lodgings near the House of Peers."

3701. Is there any further entry there relating to the Dublin Bill, or generally as to Petitions; what is the next resolution?—The next resolution is, "Ordered, That the several Petitions presented to the House this Session, taking notice of the last-mentioned Bills, or either of them, be referred to the said Select Committee, and that the Petitioners praying to be heard by themselves, their Counsel, Agents, and Witnesses against the said Bills, or either of them, be at liberty to be heard as desired, and that Counsel be heard for the Bills at the same time, if the promoters thereof think fit."

3702. Were there any Petitions against that Bill referred to that Select Committee against the Dublin Improvement Bill?—It would appear so.

3703. Now will you look at page 592, July the 18th?—I find "Ordered, That the report of the Judges in Ireland, to whom was referred a printed copy of the Dublin Improvement Bill to consider and report (presented to the House on the 7th day of this instant July) be referred to the Select Committee on the said Bill."

3704. Now will you look to the next day, the 19th July, at page 602?—"The Duke of Buckingham and Chandos reported from the Select Committee on the Dublin Improvement Bill, that they had considered the said Bill, and examined the allegations thereof, which were found to be true, and that the Committee had gone through the Bill and made some amendments thereto, which amendments were read by the clerk as follows:—Page 3, line 1, after 'may' insert 'without prejudice to any powers vested in them by the said recited Acts.' Line 3, leave out 'or persons,' and insert 'authorised by any special Act of Parliament to rate the said borough,' and in line 29 after 'bulk rent' insert 'from the commencement of said rate.'"

3705. Will you take the 26th clause of the Act in your hand, you see that that amendment does not appear in that 26th clause relating to Mr. Crampton?—Yes.

3706. Will you read what it says about bulk rent?—"And whereas the Corporation, believing that such expenditure in building would permanently improve the value of the said lands, agreed with the said Samuel Crampton to make such abatement, to commence from the said last mentioned date. And whereas, on the faith of such agreement, the said Samuel Crampton caused the said new buildings to be properly constructed.

3707. Will you look at the amendment which the Committee made, and tell me if you see any amendment made there in connection with the word "agreed"?—I find, "line 31, leave out 'are desirous of agreeing,' and insert, 'agreed.'"

3708. Does not it appear from that, that as the Bill came up originally, it said that the corporation were desirous of agreeing with them, and the Committee altered it to the shape in which it is now printed, that they had agreed?—Yes.

3709. Just read on the clause a little further, the

Mr. *Morgan*.

26 May 1876.

Mr. *Butt*—continued.

the next line?—"And whereas, on the faith of such agreement."

3710. Will you look at the amendment made by the Committee, and tell me if you find any amendment relating to that?—"Line 29, after 'bulk rent,' insert 'from commencement of said lease.'" The next, I think, is "line 31, leave out 'are desirous of agreeing,' and insert 'agreed'; line 32 and line 33, leave out 'inasmuch as,' and insert 'and whereas, on the faith of such agreement.'"

3711. Do you now see that those words, "on the faith of such agreement," are the alteration inserted by the Committee in the draft of the Bill as it was originally sent up?—It would appear so.

3712. Now will you look at the amendment, and see what were the words that the Committee inserted; do you see that the words, "on the faith of such agreement," were inserted by the Committee?—Yes.

3713. And then the result of that is, that the Bill went before Committee, and it is stated "desire to agree," then it was altered by stating the actual agreement and the expenditure on the faith of it?—Yes.

3714. And the Committee making this amendment reported that they were satisfied that the allegations were true?—Yes.

3715. And those amendments were approved by the Committee?—Yes, and they were adopted by the corporation and the tenants.

3716. In point of fact, was evidence offered before Lord Chief Justice Monahan?—Certainly; I gave evidence myself.

3717. And he then reported to the House in favour of the Bill?—He did.

3718. Are you aware that that is the usual practice of the House of Lords on all Estate Bills?—I am not very familiar with the practice of the House of Lords, but I remember that that was so to refer the case to two Irish judges if they were Irish lands.

3719. And to two English judges if it is an English Bill?—Yes.

3720. You see there Mr. Samuel Crampton; will you look at your rental at page 42, and tell me what his rental is?—The reserved rent was 107 *l.* 1 *s.* 2 *d.*

3721. Now will you look at Griffiths' Valuation; do you see at the bottom of the page "Mary Crampton"?—He had three sisters.

3722. How many acres is it in the valuation?—I find Mary Crampton No. 9; 24 acres 2 roods 7 perches.

3723. What is the valuation?—The valuation of that is 104 *l.*

3724. How is that 104 *l.* made up; that is to say, how much of it is land, and how much houses?—£. 33 15 *s.* is given as the valuation of the land, and 56 *l.* 5 *s.* of the buildings.

3725. Is that the present valuation?—I take it so.

3726. It is a valuation made long since 1855, is it not?—The house that stood on it, when I knew it first when Captain King lived there was a very snug-looking thatched cottage, and there is a very fine villa residence on it now.

3727. Can you tell me the date of that valuation which you have in your hand?—There is nothing on itself to denote when it was made.

3728. Is it the present valuation which you have in your hand?—This is the latest valuation of Griffiths.

3729. Now will you take some of those reductions of rent on the Baldoyle estate?—I find here Colonel Luke White 158 *l.*; his original rent was 192 *l.* 8 *s.* 4 *d.*

3730. And that was reduced to 152 *l.* 15 *s.* 2 *d.*?—Yes.

3731. Will you just look at Griffiths, and check that; Grange, No. 6; the rate and valuation?—Grange, No. 6, William Lane Joynt is the occupant, and the immediate lessor the Honorable Colonel Luke White; house, offices, and land, 22 acres; 33 *l.* 10 *s.* on the land, and 56 *l.* 10 *s.* on the house.

3732. What is the total valuation?—£. 89; that is 22 acres; Colonel White had two other holdings.

3733. Can you find what the valuation of the whole is; who are the other two farmers that had it?—Gerald Rice and John Gill got the rest of the land between them.

3734. Can you tell me what they are valued at?—Gerald Rice is a tenant of the Honourable Colonel Luke White for 57 acres 2 roods 2 perches; rent, 80 *l.* 15 *s.* on the land; 2 *l.* 5 *s.* for the buildings; and 83 *l.* is the total valuation.

3735. What is the other holding?—Gerald Rice also appears to hold from the Honourable Colonel Luke White 22 acres 3 roods 20 perches, valued at 32 *l.*, there is no building on that part.

3736. Will you just sum up those three valuations for me?—£. 204.

3737. If they are valued at 204 *l.*, it appears by your rental that Colonel Luke White had originally contracted to pay two sums of 192 *l.* and 191 *l.*, making together 383 *l.*?—Yes.

3738. Being valued at 204 *l.* the corporation receive under the reduction for that, 152 *l.* and 124 *l.*, making 276 *l.*?—Yes: that is right.

3739. I find that Patrick Butterly was reduced from from 138 *l.* to 129 *l.* for 52 acres, will you look at Griffiths and tell me what is the valuation there?—Butterly had been steward to Mr. Hutton, and he had received the rents for several years for Mr. Hutton; I know that he got a lease of 52 acres 2 roods 17 perches, at 129 *l.* 17 *s.*

3740. Take Mr. Henry Darley, in your rental he had 37 acres and he agreed to pay 113 *l.* which was reduced to 86 *l.*?—Yes.

3741. Will you look at his valuation at No. 8?—I see No. 8 "Captain Henry Darley, Corporation of Dublin immediate lessors, Gate Lodge and small offices, house, and land 31 acres 1 rood 7 perches," 41 *l.* is the value of the land and 4 *l.* for the buildings making a total valuation of 45 *l.*

Mr. *Kavanagh*.

3742. In what year was that valuation made?—I am not able to tell with accuracy, it is certified on the 13th of December 1866, but it was made, certainly, before 1865.

Mr. *Gibson*.

3743. As I understand Mr. Crampton's position he did not complain at all, according to the Act of Parliament, at being assessed at too high a rent?—He did, he refused to pay his rent, and I had to file a petition in Chancery against him and got a decree.

3744. Did not the section of the Act of Parliament which deals with Mr. Crampton's case, the 26th

Mr. *Gibson*—continued.

26th Section merely enact that there should be a reduction of 60 *l.* a year from his rent in consideration of his expenditure of 1,000 *l.*?—Yes.

3745. Is not that all the Act of Parliament enacts?—That is all it does. Mr. Brewster, I think it was or Baron Deasy, I forgot which, stated that, in his opinion, by the agreement with Mr. Crampton to lay out 1,000 *l.* at 6 per cent., we were not warranted in strict construction of the law in making that reduction, and it was put into the Bill in order to get the sanction of Parliament to it.

3746. Then he was bound under that section to spend 1,000 *l.*?—Yes.

3747. Under this section of the Act of Parliament, was not he given a reduction of 60 *l.*, dating back to the commencement of his lease?—Yes.

3748. So that he was to have a reduction of 60 *l.* for 31 years?—Yes, he would have it from 1864.

3749. That is to say, he would have 1,860 *l.* for an expenditure of 1,000 *l.*, and he would have the enjoyment of all his improvements at the same time?—He expended upon it 2,000 *l.*

3750. His contract with the corporation was only for 1,000 *l.*—Only for 1,000 *l.*

3751. He got a rebate from his rent of 1,860 *l.*, and he had in addition the enjoyment of the place the whole time to the end of his lease, was not that the result of the Act of 1864?—He was an old gentleman, and he died before he had his improvements finished; it was certainly great courage on the part of a man of his age to do it; he was 70 years of age before he began it.

3752. Were not all those old lettings, made in the year 1855, let under the conditions with which the corporation made all lettings, that all the biddings should be at equal acreable rents per statute acre?—Yes; the biddings were so taken, but the bulk rents were inserted in the leases. The biddings were taken by the acre. Several people did not know exactly, when they were bidding, the difference between Irish and the statute acres. There was very wild and confused bidding for those lands.

3753. Were not printed conditions of lettings by auction circulated at the place?—Yes, there were.

3754. Is not this the third of the printed conditions that were circulated: "That the lands be set at acreable rents per statute acre, according to survey made by the city surveyor; such survey to be final. New mearings to be made by and at the expense of the tenant"?—Yes.

3755. Though all those tenants were so bound to make acreable biddings, the rents were afterwards brought out as bulk rents?—They made acreable biddings to an extent beyond what are now the bulk rents. They never made any alterations in their boundaries, at least many of them did not.

3756. I assume that James Doyle, Gerald Rice, Lord Annaly, Mr. Darley, and the other parties mentioned, were all men who knew how to attend to business?—No, James Doyle was a very poor old man, he was nearly 80 years of age, and he would have bid 12 *l.* an acre for the land rather than lose the shelter of it. He had a daughter that was a servant to Lord Carlisle, and she had 150 *l.*, or something saved, which she applied to helping to keep the place, and she afterwards gave up her situation.

Mr. *Gibson*—continued.

Mr. *Morgan*.

26 May 1876.

3757. He was the smallest tenant?—Yes, much the smallest one.

3758. I see it was only eight statute acres, but Lord Annaly had over 100 acres, and he was really a large tenant?—Yes. Mr. White bid for two lots.

3759. Are you aware that none of the acreable rents that were bid for, except in one case, reached 4 *l.* per acre?—I know that they all exceeded that very much.

3760. Have you got and can you give me the acreable rents for a single lot?—They were reduced to about 4 *l.* per statute acre.

3761. According to your own principle, as passed by the corporation, the biddings were to be at acreable rents per statute acre, was there a single rent before reduction that reached 4 *l.* per statute acre?—There was one lot, the first lot, that afterwards became Samuel Crampton's, which went very high. Mr. Crampton became a tenant at a higher rent certainly than that.

3762. Mr. Crampton did not claim a reduction at all, nor is he included in the schedule of reductions. I am dealing with the schedule of reductions, which contain 13 names; is there a single one of them which has an acreable rent of 4 *l.* per statute acre when this bidding was taken?—Duffy's was more than 4 *l.*, and he has remained unreduced.

3763. What is the number of Duffy?—James Duffy is No. 8, All Hallows.

3764. He is not amongst the schedule of reduced rents at all?—No; he was offended at some very rude remarks that were made against him in the debate in the corporation, and he refused to take charity from them; he was a very independant man; he was a magistrate.

3765. I know he is the only excepted person. Do I understand you to say that his name not being in the Act of Parliament, the corporation reduced his rent without any Act of Parliament?—His name was unfortunately left out of the Bill, and the Act of Parliament has not his name in it.

3766. Did you reduce his rent?—No, it never was reduced; unfortunately they have not had the power to do it since.

3767. Do I understand that Mr. Duffy, or his representative, at present is paying 98 *l.* 6 *s.* 8 *d.*?—He may.

3768. So that he has been able to pay, at all events, the unabated rent?—He was a man of property, and a man of independence; he would not lose his time begging after it, and he paid the rent; he erected a gate lodge afterwards, and several of the corporation went down to see the place and see what could be done for him, and they promised him that they would give him a reduction in some shape or form, and he built a new gate lodge on it, and a stable, if I recollect rightly; he improved the holding very much after some time.

3769. Can you tell me what is the average rent of the neighbouring lands of Baldoyle, the immediate adjoining estate; do not they reach to 5 *l.*, 6 *l.*, and 7 *l.* per statute acre?—No, I think not; I always heard that Lord Howth's land was let much lower than the corporation land, and I believe it to be a fact. I have no actual knowledge of the matter myself, but I know I have always heard that Lord Howth's is let at less than the corporation's.

3770. With regard to Mr. Darley's valuation, the

Mr. Morgan.

26 May 1876.

Mr. Gibson—continued.

the honourable and learned Member for Limerick asked you the question, and you said it was 45 *l.* a year for 31 acres 1 rood 7 perches acreage; in your rental it is stated as 37 acres 3 roods 4 perches; how do you account for the discrepancy?—Mr. Darley held other land and a house in connection with the corporation land, but the portion that is there as the area of the corporation land is correct.

3771. Can you tell me what is the valuation attached to the 6½ acres on which the house is placed?—I do not know whether they have been separately valued.

3772. In the place where Lord Annaly lived, and where Mr. Joynt lives at present, is there not a dwelling house?—Yes; a very large old manor house; an old fashioned house with a great number of rooms in it; there is a ball-room the whole length of the face of the house.

3773. So that that reduced rent, which he paid of about 250 *l.* for the two holdings, was for over 100 acres of land and this old manor house in which Lord Annaly was able to live himself?—No, he only retained the old manor house and about six or eight acres lying immediately round it. Mr. Gill and Mr. Rice got the rest of the land of those two holdings.

3774. Were there buildings on the other holdings?—There was no building on the part that was given to Mr. Gill or to Mr. Rice either.

3775. But on each of the three holdings, were there residences on each, or not?—No; there was a residence on the one that Mr. Gill lives in. The residence that Mr. White came to, as I told you, was an old manor house, and it became quite decayed; in fact, he had leave to take it down and turn the materials into stables or farm offices. He petitioned for leave to do it, but he changed his mind afterwards, and fitted it up, and resided in it with his wife and children for some time.

3776. Who is the land agent for the corporation?—I am called the land agent.

3777. Do you act as receiver of rents?—No, I do not receive the rents at all. I do not know why I am called the land agent, for I cannot carry out my views to any great extent.

3778. Who is the person that receives the rents?—The city treasurer, I believe.

3779. Who is the person who acts as collector of rents?—The city treasurer. Notices go round half-yearly to the tenants to bring their rents into the office one half-year within another. The rents are very well paid.

3780. I find, on page 44, that the tenants pay their rents to a collector; who is the collector?—Mr. Patrick Butterly had been the land steward of Mr. Hutton, the previous owner under those leases before they fell in. He was a very respectable farmer, and he collected those rents weekly, for there were a lot of very wretched cabins on the land, but still it was thought better to get something from them than to allow them to acquire an adverse possession. Mr. Butterly was allowed 10 per cent. to collect those small rents.

3781. Is there anyone who ever goes to inspect this property and see how the tenants perform their covenants and keep their places in repair?—Sometimes I go down there, but I consider that Mr. Butterly, being resident in the town of Baldoyle, is much more competent than I am to look after that. In fact, I hear about them at every turn; anything of any importance that happens they come and tell me.

Mr. Gibson—continued.

3782. As I understand, he is only employed to collect from the small holdings at Baldoyle; taking the other holdings remaining of the corporation estates, is there anyone whose duty it is to go and inspect the property periodically, to report upon their state, repair, and so on?—That should be the duty of the surveyor.

3783. Who is he?—Mr. Neville is the city surveyor, or it may be my duty, but I never was commissioned actually to do those things.

3784. Is it any part of Mr. Neville's duty to go and inspect the farms and houses at Baldoyle?—I think he would be a most capable man to do it, but be has more important duties to perform. There is the water supply, which is of course considerable, and there is the measurement of land. That is the kind of thing that he attends to; he employs a very competent assistant, who is a very skillful land surveyor, and whenever there is any question of measurement or boundaries, or anything of that kind to be done, this man is always sent down on my requisition.

3785. In what particulars are you land agent?—Only this, that when holdings fall out of lease I advertise them to be let. I compose the advertisement; I apprise the corporation that such and such lands are out of lease, and I fix the day for their letting. I am now speaking of the past time when they were let by auction. After fixing the time for letting, I described the premises, and they were put up; and we generally had a tolerably good attendance.

3786. After the premises are let and the lease is taken, have you anything more to do with the letting?—When once the leases are made, they are handed over to the city treasurer to receive the rents.

3787. Then your duties are strictly those of a solicitor to prepare the leases for the letting?—Yes, but I drive round the lands besides and go and see them. I know what is passing tolerably well on the lands. I go there not so often as I would wish to go, because my salary does not enable me to keep such a number of horses and an establishment as I would require to be a regular land agent.

3788. You are called the Corporation Law and Land Agent, are you not?—Yes, I am called the land agent more in courtesy than anything else.

3789. Was your pay ever increased?—Not with the addition in dignity, as I suppose it was considered to be in dignity.

3790. When were you given the title of land agent?—As you will observe in the rental, I did not in 1867 call myself land agent; it says only law agent. The corporation were exceedingly kind to me when this was finished and they granted me liberal payment for it, and perhaps they have attended more to my opinions on the matter than before, that is all. I have no separate pay, and I never got any separate appointment as land agent.

3791. Am I then to understand that there is no person whose formal duty, and for which he is paid, is to inspect the corporation tenants and their holdings and to report periodically on their condition?—There is no one that answers that description at present. I never was appointed to do it, but it is a thing very necessary to be done, and ought not to be neglected, for in the course

Mr. Morgan.

26 May 1876.

Mr. Gibson—continued.

course of nature I must very soon pass away, and it will require constant looking after.

Mr. Brooks.

3792. Do you not know that the Committee of the corporation periodically inspect the property?—They do go when any particular question occurs If it happens to be summer weather they perhaps will go down to look at a particular thing in Baldoyle, but there is never much, practically, comes out of it because they scatter about the town. It would require a much more regular supervision.

3793. Do you accompany them?—Yes, I always do; I do not consider myself a land agent to this extent, that I do not get alterations and improvements made that I think are very desirable; but as I may be moving off the scene very soon, some one else perhaps will have a better opportunity.

3794. You think that the committee avail themselves of the summer to make those visitations?—I have known them go in the winter if there was any actual necessity for it; but it is more congenial to go in the summer on those visitations. As I say, I never knew them to be of much practical use; for instance, although they have gone to see the town of Baldoyle very often, and I have been entreating them to build a few new cabins on it there, they have remained in a terribly neglected state for a long long time, and I am afraid they will remain so during my time.

3795. What is the duty of the treasurer with regard to collecting the rents?—Immediately after a gale falls due or very soon after, he sends a notice out from his office to the tenants to send in their rents, and as all of them have good interest the rents are all well paid.

3796. Is it any part of his business to make treaties for reductions?—No, that is always done by a letter from the parties themselves to the committee if they want it, but they all tolerably well understand now that the reductions are more difficult than they were before.

3797. Are there any duties towards the tenants on the part of the treasurer, except to receive the rents, and to give you notice if any rents are in arrear?—His practice is this: if rent is in arrear one year or two gales, he calls on me to serve ejectments, or to take the steps that are necessary to protect the corporation; that is to say, the only thing that I am allowed to do without getting the special act of the council, is to bring ejectments to recover rents.

3798. Does he call upon you to serve ejectments, or does he simply give you notice of rents being in arrear?—He gives me a list of the rents that are in arrear; if he seems to think that they will not be paid, he sends to me, and I immediately take action upon it. My orders are to serve ejectments in any case where loss is likely to arise if there is a year's rent due. That was the practice of the old corporation before 1841.

3799. Then he has no duty towards the tenant except to receive the rents, and to inform you as law agent if a tenant's rent is in arrear?—Yes; or if he heard of any waste or anything of that kind being committed on the land he would inform me, and I would immediately go out and inquire after it.

3799*. It is no part of his duty to inform himself as to the term of the leases?—No, I think not. There is a copy of my rental in use in his

Mr. Brooks—continued.

office, and he generally looks into it beforehand.

3800. In fact, he is not the land agent or the law agent?—No, he is neither land nor law agent, but he is treasurer, which is a better thing, and more dignified.

Sir Arthur Guinness.

3801. You said that the rents of the Baldoyle Estate were satisfactorily collected?—All who hold leases pay their rent very well; it is the poor creatures that are at weekly rents in the town that do not.

3802. Was your attention called to the auditor's report of 1873; will you read it to the Committee?—"On examining the rentals, I found that arrears of weekly rents on the Baldoyle Estate, amounting to 162 *l.* 10 *s.* 11 *d.*, were outstanding at the end of the year. I think this amount excessive on an annual rental of 240 *l.*, and that it is unadvisable to allow such comparatively large arrears to accumulate on tenements of this class, owing principally to the very great difficulty of recovering them. The agent ought, I think, be urged to obtain payment where practicable, while in some cases the corporation would probably do well to remit the amount, or a portion of it, cautioning the agent against allowing a similar accumulation of arrears." That agent is Mr. Butterly, the person whose name was mentioned before. He has 10 per cent. on the gross rents for collecting them; he does not make much by the transaction. The auditor says: "The rents on the other portions of the property of the corporation have been well paid."

3803. Will you look at the auditor's report of the next year and read what he says there?—"I called attention in my report for the previous year to the large amount of arrears of rent due by the weekly tenants on the Baldoyle estate. The arrears at the end of the year under audit amounted to 163 *l.* 19 *s.* 5 *d.*, being more than 20 weeks' rent, and a slight increase on the previous year's arrears. The agent states that while some portion is due by persons who are able to pay, the greater portion is due by persons who are unable." I quite agree with him. "I would suggest to the corporation the propriety of their obtaining from the agent a list of the outstanding arrears at the end of the current year, and after scrutiny by the committee, of remitting the latter portion and directing their solicitor to take the necessary steps to obtain payment of the former, at the same time cautioning the agent against allowing a similar accumulation of arrears."

3804. Will you read the auditor's report for 1875 upon the same subject?—"The arrears of rent on the Baldoyle estate, to which I referred in my previous reports to your Board, remain unpaid, and otherwise undisposed of. The corporation appear to contemplate the sale of this property with a view to a reduction of their debt." I have recommended them to build 20 new cottages and they would then sell them and the land to advantage, but in the present wretched appearance of the town it would scare away any capitalist.

3805. Do you think that they would get as good a bidding for them if the town was sold now as they got the last time?—Yes, I think that those leases would, every one of them, fetch more. If there were 20 new cottages built, they would

Mr. *Morgan.*

26 May 1876.

Sir *Arthur Guinness*—continued.

would not only get back the money they cost, about 100 *l.* apiece, but they would get a very good fair price for the land.

3806. Has that return been made by the Baldoyle land agent which the auditor asked for?—I think it has; he has brought in his accounts; but they were to have been checked by the town clerk, and by the committee. I do not know whether the town clerk has had leisure to do so, but they were never in my department.

3807. The honourable Member for Limerick the other day took an interest in connection with the religious denominations of the employés of the South Dublin Union; do you happen to know anything about that subject?—I never was a poor law guardian, nor had any intercourse with them at either of the unions, except very slight on some matters of business.

3808. Then you are not aware, are you, that both in the North and South Dublin Unions the greater number of the officers are Roman Catholics?—I do not know at all.

Mr. *Bruen.*

3809. I think in answer to a previous question referring to some lettings in the townland of Clontuik, you said that the letting made to Blainey Mitchell of 10 acres in 1852 was not made by auction, submitting it to competition for the highest offer?—I am not aware that I said that. One of Mitchell's lettings was made, I think, in my absence; but I think that that portion which is now held by All Hallowes College was certainly let by auction, because I remember the name of the previous tenant who had surrendered it.

3810. And the lettings in 1852 of 10 acres 7 perches, to Blainey Mitchell, were made by public competition?—I identified one which belonged to Mr. Kirwan and Michael Lynch. I was absent when it was let, but the other was let, I am positive, by competition.

3811. I think you said that it was not let by public competition, because the system of competition had not then commenced; that is to say, the bye-law by which the corporation were obliged to let it by public competition had not been passed?—I would be wrong in saying that, but the system of competition, when the Rev. Mr. Hand took a large portion in 1843, had not commenced; but Mr. Mitchell's was let by auction.

3812. I see by page 39 of the rental that both of them were made the same date, namely, 1852, both the letting to the executors of the Rev. Mr. Hand and the letting to Blainey Mitchell?—The Rev. Mr. Hand's was let as early as 1843 or 1844, and then he induced the bishops, or the higher orders of his church, to adopt his lease, and then they got a new lease with the consent of the Treasury.

3813. In page 39, lots 14 and 15, you put as being the lessees, executors of the Rev. J. Hand; occupiers All Hallowes College; measurement, 38 acres 3 roods 21 perches; commencement of lease, March 1852; term 1,000 years; is that correct or is it not?—It requires explanation. The original letting to Mr. Hand was about the year 1843 or 1844; he had it and held it until his death, which was perhaps about the year 1849, and then it was given over to the Catholic Bishop, and they applied for a new lease on the terms of spending 10,000 *l.* on it.

3814. What were the terms of the original lease to the Rev. Mr. Hand?—Seventy-five years, from 1843 or 1844.

Mr. *Bruen*—continued.

3815. Did he surrender that in 1852?—His possession merged in the present authorities of the Catholic Church; then they got a new lease. He handed it over; in fact, he held it until his death, but they got a new lease as his executors. I remember it now: the Rev. Mr. Yore and the Rev. Mr. Meyler were the executors of Mr. Hand, and they got the new lease, to which Mr. Hand would have been entitled.

3816. How would Mr. Hand have been entitled to a lease for 1,000 years, his term being only 70?—He would not have been entitled as a matter of right, but the corporation considered that it was a matter of prudence, when they were offered, to have an expenditure of 10,000 *l.* on 24 Irish acres let at 10 *l.* per acre, which was the original take of Mr. Hand.

3817. Have you reason to suppose that if the law requiring the corporation of putting that land up to public auction and competition, and which had come into operation at that time, had been carried out, it would have prevented the persons who bought Mr. Hand's interest from making the offer which they did?—I can only say that I think that if it had been put up to auction it would not have brought a higher rent than the Rev. Mr. Hand undertook to pay for it, for it was principally grown with very large old timber, elm trees, and it was an unprofitable place, but very well suited for the purpose for which he got it, as a college, but no gentleman would have taken it as a permanent residence. Sir Guy Campbell had it for a time.

3818. Do you say that the corporation got very high terms?—I think they did.

3819. Have you any reason to suppose that they would not have got such high terms if they had offered it to public competition?—I do not think that they would have realised more from a solvent tenant.

3820. Would they have got less?—It might have been set less.

3821. On what plea could it be that the corporation refused to comply with a law which was then existing?—The bye-law for letting by auction was not made until 1851, which was to have everything set up by auction twice before it was set by hand.

3822. I understood you to say that in 1852 there was a new letting made to the executors of the Rev. Mr. Hand, or to the authorities of All Hallowes College?—A new lease, but not necessarily a new letting. The original letting did take place in the year 1843 or 1844 for 75 years, and he was in possession under that lease at 10 *l.* an acre, and he had been very successful in establishing a college, so much so that I heard that some other clergymen were rather jealous of him, and that he was called on to give it over for the general good of the Church, and ultimately when he died they got it, and they got a new lease. They had built a range of very large buildings on it, and they proposed to lay out 10,000 *l.*, and it was on condition of laying out that that they got an extension of the term for 1,000 years.

3823. That is, in fact, a new letting in reversion?—Yes, that is the effect of it.

3824. Do you suppose that that was a compliance with the law, which obliged the corporation to let all the new lettings by competition?—No,

Mr. *Bruen*—continued.

No, it was not; but the fact is that the bargain was made prior to the making of that rule to let by auction. The bye-law was not made until 1851, but the Rev. Mr. Hand's tenancy had commenced in 1843 or 1844.

3825. Mr. Hand's letting only extended to 75 years, and the corporation in 1852 gave a new letting in reversion on the termination of it?—Yes; an extension of the term at the same rent.

3826. And not by public competition?—Not by public competition, but they gave it with the consent of the Treasury on memorial. They are allowed, when they want to go outside the Act of Parliament or the bye-laws, to memorialise the Treasury. They did so in that case, and they got leave.

3827. Will you turn to page 42 of your rental; I see that at the bottom of the page there are entered 16 lots let next to the town of Baldoyle, held quarterly by 12 tenants; are these in the nature of town parks or town lots?—Yes, they graze their cows there. They are all in the nature of town parks.

3828. Is it or is it not the fact that town parks and town lots generally fetch a higher rate than ordinary agricultural land?—They do generally; there is more demand for them.

3829. Will you look at Nos. 22 and 24 on that same page. Patrick Butterly; what is his holding?—He has 26 acres 39 perches.

3830. The rent of that is 41 *l.* 12 *s.* 4 *d.*, which gives an acreable rent of about 1 *l.* 10 *s.*, does it not?—Yes.

3831. Is that above the average rate of agricultural land in that district?—It is not, and I can account for that. Mr. Butterly had been steward of Mr. Hutton. He was not a man of that sort, that if he wanted that land they would not be likely to oppose him. He would have got the farm from Mr. Hutton, and when he applied for it from the corporation I do not think that there was any strong desire by any others to outbid him in any way.

3832. Do you think that 1 *l.* 10 *s.* is the fair letting value of that land?—I do not. I think that it was worth more, and I do believe that when it comes to be sold, it will sell at a much higher rate than that.

3833. Does that remark apply to most of those town parks and lots?—I think those town parks are worth 4 *l.* an Irish acre all round.

3834. Has Mr. Darley any other holding in Baldoyle but that one which is put down as No. 2?—No; he had a fine house adjoining to that lot, but he has ceased to live there. He lives in London at present, and he sold his interest to Mr. Van den Eynde.

3835. I want to know whether Mr. Darley is lessee of any other land at Baldoyle under the corporation than this 37 acres 3 roods 4 perches?—No, he is not.

3836. Then that 37 acres 3 roods 4 perches, comprises the house that you spoke of?—No, the house that he occupied was on a different estate, in which he had a large interest, and he sold his residence and this land, which he rented from the corporation to Mr. Van den Eynde.

3837. Does Mr. Van den Eynde occupy it himself?—He does; he has been very successful; he has a very nice house.

Mr. *Kavanagh*.

3838. With regard to the Act of 1864, which allowed the reduction of the rents in Baldoyle, am I right in saying that it was retrospective in its action?—The letting had only taken place in 1859. I think they made it retrospective, and in settling the amount they got the full benefit of it from the start.

Mr. *Morgan*.

26 May 1876.

3839. Let me call your attention to Clause 27 of the Act: "And whereas the corporation, by resolution of council, resolve to make abatements from the said reserved bulk or rack-rents to the several reduced rents, as specified in the said Schedule A, from the 25th day of March 1859."—That was going back, to a certain extent, from 1864 to 1859. I suppose they thought that they had better do it generously if they did it at all.

3840. How was that managed; was the money repaid to the tenants?—They were all allowed it in settlement of their rents.

3841. Do you mean as a sort of credit?—They have got the allowance from that day most certainly.

3842. In page 32 of your rental you will observe, "Pitt-street, A. H. 189, Patrick Clarke, lessee; commencement of lease 1857; term 31 years; rent 14 *l.*; poor law valuation 15 *l.* Can you explain how it is that the rent and the poor law valuation are so near in amount?—Yes; it is a poor wretched house; Clarke is dead, and it has been re-let since it is in very bad order.

3843. Did not you say that the poor law valuation is generally a good deal below what the real value of the holding is?—Generally it is so, but there are exceptions.

3844. I find in the same page, in No. 5, A. H. 150, Patrick Fitzpatrick has a term for 31 years, from Michaelmas 1853, at a rental of 10 guineas, and the poor law valuation is 11 *l.*; do you know anything about that case?—Yes, I know that a person came forward as a tenant for it, and that illustrates the mischief of these public lettings, for the fellow had a good character from D'Arcy's brewery, and he immediately sold it to a brothel keeper, who established it in that line; I had to evict him some time after; the sweeps got into possession of it.

3845. Here is a later case on page 31: David McAsey, with a 31 years' lease made in 1866, for 30 *l.* a year, and the poor law valuation is 25 *l.*; that seems a very slight increase upon the poor law valuation?—I know that house very well; I think perhaps it was worth 35 *l.*, but it was an old house at the time, and he laid out a good deal on it.

3846. The next case above him is nearly the same?—Yes, that of Henry Johnston; they were let together.

3847. As a general rule, do not you consider that the lettings ought to be made with a fair increase on the poor law valuation?—Yes, a good many of them. Those that have been let such as I have already referred to, for 31 years within my own time, would generally have brought the highest price, and there would not be much increase on them; but in the case of the very old leases, the 99 years' leases, which are now about to fall in, there will be an increase, but some of the houses are very old indeed, and very ricketty.

3848. What proportion do you think the poor law valuation bears to the letting value of the property?—I think there would be a difference of 20 per cent. in the city holdings.

3849. That is to say, the poor law valuation is 20 per cent. under the real value?—I think it was.

Mr. *Morgan.*

26 May 1876.

Mr. *Kavanagh*—continued.

was. They generally made allowance for insurance and repairs; in fact, I have heard the Government valuator say so.

3850. In the case of those houses that I asked you about, they were a little below the poor law valuation?—Yes, they were. There was not a competition as regards these two houses.

3851. Would your answers exactly apply to the general valuation of property all through the city of Dublin in relation to the letting value?—It would not. I am well acquainted with the whole of the corporation estate. I cannot say what is the relative difference, but I would not wish to say as to other property upon that point; but, generally speaking, I can make a tolerably fair guess of the value of houses in all parts of the city.

3852. In page 23 there are three lettings side by side. Joseph Cass, Esther Dunne, and H. Kavanagh, in Fleet-street; do you know them?—Yes, they are three houses on a very old lease which fell in together, and the same persons who had been occupants bid for them, and they were unable to continue in the payment of the rent. Joseph Cass was a very comfortable man, a dairyman; he is since dead, and his daughter has got the lease of it.

Chairman.

3853. Some questions have been asked you as to the management of the corporation property; can you tell me whether these outlying properties at Coolock and elsewhere, are let on repairing leases or whether the corporation do the repairs themselves?—Most all these old leases are very simple, and they have not stringent covenants as to repairs. The parties having a good interest in the land has induced them to keep them in tolerable repair. At Ballycolane there is only one residence on the 600 acres, and it is only a very humble place.

3854. You spoke, I think, of the bad state of repair of the cabins at Baldoyle?—Yes; they were cabins of a very miserable class originally. The corporation built 20 cabins themselves; they have paid fairly, and they got between 5 and 6 per cent. interest upon their outlay, and there are no arrears on any of them; and that is the reason that I have pressed them strongly to build 20 more, as that would enable them to take down the 40 wretched cabins that are there, and that disfigure the place.

3855. The tenants there, I presume, have not covenanted to repair?—No; the 20 new cottages built by the corporation are held by weekly tenants, but Mr. Butterly sees to the repairs. They were well built, and they have kept very well together, and have not wanted much repair, nor are the rents of them in arrear.

3856. As to the tenants of the houses in the city on terminable leases, have they covenants for repairs?—Most of them have old leases on ground rents which were very low, and the parties have interest themselves in keeping them well together; but, of course, we will take care, in making any new leases, to have that point attended to. In every case in which a lease now expires, we make the new lessees covenant to put a new slate roof on their houses, and that insures them to stand well for 31 years. We leave the internal matters to themselves.

Chairman—continued.

3857. Who looks after the condition of that property?—I look after it; but I am still getting every year less fit for it, and I would be very glad to see a more active person that would have more authority to do it.

3858. A good deal of the house property generally in Dublin is scarcely in a good state of repair, I fancy?—There are some miserably bad, and terribly decayed dwellings.

3859. Belonging to the corporation, do you mean?—There are only a few belonging to the corporation.

Sir *Arthur Guinness.*

3860. I find in a report of yours, either in 1873 or 1874, this passage, recommending the sale of some of the corporation properties. You say that if they were sold, and a portion of the debt paid, the corporation would save annually over 1,000 *l.* a year?—I think so; I may be mistaken. The corporation think me visionary, perhaps, in some of my ideas, but those are my own notions.

3861. What estate does that refer to?—To Baldoyle; it comprises a great many denominations besides Baldoyle.

3862. Will you just read it to the Committee?—"Sale of Lands—In relation to the sale of small lots, rent free for ever, of six townlands in the county of Dublin, containing about 2,000 acres, the produce to be invested in the city of Dublin as city estate stock. Since my report of 25th May 1872, Earl Charlemont has advertised for sale his interest in the lands of Donny Carney, held under two leases from the corporation; namely, one, 50 statute acres, held for ever at the yearly rent of 113 *l.* 19 *s.*; one, 223 statute acres, to expire 1920, at the yearly rent of 743 *l.* 13 *s.* 3*d.*; total, 857 *l.* 12 *s.* 3 *d.*"

3863. Will you mention which estates you suggested?—I have advised the corporation to sell all their lands in the county of Dublin, because I do not think that they can act the part of good landlords as some gentlemen in Ireland do.

Mr. *Kavanagh.*

3864. What would they do with the money?—Pay their debenture debt in the first instance, and then invest money to pay the salaries of the officers after having paid off their debt.

Mr. *Brooks.*

3865. Will you describe the nature of the holdings in which arrears have accrued in Baldoyle?—They are of a most miserable kind, inhabited by persons to whom Mr. Hutton had set them, and the corporation did not wish to hunt them away to the poorhouse; there is but one instance, that I am aware of, of an occupant in Baldoyle dying in the poorhouse since it came into our possession.

3866. About how much are the weekly rents; are some of them as low as 6 *d.* per week?—And some of them are even put at 3 *d* in order to prevent their acquiring an adverse possession, and we sometimes, it may be, take a penny on account.

3867. It is in order to relieve the rates, in fact, that those persons are not evicted?—It is in order not to have the odium that would be cast upon us. There are many of them, I should say, who are most industrious people, and who would

pay

Mr. Murphy. 26 May 1876.

Mr. *Brooks*—continued.

pay rent for a holding that was habitable. I have no doubt they pay fairly and have paid well on those 20 new cabins that were erected, and there are no arrears.

3868. With regard to the inspection of the city property, is not the officer whose peculiar duty it is to do it the city architect?—No; whenever it happens that anything occurs he cannot go and inspect the property without an order from the committee to make a report; otherwise he would get no payment. He is paid by fees; he has no salary.

Mr. *Murphy*.

3869. Is it a fact that Lord Clifton has a very large interest in some portions of the property held by him under the corporation of Dublin?—Yes; there is property now falling out of lease.

3870. When will it fall out of lease?—In September 1881.

3871. What amount does the corporation receive now from him?—£. 36 a year.

Mr. *Murphy*—continued.

3872. What is the value of the property?—It will realise I hope 4,000 *l.* a year.

3873. Then there will be an addition to the rental of the corporation of 4,000 *l.* a year in five or six years?—Yes, after five or six years.

Mr. *Butt*.

3874. You said that Mr. Lane Joynt came to you as the agent of Lord Annaly; Mr. Lane Joynt was in the corporation of Dublin, was he not?—I do not say he was at that time.

3875. Can you not say more than that?—I am sure he was not at that time.

Mr. *Bruen*.

3876. How soon after did he get into the corporation?—His elevation was very sudden. I think it was about the year 1865 that he got in, and he was lord mayor, I think, in 1866 or 1867. He became Crown Solicitor after that, which was about three or four years ago.

Mr. Thomas O'Donnell, re-called; and further Examined.

Mr. O'Donnell.

Mr. *Brooks*.

3877. Can you state what is the origin of Pell's poundage?—I have been informed by my predecessor, who was city accountant before me, the nature of it is this: When those Royal grants were made, the first payments went through a person of the name of Pell. They were made in the Castle of Dublin, and those rents (we call them now Castle rents) are paid to us now by the Paymaster General. Mr. Pell, who first paid those rents or royal grants to the corporation of Dublin, was in the habit of deducting poundage, which was called Pell's Poundage: and every year afterwards the Paymaster General deducted it from those grants, under the denomination of Pell's Poundage.

3878. It is the Paymaster General who retains a certain per-centage of the rents, which is called Pell's Poundage?—Yes.

Mr. *Bruen*.

3879. Has he any title to retain it, except the ancient custom?—None that we know of.

Mr. *Kavanagh*.

3880. Is it for the Crown that he retains it?—I cannot answer that; we get no reason, but so far as we can look back through the city accounts we find that this deduction has been made from those particular royal grants of 500 *l.* and 300 *l.*, or rents as we call them now, because they are paid in the Castle.

Tuesday, 30th May 1876.

MEMBERS PRESENT:

Sir Michael Hicks Beach.	Mr. Gibson.
Mr. Brooks.	Sir Arthur Guinness.
Mr. Bruen.	Mr. Kavanagh.
Mr. Butt.	Mr. Mulholland.
Mr. Collins.	Mr. Murphy.
Mr. J. P. Corry.	Dr. Ward.

SIR MICHAEL HICKS BEACH, BART., IN THE CHAIR.

Mr. THOMAS WRIGLEY GRIMSHAW, M.D., called in; and Examined.

Mr. *T. W. Grimshaw,* M.D.

30 May 1876.

Sir *Arthur Guinness.*

3881. YOU are an M.D., an Honorary M.A. of the Dublin University, a Fellow of King and Queen's College of Physicians, and you hold a diploma in State medicine in the University of Dublin?—Yes.

3882. You are also a practising physician of 15 years' standing, and a ratepayer?—Yes.

3883. I believe that you are officially connected with some of the Dublin hospitals?—With Steeven's Hospital, Cork-street Fever Hospital, and the Coombe Lying-in Hospital.

3884. Your connection with those institutions has caused you to give special attention to the sanitary condition of Dublin?—Yes, especially in connection with the Cork-street Fever Hospital; I have been connected with it now for 11 years, and I have consequently found it necessary to follow up the patients to their homes and see what the causes of disease in those places were.

3885. Are you a member of the sanitary association?—I am.

3886. Have you delivered any lectures in connection with that subject?—Yes, I have delivered lectures in two or three courses; one was at the Dublin Society, a course of lectures that was organised conjointly by the Dublin Society and the sanitary association; delivered by Dr. Stokes, Dr. Hudson, Dr. Reynolds, Dr. Mapother (the medical officer of the city), myself and several others, eight or nine altogether.

3887. How often does that committee meet, and what is your mode of procedure?—The committee meet once a week, and the method which we pursue is, first of all we receive any reports of sanitary defects through the city and the suburbs, and we verify those reports by getting one or two or more members of the committee to go and examine into the truth of the complaint and the nature of the report, and if we find it to be correct we forward it to the sanitary authority of the district in which the neglect has been discovered, either the corporation authorities or the township commissioners in the suburbs; our operations have extended as far as Kingstown; I do not think that we have reported on or dealt with anything beyond Kingstown. [I have since ascertained that the committee has dealt with a sanitary defect at Ballybrack.]

3888. When was this association founded?—It was founded on the 14th of November 1872.

Sir *Arthur Guinness*—continued.

3889. What led to the establishment of the sanitary association?—The association was established in consequence of a number of gentlemen meeting to consider what the cause of the very unsatisfactory state of the public health was, and the general non-sanitary state of the houses of the poor people, and the different sanitary defects through the city. We were founded with the objects which are mentioned in the association's reports, of which I beg to hand in a set (*delivering in the same*).

3890. Will you explain what the objects were?—The objects of the association are, "First, to create an educated public opinion with regard to sanitary matters in general; secondly, direct the attention of the authorities and the public to those points in which the existing powers for the maintenance of the sanitary condition of the city, are either not duly exercised or are inadequate, or in which the machinery at the disposal of the sanitary authorities is insufficient; thirdly, to watch the course of sanitary legislation on behalf of the public; and fourthly, to form a body in which the public may have confidence, and through which they may, if necessary, act." Those are the objects of the society.

3891. What are the numbers of the association?—I refer you to these four pamphlets; the first is a preliminary report made by the provisional committee, the other three are the annual reports of the association. The number of members of the association was 272 at the end of last year, and it is more at present; the year will terminate to-morrow, so that I cannot tell you exactly without referring to the secretary of the society, but the number at this time last year was 272.

3892. What is the subscription, or how is it supported?—It is supported by subscriptions, which are not less than 10 *s.*; a good many people subscribe more than that, but the regular subscription is not less than 10*s.*

3893. What was the amount of subscriptions last year?—£. 144 *l.* 13*s.*, according to the treasurer's accounts.

3894. You have been examined as an expert on sanitary matters, have you not?—Yes, I have on several occasions; I was employed once by the

Sir *Arthur Guinness*—continued.

the Dublin corporation in the case of the water works inquiry to examine into the sanitary condition of Roundwood, and to report upon it to the corporation. I was examined then before the Local Government Board Inspector in conjunction with the corporation officers, and with another gentleman, Dr. J. W. Moore. Then I was again employed by some of the inhabitants of the Pembroke township to report on the cause of complaint there which, I believe, is about being remedied in accordance with my recommendations; and I have been employed several times to make special sanitary reports for different journals, and things of that sort.

3895. Are you personally acquainted with the unhealthy portions of Dublin?—Yes, I am. I have visited a great number of them.

3896. From your investigation of the vital statistics of Dublin, what opinion have you formed as to the health of the city?—I have formed a very unfavourable opinion of the health of the city, as compared with other towns similarly situated. On comparing the vital statistics of Dublin and the causes of death with other towns in the United Kingdom, I find that Dublin compares very unfavourably with other large towns; those 23 towns for which the weekly returns are specially made up by the Registrar General of England, and which also includes Dublin and some of the Scotch towns; Dublin compared with those towns is decidedly unfavourable. My opinions coincide with those expressed in a report on the sanitary condition of Dublin, by Dr. Burke, who is at present Assistant Registrar General for Ireland. He is a permanent officer, and is Medical Superintendent of Statistics at the General Registration Office, and he has authorised me to make use of these figures. The report was originally printed as a private document, but it has since been published in part (*handing in same*).

3897. What does it show the death rate to be?—This report shows the death rate for the Dublin district as 26·4 per 1,000. The death rate for the city, continuing Dr. Burke's report up to the present, is 28·4 per 1,000 per annum. But, according to the census returns, the death rate calculated by the burials in the Dublin cemeteries of persons who lived in Dublin at the time of their death, the rate of mortality is 31 per 1,000.

3898. How does that compare with the English statistics of towns similarly circumstanced?—The death rate for the London Registration District during the same period is 23·6; those are the registered death rates; the death rate for the western district of London is 21·8; the death rate for the central district of London is 25·; and the death rate for the eastern districts of London is 26·3 for that period. For the city of Edinburgh it is 25·; for Glasgow it is 30·2; for Liverpool it is 31·4 (that is a little higher than the Dublin rate); for Manchester 31·, and for Salford 28·7; that is an average of 10 years.

3899. What is the proportion of deaths from zymotic diseases in Dublin out of the entire number?—It is about the average of the other large towns, that is to say, about 22 per cent.; but it is very much raised in particular years. An average in this case is scarcely fair, for it is very much raised by cholera and small-pox epidemics.

3900. During epidemics, is the death rate in Dublin higher than in the other large cities?—It has been raised more in proportion than other large towns, and this is shown in Dr. Burke's return, in which he says: "The per-centage of deaths from zymotic diseases in Dublin district for the 10 years 1864–73, was 22·6, and for the nine years 1865–73, it was 23·1." (I may say that Dr. Burke leaves out the first year of registration where he takes the nine years, because it was in a preliminary stage in 1864.) "For the same periods the per-centage of deaths from zymotic diseases was higher in London than in Dublin, namely, 25·2 and 25·1. The average death rate from zymotic disease per 1,000 of the population of Dublin was 5·9 in the 10 years, and 6·1 in the nine years, against 6·1 and 6·0 in London for the same periods. On a further examination of the Tables II. and III., attention will at once be arrested by the figures, which show the greater mortality from epidemics in Dublin than in London. Thus, when cholera visited the two cities, in the year 1866, the per-centage of deaths from zymotic diseases in Dublin was 31·3, in London 29·4; the zymotic death rate per 1,000 inhabitants was in Dublin 9·0 and in London 7·8. Again, during the epidemic of small-pox in the years 1872 (in Dublin), and 1871 (in London), the per-centage of deaths from zymotic diseases was in Dublin 29·2 against 28·3 in London. The zymotic death rate per 1,000 inhabitants was in Dublin 8·4, and in London 7·0."

Mr. *T. W. Grimshaw*, M.D.

30 May 1876.

3901. Does the density of the population in Dublin account for this state of things?—No, the density of the population in Dublin, per acre, is lower than that in many of those large towns which I have quoted. The density of the population in the city of Dublin is 64·7 per acre.

3902. Have you read Dr. Cameron's report on the Fallacies in the Mode of Calculating the Death Rate?—Yes, I have. His object in writing that report on the fallacies was to show that a great number of the persons who die in Dublin are persons who come from the surrounding districts, and are admitted into the public institutions and hospitals of different kinds, and die there. The deaths of these in Dublin would reduce the mortality exactly by the same amount as there are deaths unregistered. The death rate of Dublin, 31 per 1,000, is partially due to the deaths of persons from the surrounding districts, who die in the public institutions and hospitals. These amount to not more than, for the hospitals, 374; lunatic asylums, 57; prisons, 12; workhouses, 310; total, 753. These numbers are estimated; there is no published return for them, or even a return available; the numbers are estimated by the population that supply these institutions; that is assuming, what is not strictly correct, that the country districts supply the same proportion of sick people as the town districts. It is well known that they supply less; but in making an estimate of this sort, it was considered right to take them at the same rate; and those altogether make 753; and that is almost identical with the number of deaths unregistered, so that it still leaves a death rate of 28·4, which is higher than the average of the towns referred to.

3903. Is the health of Dublin more easily affected by severe weather than any other towns?—It is. The death rate of Dublin during the first quarter of the present year was higher than that of any other town in the United Kingdom, except Salford, and the weather was less severe in

Mr. T. W. Grimshaw, M.D.

30 May 1876.

Sir *Arthur Guinness*—continued.

in Dublin than it was in any other town in the United Kingdom, with one or two exceptions. It was much more wet and cold in Salford than it was in Dublin.

3904. Do you attribute this to the unfavourable natural condition of Dublin?—No; I consider that the natural situation of Dublin is favourable to good health; it is a very open town; it is near the sea and near the mountains, and the density of the population is low. There is only one part of Dublin that is naturally situated in an unhealthy spot, and that is the part lying on low ground towards the north river, which is situated in a gravel bed, and is difficult to drain. The other parts of the city are favourably situated.

3905. To what do you attribute the high death rate?—I believe that the high mortality of Dublin depends upon the want of ordinary sanitary precautions.

3906. What are the sanitary precautions taken in Dublin with respect to organisation and control, and such things as that?—The sanitary organisation in Dublin consists of a secretary, who is styled the Executive Sanitary Officer of Dublin, a consulting sanitary officer, the combined offices, medical officers of health, and city analyst. Then there are 14 dispensary medical officers, who are employed as medical sanitary officers; and there are besides these, nine sanitary serjeants, and there were until very recently, I believe they have been withdrawn, four or five persons employed as detectors of unsound meat; and there is a clerk, an assistant to the secretary. That is the sanitary staff of the city.

3907. Under whose control is that staff?—It is under the control of a committee of the corporation, called the Public Health Committee.

3908. When was that committee first appointed?—That committee was appointed in the year 1866, and it was re-appointed after the passing of the Public Health Act, towards the end of 1874.

3909. How was that committee chosen?—I believe it is composed, according to the statement in "Thom's Directory," of one alderman, and one town councillor from each ward of the city.

3910. Has the Public Health Act of 1874 made any difference in the management of sanitary affairs?—No, the matters are pretty much the same as they were before it; and the officers are the same with the exception of the addition of the dispensary medical officers; the constitution of the sub-committee of the corporation is the same. I believe the plan of putting on of one alderman and one town councillor for each ward was modified, when the committee were re-appointed; there was some conversation about modifying it, and I believe that it was modified, but the management appears to be carried on precisely the same as it was then, so far as I can ascertain.

3911. Do you consider that that committee discharges its duties satisfactorily?—No, I do not.

3912. Have there been many complaints in Dublin concerning the conduct of this committee, in the press, or elsewhere?—I think that all the newspapers have complained of the sanitary management of the city, especially the "Freeman's Journal," because the newspapers have employed special reporters, and people of that

Sir *Arthur Guinness*—continued.

kind, to look after those matters, and investigate them. The "Freeman's Journal," in 1874, employed a medical gentleman to go round to a number of places and make reports. There were a number of those reports published, and articles appeared in the paper each day concerning the report of the previous day, and they were very unfavourable; they blamed the Public Health Committee very much for not having carried out the ordinary sanitary arrangements of the city. The "Mail" also employed a gentleman to go about at night and inspect some of those places. Some years ago (this was a good while ago), "Saunder's News Letter" sent a reporter, with a request that I would go with him and show him some of the places that were complained of, but the other reports are quite recent.

3913. Could you give any short extracts from the articles in those newspapers?—There are a great mass of them.

3914. I understand that there were very strong comments in the "Freeman's Journal," and other newspapers?—The "Freeman's Journal" spoke of the committee as the "So-called Public Health Committee;" that was one of the strongest expression that they made use of.

3915. In what sanitary state are the Liberties of Dublin?—They are in an extremely filthy state; great accumulations of filth in every possible direction, both in the streets, in the houses, and in the yards belonging to the houses.

3916. Do you think that the scavenging of Dublin is well done, and sufficient?—I think that it is very badly done, especially in the poorer parts of the city.

3917. Are there any accumulations of filth in the streets?—In the poor parts there are. It is the habit of the poor people to cast out a great deal of rubbish into the streets; that is in consequence of their not having facilities for removing it from their houses; and if they kept it it would be more injurious to the public health than throwing it into the streets, and consequently they cast it into the streets in great quantities, partly to avoid the accumulation, and partly because they have no place to put it in on their own premises.

3918. Is there any system of domestic scavenging in Dublin?—No, there is no system of domestic scavenging as it is understood by sanitarians. The mode of cleaning ash-pits and privies in Dublin is generally to employ a private ash-pit cleaner. The corporation have a small department for cleaning ash-pits and privies, but they charge for doing it, which is contrary to the practice in other towns, and the charge is 6 *s.* for the first two loads of stuff removed, and 2 *s.* 6 *d.* for every load afterwards. The result of this charge is, that the work can be done cheaper by private ash-pit cleaners, so that the citizens generally employ them. There is no system of house-to-house cleansing as there is in large towns in England.

3919. But is there not some provision for domestic scavenging in the Public Health Act of 1874?—Yes; there is power in the Public Health Act for the Local Government Board to make an order that arrangements shall be made for regular scavenging, and there is power to enforce a fine on the sanitary authority if they do not do so. The Local Government Board have not issued an order of that sort for Dublin.

3920. Have you made any calculations of the

cost

Mr. T. W. Grimshaw, M.D.

30 May 1876.

Sir *Arthur Guinness*—continued.

cost of this public domestic scavenging at the present rates?—The Public Health Committee issued an order some years ago which is in force still; this order was issued on the 1st of September 1871, and requires that all the ash-pits and privies of all houses inhabited by the members of more than one family, in those tenement houses of Dublin, shall be cleaned once a month regularly. There are 9,000 of those tenement houses, and at the rate of 6 s. for cleansing each of them, it would cost something like 30,000 *l.* a year to do the work, and the result is that the order is practically useless; it is not carried out; it cannot be done. It does not cost as much in any English town that I am aware of, or anything like it; but that only includes tenement houses, and a sum very nearly equal to that would have to be added for private houses, which would bring it up to something like 50,000 *l.* or 60,000 *l.* a year paid by the citizens for ash-pit cleansing, at the rates which are charged now, this is a very heavy cost to the city.

3921. Then that order is practically a dead letter?—It is.

3922. Has the sanitary association had any communication with the corporation upon this subject?—Yes; in the fourth of those reports, at page 28, the sanitary association wrote to the Local Government Board asking them to enforce the provision of the Act of 1874, which compels the corporation to undertake the domestic scavenging; there was a correspondence about it, and the corporation stated that they had made arrangements for doing this although they denied the necessity for any better arrangements, and the result was that the Local Government Board did not make any order upon the matter; that will be found at page 28 of the Report, marked No. 4; the Report for 1874.

Chairman.

3923. Can you tell us why the Local Government Board did not make an order about it?—Apparently, they did not make an order in consequence of the statement of the Public Health Committee, and that statement of the Public Health Committee was founded on the opinion of one single member of that committee, who was appointed to report upon the subject.

Sir *Arthur Guinness.*

3924. Has your attention been called to the state of the corporation scavenging depôts?—It has. I have visited all of them; there are three principal depôts; there is one situated at the rear of North Brunswick-street; there is another situated in Marrowbone-lane; another one situated in Clanbrassil-street, between Clanbrassil-street and Black Pits. They are, probably, the greatest nuisances that there are in Dublin. I have visited them within the last 10 days, and the stuff in those yards is piled up until it reaches the height of the first floor windows; you can stand on the top of one of those heaps and look into the first floor windows of the houses around, and they overlook the roofs of some cottages that are below the level of the heap; this is a very offensive nuisance indeed, and is a thing that would not be tolerated, I think, almost anywhere else. The result of that accumulation in those yards is, that when the Public Health Committee have endeavoured to prosecute private scavengers for collecting the manure in precisely the same way, the magistrates have declined to enforce the penalty, on the ground that the prosecutors were greater offenders than the persons who were prosecuted.

3925. Have frequent proceedings been taken by the corporation with respect to other yards?—Yes, proceedings have been taken with regard to other yards; notably, the yards situated in a place called M'Clean's-lane; and another place called Cole Alley; and another place on the north side of the town; I forget its name at present. With regard to those two places, actions were brought against the proprietors of them, and the defence set up by the ash pit cleaners was, that their nuisances were insignificant compared with the nuisances maintained in the corporation depôts, and there is no doubt that that was the case; they were perfectly right.

3926. And the magistrates agreed with them?—In the case on the north side of the town, the magistrates declined to interfere, and one of the magistrates expressed the very great difficulty he had in dealing with cases of this sort so long as the corporation depôts were maintained in the present condition.

3927. Are they in that condition at present?—They were the week before last, when I was in three of them.

3928. Can you mention, with regard to these private scavenging depôts, have the corporation recognised their existence on condition that the materials collected there were deodorised and disinfected?—Yes, and the people promise to do it, but nothing of the kind is done. It was stated that it should be mixed with dry earth, or with dry road sweepings. I went to see how this was done, and instead of dry earth, or dry ashes, or dry road sweepings, they were mixing it with stuff which they got from the corporation depôts themselves; the corporation depôt stuff was quite unfit, requiring deodorising and disinfecting quite as much as the stuff which was in the private yards.

3929. Could you give us some account of the general condition of the tenement houses of Dublin?—I have visited a great number of those houses; I made lists of the houses from whence the patients came to the Fever Hospital, and in that way I made a list of about 1,700 houses. I selected, first of all, those that furnished the most cases, and then those that furnished a number in a less degree, and then those that had furnished one or two cases. I visited a great number of them; I could not say how many, but I know that I visited a great many hundreds of them. They are generally in a most filthy condition. The houses are nearly always in bad repair, and the ash-pits and privies connected with them in a most frightful condition, totally unfit for use. The ash-pits are generally connected with what are called cess-pit privies, which are where the fluid sewage and refuse stuff is all left together, and there is not sufficient solid dry matter to neutralise the bad effect; the result is that those places are generally filled or half filled with semi-fluid matter, which is most offensive. In a pamphlet which I wrote some years ago on the prevalence and distribution of fever in Dublin, I described some of those houses. I have also made out a fever map, which I will hand in to the Committee (*delivering the same*). The worst case was No. 36, Chancery-lane, and that house is in precisely the same condition as it was when I reported it to the Public Health Committee in October

Mr. *T. W. Grimshaw*, M.D.

30 May 1876.

Sir *Arthur Guinness*—continued.

October 1871. After my report, the place, I believe, was closed; but it was allowed to be re-opened, and is just in the same filthy state as it was then. A number of these houses I have visited, and found in a most disgraceful condition.

Mr. *Corry*.

3930. Can you tell us who the owner of that property is?—I cannot say that; I do not know the owners of many of those places.

Mr. *Collins*.

3931. You have been referring to some houses as "these houses;" what houses do you mean?—The houses that I mentioned at first; those houses from whence the fever patients come to the Fever Hospital; I said that I catalogued about 1,700, and I visited all the worst; there were a great number of them that were not the very worst, but there were a large number of them congregated together.

3932. You mean by "these houses" the 1,700 houses that you were speaking of?—Yes.

Sir *Arthur Guinness*.

3933. I understand that those are the houses from which numerous patients in fever have been brought to the hospitals?—Yes; as I stated, I took down the addresses of those patients, and arranged them and mapped them out, and I visited a large number of those houses which are marked with those red dots upon the map. In every house that I visited there were accumulations of filth, and there was over-crowding, and the places were dirty and rotten to the utmost degree.

Chairman.

3934. Could you tell us where that principally prevailed?—It principally prevailed inside the circle which is marked upon the map, as the old boundary of the city of 1610. It is within that circle that the worst of those places are. The houses there could not be kept in order except by constant supervision and almost weekly visits from the sanitary inspectors. I selected some of those places that I visited in the year 1871. I took them at random, and I made a list of all the places that I had ever reported to the Sanitary Association and the Public Health Committee. I carried the list about in my pocket for the last fortnight in my walks through the town, and without going specially to visit any houses, when I came across any of the places marked on my list I visited them; a great number of them are in precisely the same state as they were when I reported them in 1871 to the Public Health Committee.

Sir *Arthur Guinness*.

3935. Do you think that there has been practically no improvement in the sanitary state of those houses?—Practically, there is no improvement since I began to look after them.

3936. Has that been for five years?—I gave that date, five years, because that is the time that I brought them under the notice of the Public Health Committee. In this pamphlet there are two lists printed of the places that I then reported to the Public Health Committee.

Mr. *Brooks*.

3937. Do you mean that there is no improvement in the condition of the fabric, or their sanitary condition?—In neither the one nor the other; but certainly not in the sanitary condition of the houses since I sent those two lists in to the Public Health Committee, with very few exceptions. There are some houses on that list which have absolutely been cleared away; those those two lists include 120 houses. I visited all of them from time to time. I visited 50 or 60 houses within the past days, which I had previously reported to the Public Health Committee.

Sir *Arthur Guinness*.

3938. Have you seen the regulations issued by the Public Health Committee with regard to tenement houses?—I have. I have referred to them already when I spoke of cleansing the ash-pits once a month.

3939. Have you ever been present when any corporation surveyors were examining those houses?—Yes, I have on several occasions been with the sanitary inspectors and the police inspectors when they have been going their rounds. They are very civil men, and very well inclined to do their work, apparently. But on two or three occasions I have brought one of those men to what I considered the most glaring nuisances, and places which had been reported by the Sanitary Association as nuisances; and I remember very distinctly at this moment that in two or three instances the sanitary serjeant said that the "Public Health Committee" would not consider that a cause for complaint. One of those instances was an immense ash-pit with a privy attached to it close to the back door of the house, and my notice was attracted to it by the smell in the street as I passed the front door. I went into it and looked about, and reported it to the Sanitary Association. We sent a report in the usual way, but there was nothing done. We went again and there was nothing done, and we went a third time, and on the third occasion we happened to meet the inspector in the street and we brought him in and showed it to him. There was another medical man with me at the time, and the inspector said that "the committee" did not consider that a cause for complaint; but it was a fearful nuisance.

Mr. *Collins*.

3940. In what state was that house at that time?—There was a great nuisance in the shape of a privy and ash-pit close to the back door of the house full of semi-fluid matter and very offensive, bubbling up under the sun in summer time; it was so bad that we smelt it when passing in the street in front of the house, and when we brought the sanitary inspector to it he said that there was no use in his reporting it, that "the committee did not consider it a cause for complaint."

Sir *Arthur Guinness*.

3941. Did he give any other reason?—He gave no other reason.

3942. Upon any occasion?—No, upon no occasion. We have frequent cases of this sort at the Sanitary Association. We send forward an account of a nuisance of this kind, and the answer we get back is that it is "no cause for complaint." Another instance was in a house in James's

Mr. *T. W. Grimshaw*, M.D.

30 May 1876.

Sir *Arthur Guinness*—continued.

James's-street; a very good house indeed; but there was one of those wretchedly constructed places just at the back of the house, and the smell passed up through the whole place. The tenants complained to me. I went to that house in consequence of going to see some poor people there in connection with our hospital, and the people all complained and asked me could not I get something done for them. I reported the case to the Public Health Committee (through the Sanitary Association); and the answer that we received was that it was "no cause for complaint," although every one was complaining of it. The sanitary serjeant, I am told, had visited it; what report he made I do not know, but we would not leave that case; we went on until we tired out the Public Health Committee, and they took away the privy and ash-pit altogether, thereby admitting that it was a cause for complaint. They tried to deny it at first, but they admitted it afterwards.

3943. Do you think that the sanitary staff is large enough?—I do not think that the inspectorial staff is nearly large enough.

3944. Are there any difficulties in the way in consequence of the state of the law, such as serving notices?—There is a complaint made by the inspectors themselves to me. When I have said, Cannot you visit this place, and cannot you look it up now and then, they say that their time is all occupied in serving notices, and that they wanted a great many more hands to do the inspecting and the notice serving both. I have brought with me the notices which it is necessary legally should be all gone through before you can finally punish a person for creating a nuisance of this sort (*delivering in the same*).

Mr. *Collins*.

3945. Are all those notices required in each case?—If a person abates the nuisance on the first notice, there would be no further notice required, but my experience in talking to these men is, that a great many require all these notices served.

3946. Do you mean in an individual case?—Yes, in an individual case, all excepting the last, which is a notice for imprisonment; they never go so far as that, I believe.

3947. If they do not act upon the ultimate one, what is the result?—The ultimate one is a warrant for their apprehension, and he is, I believe, detained until he pays fines and costs. In order to get the inspectorial work done, which cannot be done as it is with these notices, it would require a very much larger number of inspectors than there are as yet.

Sir *Arthur Guinness*.

3948. Do you think that the want of vigorous action on the part of the Public Health Committee, encourages the owners of tenement houses to violate the law in this way?—I do; I think they calculate upon this fining process never being carried out. When you ask the people in the houses, "Have you complained about this?" they tell you that they have, and when you ask why it has not been remedied, the answer invariably is, "Oh, the owner or the landlord, or the house-jobber says that he knows very well that those will not be carried out to the extremity, and that he will not abate the nuisance." That, of course, is hearsay, but the fact is that the nuisances are not abated.

Mr. *Collins*.

3949. Do you know of your own knowledge, that those facts really exist?—Yes, I have been and seen it in some cases, and I have heard of warrants being issued.

3950. And that persons have been actually imprisoned?—I do not know of any one being actually imprisoned; I cannot recollect a case; but I believe one or two people have been imprisoned, but it would be very few. For instance, I know a case, one of the most glaring instances of all, and that was a manure yard in which the notices were served, and everything was done except the arrest of the person; and all those notices were gone through to abate the nuisance; there was a fine of 10 s. a day ordered to be inflicted, but the fine was never levied, and the nuisance is there still, and has been there to my knowledge for 11 years.

3951. To what do you attribute that feeling of immunity from the influence of the law on the part of people who refuse to abate those nuisances?—They think that the thing will never be pushed to its extremity.

3952. Why do they think so?—That is their experience.

Sir *Arthur Guinness*.

3953. Do you consider that any advantage has resulted from the action of the Sanitary Association?—I do; but it has only been by the most persistent work in particular instances. We have got a number of things remedied by persistent work, but the number is inconsiderable compared with the number of reports that we have made.

3954. Are the slaughter-houses in a proper sanitary condition in Dublin?—No, they are not.

3955. Have any new licenses been granted for slaughter-houses within the city, in your recollection?—I do not know very much about granting licenses, but there was one remarkable instance in which a complaint was made by the inhabitants of North King-street, that a slaughter-house was going to be licensed next door to a bakery in a very confined place. The Sanitary Association took up the question, and after carrying on the discussion of it for some time, the slaughter-house was finally licensed next door to a bakery in a crowded neighbourhood, within about 30 feet of the windows of the dwelling houses. Another case occurred close to one of the hospitals with which I am connected, the Cork-street Hospital. There was an application made there for a slaughter-house license; this place was exactly opposite a Methodist church, and it was close to the Cork-street Hospital, and within 20 yards of a number of houses. The people in the neighbourhood protested against it, the hospital authorities protested against it, and the people of the church protested against it, and the Sanitary Association had a letter from the Public Health Committee, stating that the Public Health Committee had recommended that the license should be granted because more people had signed memorials, saying that it would not be a nuisance than those who had signed the memorial, stating that it would be. That was the ground that they alleged. The license has not yet been issued, but they have not declined to issue it.

3956. Did they make any inquiry into the facts on the spot?—Yes; a member of the Public Health Committee visited the place, and he said (this

Mr. T. W. Grimshaw, M.D.

30 May 1876.

Sir Arthur Guinness—continued.

(this is in a newspaper report) that the place itself was as clean a place as he had ever seen, and very fit for slaughter-houses.

3957. Have you visited any of them, and found them in an improper state?—Yes, I visited many of them at the end of the week before last in the immediate vicinity of South King street. The slaughter-houses belong to some of the butchers in Clarendon Market, which is a very narrow confined place. There is one slaughter-house there almost against the back wall of a large tenement house in South King-street, and it was in full working order. The blood was running out of the doorway and down the gutter in the street into Johnson's-place, opposite the Mercer's Hospital, and out into a lane in the neighbourhood, called Clarendon-row. This is a very great nuisance, and has been complained of by the people there. I saw also two other slaughter-houses quite close to this in full work. It is not only injurious to the health of the public in that way, but one very disagreeable feature is, that a number of children always crowd around those slaughter-houses. In these places, where they were killing sheep, there was a crowd of little children, from five years old up to ten, watching the process of killing those animals, and seeing the meat cut up, and all that sort of thing. I believe that that has had a very bad moral effect upon the young people in the neighbourhood.

3958. Do you think it bad for children?—I do, decidedly. I think it is very injurious to them, both physically and morally.

3959. Are there any public abattoirs in Dublin?—No, there are not.

3960. Have the corporation any power to build them?—They have.

3961. Under Act of Parliament?—They have power under an Act which they obtained themselves, the Dublin Improvement Act, as well as I remember.

3962. Have you visited any of the dairy yards in Dublin?—I have, a great many of them. They are in an extremely filthy condition. They have large accumulations of manure. Those are very much like the private scavenging depôts that I mentioned. They pile up this manure till it sometimes reaches above the walls of the yards. There have been great complaints about those yards, especially where they are near public institutions. The authorities of Mercer's Hospital, for instance, complain that there is a dairy yard situated next to the hospital, and large accumulations of manure take place in that yard; I have seen it myself. There are some 60 head of cattle kept there. It is very injurious to the hospital, and very injurious to the health of the animals, and consequently to the milk, and so on. The Public Health Committee inspected that yard, but the only action that was taken, was that the proprietor agreed to keep the manure a little further from the hospital than it had previously been kept. The dairyman promised that he would have it removed more frequently than he had previously done, but that would not abate the nuisance. And at the Richmond Hospital, the Government Hospital in North Brunswick-street, they have large dairy yards on both sides, and they complain very much of it there; and in the same way in a great many crowded neighbourhoods through the city. In many English towns a licence is required for a dairy yard within a borough.

Mr. Butt.

3963. What could be done with those dairy-yards under the powers of the corporation?—They could be dealt with as nuisances, and injurious to health, just in the same way as an accumulation of manure from any other cause.

Sir Arthur Guinness.

3964. Have any means been adopted by the Public Health Committee to guard against the spread of contagion?—Very slight. The plan pursued is, that when they hear of an outbreak of disease they visit and disinfect the place; they have a disinfecting chamber in one of the corporation depôts, where clothing can be sent to be disinfected by heat. Practically, the disinfecting chamber is so difficult to get things both to and from that it is hardly ever used. I had an outbreak of scarlatina in my own house, and I wanted my things disinfected, but I could not find out how my things were to be got to or from this disinfecting chamber. I referred to the place where I was directed, and I was told that there was a conveyance to be had; I went there, and I asked for the conveyance, and I was told that there was only one conveyance to bring the things to and from the disinfecting chamber, so that if I had sent them to be disinfected they would have been just as bad when they came back, having been brought back in the same van in which they had been conveyed. I was informed it was not in the power of the corporation, or rather, it was kept by a man called Flynn, who kept it for the corporation, and that he had to be paid by me for using it. I declined to pay a person who was not a regular official of the corporation anything, and I wrote to the Public Health Committee, and in a week afterwards I got an answer to say that the proper person to pay was the city treasurer, a thing which it was very difficult to find out. After all this work it was ascertained that the city treasurer would receive the money for the use of this conveyance for disinfecting purposes, which no person who knew anything of the subject would ever dream of allowing things to go into, because they would come back in exactly the same state as they went, or very nearly so.

3965. Is there a proper conveyance provided for the removal of patients suffering from infectious diseases?—No, there is not. The corporation at present possess only one old cab, which is quite unsuitable for the purpose, and it is very difficult to get hold of. The corporation rule is that if a certificate from a medical man is sent to this same person whom I mentioned with regard to the disinfecting van, he will get this cab for him. The process is this: the cab is kept in one part of the town and the horse in another. You apply to the man who keeps the horse, and he has then to bring it to the cab. It is not so far as it used to be; it used to be two miles off where the cab was kept, from the place where the horse was kept. However, the Sanitary Association made a piece of work about it, and finally the cab was brought somewhat nearer the horse. It is only about a quarter of a mile off now. The cab now is kept in one yard about a quarter of a mile distant or so, perhaps a little over a quarter of a mile off where the horse is kept. You take the order for the cab to the man who keeps the horse, and he gets the horse out and brings it to the cab, and then he goes for the patient and brings the patient to the hospital. This is the only

Mr. T. W. Grimshaw, M.D.

30 May 1876.

Sir *Arthur Guinness*—continued.

only conveyance and the only way of working it that the corporation have for the conveyance of the sick.

Mr. *Butt.*

3966. Then the cab and the horse do not belong to the same person?—The cab belongs to the corporation, and the horse is hired by the job. Although the corporation keep a large number of horses, they do not use them for those purposes. The corporation issued a card with regard to this use of conveyances, in which they stated that a number of cabs were available for the conveyance of patients to the hospital. This card also stated that there were cabs kept at the two unions, and that there was a cab kept at the Cork-street Hospital, which could be obtained on a moment's notice for the conveyance of patients to the hospital. This card, which was circulated largely through the town, led to a great deal of confusion. Those other cabs, beyond the one I mentioned first, are not available; they seem to belong to the north and the south union guardians, and are only available for the conveyance of persons belonging to the union; that is to say sick paupers, or for the conveyance of paupers to the union who are infirm and not able to walk. Then there is a cab kept at the Cork-street Hospital, but that is only for patients who have got orders for admission into the hospital. Being connected with the Cork-street Hospital, I can speak from personal experience with regard to this. We have had a number of applications from persons to use this cab to take patients to other hospitals; if that was allowed it would take up the whole time and we should not be able to convey our own patients: that was in consequence of the card issued by the Public Health Committee, which was altogether misleading. There was a deputation of the Sanitary Association, and a committee appointed to investigate this question; they went to all those places and made inquiries, and the result of the inquiry was that there was only one cab, and that was kept by the corporation in this way, as I tell you, separate from the horse, and the cab itself is not fit for use.

Sir *Arthur Guinness.*

3967. Is there a regular tariff of payment for the use of this cab?—There is not; there is a sum paid for the use of the horse by the corporation to this man for the hire of the horse; what that is I do not exactly know, but I am aware that demands to the amount of 10*s.* have been made by the man for conveying patients.

3968. When you were told to apply to the city treasurer, were you told what his charge was?—Yes, I was; but that was with regard to the disinfecting arrangements.

3969. What was that charge?—It is in this report. The way I got this information was this: finding that I could not obtain information by applying to this man Flynn, I first of all called twice at the Public Health Committee's Office, but could not find any one there. There was no person in charge of the place. I then wrote to Mr. Boyle, the Secretary of the Public Health Committee, and I told him that I called at his office, and not finding him, I went to him in the first instance at head-quarters, so that I took the proper course about it, and then I went to this Mr. Flynn. Mr. Flynn was not there either. I saw, I believe, his wife, who keeps a dairy shop in one of those lanes. I asked who I was to pay for it, and I was told I was to pay Flynn. I declined to pay him as he was not a corporation officer in any way. I thought myself that there was no charge made for it. I then wrote to Mr. Boyle, telling him all those facts. I wrote to him on the 21st of April, and on the 24th of April I got his answer, in which was contained the scale of charges, and the rules adopted by the Public Health Committee, which I was told are these: "That the scale of charges recommended be adopted and charged to all persons able to pay for the disinfection of their property," and "That such persons should also pay for the removal of their property to and from the disinfecting chamber." I acknowledged that letter, but the first letter did not contain a scale of charges at all; it was sent afterwards. I put in that letter of mine the following queries: "(1.) Where can I obtain in a convenient form a copy of the rules with regard to the disinfection of infected dwellings and clothing, and a list of the scale of charges referred to in Rule 15 of your letter of the 24th instant." The answer to that is: "List of charges sent herewith," and here they are: "Who is the authority which decides the question as to whether or not the person applying to have his goods disinfected at the expense of the city is or is not able to pay." The answer to that is, "The relieving officer or the sanitary serjeant of the district." Then I ask: "(3.) Does the corporation keep vehicles for the use of the citizens (with or without payment) for the conveyance of articles to and from the disinfecting chamber." Their answer to that was "Yes." The statement about vehicles I put in advisedly. The answer "Yes," so far as I have found out, is not true, for I could never find out another vehicle. "(4.) If payment for the use of the disinfecting chamber and for the conveyance of infected articles to and from the chamber is to be made, at what office, and to what officer of the corporation is application to be made and the money paid." The answer is: "The city treasurer."

Mr. *Brooks.*

3970. Surely if the corporation provided vehicles to bring infected articles of clothing to the disinfecting chamber, you do not expect that they also should also discharge the owners of the property from the duty of taking those articles which have been disinfected home?—That is the very question which I put to them; I said, "To and from the disinfecting chamber," and the answer was that they do.

3971. Surely it is not the duty of the corporation to carry disinfected articles about, after they have been disinfected?—They told me that it was; I did it to find out what was really done; but poor people could not pay for the conveyance of those things.

3972. They might fetch them away themselves, might they not?—They might, but the rule is that the corporation bring them to and from, and this is the way they do it.

Chairman.

3973. How do you mean a rule; are the corporation compelled by law to bring them to and from, or by bye-law?—By bye-law.

3974. What bye-law?—I cannot answer what bye-law, but it is one of their own rules which had

Mr. T. W. Grimshaw, M.D.

30 May 1876.

Chairman—continued.

had been sent to me. If you look at page 47 of the Report No. 3, you will see that I endeavoured to find out how this was to be done; first of all by calling upon the secretary, and then I wrote to the secretary, and the secretary in reply to the queries which I sent gives me this answer: that the corporation do keep vehicles for the removal of clothing to and from the disinfecting chamber.

Mr. *Brooks.*

3975. Is the word "vehicles," in the plural, his word or yours?—It is mine, but the words "to and from," are put in; here is my question, "Does the corporation keep vehicles for the use of the citizens (with or without payment) for the conveyance of articles to and from the disinfecting chamber?" And their answer to that query is, "Yes:" and their Rule 15 is, that persons who can afford to pay shall be expected to do so. And then, finally, they tell me that the price for conveyance to and from the disinfecting chamber is 5 *s.*, it says, "for the double journey." Here is their answer: "When parties are able to pay for the removal of articles requiring disinfection, the committee lend their vehicle; and the party using it should pay the contractor for horsing the amount he charges to the corporation, viz., 5 *s.* for the double journey."

3976. That means, that if persons having had their bundle of clothing, large or small, which may not require a vehicle, do not choose to send for it, they will put on extra charge and send it for 5 *s.*?—There is nothing about a person being willing or unwilling, or anything else in the matter.

3977. It is implied that if those persons will not come for them, the corporation will send them back?—As a matter of fact what is done everywhere else is, that there are two vehicles kept for the purpose, one for bringing them to, and the other for bringing them from the disinfecting chamber; that is the rule in Liverpool and elsewhere. I would not have minded myself; with reference to bringing those things back, I could have got the thing done, but I thought that I would test their arrangement, and I did it on purpose to test their arrangements.

Chairman.

3978. Are you aware, from your own knowledge, that other sanitary authorities convey the articles to and from the disinfecting chamber?—Yes; I am aware that it is done in Liverpool. It was considered such an extraordinary thing that it was noticed in several medical journals two or three years ago. It was written on by the "British Medical Journal," as one of the most extraordinary things that they ever met with.

Sir *Arthur Guinness.*

3979. Do you know of any case of children suffering from scarlatina, being removed in street cabs?—I do of several. For instance, at a place on the north side of Dublin, there were 16 children, suffering from scarlatina, brought in ordinary cabs. There were three cabs employed for the purpose of bringing them to the Hardwick Hospital; there were several children brought to the Meath Hospital from a charity school with measles, and there were children with scarlatina brought within the last couple of months to Cork-street Hospital in a cab, and we got the cabman reported in that instance, but it was

Sir *Arthur Guinness*—continued.

our own doing altogether. The fact of the matter is, that the public do not consider that those cabs are to be had from the authorities, so that they will not take the trouble to send for them.

3980. Therefore those school authorities were forced to take street cabs?—They were not absolutely forced, but they thought that the arrangements would break down, so that they tried the other plan. We had another instance of this kind; there was a gentleman called upon me, a clergyman, to ask me for an order for the corporation cab to remove a patient to one of the hospitals. This clergyman knew nothing about the difficulty of obtaining the cab; I did not tell him anything about it; I did not tell him that he probably would not get it; but I wrote him an order, and he took it to this Mr. Flynn at Bass-place. He asked Mr. Flynn could he get a cab to bring a patient to the hospital; this was about eight in the evening. "No," said Mr. Flynn, "it is very late; I would have to bring the horse two miles across the city to get the cab, and by nine it will be so late, that it will be too late for admission to the hospital." That is the answer he gave. We complained to the Public Health Committee of Mr. Flynn's conduct in this matter, and the answer we got was that the clergyman did not produce an order written by Dr. Grimshaw for the cab. As a matter of fact he had the order in his hand, but he did not hand it to the man, because the man told him that he would not do the work

Mr. *Gibson.*

3981. The man had not refused to supply the cab on the ground that the order was not produced?—No; he refused to supply the cab on the ground that he would have to get the horse harnessed, and lead him across the city two miles to the cab and then go for the patient.

Mr. *Brooks.*

3982. Is the man paid for doing this?—The man is paid, certainly.

Sir *Arthur Guinness.*

3983. Do you know of several cases of children being removed in street cabs whilst suffering from small-pox?—Yes, there were several cases during the small-pox epidemic. We have had very little small-pox of late. At page 51 of the last Report, No. 4, Dublin Sanitary Association's reports, which have been handed in to the Committee, you will find the correspondence with reference to this cab case.

3984. What arrangements have been made for disinfecting houses?—The disinfection of houses is supposed to be carried out by two or three people who are employed to go and disinfect them by chlorine gas developed from chloride of lime. I have gone to see how this is done, and it is done in such a way as to be utterly useless. For instance, in Liverpool the system pursued is, that a man goes with a lot of paper and pastes up all the crevices in the windows and every place, and closes up everything, and then develops the gas in the room, having turned everybody out of it. In Dublin they develop the gas with the door open, or the windows open, and hence it takes no effect whatever.

3985. Do you know the charges made for disinfecting in Dublin compared with Liverpool?—It is not charged for at all in either city.

3986. To

Mr. T. W. Grimshaw, M.D.

30 May 1876.

Sir *Arthur Guinness*—continued.

3986. To what then do you attribute the failure of the sanitary organisation of Dublin?—I attribute it more to the fact that the members of the Public Health Committee do not appear to understand what sanitary requirements are. If you speak to any of them they appear inclined to do what they can, and all that sort of thing, but they do not appear to have the mental capacity for doing the work.

Mr. *Brooks.*

3987. You think it is want of mental capacity?—I think that is about it. I know the two health officers are excellent men, and appear to understand their business. The sanitary police whom I have come across seem to be inclined to be active; but they all say that they cannot do the work; there is too much work to be done with the staff; but the extraordinary answers given by the Public Health Committee, stating of the most glaring nuisances, that they know of nothing to complain of, appears to me to show that it is not a want of desire, but they do not know what they have got to do; so far as I can see, they are not the sort of men for the work.

Sir *Arthur Guinness.*

3988. Have there been any debates in the corporation upon this subject?—Yes, there have very recently. Mr. Gray, the editor and proprietor of the "Freeman's Journal," brought forward several resolutions with regard to the sanitary organisation of the city; it was in consequence of some of the reports that he had from time to time collected for the "Freeman's Journal." In consequence of the number of articles which had been written in his journal, he thought it his duty to bring the matter before the corporation at a public meeting, as it were to pull up the Public Health Committee, which he did; and the opinion expressed there was that if there was some one responsible person at the head of the whole of the arrangements to superintend the officers of health for the whole city, who would devote his whole time to it, and not engage in private practice of his own, the whole thing would be remedied, or looked after in a better way. He suggested this, and it was referred to the Public Health Committee to consider. I think there has been no result of the debate yet; that was only recently done.

3989. Is there not such an officer in the employ of the corporation now?—No, there is no head to the department.

3990. What is Doctor Mapother's position?—He is called consulting sanitary officer. He has no duties except when he is called upon to attend the committee and give advice. He is not in any position of command; he cannot order anything.

Mr. *Brooks.*

3991. You mean that Dr. Mapother does not go himself and inspect nuisances; but he receives the reports of the sanitary serjeants and the inspectors, does he not?—He does not receive the reports; they are received by the secretary, who is called the executive sanitary officer.

3992. That is to say, they are addressed to the secretary, and then of course it becomes Dr. Mapother's duty to inspect them?—Not that I am aware of.

Sir *Arthur Guinness.*

3993. Is there any medical superintendent?—There is not. There is no officer in Dublin corresponding, for instance, to Dr. Trench, of Liverpool, who supervises everything, or Dr. Russell, of Glasgow, and men of that class.

Mr. *Butt.*

3994. Do you know whether the Corporation of Dublin have power to appoint a superintendent of that kind?—They have with the consent of the Local Government Board. I have no doubt if they suggested the thing it could be done.

Mr. *Bruen.*

3995. Do not the medical officers of the several dispensary districts in Dublin make reports to the sanitary committee?—They do if they come across instances in the ordinary discharge of their duties. When they find an outbreak of disease in a house, they report the fact to the public health committee, or if they see any sanitary defects accidentally, as it were, they are bound to report them.

3996. But is not it their duty to inspect and to make reports?—No.

Sir *Arthur Guinness.*

3997. What is the name of Dr. Mapother's office?—He is called the consulting sanitary officer.

3998. Is his whole time employed in the duties of that office?—No; they do not expect him to devote his whole time to it.

3999. He is perfectly suitable, is he not?—Perfectly suitable. There could not be a better man.

4000. What is his salary?—His salary is 300 *l.* a year.

4001. Do you think that his whole time should be taken up, and that he should be properly remunerated?—Certainly. He could not do the work for that money, if it is to be properly done.

Mr. *Butt.*

4001*. Are you acquainted enough with the arrangements to know whether Mr. Boyle is in anything like the position you have indicated; is he charged with the general superintendence of the sanitary arrangements?—I can give you exactly what Mr. Boyle's position is. Here are the rules laid down by the Public Health Committee. There was a sub-committee, of which I am a member, appointed by the sanitary association to report upon those rules to the association. You will find it at page 56 of the last Report.

4002. Mr. Boyle's office is that of executive sanitary officer?—Yes, you will see that on page 57.

4003. Would not that name imply that his duties were something such as you suggest?—But he could not do the duty for this reason, that he is not a medical man, and has not that knowledge.

4004. Would not the name "Executive Sanitary Officer," *primâ facie*, imply that he was created for that reason, and put in the very position you were speaking of?—I do not think so; for instance, you read "General secretarial duties, direction of sanitary staff and proceedings, and all duties involving civil engineering knowledge, including plans and giving evidence"; a man could not be secretary and be in his office to

Mr. T. W. Grimshaw, M.D.

30 May 1876.

Mr. Butt—continued.

to attend to his work when called upon, and be going about the town supervising duties.

4005. That was the opinion of the committee?—Yes, that was the opinion of the committee, and I may say that it was my opinion, for I happened to be on this committee; I did not write the report, but I signed it.

4006. This was your opinion: "We are of opinion that the direction of the sanitary staff and proceedings should rest with the chief medical officer of health, as is the case in most large towns, and not to be left to the executive sanitary officer, whose time ought to be fully occupied with his secretarial duties"?—Yes, that is my opinion.

4007. Would you think that that chief superintendent ought to be a medical man?—Certainly; it is the case everywhere. The rule is that this secretary is, as it were, to be always in his office to transact the general business.

4008. What objection would there be to having a person, who was not a medical man, to superintend the staff?—A great deal of the duties, in fact the majority of the duties to be performed, require professional knowledge.

4009. Would you consider it exactly the proper position to put a medical man in, to superintend the staff and to conduct proceedings against persons?—No; I do not think that conducting proceedings would be at all a proper duty for him; but he should order the proceedings to be taken. For instance, it is his business to determine whether a nuisance is a remediable thing or not. It would then be a lawyer's duty to see whether there are legal powers to remedy it, and the engineer's duty is to tell how it is to be done.

4010. Would not that part of the business be done better by a person, who was not a medical man, consulting the medical officer, and taking his opinion whether there was a necessity for law proceedings?—I think not. I think it is rather the reverse. It is the medical man who has to consult the others as to what is to be done. That is a thing which has been tried.

4011. But whether he is to be a medical man or not, you are of opinion that there ought to be such a person charged with the chief superintendence of the sanitary department?—Yes; if you take, as an example, the executive sanitary officer, he is not the head of the department, and for that reason he could not control Dr. Mapother, neither could Dr. Mapother control him; they are really both subject to the committee, and in case of anything to be done right off, there is no one to do it.

Sir *Arthur Guinness.*

4012. You think Dr. Mapother is quite suitable for that position?—Quite suitable; and I must say I fully expected that he would have been appointed to that office long before.

Mr. *Brown.*

4013. Perhaps you will correct your answer; you said that his salary was 300 *l.* a year; will you look at the corporation account, which says that his salary is 150 *l.* a year?—Yes, but this, I think, is an old report; those are the accounts of 1874. The Public Health Act passed and came into force at the end of 1874; I think when Dr. Mapother was appointed, under the Public Health Act, 1874, it was merely altering his name; his salary was raised, but it was raised on an application from himself; they were, I

Mr. *Brown*—continued.

understand, just going to pay him 150 *l.* and change his name; he would not have held office under the new Act, I think, if they had not raised his salary.

Sir *Arthur Guinness.*

4014. Are the medical sanitary officers sufficiently paid?—No; I consider that they are very badly paid, for they have a great deal of work to do.

Mr. *Brooks.*

4015. How many are there?—Fourteen. They are the dispensary medical officers, the poor law medical officers.

Sir *Arthur Guinness.*

4016. What are their salaries?—Their salaries are only 25 *l.* per annum.

Mr. *Brooks.*

4017. Is 25 *l.* the whole salary of the sanitary medical officers, or is the 25 *l.* supplemental to their salaries as dispensary medical officers?—They are different appointments; the dispensary medical officer in Ireland holds always four different appointments, under different Acts of Parliament. He holds under the Medical Charities Act, for which he is paid; he holds under the Vaccination Act, for which he is paid; he holds under the Registration Act another office for which he is paid; and then there is the sanitary appointment, and that he holds under the Sanitary Act, for which he is paid.

4018. So that, in point of fact, his salary is not 25 *l.*?—His salary as sanitary officer is only 25 *l.*, not any more.

4019. The sanitary board contribute 25 *l.* to his salary, do they not?—They do not; they only contribute 12 *l.* 10 *s.*; the Government pay half the money.

4020. Towards his general emoluments?—But this is paid him for extra work; he did not do this work before.

4021. I only want to avert any misconception on the part of the Committee as to the salaries of those 14 medical officers, as the Committee might possibly suppose that the whole of the sum that they receive for public purposes is 25 *l.* per annum?—I see what you mean; but I thought, as I understood the question, it was whether that 25 *l.* was a sort of extra payment; it is not an extra payment; it is a payment for new duties altogether, which they never had to perform before.

4022. Then it forms a part of their salary?—No, it does not indeed, with all respect; it is a separate office; it is just as if I held another appointment different from what I do, and I should expect to be paid for the extra work that I did.

4023. In fact, the dispensary doctors have had their salary lately supplemented by some 25 *l.* a year, 12 *l.* 10 *s.* from the Government, and 12 *l.* 10 *s.* from the corporation?—If you mean they have had their salaries increased to the amount of 25 *l.*, if it was shown to be an increase, no doubt, but they have not had their salaries augmented for any duties that they previously performed; it is no advance in salary, if that is what I understand you.

4024. Do not they get 25 *l.* now that they did not get before?—Yes, for new duties altogether.

4025. Do they perform new duties for the Public

Mr. T. W. Grimshaw, M.D.

30 May 1876.

Mr. *Brooks*—continued.

Public Health Committee in consideration of that 25 *l.*?—Yes, they do.

Mr. *Butt.*

4026. Is not the case this, that the medical officers of the dispensaries are obliged by Act of Parliament to discharge those sanitary duties?—They are.

4027. And as the remuneration for undertaking those duties they were to get what the Local Government Board directed?—Not exactly; it is the local authority, with the consent of the Local Government Board.

4028. Are you aware that the dispensary doctors have made great complaints of the smallness of their remuneration?—Certainly.

4029. And I believe there was a motion made in Parliament upon the subject?—There were questions put with regard to it.

4030. Was there not also a motion made by Dr. O'Leary?—Yes, he asked for a Return on the subject.

4031. Are you aware that it has been stated upon his authority that the lowness of the remuneration given to those medical sanitary officers has interfered greatly with the due execution of their duties?—I know that that has been stated. I may state this without injury to any one, that the duties are very unequally performed; some of the officers are very enthusiastic, very industrious, and very hard working, and they make as many as 200 or 300 reports every year, and each report involves an amount of work, in the mere writing, which could not be paid for with the money. But as for some of the sanitary officers now in Dublin, I know I could report as much in five days on the sanitary defects of their district as they do in twelve months.

4032. In fact the lowness of the salary almost compels the officers to do as little as they can do with a good conscience?—It is pretty nearly so, I think.

4033. Have you any reason for supposing that the Public Health Committee do not pay attention to the recommendations of their sanitary officers?—Yes, I have given some instances already; for instance, the case of those manure yards.

4034. There was a meeting, was there not, of the sanitary officers?—Yes, there was a meeting of the medical dispensary officers, and there was a meeting of the medical sanitary officers of Dublin, a meeting summoned by the Public Health Committee. They were asked to confer with the Public Health Committee as to various things, and these are the grounds upon which they were summoned. The Public Health Committee summoned them in these terms: "The subject of the high death rate which has so long prevailed in Dublin having engaged the consideration of this committee, I have been directed to convene a meeting of the medical sanitary officers of this urban sanitary authority, with a view to eliciting their opinions, and to obtaining from them suggestions as to the causes of the inordinate mortality in Dublin as compared with other cities in the kingdom. I therefore request you will be so good as to meet the medical officers of the district at this office, on the 15th instant, at 12 o'clock, in order that the subject may be considered, and that the report of the conclusions then arrived at may be prepared for the committee, by whom it may be

Mr. *Butt*—continued.

published for the information of their fellow citizens." That was signed by Mr. Boyle, the executive sanitary officer. The meeting was held in accordance with that requisition. "In accordance with which, 11 out of 14 medical sanitary officers attended the conference. There was only one member of the Public Health Committee present from the commencement of the proceedings. Two other members came in near the termination. In the first place, Dr. Mapother read his report, which had been previously drawn up, after which a discussion arose, in which nearly all the sanitary officers took part, on the following points: The great necessity of providing better homes for the working classes, expressing strongly our views that the present condition of the artizans' dwellings in Dublin is highly productive of disease; the great importance of a Building Act for Dublin, which would prevent the construction of houses in localities unsuited by the drainage low level of the land, &c. It was also pointed out that many of the houses in Dublin were unfit for human habitation, and that such should be closed forthwith. Dr. Mapother stated he would take down the points raised by us, without giving our names, and was understood to say he would give expression to them in his report. Before the conclusion of the meeting, a sanitary medical officer went round the room to ascertain the opinion of those gentlemen there, who agreed that the following views should be written down and given in to the secretary of the Public Health Committee, as representing the feeling of the majority of the sanitary officers present at the conference, viz.: That the high death rate of Dublin was in a great measure due to the unsanitary state of the houses, to remedy which a new Building Act, along with the application of the Artizans Dwelling Act, were urgently required; lastly, that all houses condemned by the sanitary officers should be closed." This is from a letter addressed to Dr. O'Leary, the Member for Drogheda, by nine out of the 11 officers who attended the meeting.

Chairman.

4035. Were you present at that meeting?—No, I am not an officer.

4036. How do you know what passed at that meeting?—This is a statement which was sent to Dr. O'Leary, the Member for Drogheda, by the gentlemen who attended the meeting, the medical sanitary officers.

Mr. *Butt.*

4037. And signed by nine out of the 11 gentlemen who were at the meeting?—Yes, I know it was signed by them; I saw the original document. They go on to say, "To our great surprise we saw by the public press a report of a meeting of the Public Health Committee, held two days after our conference (namely, the 17th of March), at which Dr. Mapother's report was read on the high death rate of Dublin, in which not the slightest notice was taken of the opinions and recommendations of the medical sanitary officers, nor did it even state that we had met with reference to the question. As members of a learned profession, and having considerable experience of the sanitary requirements of the districts we have charge of, we certainly feel this to have been a great slight. We regret very much

Mr. *T. W. Grimshaw*, M.D.

30 May 1876.

Mr. *Butt*—continued.

much that the Chief Secretary of Ireland has been misled into stating that the meeting agreed to the report of Dr. Mapother, as also that no explanation was given to or by the meeting on the subject, as to the cause of the high death rate in Dublin. The discussion which took place, and the handing in of the written recommendations by us, distinctly prove that we did not concur in the report, and also much reform was needed to improve the unsanitary condition of the City of Dublin. We remain, dear Sir, yours faithfully,—*R. F. Wilson*, No. 2 District, N. City; *Joseph E. Kenny*, No. 2 District, N. City; *Albert O'Speedy*, No. 3 District, N. City; *Wm. Dudley White*, No. 3 District, N. City; *Thomas Purcell*, No. 1 District, S. City; *Edward Peele*, No. 2 District, S. City; *John Regan*, No. 2 District, S. City; *C. F. Moore*, No. 3 District, S City; *John Short*, No. 3 District, S. City." I may mention, as an additional proof of the correctness of that document, that that meeting, although it was reported in the newspapers to have been unanimous, was, I understand, not unanimous: there was one dissentient, and that one dissentient, although he voted against these resolutions, has stated that these were the resolutions that were passed.

Sir *Arthur Guinness*.

4038. Was that report published by the Public Health Committee?—No, it was not.

4039. What was published?—Another statement that the high death rate depended upon the cold weather.

4040. Purporting to come from the meeting of medical officers?—Yes.

Mr. *Butt*.

4041. Did it purport to come from the meeting or was it Dr. Mapother's report?—It was published as the result of the meeting according to this statement.

4042. Was it published in the newspapers as Dr. Mapother's report which was handed in at that meeting?—It was published as Dr. Mapother's report of the proceedings that took place at the meeting at which he was present.

Sir *Arthur Guinness*.

4043. As to the result of the deliberation of the medical officers?—Yes.

Mr. *Collins*.

4044. Was it published officially under the authority of the Public Health Committee?—In that case, the public health committee forwarded the proceedings to the newspapers; I do not know whether you call that official. They were published by the morning papers.

4045. At all events, the report was forwarded by the Public Health Committee?—That is the usual course.

4046. Do you know anything to the contrary in this case?—I do not know anything to the contrary in this case.

Chairman.

4047. Do you know anything about the facts of this meeting beyond what appears in that report?—Except what I have laid before the Committee, but the question that that was in reply to was with regard to their attending to the reports.

Sir *Arthur Guinness*.

4048. What is the amount of money which is spent for sanitary purposes by the public health committee?—The average is a little over 2,000 *l.* a year.

Sir *Arthur Guinness*—continued.

4049. Have the corporation unlimited power of taxation for sanitary purposes?—They have practically, unlimited power; they have power to levy special rates for sanitary purposes.

4050. Have they ever done so?—They have not. With regard to their power of taxation, in the first place, the sanitary charges are on the borough rate; the borough rate, which is a 3 *d.* rate, is supplemental to the borough fund, but under the Sanitary Acts of 1866 and 1874 there is an exception put in, in which it is stated that the sanitary authority shall have power, notwithstanding anything in previous Acts, to levy the necessary expenses for sanitary purposes, and that any limit imposed upon the rate in previous Acts of Parliament was not to apply to sanitary purposes, so that they have unlimited power.

4051. Do the corporation publish the reports of the public health committee?—They do not.

4052. Is not that done by other corporations annually?—It is done by the English and Scotch towns, and by all the London districts.

4053. Do you think that the powers conferred by the Public Health Act of 1874 have been availed of largely in Ireland, and in Dublin especially?—I do not; not nearly so extensively as they should have been; there is little or no change in the state of things.

4054. To what do you attribute this?—I attribute it to the general want of capacity, as it were, of the Public Health Committee to do the work. I cannot explain it in any other way.

Dr. *Ward*.

4055. Do you think it is attributable to their unwillingness to increase the rates?—I do not think they care very much about the rates. They have been quite willing to rate us for 22,000 *l.* for the main drainage, of which we have got none yet, none of which expenditure has produced any results.

Sir *Arthur Guinness*.

4056. Do you think that the inquiries which are held by the local government inspectors are generally satisfactory?—I think not very. Some of the local government board inspectors do not appear to possess the requisite technical knowledge for holding inquiries. For instance, in Dublin when we complained about this ash-pit question, the local government board inspector, so far as we could ascertain, judged whether the work was done by going to the books of the authorities instead of going to the places that we complained of. If he had gone to the places as the Local Government Board inspector generally does in England, and seen the sanitary defects, and noted them, he would have got a great deal more information with regard to the matter than by examining the books of the authorities. There was no inquiry held. In England it is the custom when there is an outbreak of disease or a high death rate, that the Local Government Board send an inspector specially to inquire into the cause of it, and he reports to the Board, and then they issue orders for the authority to abate the state of things that is causing this high death rate.

4057. But in Dublin the Local Government Board inspector usually obtains his evidence from the Public Health Committee against whom the

Sir *Arthur Guinness*—continued.

the complaint is made?—So far as we know. We have not formally complained, except once or twice. We asked for this cleansing of the ash-pits to be enforced, but there was no inquiry held. The death rate is very high, and if that had occurred in an English town under similar circumstances, we think that an inquiry would have been held.

Mr. *Butt.*

4058. Did the local government board, in fact, abstain from complying with your application?—They abstained from complying with it.

4059. Could you tell me exactly what you mean by "zymotic" diseases?—The term zymotic is a theoretical term; it is not founded on fact exactly. We name our diseases in a very indefinite sort of way. Some of them are called according to local circumstances, some according to the way we think they are produced, and some one way and some another. The term "zymotic" is a term used in Pathology, and is from ζυμη, a ferment; and those are diseases which are supposed to be produced by the introduction of a ferment into the system. But popularly it really means "catching diseases."

4060. I want to call your attention to this statement about the cabs. I think you mentioned having given the Rev. Mr. M'Cready an order for a cab. In his letter of the 18th of July 1874, at page 51 of the Report, he describes the man having the horse, but not the cab, may I ask your attention to the last paragraph in his letter, "As I was most anxious that the patient should be removed without failure that evening, his family consisting of 10 persons, occupying but one room, I went to the South Dublin Union, where with the greatest kindness, the master instantly placed his fever cart at my service, and so enabled me to have the patient lodged in hospital by half-past eight." It was at your instance, of course, that he went to Bass-place?—Yes.

4061. Will you let me ask your attention to this at page 44 in the previous Report, the letter of Mr. Boyle to you on the 29th of November 1873, which gives this as the resolution of the Public Health Committee: "The Public Health Committee are not surprised that the Dublin Sanitary Association fell into the mistake of supposing that there were no carriages available for conveyance of persons suffering from contagious and infectious diseases within the city, inasmuch as they (the sanitary association) made the statement that there were none such previous to their having made any inquiry upon the subject." (This is the passage which I want in particular to refer to:) "The Public Health Committee, however, are glad to find that upon inquiry, the association have discovered that at each of the union workhouses there are maintained cabs, horses, and drivers for all classes of cases, and that the guardians have at all times placed the use of those appliances at the request of the Public Health Committee, their officers, and the public. The Public Health Committee, from their intimate acquaintance with the subject, know that the appliances referred to are available, and although maintained by the Guardians of the Union, and not by the Public Health Committee, are fully adequate to ordinary circumstances, both as regards the public health and the guardians in the absence of epidemics. There is therefore no necessity for the Sanitary Asso-

Mr. *Butt*—continued.

Mr. *T. W. Grimshaw*, M.D.

30 May 1876.

ciation to lay the information referred to before the Public Health Committee. The Public Health Committee have also two cabs, in one of which accommodation is provided for removing patients in a recumbent position; but the Public Health Committee would not feel warranted in maintaining in activity unnecessary appliances until circumstances should arise to justify such expenditure, and necessitate auxiliaries to the appliances of the guardians, but they were maintained in activity during epidemics. It is quite true that the committee pay to their horse contractor 6 s. for the conveyance of each patient, but the inference that the corporation charged the patient or their friends that or any other amount for such conveyance is without foundation. The fact that no applications have been made for the appliances of the Public Health Committee for the last eight months, is evidence that those of the guardians are sufficient for the present purposes." Have you got that letter of November 1873?—Yes.

4062. Do not you see now that in that letter the Public Health Committee distinctly state that the first application ought to be made to the guardians?—Yes, they do say that.

4063. And that their cab was only to be supplementary to that of the guardians?—Yes.

4064. Did you, having that letter, which says that it is first to be obtained by application to the guardians, send Mr. M'Cready first to search for the cab and horse of the Public Health Committee?—I did not, for this reason, that the statement is not true. I had previously ascertained by my inquiries at the two unions that no cabs were there available for me or for the removal of patients.

4065. Did they send the cab to Mr. M'Cready?—Yes, they did.

4066. Do you believe that if you had sent him to the guardians in the first instance they would not have sent him the cab then?—I think it is most likely that they would not; and I can tell you why; we have never stated any of these things without full inquiry. I went to the union with two of our members of the Sanitary Association once on purpose to make these inquiries. We saw the master of the workhouse, and the master of the workhouse told us decidedly that he had no cabs there for the use of the public; they were only for the use of the union, and for the use of the officers of the union; that they could not possibly be sent out in that way; but, said he, "I occasionally lend them to different clergymen, or persons of that sort, in the neighbourhood who happen to apply for them."

4067. At all events, Mr. Boyle did state the contrary to that in the letter?—Yes; but if you read the whole of the correspondence you will find that that statement is entirely refuted.

4068. Where is the statement refuted?—I do not mean to say that there is an argument entered into with regard to it, but if you will read the next letter you will see we say, "The committee would not, therefore, feel called upon to notice the resolution, were it not that the Public Health Committee have thought proper to charge this committee with 'having made statements previous to having made any inquiry,' and have also asserted that my letter was written 'partly in a needlessly fault-finding spirit, and partly in an unreasonable ignorance of the subject.' Charges such as these the committee think they ought

Mr. T. W. Grimshaw, M.D.

30 May 1876.

Mr. *Butt*—continued.

ought not to leave unnoticed. No statement is ever made by them unless as the result of careful inquiries." I was one of the persons who made the inquiries.

4069. Let me call your attention also to this: do you see in Mr. Boyle's letter that there is an additional distinct statement, that the reason why they did not keep cabs of their own was, because the guardians never refused their cabs for the purpose?—I know that they say so.

4070. Do you see that statement?—Yes.

4071. Will you show me where, in your correspondence, that statement is refuted; if you commence with the first letter, you will see that which they stated?—I must ask what you mean by refutation?

4072. Disproof?—The disproof rests on the report of the sub-committee of the sanitary association made previous to this statement of Mr. Boyle.

4073. Where is there any denial in any of your correspondence or statements subsequent to that letter; did either you or the sub-committee of the sanitary association ever deny that statement distinctly made by Mr. Boyle?—Yes.

4074. When?—Previously.

4075. After, I say?—You may see by the last letter which we wrote that we considered it unnecessary to reply to his letter.

4076. Did you ever deny that statement?—Here is the way the matter stands; we have often denied it.

4077. After this letter of his, I mean?—Not afterwards. we dropped the case.

4078. Will you tell me where you denied it before?—If you read the previous letter, you will see.

4079. Show me in any place a statement from you, that there were not cabs provided by the unions?—We never said anything about unions.

4080. Then, in fact, is not that a positive and distinct statement made upon the authority of a most respectable body of gentlemen, the Public Health Committee of the Corporation, that the unions did provide cabs?—Yes, there is that statement, but it is not true in that point.

4081. Did you ever deny it to Mr. Boyle?—Yes; I think so.

4082. When?—Here is the denial of it, I think, "The committee believe, that in consequence of the neglect of the Public Health Committee to provide such accommodation, most serious consequences have resulted to the public by the employment of hackney cabs for the conveyance of infectious cases." That is our charge.

4083. The answer given to that is, that that is not so, because no public inconvenience has arisen, because the guardians grant their cabs always?—But we have given proof that we are aware that infectious cases have been removed in hackney cabs.

4084. At all events, it was after that, that Mr. M'Cready failing to find the corporation cab, did go to the guardians, and did get it?—He did, but he got it as a matter of personal favour. If you observe, I together with others made inquiries and went and found out the facts before we made those statements; we have never made any statement of this sort as a mere matter of opinion. I went to the union and ascertained the fact, that the cabs there were not for the use of the public.

Mr. *Butt*—continued.

4085. When did you ascertain that?—I cannot exactly give you the date, but before that letter was written.

4086. You mean that it was before Mr. M'Cready went?—Yes, before that, certainly.

4087. Did you advise Mr. M'Cready to go to the union?—I did not.

4088. Then it was his own thought?—Yes.

Mr. *Kavanagh*.

4089. As a matter of fact, can you give us evidence that 16 children have been removed in public cabs with scarlatina?—Yes.

4090. Was not that really a practical denial of the ability of the public to get cabs?—It was. We found those people conveyed in ordinary cabs. People find that there is very great difficulty in getting the cab which the corporation say they have for that purpose, and the result is, that we charged them with not providing sufficient conveyances for the sick; the answer to that is, that they are provided by somebody else. We deny that they are provided by somebody else. This may be ignorance on the part of the Public Health Committee, but we were not ignorant in the matter, for we went to the unions to ascertain the facts. There is a letter in this report from the Registrar of the Cork street Hospital, stating that their cab is not available, and we ascertained other facts by personal inquiry.

Mr. *Brooks*.

4091. May it not also be accounted for by the fact that a cab can be procured in Dublin for 6 *d.*, from one end of the town to the other?—Yes.

4092. And the mother of a sick child may find it more convenient to take for 6 *d.* the child from her home to the hospital, than to go across the town for the public cab?—Yes; but as a matter of fact no cabman will bring a patient to the hospital for 6 *d.*; they generally charge 5 *s.*

4093. A cabman is not expected to perform a medical examination?—No; but if you tell a cabman to drive to the hospital he always refuses to do it.

4094. We know that they evade that by driving to a door or two away from the hospital?—I am quite aware of that; but they know too, what sort of case they are carrying.

4095. You say it is a fact that they do drive to a door or two away from the hospital?—They do.

4096. That practice is quite common, is it not?—Yes.

Mr. *Bruen*.

4097. By that means do they always impose upon the cabman?—No, they never impose upon the cabman; the cabman imposes upon the police by that; that is the only imposition.

Mr. *Butt*.

4098. What remedy would you suggest for the defective sanitary arrangements in Dublin?—We (that is the Sanitary Association) have recommended, first, a regular cleansing away of all those filthy places.

4099. My question had reference rather to the constitution of the sanitary authority?—I believe that the great difficulty in the constitution of the sanitary authority is the want of a head, well paid, and giving up his whole, or nearly his whole time to the work to supervise the whole thing.

Mr. *Butt*—continued.

thing. That is what is done elsewhere, and if any assistance is required it is given to him; but there is no head to the department in Dublin.

4100. You do not suggest that there should be a medical board superintending the matter?—No, not a medical board.

4101. You think that the superintendent should be a medical man?—I do.

4102. I believe you are aware that no borough rate is levied in Dublin?—There is no borough rate.

4103. Therefore, any expenses of the sanitary arrangements under this schedule, which you have given me, are paid out of the borough fund?—Yes, they must be at present.

4104. Generally, do not you believe that expenses which are incurred by the sewers or the nuisance authority are defrayed out of the borough fund in the city of Dublin?—Yes, I understand that to be the law.

4105. Then this sanitary expense, whatever it is, was a new charge put upon the borough fund at the disposal of the corporation by the Act?—Certainly.

4106. They have not exercised the power of levying a rate to recoup themselves any expenses that they have incurred under it?—They have not.

Dr. *Ward*.

4107. Are you aware that previous to the sanitary powers vesting in the corporation, this borough fund usually showed a large surplus?—I do not know whether it did or did not.

4108. Do not you think that there is a great deal in the surplus which the corporation feel against increasing the rates?—I do not; I think that is as true in every case.

4109. Do not you think that the local rates of Dublin are rather exceptionally high?—Yes, I do. There is a general impression that they are exceptionally high.

4110. Do you think that you would get any corporation to advocate an increase of the rates under those circumstances?—I think that the corporation often advocate an increase of the rates; I do not think the corporation are very anxious to keep down the rates.

4111. You say that you would substitute for the present arrangement a medical head of the department, who would have the sole charge of it; would that be an officer of the corporation?—Yes; certainly.

4112. What would his power be?—His power should be the general direction of the sanitary department.

4113. Would he have the power to insist that his recommendation should be followed?—Practically, he would. I think it would be absurd to give an officer power to say that his master should do what he tells them; but practically, for instance in London, in every district, whatever the medical officer of health recommends, is done.

4114. You tell us that in England when a complaint is made to the Local Government Board, they at once send a man to inspect the particular case?—Yes, to investigate it.

4115. When a complaint is made in Dublin, you charge the Local Government Board with not doing that?—I do not charge them with not doing it.

4116. Did not you distinctly say that when you complained in one special instance with regard to clearing out the ash-pits, the Local Government Board did not send any one?—No; if you thought I said that, you misunderstood me.

Dr. *Ward*—continued.

Mr. *T. W. Grimshaw*, M.D.

30 May 1876.

4117. What did you say with regard to that, did you imply any neglect on the part of the Local Government Board to go fairly into the case?—I do not imply any neglect, but I consider that the inspector went the wrong way about it altogether.

Chairman.

4118. In fact, you differ from the inspector?—No, I do not differ from him; I said that I did not consider that he went in a way that an English inspector would have gone about it. The Local Government Board inspector in England would have gone through the district to see whether the work which we thought was neglected had or had not been neglected. He went to the city hall, and asked the secretary for his books; he looked at his books which certainly said that so much work had been done. It is so stated in the return in one of these papers.

Dr. *Ward*.

4119. You make a charge as to the sanitary condition of a certain place; you draw the attention of the Local Government inspector to it; he goes and makes an examination, and finds, so he says, that it is all satisfactory; how can you blame the Public Health Committee of Dublin in a case like that?—As a matter of fact, I do not consider that in that case the Local Government Board inspector went about it in the way that we should expect it to be gone about.

4120. In that case, would any blame attach to the Corporation or to the Public Health Committee?—Yes; because the Local Government inspector is wrong in the way he proceeds about it; it does not make the authorities right.

4121. Did you report to the Local Government Board that there was a failure in that case?—No, we did not make a regular formal complaint; I believe that if we had presented a formal complaint and had petitioned to the Local Government Board they would have been bound to hold a regular court of inquiry and go into the thing. But we did not like to take such an extreme measure; that was a very serious thing to do.

4122. Did you call the attention of the inspector to it?—No, we called the attention of the Local Government Board, who told their inspector in the course of his duties to look at the books; and, as I understand, he looked at the books, and he reported that the books showed a very large amount of cleansing of ashpits, and so on. But our allegation is, that, whether the books show that or not, the ashpits are still filthy.

4123. Practically he said to the corporation committee that things were all right?—Practically he did, I am sorry to say.

4124. How would you in that case attach blame to the corporation?—But he never saw the places. His opinion upon the subject was not worth anything.

4125. But how can you attach blame to the corporation in the matter?—I do not absolve them from blame because somebody else did not do his duty.

4126. In Dublin there are a great many hospitals

Mr. *T. W. Grimshaw*, M.D.

30 May 1876.

Dr. *Ward*—continued.

pitals which people frequent from the country more than they do in London, on the average?—I do not think any more than in London.

4127. You have not large cities in Ireland as in England; there you have a sort of central hospital for the district?—No; but there is an extensive system of county infirmaries and union hospitals in Ireland more extensively than there is here.

4128. At the same time, is not there a tendency in Ireland to go up to Dublin from all the outlying districts?—Yes; but I do not think that there is any greater anxiety than there is on the part of country people to come to London. They are constantly coming to the hospitals in London from the country.

4129. In the neighbourhood of Manchester would you say so?—They would go to Manchester; it is their head-quarters.

4130. In the neighbourhood of Liverpool they would go to Liverpool, would they not?—Yes; the populations attached to those centres are not the sort of population which would be attached to Dublin as a centre.

4131. What I want to know is this, would you not say that Dublin was more a centre of the whole of Ireland in these hospital matters than London is of England; that there is a greater flow of all sorts of the worst forms of diseases into Dublin?—There is no flow of the worst forms of disease into Dublin at all; that is, diseases that raise the mortality of the city seldom come from the country at all.

4132. But surgical cases do, do they not?—Yes, but the patients as a rule do not die there, so that it does not affect the mortality. The diseases that we get into our hospitals from the country chiefly, are diseases which do not affect the mortality. They are either incurable patients sent up for final opinions and who return again immediately to the country, who go back and die at home, or else persons sent up for important surgical operations.

4133. Are you not aware that in the divisions of Dublin where there is a hospital the mortality is much higher than where there is not?—Yes, but those people generally come from the division and not from the country; poor people when they get sick in that district, go into the districts where there are hospitals and get good accommodation. I think that the figures that I mentioned accurately represent the state of things: I think the average annual mortality is 28·4 per 1,000, after allowing for all those deductions.

Mr. *Butt.*

4134. With regard to what took place with reference to the application to the Local Government Board, will you be so good as to read the 39th Section of the Public Health Act, 1874?—"Every urban sanitary authority shall, when the Local Government Board by order so direct, make due provision for the proper cleansing of streets, which such authority is obliged to maintain and repair, the removal of house refuse from premises, and the cleansing of earth closets, privies, ash-pits, and cesspools within its district."

4135. The Sanitary Association asked the Local Board, you said, to exercise that authority?—Yes, and they have not done it; I do not say that they refused to do it.

4136. It was not a complaint of any particu-

Mr. *Butt*—continued.

lar ash-pit, but a general request to them to exercise their powers?—Yes. You will see, in those reports, the letters which were sent to the Local Government Board. I should have explained, that the association had been led to believe that a good deal of the ill health of the city depended upon the filthiness of those places.

4137. Will you read that letter, and the reply of the Local Government Board?—"Dublin Sanitary Association, 16th of February 1875. Dear Sir,—The experience acquired by this committee in investigating the origin of outbreaks of zymotic diseases in this city, confirms the generally received opinion that such diseases prevail to the greatest extent in localities where house refuse and night soil are allowed to accumulate. It is almost invariably found that the houses in which such diseases occur are deficient in ash-pits and privy accommodation; indeed, the connection between dirt and disease is so well known that it is unnecessary further to insist on it. This committee are of opinion that the filthy condition of the ash-pits and privies in the poorer parts of the city, is due in a great measure to the inability of owners and occupiers of houses to make arrangements for the periodical cleansing of such ash-pits and privies. This committee, being convinced that it is the duty of the sanitary authority to make adequate arrangement for the systematic removal of filth from public and private premises, a duty recognised by the authorities of all, or nearly all, the large towns of England and Scotland, presented a memorial to the Corporation of Dublin, in the month of February 1873, in which they urged the imperative necessity of the adoption by the corporation of the following measures, amongst others: That the large accumulations of manure at present existing in the corporation dépôts should be at once removed, and that the filth collected by the corporation scavengers should be daily carried outside the city bounds. That arrangements should be made for the regular and frequent removal of night soil, house refuse, and all other accumulations of filth, from private houses in all parts of the city. As the corporation have failed to make due provision for the removal of house refuse, and the cleansing of ash-pits, privies, and cesspools, and as it is believed that so long as this most obvious and important duty is neglected all efforts to improve the sanitary condition of the city must be practically useless, the committee feel they have no alternative but to request the Local Government Board to issue an order for Dublin, under the 39th section of the Public Health (Ireland) Act, 1874. We remain, dear Sir, your obedient servant, *R. O'B. Furlong*, *C. F. Moore*, M.D., *F. W. Pim*, *J. Todhunter*, M.D., honorary secretaries." The reply of the Local Government Board is as follows, dated the 3rd of March 1875: "Sir,—The Local Government Board for Ireland have had before them your letter of the 16th ultimo, in which you convey the request of the committee of the Dublin Sanitary Association that the Board will issue an order for Dublin, under the 39th section of the Public Health Act, and I am to inform you that the Board have addressed a communication to the corporation on the subject. By order of the Board, *B. Banks*, Secretary."

4138. Did another letter come to you on the 24th

Mr. T. W. Grimshaw, M.D.

30 May 1876

Mr. *Butt*—continued.

24th of March from the Local Government Board?—Yes.

4139. Will you have the goodness to read it?—"Local Government Board, Dublin, 24th March, 1875. Sir.—Adverting to your letter of the 18th ultimo, in which you convey the request of the Committee of the Dublin Sanitary Association that the Local Government Board for Ireland will issue an order for Dublin under the 39th section of the Public Health Act, 1874, relating to the cleansing of streets, privies, and ashpits, I am directed by the Board to enclose herewith, for the information of the Association, a copy of a resolution passed on the 12th instant by the Public Health Committee of the Corporation of Dublin, acting as urban sanitary authority, adopting a report (a copy of which is also enclosed) from Mr. J. Byrne, on the subject of the scavenging and ashpit cleansing in the city. I am also to enclose a copy of a resolution of the Committee No. 1 of the Corporation relating to the depôts in use for the reception of the street sweepings. Both before and since the passing of the Public Health Act, 1874, it appears that the Public Health Committee of the Corporation have been active in regard to the cleansing of privies and ashpits, and, as an illustration of this it is shown by a return of sanitary duties and operations for the year ended the 31st March 1874, that they enforced the cleansing of such places by the owners or occupiers of 6,961 premises. It further appears from an examination of the books made by Mr. Robinson, Local Government Inspector, that from March to the end of December 1874, the privies and ashpits of 3,717 premises have been cleansed in the same manner. The Corporation afford the occupiers and owners of premises the means of cleansing their ashpits and privies on reasonable terms, by undertaking the work themselves whenever applied to, and they charge 6 *s.* when the quantity of ashes or refuse does not exceed two cartloads, and 2 *s.* 6 *d.* for every load beyond the two first. During the nine months ended December 1874, it appears that the ashpits and privies in about 490 premises have been cleansed in this way by the Corporation on the terms specified. Having regard to the arrangements that have been made and carried out by the corporation in the matter in their district, the Local Government Board are of opinion that no sufficient reason has been shown to exist at present for their interposition in pursuance of the 39th section of the Public Health Act." This was addressed to Mr. Furlong, honorary secretary of the Association.

4140. That last letter enclosed a communication from the corporation, did it not?—Yes; it enclosed this communication from the corporation. It is the report from Mr. John Byrne, which is referred to in the letter of the Local Government Board, with the resolutions of the Public Health Committee, and of Committee No. 1 of the corporation, and it is as follows:—

"Corporation of Dublin, Public Health Committee.

"City Hall, Dublin, 12 March 1875.

"REPORT in reply to the communication from Local Government Board of 3rd March 1875.

"THE corporation in, and previous to the year 1873, had so completely carried out the Sanitary Act of 1866, that the avocation of those who engaged in the business of the removal of house refuse from premises within the borough of Dublin to depôts in which same was manipulated for sale, was not only considerably increased, but at the same time seriously interfered with.

"It was increased by the action of the corporation in enforcing the removal of nuisances against the owners of premises, and interfered with by the action of the corporation against the proprietors of those depôts, in prohibiting their existence in unsuitable places within the borough of Dublin.

"These two causes acting together led to the charge for such services rendered to house owners being raised to an enormous degree, viz., to over 200 per cent. in 1873 beyond that of 1866, and in many instances the house owners could not get the work performed at any sum for weeks after same was required, and the magistrates in such cases refused to inflict fines for disobedience of their orders, under Section 14 of the Nuisances Removal Act, 1855.

"In this state of things the corporation made due provision for carrying out the work by their own scavenging carts, horses, and men, at such reasonable and fair charges to house owners as would take away from the magistrates all reluctance to inflict fines under the said section; and this proceeding on the part of the corporation had the desired effect, but moreover, in a short time, it had the effect of reducing the charge of those hitherto engaged in the work to the actual value, and thereby the staff of the corporation engaged in such work, and acting as a deterrent, had not to be augmented to any considerable extent, and it is maintained at its original experimental size, and is intended so to be, but is capable of expansion under the system then instituted, if the necessity therefor should arise, and I would here remark that this system was in full operation more than a year previous to the passing of the Public Health Act, 1874, and was and is self-supporting, and likely to be, and therefore it would be highly inexpedient and altogether unnecessary to make any change in an arrangement the working of which has proved so very satisfactory to all interests in the borough.

"Upon looking over the entire sanitary code for Ireland, I find that the cost of such work is thrown on the owner or occupier, and that it is only where the person answerable for the nuisance cannot be found that the sanitary authority may abate the same at the cost of the public. (*See* Section 21, Sanitary Act, 1866.)

(signed) *John Byrne.*

9 March 1875.

"In reference to the above, the following resolution was unanimously adopted, viz.:—

"'*Resolved*—That the report now read be adopted and forwarded to the Local Government Board as our reply to the part of their letter which relates to matters within our province as the urban sanitary authority of the borough of Dublin; and inasmuch as the matter relating to the depôts for the street scavenging is one under the Municipal Act, 1849, and the Acts incorporated therewith, and purely one of a municipal character, and of which this committee has not the

Mr. T. W. Grimshaw, M.D.

30 May 1876.

Mr. *Butt*—continued.

the charge, same be referred to Committee No. 1 of the corporation, being the body having charge of these depôts, for their action in the matter.'

"Corporation of Dublin, Secretary's Office, City Hall, Committee No. 1.

"Sir, "Dublin, 18 March 1875.

"Having submitted your letter of the 3rd instant (No. 3937, 1875, Miscellaneous), addressed to the town clerk, to the Committee No. 1, having charge of the scavenging depôts of the city, I have the honour to inform you that the committee, after careful consideration of the subject, passed the following resolution, viz.:—'That we are of opinion that the depôts in use for the reception of the street sweepings are so managed by this department as not to be a nuisance or injurious to health.'

"For reply to the remaining portion of your letter I have to refer you to the letter of the secretary of the Public Health Committee, dated the 15th instant.

"I am, &c.
"*J. C. Reynolds*, Secretary.
"per *F. H.*

"B. Banks, Esq.,
"Secretary, Local Government Board,
"Custom House."

4141. You received that enclosed document?—Yes; but you will observe that that does not end the matter. We again applied to the Local Government Board and sent a memorial.

4142. Would you wish that memorial to be in evidence?—Yes, I think it is most important.

4143. That letter of the Local Government Board was followed by a memorial of the Sanitary Association, and a letter to the Local Government Board?—Yes, it was.

4144. The next is a letter of 11th May 1875 from Mr. Pim to the secretary of the Local Government Board, enclosing the memorial to which you refer, and which answers the statements of Mr. Byrne?—Yes; the memorial is as follows:

"Memorial from the President, Vice-Presidents, and Executive Committee, D. S. A., to the Local Government Board for Ireland, 11th May 1875.

"Gentlemen,

"We, the president, vice-presidents, and committee of the Dublin Sanitary Association, beg to bring under your notice the following considerations, which we venture to think justify the opinion expressed in the letter addressed to you by our secretaries on 18th February, that necessity exists for the exercise by the Board of the power vested in them by the 39th section of the Public Health (Ireland) Act, 1874, to issue an order requiring the corporation to make due provision for the removal of house-refuse, and the cleansing of ashpits, &c., within the city of Dublin.

"I. The report adopted by the Public Health Committee of the corporation is in fact a report of an individual member of that body, whose opinion on a matter of the kind is not entitled to outweigh that of the members of the executive committee of this association, who may, without presumption, lay claim to some special acquaintance with the subject, and who have personal knowledge of the extent and magnitude of the evil complained of. Moreover the gentlemen who at present occupy the responsible positions of medical advisers of the corporation have expressed opinions in accordance with the views entertained by this committee, which were communicated to you in the letter of February 18th.

Mr. *Butt*—continued.

"Dr. Mapother, consulting officer of health for the city, in his "Lectures on Public Health," observes: 'One of the greatest difficulties in preserving the health of the city which is now experienced, is the removal and disposal of the cesspool stuff. There are quite an insufficient number of persons employed in this way on their own account, and they store it up in yards in the densest and poorest parts of the city. During some months the farmers do not care to purchase it as manure. The efforts of the Public Health Committee have as yet failed in getting contractors, who would remove it at once to the agricultural districts, and a hopper-barge to convey it beyond risk of return is extremely expensive. The scavenging depôts of the corporation have been much complained of, and the prevalence of erysipelas in an hospital was assigned to the proximity of one of them.'

"Dr. Cameron, medical officer of health and city analyst, in his "Manual of Hygiene," says, 'The 39th section of the Public Health Act, 1874, enables the Government to cause the urban sanitary authorities to cleanse the ashpits, privies, and cesspools of private houses situated within their districts. It is to be hoped that the local authorities will not wait until they are put in motion by the higher power, but that they will at once undertake the domestic scavenging of their respective districts. The cleansing of the streets, and the removal of house refuse, might be carried on simultaneously. It would be most desirable if the yards and out-offices of the houses occupied by the lower class were cleansed every day.'

"We presume it is unnecessary to remind you of the opinions recently expressed on this subject by the medical officer of the Privy Council, and of the Local Government Board of England, in his supplemental report, page 24, &c.

"II. The committee cannot accept the statement that 'the Public Health Committee of the corporation have been active in regard to the cleansing of privies and ashpits,' notwithstanding their assertion that they have enforced the cleansing of such places in 6,961 places.

"There are in Dublin 9,300 tenement houses, the ashpits and privies of which, according to the regulations of the Public Health Committee, are required to be cleansed once in every month, making a total of 100,000 cleansings per annum. In the experience of this committee, these premises are rarely cleansed without compulsion by the sanitary authority, and they therefore consider the number cleansed, 6,961, quite inadequate to the necessities of the case. Besides these tenement houses, there are upwards of 14,000 other houses in the city the refuse of which, for the most part, is removed without the intervention of the

Mr. *T. W. Grimshaw*, M.D.

30 May 1876.

Mr. *Butt*—continued.

the authorities, and at a considerable cost to the owner or occupier.

"The committee regard the means adopted by the Public Health Committee for the cleansing of ashpits and privies, and the removal of house-refuse, as extremely inefficient, and on a scale quite incommensurate with the size and population of the city. The fact that the public have availed themselves of the machinery provided by the Public Health Committee in only 490 instances is in itself a proof of this. These charges are virtually prohibitory in the case of the tenement houses.

"It is estimated that if the system were thoroughly carried out according to the present scale of charges in each tenement house, as often as required by the regulations of the corporation, the total annual cost to the owners would exceed 30,000 *l.*, while the total cost of cleansing all the ashpits in the city, at the same rates, could not be less than 60,000 *l.* per annum. In London, and in nearly all the large towns of England, the cleansing of ashpits is undertaken by the authorities free of charge, and the expense, after deducting the value of the manure sold, which in many cases is very considerable, is defrayed out of the public rates.

"The nuisance authorities should be compelled to provide a proper and sufficient machinery for the gratuitous removal of night soil, house refuse, and other like nuisances. At present, the inhabitants of the poorer parts of the city find it impossible to get rid of the accumulations of filth in their yards, ashpits, and privies, which form a most fruitful source of disease. It is in vain for the authorities to require the ashpits and privies of all houses occupied by members of more than one family to be emptied, cleansed, purified, deodorised, and disinfected regularly and periodically once every month. As a matter of fact, the directions of the Public Health Committee are treated as a dead letter, and the only way of remedying the present state of things is by requiring the nuisance authority itself to do what the owners or occupiers are, in the large majority of cases, utterly unable to do.

"In an article which appeared in the columns of the "Freeman's Journal," some time since, the following passage occurs:—

"'This question of scavenging naturally leads us to consider the still more urgent question of the removal of night soil and house-refuse. Our reports have shown that in all parts of Dublin the condition of ashpits and privies is disgraceful, a standing menace to the health of the people. The evil is increasing every day; for the present prices paid to private scavengers are, in many cases, absolutely prohibitive, and months upon months may elapse before any effort is made to remove the vast collection of filth from the overflowing ashpit, &c., of a crowded tenement house. How is this evil to be combated? Only by a system of removal of night soil by the authorities, either at a moderate cost to the landlord or occupant of each house, or by means of a special rate, for the levying of which the Public Health Committee have ample powers. In many, indeed in most of the English and Scotch towns, the authorities undertake the removal of house-refuse in addition to the ordinary scavenging of the streets. In London, owing to the system of main drainage, that marvellous work of the Victorian era, there is no night soil to be removed; but, in almost every instance, dust and house refuse are removed periodically by the local health authorities; for example, in Kensington, fortnightly; in St. Mary's, Lambeth, weekly; in Paddington, twice a week; and in Camberwell, daily, if the inhabitants so desire it.'

Mr. *Butt*—continued.

"The Legislature, in adopting the 39th section of the Public Health (Ireland) Act, 1874, which is identical with the 31st section of the Sanitary Law Amendment Act for England, appears to have recognised the necessity of the sanitary authority undertaking the duty of domestic scavenging as being a matter of too great importance in a sanitary point of view to be left to private enterprise; and this committee would again respectfully urge upon the Local Government Board the importance of requiring the sanitary authority of Dublin to provide such a system as appears to have been contemplated by Parliament."

4145. Will you read the reply of the Local Government Board?—"I am directed by the Local Government Board for Ireland to acknowledge the receipt of your letter of the 11th instant, together with a copy of a memorial from the Committee of the Dublin Sanitary Association, urging the views of the association as to the issue of an order under the 39th Section of the Public Health Act, 1874, to require the corporation, as urban sanitary authority, to make provision for the cleansing of streets and removal of house refuse, &c., from premises within its district; and requesting the Board to name a day when they will receive a deputation from the committee. In reply, I am to state that the communication of the Dublin Sanitary Association will receive the attention of the Board. The Board desire, at the same time, to observe that the proposed immediate issue of an order under the 39th Section pre-supposes the existence of circumstances which might render such an order expedient, and probably to be attended with advantage and success; and the Local Government Board must act upon their own judgment as to the existence or non-existence of such circumstances at present. In the meantime, they are obliged by the communication of the views of the association, and any further statements in writing shall at all times receive their best attention; but they must, in accordance with official practice, decline to receive a deputation on the subject of business which concerns the discharge of their ordinary duties in the administration of the law." In my evidence, I state that they had not definitely refused; that was with reference to that last letter. There is one point which I might be allowed to mention with regard to this; you see that that is a memorial of the president, vice-presidents, and executive committee of the Sanitary Association. I desire to state that that is not a mere formal thing; the meeting of the committee at which that was agreed to was attended by the president; and all the vice-presidents and the members of the committee of the association were summoned, and a considerable number of them were present at the time; it is not the mere proceeding of the ordinary working committee; it was a very large meeting; if you look on

Mr. T. W. Grimshaw, M.D.

30 May 1876.

Mr. *Butt*—continued.

on page 3 of the Report, you will see who the persons were who were responsible for that memorial; it is an important point that a document of that sort should be sent in by men of that class; it is not a mere insignificant set of fellows like myself, but men of considerable consequence and experience; I should be very glad if note were taken of the men who composed that committee.

4146. Can you tell me who were the vice-presidents and members of the committee of the Dublin Sanitary Association?—President: Jonathan Pim; vice-presidents: Sir Edward R. Borough, Bart., J.P., D.L.; Lord James W. Butler; Fleetwood Churchill, M.D.; Edward Gibson, Q.C., M.P.; Sir Arthur E. Guinness, Bart. D.L., M.P.; Ion Trant Hamilton, D.L., M.P.; the Right Honourable Viscount Monck, G.C.M.G.; George H. Porter, M.D., F.R.C.S.I., Surgeon in Ordinary to the Queen in Ireland; the President, King and Queen's College of Physicians, Ireland; the President, Royal College of Surgeons, Ireland; William Stokes, M.D., F.R.S., &c., Physician in Ordinary to the Queen in Ireland, and Regius Professor of Physic in the University of Dublin; Lord Talbot de Malahide; Colonel the Right Honourable T. E. Taylor, D.L., M.P. The executive committee are Edward F. Beatty; Charles P. Cotton, C.E.; Francis R. Davies, K.J.J.; J. Magee Finny, M.D.; Thomas W. Grimshaw, M.D.; Rev. Alfred T. Harvey, M.A.; Thomas Hayden, F.K.Q.C.P.I.; Joseph E. Kenny, L.R.C.P.E.; J. J. Digges La Touche; John M'Evoy; John William Moore, M.D.; D. Teler T. Maunsell, M.B.; George R. Price; Thomas Purcell, L.K.Q.C.P.I.; Robert Sexton; Abraham Shackleton; Edward W. Smith; Albert O. Speedy, L.R.C.S.I.; H. H. Stewart, M.D.; Rev. James Walshe, B.D.; W. Dudley White, L.R.C.S.I.; William White, Senior City Coroner.

4147. How many of those vice-presidents and executive committee were present at the meeting when that memorial was adopted?—I cannot tell you unless I had the minute books of the association, but, substantially, those people all approved of it; you see there are some of the honourable Members of this Committee on that list.

Dr. *Ward*.

4148. Would the recommendations of this Committee and your recommendations entail a very large increased expense?—Certainly they would.

4149. You would have to raise the rates considerably?—We should have to raise the rates, that I admit, but we consider that it would be cheaper to the public in the end.

Mr. *Brooks*.

4150. The Public Health Committee of the corporation of the City of Dublin was instituted, I think you said, in 1866?—It was regularly constituted in 1866.

4151. And some time subsequently the Dublin Sanitary Association was established?—Yes, it was formally established on the 14th November 1872, six years afterwards.

4152. And they have been extremely vigilant in supervising and criticising the action of the corporation of the City of Dublin?—We have done our best; but our actions are not confined to the corporation of the city. Recollect we have had frequent communication with the commissions of the townships all round. We have been in communication with the Rathmines Commissioners, we have been in communication with the Pembroke Commissioners; but I may mention that we have never quarrelled with any of them, and we have never had any material difference of opinion.

4153. Can you say whether the members of the Public Health Committee are tolerably unanimous in their action?—I cannot tell you. I do not know anything about them; of course, we could not tell that without the Minutes of the Committee.

4154. Does that Committee agree with the opinions of the Sanitary Association as to the neglect of duty?—I presume they do not, or else they would not do as they do.

4155. It is composed, is it not, of many eminent citizens?—It is composed of the usual sort of people that are in the Dublin Corporation. There is a selection of the corporation, and I believe the selection is made with a view of distributing the members as largely over the city as possible, so that all the different parts of the city will be represented on the Public Health Committee. I think that was the object in its constitution.

4156. You think that the shortcomings of the Public Health Committee are due to the mental incapacity of that body?—I do not like to charge any one with mental incapacity, but certainly they do not act in a way that we think shows any very great ability.

4157. Being asked before as to the reason of the unhealthy condition of the City of Dublin, you said you believed that this was one of the reasons?—I said that there seemed to be a want of capacity to discharge the duty; when a man does not do his duty, you must either say that he will not do it or that he cannot do it; and I think it preferable to say that he cannot, than to say that he will not.

4158. Is not the Lord Mayor of Dublin a member of the Public Health Committee?—I believe he is an *ex officio* member of all committees; he is not the chairman of that committee, but I presume he is a member of that committee.

4159. He himself is a medical man, is he not?—Yes.

4159*. In large practice?—No, I should say not; but I do not know; I do not think that he has any very large practice. He is not a hospital physician or surgeon; he is a general practitioner. I do not know that he has got a large practice; in fact, I do not know anything about his private affairs.

4160. Do you know whether he is on the Boards of any of the Dublin hospitals?—I think he is a member of the Board of the Meath Hospital, but I am not quite sure about that.

4161. And on the Board of Superintendents of Prisons?—I do not know.

4162. Do they elect members to the Board of the Meath Hospital persons who are of mental incapacity?—I should be very sorry to say that the mental capacity of all the members of any hospital Board in Dublin was very high.

4163. Do you continue to think that the Lord Mayor is a man of mental incapacity?—I make no charge against any individual person's capacity, but the mental capacity of a Board is not always the compound mind of the individuals.

4164. If we are to judge collectively of the Public

Mr. *T. W. Grimshaw*, M.D.

30 May 1876.

Mr. *Brooks*—continued.

Public Health Committee we must judge of the members individually, must we not?—I do not know whether the Chairman will require me to criticise the mental capacity of each member of the Public Health Committee; I should be very sorry to do it.

4165. Do not you know that there are other medical men upon the Public Health Committee, being members of the corporation?—There are two others; one is Dr. M'Cormack.

4166. With regard to Dr. M'Cormack, is he a man of large practice?—I believe he has a considerable practice of a certain class.

4167. Among the poorer people?—Yes.

4168. Is Dr. Long a member of the Public Health Committee?—He is, I believe.

4169. He is one of the medical officers of the Dublin metropolitan police, is he not?—I do not know. I think he is apothecary to the police. I think he is assistant to Dr. Nedley, who is the medical officer of the police.

4170. Would you say that he was a man of mental incapacity?—I must say that I will not bring any charge of incapacity against individuals.

4171. The next name that I have here is Councillor Byrne; is not Councillor Byrne generally considered to be a man of remarkable activity and intelligence?—I only speak generally of the members of the committee with regard to sanitary matters. Mr. Byrne may be a very good man of business, as may all those other gentlemen. I do not say anything about their qualifications or their business capacity, but that very thing which has just been put in evidence, the statement of Mr. Byrne with regard to the action of the ashpit and privy cleaning, I think, shows that the man is not fit to write a sanitary report at all; that is my impression about it; in fact the language is almost unintelligible.

4172. Would not the Committee infer from your evidence that the members of the Public Health Committee were not persons either of activity or intelligence?—I said in sanitary matters. I did not refer to their own affairs, nor to their own business. I say that the impression that we have from our experience of the work of the Public Health Department is that the department is worked by men who have not the capacity for doing the work; it is either that or else a charge that I should be very sorry to bring against any men, that they will not do that which they know they should do.

4173. Is not Councillor Byrne remarkable for activity and intelligence in the public affairs of the city of Dublin?—He is remarkable for great activity, but so far as public health matters are concerned, the statement which he has put down, and which I have put in, to my mind shows a great want of intelligence in sanitary matters.

4174. Is not intelligence required of a kind that would lead to the proper selection of medical officers amongst the various candidates?—I think so, but there never has been a question raised as to the competency of the medical officers.

4175. We are dealing now with the capacity of the members?—Let me understand exactly what you mean. I understand that if a man of great business ability wanted medical work, or legal work, or anything else done, his mental capacity would show itself, not in his trying to do work of that sort himself, but in his employing a first class medical man, or a first class barrister, or someone of the sort.

4176. Is not Councillor Byrne assisted by those other medical gentlemen competent to select the medical officers of the corporation?—Yes. I do not say that the medical officers are not competent; I say that the men appointed are competent. Dr. Mapother is a very eminent sanitarian, and in every way qualified for the office, but he has not the power that he ought to have. For instance, Dr. Mapother objects to the corporation depôts; he has put his objection in writing, and published it, but they are still there. It appears to me that they wholly disregard the opinion of highly competent men. Both Dr. Cameron and Dr. Mapother have objected, and I might, perhaps, be allowed to give their opinions, as I have them here. For instance, Dr. Cameron has distinctly stated that he trusts that the Local Government Board will never be asked to enforce the 39th section of the Act, for he takes it for granted that an enlightened sanitary authority would cleanse daily the ashpits and privies of all the houses in their district. That is the opinion of one of their own officers. I know, from what I know of Dr. Cameron's ability and experience, that if he were asked, "Do you think it is a thing which ought to be done?" he would say, "Certainly, you ought to clean out all those places."

4176*. Several honourable Members of this Committee are not themselves resident in Dublin, and in order to correct what I believe to have been a mis-statement, not a wilful inaccuracy on your part, with regard to the mental capacities of the members of this Public Health Committee, I must bring you through the members. Councillor Norwood; he is a member of the Public Health Committee; would you describe him as a man of mental incapacity?—I really cannot possibly describe him; I believe he is a very good barrister, but I know nothing of him as a sanitarian.

4177. The medical sanitary branch of the Public Health Committee, I think, consists of two medical men, Dr. Mapother and Dr. Cameron; they are always at the disposal of the Public Health Committee for consultation, are they not?—Yes, I should think so. Dr. Cameron has other duties besides. He is the analyst, and he has to analyse anything that is sent to him from all the country. If I want an article analysed, he is bound by our rules to analyse it for me at fixed charges.

4178. The Public Health Committee have also to discharge the duties of the analysis of food, and the inspection of unsound meat?—Yes, that is under Dr. Cameron; he is the referee in cases of that sort.

4179. Can you say whether the duty of the inspection of meat and unsound food is performed by the Public Health Committee?—I believe that is better done than any other part of their duty, as well as I can ascertain. I cannot say positively that it is well done, but my impression is that it is well done; but I have not inspected the markets in the same way as I have done in the case of poor people's houses; I have not gone into that work in the same way, but my impression is that the work is very well done compared with the other.

4180. How many sanitary serjeants are there?—There are nine according to the published list.

4181. Are

Mr. T. W. Grimshaw, M.D.

30 May 1876.

Mr. Brooks—continued.

4181. Are they selected by officers of the police on account of their special knowledge of the city?—I am not aware.

4182. What are their duties?—The rules are, First, the inspectors to have charge of the entire city for sanitary purposes, one to each side, viz: north and south of the river. Inspector Halligan, as being the senior, to have the first choice. Secondly, to see that each sanitary serjeant shall go regularly, and not intermittingly, through his district, and also to see that he shall make a daily record, available for future reference, of every nuisance, or non-observance of sanitary law discovered by him, and his action thereupon, up to the result. Thirdly, to see as far as practicable that a list be made by each sanitary serjeant, of the houses, yards, and places in his division which require frequent visits, and to see that the periodic visits deemed necessary and noted in the list, be paid, reporting the result of each visit, and the necessary proceedings carried out to abate the nuisance, and enforce sanitary arrangements. Fourthly, to be accountable to the committee for faithful reports as to repairs, drainage, supply of water, privies, ash-pits and water-closets of houses, state of manure repositories, dairy yards, piggeries, pigs, and animals in houses and adjoining dwellings, cleanliness of tenement houses and yards; state of streets, lanes and alleys, as regards flushing, scavenging, &c., to the committee, whether made by the inspector of sanitary serjeants."

4183. Do you know if any complaints have been made of neglect in the performance of their duty by the sanitary serjeants?—I do not know of any individual complaint, such as I have mentioned. One man told me that such a thing would not be considered a nuisance, in which I differ with him; I believe there are not enough of them, but I believe that they are a very good class of men willing to do the work, but they cannot do the work.

4184. Do the Public Health Committee appoint inspectors of unsound meat?—I do not know; I believe they do; that is a part of their duty, and I presume they have, because they have stated here that more than four officers, namely, two acting serjeants, and two constables charged with the detection and confiscation of unsound meat, fish, fruits, &c., I presume they are appointed by the committee; I do not know.

4185. Can you say when they were appointed?—All these appointments date from the enforcement of the Public Health Act.

4186. How many medical sanitary officers are there?—Fourteen.

4187. Do those fourteen gentlemen do their duty collectively?—I think collectively they appear to do their duty, except what appears from the statement which Mr. Gray made in the corporation.

4188. Is that your own opinion?—I do not exactly understand what you want me to give my opinion upon.

4189. Have any complaints been made of neglect of duty on the part of those 14 medical gentlemen who are the medical sanitary officers?—Not that I am aware of, except so far as Mr. Gray has complained, that he considered that the work done by some of them does not appear to be sufficient; he has said so in the corporation, but further than that I do not know.

4190. Taking that reply in connection with what you said to the honourable and learned gentleman the Member for Limerick, may I ask you if you now say that since the institution of the Public Health Committee there has been no improvement in the sanitary condition of the city of Dublin?—With the single exception that the surface of the streets in the back streets is better cleansed than it used to be, I do not know of any change whatever.

4191. Have the medical men anything to do with the cleansing of the streets?—Certainly not.

4192. You say that there has been no improvement whatever, notwithstanding the appointment and the reports of all those medical men?—There is no apparent result. As I said at the commencement of my evidence, I took at haphazard somewhere about 60 houses, and I found that the general condition was the same as it was formerly. There were a few exceptions. Some few have been closed up chiefly through being condemned by the city engineer as dangerous. I saw houses that were shut up in that way, but the general aspect of the houses that I visited within the last fortnight has been the same as they have been within my recollection.

4193. Your remedy, the appointment of a superior medical officer, could hardly enforce that?—It would do something towards it.

Dr. Ward.

4194. You would give him the power?—Yes. I might explain this. If you will take, for instance, Liverpool and Glasgow, the plan pursued there is that there is a census taken of all the streets, and each house, in fact, in those back slums. They do not keep a census of the better parts of the towns. When the mortality rises in any particular place, or whenever the medical officer of health hears of anything occurring in the way of outbreak of disease, he goes down and looks at the place himself, and if he finds that the reports have not been made to him regularly by the persons whose business it is to inspect them, they are punished severely; but there is no one to do that in Dublin.

4195. Do not the four serjeants do this?—These four serjeants have got no sufficient staff.

4196. Do not the 14 medical officers do it?—Those 14 medical officers go on reporting, and their reports are left unattended to, I am sorry to say. I have seen many of the report books of many of the medical officers, and if you summon them here they will show you that they reported over and over again the same nuisance, but the nuisance remained. I have seen as many as seven reports made in a particular instance at long intervals, and there the nuisance still remains.

Mr. Brooks.

4197. One of the difficulties in the way of the Public Health Committee you have stated to be the want of a sufficient number of inspectors?—The want of a sufficient number of men to do the work. In fact those men have told me so often, and that a vast amount of the work they have done is useless, because they cannot come back to the place and watch it.

4198. Have you seen any return of the number of pigs that have been removed from human habitations by the action of the Public Health Committee?—I have papers of that sort here; but

Mr. *T. W. Grimshaw*, M.D.

30 May 1876.

Mr. *Brooks*—continued.

but I am sorry to say that most of them have come back again, and the same pig appears frequently in the return, although he has been removed. I have here the report of the work done for the year 1874, the last one that I have.

4199. Does that give the number of houses and rooms disinfected and whitewashed?—Yes.

4200. And the pigs removed?—Yes.

4201. Where did you get it?—This was given me by Mr. Boyle some time ago.

Dr. *Ward*.

4202. I think you said that the expenditure by the corporation last year was something like 2,000 *l.*?—As well as I remember, it was 1,800 *l.* the year before last.

Mr. *Collins*.

4203. I believe the control and management of sanitary matters is altogether in the hands of the Public Health Committee of Dublin?—It is.

4204. That is a committee of the corporation?—Yes.

4205. You said, from your own experience of the proceedings of this committee, that they do not seem able to execute the duties of their office very efficiently?—Yes, I said so.

4206. That is your own experience of them?—Yes.

4207. Are not the proceedings of the Health Committee under the direct supervision of the Local Government Board?—They are under their supervision, of course.

4208. Not under their direct control or supervision?—If I understand the honourable Member to ask whether the Local Government Board interferes with them in any way, they have probably just the same power with regard to them which they have over the Boards of Guardians, Dispensary Medical Committee, and so on. Of course they have that general control that they have over all the local governments of the country, and their inspector can go and attend the meetings if he desires.

4209. Are there no other public bodies in Dublin who have charge of sanitary matters?—Not in the city.

4210 Are there no parochial authorities?—No, not that I know of.

4211. The boards of guardians do not occupy themselves with sanitary matters?—In Dublin we are somewhat peculiarly situated with regard to that; there are two unions in Dublin, the North Dublin Union and the South Dublin Union. Under the Public Health Act the guardians are the local sanitary authority for the district, but if the urban sanitary district runs into the union, that part is not under the control of the guardians.

4212. They have authority only within their own districts?—Yes, they are sanitary authorities, because they have their own rural sanitary district, but are not sanitary authorities in the city.

4213. When outbreaks of disease take place, what are the initiatory steps taken to inspect the districts that are affected?—I really do not know that there are any; so far as I am aware there are none. If a case of infectious disease comes into one of the Dublin hospitals, that is returned to the Public Health Committee from the hospital authorities. For instance, I am connected with two hospitals, one of which is the Fever Hos-

Mr. *Collins*—continued.

pital, and there the registrar, whenever a patient is admitted, gives the address of that patient to the Public Health Committee, but what becomes of it afterwards I do not know, and that is only a recent arrangement. It is right here to state that various arrangements had been entered into from time to time but generally fell through. The next arrangement at present is, that one of the sanitary inspectors calls at the hospital for the addresses of the patients.

4214. What you mean to say is this, that in the event of an epidemic breaking out in any part of Dublin, there is no regular authority within your own knowledge that will take the initiatory steps for the purpose of inspecting the district, and providing against the spread of the epidemic in that district?—I am not aware that there is. I may mention, to show the sort of thing that is done, that during the last epidemic of scarletina, which is in fact going on at present in Dublin, the Sanitary Association asked the Public Health Committee to do what is done in many English towns, that is to say, to find out the district where the disease was prevalent, and to put up notices calling the attention of the people to the fact that there was a disease abroad that was dangerous, and warning the people against it, and telling them what to do; but the Public Health Committee of the corporation declined to do that, on the ground that it "would produce unnecessary alarm." That has been done in Leeds. First of all, the Public Health Committee did not think it was a thing that was ever done anywhere. However, we were determined to show them that it was practised in well regulated towns, and we got notices from different towns in England. The one that we considered the best was Leeds, and we sent it to them; but they still thought that it was a thing which should not be done in Dublin.

4215. I observe that you spoke of your experience of Liverpool, and the information that you have derived from Liverpool?—My personal experience of Liverpool is not great; it is from Dr. Trench's reports and correspondence with him that I know so much about it.

4216. In devoting so much of your attention to sanitary matters in Dublin, was your attention at all directed to the manner in which those matters are dealt with in London?—Yes.

4217. You know that in London the practice is for the parochial authorities and vestry boards, when there is a report from their sanitary officer, that epidemics are likely to break out, or having broken out, the vestry boards take initiatory steps immediately for the purpose of seeing how the disease or epidemic is to be dealt with?—I believe that is the practice.

4218. There is no such mode of dealing with epidemics in their initiation in Dublin?—There does not appear to be; so far as we can see, there does not appear to be any special measures; there are no notices sent out; in fact, they say, "We do not wish to publish this fact, because it would create unnecessary alarm;" we have been told that several times.

4219. You have stated that the excessive rate of diseases and mortality is to be attributed, to a great extent, to the want of attention to the corporation manure depôts?—I enumerated that more as one of the largest of the unsanitary conditions; they are the largest nuisances.

4220. You did not intend to dwell very much upon it, but there were complaints against the others?—I believe so; but these are larger accumulations;

Mr. T. W. Grimshaw, M.D.

30 May 1876.

Mr. Collins—continued.

mulations; and in proportion to their size, the constant carrying to and from of the manure is more dangerous than the smaller accumulations; and in that way they are worse than the others.

4221. But, with the existing staff of inspectors and sanitary serjeants, and with the existing medical staff, such as it is, is it possible that any great nuisance of that kind can exist without having the attention of the authorities directed to it?—Yes, the attention of the authorities has been directed to this thing over and over again.

4222. Nevertheless, they allow the nuisances to remain?—Nevertheless, they allow them to remain. They promote them themselves; they carry on their own nuisances; they have two or three of the largest manure depôts in Dublin.

4223. When you say that they promote the nuisances, do you mean to say that they are indifferent to the consequences that may result?—I cannot say that they are indifferent, because that is going into their own minds, but they have been told over and over again that those things should be abolished, and it is the opinion of their own health officers, and yet they are maintained.

4224. But those nuisances, I believe, are recognised by nearly all the medical authorities as generating disease and epidemics to a great extent?—They promote them, and in some cases generate them, no doubt.

4225. With the knowledge of that fact, would you say that they would not contribute to the promotion of disease when they promote the existence of these depôts?—Certainly; most undoubtedly.

4226. You stated that there was only one public vehicle for the removal of patients suffering from whatever nature of disease they may be afflicted with, contagious diseases of various kinds, such as fever, or smallpox, or anything of that kind?—There is one vehicle maintained by the Public Health Committee, for the use of the public, but there are vehicles maintained by the unions; they (the guardians of the unions) have got as many as half-a-dozen machines, and a person afflicted with fever is brought in one cab, and another person afflicted with bronchitis is brought in another.

4227. Even in cases of epidemic, is there no organisation of any kind for removing patients to the hospitals?—During the smallpox epidemic, they increased the number of cabs. There was one I know in a hospital of which I have been a governor (Sir Patrick Dun's Hospital); the Public Health Committee applied to the governors of the hospital to permit them to use a portion of the hospital premises for a cab, and there was a cab placed there for the purpose of conveying smallpox patients to the hospitals, but that is the only one that I am acquainted with.

4228. In the case of that epidemic, have you any idea of the number of vehicles that might have been engaged for the removal of patients in that particular case, belonging to the sanitary authorities?—I only know of two; I do not say there were only two, but I am only aware of two; I know that there was a great difficulty in getting them. The Rev. Dr. Haughton stated publicly that he was obliged to get patients carried on the backs of their friends, and that that was the way they were taken to the hospital when they were suffering from smallpox, for the want of cabs to carry them.

Mr. Collins—continued.

4229. Is there no penalty of any kind provided by the Local Acts in Dublin to punish cabmen who carry patients afflicted with contagious diseases?—Not by the Local Acts, but by the Public Health Act there is.

4230. Is that often put into force?—It has been enforced sometimes, but not very frequently; however, it has been tolerably effective. Cabmen are afraid of it, they evade it, but they are afraid of it.

4231. According to your view, assuming that the organisation of the sanitary department is so bad, you believe that an effective remedy might be found by adopting Mr. Gray's suggestion, of appointing a medical head to control the management of these sanitary matters?—That would be the first thing that was necessary, but it would be necessary to act on his recommendations; for instance, in removing nuisances, providing for ash-pit cleaning, and all that kind of thing.

4232. Do you believe that the appointment of a chief medical officer would go a great way to accomplish the objects which you contemplate?—I do.

4233. That would involve, would it not, an increase of taxation for the purpose of providing funds to enable him to carry out those duties?—Yes.

4234. How do you reconcile those statements, or have you thought of doing it, in the two reports which we have had from the Local Government Board, that they saw no cause of complaint against the Public Health Committee of neglecting their duties, with your own views; do you agree with the Local Government Board in their interpretation, or do you disagree with them?—It appears to me that that is not the interpretation of the result of the whole of the correspondence with the Local Government Board.

4235. In one of the reports that has been read, we have had it that they saw no complaint against the Public Health Committee of the neglect of their duty, and it struck me that your views and those of the Local Government Board conflicted to a certain extent, and that you might possibly be able to reconcile them in some way?—I think I can reconcile the statements; it was a point which was put to me before, whether I thought that the inspection of the Local Government Board was efficiently performed. The point is this, we asked the Local Government Board to enforce those provisions about ash-pits; the Local Government Board acknowledged our letter, and said they would communicate with the Public Health Committee of the corporation. They communicated with them, and the inspector went to the corporation books and there found that there was a very large amount of sanitary work reported to be done, but the inspector did not go through the district to see what it was in the result; he merely took the statement as it appeared upon the books. Then we wrote again and we explained how this is recognised as the duty of the sanitary authorities in every town elsewhere; the Local Government Board in reply to that, do not decline to enforce the 39th section; that is the way the matter rests at present. I do not consider it by any means settled, in fact, though I cannot help thinking that there has been blame to a certain extent; their opinions are evidently shaken by the information which they have obtained.

4236. I presume

Mr. *Collins*—continued.

4236. I presume that I am correct in gathering from your evidence, that there is a very large amount of house property in Dublin, that is quite unfit for human habitation?—Certainly.

4237. And therefore you endorse the evidence which was given on a former occasion, that a great deal of this property should be cleared away entirely?—I do think so.

4238. Are you aware whether any steps are being taken by the Corporation of Dublin, under the provisions of the Act which was passed last year, to clear away any of that property?—No; the way that that question stands at present, is this: Mr. Gray who is a junior member of the corporation, but a very active member of it, has taken up the whole question of the sanitary condition of the city, and he proposed a number of resolutions to the corporation upon the subject; one of those resolutions was, that the corporation would be willing to enforce the Artizans' Dwellings Act as soon as they saw that there were private companies or private persons willing to rebuild on any property which they cleared. I dareeay you are aware, that the Act provides that they may let land, and so on. Mr. Gray's opinion was, that as the Act provides that the sanitary authorities were not to hold the houses longer than 10 years, except under exceptional circumstances, that it was not the intention of the Act that they should build, but they should clear the ground and get other people to build for them. Mr. Gray brought forward a resolution to the effect that they should, as soon as they found anyone willing or capable of building, commence clearing. That question has never been settled. In the corporation, when the division was taken, there were two people voted against Mr. Gray's resolution, and five people voted for it; but there was no quorum, and the resolution fell to the ground. I believe he intends to bring it forward again, but that is where the matter rests at present. They have not declined to enforce the Act, but in the evidence given by either the secretary of the Public Health Committee or one of the health officers before the Factories Commission, which sat in Dublin last autumn, he said that there were great difficulties in the way of enforcing the Act in Dublin, which I am not aware of for my part.

Mr. *Bruen*.

4239. I think you said that there was an impression in Dublin that the rates are exceptionally high?—There is.

4240. Is there a concurrent impression that the results which could be produced by the effect of an efficient application of those rates could be much more satisfactory than the results now are?—Certainly; the public impression in Dublin at the present moment is, that the work done for the rates paid is not sufficient.

4241. And that, even with the existing income, many of the serious evils which you complain of might be removed?—That is the general opinion. I think that they could do more than they do, but it is very hard to answer a question of that sort right off. I am quite aware that to do all that I have stated to-day, clean up all those places, and to do all those sanitary works, certainly an increased expenditure would be necessary; but I am under the impression that if the money was not wasted on other things, we might get the work done without any very great general increase in the rates.

Mr. *Bruen*—continued.

Mr. *T. W. Grimshaw*, M.D.

30 May 1876.

4242. I suppose I may also assume that the refuse which is collected is capable of being disposed of for a good deal of money?—Yes, it is capable of being disposed of for a good deal of money.

4243. Do you think that that is done in the case of Dublin?—The corporation, I believe, sell this stuff that they collect in their depôts; in some of the depôts it is sold at 2 *d.* a load. There is another depôt where it is given away gratis; and in a third depôt it has been sometimes sold and sometimes given away. I cannot exactly say what they are doing with it at present, but my inquiries have led me to believe that they gave it away in the third place, and that it was only sold in one of the depôts, but the ash-pit cleaners and privy cleaners in Dublin, the private contractors, do not think in that way, apparently; they consider it a very good trade, and they make it a trade.

4244. And they dispose of this refuse and stuff?—Yes, and they do dispose of it.

4245. And they can work by that means on lower terms in the way of cleaning out ash-pits than the corporation do?—Yes; they do it as a matter of fact lower. In the case of my own ash-pit, which I have isolated from my house, I had to pay 15 *s.* the other day to get it cleaned out. If I had employed the corporation to do it, it would have cost me 23 *s.*

4246. As regards the general question of the local government of towns connected with sanitary questions, do you think it is advisable that the upper classes, the owners of property, should have a voice in these matters, as well as the occupiers?—Certainly I do.

4247. Is it the fact that in Dublin now the owners of property are practically excluded from having such a voice?—I believe they are. I have not studied the question of the franchise very closely, but I know that they have very little influence.

4248. You are aware that complaints in that direction are made?—Yes, certainly that is the general impression.

Mr. *Kavanagh*.

4249. Do you consider that the present state of the Liffey contributes to the health of the city?—I consider that it is very injurious to the health of the city; it might be an advantage, but it is a great disadvantage at present.

4250. I suppose that subject has been brought under the notice of the Public Health Committee of the corporation?—They have had it under their notice constantly, and it has been discussed for many years.

4251. Has anything been done to abate the nuisance?—Nothing up to the present.

4252. Is there not some scientific or geological opinion held that there is a gravel bed, as it were, beneath the Liffey, which holds the sewage of Dublin like a sponge?—The recent map of the geological survey shows that there is a large gravel bed, an old raised sea beach, which the Liffey flows through for a considerable way at the east end of the town, and which spreads out into a considerable width; and that gravel bed is of necessity saturated with sewage; any soakage that gets into the Liffey must extend

Mr. T. W. Grimshaw, M.D.

30 May 1876.

Mr. *Kavanagh*—continued.

tend and saturate this for a considerable distance along both sides of the river, especially in the low ground beyond the quay wall. Where the quay has been raised it would not affect it so much, but beyond that this sewage filteration is supposed by geologists to be a very serious matter; and there is no doubt that the public health of those districts is very bad.

4253. Does there exist a body in Dublin called the Citizens Main Drainage Committee?—There does.

4254. How did that come into existence?—That body came into existence in consequence of a public meeting being held. There was a requisition signed by 2,000 ratepayers of Dublin, nearly all the large ratepayers calling upon the Lord Mayor to hold a meeting to consider what was to be done with regard to the main drainage of the city. That meeting was held in the Mansion House, and a committee was appointed to see what could be done. That committee was appointed on the 11th August 1874, and the instructions to the committee were, "To inquire and report upon the advisability of memorialising the Government, and for the appointment of a Royal Commission or otherwise, to ascertain whether a scheme of Liffey purification may not be devised which, while efficacious for the purpose, should be better suited than that sanctioned in 1871 to the financial circumstances of the city."

4255. Did they pass any other resolutions?—There was a resolution passed at the same meeting, inviting the co-operation of the corporation with that committee to help them to try and devise some means for improving the state of things.

Mr. *Kavanagh*—continued.

4256. Did that committee succeed in obtaining the co-operation of the corporation?—They did not; the corporation did not co-operate.

4257. Was there any other meeting consequent on the failure in obtaining the co-operation of the corporation?—There was another meeting held in the same year, on the 13th of November.

4258. What was the result of that?—The committee made a report to that meeting in which it was stated that they had failed to obtain the co-operation of the corporation, and recommended that they themselves should be re-appointed, and that they should memorialise the Government with the view of obtaining a Royal Commission to see what could be done in the matter.

4259. They did memorialise the Lord Lieutenant, did they not?—They did.

4260. Is the memorial a long one, or is it such that you could read to the Committee?—It is rather a long document, it gives an account of the whole transaction.

4261. In your opinion, did the resolutions passed by the ratepayers show any want of confidence in the corporation, in their way of managing sanitary matters?—There was a third meeting held after the memorial was presented, which was very fully attended, the Lord Mayor in the chair, at which the citizens passed a resolution appointing a committee, requesting them to draw up a bill, and to apply to Parliament for power to supersede the corporation and appoint a new main drainage board in Dublin; it appears to me that that showed a want of confidence in the authorities of the city.

Tuesday, 13th June 1876.

MEMBERS PRESENT:

Mr. Assheton.
Sir Michael Hicks Beach.
Mr. Brooks.
Mr. Bruen.
Mr. Collins.
Mr. J. P. Corry.
Mr. Gibson.
Mr. Kavanagh.
Sir Joseph M'Kenna.
Mr. O'Shaughnessy.
Dr. Ward.

SIR MICHAEL HICKS BEACH, BART., IN THE CHAIR.

Mr. GEORGE WILLIAM FINLAY, called in; and Examined.

Mr. *Finlay.*

13 June 1876.

Chairman.

4262. I BELIEVE you are an Auditor of the Local Government Board?—I am.

4263. Will you tell the Committee what your district is?—My district comprises 16 unions in the Province of Leinster, and the City of Dublin; the unions of Rathdown, Rathdrum, Enniscorthy, Shillelagh, Wexford, Carlow, Athy, Celbridge, Tullamore, Naas, Castlecomer, Edenderry, Abbeyleix, Baltinglass, Mountmellick, and Gorey.

4264. The inquiry of the Committee is confined to towns where there are municipalities or towns under various Local Government or Private Acts; and the questions which I ask you will relate to your duties simply with reference to towns; I believe you audit the accounts of the City of Dublin?—I do.

4265. Under what Act?—Under the Local Government Act of 1871, which imposes that duty upon the Local Government auditors.

4266. For how long have you audited those accounts?—This is the fourth year. I have not quite concluded the audit for the last year; I have concluded three audits, and I am engaged on the fourth.

4267 Can you explain to the Committee your system of auditing those accounts?—I get the cash book, and I go through all the items that are entered upon the receipt side of it; and I ascertain the items that ought to be received, but have not been received. Having ascertained the receipts, I examine the payments, and I see that each payment is legal, inasmuch as the Act of Parliament requires me to disallow all payments that are contrary to law, or that I may deem to be unfounded. I examine the payments to see that they are not contrary to law, and that they are not unfounded; and having satisfied myself upon that point, I see that the payments are sustained by adequate vouchers that they have been duly authorised by the corporation; that is to say, that the cheques are drawn and signed by three members of the corporation, and countersigned by the treasurer and by the town clerk before being presented to the bank; I then see that the party to whose order the cheque is made payable has given a receipt for the money.

4268. First as to the receipt side; can you tell us anything from your different reports upon the City of Dublin accounts of your impressions with regard to the correctness of that part of the account?—My first report will show that when I went first to audit the accounts of the corporation, I found that certain monies that ought to be received from the tolls of the cattle market on the North Circular Road had not been duly accounted for by the superintendent of the market. I found that he had been falsifying his accounts for a series of years previously. I ascertained the amount withheld from the corporation for the year under audit, and that amount was paid by members of his family; they were not under any legal obligation to pay it, inasmuch as there was no bond, and he had fled the country.

4269. Did you make any recommendation to the corporation for a change of system consequent upon that discovery?—I did.

4270. What was it?—It was not to accept the return of the superintendent of the cattle market, or of any other accounting officer, as correct, without going back to the foundation, and having an examination of the returns and other documents from which the account is made up, and the accuracy of the latter certified before the money is paid in.

4271. Was your suggestion adopted?—Yes, fully as regards the cattle market returns, and partially as regards other returns. That was a defalcation which could not have occurred if certain officers of the corporation had discharged their duty.

Mr. Gibson.

4272. What date was that?—That was the audit for the year 1872.

Chairman.

4273. Which were the officers who you consider failed in their duty?—The officer, in the first instance, who failed in his duty was Mr. Robinson, who was then the Secretary to the committee No. 2 having charge of the markets; he was the gentleman who was afterwards treasurer.

4274. Was there any other officer to whom your remark would apply?—There was a question about

Mr. *Finlay.*

12 June 1876.

Chairman—continued.

about fees payable by the town clerk; I mean fees received for the corporation; he has not lodged those fees to the credit of the corporation; he claims them as his own in virtue of his office, and that he is entitled to them. His predecessor, I find, had always lodged them.

4275. In what year did that question arise?—Ever since the appointment of Mr. Henry to the office of town clerk; that is about nine years now; those fees have not been lodged. For five or six years before his appointment they were regularly lodged by Mr. Farquhar, who preceded him in the office of town clerk. They were lodged in pursuance of a resolution of the Council in 1860, which resolution was to the effect that the salary paid to the town clerk should be in lieu of all fees, or allowances, or presentments connected with his office; and that all such should be paid in future into the borough fund. Mr. Farquhar was thereupon appointed to the office of town clerk, and lodged all fees and presentments received by him; but Mr. Henry contends that, inasmuch as the resolution was passed immediately prior to the appointment of Mr. Farquhar, and was not renewed when the office was vacant through his demise, he, Mr. Henry, was not bound by the resolution.

4276. Do you know what the annual amount of those fees was?—No; they are small. I can tell you what Mr. Farquhar lodged. In 1861 he lodged 61 *l.*; in 1862, 66 *l.*; in 1863, 57 *l.*; and in 1864, 52 *l.*

4277. What were those fees received for?—£. 50 was received for services rendered by him under the Parliamentary Voters' Act which entitled the town clerk to be paid. The remainder were fees received on the admission of freemen, for the sealing of burgess rolls, and some other small matters.

4278. For what services under the Parliamentary Voters' Act are fees paid?—For the annual preparation of the Parliamentary Voters' List, the town clerk is entitled to receive the money, but the corporation made it, by their resolution of 1860, a condition that whoever should be town clerk should lodge that fee and the other fees received by him to the credit of the corporation, they paying him a fixed salary.

4279. Then Mr. Henry contends that as that condition was not renewed with him, he is entitled to those fees?—Yes.

4280. Have the corporation taken any steps in the matter?—No, they have taken no steps. It was under the consideration of the corporation some five or six years ago, I think, but the matter was allowed to rest. An explanation was asked of Mr. Henry; he gave an explanation, and there was nothing further done in the matter.

4281. You have called the attention of the corporation to the matter, have you not?—I have called the attention of the corporation to it every time that I have audited the accounts.

4282. Can you make any statement to the Committee with respect to the rental of the corporation?—The rents appear to me to be very fairly collected, with the exception, perhaps, of the Baldoyle rents. There are a lot of wretched tenements in Baldoyle, and the arrears on those tenements are yearly increasing.

4283. What is the annual rental of those tenements?—The annual rental is about 220 *l.* or 230 *l.*

Chairman—continued.

4284. How many tenements are there?—I think there are about 100 tenements.

4285. Is the rental fairly collected, and properly accounted for on the other property of the corporation?—I think it is.

4286. Are there not very considerable arrears besides those on that Baldoyle property?—Nothing unreasonable, I think; there were somewhere about 7,000 *l.* arrears on the 31st of August 1875; the arrears are diminishing; they were higher by 1,000 *l.* or 1,200 *l.* the preceding year. Those arrears are collected half yearly; immediately after August they would be diminished considerably, or perhaps nearly altogether paid off. The tenants pay one gale within another.

Mr. *Kavanagh.*

4287. That means a hanging gale?—Just so.

Chairman.

4288. Have you made any recommendation to the corporation with reference to the Baldoyle property?—Yes; the recommendation I made was simply that as those arrears had been increasing year after year, the corporation should ascertain what was recoverable, and collect it, and declare the remainder irrecoverable.

4289. I do not think you told us what the total amount of arrears on the Baldoyle property was?—The total amount of arrears on the 31st August last was a little over 200 *l.* They were about 160 *l.* the year before. I spoke to the agent who collects the rents about the matter, and he seemed to think that the arrears would continue to increase; he told me there was no getting the money, and that the houses were rapidly falling into ruin; that they were utterly neglected.

4290. Are you aware why that property is so neglected and the houses left in such a state?—I do not know; the corporation, perhaps, are bad people to deal with property at a distance of 10 miles from Dublin.

4291. Are you aware whether it rests with the corporation as lessors or with the lessees to repair that property?—I should say that it rests with the corporation altogether, as they are tenements let to weekly tenants on which that arrear is.

4292. Are you aware whether it has been suggested to the corporation that that property might be sold with advantage?—Yes; some members of the corporation have considered that question; I know it is the opinion of the law and land agent, Mr. Morgan, that the property ought to be sold and applied to the liquidation of some of their debts. They would be bound to apply it in that way if they should sell it. I think Mr. Morgan submitted his views to the corporation in a report.

4293. Then, I suppose, you have made no recommendation upon that point?—I did not think it within my province.

4294. Are there any other points with reference to the receipts of the corporation on which you have made any recommendation for a change in the system?—Finding that a sum of 9 *l.* 10 *s.*, the price of old stores sold in December 1873, was not lodged with the treasurer down to the time of audit (July 1874), and that the sale was not attended with sufficient publicity, I suggested that tenders be invited on such occasions, through the

Chairman—continued.

the medium of the newspapers. The money was lodged immediately after my inquiries. I made a recommendation with reference to some moneys that are lying in the hands of the gas company; there is 500 *l.* lying there for the corporation, and the corporation will not take it.

4295. How is that?—That I cannot say. The gas company two or three years ago applied for an Act of Parliament, and the corporation opposed them, and they came to an arrangement in the House of Commons about it, the gas company agreeing to pay the corporation 500 *l.* as their costs of the opposition. The secretary and the chairman of the gas company have both told me that the money is there, and that the corporation have only to ask for it to obtain it. The corporation have paid about 325 *l.* to their own agents, the Parliamentary agents, and the gas engineer, as the costs of that opposition.

4296. And no steps have been taken by the corporation to get out the money?—No steps have been taken by the corporation to get the money.

4297. Is there any other point which occurs to you?—The fees receivable by the secretary to the Lord Mayor are paid now into the funds of the corporation; they were always considered the private property of the secretary until about two years ago; when Mr. Brooks was Lord Mayor, there was a change made for the first time, increasing the Lord Mayor's salary by 262 *l.* a year, the amount to be applied as salary to his secretary, the latter being paid up to that time by fees. The arrangement then made was that the secretary should hand over to the corporation certain fees, but not the whole of his fees, and the result is that a very bad bargain has been made for the citizens, inasmuch as they pay 262 *l.* as salary to the Lord Mayor's secretary, and receive in return fees to the amount of 50 *l.* a year.

4298. Do you know what the amount of the fees still received by the Lord Mayor's secretary is?—I do not know what the entire amount of the fees is. I have no power to inquire, the portion that he receives being his own property. I understand that they are somewhere about 100 *l.* a year, but I am not certain about that; at all events I know that all that he gives up to the corporation of the fees received in the Lord Mayor's Court amount to 50 *l.* a year or thereabouts.

4299. Turning to the expenditure side of the accounts, the accounts are divided under several heads, are they not?—Yes, there is an account for each fund administered by the corporation.

4300. Are those funds kept properly separate?—They are kept properly separate in the accounts of the corporation, but they are not kept properly separate in the bank. The monies are thrown into a common purse in some cases.

4301. Will you explain to the Committee how that is done?—The improvement rate and the grand jury rate are put into a common fund, called the Improvement Fund, and drawn from indiscriminately for the purpose of either. The improvement fund may not have a balance, and very often has not a balance, to its credit, and the monies of the grand jury would be used in that case, and *vice versâ*, if the grand jury wanted money. Then there is the borough

Chairman—continued.

Mr. *Finlay.*

13 June 1876

fund, which is composed of the rents of the corporation property, amounting to about 18,000 *l.* or 19,000 *l.* a year; these and the waterworks' moneys, and the main drainage rate, are thrown into a common fund, called the Borough Fund, in the bank, and are drawn out indiscriminately, the one for the purposes of another; and at the present moment of a sum of 35,000 *l.* received by the corporation under a recent Act of Parliament, for the purpose of paying off some Lloyds' bonds that they owed, and for making filter-beds, at Stillorgan, and doing other works in connection with the waterworks, 6,000 *l.* has been drawn away, without the knowledge of the Waterworks Committee, by No. 3 committee, for borough fund purposes. The waterworks people are complaining of this, as they will want that money very shortly for the purpose of making those filter-beds.

4302. Do I understand that each of those committees, although administering funds properly separate, and keeping separate accounts, have yet power to draw upon the whole of this money which is placed in one fund in the bank?—Yes; No. 3 committee is charged especially with the administration of the borough fund, and yet they have power to draw upon the common fund in the bank provided for the waterworks and the main drainage purposes.

4303. Do you consider that that is in accordance with the law?—No, it is directly at variance with it.

4304. Will you tell us the provisions of the law with which you consider it is at variance?—The Waterworks Act and the Main Drainage Acts specify that the funds to be raised thereunder shall be applied only to the purposes of those Acts.

4305. You consider the practice illegal; do you consider it also objectionable?—I consider it illegal and objectionable, and I have called attention to it, I think, in every one of my reports.

4306. Will you read to us the terms in which you have done so?—In my report on the accounts for the year ending the 31st August 1873, I say, "I would suggest that an arrangement be made with the Bank of Ireland for the keeping of a separate account for each fund administered by the corporation. At present all lodgments on account of the Borough Fund, the Waterworks Fund, and the Main Drainage Fund, and all payments made in respect of those funds, are placed by the bank to the credit and debit of but one account, entitled 'The Borough Fund Account.' In like manner all lodgments and payments in respect of the Improvement Fund, the Grand Jury Fund, and the North and South District Sewers Fund, are placed to the credit and debit respectively of one account, entitled 'Improvement Fund Account.' The proposed change would facilitate the ascertainment of the balances on foot of each fund, at any time, and would in other respects be desirable. It would also render it impossible that money belonging to one fund should be drawn in ignorance for the purposes of another." There was nothing done. Then, in my next year's report, I say "The suggestion I made last year that an arrangement be made with the bank for the keeping of a separate account for each fund administered by the corporation has not been adopted. As a consequence of the existing arrangement whereby moneys belonging to

Mr. *Finlay*.

13 June 1876.

Chairman—continued.

to other funds on being lodged in the bank are placed to the credit of either the Borough Fund account, or the Improvement Fund account, the balance of 3,227 *l.* 13 *s.* 7 *d.* due by the Improvement Fund at the end of the year under audit, represents so much of the moneys collected and lodged for the purposes of the District Sewers Fund, but applied in payment of claims on the Improvement Fund. This application of the sewer rates is directly opposed to the 113th and 114th sections of the 12 & 13 Vict. c. 97, which prescribe very clearly the objects to which they are to be applied. It is undoubtedly the policy of that enactment that these two funds shall be kept altogether separate and distinct. The balance against the Improvement Fund would, moreover, have been vastly increased had the Corporation observed the conditions (as prescribed by the 116th section) on which they have, between January 1866 and March 1875, obtained loans to the amount of 28,550 *l.* on the security of the improvement rate, 2,900 *l.* of which only have been repaid. Those conditions are, that the corporation shall set apart and appropriate 1-20th part of the Improvement Fund 'in payment off of the principal moneys which shall have been borrowed or secured on the said improvement rate.' From the commencement of the year 1866 down to the 31st August 1874 the receipts which go to form the 'Improvement Fund,' namely, the improvement rates, collected and lodged, and cattle market receipts, amounted to 473,804 *l.* 1-20th of this sum would amount to 23,690 *l.*, 22,150 *l.* of which would be required to pay off the balance due on foot of these loans to the 31st August last, and to which purpose it is clear it should have been applied. I have to repeat my recommendation that there be a separate account kept in the bank, and a separate pass-book provided for each fund administered by the corporation." I have understood that the corporation object to separating them on the ground that it interferes with what is termed financing, that is, applying the moneys in the common fund for the purpose of some fund that is in debt.

4307. That is a process to which you, as auditor, object?—Certainly.

4308. Can you give us any other instances besides the one you spoke of, in which that has carried out?—I have mentioned the recent been application of 6,000 *l.* of the waterworks money; I do not know of any other; nothing else has come before me, but there is no doubt that it frequently happens that they use money in that way as they want it. This waterworks business is one of the evil results of the present system which I have done my best to remedy. Some steps should be taken to compel the corporation to keep the funds separate in the bank.

4309. If the corporation are acting illegally in the matter, has no one the power to compel them to act according to law?—That is a question which I cannot answer positively; I should say that the burgesses would have power, and I know that in some cases the burgesses are entitled to come to the Court of Chancery to compel the corporation to act within the law.

4310. Has any question arisen since you have audited the accounts of the corporation as to the security given by the officers?—The only question was in the case of M'Cann, the market superintendent, which I have mentioned. There was no bond for him, although he had been in office for some years. The corporation at the time of his appointment required him to enter into a bond, I think in a sum of 500 *l.*; they afterwards reduced the amount considerably, but still no bond was executed. His successor has given a bond, but I do not know to what amount. I am satisfied as to its sufficiency.

Mr. O'Shaughnessy.

4311. Was M'Cann a defaulter?—Yes.

Chairman.

4312. To what extent was he a defaulter; do you know?—I ascertained that during the year under audit the sum misapplied by M'Cann amounted to 114 *l.* 16 *s.* 6 *d.*; and on his accounts for the previous year, and for the period subsequent to the 31st of August, at which date the year closed, being examined, a number of defalcations, amounting to 222 *l.* 10 *s.* 11 *d.*, were discovered; making altogether 336 *l.* as the amount of M'Cann's defalcations. The first-mentioned sum was lodged during the audit, but owing to the absence of security the larger sum of 222 *l.* 10 *s.* 11 *d.* was lost.

4313. Since that time have the corporation taken, in your opinion, proper security from the officers that they have appointed?—I think they have; I suggested it to them, and I pointed out the necessity for an examination of the bonds periodically, say once a year, to see that they have them all right, as is the case with boards of guardians.

4314. Have they taken steps for that purpose?—I do not know whether they have done that or not.

4315. Have you made any other recommendations to the corporation, with the view of guarding against loss by defalcation on the part of their officers?—No, I have not, beyond, as I stated, the necessity for having the returns sent in by the different accounting officers examined by the proper officer of the corporation, to see that the corporation have received all the money that they were entitled to receive from them.

4316. Who would be the proper officer to examine them?—There is some doubt about that. I have been always inclined to think that the proper officer would be the secretary of the committee having charge of the peculiar source of revenue, and that as regards the markets and toll-houses, &c., the proper officer would be the secretary of No. 2 committee. The secretaries do not appear to be satisfied that it is a part of their duty; they seem to think it is the duty of the accountant, or some person in the treasurer's department, and the treasurer's department say that it is not their duty; that their duty is to receive the monies that are brought to them. However, I mean to recommend, in my report at the close of the audit on which I am now engaged, that all the accounts of the several committees be transferred to the city accountant, and a suitable staff be given him, which are in existence in other departments, and that all the accounts of the corporation be kept by him, and all accounts of receipts and all bills presented for payment be examined by him, and their accuracy in every case be certified before either the money is received from the accounting officer or payment is made to the party to whom the corporation are indebted. This will necessitate the keeping by the city

Chairman—continued.

city accountant of personal legers for the money transactions of each committee.

4317. Do you consider that that would be a safeguard against defalcation?—I consider that it would be a great improvement upon the present system, and I know it is the opinion of many members of the corporation. Mr. Dockrell has been very anxious to have it effected for a long time past; he and some other members of No. 1 committee have succeeded in bringing the accounts of that committee into a satisfactory state from a state of great confusion.

4318. Has there been any deficiency in the collected rates during the last few years within your knowledge; has the amount in the bank represented the amount collected?—So far as I know. I have no power over the collection of rates in the city of Dublin.

4319. I am asking you whether you have been satisfied that the amount in the bank to the credit of the rate has represented the amount collected?—Yes, invariably.

4320. Of course with the question of collection you have nothing to do?—No. The Collector General's accounts have been audited by Master Fitzgibbon, the Receiver Master of the Court of Chancery, up to the present time.

4321. Besides auditing the accounts of the city of Dublin, you also audit, do you not, the accounts of towns under the Act of 1854, and I think under the Act of 9 Geo. 4?—I do not think there is any town in my district now under the Act of the 9th of Geo. 4. All, or very nearly all, the towns of Ireland have adopted the Act of 1854.

Mr. Gibson.

4322. Is not Wicklow under the Act of George the 4th?—Yes, Wicklow is under that Act.

Chairman.

4323. As that is the earlier Act, will you tell us the mode in which you audit the accounts of Wicklow?—On my first visit to the town of Wicklow I found matters in a very unsatisfactory state as regards the accounts, and the course of procedure in regard to receipts and payments altogether at variance with the law. The first year is the year ending the 31st December 1872, at which time I found a balance in the hands of the agent of the Commissioners amounting to 385 *l.*; and I objected to the manner in which they dealt with the funds which he received. He is a very respectable man, and received the rents of the corporation, but instead of lodging the amount with the treasurer to the credit of the Town Commissioners, and of having the payments made by cheque drawn by the Town Commissioners, there were certain payments that he was authorised to make, and he regularly made them, and the result was that he had this large balance in hand, while at the same time the legally appointed treasurer, the manager of the bank, was charging the Commissioners with interest on over drafts. I got the system changed, and all the money received by the agent regularly lodged in the bank in Wicklow, and all payments made on the cheques of the Town Commissioners.

4324. What was the annual amount of the receipts, taking that year as an example?—The rents received amounted to 1,224 *l.* that year. The entire income of the Town Commissioners of Wicklow is derived from rents; they make no

Chairman—continued.

rate, and are not under the necessity of making any, for they have a very good property, but they are very heavily encumbered with debt; and the interest they pay during the year absorbs nearly half the amount they receive.

4325. What was the debt incurred for?—The debt, amounting to 12,000 *l.*, was incurred on mortgage with the consent of the Lords of Her Majesty's Treasury, for the purpose of lending the money to the Harbour Commissioners, who were desirous of improving the port of Wicklow, which was represented as being much in need of improvement. The Harbour Commissioners were to pay the interest, and to repay the principal; but they have never been able to do either the one or the other, and the consequence is that this heavy burthen of interest of 540 *l.* a year has fallen upon the Town Commissioners, and I do not see any prospect of a release from that burthen.

4326. Can you tell us where this property is situate?—It is situate in and about the town of Wicklow.

4327. Is the system of accounts of the Wicklow Town Commissioners now satisfactory, in your opinion?—Satisfactory so far as that the monies are lodged in the bank regularly, and the payments made, as I have stated, on the cheques of the Town Commissioners, as in other places.

4328. Have you any improvement to suggest in the system of account keeping which towns in the position of Wicklow adopt?—Not in Wicklow. I think that the system of accounts is satisfactory there now. The rents are regularly paid. There was something very peculiar in the mode in which the Commissioners dealt with the lands that had fallen into their hands up to that time. A portion of their property had been for a very long time, 99 years, in the hands of Colonel Gun Cuninghame's family. The lease expired about two or three years ago; and instead of letting the tenements to the highest bidder, or, at all events, letting them at somewhat about the tenement valuation, they let them, in some instances, to members of their own body, and to their agent, very considerably below the letting value.

4329. Could you give us the figures showing that?—Yes, I can. At the audit for the following year, 1873, some ratepayers appeared before me, and objected to the insufficiency of the receipts, owing to the mode of dealing with the corporate property. As the matter was not strictly before me at that time, I felt that I could not take cognisance of it, and I postponed the consideration of it until my next audit, when I went very fully into it, and I can give you the result from my report to the Local Government Board. "It was represented to me at the audit that, owing to the manner in which the Commissioners dealt with the property which came into their hands in the course of last year, on the expiration of the lease for 99 years, made by the old corporation of the borough of Wicklow to an ancestor of Colonel Gun Cuninghame, the Commissioners' receipts during the year were less than they ought to have been. The property in question, which consists of houses and building sites in the town, was leased, in the year 1775, at a rent of 3 *l.* 13 *s.* 10 *d.* per annum, and by virtue of the Act 3 & 4 Vict. c. 108, which abolished the old corporation, the ownership became vested in the Town Commissioners, who are constituted under the Act 9 Geo. 4, c. 82. Colonel Gun Cuninghame derived from his under tenants, at the

Mr. *Finlay.*

13 June 1876.

Mr. *Finlay.*

13 June 1876.

Chairman—continued.

the time the lease expired, an annual rent in respect of this property of 167 *l.*, and Griffiths' valuation of it amounts to 300 *l.* 10 *s.* per annum. The Town Commissioners, in the course of last year, leased this property for 75 years to Colonel Gun Cuninghame's tenants, who were in possession" (those were sub-tenants who were in possession at the time the property fell into the hands of the Commissioners), "among whom were four members of their own body, and the Commissioners' agent, at rents amounting in the aggregate to 66 *l.* 5 *s.* per annum, being 234 *l.* 5 *s.* under the tenement valuation, and 100 *l.* 15 *s.* less than was received by Colonel Gun Cuninghame, whose tenants held only from year to year." They undertook to keep the premises in repair although they were only yearly tenants. "It was asserted on the part of the Commissioners and their agent that the rents were only fair and reasonable, and that the lettings were made in accordance with an arrangement or promise made many years ago by the Town Commissioners, and ever since acted on by them, that the occupying tenants of properties leased by the old corporation should, on the expiration of those leases, receive leases for 75 years, as an inducement to them to maintain their respective tenements in a proper state of repair, and prevent dilapidation of the property; and that this arrangement has been beneficial to the town. Some of Colonel Gun Cuninghame's tenants no doubt erected buildings and otherwise improved their holdings, and all were expected to keep their tenements in repair, although only yearly tenants, and were content to pay rents amounting in the aggregate to 167 *l.* per annum; yet, when the Commissioners got the management of this property they reduced those rents by very nearly two-thirds, while granting leases for the longest period for which the law enabled them to lease the property. The Commissioners had previously been advised, by counsel whom they consulted, that as trustees for the public they should set up the premises separately to public competition, and procure the most favourable terms they could; that members of their own body could not legally take leases from them; and that any such leases would be void in law. On receiving this opinion, the Commissioners published a notice in the local newspaper on the 2nd of May last, intimating that they would receive tenders on the 11th for the several holdings. The objects the Commissioners would appear to have had in view in publishing this advertisement were the rendering a formal compliance with the law, and the ascertaining of the letting value of the holdings, rather than the throwing of the latter open to competition. All the parties in occupation tendered, but the Commissioners' determination to let only to Colonel Gun Cuninghame's tenants being publicly known, only a few tenders were received from other parties, containing offers, however, of very much higher rents than the premises were subsequently leased at. Four of the Commissioners who were tenants in possession resigned their offices at the same time, and then obtained leases of their holdings at a large reduction of the rents which they had been previously paying. Two of the number were, in a couple of months afterwards, re-elected as Commissioners. All the property was leased simply as building sites, the Commissioners taking no account of the value of the buildings erected thereon. Granting that the tenants who invested money in increasing the value of their holdings by buildings or other improvements (and only a portion of them did so) were entitled to a preference from the Commissioners in consideration of their expenditure, and that the law enabled the Commissioners in their capacity of trustees to grant such preference, their interests would probably be considered to have been sufficiently respected, having regard to the present yearly net annual value of the tenements, and the income derived from them by Colonel Gun Cuninghame, by leasing their holding to them at rents not less than they had been previously paying as tenants from year to year. The rents at which the premises have been leased would appear to be altogether inadequate and unreasonable, and consequently the complaint of the insufficiency of the Commissioners' receipts during the year appeared to me to be well founded. The manner in which the Commissioners have dealt with this property, is, I understand, likely to be brought before the Court of Chancery by burgesses of the borough, who feel aggrieved by the proceeding."

4330. Was any action subsequently taken upon that subject?—No.

4331. It was not brought before the Court of Chancery?—Not that I am aware of, and I think I should have heard it if it were

4332. You have no power to do anything but to report the matter?—No further power. I believe the law is, that any two burgesses could have brought the matter before the Court of Chancery.

Mr. Kavanagh.

4333. Would it have cost much to do so?—I do not know. I am afraid that Chancery proceedings always cost a great deal.

4334. Would the burgesses who brought it before the Court have had to bear the cost?—I do not know. If they had succeeded, I doubt if they would have had to bear the costs.

Mr. Brun.

4335. But they would have to run the risk?—Yes, they must run that risk, of course.

Chairman.

4336. Could you make any suggestion to the Committee with regard to an amendment of the law which, in your opinion, would prevent such a state of things as your report discloses?—I do not know that any amendment would be necessary. I think there are sufficient powers to persons entitled to move in the matter, and that the law provides sufficient remedy.

4337. Is there any other point in the case of Wicklow which you wish to mention to the Committee?—No, beyond that the Commissioners have placed an unnecessarily large amount in their town clerk's hands for petty expenses during the year. I objected to this, and presume it will not be repeated. The accounts are in other respects kept in a satisfactory manner.

4338. So far as the expenditure is concerned, you have no fault to find with the conduct of the Commissioners?—No, I have not.

4339. Turning to the towns under the Act of 1854, what towns are there in your district under that Act?—I think all the other towns in my district are under that Act. In the town of Trim

Mr. *Finlay*.

13 June 1876.

Chairman—continued.

Trim I have had reason to complain of the manner in which the Town Commissioners deal with their landed property. They make no rates there; it is a similar case to that of Wicklow; the property is sufficient for their purposes.

4340. What is the annual value of their property?—The receipts from property are a little over 600 *l.* a year.

4341. Is the property situate in or near the town?—In and about the town; it is property derived from the old corporation.

4342. What was your complaint with reference to that?—I stated in my report, "The principal source of revenue is a property derived by the Commissioners from the old corporation of the borough of Trim, (styled the Portreeve, Burgesses, and Freemen of Trim), which was dissolved by the Municipal Reform Act of 1840, and consists of 'common lands,' comprising 450 acres. I understand that the property was, at a distant period, of much greater extent, but was reduced to its present dimensions by portions having been alienated for ever by the old corporation. These common lands were divided into a large number of 'portions' or holdings, which were granted by the old corporation to freemen of the borough, at the nominal rent of 1 *s.* per annum, to be held for the life of the grantee in each case, and on his demise by his widow for one year additional, and at the expiration thereof to revert to the corporation. Accordingly, from time to time a considerable number of these portions have fallen into the hands of the Town Commissioners, who, on such occasions send a committee, consisting of three of their members, to inspect the premises and determine their letting value. The portions have been, in many instances, sublet by the grantees, and if the tenant in occupation be willing to hold at that rent, he is understood to be entitled to a preference; if not, the holding is let on proposal to some party approved by the Commissioners. In numerous instances individual Commissioners have become the tenants, and in some cases such Commissioners have sold their interest to other parties, who shortly after have had their rents reduced on the ground that they were fixed too high by the committee of valuation. This practice of the Commissioners of letting the lands to members of their own body in preference to persons who are not connected with them is complained of as unfair, if not illegal. It would appear to be at variance with the policy of the law, which is to prohibit members of municipal corporations from having or deriving any personal advantage from the management of the trust confided to them, and in a purely agricultural district such as Trim, where land is so much desired by the people, and so difficult to obtain, it does appear to be calculated to raise unpleasant feelings and suspicions unfavourable to the Commissioners, even though as high a rent were obtained from a member of their body as any other solvent tenant would be willing to give. There is no map of the Commissioners' property, and no rental except that kept by the agent, which only shows the portions that have fallen into the hands of the Commissioners, but of the tenements yet to fall in there does not appear to be any record. The town clerk, who ought to be in a position to supply authentic information on the subject, could give none, and the agent who receives the rents seemed to be in doubt as to their number, but he said he thought there were about five or six," that is, of tenements yet to fall in. "He told me that no other person could give any information on the subject. A survey and a map of the property, showing the different buildings and extent of each, as well those in the Commissioners' possession as those yet to fall in, ought to be prepared at once, and hung up in the board-room at the town hall."

4343. What was the date of that report?—I made that report in 1873.

4344. Were any steps taken in consequence of it?—I ceased to be auditor after that. On the appointment of an additional auditor to the district, the town of Trim was transferred to one of my colleagues; but, I believe that no steps have been taken by the Commissioners with the view to carrying out that suggestion.

4345. Was that report made public in the town?—I remember it happened to get into the "Freeman's Journal," and was published very extensively.

4346. Did none of the inhabitants take any steps with reference to that?—No.

4347. I suppose you are not aware whether the practices to which you have alluded still continue?—I should say they do; I have no reason whatever to suppose that they have ceased, or that there is any chance of their being discontinued.

Mr. Bruen.

4348. Who is the auditor now?—Mr. Collett; I am pretty sure there has been no change.

Chairman.

4349. Have you anything to mention with regard to the expenditure of the town of Trim?—Yes; I had a great deal of litigation with the Commissioners, and even with the magistrates of Trim Petty Sessions Bench, with reference to disallowances that I made there. I found that the Commissioners had given a sum of money to the parish priest to enable him to provide gaseliers and gas-fittings for his house, and for the parish chapel, and at the same time they gave a certain sum to the Wesleyan Methodist body for the purpose of providing a gaselier for their house of worship. They gave some other moneys; for instance, a contribution to the Flower Show Committee of 5 *l.*; for scouring the Boyne, as they called it, as a sanitary work. It was, in fact, for clearing the stream, which is sluggish at the bridge of Trim, for the purpose of a boatrace. At the flower show every year there are boatraces, but a lot of flaggers had grown up in the water, and with a scythe or reaping-hook they were cut down a foot or so under the surface so as to admit of the boats passing; and the Commissioners called that a sanitary measure. They handed 5 *l.* over to the Flower Show Committee, who spent only 4 *l.* upon clearing the water, and 2 *l.* was given to the Chairman of the Town Commissioners for presiding at the election of Commissioners in June and October 1871. I disallowed all those payments. They appealed to the Local Government Board against my disallowances; but my decision was confirmed in every case by the Local Government Board, and thereupon the money given to the Flower Show Committee, and the money paid to the chairman of the Town Commissioners for presiding at the election, and the money given to the Wesleyan body, were refunded; but the money given to the parish priest was not refunded, and I was obliged to proceed to

Mr. *Finlay*.

13 June 1876.

Chairman—continued.

to enforce it under the Act, by summoning the three Commissioners who had signed the cheque, and who were the parties surcharged. They defended it; they had counsel at Trim, and there was a long argument about it; there were two magistrates on the Bench, and as they differed in opinion there was no decision; then I issued another summons, and I went again to Trim; at that time there were, I think, five magistrates on the Bench, and they were unanimous in dismissing the case. They held that it was all right, considering that it was a Roman Catholic district, they seemed to think that it was a proper application of the funds, and that I ought to have allowed the expenditure. My counsel pointed out the provisions of the Act of Parliament under which the proceedings were taken, provisions so clear that the Lord Chief Justice of the Queen's Bench said, when the case went into his court, that they were level to the most rustic intellect. The Act of 10 Vict. c. 31, directs the magistrates, on the auditor submitting his certificate of disallowance, to inquire whether the amount has been paid, and if they find that the amount has not been paid, to make an order for it, but notwithstanding that the magistrates would go into the merits of the case, and they dismissed the case, as they stated, without prejudice. My counsel wanted to have it dismissed on the merits, so as to admit of an appeal to the Superior Court, but they would not dismiss it on the merits. My counsel said, You will give us another summons, if you dismiss it without prejudice; but they would not do that, unless on a new complaint, which it was too late then to make, so that the position I occupied was, that I was put out of court without any chance of coming into court again, so far as the action of the magistrates could prevent me.

Mr. *Collins*.

4350. Were the magistrates unanimous?—They were.

Mr. *Gibson*.

4351. Who were the magistrates?—One of them was the stipendiary magistrate, Captain Butler; I do not remember the names of the others. There were four justices of the peace and one stipendiary. It was with great difficulty that we succeeded in getting a rehearing. We were obliged to go the Court of Queen's Bench to compel the magistrates to issue another summons. There was a conditional order obtained, and the magistrates answered it. The case was fully argued in the Court, and the conditional order was confirmed, and they were obliged to issue another summons.

4352. Were they the same magistrates?—I think the same magistrates were present; the order of the Court of Queen's Bench, I think, was addressed to them personally, requiring them to rehear the case. They ultimately made the necessary order.

Chairman.

4353. Was the money eventually paid by the Commissioners who signed the cheque?—It was paid, but I believe by the parish priest. In fact, some of the Commissioners who signed the cheque told me they were prevented by him from paying it. I spoke to them about it and said, "You are wasting the funds of the town in this litigation; it must ultimately go against you, and you are recklessly wasting the funds of the town." They gave me to understand that it was the parish priest who would not allow the money to be repaid.

4354. Do you know what the costs of that case were from beginning to end?—I should say that the costs of the whole of the proceedings upon the town were nigh 100 *l.*

4355. What were your costs?—I speak now of my costs.

4356. Your costs were paid out of the town funds?—Yes; they were paid out of the town funds, under the Act of 1871. The Town Commissioners drew a cheque afterwards in payment of their own solicitor's costs in the case, and that payment was disallowed by my successor when he went to audit the accounts, and the amount has since been paid, but not until proceedings were threatened; they got so much of litigation in the other case that they were not disposed to fight it with him.

4357. Is there anything else which you think it necessary to mention to the Committee with regard to Trim?—No; my connection with Trim ceased then.

4358. What other towns in your district are under the Act of 1854?—Perhaps I may mention that in some of the towns in my district the Report of the Municipal Corporation Commissioners of 1835 showed that the old corporations had property of which there is no trace now.

4359. Could you tell us which those towns are?—Yes, Athy is one. The Corporation Commissioners returned a revenue there of 154 *l.* a year; but there is no trace of it, except the tolls for weighing at the public crane and could can be considered identical with it. They do not describe what the property is, they merely put it down as so much per annum.

4360. What do those tolls amount to now?—About 140 *l.*, at present.

4361. And you do not know whether they existed at the time of the Report of the Commissioners?—I do not. At Kilbeggan there was 50 *l.* a year paid to the portreeve from the public crane; there is no trace of that. In Naas there was 322 *l.* a-year, and the Commissioners stated that it should be more. That property, it appears, has been handed over to the trustees of the Protestant Orphan Society of Kildare. The Act of Parliament, 3 & 4 Vict. c. 108, enacted, that on the abolition of the old corporations, wherever a town had adopted the provisions of the 9th of George the 4th, the revenues of the old corporation should go to the Commissioners appointed thereunder, and wherever there were no such Commissioners, the revenues should go to the board of guardians of the union in which the town is situate for the benefit of the electoral division; but the property of the old corporation of Naas appears to have been handed over to the Protestant Orphan Society of Kildare, under what authority I do not know.

4362. When was that done?—It must have been done about 1840, I should say. The only case that I know of in which there was property at the suppression of the corporation, which property is now held and enjoyed by the board of guardians, is that of Portarlington. The revenue of the old corporation, amounting to about 55 *l.* a year, is handed over to the board of guardians of

Chairman—continued.

Mr. *Finlay*.

14 June 1876.

of Mount Mellick Union by the Earl of Portarlington, who holds the property. The Towns Improvement Act, 1854, superseded the 9th of George the 4th wherever its provisions were adopted.

4363. Are there any other towns that you could mention?—Yes; there are Bagnalstown, Athy, Carlow, Enniscorthy, Gorey, Maryborough, Mount Mellick, Newbridge, Tullaghmore, and Wexford, in addition to the towns that I have already mentioned.

4364. Are those towns which you have mentioned in your district under the Act of 1854?—Yes.

4365. Have you told us of all of those which, being old boroughs, were possessed of property at the time of the passing of the Act of the 3 & 4 Vict. and the Act of 1854?—Yes, all in my district.

4366. Is Kilbeggan now under the Act of 1854?—Kilbeggan is one of the suppressed boroughs: it has ceased to have any existence as a corporate town in any sense.

4367. That was a place which had property as an old borough, but which now is under a board of guardians, the property not having been handed over to them?—Yes, it is a case in which the property should have gone to the board of guardians if there was any.

4368. Have any of those towns, putting aside Portarlington and Kilbeggan, any property in the possession of Town Commissioners?—No, with the exception of Wicklow and Trim which I have mentioned, none of those towns have possession of property. The funds are derived from the rates that they are empowered to levy under the Act.

4369. The rates are limited, are they not, by the Act of 1854?—Yes, to 1 *s*. in the pound for ordinary purposes, and 1 *s*. 6 *d*. in the pound where they supply water.

4370. What is your experience as an auditor of the working of that limit?—My experience is favourable to it. The Act appears to me to provide for the cleansing, lighting, paving, and water supply, if they choose to have it, and to provide for nearly all the wants of the town.

4371. With regard to the limit of 1 *s*. in the pound, have you found, as a matter of finance, that the Town Commissioners keep within it?—Yes.

4372. You spoke, did you not, of certain disallowances which you had made in Wexford?—No, not in Wexford. I began with Bagnalstown, in the county of Carlow, and I disallowed at my last audit 16 *l*. 12 *s*. paid to the sanitary and nuisance inspectors subsequently to the date, October 1874, on which the Public Health Act came into operation, when the powers of the Town Commissioners, &c., as the sanitary authority of the town, were transferred to the board of guardians, and the sanitary officers appointed and paid by the latter, but I have not taken any steps to enforce my disallowance. I did not think it right to take any steps, because the payments were evidently made in ignorance of the Commissioners' powers. They had overlooked the fact of the recent introduction of that Act. I found, in a considerable number of cases, small sums, amounting altogether to about 6 *l*. or 7 *l*., were retained by the town clerk, acting in his capacity as clerk of the petty sessions. No return was made of them to the Town Commissioners. They are entitled to the fines inflicted under the Act of 1854, for drunkenness and offences under that Act. The particulars were ascertained by me at the audit with much difficulty, and I presume that the town clerk has lodged the money since. Mr. Newton, the chairman, undertook to see that he did so. I disallowed in the Blackrock case, at my first audit, 6 *l*. paid out of the improvement rate to the Rathdown Board of Guardians for the interment of poor persons, on the ground that the Commissioners had no right to apply the funds provided for improvement purposes in that way. On my intimating that if the Town Commissioners would make a burial rate, there would be no further steps, the secretary undertook that it should be done. I disallowed at a subsequent audit a further sum of 2 *l*. 5 *s*. expended in like manner. The Town Commissioners then appeared to hold that they were not a Burial Board, and that they had no power to make a burial rate; and that they were empowered to expend this money in the interment of poor persons under the Sanitary Act of 1866. I differed from that view, and I disallowed the money, but again stated to them that if they would make a burial rate, to provide for the future expenses of that kind and to recoup the improvement rate, there would be no proceedings. However, they did not make a burial rate, but appealed against that disallowance, as also against the disallowance of 43 *l*. 15 *s*., which they gave to their secretary on his retiring from office on the ground of ill-health after less than three years' service. He got into a very bad state of health, and the Commissioners gave him four months' leave of absence, and at the end of that period, finding that he was utterly unable to resume his duties, they paid him his salary up to the date of his retirement, and a gratuity of 43 *l*. 15 *s*. as compensation for resigning his office. The Court of Queen's Bench decided that both payments were illegal, but suggested that under the peculiar circumstances, the action of the Town Commissioners being *bonâ fide*, perhaps it was desirable that the payment should not be enforced against individuals, and of course I acted upon that suggestion, and refrained from enforcing payment.

4373. Generally speaking, are you satisfied with the mode in which the accounts of the towns under the Act of 1854 are submitted to you?—Yes, I am now. There was irregularity at first, but I found that the Town Commissioners, as a rule, were very willing to adopt any suggestion that was made to them, and generally speaking the accounts are in a satisfactory state now.

4374. What towns under special acts in your district are under your audit?—There is Blackrock, which I have mentioned. Bray is under a special Act also. I made a disallowance there at the audit of 1873 of 337 *l*. There was a good deal of agitation in the township about the expenditure; and some of the ratepayers complained of items to the amount of about 1,400 *l*., which they called upon me to disallow. On investigating the matter, about 1,100 *l*. appeared to me to be perfectly legal expenditure, and I allowed it; the balance of about 330 *l*. I disallowed; 283 *l*. of that sum represented the cost of making sewers. The disallowance of this latter sum was made on the ground that the cost should have been borne by a separate district sewer rate, in accordance with the provisions of the Towns Improvement Act and the Towns Improvement Clauses Act. My

Mr. *Finlay*.

13 June 1876.

Chairman—continued.

My decision in that case was appealed against to the Local Government Board, and on the appeal being sent to me for my observations, I found that one of the points made, and made then for the first time, was that the money was paid, not out of the rates, but out of the balance of a loan obtained for the purpose of making those sewers. I went down to Bray and ascertained that this was the fact, and it appeared to me to alter the ground so completely, that I told the Local Government Board that my disallowance could not be sustained, and the matter ended there. A further disallowance of mine at Bray was the payment to the grand jury of the county of Wicklow of a portion of the salary of the county surveyor and his assistants. The payment of this salary was clearly at variance with the local Act of Parliament, in which there was a clause exempting the town from contributing to the salary of the county surveyor appointed by the grand jury. The payment was defended on the ground that the county surveyor was not appointed by the grand jury, but by the Lord Lieutenant. I inquired whether there were two county surveyors, one appointed by the grand jury and the other appointed by the Lord Lieutenant, and the answer was no. I thereupon held that the officer in respect of whose salary the payment was made was the county surveyor referred to in the Act of Parliament, in which there was a verbal mistake of no importance, and I disallowed his salary. The grand jury of the county of Wicklow subsequently repaid the Town Commissioners the sum of 338 *l.* in consequence of that disallowance. There have been very heavy legal expenses in that township of Bray. Large payments under this head have been made from time to time, and I apprehend that a large amount is still due, but I do not know what the amount is, as the costs have not been furnished for some years. I have at each audit urged the Commissioners to get them furnished, taxed, and settled, but they have not been furnished as yet. I understand, from a conversation that I had with the solicitor recently, that he is now about furnishing them, and the Commissioners should see that this is done without further delay. The collection of the rates has not been very satisfactory.

4375. What were the legal expenses for?—There were some actions taken against the Commissioners by some parties with reference to the esplanade, and there were Parliamentary costs, I think, in opposing Bills promoted by the Gas Company, and the Bills of the Corporation of Dublin in relation to the Waterworks and the Gasworks and some other Bills; as also costs of a miscellaneous character.

Mr. *Brooks*.

4376. Is the solicitor Mr. Keogh?—Yes, Mr. George Keogh.

Mr. *Gibson*.

4377. And Mr. Toomey also; I believe they had two sets of solicitors?—They had either three or four solicitors. They had Mr. Octavius O'Brien, Mr. George Keogh, Mr. Toomey, and Mr. Brownrigg. I think they paid off Mr. Toomey and Mr. O'Brien, but Mr. Brownrigg's costs, which cannot amount to much, are still due. It is Mr. Keogh's costs that are still unfurnished.

4378. Some of those solicitors were acting concurrently at the same time in different transactions?—Yes, in different cases.

Chairman.

4379. Were any of the solicitors Commissioners?—No. I was not satisfied with the collection of the rates in Bray; I urged them to scrutinise the list of outstanding arrears; I do not know that it had ever been done. It is always a good plan for the Commissioners to get a return containing the names of the different parties and the amount due by them, and scrutinise them as a check upon the collector, to see that he is discharging his duty and accounting for all moneys that he receives.

4380. The rates in those towns are collected by the collector of the Commissioners, are they not?—Yes.

4381. Therefore in those towns you audit the collection as well as the expenditure?—Yes, I audit the collection in every place that I audit, except the Corporation of Dublin.

4382. Generally speaking, are you satisfied with the collection?—Yes, I am, generally speaking.

4383. When you spoke of the arrears being heavy in Bray, what proportion of arrears is there?—I think I found on my first audit one-third or nearly one-half of the rates outstanding; I urged them to collect at the proper period. The best period for collecting the rate there is from this time down to the end of September, when every house in Bray is occupied. A great number of them are let furnished to seaside visitors, and the time for collecting the rate is during the summer and autumn. I found great irregularities in respect to making and collecting the rates in Dalkey township, which is another township under a special Act, and I found defalcations and frauds there by the rate collector; the accounts were in the greatest confusion; proceedings had been instituted against him in the police court; I do not know any town or township in which matters were at all in so bad a state as in Dalkey township, so far as the collection was concerned.

Mr. *Gibson*.

4384. Is not the population of Dalkey under 3,000?—I do not know what the population is. The collector had been receiving moneys for a considerable period before I went there, and not lodging them with the treasurer of the Town Commissioners, but making use of them for his own purpose. I found that several rates, I think three or four different rates, were in course of collection concurrently, instead of winding up each rate and carrying the arrears into the next, and balancing every rate before they gave the books to the collector for another rate. I pointed all this out to the Commissioners. He seemed to be an exceedingly slippery and sly officer, and I suggested to the Commissioners to put him into a corner by withholding his warrant, and not giving him any power to collect more money, and by getting a return made out of the arrears that appeared to be outstanding. They did so, and they were enabled in that way to ascertain how he had been working, getting payment in some instances of large sums, and filling up the block of the receipt, which is the ordinary check upon him, for a smaller sum, getting perhaps from one man 10 *l.*, the amount of his rates, and filling up the block as if it were 10 *s.*, the amount assessed on another ratepayer, for which the counterpart was issued. They have been proceeding against him for the last

Mr. *Finlay*.

13 June 1876.

Mr. *Gibson*—continued.

last year and a half, I think, in the police court, and the long delay in bringing matters to a close is most unaccountable.

Chairman.

4385. What is the deficiency there?—Allow me to read from my report, "In my report to your Board of the 7th of March last I referred to the large arrears of previous rates amounting to upwards of 1,100 *l.* outstanding, and stated that I considered it desirable that the collector should be required to furnish the Commissioners, as soon as possible, with lists of the arrears on foot of each rate, giving the necessary particulars in each case, with a view to the lists being scrutinised by the Commissioners. I further recommended that the collection of each year's rates should in future be closed before a new rate be put in course of collection. The Commissioners acted on this advice, and the result has been that 743 *l.* 14 *s.* of the arrears were collected and lodged during the year under audit; the collector referred to has been removed from office, and after great delay and with much difficulty the scrutiny of his lists of arrears has brought to light sufficient facts to compel the Commissioners, in fulfilment of their trust, to institute proceedings against him in the police court. As these proceedings are still pending, I think it right to refrain at present from further comment on the late collector's dealings in connection with the collection of the township rates. One of the consequences of this state of things has been the embarrassment of the affairs of the township to a very considerable extent, as the Commissioners were obliged to defer placing the rates made in May 1874, amounting to 1,574 *l.* 9 *s.* 1 *d.*, in course of collection until the appointment of a new collector, which did not take place until the end of the year. Meanwhile they were left without sufficient funds to meet their engagements. These latter were of formidable proportions, comprising amongst other items a claim of 473 *l.* 5 *s.* 4 *d.* for the costs of the Commissioners' opposition to the Bill promoted in Parliament by the Kingstown Commissioners in 1873, which affected the Dalkey township, and 149 *l.* 9 *s.* 10 *d.* due to the grand jury of the county of Dublin for the second moiety of the proportion of the county at large charges, payable by the township for the year 1873; and 250 *l.* due on foot of the sinking fund account. The costs of opposing the Kingstown bill appear to have been duly taxed and ascertained, and a copy of the taxing officer's certificate was laid before me, but I felt unable to accept that document as sufficient evidence of the amount to which the Commissioners were liable in respect of those costs. The Commissioners were not able to pay the amount claimed, but they passed a bill for it to Messrs. Casey and Clay, the solicitors, who conducted the proceedings, which on arriving at maturity (the Commissioners being still unprepared with the amount) was taken up by Alderman O'Rorke, one of the Town Commissioners, who thereupon took Messrs. Casey and Clay's place, and to whom payments on account, amounting to 113 *l.* 5 *s.*, have been made in the course of the year. This bill has been renewed to the firm of which Alderman O'Rorke is the head for the balances remaining after each payment and interest or discount thereon at 6 per cent. paid by the Commissioners.

Chairman—continued.

The original certificate of the taxing officer will have to be produced before payment of the balance due on foot of those costs can be allowed. In like manner, in respect to the sum due to the county grand jury, for payment whereof the Commissioners were threatened with legal proceedings, Alderman O'Rorke again came to the Commissioners' aid, and paid the amount for them, receiving the town clerk's acceptance, which is also renewed for the balance at the same rate of interest; 20 *l.* of this sum has been paid to Alderman O'Rorke during the year, as standing in the place of the grand jury. The sum of 250 *l.* which the Commissioners are bound, under the 51st section of their local Act, to set apart annually in order to provide a sinking fund, not being in hand, Mr. Fleming, another of the Town Commissioners, came forward and with his own funds purchased stock to that amount in the names of himself and two other Town Commissioners. The practice on the part of a corporation of issuing bills and paying interest or discount thereon, appears to be of questionable legality, but under the very exceptional circumstances in which the Commissioners found themselves placed during the year, I have thought it prudent to follow the course adopted at the previous year's audit, and allow the payments coming under these heads, in the expectation that in the course of the current year all such transactions will cease, as the Commissioners will have ample funds from the rates of 1874, the collection whereof is satisfactorily progressing; and the arrears of previous rates either uncollected or in the hands of the rate collector, and for which he and his sureties are liable, together with the new rates which the Commissioners are entitled to assess for the current year." Some money was got from that collector, but the proceedings are still pending.

4386. Had he sureties?—Yes, he had.

4387. In those small towns which you are speaking of, as a rule do the Commissioners take security from their officers?—Yes, it is the rule; there have been some exceptions to it. I found, perhaps, in half-a-dozen cases they had not had bonds from their officers. The Act of Parliament requires them to get security from every officer having the custody or control of moneys; and whenever I have found that there was no bond, I have urged them until I have succeeded in getting them to obtain security. As regards Dalkey, in my report to the Local Government Board of the 12th of February 1876, I said, "The proceedings in the police court to which I referred in my last report as then pending, resulted in an order being made for payment by Mr. O'Dowd" (the defaulting collector), "of 99 *l.* 4 *s.* 2 *d.*, ascertained to have been collected by him, but not lodged with the treasurer, or on failure of payment, that he should be imprisoned for three months. Mr. O'Dowd has lodged 96 *l.* 19 *s.* on account of this sum, and it has since been ascertained that he and his sureties are liable for a further sum of 158 *l.* 18 *s.* 1 *d.* There still remains of rates entrusted to Mr. O'Dowd for collection, the sum of 231 *l.* 11 *s.* 6 *d.* His liability in respect of these rates has yet to be ascertained, which can only be done by application to the individual ratepayers appearing to be in arrear. It is to be hoped that no further time will be lost in ascertaining this, and in recovering the entire amount from Mr. O'Dowd or his sureties."

Mr. *Finlay*.

13 June 1876.

Chairman—continued.

sureties." Those proceedings are still pending. The delay in bringing them to a satisfactory conclusion is most unaccountable. It would look as if the Commissioners were not in earnest in the matter.

4388. Have the Dalkey Commissioners adopted any means, besides bonds from their officers, which in your opinion will obviate this state of things?—Yes, and as regards the current business, everything is going on in a very satisfactory manner now. There was the grossest irregularity formerly with regard to making the rates, I say in my report, from which I have just been reading. "There have been very great irregularities in former years in reference to the making of rates in the township, the provisions of the Act of Parliament on the subject having been quite disregarded. Section 61 of the Towns Improvement Act, which is incorporated with the Dalkey Township Act, requires the Commissioners to cause to be made up each year a rate book, or 'Book of Assessment,' to be signed by the chairman and two other Commissioners, and directs that a copy of such book of assessment be delivered to the collector for the purpose of collecting. For the year 1871, the only book that appears to have been prepared was a collecting book, which, however, contained all the necessary particulars. In 1872 there was no assessment book prepared, but a collecting book was made out by the former collector, Mr. O'Dowd, in which the only column filled up is that showing the net annual value of the several tenements. No figures whatever were inserted in the rating columns, yet at the end of the book the chairman and three Commissioners certified that 'the particulars required by the Act have been set forth in the pages and several columns of the foregoing rate book.'" They signed a skeleton book for him, and they left it to him to put in what he pleased.

4389. Do you audit the accounts of Rathmines?—No; Rathmines is exempt from the operations of the Act.

4390. How is it exempt?—It is specially exempt, being a town in the county Dublin under a special Act of Parliament. The Act of 1871 exempted certain towns in Ireland; Cork, Waterford, Kilkenny, and the townships in the county of Dublin, unless the ratepayers in the latter choose to apply to put themselves under its provisions. Some of those townships have availed themselves of the advantages of the Act of 1871, but Rathmines, Pembroke, Clontarf, and Kilmainham have not.

4391. Dalkey has?—Yes, Dalkey, Blackrock, and Kingstown have.

4392. Dalkey has, with the result which you have told us?—Yes. I may mention that when the Dalkey collector's book was withheld from him, and he had no longer a legal authority for going about collecting rates, he took upon himself to collect rates, and one of the first ratepayers that he attacked was Judge O'Brien, one of the judges of the Court of Queen's Bench, from whom he got, I think, 15 *l.* or 20 *l.* He did the same with some others; but although he has stood his ground, there has been no criminal prosecution.

4393. Have you any remarks to make with regard to Kingstown?—Yes; I disallowed 38 *l.* 12 *s.* for the year 1872 in Kingstown under similar circumstances as the Blackrock disallowance, being the sum paid for the interment of poor persons, on the ground that they had no power to employ the improvement rate in that manner, but they made a burial rate since, and recouped the improvement rate, so that there was nothing more about it, and matters are going on all right there now. I found that they had been paying an annual premium to the guarantee society on the guarantee bond of the town clerk. I considered that it was a payment which should be made by the officer himself, and not be charged upon the funds of the town. It was his business to provide a security, and if instead of getting personal security, he chose to go to the guarantee society, he ought to pay the cost himself.

4394. How much was the amount paid to the guarantee society?—It was only a small sum, 2 *l.* 12 *s.* 6 *d.* annual premium on his guarantee bond; I disallowed it, and it was repaid. There was a very curious state of things there with regard to the payment of the former secretary, which I referred to in my first report to the Local Government Board in these terms: "There is a sum of 166 *l.* 13 *s.* 4 *d.* standing in the accounts as an asset of the Commissioners, and described as a debt by 'Mr. James Murray or defendants (or some of them) in the case of the Attorney General *v.* Barrett and others.' As the circumstances connected with this item are somewhat peculiar, I shall briefly state them for the information of your Board. By the Kingstown Improvement Act of 1861, the then Commissioners were authorised to pay Mr. Murray, who was their secretary, a superannuation allowance to the extent of two-thirds of his salary 'on account,' as stated in the Act, of 'ill health, and being thereby permanently incapacitated to discharge the increased duties which would be imposed upon him by the passing of the Act.' Accordingly, on the Act coming into operation in July 1861, Mr. Murray was awarded by the Commissioners a pension of 66 *l.* 13 *s.* 4 *d.* per annum, but he continued, notwithstanding, to hold the office of secretary, and for two and a half years after that date to draw his salary at the usual rate (100 *l.* per annum), and his pension as well. This double payment led to proceedings in the Court of Chancery against the Town Commissioners by one of their former officers, for recovery of the amount of either the pension or the salary paid during that period, when the Lord Chancellor gave a decree for the amount of the pension (166 *l.* 13 *s.* 4 *d.*). An obstacle to its recovery by the present Town Commissioners has, however, arisen owing to the omission from the Act of 1869 (32 & 33 Vict. c. 133) amending the Towns Improvement Act, 1854, in regard to the township of Kingstown, of an enactment transferring the rights of the then existing body of Commissioners (which were under the Act to go out of office on the 1st of January 1870) to their successors, the present Board of Commissioners. This being the case, the only party entitled to enforce the decree is the relator in the Chancery suit, but he is unwilling to do so. Under these circumstances, I would suggest to the Commissioners to take into consideration the propriety of removing the item from their accounts." That double payment had been going on for two-and-a-half years, the Commissioners treating the man at the same time both as an officer discharging a duty, and as a pensioner incapacitated

Mr. Finlay.

13 June 1876.

Chairman—continued.

tated from ill-health to discharge that duty, and paying him the full amount he was entitled to receive in both characters. My attention was called, at the succeeding audit, to an arrear of 5 *l.* odd of rates returned by the collector, and declared irrecoverable by the Town Commissioners. I found that this arrear was on a house which had been purchased by one of the Town Commissioners. In making the purchase, the rates being due at the time by the party from whom it was purchased, the Commissioner referred to stipulated that he should be allowed to deduct the amount, inasmuch as it was the property of the Commissioners, from the purchase-money, and he was allowed to do so. Thereupon he got the Town Commissioners to declare the amount irrecoverable, and withheld the money. I expressed a desire to see him at the audit. He did not attend, but an agent attended for him, and handed in the 5 *l.* odd, which was placed in the hands of the treasurer, but he made no explanation whatever about the matter. The Town Commissioners were rather indignant at my having commented upon it in my report, and they complained to the Local Government Board about it, but the Local Government Board did not see anything objectionable in my report.

4395. What ground of complaint did the Town Commissioners allege?—The ground of complaint, I think, was the manner in which I spoke of the transaction in my report to the Board, namely, "On investigating this matter it appeared that the tenement in question was sold about the middle of the year 1872, to one of the Town Commissioners, the rates being then due and payable, and that on paying the purchase money the purchaser stopped the amount of rates due, but failed to pay it over, as he should have at once done to the Commissioners. Subsequently, at the end of the same year, the arrears of rate were remitted by the Commissioners. I was informed that the commissioner referred to was prepared to give a satisfactory explanation on the subject; and being desirous to afford him an opportunity of doing so, I intimated to him that I would be prepared to hear whatever he had to say in support of his right to retain this money. On my resuming the audit on a future day, a messenger attended from the Commissioner, and handed in the amount to the town clerk without any explanation. Of the impropriety of the proceeding of the Commissioner referred to in withholding this money from the Commissioners there can, I apprehend, be no question; and it is to be hoped that his colleagues, when remitting the rates, and the collector, when returning them amongst the irrecoverable arrears, were unacquainted with the circumstances of the case; otherwise their action in the matter would be considered equally censurable, and as manifesting a disregard of the responsibilities devolving on them, and of the interests of the ratepayers." This last sentence has been objected to.

4396. What did they object to in it?—The reflection that was conveyed in it, and that I exceeded my duty.

Mr. Collins.

4397. In what form did they state their complaint?—In a letter to the Local Government Board.

Mr. Collins—continued.

4398. Have you got a copy of that letter?—No.

4399. How did the Local Government Board treat the letter?—The Local Government Board saw no reason to interfere with the auditor.

Chairman.

4400. Did the Commissioners dispute the facts?—No, not at all; they could not dispute them; they did not attempt to do so.

Mr. Corry.

4401. They only found fault with the terms in which you expressed yourself?—Yes; that is all.

Chairman.

4402. Have you any other statement to make with respect to Kingstown?—I disallowed at the last audit a sum of 62 *l.*; 52 *l.* was for advertising in the newspapers, and 10 *l.* for costs; both items being in relation to an abortive Bill, which the Town Commissioners had been promoting, and in respect of which an injunction was obtained from the Court of Chancery, to prevent them in their corporate capacity proceeding with the Bill or expending any rates in its promotion. I found they published notices within the period during which they were prevented by the Towns Improvement Act from incurring any expense. That disallowance was appealed against to the Local Government Board, who confirmed my decision, and the money has since been lodged with the treasurer.

4403. Have you found, not only in the case of Kingstown, but in Dublin, or in the cases of other towns whose accounts you audit, considerable sums paid to newspapers for advertisements?—Yes; sometimes there have been considerable sums paid to newspapers with regard to the promotion of Bills. There are very long notices that must be inserted at certain periods of the year when they are about to promote a Bill in Parliament.

4404. Have you had reason to object to the amounts paid?—In the payments that have come before me I have not had reason to object, except in regard to the costs of publishing copies of my report, which is not authorised by the Act, but there is a great deal of money due to newspapers by the Dublin Corporation for notices of Bills in Parliament, but the payments have not been made, and consequently they have not come before me officially.

4405. How are you aware that a great deal of money is due?—I am aware of it in this way: Some very small items in the case of the Dublin Corporation came before me with respect to abortive Bills that they have been promoting in Parliament. I disallowed those small items, and an appeal has been made in the case of one sum I disallowed, which was about 1 *l.* 18 *s.*, and another sum was about 12 *l.*, being 13 *l.* or 14 *l.* altogether. The Act of Parliament entitles parties who are surcharged to appeal to the Court of Queen's Bench or to the Local Government Board; but it does not give them two appeals, an appeal to each tribunal; at all events they managed to secure two appeals in the case of those two items; they went to the Local Government Board with an appeal with regard to the item of 1 *l.* 18 *s.*, the parties who were surcharged being different from the parties who were surcharged in respect of the item of 12 *l.* The Local Government Board confirmed my decision.

Mr. *Finlay.*

13 June 1876.

Chairman—continued.

cision. They then went to the Court of Queen's Bench with regard to the 12 *l.* disallowance, but after trying for two terms to get a Conditional Order against me they did not succeed, and the matter is now at rest. There is a peculiarity with regard to this 12 *l.* item. The secretary to the gas company, who was at the time the expense was incurred the secretary to the gas committee, and an officer of the corporation, felt that he was in some way or the other bound in honour to repay this money, and not to allow the members of the corporation who were surcharged pay it, and he accordingly sent a cheque for the amount to the corporation. I concluded that the matter was then at an end, and that there would be no litigation about it. However, the corporation committee, No. 1, passed a resolution calling upon the treasurer not to turn that cheque into cash, inasmuch as one of its members was about instituting proceedings which might be damaged by his doing so. The member referred to, then went to the Court of Queen's Bench, as I have stated, for a Conditional Order, and failed two separate terms in getting it. I applied to the treasurer of the corporation, at the end of the third term, to turn the cheque that he had into cash, and he applied to committee, No. 1, for instructions as to what he should do in the matter; the answer that he got simply was that the letter was marked "read." I then instructed my solicitor to serve a notice upon the parties who were moving in it, either to go on with the case and get their Conditional Order, or to abandon it; and the proceedings were abandoned. I was obliged then to proceed before the police magistrates to enforce the payment from the parties whose name were on the cheques, and who had been surcharged with the amount. On receiving the usual letter from my attorney, No. 1 committee at length changed their mind, and allowed the cheque to the secretary to the gas company to be placed to the credit of the fund, so that in that way the matter has been settled.

4406. On what do you ground your opinion that there are large sums due by the corporation?—Because I am aware of their proceedings. I am aware that they were proceeding to get a Gas Bill, and that those proceedings failed here. There was a long battle before a Committee of the House of Lords, or the House of Commons, and after several days the preamble of the Bill was declared not proven; those costs have not been paid.

Mr. Collins.

4407. How do you know that they have not been paid?—They could not be paid without my knowledge, unless there was a fraudulent falsification of the accounts and vouchers, by representing payments made for such purposes as having been made for purposes that were strictly legitimate. Such a falsification would render the parties concerned liable to severe punishment under a recent Act of Parliament.

Chairman.

4408. You know what has been paid by your examination of the accounts, and you know by having seen those notices in the newspapers that those advertisements have not been paid for?—Yes; and there are very heavy costs to counsel, and costs to attorneys, and costs to Parliamentary agents, and fees to gas engineers and others; in fact, one of those gas engineers recently took action against the corporation for his fees, which amounted to several hundred pounds.

Chairman—continued.

4409. When were those expenses incurred?—They were incurred in the year 1874.

4410. Are you aware of any other expenses of this kind which have been incurred in previous years, and which have not been paid?—I am not at present aware of any.

4411. How is it that those expenses which were incurred in 1874, have not yet been paid by the corporation?—They are afraid to pay them; they are willing to pay them. Many persons are deeply interested in them, but they are afraid of the auditor. They say, if we pay them, the auditor will disallow them; and with a view to get over that difficulty, Mr. Clemenshaw, the gas engineer employed on that occasion, sued the corporation for the amount of his fees, and got a verdict against them, subject to the decision of the full Court on a question of law, namely, as to whether having failed to get their Bill, the corporation could apply any portion of their funds in the payment of costs. The Court were unanimously of opinion that they had no power to do so.

4412. Do you know at all what the corporation may be liable for on that account?—No, I do not know, but it must be many thousands of pounds.

4413. Have you any general remarks to make or suggestions to offer to the Committee with regard to the improvement of the system of audit which you administer?—I have not; but in a case in which I proceeded in the Court of Queen's Bench against the town clerk for the recovery of those fees of which I spoke some time ago, the court decided unanimously that I had no power to recover; that the law did not empower me. I proceeded at the suggestion of the Local Government Board; they told me that I had no option in the matter but to proceed; I had a good deal of doubt as to whether I had the power or not. However, the Local Government Board thought that I had, and I proceeded accordingly. Judge Fitzgerald, in delivering his judgment, stated that he thought it would be highly desirable that in any future amendment of the Local Government Act power should be given to the auditor to recover moneys withheld by an officer of a public body whose accounts he has audited. At present where an officer withholds money which he ought to pay, we have no power to move in the matter; the power is altogether in the hands of the corporation or Town Commissioners, and they are slow to exercise it. I have referred to this matter in one of my reports to the corporation, in which I say, "In my report on the audit of the previous year's accounts, I informed your Board that I had debited the town clerk with the sum of 121 *l.* 12 *s.*, received by him as 'fees and presentment,' which I conceived, for the reasons therein stated, he should have lodged to the credit of the borough fund. My decision formed the subject of appeal to the Court of Queen's Bench, on the grounds, as set forth in Mr. Henry's affidavit, that the resolution of the town council of the 14th June 1860, to the effect that the annual salary paid to the town clerk should be in lieu of all fees or allowances, and that all fees or allowances

Chairman—continued.

lowances or presentments connected with that officer or his office should be paid in future into the borough fund, was rescinded by the town council by their paying over to him the amount of the annual presentment of 100*l*., and that from the continued annual payment of this presentment, his appointment at a fixed salary was in no way governed by the resolution in question. That the presentment was in fact a personal allowance to him for actual labour in connection with the preparation of the Parliamentary Voters' Lists, and that I should not have debited him with the amount, as he was not the person making, or authorising the making, of the payment. As regards the 'fees,' amounting to 21 *l*. 12 *s*., Mr. Henry did not, in his affidavit, set up any claim to retain them, but, on the contrary, stated as follows:—'I have never refused, or wilfully neglected to make payment of any of the moneys remaining due by me to the treasurer, within three days after being thereunto required, by notice in writing, under the hands of any three or more of said council.' The judges, after hearing counsel on both sides, were unanimously of opinion that I had no legal power to recover from the town clerk the sums so received by him as fees and presentment, nor to debit him with the amount, and directed that on this ground my certificate should be quashed; at the same time expressly guarding themselves against being supposed to give any opinion respecting Mr. Henry's right to retain those moneys. Mr. Justice Fitzgerald, in delivering his judgment, referred to the expediency of amending the Local Government (Ireland) Act, 1871, so as to enable an auditor to recover moneys withheld by the officer of a public body whose accounts he has audited." Then I point out that the Act of Parliament imposed the duty of recovering any fees on the corporation, and I say, "It now remains for the corporation to discharge their duty, by requiring the town clerk to account for, and pay over to the treasurer, all moneys received by him as fees, &c., under colour of his office."

4414. Was not there a case decided the other day bearing upon this matter, of Michael Angelo Hayes?—Yes, there was apparently, but in reality only very remotely bearing on it.

4415. What was the decision in that case?—The decision was that Mr. Hayes was entitled to the fees of his office of marshal, received in his other capacity of registrar of pawnbrokers. "His Lordship, Chief Justice Morris, said that the Court were unanimously of opinion that the verdict had for the defendant should stand. The defendant was City Marshal, and, as such, was Marshal of the Borough Court, and Marshal of the Court of Conscience. He was also, under the Statutes 26 Geo. 3, c. 43, and 28 Geo. 3, c. 49, registrar of pawnbrokers, and in that capacity received fees much exceeding the salary at which he was appointed by the plaintiffs. The bond entered into by him on his appointment by the plaintiff, provided that he was to pay over the fees and emoluments of his office to their treasurer. It had been admitted during the argument, that such an arrangement would have been clearly illegal prior to the 3 & 4 Vict. c. 108; illegal as a bargain of an office of trust, by which the plaintiffs, in appointing the defendant, were to obtain a large benefit by the receipt of the fees appertaining to the office. It had been, however, argued that the 93rd and 95th sections of that Act enabled the plaintiffs to enter into such an arrangement. The Court considered that this was not so. The plaintiffs could, it was true, fix the salary of the City Marshal, as an officer appointed to discharge that which the corporation required to be done by virtue of that Act, but, as registrar of pawnbrokers, there was no privity between the defendant and the plaintiffs. No doubt his appointment as marshal constituted him registrar of pawnbrokers, and entitled him as such to certain fees. But in the opinion of the Court, it would be to the last degree against public policy to allow the plaintiffs to bargain for the fees of an office with which they had no connection, and to which they had not a shadow of claim. The defendant also relied upon another defence, that his appointment was void, as being only for a year, whereas it was contended that the office was a freehold one. It became unnecessary to decide upon the validity of this defence, but his Lordship retained the opinion he had expressed at the trial, that the appointment was by usage an appointment during pleasure or by the year." The appointment of marshal was made after an undertaking had been signed by the different candidates pledging themselves to accept a salary, and to pay over to the corporation weekly all fees received. The Court held, that notwithstanding the agreement, and the bond to the same effect entered into by Mr. Hayes on his appointment, the transaction was illegal, being opposed to public policy.

Mr. *Brooks*.

4416. Notwithstanding that, they found that Mr. Hayes was not liable to refund?—Yes, that the fees were his own, having been received by him as registrar of pawnbrokers, an office with which the corporation had no connection.

4417. Does not that rather lend a sanction to Mr. Henry's view of the case?—At first sight Mr. Henry's case would appear to be similar, but on carefully reading the judgment of the Court, there appears to be a distinction between the two cases.

4418. You recommended in each of those cases that the corporation should claim the refund of those fees?—Yes, in both cases. In Mr. Hayes' case we acted under very peculiar circumstances upon an opinion given by the late Sir John Rolt, when he was Attorney General of England. There was a case submitted to him by the late Alderman Reynolds on the death of his brother Mr. Thomas Reynolds, who held the office of City Marshal for a great number of years. At the time of Mr. Thomas Reynolds' death, there was a sum of 800*l*., or so, in the hands of Mr. John Reynolds, as his executor, and he submitted the case to Sir John Rolt to ascertain whether he was bound to pay over this money to the corporation. Sir John Rolt gave an opinion to the effect that Mr. Thomas Reynolds had no right to the fees received by him as registrar of pawnbrokers, and that the corporation could recover the amount. Then there was an opinion obtained from Mr. Brewster at variance with that, and there was a further opinion obtained from Mr. Gibson taking the same view as Mr. Brewster took, and also at variance with Sir John Rolt's opinion. The corporation were anxious to know exactly how the matter

Mr. *Finlay*.

13 June 1876.

Mr. *Brooks*—continued.

matter stood between those conflicting opinions, Mr. Hayes having commenced to withhold the fees from them, and they submitted the whole of the cases and opinions to the present Lord Chief Baron of the Court of Exchequer, who was then at the bar. Mr. Palles stated that he gave his opinion, after the most careful consideration, owing to the conflicting opinions of such eminent lawyers, in favour of the view taken by Sir John Rolt, that the corporation were entitled to the fees. Under that state of circumstances I conceived that I should treat the case as one in which the fees were payable to the corporation.

Chairman.

4419. You told us, I think, that certain places in Ireland were specially exempt from your system of audit; what was the reason for that exemption?—Mr. Cruise, who at the time that the measure was passed was private secretary to Lord Hartington, who was then Chief Secretary for Ireland, told me that the reason for exempting those places was that the Session was very nearly run out, and the Government found it very difficult to get the Bill passed; that it was strongly opposed in the interest of the places referred to, and the opposition would have had the effect of throwing it out if it was continued.

4420. Have you acquainted yourself with any difference in their condition from that of the other towns, or any reason why they should be exempted?—I do not know of any grounds whatever for exempting them. There was an objection made on the part of some of those towns and townships to the charge made by the Treasury for auditing the accounts; the Kingstown Commissioners had objected to it very strongly.

4421. What is the charge that is made by the auditor?—It varies; I think it is about 30 *l.* in Kingstown.

4422. How is it calculated?—It was calculated in the office of the Local Government Board by the amount of time occupied, so much a day, and by the amount of expenditure.

4423. What is paid by the Corporation of Dublin for your audit?—One hundred guineas was the sum originally paid; but the Local Government Board, on the appointment of a seventh auditor, has increased the amount to somewhere about 120 *l.*, I think. It has been contended that there is no ground for maintaining this charge. It is certainly very curious. The auditor goes down to a union, and spends perhaps six days in the year, auditing the accounts of an expenditure of some 8,000 *l.* or 10,000 *l.*, and there is no charge whatever made against the union for his services. He goes to a town in the same union where the expenditure is 100 *l.*, the auditing of which occupies him an hour, and there is a charge of four or five guineas made upon the town in respect of his services.

4424. I presume that that is because the audit of the town accounts was not a part of the original system?—I presume so.

4425. You were originally the poor law auditor only, were you not?—Yes; the poor law unions originally paid a portion of the auditor's salary, some 30 years ago; but owing to the passive, and in some cases the active, resistance of the boards of guardians, they got rid of the charge.

Mr. *Bruen.*

4426. The audit of the accounts of lunatic asylums is also paid out of the rates, is it not?—Yes, it is paid out of the grand jury fund.

Mr. *Brooks.*

4427. With regard to the arrears of rent, can you say if there are any standing arrears, excepting those of the poor villagers at Baldoyle, I mean beyond one-half year within the other?—Yes, in some cases I have observed that there have been a couple of years due.

4428. Are you aware of any being allowed to remain over so as to become irrecoverable?—No, I do not know whether they are recoverable or not. I have no personal knowledge of the property. I suggested a short time ago, since the affair of the treasurer turned up, that application should be made in every case to the tenants to produce their last receipts, and an examination should be made so as to test the perfect accuracy of the outstanding arrears as shown on the rental, and I hope they will do that. I think it would be very satisfactory to do so.

4429. Whilst we are upon the subject of the treasurer, can you say that the corporation have neglected any ordinary precautions with regard to the security to be given by the treasurer?—No, I do not think they have. I think that they have acted with perfect correctness.

4430. They have done as much, have they not, as Poor Law Boards and others do?—Yes, certainly.

4431. You have no reason to think that there has been any shortcoming on the part of the corporation with regard to the security obtained from their officers?—No, except in that case of McCan's of which I spoke. I do not think there is any neglect.

4432. Do you know anything of the circumstances of Baldoyle?—Not at all. I never saw the corporation property. I know the place, but I do not know their property from any other property.

4433. Do you know that Baldoyle was a decayed fishing village?—Yes.

4434. And do you know whether the allegation is correct, that the tenements in which those people live are allowed to go on in that condition, in order that the poor rates may be relieved, and that the poor rates would be augmented if those wretched tenements in which they lived were destroyed?—That is to say, that they would be driven into the workhouse if they were shut out of their holdings. I do not know how that would be. I have no knowledge whatever of the tenantry. I do not know of what class they are; but they must be very poor.

4435. Of course 100 tenants paying a rent of 200 *l.* a year must be very poor?—Yes, they must be very poor indeed.

4436. With regard to increasing the salary of the Lord Mayor, do you know under what circumstances, or by whom, that increase was made?—It was made by the council.

4437. Do you know whether the fees that were formerly received by the secretary from the Lord Mayor's Court have fallen off of late years?—I do not know that. I doubt that they have fallen off, and my reason for saying that is, that I have spoken to Mr. Carroll, who for two years held the office of secretary to his father when Lord Mayor, and I found that his statement regarding the fees, tallied with the amount now received.

4438. Do you know that Sir William Carroll was

Mr. *Brooks*—continued.

was Lord Mayor during the time of the American War?—I do not remember whether it was at that time or not.

4439. Then you do not know that the fees received by Sir William Carroll's secretary were fees received for affixing the city seal to commissions from Irish soldiers in America to their friends in Ireland?—Yes, part of them were those fees, and part of the fees still received by the Lord Mayor's secretary is for similar business; but those fees he is allowed to retain, whatever the amount may be. I do not know the amount; I have no means of knowing what the amount is beyond what I stated. I think I understood it was somewhere about 100 *l.* a year.

4440. Can you give the Committee any reason why the corporation do not adopt your suggestion for having separate pass books and separate accounts in the Bank of Ireland for the funds of the separate committees?—Yes, I understand that it is to enable them to avail themselves, whenever there is a balance in the Bank belonging to a particular fund, and money is wanted for the purposes of another fund, the latter being very hard pressed, of the power of making use of the money temporarily for, say, improvement purposes.

4441. Do you mean money lying to the credit of the waterworks?—Yes, the money belonging to the waterworks or any other fund.

4442. Supposing that No. 1 committee did not draw from the waterworks upon the sum of money lying to the credit of the Waterworks Committee, would they not, as a matter of fact, have to pay the Bank of Ireland interest for the overdraft?—There would be two courses open to them, either to diminish their expenditure, or, if they continued it, so as to render it necessary to obtain money beyond the amount of their income, to borrow at interest.

4443. Is it not more feasible that they should draw upon the money in their power which is lying to their credit under the head of the Waterworks Fund?—It would be more economical than to pay interest upon it; but there is an Act of Parliament declaring that money received for the purposes of a particular fund shall be applied only to those purposes. It is contravening the Act of Parliament.

4444. In the end it is really applied to waterworks purposes, although temporarily it may be availed of for the benefit of the citizens?—But here is the state of things now with regard to 6,000 *l.* taken from the waterworks and applied to borough purposes, that the waterworks people are going to set to work now to form new filter beds at Stillorgan, and they are complaining that the money which they thought they had in the bank for the purpose is gone to the extent of 6,000 *l.*

4445. You mean to say that it has been misapplied?—Applied to the purposes of another fund.

4446. But only to corporation purposes?—Yes, certainly.

4447. You said that Mr. Dockrell had made to you, as auditor, certain suggestions with regard to the mode of keeping accounts; do you find that the members of the corporation are ready at all times to afford facilities to the auditor?—Quite so; both the members of the corporation and the officers.

4448. Is there any desire to withhold any information from the auditor?—I think not.

Mr. *Brooks*—continued.

Mr. *Finlay*.

13 June 1876.

4449. You say that in Wicklow the Commissioners have refrained from taking proceedings, because there is no fund from which they could be indemnified from costs; can you suggest any mode of indemnifying the members of corporations who *bonâ fide* incur costs in their capacity as members of the town council?—I do not think that I gave a reason for their not proceeding, for I never heard any reason, and I do not think that I assigned any. It was suggested by some Member of the Committee, but I do not know the reason.

4450. The members of the town council of the City of Dublin are liable, are they not, for costs in promoting the gas company?—Yes, that is they would be if they pay them; I do not know whether they are personally liable, say to the gas engineer that I have mentioned, or to the newspapers, or to counsel, or attorney, or Parliamentary agents; but I understand legal opinions have been obtained to the effect that there is not any personal liability.

4451. Although their proceedings were strictly *bonâ fide* they would still be liable?—I understand that they would not be personally liable. Some proceedings have been threatened against them individually by parties to whom the corporation are indebted, as the Court was unanimously of opinion in Clemenshaw's case that they could not pay their claims out of the rates, some parties are seeking to make them personally liable.

4452. With regard to the proceedings by the town council for promoting the purchase of the gas company, are you able to inform the Committee of the sum agreed to be paid for each share by the corporation to the gas company?—No, not with accuracy. My memory is not very clear about it, because it is not a matter in which I take any interest.

4453. May I remind you that it was 13 *l.* 5 *s.* a share?—I do not know; it never came before me. Anything I know in that way would be derived from the newspapers as an ordinary reader.

Sir *Joseph M'Kenna*.

4454. Have you anything to do with, or do you know the circumstances of, the collection of the rates in Rathmines?—No.

4455. That is not brought under you?—Not at all.

4456. Can you explain why it is not?—It is, as I have stated, one of the townships in the county of Dublin which are exempted by Act of Parliament.

4457. Do not you think it is very desirable that it should be brought within the scope of the audit?—It is a strange thing that the Act should be applied to nine-tenths of the towns in Ireland, and that one-tenth should be excluded from its operation. I cannot understand the propriety of such an arrangement.

4458. You can suggest nothing as being a proper and sufficient reason for the exclusion of Rathmines?—No, the only reason I am aware of is the one that I saw assigned by the chairman of the Rathmines Commissioners recently.

4459. Is that a sufficient reason in your mind?—No; the reason he assigned was, that if they had a Government audit, the Government auditor would prevent their doing many acts which were illegal, but which were considered by the Commissioners beneficial to the township.

Mr. *Finlay.*

13 June 1876.

Sir *Joseph M'Kenna*—continued.

4460. Do not you think that that very fact which he alleged is a very good reason for extending the audit to Rathmines?—I should say so, certainly; I thought when I read it that it was a very strong reason for extending it.

Mr. *O'Shaughnessy.*

4461. You spoke of towns in which the ordinary rate was confined to 1 *s.*, and an additional rate of 6 *d.* allowed for water purposes; do you find in the majority of towns that they have had to add to each of those rates?—They are generally confined to the 1 *s.* There are some places as low as 6 *d.* In Athy it is only 6 *d.*

4462. Do you mean to say that they only go as far as 6 *d.*?—Yes; in Enniscorthy they only go to 8 *d.*, and in Gorey to 6 *d.*

4463. Would you say that in the generality of those small towns they have left themselves still some margin for further improvements, and for further expenditure?—I think not in the majority. I think in the majority of cases they go to the 1 *s.*

4464. Is it your experience that in those cases it is likely that other public necessities may arise requiring further taxation than could be met by the 1 *s.*?—Yes.

4465. Therefore it would be necessary either to leave those public duties undischarged, or to increase the power of taxation?—In a great number of the towns to which you refer, the portion of the expenditure for sanitary purposes, which is a growing expenditure, has been transferred from the town funds to the union fund, so that the former would be eased to that extent; and perhaps the shilling may be found to be sufficient.

4466. But if any other public necessity arose, chargeable upon the rates, it might be necessary in many cases to increase the power of taxation?—It might.

4467. With regard to the property belonging to the old corporation of Naas, which has become vested in some way or another in the Protestant Orphan Society, do you know whether that property still exists?—I know that I had a letter on the 27th of April from the town clerk of Naas, in reply to an inquiry of mine in which he says, "I have made inquiry as to the old corporation property, and ascertained that it was handed over to the trustees of the Protestant Orphan Society of Kildare. Lord Mayo, I am told, receives a yearly sum in lieu of tolls." That is my source of information.

4468. Are there Commissioners in Naas?—Yes.

4469. Therefore in Naas, it is in those Commissioners and not in the union that property would vest now?—Quite so, under the 3rd and 4th Vict. c. 108.

4470. You say that you took proceedings once at the suggestion of the Local Government Board against Mr. Henry to recover certain fees received by him, and you were defeated in those proceedings, were you not?—Yes.

4471. Who bore the expense of your defeat?—The City of Dublin.

4472. Am I to assume that in all proceedings instituted by you in your capacity of auditor against people like Mr. Henry, you calculate that the expense of them is to be borne by the community if you are defeated?—Yes; if it were not for that you would not see many disallowances. Of course, since that decision, no similar proceedings would be instituted in the present state of the law.

Mr. *O'Shaughnessy*—continued.

4473. Have you to obtain the permission of the Local Government Board in every instance before instituting such proceedings?—No.

4474. As a matter of fact, I believe the auditors always take counsel of the Local Government Board?—As a rule we do.

4475. Did I understand you to recommend the extension of the system by which, instead of the auditors being paid as they now are in the towns for their audit of the towns, they should be paid as they are in the case of unions?—Yes. In other words that there should be no charge upon the towns; that the Treasury should bear all the cost of the auditors' salaries instead of imposing a portion of it on the towns.

4476. Have you ever, in any of the places in which you have audited, had to deal with cases like that of the expenses for the Gas Bill in Dublin, cases in which a corporation have undertaken Parliamentary proceedings which proved futile?—Yes; I gave the instance of Kingstown, where a disallowance was made by me of 82 *l.* for proceedings in the case of an abortive Bill.

4477. Did you decide there that the Corporation of Kingstown or the Commissioners of Kingstown were not liable?—I decided that it was not a charge which could be inflicted upon the ratepayers.

4478. You have told us in the course of your examination that where you find a commission or a corporation claiming as an asset a debt which had been allowed to remain outstanding a long time, and where the recovery was hopeless, you have recommended them to strike it off?—Yes.

4479. Where you find the converse case, where you find a debt hanging over a corporation, or a claim hanging over a corporation, remaining unprosecuted, what course do you adopt in those cases; supposing you find a claim, we will say, against the Dublin Corporation hanging over them for three or four years, one after another, do you make any recommendation with regard to the payment or settlement of that claim?—Certainly not; in a case in which if payment were made it would be held to be illegal, I should not recommend the corporation to do anything of the kind, inasmuch as when the payment should come before me at the audit, I should have to disallow it.

4480. With regard to the mixing up by the different committees of the Dublin Corporation of the funds which they have received for different purposes, whereas you have recommended them to separate those funds, and strictly to draw on a particular fund for the purposes of that fund only, have you any power to enforce that recommendation?—No.

4481. You can only report to the Local Government Board that you have recommended it, and that your recommendation has not been followed?—That is all.

4482. Do you recommend that the auditors of the Local Government Board should receive any power, subject, of course, to appeal, for the purpose of enforcing advice of that kind?—I do not.

4483. Do not you think that a system is defective which would leave you merely with a power of

Mr. *O'Shaughnessy*—continued.

of recommending a change of the law, but no authority in the country with the power of enforcing it?—Yes, I should say so, certainly.

4484. Do you make any suggestion for remedying that defect?—I do not make any suggestion beyond what I have made, that some steps should be taken in the case of the Corporation of Dublin for keeping separate accounts in the Bank of Ireland for those funds, to prevent them being mixed up.

4485. Do not you regard the powers of the Local Government Board as defective, in that they can merely take notice of the existence of such a state of things as that?—I do not know. When an Act of Parliament prescribes that certain funds shall be applied to certain purposes, I presume that there must be some power to enforce compliance with the law; the burgesses I should say would have the power to enforce it.

4486. You have mentioned the case of the fraudulent leases made by the Wicklow Corporation to members of the corporation; do you know whether there were in the new leases any obligations thrown upon the new tenants which would account for there being those small rents reserved?—I think there was an obligation as to building, but I do not think that those obligations have been complied with in every case.

4487. Would the obligation thrown upon them of building be sufficient to account for the very low rents imposed, taking into account the length of the leases being 75 years?—I do not think it would.

4488. Have you any further specific recommendations to make about the increase of your powers?—No; I have no desire to see them increased.

4489. Have any of the towns which were originally exempted from the Audit Act come, since the passing of that Act, under the operation of the audit?—Yes, voluntarily.

4490. Involuntarily, have any?—No; they voluntarily adopted the provisions of the Act with regard to the audit.

4491. What towns have adopted the provisions of the Act?—There are the townships of Kingstown, Blackrock, and Dalkey; those three have adopted them.

4492. Was Dublin exempted in the first instance?—No; the only exemptions of towns (putting aside the townships in the county of Dublin) were Cork, Waterford, and Kilkenny.

4493. When you came to deal with the towns which had been first exempted, and which came voluntarily under the system of audit, did you find frauds or misapplications, or misconduct of any kind in the prior accounts, which would account for their unwillingness in the first instance to come under the audit?—I have given an instance in Kingstown of the payment to a late secretary, concurrently of salary and pension for two and a-half years; and I have given an instance in the case of Dalkey of great irregularities in respect to the collection of rates. There had also been serious irregularities and misapplication of funds by a former secretary of the Blackrock Commissioners. In the case of each of these townships, the bringing of the township under the operations of the Act was the act of the ratepayers.

4494. Do you believe that these misapplications and irregularities were probably one motive that led those people in the first instance not to submit themselves to the Act?—I cannot go that length; I do not know what the motives were. I can only say that they would not have occurred if they were under a system of Government audit, or had they occurred, they would not have continued.

Mr. *Gibson*.

4495. Have not one of the excepted towns, Waterford, a very large amount of corporate property?—I do not know anything about Waterford; neither it, nor Cork, nor Kilkenny has ever been in my district.

4496. I think you stated to the Right honourable Chairman, when he asked you the question whether you thought on the whole that the towns under the Act of 1854 were fairly audited, that their accounts had been kept with reasonable fairness?—Yes, I think so.

4497. Are you aware that under the 59th section of the Act of 1854, it is provided "That the Commissioners shall in all cases appoint some bank or banking company to act as their treasurer, and that it shall not be necessary to require from such bank or banking company any security for the due execution of such office as required by said Act"?—I am.

4498. And that consequently no towns under the Act of 1854 have any treasurer at all other than a banker?—Yes.

4499. Are you aware that legislation has moved in that direction in the case of the grand juries within the last six or seven years, and that none of the grand juries of Ireland have treasurers of their own, but are exempted from the necessity of appointing a treasurer, and can appoint a banking company in the neighbourhood?—I am aware of that.

4500. Are you aware that that system of appointing a banker and not a treasurer works sufficiently well in those towns under the Act of 1854, and also that the grand juries have adopted it?—Yes; and you may add the Poor Law unions are all under the same rule.

4501. And they have found that the system of no treasurer, but a banker to act as treasurer, works efficiently?—Yes, certainly.

4502. Are you aware that it is by virtue of the provision, I think, of the 93rd section of the 3rd & 4th Vict. c. 108, that it is assumed that it is necessary for towns and for boroughs to appoint a treasurer, and that it is compulsory?—It is compulsory. The word is "a person"; they must appoint a person.

4503. Are you aware that any of the towns in Ireland have endeavoured to get the benefit of appointing a banker, and nominally complying with the provisions of the Act of Parliament?—Yes, I am aware that that is the case in Derry, and I believe it is the case in Belfast. I have heard so. What they did in Derry was this: They appointed the manager of one of the banks there to be their treasurer, at a nominal salary of 5 *l.* or 10 *l.* a year.

4504. Are all the accounts there paid into the bank?—Yes, they are all paid into the bank.

4505. The salary paid to the treasurer of the city of Dublin is 600 *l.* a year: do you see any difficulty at all in the corporation applying this general principle to town accounts of appointing a banker as their treasurer, and saving this large salary?—It occurs to me that there might be a difficulty with respect to the collection of the rents. The corporation have a very large number of tenants, and

Mr. *Finlay*.

13 June 1876.

Mr. *Finlay.*

13 June 1876.

Mr. *Gibson*—continued.

and they are thinking of getting the tenants to pay their rents into the bank since that business of Mr. Robinson occurred, but I do not know whether they have seen their way to it.

4506. That is to say, to apply the system of receivable orders that were invented by the Irish Church Commissioners?—Yes; the corporation have about 700 tenants.

4507. And you think that there would be more difficulty in the case of a corporation like that of Dublin, which has many tenants?—Yes; I think there would be a difficulty. I give that opinion with much hesitation, because the difficulty may be got over. You would require to have agents who would look very sharp after the collection of the rents. If they were not coming into the bank, you would require an agent who would go to the tenants and hunt them up, and the solicitor to proceed against them.

4508. You are no doubt aware that the late treasurer was not in the habit at all of attending to collect the rents from the tenants; do you see any difficulty in having collectors like the poor rate collectors to pay the rents into the bank, and no treasurer; might not that save a very substantial part of the 600*l.* a year salary?—I doubt it, for this reason; you must have an officer, no matter whether you call him treasurer, or cashier, or paymaster; as there is a very large sum of money paid out of the office, and which must continue to be paid out of it. Look at hundreds of the scavengers, and other men employed by the corporation. They have waterworks extending from Dublin to Stillorgan, and on to Roundwood, and there are a great number of men employed on those works, and those men are paid every week, and their money must be brought to them; a large number of the employés are paid their wages in the city hall.

4509. Could you give an idea of the weekly outgoings that must be paid in that way by the treasurer?—I would not venture to say, but it is, of course, a very large sum.

4510. Would it amount to several hundreds of pounds?—Yes, certainly.

4511. So that, in your opinion, it is necessary that some person should be trusted with the manual receipt and management of the money, and your only safeguard is to look to the sureties?—Yes, there must be such a person, even if the rents were brought to the bank.

4512. With regard to the Act, under which you yourself audit these accounts, are you aware that there is ample power given to the Chief Secretary, who is at the head of the Local Government Board, to give Provisional Orders to deal by way of repeal and amendment with all the special Acts?—Yes.

4513. Are you aware that that power does not enable the Chief Secretary to deal in any respect with any of the towns that are under the Act of 1854, that being a public Act?—Yes.

4514. Do you think it would be desirable to declare that the towns under the Act of 1854 should be regarded as under a special Act, and to give them the benefit of this power of having Provisional Orders?—I think it would.

4515. It would save them the expense of going for a new Act of Parliament, would it not, whenever they wanted a slight change in the law?—It would save them the expense where all the parties concerned are of one mind, but the power of proceeding by Provisional Order has in some

Mr. *Gibson*—continued.

cases led to a very large increase in the cost of obtaining an Act of Parliament, because you have an inquiry before an Inspector of the Local Government Board; you have counsel, attornies, and skilled witnesses, and you have a report to the Local Government Board, and a Provisional Order is issued. There has been an opposition on the part of some of the parties interested, before the Local Government Inspector, and that opposition is carried into Parliament, and the whole of the proceedings are gone over again before a Committee of Parliament, just the same as if there were no Provisional Order. This would appear to point to the necessity for a change in the law, whereby the evidence taken in Ireland would be deemed to be sufficient to justify Parliament in legislating on the subject.

4516. But, at all events, if the parties who chance to be in towns under a special Act, agree upon a certain application, they can have it carried out by Provisional Order?—Yes.

4517. Whereas they may be all quite united and agreed, but if they chanced to be under the General Act of 1854 they would have no alternative but to go to the great expense of getting an Act of Parliament?—Yes, that is so.

4518. And you state that it would be desirable to remedy that by the way suggested?—Yes, I think that it would be desirable to give the power to every place to apply for a Provisional Order.

4519. In towns other than Dublin, where the collector general of rates has his accounts audited by Master Fitzgibbon, you audit also the collection of rates?—Yes, invariably.

4520. Have you got any power under the Act of 1871 in dealing at all with the rates that have been neglected to be collected?—No, we have not.

4521. If the rates of a town, taking an arbitrary figure, should amount to 3,000*l.*, and you find that only 2,000*l.* has been collected, have you absolutely no power of inquiry into the 1,000*l.* which has been left uncollected?—Yes, we have power to see, and we do require to see, how it has happened, and why it has happened; and then we report to the Local Government Board at the close of the audit.

4522. Supposing you found that it has been by the grossest negligence and culpable carelessness that the 1,000*l.* has not been collected, you have no power other than that of reporting them to the Local Government Board?—I have no other power. I had such a case in Dalkey, which I mentioned.

4523. You mentioned that Mr. Justice Fitzgerald suggested an amendment in the powers of the auditor in one direction; do you think it would be also desirable to give you a further power of dealing with uncollected rates when you were satisfied that they had been improperly and negligently left uncollected?—It would be a difficult matter for us to ascertain particular cases in which the rates ought to be recovered, but have not been recovered. It requires a local knowledge which we do not possess, going as we do, as strangers to the place. The course that we pursue, I think, answers all the purposes, and that is, to get the collectors to furnish a list of the outstanding arrears, and get the Town Commissioners to scrutinise them, and in that way to keep a check upon the collectors; and I think, on the whole, that our recommendations are attended to sufficiently by the Town Commissioners.

4524. I

Mr. *Gibson*—continued.

4524. I find, in the 12th section of the Local Government Act, 1871, which is one of the sections regulating your powers, that a power is given to a person who feels himself aggrieved, of taking what he wishes to question into the Court of Queen's Bench by *certiorari*, or else to apply to the Chief Secretary to inquire into the matter; have you found that many people apply to the Court of Queen's Bench?—No, very few; I think I have had only two appeals, or three at the outside, to the Court of Queen's Bench.

4525. Are they all from Dublin?—One was from Blackrock, which was decided last term, about the money given to the late secretary, and the small burial expense; there were two from Dublin.

4526. Are there any appeals made to the Local Government Board itself?—Yes, several appeals.

4527. Those are commoner than to the Court of Queen's Bench?—Yes, much more numerous.

4528. Are they quite inexpensive?—They ought not to cost more than the sheet of paper on which they are written.

4529. As to the appeals to the Local Government Board, are they contained in writing without the intervention of a solicitor or a barrister, or law costs?—I do not think so in some cases. The appeal is in writing, but in some cases that I know of, and perhaps in numerous cases, the appeal has been framed by an attorney or some legal man. They set out all the grounds on which they object to the auditor's decision. The appeal is sent to the Local Government Board, and forwarded by the Local Government Board to the auditor for any observations he may think proper to make upon it. They hear our observations, and they weigh the arguments on both sides, and decide the matter in writing.

4530. But there is no argument before them, is there?—Except on paper.

4531. And that, of course, is a very inexpensive system?—Yes, quite inexpensive, at least it ought to be so, as an intelligent town clerk could prepare the document in almost every case.

4532. Are you aware that at the present time the audit before you is open to this observation, that if a person wishes to make a large payment, say for a beneficial object, but whose legality may be doubtful, he has no mode beforehand of ascertaining its legality; but he must run the chance of incurring the expense, and then seeing whether you will pass it or not?—Yes; he has no mode except the ordinary mode that everybody has of ascertaining whether the step that they are about to take is legal or not, by seeking legal advice.

4533. That advice may be wrong, because opinions vary on doubtful points; you are aware, I presume, that in the case of a grand jury presentment the opinion of the judge can be got for asking, which is conclusive as to the law?—Yes; that is by the judge's fiat on the presentment.

4534. Have you any suggestion to make as to power being given of applying to a judge, or to some tribunal that would have the power, beforehand of finally determining whether an expense should be legal or not?—That is an expense about which they have a doubt?

4535. Yes. You may be aware that if a person has a doubt about what stamp to put upon a document he can get the opinion of the Stamp Office upon it, which is conclusive; can you suggest any analogous course to be adopted with reference to an expenditure which will afterwards have to be audited by an officer of the Local Government Board?—I have not any suggestion to make, but I would merely observe with regard to the grand jury powers, that I do not think they work very satisfactorily. I had a case, to which I called attention sometime ago, in the city of Dublin, in which a payment was made to the sheriff under the Grand Jury Laws for the printing of summonses to the jurors. He is entitled under Lord O'Hagan's Act to post the summonses. I think prior to that they were delivered by hand; he is entitled now to post them, and he is declared entitled to whatever charge he may incur in posting, but I found that in addition to postage there was a charge made for printing the summonses. That appears for the first time in the year 1873 or 1874, and I called attention to the absence of anything in the statute respecting printing: it applied merely to posting, and I suggested that the attention of the Court should be called to the matter at the next presentment sessions, because as I need not tell you, these items do not come in detail before the judge.

4536. What did the judge do then?—The matter was not brought before the judge, and has never been so up to the present time, although the charge continues to be made; I was very anxious that the judge's attention should be called to it in order that he might say whether it was or was not legal.

4537. You cannot call that an illustration of the unsatisfactory way in which it works, because the opinion of the judge never was asked?—No, the opinion never was asked, but the expenditure was incurred.

Mr. *Finlay*.

13 June 1878.

Mr. *Collins*.

4538. In auditing the accounts of those municipal bodies, what books do you usually require to be produced to you?—We require the ledger and the minutes when it is necessary to refer to them, and the banking book.

4539. Are those sufficient to show you the amount of payments actually received?—Yes.

4540. How do you ascertain the amount of payments that ought to be received to which you refer in your evidence?—We ascertain that from our knowledge of the funds usually received in the town. We find, for instance, that there are funds received in a certain place from the market tolls, and the weigh-bridge. We know that last year there were funds from these sources, and if we find none this year we inquire why that is. We have the officers before us, and they are bound to produce their accounts to us.

4541. Where do you find those items; is it in the previous audits, or from the books?—Both; we know, of course, the officer in charge of the markets, who receives the fees, and we require to have his accounts, and we should know from those what he had received.

4542. The ledger would not supply that information?—The ledger would, of course, supply information as to monies which have been received. It does not show monies which have not been paid.

4543. Then the banker's book would not supply that?—No.

4544. Is there no book held by corporate bodies

Mr. Finlay.

18 June 1876.

Mr. *Collins*—continued.

bodies that would specially direct your attention to a subject of that kind; is there no record of description?—There is no record in that way; but I do not think that the accounting officers could escape, as we know who the accounting officers are.

4545. Does not it greatly increase the difficulties of an auditor if he must ascertain the amount of payments which ought to be received, if he has not a document that would direct his attention to the subject?—I think not; we know them, and we keep them in view. I suppose, in the case of a body misapplying money coming into their hands, they could keep it out of the book which you have in view.

4546. I could understand that of money that has come into their hands, but I mean moneys that ought to come into their hands?—In the case of money that came into their hands and was misapplied, what they would have to do would be to keep back the record of it from the auditor.

4547. But in the case of money that ought to be received, the question I ask you is this: how are you, as an auditor, able to deal with funds which you believe ought to be received if there be no public document or no book that will direct your attention to such funds?—I never felt any difficulty about that; and I do not think there is, practically, any difficulty.

4548. Then you would be guided simply by your own experience, and by your knowledge of the circumstances of each town?—Yes.

4549. You could be misled upon that point, could you not?—It is quite possible, but I do not think it is likely.

4550. Does not your experience suggest to you that it would be desirable that there should be a record of money of that description which should be brought under your consideration as an auditor; would you not suggest that a certain class of books should be kept by municipalities, that would at any time put before you or any other auditor a list of payments that ought to be collected by the municipalities?—I see no objection to that.

4551. Would you not consider it very desirable?—I think that parties about to commit a fraud would take care to omit those items from such a book, and if I were guided by that book I might lose sight of the thing altogether.

4552. It might have the effect then of deceiving you?—Possibly in that way.

4553. When you object to payments, if your objections are sustained, do you find that the moneys so objected to are reinstated on the occasion of your next audit?—Generally they are reinstated; in some cases they are not.

4554. In cases where they are not reinstated, what proceedings do you take?—A proceeding before any two magistrates of the petty sessions district.

4555. Would you do that in such a case as you mentioned with regard to Trim?—Yes.

4556. How often during the year do you visit towns to make audits?—We are required by the Act of 1871 to visit them once a year.

4557. Do you ever make your visits more frequent?—No; "shall be audited and examined once in every year" is the language of the Act.

4558. You stated that in the case of Wicklow the ratepayers brought before you, as auditor, complaints respecting the disposal of the town property, that the municipality, in fact, leased to members of their own body property valued under Griffith's valuation at 300 *l.* a year, and leased it for a period of 75 years at 66 *l.*, or thereabouts?—Yes.

4559. In the case of a misappropriation of that description, is there no power on the part of the Local Government Board to take proceedings?—None whatever.

4560. Nor on the part of any authority whatsoever?—No, there is no authority to move in the matter. The only parties, I believe, who can move as the law stands at present are two burgesses of the place, who can proceed in the Court of Chancery. I believe that that is the state of the law.

4561. Then, practically, the public has no redress at all in the case of being robbed by corporations of that description?—I think not. I think there is no remedy, except as I have stated; at least none that I know of. There is none certainly in the Local Government Board, nor in any of their officers.

4562. The Local Government Board is not aware of any mode of obtaining redress in cases of that kind?—No.

4563. If burgesses take proceedings in the Court of Chancery, of course they can open up the case?—Yes.

4564. But it must be done, must it not, at their own personal expense?—It must be done at their own risk. If they succeed, I take it as a matter of course, the costs will follow the result.

4565. However, the risks attending proceedings of the kind would be likely to be so great as to deter them in fact from proceeding to obtain redress?—It would deter them no doubt.

4566. Does any mode suggest itself to your mind for applying a remedy to so great an evil as that?—I have not considered that question.

Mr. *J. P. Corry*.

4567. In auditing the accounts of the corporation, do you require all the vouchers for the payments to be produced?—Invariably.

4568. In the case of the corporation of Dublin, do you require the weekly pay-sheets for scavengers and others to be produced?—Yes.

4569. Do you check them?—Yes.

4570. The honourable Member for Dublin asked you with regard to one committee drawing money from the credit of another, and that it was an economical way of proceeding, because if one committee had not the money to its credit it would have to pay interest; would not it be easier for a corporation to make arrangements with a banker that in the banking account kept with him, the interest should be charged on the one account and incurred on the other?—Yes; they might make an arrangement of that sort if the funds were separated; but my desire is to have the funds so separated with the view to prevent their drawing from one fund for the purposes of another.

4571. You think that it would be quite possible for them to make an arrangement with the bank that upon the money to the credit of one fund, interest should be allowed as against the interest that would be due on the overdrawn part of the other account?—Yes.

4572. Have you ever heard of members of a corporation having to pay the cost of proceedings with

Mr. *J. P. Corry*—continued.

with reference to abortive Bills in Parliament?—I do not know of any such case; none has come under my notice. I have already stated that the corporation of Dublin have been advised that they are not personally liable to the parties to whom the costs are due.

Mr. *Brooks*.

4573. Did not you say that at Kingstown they paid 68 *l.*?—That was through the agency of the audit. I understood the last question to be, whether I knew of any case in which payment was made direct to parties who rendered the services, by individual members of a governing body; in the case that I spoke of in Kingstown, the payment was made by the Town Commissioners in the first instance in their corporate capacity and was disallowed by me, and the amount subsequently refunded by the three Commissioners who signed the cheque, owing to my disallowance.

Mr. *J. P. Corry*.

4574. Do you find the accounts of the corporations, as a rule, kept in a satisfactory way?—I do.

4575. But you think that it would not be possible to deal altogether with a treasurer in a corporation like Dublin, where there are so many tenants?—Supposing you got over the difficulty about the tenants, and got them to go to the bank and lodge their rents there regularly, you must have a person who would pay out moneys for the corporation from day to day and week to week. There is a very large number of persons who are in the receipt of weekly wages, and there must be somebody to be entrusted with the payment of the wages.

Mr. *Bruen*.

4576. You were asked some questions by the honourable and learned Member for the University of Dublin with regard to doing away with the office of city treasurer, and you stated that you saw a difficulty in doing so, on account of the city treasurer receiving the rents of the corporation estate?—That was one of my reasons.

4577. Dealing first with that reason, do not you think that the Collector General of Rates, having a staff in his office accustomed to the kind of duty involved in collecting rates and looking after property, could very well undertake the collection of the rents of the corporation estate in Dublin?—I am not able to answer that question, because I have no knowledge of the extent of the labours which are imposed upon the collectors in the office of the Collector General; in fact, I do not know anything about them.

4578. You do not audit the Collector of Rates' accounts, but would you mind giving an opinion to the Committee as to whether you think it would be desirable that the accounts of the Collector of Rates should be brought under the same system of audit as the accounts of the corporation?—I do think it would be desirable; more especially as the office of Receiver Master in the Court of Chancery is about being abolished. There is a Bill at present in Parliament for the purpose, and some provision must be made for the discharge of the duties in connection with public accounts, which heretofore devolved on Master Fitzgibbon.

4579. You mentioned, in answer to a question

Mr. *Bruen*—continued.

of the Right honourable Chairman, certain costs that were not paid; can you state whether they were incurred in respect of one Bill which you mentioned, namely, the Gas Bill of 1874, or whether they were incurred in respect of different other Bills?—There were two Gas Bills in two different Sessions that fell through; one Bill was defeated before the Committee of the House of Lords after a long battle. In the next Session the corporation promoted another Bill, and after getting a first reading, I think the Bill was about being taken before a Committee, when the corporation got an opinion from Mr. Serjeant Armstrong, to the effect that they had no legal power to proceed, and that any expenditure incurred by them would be illegal, and they withdrew that Bill; and the costs in respect of neither of those Bills have been paid.

4580. Supposing that they had paid those costs out of the rates, do you feel that it would have been your duty to have disallowed them?—Certainly.

4581. Of course you do not wish to extend the opinion which you have so given, so far as to say by whom it should be paid?—If an auditor makes a disallowance the Act requires that he shall surcharge the persons who authorised the expenditure, in other words, those who signed the cheque; the three members of the corporation who signed the cheques would be the parties liable.

4582. But you would not go further, and say who were primarily liable to the payment of those costs?—No.

4583. In going through the receipts in the different boroughs, whose accounts you audit, you have given a strong expression of opinion as to the sufficiency of the proceeds derived from the estates of those towns; for instance, in Wicklow, you had occasion to find fault with the amount of the rents received as being too low?—I found fault with it in consequence of the objection of some ratepayers that the receipts were not sufficient, owing to the property being let in the manner that I have stated.

4584. If those people had not made such objection, would it have been within your province to have inquired into the subject, and to have ascertained whether the rents were adequate or not?—I should have known nothing about it. I should have seen 66 *l.* a year brought into the rental, and I should not have known whether it should have been that sum, or a lower or a higher sum.

4585. You do not then compare the rents received with the valuation of the property?—No, we do not do that. It is a power which we do not possess.

4586. I think that in the earlier part of your examination you stated that you ascertained the items on the receipt side of the cash books?—Yes.

4587. And that you also inquire what ought to be there?—Yes.

4588. Would not that inquiry extend to the question of insufficient payment of rent?—No, I think not, because a tenant takes a place, say, for 66 *l.* a year rent, the value of which is fairly double that, but all that I should expect to find is that the sum for which the tenant is liable, namely 66 *l.*, is placed among the receipts.

4589. So that unless the question is raised before you by one of the ratepayers who has an interest

Mr. *Finlay*.

13 June 1876.

Mr. *Finlay*.

13 June 1876.

Mr. *Brunn*—continued.

interest in the matter, you do not inquire into it?—I do not inquire. I do not know what ought to be the rent.

4590. Has any question of that sort ever been raised before you with respect to the property of the city of Dublin?—No such question has ever arisen before me.

4591. Has any disallowance been made by you in the city of Dublin accounts of payments by way of advance of salaries to officers, that is to say, payments made in advance of what was due to them?—Yes, such matters have come under my notice.

4592. Do you consider that to be illegal?—Certainly.

4593. Has it been done more than once?—It has.

4594. Since you have drawn attention to it and disallowed it?—Yes.

4595. You have occasion to audit a good number of towns in Leinster; in the case of Enniscorthy, for example, did you meet with anything to find fault with in respect to the Town Commissioners accounts there?—I found when I went there first, that the payments made were not authorised on the Minutes. We expect to find authority on the Minutes so as to insure that the cheques are not drawn without the knowledge of the Board as a body. I found that it was not so there, but the expenditure is very small; not I think over 130*l.* a year; and, on my pointing out to the town clerk the necessity for having the Minutes made in the first instance, the thing was remedied, and there has been no further complaint.

4596. I find in Thom's Directory that the revenue of Enniscorthy in 1873 was 270*l.* a year, so that I suppose since that time their taxation must have been reduced?—Yes, they have been relieved of the sanitary expenses, which have been transferred under the Public Health Act of 1874 to the board of guardians of the Enniscorthy Union, the town not containing 6,000 inhabitants.

4597. Would that account for the difference?—I think it would.

4598. As regards the borough of Wexford, is there not a debt there?—Yes, there is a debt.

4599. Can you tell the Committee what that debt amounts to?—I cannot; I do not think I have got the particulars for Wexford here.

4600. Is there any property belonging to the Corporation of Wexford?—Yes, they have property, and an agent who collects the rents.

4601. Did you find the management of that property satisfactory?—So far as I could see the management was satisfactory; the agent appeared to me to discharge his duties in a very satisfactory manner.

4602. There has been no ratepayer who has directed your attention to any malfeasances on the part of the Commissioners, as was the case in Wicklow?—No, not in that way; there has been a complaint regarding an expenditure which is alleged of an illegal character, but I have not investigated it as yet. I shall be going down there as soon as I get done with the Dublin Corporation.

4603. Do you know whether the rates in the borough of Wexford are very much lightened by the receipts from the corporate property?—They must be a good deal lightened; I find in my abstract that the rents of the corporate property are 327*l.*, and the pipe water rents 125*l.*; they must be lightened to that extent.

Mr. *Brunn*—continued.

4604. Do they furnish you with a rental of the corporate estate?—Yes, I always examine the rental.

4605. I find by a Return which has been made to an Order of the House of Commons of last August, that in the year 1873 the rates were 1*s.* in the pound in the Wexford town and borough; in 1874 they were 2*s.* 10*d.* in the pound; and in 1875 they were 2*s.* 6*d.* in the pound; how do you account for that increase?—They got a Provisional Order in the meantime enabling them to do certain works and increase their expenditure.

4606. But in this Return there is no mention made of any property belonging to the corporation, although in other boroughs there is mention made of it?—There is a distinct entry in my own handwriting, "Rents of corporate property, 327*l.* 9*s.* 7*d.*"

4607. To go on with the list of the towns, Carlow is another town in your district, is it not?—Yes.

4608. Have you been satisfied with the manner in which the management of the rates of the town has been carried on there?—No, I have not been satisfied about it, nor my predecessor either, but they have changed their collector; they had a very unsatisfactory collector. When I was last in Carlow there was a small balance of 10*l.* or 12*l.* in his hands. I called attention to this matter, and suggested to the Town Commissioners to put a decree which they had against him in force. I find that matters are going on much more satisfactorily in Carlow.

4609. But the whole of the money has been recovered, has it not?—Yes; I think the whole of the money has been recovered. If they have have recovered that sum they will then have had it all.

4610. In fact, they complied with your suggestions?—Yes, they complied with my suggestions; they seemed to be very anxious to do right.

4611. There was no complaint made by any of the ratepayers there?—No complaint was made; they seem to me to be very anxious to do what is right.

4612. With regard to Athy, did you say that there was a small property belonging to the old corporation of Athy long ago?—Yes; amounting to 154*l.* a year.

4613. And that has disappeared altogether, I think?—Yes; possibly it may be the tolls for weighing at the public crane and council, but if that is not the property that was referred to in the Report of the Commissioners in 1835, there is now none of it.

4614. Is there much revenue derived from that now?—About 140*l.* a year.

4615. That would very nearly correspond with the market tolls?—Yes, very nearly.

4616. I see that in Athy the expenditure is put down in 1873 as 288*l.*; is not that rather large for a town of 4,000 inhabitants?—No; they appear to me to do matters very well in Athy town.

4617. Comparing that with the expenditure in Carlow, it appears a large sum, seeing that in Carlow the expenditure is only 127*l.*, and it is nearly double the size?—The expenditure in the abstract that I have for Athy for the year ending the 1st of May 1875, is 291*l.* 17*s.* 7*d.* The balances

Mr. *Bruen*—continued.

balances may explain the difference between the expenditure in both places. I will see how the balance stood in Carlow. My expenditure in Carlow for the year ending December 1874, was 473 *l.* 1 *s.* 2 *d.* The 1875 abstract I have not got here. There was a question about it in the Local Government Board, and that paper has been kept there.

4618. Does not that include the sanitary expenses in Carlow?—Yes, it does.

4619. The entry made in Thom's Directory of the expenditure in 1872 appears to be only 127 *l.*?—The expenditure, taking any one year, may be misleading in this way. Certain accounts are allowed to hang fire sometimes for two or three years, and even for six years I have found them unpaid. If those are all paid in one year, up jumps the expenditure as compared with the preceding or succeeding year, and that may have created the discrepancy.

4620. The nominal expenditure for the purposes for which those rates are levied in those different towns does not vary very much, and ought very much to depend upon the size, the population, and the circumstances of the town, ought it not?—The size of the towns ought to have a great deal to do with it, seeing that it is in the paving, lighting, and cleansing, that the principal expenses are incurred. But some Town Commissioners carry on very much more works than others; some of them are more desirous of effecting improvements than others, and of course that makes a great difference in the expenditure in towns.

4621. Did you find that in Wicklow there were very great improvements made in the town?—Indeed I did not.

4622. I find here that they have a very large income and a very small population?—Yes.

4623. The inference seems to be that they must squander their income if they do not make very large improvements?—You must bear in mind that they pay between 500 *l.* and 600 *l.* a-year for interest alone.

4624. But even making allowance for that, they would have in Wicklow an income of over 800 *l.* a-year, their population being only 3,400; and comparing that with Athy, which has about the same population, their expenditure is only 280 *l.* a-year?—The state of things in Wicklow is not by any means satisfactory. There is 1,663 *l.* under the head of expenditure; out of that must be taken the balance due to the treasurer at the close of the previous year, and the balance in the treasurer's hands at the close of the particular year, amounting in all to 600 *l.*; that would give a nett expenditure of 1,000 *l.*

4625. From that they must deduct 600 *l.* interest?—£. 546 interest on the mortgage and bonded debt; the balance was expended thus: on new works and repairs, 146 *l.*; water supply, 76 *l.*; rent and taxes, 66 *l.*; cleansing and scavenging, 82 *l.*; salaries, including agent's fees, 166 *l.*; printing, stationery, postage, and incidental expenses, 30 *l.*; that is the way the balance is accounted for.

4626. Did you inquire whether it was possible to obtain from the Harbour Commissioners any assistance towards the payment of this interest?—I did inquire with that view, and I stated to the Local Government Board, with respect to the money lent by the Town Commissioners to the Harbour Commissioners, that "owing to the

Mr. *Bruen*—continued.

dues received by the Harbour Commissioners being barely sufficient to pay the moderate expenses of management, they have been unable to contribute a shilling towards payment of either principal or interest, which remain a dead weight upon the funds of the Town Commissioners, the interest absorbing nearly half their present gross annual income, and it is to be regretted, for many reasons, that there does not appear to be any hope of release from this heavy burthen."

4627. I suppose that absence of revenue is owing to the small amount of shipping done in the harbour?—Owing to the small amount of shipping, which I understand is owing to some obstruction in the bar which they have been trying to remove, and which would improve the harbour.

4628. You have nothing to do, I presume, with auditing the accounts of the Harbour Commissioners?—Nothing.

4629. Do you know whether they are audited by anybody?—I do not know.

4630. Is Tullamore in your district?—Yes.

4631. Are you satisfied with the care that is taken by the Commissioners in discharging the duties committed to them in Tullamore?—I am; they have got a very careful clerk.

4632. At Naas, another of your towns, are you satisfied with the management there?—Yes.

4633. As to Gorey, another of your towns, do you give the same report?—Yes, the same answer.

4634. As to Maryborough and Mountmellick, which are also under you, have you found any fault there?—Not as regards Mountmellick. In Maryborough I had reason to complain of irregularities in the mode of conducting their fiscal affairs, allowing accounts to run on for years, the accounts containing numerous items, which of course it was impossible for anybody to certify with accuracy; owing to that state of things, the accounts were not at all in a satisfactory state.

4635. I find they are returned in Thom's Directory for the year 1872, as obtaining a revenue of 39 *l.*, and expending 43 *l.*; I suppose that can hardly be correct?—I find that in September 1875, I reported that the Town Commissioners received during the year, 202 *l.* 5 *s.* 9 *d.*, and they expended under various heads of accounts, 120 *l.* 13 *s.* 3 *d.*, leaving at the end of the year a balance in their treasurer's hands of 82 *l.* 3 *s.* 8 *d.*

4636. That includes expenditure for sanitary purposes; are rates levied there for those purposes?—They are not a sanitary authority now, being under 6,000 population, their powers are transferred to the Mountmellick Board of Guardians.

4637. Then, I understand that this, which purports to be a return of the union expenditure for 1872, can hardly be correct, namely, 39 *l.* revenue, and an expenditure of 43 *l.*?—It may be correct, because I remember one year the expenditure and the receipts were very small. I made a disallowance of a few pounds, being the costs incurred in presenting an address to a deputation, I think, from the French nation that came over to Ireland. They were on their way to Cork, and they stopped at Maryborough Station, and the Town Commissioners availed themselves of the opportunity of presenting them with an address. The cost was trifling.

Mr. *Finlay.*

13 June 1876.

4638. When

Mr. *Finlay.*

13 June 1876.

Mr. *Bruen*—continued.

4638. When you inquired into the case of Trim, I think that there the receipts from the corporation lands were brought to your notice as being insufficient; there was a complaint made to you, was there not?—Yes, there was a representation made to me respecting it.

4639. Do you recollect the value of the common lands by Griffith's valuation?—No, I do not.

4640. Did they give to you, or place before you, any rental, or any sort of statement, of what the corporate property was?—Yes; the agent put before me a rental.

4641. Is it mentioned in your report?—What I mentioned in my report is, "There is no map of the Commissioners' property, and no rental except that kept by the agent, which only shows the portions that have fallen into the hands of the Commissioners," so that it is clear that a rental was before me.

4642. I believe that the town of Cashel is not now in your district?—It never was.

4643. And you never audited any of the accounts of Cashel?—No. Cashel is in the district of Mr. Pelly.

4644. Your reports are made to the Local Government Board; they are not made public, are they?—They are made public in this way. We are bound, under the Act of 1871, to send a copy of our report to the governing body for their information, and they may, or may not, publish them in a newspaper; sometimes they do.

4645. I suppose you refer to Section 18, which says, that "Within 14 days after the completion of the audit of the accounts of any town, the auditor shall report upon the accounts audited and examined, and shall deliver or transmit such report, with an abstract of the accounts, to the Chief Secretary, and a copy of the same to the governing body of such town, and the said governing body shall cause the same to be deposited in the office of the town clerk, or other proper officer of such town, and shall publish an abstract of such accounts in some one or more of the newspapers circulated in the district in which such town is situate." But that only refers to the publication of the accounts?—To the publication of the abstract, that is all.

4646. In your opinion, would it be advisable that the report should be placed somewhere where it could be accessible to the public?—They are in the hands of the governing body and the town clerk.

4647. But there is no provision for their being seen by anybody?—There is not.

4648. And they can be withheld, can they not?—No doubt the governing body can refuse to show them to any person if they choose.

4649. Do you think it desirable that they should be accessible to the public?—I should think it would be desirable.

Mr. *Brooks.*

4650. Do you know whether any reason has been offered why the accounts of the Collector General's office have not been subjected to a Government audit?—They are subject to a Government audit, inasmuch as they are audited by Master Fitzgibbon, the Receiver Master of the Court of Chancery, and they have been always audited by him.

4651. Are your audits public?—Perfectly public; quite open.

4652. As I sometimes read in the papers, I think Mr. M'Evoy and others attend, and they have full power to criticise the items that come before you?—Yes; during the audit the apartment in which the auditor sits is open to the public and to the representatives of the public press.

4653. Therefore the audit is of a most public character in the city of Dublin?—Yes, of the most public character.

4654. Have you read the evidence given by Mr. Frederick Stokes, the chairman of the Rathmines Commission, before this Committee?—I have read it as given in the "Freeman's Journal"; that is the only source from which I have obtained information about it.

4655. Can you give the Committee any reason why the Rathmines Commissioners should continue to be exceptionally treated in the matter of exemption from Government audit?—I do not think there is any good reason for it.

4656. Do you think that the same necessity exists with the Rathmines Commissioners as exists in the case of other public bodies?—Quite so, and I think that the reason given by Mr. Stokes for exempting them was a reason not for exempting them, but for imposing the audit upon them.

Friday, 16th June 1876.

MEMBERS PRESENT:

Mr. Assheton.	Sir Arthur Guinness.
Sir Michael Hicks Beach.	Mr. Kavanagh.
Mr. Brooks.	Sir Joseph M'Kenna.
Mr. Bruen.	Mr. Mulholland.
Mr. Collins.	Mr. O'Shaughnessy.
Mr. J. P. Corry.	Mr. Rathbone.
Mr. Gibson.	Dr. Ward.

SIR MICHAEL HICKS BEACH, BART., IN THE CHAIR.

Mr. ALEXANDER M. SULLIVAN, a Member of the House; Examined.

Mr. A. M. Sullivan, M.P.

16 June 1876.

Mr. *Brooks.*

4657. You have been a member of the Municipal Corporation of the city of Dublin, have you not?—I was for a period of about eight or nine years.

4658. Were you upon any, and upon which, of the committees?—Throughout that period I acted upon nearly all the committees. I was also for a good part of the time a member of the Board of Superintendence of the city prisons; I was trustee of the Newgate Buildings; and for some five years of the time I was a Poor Law guardian in the city.

4659. You would, therefore, be thoroughly acquainted with all the details of all the departments that are under the control of the corporation?—I would not like to say that, but I would say that I ought to be able to give the Committee a pretty good idea of the general working of the system and its faults, and where it needs amendment.

4660. Will you inform the Committee as to the composition and mode of working of the municipal council?—I entered the corporation of Dublin with a very strong prejudice against it, but I found it on the whole a body of gentlemen, discharging very difficult duties with a good deal of zeal and attention.

4661. You are not any longer, I believe, a member of the corporation?—No, I am not; I was turned out of the corporation; I failed to be re-elected; I was expelled by the constituency that I represented.

4662. When did you leave the corporation?—In 1870 or 1871, I think. It was on re-election that I was defeated.

4663. Will you proceed to inform us of the mode of working of the council?—With regard to the municipal council of Dublin, as I have said, after watching very attentively and rather critically its inner working in its committees, I found that there was a good deal of want of capacity in some respects, but I never saw a want of zeal; I always saw great honesty and integrity in the matter of the accounts and the expenditure; but there is some need of a reformation to facilitate the transaction of public business in the corporation.

4664. Was that want of capacity that you speak of owing to the inexperience of new members, or what?—I complained very much when I was in the corporation, that the burden of the work fell upon some eight or ten gentlemen who, let me remark, did not all belong to one political party; on the contrary, many of them being Conservative gentlemen; and that the corporation was abandoned very much by men who should come and take their share in the public work there.

Mr. *Brooks*—continued.

4665. What means suggest themselves to you which could be adopted for bringing in a better class of men into the corporation?—The city of Dublin is badly managed to this extent, that the real origin and source of the present difficulties is this, that it is in a state of chronic impecuniosity.

4666. Does that deter men of property and merchants of the better class from entering the corporation?—I gave, during those eight or nine years, or at least the last six of them, very close and serious attention, and I think I might go so far as to say very laborious effort, in the work of the city myself, and I endeavoured to find out exactly why we could not get men of greater capacity, or rather men of capacity, and of higher mercantile position in the city, to come in in greater numbers, and I arrived at conclusions that are to my own mind irresistible, as to why they do not come into the corporation.

4667. Will you explain them to the Committee?—In the first place, men of that position who were in the corporation found it an exceedingly unpleasant duty to be managing a city that was so straightened for means; and they did not like to belong to an institution that was out at elbows. I saw myself how irksome it was to those gentlemen to be facing in committee No. 1, with myself and others every Saturday the disagreeable problem of how to make sixpence go so far as half-a-crown; and the pecuniary difficulties of the corporation were found to be so great, and the work so hard, and the censure outside the doors so great, that those men, or a great many of them, fell off.

4668. This impecuniosity that you describe arose during the period when no doubt that class of men of position, of large property and large mercantile experience, had control of the corporation?—I must tell the Committee that the corporation

Mr. *A. M'Sullivan*, M.P.

16 June 1876.

Mr. *Brooks*—continued.

Corporation of Dublin is greatly embarrassed in effective civic government by the circumstances under which it came into existence. The constant cry in the city now is that the present corporation has increased taxation enormously, whereas the good old corporation had hardly any taxation. On looking into that while a member of the body, I found it was true in this sense, that the old corporation had no limit to its borrowing powers, and caring nothing about posterity, it borrowed away instead of taxing the city, and as long as its debentures could be floated it made no taxation. When the present or the reformed corporation came in they found the city loaded with debt, and with scarcely anything to show for it, as I shall satisfy the Committee. We had for ourselves to create in our own time all those necessary public works in the city which ought to have been represented by the enormous debt bequeathed to us, whereas, on the contrary, we had scarcely anything to show for the debt bequeathed to us. On the day the reformed corporation came in, the sheriff's officers were in seizure of the mansion house; and the Lord Mayor's coach was under seizure, and civic bankruptcy had virtually ensued. All this I am stating from a knowledge of actual corporate records. Other things which I am now about to state are outside of that, and I do not know whether it is evidence; that is to say, I am aware from other sources, not corporate records, that the incoming corporators had themselves to subscribe out of their private fortune the means to rescue the corporate property that was under seizure; and then in order to carry on the city, and to restore the city credit, the debentures at that time being at a very low figure, taxation had to be struck, consequently the cry of taxation was raised in the city, and the taxpayers were very unreasoning when they found that the taxes were being increased. It was a great calamity for the city—and I hope in any legislation which the Committee may recommend, that the evil may be averted in the future—that a very influential, though numerically small, section of our citizens early assumed an antagonism, on political grounds more or less, to the reformed corporation, and up to 1851 it was not considered respectable to belong to the reformed corporation. Since then, under these difficult circumstances, the council has been going on, but we never attempted to carry out a useful reform in the city that we were not stopped for the want of means. Having given some attention to the question of why Dublin is not thoroughly swept, as I believe that is the most general complaint in the city, I gave myself, I think, five years of my time to that particular committee, No. 1 committee (it was my wish so to do), which had to do with those practical matters of the sweeping and cleansing and lighting of the city. I should say that in their rotation I had a right to go the round of No. 1, No. 2, and No. 3, each year, but at the request of Councillor Byrne and Mr. Norwood, I remained on this committee particularly for four or five years. There are two reasons why Dublin is badly cleansed. I suppose the Committee will be amused if I say, that one is a geological, and the other is a financial, reason. Individually, quite outside their action as a committee, members of the committee have taken enormous trouble to find within cheap and easy access of our city some stone material better than that which we are obliged to use, but there really is none nearer than Wales, which is enormously costly to us.

4669. When you say nearer, do you mean really none so near, or so cheaply transported to Dublin?—The Welsh stone is quite superior to any within a reasonable distance of Dublin as a material for macadamising our streets, and that is very costly.

4670. Is it not accessible by water from the quarry to the roads on which it is placed?—Yes, but the cost of transport from Wales to Dublin makes it a very serious matter, so that the corporation being straightened for money we have to take the bad material which is at hand in Dublin, this black calp, which is nothing but indurated mud; the slightest wet in our city makes the streets muddy, and the least dry weather makes them inordinately dusty, and nothing but a loan to the city on easy terms, enabling them to pave or asphalte Dublin, will solve that difficulty. I wish very strongly to give the Committee my evidence upon this one point, at all events as a matter of my actual personal observation, that the failure, if it can be called a failure, to keep the streets as they ought to be arises from no want of earnest attention on the part of the corporation.

4671. I think we passed on from the composition of the municipal council rather more rapidly than I intended; you have not favoured us with your statement as to the composition of the council?—I thought I stated something as to the composition of the body; it is composed not so largely of men of mercantile standing in the city as I should like it to be, but I do not know in Ireland, and on inquiry I have not been able to hear in England, of any body that at all approaches the corporation of Dublin in its fairness of spirit and in its tolerance of minority dissent; in this I refer to the reformed corporation. I should state that the old corporation in which one political party greatly dominated, never allowed any minority representative to fill an office, whereas under the present corporation I believe it is singular in this fact (I do not know of any instance in England), that it voluntarily confers its highest offices from time to time upon members of the political minority.

4672. Can you favour the Committee with your opinion as to the taxation of Dublin, as to whether it is higher or lower than the taxation of other cities?—At one time while in the corporation I had accepted the current theory that our municipal taxation was enormously high, but I collected some information from Belfast, Glasgow, and other towns. The figures I do not undertake to give the Committee, because I do not come prepared, but I should say that the corporate officers should be able to give you the exact figures; I only undertake to give the Committee general evidence as a member of the body for eight or nine years; but I find, and know it to be the case now, that the municipal taxation is not very high as compared with most other large towns. When speaking of taxation in Dublin, most persons talk of the taxation as being 9 *s.* or 10 *s.* in the pound; but of the 9 *s.* 6 *d.* in the pound, strictly speaking (I will not take the present or the last year), there is only about 4 *s.* in the pound of municipal taxation, it is 3 *s.* 7 *d.* accurately; the grand jury tax is about 1 *s.* 10 *d.* or 2 *s.*, so that even

Mr *A. M. Sullivan*, M.P.

16 June 1876.

Mr. *Brooks*—continued.

even including the grand jury tax, all the taxation that we in my time had the administration of did not amount to more than about 5 *s.* in the pound upon the valuation. Now, if our valuation was anything near the rental the total of the civic taxation would be about 3 *s.* 4 *d.* in the pound. The Committee, no doubt, has it from other witnesses, and I do not like to be repeating anything which I imagine you have got already, but the improvement rate in the city is limited to 2 *s.* in the pound, and that was an estimate formed upon the valuation of the city which then prevailed, and which was estimated by Parliament to yield 10,000 *l.* or 12,000 *l.* a year more than the reduced valuation gives the corporation; the result of it is that the lack of that 10,000 *l.* or 12,000 *l.* a year is, from year's end to year's end, plunging the committees into begging and borrowing, and paying a higher price for materials than they would need to do if they had ready money. Our city taxation at present would be much less than it is if our city estates were intact. Up to the time of my own personal investigation, I had not been able to get any accurate information upon the subject, and I investigated for myself what had become of the city estates, and why they were not now producing to the corporation a larger sum in aid of the city taxes; and I found that the cream of the city estates had been jobbed away, and virtually bestowed under the pretext of leases by the old unreformed corporation. Some of those alienations are of very old date; the first instance that I give, and I wish all the others were equally meritorious in character, is, that the best piece of ground and most valuable in all the city of Dublin, Trinity College has got free from the corporation of Dublin; that is to say, all the grounds covered by the college and park, which if let now for building (and I am glad it cannot be in one sense), would be valued at about 15,000 *l.* a year, at a very moderate estimate. That is a fact which does not seem to be remembered sufficiently between Trinity College and the corporation. Whenever the old corporation was disposed to reward any official of their own body or otherwise, they made them a lease of a slice of the city lands mostly for ever, making them pay a rental of generally a pair of gloves or sometimes two. I inquired what had become of our property at Inns Quay, which would now be valued for considerably over 10,000 *l.* a year, and I found that it was leased away in this manner to Lord Santry for 7 *l.* 7 *s.* 8 *d.* I should say that that was about 100 years ago; this particular property, and some in the street to the west, the corporation expect will fall in within the next 10 years.

4673. Is that the property called Ellis's Quay?—Yes. I should inform the Committee that the notes which I made from my investigation amongst the city leases and records were not made with a view to this examination at all, but for my own private information as a member of the corporation; for without the slightest political or other object of that character, I spent nearly whole days at a time while I was a member in looking into these matters to try and find out exactly why the city was in its present state. The Marquis of Ormonde got in this way a property worth now 2,500 *l.* a year for a pair of gloves. Those leases were granted in the period from about 1720, as well as I could make out, up to 1818; I think the latest was about the early part of this century.

Mr. *Collins.*

4674. Was the grant to the Marquis of Ormonde a lease for ever?—Yes.

Mr. *Gibson.*

4675. Will you give the Committee an intimation of where you got this from; what the return is?—It is not a return: I wish the Committee to understand, as I stated to the Chairman, that it is from the city leases and rental.

4676. Are you quoting from any published or authorised statement, or only giving your own private reading of those documents?—I am giving to the Committee, who will take it at its value, the information which I gathered myself from those several documents. It is some seven or eight years ago that I acquired this information; it is all in the "Rental," except the valuations; all the names that I gave you are in this record. I could verify in this document any of the facts I have mentioned to this Committee, but it would shorten the matter by not delaying to do so now, and I will undertake to make a reference to the rental.

4677. I presume you are familiar with the rental, and have read it up carefully?—Not familiar with it now, but at that time I was.

4678. Does your evidence differ from the conclusions that are stated there by Mr. Morgan, or go beyond them, or fall short of them?—They do not at all differ.

4679. Then, substantially, from your recollection of that time, do you adopt the conclusions of Mr. Morgan?—Certainly.

4680. Are the Committee to take it, that your evidence is all covered by the ground which Mr. Morgan has traversed in the preparation of that report?—Certainly; in fact, if this is given in evidence, I am anxious to be as brief as possible, and so perhaps I may pass on from that; I was not aware before that this information was accessible to the Committee.

Mr. *Brooks.*

4681. Are you of opinion that the action of the corporation is in anywise impeded by the amateur associations in Dublin; may I remind you of the so-called Non-political Ratepayers' Association and the Citizens' Committee?—The dissatisfaction of various parties from time to time with our action, I noticed, took the ground of objecting to "politics in the corporation." Sometimes, as it seemed to me, it was perfectly honest and genuine, but very often it was the reverse. In 1865 and 1866, some of us in the corporation had to fight a two years' battle in order to put into force the sanitary laws affecting tenement lodging-houses. I am not sure, but I think some of the corporators lost their elections upon the head of it. An association was formed at once in the city to resist this sanitary action on the part of the corporation. It was composed of the owners of tenement house property, who objected to the corporation putting these sanitary laws into force, and the title that they gave themselves was, The Anti-political Ratepayers' Association. The ostensible ground of objection to us was, that they objected to "politics in the corporation; but all their resolutions really took the shape of objecting to our compelling them to have ash-pits

Mr A. M. Sullivan, M.P.

16 June 1876.

Mr. *Brooks*—continued.

ash-pits and house drains in their tenement houses. There always is in Dublin an association or two of what are called amateur corporations, or amateur public health committees; and although they are some of them most laudably endeavouring to help the public interests, yet they are free from all responsibilty, and very often not in the way of ascertaining the correct facts. They publish their statements however, and as the corporation does not enter into controversy in the newspapers, the public mind is very often injuriously misled. There is the matter of the cleansing of the Liffey, which I may mention. I believe in the House of Commons, and generally out of doors, the delay of the corporation in cleansing the Liffey is considered a great reproach to the civic government of Dublin; but as in the case of the Varty Waterworks and other great public improvements, parties in the city that ought to facilitate the corporation, considerably obstruct them. In order to protest against the main drainage scheme, what was called a citizens' committee was formed in Dublin. I attended a meeting of the citizens at which that committee was formed; it was held in the Round Room of the Mansion House, at about one or two o'clock in the afternoon. About 200 or 300 citizens attended. On the platform, however, were several of our most respected and influential citizens who do not belong to the corporation, but who are generally supposed to be opposed to it. The meeting was strongly protesting against Sir Joseph Bazalgette's scheme for cleansing the Liffey, and there seemed a wondrous unanimity in the body of the meeting in declaring this scheme to be a corporation job; I pointed out, I am not sure, but I think it was to Sir Arthur Guinness, who was on the platform somewhere near me, that in the body of the meeting I was able to identify personally some 30 or 40 disappointed plan-makers of Liffey cleansing, whom I had the misfortune to come in contact with in the corporation, and who plainly came there because their own plans, which they honestly believed to be quite perfect, had not been adopted by the corporation. There are two parties in the city on the matter of the cleansing of the Liffey, one prevails in the summer and the other in the winter. Whenever the weather gets hot, and as the thermometer rises, the cry of "Cleanse the river at all hazards," resounds in Dublin, but whenever the weather gets cold it is most unpopular in the city to propose an additional taxation even for cleansing the Liffey. The corporation is buffeted between these conflicting parties, and nothing has been done; I think there is a want upon the corporation of Dublin of men who could afford to defy what would be called unpopularity in firmly and courageously carrying out some necessary reforms; and although I think the body on the whole exceedingly honest and fairly capable, I think its character has been greatly injured by the fear of men that these passing cries would defeat them at their election. I think what is called the popular party in the city of Dublin ought to be ready to make some concessions, and even large concessions, to endeavour to turn over a new leaf so as to bring into the corporation the co-operation of the influential elements in the city that now are outside of it.

4682. What shape would you recommend that those concessions should take?—I would be able to give the Committee an idea of what I think is wanted in that respect, and others for reforming the whole state of affairs as regards the civic government in Dublin. In the first place, I think the franchise ought to be developed; not that I approve of the following principle, but that under the circumstances I have just stated, of the necessity of some compromise in the city of Dublin, I think that property owners non-resident in the city of Dublin ought to be allowed to vote; I think also, that the power of any political party to seize all the seats in a ward in the city ought to be checked; I wish the Committee to understand that, in making these suggestions, I want to guard myself against approving of these principles in the abstract which I am now stating, because it may be that elsewhere I would advocate sincerely other views; but I mean to say, that this is my view of a compromise in the city. I think that the election for the representatives of each ward ought to be simultaneous to allow of a cumulative vote which would enable the minority to return a member; at present, about two-thirds of the corporation are Liberals, and about one-third are Conservatives; still there are wards in the city in which Conservative property holders and residents might fairly expect to be represented, and I should like, if it would lead to a better system of government in our city, to see this concession made so as to enlist their interest and sympathies with the civic government. In the next place, and this is really indispensable, as I shall show the Committee, the boundary of the municipality must be enlarged. The present boundary was fixed long ago; they put an unnatural girdle around the city; the city has grown entirely beyond the arbitrary limit then fixed, and in place of advancing or enlarging the municipal boundary, a number of what I call parasitical townships have been created, the residents of which are really Dublin citizens, and they enjoy all the advantages of the city proper without taking any share of the burdens or the responsibilities. I think that such an extension of the boundary would be a great solution of the financial difficulties of the corporation along with a new valuation of the city, or rather an adjustment of the existing valuation. English members of the Committee may not understand what is meant by an adjustment of the present valuation. It is this: the Commissioners of Valuation have, I believe, no power to alter the valuation of a house that is unaltered structurally; but whenever a house is knocked down and rebuilt or improved, they raise the valuation, and thus glaring inequalities prevail in our city valuation. A fair valuation of the city would assist the corporate funds by about 15,000 *l.* a year; and I should like some legislation to secure that this increase would be devoted solely to the matter of our streets. In the next place, wide street powers, as I will call them, are required to enable the corporation to improve the streets.

4683. Do you mean the powers formerly exercised by the Wide Street Commissioners?—Yes; but more than that, the corporation at present, at all events when I was upon the corporation, and I am not aware of any change since, had the power no doubt to take lands and houses for wide street uses, but we had no power on earth to do so unless we were able to agree with the property holders. We could not, as in the

Mr. A. M. Sullivan, M.P.

16 June 1876.

Mr. *Brooks*—continued.

the case of a railway, take Bull Alley for instance, a place which is a disgrace to the city, and clear it away, which the corporation would have cleared away and built a decent street there, but whenever it got out that the corporation had an idea of such a thing the property holders wanted a larger price for their property than it was worth. The corporation has neither borrowing powers, nor compulsory purchasing powers, so that their wide streets powers are worthless at present, and there are quarters in the city that on purely sanitary grounds are disgraceful to the city, for the want of some powers of this kind.

Sir *Arthur Guinness*.

4684. Might I ask how it was that the Wide Streets Commissioners were able to effect such very large improvements, and whether their powers were not conveyed to the corporation?—Not the whole of them, so far as I could ascertain at that time. I think it will be found that my evidence is correct. I am giving the Committee, to the best of my ability, my experience, and any information that I acquired at that period. I have not, since I left the corporation, watched, perhaps, so closely as I ought, any changes in the law, but I know that at that time we had no such powers.

Mr. *Brooks*.

4685. Were you concerned in any negotiations for inducing men of property, and men of a higher standing, to enter the corporation?—Yes, I was. I believe there can be no objection to my stating, although the matter was private at the time, that a most respected and influential Conservative gentleman in the corporation appealed to me to make an endeavour on one side and on the other to bring, as it is said, better men into the corporation. This was Mr. Maclean, the chairman of the Public Health Committee; a gentleman for whose labours, as I can testify, on the Public Health Committee, the citizens of Dublin must be for ever grateful. He came to me as a Conservative, to say that we ought to try on both sides to bring better material into the corporation. We agreed upon it in this way, that if the Liberals, in what were called Liberal wards, put up mercantile men in a large position against some of the men that perhaps were not as good as we desired to see in the corporation, the Conservatives would not run a man between the two, and that we would act in the like manner towards the Conservatives in the Conservative wards. I immediately waited upon some influential gentlemen connected with the Chamber of Commerce, and there is no man more respected than Mr. Latouche, the President of the chamber, and I used all the exertions that I could to induce that class of gentlemen even, on this compact, to come into the corporation; but Mr. Maclean's endeavours and mine failed. I noticed that the gentlemen who would not come into the corporation, and some of those even who were virtually offered seats in it, were very prominent on what is called the Citizens' Committee, in pursuing a course of censorious criticism upon the body which they abstained from helping.

4686. Was it on the score of politics that they objected to become candidates?—No; the answer given to me was, that really their business was so large that they had not time. To that I always gave them the warning derived from my personal observation and inquiry in the City of New York. I warned them then what fate would overtake Dublin if the wealthy citizens abandoned to men of less ability, and perhaps of less honesty, the care of public business. I think that the corporation requires a Building Act. We fought out a Building Act when I was in the corporation as far as the Parliamentary notices. Belfast has a Building Act, I believe, and it is a reproach that Dublin, the metropolis, is to this hour without a Building Act, and generations to come will pay the penalty in the prevalence of disease in parts of our city from the buildings that are now going on, owing to the want of a Building Act. I know that, and I know the evils that are occurring from the want of a Building Act.

Mr. *Bruen*.

4687. Are you now referring to new buildings?—Yes, to new buildings, as regards sanitary matters; but as I was saying, Parliamentary notices having been given after a year's struggle in the council, we were defeated on a vote, and the Bill was strangled in the corporation itself, I am sorry to say.

Sir *Arthur Guinness*.

4688. When was that?—That was, I think, in 1867. Every November, 20 men are going out of the corporation, and consequently any endeavour to reform affairs in Dublin will have 20 men in the corporation under the menace of any small band of their constituents who are personally interested in obstructing the reformation. If it is not tedious I would like to give the Committee a little of my own personal experience upon that, when I was defeated in my own ward. There is a law unenforced in Dublin, and I have been always fearing that some Chief Secretary for Ireland would step in and deal very sharply with the corporation for not enforcing it. I refer to the law as regards the registration of marine-store dealers, which is enforced in England, and I thought myself that it ought to be enforced in Ireland. The marine-store dealers rose in arms against such an attempt to cause them to keep a registry of the property that they received; and it was virtually upon that issue, and my voting for those obnoxious reforms, that I was put out of the corporation. The sellers of intoxicating drinks of course had long been violently opposed to me, but numerically they were quite unable to put me out of the corporation; but my ward, which was the Inns Quay Ward, comprising all that district round the Four Courts, Charles-street, Mary's Abbey, Pill-lane, and so on, as some honourable Members of the Committee may know, is full of marine-store dealers, and when I went round on my canvass I of course could not expect the publicans to vote for me; but when I entered a dairy shop I thought I was safe, until the proprietress called out that I was the man who had appointed that villain Cameron to go round inspecting their milk. It is quite true that that was done, after a desperate struggle indeed, in the corporation, and it was I who took a prominent part in getting Dr. Cameron's office to become a reality. The butchers all voted against me, or nearly all, because I had promoted the Abattoirs Bill. The market owners voted against me because I was for abolishing a very vicious system in Dublin, that of private-public markets, if I may so call them, that is to say, public markets

Mr. A. M. Sullivan, M.P.

16 June 1876.

Sir *Arthur Guinness*—continued.

markets owned by private individuals. As being a trustee of the Newgate property I joined other gentlemen in projecting a large city market on the site of the old Newgate. That is enough. I will not pursue the matter any further, and take up the time of the Committee, but I wish to impress the Committee with this fact, that the reforms which are needed in Dublin require a strong hand just now, and that the corporation itself can hardly be trusted to undertake them. If the corporation were to promote a private Bill for the carrying out of those necessary reforms in the city, they could not carry the Bill through in the corporation itself by reason of the personal and sectional interests that would be up in arms against them, and it is therefore that I respectfully suggest to the Committee that nothing but a public Bill for reforming the affairs of the Corporation of Dublin will ever carry out what is needed to be done there. That is all I have to say.

Chairman.

4689. Do you think that any of the evils which you have pointed to in detailing your personal experience when a candidate for re-election would be obviated if, in addition to the reforms which you have suggested, the elections were less frequent and seats were held for longer periods?—I hardly think so, because it is not the frequency of election that is so great an evil, I think, except in this instance, that one-third is too large a proportion of the corporation to be in peril of their seats every year.

4690. If any plan of the cumulative or minority vote were to be adopted, it must be accompanied with an increase in the number of the corporation to be elected at one time, and therefore if you are to obtain the additional advantage of a smaller proportion of the town council appealing for re-election at once, you must have the election less frequent if you adopt the cumulative vote?—Not necessarily so, because, for instance, what I have had for some time in my mind is this; that in five wards in the city alternately three members might go out. Let me say that I think the number of representatives from each ward is too large.

4691. How many are there at present?—Four; one alderman and three councillors. If the city boundary were extended I would still have but 60 representatives of the whole, including the new districts, and that would take away one councillor from each of the present wards; and if five of those wards year by year elected simultaneously each of them three members, that would give you but 15 men as at present, and yet the whole three would stand together. You might take any number, but it does not necessarily follow electing a number of men together would increase the number of elections.

4692. You would only have elections in five out of 15 wards?—I am merely suggesting that as a possible solution.

4693. In considering the question of enlarging the municipal limits of the city, have you at all considered how far you would go, and what you would include?—Yes; there is a great advantage in any case of the kind in having a natural frontier. I think that the lines of the River Dodder and the River Tolka afford that very reasonably, striking from the Dodder River about Terenure, and going all round the town northward by

Chairman—continued.

Island Bridge to the River Tolka, about to the north of the east end of Phœnix Park.

4694. That would not represent any existing boundary, would it?—It would not. The other plan would in another sense be more simple, and that is to take in the townships of Rathmines, Pembroke, and Kilmainham. My objection to this, however, would be that it would give at some points a larger increase to the city than I think would be necessary. The sweep of the rivers would be a smaller area, but it is certainly a great advantage to take the recognised and existing boundaries of those townships.

4695. Such a question, perhaps, might best be settled by the inquiry of a commission upon the spot?—Yes, I think so.

4696. In suggesting the cumulative vote, do you mean the cumulative or the minority vote?—I mean the cumulative vote; that is to say, that a person may vote for each of the three, or for any one, and give him the three votes.

4697. That is the system in England which is adopted in the School Boards, but not in the Parliamentary elections?—Yes, that was my idea; I am not wedded to any particular form, but I think that some facility should be given in Dublin under those circumstances, and some offer should be made to an influential but numerically small minority in our city to enter heartily into civil affairs.

4698. In suggesting a vote to non-resident owners of property, have you considered what limit of value you would fix?—I would say 50*l.* a year. I would give a person one vote for that; not voting as a rated occupier.

4699. You do not contemplate a plurality of votes?—No, certainly not; I object very strongly to that.

4700. Have not the town council of Dublin, acting as a grand jury of the county of the city, power at present to obtain a re-valuation of the city, if they choose?—No; they have made endeavours to obtain it, if my memory be correct, but Sir Robert Griffith declined to undertake it. But I know that a new valuation of the city is objected to very strongly by a considerable number of persons in the corporation; they say that the Imperial Government would come in and avail of it for income-tax purposes. I know that they object to it; but, however, when I was in the corporation I urged that they should discard those views, and get the city properly valued.

4701. Are you aware whether they ever applied to the Government for that?—They did not apply in my time; but I heard in the corporation that before my time they did ask for it.

4702. There is a limit, I think, fixed in the Valuation Acts before which a re-valuation could not be carried out, but after which any grand jury may apply for a re-valuation, and obtain it?—I was not aware of that.

4703. Perhaps the first application was made before that limit?—I am very certain that an application from the Corporation of Dublin for a re-valuation which would raise the valuation of houses in the city would expose them to one of those spasms of unpopularity which, as I have testified here, have been so fatal to improvement in the city.

4703.* Your attention has been turned a good deal to the sanitary state of Dublin, has it not?—Yes;

Mr. A. M. Sullivan, M.P.

16 June 1876.

Chairman—continued.

-Yes; although I did not belong to the Public Health Committee for so long a time as I did to the Streets Committee, yet I took a good deal of part with Mr. Maclean in working it at its earliest stages.

4704. Are you acquainted with the evidence which was given before this Committee a few days ago by Dr. Grimshaw?—I have not read it; I saw a slight sketch of it, I think, in the "Daily Express," in Dublin, but I should not like to give any evidence with reference to Dr. Grimshaw. I should say that the Secretary of the Public Health Committee would shorten the time of the Committee upon that.

4705. Having regard to your own impressions upon the subject, do you consider that the Public Health Acts are efficiently worked in Dublin by the Public Health Committee of the Corporation?—I can certainly and clearly state to the Committee that the Public Health Committee of the Dublin Corporation is the most irreproachable part of our civic government; that is my belief. It was the one committee with which I myself never was able to find any fault as regards its working. It early got into capable and competent hands; Mr. Norwood, Mr. Byrne, Alderman Redmond, and Mr. Maclean early took it in hand, and I do not believe that any four gentlemen in the city of Dublin could bring to that committee more zeal and ability than those four gentlemen seemed to me to have brought to it.

4706. I think Dr. Grimshaw made some suggestions as to the deficiency in the official staff under the orders of the committee, and as to the want of a head to superintend generally the sanitary work, rather than any objection to the composition of the committee itself; what are your views upon that subject?—I know a little about it; and I know of my own knowledge that the delays incidental to carrying out the sanitary laws in the Public Health Committee largely arise from some little defects in the legislation upon the subject, owing to the number of notices, and the number of hearings that are necessary before the magistrates. Really in dealing with disease and health in a crowded city, I am afraid to use the word, but a little more of despotic authority must be vested in the hands of the Public Health Committee. The public seeing a nuisance in a certain spot get easily impatient, and think that the Public Health Committee is dilatory, when in fact they are arrested by the necessity of certain forms of procedure. I should say also, as regards the want of a head, that from my personal observations when in the corporation, the secretary of the Public Health Committee, Mr. James Boyle, who was a civil engineer by profession, and who seemed to me to be one of the most zealous and capable officials I ever met with in connection with public health affairs, seemed to me to convert his *quasi* leisure hours at home into the hardest working portions of the day; for I found him bringing to the committee in the morning most laborious returns and information which he must have been doing at home, and, unless he has degenerated since I left the corporation, I consider him an efficient head of the staff.

4707. You spoke of a large debt which had been incurred by the old corporation before the Municipal Reform Act; are you aware what it amounted to?—About 230,000 *l.*, I think; that would not be a great debt for a city, but I would ask the Committee just to consider what Dublin has and what it had not; we had not a fire brigade, and the several civic institutions provided by the present corporation represent an enormous outlay; we had not waterworks; we had a state of protection against fire that was utterly inefficient. We had not sewers; all the sewers in Dublin, miles and miles of sewers, have been constructed within the last 30 years. The flagways of Dublin have all been constructed inch by inch slowly, according as the means allowed, so that we have now very good flagways; and the whole city is being gradually reformed in this way, kerbstones being pushed out, and the flagging by degrees improved. We had nothing of these things in the city when the corporation was reformed, and we had 230,000 *l.* debt.

4708. You do not complain so much of the amount of the debt?—No; but besides having to pay interest upon it, we had to begin all these things.

4709. I suppose you do not know for what that debt was incurred?—There were debentures for various purposes, but I only know, so far as I could ascertain by inquiries of my own, and investigating the old rolls and all that, that they never levied a tax while they could borrow.

4710. Whilst you were a member of the corporation, did you make it your business to inquire into the mode in which the accounts of the corporation were kept at the bank?—No, that was in the city treasurer's office; and the old city treasurer in my time, previous to Mr. Robinson (Mr. Robinson was appointed since I left), was an old gentleman of whose department I heard every one speaking very highly, and I never went into that matter at all.

4711. Were you on the Finance Committee?—I was for a period on the City Estate Committee; it was from my private notes and investigations while I was on the City Estate Committee, that I found amongst my papers at home some old notes, which I made about 10 or 12 years ago, and from which I was speaking in the early part of my examination.

4712. My question rather had reference to the evidence given here by Mr. Finlay, the auditor, as to the fusion of all those which were properly separate accounts of the city into one general account?—I think there is room for improvement in that. When I was in the corporation I found a system of robbing Peter to pay Paul, of borrowing from one committee and lending to the other, which seemed to me frequently to lead to dangerous confusion, and at that time I thought it rather objectionable. I should think that there is hardly a committee in the corporation that has not a cross-account with some other committee of the corporation.

4713. Might not an evil of that kind be remedied without the risk of incurring unpopularity on the part of the town council?—It would require an Act of Parliament.

4714. Surely the provisions of the Acts are now that separate accounts shall be kept?—Yes, that is what I say; that to improve or to consolidate the keeping of accounts will require an Act of Parliament, if my impression of the law be correct.

4715. The fact, I think, is this, that the law requires for obvious reasons that separate accounts shall be kept for any separate purposes to which the funds are devoted, but that the corporation instead

Mr. A. M. Sullivan, M.P.

16 June 1876.

Chairman—continued.

instead of obeying the law keep all their accounts in one, and lend and borrow from one to another as you have stated?—I was not aware that they kept all their accounts in one. In my time the accounts were certainly kept separate, but the accounts of committee No. 1 were always before us, and we never saw any other account. The waterworks accounts were certainly kept strictly separate.

Mr. *Collins.*

4716. Probably you are not aware of the fact that the existing Acts of Parliament require the various accounts to be kept separate?—I am aware of that.

4717. And that is evaded under the present system by the way in which things are managed?—I am not aware of that latter incident, but 10 and 12 and 14 years ago the accounts were kept separate.

Chairman.

4718. Perhaps there is some confusion between accounts and funds; the accounts as they appear in the published accounts of the city are separate, but I asked Mr. Finlay at Question 4300, "Are those funds kept properly separate?" and his answer was, "They are kept properly separate in the accounts of the corporation, but they are not kept properly separate in the bank. The monies are thrown into a common purse in some cases," and then he explains how one committee lends to another?—Then I am right in saying that the the accounts were kept separate in the books, but it seems not in the bank. In point of fact in my time the payments were made by the treasurer's own personal cheque, but no old office ever fell out in my time that the corporation did not instantly take some means to make matters better, generally to reduce the salaries and to economise and to provide greater checks and safeguards than had been in the old system. I never knew, when I was in the corporation, an old office to fall out that a committee was not appointed to see what better provisions could be made before they appointed a successor, and they invariably economised in so doing.

Sir *Joseph M'Kenna.*

4719. You consider, do you not, that the chief difficulty of the present corporation is one of ways and and means?—Yes.

4720. The remedies which I understand you would apply to that would be by law to widen the area of the city taxation, and to re-value or re-adjust the present valuation?—Yes.

4721. And you require a Building Act?—Yes, and an Abbattoirs Act.

4722. Is it your decided opinion that the requisite Act to effectuate the reform or reforms which are now needed, must from the nature of things originate outside the corporation, and not from it?—Yes, it never can be carried out by an Act promoted by the corporation itself.

Sir *Arthur Guinness.*

4723. Do you think that your answer that the corporation were unable to cope with the affairs of the city, and improvements of various kinds, may be owing to the owners of property being so badly represented, the consequence of which is the return of representatives who are liable to influences such as you have described?—Yes, I think it is a great evil in Dublin; whatever be the cause of it, that the owners of property, and large mercantile men, are not in greater numbers in our corporation.

4724. You spoke of amateur committees not being in the way of ascertaining facts; do you think that the citizens should be afforded such information about their own affairs as facts?—Certainly.

4725. Are you aware that they have been frequently refused facts?—I am not aware that they have ever been refused information when it has been properly applied for, or when the information was in that stage that it could be given. For instance, I do know of information being refused in the case of a report upon our tenements at Baldoyle, written by our agent; but as well as I recollect now, at this distance of time, application was made for it, before it had been laid before the committee, and it was refused. I merely instance that; but I do think that the corporation and its committees ought never to refuse information when once it had been legitimately before the public.

4726. Are you not aware that on many occasions letters from those amateur associations have been marked "Read," and no other notice taken of them?—I am not aware of that.

4727. I think you mentioned the main drainage scheme; you are aware, are you not, that there were two public meetings at which the Lord Mayor was in the chair?—Yes, I was at both.

4728. And you probably recollect the result of those meetings?—Yes.

4729. Was not a resolution carried, asking the corporation to co-operate with the citizens' committee?—Yes; and I thought it a very extraordinary resolution.

4730. Was not it rather pointing towards giving information to the citizens, which was only in the hands of the corporation at the time?—Whatever might have been the intention in the minds of the movers of such resolution, I thought it most offensive towards the city government, asking them to come and assist this other body, instead of the other body passing a resolution that they would assist the corporation.

4731. Are you aware that those were the words of the resolution, asking the corporation to come and assist the other body?—Yes, I believe so.

4732. To co-operate, was it not?—Yes; that is, to assist. I remember the tenor of the resolution, and I thought it very nearly as absurd, as if some political or other committee in England were to call upon Parliament to co-operate with them.

4733. Do not you think that representatives, whether municipal representatives or Parliamentary representatives, should communicate with those that they represent in matters of that kind?—Yes, certainly.

4734. If they do not answer their communications, or if they declined to co-operate with them, that is hardly doing what you think they ought to do?—I am now talking of the representatives in their individual capacity, but if I had been in the corporation at the time, and such a letter were received, I would say, "*We* are the representatives of the citizens, and if they will inform us what is necessary to be done, it is our duty to do it;" but I think it very objectionable that there should be two corporations sitting in Dublin, one

Mr. A. M. Sullivan, M.P.

16 June 1876.

Sir *Arthur Guinness*—continued.

one responsible and the other irresponsible, one elected and the other self nominated.

4735. Are you aware that, so far from the citizens' committee asking the corporation to come to them, the citizens' committee went to the corporation, on one occasion at least?—I am not aware of that; I am very glad to hear that they did. I should say that one resolution passed at a meeting at which I think you presided was a most excellent resolution; it was a resolution asking the Government to appoint a commission.

4736. What was the result of it to the corporation?—I am not aware; but I should state at once to you that I heartily disapprove of a good deal of the action of the corporation on the matter of the main drainage, that is to say, its hesitancy to carry out the Bazalgette scheme.

4737. Are you aware that a deputation of the citizens' committee waited upon the Lord Mayor at the Mansion House, three of the principal members of it, and that he appointed a day to receive the deputation, and that some members of the corporation did assist in the deliberation for co-operating with, or at least ascertaining the views of the citizens' committee on the main drainage scheme?—I never heard what the Lord Mayor individually did in that case.

4738. You also perhaps are not aware that the deputation waited on him at the Mansion House, and that he had gone to the country?—I am of course quite unable to testify to the Committee as to what the Lord Mayor privately did in his individual capacity; he never let me know of all those movements.

4739. What is your opinion of the Bazalgette scheme?—I am not a civil engineer, but the reason I have long censured the corporation for hesitation to carry it out is this: I am of course aware that it is a very costly scheme, but I think that after the corporation sought the best professional advice in the British empire, and obtained that advice at great cost, they ought to resolutely act upon it, and not to be moved by every current and breeze of different opinion in the city of Dublin.

4740. What were those currents; were they not in consequence of the estimates for the work turning out to be twice the amount of what the engineer originally estimated for?—That was a misfortune; but there was no reason why the necessary work of purifying the river should not have been carried out, even at the increased cost.

4741. Do you think that when Parliament authorised an expenditure to the amount of 350,000 *l.*, if it turned out to be 800,000 *l.* or 900,000 *l.*, the citizens should not have a right to object to such an amount being spent?—Certainly, I admit that they have a perfect right to object, and I do not blame them for objecting, but what I stated to the committee was, that I complained of the corporation of our city being blamed in one breath for not carrying out the works, and in the next, being prevented from carrying them out, because if this be a necessary work, and if this be the best and really efficient plan (and on that I take Sir Joseph Bazalgette's professional opinion, and have none of my own), I say that the city, in such a matter, is bound to carry it out, as cheaply as possible, but still to carry it out.

4742. Did not the citizens' committee, before the specifications were sent to the contractor, foretell that it would cost a great deal more than

Sir *Arthur Guinness*—continued.

the amount taken under the Act of Parliament?—I foretold it also. And anyone could have have foretold it, because I never heard of an instance of a Parliamentary estimate for public works being within the figure.

4743. You were not surprised at its turning out nearly double?—I was surprised at its being double, but I always thought it would be about half as much again.

4744. You admit that it was rather alarming to the ratepayers?—I do not blame the ratepayers for being alarmed, but in no other way than by intercepting sewers can the Liffey be cleansed, and we shall have to pay an enormous sum for it, but although we shirk the difficulty for 10 years more, we shall have to come to that.

4745. With regard to the gas scheme, to which the Dublin Citizens' Committee objected, can you tell me what was the result of the action of that committee; but first of all, what was the corporation scheme?—The corporation scheme was to purchase from the present gas company their rights and interests for the Corporation of Dublin, and as is the case with many corporations in England, to supply the gas themselves.

4746. Do you know what the amount of the proposed capital of this gas company was to have been?—Upon this matter I should like to tell the Committee that all this happened since I left the corporation, and therefore my evidence upon it cannot be taken as from any knowledge that I have as a corporator; I am now a pure outsider upon all this, and therefore I may not answer you as correctly as I should like; it did not happen while I was in the corporation, otherwise I could give you information.

4747. Are you aware that it was as much as a million?—I was not aware, but I have no doubt that if it was a million there would have been property to represent that; I thought myself that the corporation ought to have not only the water of the city but the gas of the city in its hands; but I did feel great uneasiness as to whether there was intellectual capacity enough in the corporation to manage that department in addition to the others.

4748. Do not you think that the corporation have already enough on their hands, judging from the results of their efforts in the failure of the main drainage scheme, and various other things of that kind, without entering upon such an enormous undertaking as the manufacture of gas?—No, I do not think they have enough upon their hands in this sense, that they are not doing, and are not enabled to do, half the work that the city requires. I think that we want public markets, public abbattoirs, and we want many other things; the corporation would be well able to take care of all those things if it had the financial means, and if some effort or means could be adopted to bring into the corporation our citizens of ability and character.

Mr. *Gibson*.

4749. I think you traced the evils of the present civic government in Dublin to poverty as its radical source?—Yes, I decidedly traced nearly every one of our existing evils to that; all the lines of pursuit of information brought me very nearly to that.

4750. Are you aware that notwithstanding that poor condition, there is hardly one of its officers

Mr. A. M. Sullivan, M.P.

16 June 1876.

Mr. *Gibson*—continued.

officers whose salary it has not raised in the last ten years, including that of the lord mayor?—I am aware that the salaries in the corporation are entirely too low; I conceive that it is a great evil that the corporation does not pay higher salaries to its officers; the salary of the lord mayor is too low; the salary of the town clerk is shamefully low; increases have taken place, but it is necessary that I should inform the Committee that they were increased because they began at a minimum. In nearly every case when I was in the corporation, when an office fell out either in the city prisons or in other departments of the corporation, which was, say 200 *l.* a year, we started the man who came in at 120 *l.*; then, of course, after he had been with us some years, and he asked for 20 *l.* more, and the economy party cried out, "Here you are making an increase to the salary," but they never took into account that we started the man at a low salary; but the maximum salaries now in the corporation are, if anything, I conceive too low. We ought to pay salaries not extravagantly, but yet salaries that would enable our civic functionaries to be men of reasonable social position and ability; a mercantile man would pay more in his employ. There is not a merchant in Dublin with dealings of large magnitude who would not be ashamed to offer the town clerk's salary of 500 *l.* or 600 *l.* a year to a man comparatively in his position in his employ.

Sir *Arthur Guinness.*

4751. Could you tell me, as you were on the committee that managed the streets, who is the authority which supervises all that?—The city engineer is supposed to do that; and upon that point there were numerous resolutions and negociations and efforts pursued by myself and others to try and get it under some one else, because we found that while the Vartry works were being conducted the personal attention of the borough engineer was diverted from our streets.

4752. Then you are of opinion that the same officer who is in charge of the streets should not have the power of paying the men, and superintending the work?—Perhaps now there may not be the same necessity as the Vartry works are over, but if the main drainage operations commence the borough engineer cannot attend to our streets.

4753. And you are not satisfied with the state of things?—Very much dissatisfied with them.

Mr. *Gibson.*

4754. You stated that you look upon it as one of the most desirable things for Dublin to pass a Building Act; do you know if any attempt has been made to get a Building Act?—Yes, I stated to the Committee that we fought a Building Act, I think for two years, in the corporation up to the necessary point of ordering it to be prepared and getting the draft before us. The committee who came to consider the draft took three weeks adjournment for amendments to the draft and 10 weeks debating over the draft; and then there was the insertion of the notices and advertisements in the papers and the lodging. If my memory be correct, and I think it is, we went so far as even to lodge our Bill, but we were defeated over a vote in the corporation ultimately. It was said that we were going to bring an Algerine despotism into the city, and that no poor builder would be allowed to take a handsaw in his hand unless the borough engineer would allow him.

4755. Am I right in saying that in the whole period of the existence of the reformed corporation they never passed a resolution in favour of a Building Act?—It has passed a resolution, and it ordered the Bill to be prepared, and I have, although not amongst my papers in London, a copy of that Building Bill.

4756. At all events, nothing was even done in the way of making application to Parliament?—Advertisements were issued for a Bill in Parliament, and the Bill was lodged in Parliament, and yet the corporation were induced, I am sorry to say, to go back upon it, and they did not push it.

4757. You are of opinion, are you not, that the duties of the corporation are principally non-political?—Principally non-political.

4758. Do you think that anything that would tend to make the constitution of the body non-political would be desirable?—I do not know that, because when the Municipal Reform Act was being passed through Parliament, the Member of the Government who had charge of the Bill deliberately stated to Parliament that one of its great objects, and he and the Government fervently hoped that one of its best results would be that those reformed municipal corporations in Ireland would tend "to create and foster public opinion in Ireland, and make it racy of the soil." I think myself that although in Ireland what are called the political aspects or turmoils in our local bodies are evils, they are not so great as they are supposed to be, and that we manage these things more good humouredly, with a certain excellent public result. I think that the Government of the country ought to greatly rejoice, although there are some inconveniences in it, at having some means in the country through which the Government in Dublin Castle can ascertain how the current of public opinion is running in the country. It may be in a direction that they may not like, or it may be the contrary, but I should say, that although there is much noise made about the occasional incident of a political episode in those bodies, people outside exaggerate the frequency of them.

4759. Do not you think it would be desirable to obviate that criticism as much as possible, and let them adhere to their non-political business as much as possible?—The Committee should receive the answer which I am about to give with a perfect knowledge that I am a strong partyman and a strong politician. I think it would be a great public evil in any way to infringe upon the municipal spirit, and upon the traditional and historic functions of municipal government, especially in Ireland. I think it is most desirable that in a country like Ireland the people should be trained, even although they may rather roughly use the machine at first, to habits of public life and of meeting their neighbours and fellow-citizens of different politics and different religious opinions from time to time; I can say that in the corporation of Dublin this political conflict or friction invariably has had the result of softening political feeling, and I may say almost of abolishing anything like sectarian prejudice in the assembly.

4760. May I take it that it is your opinion that the adjustment and distribution of the rates and

Mr. *Gibson*—continued.

and the public expenditure in the city should at all events occupy the first place?—I should certainly say that it should occupy nine-tenths of their attention at the very least.

4761. And that that is the primary and the highest duty of a corporation?—I think it a primary duty, though I would not call it the highest duty; I say that the highest duty of a municipal body is to reflect within the municipality the opinions and the interests of the municipality, just as a man may consider it his primary duty to provide himself with food and clothing; but I would not call that the highest duty of a man.

4762. Would you say that the disbursement of a rate, for instance, or looking after the public health and attending to the sanitary condition of the city, and the paving and scavenging, and all other matters of that description, should be regarded as the most important duties of a corporation?—I think that they are matters of practical every day life, and most important, and that they are so treated at present in our corporation.

4763. When you say that there is a tolerance of the minority in the Dublin Corporation, are you aware that the Dublin Corporation appointed a committee of their body to attend here?—I read in the newspapers that they appointed a committee of their body whom they would consider qualified to express here the opinion of the body as a whole.

4764. Are you aware that they refused to include in that any member of the corporation that was not in favour of the honourable and learned Member for Limerick's Bill, and that they refused to allow the Lord Mayor to join the deputation on that ground?—I could only give the Committee my personal evidence as a reader of the newspapers on this subject; but I am aware from what I saw in the newspapers, that they, as it seemed to me, very properly refused to send to represent the whole body as a body any one who would not represent the whole body in its concrete character; for, of course, to send individuals here to give evidence to this Committee in the name of the corporation who would only give evidence of their individual views, would be a very great absurdity.

4765. Do you think it would be reasonable if, as you say, one-third of the corporation represent views different from the majority, that they should have an opportunity of being represented here as a deputation from the corporation, or that only one side should be sent here?—Certainly, I think it would be absurd. If Her Majesty's Government were sending representatives of the Government to a foreign country, if I might so express it, they would not go to the front opposite bench and send one of them to act against their own more immediate representative; I am sure I would not.

4766. You stated that in the appointment or distribution of their officers the corporation also forgot political distinctions; could you tell me of any officer of the corporation, except the Lord Mayor occasionally, who does not profess the politics of the majority?—It is due to the Committee that I should stick as much as possible to my own period in the corporation, because otherwise my evidence has no right to be given here rather than that of an outsider. I will take Mr. Alexander Farquharson, who was elected town clerk; he was a Protestant and a Conservative, and there was not a man in the corporation that I ever met who ever thought of making any objection to him, although he was the chief executive officer. He was a man of politics and religion different from the bulk of the council, and the regret on his death was universal. The next town clerk, the present gentleman, is no doubt a Liberal and a Catholic, but his chief assistant in the office, and who, I should hope, will eventually rise to his position, or to some position equally high, is Mr George Grice, a gentleman of the very strongest political opinions, opposed to the bulk of the corporation. Then there is Dr. Cameron, our city analyst, an officer of the first importance and of the first ability; Captain Ingram, chief of our fire brigade, whom we would not swop with any city in the empire; Mr. Boyle, of our public health committee, of whom I have already spoken; Mr. Neville, our city engineer, a gentleman worthy of much higher position than we can give him; Mr. Andrews, waterworks engineers, and several others. I am taking those at random, and I can only say, that although the corporation of Dublin are party men, and may be by no means devoid of reproach on this ground of party; but, as I have stated in my evidence, compared with any other body in Ireland or in England, they are the most liberal and tolerant body that I have ever been able to hear of. For instance, in the matter of the mayoralty in 1862, I obtained a committee of inquiry to inquire into the alternate system of appointing Liberal and Conservative mayors, in order to know whether such a system prevailed in any other city in Ireland, England, or Scotland, and more especially whether anything like such a system as a majority of two-thirds allowing a one-third minority to appoint its man every second year or even every third year obtained in Belfast, in Londonderry, in Coleraine, or in any place where the majority party were double the minority. We sent inquiries to Liverpool, to Manchester, to Birmingham, to London, to Belfast, to Londonderry, and all round the three kingdoms, and we found that nowhere was such a system known except in Dublin.

Chairman.

4767. Did you ascertain that the election of the Lord Mayor in the City of London depended upon his politics?—The reason that we sent to London was this: although the inquiry was particularly with regard to Ireland, and although I myself said individually that there was no need sending to London, yet London came within the scope of the resolution of the corporation; but we know that in Liverpool it did, and we know that in Birmingham it did depend upon political considerations.

Mr. *Gibson.*

4768. Did I understand you to say that the alternation was between Conservative and Liberal or between Catholic and Protestant?—Between Conservative and Liberal; but in the Corporation of Dublin, naturally enough, as might be understood, the Liberals are nearly all, although not quite all, Catholics, and the Conservatives are all Protestants; it works out very much the one thing or the other.

4769. Occasionally you elected a Protestant who might not be a Conservative?—Occasionally we took Protestants, who were not Conservatives, since that Committee of Inquiry, but not before.

Mr. A. M. Sullivan, M.P.

16 June 1876.

4770. Are

Mr. A. M. Sullivan, M.P.

16 June 1876.

Dr. *Ward.*

4770. Are you aware that in England it is quite common for politics to enter into corporate elections?—I should like the Committee not to ask me anything about England; I will stick to what I know. I am not aware of anything, except from ordinary hearsay, about what is the state of things in England; I know something about the Dublin Corporation but nothing about English Corporations.

4771. Are you aware that the Home Secretary stated as a matter of fact in the House that politics are usually regarded in these cases?—I have heard of it, but I do not know of it.

Mr. *Rathbone.*

4772. You stated that you considered that the great difficulty that you had to deal with in Dublin, was the want of interest on the part of capitalists and owners of property in the government of the city?—Yes, that is one evil; I think it is an evil in the city of Dublin, that from one reason or another that class do not come and cordially take their share in the responsibility and disagreeability of civic government.

4773. I suppose it is the case in Dublin as in other places, that the capitalists in Dublin pay a very small contribution to the government of the town in proportion to their wealth?—Yes; in proportion to their wealth an enormously small contribution; and in Dublin, peculiarly so; because what is done is this: a man of enormous fortune keeps a little counting-house in the Commercial-buildings, and he has his residence in Rathmines, and he is rated at perhaps a few pounds a year in the city. That is all he pays to it.

4774. Then, again, the mode of taxation in Ireland is the same as it is in this country; that is to say, that the rates paid are paid by the occupier?—Yes, by the occupier; and I strongly hope that in any legislation on the subject of the rated property the owner will be made responsible for the public rates in Dublin, in the last resort, at all events. A considerable sum used to be lost by reason of fly-away occupiers.

4775. That being the case, do not you think it not unnatural that men who do not feel immediately, at any rate, the rise and fall in the rates, should not be so attentive to the expenditure of those rates as they otherwise would be?—Perhaps, in one sense, natural, but I think it very unnatural, for a man is bound under a sort of public obligation, that if in a community or a town, he is acquiring wealth and fortune, and station, he ought to pay his toll upon the road to fortune, by giving his time and interest to the affairs of that community.

4776. That is so, no doubt, but on the other hand, is it not rather natural in this world that where things are not brought under the notice of people, they do not give the same attention to them, as where they are brought home to them by the direct demands of the tax-gatherer?—That is true; but then those gentlemen to whom you refer in Dublin, although they have a very small interest at present in the city as occupiers, have considerable interests, many of them as owners of house property in the city; and it is, therefore, that I would make an exception to the principle which I hold myself as regards the franchise, to compromise with them by giving in our municipality a vote to non-resident property owners, in order to give them that interest which your question suggests they would acquire.

Mr. *Rathbone*—continued.

4777. What I wanted you to consider was this: probably you are aware that the law in Scotland is somewhat different from that in England, and that in Scotland the owners of property pay to the tax-gatherer, one-half of the rates levied in any year for local government purposes?—I was not aware of that being the fact in Scotland.

4778. And that in Scotland the owners of property are represented, and take a very active part and interest in local government?—I think it would be an almost unmixed calamity if it were introduced into Ireland, more especially, because it would lead to grave evils, and to further increase the lines of demarcation between social classes who would always take one view, and political classes. In addition, I think it would be a great evil in Ireland to have one half members of a sort of House of Lords, and the other half members of a House of Commons, really sitting together, as in the Scottish Parliament; the one-half would be aristocratic, so to speak, and the other half would be democratic, and they would feel bound to oppose each other.

4779. Is it not the case in Ireland, that the Irish are rather peculiarly susceptible to social influence?—Yes; there are few people, I believe, in Europe who, on the whole, pay such deference and willing deference to social position, and especially old family position, as the people of Ireland; often extravagantly so.

4780. Do you not think that if they found the owners of property coming and taking an active interest in the affairs of the country, and working side by side with them on the same board, that influence would have a natural effect; that those lines of demarcation would be rather removed by such a process than increased?—In my opinion not; but if they found those gentlemen coming as ordinary members, returned and taking their share in the public work as representatives, it would have a wonderfully healing and good effect; but I think that if they were to come in as a sort of superior human nature upon our municipal boards, it would have an evil effect. I am not at all advancing to the Committee that if you were newly inventing or creating municipal institutions in Ireland, you might not try that. I am merely saying that if you were to go back from the present system into allowing one half the body or a part of the body to be elected by an aristocratic franchise and the other half by a democratic, you would introduce into our municipal bodies irretrievable evils and mischief.

4781. Have you quite considered that with the coming into those municipal bodies of those owners of property, would be combined their coming forward to take their half share of the burdens which no doubt the occupiers feel strongly, and that therefore a very considerable relief from a sense of injustice would accompany their introduction?—I have not yet been informed by any one on what ground one-half of the representation of the municipal body in Ireland should be given to property owners.

4782. That they paid one-half the expenses?—I think that importing such a feature is perfectly foreign to the British Constitution, or at all events any fragment of it that is known in Ireland.

4783. But as I understand you to say, you are not at all satisfied with the working of the fragment of the British Constitution that is known in Ireland, whereas the Scotch people we have understood

Mr. A. M. Sullivan, M.P.

16 June 1876.

Mr. *Rathbone*—continued.

understood seem to be very well satisfied with the working of their little fragment of it; might it not be well to try in one part of the British Empire what has been so very successful in another part?—That would lead me into a line of answer which I am very reluctant to trouble the Committee with. But what I want to point out to you is, that a system which may work well between proprietors and non-proprietors in Scotland would work mischievously in Ireland. It would lead me into what would be considered semi-historical, and I think we had better avoid that.

4784. Without having that distinct line of demarcation drawn between the representatives of owners and occupiers, supposing the owners and the occupiers voted on the same list for representatives together, do you not think it would be a very good thing, and that it might not tend to increase the interest, that the owners would take in the management of local affairs if they were directly rated for a certain proportion, whether one-half or otherwise of the local rates, and therefore felt from year to year the rise and fall of those rates?—It might. I should not like to commit myself at once to a decided pronouncement of judgment upon that; but I may say this, in answer to the question, that I myself would be prepared to go very far in making any concession which would give property owners an interest, seeing especially that they are, although a political minority, yet socially and otherwise an influential minority, in our city. I would go very far to conciliate them and give them an interest in our civic government.

4785. I do not know how far taxing would conciliate them?—It would give them an interest in the city.

4786. My object would be to put a certain pressure upon them to do their duty, as you propose that they should do; but the point which I wanted your opinion upon was this, that seeing that they do not now bear their share of direct taxation, and seeing that they are just the parties who do not take, as you have just told us, the interest that they should take, whether it would not be desirable to try the experiment of putting taxation on them in order to induce them to do it?—Although I have in my evidence to the Committee been very anxious to avoid blame or recrimination, I must say that upon the facts of the case, as known to me in the corporation of Dublin, I must distribute blame a good deal upon that class for their abstention. Up to the Vartry scheme we had men like Mr. George Woods Maunsell in the corporation of Dublin; and, incomprehensible as it may seem, the fact is on record that over a fight against the Vartry scheme we lost nearly the last of those men. The late Sir John Gray was a leader in the scheme, and we are getting better in this respect in Ireland every day; but even the Vartry scheme seemed to be made a sort of party battle of, and those gentlemen like Mr. George Woods Maunsell and others, retired from the corporation over a squabble or battle on the Vartry scheme, which was violently opposed by what is called the Chamber of Commerce party in Dublin. Even up to the very last, the statement that the Vartry would never be seen in the streets of Dublin was firmly believed. Then they discovered that the valley of the Vartry contained copper ore, and would be arsenical and would poison all the city. I do not like to say anything hard of those gentlemen, for they are entitled to have their prejudices and feelings as well as anyone else, but I think that their conduct in deserting the Corporation of Dublin is deserving of great censure.

Mr. *Collins*.

4787. You said that your debt of 230,000 *l.* or thereabouts was bequeathed by the old or unreformed corporation?—Yes; and no interest having been paid on it then, it was at a very low price in the market. It is now nearly as high as consols.

4788. Against that 230,000 *l.*, had the old corporation issued debentures?—Yes, for the greater part of it.

4789. You say that those debentures had fallen to a very low price, are you able to state from your own knowledge or belief what the price of those debentures was at the time that the new or reformed corporation took office; for instance, could you tell us what the price of the 5 per cent. debentures was, or what the price of the 4 per cent. debentures was, or whether there were different debentures, or whether they were all under one denomination?—That is a question which the city treasurer would have been able more accurately to give the Committee an answer about; but my belief is that the debentures in the years 1839 and 1840 were very nearly unsaleable; they were about as marketable as Turks or Egyptians.

4790. I suggest the question because you grounded many of the difficulties attached to the new corporation upon their financial difficulties, and you knew the low value of the debenture stock when they took office, and therefore the question bears very much upon the subject of the financial difficulties of the new corporation, or does it bear upon it in your opinion?—What the price of city credit was at in the market at the time does not bear so much, but it does bear upon the amount of debt upon which they have to pay interest. They instantly cleared off by cash payment on the spot, the more pressing debts, and they have since continued to pay with rigid punctuality the dividends on the city debt so as to bring its value up to 80 or 90 in the market; and not only that, but, in addition to paying the interest, they have considerably reduced their debenture debt.

4791. If the value of the debentures had fallen so considerably at the time the reformed corporation came in, did the discredit into which they fell for this reason have the effect of preventing their raising money on debentures to carry out improvement?—No, it had no such effect, because the new Reform Act and the Improvement Act had subsequently come in to force, which in the face of the financial public gave them greater powers of security, on the faith of which they were able to go into the market for any money that they wanted in the future.

4792. Altogether irrespective of the old debt, and the condition of discredit into which the old debt represented by debentures had fallen?—No doubt that discredit for a long period hung about the corporation, and did affect their financial credit to some extent, but still they were given certain means, or were proposed to be given certain means, by the 2 *s.* rate, for instance, which any

Mr. A. M. Sullivan, M.P.

16 June 1876.

Mr. *Collins*—continued.

any capitalist wanting to invest his money could see would not be touched by the disrepute of the old debt at all.

4793. I think you said that the financial difficulties of the reformed corporation was in fact the principal reason why merchants of standing and owners of property were unwilling to become members?—Many of them did become members, especially after the Improvement Act of 1850 or 1851, but I say that when they had been a few years at it, and finding how very odious and unpleasant it was to be out at elbows, and every Saturday trying to raise the wind, I know that they fell away from the corporation by degrees. The Committee ought to know that it seemed to be an occasional feature of committee work on the corporation, at all events in some of its committees, for individual members to put their names on a bill to raise money, so that that will enable the Committee to see whether I am correct or not in saying that this financial distress on the corporation tended to make men withdraw from it.

4794. From your very large experience of municipal matters in Dublin, have you formed any opinions as to any mode by which funds might be found by the corporation on moderate terms to enable them to carry out the necessary improvements?—I think that they would have plenty of funds if the area were enlarged, and if the valuation of the city were reformed; and if anything were wanted in addition to that, although I doubt whether they would want anything more, I think that in view of all the circumstances of the case the Government might lend them, on easy terms, as it did for the Vartry waterworks, and which has been regularly paid up, on easier terms than they could get in the ordinary money market, a sum of money for certain specific public improvements.

4795. Then, in your opinion, it would be a much more desirable mode of raising money to apply to the Government for aid, at a moderate rate of interest, rather than endeavouring to raise money by the issue of city debentures?—I do not think either Government aid or city debentures would be needed. If the other steps that I pointed out were taken, the widening of the area of the city and the reformation of their valuation, I doubt whether they would require the aid of the Government, or even further borrowing, at all.

4796. That would be a different phase of the case. I began by asking whether you had thought the subject over, and you then suggested that loans might be obtained from the Government for the purpose of carrying out all the important works; and the question that I put now is this, whether in your opinion it would be more desirable to go to the Government for those loans rather than raise the money by the issue of city debentures?—Clearly so; and specifically I would mention certain sanitary works that are needed in the city, clearing away blocks in certain squalid and unhealthy localities that can never be set right, unless we abolish them. I should say that the corporation ought to get borrowing powers for such works, or that the Government might advance them upon easy terms the necessary money for that specific purpose.

4797. When you say that the Government might lend upon easy terms, are you aware that it is the practice of the Government to advance considerable sums of money in England at rates of interest something like 3¼ or 3½ per cent. per annum?—I have heard of that; I only know that if the Corporation of Dublin could get money at 3½ per cent. from the Government for certain specific necessary public works in the city it would be an immense boon.

4798. Have you heard of the fact that the Government does lend money in England largely, at rates of interest not exceeding 3½ per cent., for public improvements?—I heard that one night in the House in a discussion upon the Estimates.

4799. Are you aware at all of what the general rate of interest demanded upon loans by the Government is in the case of Irish loans?—Four and a half or five per cent., so far as I recollect, to cover a sinking fund, I think, but I am not sure.

4800. In the case of interest being charged at 5 per cent., are you aware of the fact as to the number of years that loans bearing 5 per cent. are spread over so as to provide for a sinking fund?—No; upon that matter I am not just now able to give any information.

4801. Taking into account the deduction or allowance for a sinking fund which is calculated according to the period of time in which the capital is to be refunded, have you ever heard what the rate of interest charged upon Irish advances would be, minus the amount allowed for sinking fund?—I always thought it was 4½ per cent.

4802. You believe that under good management, and with an extended area of taxation, a sufficient revenue might be raised to pay the interest on loans, and to elevate Dublin from its present condition of financial difficulty?—I think so. There is another point in connection with this matter of the finance of the city which I have very strong opinions formed upon, and that is, that the Government ought to give up to the city of Dublin the cab and carriage rents of the city. Those cabs wear down our streets, and yet the revenue derived from those cab licenses is taken away from our city; it is purely a local revenue, carried away to the Government from us. I think it would greatly assist the city if the Government would give up the carriage rents to the city. On the other hand, the city has a revenue that I think the Government of the country at large ought to take away from the city, and that is the pawnbrokers' licenses all over Ireland, which go to pay the salary of the city marshal in Dublin, a perfectly needless office that might well be abolished; and I think the city of Dublin has no right to tax all Ireland in this matter of the pawnbrokers' licenses; I think, putting one against the other, that the city ought to give up the pawnbrokers' licenses tax all over Ireland, and it ought to obtain from the Government the carriage rents.

Chairman.

4803. Are you aware that the carriage rents go towards a proportion of the expenses of the Dublin metropolitan police?—I know that they do; but the expenses of the Dublin metropolitan police are, of course, partly paid by those and partly by the one shilling in the pound police tax; but really the Dublin metropolitan police are not a civic body at all, they are a Government force, and a very excellent body they are. I do not believe that in the empire there is a better body of men for their duties.

4804. In

Mr. *A. M. Sullivan*, M.P.

6 June 1876.

Mr. *Collins*.

4804. In addition to the extension of the area of taxation that you have mentioned, you also recommend that there should be a revaluation?—Yes, or a readjustment of the present valuation. I think that would add about 10,000 *l.* or 12,000 *l.* a year to the city revenues.

4805. A re-valuation is greatly objected to in Dublin, is it not?—Yes; a general re-valuation would call forth, certainly, some reclamations in the city.

Sir *Arthur Guinness*.

4806. But you would approve of it?—Yes; I should, certainly. I have come, from my nine years' experience of the work of the city business, to the conclusion that people cannot have value in the world now without paying for it, and if the people want their city cleansed, and sanitary laws enforced, and other things, they must pay for it.

Mr. *Collins*.

4807. Why did Sir Richard Griffith object to the re-valuation?—I do not know; I only heard in my time that he had been previously asked to re-value the city.

Dr. *Ward*.

4808. Are you aware, of your own knowledge, whether a re-valuation would add largely to the income of the corporation?—Certainly, I know it would.

Mr. *Collins*.

4809. Do you recommend that the re-valuation of Dublin should be made compulsory?—Yes, I do.

4810. By what authority?—It should be carried out by the General Valuation Office. I hear from the right honourable Chairman that Parliamentary powers are not necessary, but I think that if necessary they might be given. I am afraid that the corporation will never ask for a general re-valuation of the city; it would be as much as a man's seat would be worth.

4811. In respect of the Building Act, you endeavoured to promote a Building Act yourself?—Yes.

4812. You said that you regretted that the corporation opposed it?—No; that the corporation, after deciding to introduce it, and going a long way in the contests, eventually upset it, rescinded and abolished it; or else, what was more efficacious, and a matter productive of real evil in the corporation owing to the obstructive policy pursued by a few members, who succeeded in counting out the house, and thus threw it off from the time within which they could either lodge their Bill or appear in Parliament; and that is why I would greatly urge that the quorum of the corporation should be reduced. At present it is one-third of the whole body, 20 out of 60, which is very large; and two or three men would be able to obstruct any business, seeing that on the 20th of November is the time when we must have a certain step taken, if they can dodge it beyond the time all is lost.

4813. Do you know why it was that they objected to a Building Act?—Because all the parties interested in buildings in the city in the various wards stirred themselves up, and declared that this was a most Algerine Act whereby a man would not be allowed to build his house as he liked himself.

Dr. *Ward*.

4814. What number of the corporation would you recommend for a quorum?—I would say 13, in the place of 20. I think that would be abundantly large. It is a mistake to assume that fixing a large quorum is a protection to absentees. I found that the contrary was the case, from my experience at the North Dublin Union board of guardians, on which I had a seat for some years. The number of guardians is 60, the same as the number of the municipal corporation, and yet the quorum is only three, the quorum being 20 in a corporation of 60, but, as the result, we never had to wait a moment for a quorum in the North Dublin Union; and not only was a quorum present when the clock struck the hour, but five times the quorum; and why? Because most men said, as three can do injustice, I had better be there to watch; whereas in the corporation a man argues the other way. He says it will be so hard for them to keep a house that I do not need to go; nothing will be done. The large quorum is a powerful obstruction to the transaction of business in Dublin.

Mr. *Collins*.

4815. You stated, did you not, that you would make a concession to the extent of introducing owners of property into the corporation by giving them the franchise?—I did not say by introducing them, but by inducing them, as far as possible, to take their fair share in the civic government. I would make great concessions from what I would otherwise consider the strict rules of public principle.

4816. You would give the owners of property the franchise?—Yes, I would do so.

4817. What would be the qualification?—£. 50 beneficial interest.

4818. You would not enforce the payment of taxation in such a case as that?—No, I do not propose that in my own mind. I do not take that view of it which I have heard suggested here, although it might be very useful.

4819. You would be content with a beneficial interest of 50 *l.* a year?—I would give him a vote if he had a beneficial interest in it. If that suggestion were carried out, you would ultimately have a certain portion of the ratepayers men of property, responsible, at all events, in the last degree, for the payment of the rates.

4820. If there were any difficulty respecting this property franchise, would you abandon any opposition to the necessity for the payment of rates rather than lose the benefit of the introduction of this class of representatives?—I really think I should be ready to deviate so far from mere abstract general principles, under the peculiar state of circumstances in Dublin, I should be ready to go as far as that.

Chairman.

4821. Do you mean that you would go so far as to give the owners representation?—So far as to give the owners a vote without their paying direct taxation in respect of their qualification.

Mr. *J. P. Corry*.

4822. In what year did you enter the corporation of Dublin?—In the year 1861 or 1862; about the end of 1861, I think it was.

4823. Was that prior to the Vartry scheme being introduced?—No, the works were beginning

Mr. A. M. Sullivan, M.P.

16 June 1876.

Mr. *J. P. Corry*—continued.

beginning to be undertaken at the time; the Bill had passed.

4824. I presume that it was prior to that time that the gentleman whom you refer to left the corporation?—Just a year before that, I think, Mr. George Woods Mannsell left the corporation, and some two or three of those gentlemen.

4825. You told the Committee that you entered the corporation with a very strong prejudice against the management of the corporation?—I did.

4826. And that the result of your investigations was to show you that those prejudices were ill-founded?—In a great degree ill-founded.

4827. I presume that the Committee may gather that you have changed your mind with reference to the representation of property from the views that you held prior to the time of your entering the corporation?—Yes; I remain, of course, of the same opinion still on the general principle, but I think I would make an exception in the case of Dublin; I should be very sorry to propound it as a general principle that in municipal governments such things should be done; I am only asking the Committee to take my evidence as regards the city of Dublin, I do not profess to speak from any personal or peculiar knowledge of any other municipality in Ireland.

4828. You do not wish to speak for them generally?—No, I do not.

4829. You are aware of the Artizans' Dwelling Act which was passed last Session; do not you think that if it were applied to Dublin it would have a very beneficial effect?—I think so.

4830. Do you remember what were the principal things in the Building Act which you referred to which you wished to get?—It was upon the Belfast Building Act that we modelled our Building Act. Mr. Norwood got the Belfast Act for us, and we modelled our Bill very largely upon it. I should state to the Committee that as regards Belfast and Dublin, bearing upon my suggestion of the extension of the area, the area of Belfast is twice as large as the area of the municipality of Dublin, showing that Dublin really needs extension although the population of Dublin, I should say, is twice the population of Belfast.

4831. The difference is this, is it not, that we have not any townships outside Belfast?—Fortunately that is the case.

4832. You stated with reference to the question of salaries, that when an office became vacant the corporation at once appointed a committee to look into the duties of the office, and the result was that you got a new officer at a lower salary than the old one?—That was the general practice, and I believe it is so still, and also they endeavoured in some way to secure benefits to the corporation in the new arrangement. Upon that subject I would refer the Committee to what has just happened in the law courts in Dublin last week, with reference to the appointment of city marshal in Dublin. When it fell out within my time when Mr. Thomas Reynolds died, and it came into the possession of the present marshal, they made an agreement that those fees leviable all over Ireland on the pawnbrokers, which amount to a very considerable sum, and which previously went altogether into this official's pocket, should be given over to the corporation, and that he should take in lieu thereof a salary, which would be about one-half of the value which those fees would amount to. The corporation wished to bring this 400 *l.* or 500 *l.* a year to the aid of the rates, but the late city marshal, although he entered into that agreement and signed a bond to the corporation to that effect, has gone into the law courts and obtained a decision that the bond being in opposition to an Act of Parliament, he has a claim to the whole of the fees. I merely instance that as showing how the corporation has always endeavoured in this matter of salaries to economise and bring money to the aid of the rates.

4833. I think you told the Committee that you considered the salaries paid by the Dublin Corporation as miserably low?—Indeed, I think so; that is my opinion.

4834. Would you consider it good policy, when an office becomes vacant, to ask for candidates for that office at a much lower salary than the previous officer enjoyed?—I think it is good policy to have a minimum and a maximum salary in those cases. I think a man who has served 40 years has acquired for that public service in the course of the 40 years certain capacities, and knowledge, and experience, and is giving greater value than he did before, and I would increase his salary, but I would always start a fresh man at the minimum, and let him work gradually up to the maximum.

4835. We have had a great deal of evidence with regard to the franchise in Dublin, whilst you have been looking into other matters, have you considered the relative proportion of the citizens of Dublin who are upon the rate books and who are entitled to the franchise?—I have; I think that the proportion is enormously small in Dublin as compared with the English cities, and I think that the mode of getting on the franchise list in Ireland is very obstructive, and practically keeps numbers out and throws us into the hands of party agencies. You have no chance of getting on the Burgess Roll in Dublin, unless the Conservatives believe you to be a Conservative or the Liberals a Liberal, and unless they will take the trouble through their agencies of getting you on, it is almost impossible to get on.

4836. After the evidence which you have given us, and the investigations which you have made yourself, do you think that the increasing the number of electors would tend to give you a more respectable town council?—I think it would by extending it, as I proposed, in both directions. I think by broadening it, as regards giving the household franchise, virtually the municipal franchise on the English basis, you would give a broad and popular basis to the franchise, and on the other hand the proposition I make in the other direction of the property owners, I think, would give it another very necessary element for its stability and position.

4837. Your opinion is, that the one would require to be blended with the other?—I should say in Dublin, that would be so.

Mr. *Brown*.

4838. Have you formed any calculation as to the number who would be admitted to the franchise by your proposal of giving votes to property owners of 50 *l.* valuation?—No; I have not gone into

Mr. *A. M. Sullivan*, M.P.

16 June 1876.

Mr. *Brun*—continued.

into any figure calculation, except that in my own mind I worked out this problem; that in the City of Dublin, apart from general abstract theories, it was very necessary to enlist the sympathies and the interest of a certain very influential social class.

4839. Do you think that you would enlist their sympathies simply by giving them votes, unless they were able to exercise influence upon the elections?—I think that the giving a man the franchise as a property holder, as I suggest, would by itself amount to very little, but that giving it in conjunction with the minority representation, which I have already suggested to the Committee, it would count for a very great deal indeed in Dublin.

4840. You have already said that you do not wish to give any opinion to the Committee with regard to other municipal bodies besides Dublin; but assuming the case of a municipal body in which the same reasons existed for obtaining the co-operation of the propertied classes, I suppose you would in that case extend the same privileges to them?—Certainly.

4841. You are of opinion, are you not, that in municipal government as in other governments, it is good policy to erect the system of government upon as broad a basis as possible, and to enlist the sympathies of as many different classes of interests as there are within the municipality, and to give them some power in exercising the franchise?—Yes, I do certainly think so; I think at all events, in municipal matters, that this disregard of the feelings or interest of the minority is a great evil.

4842. And any system which absolutely excludes and disqualifies any special class or interest requires reform?—I should say so far—*pro tanto*.

4843. With regard to valuation, you say that you are in favour of a re-valuation of the City of Dublin; are you also in favour of a re-valuation of the property over the whole of Ireland?—That is a very broad and very serious question, and hardly within the lines of this Committee but still I should like to answer the honourable Member by saying, that there are special reasons which I mentioned to the Committee about the valuation of the municipality of Dublin, namely, that it was reduced after the passing of the Improvement Act, which gave certain funds on the faith of a general valuation, and, consequently took away 10,000 *l.* a year from the corporation, and looking at the 10,000 *l.* a year which had been taken into their estimates, that really left them in a lamentable difficulty. The valuation of the city was reduced since the Improvement of Dublin Act was passed. In that Improvement of Dublin Act, a limitation of 2 *s.* in the pound on the then valuation of the city was placed; that estimate of 2 *s.* in the pound being formed on the then valuation, would give them enough wherewith to sweep the streets; but 10,000 *l.* a year being so taken from them, that is to say, the valuation of the city being reduced by a larger amount than that; 10,000 *l.* a year will be the money needed to sweep the streets of Dublin.

4844. Does the Valuation Act in Dublin cause this to take place, that the valuation of the buildings is reduced?—Of course in what are called the revisions, and revisions are constantly going on under Mr. Greene, the Chief Commissioner, a reduction is occasionally made, but that reduction is from a certain basis.

Mr. *Brun*—continued.

4845. You complain that buildings to which any structural addition or improvement is made, are at once valued at a higher rate than buildings to which no addition is made?—That was hardly my complaint or observation. My observation based on such information as I have, is that the commissioner is allowed to have a new valuation, disregarding what is really the starting point or basis of the general valuation, in the case of a structure which is sufficiently taken down or broken in upon, or removed, to constitute in the eye of the valuation office a new building. It is then valued on data quite different from the old existing standard.

4846. And owing to the operation of that rule, is it not a fact that the general valuation of the City of Dublin is constantly increasing?—To some extent it is increasing as new buildings go on, and plate-glass windows are put in, and insurance offices spring up.

4847. That increase of valuation considerably more than counterbalances any decrease that may take place by the possible deterioration of buildings?—I think that the balance is on the side of some gradual increase.

4848. As to the re-valuation which you wish to take place, do you wish it to be made upon the basis upon which the commissioner values new buildings, or that the whole of the city shall be gone over and the general rate of valuation increased throughout the city?—My answer to that is this: that I wish the valuation of the city to be more real and genuine than it is now. It is very patchy, if I may be excused such a phrase at present, by reason of those new buildings being valued upon different data from the generality of the city besides.

4849. And it is only on that account, and because of the reduction of the valuation that was made from time to time, that you wish a new valuation?—Quite so.

4850. Those are the reasons upon which you advocate this re-adjustment?—Quite so.

4851. In cases in which those reasons do not exist, you would not advocate a re-adjustment?—That is exactly my position in these Dublin matters.

Mr. *Kavanagh*.

4852. I think you said you experienced a good deal of difficulty when you were on the corporation in carrying out the sanitary law?—Yes, we were obstructed a good deal at first, but eventually in the corporation we got a majority and had it put into force, and it has been very strongly and firmly enforced since then.

4853. I think you said that you had to fight a two years' battle?—I think we were two years fighting, led by the late Sir John Gray; indeed, he led in most of these things. At one time we were in a minority, but we carried the majority of the corporation with us ultimately.

4854. I think also you said that with the people in the town you had difficulties when you wanted them to build ash pits, and make sewers, and that sort of thing?—We had considerable difficulty from the parties who were personally interested in not laying out this money, but the bulk of the citizens, I must say, heartily approved of the Sanitary Act.

4855. But still the poor individuals who were actually affected by your orders, did not like them?—They were not poor; they were the tenement-house owners, who are a very well-to-do

Mr. A. M. Sullivan, M.P.

16 June 1876.

Mr. *Kavanagh*—continued.

do section of our community, they were not poor at all, and I am sorry to say, that if judged by their means, they ought to have had more public spirit. They are an influential class of men in Dublin who are called house jobbers, who take old tumble-down houses and send in a plasterer and glazier and just cobble them up a little, and let those houses out to tenement holders who pay them weekly sums, and before the enforcement of the Sanitary Act this class of houses in Dublin were disgracefully deficient in the decencies of home life.

4856. Why did these house jobbers object?—We called upon them by this Act to provide water closet accommodation, for instance, not only for males but for females, and for cleansing and whitewashing, and ashpit accommodation; I am able positively to state to this Committee, for I myself went personally into the matter, we found the most astounding deficiency in the case of the working classes, who were living in those rooms in what I will call no provision for absolute decency in their houses until this Act was passed, and we experienced great resistance from this section of people, who said that the people were getting on very well, and the result would be that if they laid out all this money they should charge 1 *s.* 6 *d.* a week more, and that we, the corporation, were thus virtually taxing the poor people who were getting on very well as things were.

4857. In fact, the real objection was that they were obliged to spend their own money in doing it?—Precisely.

4858. It was a money objection?—Yes.

4859. Did the parties who lived in these houses approve of what you wanted to have done?—They highly approved of it.

4860. Even at the increased 1 *s.* 6 *d.*?—Even at the increased 1 *s.* 6 *d.* My experience upon the corporation satisfied me distinctly; the testimony of Mr. Lombard and other gentlemen of means, who have been building small houses for the people in Dublin, satisfied me that the working classes in Dublin would gladly pay an additional sum if they could get decent and cleanly homes.

4861. Then, really the summary of what you have said is this, that the objection of house jobbers to this sanitary improvement was so strong that they influenced the corporation, and made it difficult to pass them?—Yes, to a certain extent. They made out wonderfully plausible cases to those members who were going out in the following November, but I noticed that when those members had got in in the ensuing November, they became advocates of all sorts of sanitary improvements in the following January, for they had three years before them then.

Mr. *Collins*.

4862. Those people succeeded in throwing you out of the corporation, did they not?—No, it was not upon that issue that I was put out.

4863. I think you enumerated that amongst other causes?—Yes, I was exposed to some unpopularity on this issue in the corporation, and a good deal out of it. Some of my supporters in the ward were interested in this matter, but I must do them the justice to say that they did not try to put me out, although I know that I incurred a good deal of unpopularity at the time by it.

Mr. *Mulholland*.

4864. I think you suggested that the arrears of rating should be made a charge ultimately against the owner of house property?—I think something of that kind is needed in Dublin.

4865. In that case would it not be reasonable that the owner of property should have an adequate representation when the question of expenditure is considered?—Not necessarily, because protection could be afforded to them, if sufficient notice was given that the rate was unpaid, to collect it in his rent.

4866. But you are aware that that must affect the rent ultimately?—So it would; it would settle itself in that way. If the landlord pays the tax, it is only another name for the same thing.

4867. Besides the reasons that you suggest, is it not the fact that the present expenditure for municipal purposes tends to be of a more permanent nature than the expenditure was formerly, and that there is more money spent in sanitary improvements and bringing water into Dublin, and so on?—Enormously more.

4868. And that will become ultimately a charge upon the property?—All of it, in one way or another, reaches the property. It is not sufficiently borne in mind that the increase of taxation all over the country, and in Dublin as well, is largely represented by Parliament extending the powers of causing things to be done which, in our grandfathers' time were never dreamt of being done by public money.

4869. You say that under those circumstances you think, with reference to Dublin, that property ought to be represented, but because the same circumstances do not apply equally to other towns, you would not extend it to other towns; but ought not property to be adequately represented everywhere?—I am afraid that you hardly caught my answer upon that. I never said that property should be represented as such upon the council; what I have been urging is, that that is a class which should have a vote, though it has not at present.

4870. But would not the same reasons apply in other places as well as in Dublin?—Wherever they apply, as I have stated throughout my evidence, I should unhesitatingly apply the same principle.

4871. Have any attempts ever been made to extend the area of taxation?—I am not aware of any; I think the corporation in my time was deterred from doing so; their idea was to promote a private Bill, but they were deterred by the certainty that the townships that have been unfortunately allowed to grow up around us would wage such an expensive war, in the matter of a private Bill, that the corporation, having no funds properly applicable to such a hazardous enterprise, were powerless; they were apprehensive that the members would have to pay out of their own pockets, if the Bill should not pass, the 10,000 *l.* or 20,000 *l.* that was spent; and thus they were deterred from attempting it.

4872. Was it considered that those townships ought to share in the taxation equally with Dublin?—Yes, they have no claim to a separate existence except the accident that they were allowed to constitute themselves separate townships.

4873. There is no real reason why they should not bear their share except that they have been erected into those townships?—None, for it is simply

Mr. A. M. Sullivan, M.P.

16 June 1876

Mr. *Mulholland*—continued.

simply the growth outward of the city; there is no real separation at all, the city simply grew in those directions.

4874. With reference to an answer which you gave to the Member for Carlow, is there any reasonable objection to re-valuations where the values of properties have changed?—That is a general question extending to the whole of Ireland, I take it.

4875. Would not the same causes apply elsewhere to places which have changed in value that have applied in Dublin?—I daresay that, as a general and abstract question, it might be so.

4876. But as a question of justice could any reason be urged against periodical valuations where the values have changed?—I should say not.

Chairman.

4877. Do not the corporation transact a great deal of their business in Committees of the whole House?—The business of the corporation is transacted in Committees of the whole House, and a very objectionable form of committee in my opinion it is, because the responsibility is not fixed upon a definite number. Not a good deal of administrative duty, but a good deal of what would be called deliberative duty is remitted to a Committee of the whole House?—A Committee of the whole House in my time never undertook what I would call administrative duties, but it always investigated more freely and conversationally than it could in the public council in a matter requiring the attention of the public council. For instance, a Committee of the whole House would inquire into some special report of Committee No. 1, saying that scavenging needed a certain change; that could be better and more freely debated in a Committee of the whole House than in a public council. This Committee of the whole House I always thought was very useless, I like where administration is to be done, to fix some three, five, or seven men, specifically with the responsibility, and then they will do it, but when you fling the responsibility broadcast among 60 men that any may come or any may stay, it is generally neglected.

4878. But the difference between a Committee of the whole House and the deliberations in council is this, is it not, that in one they are private and in the other they are public?—Yes, a man may speak as often as he likes in a Committee of the whole House, whereas he must only get up under certain bye-laws and address the Chair in a more formal manner at a public sitting; the business is not so rapidly done in a public sitting.

4879. I apprehend that you would not wish that the sittings of the Town Council should be private?—Certainly not.

4880. Even although it might tend to the more rapid transaction of business?—Privacy would not so much tend to the more rapid transaction of business, as absolutely freeing the members from certain formalities in the transaction of public business. For instance, in a public sitting of the corporation at present, the objection of one individual to suspending the bye-laws, has very often been efficacious to stop some most urgent necessary business that had cropped up within the 24 hours, and that needed to be done. For instance, some order about the Public Health

Chairman—continued.

Committee is needed to be given to appear before the magistrates or something of that kind, and if one man gets up and objects to the suspension of the Standing Orders, the matter is thrown over to go through first reading, and second reading, and such formalities; that is what wastes a good deal of the public time.

Sir *Arthur Guinness.*

4881. Are Committees Nos. 1, 2, and 3, public?—No, they are private; the committee meetings are the best phase of the corporation action that exists in Dublin, and it would be impossible to overrate the industry and attention exhibited at the committee meetings of the corporation, by the business men of the city who attend them, such as they are.

Mr. *Brooks.*

4882. Do not the citizens sometimes attend those committee meetings?—I never saw anyone except members of the corporation present at the committee meetings; they are not allowed to; they are private.

4883. Every member of the corporation may attend, may he not?—Yes, every member of the corporation may attend whether he belong to the committee or not, but he cannot vote unless he is on the committee; at a committee of the whole house every member of the corporation can vote.

Sir *Arthur Guinness.*

4884. But there is no place for the public at the committee?—No, not at the committee.

Mr. *Brooks.*

4885. Arising out of the questions of the honourable Baronet, with regard to the estimates of Sir Joseph Bazalgette for the main drainage, I think the works were estimated to amount to about 350,000 *l.*?—About 400,000 *l.*, I thought it was.

4886 Those estimates were made, I think, immediately before the advance in iron and other materials, and labour, about four or five years ago?—Yes.

4887. The main drainage pipes as designed by Sir Joseph Bazalgette, were intended to be of iron, were they not?—Yes, and of a certain diameter which had also to be increased, I think.

4888. Am I correct in saying that, in the interval between making his estimate and the receipt of the tenders for carrying out the work by the corporation, iron increased in value from about 4 *l.* to about 11 *l.* per ton?—I know that it increased enormously in value at the time, but I cannot give the Committee the exact figures.

4889. And that the increase in the cost, if the work had been carried out at that time, would have been due not to miscalculations on the part of the corporation or of Sir Joseph Bazalgette, but in consequence of the advance in the price of materials, which was common to all the country at that particular epoch?—I am quite satisfied that the bulk of it was in consequence of that, and I have already remarked upon the almost invariable excess of the reality over the Parliamentary Estimate in such cases.

4890. If the main drainage of London had been carried out at that particular period the cost would have been increased in the same proportion?—Naturally and inevitably so.

4891. You were asked also with regard to a deputation

Mr. A. M. Sullivan, M.P.

16 June 1876.

Mr. *Brooks*—continued.

deputation from the corporation to attend on this Committee; do you know if there is any fund at the disposal of the corporation for sending its private members here upon any public business?—Since the public auditor was appointed, I know that they are prevented from doing things of that kind very considerably, but I know that the amount of personal payment that a member of the corporation is called upon to bear for going on citizens' business, even in my time, was most unfair. For instance, I objected when on the Estates Committee to go away and visit the city property at my own expense, miles and miles out of Dublin; I said I was willing to do it, and I did not care about the pound or two that it cost me; but as a matter of principle, I objected to go out; I said, that within the city, I would be at a fair charge to do that civic duty, but I would not be putting my hands into my pockets for the citizens in that way.

4892. The honourable and learned Member for the University of Dublin has been informed that the majority of the Liberal members of the corporation have declined to select and send here a Conservative member of the corporation; must not it be fallacious; is it not the case that any member of the corporation may come here at his own expense, and that no member of the corporation can come here on a deputation except at his own expense?—That is quite so, I believe; but I would say this, with great respect to the Committee, that whilst it is very proper that the corporation should select to speak its mind as a unit, men who will speak its mind as a unit, I would strongly and respectfully urge on the Committee to summon here Mr. John Byrne, or Mr. Norwood, who although they are as strong party men on the one side as I am on the other, are about the most competent men that I know in Dublin to give evidence upon this matter, who will give it honourably and fairly, utterly irrespective of party feelings. These gentlemen might not represent the mind of the corporation as a whole body, but I say nevertheless, they are acquainted with all the facts, and their vast experience, and the capacity they have displayed in transacting their business in Dublin, qualify them pre-eminently to give this Committee information.

4893. If the Committee were to form an opinion based upon the question of the honourable and learned Member for the University, that the corporation had acted illiberally in its selection of members upon the deputation, they would be under a misconception?—Quite so. I am very confident that if the honourable Member was himself a member of the corporation in like circumstances, he would do exactly what the corporation have done, because it was the common sense thing to do, and I am sure he would act from common sense.

Mr. *Brooks*—continued.

4894. Do you know the price that was agreed upon between the corporation and the gas company for the shares which it was proposed that they should buy for the citizens?—I thought it was about 12 *l.*, but that was since I was in the corporation, and I am reluctant to trouble the Committee with any precision in answers upon anything that happened about the corporation since I left it.

4895. Do you know from the public prints, and as a matter of public notoriety, that the value of the shares of the gas company have since increased something like 25 per cent.?—I am very well aware of that, and I am very well aware that it seemed to me at the time that even financially the corporation would have made as good a thing of the gas undertaking as under the present new régime in the gas offices they are doing it now; but I still qualify that answer as I qualified it awhile ago, by expressing my apprehension as to whether, constituted as the corporation is at present, it would have time and capacity within it sufficient for managing so serious a new department, but such a department ought to belong to the corporation, in my opinion.

4896. You give that as your opinion?—Yes, simply as my opinion.

4897. But as a matter of fact beyond controversy, if the corporation had not been obstructed at that time by amateur citizens' committees, would not the citizens have obtained the property of the gas company at a sum less by 100,000 *l.* than the market value of to-day?—I know that, taking what the gas company at present is doing, and for reasons which I will explain to the Committee, the corporation would have benefitted by several thousands a-year in aid of the rates, because the corporation, in making its proposition, were acting largely upon information supplied to them by an officer then in their employ, Mr. Cotton, who would have to do with the gas under the corporation. What the gas company did was to get this officer away from the corporation and employ him themselves, and he is enabling them now to do that which the corporation had calculated upon his enabling the corporation to do, whereby they would have made from 10,000 *l.* to 20,000 *l.* a-year for the citizens.

Tuesday, 20th June 1876.

MEMBERS PRESENT:

Sir Michael Hicks Beach.	Mr. Kavanagh.
Mr. Brooks.	Sir Joseph M'Kenna.
Mr. Bruen.	Mr. Mulholland.
Mr. Collins.	Mr. Murphy.
Mr. Gibson.	Dr. Ward.
Sir Arthur Guinness.	

SIR MICHAEL HICKS BEACH, BART., IN THE CHAIR.

Mr. JAMES BOYLE, called in; and Examined.

Mr. *Boyle.* 20 June 1876.

Mr. *Brooks.*

4898. YOU are a Civil Engineer, are you not?—I am.

4899. Have you been employed in that capacity by the Government?—I have; I was employed as Government engineer for the counties of Wicklow and Waterford during the years 1846, 1847, and 1848, and subsequently in other capacities.

4900. How long have you been in the employment of the corporation of Dublin?—Since the inception of the Sanitary Act of 1866.

4901. What is your office, and what is the nature of your duties?—I am secretary and engineer to the Public Health Committee of the Corporation of Dublin, and I act as executive sanitary officer under the Local Government Board.

4902. Have you read the evidence which has been supplied to the corporation, as given by Dr. Grimshaw?—I have.

4903. Do you concur in his statement as to the excessive mortality from zymotic diseases in Dublin?—By no means.

4904 As a matter of fact, has this mortality increased or decreased?—The mortality from zymotics, that is from preventible diseases, has steadily decreased since 1866, and I refer to the Registrar General's returns in proof of this.

4905. Dr. Grimshaw stated the death-rate of Dublin to be 28·4 per 1,000, and therefore higher than in a great many other towns that he spoke of; is that so?—No; the Registrar General's returns show the maximum death-rate to have been in one year, the year 1875, for instance, 27 per 1,000; in 1874, 28·6 per 1,000, and in 1873, 26 per 1,000. I will take the most unfavourable of those years, 1874, and I will refer to the report of the Registrar General, if you desire it, which states that Dublin was not exceptional in respect of a high death-rate in that year, but that it applied equally to all Ireland.

4906. Will you state to the Committee what the sanitary staff in Dublin consists of?—I have a return of them, but I will shortly state that it consists of the secretary (that is myself), the consulting medical officer, the medical officer of health, who is also the city analyst, and 14 medical sanitary officers, who are the dispensary medical officers in the city, appointed under the provisions of the Public Health Act, 1874. By virtue of their offices the medical officers of dispensaries, by the provisions of the Public Health Act, 1874, became sanitary medical officers; they were not appointed by the corporation. We have nine sanitary police now; formerly we had 15.

4907. Is there not a short printed return of the sanitary operations and duties of those officers?—Yes. (*The same was delivered in.*)

4908. Will you state the composition of the Public Health Committee?—It consists of 30 members, two members being taken from each of the 15 wards of the city. The members comprise six borough magistrates, two governors of hospitals, 17 are members of boards of guardians, and six are members of the dispensary committee of the city, and there are three medical men; there were formerly four medical members of the committee.

4909. It has been stated that the sanitary condition of the tenement houses in Dublin remains unchanged, and that thereby the health of the city remains unimproved since the formation of the Public Health Committee; is that so?—No, the Return that I have given in shows that upwards of 3,000 houses have been provided with house drains; 2,706 with privies or water-closets, and 2,302 with ashpits; 646 dwellings have been condemned and closed, as being unfit for human habitation, and 457 dwellings have been reported to the city engineer as being dangerous to the public.

Chairman.

4910. Could you tell us how many there are that are under the jurisdiction of the Sanitary Committee?—There are 24,000 houses in Dublin; of these 9,700 are occupied as tenement houses, and are specially under the control of the Sanitary Committee, but the proprietor of any house becomes amenable to it should a nuisance exist in it.

Mr. *Boyle*.

20 June 1876.

Mr. *Brooks*.

4911. Referring to the evidence of Dr. Grimshaw, did you, in 1872 receive from Dr. Grimshaw two lists of houses designated as fever dens?—I did; I recived from him two lists of houses, numbering in all 115. I had an immediate inspection made of those houses, and they have been subject to our supervision ever since. I produce a detailed report of the condition of each house at the time, and of the proceedings taken against each of those houses from time to time as circumstances required. I can give the details in each case. I will give an abstract of those 115 houses: 211 summonses have from time to time been issued against their owners; 26 owners were fined; the amount of penalties imposed on and levied from the owners of those houses was 25 *l.* 5 *s.*; the number of owners imprisoned was two; the number of dwellings closed was four; the number of dwellings taken down was four; and the number that are now only occupied by caretakers is two. The condition of those houses on the 8th of June of the present year was as follows: 60 of them were very good, 39 were fair, and six were bad. One of those six was ordered to be closed, and the others have been proceeded against; the details in each case are given in this return.

4912. Is their condition, as was alleged, unchanged?—Quite the reverse. I had an inspection made of them by the consulting sanitary officer, and he concurs in the report which I have now given. Some of them were in a bad condition at the time, viz., in 1872, but their condition at the present moment is as I describe. None of of them are unfit for human habitation with the exception of six, which are only partly occupied, and against which proceeding shave been taken.

Dr. *Ward*.

4913. Who inspected those houses?—I inspected every one of those houses.

4914. Who was the sanitary officer?—Dr. Mapother.

4915. When did the inspection take place?—During the week before last; and since reading Dr. Grimshaw's evidence I inspected all those houses, with two exceptions.

Mr. *Brooks*.

4916. In how many instances has the occurrence of fever in these houses been reported to you by the medical consulting officer?—Since 1874, when the medical sanitary officers were appointed, but three cases of fever were reported by them as occurring in those houses. I produce he reports of those three cases.

4917. Will you describe them shortly to the Committee?—With reference to Dr. Grimshaw's two printed lists of fever dens, I have here an extract from the official reports of the medical sanitary officers on the south side of the city to the 1st of May 1876. The object of this return is to show that inasmuch as but three of the houses noted in Dr. Grimshaw's lists are included in this return, they have ceased to be fever dens. These three houses are marked with an asterisk. If there had been fever in them, it would have been the duty of the medical sanitary officer to have reported them to me.

4918. Do they still continue to call those places fever dens?—No, they are not known as such, nor do they furnish cases of fever. In order that the Committee may know the opportunities we have of knowing where fever exists, I beg to state that on each morning the sanitary sergeant calls at the dispensary in his district, in order to receive from the medical officer a return or list of any cases of infectious disease that may have occurred during the previous 24 hours; this he reports to me on the same morning. I receive from each medical officer of a dispensary a statement of all cases of fever occurring within his district. I receive, from each of the hospitals in the city receiving fever patients, a return twice a week of the names and addresses of patients admitted, in order that I may take means for prompt disinfection of the premises, and for the removal of anything that is calculated to communicate disease. I have, since 1874, received but three reports of fever occurring in the houses reported by Dr. Grimshaw as fever dens.

Mr. *Brooks*—continued.

4919. What steps have you taken in consequence of those reports?—The clothes, and bedding, and other articles are at once sent to the disinfecting chamber and disinfected, and every effort is made to induce the parties to go to the Fever Hospital. The house is limewashed, and it is also chemically disinfected by fumigation with chlorine gas.

4920. Do you find that your recommendations are adopted by the inhabitants of those houses?—They are invariably enforced, but we have much difficulty in inducing parties to proceed to the hospital, and very frequently they will not go; but in the great majority of instances articles of bedding and clothing are sent to the disinfecting chamber, and we have never failed to obtain a disinfection of the house.

4921. By whose assistance are the recommendations for removal to the hospital enforced?—They are executed under my direction through the instrumentality of the sanitary police, and also through the assistance of the medical officers of the dispensaries.

4922. Is there any resistance to the efforts of the Public Health Committee?—No, we find that the humbler classes are very willing as a rule to accept of our intervention.

4923. Are all the necessary steps taken by the sanitary police and the sanitary medical officers to give you information regarding the existence of fever in those dens in those districts?—Invariably. It is almost impossible for a case of infectious disease in a tenement house or amongst the humbler classes to escape observation or detection.

4924. The house 36, Chancery-lane, was referred to; what statement have you to make with regard to that house?—On reading the evidence I immediately went to it, and I will give you also the report of the consulting sanitary officer, whom I asked to go to see it. It is one of the most wholesome houses in Dublin; it is clean, it is staunch, it has got an exceedingly good yard, a large air space at the rear, a water closet detatched from it; an ashpit detached from it; and a water supply. The yard was quite clean. I may mention that in 1872 that house attracted our attention; it was then in a very different state. The yard wall was taken down and the yard enlarged; the filthy privy that existed was replaced by a clean, excellent, and effective water closet at one point, and the ashpit in the other; and we also got the water laid on at the time. I saw that house on the 8th of June.

4925. Was

Mr. *Boyle.*

20 June 1876.

Mr. *Brooks*—continued.

4925. Was any time lost by the Public Health Committee in endeavouring to have the faults in that house rectified?—Certainly not. The moment we heard of it, immediate steps were taken to put it in the condition which the sanitary laws would require, and it has remained such since the year 1872.

4926. Do you consider that the sanitary police are qualified for the duties that they have to perform under the Public Health Committee?—Beyond all others, and for many reasons which I will mention. They are thoroughly competent, and most thoroughly qualified. They are not open to any influence, or to any intervention. They receive no orders except from me; not only is their appointment in danger if they neglect their duty, but their superannuation afterwards. The Commissioners of Police exercise a strict supervision over them as regards sanitary matters, for they report directly each week to the Commissioners of Police, as well as to the Public Health Committee, and they receive their orders from me every morning. I believe that we never could in Dublin, circumstanced as it is in many respects, socially, morally, and otherwise, carry out the Public Health Act through the instrumentality of any other force or body of men. There is an obedience to anything that they may say, which certainly would not be paid to any other individuals.

4927. Do they do their duties in their police uniform?—Yes, and that carries great weight with the people.

4928. Are you enabled to say that the sanitary sergeants are selected by the Commissioners of Police for those duties on account of their special steadiness and good character?—I am enabled to state from my knowledge of them, and also from my acquaintance with Sir Henry Lake, that they were specially selected for the purpose by reason of their intelligence, their discretion, and good temper, their firmness, and also their integrity. I have had, I think, very nearly 60 under me, and with two exceptions, who were not suited for the purpose, although very good men in other respects, they have proved exceedingly valuable men. I should prefer half the number of sanitary police to double the number of civilians.

4929. Can you say that any persons have been fined, and that any have been imprisoned for infraction of the sanitary regulations in consequence of the action of the Public Health Committee and the sanitary officers?—Yes; the amount of the penalties imposed was 3,004 *l.*, and the costs 521 *l.*, making a total of 3,525 *l.*; of which sum, 3,395 *l.* was levied and paid in to the treasurer of the Corporation of Dublin. The number of persons imprisoned for ordinary sanitary offences was 15; the number of persons imprisoned for the sale, or the possession for sale, of unsound meat, &c., was 27, making the total number imprisoned 42.

4930. Is there any unwillingness on the part of the magistrates to enforce the recommendations of the Public Health Committee?—On the contrary, the magistrates afford us every assistance; they have thrown their whole heart into the matter, and assisted us in every possible way.

4931. With regard to those reports of the medical sanitary officers, will you state to the Committee what the action taken by the Public Health Committee upon those reports has been?—I have a number of them here; I receive those reports from the several dispensary doctors, and the moment those reports are received they are immediately handed to the sergeant of the district, and he produces them the next morning with his report of the state of the premises, as the case may be, and the action taken on it; that is submitted to the committee upon each Friday morning for their information. The case is followed up, if necessary, by a summons, and if the nuisance has been abated there is nothing more about it; but on the day they are received action is invariably taken on them.

4932. Are the recommendations of the consulting sanitary officer carried into effect?—Invariably; there has never been an instance in which his suggestions or recommendations have not been strictly carried out with equal diligence and alacrity. He consults with me almost every morning as to the business of the day.

4933. Are his services usually available?—They are at all times available; his entire time, if necessary, is given to the duty; he inspects the premises where medical advice is required, he furnishes the certificates that are necessary for obtaining convictions, and he attends the police court in order to give evidence in cases where medical evidence is required.

4934. Is his entire time occupied?—It does not involve his entire time, nor quite one-half of it; but if it is required it is available.

4935. Will you state to the Committee what are the available means for the removal of the sick to the hospitals?—We have two cabs for the removal of the sick, and by an arrangement with the guardians of the North and South Dublin Union, we also have the use of their cabs in the event of a case of sickness occurring more convenient to the hospital than it is to the stations of our cabs. I will read to the Committee the circular that was sent out at two different periods: "Six cabs with horses for the removal of sick to hospital are kept at the following places, and can be had at a moment's notice on the certificate of any qualified medical man, by applying to Mr. Flynn, 13, Bass-place, or at the union workhouses, north and south, or at Cork-street Hospital, and Sir Patrick Dunn's Hospital; a van for the removal of infected clothing, bedding, &c., to the corporation disinfecting chamber, Marrowbone-lane, may be obtained on application at 13, Bass-place." I sent that card to every medical man in Dublin in September 1872; and again at a more recent period I sent out a circular of a somewhat similar description, in order that every information might be had with reference to the stations of the sanitary police, and of the several medical officers, and that no delay might occur in any department as to facilitating the removal of the sick to the hospitals. (*The Circular was handed in.*)

4936. To whom was that circular sent?—To every medical man in Dublin, every man connected with medicine or surgery there; 482 cards, I think, were sent out.

4937. To any other persons than those?—Yes, to members of the charitable societies, the members of the Society of St. Vincent de Paul, to the Sick and Indigent Room keepers Society, and others.

4938. What was the nature of the arrangement

Mr. *Boyle.*

29 June 1876.

Mr. *Brooks*—continued.

ment that was made between the Public Health Committee and the boards of guardians with regard to the joint use of these cabs or vehicles?—The members of the boards of guardians who are on the Committee arranged that their cabs should be always available for us in any emergency, either during the prevalence of an epidemic, or when a case of sickness requiring instant removal demanded their use, and they have been repeatedly availed of.

4939. That is by an arrangement of the members of the poor law guardians being members of the Public Health Committee?—Yes.

4940. And made at the Public Health Committee?—Yes, made at the Public Health Committee, and acted on by the boards of guardians as a body.

4941. Are you enabled to inform the Committee if those means are sufficient in all ordinary times?—Amply sufficient.

4942. Can you inform the Committee as to the means available for the disinfection of dwellings?—A person is specially employed throughout the year, and when epidemics exist an additional man is employed in the disinfection of dwellings according to a method prescribed by Dr. Cameron, the city analyst. On receiving information of the occurrence of a case of infectious disease in any dwelling, the sanitary inspector immediately puts a man into the dwelling, and sees that the directions given by Dr. Cameron are carried out by fumigation with chlorine gas, besides enforcing whitewashing by the landlord, and by the removal, if necessary, of infected clothing, or other articles of furniture, to the disinfecting chamber.

4943. And that is done according to the directions of a qualified medical officer?—It is. Dr. Cameron is a chemist of considerable ability, and it is under his direction that it is done.

4944. As to infected articles, how are they treated?—We have got a disinfecting chamber, which was built after the most approved model. I believe there had been only one at the time built in England in 1867. It is available gratuitously for those of the humbler class who cannot pay for the disinfection of any article that may be sent to it by them, or conveyed to it by our van. There is a van for the purpose of conveying articles to and fro. The chamber is available every day in the week.

4945. If persons bring infected articles to the disinfecting chamber, they are disinfected without charge, are they not?—Yes, if they reside within the city. In a few instances rich people have paid for them, but that is an exception.

4946. With regard to the articles that are disinfected, may the owners carry them away without charge?—They may.

4947. You do not insist upon sending them back and making any charge for it?—No, we do not. We have a chamber utterly apart from the disinfecting chamber, to which articles on their disinfection are immediately removed, lest they should come in contact with others that are awaiting disinfection.

4948. Do you approve of the action as it is stated by Dr. Grimshaw, of returning to the owners articles that are disinfected, in the same van in which infected articles are brought to the disinfecting chamber?—I do, for this reason that the articles are carried in the inside of the van when coming to the chamber, and they are

Mr. *Brooks*—continued.

carried on a crib on the outside when returning, but in the interval the van is washed with a solution of chloride of lime, or chloralum. I have never known a second instance of infection occurring in houses to which articles have been returned; that is to say occurring within any reasonable time, within a year or 18 months.

4949. Would it be unreasonable to provide a cab for conveying disinfected articles home?—It is unnecessary.

4950. In the event of any epidemic occurring in Dublin, what provision is available for preventing its spread?—Under the 8th section of the Public Act, 1874, in the event of an epidemic breaking out, the Diseases Prevention Act would be put in force by the orders of the Local Government Board, and then all our sanitary appliances would be transferred to the Board of Guardians who would be solely entrusted with the duty of carrying out that Act, and the corporation would have nothing to do with it.

4951. Is that in consequence of the very large medical staff possessed by the guardians?—Yes, the 14 medical officers are paid from the poor rates, and they are appointed under the Medical Charities Act. Formerly when the Diseases Prevention Act was put in force it was put in force by order of the Privy Council; it would now be put in force by order of the Local Government Board, and as soon as it comes in force the Public Health Committee cease to have anything to do with the prevention of that epidemic.

4952. Their medical officers are in point of fact the medical officers of the Public Health Committee, and the boards of guardians, are they not?—Yes.

4953. As to the condition of the corporation depôts, have you read the evidence?—I have.

4954. Can you give the Committee any information as to those depôts?—Yes, I am responsible for their condition, and therefore I necessarily know something of them.

4955. Will you describe their condition to the Committee?—Their condition is that they are inodourous and inoffensive.

4956. That is, as far as from the nature of things they can be made so?—Beyond their own limits you cannot discover their existence by reason of any odour. They were in a very bad condition some six or seven years ago, but their condition has been materially improved by scattering ashes and other deodourants, such as the scrapings of the streets. Pulverised macadam constitutes a very powerful deodourant, and it is a deodourant which is used elsewhere; in Manchester, for instance. That is spread over the decaying and decomposed organic matter, which finds its way into the depôts.

4957. Is that carefully and regularly performed?—It is; and still more, there is a number of persons who manufacture manure by drawing away the decayed animal and vegetable matter coming from the markets and tempering it with thin calp and ashes, and such like deodourants, and sending it away by boats from the city. These depôts had been so frequently complained of that at last the Local Government Board sent their inspector to examine them. He called on me, and I accompanied him on two occasions over them, but he found no cause for complaint of their condition.

4958. Can you say that sickness prevails more in the vicinity of those depôts than in other parts of

Mr. *Brooks*—continued.

of the city?—There is no undue amount, or unusual amount, of either sickness or mortality in the vicinity of those depôts. In consequence of the complaints that were made of them, I personally inquired into the subject and on several occasions had a house-to-house inspection made throughout their neighbourhoods, and I found that there was no undue or unusual amount either of preventible disease or of mortality in that neighbourhood.

4959. Would not it be better, on the part of the corporation, to have those depôts outside the city?—The corporation made repeated efforts to obtain a site for them in an extra-municipal district, but they failed to do so. The commissioners of Pembroke and other outlying townships, refused to have them within their districts; and although it was attempted, on several occasions, to get up the means for sending the manure out of the city directly, and for establishing depôts remote from the population, we failed to do so, simply for the reason that there is no demand for the manure. It is now given away gratuitously.

4960. Will you state to the Committee why it is that the manure and street sweepings of the city of Dublin are not worth anything, whilst in other towns they are?—The amount of tillage land in the vicinity of Dublin is much less than that in other towns, especially in England. I may mention, as a fact, that a man who paid 40 *l.* a year for many years for portions of the sweepings of the lanes where a large quantity of refuse is cast forth, gave up his contract. It is given to him for nothing, as he is obliged to take it to Kilcock before he can find a market for it.

4961. What is the condition of the private manure yards?—There are only four of them in Dublin, and they are inoffensive, they facilitate the removal of night soil from the yards of tenement houses. There are parties who trade in the manufacture, mixing night soil with ashes, mould, other deodorants, and sending it away at once. There are only four of them, and they have been under strict supervision. They are visited daily by the police, and the moment that they are found to be offensive, or that carelessness in the management occurs, the parties are summoned. In two instances the parties were imprisoned, and in other instances they were fined. They have now from habit got into a method of managing them so carefully that they create no offence, and they facilitate the removal of night soil from the city.

4962. Would not it be better that the night soil should be conveyed at once to our agricultural districts, and not deposited in any yards in the town?—There is a great objection on the part of farmers and others to remove it as it comes from the cesspools; they wish it to be deodorised or tempered with something else; it is less offensive. They do not wish to use their carts for conveying it in its original state.

4963. How long does it remain in those private depôts?—Not more than from two to three days. There is a continual supply and a continual removal going on.

4964. Does it remain there longer than it is necessary to mix it with the deodorising material?—No; those depôts are very near the corporation depôts, where they get a quantity of sweepings, with which they at once temper it and send it off as soon as it is mixed.

Mr. *Brooks*—continued.

Mr. *Boyle*.

20 June 1876.

4965. Will you inform the Committee as to the arrangement made by the Public Health Committee for domestic scavenging?—In consequence of the pressure put upon the owners of tenement houses by the Public Health Committee in compelling them to cleanse their premises, those parties who follow the occupation of cleansing ashpits, and removing the stuff from the yards of the tenement houses, raised the prices to such an enormous amount that the Public Health Committee felt it their duty, in the protection of the public, to interpose, and they then undertook domestic scavenging rather for the purpose of preventing exorbitant prices being charged, and which had the effect, of course, of inducing many people to retain the refuse longer than it should be retained. They, therefore, fixed a tariff of 6 *s.* for the cleansing of each ashpit when the amount to be removed did not exceed two loads, and when the amount exceeded that, they fixed 2 *s.* 6 *d.* per load for the removal of the stuff. The result of that was that the prices which had risen from about 5 *s.* or 6 *s.* for cleansing an ashpit up to 18 *s.* or 20 *s.*, suddenly fell back to about their original amount, and is is now executed for about 8 *s.* The object of the corporation, has thus been accomplished, and they have not, therefore, been called upon to any great extent to carry out domestic scavenging by their own instrumentality.

4966. Have you any further information with regard to domestic scavenging, or any documents in relation to it?—Nothing further than to state that our domestic scavenging department has been utilized in about 2,500 houses.

4967. In the case of a difficulty with regard to what are called night-men in the city of Dublin, the Public Health Committee provided a moderate charge for the cleansing of ashpits and privies, and other receptacles for domestic refuse?—Precisely. I should have mentioned another object that we have accomplished, which was that when parties were summoned before the magistrates for not having their premises cleansed, or for sanitarily neglecting them, they stated that they could not get the work done, that there were not the parties to do it. The getting up of the corporation establishment took away that pretext, and as a consequence the tenement houses are much more rapidly cleansed than they had previously been.

4968. You have in Dublin an amateur sanitary association, have you not?—Yes.

4969. And that has upon its roll many of the most eminent of our citizens?—Yes.

4970. Are you open to any complaints from that body?—Most certainly, and we very gladly receive them from them, or from any others.

4971. Do you attend to those complaints?—We pay the same attention to those complaints as we do to the complaints made by the medical officers of the dispensaries, namely, that the moment they come in they are immediately referred to the sanitary sergeant of the district; his report is endorsed on them, and the complaint and the report come before the committee at their next meeting, when the action taken is considered by the committee in order to ascertain whether sufficiently prompt and satisfactory measures have been taken.

4972. Do you refer them also when necessary to the sanitary medical officer?—Dr. Mapother is our consulting sanitary officer, and when any difficulty

Mr. Brooks—continued.

Mr. *Boyle*.

20 June 1876.

difficulty occurs that requires medical intervention, we immediately refer to him.

4973. Are you aware of any complaints from the Dublin Sanitary Association that have passed without attention?—I have known of no instance being disregarded where the circumstances demanded it. I have very often differed from them as to the existence of the cause of complaint. I have some complaints here, just as illustrations of the manner in which we deal with them (*producing the same*). Those complaints began on the 14th of October 1873, and I take them at random. I attended to No. 1 myself. "No. 2. rear of 80, Meath-street, ashpit and privy filthy; drain in bad order; choked up and almost useless." The endorsement of the sanitary inspector on that item is, "Attended to before receipt of complaint." "No. 3. Neill's-court; houses in this court filthy and dilapidated; need whitewashing; open drain lately put in, but the whole place wants a thorough overhauling. Febrile disease, and diarrhœa, constant here." The endorsement on that is, "Attended to before receipt of complaint."

Mr. *Gibson*.

4974. Is there the date of the reception of the complaint and the date of the report, showing the interval between them?—This was dated the 14th of October 1873, and I have marked it myself: "Received 15th October 1873;" and it was acknowledged by me on the 20th of the same month.

4975. What is the date of the report of your sanitary serjeant?—Before the 20th.

4976. So that there was an interval of five days?—No, pardon me; I do not convey myself properly. That was received on the 15th, and it was acknowledged by me on the 20th; it could not be acknowledged until the next Wednesday; or until the sanitary sergeant had made a report.

4977. There was an interval of five days between the receipt of the complaint and the statement sent back to the Sanitary Association, that the subject of complaint was redressed before the receipt of the complaint?—Yes.

Mr. *Brooks*.

4978. Does the Sanitary Association sit daily?—No, they sit on Thursdays.

4979. If their report came to you on the Friday, the day after their sitting, it would be quite useless to send any reply to it until their next meeting?—Yes; also I should not reply to it until I had submitted it to my own committee.

4980. But it would be useless to send it to them until they met again?—Yes, certainly.

4981. And by that time you would have the opportunity of giving the latest information?—Yes; besides it is an order of the committee that all such statements be submitted to them.

4982. A reference has been made to the house No. 18 in Ardee-street; have you had many complaints of that house?—Yes, that has been a very fertile source of complaint.

4983. Ardee-street is in the very worst part of the city, is it not?—Yes, in a very bad portion of the city. We had so many complaints from the sanitary association with regard to No. 18, Ardee-street, that at last I urged the attention of the committee to it, saying that I could not find any cause for complaint. Dr. Mapother was unable to discover any cause of complaint.

Mr. Brooks—continued.

4984. Have you any report from Dr. Mapother?—I have not a report from Dr. Mapother, but I have a report from a sub-Committee of the Public Health Committee, who inspected the premises in consequence of the repeated complaints which came from the Sanitary Association with reference to No. 18, Ardee-street. I asked the Public Health Committee to visit the premises and they did so, and I will read their report: "Read letters of 3rd and 7th July 1873 from Dublin Sanitary Association, transmitting list of six alleged nuisances of which one had been acted on before, and three since receipt of letter; in two cases no cause existed." The letter of the 7th contained the following statement, viz.: "18, Ardee-street. In the usual state frequently reported to the Public Health Committee; is always a hot-bed of disease; was severely visited by cholera in the year 1866; furnished three cases of fever to hospital, 1869-70; seven cases of small-pox, 1871, and since two cases of enteric fever. The room in which fever has occurred has been disinfected. That the committee, having heard of the report of the inspection committee in the house 18, Ardee-street, and having considered the previous history of the house, and the opinion expressed in the letter of the secretary of the Public Health Committee of the 27th November 1872, 'demolition and re-construction of the house alone could render it as perfect as could be desired,' are of opinion that it is the duty of that body to have this house permanently closed as a place unfit for human habitation." When I received that report, I made a report upon it myself, which was as follows: "There is not, in my opinion, anything in this house to warrant an application to have it closed, and the amount of disease occurring in it is not greater than that, to my knowledge, in houses in more favoured localities and occupied by more favourable families. It is a fair sample of about 1,600 or 1,700 houses in the city, for whose occupants, numbering fully 20,000 souls, provision must be made, if all houses, even inferior to this, shall be closed. The house in question possesses no inordinate attraction for disease; it is reasonably clean, water-fast, and, save the windows, in a moderate state of repair. It is provided with proper sanitary accommodation. I adhere to my report, referred to by the Sanitary Association." Signed "James Boyle." In reference thereto, it was moved by Councillor M'Cormick, M.D., "That Councillors Byrne, Reilly, and Lawlor be appointed a sub-committee, with request that they will favour the committee by at once proceeding to 18, Ardee-street, and by immediately reporting on the condition of that house and premises. Motion put, and carried." The request of the committee having been complied with, the sub-committee presented the following as their report, viz.: "Upon reading the report of the Sanitary Association of 7th July 1873 in relation to 18, Ardee-street, we, the undersigned, went to the premises and visited them from top to bottom with the surroundings. We found the house old and decayed, but the rooms were clean, the walls were limewashed, including the walls of the staircase; the inhabitants are very poor, and pay very small rents. We found no nuisance or offensive odour on the premises; the floor required repair, but their

Mr. *Brooks*—continued.

their state, although worn out, was clean, and we consider the report of our officers fully borne out in relation to this house. None of the inhabitants are sick, nor do they complain of the owner of the house having neglected any sanitary requirement. The house is provided with privy, ashpit, and house drain." That is dated the 11th of July 1873, and signed by John Byrne, James Reilly, and W. T. Lawlor, and then there was the following order: "Report to be forwarded to Sanitary Association, and to be given to the press."

4985. With regard to those gentlemen who signed that report, are they not amongst the most active and intelligent members of the Public Health Committee?—They are; not only are they amongst the most active, but one of them, Mr. Byrne, I should say, is the ablest member that we have; he was one of the most able supporters of the introduction of the Sanitary Act, and he has a great knowledge of sanitary jurisprudence and the science of every-day life; he has been one of our most valuable aids in promoting sanitary matters throughout the city; he is most anxious for it, and he has given a large amount of time, care, and attention to it, and has a most intimate knowledge of the subject.

4986. May the same be said with respect to Mr. Reilly and Mr. Lawlor?—Yes; all these are gentlemen who are intimately connected with the local and charitable institutions, and have a great knowledge of the social habits of the people.

4987. Have you any copies of the correspondence with the Local Government Board with reference to domestic scavenging?—Yes.

4988. In consequence of the corporation having refused the request of the Sanitary Association to carry out the domestic scavenging, and to cleanse the ashpits and privies of the citizens without charge, the Sanitary Association addressed the Local Government Board upon the subject, and a correspondence ensued between the Local Government Board and the Public Health Committee. Soon after, the Local Government Board forwarded their reply to the Sanitary Association and to the Public Health Committee, stating that the corporation had been active both before and since the Public Health Act of 1874, in putting the Sanitary Act in force in cleansing ashpits and privies, and they did not feel called upon to require the corporation to put the 39th section of the Act in force for cleansing ashpits and privies. The Sanitary Association made another attempt with the Local Government Board by a memorial, and they received a somewhat similar reply.

4989. Will you confine yourself to the correspondence between the Public Health Committee and the Local Government Board, because what has been done between a certain Sanitary Association and the Local Government Board, is not the subject of inquiry here?—The correspondence is dated the 14th of May 1875, when there was a letter addressed by the Local Government Board to the Public Health Committee.

4990. This letter has been already referred to; had you any other correspondence with the Local Government Board?—Nothing in relation to domestic scavenging. We had two letters from them on the occasion of the application to put the 39th section in force, and a renewed application on the same subject.

Mr. *Brooks*—continued.

Mr. *Boyle*.

20 June 1876.

4990.* As to the operation of the manure depôts; had you any correspondence with the Local Government Board?—No, we have had no correspondence with the Local Government Board. The inspector called upon me, and I accompanied him to several depôts in the city, and minutely inspected them all, and ascertained that they were inoffensive, and he expressed himself to that effect to me. There was no communication or complaint addressed to us. He unexpectedly called on me, and I immediately accompanied him to all the depôts, and although he saw them under unfavourable circumstances he expressed his opinion that they were inoffensive.

4991. What was the name of that gentleman?—Captain Robinson, who is now the Assistant Under Secretary for Ireland.

4992. With regard to the condition of the dairy yards; have you read the evidence of Dr. Grimshaw?—Yes.

4993. Have you any information to give the Committee upon that subject?—I have. The only means that we have of dealing with the dairy yards is when, by reason of the accumulations of manure, they become offensive, and then we can deal with them as with any other accumulation, but we have no power or means of dealing with the manner in which the cattle are kept, so long as they are not kept in an uncleanly state; but they are nevertheless in a most unsatisfactory condition. So much so that I personally reported to the Public Health Committee; perhaps I may be allowed to bring this matter before this Committee. In July 1875 I called the attention of the committee to the dairy yards; I measured a very large number of cow-houses, and I found that the average cubic space that the cattle had was little more than about 250 feet, whilst in London the minimum space is fixed at 600 feet. I asked that some legislation should be suggested in relation to that, and the Committee adopted my recommendation. I will hand in to the Committee a document, containing reports, correspondence, and resolution, in relation to dairy yards, a sanitarium for sick cattle, their slaughter, and sale; the keeping of pigs, and also as to the deficiencies in the existing powers of sanitary authorities in Ireland; the report is dated July 1875 (*delivering in the same*).

4994. Has this report been published?—Yes.

Mr. *Collins*.

4995. To whom was that report made?—It was made by me to the Public Health Committee, when calling their attention to the necessity of legislation with regard to the dairy yards.

Mr. *Brooks*.

4996. Will you state what legislation it was which you suggested?—That a minimum amount of cubic space should be assigned for the cattle, because at present they are so packed together that two adjoining cannot lie down at the same time; the head room is utterly insufficient; they absorb from each other's bodies their impurities; they inhale each other's breaths, and there is not sufficient head room to permit of the escape of the exhalations from their lungs or from their bodies. There should be more strict provisions also for the flooring, draining, and sewerage of the yards.

4997. What is the condition of the health of the

Mr. *Brooks*—continued.

Mr. *Boyle*.

30 June 1876.

the cattle which are kept in those yards?—I think there is an undue amount of pleuro-pneumonia arising from the manner in which the animals are kept; I consider that the amount of pleuro-pneumonia would be greatly diminished if the animals had a greater amount of air space.

4998. Is not the risk to the property of the owners in itself a guarantee that the health of the animals will not be neglected?—They do not seem to consider it so; I was obliged myself to thin out about 140 head of cattle from the dairy yards adjoining the House of Industry Hospital. I found there 143 or 144 animals greater than I thought the space could possibly contain. The parties were summoned and brought into court, and we obtained a magistrate's order for the removal of the animals, but it was with very great difficulty that we obtained a conviction.

4999. Is it your opinion that although those dairy yards are over-crowded, they are not in such a condition as to demand the interference of the magistrates?—The magistrates cannot interfere in that particular point; there is a want of authority for their interference, because the law does not enable them; we got those removed under very peculiar circumstances. We brought an amount of medical evidence to bear upon it, and the parties found that we were too strong for them, so that we could ensure the removal of the animals from the place. They found that it would have involved them in continual litigation with the corporation if they had not submitted.

Chairman.

5000. You have obtained what you require under the present law?—Yes, but we cannot now effect the removal when the animals are crowded, though a nuisance is thereby created.

Mr. *Gibson*.

5001. What section did you proceed under?—It is under the head of nuisances; I cannot refer to the section at the present moment, but I think it is the 20th Section.

Mr. *Collins*.

5002. In what year did you institute those proceedings?—In the year 1868.

5003. The law affecting inquiries of that kind has been altered since that time, has it not?—No, it remains as it was.

Mr. *Brooks*

5004. Did you go as far in your attempts to remedy the over-crowding in the dairy yards as the law enabled you to do?—Yes; this case was an exceptional one; there were not merely dairy cattle there, but parties were in the habit of bringing in bullocks for fattening, and the authorities of the hospital found such an offensive odour emanating from them, that they interfered, and we were enabled to make out a case against them; we have failed in other somewhat similar cases, perhaps not quite so strong.

5005. Then do I understand you that the present condition of the dairy yards is offensive still, but that it is not of such a nature as to warrant you to engage the interference of the magistrates?—We could not remove them unless they are in such a condition as to be injurious to health, and that is the reason why we do not proceed against them.

5006. Has anything further been done in that direction?—Yes; about four years ago we made an effort in one case, and failed in it; we knew that we had not the power, unless we could prove that the condition of the dairy yard was directly injurious to health by reason of the manner in which the cattle were kept in them; we knew that we should fail, and therefore we have not attempted it.

Mr. *Brooks*—continued.

5007. You were not able to prove that the condition of the dairy yards was injurious to the public health?—No.

5008. Do you recollect what was said by Dr. Grimshaw with regard to the existence of the dairy yard in the immediate vicinity of Mercer's Hospital?—I do; I prosecuted in that case myself; the report which I have put in refers to it; a description and a plan of the yard is given in it. It was that dairy yard that called forth that report which I have now put in.

5009. Dr. Grimshaw in his evidence, in reply to Question 3962, said: "I have visited a great many of them; they are in an extremely filthy condition; they have large accumulations of manure. Those are very much like the scavenging depôts that I mentioned; they pile up this manure till it reaches above the walls sometimes of the yards;" do you think that is correct?—I have never seen anything of that kind.

5010. He went on to say: "There have been great complaints about those yards, especially where they come near public institutions; the Mercers' Hospital, for instance, complain that there is a dairy yard situated next to the hospital, and large accumulations of manure take place in that yard, I have seen it myself;" what have you to say with regard to that?—I have made a report on that.

5011. Will you read your report upon it?—The report was called for by a letter addressed by Dr. Morgan, the surgeon of Mercers' Hospital, to the Local Government Board, by whom his letter was sent on to the Public Health Committee. The committee desired that I should report upon it, and I presented a report dated 22nd of July 1875, in these terms: "Gentlemen,—Pursuant to your order of the 16th July, that I should report on this subject, I have the honour to submit the following statement for your information, and to refer you to the accompanying sketch plan. On the 23rd March 1875 a complaint was made by the authorities of Mercers' Hospital of the nuisance and injury caused to the patients by the condition of an adjoining dairy yard, the property of Andrew Moore. The dairy yard was at once inspected, and found to contain 70 cows, four pigs, and four horses, all of which were kept in a fairly clean condition. The yard was paved, sewered, and, with the exception of a heap of manure, amounting to about 30 loads, was in a cleanly state. The heap was situated at a point A. (on sketch plan), about 26 feet from the hospital grounds, and 35 feet from the window in the corridor referred to in Dr. Morgan's communication. On visiting the hospital (on same day) I found that the odour from the manure (then in process of partial removal) entered the window referred to, and that it was disagreeably perceptible in this portion of the institution. A notice to remove the entire heap of manure within 48 hours was served on the 24th March, and being disregarded, a summons followed, and a magistrate's order to remove the manure

Mr. *Brooks*—continued.

manure within 48 hours, and to remove all future accumulations on every second day, was obtained on the 14th April, when the law agent attended and prosecuted. An order was also made that all future accumulations should be deposited wherever I might direct, and I fixed the point B. as being the most remote, viz., 46 feet from the hospital grounds and 85 from the windows in question. These orders have been carried into effect. Early in May the cattle were removed to the grazing lands, and since then a pig and two horses have been the only animals kept here, save occasionally during the night preceding or succeeding a market. This dairy yard is entered from Digges-lane, and for its entire length on its northern side (108 feet) is bounded by the hospital grounds. It possesses ample air space, and has a good fall westward. Its condition is above an average. In point of fact there are not any dairy yards in the city in better condition. As the course therefore to be pursued with respect to the dairy-yard in Digges-lane should be applied to many others, I would beg to direct the attention of the Committee to Section 8 of 18 & 19 Vict. c. 121, by which, as the law now stands, they are empowered to deal with the keeping of animals, and to suggest that so long as this dairy yard continues to be maintained as it has hitherto been, they are utterly powerless, except in respect of accumulations of manure, inasmuch as that it is perfectly possible, by keeping the animals in a cleanly state, to exempt them from any interference; and, therefore, that should an "accumulation" exist, it is the "accumulation," and not the "animals," against which proceedings should be instituted. This is to be regretted, for in Dublin hundreds of dairy cattle are, through the absence of power to interfere, maintained in a condition which, by reason of insufficient cubic space, must, in a variety of ways, affect their own condition, and necessarily, therefore, the health of those by whom their milk or their flesh is consumed. By referring to the sketch, it will be found that the cubic space allotted to each cow varies from 195 to 399 feet, and that in the majority of cases it does not exceed 240 feet, while I have ascertained that in London the minimum cubic space is fixed by law at 600 feet. I have in Dublin calculated the cubic space in nearly 400 cases, and found it to average about 268. Whatever objections may apply to the dairy yard in Digges-lane, they are trivial when compared with those which are applicable to the dairy yards which adjoin the House of Industry Hospitals, and especially to those which adjoin the Richmond (Surgical) Hospital on the south, and the Hardwicke (Fever) on their eastern sides. In these yards an average number of about 470 head of cattle are kept during winter, and in a condition that urgently demands an amendment, in this respect, in sanitary legislation. The cubic space allotted to the animals in these yards averages about 230 feet; through the insufficient space of three feet in breadth, no two adjacent animals can at the same time lie down; their close proximity renders it impossible to cleanse their bodies; through the same cause they absorb the exhalations from the bodies of each other, from their lungs, the ammonia from their urine, and also the effluvia from their manure. Their sheds are barely 6 feet 6 inches in height under the lintels; they are not ventilated, and their thatched roofs are saturated with the exhalations from breath; their standings are insufficiently long, and they are imperfectly floored. Animals thus kept cannot be in a healthy state; their blood, and therefore their flesh and their milk, must be in a more or less unhealthy condition, and predisposed to pleuro-pneumonia, lung distempers, and other diseases. I would, therefore, submit that, as the existing law is insufficient to remedy such a state of things, increased legislative power in this respect is urgently required, and should be sought for by sanitary authorities in Ireland. In connection with the subject of dairy yards, I would suggest the establishment of a sanitarium for the reception of cattle suffering from lung distemper, for those suspected of being affected, and those in the incipient state of disease;" and so on.

Mr. *Boyle*.

30 June 1876.

5012. Then the object of this report is to obtain further remedial legislation?—It is.

5013. Did the Public Health Committee exercise such powers as they had to their utmost extent?—Yes, to their utmost extent.

5014. Have you any return of the quantity of unsound food that is confiscated?—Yes; the return which I have handed in sets it forth.

5015. Would the confiscation be increased if the sanitary staff was larger?—Yes, we require an increased sanitary staff; I think that the confiscations would probably diminish from an increase of the sanitary staff, as it would act more as a preventive measure. Until the establishment of the sanitary staff, there was a systematic trade carried on in the sale and preparation from a sale of unsound and diseased meat bought up from a distance of some 30 or 40 miles around Dublin. Latterly our operations have been more of a preventive character than of actual confiscation.

5016. Your sanitary staff at present is limited, is it not, by the funds at your disposal?—Yes, the funds are insufficient to maintain a proper sanitary staff.

5017. Do you maintain a staff quite as large as your funds enable you to pay?—Yes, and the fund from whence we derive our resources is in debt.

5018. From what source do you derive your funds?—From the borough fund; the fund indicated by Act of Parliament.

5019. Has the borough fund been supplemented from any sources since the institution of the Public Health Committee?—No, it has not.

5020. And therefore the sum expended by the Sanitary Committee and drawn from the borough fund lessens to that extent the fund at the disposal of the committee for other purposes?—Yes. It has been officially reported to me that the borough fund has been overdrawn.

5021. Have there been any official reports as to the sufficiency or insufficiency of the borough fund?—Yes, it has been reported to the committee that greater economy must be practised, for the fund was not equal to the demands upon it.

5022. When you say "economy," what do you mean?—When I speak of economy, I know that it is unable to meet the requirements of the Public Health Committee, and our requirements are every day increasing.

5023. You mean the withdrawal of the funds from other objects of expenditure?—Yes.

5024. What has been the amount expended by the Sanitary Committee?—£. 21,546., as appears in the return which I have handed in.

5025. A statement

Mr. *Brooks*—continued.

Mr. *Boyle*

20 June 1876.

5025. A statement was made here by a witness, Mr. Pim, that persons habitually dwell over slaughter-houses in Dublin; is that so?—That is not the fact. I was present when Mr. Pim made that statement, and I immediately wrote to the sanitary inspector of the district, and desired him to search every slaughter-house on the south side of the city. Mr. Pim referred to a particular place, and I have got the report of the sanitary inspector here in which he denies it, and says that it is not possible to have slept in the place which Mr. Pim mentioned, for the simple reason that there is no loft over it.

5026. Do you know whether there are any dwellings over slaughter-houses in the City of Dublin?—No, there are not.

5027. Have you made any inquiry of the sanitary sergeants or inspecting officer?—I have. I will read his report, dated the 19th of May 1876: "With reference to Mr. Pim's evidence, referred to in your letter, I beg to state that on this day I inspected the several slaughter-houses in Castle Market, and I find that there is no dwelling place, or even a loft over any slaughter-house there. Consequently it would be impossible for any person to sleep over them. And I may add that I have known these slaughter-houses and all the slaughter-houses on the south side of the city since the year 1861, and I have never known an instance of people sleeping over a slaughter-house, and it could not have occurred without my knowledge. I beg to remark that the access to Quinn's slaughter-house, in Joseph's-lane, is by a gateway under a dwelling; but the slaughter-house, which is well kept, is beyond 16 feet from the back wall of the dwelling-house." I went up myself to see the slaughter-house, and I found that report to be accurate.

5028. Have you, as secretary to the Public Health Committee, any suggestions to offer as to amendments in the Sanitary Act?—Yes, I have.

5029. Have you some report which has been adopted by the corporation upon that subject?—Yes; in consequence of this inquiry the corporation passed a resolution directing the several committees to report to them what amendments in their several Acts and laws affecting the discharge of their duties would be desirable; and I drew up a report, which was adopted by my own committee, the Public Health Committee, and which was also ratified by the council; I will put it in (*delivering in the same*).

5030. Will you state to the Committee the nature of the suggestions which you offered; first, will you give us the requirements?—What presses most upon us and impedes us most is the complex proceedings that we are obliged to adopt for the abatement of the simplest or the most serious nuisance. A period of six weeks has on several occasions occurred in the suppression of a nuisance. Under the existing law so many as eleven forms are required, and the expenditure of time and of money is proportionately great. Our diminished sanitary staff would accomplish a greater amount of work if their proceedings were shortened; and as the prosecutions take place under my direction, and the sanitary staff is under my control, I offered them my experience in the matter, and suggested that the forms now in use should be reduced from 11 to six, and that all sanitary offences should be treated as ordinary police offences, that when the penalty was imposed, it should be either levied or the party imprisoned. At present we are hampered by the number of forms, which account, especially in the case of tenement houses, for the long delay which often occurs in abating a nuisance. I have brought copies of those forms which I suggest should be discontinued, and also of those which I suggest should be retained (*producing the same*).

5031. Can you state shortly the nature of the amendments which you suggest?—First of all, I would simplify the proceedings by a reduction of the number of forms, and thereby enable the magistrates to deal more promptly with those complaints.

5032. Could those amendments be effected without a change of the law?—The intervention of Parliament is necessary in dispensing with any of the forms.

5033. As to the nature of the changes which you suggest to be made in the law, what are they?—"Under the present state of the law a period exceeding six weeks has on several occasions elapsed through the vexatious contumacy of individuals before the abatement of the nuisances could be effected. In the time expended by the sanitary staff in repeated inspections in the service of the numerous forms required, and by their attendance at courts, &c., some of these cases involved an expense exceeding 3 *l.*, while in the majority of the cases brought before the magistrates, three hearings of each case have been necessary to ensure convictions, and more than double the amount of time which should be required has been needlessly wasted. When it is borne in mind that over 4,000 cases are annually adjudicated, some idea may be formed of the economy of time that may be accomplished by a reduction in the number of forms and of inspections. Your committee beg to submit some other amendments which their experience of the working of the Sanitary Acts has suggested."

Chairman.

5034. There are some points in your evidence about the dairy yards which I should like to have rather more clear. The Act under which the Public Health Committee can take proceedings against such yards is, I believe, the 18 & 19 Vict. c. 121?—It is.

5035. I notice that the 8th section of that Act defines a nuisance as including "any animal so kept as to be a nuisance or injurious to health; any accumulation or deposit which is a nuisance or injurious to health;" and some subsequent sections authorise the local authority, in this case the Public Health Committee, to proceed before the justices in such cases, and allow the justices to make an order for the abatement of the nuisance by carrying away the accumulation or deposit which is a nuisance or injurious to health, or by providing "for the cleanly and wholesome keeping of the animal kept, so as to be a nuisance or injurious to health, or if it be proved to the justices to be impossible so to provide, then to remove the animal," "or to do such other works or acts as are necessary to abate the nuisance complained of." I do not quite understand what point it is in which the existing law is in your opinion deficient?—As to cubic space.

5036. Your suggestion was, I think, that the law should lay down a certain number of cubic feet as necessary for every animal?—Yes.

5037. But under those sections the justices may

Chairman—continued.

may, if they are convinced that the animals in question have not a sufficient number of cubic feet of space allotted to them, convict those animals as injurious to health?—They will not do so.

5038. Have you tried that question, and have you failed?—Perhaps you will allow me to answer that question by stating that we brought it under the consideration of our law agent, and I have got his opinion here.

5039. Will you read his opinion?—"Pursuant to your order of the 17th instant, I beg to report (having ascertained from your secretary) that the section already adopted by your committee in reference to the case, the subject of Dr. Morgan's communication to the Local Government Board, consisted of the proceedings taken by summons against Andrew Moore on the 14th April 1875, for suffering an accumulation of manure in the dairy yard at Digges-lane, when an order was made for the collection of the manure at a remote part of the yard from the hospital, and for its removal every second day. If strict compliance with this order, which can be enforced by close supervision, has not the effect of abating the nuisance complained of, I cannot suggest any other action to your committee. As, however, it would appear from Dr. Morgan's communication, page 7 of copy, that even 'cleanliness strictly enforced would not remedy the evil,' the case seems to me to come within the 13th section of the Nuisance Removal Act, 1855; and if it be 'proved' to the magistrates that it is impossible so to provide for the keeping of animals in this place as to prevent their being a nuisance, or injurious to health, they have power to order the removal of the animals, I beg to remind your committee that the magistrates are slow indeed to make orders calculated to affect the means of livelihood of persons engaged in more noxious occupations than that of dairy keeper; and on this account the proof to be offered in any proceeding, because the removal of animals in this or like cases should be convincing upon the reference as to the powers of your committee to control cubic space for animals, I beg to report that no such powers exist."

5040. Did the Public Health Committee try whether, in accordance with that opinion of your law agent, the magistrates would convict the animals in those cases, on account of its being impossible to provide for their being kept there, so as to prevent their being a nuisance or injurious to health?—We did not, and for this reason, that our consulting sanitary officer would not certify that the manner in which the animals were kept, or that the cubic space constituted a nuisance injurious to the public health.

5041. Then in suggesting that the law shall define 600 cubic feet at the least to be allotted to each animal, you are suggesting a number far in excess of that which your sanitary officer considered necessary for the public health?—No, I would suggest, not the extreme cubic space that they have taken in London where the air space is less, but having regard to the circumstances of Dublin I should say 400 feet in Dublin would be equal to 600 in London.

5042. But even that would be considerably in excess of what, in this instance, your sanitary officer considered sufficient?—Yes, he had regard to the surroundings of that dairy yard. It is a

Chairman—continued.

dairy yard with an unusually large amount of air space; the sun's rays have access to it. It is on the slope of a hill, and lies exceedingly well with great facilities for drainage. Having regard to all those surroundings he thought that in that part a diminished amount of cubic space was less objectionable than a greater amount of space where the place was more confined.

5043. Would not the same reasoning apply to other cases also, that supposing you were to fix any limit, and govern yourselves entirely by that, that limit would apply in some cases and not in others?—That is so, but the magistrates are very slow to act on it in Dublin.

5044. One of the yards in question is within a very few feet of the corridor and corner window of the Mercers' Hospital?—Yes.

5045. In the other case which you have told us of, the dairy yards adjoining the House of Industry Hospitals and the Richmond Surgical Hospital, were even in your opinion worse than that adjoining the Mercers' Hospital?—Yes.

5046. In those cases also did your consulting sanitary officer consider that the cubic space allotted to the animals was sufficient for health?—He was unwilling to give a certificate in that case. He gave evidence, and so did several other medical men previous to the reduction of the number of animals, but he could not go any further than that. We reduced the number of animals by 148.

5047. Did I understand you to say that any further powers were necessary to be given to the Public Health Committee to prevent accumulations of manure?—No; we have ample power under our existing Acts, and we enforce it.

5048. You told us that you have a system of cleansing ashpits and privies, and in the report which you have handed in you gave us some figures as to the number of cases in which that system had been applied; in the Report for 1875 I see that 6,708 cases of that kind are stated?—I refer to enforced cleansing by the owners; notices having been served upon them.

5049. In how many cases did you carry out your system?—In none of those. In 1875 I think there was 212. It was carried out by a separate department, but I get copies of the Returns.

5050. This Return does not show that, does it?—No.

5051. Then in fact, practically speaking, there is no public system of cleansing ashpits and privies in Dublin?—No, only so far as this, that while our system exists it prevents those parties who are employed in the business from charging exorbitant sums. It also takes away the pretext which has been frequently set up by the owners of tenement houses before the magistrates, that they cannot get their work done by anyone, and that they are obliged to wait. That need not be so when the corporation has the means available for the purpose.

5052. Dr. Grimshaw told us that your charges were so high that the system was practically inoperative, and that private persons could do it cheaper, and those figures appear to carry out that charge?—This is a circular (*producing the same*) which has been put forth by No. 1 Committee who execute this work, in which they state that the charge is 6 *s.* for cleansing an ashpit containing two loads; that charge, I think, cannot

Mr. *Boyle.*

20 June 1876.

Mr. *Boyle.*

20 June 1876.

Chairman—continued.

cannot be considered as too high. I believe it is a moderate charge.

Mr. *Kavanagh.*

5053. Are the people able to pay it?—Yes. The parties who own tenement houses are amongst the richest people in Dublin. It has now become a business of itself. There are about 1,207 tenement houses in Dublin owned by five individuals.

Chairman.

5054. There are 24,000 houses in Dublin altogether you told us, and there were 8,700 of those places cleansed by private individuals, and rather more than 200 by your own agents; what happened to the rest?—They were cleansed voluntarily without our interference. The continued visits of the police induced the parties to be more prompt in cleansing them; but in those 8,000 cases it was necessary to proceed by notice or by summons against them. Some parties cleansed them on receipt of the notice, but it was necessary to bring others into court.

5055. Are we to take it that, in your opinion, all the ashpits and privies of those 24,000 houses are properly cleansed by private parties, and that in only 8,700 cases it was necessary to compel this cleansing?—That is the fact. Of course there may be some exceptions, but as a rule, in the private houses, they are properly cleansed. As to those 8,700 houses, I would go further and state this, that I know several cases in which it has been necessary to proceed against them in three or four instances within the year to compel them to cleanse them, so habitually negligent were the parties. So that you cannot take it as being 8,700 houses. Probably there would not be more than 7,000 houses, but there were 8,700 cleansings.

5056. What has been the result of those proceedings?—In some instances it was only necessary to serve a notice; in other instances, where the magistrate's order was served on them, they did the work. A sanitary offence does not become penal till the magistrate's order is disobeyed. The disobeying of the sanitary notice does not entail any consequences of a penal character whatever. But if the magistrate's order is disobeyed the penalties are levied. But with regard to cleansing, it very rarely goes so far as the imposition of a penalty.

5057. What means have you of knowing that this cleansing is properly done?—I should know of it directly from the supervision that I exercise over the city, and from the complaints from the neighbouring parties who would complain of the nuisance.

5058. So far as your officers are concerned, am I to understand that the nine sanitary sergeants are the only persons whose duty it is to inspect those 24,000 houses, and see that the work is properly done?—I am aware that we have only nine inspectors of nuisances now, but the medical sanitary officers report all nuisances which in the course of their duty they perceive. We have received from them altogether about 2,000 sanitary reports, and about one-half of those refer to nuisances. We had 15 sergeants until recently, when Sir Henry Lake removed six of the men whose services he had given gratuitously; he was obliged to remove them in consequence of the corporation not being able to

Chairman—continued.

comply with his desire that we should pay them. We had had them gratuitously for several years.

5059. They were not removed because their services were not required?—No, their services are much required.

5060. In your opinion is a much larger staff required than exists?—Decidedly so.

5061. What sort of staff do you consider competent to carry out all this work?—I prefer one policeman to two civilians; it is sanitary police as the inspectors of nuisances that we require.

5062. How many?—Fifteen would be quite sufficient for the purpose.

5063. Has the corporation any power to levy a special rate for sanitary purposes?—They have power to levy a rate in aid; but raising that rate in aid is surrounded by a great many difficulties. The subject has been frequently considered by them, and my opinion is that a direct and distinct sanitary rate would be preferable to a rate in aid.

5064. They have never done so, have they?—No.

5065. But in your opinion the power that they have now, I understand, should be exercised?—Yes.

Mr. *Brooks.*

5066. Besides the nine sanitary sergeants, I would ask if the police generally have not duties with regard to public nuisances, that is to say are they not bound to make reports?—They are not bound to make reports; but through the very great assistance that we have derived from Sir Henry Lake, he has given instructions to the police force generally, as a body, to assist us in every possible way, and they have furthered us very greatly. They go so far as to regard it as a portion of their duty to report anything that they hear or see that is in contravention of the sanitary law. The execution of sanitary duties is not imposed on the police by any Act of Parliament.

5067. To supplement the action of the sanitary sergeants, do you mean?—No, only so far as mentioning the occurrence of a nuisance or anything that requires attention. They have been the means of seizing very large quantities of diseased meat in the streets while on their beat.

Sir *Arthur Guinness.*

5068. Do you consider that 1,800 *l.* a year is sufficient for the sanitary purposes in Dublin?—Certainly not.

5069. How much do you think would be a proper estimate?—My estimate would be 3,100 *l.* a year.

5070. You are aware that the corporation could supply that money if necessary, and if they desired to do so?—They could; but the difficulties of supplementing the borough fund by a rate are very great. The corporation have had it under their consideration on many occasions. Taking into consideration the preparation of estimates, and looking beforehand, and a variety of other matters in connection with it, I think that there would be a great deal of trouble and difficulty in connection with it, and I think it would be much more satisfactory to have a distinct sanitary rate.

5071. What are your duties as executive sanitary officer?—My duties as executive sanitary officer are to communicate with the Local Government Board

Sir A. Guinness—continued.

Board our proceedings, sending them copies of the minutes, communicating the orders of the committee, and seeing that they are carried out.

5072. Is this a correct description of your duties: "General secretarial duties, direction of sanitary staff and proceedings, all duties involving civil engineering knowledge, including plans and giving evidence"?—Yes.

5073. Do you think that one person is able to undertake and carry out all these duties satisfactorily?—It gives me a great deal to do, but I find that I am quite equal to the work.

5074. Who is your assistant?—I have a clerk.

5075. What is his name?—Robert Alcock.

5076. Could you tell me what his hours at the city hall are?—He is supposed to be there from 10 till four; those are the corporation hours.

5077. You would be surprised, perhaps, to know that very often there is no one there to represent you?—I should say not very often; my duties require me frequently to go about town about cases wherein structural works are involved; but it is very seldom indeed that I have not some one to represent me in my office.

5078. What is this gentleman's salary?—£ 52 a year.

5079. Are you satisfied with the way in which the public health committee carries out its duties?—I am.

5080. Have you ever expressed a contrary opinion?—I have never expressed a contrary opinion; we may have differed on very slight matters; they accord to me the privilege of expressing my opinion upon all occasions; but I believe it is impossible for any body of men to have brought to bear a greater amount of unanimity, exertion, and intelligence in the discharge of these very difficult duties than the Public Health Committee have done.

5081. Can you state, as a fact, that the officers of the Public Health Committee court assistance from the public in supplying them with reports of nuisances?—Yes.

5082. I think you said that you valued the assistance of the sanitary association?—I am exceedingly grateful to any person who gives information of nuisances where our staff is so small, for it directs attention to the spot and saves the time occupied in looking for nuisances.

5083. Are you aware that a great many reports of sanitary associations were not attended to by the corporation?—I am aware that some were not.

5084. For what reason?—There were various reasons; I will mention some of them; some of them were couched in a spirit that was considered scarcely courteous, and which seemed to invite newspaper correspondence rather than the abatement of nuisances, and the Public Health Committee do not care for such correspondence.

5085. Did the Public Health Committee refuse to give the Sanitary Association any information upon the subject of the slaughter yards of Dublin?—Yes, they did.

5086. Does that exactly agree with your statement that you were glad to have their assistance?—Yes, having regard to the circumstances it does not bear upon my statement at all; my statement was as to information with regard to localities of nuisances and the existence of nuisances; with regard to slaughter-houses, that is a totally different question.

Sir A. Guinness—continued.

Mr. *Boyle*.

20 June 1876.

5087. Might there not be very great nuisances in connection with slaughter yards?—There might, and I regard slaughter-houses as nuisances, as a rule.

5088. Then they were only inquiring on the subject of nuisances, which seems to have been part of their duties; you are aware, no doubt, that they were refused their Report that was asked for?—They were.

5089. Or any information upon the subject of slaughter-houses?—I do not know if they were refused any information upon the subject of slaughter-houses, nor do I recollect their applying for anything more than that Report.

5090 You will perhaps recollect that they wrote three letters, and that the only answer which they received from the Public Health Committee was that they were marked "Read"?—Yes, I recollect the circumstance to which you allude.

5091. Do you approve of manure being manufactured within the city?—Under the circumstances in which it is manufactured I have no objection to it. I think that those manufactures facilitate the abatement of nuisances and remove foul matter from the rears of tenement houses that otherwise would remain there a longer time. I consider the private manure depôts as auxiliaries to the operations of the Public Health Committee.

5092. And no nuisance to the neighbourhoods in which they are?—They do not constitute nuisances; our consulting sanitary officer does not consider that they do.

5093. And you do not perceive any disagreeable perfume from those manufactories of manure when you visit them?—I do not, excepting on those occasions in which they were punished for the offence. They have ceased for more than a year to be nuisances.

5094. Do you know how many there are in Maclean's-lane?—Either three or four; you might call it four; one of them is a joint property.

5095. Does this lane run through a densely populated lot of tenement houses?—No, it does not.

5096. Are there any houses there?—I can tell you every house in it. I think there are five houses in that lane.

5097. What population might there be in the immediate neighbourhood of those three manufactories of manure?—Taking a distance of 100 feet from them I should suppose about 80 to 90 souls.

5098. How many convictions were there under the Sanitary Acts?—Of convictions for ordinary sanitary offences there were 24,749 in 10 years; the others were for the possession or sale of diseased meat, and for offences under the Adulteration of Food Act. There were altogether 26,435 convictions.

5099. And there was only 3,395 *l.* collected from fines and costs?—Yes.

5100. That represented, did it not, a very small average sum of fines?—It is right to mention that, at the commencement of the Sanitary Act, the penalties imposed were very few. Parties were ignorant of the sanitary law, and for a long time there was a reluctance on the part of the committee to apply for heavy penalties, and a reluctance on the part of the magistrates to punish parties for offences that really constituted a portion

Mr. *Boyle*.

20 June 1876.

Sir *A. Guinness*—continued.

a portion of their habits from their earliest days.

5101. Can you tell me how many shillings the average fine would represent?—About 2*s.* 8*d.*

5102. Do you think that a sufficient amount to deter those who were breaking the sanitary laws?—The magistrates considered it so.

5103. Do you know of any instance in which Colonel Torrens's Act with regard to dilapidated houses, which was passed in 1868, was enforced in Ireland?—It has not been put in force in Dublin.

5104. Let me call your attention to an order of the Public Health Committee with regard to tenement houses, dated the 4th of December 1866, which says that, "They require that all ashpits and privies of houses occupied by members of more than one family be emptied, cleansed, purified, deodorised, and disinfected regularly and periodically once in each month, viz., on or before the last day of each month," was that enforced?—Yes, I recollect that order.

5105. Are those provisions enforced?—They are not strictly enforced; they are fairly enforced so far as our staff will permit of it.

5106. Then you attribute their not being fully enforced to your staff being insufficient?—Yes.

5107. You had a long correspondence, had you not, about the conveyance of sick people between the sanitary committee and Public Health Committee?—Yes.

5108. Is there a cab kept for removing the sick at Sir Patrick Dun's Hospital?—There were two of them there during the epidemic of small-pox. We got leave to keep one there during the epidemic, and subsequently removed it. It was only pending the epidemic that we kept it there.

5109. Does that notice which you have put in state that it is there now?—I have put it in evidence that the position has been altered. There are two cabs fitted up specially for the purpose.

5110. Can you tell me how often those two cabs have been used this year?—On 43 occasions our cabs have been used.

5111. Something has been said about the unions having cabs; do you know that it is no part of their duty to provide conveyances for the city?—In consequence of its having been stated by Dr. Grimshaw that the union masters had denied the facilities afforded by their cabs, I wrote to each of them, and I have received from each a reply, dated, the one on the 14th of June, the present month, and the other the 15th.

5112. That is not quite an answer to my question; do you think it part of their duty to provide conveyances for the city?—I do not know whether it is their duty or not; but I know that the guardians readily afford the use of those cabs for the purpose.

5113. Do you know that many respectable people would object to go to a hospital in workhouse cabs?—I think so; or in any cab for the conveyance of the sick.

5114. But they would particularly object to a workhouse cab?—I think they would object either to a workhouse cab or to a cab provided by the corporation, and much difficulty has arisen by their objecting to using our cabs.

5115. Do you think that they would not prefer a cab provided by the city to a workhouse cab?—I think they would, but I have known of our cabs being objected to.

Sir *A. Guinness*—continued.

5116. Can you mention any case in which your committee have prosecuted persons for carrying persons with an infectious disease in cabs?—Yes; and the committee have obtained a conviction under penalty.

5117. On how many occasions?—In one instance, when I found that this was the case, I immediately communicated with the Commissioner of Police; and he was good enough to station a policeman, during the epidemic of small-pox, at every hospital in the city, for the purpose of preventing the use of public cabs by infected patients; but we found the desire of the public was to take the nearest cab or vehicle they could possibly get, and to drive towards the hospital, and to stop short of it by a few yards, and then get off, so as to escape the policeman.

5118. Do not you think that that was caused in any way by the corporation cab being so far away?—No, it was a question of the facility of access. If they had a cab in the next street, or near their own house, they prefer it to sending 100 or 200 yards for the corporation cab.

5119. Had they any difficulty in getting this cab?—None.

5120. Was not the horse kept at a different place from the cab?—Yes, and it was only necessary to apply where the horse was in order to obtain the cab.

5121. Did you never know of a refusal?—Never; I heard of an alleged refusal, and I investigated the circumstances, and I found that it was not so.

5122. Do any members of the public health committee or the corporation, to your knowledge, own tenement houses?—I cannot call to my mind a single member of the corporation owning tenement houses.

5123. Was there any complaint made to the committee about the premises of one member of the committee, and an attempt made to abate the nuisance?—I recollect a circumstance which occurred with regard to a member who died about six years ago, and I proceeded against him. The committee did not hesitate for a moment to proceed against one of their own body for the non-abatement of a nuisance; they summoned him, and eventually the nuisance was abated.

5124. Which member was that?—Mr. McGrath, he died about six or seven years ago.

5125. Did they obtain a conviction against Mr. McGrath?—Immediately on his being summoned he abated the nuisance; he was coerced to abate the nuisance by his own colleagues.

5126. Was there any other case of that kind?—I am not aware of any. I am quite satisfied that if there had been another I should have remembered it. I might almost say that there was not.

5127. Was there any case of prosecution against Mr. McAnaspie?—Yes.

5128. Did you obtain a conviction?—We did, we obtained a magistrate's order against him.

5129. Not a fine?—No; it was principally on Dr. Mapother's evidence and mine.

5130. Was the prosecution not pressed?—The prosecution was pressed, and the nuisance was partly abated. The reason it was not entirely abated was this. It was about four years ago. It formed a portion of a heap in the lane, which was removed; it was merely a quantity of gravel which

Sir A. Guinness—continued.

which had constituted a portion of the surface of the road; some of the gravel was taken off, and was wheeled in this lane, and being inodorous it was inoffensive.

5131. What was the largest number of nuisances which you have known to exist in any one house or premises?—It is rather a difficult question to answer.

5132. Do you enter five or six nuisances at the one house as separate nuisances?—No, unless they occur at different periods.

5133. Taking the case of a tenement house, do you enter it as one nuisance, even supposing there were a nuisance found in each room?—As one nuisance. The number of houses we take rather than the number of nuisances.

5134. It is only to be understood that each nuisance represents a house or premises?—Yes.

Mr. Gibson.

5135. Are you aware that there is power given to the Corporation to erect public clocks and public privies?—I know that they have power to erect clocks under the Improvement Act of 1849.

5136. Is there a single clock erected anywhere in the city of Dublin by the Corporation?—Nowhere.

5137. Is there a single public privy erected in the city of Dublin by the Corporation?—Yes, there is.

5138. Where?—At the further end of Sir John Rogerson's Quay. I may mention that there has been an attempt to get them erected.

5139. There is one at Sir John Rogerson's Quay; what are its dimensions?—It was for the use of the sailors frequenting the port that it was erected. I should suppose that its length is about seven feet by about five feet or thereabouts.

5140. And am I to understand that that is the only public privy erected in the whole of Dublin?—The only one.

5141. And that was erected, not for the population of Dublin, but for the migratory sailors who come there with ships?—Yes.

5142. Do you know if any attempt was made to remedy this, which I suppose you conceive to be a disgraceful state of things?—Yes.

5143. When was the attempt made?—It was made by me in 1869 or 1870.

5144. What was the result?—That the erection of one of those privies constituted one of the most frightful nuisances that I ever beheld.

5145. Where was it erected?—At a place called Blessington-place, eastward of Blessington-street, at the head of White's-lane.

5146. Is it your evidence that it is impossible to do it, and that that section of the Act of Parliament must always remain a dead letter?—I will give you my experience if you will permit me.

5147. I want you to say, speaking from experience, whether you think it is impossible?—No, not at all. You may erect any structure, but the question is, what is the result of the erection of that structure.

5148. How long was it up?—About four months.

5149. What month was it put up, and when was it taken down?—I cannot speak with sufficient accuracy as to that.

5150. Was it summer or winter?—I cannot tell that.

5151. Could you give me the dimensions in

Mr. Gibson—continued.

that case?—It contained four distinct seats, separated from each other. I suppose each of them was about two feet three or two feet four.

5152. I suppose the nuisance to which you refer is that there was rather a crowd about the place, and that the accommodation was not found sufficient, was that so?—Quite the reverse.

5153. Then in what respect was it a nuisance?—It became a nuisance in the same manner as the privies attached to tenement houses become nuisances. They are scarcely erected before they become so foul and so filthy, no matter how ample the provision may be, that they soon constitute nuisances much worse than the previous state of things.

5154. Are you able to cope with the difficulty of tenement houses?—We are not.

5155. Are you in favour of taking away privies altogether from tenement houses?—Certainly not; it is one of the greatest difficulties that the Public Health Committee have to contend with.

5156. Except in that particular case of the accommodation for four, which was erected in Blessington-street, for a population of 300,000, have you ever tried to cope with the difficulty?—There is the one on Sir John Rogerson's Quay.

5157. That is for the sailors, not for the inhabitants of Dublin; do not you think that this is a sanitary matter of the very highest and first importance?—I do not think it is.

5158. Do you think it is of any importance?—No.

5159. Are you of opinion that not only is that section a dead letter, but that it should remain a dead letter?—Distinctly so.

5160. Will you give us some reasons for that?—In the first instance there are about 730 dwelling houses in Dublin unprovided with internal or external space for the construction of privies or water closets; and we have endeavoured, by getting accommodation in adjoining yards, and putting up privies with two, three, or four seats, as the case may be, to accommodate the parties giving a separate privy for the women, and thus they have been made available for four or five houses; but we have been obliged to abandon this course by reason of the habits of the people. The condition in which these places were, within a few days after they had been erected in the best manner, and fitted with all that decency or comfort could suggest, was something almost incredible.

5161. Do not you think that those are the very habits that require to be fostered by a little encouragement and a little attention?—And those habits are being fostered at the expense of the landlords of those houses; I have obliged them myself on many occasions to provide sanitary accommodation, and they have done it thoroughly to my satisfaction, but they have come to me a week afterwards and said, "Come and see those places which are positively abominable by reason of the habits of those people, and what are we to do."

5162. You still coerce the landlords to do this?—They are obliged to provide sanitary accommodation, and look after the premises as well as they can.

5163. Do you oblige the landlords to do this, believing it to be a sanitary reform?—Yes, we do.

5164. Why then do not you oblige your own corporation to do for the public what they are obliged

Mr. Boyle.

10 June 1876.

Mr. Gibson—continued.

Mr. Boyle.

20 June 1876.

obliged to do under another section of another Act of Parliament?—I should fail in my duty if I were to oblige the corporation to become the cause of nuisances.

5165. If there is a sanitary reform which is necessary to be enforced in relation to landlord and tenant, why should there not be the same sanitary reform on the part of the corporation in relation to its duties to the public; where is the distinction?—I believe the circumstances are quite different.

5166. Why?—There is a control as between the landlord and the tenant which never could exist as between the corporation and the public.

5167. Is not the control in each case the controlling power of your sanitary serjeants?—No, unless you station a man at each of those houses.

5168. Have you not people enough to look very closely after those tenements?—Not to station a man at each house; that is a subject which has engaged the attention of the corporation and the Public Health Committee very much indeed.

5169. What exactly is the figure which you would put as the proper number of your staff?—Fifteen.

5170. Do you think that is enough?—I do; I think we could manage the city with 15 policemen.

5171. And that would be quite enough?—I should say so; I should be perfectly content to take the responsibility of carrying on the sanitary duties with 15 men.

5172. Do any of those returns which are mentioned here comprise those which are known as double entries; for instance, I find in the report of 1875 the number of privies and water closets repaired was 1,294; then I find the number of privies and ashpits cleansed was 8,708; are any of the 1,294 included in the 8,708?—They are utterly distinct operations; one is the repair of structural works and the other is cleansing and removal.

Chairman.

5173. Are they in relation to the same thing?—No; they are in different places.

Mr. *Gibson.*

5174. Have you added together all those figures for any one year so as to give the Committee a statement of the number of operations for any one year?—I have never done it, and have never thought of doing so.

5175. When was the Public Health Committee formed?—It held its first meeting on the 24th of August, 1866.

5176. And it has been in operation ever since, has it not?—Yes.

5177. When did it first begin to publish reports?—Seven months after the constitution of the Committee.

5178. Have they published annual reports ever since?—I believe they have. I have a very large number of them here for almost every year.

5179. When was this yellow document compiled, showing the work for ten years?—That was compiled about a month ago.

5180. I suppose since this Committee sat, and with reference to the evidence which has been given here?—Yes.

5181. Have you any document showing the result of each year with regard to the number of prosecutions?—Yes, they are all here.

Mr. Gibson—continued.

5182. Is it the fact or not that there used to be more prosecutions at Green-street with reference to misconduct on the part of tradespeople about mixing milk and other matters, about four years ago, than there are now?—No.

5183. Used there not to be many more prosecutions and greater activity against the same classes of trader in Dublin than has been continued to the present time?—No. Our prosecutions have largely increased. I will give the facts. Up to about three years ago the average number of summonses which were weekly sanctioned by the Committee was 54, and now they average 87; they range from about 81 to 105 a week.

5184. Do you deduce from that, that through the activity of your officers they discover offences now that they omitted to discover before?—That as the people become acquainted with the sanitary law, and with sanitary requirements, we trust that we shall have less occasion to prosecute them for breaches of the sanitary laws.

5185. May we take it that there are more prosecutions with nine serjeants than there were with 15?—There have been more prosecutions by 30 per cent. within the last two years over those of the previous two years.

5186. When were the 15 serjeants reduced to 9?—On the 1st of April of this present year.

5187. Have the prosecutions fallen off since that?—They have not.

5188. So that, according to the prosecution test, you have no inconvenience from the diminished number?—So far as prosecutions are concerned, they have not diminished, but the number of notices served is less than it was.

5189. Had your sanitary serjeants districts?—Yes.

5190. And did you extend those districts that they each had?—Yes, we were obliged to enlarge their various districts.

5191. Have you a system of rewarding the men for vigour in finding out nuisances?—No.

5192. So that there is nothing in the way of payment by results?—No; but we reward them in another manner, that is, by bringing their conduct under the notice of the Commissioner of Police, who very thankfully receives such testimony; it stands to the man's credit, and the police accept it more gratefully than they would a small pecuniary reward.

5193. It is a record of good conduct?—Yes.

5194. The police, of course, know that you have got this power?—Yes, it is always notified to them when they are recommended.

5195. Do they get anything beyond their ordinary pay as police serjeants?—Yes, two of them do.

5196. Have you got the power of selecting the men who are to get that?—No, Colonel Lake reserves to himself everything with reference to the remuneration of the police.

5197. Does it depend upon your reports whether a man will get the extra pay?—There is no extra pay. Colonel Lake fixes the pay of the men, and in the case of two who have been with us for a long time, about five years and seven years respectively, he gave them a considerable increased amount of pay, without any suggestion on the part of the Public Health Committee, but when the sanitary police, or the police on

Mr. Boyle.

20 June 1876.

Mr. *Gibson*—continued.

on the beat, distinguish themselves in any remarkable way, the policeman's name is brought before the Committee, and it forms a matter of record on our minutes, and is communicated to the commissioner.

5198. You wish to compel all the houses which have got ashpits and privies to be properly cleansed; you do this, of course, in relation to houses in good localities if it is necessary?—Yes.

5199. But your principal attention, I assume, is directed to tenement houses?—It is.

5200. Do you see that the privies and ashpits are kept cleansed?—Yes.

5201. Do you ever yourself direct the Corporation, or carts, or anything in that way, to go and clear them out?—Never.

5202. What do you do?—I make periodical inspections of the different districts, with a view to ascertain that the police fairly discharge their duty efficiently.

5203. If you go into a tenement house inhabited by poor people, how do you look after the cleansing of those ashpits and privies?—By the sanitary police inspection.

5204. All the inspection in the world will not cleanse them; what do you do to cleanse them?—Notices to cleanse them are served on the spot; the parties are summoned before the magistrates in default of doing so.

5205. Have you anything to show the number occupying tenement houses that you have summoned for this offence?—Not as contradistinguished from others in the report.

5206. Not the particular offences; it is the number of general convictions, I think?—The inspections of tenement houses amounted to 41,843, and it gives you then the different descriptions of nuisances that we have to deal with; there is not a single description of nuisance that is not set forth in detail.

5207. Can you tell me what is the number of convictions for non-cleansing of privies and ashpits in tenement houses?—It does not give the number of convictions in each particular case.

5208. Is not that an important point; how do you work it in Dublin where there are thousands of those wretched tenement houses; how do you manage the cleansing of the ashpits and privies?—When premises are filthy, a notice is served on the spot, giving a certain number of days, and if that notice is disregarded, the party is summoned before the magistrate who makes an order, giving him a certain number of days beyond that, and if that order be disobeyed, the man is then summoned, and a penalty is inflicted.

5209. Have you any document showing how many penalties were put on for the non-cleansing of those tenement houses?—We have in the City Hall a record of every summons that is served, and of the offence.

5210. Are you able now to tell the Committee the figures?—I am not.

5211. Do they amount to hundreds?—About two-thirds of the convictions are for non-cleansing.

5212. The report which you have handed in gives a record of all the detections, confiscations, and convictions, and so far as I can see, here is no record of what I am asking for, unless it is under the head of "convictions for ordinary sanitary offences"?—Yes, it is under that head; two-thirds of those that are mentioned there are for failing to cleanse or to remove nuisances.

Mr. *Gibson*—continued.

5213. In any cases at all have those tenement houses availed themselves of the corporation carts and machinery for cleansing their ashpits and privies?—Yes; but not more, I suppose, than about 700 or 800.

5214. Not in the whole of the ten years?—It has only been in force for about four years.

5215. As a rule, may it be accepted that the tenement houses do not use the corporation machinery for emptying the night-soil?—They do not.

5216. Is not that the best and strongest evidence to show that the tariff of the corporation is beyond the reach of ordinary people?—I do not think so.

5217. Is it not only the better class of people who use them?—I cannot answer that question distinctly or directly, but I believe that is not the reason.

5218. Never mind the reason, I want the fact; is it not the fact that a great number of people who use the corporation machinery for emptying their ashpits and removing their night-soil, and all that kind of thing, belong to the better class of citizens and people of wealth?—Yes.

5219. Is it not the fact that it is only a very trivial number of tenement inhabitants who ever dream of it?—Yes.

5220. I ask you, as the sanitary officer of a great city, would not it be desirable, if possible, that the use of the machinery for the emptying of those ashpits should be fixed at such a rate that it would be within the reach of the humbler inhabitants?—I believe it is within their reach.

5221. At all events they do not use it?—No.

Dr. *Ward.*

5222. What was the date of that epidemic in which the great difficulty arose about conveying patients to the hospital?—It was during the small-pox epidemic of 1872.

5223. That was previous to the passing of the Health Act of 1874: if you look at that Act, is there not a section in it which would now remedy all that, by compelling unions, if the Local Government Board thought fit, to provide cabs?—Yes, under the 8th section of the Public Health Act of 1874, in the event of an epidemic breaking out, the Local Government Board may put the Diseases Prevention Acts in force, and declare it to be in force, and then the prevention of the spread of epidemics rests entirely in the board of guardians.

5224. The unions would now be obliged, if the Local Government Board thought proper to direct them, to provide conveyances, would they not?—Yes; not only that, but all the other appliances, the conveyance to the disinfecting chamber and everything, is transferred to the board of guardians.

5225. What is the amount of expenditure which would be necessary to carry out these sanitary arrangements?—About 3,100 *l.* a year.

5226. What was the actual expenditure last year?—The actual expenditure last year was 3,003 *l.*, I think, and the year before 4,100 *l.*

5227. Is it correct to state, as Dr. Grimshaw stated, that the year before last, the expenditure was 1,800 *l.*?—No; as I have stated, it was 4,100 *l.*

5228. You think that an expenditure of 3,100 *l.* ought to be sufficient to carry on the sanitary arrangements of Dublin?—Yes.

5229. With

Mr *Boyle*

20 June 1876.

Dr. *Ward*—continued.

5229. With regard to the number of convictions upon which the honourable Baronet asked you, was not it the case that in the great mass of convictions at the beginning, people were let off easily because they did not understand the law?—Yes.

5230. Therefore it is unfair to take 2 *s.* 8 *d.* as the average of the present fines, because the fines at present are larger?—Yes, the fines at present are never less than 10 *s.*

Sir *Arthur Guinness.*

5231. That is including costs, I presume?—Yes.

Dr. *Ward.*

5232. Up to the year 1874 you were under the Act of 1866, with limited powers, were you not?—Yes.

5233. You stated, I think, that you differed from Dr. Grimshaw as to the excessive mortality from zymotics in Dublin?—Yes, I differ from him very decidedly.

5234. And you stated, I think, that you differed from him with reference to the Report of the Registrar General?—Yes.

5235. What does the Registrar General say, in a few words, with regard to zymotic affections in Dublin?—That they are greatly decreased. Taking the last year, he says, "The number of deaths from zymotic diseases registered during the year 1875 was 1,396 or 4·4 in every 1,000 of the population, being considerably under the average for the previous 10 years, which amounted to 1,917, a number equal to 6·1 per 1,000 inhabitants."

5236. So that they have been reduced two per 1,000?—Very nearly two per 1,000.

5237. That would, therefore, be a reduction of one-third?—Yes.

Sir *Arthur Guinness.*

5238. When you say that 3,100 *l.* would be a sufficient amount for sanitary purposes, are you sure that there was over 4,000 *l.* spent last year?—It was the year before last.

5239. Do you think that there was too much spent then?—It was owing to a circumstance which occurred at that time; we were obliged to pay 1,100 *l.* as our contribution for a floating hospital, which made it an exceptional year.

5240. In fact you think that there is enough money spent upon the sanitary improvement of Dublin?—£. 3,100 would give us what we would require, less would not suffice.

5241. Then so far as sanitary affairs are concerned, the usual plea of want of funds cannot be urged?—No, the corporation are very willing to expend money for sanitary purposes, if they only saw their way to getting it.

Dr. *Ward.*

5242. Would it be correct to say, as has been stated, that the Sanitary Committee do not pay attention to the reports that are sent to them?—No, I am obliged to produce every complaint that comes to me with the Report of the sanitary inspector or serjeant on it, at the next meeting of the committee, when action is taken upon it.

5243. If there is anything involving the necessity of a skilled opinion, do you refer to the sanitary medical officer?—Instantly; he is always available for the purpose.

5244. It is quite optional, is it not, with any ratepayer in Dublin, if they are not satisfied with the sanitary condition of the city, to draw the attention of the Local Government Board to the lapses of the Sanitary Committee?—Yes.

5245. And that has been done, has it not?—Yes, that has been done.

5246. And the Local Government inspector has come to you, has he not?—Yes, he has.

5247. Would it be correct to say when he came to you, as has been said, that when he came to you the Local Government inspector, instead of doing what they do in England, namely, going through the district about which each complaint was made, went to you at the City Hall, and merely looked at your books to know what was the state of things, and expressed himself satisfied?—No.

5248. The reverse of that is the case, is it not?—The reverse of that is the fact. I received a note from him in the morning saying that he would come to me at 11 or 12 o'clock, and he immediately proceeded with me to all the parts of the city with reference to which complaint had been made.

5249. Therefore Dr. Grimshaw, in stating that the Local Government inspector did not really see into the cases that were referred to him, was incorrect?—Yes.

5250. The sanitary police report to the Commissioner of Police as well as to you, do they not?—Yes, weekly.

5251. With what object?—The Commissioner of Police does not wish to abandon his control of the police in any respect.

5252. What do they do with those reports?—They are sent back to the Public Health Committee with a memorandum that they have been received and read.

5253. Now we come to the matter of the disinfection of houses, and that portion of the evidence by Dr. Grimshaw, at Question 3984, where, in answer to Sir Arthur Guinness, he said, "The disinfection of houses is supposed to be carried out by two or three people who are employed to go and disinfect them by chlorine gas developed from chloride of lime. I have gone to see how this is done, and it is done in such a way as to be utterly useless;" and then he says, "I attribute it more to the fact that the members of the Public Health Committee do not appear to understand what sanitary requirements are." Do you not state, as a matter of fact, that when they carry on this disinfecting, they carry it on under the superintendence and direction of one of the medical officers of the corporation?—Distinctly so. The instructions are drawn up by him.

5254. As to the statement that the disinfection is not a *bonâ fide* disinfection, that is a mere matter of the opinion of Dr. Grimshaw as opposed to that of Dr. Cameron?—No; I would go a little further than that. If you judge by the results, the disinfection has been perfect.

5255. But when a statement has been made that such disinfection as is carried out under Dr. Cameron's orders is a perfectly worthless disinfection, it is a mere difference of opinion between Dr. Grimshaw and Dr. Cameron as to what disinfection is?—Yes.

5256. Therefore his charge against the Public Health Committee, that because of this disinfection they are incapable of understanding what sanitary requirements are, falls to the ground. It is a mere difference of opinion between those doctors?—

Mr. *Boyle*.

20 June 1876.

Dr. *Ward*—continued.

doctors?—Yes. Besides, we have got three medical members on the committee who take a very anxious interest in the working of the committee, and who have a sufficient knowledge of the laws of chemistry to be aware that the application of chloric gas must prove effectual.

5257. Your point is, that you carry out your disinfection under medical superintendence and by medical direction?—Yes.

5258. Have you seen the recommendations of Dr. Grimshaw, and his statement, that it would involve a very great increased cost to the city to carry them out?—Yes.

5259. Do you agree with him in the necessity for that?—No; we have at the present moment more medical aid than we require; we could not utilise any further amount of medical aid.

5260. You were here the other day, I think, when the honourable Member for the University asked the honourable Member for Louth, who was a witness here, with reference to the appointment and distribution of officers, and he asked if they forgot political distinctions in that; would you object to say what you are yourself in religion and politics?—I am a Protestant, and I believe I am what is generally understood as a Conservative.

5261. Are there many of the first officers of the corporation in your position?—There are eight who are.

5262. Are not all the largest paid officers, or nearly all of them, of the same politics as you?—Yes; the majority are.

5263. From your knowledge of the appointments made by the corporation, what is your opinion of the allegation that has been made, that the corporation have been unduly influenced by the religion and politics of the candidates?—I state as a fact that no such influence operates with regard to any officer. I state as regard myself that I never could have known in the case of any member of the corporation by his demeanour towards me what his religion was; and with regard to the conferring of appointments, there are eight superior officers, almost all of whom are Protestants and Conservatives.

Mr. *Collins*.

5264. You appear to be satisfied with the existing sanitary condition of the town?—No, I am not.

5265. In what respect are you dissatisfied?—I am dissatisfied with the sanitary condition with regard to cleanliness by reason of the insufficiency of our sanitary staff; but it is a question of money.

5266. You stated that, to make the staff of sanitary inspectors perfect or efficient, it would be sufficient to increase the number from nine, as it exists at present, to 15; would that change, in your judgment, be sufficient to enable Dublin to be put into an efficient and satisfactory sanitary condition?—It would, so far as the Public Health Committee are concerned, and for this reason, that the people have become more amenable to sanitary law, and more conscious of the results of sanitary operations than they were formerly, they are beginning to appreciate sanitary reforms.

5267. You think that an expenditure of 3,100 *l.* a year would be sufficient to defray the expenses of administering the sanitary matters of Dublin?—Yes.

Mr. *Collins*—continued.

5268. And that 3,100 *l.* a year would be about the average expenditure, would it not, of the last three years? Yes, it would be about the average of the last three or four years.

5269. Then it would not be necessary to increase the expenditure in order to make the administration effective?—No, not beyond the expenditure of the last three or four years.

5270. You suggested, did you not, that it would be desirable to raise a special sanitary rate instead of taking the amount which is necessary for sanitary purposes out of the borough fund as it exists at present?—That is my opinion; there are some who differ from me.

5271. Is it a matter which admits of much difference of opinion in the municipal council?—No, it is not so much a difference of opinion; but there are many reasons why I have suggested it. So long as you take from a fund from which others are drawing, the public have no idea what you are spending; whereas if you take from a distinct and separate fund, and apply it to your own purposes, it is then known what you are expending, and the public take a greater interest in it.

5272. From the different reports the public can derive that information, can they not, if they wish to refer to those reports?—They do not take an interest in reading them.

5273. With reference to the cleansing arrangements of Dublin, have you found them very fairly carried out by the Public Health Committee?—They are carried out as far as our staff enables us, but it requires a larger staff to carry them out as fully as I should wish.

5274. Upon the subject of those manure manufactories, you say that the existing proceedings for the purpose of suppressing nuisances are very complex and interfere very much with your carrying out your operations satisfactorily?—Yes.

5275. And the General Act of the 18 & 19 Vict., does not at all aid you?—It might be greatly simplified.

5276. In what respect might it be simplified?—In diminishing the number of forms, shortening the proceedings before the magistrates, and making the disobedience of their order a matter to be immediately punished as you punish any other offence.

5277. Are those numerous forms necessary under the General Act?—They are rendered imperatively necessary.

5278. And that is the remedy which you would suggest?—Yes, it would be equal to an addition of 25 per cent. to our sanitary staff.

Mr. *Kavanagh*.

5279. You were asked some questions about the slaughter-houses, and you referred to some evidence which Mr. Pim gave; I have looked into his evidence, and I find that his answer which refers to that subject is number 2,458, in which he says, speaking of the state of the slaughter-houses in Dublin, that "It is a frightful condition of things having slaughter-houses scattered through the city, and usually in places where they are surrounded by the dwellings of the poorer classes"; is that the case?—That is the fact.

5280. I think the question that was asked you was whether there were any cases of dwelling-houses

Mr. Boyle.

20 June 1876.

Mr. *Kavanagh*—continued.

houses over slaughter-houses?—I was asked whether parties slept over slaughter-houses, and I said that there is nothing of that kind.

5281. But you allow that it is a frightful thing to have slaughter-houses scattered through the city, and surrounded by dwelling-houses?—There can be no difference of opinion upon that.

5282. And still it is the fact?—It is the fact.

5283. Do you know whether, in some of those houses in Dublin that are not actually butchers' shops or slaughter shops, they do slaughter animals?—Unlicensed slaughtering is a crime which the magistrates punish very severely, and our means of detection are very ample in relation to it; it is therefore of very rare occurrence. It may be that in the hurry for Saturday's provision a sheep is sometimes killed at the rear of a butcher's shop, but the slaughtering of horned cattle does not occur. There have been several parties punished for it, and it has been put a stop to.

5284. And you think it does not exist?—No; I do not think it does.

5285. I merely ask you the question, because from my own knowledge of towns in the country, I know there are a great many places where kids, sheep, and those sort of animals are slaughtered which are not the owners' regular shambles?—That does not exist in Dublin.

5286. However, the main statement which Mr. Pim made in that answer to which I have referred, you say is correct?—Quite correct.

5287. Could you tell me about Ardee-street, to which you have referred, who is the owner of the house, No. 18, Ardee-street?—A man named Terence May. I know his name from the fact of having had him imprisoned for non-payment of penalties for the condition of his premises.

5288. What is his position?—I do not know what he is. I think he had been a soldier at one time, but I am not quite sure.

5289. He is not in a wealthy position?—No.

5290. Is he a poor man?—He is, comparatively, poor. I think there are eight tenancies in that house of his, and they pay him, on an average, about 2 *s.* a week each.

5291. With regard to the expense of domestic scavenging, which amounts to 6 *s.* a load for an ashpit of two loads, and 2 *s.* 6 *d.* a load on anything beyond, who pays that; is it the occupier, or the owner of the tenement?—The party applying at the city hall is generally the owner, and he is responsible, unless the house is held by the year. In a tenement house it is invariably the owner who pays.

5292. Supposing that an application is made to have an ashpit cleaned out, and that you were obliged to take proceedings to punish the parties, from whom is the penalty levied?—From the owner, not the occupier. A house may be occupied by seven or eight families, and you could not fix it upon any one particular party; the owner is the person indicated in the Act as the party from whom it is recoverable. The owner is described in this manner, as the person next in receipt of the rent.

5293. That is to say the immediate lessor?—Yes.

5294. From your general evidence at the commencement, I gathered that you were rather inclined to disagree with Dr. Grimshaw's statement as to the sanitary state of Dublin?—Yes.

5295. His general evidence was, I think, to the effect that the sanitary condition of Dublin was not satisfactory?—So he stated.

Mr. *Kavanagh*—continued.

5296. And I understand your general evidence to be to the effect that it is?—It is not so satisfactory by any means as I could wish, or as it ought to be; but I referred particularly to his lists, in which he described the condition of several houses, numbering about 115, and he subsequently described the condition of the tenement houses in Dublin as being very bad. With regard to his list, I gave evidence as to the condition of the houses now, and I am also prepared to put in the evidence of the consulting sanitary officer, who saw them since Dr. Grimshaw gave evidence, as to what they are now.

5297. Then, as a general statement, I may take your evidence as really practically verifying his?—No.

5298. You think, then, that the sanitary condition of Dublin is practically satisfactory?—Whilst it is not satisfactory, it is not nearly so bad as he described it.

5299. Then it is not good?—No.

5300. You admit that?—It is not so good as it ought to be.

5301. Of course "as it ought to be" is comparative, and rather an indefinite thing, but you admit that the sanitary condition of Dublin is not good?—I could not go so far as that, because if I did, I should be confuted by the results, for Dublin is not an unhealthy city.

5302. If you considered that it is good, might I ask you why you consider that a sum of 3,100 *l.* per annum should be spent upon the sanitary arrangements, instead of 1,800 *l.*, if double the amount of money, or very nearly double the amount of money, is required to be spent upon carrying out the sanitary arrangements that is now spent, how do you still, in the face of that statement, consider that the sanitary arrangements are good?—I will give you the reason. Dublin contains 2,360 houses of very great antiquity, which may be kept in a perfectly sanitary state if carefully looked after; but leave them alone, and by reason of their age, and by reason still more of the class of people by whom they are inhabited, a nomadic race of the poorest class coming in from the west and north-west of Ireland, it requires continued surveillance to be exercised over the people as well as over the houses. It is with the habits of the people that we have most to contend with in Dublin.

5303. Still, if the state of affairs requires something to be done which is not done, you must allow that the state of affairs is not satisfactory?—It is the prevention of their being unsatisfactory that we look at. Our measures are more preventive than otherwise.

5304. Then in Dublin the 3,100 *l.* which you expend is only for the purpose of prevention?—Yes, and for continual supervision over the parties who occupy those houses.

5305. That would seem to be a large sum, would it not?—No, I think it is a very small sum; it is not 1½ *d.* in the pound on the rateable property in the city.

5306. Three thousand one hundred pounds spent in mere supervision and for prevention would, you think, not be large?—No; one-fifth of the population of Dublin are not natives of Dublin.

5307. But that does not alter the circumstances whether they are natives or not. I am merely dealing

Mr. *Boyle.*

20 June 1876.

Mr. *Kavanagh*—continued.

dealing with the locality. The locality is unhealthy or it is healthy?—It is not unhealthy, but it is necessary to take these precautions to prevent its becoming unhealthy.

5308. Then its condition is not satisfactory?—Not quite, though comparatively it may be.

5309. You contradict Dr. Grimshaw's evidence, do you not, as to the death-rate?—Yes.

5310. Was not his evidence as to the death-rate founded upon the Registrar General's statement?—I cannot tell you from whence he derived his evidence, but I put in the Registrar General's statement, which is to the very contrary effect. He states in his evidence also, that in London the death-rate by zymotics is 6·1, and that in Dublin it is only 5·9 (I think you will find that in his evidence), thereby proving that the mortality from zymotics in Dublin is less than it is in London.

5311. You dispute the figures in the return to which Dr. Grimshaw alludes?—I do.

5312. They are not Dr. Grimshaw's figures, are they?—I do not know. I gave in the printed return which I received from the Registrar General of Ireland.

5313. You also said that you did not believe that so many cases of fever as were reported by Dr. Grimshaw existed?—I contradict that so far as this, that in his evidence he quotes the houses, of which he gave a list in 1872, as being fever dens. I quote the returns which I receive from the medical officers of the dispensaries, whose duty it would be to report to me every fever den in the city, or every house in which a case of fever occurred, no matter what class. I have the reports since October 1874, and I find that but three of those houses have been reported by them as houses in which infectious diseases have occurred.

5314. Therefore your contradiction of Dr. Grimshaw's evidence is not from your own knowledge; it is from hearsay?—Not from hearsay, but from written reports sent in on that list. I inspected every one of those 115 houses. I was so struck by the statement that I not only did so, but I also got the consulting sanitary officer to inspect them; I will give you his letter, which I have got here. "No. 6, Merrion-square, North, Dublin, 15th June 1876. I have this day inspected fully the following houses" (then he gives the houses referred to in Dr. Grimshaw's report), and he says, "I could not certify that any of above houses are now unfit for human habitation."

5315. He did not certify that they were fit for it?—I take the context as certifying that they are fit, because they must be either fit or unfit, I take it.

5316-7. It strikes me that there is a slight difference between a medical officer refusing to certify that a dwelling is unfit for human habitation, and agreeing to certify that it is fit; however, that is a matter of opinion?—He describes each house, and he says with regard to Cathedral-lane, for instance, "Majority of houses sound, with good rears; free air-space on east side. (3.) Court behind 21, Golden-lane; the room over privy has been emptied, and closed permanently; court much cleaner lately. (4.) 36, Chancery-lane is a sound house with free air-space at rear. (5.) Derby-square; three houses are permanently closed; the rest are sound and clean. (6.) Tennis-court; three houses on the west side are closed; the rest are fairly clean, but want of rears causes filth to be thrown on surface; far better than 1866, when cholera raged there. (7.) Northern end of Magninness's-place; the privy and ashpit accommodation far better; the houses are very old but staunch; I could not certify that any of above houses are now unfit for human habitation."

Mr. *Murphy.*

5318. You referred, as accounting for the additional expenditure of 1,100 *l.* two or three years ago, to its being caused by the expenditure upon the floating hospital, which was provided by the sanitary authorities in Dublin; what was the special object of providing that floating hospital?—The floating hospital was provided under the Sanitary Amendment Act of 1871, whereby the local government were empowered in such places as Cork, or Belfast, or Dublin, where two or three sanitary districts conjoined, to designate the particular sanitary authority which should have the charge during epidemics of the port, and provide hospital accommodation for it. In this case the Local Government Board designated the South Dublin Board of Guardians as the sanitary authority, and they got up this hospital irrespective of the opinion of the city of Dublin, or of any other maritime sanitary authorities. They got this hospital constructed, and they sent a precept to us, which they were empowered by the Act to do, quoting our proportion of the costs at 1,100 *l.*

5319. Have you any means of stating what the total cost of the hospital was?—I think it cost 2,700 *l.* I am not sure.

5320. Am I correct in assuming that this vessel was specially built in Dublin for the purpose?—Yes, it was built especially for the purpose.

5321. Can you mention what the tonnage is?—No; it does not resemble any other vessel; it is a large quadrangular mass.

5322. Are you in a position to tell me whether upon a consideration of the various modes of providing hospital accommodation for this epidemic of small-pox or something of that kind, they considered that a floating hosipital was better than one upon land, or one in any other position which they could take, such as a lazaretto or any thing of that kind?—I may state that previous to the construction of this floating hospital, with which I had nothing to do, inquiry was made by myself and a great many others in every direction round Dublin to endeavour to procure a site whereon to erect a hospital, but we failed to get one. I was most anxious that we should get one on land, that we might combine those purposes with others, but there was some objection raised by the neighbouring owners, and failing in this, the Local Government Board put the South Dublin Union Guardians in motion, and after that the corporation were never consulted; we only knew of it when we had to pay the money.

5323. Are you aware whether the authorities had power compulsorily to take the land which was required for the purpose of making an hospital?—No power to take lands compulsorily. Under the Act of 1866 we had power to treat for and take land, but not to take it compulsorily.

5324. How many hours a day do you devote to the duties of your office?—The corporation hours

Mr. *Boyle.*

20 June 1876.

Mr. *Brooks.*

hours are six, but my duties occupy an average of about from nine to nine and a half hours throughout the year, and sometimes a great deal more. I do not feel myself bound to hours; therefore I am the more willing to work.

5325. What reasons operated upon the minds of the Public Health Committee which induced them to refuse to give to the Sanitary Association a report on slaughter-houses?—The communications of the Sanitary Association were not considered courteous; they were considered and framed in a dictatorial spirit, and less with a view to assist the Public Health Committee than for other purposes. They might have rendered us very great assistance.

5326. Was there anything upon the face of those communications which was disrespectful?—They were considered discourteous.

Sir *Arthur Guinness.*

5327. Have you any of them that you could show the Committee?—No, I did not bring any of them here.

Mr. *Brooks.*

5328. Do you know whether there are any public privies in London?—I have been thinking since I have been here, and I have never heard of them.

5329. Have you in any other large towns?—I am not aware of them. I have been in a great many large towns, and I have never heard of them.

5330. Or with regard to public clocks provided by the corporation, do you know if there has been any demand for public clocks in Dublin?—No.

5331. With regard to the sanitary rate, may I ask you if already there are not grave complaints on the part of our largest manufacturers and our gentry, that the burthens of taxation in Dublin are already so high that we cannot afford a further rate?—It is a universal complaint.

5332. Are you able to say whether those complaints proceed as much from the poorer inhabitants as from the more wealthy?—The complaint is a general one; it proceeds from all. I have heard in all quarters the complaint that the necessary burthens are very great.

5333. Do you think that if a rate for sanitary purposes were struck in Dublin, it would be opposed by the citizens?—I feel assured it would meet with a great deal of opposition.

5334. And it is the feeling that it is better to endure the ills we have than fly to further taxation?—I am sure it would meet with very great opposition; however, I give that as my opinion, as the only way of meeting the difficulty.

5335. You think that the complaint of the citizens that you have heard, as to the taxation of the city, has operated upon the corporation, in preventing them from raising a rate for sanitary purposes?—Yes; in point of fact, it is the act of the citizens, and not alone the corporation.

Sir *Arthur Guinness.*

5336. I think you said that you were quite satisfied that the amount now spent for sanitary purposes was quite adequate?—I stated that 3,100 *l.* would be amply sufficient.

5337. The amount spent last year was 4,000 *l.*?—In the last year it was 3,093 *l.* In the year before it was 4,000 *l.*

Mr. *Brooks.*

5338. The meaning of that is, that a demand was made upon the Public Health Committee for payment for an hospital ship, and that that claim was charged upon the outgoings of the Public Health Committee?—Yes.

5339. It was not one that was occasioned by any act of the Public Health Committee, or that was at all under their control?—They had no voice in the matter; it was imperative on them to pay that money.

5340. It was not their act?—No; they had nothing to do with it.

Dr. *Ward.*

5341. Was not it an abnormal expenditure?—It was an unprecedented expenditure.

Mr. *Brooks.*

5342. Is there not a class of persons in Dublin whose occupation and avocation it is to clean ashpits?—Yes, their exclusive occupation.

5343. Was it ever contemplated, do you know, that the corporation should clean out the privies and ashpits of the inhabitants?—Not at all.

5344. They never admitted that they were bound to do it?—Not at all; and it would be generally complained of by the poorer householders in Dublin if the corporation cleansed the ashpits in Merrion-square, and Mountjoy-square, and Fitzwilliam square, at the expense of the others; they would much prefer the state of things as it is. They are prepared to pay for cleansing their own ashpits, but not for the cleansing of others.

5345. Also could not those persons in Dublin whose avocation it is, clean the ashpits more cheaply than the corporation could?—Much more so. The corporation cannot do the work on nearly so economical terms, but the reason why the corporation are resorted to by the richer class rather than the poorer is this, that the corporation employés are a more respectable class to go about their places; they are not likely to steal or abuse their positions, but they will execute their work at once.

5346. When you say that the sanitary condition of the city of Dublin is defective, bearing in mind that all the sanitary authorities in the public meetings declaim on what they agree to be the defective sanitary condition of Dublin, do you mean that the defective sanitary condition of the city of Dublin is positive or comparative?—Comparative; but I have been in all the large towns in the kingdom, and I know some of them very well; and since I came to London I have visited several of the districts in London, and I am much better pleased with Dublin than when I left it.

Mr. *Murphy.*

5347. With reference to this floating hospital which has been spoken of, how long has it been in existence?—I think between three and four years.

5348. Have you the means of letting us know what the annual cost of it has been since that time?—I think it is somewhere about 100 *l.* a year.

5349. That pays for the staff, the watchmen I suppose, and everything else?—Yes.

5350. What use has been made of that hospital since it was erected?—It has had one patient.

5351. Has

Mr. *Boyle.*

20 June 1870.

Mr. *Murphy*—continued.

5351. Has it never been put to any further use since that time?—No.

5352. It costs 100 *l.* a year to keep it up?—I have heard so. I have no official cognisance of it.

5353. Under those circumstances would your opinion be, that if you had got a proper site on land, and if the money that had been expended in building that floating hospital had been laid out in building an hospital upon land, the ratepayers, and the citizens at large of Dublin, would have had more advantage from it than from the floating hospital as it exists now?—Unquestionably; so much so that I myself went in every possible direction along in the neighbourhood of the port where the vessels arrive, with a view to procure a suitable site.

5354. From your experience, taking it on the whole, do you conceive that a floating hospital is such a substitute for a land hospital as ought to be adopted, unless it could not be helped?—I take the experience of the cholera of 1866. I think that the isolation afforded by a floating hospital possesses great advantages under such circumstances. I think that there are cases in which isolation is everything to the prevention of the spread of disease, especially in the case of small-pox.

5355. Supposing you could get that isolation on land as well as on the water, and have a permanent hospital built that could be put to other purposes besides one special one, for an epidemic or a passing disease, which would you prefer?—I would prefer an hospital on land, except in the case of cholera. I need not tell you that the circumstances connected with the spread of cholera are very different from those connected with any other disease.

Dr. *Ward.*

5356. Are you not aware that hospitals on the water, *qua* hospitals, are not so good as those on land for the purpose of hospitals?—No, not nearly so good.

5357. Then it is simply in the case of people who are affected with such diseases as cholera that you would make use of them to preserve the population from infection?—Yes.

Mr. *Murphy.*

5358. What was the character of the disease of the one patient in this hospital?—Speaking from memory, there was an Order in Council on the subject. At the time it was supposed that there was an outbreak of cholera in Bremen, and also in some of the ports of the Baltic. A man came who was supposed to be affected with it, and he was immediately put on board, but I believe it turned out that it was not cholera at all.

Friday, 23rd June 1876.

MEMBERS PRESENT:

Sir Michael Hicks Beach.
Mr. Brooks.
Mr. Bruen.
Mr. Collins
Mr. J. P. Corry.
Mr. Gibson.
Sir Arthur Guinness.
Mr. Kavanagh.
Sir Joseph M'Kenna.
Mr. Murphy.
Dr. Ward.

SIR MICHAEL HICKS BEACH, BART., IN THE CHAIR.

Mr. PARKE NEVILLE, called in; and further Examined.

Mr. P. Neville.

23 June 1876.

Mr. *Brooks.*

5359. You are the Engineer to the City of Dublin, and a Civil Engineer?—Yes.

5360. And a member of the Institute of Civil Engineers in London?—Yes, both in London and in Dublin.

5361. How long have you held this office in Dublin, which you now hold?—Twenty-five years. The reformed corporation of Dublin came into office in 1851, and I was elected local surveyor and engineer the April of that year.

5362. Will you inform the Committee, as shortly as possible, when the Dublin Improvement Act was passed and came into operation in Dublin?—The Dublin Improvement Act was passed in the year 1849, and it came into operation on the 1st of January 1851, when the duties and functions of the late Paving Board, of the Wide Streets Board, and of the City or Term Grand Jury were transferred to them.

5363. Did the corporation, when they came into office, dismiss or retain the officers of those boards?—The corporation retained all the officers whose duties could be made available; for instance, all the officers connected with the Paving Department were retained excepting the tax collectors, whose duties were transferred to the Collector General. Each board, namely, the Paving Board, the Wide Streets Board, and the Term Grand Jury under the old regimen, up to 1851, collected their own taxes, and had their own staff of tax collectors; those all became useless on the Collector General's office being established; some few of them were transferred to him, and the remainder were removed on compensation about this period.

5364. Did the corporation retain any or every one of those whose services could be made available?—The corporation retained the entire staff of the Paving Board, connected with the repair of streets, also their secretary.

5365. And then they dismissed others, such as those who were incapacitated by age, and so on?—There were a large number removed; for instance, five pipe-water collectors and three Commissioners of the Paving Board, whose duties ceased. There was also the secretary of the Grand Jury, Mr. Stanley, and of the Wide Streets Board, Mr. Sherrard, and a solicitor, Mr. Darley, who were removed on compensation, and there were several collectors. Altogether, there was 4,346 *l.* per annum given as compensation to officers whose duties ceased.

Mr. *Murphy.*

5366. Do you mean that there was that saving?—Yes; they were not required under the new regimen.

Chairman.

5367. They pensioned some of them, I suppose?—Yes; those who were put out on compensation, their services not being any longer required, got retiring allowances or pensions.

Mr. *Brooks.*

5368. Can you tell the Committee what is at present paid on the foot of those retiring allowances, to persons yet alive?—At the present moment I make it out that the total retiring allowances of the old annuitants of 1841, when the first Reform Corporation came into office, amount to about 485 *l.*; and of the annuitants from 1849 to the present time on the list, including Mr. John Reilly, the secretary of the Paving Board, and Mr. Denis Costigin, the late treasurer, is 1,956 *l.*, making a total of 2,442 *l.*

5369. Were the powers of the Wide Streets Board limited?—The powers of the Wide Streets Board were limited; they had only two officers, one the secretary and treasurer, and the other the law agent and surveyor; the secretary, Mr. Sherrard, was continued in office for some time; finally, he was also, I believe, put upon compensation, but their powers were limited so far that they were obliged to apply for Acts of Parliament to effect the improvements they desired, and to get the power to levy rates; and their powers in every respect, except that of levying rates, were transferred to the corporation.

5370. But the corporation have no power to levy rates under the Dublin Improvement Act, except the 2 *s.* rate and the 4 *d.* sewer rate?—No,

Mr. P. Neville. 23 June 1876.

Mr. *Brooks*—continued.

No, they are limited to those rating powers under the Dublin Improvement Act.

5371. Is the staff of officers at present in the employ of the corporation, in your opinion, excessive?—Decidedly not, but quite the reverse. If they are compared with the staff officers employed in any other city, Liverpool, Manchester, or elsewhere, that can be very easily ascertained.

5372. Has there been any increase in the rates of wages and salaries in the city of Dublin since 1851?—Yes, there has been an increase in the salaries, a statement of which has been handed in, I think, in this inquiry, and of which I have a copy in my hand, and which shows that the total increase of salaries from 1851 up to the present, so far as I can make out, is 3,619 *l.*, not 5,000 *l.*, as stated by a witness.

5373. Is that in consequence of the necessity for employing a larger number of persons?—It is partly brought about by the New Corporation Waterworks, which rendered it necessary to employ a much larger staff of officers than were in existence in 1851. Then my own salary was increased in consequence of that, and that of other officers also. The Law Agent has been a recent appointment, he is now on a salary of 800 *l.* a year. Formerly they had a small salary for doing the ordinary business, but they had power to charge for their Parliamentary business. Now the present solicitor got 800 *l.* a year, and he is obliged to do all the business, Parliamentary and otherwise.

5374. What was the income of the late Paving Board?—Thirty-nine thousand pounds, or close on 40,000 *l.* a year.

5375. What was the mileage of the streets under their charge?—Eighty-eight miles.

5376. Are you able to say what they expended on scavenging and watering?—They expended on an average of six years about 11,000 *l.* a year on scavenging and watering.

Chairman.

5377. Does that include maintenance of streets?—No, that is only for scavenging and watering; they scavenged the streets out of the rates they levied for paving, lighting, and cleansing, but the watering was paid for by a special rate on the inhabitants of each street watered. I think it was in this way: if two-thirds agreed to pay the cost and memorialised the Board to water the street, the other third were compelled to pay.

5378. Does the corporation now in office operate upon a larger area, and have they a greater mileage of street to maintain, than the Paving Board had?—I should tell you that the Paving Board spent on macadamising and paving 11,154 *l.*, on flagging, 1,450 *l.*, and on lighting the public lamps, 8,863 *l.* per annum. That is on an average of the last six years.

5379. How much per mile can you tell us did it cost the Paving Board for the maintenance of those streets?—I have not got that made up. Besides that would not be a very fair criterion, because some of the streets cost four or five times the amount for maintenance that others do.

5380. I suppose the streets which were under the old Paving Board were those in the centre of the city, were they not, over which most of the traffic goes?—Yes (*The Witness produced a map to the Committee, showing the limits of the jurisdiction of the old Paving Board*).

5381. In fact, I conclude from this map that the additional streets which are now under the control of the corporation, and which were not under the control of the Paving Board, comprise streets extending quite to the outside of the municipal limits?—Generally speaking a great number of those outside have been built since the corporation got that district. The population of the new district at that period was very small compared with what it is now.

5382. So that the streets which always have been expensive were maintained by the Paving Board just as they are by the corporation?—Yes, they were. I may mention that at the present moment the additional streets that are under the jurisdiction of the corporation comprise about 22 miles.

Mr. *Bruen.*

5383. Is that in addition to the 88 miles which you mentioned just now?—Yes, that is what has been added to the city—the new district, as it was called in 1851.

5384. That will make 110 miles?—In round figures about 110 miles.

Mr. *Brooks.*

5385. What was the valuation of the city of Dublin in 1851?—In the years 1847 and 1848 there were local inquiries held in Dublin by surveying officers, and extensive evidence given as to the various duties of the Paving Board, the Wide Streets Commissioners, and the grand jury, and at that period the valuation was given as 663,048 *l.* In 1851, on the corporation coming into office, the valuation was 634,848 *l.*; but from this there were certain exemptions in cases of public buildings, &c., which reduced the valuation, so far as I remember, on which the assessment could be made to something a little over 600,000 *l.*

5386. Was that further reduced in 1852?—In 1852 the valuation was reduced by the Government by, in round figures, 100,000 *l.*, which took 10,000 *l.* a year off the rates which the corporation had a right to expect for the repair and maintenance of the streets, which has placed us in difficulties almost ever since.

5387. What was the annual sum at the disposal of the corporation for the 10 years following 1852?—About 41,000 *l.*, or 1,100 *l.*, a year more than the Paving Board had on an average.

Dr. *Ward.*

5388. That is to say, you had only 1,100 *l.* a year for the additional 22 miles of streets?—Yes.

Mr. *Brooks.*

5389. From 1860 down to the present time, what is the amount at your disposal for those purposes?—For the ten years up to 1870 the sums available for those purposes averaged about 47,000 *l.*, and for the five years ending 1875 it has been something under 50,000 *l.* per annum. There has been a gradual rise going on in the valuation, and then in this last year there was a grant from the Government called a bounty in lieu of the rating on Government buildings. I think, on the whole, it is about 7,000 *l.* a year, but I cannot speak as to the exact figures. That amount is spread over the different rates, and if I remember rightly the sum apportioned to the improvement fund is something about 3,000 *l.*

Mr. P. Neville.

23 June 1876.

Mr. *Brooks*—continued.

5390. Has the price of labour and materials increased since 1851?—Enormously.

5391. Have you any particulars which will show the extent of the increase?—This Table (*producing the same*) shows the price of wages and labour in 1851, 1860, and 1875, and you will see by it that the paviors, in 1851, ranged from 12 *s.* to 18 *s.*; in 1860, from 15 *s.* to 21 *s.*; and at the present time their wages are 30 *s.* per week.

5392. So that, in point of fact, you spend more in Dublin per week than at that time?—Yes; from 1851 to the present period, on the whole, the rise in wages has been about 75 per cent.

5393. What were the wages of labourers?—They were only 8 *s.* a week for some three or four years after the corporation came into office; they are now 13 *s.* to 14 *s.* Scavengers get 14 *s.* a week; that is a rise of 75 per cent.

5394. What were the wages of a horse and driver in those days?—A horse and driver, when I first came into office, were hired at from 4 *s.* to 4 *s.* 6 *d.* per day. In 1860, the cost was 4 *s.* 11 *d.*; and the cost now is about 7 *s.* 6 *d.*

5395. Is that by contract, or is it a computation?—The corporation found that they could not get contractors to do the work satisfactorily, and we were obliged to provide our own horses, and following what has had to be done in Liverpool, Manchester, &c.

5396. Are you able to say, as a matter of fact, what is the contract rate in London for horses and carts employed by the Metropolitan Board of Works?—I saw the metropolitan contract the other day, and it is 10 *s.* a day. I saw their schedule of prices attached to contract.

5397. With regard to materials, to what extent has Bonabreena-green stone increased in price?—It has increased from 6 *s.* to 6 *s.* 6 *d.* a ton. It fell in 1860, when we got it for 5 *s.* 4 *d.*, but it has risen since to 6 *s.* 4 *d.* and 6 *s.* 6 *d.* The delivery is 2 *d.* cheaper on the south side of the city, because it is nearer to contractors than on the north.

5398. As to calp or limestone, what was the price in 1851?—When I came into office it was 2 *s.* 8 *d.* to 2 *s.* 10 *d.*; it continued at 2 *s.* 10 *d.* up to 1860, and it is now 3 *s.* 10 *d.*, 4 *s.*, and 4 *s.* 3 *d.*

5399. About how many tons do you require in Dublin annually of the limestone?—A very large quantity; from about 30,000 to 40,000 tons. I have not got the figures with me. There is round shingle, from 1 *s.* 6 *d.* to 1 *s.* 8 *d.*, which is used in the outskirt streets a good deal; that rose to 2 *s.* in 1860, and it is from 3 *s.* to 3 *s.* 3 *d.* now. The same thing affects the gravel that the paviors use; it has risen in exactly the same way.

5400. Have the granite flags risen from 25 to 50 per cent.?—They have risen from 5 *s.* 10 *d.* to 6 *s.* 9 *d.* per superficial yard.

5401. As to brick, what was the price of Dublin stock bricks?—They have increased enormously; they used to be got, on an average, at 36 *s.* per 1,000; they rose to 46 *s.*, and they now are up to from 50 *s.*; 55 *s.*, I believe is the price for them. Athy bricks are what we chiefly use now for sewers; we used to get them at 30 *s.* as an average price; sometimes they were a little higher, and at other times lower; they rose to 34 *s.* in 1860, and I am now paying 40 *s.* per 1,000 for them.

Mr. *Brooks*—continued.

5402. You use a great deal of brick also from Tullamore, do you not?—No; I do not use the bricks from Tullamore; they are only used for building the interior walls of houses.

5403. As to Portland cement, do you remember the price of that in 1860?—It was about 50 *s.* a ton down to 1855; it is now from 70 *s.* to 75 *s.*

5404. Then as to the Welsh paving-stones with which the greater part of our streets are paved that are paved, what have you to say about them?—The first pavement laid down in the town with Welsh sets, was in 1857 and 1858. We then got paving-stones at 14 *s.* 6 *d.* a ton, delivered on the quays in Dublin, and they remained so for a long time; but two or three years ago they were raised to 22 *s.*, and now they are 25 *s.*; for the paving which we are executing at present we are paying 25 *s.* a ton for the sets.

5405. Have channel stones advanced in the same manner?—They have advanced in the same way. We used to get them for 1 *s.* 11 *d.* per lineal yard, and now they are 3 *s.*

5406. What was the price of lime?—Lime used to be 6 *d.* per hogshead, but it is now 7 *d.*

5407. What is the difference in building stone?—It used to be from 2 *s.* 10 *d.* to 3 *s.* for ashlar stone; that is to say, stone for making ashlars; it is now 4 *s.* 6 *d.* Wallers we used to get from 2 *s.* to 2 *s.* 2 *d.* per ton, it is now 3 *s.* 6 *d.* I may mention, with regard to watering and scavenging, a curious fact, that the corporation have expended on an average 15,715 *l.* a year for the last three years on scavenging and watering; that would appear to show an excess of 4,700 *l.* a year over what the Paving Board spent, which was 11,000 *l.*; but in reality, if you make allowance for the increase in the price of labour and horse hire, it is 3,500 *l.* a year less; that is, if we employed the same number of horses and carts as the Paving Board did, it would cost 3,500 *l.* a year more.

Dr. *Ward.*

5408. Do you state to the Committee that the Paving Board, with 88 miles of streets, employed more men and carts than you do with 110 miles?—They must have done so on account of the price, because if you increase the 11,000 *l.* 75 per cent., which is three-quarters, it would make a sum of 19,250 *l.*, which the corporation ought to spend per annum now on the streets for scavenging and watering, supposing they employ the same number of men and horses as the Paving Board did.

Mr. *Gibson.*

5409. You say that they spend now less for scavenging, making allowance for the difference of price, than the Paving Board did?—Yes, we must employ less men and horses.

5410. As you are going on upon figures, have you got here the number of men and horses that the Paving Board employed?—No, I have not; I am only taking the expenditure.

5411. May not this be the explanation, that inasmuch as the expenditure of the Paving Board was higher, making an allowance for the difference in prices than that which you now spend, they may have employed more men and carts with the larger sum of money?—No, I think the meaning is this, that they spent on the average of their returns 11,000 *l.* a-year during

Mr. *Gibson*—continued.

during the last six years of their administration, and supposing that the work was to be done now at the present prices, the increase of price would be 75 per cent., and that would make that 11,000 *l.* a-year 19,250 *l.*; it is a very startling figure, and that is without taking into consideration the extended area. If you go on further and include that, it would show that the corporation would require in reality to expend 21,000 *l.* on the scavenging and watering. I may say that the price of macadamising materials has increased on an average about 12½ per cent., and the corporation now light 3,459 public lamps, being an increase of 570 since the year 1851.

Chairman.

5412. What is the relative cost of lighting then and now?—Formerly the price used to be paid by the lamp; it is now paid by the 1,000 feet.

Mr. *Brooks.*

5413. How much did it come to per lamp then and now; how much per annum for the whole?—The public lighting for the year 1875 cost 8,807 *l.* 13 *s.* 7 *d.*

Chairman.

5414. What was it in 1851?—The Paving Board spent 8,803 *l.* on the average for their last six years; there were 2,800 lamps lighted by the Paving Board for which they paid 3 *l.* 1 *s.* 8 *d.* per lamp for; and for 89 they paid 3 *l.* 12 *s.* 2 *d.* per lamp. That was for 12-candle gas, and it was on a contract which lasted up to the year 1865, that went on for 15 years after corporation came into office.

5415. What I want to ascertain is the comparative cost of lighting in 1875 and in 1851, taking the same items; perhaps the average expenditure of the Paving Board might include replacing a considerable number of lamps, or something of that kind?—The corporation light 570 lamps more than the Paving Board had, and the sum is very nearly the same annually; therefore the corporation lighting at present must be cheaper per lamp than it was before, it is, in fact, about 2 *l.* 11 *s.* 3 *d.* per lamp.

5416. That is if it includes only the same items?—It only includes the same items.

Mr. *Murphy.*

5417. How many lamps do the corporation light now?—Three thousand four hundred and fifty-nine.

Mr. *Brooks.*

5418. Have the corporation, since the year 1850, constructed new side pavements?—They have expended, between 1867 and 1869, 25,000 *l.* in paving with square sets many of the leading streets; since that they have paved Castle-street, part of High-street, part of Great Brunswick-street, part of Nassau-street, and Wormwood Gate, besides this, out of money raised by presentment, amounting to about 10,000 *l.* They have paved the North Wall, the Custom House Quay, the City Quay, and a large portion of Sir John Rogerson's Quay. This money was raised under the provisions of a clause in the old Ballast Board Act passed in the year 1792, and which was copied by the promoters of the Port and Docks Act in 1869, and is now in force. It was not smuggled into the Act by the corporation, as stated by Mr. Stokes, and it has been fiated for three years in consecutive presentments by the judges; each year there was a certain quantity of work presented, for I have with me the clause in the Act of 1792, 32 Geo. 3, c. 35, and it is the clause as copied by the Port and Docks Board.

Mr. *P. Neville.*

23 June 1876.

5419. Do you hand those clauses in to explain the statement as to the smuggling?—Yes; the clause in the Act of 32 Geo. 3, c. 35, is as follows: "And be it enacted that it shall and may be lawful for the grand jury of the city of Dublin in every Easter Term in each and every year for ever hereafter, to cause to be presented and raised upon the county of the city of Dublin at large in the manner prescribed by the laws now in force for raising money by presentment, for repairing roads in counties or counties of cities, a sum of money sufficient for repairing the roads upon the said north and south walls bounding the said river." The clause in the Dublin Port and Docks Act, 1869, 32 & 33 Vict. c. 100, is as follows: "The municipal corporation shall from time to time cause to be presented and raised upon the county of the city of Dublin at large, in the manner prescribed by the laws for the time being in force for raising money by presentment for repairing roads in counties, or counties of cities, a sum of money sufficient for repairing the roads upon the north, south, and east walls bounding or near the river Liffey." The first clause was copied in my office from the Act of 1792, and the other is copied from the present Port and Docks Act, 1869.

Chairman.

5420. Was this clause in the Act of 1869 when it was introduced?—Yes, certainly.

Sir *Joseph M'Kenna.*

5421. Was it in the original print of the Bill?—Yes, to the best of my knowledge.

Mr. *Brooks.*

5422. Will you inform us as to the main sewers that have been constructed in the city since you came into office?—When the corporation came into office, the sewers of the city were in a very bad state indeed, both as to the number of streets having no sewers, and the existing sewers being in a very bad state, a large portion of them being choked up with deposit.

5423. The present water-closet system has necessitated in Dublin a system of main sewerage that was formerly not in existence?—Yes; the corporation got power to levy a 4 *d.* sewer rate by the Act of 1849; and since 1852, there have been 52¾ miles of new sewers built, and 15½ miles have been repaired and had their levels adjusted, and brick invert bottoms put into them. All the old bottoms were flat, or in the clay, and we have had egg-shaped bottoms put into them, and had the sewers repaired. The total expenditure has been about 104,000 *l.*, and that has been paid for out of the rates from year to year, and no money has been borrowed. The works at present in hand this year are estimated to cost about 5,800 *l.*, and there will not remain very much to be done afterwards. Probably from about 15,000 *l.* to 20,000 *l.* will finish the whole system; a great deal of what has to be done now is putting inverts into the old sewers.

5424. Have you any further facts for the Committee

Mr. *P. Neville.*

23 June 1876.

Mr. *Brooks*—continued.

Committee on the subject of the sewers?—No, I think not.

5425. Have the corporation effected any improvement in widening the streets?—At present the corporation have no power to levy money for widening streets, but there have been two or three small improvements effected. There was an old house purchased in Kevin-street, to widen Bride-street, and they caused a house to be set back in Henry-street, at Ball's Bank last year; and they made a small improvement in Grafton-street, at the corner of King-street. Those were merely accidental things that occurred, and they took advantage of them, but they have no money available for the purpose of widening streets.

5426. It is alleged that the corporation have neglected its duty in not clearing away tenement houses that are unfit for human habitation; can you give the Committee any information on that subject?—The power that the corporation at present possess, so far as the Improvement Act is concerned, and that I am connected with, is simply limited by the Dublin Improvement Act and the Towns Clauses Improvement Act incorporated therewith, which provides that the surveyor or his deputy may, under the authority of the Lord Mayor, cause any building to be shored up or otherwise protected for the protection of passengers; in fact the house must be in such a dangerous state that it is dangerous to life and limb of people passing along the street; in that case I can, for the protection of the public, put up a fence or hoarding in front of the building, and then I can summons the parties before the magistrate after seven days' notice, and the magistrate then makes his order for the owner to take down or repair the premises, and gives him certain time (it is generally taken from me what time is allowed), and if the owners do not do it in that time I have power to take down the house or make it safe so far as the public are concerned. During the last year there were reported at my office, by the police, whose special duty it is, and by others, 359 houses, all of which were examined. Of those about 108 were not considered in such a state as to bring them within the meaning of the Act which I have described; 64 were taken down by the owners, 116 were secured or repaired; seven were taken down by the surveyor, and 74, up to the date of the return, were either hoarded up or in hand to repair.

Mr. *Kavanagh.*

5427. What you mention does not include the three houses that fell last year?—There were two houses that fell in George-street, opposite Messrs. Pim's; that was from the giving way of some of the internal walls or beams; I think it was a beam that gave way inside, and it fell and collapsed inwards. There was one in Sackville-street, which was owing to the cutting through the wall to make a passage some years ago between that and a house behind it, and then the owners got into a law dispute, and the house was shut up altogether for years, but those houses were not included in this number.

Mr. *Brooks.*

5428. They were not reported to you?—They were not reported before they fell. On consideration, probably they are included in the 359 houses, because there were the remains of them which we should serve notice, on the owner to clear away, therefore we must have served the necessary notices, and I dare say they were included.

Mr. *Brooks*—continued.

5429. No doubt if there were external indications of defects in the structure, such as would warrant the police in reporting to you, they would do so?—I can only say that my attention was not called to them; I cannot say more than that.

5430. There were no indications of danger?—I presume that there was nothing to attract the notice of the police. The Police Commissioners kindly allow them to report these things.

5431. The inhabitants of the houses that live on the opposite side of the street did not call your attention to them?—No; I know Messrs. Pim and Company very well, and am often in their establishment in George's-street, and members of the firm have spoken to me, abusing the houses for being very old and dilapidated, and saying that the corporation ought to remove them for the purpose of widening the street; but I do not remember the circumstance that Mr. Pim referred to.

5431*. Have you a Building Act in Dublin?—No, there is no Building Act in Dublin.

5432. Is a Building Act necessary for Dublin, in your opinion?—It is very necessary indeed. The corporation have given directions to myself and the law agent, and we are at present engaged in framing a Building Act, and considering it in connection with the London Metropolis Building Act.

5433. Was not a Bill for that purpose promoted in 1867?—There was; I have the Bill in my hand which was promoted in 1867, but it has also included in it power to construct abattoirs; against which there was great public commotion got up as to its interference with the butchers' rights, and somehow or other the influence was so great that it dropped through. It was not proceeded with. The corporation have decided upon promoting a Building Act next Session.

5434. Are you now engaged in drafting the Bill?—I am, in connection with the law agent. I wish to state, with regard to dilapidated buildings, that a very large proportion of the tenement houses in Dublin are in a most dilapidated and filthy state; they are held by a class of people who do not repair them, but I have nothing to say to that; I may mention that with respect to the removal of houses, the corporation have no power, so far as my information goes, of dealing with anything but those terribly ruinous places which are in danger of falling down, endangering the lives of the public passing through the streets.

5435. Are you able to say, as the city engineer, whether the funds at the disposal of the corporation, expended with the utmost regard to frugality and economy, are sufficient for the proper maintenance of the streets?—They are not; the figures which I have given show, that although the valuation which was made in 1851, and which was reduced in 1852, has increased by a small amount since that period (it has increased probably 15 to 20 per cent. between that period and this), yet the price of materials and the cost of labour have gone up 75 per cent.

5436. But the funds may have been excessive in 1850?—No; they were never excessive; they were never able to meet the demands.

5437. At present they are insufficient, in your opinion?—Yes, they are very much so.

5438. How

Mr. P. Neville. 23 June 1876

Dr. *Ward.*

5438. How many men would you require to do efficiently the work of Dublin streets?—That depends upon what would be required.

Mr. *Brooks.*

5439. After your experience of 25 years in the corporation, and as an officer of the corporation, I ask you if the valuation of the city is too low or if it is unequal in its application?—I think it is very much too low and it is very unequal; I do not know whether I ought to mention that I was speaking to Mr. Ball-Greene, the Government valuator, quite recently upon the subject. The fact is, I believe, that the old valuation which stands for many years back is entirely too low, and it wants an entirely new valuation. Mr. Ball-Greene told me that he considers the valuation in such a state that it requires to be revised, and the people in Belfast are actually applying to the Government for a re-valuation.

5440. Have you read the evidence given before this Committee by Mr. Pim, Mr. Stokes, and Mr. McEvoy, which has been supplied to the Town Clerk's Office?—I have.

5441. Do you, as the city engineer, and as an officer of great experience, concur with those gentlemen?—I entirely concur in their views about the valuation. I may mention an instance that I heard myself the other day. There was a house in Grafton-street, which used to be Goggin's bog-oak shop, and Mr. Gillman, who removed from the corner house of Essex Bridge on account of that house being condemned, paid 275 *l.* a year for the house in Grafton-street, and took it for the remainder of the term; he has only just got rid of it a few days ago, and that house, in the best part of Grafton-street, is valued by Thoms' Directory at 85 *l.* a year.

5442. Are you of opinion that the corporation should have greater borrowing powers?—Yes.

5443. Will you tell the Committee why?—The corporation have borrowing powers under the Improvement Act to the extent of 100,000 *l.*; of these they have spent about 25,000 *l.* on the new Cattle Market in Prussia-street, which has been a great success; they have borrowed 2,000 *l.* for improving the college railings, and recently they have borrowed 50,000 *l.* to substitute square set pavement for macadam in the streets of great traffic, a part of which work is in progress at present; so that that reduces their borrowing powers at the present moment to about 23,000 *l.* I think that if the valuation is raised, that they ought to have power given to them to borrow money to enable them to construct, if they are to be called upon to do it, which I think they ought to do, new markets and abattoirs; and it would be very desirable indeed if the floating debt on the Improvement Rate, which amounts to about 14,000 *l.* or 15,000 *l.*, could be paid off, and then committee No. 1 could pay for materials in cash, and they would have a better command of the market than they have at present, and get materials cheaper.

5444. Does that want of funds compel you to pay a somewhat higher rate for your materials than if you had funds?—It does; I do not go the length that Mr. Stokes does, because I know the prices that they are now paying at Rathmines; I have got them here, and there is not very much difference; but there is no doubt in the world that our not being able to pay our contractors regularly, so as to enable them to calculate with certainty, on receipt of their money to a day, in place of not getting it perhaps for two or three months, has the effect of giving the out townships the preference of getting material a little cheaper than the corporation, and more promptly; and besides that there is a little difference in the distance; the stone chiefly comes in from the country district on the south-western side of the city, and consequently it has to pass through the township of Rathmines to come into the city.

Mr. *Brooks*—continued.

5445. It has been stated, I think, that the department over which you preside does give as much as 25 per cent. to the contractors beyond what is paid by the commissioners of the outlying townships; is that correct?—I do not agree that there is anything like that amount of difference.

5446. Will you state to the Committee what the difference may be as closely as you can do?—The difference at present is very small.

5447. What do you mean by very small?—It is not more than 5 per cent.

5448. What credit do you get?—Very often the contractors do not get paid for three or four months; for instance, an account due in April may not be paid until June or July; the accounts are all balanced up to the end of each month.

5449. If the corporation pays 5 per cent. more for its materials on account of its taking three months' credit, that would be equivalent, would it not, to paying interest at the rate of 20 per cent. per annum?—I do not see that exactly; we do not pay interest for that debt; the only thing is that the men do not get their money.

5450. If you do pay 5 per cent. more than Mr. Stokes does, and you only get three months' credit, that is really equivalent to 20 per cent. per annum?—Putting it in that way it is, but I think that is not the right way; the fact is, as I have stated to you, that the corporation do not pay regularly.

5451. Are those a very poor class of contractors?—Some of them are poor.

5452. To whom a little money is a great object?—Yes.

5453. It is therefore you think that we require borrowing powers in order to pay off our floating debt, and to pay ready money for our materials to poor contractors?—That is so; the township is paying for green store at this moment within 1 *d.* or 2 *d.* of what we are paying.

5454. But they do buy that 1 *d.* or 2 *d.* cheaper than we do?—They are buying green stone at 6 *s.* 8 *d.*; we are paying 7 *s.*; that is rather a high price, and I think it should be lower; they are paying for Shank Hill stone 6 *s.* 1 *d.*, and for round stone 2 *s.* 6 *d.*, and an advance of 6 *d.* per ton was applied for, and it has been obliged to be given. This is a return signed by Mr. Evans, the secretary of the Rathmines township.

5455. Does the Committee, having the charge of the purchase of these materials, do all that it is in their power to do with the funds at their disposal to purchase those materials at the cheapest rate?—They do all that, I believe, they can do (that is by public advertisements) to seek for tenders.

5456. Do they invariably make their contracts with those who supply their materials at the cheapest price?—Yes.

5457. With regard to the extension of the boundary of the city to the extra municipal townships; is it the fact that the city is extending southwards and leaving the northern part to decay?

Mr. P. Neville.

23 June 1876.

Mr. *Brooks*—continued.

decay?—Yes, I may say with regard to a statement that was made in evidence to the Committee as to the extended area that is shown in the map before the Committee, being a loss to the corporation that I must dispute the fact altogether: it is no loss to the corporation; it has been a great gain to them; for the first couple of years there was a considerable expense incurred in putting those out districts in repair; it was a sort of *terra incognita*, disowned by both parties; and there was a considerable expense for a couple of years, but since that they have been bringing a large income to the corporation, particularly latterly since there have been several new streets opened in those districts which have been built on by private parties, Mr. Stokes himself amongst the number, and those all bring in rates to the city; as for that district which used to be called the North Lots, in which the land has been selling at such extraordinary high rates for railways, and where arbitrations have been going on lately, that is all being built and covered with most valuable property, and will tend very largely to increase the rates; if I had had time I should have made it out for the Committee, but I had not time to get the figures.

5458. Then you do not agree with the evidence which has been given as to the extension of the area of the city in 1850, being a misfortune and a loss to the corporation?—Decidedly not, looking at it with regard to its gradual increase in value up to the present time, just at the moment for two or three years, it led to a considerable increase more than the value of any rates that could be got out of them for those two or three years, but since then it has been altogether different.

5459. What is your opinion with reference to the present system of collecting rates, having regard to Mr. Stokes' evidence upon that subject? From what I have heard from Mr. Stokes, and from the evidence, I consider that there is a loss one way or the other to the corporation of about 12½ per cent.; that is to say, we only get 1 *s.* 9 *d.* out of the 2 *s.* rate, and therefore I think that any system which would reduce this loss by collection would be desirable. Mr. Stokes gave an account of their collection in Rathmines, which appeared to be of a most satisfactory character; however there is little poor property, such as tenement houses there.

5460. Have the corporation expended any money in building markets?—Yes; they have built a cattle market which cost about 25,000 *l.* or 26,000 *l.*

5461. Have the corporation any funds to carry out an effective system of domestic scavenging?—No.

5462. Can you inform the Committee what the cost of this work is in Liverpool and in Manchester?—In Liverpool, the domestic and street scavenging costs over 50,000 *l.* a year; in Manchester it costs over 25,000 *l.* for the domestic scavenging alone.

5463. Can you say anything as to the sale of scavenging products?—In Dublin it can hardly be sold; the street sweepings are almost unsaleable; it is almost impossible to get rid of them; that is one of the great difficulties of the corporation to get rid of these sweepings.

5464. Can you say whether, in Liverpool or in Manchester, the scavenging products are saleable?—I know, from my own knowledge, that they have a better market for it; it is carried by the canals into the country, and is more appreciated as manure in both Liverpool and Manchester than it is in Dublin.

Mr *Brooks*—continued.

5465. Have you anything further to say regarding the domestic scavenging in Dublin?—The domestic scavenging is not exactly in my department.

5466. It has been stated in evidence that the corporation have expended large sums of money in promoting and opposing Bills in Parliament; you have had considerable experience, have you not, with regard to those Bills which were endeavoured to be passed through Parliament?—Yes.

5467. Can you tell me from your official position, whether that was done with the intention of benefiting the city?—In almost every Bill that has been either promoted or opposed, I have been professionally engaged on the part of the corporation, and certainly in any Bills that have been promoted or opposed, I consider that the action of the corporation has been absolutely necessary for the benefit of the public. The Bray and Enniskerry Bill has been referred to here as a Bill which the corporation petitioned against. The reason why the corporation petitioned against it was, that it interfered with the Vartry main pipe which conveyed the water of the Vartry to Dublin.

5468. That was opposed, was it not, at a cost of 67 *l.*?—It was opposed at a cost of something about that; I have brought with me a map (*producing the same*), which shows the works of the railway and the main pipe (*the Witness explained the same to the Committee on the map*). The line of railway proposed to interfere with our pipe very seriously, and we were obliged to protect ourselves, and to compel works to be made in connection with the railway for the protection of the corporation property. With regard to Stephen's Green, which was the other case referred to, there was a Bill promoted in 1866, which I have here, and which the corporation petitioned against also. The chief ground of opposition was, that the company then about to be formed proposed, compulsorily, to take away a rent of the corporation of 300 *l.* a year Irish, and that was opposed by the corporation. With regard to a large expenditure which was incurred before 1864, a very large proportion of that was incurred in the great water fight in 1860 and 1861, which was one of the heaviest Parliamentary fights on record.

5469. It has been given in evidence here that all parties in Dublin joined in order to promote a scheme for a better supply of water for the city, and that the hatchet was buried; will you inform the Committee what were the facts with regard to the opposition on the part of the outside committees?—There was evidence given as to the defective supply of water to Dublin before the surveying officers in 1847 and 1848. The present corporation took up the subject about the year 1854, and from that time up to 1859 had various plans under consideration, and employed Mr. Thomas Hawksley as consulting engineer, and every plan submitted was examined into by him and myself, finally, on our advice. In 1859–60, the corporation came to Parliament for a scheme which was called the Coyford scheme. Having given the usual notices, and lodged the plans and passed the Standing Orders, there was a most terrific opposition got up by the citizens at large, comprising the leading men, the railway companies, and the canal proprietors, against

Mr. P. Neville. 23 June 1876.

Mr *Brooks*—continued.

against the scheme, which was subsequently altered in design (there was some clause in the Bill which gave power to do so) into a canal scheme, by which it was proposed to take water from the canal, supplemented by a supply from the Liffey. Then after we had lodged our plans, that was opposed, and finally we were thrown out on Standing Orders; but, however, it never would have been carried out, for the canal company would not come to terms, or guarantee the quantity of water that we wanted. At that period the city Members of the day, Mr. Grogan and Mr. Vance, and others, proposed that there should be a Royal Commission; the corporation accepted it, and it was agreed that there should be a Royal Commission, and all parties agreed to bind themselves that whatever plan the Royal Commissioners recommended should be carried out. The Government appointed Mr. Hawkshaw, now Sir John Hawkshaw, as the Commissioner. He held an inquiry, extending over several days, in Dublin; he received and heard the evidence, and examined all the districts, accompanied by myself and Mr. Hawksley, from which it was proposed to take water. In October 1860 he made his report, recommending the Vartry scheme as being the best; it was the most expensive, and it took the corporation altogether by surprise; but they felt themselves bound to adopt it, and they did adopt it. They went to Parliament in the Session of 1860–61 for a Bill, and when the Bill came before Parliament it was opposed fiercely by the very same parties that opposed before. There was a five weeks' fight before the Committee in the House of Commons; and then on the third reading there was an attempt made to throw it out, and there was a division taken, and only for the energy of the late Sir John Gray, who happened to get hint of it, that Bill would have been thrown out on the third reading, after an expenditure of several thousands of pounds. It was then opposed in the House of Lords, and there was a six days' fight, I think, in the Committee of the House of Lords, but it was finally passed. Both the Committees of the House of Lords and the House of Commons, I may say, were unanimous in passing the Bill. However, the opposition did not stop here, for they continued opposing it and writing against, and frightening the public about it for two or three years, and at last Sir John Gray was called upon to make a statement in answer to the allegations, which he did in a speech (which was afterwards printed in the shape of a report), to allay the excitement of the public mind upon the subject, which he did in the year 1864. Subsequently the works were completed, and I believe I may say its bitterest enemies have no fault to find with it, except what Mr. Stokes may say; and the Committee heard what he said. The cost of the Vartry Waterworks has been 541,400 *l.*, and not between six hundred and seven hundred thousand, as stated by Mr. Stokes. The increase of cost over the Parliamentary Estimates was owing to the service reservoirs being increased in size. The mainpipe from Roundwood to Stillorgan was increased in size; there was a double line of main laid between Stillorgan and Dublin; instead of a single main there were two mains laid, so that in case of one coming to grief the other one would act whilst it was repairing. Also the repiping within the city cost 66,000 *l.* We were

Mr. *Brooks*—continued.

tremendously salted by the verdicts of the county of Wicklow juries, upon claims made chiefly by the riparian proprietors. The total sum which had to be paid in compensation for land, wayleave, and water rights, was 81,180 *l.*

5470. The Coyford scheme, which Mr. Stokes told us would have been a better scheme than the Vartry, was actually proposed, was it not, in the House of Commons by the corporation?—It was proposed by the corporation originally.

5471. And it was rejected by the House of Commons, was it not?—No, it was not rejected by the House, for it never came on to that stage, but it was dropped by the corporation on account of the opposition to it.

5472. It was opposed by various parties in Dublin?—It was.

5473. Would you say, as an engineer, that if the Coyford or the Ballysmutten scheme had been carried out they could have supplied the extra-municipal districts with water so advantageously as by means of the Vartry?—No, it is quite absurd to suppose so. (*The Witness produced a map, and explained to the Committee the course of the pipes of the waterworks from the reservoir to the city.*) We supply Blackrock and Pembroke without any expense at all from the pipes on their passage to Dublin from the works.

5474. Is the water supplied from the Vartry ample?—It is.

5475. Have you, as engineer, any fear of its failure?—No. I may also mention that the Ballysmutten scheme could not be carried out for 300,000 *l.*, if constructed upon the same system of enlarged proportions as the Vartry was. It might have been done something cheaper, but we would have lost the supply of the extra municipal townships.

5476. From whence is Rathmines township supplied?—Rathmines township is supplied from the Grand Canal.

5477. From the open canal?—Yes.

5478. Upon which the traffic from that part of Ireland is carried?—Yes.

5479. Do you know anything of the quality of the water?—The quality of the water is very hard, and it is liable to pollutions. It was condemned by the Royal Commissioner, strong evidence having been given against it.

5480. And yet that is one of the sources from whence the city of Dublin derived its water supply before the Vartry scheme was promulgated?—Yes, before the Vartry scheme was carried out Dublin was supplied with water from the Grand Canal, from the Royal Canal, and from the River Dodder, which latter was the ancient supply of the city. For centuries back, before the canals were made, the supply was altogether from the Dodder.

5481. Is the pressure of the water supply in Rathmines sufficient for the prevention of fires?—No, the pressure is not good; the mains are small. There were fires there lately, and people made great complaints of the want of water.

Sir *Joseph M'Kenna.*

5482. What is the height and pressure, as a rule, at Rathmines above the level of the main streets?—I think that the level of the water in the canal from which they take it, speaking from recollection, is about 160 to 170 feet above ordnance datum, or on average 90 to 100 feet above the main street of Rathmines.

Mr. *P. Neville.*

23 June 1876.

Sir *J. M'Kenna*—continued.

5483. Do you know which lock that is at?—It is above the sixth lock.

Mr. *Brooks.*

5484. Was there any medical evidence as to the quality of the canal water?—There was a great deal of evidence given about the quality of the water from Dr. Apjohn, Professor Sullivan, and others at that local inquiry.

5485. And it was condemned as unwholesome, was it not?—Yes.

5486. But is now used by the Rathmines Commissioners?—Yes.

Sir *Joseph M'Kenna.*

5487. It was the water that was taken from the basin at Portobello that was condemned. I believe the Rathmines Commissioners take their water from a higher level of the canal where it is not polluted?—They take it above the sixth lock.

Mr. *Brooks.*

5488. Have you anything further to say with regard to the Vartry water scheme?—It was stated that the citizens were dissatisfied with the terms on which the townships got the water. I do not know that there is any complaint of the sort beyond this, that Pembroke and Blackrock get their water probably a halfpenny in the pound cheaper on the valuation than the others; but the corporation derive an income from those out-townships at the present moment of about 4,800 *l.* a year. I wish also to mention, as it was stated that the corporation got no payment for the extra water that, under the local Acts of Parliament of the townships, we are bound to provide them a supply equal to 20 gallons per head upon the populations. They have been disputing as to what census the populations should be calculated upon. We hold that they were bound by the census taken in 1871, being the last, and they say, that the populations have increased very largely since that, and they want another datum to go on than that of the census of 1871. I may say with respect to Blackrock and Pembroke, that this dispute has been settled, and I hope the others will be settled amicably. We calculate upon getting 2,000 *l.* a year for that extra water in addition to the 4,800 *l.* that we receive at present; in fact, the Pembroke township has paid 500 *l.* on account of their debt. I wish further to mention that so ample is the supply of water from the Vartry catchment basin, that two-fifths of the rainfall passes annually over the bye-wash; if the city ever wants more water this could be utilised by the construction of an additional reservoir at a cost of 30,000 *l.*, and the corporation own all the water up to the source.

Mr. *Murphy.*

5489. How many gallons do they deliver in Dublin in the 24 hours?—Between 14 and 15 million gallons altogether, including the townships.

Mr. *Brooks.*

5490. With regard to the main drainage scheme which was proposed by Sir Joseph Bazalgette and yourself, will you state whether that scheme which passed both Houses of Parliament is now abandoned?—I should be sorry to think that it was abandoned; the Act does not expire for two years so far as the construction of works is concerned. So far as the compulsory purchase of property goes, the powers expire, I think, in August; but it would be a very deplorable thing if the scheme were to drop through after costing so much money as it has done.

5491. Will you inform the Committee why that scheme is not now in progress?—The Parliamentary estimates were made in the year 1870, and between that and the year 1873, when the first tenders were advertised for; there was an enormous increase in the price both of labour and materials which was one main cause of the great difference. Then, again, there was a variety of causes at work; there was a great derangement in the labour market, and the contractors put on very large sums for contingencies to meet possible disappointments; in fact, it was almost impossible to get tenders at the time within a reasonable figure.

5492. Then it was not because of any engineering difficulties?—No. I may say that Parliament passed a Bill last year authorising the Exchequer Loan Commissioners to lend them 500,000 *l.*, and the corporation have had estimates sent in that would complete the works, including every item, for 468,960 *l.* Since that, with a view of reducing the expenditure more, and to bring the contracts within the means of contractors of moderate means as much as possible, we divided the works into nine different contracts; and on revising the estimates, I think we can now complete the works for about 430,000 *l.*, including everything.

Sir *Joseph M'Kenna.*

5493. Then there is a difference of 20,000 *l.* odd made by splitting it into nine contracts?—I do not know the result, but according to my estimate there is a difference of over 30,000 *l.*

Mr. *Brooks.*

5494. Will you tell us why the tender for the main drainage works so far exceeded the Parliamentary Estimate?—That is the main cause which I have just mentioned.

5495. The levels of the main drainage scheme were stated to be erroneous; were they so considered by you?—Decidedly not; there was no error whatever in the levels. The fact is, there was a portion of the Pembroke district, which comprises Irish Town and Sandymount, lying east of the Dodder, on so low a level that it was not embraced in our scheme; and it was always contemplated that the sewage from it should be lifted up into our sewers by a separate pumping system. Here is the evidence given by Mr. John Vernon, the chairman of the township commissioners of Pembroke, on the main drainage scheme. He was asked, "You are a petitioner against this measure on behalf of the Earl of Pembroke? (*A.*) I was; and on behalf of the township of Pembroke as well. (*Q.*) Having a strong interest in the question, not only directly, but indirectly, what would be your feeling as to the abandonment of the present scheme? (*A.*) I should be very sorry to see it thrown out on public grounds. (*Q.*) You have been attending the Committee during the investigation pretty constantly? (*A.*) I have been a good deal here. (*Q.*) From what you have heard, do you believe the scheme to be a good one. (*A.*)

Mr. *P. Neville.*

23 June 1876.

Mr. *Brooks*—continued.

(*A.*) As far as I am able to form an opinion. (*Q.*) You are of opinion that it is absolutely necessary for the city that it should be carried? (*A.*) I think, they must carry a scheme, and I think postponing it would be a very great misfortune to Dublin. (*Q.*) You made an arrangement on behalf of your townships with the persons having the carriage of this Bill? (*A.*) I did. (*Q.*) For what reasons did you make that arrangement? (*A.*) Because I was advised that the Bill as a whole, could not be successfully opposed on engineering grounds, and I was very anxious that the Bill should be passed, and I was anxious also to derive some benefit from the Bill, which we do by the arrangement that has been made with the corporation. (*Q.*) Then you think the scheme from what you have heard and what you have been advised, is a well-devised and a well-considered one? (*A.*) Yes; so far as I am capable of forming an opinion. The engineering question is beyond me? (*Q.*) Your engineer has advised you, that on engineering grounds it could not be opposed. (*A.*) I was so advised as regards the city, not as regards the township. (*Q.*) That so far as the city was concerned, and the objects to be effected by the scheme, it was well devised? (*A.*) I was so advised. (*Q.*) Do you think the people of Dublin and the suburbs in general understand this main drainage scheme? (*A.*) I think they do. We quite understand it," and Mr. Stokes in his evidence before the Committee was asked, "You were a few days ago of opinion that this was not a good scheme? (*A.*) We did not enter into the scheme at all, but we were advised by our engineer that we could make no practical objection to the scheme; they advised us that it was one that could be carried out for the money the corporation wanted, and that there was no engineering difficulties. We never objected to the scheme, we only objected to pay more than our fair proportion towards it. (*Q.*) Your engineer has been your adviser? (*A.*) No, we employed independent engineers in London, Mr. Hassard and Mr. Hawksley." Then the question was put to him, "And you have been advised by them that it is right and proper that you should join this scheme?" to which his answer was: "We did not want them to advise us as to that. We consulted them about an alternative scheme; we were prepared to drain ourselves, and have nothing to do with the corporation. We never requested them to investigate the corporation scheme. Mr. Hassard in fact could not object to it, because he proposed the same scheme, but they proposed a scheme which we thought could be carried out with a rate of 3½*d.* in the pound, and which would have discharged the sewage without annoyance to anyone. In that we had this advantage, that we joined with the township of Pembroke, and in the township of Pembroke all the sands belong to Lord Pembroke, and therefore we had great facility in discharging on that side." That went to show that there was no allegation that the levels were wrong, and all that, and here is their own engineer's evidence upon the subject.

5496–8. Will you explain the surcharge of the Public Auditor of 6,000 *l.* for the construction of the low level sewers at Grattan Bridge?—When the corporation decided upon rebuilding what was called Essex Bridge, now Grattan Bridge, I advised them that it would be very desirable if they would make a portion of the two low-level sewers which were designed to run on either side of the quay, so as to avoid any interference with the streets afterwards, and Sir Joseph Bazalgette also agreed to that, and we both recommended it; and consequently the corporation applied to the Port and Docks Board to include the building of those two pieces of sewer in the rebuilding of Grattan Bridge; they did so, and that increased the cost of the work by 6,708 *l.*, which, I think, was the figure. The work was carried out and completed, and the council ordered the Main Drainage Committee to pay this money out of the moneys that they had in their hands; the Main Drainage Committee did so, but it was out of the rates, and then when it came before the auditor, he expressed his opinion that in law he could not allow it, for, although it was a very proper and just expenditure, and he would be very glad to allow it if he could, he would be obliged to report against it on the grounds that the works should have been executed out of loan instead of out of rates; but the corporation expect that it will come before the Local Government Board by-and-bye, and they have good reason for believing that it will be then set right.

5499. As to the cost of feeding the horses employed by the corporation, what is the weekly cost?—For the year ending December last the scavenging horses cost 1 *l.* 0 *s.* 4 *d.* a week, and the gravel horses cost 18 *s.* 10 *d.*, for the five months; this year, on account of the fodder being cheaper, the cost of the scavenging horses on an average is 17 *s.* 8 *d.*, and of the gravel horses 16 *s.* 8 *d.*

5500. Does that include straw and everything?—Yes, it includes everything in way of forage; the total cost is about 7 *s.* 6 *d.* a day at the present moment for the horse and the driver.

5501. Does the man who drives the horse also groom the horse?—Yes, he does; he takes care of the horse, the harness, and everything else. What I mentioned before was the mere cost of feeding the horse, the forage.

Mr. *Kavanagh.*

5502. How will that agree with Mr. Robinson's evidence that the forage of the horses per annum was 4,051 *l.*?—I really do not know; I cannot answer that question, but I have here a return made to me from our horse inspector, in White Horse Yard, dated the 3rd of June 1876, which gives the cost exactly: the rations of the scavenging horses are returned as 21 lbs. of hay, 6 lbs. of straw, oats 10 lbs., Indian corn 10 lbs., and bran 2 lbs.; and of the gravel horses, hay 21 lbs., straw 6 lbs., oats 8 lbs., Indian corn 8½ lbs., and bran 2 lbs.

5503. Mr. Robinson in his answer to Question 2725 says: "Then the horse account is, purchase of horses 599 *l.*, forage 4,051 *l.*, veterinary expenses 252 *l.*, harness and repairs 72 *l.*, miscellaneous 123 *l.*, stable expenses 513." I suppose that the weekly wages which follows applies to the 7 *s.* 6 *d.* a day for the horse and driver?—Yes it includes that; and also of some stablemen who have to keep the stables clean, and the yards, and so on.

5504. We have in an answer to the Chairman a very different statement, for at Question 2765, the Chairman asked him: "And in the same way, taking the various items which you have given us on the horse account, amounting altogether to 6,143 *l.*, that is spent in work in the year?

Mr. P. Neville.

23 June 1876.

Mr. *Kavanagh*—continued.

year? (*A.*) Yes. (*Q.*) How many horses do the corporation keep? (*A.*) 80." If you divide 6,143 by 80, it gives a rate for each horse, that is for working them as well as feeding them of 76$\frac{43}{80}$ *l.*? I am giving you the actual figures which are returned to me; I have got here the return of the horses in the year 1875. There has been some confusion between the financial year of the corporation ending the 31st of August and the year proper from from the 1st of January to the 31st of December, besides Mr. Robinson's figures, are payments made on this account within the year, which will differ from the actual expenditure, within the same. I have here the cost of everything for the year commencing the 1st of January and ending the 31st of December 1875.

5505. Could you give us, according to your Return, how much the cost per horse per annum?—I could, and I will prepare it for you, and give it to you the next day of the meeting of the Committee.

Chairman.

5506. Those figures which Mr. Robinson gave us were taken from the accounts of the corporation, and therefore they must be correct, must they not?—I have no grounds for saying that they are not correct, but this is the actual cost of feeding for nearly two years (*delivering in the same*).

5507. We are speaking of the year ending the 31st of August 1875?—I suppose so; that I have not got the particulars of.

5508. Mr. Robinson gave us all the details for that year, and they of course ought to tally with your accounts?—This return commenced October 1874, and it gives the weekly cost of the scavenging horses and the gravel horses.

Mr. *Murphy.*

5509. Did I understand you to say that the daily cost of the horses was 7 *s.* 6 *d.*?—The horse and the driver.

5510. Could you take out the cost of the driver and separate them?—The driver is 2 *s.* 6 *d.*, leaving 5 *s.* for the horse. Of course there are some other items; there are the shoeing, veterinary, and stable expenses, and things of that sort.

Mr. *Brooks.*

5511. I asked you to give the Committee the cost of feeding of the horses employed by the corporation; what is the present weekly cost?—I have totted it up for the year commencing January 1875, to December 1875, and I make the average cost for the scavenging horses 1 *l.* 0 *s.* 4 *d.* per week per horse for feeding, and 18 *s.* 10½ *d.* for a gravel horse; that is a lighter horse, and has not such heavy work to do. For the five months of this present year, from January last to May inclusive, the average cost of the scavenging horses is 17 *s.* 8 *d.*, and of the gravel horses 16 *s.* 8 *d.*

5512. What charges are included in those figures which you have named; do those charges include veterinary advice and shoeing?—No; this return is simply the cost of food.

5513. Does it include bedding?—No; but if you will allow me, as there appears a difficulty about this, if you will tell me exactly what I am to get, I will have it in proper form by the next day. I believe that the 7 *s.* 6 *d.* is what is now computed to be the cost of a horse and driver,

Mr. *Brooks*—continued.

including everything, veterinary, bedding, stabling, care of yards, shoeing, and all the various items.

5514. Will you be able to give the Committee on Tuesday next any details as to that 7 *s.* 6 *d.*?—Yes, I will write over for them, and get them in detail. I may mention that in London the contract of the Board of Works for horses is 10 *s.* a day: I saw it in the schedule the other day in Sir Joseph Bazalgette's office.

5515. Can you offer any explanation of Mr. Stokes' statement with reference to the Waterworks Committee, who, he said, by a scratch of the pen got rid of a deficiency of about 19,000 *l.*?—The explanation of that is, that up to August 1870 there were separate accounts kept of receipts and expenditure, one being called the Waterworks Rate Fund and the other the Waterworks Loan Fund. Pursuant to the Waterworks Act of 1870, Clause 16, the two accounts were amalgamated, and from that time to this there has been only one account kept. The balance which, upon the 31st of August stood to the credit of the Waterworks Loan Fund, was 18,695 *l.* 8 *s.* 5 *d.*, and to the debit of the Waterworks Rate Fund 18,399 *l.* 3 *s.* 10 *d.*, leaving, as between the two sums, a balance of 296 *l.* 4 *s.* 7 *d.*, which was carried on the 1st of September 1871, in the treasurer's return, to the credit of the Corporation Loan Fund, there being only one fund from that time to this.

5516. To pass on from that subject to another, you are, as well as being one of the oldest officers of the corporation, one of the most highly paid and trusted, I think?—I am one of the highest paid, although my salary is small when compared with what is paid in Liverpool, Manchester, and other places.

5517. What is your salary?—£. 750 a year.

5518. Some time ago it was not so much?—No, it was raised about five years ago.

5519. You have been 25 years in the employ of the corporation?—Yes.

5520. May I ask you what the corporation of Glasgow, or of Manchester, or of London, pay the officers who fill situations similar to yours?—They pay very much more; I cannot give the exact figures; I think formerly, in Liverpool, Mr. Newlands, the borough engineer, had 1,200 *l.* a year, and the waterworks engineer the same amount; they are amalgamated now, and Mr. Deacon holds the office, and I think he has 1,200 *l.* a year.

5521. The subject has been introduced here, and I am compelled, in order to vindicate the corporation, to pursue it, although I do it with some reluctance; may I ask what is your religion?—I am a Protestant.

5522. Do you know whether your co-religionists, Protestants, are excluded from office by the corporation on account of their creed?—No, not necessarily; at least not to my knowledge; I know that several of the officers are Protestants.

5523. Have the corporation any power of re-valuation of the houses and the property in the city of Dublin?—No. I believe that any person, if they consider their premises valued too low or too high, can go individually to the Valuation Office and demand a re-valuation of that particular tenement, but there is no power in any public body, I am informed, to call upon the Valuation Office for a general re-valuation.

5524. There

Mr. *P. Neville.*

23 June 1876.

Sir *Arthur Guinness.*

5524. There would be nothing, would there, to prevent the corporation petitioning Government in favour of it if they chose?—I do not know that they have the power. I was asking Mr. Ball-Greene that very question last week, and he said that they had no power.

Mr. *Brooks.*

5525. Do not they know that if they were to re-value, that the valuation would be totally inoperative as a mode of increasing the taxation of any individual?—I do not exactly understand how that would be.

5526. Have the corporation the power of increasing the valuation of any premises in Dublin, and obliging the tenant or ratepayer to pay increased rates?—No, not on the city at large. I do not know about any particular individual case, but as a general principle, and as to increasing the valuation, as proposed in evidence given before this Committee, they certainly have not the power.

Sir *Joseph M'Kenna.*

5527. Can they on the request of any particular householder, re-value his house?—It is not the corporation that makes the valuation; it is done by the Government under Mr. Ball-Greene.

5528. Have the corporation the power at the request of any householder or proprietor, of ordering a re-valuation?—I think not; I am quite sure they have not; the corporation have nothing to say to such a person. He may go himself to the Valuation Office if he is dissatisfied with his valuation.

Mr. *J. P. Corry.*

5529. Is not this the state of matters, that provided any change is made in any property, the Government valuators at once change the valuation?—Upon their becoming acquainted with the fact of a house being rebuilt, or anything of that sort, or any improvement in it, I believe they re-value it; and as Mr. Stokes said, the scale of valuation which they have adopted lately on those new buildings (he mentioned particularly two houses in Sackville-street) shows that it is a different scale from the general scale, which was adopted some 30 years ago, when first the valuation was generally made.

Mr. *Brooks.*

5530. Passing on to another subject, I will ask you whether the rate which was levied for re-building Grattan Bridge was leviable upon a much more extended area then the municipal district?—It was assessed over a very much larger district. It is levied off what is called the metropolitan police district in the map which I hold in my hand, and which I produce to the Committee; the part coloured red shows the present municipal borough of Dublin; the part coloured yellow is Clontarf; the part coloured blue is Kilmainham; Rathmines is left white, and Pembroke, and Blackrock, and Kingstown, and portions of Dalkey, a part of county Dublin, Phœnix Park; indeed, the entire of the district surrounded by the hard red line is the police district, and it embraces a great many townships and a considerable portion of the county of Dublin immediately adjoining the city.

5531. Will you give us the names of those districts from which this bridge rate is leviable, and what is outside the municipal district?—As I have mentioned, it embraces as shown on this map, the entire of Clontarf, the entire of Kilmainham, the entire of Rathmines, the entire of Pembroke, Blackrock, Kingstown, Dalkey, and a part of Killiney townships; also those small ports of the county Dublin.

5532. Does the bridge rate extend to Dalkey?—It does, and it embraces also certain portions of the county of Dublin immediately adjoining.

5533. Did the Rathmines commissioners object to this bridge rate being leviable over their district?—They did.

5534. That objection was overruled, was it not?—It was.

5535. Is it your opinion that the districts included in the metropolitan district should also contribute towards the expenses of paving and scavengering the streets leading to those bridges, and for the same reasons that they contribute to the bridges?—Yes; this map, I think, will show it (*producing another map*). You will observe that Rathmines and Pembroke are all one continuous town with the City of Dublin, as much so Parliament-street and Whitehall; they are only separated by an imaginary line, I may call it, of the canal; and the streets are just as thickly inhabited as the city adjoining, and I contend that the boundary should be extended so as to embrace almost the entire townships of Pembroke, Rathmines, Kilmainham, and Clontarf.

5536. And that the liability for the construction of the bridges should extend to the scavenging and repairing of the streets leading to those bridges?—I consider that they should be incorporated in the city for general purposes, for the reason that the city of Dublin is travelling or extending almost entirely in one direction, that is from the north to the south, and that leaves the north side of the city in an impoverished condition. The best private streets, such as Gardiner-street, Gloucester-street, and such streets, were formerly inhabited by the very first class professional and mercantile men, but now they are almost all lodging-houses, or let as tenement houses. The class of people that used to occupy them now are all gone in the direction of the Rathmines and Pembroke townships, and the consequence is that the repair and maintenance of the streets remain the same, although the people who paid high rates have gone outside the boundary line; I, myself, live in Pembroke-road, which is only a simple continuation of Baggot-street, the canal dividing the streets, the former being outside, the latter inside, the city.

5537. As a matter of fact, have all the rates leviable by the corporation been at their maximum since 1870?—Yes, they have been all at their maximum, except that for two years the sewers rate was not quite up to the maximum, in 1874 or 1875, I think it was; but otherwise they have been all up to their maximum.

5538. Amongst the items of increased nominal revenue of the corporation, is there not a very large sum receivable from the corporation itself for a tax on their own water-mains?—Under a recent decision the corporation water-mains have been valued, and a very heavy rate struck on them, and of course a portion of the water rate, which is 1 *s.* 3 *d.* in the pound, is payable in that queer way. The rating on the mains outside the city for 1875 is 1,692 *l.* 9 *s.* 10 *d.*, and within the city it is 4,073 *l.* 16 *s.* 7 *d.*, making a total of 5,766 *l.* 6 *s.* 5 *d.* The water carried through

Mr. P. Neville.

23 June 1876.

Mr. *Brooks*—continued.

through these mains is, with exception of the quantity, sold for manufacturing purposes for the supply of the city, and the citizens who paid for the works. There might be some ground for levying a rate on the income derived for manufacturing supply, which is about 13,000 *l.* a year at present. Of course it might be considered that it ought to be taxed; but the general rating on all the mains that supply the city, is, I think, hard lines. However, that appears to be the law.

5539. How much is so levied?—There has been a lawsuit going on about it. The corporation have been disputing the claim, and it was decided by the Court of Exchequer against the corporation last week, in favour of the Collector General, who is the plaintiff.

Mr. *Murphy.*

5540. Has it been decided that it being the property of the corporation out of which profit is made, it is taxable for general purposes?—The way it is put in the valution is, that it increases the value of the land, and to have mains laid through the streets; it is very curious.

Mr. *Brooks.*

5541. Is it a fact that under the Waterworks Act the corporation can receive no beneficial revenue from the water rates, either the public rate or the private rate, and that they are bound to devote any surplus, after paying the interest and the charges, to the reduction of the water rate alone?—That is the law. If the income from the water rate was over the cost of paying the charges on it, for instance, interest on borrowed money and the maintenance of the works, they should reduce the rate. They could not spend that money for sewerage purposes, or for any other purpose.

5542. And they cannot devote it to scavenging?—No, nor for any other purpose.

5543. No matter how short the fund may be?—No matter how short the fund may be they have no right to do it.

5544. It is not considered a hardship to make them pay poor rate and police tax for property in which they have no beneficial interest?—That is the very question which has arisen upon this rating of the mains; that is the ground upon which the question was raised.

5545. I will direct your attention to the fire brigade; how is the fire brigade supported?—It is supported by a rate of 1½ *d.* in the £., which is taken out of the public water rate. Originally by the Waterworks Act of 1861, the rate was limited to 1 *s.* in the £. for the domestic rate, and 3 *d.* in the £. for the public rate. The year following, I think it was, the corporation went for a Fire Brigade Bill, and they got authority to spend 1½ *d.* in the £. of the public rate to support the brigade; that was for 10 years from the passing of the Act, after which it dropped to 1 *d.*; however, when the 10 years elapsed it was found the 1½ *d.* was barely sufficient to keep up the brigade, even with a limited number of men, in an efficient state, and when it was reduced by the other halfpenny, which represented over 1,000 *l.* a year in Dublin on the valuation, it was quite inefficient, and they were obliged to diminish the force of the brigade. About a year afterwards there was a Bill promoted by the corporation, by which, among other powers, they got power to re-enact the old charge of 1½ *d.* for the fire brigade in the place of 1 *d.*; but it was actually down to 1 *d.* for a couple of years.

5546. So that taking from the water rate 1½ *d.* for the fire brigade, the water rate practically remains what?—One shilling and three halfpence, being 1 *s.* domestic rate and 1½ *d.* for the public rate.

5547. It has been suggested that the sewer rate having reached its maximum, now charges for it are put upon the grand jury cess; is that so?—I can only say that the sewer rate is a rate separate to itself, and that no part of the sewer rate was ever applied for grand jury or other purposes.

5548. Is there power to levy a borough rate in Dublin?—I believe there is. I have always understood that there was power of levying a borough rate to the amount of 3 *d.* in the £.

5549. Has that power been exercised?—No, I think not. I am not very well up in the rating powers of the corporation, except the part that comes immediately under my own department.

5550. Is it quite erroneous to suggest that the corporation have levied all the rates up to their maximum, and have levied every rate that they possibly could?—They have not levied the borough rate, and there were two years in which the sewers rate did not reach the maximum.

Sir *Arthur Guinness.*

5551. Are there any other rates that are not at their maximum?—I am not aware. I think that they are all at their maximum. The corporation have nothing to do with any rates in the city, in the way of collecting them or spending them, except the improvement rate of 2 *s.*, the sewer rate of 4 *d.*, and the water rate, domestic and public. There is a vestry cess, which is something very small. There is also the Grand Jury Fund levied for the support of the city prisons, reformatory schools, paying interest, and on former loans, &c.; but most of those charges are compulsory on the corporation to levy.

Mr. *Brooks.*

5552. They have levied the improvement rate, which is devoted to paving, lighting, and scavenging, and that one is up to its maximum?—Yes.

5553. Have they power to raise additional funds for those particular purposes?—Not that I am aware of; the borough fund is chiefly formed by the city estate, and any surplus from that I believe they could apply to the improvement of the streets or paving, or anything else; but there is no surplus.

Mr. *Kavanagh.*

5554. One of the witnesses said, in reply to an honourable Member, that the corporation have only power to dispense certain rates which he named; who has the power to dispense the other rates?—There are the poor rates, which go to the poor law guardians. There is the police tax of about 8 *d.* in the £., which is entirely a Government tax, and then there is the grand jury cess, a large proportion of which is mandatory on the corporation. They are bound to do it, it is for the support of the gaols and other purposes, and if they did not present the judges would do so I have always understood.

5555. The grand jury are practically the corporation, are they not?—There was a term grand jury

Mr.
P. Neville.
23 June 1876.

Mr. *Kavanagh*—continued.

jury originally in Dublin, and their powers were transferred to the corporation.

5556. Then really the grand jury means the corporation?—Yes, the grand jury means the corporation.

Mr. *Brooks.*

5557. Does not the corporation levy the grand jury cess which is handed over to the grand jury, say for Rock-road and other purposes?—It may be seen in the accountant's returns that there is a grand jury cess levied chiefly for the maintenance of the prisons, and there is also a sum levied towards the repair of the Rock-road.

5558. Is not that money distributed by the grand jury?—The prison part of it is distributed by the Board of Superintendence, which is a board appointed by the corporation. Then there is a portion goes to the reformatory and industrial schools, and things of that sort. I am not very well up on this subject. I daresay that other witnesses will afford the information; but here it is in the accounts. There are the expenses of provisions and all that for the support of the prisons. That is one, of course, under the direction and authority of the Board of Superintendence, which is a branch of the corporation. Then there are witnesses attending commissions, chaplains' salaries, inspectors of prisons, registration of voters, and so on.

5559. Are there any special circumstances which make the scavenging of Dublin streets a matter of exceptional difficulty?—One of the difficulties is the great length of carriage to get rid of the soil, and the non-sale of the soil, there being no market for it. Another difficulty is that Dublin is proverbially a very damp city, and of course it is more difficult to keep it clean than a city where there are a greater number of dry days in the year than there are in Dublin.

5560. Besides its humidity, and the cost of carriage, and the waste of material, are there any other circumstances?—Those are the principal ones; I do not remember for the moment anything else.

5561. With regard to the road material that we raise in the vicinity of Dublin, is that good or bad material?—The material that we have in the neighbourhood of Dublin is not by any means a first-class material for macadamising.

5562. Does that cause any difficulty as compared with London?—If we could get Guernsey granite, which costs the great price that it does in London, it will make better and smoother streets than the material which we have got in Dublin will do.

Sir *Joseph M'Kenna.*

5563. Is there no granite to be had in Dublin?—No granite fit for macadamising material.

Mr. *Brooks.*

5564. With reference to the disgraceful condition of Rock-road, near Dublin, about which we are all agreed, and which was referred to by Dr. Hancock, will you inform the Committee whether the grand jury of the city has any power to keep that road in order?—The part of the Rock-road from Baggot-street Bridge to the cross in the Blackrock was, by some old Act of Parliament which I am not acquainted with, placed under the Grand Jury of Dublin, and the City of Dublin, and what was called the Barony of Dublin, each of which were to pay one-third of the cost of keeping that road in repair. It was placed under the care of the grand jury for many years, and the grand jury still have charge of it. For many years it was kept in repair at the expense of 1,200 *l.* a year, of which the corporation paid its third. Latterly it was taken by a contractor for a very low figure.

5565. Have the corporation any power to repair that road?—They have not, beyond what I have mentioned before.

5566. One of the judges lately threatened to stop your salary, I think, in consequence of the condition of Rock-road?—He made a mistake, and he has since told me so; the corporation have nothing to say to it.

5567. Can you tell me what are the respective limits of the jurisdiction of the Port and Docks Board, and of the corporation?—The duties of the Port and Docks Board are entirely confined to the maintenance and keeping in repair of the Port of Dublin; they have the charge of the quay walls and bridges up to Victoria Bridge, which used to be called Barrack Bridge before it was rebuilt.

5568. Do you know whether the ratepayers of Dublin are in the habit of attending before the public auditor and inquiring into the expenditure?—They are; I have been in the room when the auditor has been sitting, and there have been ratepayers there.

5569. Do you know if any of Mr. McEvoy's objections have been allowed?—He has made several objections at each audit, and I think they have been mostly disallowed; there were one or two about the gas supplied for lighting the public lamps which were disallowed, I know, lately. The gas to the public lamps is now supplied by meter; there is a meter, I think, on every tenth lamp. It was alleged that the company consumed more gas in those lamps than they did in the other lamps, and consequently, of course, the average showed a greater amount of gas than was really consumed. That charge was investigated before the auditor, Mr. Finlay, and he heard evidence on it, and he came to the conclusion that the allegation was erroneous.

5570. And the result of that was published in the newspapers, was it not?—Yes; his observations were published in the newspapers, and they have been sent to me.

5571. He stated, I think, that those charges were disproved?—Yes.

Sir *Arthur Guinness.*

5572. Was it an objection, or was it an endeavour to obtain information on the subject, or in what form was it?—I understood that it was what I mentioned; it was more against the gas company than the corporation; but, of course, the corporation paid for the gas.

5573. Did Mr. McEvoy ask the auditors to decide the question, or only ask for information?—There was an inquiry before the auditor into it, and here is the report of it in the newspapers. "Mr. Finlay (the auditor) said: This matter had come before him on objections to portions of the payments, amounting to 5,000 *l.* or 6,000 *l.*, made by the corporation to the gas company for gas represented to have been supplied to the public lamps. He had taken all the evidence that was submitted to him in support of the allegation

Mr. *P. Neville.*

23 June 1876.

Sir *A. Guinness*—continued.

allegation that that charge by the company represented money for gas which was not in fact supplied to the corporation. In other words it was an imputation—a very serious imputation indeed—against the gas company. He had considered very carefully the evidence in support of the objection, and that on the other side, as well as the statements made, and he was glad to find that Mr. McEvoy had not felt it necessary to press for a disallowance in this case, for if he were to have done so the application was one to which he could not possibly accede."

5574. Then he did not press for it?—He did not press for it.

Sir *Joseph M'Kenna.*

5575. As to the estimate of the proposed main drainage works, was that estimate formed upon a specification, and detailed prices?—Not the first estimate. Of course the first was merely a Parliamentary estimate made upon the Parliamentary plans.

5576. I mean those that you got for the purpose of ascertaining what the cost would be if the works were carried out?—The tenders that the corporation received were based upon regular specifications and working plans.

5577. Did they give a specification of the prices for each head?—They all got specifications, no doubt, to arrive at their estimates.

5578. But did you get specifications of prices for each description of work?—No, the tenders came in to the corporation in a lump sum.

5579. If we find that the prices of materials, and a certain class of prices of labour, have fallen between the time that you got that estimate and the present time, inasmuch as the prices were not furnished on detailed specifications, you could not now, upon the basis of the former proposals, re-estimate what would be the reduction in the cost?—No, only from our own knowledge of the price of things at that period, and the price now.

5580. That is in a general way, but you could not with an estimate made in such a general way replace it before the contractors who tendered in the first instance, and say to them, "You asked us at a particular season 450,000 *l.* for doing such-and-such work on such-and-such a scale of prices, can you review those prices, and say what it will come to now"; you could not test the reduction in that manner?—We had no detailed prices from the contractors; we furnished a bill of quantities, but they were not priced.

5581. When a new house is built in Dublin, it is valued, is it not, strictly according to what is its fair valuation at the day?—I am informed that the scale of valuation on which a new house is now valued, by the valuator, is a very much higher scale than that which was adopted in the valuation of houses of a similar class, when the valuation was made some 30 or 40 years ago.

5582. Then the builder of a new house has to pay a taxation in proportion, not merely to the value of the house, as compared to its actual valuation at the present day, but he has to pay in a greater ratio than the owner of a house of a similar value that is next door to him that happened to be an older house?—That I believe is so, and that is one reason why it has been said here by others that it is an unequal valuation.

5583. Does not that condition of things

Sir *Joseph M'Kenna*—continued.

operate as a penalty upon improvements?—It would do so, but at the same time I do not think that it would stop any man that wanted to improve his property.

5584. If a man takes a house in Grafton-street, which was valued on the old valuation at 85 *l.* a year, and he chooses to build a new house, and a more suitable house, on the same area, he would have to pay relatively and actually three times as much taxes as he would have to pay if he managed to get along with the old house?—It would appear so. I do not know whether it is exactly the same rule that is adopted, but it is notorious that the scale is higher.

5585. Subject to any variation that may happen to be found out on experiment, it certainly is the case that he would have a direct interest, so far as the taxation of the premises is concerned, in living as long as he could in the old premises, and not building a new or improved house?—Looking at it in that point of view, of course, it would be so, but I doubt very much whether that would stop a person wanting to rebuild.

5586. Have you estimated what would be the relative increase of area of the extended boundary, which you have recommended to the Committee, as compared to the old?—I think it would double it.

5587. You estimate that it would nearly double the area; have you estimated what would be the additional value upon the area?—I have not.

5588. It would be considerable, would it not?—It must be very considerable.

5589. But nothing like double?—No.

5590. What would be a gain to the corporation by extending the area, subject to the city taxation, would be imposing upon those outlying districts that portion of the taxation of the city which they now escape?—Yes.

5591. And the question that arises here is simply whether they are not equitably liable as members of the same large community to a very large proportion of the metropolitan expenses which they now escape?—Yes, that is my opinion, and also I may add that with regard to the poor rates, those outlying townships have a very moderate poor rate; I think it was stated here as 10 *d.*, while Dublin is 1 *s.* 10 *d.* And in addition, when the people there are out of employment and cannot get employment, they come into the city and fall upon our poor rates. I think that is another ground on which they should be included.

Mr. *Kavanagh.*

5592. In your examination with regard to the Bill which was brought into Parliament and afterwards dropped, you said that Mr. Stokes mentioned something about a clause being smuggled into the Act, and you were rather inclined, I think, to contradict his evidence about that; did you ever see the original draft of the Bill as it was prepared?—I cannot say that I did.

5593. You never saw the Bill in the shape in which it was introduced into Parliament?—I could not say; I might have done, but I could not say for certain.

5594. Then you cannot speak positively as to whether that clause, whatever it was, was in the Bill when it was introduced into Parliament?—I know as a fact that the clause was copied from the

Mr. *P. Neville.*

23 June 1876.

Mr. *Kavanagh*—continued.

the old Ballast Board Act, and I went to the Act, and found it there, and I got the two clauses copied for the information of the Committee.

5595. Still you cannot say that that clause appeared in the original draft of the Bill as it was introduced into the House?—I could not say that.

5596. Therefore you cannot say whether it was introduced afterwards?—It may have been; but I do not think it was.

5597. I asked you a question with regard to the falling of the houses, and you said that you rather disagreed with some of the evidence which Mr. Pim gave. I find that Mr. Pim was asked about this by the honourable Member for Dublin at Questions 2410 and 2414, "Are you aware that the commissioner of police has 1,000 men continually patrolling the town, and that it is the duty of the police to inform the city engineer when the houses are in that dangerous condition?" His answer was: "I do not think myself that there are many policemen that know anything about architectural buildings." Then he goes on about those houses afterwards that fell, and he is asked: "Did you call the attention of the police or the corporation to them?" And this is his answer: "Several years ago a gentleman asked Mr. Neville to come there, unfortunately he is no longer living, and therefore I cannot produce his evidence; but I was informed the other day that Mr. Neville had been asked several years ago, by him, to come into our part, and get up to the roofs of those houses to see the state they were in; that may be six or eight years ago, I daresay"?—I have not the least recollection of that circumstance. I am constantly in Messrs. Pim's establishment. I have known Mr. Pim, and I have known the other partners for a long time, and they have frequently spoken to me, generally about the state of those houses opposite. They project beyond the general line or range of the street some five, six, or eight feet, and there are some of them very old, and very bad houses. The gist of the conversation was always this: they used to say that it was a shame on the corporation not to pull down those houses, as they were disfiguring the street, and that they should widen the street. The fact was that the portion of the street that jutted out happened to be the city estate. But with regard to the other assertion I have no recollection at all.

5598. Are you speaking of the houses that fell?—The two houses which fell were part of those houses which I mentioned; there were several houses extending from Exchequer-street down to where the street widens, I suppose six or seven houses altogether; I could see no appearance of any danger externally from the street.

5599. Then your evidence with regard to that statement of Mr. Pim's is this, that he had called your attention to the houses with regard to removing them?—Yes; certainly with regard to removing them for the improvement of the street.

5600. And not as regards their being dangerous?—No; they were very bad-looking houses some of them, with very bad roofs; and they were very discreditable, and I support his evidence to that extent.

5601. There was another part of Mr. Stokes's evidence which I gather from you you do not agree with, and that is, as to the cost of the Vartry Waterworks; I think you said that the cost of the Vartry Waterworks was only about 454,556 *l.*?—If I said so, it was a mistake; the cost of the Vartry works was 541,400 *l.*

Sir *Joseph M'Kenna.*

5602. Did that include 81,180 *l.* to the riparian proprietors?—Yes, the cost of the works was 321,000 *l.*, and the compensations given, including the riparian proprietors, amounted to 81,180 *l.* 5 *s.* 9 *d.*

5603. The total cost of the Vartry Waterworks was, in the first place, "Expended on all works outside of the city boundary, including the superintendents' houses, lodges, planting, road-making, and forming grounds, 331,000 *l.*"?—Yes.

5604. Then under the heading of "Compensations and purchase of lands, way-leave, and water rights," there is the sum of 81,180 *l.* 5 *s.* 9*d.*?—Yes, that is right.

5605. Then under the head of engineering staff, draftsmen, surveyors, valuators, &c., 18,933 *l.* 1 *s.* 9 *d.*?—Yes

5606. Then there is an item for Parliamentary costs, 27,186 *l.* 13 *s.* 4 *d.*; what were those costs?—That was Parliamentary and law costs extending for nearly 10 years, but they were connected with the completion of the Vartry scheme; there were the costs of arbitrations, and all that sort of thing.

5607. Then there was damages paid for injury to property by burst of pipes, 1,100 *l.*; and the cost of works in altering, extending, and relaying pipes, &c., 70,000 *l.*?—Yes, that is correct.

5608. Cost of laying mains from the Corporation Works to the boundaries of Bray, Kingstown, Dalkey, &c., 12,000 *l.*?—Yes.

5609. Then the two items which are mentioned in this page, but not primarily included in the expenses of the Vartry Waterworks, are two-thirds of the expenditure in laying a main from the canal, 7,040 *l.*, and the debt due by the corporation on monies borrowed in 1809, 72,000 *l.*, is that so?—Yes, that is correct.

5610. Mr. Stokes in his evidence stated, did he not, that the cost of the Vartry Waterworks, in round figures, was something about 600,000 *l.*?—He said it was between 600,000 *l.* and 700,000 *l.* You will observe with respect to this 7,040 *l.* for laying a main from the canal to brewers and distillers, and so on, that money was expended in laying the main down for them, and of that the canal company paid the other-third, and the profits of the water is divided between the corporation and the canal company; that 72,000 *l.* is the old pipe-water debt, which was incurred in the year 1809, with the interest on it.

Mr. *Murphy.*

5611. That leaves 550,000 *l.* as the cost of the waterworks, exclusive of the pipe-water debt?—Yes; the figure which I gave you before.

Tuesday, 27th June 1876.

MEMBERS PRESENT:

Sir Michael Hicks Beach.	Sir Arthur Guinness
Mr. Brooks.	Mr. Kavanagh.
Mr. Bruen.	Sir Joseph M'Kenna.
Mr. Butt.	Mr. Murphy.
Mr. Collins.	Mr. O'Shaughnessy.
Mr. J. P. Corry.	Dr. Ward.
Mr. Gibson.	

SIR MICHAEL HICKS BEACH, BART., IN THE CHAIR.

Mr. PARKE NEVILLE, C.E., called in; and further Examined.

Mr. *Neville*, C.E.
27 June 1876.

Sir *Arthur Guinness*.

5612. HAVE the Corporation received all the power that the Wide-street Commissioners had?—I presume that they have, except the power of rating; that is my impression.

5613. In carrying out the improvements which are called private improvements, in your account, is there any loss upon them, or is the expense altogether paid by those who have those improvements effected through the corporation?—You mean what is called licensed work. If a person wants to effect an improvement in the way of flagging, or that sort of thing, which is not public work, it is done for him on his paying the estimated cost.

5614. Will you explain the mode of procedure, supposing there is any improvement required, either in flagging, or in connection with an alteration of the coal vaults, or anything of that kind?—The flag in which the coal stopper is fixed and used for the purpose of passing coal from the street into the coal vault underneath, is the property of the householder, and he is bound to supply it, and keep it in repair, and if it gets out of order he is noticed by the corporation to lodge a sum of money sufficient to renew the stone, to prevent accidents to the public; also the iron gratings that give light into the areas underneath the footpaths are private property, and the stone in which they are leaded is the property of the owner, and if he wants them either put down new or have the old repaired he has to pay the cost of doing it. Those are what we call licensed works. Then in the same way with regard to sewers; if you want to get your house drained, either by putting in a new one, or if the drain has become stopped, and you want to get it cleared, or to get the street opened from the house into the main sewer of the street, the drain being the property of the owner of the house, and he has to pay for repairing it, renewing it, or clearing it.

5615. In any improvement of that kind, is all the expense invariably paid by the owner of the house?—I think so; that is my experience.

5616. How are the men who are sent to carry out that work, superintended?—By an overseer, either a flagging overseer, or a sewer overseer, or a ganger.

Sir *Arthur Guinness*—continued.

5617. Have you never known an instance in which the whole amount was not paid by the individual?—I cannot say; there might have been some exceptional cases. For instance, if the owner of a drain alleged that there was some defect in executing the work originally, or if, in the case of house drains, it is found that the stoppage of a house drain was caused by deposit in the main sewer, he is not charged for the opening of the street.

5618. I ask these questions, because it is the general opinion, in Dublin, that the men, carrying out these works are very insufficiently watched and checked?—I think they are as well watched and checked as they can be or are in any other place, but when you have to scatter men in gangs of two or three, it may be in 10 to 20 jobs in different parts of the city each day, you cannot have an overseer constantly with each set of men.

5619. Who values the cost of each of the works?—The work is charged for according to the time that the men are engaged upon it, and any materials used is charged for at cost price. They pay so much a yard for the flags, sewer pipes, &c., as I mentioned in my evidence the last day.

5620. As to the paving of the streets, and the stone for the repairs of the streets, do you think that the streets are at present in a satisfactory state?—No, not the macadamised streets; and, as to the paved streets, some of them want to be taken up and re-done. They have not been done for 16 years. For instance, in the case of Dame-street and College Green, it is 17 or 18 years since they were paved.

5621. How do you get your stone for macadamising?—There is some portion comes from the neighbourhood of the Dublin mountains, from Friarstown, and Bonabreena.

5622. Are they good stones?—They are the best we can get, but I do not think they are a very

Sir *Arthur Guinness*—continued.

very good stone for the purpose. It is a hard stone, but they do not bind well.

5623. Will you read to the Committee what you recommended in your report in the year 1869, with regard to obtaining stone for the streets?—"The present system of obtaining macadamised material is also most objectionable, and tends to great inconvenience, and is much to the detriment of the proper maintenance of the streets. The stone is got from a number of contractors of very small means, who either quarry the stone on their own farms, or buy it from parties having quarries. Each of these have a limited number of horses, one, two, three, or a few more; and as they cannot afford to allow those horses to be idle (having no other work for them), their object is to force the macadamising material in equal quantities on us all the year round, whereas, that is not the way we want it, having reference to the proper repair of the streets, which require double the quantity of material during the winter and spring than in the summer seasons; and whenever it is found expedient to diminish or increase the quantity, there is always great difficulty, trouble, and annoyance with the contractors."

5624. Will you read what you recommended as a cure for that?—"The only remedy for this state of things would be for the corporation to contract with some party or parties having the command of quarries of the best stone, and storing a large quantity of the material ready to draw out as required."

5625. Has that which you recommended been done?—No, it has not; we have one large contractor, a Mr. Worthington, who has a contract with the Dublin, Wicklow, and Wexford Railway Company, who supplies a large quantity of stone from Bray Head; this we can get pretty nearly as we want it, but not so well from the small contractors.

5626. What is the cost of the Bray stones?—The present cost is 7 *s.* a ton.

5627. Laid in the streets?—Yes, laid down on the streets.

5628. Are you aware that the Rathmines Commissioners get this stone at 6 *s.* 1 *d.* per ton?—Six shillings and eight pence is the present price, I gave that in evidence on Friday. I think 7 *s.* that we pay is too high.

5629. What is the reason you cannot get it on the same terms as the Rathmines Commissioners?—One reason is, that a good deal of it has to be brought to the north side of the city. It comes in at the back of the Harcourt-street Station, and driving it to the north side of the city makes a longer carriage on it, and also at the time we were hard up for stone, and were obliged to get it where we could.

5630. As to asphalting the streets, has the asphalte which has been laid down on the carriage-ways and footways been successful?—The only asphalting on the carriage-ways in Dublin has been laid in Grafton-street, a portion of which was done by the Val de Travers Company, and the other portion by the Limmer Company. Then there was a piece done in Henry-street by the Val de Travers Company, those are the only pieces of carriageway that have been asphalted.

5631. Has it been quite successful?—The Limmer asphalte has answered the best. The Val de Travers had to be repaired in Henry-street more than it has in Grafton-street, but the Limmer is the better of the two, being laid down in a liquid state, whereas the other is laid down in a dry state.

Sir *Arthur Guinness*—continued.

Mr. *Neville*, C.E.

27 June 1876.

5632. You also state in your report at page 34, "The next place on which the asphalte has been laid down was Suffolk-street. This was most carefully done, and the street opened for traffic on 14th September last, since which it has remained in admirable order, and is the best bit of street in Dublin at present;" what has become of that asphalte, is it there now?—No.

5633. Then it was not a successful experiment in asphalte?—I remember it now, we called it asphalte, but it was made by mixing macadam with a preparation of tar; a sort of grouting of tar and lime. It lasted pretty well for a time, but it did not answer expectation, and was macadamised over again in the ordinary way; it was, in fact, a laying down of a sort of concrete instead of dry macadam, and it was not exactly right to call it asphalte.

5634. What do you pay for gravel at present?—From 3 *s.* to 3 *s.* 3 *d.* a ton.

5635. Do you know that the Rathmines Commissioners are getting the same gravel from the same contractor at 2 *s.* 6 *d.*?—I have it here in a letter from Mr. Evans, the secretary, saying that they are now asked and cannot get it under 3 *s.* I produced that letter the last day I was here.

5636. They have been obtaining it at 2 *s.* 6 *d.*?—Yes, they have been obtaining it; but it is only within the last six or eight months that we have been paying more than 3 *s.* for it; we used to get it at 3 *s.* and 2 *s.* 10 *d.*

5637. They have got it for a considerable time, have they not, less than you have?—Yes; but it must be remembered that the material that comes into Rathmines involves much less carriage on the contractor; that is one reason; and I have also stated that I have no doubt but that Rathmines and those other townships which are able to pay ready money, have a preference over the corporation, and therefore they are able to get it somewhat cheaper.

5638. I find in your report of 1869, at page 40, a recommendation on the subject of scavenging. In speaking of the manure depôts in Dublin, you made this recommendation: "To meet this difficulty," that is the nuisance caused by the smell from those depôts, "it has been suggested by Mr. Sullivan, town councillor, to employ barges or hoppers to be moored along the quays at certain points, and to discharge the scavenging soil of adjoining districts into them and, as filled, to tow them out into the bay by a tug boat to such a distance that no objection in any point of view could be raised to emptying their contents into the sea, as is done by the Ballast Board with the deposit of sand and sludge dredged out of the Liffey. This plan is adopted, I believe, in other places, and is one I have often thought of. It is decidedly practicable, and if the scavenge cannot be got rid of at a reasonable cost otherwise, will probably soon have to be resorted to;" has that been done?—That has not been done; but I have very little doubt that it will have to be done, because, putting aside the nuisance of the depôts, which is not referred to in my report, and is a statement I do not agree with, it has been a most difficult matter to get them. We used to be able to deposit it on private grounds, but they are all filled up and built over, and we are so crippled for space now that the corporation must adopt that or

Mr. *Neville*, C.E.

27 June 1876.

Sir *Arthur Guinness*—continued.

or some other plan. but it will be enormously costly. The barges must be of large size, flat-bottomed, and able to hold a very large quantity of stuff, and would have to be towed out to sea by a steam-tug seven or eight miles to where they could drop it.

5639. You recommend that, and you consider it to be more economical than the present plan, which you say is bad?—With regard to economy, it would get rid of the thing altogether, and get rid of a good many complaints that are made at present.

5640. Are you able at present to sell the manure in those depôts?—No, there is little or no sale for it.

5641. You have to pay to have it removed in any case?—We give it for nothing; it is taken out from the depôts for nothing, except in one or two places where they pay 2 *d.* a load.

5642. Have you changed your mind on that subject since you wrote that report about the barges?—No; in fact it is the want of means which is our great difficulty in this matter. I think I made an estimate of the cost; and speaking from recollection, I think it would cost some 8,000 *l.* or 9,000 *l.* to buy four of those big barges, which would be 1,500 *l.* a piece, at least, to start with, and the annual cost for tugs, labour, &c., was estimated at 800 *l.* to 1,000 *l.*

5643. You think this a costly and an undesirable plan?—No; I think it will have to be come to in the end.

5644. Do you think it will be cheaper in 1875 or 1876 than it was in 1869?—Everything is dearer in 1875 and in 1876 than in 1869. We should have to pay a great deal more for the barges, &c., &c.

5645. On the subject of the markets, I find in your report that you say that in 1862 Dublin was in a very unsatisfactory state as regards markets, because, at page 57, you say, "There is no city, I believe, in the United Kingdom worse off for good general markets than Dublin. When it is observed the fine markets that are erected in Liverpool, Manchester, Birmingham, Newcastle, Glasgow, and in all the large towns and cities in England and Scotland; also that Cork and Belfast have good markets, it appears strange that Dublin should be an exception; Castle Market, Clarendon Market, Ormond Market, and Cole's-lane Market are all fast falling into decay, and the best class of butchers, &c., leaving them and establishing themselves in the streets, which is not considered desirable;"—from this book I gather that you are very well up on the subject of markets; can you tell me the history of Mr. Malley's Bill for the establishment of a market on the North Lots?—Mr. Malley proposed to establish a cattle market, and got up a company for the purpose of establishing a cattle market on the North Wall, nearly where the present terminus of the Liffey Branch of the Midland and Great Western Railway is; on the very site, in fact.

5646. That Bill was carried through both Houses of Parliament, was it not, although opposed by the corporation?—It was opposed by the corporation, because it was an attempt on the part of the promoters of that Bill, who were chiefly persons connected with the Midland and Great Western Railway Company of Ireland, for the purpose of taking the cattle trade from Smithfield to them. It was also opposed by the sales' masters.

Sir *Arthur Guinness*—continued.

5647. But it was carried through Parliament?—It was carried, no doubt, but in three days after it passed the House the sales' masters subscribed 14,500 *l.* in cash down to the corporation to enable them to construct a new cattle market in Prussia-street.

5648. Do you know what the cost of the opposition to making that market was to the city?—I cannot tell you.

5649. Will you read from that Parliamentary Return what the cost was (*handing a Paper to the Witness*)?—I see here 2,108 *l.*

5650. Having failed to prevent that Bill being obtained, the corporation got up a market in opposition to that; is not that so?—The sales' masters and the Corporation of Dublin got up the new cattle market in Prussia-street, which has been a great success; it is one of the finest markets in the United Kingdom.

5651. That was immediately after the Bill passed, was it not?—It was immediately after; the very day that the Bill passed the House of Lords the groundwork for getting up that market was begun. The corporation and the sales' masters thought it would be a very injudicious thing, and very bad for the cattle trade of the country at large, if it was to be transferred altogether into the hands of the railway company.

5652. Is it not the case that from the year 1849 to the year 1862 the corporation did nothing about establishing markets until this Act was obtained?—There was great complaints about the Smithfield Market from time to time, but there was no new market actually constructed; there were sites spoken of, and it was proposed to purchase property to enlarge Smithfield.

5653. But under their Act of 1849 they had power to make markets, or to promote Bills for them?—Yes, they had.

5654. But until 1862 nothing was done?—No actual work was undertaken from want of funds.

5655. On the subject of the main drainage in the year 1866 I find, in this book of yours, at page 9, that Mr. Bazalgette sent in his report with plans and sections, on October the 13th, to the special committee, but is it not the case that there was nothing done from the year 1866 until the year 1869, when surveys and estimates were made?—I think so.

5656. I find at page 23 you say: "With regard to the cost of carrying out the works as recommended by Mr. Bazalgette and myself, I have had careful surveys made, and estimates prepared, and am of opinion that to complete them, including provisions for carrying off the extra-municipal sewage through the city sewers, and main outlet sewer to reservoir, the cost will be 230,000 *l.*; that was in 1869; what was done between 1869 and 1870?—I do not know that there was anything done. It was in 1870 that the Government passed a Bill enabling them to lend the corporation 350,000 *l.*, on condition that they would promote the Bill of 1871, the present Main Drainage Act, which the corporation did.

5657. When they applied, in 1870, to the Government, did they not, for a public Bill?—Yes; there was an injunction, or some other legal proceeding taken against the corporation to abate the nuisance of the Liffey; I forget exactly what the technical name of it was.

Mr. *Neville*, C.E.

27 June 1876.

Sir *Arthur Guinness*—continued.

was. There was an examination before the Lords Justices in Dublin, and the corporation were obliged to undertake to do this work, and they were given a time to do it. Then the want of funds was made right by the Government undertaking to introduce this Bill, enabling them to lend the money, which was upon the condition of the corporation going for a Bill the following year to construct the works.

5658. In 1871 what was done?—There was a Bill obtained, the Dublin Main Drainage Bill.

5659. In 1872 what was done?—From that time until 1873 the working drawings, surveys, and all the necessary details for getting up the work and enabling tenders to be got, occupied the time.

5660. Were not the working plans complete before that?—No, it takes a long time to get up working surveys, and estimates, specifications, quantities, and other details necessary.

5661. In 1873 what was done?—There were advertisements for tenders.

5662. Was that before or after the corporation promoted the Bill for obtaining a gas supply for Dublin?—I really cannot say at this moment. I forget when the corporation promoted the Gas Bill.

5663. It was in 1873 that the corporation went for a Gas Bill, and they had not at that time advertised for tenders; is not that so?—My recollection is that it was July 1873 when the first tenders came in for the main drainage works.

5664. You are, no doubt, aware that when the Corporation endeavoured to obtain this Gas Bill, they were then taunted with the fact that they had done nothing about the main drainage, and I will ask you to read Section 22 of the Petition which was presented against the Bill?—"That the Corporation of Dublin does not possess sufficient claims upon the confidence of the Legislature to entitle it to the wide extension of powers which is now sought for at the hands of your honourable House."

Mr. *Brooks*.

5665. What is that which you are reading from?—It is the Petition against the Dublin Corporation Gas Bill of 1873, from the Commissioners of the Township of Kingstown. As I was observing, the first tenders for the main drainage works were received in July 1873, and they must have been advertised in the papers for some time before. I can state, from my own personal knowledge, as the engineer of the main drainage scheme, that it was in my office the main drainage plans were prepared; and that the Gas Bill had nothing to say, directly or indirectly, to the proceedings of the main drainage, nor had I anything to do with the Gas Bill.

Mr. *Gibson*.

5666. Was there any tender received until after the complaint was made in the Petition of the Kingstown Commissioners, that the Corporation could not be trusted with the Gas Bill because they neglected their business under the main drainage scheme for a year; was it a fact that any tenders had been received?—Tenders were received, as I tell you, in July 1873.

5667. Was it after that?—There is no date to this document that I see, but I state of my own knowledge that the Main Drainage Committee had nothing to say to the Gas Bill; the main drainage tenders were advertised for as soon as the plans were ready, and it takes fully a year or a year and a half after the Bill is passed before you can get ready to advertise for tenders for such a large work.

Sir *Arthur Guinness*.

5668. When were these plans perfected?—They were perfected about March 1873, I think. The working drawings are not made until after the Bill was got.

5669. Will you read the first paragraph at the top of page 8 of the Report of the Main Drainage Committee, dated 2nd September 1870?—"The corporation has been in consultation with Mr. Bazalgette, the engineer of the Metropolitan Main Drainage of London, and in conjunction with him has prepared plans for the requisite works, which have been revised in accordance with the results of a series of experiments, and are now deemed perfect for all the objects to be accomplished." That means that the Parliamentary plans would be ready to lodge in Parliament, and the details necessary to give evidence in support of it, but after that is done, and after the Bill has received the Royal Assent, and has become an Act, those working drawings, surveys, and other details have to be made.

5670. That Bill was obtained in 1871, was it not?—Yes.

5671. What is the date of that report?—September 1870; it was in November 1870 that the Parliamentary plan for the main drainage scheme had to be lodged, as directed by Standing Orders, and they were not lithographed at the time that report was made.

Mr. *Collins*.

5672. How long an interval elapsed between the time when the tenders were received in June 1873, and the time when the advertisements first appeared?—I cannot exactly say the date, but I should say that, for a large job of that sort, we should give two or three months to the contractors to tender.

Sir *Arthur Guinness*.

5673. Have you seen the requisition which was signed for a Mansion-house meeting, presided over by the Lord Mayor, upon the subject of the main drainage in 1874 (*handing a Paper to the Witness*). Will you look over those names and see if there are 22 members of the Corporation of various politics who signed that requisition?—I knew that there was an agitation got up against the main drainage scheme. It was stated that it would raise the rates on the city 5s. in the pound, and all that sort of thing.

5674. Will you read that requisition?—"We, the undersigned, request your Lordship to convene a meeting of the ratepayers of the City of Dublin, to take into consideration the advisability of calling upon the corporation to discontinue all further expenditure in respect of their Main Drainage Act of 1871, and to join with the citizens in a memorial to the Government for the appointment of an engineer of eminence and experience, not previously consulted in the matter, to investigate and determine whether a scheme of Liffey purification may not be devised, which, while efficacious for the purpose, shall be better suited to the circumstances (financially) of the City

Mr. *Neville*, C.E.

27 June 1876.

Sir *Arthur Guinness*—continued.

City of Dublin, than that sanctioned under the Act of 1871."

5675. What was the result of that petition, did the corporation accept it?—I do not remember.

5676. Do you recollect that they declined to entertain it?—I should think they did.

5677. Then there was a second meeting, presided over by the Lord Mayor, also?—The Lord Mayor presided over it because he was called upon to do so in his official capacity.

5678. But it was a fact that he did so?—Yes.

5679. And at that second meeting, it was carried unanimously that the corporation be requested to ask the Government to appoint a Royal Commission?—I think so.

5680. And that was declined by the corporation also?—It may have been, but they have since agreed, I think, to ask for a Royal Commission.

5681. And have they done so?—I do not think that has been done yet. I think there is a report from a committee of the whole house upon the subject recommending it.

5682. Then there was a deputation to the Lord Lieutenant, and the Government consented to increase the borrowing powers of the corporation by an Act of Parliament to 500,000 *l.*?—Yes, they passed that Act last year.

5683. On condition that the corporation obtained a Bill for carrying out the works?—Yes.

5684. Did the corporation take any steps towards doing this?—They attempted it last Session, but there were proceedings taken against them in the Court of Queen's Bench to stop them.

5685. Then the corporation did not promote this Bill legally?—There were the usual advertisements inserted in the papers in November last of their intention to apply for an Act; and then upon that there was immediately an injunction, or some legal proceedings taken against them in the Court of Queen's Bench, which was decided against them, and they were obliged to abandon it.

5686. The Court decided that the proceedings were illegal?—I suppose so.

5687. You are aware that the citizens committee stated to the corporation that it was necessary to give notices in order that their action should be legal?—I do not know; it is very likely they did. I do not say that they did not; they were in correspondence last year, and there was disputing going on between the citizens committee and the corporation.

5688. Will you read to the Committee the passage at page 13 of the Report of the Main Drainage Committee for 1875?—"The committee not wishing to assume the responsibility of recommending the acceptance of even the lowest of these reduced tenders, passed the following resolution, and referred the matter for the consideration of the town council, namely: 'That it appearing manifest that under any circumstances it is not possible to execute the works for the sum, the corporation are authorised to borrow, and that it is undesirable to require the committee to incur a personal liability, a special report to this effect be made to the corporation, in order that they may, if they think it desirable, seek further powers from Parliament, and offered the citizens an opportunity of considering whether they will sanction the increased taxation, if necessary.'"

Sir *Arthur Guinness*—continued.

5689. Did they afford the citizens the opportunity mentioned there; do not you know that those notices were the way in which the citizens were to be afforded an opportunity of judging, which opportunity they did not receive?—The complaint was that the corporation did not adopt the plan pointed out in the Towns Clauses Improvement Act, which requires certain notices to be given two or three months before inserting the Parliamentary notices; but the corporation were prevented doing it from want of time. There was everything running one against the other, and they could not do it; but that is more in the law agent's department than mine.

5690. Does not that show that the corporation were aware that notices were necessary?—I cannot tell what notices you refer to.

5691. Giving the citizens an opportunity of judging?—There were the notices which they did take the opportunity of, which were given them in November last year, 1875; and the corporation were stopped by proceedings in the Court of Chancery.

5692. You mean that their illegal Bill was stopped by an injunction?—The Bill was stopped by legal proceedings.

5693. The Government carried their Bill, did they not?—Yes, last year they did.

5694. Then from that reply of the Main Drainage Committee, it is not much more advanced now than it was in the year 1853, when you first called the attention of the corporation to it?—That is not the fault of the corporation.

5695. With reference to the water supply of Dublin, I find in the Report of the Waterworks Committee, at page 26, some remarks on the subject of the purity of the water of the Coyford scheme, which I think you said, the other day, was not pure?—No; I said that the canal water was not pure; I said nothing about Coyford.

Mr. *Brooks.*

5696. What is the date of that Report?—1859. We were speaking upon the subject of the supply to Rathmines by the canal; and I said that the canal water had been condemned by the Royal Commission.

Sir *Arthur Guinness.*

5697. I find that you reported to the Waterworks Committee, No. 2, in February 1859, on the subject of the purity of the canal water; will you read it to the Committee?—This was before the Royal Commission reported, or that inquiry was held. "That the waters of the canals, as proved by the analysis, are of a good wholesome quality; and when taken at a proper distance from the city, and after being subject to the process of filtration, will be unobjectionable waters for domestic use, quite colourless, and of but a moderate degree of hardness."

5698. Then at that time it appears that the water of the canals was purer than subsequently?—I do not think there is much difference. It is right to mention with regard to this that this was before the inquiry in which all the analyses were made and the whole thing threshed out by Mr. Hawkshaw as the Royal Commissioner.

5699. I think in your evidence the other day you said that there was great opposition got up on the part of the principal citizens to the Coyford scheme; will you explain what that was?—Yes, the Coyford scheme was the one that was first

Mr. *Neville*, C.E.

27 June 1870.

Sir *Arthur Guinness*—continued.

first recommended by Mr. Hawksley and myself to get a supply of water from the Liffey.

5700. I think you told the Committee that you attributed it to the leading citizens' opposition at that time; you say in your book that the opposition was got up against it by parties in the canal and railway interest?—It is pretty nearly the same thing.

5701. Did not the Report of Sir John Hawkshaw and the Vartry Act, contemplate providing for the townships by contributions enabling the city to undertake the expense?—In Sir John Hawkshaw's adoption of the Vartry scheme he stated that one of his reasons was that it gave facilities for supplying the out townships; in fact, greater facilities than any other scheme.

5702. But it was contemplated under the Act to supply these townships?—Yes.

5703. Was not a borrowing power of 75,000 *l.* given in the Vartry Act to enable the corporation to pipe the townships, and the other extra-municipal districts?—In the original Act I think there was that power.

5704. The corporation did not supply the townships with water, did they?—They did, but they did not pipe them; they supplied each of the townships in bulk, at so much a thousand gallons under the provisions of the Local Township Acts that were obtained subsequently to the passing of that Waterworks Bill in 1861. The first of these Acts was the Pembroke township and the Blackrock township, who got separate local Acts of Parliament themselves, in which were embraced clauses for an arrangement between the corporation and themselves for the supply of water in bulk at so much in the 1 *l.* on the valuation for 20 gallons per head of the population.

5705. Then the corporation did not pipe the township?—They piped none of the townships.

5706. Was not this 75,000 *l.* for that purpose, for supplying water to the townships?—It was; I ought to say that this sum which I mentioned in my report about the 12,000 *l.* was spent not in piping the townships, our mains passed through the townships of Pembroke and Blackrock on the high road to Dublin, so that there was no expense necessary beyond merely the connections and the necessary valves. But with regard to supplying Bray, Kingstown, Dalkey, Killiney, and Ballybrack, the corporation had to expend about 12,000 *l.* for bringing the mains from their trunk mains to the boundary of the townships.

5707. I think you say that under this Act the corporation had no right to raise that 75,000 *l.* unless they also supplied the townships with water. I will read from the Act of 1861, Section 63. "The corporation may from time to time extend their distributory and other works and pipes within the borough of Dublin and the extra-municipal districts when and as occasion may require, and for such purposes may take up at interest any further sums of money, but any sums of money which may from time to time be required for the purpose of making and extending the distributory and other works and pipes for the supply of the extra-municipal districts, or any part thereof, shall be raised only on the security of the income arising, or to arise, from the supply of water in the said extra-municipal districts"?—It was considered more desirable to supply those townships in bulk, and a subsequent

Sir *Arthur Guinness*—continued.

Act was obtained by which the clause you refer to was altered.

5708. What was the subsequent Act?—I really cannot tell you, but I know such was the case.

Mr. *Gibson*.

5709. I believe there are eight or nine amending Acts of the original Water Act?—There are seven; the first amended Act was in 1863.

Sir *Arthur Guinness*.

5710. When was the Pembroke township created?—I think it was in 1862 or 1863, a year or two after the Waterworks Act was passed

5711. Did the corporation oppose the Bill, so as to secure the rights that they had?—Yes; but the parties representing the townships, Mr. Vernon and other parties, having agreed to the terms as to which the corporation would give the water to them, there was no opposition of the corporation to the Bill beyond looking for the necessary clauses, and to see them inserted.

5712. But were the rights of the corporation, so far as supplying with water, interfered with by allowing that Bill to pass?—I think not, because the corporation reserve the right to supply the district; there is nothing to prevent us laying a pipe through the township now under our general Act.

5713. Why was the water supplied at such a low rate as 3½ *d.* to the townships of Pembroke and Blackrock?—I cannot exactly say; it was arranged between the corporation and the late Sir John Gray; I know there was a compromise between two figures, and that happened to be the average, or something of that kind; they ought to have been made to pay a halfpenny more. When it is said that the townships have water at 3½ *d.*, or 4 *d.*, or 5 *d.*, as the case may be, that is not the case, because there must be added to that the capital monies expended in piping.

5714. But that does not come from the corporation?—No: but if the corporation did the work they would have had to pay for it.

5715. With regard to the township of Clontarf, Dalkey, and Kilmainham, did the Corporation oppose their obtaining exclusive power for the supply of water?—My recollection is that the corporation lodged a petition against each Bill for the same purpose, to preserve their rights and to get clauses in for the purpose of protecting and preserving their rights for the supply of water to the district. For instance, in the case of Kingstown, the Kingstown Commissioners had actually a plan for getting an independent supply.

5716. Kingstown pays more than the other townships, does it not?—Kingstown pays 5 *d.*

5717. In your evidence upon the subject of the bridges in connection with the townships, you seem to think that the townships should pay for the repair of the streets and bridges equally with the city?—My idea is, that with regard to a large proportion, if not the entire of Pembroke, Rathmines, Clontarf, Kilmainham, and a part of Crumlin and Drumcondra, they should all have to pay, and that the circle of the city should be enlarged.

5718. Do not you think that the same thing would hold good as regards water; do not you think that they ought to pay an equal rate for water if they are to be equally rated to the city for

Mr. *Neville*, C.E.

27 June 1876.

Sir *Arthur Guinness*—continued.

for the repair of roads and bridges?—If they were amalgamated with the city, that is a question which would arise, but I have not considered it at present.

5719. But as they are not amalgamated now, you think that they should still as townships contribute towards the streets and bridges?—I think that the boundary of the city of Dublin should be enlarged because the town is travelling south from the north.

5720. Would it not then follow that they should pay an equal rate for water too?—I dare say it would.

5721. Then you think that the arrangement for giving the townships water at a very much lower price than the city, was an erroneous one?—I say that they have to pay for their own pipes, and to pay for the maintenance of their works, and taking care of them and everything else. The corporation have nothing to do but to give them so much water at so much on the valuation, and they are not responsible for accidents, or bursts, or anything at all. It is the same way I know at Salford, near Manchester, and other places in England, where they are supplied from other companies, they take the water in bulk in that way; I believe it is quite the usual way.

5722. If they were rated equally with the city, would not they pay 9 *d.* in the pound for water more than they do at present, allowing you the cost of piping?—No; and they vary.

5723. Would not it about average 9*d.*?—I think that at present the Pembroke rate would be between 7 *d.* and 8 *d.*, including everything, and Blackrock would be a fraction less. Kilmainham and Kingstown would be about 9*d.*; there is the difference between that and 1 *s.*, the domestic rate.

5724. Are you acquainted with any city where the extra municipal districts are supplied by the corporation at a lower rate than the municipal district?—I cannot say that I am.

5725. Are you not aware that the townships outside Glasgow pay more than the city, and in Belfast and Manchester also?—No; but then there are two ways of looking at that. For instance, the corporation have a profit that is on the actual cost of the water of 66 per cent. in Pembroke, that is by taking the gross cost of the work upon the actual water, not putting it as a rate at all, but simply as the value of a thousand gallons of water.

5726. Would you take the case of Liverpool, from your own book?—This is the price paid for water for manufacturing purposes, which is quite a different thing.

5727. How is it that the manufacturers do not pay more for manufacturing purposes?—They pay on a graduated scale made up in that way.

5728. But for manufacturing purposes, with Vartry water, you charge the same amount?—It is a varying scale; the largest consumers pay 3 *d.*, and the price goes up to 1 *s.* per 1,000 gallons.

5729. I think you said that the extra-municipal districts in other cities were charged more for water than the municipal districts, and so far as you were aware, the townships near Dublin were the only instances where they pay less than the city for water?—Yes, that is so.

5730. In Liverpool, Glasgow, Belfast, and Manchester, the out-townships pay more?—I do not know what the out-townships pay in those cases.

Sir *Joseph M'Kenna.*

5731. What was the object of their letting them pay less than the citizens?—The water was supplied in bulk at so much in the 1 *l.* on the valuation to those out-townships, affording them a supply equivalent to 20 gallons per head upon the population of the township, and then they had to do all the work inside. We simply gave them the water at the boundary of the township.

5732. That does not mean but that the water may cost the inhabitants as much in those townships as it costs the inhabitants in Dublin?—It might, but it does not. As I was saying, it varies from 7 *d.* to 9 *d.* in what are called the out-townships; the water costs on an average, 7 *d.* to 8 *d.*

5733. You supply water to the neighbouring townships, on the whole, on more favourable terms than you supply it to the inhabitants of Dublin?—In point of rating we do, but we get a great deal more for that water than what it costs the corporation.

5734. But you do not get more for it than you charge your own people?—No.

Mr. *Brooks.*

5735. In fact we charge the citizens a sum equivalent to the cost of the works and the wiping out of the debt to the Government, the sinking fund of the loan?—I think that the way that those figures were arrived at, in the first instance, was this: Those townships represented that they could execute works and get an independent supply of water for themselves at a certain price, and that they would not give more to the corporation, and that that was the basis upon which those figures were struck, particularly with reference to Pembroke, Blackrock, and Kingstown. I think that Mr. Hassard was the engineer in both cases, who had a plan for supplying them from the canals at 4 *d.* or 3 *d.*, and then they came to us, and they said: Well, if you do not give us water on equal terms as we can supply ourselves, we will fight.

5736. You had to make the best terms you could?—Yes, we had to make the best terms that we could; there was no one more able or anxious to make good terms for the citizens than the man who negotiated all this; that was the late Sir John Gray, Chairman of the Waterworks Committee.

5737. Then, although there is a disparity apparently against the inhabitants of Dublin, you were enabled to sell water to those townships at terms which, on the whole, were a relief to you, although you did not charge them as much as you charged the inhabitants of Dublin?—Certainly it was a relief to the citizens so far that at the present moment they get 4,600 *l.* a year, with a prospective increase of 2,000 *l.* a year on account of this extra water.

Sir *Arthur Guinness.*

5738. That was not the system recommended by Mr. Bazalgette for the main drainage, for he says, on the subject of the main drainage: "The remedy which I should recommend as the most natural and perfect would be an extension of the limits of the borough, so as to include the drainage of these populous suburbs with that of the city under one management, and to defray the cost of the drainage works, by which all parts are equally benefited, by a uniform rate upon the whole." Do not you think that that would apply

Mr. Neville, C.E.

27 June 1876.

Sir *Arthur Guinness*—continued.

apply in the case of water where they were equally benefited too?—Looking at it in that way probably it would; but I have explained to the Committee under what conditions those bargains were made; and the same thing may be said with regard to the main drainage of Rathmines and Pembroke. There has been a great deal of talk about it, and I suppose it will come on by-and-by; but there was a great deal of discussion about our undertaking to drain them at 4 *d.* in the £. on their valuation, the citizens' committee objected to that on the same grounds; but the fact was, those townships brought forward a plan prepared by Mr. Hassard and Mr. Hawksley to show that they could drain themselves for the sum of 3½ *d.* or 4 *d.* in the £.

5739. In point of fact the corporation yielded to the townships better terms, both as to main drainage and as to water, than to the citizens?—The supply of water is profitable to the corporation, and so will be the main drainage if carried out.

5740. It could not be so great a profit as if the charge was equal?—Of course not.

5741. Mr. Donnelly was a member of your main drainage committee, was he not?—No, I think not.

5742. He has had very considerable experience in corporation affairs?—Yes.

5743. Do you recollect his finding considerable fault with some of the sewers of Dublin?—Yes, quite recently.

5744. Did he not bring before the committee the state of Mountjoy-square and Gloucester-street as to drainage?—He brought forward a complaint about Mountjoy-square, and he grounded his complaint on an estimate made in 1869, I believe. It was to have been repaired and under-pinned. However, on balancing the accounts in, I think, 1870, it was found that the sewer rate was so much in debt that the committee were obliged to postpone the execution of all works, and this was among them, although it was included in the schedule of my report of 1869 as intended to be carried out that year; the work was taken in hands this spring, and is just finishing at this moment. It is merely putting an invert bottom into the Mountjoy-square sewer.

5745. Has any action been taken against the corporation for damage to property caused by the defective construction of the sewers?—There have been actions taken for flooding, but that is not owing to any defective construction of the sewers. One might as well say that the flooding of Lambeth the other day was owing to the defective construction of the sewers. It is impossible to make sewers to meet every contingency.

5746. Were there any verdicts against the corporation?—Yes, there were; there always are, I think, against a corporation.

5747. On what ground did the judges hold the corporation liable?—That they were bound to prevent the flooding. I think that was the broad principle laid down by the Chief Justice.

Sir *Joseph M'Kenna.*

5748. What is the form of the action?—It was Messrs. Martin's timber-yard on Sir John Rogerson's quay; and another case was Cherry & Smallridge's works in Seville-place. In both cases there were extraordinarily heavy rains and floods; the sewers got surcharged, and the ground being exceedingly low the water rose up through the gullies and flooded the premises. The fact is, that both those premises are situated in what were the swampy waste grounds; on both sides of the Liffey those have all been filled up now; they used to form a reservoir to hold those extraordinary storm waters; but this area being now filled up and partly built on, there is no place for the storm-waters but the sewers themselves. However, we are trying by storm overflows and every means that we can adopt to meet that difficulty now.

Sir *Arthur Guinness.*

5749. Were those arguments mentioned in the trials before the Chief Justice?—Yes, but the fact is, the law appears to hold that in the case of floods the city sewers ought to be of sufficient capacity to meet all contingencies.

5750. Is not the gas now dearer in Dublin than in any other similarly circumstanced city?—I cannot answer anything at all about the gas.

Mr. *Bruen.*

5751. You gave some evidence on Friday last with regard to the price of materials and especially about the price of brick, and I think you said that bricks had increased very much indeed in price in the last few years?—Yes, that is so.

5752. And that you are paying now 54 *s.* per thousand for bricks?—That is the price for county of Dublin stocks; the Athy bricks are not quite so high; it is the Athy bricks that I am using for the sewers, and I am paying at the present moment 40 *s.*, and I had to send one of my assistants down to Athy to try and make a bargain for them. The fact is, that brickmaking in Dublin and the brick trade generally, is in the most unsatisfactory state; we are completely at the mercy of two or three parties who can charge what they like.

5753. Have you taken any means to ascertain whether you could get bricks as cheap and as good elsewhere?—Yes, the place where the bricks are got for use in Dublin are either the county of Dublin, Tullamore, or Athy. The Tullamore bricks are not suitable for any works that I have to do with, and we have only a choice between the Athy and the county of Dublin.

5754. Did you ever try the bricks made in the district near Athy called Kilabelan?—I do not remember the townland where the bricks come from, but I think it is along the canal, about two or three miles from the town of Athy.

5755. If you were to hold that you could get a good hard brick, as large as the Athy brick and of as good quality, though perhaps not so smooth-looking a brick, delivered on the railway or canal at 1 *l.* per thousand, should you think that was cheaper than the price you are at present paying?—I daresay I may; of course what the railway may charge I do not know, but I should be very glad to get a hint as to where I could get cheaper bricks, for I pay that money on the part of the corporation with great regret, for the bricks are not worth the money at all.

5756. With regard to the Ashlar that you spoke of, is the Ashlar cut stone for building?—The Ashlars are large-sized stones that we can hammer and dress for quoins, &c., and are used in building walls, &c.

5757. I think you said that the rate you paid for

Mr. *Neville*, C.E.

27 June 1876.

Mr. *Bruen*—continued.

for Ashlar stone was 3 *s.* 6 *d.* per ton?—It has risen from 2 *s.* 10 *d.* and 3 *s.* to 4 *s.* 6 *d.*

5758. From what quarries do those come?—They are got from the neighbourhood of Dublin. They are the Calp stone, a black sort of limestone; it used to come from the neighbourhood of Crumlin, but those quarries are chiefly given up. It is very hard to get stone in Dublin now, although the city is surrounded by stone quarries.

5759. Is that limestone?—Yes, it is a sort of inferior limestone known by the name of Calp.

5760 In laying the streets with macadam material, do you employ machines for breaking the stones, or is that done by manual labour?—We buy the stones broken; we do not break them; they are delivered on the streets broken by the contractors.

5761. Are you aware whether the contractor employs machinery or manual labour for the purpose?—Mr. Worthington, who is one of our largest contractors, bought a stone-breaking machine the other day, and has just got it to work. It is a new machine that was shown in the Exhibition of the Dublin Society last April, and it did its work then very well.

5762. Do you anticipate a considerable saving of expense from the use of machinery in breaking the macadam materials as compared with manual labour?—I expect there will be a considerable saving.

5763. Do you not think that the corporation could save a good deal if they were to take those contracts themselves, and keep machinery, and break the stones themselves?—I do not think it would be prudent for the corporation to go into the quarrying of stone. If they were to get their own breaking machinery, and if they got the stone unbroken, there would be a saving upon the breaking of it; but I am afraid that quarrying stones for themselves would probably not be economical.

5764. It is your opinion, is it not, that there ought to be a re-valuation of the property in Dublin?—I think so.

5765. Have you ever pressed that opinion upon the corporation?—I do not remember that I have made any written reports upon it, but I have always spoken of it as necessary.

5766. In the original Valuation Act, I believe, there is a provision for re-valuation at the request of the grand jury of the county?—I really am not able to state exactly about that. As I mentioned the other day, I was asking Mr. Ball Greene, a few days ago, upon the subject, and he told me that it could not be done, except by order of the Government, but how that order is to be got I cannot tell you. He mentioned the case of Belfast. That Belfast Corporation had applied for it, and threatened that if they did not get it they would go for a private Bill.

5767. I will read you the clause of the Act of the 15 & 16 Vict. c. 63, s. 34, which says, "For the purpose of providing for the necessary revision of the valuation of the land, in consequence of changes that may have taken place in the gross amount of the value of the several townlands from time to time;" and then it goes on to say, "It shall be lawful for the Lord Lieutenant of Ireland, on application by the grand jury of the county, if he shall think fit so to do, to direct the Commissioner of Valuation to make a general revision of the valuation of any such poor law union, county, or barony, and so from time to time at or after the expiration of every subsequent period of 14 years, from the final completion of the preceding general revision of the valuation to cause a new revision to be made;" does not the Corporation of Dublin stand in the position of the grand jury?—I believe they do; they succeeded to what was called the Old City Grand Jury.

Mr. *Bruen*—continued.

5768. Does not the reading of that appear to be that the corporation really have the power to apply to the Lord Lieutenant for a revision?—That may be so, but I am not able to say.

5769. In fact it is in their own hands?—It may be so, but I am not able to offer an opinion about it; it is a legal question.

5770. With regard to houses in a dangerous state in Dublin, you stated that 353 houses have been reported to you; were they all reported by the police?—Almost all. That is the general rule. Occasionally there is a letter, sometimes anonymous, and sometimes with a name to it; but I should say that nine-tenths, or even more than that, came through the police.

5771. Is this duty of the police almost a voluntary duty, or are they paid for it?—They were asked to do it; they are not paid for it, but they are always patrolling the streets. I should mention that a large number of those are reported by the serjeants of police, who are employed as sanitary serjeants, and who are paid extra for that duty.

5772. They have, of course, various duties to perform as regards sanitary matters, unconnected with the condition of the structure of houses?—Yes, but still having to go through houses and to examine them, of course their attention is more likely to be called to it. It is a fact that they do report a great number of cases.

5773. I suppose that the duties of those sanitary inspectors would rather lead them to look to the drainage, and to the lower part of the house, than to investigate the upper portions?—The fact is, that when they come to look at a house if it is bad enough for me to proceed against it under the law, it must be in such a state that almost anyone would see it, and would be able to form an opinion that it is necessary to have it condemned, because it must be as bad as that for me to intervene.

5774. Is it a fact then, that unless the wall of a house is so much out of the perpendicular as to attract the attention of an unprofessional person, you would get no report about it?—I think I would not, because unless the sanitary serjeant sees anything rotten or dangerous in the roof or things of that sort that are not obvious to ordinary inspection or observation, there would be no probability that any person could see it. The fact is that the law is for the protection of passengers in the streets.

5775. So that if the wall facing the street was plumb, probably the police would not report anything, although that wall might be far out of the perpendicular?—They might not, unless it was bad enough to attract attention as being in danger of falling.

5776. Would a back wall come under the notice of the police at all?—Sometimes it would. As I have before mentioned the great bulk of the reports are from those sanitary serjeants.

5777. Did not a house fall a short time ago in the

Mr. Neville, C.E.

27 June 1876.

Mr. *Bruen*—continued.

the neighbourhood of Georges-street?—Yes, opposite Mr. Pim's.

5778. I mean within the last few weeks?—No, it was last year that those houses fell.

5779. Have you had a report of a house falling within the last three weeks?—I think that the last we had was a house that was rebuilding in Golden-lane, and two houses fell quite recently in Meath-street. Those were two houses that had been re-fronted and repaired last year. The front walls of the adjoining houses were rebuilding; about three weeks ago there was a party-wall between them, and they were doing something to this divisional wall; and whatever they did, it all came down, and those two houses collapsed. There is no doubt in the world that we are very much in want of a regular Building Act in Dublin, because in these cases there is no power to interfere. You may see the worst materials used; old bricks put together with mud, and old timbers and old materials of the worst description, all worked up without any check upon it; they do just as they like.

5780. Are you satisfied with the present means that are taken for the inspection of houses supposed to be in a dangerous state; are they sufficient for the safety of the public?—No; I think that if there was a Building Act the building surveyors appointed under it would be much more competent, and would have nothing else to do but to attend to the buildings.

5781. Do you mean with regard to new works?—Both with regard to new and to old works. For instance, a great many of those ruinous houses are injured originally by the cutting away of the chimneys to make handsome shops. There was no proper examination of the plans for doing it, and if it has been done badly and scamped, in a few years the house begins to settle down. If there was a Building Act, they should lodge the plans with a building surveyor, who would have the approval of them as to how the work should be done, and as to the scantling and the materials, and inspect the work during its progress.

5782. I think you have been conversant from the first with the attempts that have been made to open Stephen's Green to the public?—Yes.

5783. Did you report upon the subject in 1865, and attend before the Parliamentary Committee that inquired into it?—I know that I attended before the Parliamentary Committee; I think it was in 1866.

5784. Were you in favour of opening Stephen's Green to the public at that time?—Yes, I have always been in favour of opening it to the public.

5785. The first proposal for opening Stephen's Green came, did it not, from the Prince Albert Testimonial Committee?—I really cannot say; I have the Bill here of 1866, and I know that the corporation petitioned against it. Looking over their petition, I see that one of the chief grounds of opposition was the loss of 300 *l.* rent Irish.

5786. Was that the ground of their opposition?—Yes; that was going to be compulsorily taken away from them by a private company.

5787. Was there any other ground of opposition?—I do not see anything further, but I really cannot say; I am not certain.

5788. Will you have the goodness to read the last clause but two of the petition?—"It would not be just or fair towards the public creditors to remit or relinquish said rent; and that your petitioners or their council ought not to be exposed to the demoralising influence of popular clamour or to the undue pressure which would be put upon them from without if such permissive but inoperative power were to be conferred upon them as that proposed by the 34th section of said Bill.

5789. The corporation protested against the demoralising influence of popular clamour?—I really do not know about that; I know that I was in favour of opening the green.

5790. And I believe that the citizens of Dublin were in favour of it?—I suppose so, but I really cannot exactly say.

5791. You have no recollection of the circumstances?—I think it is very likely that the citizens were in favour of it.

5792. Was not there a public meeting called?—I cannot remember.

5793 At all events the responsibility for closing the Green, and depriving the citizens of Dublin of whatever advantages they might have derived from its being used as a people's park, rests with the corporation, does it not?—The corporation, I think, considered it their duty to protect their property, and that an outside body should not take away this 300 *l.* a year from them; that is the substance, I think, of the petition.

5794. From whatever cause or motive the opposition proceeded, it is a fact, is it not, that the corporation are almost the only influence which has prevailed to keep the Green shut?—I forget how the commissioners felt at that time. I think, speaking from recollection, that the commissioners were against it.

5795. Did they petition Parliament?—I remember there being some of them here: it is a good while ago and I forget the details, but I am pretty sure that the commissioners opposed it.

5796. At present the commissioners are not opposing it, are they?—I believe they agreed to the terms of opening it, provided it was placed under the Board of Works.

5797. At present then the corporation are the obstacles?—The corporation consider that the management of it should be in the hands of the citizens.

5798. But from whatever motives they are opposing, they are the only opposing parties to the opening of the Green?—I believe so.

Mr. *Gibson*.

5799. I want to know exactly what is the staff of your office; how many assistant surveyors have you?—In the waterworks there are Mr. Andrews, Mr. Harty, and young Mr. Crofton, and there is Mr. Gartland in my own office. I have four assistant surveyors.

5800. Does the appointment of those rest with the corporation?—The corporation have appointed them. With regard to those gentlemen who are employed on the waterworks, they were originally employed when the surveys and plans for Parliament were getting up, and in that way they were employed by me, and then the corporation subsequently confirmed their appointment.

5801. What salaries do they receive?—Mr. Andrews has 350 *l.*; he got an increase of 50 *l.* a year about six or eight months ago; he came in at 300 *l.* a year in 1862. I got him, through the influence of Mr. Hawkshaw, from Mr. Walker,

Mr. *Neville*, C.E.

27 June 1876.

Mr. *Gibson*—continued.

Walker, the engineer. Mr. Harty has 250 *l.* a year; he has charge of the city works from Stillorgan to Dublin. Then Mr. Crofton has charge of all the licensed work, the plumbing work, and that class of work in the city, his family have been in the corporation in connection with the waterworks as overseers or one thing and another for a century. His father was only retired from ill-health about a year ago. Mr. Gartland prepares the working plans, levels, &c., for the same work, and assists as a surveyor and draughtsman in my office. I think he has only 150 *l.* a year, and he came in at 100 *l.* a year.

5802. I presume that your salary has been increased as you have been a long time under the corporation?—Yes.

5803. From what to what?—I went in at first at 300 *l.* a year; now my salary is 750 *l.*

5804. With regard to all this large expenditure under the waterworks and the main drainage, and so on, are you given anything for that, that is to say, are you bound to carry those works out for your ordinary salary?—I carry them out for my ordinary salary. In the case of the waterworks when the Bill passed, the corporation gave me 300 guineas as a present.

5805. For labour and supervision?—Yes.

5806. But you get no commission upon the expenditure?—Nothing whatever.

5807. And is it the same with regard to the main drainage?—Yes, precisely the same. The last increase that I got was 250 *l.* on account of the successful completion of the Vartry Waterworks and the additional labour I would have on the main drainage works.

5808. When they added so much to your duties they gave you a fair increase to your salary, but you did not get any commission out of the large expenditure on the waterworks, or out of the expenditure on the main drainage?—No.

5809. Or if your time was taken up in the erection of bridges would you get any commission on it?—No.

5810. In point of fact your whole time is given up to the work of the corporation?—Yes.

5811. Are you allowed to take any private practice or pupils?—I may take a pupil, or I may give an opinion as consulting engineer, but I could not undertake works elsewhere.

5812. The understanding of your office is that your whole time is occupied by the corporation?—Yes.

Mr. *Brooks*.

5813. Who holds the keys of St. Stephen's Green?—I suppose the commissioners and people who subscribe by paying a guinea a year. I lived for a long time in York-street, and I know that I paid a guinea a year for the key.

5814. Who are the acting commissioners?—I do not know them; I know that Mr. Robert Smith is one, but I really do not know who they are.

5815. Have you seen a letter which has been recently published in the Dublin newspapers, signed by the honourable Baronet the Member for the City of Dublin, regarding the refusal of the commissioners?—I do not think I have; I do not remember it.

5816. Are you aware that the Corporation of the City of Dublin have recently offered to forego the rent if the commissioners will open the Green to the public?—Yes.

Mr *Brooks*—continued.

5817. Are you aware that they have also proposed to contribute at the rate of 600 *l.* a year for the maintenance of the Green, if the commissioners will open it to the public?—Yes.

5818. Are you aware that those offers of the corporation have been refused by the commissioners?—I believe they have refused it from what I hear.

5819. Do you know that the Lord Mayor, the Sheriffs, and the Members for the city are themselves commissioners of the Green?—I really do not know the constitution of the commission at all; it may be so, but I am not able to answer the question.

5820. Are you aware that as a condition sought to be imposed by the commissioners for opening St. Stephen's Green, it was required that the rights of the Lord Mayor and of the Sheriffs and the Recorder should be alienated?—I do not know anything at all about that; but I understood that the main point that the corporation object to is on the grounds that the management and control of the Green was not to be left with them in case it was opened, but that it was to be transferred to the Board of Works.

5821. And on those grounds the commissioners refused to open the Green?—I believe so.

5822. Being the engineer having charge of the streets of Dublin, and being responsible for their condition, I will ask you whether the stone that is used for macadam is not excessively hard, and not so liable to breakage by wheels as some other stone?—The stone got from Bennbreena; it is a sort of porphyry, and is a very hard stone, but as I have said before, it does not bind well; it rolls round instead of knitting into a sort of pavement; it is liable to get disintegrated and to ravel up.

5823. The wet condition of the streets is increased, is it not, by the hardness of the stone, and its want of binding quality?—The dampness of the streets depends very much upon the great number of damp days that we have in the year, and of course that increases the scavenging of the streets, and as the stone does not bind so well, as for instance, the Guernsey granite in London, this increases the mud.

5824. And contributes, in fact, to the mud?—Yes.

5825. Will you read from page 40 of your report, the remainder of your recommendation with regard to the barges?—"This plan is adopted, I believe, in other places, and is one I have often thought of; it is decidedly practicable, and if the scavenge cannot be got rid of at a reasonable cost otherwise, will probably soon have to be resorted to. The necessary hoppers and plant I estimate would cost about 8,000 *l.*, and the annual expense for wages to men, to man hoppers, the hire of a steam tug-boat, provision for repairs and casualties from 600 *l.* to 800 *l.*, and this latter is, calculating that during the summer months there would be little or no necessity for working the hoppers."

5826. And to the present day you have been able to induce persons to remove the scavenging materials without charge?—A great deal of it is removed without charge.

5827. With reference to the Kingstown petition, do you know if the taunts referred to proceeded from those who obstructed the main drainage; who was the chairman of the Kingstown

Mr. *Neville*, C.E.

27 June 1876.

Mr. *Brooks*—continued.

town commissioners that presented that petition?—I cannot tell who was the chairman at that time. Mr Crossthwaite is the chairman now.

5828. Was Mr. M'Evoy the chairman at the time?—I think he has been the chairman, but I cannot say whether he was the chairman then or not.

5829. Has Mr. M'Evoy habitually opposed all the schemes proposed by the corporation?—I think he has as a rule.

5830. I mean in his public capacity?—Yes, certainly.

5831. Have not the great manufacturers in Dublin obtained water on contracts made now within the last month at less rates for manufacturing purposes than that at which the townships were supplied by agreement?—Yes, they are supplied on a different basis; they are supplied by the 1,000 gallons, whereas the townships are supplied at a per-centage on the valuation.

5832. The supply per head to the townships is limited, is it not?—Yes, it is limited to 20 gallons per head.

5833. Is the supply to Dublin limited?—No.

5834. What rate do the townships pay for any water that they may take in excess of the 20 gallons per head?—Threepence-halfpenny per 1,000 gallons was, I think, the arrangement made with some; there has been no arrangement made with others.

5835. With regard to St. Stephen's Green, do you know any instance of a people's park (not a royal park) in any town in England where there is a corporation, being handed over to the Commissioners of Public Works? I really do not know anything at all about it.

5836. Do you know that there is a public park in Halifax?—I have no knowledge on the subject; I know that there are public parks here in London, and I know that there are public parks in Chester and Manchester, and other places, but as to who manages them I do not know. I believe as a rule they are managed by the municipalities except the royal parks. I see parks presented by wealthy citizens to towns occasionally, and I was at the opening of one in Paisley some years ago.

5837. Do you know that that was given to the corporation?—It was presented to the corporation by Mr. Coates, the great manufacturer of cotton thread.

Mr. *Butt*.

5838. Is not the reason of the main drainage scheme being at present in abeyance in consequence of the Public Loan Commissioners not considering the security sufficient?—That is the case.

5839. Was there any attempt made in any way to remedy that?—No, I think not.

5840. Did not the corporation go on a deputation to the Chief Secretary somewhat after that?—I think they did.

5841. Were you on that deputation?—No, I think not.

5842. Then you are not able to tell me about it?—No, to the best of my recollection I know that in the first place the Exchequer Loan Commissioners sent in a number of questions as to the financial condition of the corporation; those were answered in great detail by the corporation, and that is referred to in my report. Then the Exchequer Loan Commissioners wrote back raising objections as to the security proposed by the corporation, and I think the corporation took measures to try and arrange the matter by communicating with the Government to remove the difficulty raised.

Mr. *Butt*—continued.

5843. Am I right in supposing that there was a deputation, or a meeting at all events, between the Chief Secretary and the corporation, and some of the commissioners of the townships, and are you able to tell me what did take place?—I think you are, but I am not quite certain.

5844. The Main Drainage Act passed in 1871, did it not?—Yes; the plans were lodged in 1870, and the Bill was passed in 1871.

5845. In the petition which the Kingstown commissioners presented against the Gas Bill which the corporation promoted in 1873, they alleged as one ground of their opposition that the corporation had done nothing in the matter from 1871 to 1873 beyond levying rates annually under the Act for the payment of the costs of obtaining it, and for the salaries of the officers of the Main Drainage Committee; do you remember that allegation?—I see it in their petition.

5846. And they appeared by counsel against the corporation; is it true that from 1871 to the presentation of the petition, nothing was done?—No; as soon as the corporation obtained their Act in 1871, they at once ordered the necessary working drawings and surveys to be made, which are things which must be done over again, because the Parliamentary plans would not do at all. This is a very laborious operation, requiring borings and all sorts of surveys and examinations to be made. Of course that occupied time, but the moment they were ready, the Main Drainage Committee advertised for tenders, and that advertisement, to the best of my belief, was in March 1873, or thereabouts.

5847. In fact, the accusation made against the corporation in that petition was not well founded?—It was not. Besides, they had to pay their costs. The corporation had made progress; they never lost a moment up to the time of lodging the plans.

Mr. *Gibson*.

5848. You are aware, from your residence in Dublin, and as a citizen, that it would be very desirable for the people in the neighbourhood, and for the inhabitants round Stephen's Green, to be able to use it as a people's park?—I believe that it would.

5849. And that it would largely contribute to the health of that locality?—Yes, I think so. I think the area is 22 acres within the railings, and it is too large a space to be shut up as a private square, especially now that one half of the houses around it are turned from private houses into public buildings, clubs, shops, and establishments of that kind. It is not now, as formerly, surrounded by private houses the residences of gentlemen, as Merrion-square is at present.

5850. Are you aware that every Sunday the Green has been provisionally opened; that is to say, the gates have been left open?—I am aware that to a certain degree it has, because any person passing can see it.

5851. Are you aware that it has been largely used by the inhabitants of the locality whilst it was provisionally opened?—It is. I constantly pass it, and I observe it.

5852. Are

Mr. *Neville*, C.E.

27 June 1876.

Mr. *Gibson*—continued.

5852. Are you aware also, from the ordinary channels of information, as every citizen is, that the Commissioners of Stephen's Green agreed to give up their own control, and to hand it over to the Commissioners of Public Works on certain terms?—Yes.

5853. And that Sir Arthur Guinness agreed to give 7,000 *l.* for the improvement of the Green as a people's park?—Yes.

5854. Conditional on its being so handed over?—I believe so.

5855. Are you aware that the Government, on the same condition, agreed to give 600 *l.* a year to assist in keeping it in order?—Yes.

5856. All similarly conditioned?—Yes.

5857. Are you aware that the corporation, at one meeting, agreed that they would assent to handing it over, and that they further agreed that they would abandon their right to the rent of the Green, and that they would contribute another 600 *l.* a year in the interest of the citizens also to keep it as a people's park?—Yes; there was a meeting, at which it was agreed, by a majority of one, to agree to Sir Arthur Guinness' terms.

5858. Are you aware that, at a subsequent meeting of the corporation, that resolution was rescinded, whereupon the Commissioners of Stephen's Green declared that the condition on which their consent was offered having been broken, they withdrew it, and that Sir Arthur Guinness did the same, and that as a matter of fact Stephen's Green now will not be opened?—I know that there was a second meeting of the corporation, at which they refused their consent to open the Green, on the ground that they considered that it should be placed in the hands of the citizens, and not in those of the Board of Works.

5859. Is the result of it now that the whole affair has broken through?—So I hear.

5860. Do you consider that that is a great calamity for the citizens of Dublin, and for the health of the locality?—I think it is a great pity that the Green should not be open, and I have no doubt that it will be so, for I understand that the corporation are going to take measures to open it by means of a private Act of Parliament.

5861. Are you aware that, on a previous occasion, it was attempted to get a private Act of Parliament to open the Green?—Yes, there was; what I allude to was some sort of private company in 1866.

5862. That was an attempt to open the Green?—Yes.

5863. Did the corporation then oppose the Bill?—They opposed it, as I mentioned before, so far as I can judge, upon the ground of the loss of rent.

5864. Now they have rescinded their first resolution on the ground that they themselves will not abandon the control?—That appears to be the case.

Mr. *Brooks*.

5865. Do you know that it was stated that the majority of the council was obtained by the chairman voting twice?—I do not know it to be so; I heard a good deal of argument about it, but I cannot say that it was so.

5866. And that there was an exact quorum, and only the exact quorum necessary?—I heard that there were only 11 on each side. I think the Lord Mayor voted, but whether he voted twice or not, I cannot tell.

5867. Are you aware that the corporation are most anxious to open the Green?—I believe they are.

Mr. *Gibson*.

5868. If they opened the Green themselves out of their own resources should they bear the entire cost of keeping it up as a people's park?—That is a matter which I am not prepared to answer.

5869. Was not 1,200 *l.* a year estimated as the figure for keeping it in order?—I think that where there is so much money spent in London on parks the Government might give 600 *l.* a year towards a people's park in Dublin.

5870. Was not the sum estimated at 1,200 *l.* a year?—Yes.

5871. Is not this the present position of things, that the corporation prefer keeping the control in their own hands and putting the entire cost of maintenance on the city at large rather than take the contribution of 600 *l.* a year from the Government and 7,000 *l.* from a private citizen, and give the control up to a great public department?—That would appear to be the state of things.

Mr. *Butt*.

5872. Do not you think that if municipal institutions are to exist at all in the county they are quite right?—Yes, but I think it is a pity to give up that 600 *l.* a year.

Mr. *Brooks*.

5873. Is not it a fact that the corporation are prepared to contribute 1,000 *l.* a year to open the Green and to keep it under their own control?—I really did not hear the figure of a thousand a year, but I understand that they are going to propose asking for a contribution of 600 *l.* a year from the Government, and that they will undertake to maintain it as a people's park and to pay all the costs.

5874. Who is it that proposed to take it from the corporation and to hand it over to a public department; do you know?—I think it was Sir Arthur Guinness and the Commissioners of Stephen's Green.

Mr. John Norwood, LL.D., called in; and Examined.

Mr. *Norwood*, LL.D.

Chairman.

5875. I believe you have been a Member of the Town Council of Dublin for some years?—Yes.

5876. Your are now Chairman of the Main Drainage Committee, and member of the Waterworks, Public Health, and Law, Lease and Finance committees?—Yes, a member of No. 3 standing committee of the council.

5877. Do you hold any other offices?—I am on several public boards. I am *ex-officio* member of the board of guardians of the North Dublin Union, and was an elected guardian both of

Chairman—continued.

of that union and of the South Dublin Union for several years.

5878. And also a magistrate for the county of, and also for the city of, Dublin?—Yes.

5879. Are you a member of the Board of Superintendence of City Prisons?—For four years I was on that board.

5880. Have you been deputed by the corporation of Dublin to give evidence before this Committee?—Yes, in consequence of some observations that were made by an honourable Member, the corporation passed a resolution asking me to attend before the Committee, and in accepting that trust I stated that I would state their views to the Committee, but that I held myself quite independent to state my private opinions with reference to any matter that the Committee might wish to ask me about.

5881. I think, besides what you have told us, you have acted as Parliamentary counsel in drafting and passing a considerable number of local and personal statutes, have you not?—Yes, that is so.

5882. And have taken a considerable interest generally in matters relating to the local government of towns in Ireland, particularly on sanitary points?—Yes.

5883. Do you consider that any change is required in the present constitution of the corporation of Dublin?—I think that like all bodies after the lapse of so many years a reformation is necessary, and I gather that from the prevalence of public opinion. Whether that public opinion be founded on right data or not, still it exists, and in deference to that public opinion I think some changes should be made, and I believe that that is the general opinion of the majority of the members of the corporation.

5884. Do you think that the public opinion against the present corporation is justified by the facts?—I think that it is not; that many charges which are brought against them are quite unfounded; and that that adverse opinion has been fostered by mis-statements, in many instances, which I know to be unfounded, and they, principally, judge of the conduct of the corporation from their public meetings, never for a moment remembering that the real business of the corporation is transacted in committees; and I may add, once for all, that although I have been on many public boards, and although I entered the corporation somewhat prejudiced against that body, I have never found any committees discharge their business with a greater anxiety for the welfare of the ratepayers in dealing with the taxation of the city than the corporation has done.

5885. Then am I to gather from that answer that, in your opinion, a change should be made rather in response to a considerable desire on the part of the public for it than because that desire is well-founded?—Yes, I may say that, of course, there are on the corporation less efficient and less desirable members than others, but that happens in every public body, and the House of Commons itself is not free from that difficulty, but I should be very sorry that the public should judge of the entire body from some of the members of the town council.

5886. What is the first point on which you think improvement is necessary?—In order to get a sound constituency it should be founded upon a right and proper valuation; I do not think

Chairman—continued.

Mr. *Norwood*, LL.D.

27 June 1876.

that the valuation of the city is at present in a healthy or desirable condition; the last primary valuation under the 15th & 16th Vict. c. 63, took place in 1853, and since that there has been no primary valuation; from time to time, as improvements are made in dwellings and premises within the city boundary, the Commissioners of Valuation send their valuator, who values them, but it increases the value of that particular house, but the houses beside it, although perhaps equal in value (with the exception of the improvement which an enterprising citizen has undertaken), remain at the same amount, and that is an injustice to the neighbours, and it checks improvement, because if a person knows that by improving his premises, putting in plate glass or any minor improvements of that sort, it will result in a large increase to his valuation, he hesitates before doing so.

5887. Have the corporation passed any resolution on that subject?—They have. Since this Committee met there was a "committee of the whole house" of the corporation appointed to consider what suggestions they should lay before this Committee, and each one of the committees was summoned to consider that resolution of the council, and each of them framed reports which were sent forward to the council, stating what improvements they would suggest; improvements not only to enable them to carry on the business of the corporation with greater efficiency, but improvements which would contribute to the advantage of the city. They hesitated, I should say, directly to ask for a valuation, as they thought it would be an unpopular measure; but they suggested that a just revaluation might, with propriety, be asked for. The same point was considered both by No. 1 Committee and by No. 3 Committee. I cannot lay my hand upon it just at present; but the report of one of the sub-committees is that it would be expedient that a just and equitable valuation of the city should be made, and that that valuation should extend to the townships and to the county as well, because they were of opinion, as I may gather from some of the statements of the gentlemen who spoke, that to raise the valuation of the city justly and fairly, and to leave the surrounding townships unrevised, would, in the event of the income tax being increased, result in a larger burthen being placed upon the citizens than upon the neighbouring townships. One of the principal reasons why they did not ask for a valuation, that is to say, if they had legal power to do it, was that they thought it unpopular to raise the valuation, and thereby increase the general taxation upon the citizens.

5888. The resolution which you have referred to was a resolution of the committee, and not of the corporation?—It was a resolution of the committee. Those reports have since been confirmed by the corporation.

5889. Are you aware from your legal knowledge whether the corporation, acting as the grand jury of the county of the city of Dublin, have the power to ask for a revaluation?—I rather think they have not. The question arises under the 12 & 13 Vict. c. 97, the Dublin Improvement Act; and in order to see what Sections 40 and 41, which refer to the transfer, mean, it is necessary that I should refer the Committee to the preamble of the statute, which says, "And whereas it is expedient that the fiscal powers of the

Mr. *Norwood*, LL.D.

27 June 1876.

Chairman—continued.

the grand jury of the county of the City of Dublin and the sessions grand jury of the City of Dublin, so far as they relate to matters required to be done within the borough of Dublin, should be transferred to the Right honourable the Lord Mayor, Aldermen and Burgesses of Dublin," and then that preamble is carried out in the 40th and 41st sections. The marginal note to Section 40 being this, "Fiscal powers of grand jury and sessions grand jury in the borough of Dublin to cease;" "and whereas the powers of presenting and levying rates or cesses for divers local purposes are now vested in the grand jury of the county of the City of Dublin, and in the sessions grand jury of the City of Dublin, and it is expedient that the same powers, so far as they relate to matters to be done within the borough of Dublin should be transferred to the Right honourable the Lord Mayor, Aldermen and Burgesses of Dublin. Be it therefore enacted, that on and after the day on which this Act shall come into operation all the powers and duties of the said grand jury of the county of the City of Dublin, and the said sessions grand jury of the City of Dublin, in relation to the presenting and levying of rates or cesses as aforesaid shall cease and determine within the said borough." Then the marginal note of the 41st section is, "And to be transferred to corporation;" "and be it enacted, that from the time aforesaid all the powers theretofore exercised by or vested in relation to the presenting and levying of rates or cesses for local purposes within the borough of Dublin in the said grand jury and the said sessions grand jury shall be transferred to and be solely exercised by the council of the said borough, and all things by any Act theretofore in force authorised or required to be done by the said grand jury of the county of the city aforesaid, and of the said sessions grand jury in relation to the said fiscal matters, rates or cesses shall, save where altered by this Act, be done by the said council." The Committee will observe that throughout the preamble, and throughout those two sections, the transfer of powers is conversant only with fiscal matters, the collection of rates and cesses; and in point of fact the question was raised upon the occasion of the decease of one of the medical officers of one of the prisons when the corporation did appoint a medical man to that office. But upon a consideration of the Act the term grand jury appointed a doctor, and then the question was raised in the courts, and it was decided that although fiscal matters relative to cesses and taxes, and so on, were transferred by that Act, still that the powers of appointment to external officers of city prisons (the appointment of internal officers being provided by another statute) were not transferred to the corporation, and the medical man appointed by the grand jury was installed in office, and the other gentleman was held not to be legally appointed. That shows that all the powers of the grand jury are not transferred; and in point of fact the grand jury is still summoned or would have been summoned from time to time, but that by a recent statute they are only to be summoned when necessary.

5890. Are they ever summoned now?—Not for some time; it is only for criminal business or, I take it, if a situation like this became vacant, it would be necessary to summon them.

5891. From your answer I rather gather that it is probable that the power of requesting a re-valuation is not vested in the town council?—That is my opinion.

5892. Have the town council ever taken formally legal opinion upon that subject?—Not to my recollection.

5893. Let me call your attention to the 34th section of the General Valuation Act, 1852, c. 63; will you read that section to the Committee?—"And for the purpose of providing for the necessary revision of the valuation of the land in consequence of changes that may have taken place in the gross amount of the value of the several townlands from time to time, be it enacted, that at or after the termination of 14 years from the period of the final completion of the first general tenement valuation of any poor law union, county, or barony, under the Act of the 9th and 10th years of Her present Majesty, c. 110, or under this Act, it shall be lawful for the Lord Lieutenant of Ireland, on application by the grand jury of the county, if he shall think fit so to do, to direct the Commissioners of Valuation to make a general revision of the valuation of any such poor law union, county, or barony."

5894. From what you have told us, then, we may gather that it is very probable at any rate that the power which is contained in this clause of applying to the Lord Lieutenant for a new valuation is still vested in the grand jury of the county of the city of Dublin which hardly ever meets?—That is my opinion.

5895. You have suggested a re-valuation by way of a basis for arriving at the formation of a new constituency; what other changes would you suggest with regard to Dublin?—I think it would be a proper measure to give the owners of property as well as the occupiers of premises the right to vote. Constitutionally their claim to that power has only arisen since the imposition of the water rates, because there the owners are directly taxed, that is to say, the owner of the rack rent is directly taxed. But indirectly the owners of property are very deeply interested in the due disposition and disbursement of the rates, and for this reason, that recent legislation has given town councils and other municipalities the power of charging the rates for 30, 40, or 50 years for public improvements. Now the owners of property are subjected to those rates during the entire period of the repayment of the loans, whereas a yearly tenant or a person having a short lease is one rated with the burthen only during the period of his lease or of his annual tenure, and is not in any way interested (and is, of course, careless) as to what comes after the termination of his lease. So that in justice and fairness to the owners they ought to have a controlling power over the taxes, and that is only to be obtained by giving them the power of voting.

5896. Would you make both the owner and the occupier vote at the same time on behalf of the same representatives, or would you allow them to meet separately?—I would adopt the former mode. I saw by the Bill introduced by the Right honourable Baronet, the Member for Dublin, and other Members, that there were to be owners' representatives as well as occupiers' representatives. From what I know of public boards I think that might give rise to invidious comparisons in the town councils elected under that system, and I think simplicity is a great desideratum

Mr. *Norwood*, LL.D.

17 June 1876.

Chairman—continued.

desideratum in such matters, and that you should proceed upon the old lines as far as possible.

5897. Have you formed any idea how many persons would be qualified as owners to exercise the franchise in Dublin?—The only way in which I could form an opinion upon that would be by considering that the persons who vote by proxy for poor law purposes, and who are landlords, are in most of the wards nearly equal to the number of persons who vote as occupiers; I have never gone into an arithmetical calculation in the matter, but that occurs to me as being a fair way of ascertaining in the event of the owners of rack rent being given the power of voting, how many would come in under that system.

5898. What limit of value would you put to the owners' vote?—As to the valuation of their premises you cannot put any limit to that, but I would give the same value to the owner as to the occupier. It is so in the poor law.

5899. What view do you think would be taken by the corporation of the proposal for a cumulative or a minority vote?—A number of the members of the corporation have expressed themselves in favour of giving the minority the power of electing a representative on the "three-cornered constituency" system.

5900. Is that your own opinion?—No, I much prefer to adopt the poor law principle of giving a plurality vote, because I think it is a very unjust thing that a person owning a 4 *l.* or 5 *l.* tenement should have the same control over the disbursements of the taxes to which he contributes an infinitesimally small amount, as the owner of premises valued at several hundred pounds; and the principle having been admitted in the Poor Law Acts, I think it should be carried out with reference to other municipal affairs.

5901. Are you in favour of the female franchise for municipal purposes?—Yes, they vote for poor law purposes, and there are a great number of them who are householders. For instance, in the township of Rathmines, I saw from Mr. Stokes's evidence that there are upwards of 700 females who are in the position of occupiers, and therefore who are deeply interested in the disposition of the taxes; and I say they ought to have some controlling power.

5902. What is your view of the present residential requirement of the seven miles limit?—That was provided for by the statute under what I conceive to be a totally different state of affairs from what obtains at present. It was desirable in former days that residents only in a municipality should have the control of the taxes and of the municipal affairs, but, under the present system of mercantile business in towns, most of the merchants and traders reside outside of the borough boundaries both in Dublin and in Belfast, and in various other towns. The railways, and other means of locomotion, have brought 20 miles practically as close to the city as formerly seven miles were, and I know that many of the best citizens, both in Belfast and in Dublin, live beyond the seven miles circuit, and I do not see any reason why, if they pay rates and taxes for premises in their occupation within the boundary, they should not be permitted to vote.

5903. You have some special knowledge of the borough of Belfast, and the county of Antrim, have you not, as borough assessor and revising barrister for the county?—I was revising barrister for the county of Antrim under the Representation of People Act, 1868, when the constituency was first formed under that Act, and I was borough assessor for several years in Belfast itself.

Chairman—continued.

5904. What limit would you substitute for the seven mile limit?—I would leave it unlimited. In Belfast many of the merchants reside below Carrickfergus, and below Bangor, on each side of the shores of Belfast Lough, and their villas stud both shores for a distance of 20 miles down, and inland very nearly to the same extent. With regard to Dublin, Bray, which is a very populous and attractive township, is 10 miles from Dublin, and I think that 20 miles round Dublin would bring in all the persons who are entitled to the franchise; but in other towns it might be necessary to extend it even further.

5905. What is your view of the present municipal boundary of the City of Dublin?—I would extend the boundary in the same way as has been done in Belfast, and I would bring in the townships.

5906. Which townships?—Rathmines, New Kilmainham, Clontarf, Pembroke, and, perhaps, Blackrock.

5907. Was any part of those townships formerly within the City of Dublin?—The boundary of the City of Dublin, for Parliamentary purposes, extended to the Cross in Blackrock, which is in the centre of that township.

5908. What is your reason for desiring that extension?—Upon the principle that those townships have, with the city, "a community of interest" in many fiscal matters; they are directly bound up with the interests of the city. The principle has been sanctioned by the Legislature, in passing the 17 & 18 Vict. c. 22, a statute which provides for the contribution by the owners of premises in the Dublin Metropolitan Police District towards the maintenance of the quay walls and building of bridges within the City of Dublin. That Metropolitan Police District extends as far as the southern end of the township of Killiney and Ballybrack from the City of Dublin. And, with regard to that, I may be permitted to observe that the Dublin Metropolitan Police District is a most uneven and, apparently, arbitrarily constructed district. It was framed, under an Order in Council, by my Lord Clarendon, in May 1850; and from the buildings and extensions of streets and villas through the county, it is almost impossible to define the exact points to which it now extends. It should, in justice, have embraced a great portion of the northern side of the county, whereas, it entirely goes to the south of the city, and compels the dwellers in the county of Dublin, south of the city, to contribute towards those taxes; whereas it leaves exempt the ratepayers at the northern side of the city, who are just as much interested in the construction and maintenance of the bridges and quay walls as the others. However, that injustice has been repaired by a Bill, introduced by the Port and Docks Board, in the present Session of Parliament, which provides, practically, for a 10 mile circuit within which the ratepayers shall contribute towards that particular tax for the maintenance of the bridges and the quay walls.

5909. Are there any matters in which those townships are now united to some extent with the city?—Yes; in the matter of the maintenance of bridges and the quay walls, as I have mentioned; also, one gas company supplies the entire

Mr. Norwood, LL.D.

27 June 1876.

Chairman—continued.

entire district; and, in the next place, the Vartry Waterworks supplies most of the townships and districts of the county of Dublin with water, and they contribute to the support of the Metropolitan Police, who are under the one set of Commissioners; and, in my mind, they ought to contribute to the maintenance of a single fire brigade, and they also should, in justice, contribute to the grand jury rates, which provide for the maintenance of the streets and roads within the borough, because they use our streets and roads, and have all the advantages of living near to a great capital—and, in point of fact, Rathmines, Pembroke, and Blackrock, are almost one continuous city with Dublin.

5910. Is there any point in which you think the city suffers injustice by the present state of affairs?—There is one very striking example, and that is with regard to the unequal burthen of the poor's rate. In those townships that have been recently built, the houses therein are occupied by the middle and upper classes, and there are no dwellings within their boundaries, or but few dwellings, for the accommodation of the artisan class The artisans and labourers who build those houses and do the work in those townships, are compelled to reside within the borough boundary, and when they are used up and become unable by sickness or old age to labour, they are charged directly upon the rates of the city, whereas the persons who have had the benefit of their labour during all their days escape scot free. That injustice might be repaired by union rating in place of ratings by electoral divisions. The difference in the rating, for instance, between Rathmines and Dublin is as 10*d.* or 1*s.* to 1*s.* 10*d.* or 2*s.*

5911. In proposing to unite those townships so as to form one great corporation, have you formed any idea what representation you would give them?—The present number of the town council is 60. Rathmines, I think, has 20, and I would give them 10. I would give New Killmainham four, Clontarf three, and Pembroke perhaps 12; and, I may add, that such united board would not form too large a body for the discharge of the affairs of the districts so to be brought in, for the business of the corporation has within the last few years increased almost fourfold. I have a return here, which was given me by the town clerk, which shows that this is shown even in the matter of the minutes of the corporation, whereas the six years of the minutes of the council between August 1845 and July 1851 only occupied three volumes; in subsequent, and recent, years the number of volumes had increased to five and six for the same period.

5912. What would be the total number of the corporation under your proposal?—I think that they would amount to 90. When you consider that there are 65 on the board of guardians of the South Dublin Union, and 60 on the board of guardians of the North Dublin Union, and that they manage a much less annual amount of rates, and that they only manage one single establishment each, I think it would not be too large a board to manage the many matters that are entrusted to the care of a corporation.

5913. Possibly, if the business of the corporation increased to so great an extent as you have told us, it may be one reason why the citizens who are engaged in business are reluctant to join it?—I believe that that is one principal reason; in fact, many citizens have told me so. For instance, there is one leading citizen whom we all would desire to see in the corporation, Mr. Parker; he is a commissioner of Rathmines, and he was a member of the Main Drainage Board, but he declined to permit himself to be re-elected on that board, although it meets much less frequently than the other committees in the corporation, and the reason he told me was that it was impossible, consistent with the many duties which he had to discharge elsewhere, to assume the responsibility of sitting upon any more committees; and other leading citizens have told me the same.

Chairman—continued.

5914 Of course the management of the Waterworks Department has made a great addition to the business of the corporation?—A very large addition. The honourable Member for the city knows that we meet once a week ordinarily, and that the business of that department, although it has an excellent chairman, occupies from half-past one generally until four, or sometimes until five o'clock, and they have to meet specially sometimes to finish the business.

5915. Do I gather from your suggestion for the new constituency that you would propose any alteration in the present occupation franchise in the City of Dublin?—I would rather leave it as it is at present, and give the plural vote according to the poor law system, giving the owner the right to vote. A good deal would depend of course upon whether Parliament would consider it right to deal exceptionally with Dublin. Dublin is an exception to other municipalities throughout the country. They are under the 3 & 4 Vict. c. 108, unaltered, whereas a subsequent statute altered the franchise with regard to the City of Dublin.

5916. Would you leave the term of residence that is now required, three years, as it is?—That was very well considered when the 3 & 4 Vict. c. 108, was amended in the direction mentioned, and that was advisedly put in after deliberation as a counterpoise for the lowering of the qualification.

5917. What qualification would you propose in the townships if they were included in the city?—If the townships were included, I would rather adopt the qualification of the different townships rather than lower them to the qualification of the city. I think you would have a better constituency, and a more satisfactory one in every way.

5918. You would not have them in one part of the municipality voting under one franchise and the rest under another, would you?—No, I say I would rather adopt throughout the whole of the municipal district the one single franchise.

5919. What is the township franchise?—It varies; in Kingstown, I think it is 4*l.* and upwards; in Rathmines, I think it is 10*l.* and upwards.

5920. Which would you adopt?—I would prefer the 10*l*, but I would be content with the 4*l.* and upwards, of course having the other principle introduced of giving the plural vote.

5921. I think that a former witness suggested to the Committee that, in his opinion, the town council were elected for too short a term; what is your view upon that point?—I think so, and for this reason, it is only when he is leaving the town council by the termination of the period for which he is elected, that a town councillor has really become efficient by the acquisition

Chairman—continued.

sition of the knowledge of his duties. The aldermen are elected for six years, and I think that an uniform period of five years for both aldermen and town councillors would be preferable to the present shorter period of three years for councillors.

5922. Have you observed any bad influence exercised over a corporation, such as has been alluded to here, by the dread of the loss of popularity when the time of re-election comes?—Yes, that is so; I remember one instance of that, which led to the withdrawal of a very excellent measure which had received a great deal of consideration by the town council, namely, the "Dublin Abattoirs, Markets, and General Improvements Bill," of 1868, which was lodged in 1867, and was withdrawn in consequence of the opposition offered to certain members who had voted for some of its provisions when the re-election was approaching.

5923. Would you wish to see any change in the present department of the Collector General of Rates?—In my opinion, the suggestion that the collection of taxes should be transferred to the corporation and other boards would be a retrograde movement. The present system works well, and it is much more convenient that the citizens should have a central office and should have one collector calling at their premises, rather than have different collectors for each of the boards; I have always heard that the present system gives satisfaction.

5924. Are you satisfied with the amount of rates that is collected?—I think, considering the poverty of many of the inhabitants and ratepayers of Dublin, and the difficulties that they labour under, the taxes are collected very fairly. I think that is shown by the increase in the poundage. The rate collectors are persons of great intelligence, and I think they discharge their duty with great forbearance and with great success.

5925. Have not the corporation taken much interest in the topic of a possible improvement in the system of Private Bill Legislation?—Yes, they had that matter under consideration, and they passed a Resolution to present a Petition to the Houses of Parliament praying for an improved system.

5926. Was this a Resolution of the corporation or of the committees?—A Resolution of the corporation.

5927. Will you state the principal points which they desire to see carried into effect?—They state, "That the present system of Private Bill Legislation entails on the promoters and opponents of Private Bills, costs and charges so heavy as to present serious obstacles to social progress and local improvements, and tends to prevent the introduction into Parliament of many desirable and useful measures. It says, "That the difficulties and expense in procuring" such Acts increase directly as the distance of the localities from the metropolis, and that, "consequently the obstructions to local improvements operate unjustly against the more remote localities and people. The cost of the carriage of Private Bills bears especially hardly upon the people of Ireland." It says, that while they "acknowledge the advantages arising from the introduction of the system of Provisional Orders under the provisions of the Local Government (Ireland) Act, 1871, and the Local Government (Ireland) Act, 1872, as insuring a more satisfactory investigation into the merits of any proposed measure in the locality and at a less cost, yet they submit that serious defects still exist in the working of the Provisional Order system which require amendment." Then they state: "That it is unsatisfactory that the persons who under the provisions of the Local Government (Ireland) Acts, 1871 and 1872, hold the inquiry, examine the witnesses, and hear the merits of any proposed measure, are not the persons who ultimately decide on the propriety of granting or refusing the Provisional Order. That the powers conferred by these statutes on the Local Government (Ireland) Board are insufficient. That there are no general orders or regulations for the guidance of such inquiries, and there is no uniformity of procedure in their conduct, and the persons appointed to hold them are in many cases unacquainted with judicial proceedings, with legal forms, or the rules of evidence. That the tribunal is defective in not possessing the exactitude and sanction of a court of justice, and cannot in certain cases enforce the attendance of witnesses;" and that, therefore, "full relief cannot always be granted, and thus the expenditure of additional time, trouble, and costs is rendered necessary." Then they say that there is no finality under the system, and that the Corporation of Dublin and other local authorities have been subjected to heavy costs and charges by reason of those defects. Then they give suggestions for adopting "the precedent afforded by the Parliamentary Elections Act of 1868, for holding inquiries into the validity of elections for Members of Parliament before judges of Her Majesty's superior courts within the borough or county where the election took place." They say that is a convenient and facile precedent, inasmuch as the inquiries have been held before persons "acquainted with the laws of evidence and regulated by well-arranged general orders, and because, in the majority of instances, the inquiries are held at a reasonable cost. That the adoption of some such system would facilitate local improvements, by enabling investigations to be holden in the respective localities, and obviate the necessity of bringing witnesses, documents, &c., to London, and there maintaining them at heavy cost." I may state that the Corporation of Dublin have directly suffered from that because, in many instances, where they have applied for Provisional Orders, the defects in the Acts have been such, that they have had to go, *pari passu*, for Private Bills in Parliament. "That, in order to prevent the loss of time and the heavy costs and expenditure consequent on re investigations before Parliamentary Committees, in cases where petitions are lodged against the confirmation of Provisional Orders, arrangements should be made for securing that the decision of the tribunal proposed to be established for adjudicating on local and personal Bills, should, as far as possible, be final." By reason of want of power in the Local Government Board, they have been obliged to supplement Provisional Orders by Private Bills brought, in the ordinary way, into Parliament, and thus they have been subjected to double costs. That occurred in the case of the Waterworks Amendment Act of 1874.

5928. Did they obtain an Act then?—Yes. The Town Council of Dublin found it necessary, from

Mr. *Norwood*, LL.D.

27 June 1876.

Mr. Norwood, LL.D.

27 June 1876.

Chairman—continued.

from the experience of several years, and the extended area of water supply, to seek for enlarged powers and amendments in the Waterworks Acts, and the construction of additional works. They presented a petition, under the Local Government Board (Ireland) Acts, 1871 and 1872, in which they stated all their requirements. The Local Government Board directed an inquiry, which was held in the City Hall, and all parties interested having been, by public advertisement, apprised of the holding of same, and invited to attend, the inquiry lasted several days. The town council fully proved their case, and the petititioners, against the Provisional Order sought, were fully heard. After grave consideration, the Local Government Board determined that they were not empowered, under their statutes, to grant certain of the required provisions, which were accordingly eliminated from the Order; and the town council, who had, fortunately, taken the precaution to serve the necessary Parliamentary notices, and deposit a Private Bill, embodying similar clauses as were prayed for in the petition for the Provisional Order, were forced to incur all the costs of a Parliamentary contest to secure the complementary clauses left out of the Order, and the very persons, who had been fully heard before the Local Government Board Inspector, fought the case before the Select Committee of the House of Lords, and would have renewed the fight before the Select Committee of the House of Commons, but that they were excluded on Standing Orders from opposition. Upon that inquiry I may state that the very authority and powers of the Local Government Board itself were put in issue by the petitions filed by the opponents; and the officials in that department, including Sir Alfred Power and Mr. Monahan, their counsel, were summoned over here to sustain the validity of their proceedings before Parliament. It would have been less expensive for the town council to have at once sought for a Private Bill.

5929. What were the points on which the Local Government Board considered they were not empowered to decide?—I cannot at the moment tell you without looking at the Provisional Order, and also at the Bill; but about one-half of the provisions only were included in the Provisional Order.

Mr. *Gibson*.

5930. Had you not a conversation with the Attorney General of the day on the subject?—Yes, and he admitted that the Act was defective, and that it must be remedied.

Chairman.

5931. Did the corporation eventually obtain the Act which they sought?—They obtained both; they secured all that they wanted, but they had to do so by the double method. There was a neighbouring sanitary authority which had caused a pollution of the source of the Vartry water supply by defective drainage and sewerage, and the corporation presented a petition praying for relief, and an inquiry was held at Roundwood, and after the inquiry had been held, and all the cost gone to, the Local Government Board were advised that the granting of the relief sought would be *ultra vires*, and the corporation, the petitioners, were left without remedy.

5932. Did the corporation apply to Parliament for an Act to remedy that?—No; but Sir John Gray spoke to the Chief Secretary at the time, and represented the difficulties which were presented by the defective working of these statutes; and I suppose, if he had lived, he would have carried out his intention, as expressed to me, of bringing in of a Bill for the general regulation of these matters. But I can only say, from my knowledge of what has occurred in other towns, that a greater boon could not be granted than a proper system of Private Bill legislation. I may state that I was counsel for the Kingstown Commissioners, who found a great many defects in their Acts, and I received instructions to prepare a petition praying for the amendments that they required, and in a measure codifying their Acts. After the petition was presented, Mr. Monahan gave it as his opinion that but very few of their requirements could be granted or the evils rectified in consequence of the defects in the Local Government Acts of 1871 and 1872. The principal reason for that was, as he holds, that the Local Government Board have only power to deal with local Acts, and they cannot modify or amend, or repeal any portions of a public general statute. For instance, he holds that they could not deal with any of the provisions of the Towns Improvement Act of 1854, as applying to Kingstown or other townships. Mr. G. Fitzgibbon and myself were of opinion that that was too narrow a construction of the Local Government Acts; for this reason, that we held that, so far as each township was concerned, the Towns Improvement Act of 1854 was to all intents and purposes a local and personal Act; and that when a Provisional Order sought only to deal with the provisions of that general statute, only as related to that particular township, it should have been granted under the Local Government Acts.

5933. You have called our attention to this point; but, as I understand, the corporation of Dublin have incurred very great expense in consequence of being obliged to apply directly to Parliament under the present system?—Yes; I may state another instance that occurred, I recently prepared a petition, upon instruction from their solicitor, for the Rathdown Union Board of Guardians, who sought for a system of drainage, and in consequence of a defect in the Act, Mr. Monahan held that no relief could be given.

5934. The corporation have prepared certain suggestions for the consideration of this Committee, have they not?—Yes. If the Committee will permit me I will state what they are.

5935. Have those suggestions all been agreed to by the corporation, or do they simply emanate from the separate committees?—The majority, if not all, have been passed by the corporation.

5936. Will you state in general those which have been passed by the corporation?—Committee No. 1, that is the committee which has charge of the paving, cleansing, and lighting, "are of opinion that with a view to the more efficient discharge of the functions committed to their charge, measures should be taken to increase the powers and augment the revenue applicable to the cleansing, paving, maintaining, lighting, and improvement of the thoroughfares." They state "that the average annual sum of 39,936 *l.* available for lighting, cleansing, repair and maintenance of streets, was at the disposal of the late Paving Board Commissioners during the last

Chairman—continued.

last five years they held office, 1845 to 1850, and that at the end of that period the streets were handed over in the worst possible condition, requiring an immediate and large outlay to put them into passable repair, and that the extensive portion of the present city, outside the district of the Paving Board Commissioners, handed over to the corporation in 1851, no repairs had been done for years; that the footways were defective, many of the flagged portions having been laid for upwards of 32 years; and that the number of lamps in the city was 2,889, supplied with 12-candle gas, under a contract made by the Commissioners, to which the corporation were bound until 1865. That the valuation in 1847 was about 663,000 *l.*, and it was on this estimate that 2 *s.* was fixed as the rate that could be levied for the repair, scavenging, lighting, and improvement of the thoroughfares by the corporation, under the Dublin Improvement Act. That in 1857, on the corporation coming into office, the valuation of the city was found to be only 634,848 *l.*, being less than the previous estimate by 28,000 *l.*, representing a reduction of income amounting to 2,800 *l.*, and this was still further reduced by the deduction of valuation on buildings exempted from taxation; and that consequent on the general revision of the valuation in 1851, a further reduction on the valuation was made to the extent of about 100,000 *l.*, further reducing the available income of your committee by 10,000 *l.* per annum. That the amount at the disposal of your committee for the foregoing purposes in the 10 years ended 1860, after allowing for charges to which the Paving Commissioners were not liable, was on an average annually 41,000 *l.*, or only 1,100 *l.* more than the amount at the disposal of the Commissioners; your committee having in charge some 20 more miles of streets, and the rate of wages and cost of horse-hire having increased. That in the 10 years ended 1870 a further increase of prices took place, and the average income of your committee nominally applicable to these purposes, after making similar allowances, rose to 47,100 *l.*, owing partly to the extinguishing of the wide street debts, but chiefly to the increasing amount of money deposited for private works and solely applicable thereto. That in the five years ended 1875, the available income was under 50,000 *l.*, while wages, horse-hire, and materials have still further and very largely advanced in price. So that the average amount applied by the paving board to the scavenging and watering of the city would no longer suffice for the purpose. That the increase of prices extends to all departments in charge of your committee. That it should be borne in mind that public requirements are greater than they were formerly, and that since the introduction of railways the wear and tear of the streets from increased and more rapid traffic has become excessive. Your committee wish also to draw attention to the fact that there are now 3,459 public lamps in the city, being 570 more than the number maintained by the paving board. Your committee, in view of these facts, are of opinion that the effective and satisfactory discharge of their functions in regard to cleansing, maintaining, and lighting of the thoroughfares, imperatively demand an increased income, and they submit that this should be obtained by the means suggested, or by such other equally equitable means as may be found most advisable. That the use of the streets by the rapidly increasing population of the outlying townships causes a large and considerably increasing additional cost in their repair and maintenance, therefore it is necessary to obtain the extension of the civic boundary to include adjoining townships, the inhabitants of which are drawn thereto by the improved and economic construction of modern dwellings, and who reside in the vicinity of the city, and, but for this consideration, would reside within the boundary, some because their avocations lie in it, and others on account of the advantages to be derived from living in or near a city, but all having a direct interest in the cleansing and maintenance, lighting and watering of the thoroughfares, to which they should, therefore, contribute their share of the expenses." The next point that they deal with is the question of carriage rents, and upon that they say: "That your committee are of opinion that the duties, fees, rents, or sums paid in respect of licenses granted for hackney and other carriages, carts, and job horses within the metropolitan district of Dublin, should be transferred to the corporation in aid of the Improvement Fund, and that the Dublin Carriage Act, 1853, and Amendment Acts, in so far as they deal with the application of these sums, should be amended accordingly. The revenue, drawn into the Imperial Exchequer from this source, in 1874, was over 5,000 *l.*, and your committee are of opinion that this sum is fairly applicable to the repair and maintenance of the thoroughfares. That, in regard to buildings to be erected within the city, and alterations of, or additions to, old buildings, the powers of the corporation are altogether inadequate, and that the city engineer and the law agent are at present engaged, under the directions of your committee, in preparing for your approval a draft Bill to deal with this subject similar in its provisions to Acts in operation in other cities." I may state for the information of the Committee, that the building clauses providing for the very matters alluded to in this paragraph were included in this Bill, which I framed for the corporation in 1867, and those building clauses were modelled upon the best ones I could find in England, and upon the excellent set of building clauses in the local Act in Belfast, which is now worked admirably in that town. The next suggestion is, that "Your committee desire to direct special attention to the desirability of extending the Scotch law as to ruined houses to this country." In Scotland a person whose title is doubtful may obtain from the local authority a warrant to rebuild or repair, and charge the expense on the premises in case of dispossession; and when the owner of dilapidated premises is not known, the local authority can, after due notice, sell the site, and invest the price for the owner. An attempt is being made to introduce similar reforms into Ireland, where they are most necessary, and would prove very beneficial.

Mr.
Norwood,
LL.D.

27 June
1876.

Mr. *Gibson*.

5987. Is not that the Act of Parliament referred to by Dr. Hancock?—Yes. I may mention that at present it is impossible for the corporation to take down or deal with ruined dwelling-houses, unless they are actually dangerous to the passers by in the street. They may be internally as dangerous as possible, or ruinous in the

Mr. Norwood, LL.D.

27 June 1876.

Mr. *Gibson*—continued.

the rear, but unless they are dangerous to passers by in the street, the corporation cannot deal with them. That arises from the defective provision in the Towns Improvement Act of 1849. This suggestion, however, goes further, because it provides for cases which have arisen in Dublin similar to the case in Sackville-street, where in one of the best localities in the city a house has been left derelict, and in a ruinous state for many years, and ultimately it tumbled down within the course of the last few months, and the reason of that is that no person would repair it in consequence of the defective title, and this suggestion, which was first given to the corporation by Dr. Hancock, and adopted by them, would repair that defect. The next suggestion is, "That in regard to the erection of abattoirs and of markets, and the widening of thoroughfares, more enlarged powers are required, enabling the corporation to purchase and take by compulsion such lands as they may decide to be most suitable for these purposes, subject to the usual restrictions and provisions with respect to the taking of lands otherwise than by agreement." At present, under the Towns Improvement Act of 1849, they can only widen streets by agreement with the owners of premises which stand in the way. The wide-street commissioners had, I think, in 1837, obtained an Act dealing with a great number of local improvements, the opening of wide streets, and so on; but the powers of that Act expired in seven years, and nothing was done subsequently in that direction.

Mr. *Murphy*.

5938. Was any application made upon the passing of the Act of 1849 for the renewal of those powers?—I cannot speak from my own personal knowledge, but I know that that Act had expired, because I had to consider it so far back as the years 1852 and 1853, and I know that the powers expired under that Act of 1837.

5939. But are you aware whether or not any application was made to Parliament, in the Act of 1849 which you spoke of, which was, I believe, "the Dublin Improvement Act," to extend the similar powers in that Act to what had existed in the Act of 1837?—Not that I am aware of. At the present moment there is a ruinous building which obstructs one of the most considerable business thoroughfares in the city, Talbot-street, leading from Sackville-street to the Great Northern Railway Terminus, in Amiens-street. The corporation cannot deal with that save by agreement with the owner of the premises, who requires a very large sum. That is an improvement which the corporation have been asked by a very influentially signed requisition to effect, and they cannot do it otherwise than by an agreement, and consequently at a much less reasonable rate than they would if they had the proper powers.

5940. Then it is almost unnecessary to ask you if it be your opinion that it would be most advantageous in any legislation for Dublin, or any other corporate town of similar kind, that compulsory powers should be taken and vested in the corporation for making new and convenient streets, widening them to a certain specified width, and that they should have powers to take down houses, and purchase them for that purpose?—Certainly, it is absolutely necessary; for instance, there is one improvement which the corporation have been most desirous to effect, and for which they would obtain assistance from citizens interested in the matter. At present the city is practically divided into two by the steep gradient of Cork-hill, and the corporation have long contemplated the making of a new street, with a convenient gradient, from Dame-street to Thomas-street, which has become now a very thriving business neighbourhood, but they are unable to effect this, and that was one of the improvements in the Act of 1837, to which I have alluded. In Francis-street there is a narrow passage, caused by three or four houses, which, if removed, would be a great advantage to that commercial locality. That was another of those improvements that was uneffected, and there was also a wide street from the Midland Railway terminus to the quays, which would have been a very great advantage not only for the traffic, but also that opening through a most ruinous district, inhabited by the very lowest characters, and unwholesome to a degree, it would have cleared them away.

Mr. *Murphy*—continued.

5941. From your knowledge of the law, and from the attention which you necessarily have paid to this branch of the subject, is it or not your opinion that there is anything disadvantageous either to public policy or to the improvement of a town, or any just obstacle existing, why powers such as you have been asking for making wide convenient streets, and compulsorily taking houses for that purpose, should not be granted to corporations such as Dublin, Cork, and Belfast?—No, no reason that I know of; it would be most desirable that they should be granted.

5942. And are you not aware that Parliament have refused to grant those powers in certain instances?—Parliament granted them to the Wide Street Commissioners in Dublin, and would, I have no doubt, have granted them to the corporation if they had applied for those powers, and I have no doubt that if a Bill was brought in for that purpose Parliament would grant it now.

Chairman.

5943. Does that close the recommendations of No. 1 committee?—There is one more in which they say: "That the borrowing powers of the corporation, limited by the 24th section of the Improvement Act of 1849, should be supplemented by an enactment rendering it lawful to re-borrow, on credit of the improvement rate, such sums as may be paid off or redeemed." That Act of Parliament enabled them to borrow a sum of 100,000 *l.* for local improvements, but the amount of borrowing powers has been nearly exhausted, and it would be necessary if any public improvements are to be carried out in future, that power should be given for them to re-borrow that sum; they have repaid a considerable portion of it, "and by powers to borrow further sums on the credit of the improvement rate, and of the rates, rents, and other sources of income arising from new abbatoirs and markets, and on the security of lands to be purchased for them, and on land and holdings which may become the property of the corporation in the making of new streets or widening of existing streets. That these powers are desirable for the proper conduct of the public works under charge of this committee, in order that outstanding liabilities may be discharged, and cash payments

made

Mr. *Norwood*, LL.D.

27 June 1876.

Chairman—continued.

made in all cases, and that they are further necessary to enable the corporation to effect the desirable improvements alluded to; that a sufficient capital may from time to time, as occasion requires it, be commanded for the prompt execution of extensive works of necessity, and for the acquiring of lands and hereditaments where a money compensation has been arrived at by arbitration. All which we submit as our report, this 3rd day of June 1876, signed *E. Dwyer Gray*, Chairman." That was adopted by the town council.

5944. Are you aware that Belfast has obtained a Building Act?—Yes, and I know that it works very well there; there are from 1,200 to 1,500 houses built within the borough boundary annually in Belfast for the last few years, and the plans of those houses have to be submitted to the borough engineer; and the corporation do not allow of buildings to be erected unless all the necessary provisions are made to the satisfaction of the city architect and their engineer, for ventilation, drainage, water supply, and other requirements necessary for the health of the in-dwellers.

5945. Was that Act obtained by the Provisional Order system?—No, it was before 1871.

5946. Why cannot Dublin follow the example of Belfast?—They are applying now for it, and as I mentioned to the Committee, they did try in this Act of 1867 to obtain those powers, and it was abandoned for the reasons I have told you.

5947. What are the suggestions of the No. 2 committee?—They state, "Your committee beg to report that, upon receipt of the Order of Council of the 29th day of May 1876, they gave the subject the best consideration, and having conferred with Mr. Morgan, your law and land agent, they requested that gentleman to carefully examine into the several subjects referred to in the Bill promoted by the corporation in 1868"; that is the Bill to which I have alluded, and the following report has been furnished by him: "Report of Francis Morgan, Law and Land Agent." That was the gentleman who was a witness before this committee. He says, "Pursuant to the order of the municipal council of 29th May 1876, I had on 5th June instant, forwarded to your committee from Buxton a few written suggestions of such additional powers as are required by the municipal corporation of Dublin in the departments under administration of your committee." It appears that he refers to the clauses in this Bill which were prepared at the suggestion of No. 2 committee in 1868, and in that way it is laid before the council. In 1867 all the committees of the corporation prepared suggestions in this way, and they were all embodied by me in this Bill. The suggestions of No. 2 committee are contained in this Bill, and they are alluded to by reference by Mr. Morgan in his report, and that is why No. 2 committee lay their suggestions, in the form of reference, before the committee. But it will be necessary for me to see what clauses No. 2 committee framed in 1867 in order to tell you the exact requirements.

5948. Do you know on what points they were?—They were points connected with the markets and the proper regulations of Smithfield and the proper regulations for driving cattle through the streets, and I observe that one of the questions by the honourable Member for Cork as to whether the corporation had ever considered the question of the proper shipping of cattle, was dealt with by a suggestion from No. 2 committee in this very Bill. It is Clause 17, and it says, "No railway company, steampacket company, or other body, person, or persons, public or private, engaged in the carrying and transportation of cattle, sheep, or swine, to or from the said city or suburbs, by land or water, shall confine the same in cars, waggons, ships, or vessels for a longer period than 24 consecutive hours, unless delayed by storms or other accidental and inevitable causes, without unloading for rest, water, and feeding, for a period of at least 10 consecutive hours, under pain or penalty of 3 *l.* for every live animal that may be so confined beyond the prescribed period; and in estimating such confinement or confinements, the time the animals may have been confined without such rest, water, or food, on connecting roads from which they are received, shall be computed, it being the intention to prevent their continuous confinement beyond 24 hours, except upon the contingencies herein stated." That was one of the requirements which I believe was alluded to by the honourable Member for Cork.

Mr. *Murphy*.

5949. I suppose that clause applies as well to the land as to the sea?—Yes.

Chairman.

5950. With regard to driving cattle through the streets, was not that dealt with by the Traffic Regulation Act of last Session?—It was; that point is completely dealt with by the Act of last Session, and by the rules framed by Sir Henry Lake and the town council under that Act.

5951. What were the suggestions of No. 3 committee?—They say: "The committee desire to observe that the suggestions in the schedules numbered 1 to 12 inclusive have already received the sanction of the town council, and were embodied in clauses contained in 'The proposed Dublin Abattoirs Markets and Improvement Act, 1868,' being a Bill prepared by directions of the town council in the year 1867." They state that "the term of 75 years, for which the council is at present empowered to grant building leases, is felt to be too short to induce persons to erect substantial buildings on the corporate estate, and operates prejudicially in preventing the obtaining of more remunerative rents for building sites; and it is therefore recommended that the term for which the corporation shall in future be enabled to grant building leases be extended to 150 years, with the sanction of the Lords of the Treasury." Then the report states, "that it is of importance for the better administration of justice and the speedy recovery of small debts that the jurisdiction and procedure in the Lord Mayor's court should be more accurately defined and extended." It says: "The town council have frequently affirmed the principles conveyed by resolutions and in addresses to Parliament and the Irish Executive that the carriage rents and licenses should be paid to the corporation in aid of the rates for repairing, cleansing, and lighting the streets." That is a suggestion dealt with also by No. 1 committee. Then it says: "The injustice of levying a tax on the citizens of Dublin for the repair and maintenance of the Rock-road, situate outside

Mr. Norwood, LL.D.

27 June 1876.

Chairman—continued.

outside the borough boundary, has long been felt, and the committee recommend the amendment or repeal of Sections 117 and 118 of the 7th and 8th of Vict. c. 106, and that the care of the road be transferred to the townships of Pembroke and Blackrock, in the county of Dublin." Then it says: "The town council has been prevented from effectuating many desirable improvements in the widening of streets and the removal of houses, obstructions, &c., by not possessing the requisite powers for compulsory purchase of lands and tenements under the Lands Clauses Acts, and by not having the necessary facilities for borrowing monies for such purposes, without having to incur the expense and delay of an application to Parliament for a Private Bill. It is doubtful whether a Provisional Order under the Local Government (Ireland) Acts, could be obtained for such purposes. The committee desire to refer the council to the Act which was obtained so far back as the year 1837, and which was passed for the carriage of some most valuable improvements. But the period for the effecting of the majority of those improvements was too short, and the powers conferred by that statute were, from want of means, suffered to expire. If the powers contained in that Act were revived, such improvements could be carried out in connection with the 'Artizans' Dwellings Acts' as would greatly improve the sanitary and social condition of the people. The committee append in the schedule a list of the improvements sanctioned by the Legislature by the Act of 1837."

5952. Did the corporation apply for a renewal of those powers that were contained in the Act of 1837 and in the Act of 1849?—No.

5953. Do you know why they did not?—I do not know anything about the circumstances attending the application for that Act of Parliament. Then they say: "Your committee recommend that, with the view of the more satisfactory keeping of the accounts and the more effective carriage of the Sanitary Acts, that facilities should be given for the raising of monies for sanitary purposes by levying a distinct sanitary rate, and that the town council should apply, under the Local Government Acts, for a Provisional Order to enable them to levy a distinct rate for all sanitary purposes." That I should state was a matter referred to by Mr. Finlay in several of the reports made by him as auditor of the corporation accounts. The way in which this matter arises is by the Public Health Act of 1866. The fund applicable for sanitary purposes is stated to be the borough fund, or the borough rate. The borough fund is composed principally of the rents of the corporation, and it is under the control of No. 3 committee; but the Public Health Committee is another department of the corporation, and it has been found highly inconvenient that one department should draw for its purposes upon a fund not under its control, and of which it does not know the condition at the time of its drawing the drafts. The same thing happened with regard to the waterworks accounts, and the borough fund; they were all mixed up together in the bank account, and within the last few days, No. 3 committee had an interview with the Governor and Company of the Bank of Ireland, and arrangements have been made by which each department will have its separate fund, a distinct account being opened in the Bank, and each department drawing upon its own fund, so that all difficulty upon that head will be obviated. Then it says, "That any doubts which may exist as to the rights of the corporation to receive fines and penalties by the city treasurer under the Dublin Improvement Act, 1849, should be set at rest by specific enactment or amendment of the Fines and Penalties Act." That is in consequence of a suit being instituted by the board of guardians of the North Dublin Union to recover such fines, and upon argument it was then found that neither the corporation nor the board of guardians were entitled to them, but that they ought to be paid in to the Treasury. It says, "That with the view of the prevention of frauds in the coal trade, and the protection of the humbler classes of citizens, provisions should be obtained for declaring the quays of Dublin a public market for coals, and for enabling the corporation to make bye-laws regulating the sale of coals and other commodities on said quays." The Dublin Improvement Act deals with fraudulent sellers of coals; its provisions require that they shall have on their carts appliances for weighing coals; but that is when they are at a distance from the coal quay, and there are no means of preventing the frauds of shipowners, or their employés on the quays, by giving short weight, or otherwise defrauding the purchaser of coals, and it is desirable that the clause should be passed for that purpose. Then they say: "It is desirable that the questions which have been raised as to the powers of the town council to deal with the fees payable in connection with the office of city marshal and other officers should be definitely settled, and power should be given, if necessary, to enable the corporation to commute the said fees into a fixed salary. Also that the citizens should be relieved in future from the burthen of contributing fees to the sheriffs and Clerk of the Crown for prisoners at commissions or quarter sessions, and also from the fees to court criers." Those fees they present for. Then there is this matter, which I crave leave to mention to the Committee: "The committee recommend for the protection of members of municipalities discharging public duties *bonâ fide* and gratuitously, that provision should be made for submitting contemplated raising and levying (by corporations) of moneys for all purposes to the Court of Queen's Bench for approval and fiat, in the same manner as moneys to be raised and expended by grand juries are submitted for the opinion of that tribunal. The machinery at present existing under the Local Government (Ireland) Acts for ascertaining the legality of payments on the part of the corporation and of surcharge by the auditors is inefficient and unsatisfactory." It is only after a surcharge is made that an inquiry as to the legality of the payment is raised, and the corporation think that if a power of surcharge is granted they should have an opportunity, previous to making the payment or signing the draft, of obtaining the opinion of a court of law upon the matter. It says: "That the financial year should terminate in all departments of the corporation on the 31st of December, and that such sections of statutes as require corporate accounts to be closed at other periods, should be repealed. That buildings and institutions, such as Trinity College, at present exempt from grand jury and other rates, should

Mr. Norwood, LL.D. — 27 June 1876.

Chairman—continued.

should in future be required to pay same." Trinity College is exempt from the grand jury rate under the words of an old charter. Then it says: "That the borough boundary should be extended; that larger powers should be conferred on the corporation for the inspection and compulsory repair or demolition of ruinous and dangerous dwellings, and that the sections of the Dublin Improvement Act, 1849, and other statutes dealing with such matters should be amended with that object." Then that building clauses should be introduced, and "That the accounts of the Richmond District Lunatic Asylum should be forwarded half-yearly to the council, and also that all estimates and projected expenditure of moneys on account thereof should be submitted for the consideration and fiat of the Court of Queen's Bench, in the same way and in the same term as Grand Jury Presentments are now brought before that Court, and that the ratepayors be adequately represented on the board of governors of said asylum." I should mention, with regard to that, that the corporation feel that if they are compelled to levy such large sums for the Richmond Lunatic Asylum, they ought to have some control over the expenditure. The expenditure has risen in 11 or 12 years from 8,000 *l.* a year to something like 18,000 *l.* a year, and the corporation have not even the estimates or the accounts laid before them until the accounts are all paid and printed, and they think that, being the authority to levy that large sum, they ought to have some information as to why the estimates are continually mounting up for the support of that asylum.

5954. Do they complain that the asylum is extravagantly or ill managed?—They do not complain of its being ill managed, because they know very little about the management; but I understand that some of the governors of the asylum feel that they have little or no control themselves over the expenditure.

5955. Are any of the governors of the asylum members of the corporation?—There are three, I think; Sir John Barrington, the late Alderman Redmond, and Alderman Campbell. This matter formed the subject of a deputation to the Chief Secretary, and also to his Excellency the Lord Lieutenant on the part of the corporation, asking that some control should be given over this expenditure, for the reasons that it had increased so much within the period I have mentioned.

5956. Have those governors of the asylum, who were also members of the corporation, made any representation to the corporation as to bad management or extravagance in the asylum?—I have not heard of any such representations, but they feel that they have no control. When the resident physician or physicians order improvements in the place, they feel that they have little control over the payment of much of the expense. The only complaint that I have heard them make was that buildings of an extravagant character were erected when others of a less expensive description would have sufficed for the purposes of the institution.

Mr. *Murphy.*

5957. Has the corporation any direct representation on that board?—None, except by virtue of the appointment of the Lord Lieutenant of a member of the corporation.

Mr. *Gibson.*

5958. Is not the Lord Lieutenant bound to appoint a member of the corporation?—No.

5959. Then it is a pure accident that he chances to be a member?—Yes; it is by the grace of the Lord Lieutenant.

Mr. *Murphy.*

5960. There is no *ex officio* representation of the corporation?—None; they say, "The committee desire to call the attention of the council to the importance to the commercial and trading classes of Dublin, that there should be more frequent sittings of the recorder's hours, and the appointment of a successor to Sir Frederick Shaw would be a convenient opportunity for making the necessary arrangements." That has been partly dealt with in the Civil Bill Courts Act, but it is a matter upon which the corporation think that the commercial and trading classes of the city would be greatly benefited if more frequent sittings of the Recorder's Court were held, as in Belfast

Chairman.

5961. Are those the suggestions of No. 3 committee?—Those are the suggestions of No. 3 committee; and they are accompanied by a schedule in which they give the clauses of the Bill of 1867, which they deem desirable should be embodied in an Act of Parliament.

5962. Their recommendations were adopted by the corporation, I understand?—Yes.

5963. Have the Public Health Committee made also some recommendations?—Yes; it will not be necessary for me to read them, as I understand they were laid fully before the Committee by Mr. Boyle, the secretary of the Public Health Committee, so that I will merely hand them in; and also the Schedule of clauses from the Bill of 1867, adopted by No. 3 committee.

5964. Have the Waterworks Committee made any recommendations?—Yes, it was resolved by the committee: "Understanding that Mr. Norwood will probably be summoned to give evidence before the Select Committee of the House of Commons on the Local Government of Towns (Ireland) Bill, that he be requested to explain the present position of the Waterworks Committee with reference to the rating of the mains and other works and property belonging to the corporation, and the necessity for legislation thereon, if necessary, as soon as possible, for the purpose of relieving the corporation of the liability to be rated for said mains, &c.; and that the law agent do prepare a short explanatory report on the subject for the information of the Select Committee; that a copy of this resolution be posted to Mr. Norwood, and that the result be reported to the council."

5965. Is not the position of that matter something of this kind, that the corporation are rated for their mains, but that on the other hand they have no power to apply any profits that they may make from the waterworks to the general benefit of the citizens, those profits being compelled by law to be applied to reducing the water rate?—Yes, that is shortly the state of the case, and they feel it an additional grievance, inasmuch as the property of the Port and Docks Board being public docks, which were subject to the rates and paid the taxes during the occupation of the docks by the lessees of the Port and Docks Board, Messrs.

Mr. Norwood, LL.D.

27 June 1876.

Chairman—continued.

Messrs. Scovell, the moment they came into possession of the Port and Docks Board they then became exempt from taxation; while they see on the one side that there are no profits from the water mains, which are works of a public nature, yet that there are profits from the Port and Docks Board's premises which ought to be subject to taxation

5966. It is the poor rate that they complain of, is it not?—Yes.

5967. What are the rates on the city mains this year?—£. 4,073.

5968. Have the Waterworks Committee made any other suggestion?—None, except that one, and for this reason, that they say they recently obtained a Provisional Order and an Act of Parliament amending the Waterworks Acts to which I have alluded, and it is not necessary that any legislation should take place in any other matter save the one to which I have called attention.

5969. Have the committee of the whole house offered any suggestions?—The committee of the whole house, I think, only suggested that it was desirable that powers should be given to the corporation for the unification or consolidation of all their loans, in the same way that the Metropolitan Board of Works have obtained the consolidation of their loans. That debenture stock should be issued at a low rate of interest, and they think that a matter of very great importance. The Board of Superintendence of City Prisons have also made suggestions, but I observe that there is at present pending in Parliament a Bill dealing with prisons generally throughout Ireland; and I do not know whether it would be necessary to do more than what I was asked by the corporation, namely, to hand in those suggestions for the information of the Committee. They state, "That every board of superintendence in Ireland has the appointment and dismissal of prison officers, except the Board of Superintendence of the City of Dublin Prisons. Every grand jury of a county, and every council in a county of a city in Ireland, has the power to fix the salaries and emoluments of prison officers, except the council of the City of Dublin." It then says, that "This exceptional legislation was not initiated when the city prisons were given in charge to the present corporation in 1851. It began in 1826, under the 7 Geo. 4, c. 74, the second section of which Act gave to all the grand juries in Ireland, except the grand jury of the City of Dublin, the power to appoint a board of superintendence to govern their prisons." Then it requires that the Dublin Improvement Act, the 12 & 13 Vict. c. 97, should be amended, in order to vest in the municipal council the appointment of the extern officers for the prisons.

5970. As a matter of fact does not the Board of Superintendence of City Prisons now appoint to those offices with the sanction of the Lord Lieutenant?—No; they send forward the names to the Lord Lieutenant and he appoints.

5971. He appoints those whom they recommend?—Or declines to appoint them, as sometimes happens, of course upon the report of the Inspectors of Prisons.

5972. Was not some charge made about four years ago in this matter?—There was. Previous to that appointments were made directly by the authorities at the Castle, but, subsequently, the system was adopted of the Board of Superintendence sending forward the names of persons whom they thought eligible, and selections from them were made by his Excellency.

Sir Arthur Guinness.

5973. Why was that change made?—I think it was made upon the remonstrance of the Board of Superintendence to the town council.

5974. What reason was alleged?—They thought it was an exceptional arrangement that the corporation or the committee of the Board of Superintendence should not have the same power and authority in the appointment of officers as other Boards of Superintendence throughout the kingdom had.

Chairman.

5975. Were there not certain circumstances before that period which happened with reference to an important officer in one of those prisons, which might give some ground for retaining the appointment of the officers in the hands of the Government?—I think so; that was before I held a seat upon the board, but I believe there were circumstances. It then says that, "To place the council and the board in the same position as all the other councils, grand juries, and boards in Ireland, it will be necessary (1.) To repeal the third section of the 6 & 7 Will. 4, c. 51, so far as regards the appointment and payment of officers. (2.) To repeal the words 'with the exception hereinafter in that behalf specified,' in the 6th and 7th lines of the 18th section of the 19 & 20 Vict. c. 68. (3.) To repeal the whole of the two provisoes at the end of each of the two sections, 18 and 22, in the 19 & 20 Vict. c. 68, as far as they exclude Richmond Bridewell and Grangegorman Prison from the application of each section. (4.) To repeal the 6th section of the 12 & 13 Vict. c. 55, so far as it limits the salaries of chaplains." Then it says, "It is desirable that a section of any new Act of Parliament shall declare it illegal to plant trees, or erect any structure within a certain distance from the outside of the boundary wall of any prison, giving a summary mode of abating any breach of such law, also inflicting penalties" for planting trees, or making such erections, "and giving a summary mode of recovering the penalties. It is also desirable that in case a vacancy occurs in the board from resignation or otherwise, the council should have power to appoint a member to fill the vacancy. The fines received in the prisons should be retained by the board and applied to the support and maintenance of the prisons; a clause to effect this object is required." Those are all the recommendations of the Board of Superintendence.

5976. Have you stated to the Committee now all the suggestions which you were requested, as representing the corporation, to bring before them?—Yes, with the exception that I was asked to mention that although it has not yet been adopted by the council, it was passed by a committee of the whole house that a requisition should be sent forward to Her Majesty's Government, asking for the appointment of a Royal Commission for the purpose of inquiring into and reporting on the question of the main drainage of Dublin and its vicinity. This is the resolution: "Pursuant to the Order of Council of the 13th March 1876, referring the letter of Messrs. M'Evoy & Inglis, of the 11th March, to this committee

Mr. *Norwood*, LL.D.

27 June 1876.

Chairman—continued.

committee for consideration and report, your committee now beg to report that, having considered this matter, they beg to recommend that your council do request Her Majesty's Government to appoint a Royal Commissioner for the purpose of inquiring and reporting on the question of the main drainage of Dublin and its vicinity free of cost to this corporation, inasmuch as no funds of the corporation are at present applicable to meet the expenses of such Commission. All which we submit as our report, this 19th day of April 1876."

5977. Might not a very large majority of the suggestions which you have stated to us, of those coming, at any rate, from No. 1 and No. 3 committees, be met by such a Bill as was introduced by the corporation in 1867?—Certainly.

5978. Why do not the corporation introduce a Bill to carry out the suggestions to which they have agreed?—There are very great difficulties in introducing a private Bill by corporations. Under the 11th & 12th of the Queen, it is necessary that notices should be published early in the year, and the corporation have been opposed in a great many of their applications to Parliament by the citizens, who seem to treat every suggestion coming from the corporation as being one to be viewed with suspicion.

5979. But other corporations, such as Belfast, obtain Acts of this description?—Yes, and the corporation of Dublin endeavoured to obtained Acts in the same direction. I may mention one; for instance, the corporation of Belfast obtained an Act for transferring the undertaking of the local gas company to the corporation, following the example of many towns in England and in Scotland, which had done so with great advantage to the ratepayers. The corporation of Dublin obtained the opinion of leading gas engineers and others, that the transfer of the Alliance Gas Company's undertaking to the corporation would be beneficial to the citizens, both in the way of getting cheaper public lighting, and also with the view of utilisation of the profits arising from the undertaking in local improvements. A Bill of that nature passed for Belfast, I believe, unopposed. When it was proposed in Dublin, although it had the adhesion of the Chamber of Commerce and of a number of leading citizens placed upon the committee, for the purpose of promoting the Bill, it was bitterly opposed and was thrown out. It subsequently turned out that all the anticipations of the engineers and of Mr. Cotton, the borough gas engineer, who suggested the promotion of that Bill for the advantage of the city and citizens, have been fully realised, and the shares of the gas company are now sold at a much higher rate than the corporation undertook by that Bill to pay for them, and the profits of the concern are very large indeed, and likely to increase.

5980. Why, in your opinion, is there such an influential body of persons in Dublin, who oppose these kinds of measures when proposed by the corporation?—I think that there is a very great want of confidence in the corporation; I do not believe that such want of confidence is fully warranted, but it does prevail in Dublin, and has prevailed in Dublin for several years, and it operates very prejudicially against the due working of the corporation, and prevents their promoting Bills for improvements of the character which I have suggested.

5981. Do you think that that want of confidence would be removed by such alterations in the constitution of the corporation as you have suggested to this Committee?—I think that anything that would improve the *personnel* of the members, and anything that would give a more direct control to the owners of property, would tend to restore confidence to the body.

5982. Do you think that the alterations which you have suggested would be sufficient to restore that confidence?—I think that if we could induce the leading citizens to take a part in the affairs of the corporation that would restore confidence.

5983. Do you think that the alterations which you have proposed would be sufficient to restore that confidence, and induce the leading citizens to take their part?—I think so; if the Committee will permit me, I was asked to mention to the Committee with reference to a point which had been made against the corporation, that the corporation estates have been badly managed, inasmuch as large arrears have been suffered to accrue of rents from year to year. That is a matter which was under the consideration of No. 3 committee, so far back as December 1870, and the attention of that committee was called to the matter by Mr. Read, who, at that time, was borough auditor, under the 3 & 4 Vict. c. 108, and he says, "I would feel obliged by your calling the attention of the council to the large arrears of rent due to the corporation as appears by the rental placed before me for audit, amounting to 6,872 *l.* 12 *s.* 2 *d.*, exclusive of the half year due 29th September." He then complains that those arrears should have been suffered to accrue, and then the committee took the matter into consideration, and referred it to the city treasurer, Mr. Costigin, to report upon the matter, and Mr. Costigin reported thereupon, and stated that, at the date alluded to by the city auditor, "the actual solvent arrears did not exceed 1,000 *l.*, there having been collected fully 5,000 *l.*," and that the city auditor was made acquainted with that fact. The treasurer goes on to say: "That at this moment there are not 800 *l.* remaining to be collected; and permit me to observe, it was essentially necessary that the arrear appearing on the 31st August, which he refers to on the 19th December, should be in hand early in September and October, to meet the large gale of interest due upon the debentures (4,500 *l.*), the quarter's salaries, and compensation, at the same period, besides the heavy monetary arrangements of the house." He says: "It will be recollected that the custom has been, from time immemorial, to allow the tenantry on the city estate to pay one gale of rent within another, which affords a sufficient reason for the presence, on the 31st August, of the 6,800 *l.* appearing on the city estates, due from the previous March, and, on so large an estate, as nearly 20,000 *l.* a year, the solvent arrears at this moment being so low as 800 *l.*, the treasurer hopes will be deemed a creditable collection." The matter then was referred by the No. 3 committee to a sub-committee, to investigate the arrears, and the sub-committee states: "The accompanying list of arrears, though showing 668 *l.* irrecoverable, has a credit against it, in the borough fund, of 180 *l.* 10 *s.*, the last year's rent in advance on several of the holdings paid in at letting, which reduces the amount to 477 *l.* 10*s.*" The custom of the corporation, in letting their estates, is that the persons bidding at an auction, and taking the premises

Mr *Norwood*, LL.D.

27 June 1876.

Chairman—continued.

premises from the corporation, pay the first quarter's rent in advance. "This 477 *l.* 10 *s.* is again reduced by 141 *l.*, remitted by committee, from time to time, with the view of obtaining quiet and inexpensive possession of property dependent on lives, ascertained by the law agent to be dead, when the rents accrued due, so that, in fact, the bad arrears do not exceed 336 *l.*, these latter originating from insolvencies and consequent ejectment for non-payment, every effort, however, being made at the time to recover some portion, but without effect. These arrears have been annually accumulating, and extend over 11 years. Within that period," Mr. Costigin says, "I have actually collected 220,000 *l.* in rents, and I should hope the committee will regard so very small a loss on so large a collection satisfactory, as indicating good and careful management of the estate." Then the sub-committee "proceeded to examine into the special circumstances connected with each of the cases" in the schedule which was laid before them by Mr. Costigin, the arrears amounting, as I before mentioned, to 645 *l.* 16 *s.* 8½ *d.*, and the committee state, "Having examined each of the foregoing items, and heard explanations from treasurer and law agent relative thereto, and on reference to the city rental and ledgers, we are of opinion that the said several items of arrears should be removed from the rental of the corporation estates, as being insolvent and irrecoverable. We would add, that having regard to the facts, that during the lengthened period of seven years a net sum of 645 *l.* 6 *s.* 8 *d.* only has been lost as irrecoverable out of the large sum of 220,000 *l.* collected during that time, we are of opinion that the rents have been collected in a most satisfactory manner." No. 3 committee were anxious that I should lay that before the committee, as some stress had been laid upon the arrears appearing in the books upon the 31st of August in each year.

Friday, 30th June 1876.

MEMBERS PRESENT:

Mr. Assheton.	Sir Arthur Guinness.
Sir Michael Hicks Beach.	Sir Joseph M'Kenna.
Mr. Brooks.	Mr. Murphy.
Mr. Collins.	Mr. O'Shaughnessy.
Mr. J. P. Corry.	Dr. Ward.
Mr. Gibson.	

SIR MICHAEL HICKS BEACH, BART., IN THE CHAIR.

Mr. JOHN NORWOOD, LL.D., called in; and further Examined.

Mr. *Norwood*, LL.D. — 30 June 1876.

Chairman.

5984. WITH reference to your evidence on Tuesday, I put into your hands a letter from Dr. Lalor, of the Richmond Lunatic Asylum; have you any remarks to make about it?—Yes; there has been a misapprehension about my evidence; I did not state that Dr. Lalor had ordered those buildings, because he is not the party to give directions for the erection of any buildings; I merely stated what has been mentioned in the town council as a cause of complaint, that buildings of a more ornate character had been erected where ones of a more modest architectural description would have sufficed for the purposes of that department. I do not know that of my own knowledge as I have never been through the asylum, but it was a complaint made in the corporation. When they were complaining that the amount presented for the support of that department had in a comparatively few years risen from 3,000 *l.* a year up to 17,000 *l.* and 18,000 *l.*, that was one of the reasons given why the increased expenditure took place. I see in his letter, and I should state it in justice to Mr. Lalor, that the number of beds in that asylum has been increased from 615 to 1,100, which, of course, would account for the very large increase in the expenses of maintenance of the establishment.

5985. I think he adds that the asylum is now nearly full?—Yes, I think it is nearly full; I find that in an answer which I made on Tuesday, I stated that the suggestions of several of the committees had not been adopted by the council. It appears that they have been adopted by the council, and I hand in the suggestions of the various committees, as amended by the council, and authenticated by the signature of the town clerk.

5986. Would you correct the evidence you have already given upon that point, so that it may show the reports as they were agreed to by the town council?—Yes. In the course of giving evidence of a number of documents, one can very well understand that I cannot carry everything in my head.

Mr. Brooks.

5987. Have you read the evidence which has been supplied to the corporation of the City of Dublin given before this Committee?—I do not know whether I have read the entire, but I have read the greater part of it.

5988. In the evidence of Mr. M'Evoy, it is stated that the change in the audit system was made because the state of things was so bad in Dublin; can you say whether that change in the audit system was not in consequence of an application from the corporation itself to the Government?—It was; there was a resolution moved by Alderman Campbell, and adopted by the council, asking for the appointment of an independent Government auditor, and that proposition came from the council in the first instance.

5989. Was that because the state of things was so bad?—It first arose from a conversation between Alderman Campbell, Sir John Gray, and myself; some imputations had been made in some of the public journals with reference to the corporate extravagance, and we thought that it would be much more satisfactory for the members of the council, as also for the public, that an independent audit should be made annually of the accounts.

5990. And that change was made from within?—Yes, that change was made at the suggestion of the council, and Sir John Gray and myself had the honour to wait upon the then Chief Secretary to ask that the Government should grant that audit; it was said that the corporation obtained a postponement of the Government audit for a year, in consequence of their desire to evade a surcharge of the sum of 500 *l.* for a contribution towards the relief of distress in France; that was not so; the reason the audit was postponed for a year was this: under the 3 & 4 Vic. c. 108, s. 70, the corporation were bound in December of each year to elect two auditors; they did so, and in the subsequent Session an Act of Parliament, giving an independent audit, passed the Legislature, and the auditor gave notice of his intention to sit in the month of September or October, I do not know which, for the purpose of auditing the corporation accounts; the two auditors that had been appointed at the close of the previous year were also about to sit and audit the accounts, and the corporation were bound by the terms of their appointment to pay those two gentlemen. The corporation thought it rather hard that they should

Mr. *Brooks*—continued.

Mr. *Norwood*, LL.D.

30 June 1876.

should have to pay two sets of auditors, and accordingly they suggested that the auditors for that year should be paid and suffered to complete their audit; at the same time they said that if the Government wished to audit the accounts by the independent auditor under the Local Government Act they were perfectly willing, but they thought that the citizens ought not to be charged with the payment for the double audit; and further than that, as the auditor requires the attendance of the accountant and other officers of the treasurer's department for two or three months, if the other auditors also required that attendance, the books would have been withdrawn from those departments for between four and five months, and consequently the entire accounts would have been thrown out of gear. The Government yielded to that suggestion, as they thought it but reasonable that but one audit should be paid for out of the rates, and that was the reason that it was postponed for a year, and not for the other one suggested.

5991. What are your opinions as to appeals from the decisions of the auditor?—I think that they should be to a court of law, because the majority of questions that arise before him are legal questions; at least, hitherto it has been so.

5992. Have you any suggestions to offer upon that subject?—Yes. Dr. Hancock made a suggestion, which I think an excellent one, that corporations generally should have an opportunity of obtaining, previous to incurring any expenditure, the opinion of a court of law, if they should think that there was any doubt upon the legality of the expenditure.

5993. Have the corporation considered this question of appeals?—They have, and they also think it rather hard that if a person should appeal against a surcharge and should be successful, the corporation or the party should have to pay the auditor's costs.

5994. Are you of opinion that it is better to have an independent auditor for the other Boards in Ireland as well as for Dublin?—Certainly; it is more satisfactory for the Boards, for the public, and for everybody.

5995. You are aware that Rathmines is exempt at present?—Yes.

5996. You would extend that system of audit to Rathmines and to Waterford?—To all municipalities; and I have seen a section in the Public Health (Ireland) Act, 1876 (a Bill which is at present pending in the Legislature), which provides that the public audit should be extended to those cities.

5997. Mr. M'Evoy asserted that the corporation extravagantly expended their rates in promoting and opposing Bills; will you describe the course pursued in dealing with Private Bills?—Notice under the Standing Orders is served upon the town clerk, of the intention to apply for Bills affecting Dublin, and it is his duty to report them at once to the council, which he does; and when a copy of the Bill is furnished, he sends it forward to the next meeting of the council. It is then referred by the council to the consideration of whatever committee has charge of the department to which the Bill refers; if it relates to the streets, or anything connected with the town or the bridges, it is referred to No. 1 committee; they direct the law agent to report upon it, and if he says that it is necessary that the corporation should obtain a *locus standi*, he reports to that effect to the committee. The committee then report the result of their inquiries to the corporation, and the corporation then finally decide whether there is to be an opposition or not.

Mr. *Brooks*—continued.

5998. As in duty bound?—Yes. It is necessary for many reasons that the corporation should obtain a *locus standi* on those Bills, inasmuch as they being a governing municipal body, are the only parties legally entitled to obtain a *locus standi*. I may add that it is not the fault of the corporation that they have to expend the monies of the ratepayers in lodging petitions against local Bills, because in many respects they have been of an objectionable character, and unless a petition was lodged, there would be no means of amending a Bill in passing through the House, or obtaining clauses for the protection of the inhabitants and ratepayers.

5999. The adjoining townships, such as Kingstown, have also been put to considerable expense in the matter of Bills before Parliament, have they not?—Yes. A member of the Town Commission of Kingstown told me that that township and the neighbouring ones and the ratepayers, had within a very few years been put to an expense of something like 17,000 *l.*, in promoting and opposing private Bills.

6000. Are you acquainted with the mode of revision in Belfast?—Yes. There must be an amendment of the 3 & 4 Vict. c. 108, with regard to the appointment of borough assessor.

6001. Did you not occupy an official position in the revision of Belfast?—Yes, I was borough assessor for eight or nine years. At present the burgesses elect two borough assessors, and they are not necessarily legal men; the only qualification under the Act is that they must be burgesses. Formerly, those two burgesses used to name each a Member of the Bar, and that system obtained for very many years, and the borough assessorships were filled by men of very great distinction at the Bar, such as Sir Joseph Napier, afterwards Chancellor, and Mr. Lowry, Q.C., and persons of that character; but after awhile it was discovered that there was no authority under the Act to pay the fees for the barristers so acting; and consequently the town council or the borough assessors elected by the burgesses could not appoint barristers; and the next best thing to be done then in Belfast was, that they appointed two local solicitors of position, and they revised the burgess list. But it is necessary, in my opinion, that it should be a legally qualified person. I would suggest in Dublin and elsewhere, that the barrister who revises the Parliamentary lists should likewise revise the municipal lists and also the juror's lists. That would be a saving of time and a saving of expense, and all legal points could be fairly argued before him, and legally and satisfactorily decided. All notices of claims and objections should be sent through the post, as the notices connected with the Parliamentary voters' lists are.

6002. Have the corporation considered this subject?—Yes, I think I handed in a resolution to say that it would be a saving of time and expense if that system were adopted.

6003. It was suggested that our corporate officers should should be appointed by a competitive or qualifying examination; have you any opinion upon that?—I do not think that that is possible; so far as I know of the appointments of the officers in the corporation they are very fairly appointed, and I think, taking them on the whole, they are a very

Mr. *Brooks*—continued.

a very fair set of officers, and do their duty very properly.

6004. Do you know whether the corporation have been guilty of any extravagance with regard to the salaries of their officers as was alleged?—I think not; I have to hand in a return, a comparative statement, showing the salaries paid by the Corporation of Dublin to their officers in the years 1863–4 and 1875–6, with an analysis showing first the salaries in those two years; next showing the simple increase in the salaries; next whether those increases are for new duties; thirdly, new appointments, and a fourth column showing any decreases which have taken place during those years. The salaries in 1863–4 amounted in the total to 10,893 *l*., and in 1875–6 they amounted to 15,250 *l*. The simple increases in the salaries during that period amounted to 1,380 *l*. 10 *s*., and 1,000 *l*. was for new duties in new departments; 2,828 *l*. for new appointments, and there have been increases to the amount of 930 *l*., and the net actual increase, irrespective of new duties, amount to 430 *l*. 10 *s*., showing a per-centage of increases in 12 years, irrespective of new duties, of 3·2 per cent.

6005. With regard to superannuations, have they been of a moderate or an extravagant nature?—They have been of a moderate character, and I beg to state that all those superannuations are subject to the supervision and approval of his Grace the Lord Lieutenant. I have here a report as an example of one of them from the Board of Superintendence. The Board determine upon the report of the medical officer of the prison whether any officer is to be superannuated or no; that is sent forward, and it is reported upon by the Inspector General of Prisons, who certifies whether a superannuation allowance ought to be granted, and at what rate, and that is verified by the local inspector, by the governor, and finally sent on to the council, and if approved by them is forwarded to the Lord Lieutenant, who has the power of veto or of sanction.

6006. Have you compared the salaries of the corporate officials in Dublin with those of other large towns elsewhere, or with the salaries to officials in other institutions in Dublin?—I have; and I find, without going through them, that in Bradford, in Birmingham, in Bristol, in Leeds, in Liverpool, in Manchester, in Sheffield, and in Edinburgh, the salaries to officers discharging similar duties are much higher.

6007. With regard to the salaries paid by the Port and Docks Board to their engineers and chief clerks, what observation have you to make?—I find that the secretary of the Port and Docks Board, who discharges duties somewhat similar to those of the town clerk, gets 800 *l*. a year; he has an assistant at 140 *l*., and in his department the amount of salaries is 1,609 *l*. 7 *s*. 9 *d*. I find that the engineer of the Port and Docks Board gets 1,500 *l*. (while Mr. Neville gets 750 *l*.), and that the assistant engineer has 400 *l*., and there is another assistant engineer at 250 *l*., and a draughtsman at 210 *l*.

6008. How do the salaries of the corporation compare with the salaries of the Poor Law Boards?—They are very little more than the salaries of the Poor Law Boards for persons discharging similar duties. I may add this, that under the Dublin Improvement Act they are entitled to the appointment of three secretaries

Mr. *Brooks*—continued.

for each "standing committee," at 400 *l*. a year; but in order to save expense, the corporation have appointed the town clerk as secretary to No. 3 Committee, without giving him a separate salary for it, and the duties of the secretary to No. 3 Committee are discharged by him, as well as the duties of town clerk. The secretary of No. 1 Committee has 300 *l*. a year, whereas, under the statute, he might have 400 *l*.; and the secretary of No. 2 Committee has only 100 *l*. a year, because the corporation appointed the secretary of the Waterworks Committee to discharge the duties of the secretary of No. 2 Committee along with those of the secretary to the Waterworks Committee, and gave him, in addition to his salary of 200 *l*. a year, 100 *l*. a year for discharging the duties in No. 2 Committee.

Mr. *Norwood*, LL.D.

30 June 1876.

6009. With regard to the imputation of nepotism in the election of officers, have you any observations to make?—I saw some curious statements with regard to that; I saw that Mr. Murphy's son had been appointed to this office. Mr. Murphy is a town councillor, but he has no son.

6010. We have but one Mr. Murphy, I think, in the council?—That is so. It was stated that Mr. Barlow was appointed because his father was in the town council. Mr. Barlow says that his father died 21 years before he was elected mace-bearer, that his uncle had been a member of the town council, and had left Dublin for many years before he ever was appointed. I need not go through them all, but most of those statements were erroneous.

6011. Will you explain the causes of any falling off of the duties in the marshal's office?—Yes, I have got a statement from the marshal here in which he states that the trade of pawnbroking is subject to great fluctuations. The years 1863 and 1864 were exceptionally good years on account of the American War and other reasons that operated with regard to that, and the sales in one divisional sale-room alone, in 1864, amounted to 69,000 *l*. whereas in a very few years after, in 1874, they fell off to 26,000 *l*., and it appears that the number of pledges in 1874 amounted to 3,128,684, the amount lent upon which was 591,640 *l*. 11 *s*. 5 *d*., whereas in 1875 the pledges had diminished to 2,715,555, showing a decrease of 413,129 and a decrease in money value of 54,108 *l*. 0 *s*. 10 *d*., showing very great fluctuations indeed, and also it is stated that one of the causes why they do not send in their fees and annual returns, as they are bound by statute to do, is that the feeling has prevailed for some three or four years that the laws respecting pawnbrokers are about to be altered at the suggestion of Dr. Hancock, and for that reason the pawnbrokers have been careless in sending in their returns.

6012. Mr. M'Evoy stated that the last Waterworks Act was virtually a dead letter, inasmuch as the corporation have never received a shilling under it for extra water supply; will you state the facts with regard to that?—That is not a fact. We have received one sum, I know of 500 *l*., from the Pembroke township, and the other townships have to contribute large sums; but there have been negotiations pending between the Waterworks Committee and the townships with regard to the amount of excess water, and those negotiations are very nearly closed with

Mr. Norwood, LL.D.

30 June 1876.

Mr. Brooks—continued.

with Pembroke, Blackrock, and the other townships, and, as soon as the amount is adjusted, the township will pay their respective quota for excess of water.

6013. Do you desire to state anything as to the alleged neglect of the corporation in sanitary matters?—My own experience is, that every complaint is promptly and carefully attended to, and whenever I myself have suggested to Mr. Boyle any matters, they are at once attended to by him or by the constabulary, and the constabulary are subjected to the double check of having to report to Colonel Lake and his staff, as well as to report to Mr. Boyle and the Sanitary Committee. I think nothing can be more satisfactory than the way in which they discharge that duty. At the same time it has been a serious loss to us that Colonel Lake felt it to be his duty, consistently with the discharge of other public departments connected with the police, to withdraw six constables from us, and the Public Health Committee would willingly pay the salaries of those constables if the department would only let us have them.

6014. Have you considered the subject of the difficulties in the way of sanitary work in Dublin?—I have; and I have laid before Sir Alfred Power, and also before the Right Honourable Baronet, the Chairman of this Committee, my suggestions in a paper which I read before the Statistical Society showing the difficulties in the way presented by the defects in the sanitary laws; and since I came over here I have had an opportunity of seeing the Bill introduced by the Government in the present Session for the amendment and codification of the Public Health Statutes; and I think that most of the suggestions which I had the honour to make have been carried out.

6015. Do the Public Health Committee neglect any complaint or suggestions made by the citizens?—I never knew them to do so.

6016. Or any suggestions?—Or any suggestions. The very moment they come in they are at once acted on. Those are the directions of the Public Health Committee.

6017. Have you any suggestions to make with regard to the improvement of the sanitary arrangements?—None, except those that I have mentioned.

6018. Would you not recommend that there should be a sanitary magistrate for the whole metropolitan district?—It would be a very great improvement, because the sanitary sergeants, when they attend for the prosecution of cases before the magistrates, have to wait until the custody cases and the night charges are disposed of, and that very often entails the loss of several hours during the day (which, in the case of a limited staff, is a matter of very great moment), as they should remain in court, whereas they might be attending to their inspections throughout the city. I think that if there were a magistrate for the entire metropolitan district, including the townships and the county, it would be matter of very great importance for the speedy and satisfactory discharge of the duties of that Board.

6019. Then, by a re-arrangement of the duties of the magistrates, no additional expense need necessarily be entailed by the adoption of your suggestion?—I should say not. I think the magistrates themselves might make some arrangement for that purpose.

Mr. Brooks—continued.

6020. And the convenience of the public would be more advanced?—Yes. The per-centage of cases prosecuted have very largely increased since the passing of the Public Health Act of 1874, and will necessarily increase, in consequence of the very great attention now given to sanitary matters and sanitary legislation.

6021. Do you suggest anything as to the removal by the corporation of nuisances from dwellings?—That was a matter which was pressed upon the Sanitary Committee by the Sanitary Association; but as far as matters are concerned connected with it at present, I think that the removal of nuisances from dwellings is very fairly attended to. If the nuisances were removed at the public expense, it would merely be for the advantage of a large number of house jobbers, and so on, and the expense upon the ratepayers would be enormous, and I do not think there would be a corresponding advantage as compared with the cost over the present system.

6022. Will you explain why the corporation have not put the Artizans' Dwellings Act into operation?—Their principal reason is the avoidance of expense, and they think there would be considerable delay in it. I may add, with regard to that Act of Parliament, that Dublin is somewhat differently situated from those cities for which, as I understand, the Public Artizans' Dwellings Acts were first intended; they were intended for places like London and Manchester, where there is but little space for building within the borough boundaries, whereas there are large spaces in Dublin available for building artizans' dwellings. At the same time, I think it is most desirable, not only with a view to the erection of proper artizans' dwellings, but also with the view of running streets and wide passages through unwholesome districts, that the Artizans' Dwellings Act should be put into operation, but the citizens must understand that it will entail very considerable expense upon the rates.

6023. In fact, there are spaces now occupied by houses that are thoroughly dilapidated, and uninhabitable and ruinous, that would be available for the erection of artizans' dwellings without the demolition of any that are now occupied?—Yes; I may state that, as far back as the year 1853, I advocated very strongly the running of a wide street through a portion of St. Michan's parish for the very purpose of opening an air space, and for the prevention of disease in a district which was then in a most unwholesome and filthy condition; and although it is somewhat better now, still it would be most necessary to open air spaces through that district.

Sir Joseph M'Kenna.

6024. From what point would that street start to which you refer, and at what point would it finish?—From the terminus of the Midland Great Western Railway to Richmond Bridge and the Four Courts.

Mr. Brooks.

6025. I think it was stated by a witness to whom I have already referred, that the corporation have, in point of fact, too large a staff of officers; do you agree with that?—No; considering the increase in the business of the various departments, I do not think that they have too large a staff. Whenever they have a pressure they appoint temporarily a clerk, or a couple of clerks

Mr. *Brooks*—continued.

clerks, at 30 s. a week, or something of that sort, and then as soon as the pressure goes off the department the services of those officers are discontinued.

6026. And it is necessary to appoint those temporary officers?—Certainly.

6027. Will you explain the circumstances as to the dismissal of officers by the corporation in 1844?—I do not know as to that; there were a great number of officers dismissed after the 3 & 4 Vict. c. 108, came into operation, and at at that time I believe there was a good deal of public animadversion about the matter: but what led to the dismissals of the officers, or the reasons assigned by the corporation of that day, I do not know.

6028. Have you read also the evidence given by Mr. Pim as to the management of the financial affairs of the corporation?—Yes.

6029. Have you also read Mr. Finlay's evidence upon that subject?—I have.

6030. Will you give us your own opinions, based upon your knowledge and experience?—I think they are most carefully looked after; the accountant's department is very well managed, and the other accounts of the corporation are very carefully kept; I think Mr. Finlay has stated his opinion of the accountant and the other officers connected with the financial affairs of the corporation, as being favourable to their efficiency and the way in which the accounts are kept.

6031. Can you say anything as to the alleged irregularities in the attendance at the meetings of the corporation?—Nothing can be better than the way in which they attend at the committee meetings; a return has been prepared, showing the number of attendances of members of the council on committees in 1875, which I have here (*producing the same*).

6032. The work has very largely increased, has it not?—Yes.

6033. If there was a smaller quorum, do you think the business would be facilitated?—Immensely. The large quorum of 20 members is a great hinderance to business. The quorum of the committees, which are composed of 20 members, is but three, and if that proportion were carried out, as 3 is to 20, so would 9 be to 60, we should get through the business at once, and we would not allow an opportunity to the gentleman, who holds very peculiar notions about quorums, who is always on the watch, and the moment he sees that, the number of attendances drops to 19, he immediately counts the house, and the whole business of the day is knocked up.

6034. Are you referring to a member of the corporation?—Yes.

6035. That example is not followed by the others as a rule; it is deprecated by the other members, is it not?—Certainly; and it is the greatest possible loss of time to business men. When you consider that the business of the Poor Law Boards is discharged by some 60 or or 65 members, and that their quorum is three, I think that nine would be a very fair quorum for the corporation, and certainly would prevent many days' loss to the business men of the corporation.

6036. And you advocate the lessening of the quorum?—Certainly.

6037. The Committee have heard a great deal of evidence with reference to political discussions in the corporation; will you inform us as to your experience on that subject?—I have never myself taken part in political discussions in the corporation, because my own notion is that I was sent there by my constituents for other purposes; but whenever they do discuss politics, I go down to court and attend to my business. They generally appoint a special day for the discussion of those questions, and it does not practically interfere with the discharge of the duties in the committees which are really the meetings for business. Of course, other gentlemen think it is the business of the corporation to discuss political affairs, but I do not.

6038. Have you anything to suggest with regard to the prevention of discussion on political subjects at the meetings of the council?—No, nothing, except that the good sense of the members would cause them to avoid political discussions if they should interfere with the public business.

6039. Do they as a matter of fact interfere with the public business of the corporation?—Practically they do not, because, as I have said, they appoint special days for the discussion of those political matters; and those members who take an interest in them, attend and discuss the matter in hand, whatever it may be.

6040. Do the corporation show any disposition to reduce as far as in them lies, the taxation of the city?—Certainly. I think I have shown that so far as salaries are concerned and superannuation allowances, they are most carefully looked to with a view to the saving of expense to the public. The vice of the corporation, so far as I see, is rather the other way, that, in place of being extravagant, they are more inclined to be parsimonious.

6041. Is it true that the members of the corporation pay themselves but a small amount of taxation?—No. A return has been handed in, I understand, during the progress of Mr. Stokes's evidence, which shows that the majority of the members of the corporation are very large ratepayers indeed.

6042. Can you inform the Committee why it is that so few men of the higher mercantile classes come into the corporation?—There are many reasons for that. Take the members of the council of the Chamber of Commerce who are selected, and very fairly so, as being a type of the leading mercantile gentlemen in Dublin; for the majority of those gentlemen it would be impossible, consistently with their other avocations, to attend to corporate affairs, and so several of them have informed me. Yesterday morning I took down the names of three or four gentlemen who are leading members of the Chamber of Commerce, and whom I should greatly desire to see members of the corporation. And I find, taking Mr. Parker for instance, he is the head of a large firm; he is one of the Rathmines Commissioners; he is one of the council of the Chamber of Commerce; he is a Commissioner of Irish Lights; he is a director of the Irish Civil Service Building Society, a director of the Dublin and Glasgow Steam Packet Company, and of the Liberal Annuity Company; he is *ex officio* guardian of the South Dublin Union; he is a director of the Royal Bank, and he is a director of the Dublin, Wicklow, and Wexford Railway Company; then there is Mr. La Touche, who is a director of the Northern Railway Company, managing

Mr. *Norwood*, LL.D.

30 June 1876.

Mr. *Norwood*, LL.D.

30 June 1876.

Mr. *Brooks*—continued.

managing director of the Munster Bank, chief manager of the Royal Exchange Insurance Company, governor of the Richmond District Lunatic Asylum, and on several railway boards. In the same way Mr. Boyce is on a great number of public boards; Mr. Colville, another gentleman, is on a great number of public boards, and all those gentlemen could not possibly attend to the business of the corporation, which is very heavy indeed.

Sir *Joseph M'Kenna.*

6043. And not remunerative?—And not remunerative. Those gentlemen, I suppose, get their fees as directors for all those companies for whom they act, and it would not pay them to attend to the corporation business.

Mr. *Brooks.*

6044. But you have upon the corporation many men who are largely engaged in public avocations, such as, for instance, Alderman O'Rorke?—Certainly; he is a leading merchant and a poor law guardian. There are Sir James Mackey, Alderman Manning, Alderman Jamieson, Alderman Gregg, and Alderman M'Swiney; those gentlemen are all largely engaged in business and directors of public companies.

6045. Have you any observations to offer with reference to the statement of Mr. Pim, that a person must be a political partisan to remain in the corporation?—I think not; I have never taken part in politics since I went into the corporation, and I think I am as well received by all the members there as anybody in the corporation, and if I chose to seek re-election I have no doubt that I would be re-elected.

6046. As a gentleman of large experience in the corporation, you would say that in your opinion the evidence given by Mr. Pim on that subject is inaccurate?—So far as that is concerned, but at the same time I am bound to add this, that I think that the election of many of the members of the corporation is due to political influences; I do not say that that has operated in my case, because I know that it has not.

Mr. *Gibson.*

6047. I suppose that you represent a Conservative ward?—I do.

Mr. *Brooks.*

6048. Who are your colleagues?—Alderman Harris (who is, I believe, a Liberal in politics, but so far as the corporation is concerned, in his address he stated that he would know no party), Sir John Barrington, and the Honourable Mr. Vereker are my colleagues.

6049. With regard to complaints of jobbery of which Mr. Pim spoke, can you give the Committee any information?—I do not think that Mr. Pim or any other gentleman made any charge directly of jobbery, but they stated that there were rumours and suspicions. If there be rumours and suspicions I do not know what foundation they rest upon, for I have never seen anything of that character in the committees of the corporation.

6050. Mr. Pim compared the punctuality and the good style in which the Port and Docks Board conduct their business, with the mode in which the corporation conduct theirs; can you tell us anything with regard to that?—I think that if the quorum were reduced in the corporation, they would meet with more punctuality, and so far as the committees are concerned, I do not think that the Port and Docks Board can possibly discharge their duties with more care and assiduity than the members of the committees do.

6051. The financial business of the Port and Docks Board is of considerable extent and importance, is it not?—Yes, certainly; and they discharge it, I believe, most satisfactorily to the citizens of Dublin.

6052. Do you know the number of their quorum?—Their quorum is five.

6053. You have also read Dr. Grimshaw's evidence, have you not?—Yes.

6054. Can you give us any particular instance of the watchfulness of the corporation with regard to the expenditure of money?—Generally I may state that they scrutinise most carefully the expenditure of any moneys, and there are members of the corporation whose business appears solely to be, and very properly so, to scrutinise the expenditure of every farthing.

6055. With regard to the imputations upon the manner in which the police discharge their duties, can you give us any information?—I have been myself a most active member of the Public Health Committee since its establishment, and nothing can be more satisfactory than the way in which the constabulary discharge their duties.

6056. What do you say with regard to those who are employed by the Public Health Committee more particularly?—They are officers, of course, of very great intelligence, and most anxious to fulfill all the duties imposed upon them by the Public Health Committee. They have frequently been recommended to Colonel Sir Henry Lake for reward by the Public Health Committee, and he has always expressed his approval of the way in which they have discharged their duties. A return of the sanitary duties discharged since the establishment of the Public Health Committee in 1866, shows a mass of duty fulfilled, and a number of prosecutions successfully conducted, which certainly would tend to show that the public interests are not neglected by that body.

6057. With regard to the opinion vouchsafed to this Committee, that there has been no improvement in the sanitary condition of Dublin since the institution of the Public Health Committee, have you anything to say?—I have known Dublin all my life, and as I have shown by that pamphlet, written in 1853, to which I referred last Tuesday, I have taken very great interest in sanitary affairs, and I say that Dublin has improved in its sanitary condition, and that it could not possibly have done otherwise when you consider the mass of sanitary works which have been carried out under that committee since 1866. I do not for one moment say that they have done all that they ought to have done. Like other public bodies, they have their shortcomings, but I think that the wholesale charges that have been made against them are perfectly groundless, and it is certainly very hard for persons who seek to discharge their duties honestly and fairly to be subjected unjustly to imputations of that character.

6058. Has there been any improvement in the sanitary condition of those houses of which complaints

Mr. *Norwood*, LL.D.

30 June 1876.

Mr. *Brooks*—continued.

plaints have been made?—Certainly; I have visited many of them myself; whenever I have heard of houses which have not been cleansed or improved in accordance with the orders of the Sanitary Committee, I have gone there myself. I have conducted several hundred cases on behalf of the Public Health Committee as counsel, and in many instances I have gone myself previously to the houses in question in order to inform myself fully about them.

Sir *Arthur Guinness*.

6059. The honourable Member for Dublin, I think, said that Dr. Grimshaw had given evidence that there was no improvement in the sanitary state of Dublin; I must refer you to his evidence at Question 3935, where he was asked, "Do you think that there has been practically no improvement in the sanitary state of those houses?" referring to certain houses which had been mentioned before; and his answer was: "Practically there is no improvement since I began to look after them;" it is not with regard to Dublin generally?—With regard to those particular houses, I believe that Mr. Boyle gave evidence as to them.

6060. You are not aware what houses this refers to; you have not visited them?—No, certainly not; but the Public Health Committee have done certainly as much as their means enabled them to do. I may add that they have carried out those sanitary operations without the imposition of a sanitary rate or any additional taxation.

Mr. *Brooks*.

6061. Can you say whether the fines imposed by the magistrates are levied as far as possible?—Certainly; I have been engaged myself as counsel in very many cases in which heavy fines were imposed, and they were subsequently levied, as the accounts will show.

6062. Can you state whether the slaughter-houses are duly inspected?—Every week they are inspected by the officials of the Public Health Committee.

6063. Can you say so to the fact that Dr. Mapother has no duties; does he inspect?—Certainly; I have frequently examined him in court, and whenever his attendance in court is necessary he always attends, and he reports weekly to the committee. Day by day he makes his inspections, and he reports on Fridays at the meeting of the committee, and he is a most valuable officer.

6064. Are the medical sanitary officers in your opinion insufficiently or sufficiently paid?—I think that they are very fairly paid. The Public Health Committee did not propose at first to give them as much as they have now, but the Local Government Board, after some correspondence, sanctioned the amount which they get at present, which is 25 *l.* in addition to their salaries as poor law medical officers.

6065. Does the Public Health Committee publish reports periodically?—Every month, and they publish an annual resumé of all the operations during the year since 1866.

6066. Do those reports circulate?—Yes, certainly; they are circulated in the first place among the members of the council and among persons interested in sanitary affairs in Dublin.

6067. Can you say of your own experience

Mr. *Brooks*—continued.

whether due attention is paid to the reports of their officers?—Certainly, at once.

6068. Do you think that the late Local Government Board Inspector, Mr. Robinson, is not a gentleman of great capacity and experience?—Certainly he is; he is now Assistant Under Secretary for Ireland, and a gentleman of the very highest capacity. With regard to a matter which he investigated connected with the corporation depôts for the deposit of scavenge, and so on, he took the utmost pains about it, and not only examined the books, but went himself and visited the depôts, and reported to the Local Government Board, as I am informed, on the matter.

6069. Would it be true to say that there are no cabs at the unions available for the general public?—Mr. Boyle has explained that fully; there are cabs there.

6070. You being one of the poor law guardians, is that your experience?—Yes, they are there certainly.

6071. Can you say of your own experience whether there are not a number of gentlemen upon the Public Health Committee who are of the most intelligent of our citizens, and who are competent to look after the sanitary condition of the city?—Certainly.

6072. They have been described as gentlemen "of mental incapacity;" you probably would not agree with that?—I do not know whether I would be competent to form an opinion upon that, for I may be myself labouring under that difficulty.

6073. May I ask whether, in your opinion, they fairly represent the average of the citizens of the city?—Very fairly, I think. I think they are a very fair set of men.

6074. You are a member also of the Waterworks Committee?—Yes.

6075. Have you heard a complaint made that the corporation have given the Vartry water supply to the townships at an unreasonably low rate?—Yes.

6076. Will you give us the reason for that?—At the time that the negotiations were pending between Sir John Gray and the Pembroke township and other townships, there was an offer made by the Rathmines township to supply the Pembroke township with water at a much less rate than Sir John Gray was asking for a supply per 1,000 gallons from the Vartry source, and Sir John was compelled, by being underbid by Mr. Stokes, to give it at a much less rate than he otherwise would, and many of the persons who belong to Rathmines and to the City of Dublin complained that it was so done; but they were not aware of the circumstances that Mr. Stokes would have supplied water to Pembroke for nothing, rather than let the corporation get an adequate price for it.

6077. What has been the consequence to the ratepayers of Rathmines of the policy of their Board with regard to the water supply?—If they had taken the water supply from the Vartry source, they would have had a much better and purer supply, much more copious and at a less cost, and at the present moment there are complaints made of the quality of the water supplied from the canal to the Rathmines district. The Vartry water pipes are now laid through the township to Rathgar and Rathfarnham, and the inhabitants of that district are applying day by day for supplies from those pipes.

Mr. *Norwood*, LL.D.

30 June 1876.

Mr. *Brooks*—continued.

6078. Is that because they allege that the water is bad or insufficient?—The water is much purer from the Vartry supply, and the supply is ampler and the pressure greater.

Sir *Joseph M'Kenna.*

6079. What is the difference in the altitude of the two basins of supply?—I cannot tell off-hand, but the pressure of the Vartry is far away in excess of that from the canal.

Mr. *Brooks.*

6080. Have there been any evil effects from insufficient pressure recently?—The extinguishment of fires in the Rathmines district is not so rapid as in the City of Dublin.

6081. You were also, I think, for several years on the Main Drainage Committee?—I was; I am chairman of that committee since Sir John Gray resigned the chairmanship at the end of the first year of the establishment of that committee.

6082. Being the chairman, have you ever heard that political questions have deterred citizens not members of the corporation from joining that committee?—There never was any political discussion in that committee that ever I heard of. Mr. Stokes and Mr. Parker and other gentlemen belong to it from the different townships, and we discuss nothing but the business of the committee.

Mr. *Gibson.*

6083. As I understand you, there are no political discussions at any committee meeting?—No.

6084. And no reporters are present at any of the committee meetings?—None; as chairman I would not suffer the discussion of any political matter, or of any matter excepting the business in hand of the committee.

Mr. *Brooks.*

6085. With regard to Mr. Stokes, he himself is a member of the Main Drainage Committee, is he not?—He is a very efficient member.

6086. Are you aware that Mr. Stokes gave, as one of his reasons for not joining the corporation, the prevalence of political discussions?—So far as my experience of the Main Drainage Committee is concerned, there is no foundation for his apprehension.

6087. Have you any observations to make as to the surcharges by the corporation auditor?—Further than this, that although something like 250,000 *l.* a year is administered by the corporation, either directly or indirectly, the amount of surcharge since 1871 is infinitesimally small, and would show that the business is very fairly attended to.

6088. Have those arisen from any malversation?—Certainly not; they have been on mere technical points.

6089. To what cause do you attribute the desire of many persons to avoid being placed on the burgess roll?—The present operation of the jury laws in Dublin has a good deal to do with it. Gentlemen who live in the townships and outside the borough boundary, and occupy houses there and also occupy premises and warehouses, counting houses, and shops within the borough boundary, are unwilling to allow themselves to be put upon the burgess roll, inasmuch as they would thereby be subjected to serve on both county and city juries; and I think it would tend very much to obviate that unwillingness to go upon the burgess roll if there was, as in Middlesex, but one venue for the city and county; because then they would be only subjected to be summoned on the one jury. Gentlemen have told me that one of the reasons why they avoided going on the burgess roll was that they would have to serve on the city juries, whereas they felt that they discharged sufficiently their civil requirements by attending upon the county juries.

Mr. *Brooks*—continued.

6090. Are the corporation in favour of a revision of the valuation?—Yes; I stated that on the last day of my examination; but they hesitated to recommend it, inasmuch as they thought it would not be fair towards the city to have the valuation of the city adjusted without having the same process extended to the townships and the county.

6091. Could you explain about the transfer of the rate from the sewer fund to the improvement rate?—That was a mere question of account. What are called sewer openings in the different streets, of course caused an expenditure upon the improvement fund necessary for the restoration of the surface of the streets. No. 1 Committee took the opinion of Mr. Gerald Fitzgibbon, Q.C., who was of opinion that the improvement fund should be recouped by the sewer fund for the purpose of compensating the improvement fund for the reparation of the street surfaces consequent upon the openings for sewer purposes. The same process goes on with reference to the waterworks account, which is charged with the amounts necessary to restore the surface of the street after openings have been made by the Waterworks Committee for the laying of pipes, and such purposes.

6092. Will you explain how it was that the sum expended upon the waterworks exceeded the original estimate?—The original works were executed within the original estimate; but, although that was so, in consequence of unexpected difficulties in quarrying and making the tunnel at Callow-hill, the contractors lost considerably, and became insolvent, but their sureties completed the original works within the original estimate. Subsequently, when the township came to be supplied, the works had to be enlarged, and additional works constructed, and that made the additional sum over and above the original estimate.

6093. With regard to filtration, has the system of filtration been adopted in consequence of the Vartry water being impure, or as an afterthought?—Certainly not; it was always originally intended that there should be filter beds, and in every properly constructed system of waterworks, no matter how pure the water is, there must be filtration.

6094. Will you explain to the Committee the mode of contributing to the repair of the Rock-road?—That was first provided for, I believe, in the Pembroke Township Local Act; the corporation petitioned against that Act only so far as it affected the water supply; they did not petition generally against it, and that clause was put in, as I am informed, in the absence of the corporation; the clause requires that the corporation should contribute a sum towards the repairs of the Rock-road, the townships of Blackrock and Pembroke contributing a certain proportion, and

Mr. Norwood, LL.D.

30 June 1876.

Mr. *Brooks*—continued.

and a portion of the county of Dublin; the barony of Rathdown also contributes towards it; but the corporation have no control over the Rock-road after they have paid their contribution towards it.

6095. Are you able to offer the Committee any explanation concerning the alleged misappropriations in the marshal's office?—In justice to the late marshal, it should be stated that the defalcations were caused by the subordinates in his office.

6096. That is all you wish to say?—That is all I have to say about that.

6097. Do you think it satisfactory, or otherwise, that the assessors in the revision court should be elected annually?—I think not; I do not think that any person exercising judicial functions should be subjected to annual popular election.

6098. Would you wish to have the law amended in any other respect?—Yes, in the direction which I have already explained; the same barristers that revise the Parliamentary voters' lists should also revise the municipal lists and the jurors' lists, for the purpose of saving expense and time, and also for the more efficient discharge of the duty of revision.

6099. Do you think that power should be given for extending the time of revision?—Yes, in some cases. It is too limited, and there must be an amendment of the last Election Act, inasmuch as they did not observe the requirements of the 3 & 4 Vict. c. 108, with regard to the period of the completion of the revision of the voters' lists. A difficulty has arisen about that, and although it has been got over, still it will probably form the subject of judicial inquiry hereafter, unless it be amended.

6100. With regard to the collector-general's department, can you say whether the expenses have been unnecessarily or extravagantly increased?—They have not. I observe it was stated that the expenses have risen from 3,000 *l.* and some odd hundreds up to 7,000 *l.* Whoever stated that forgot to state that the increase is in the poundage, which makes a most material difference, because it shows that larger sums were collected, and that the increase arose in consequence of the much larger sums put in collection by the operation of presentments, and otherwise. The sum of 1875 for the office account is 6,767 *l.* 11 *s.* 3 *d.*, and not 7,000 *l.*, and that includes a sum of 987 *l.* 14 *s.* 6 *d.*, which was re transferred to the several boards after the payment of expenses. So that that reduces the 6,767 *l.* to 5,700 *l.* and odd; and the salaries remain in many respects the same as in 1850, when the collector-general's salary was fixed at 800 *l.* by Act of Parliament, and it remains the same, and cannot be increased unless the Act be amended. Besides that, the salaries in the office are fixed by the Lord Lieutenant, or they are subject to his sanction and revision, and it does not appear, so far as I can see, that the salaries are too high. There is one chief clerk at 252 *l.*, rising to 350 *l.*; there are three first-class clerks at 150 *l.*, rising to 200 *l.*; and three second-class clerks at 90 *l.*, rising to 140 *l.* But whether they be large or small, they are fixed by his Excellency the Lord Lieutenant, and of course with a due regard to economy. I may state, as showing the increase of poundage, that in the first year of the establishment of the collector-general's department, the amount collected was 150,000 *l.*; it has now risen to 290,000 *l.*, passing through the office, and as the collectors are paid by poundage, of course it is their interest to collect as much as possible.

6101. With regard to the burgess list, do you wish to make any suggestions concerning the extension of time for the completion of the lists?—I have mentioned that already. Sometimes the assessors have to sit by night in addition to sitting from 11 to 4, and that is extremely objectionable.

6102. Do you agree with Judges Barry and Warren that it is legal to put weekly and monthly tenants upon the burgess roll?—I have always contended against it when acting as counsel before the revision court, and I have always deferred to the opinion of those eminent judges.

Sir *Joseph M'Kenna*.

6103. On what authority is the quorum of the corporation fixed at 20?—It is fixed by a bye-law under the Act of Parliament, and it therefore has the force of a statute.

6104. But has the corporation the power of making a bye-law to alter the quorum?—Not without 40 members being present, or without the sanction of his Excellency the Lord Lieutenant.

6105. If you had a meeting of 40, and a majority, say 25, of the 40 present fixed the quorum at less than 20, that is to say, at nine or ten, and the Lord Lieutenant gave his sanction to it, would that make the new quorum legal?—There are very great difficulties in getting the number sufficient to alter a bye law; there are so many difficulties in the way that one trifling alteration in a bye-law took very nearly two years before we could get the necessary formalities completed under the statute and the bye-law, and consequently the simpler way to do it would be by amending the statute.

6106. Does it appear to you that the requirement of the presence of 20 citizens for the ordinary corporate business, in order to constitute a quorum, is somewhat oppressive in its working?—It is certainly most oppressive on business men.

6107. You have suggested already the number which you would have instead of 20 as a quorum?—Yes; the Standing Committees' quorum is three. The Standing Committees, numbering 20, and the other committees, with the exception of the Main Drainage Committee, have their quorum fixed at three. The Main Drainage Committee's quorum was fixed at seven, but that was in consequence of that committee being a mixed committee, composed of members of the corporation and members of the different township boards outside; and the corporation thought that seven would be the proper quorum for the meetings of that particular committee. I did not agree with the majority in fixing that quorum, because I thought that three would be sufficient, and I did so because three is the quorum of the Poor Law Boards throughout the country, and is quite a sufficient number.

6108. Would you not think that seven would be a sufficient number for the corporation at large?—I should say nine. As three is to 20, so is nine to 60, the full number of the corporation.

6109. You are aware that the quorum of this House

Mr. *Norwood*, LL.D.

30 June 1876.

Sir *Joseph M'Kenna*—continued.

House is 40 out of upwards of 600?—Yes, that is a less proportion than I have mentioned.

6110. It appears to me that for the ordinary business of the corporation a quorum of seven would be very efficient; have you anything to say against it?—Nothing whatever. I should be delighted to see it, and the members of the corporation, with perhaps one or two exceptions, would be delighted to see the quorum reduced.

6111. Are your acts legal, although you have less than a quorum, unless the deficiency is noted by some one counting the house?—They are quite legal.

6112. Then it ordinarily arises from the solicitude of an individual member that a smaller attendance does not suffice?—Quite so; unless the attention of the Lord Mayor or the chairman is called to it, the business proceeds.

6113. But there is generally speaking some one person whose business it is to observe the fact and act upon it?—There is a gentleman whose peculiar idiosyncrasy it is to watch the quorum, and the moment he sees 18 or 19 only present, he jumps up and calls the attention of the Lord Mayor to it, and unless somebody comes in before the roll is counted, the business is closed, *solvuntur risu tabulæ tu missus abibis*.

6114. If you were to sum up all the defects of the corporation and all the causes of complaint against them, would you ascribe them to deficiency of ways and means?—Certainly; they have endeavoured to make 6 *d.* go as far as 2 *s.* 6 *d.*, and the difficulties in the way of that arithmetical process are very great. They would do a great deal more if they had more funds at their disposal.

6115. Do you think if there was a new plan by which your revenue would be fairly recruited, it would be a good and efficient corporation?—I think so. Taking them as a body, I think they discharge their business very fairly. But in the course of a few years their resources will improve. There are leases shortly to drop in under which they derive now merely a small head-rent, and they will then derive the rack rent from those premises, and will get a large increase in their revenue. If the valuation were properly adjusted, I think they would be in a better position in a few years. Then there is this also to be said, that so far as the repairs of the streets are concerned, they are getting this advantage, that the tramways company have relieved the corporation from the repairs of a considerable portion of several miles of streets through the borough; and the corporation have lately borrowed 50,000 *l.*, and are paving with Welsh setts a considerable portion of the most frequented business streets in the city. All that will tend to relieve the expenses of the repair of the streets in coming years; the less Macadam they have the less repairs will be required.

Sir *Arthur Guinness*.

6116. I presume you have heard of what was called by a witness here the "Amateur" Corporation of Dublin; I mean the citizen's committee?—Yes.

6117. Are you aware that it is composed of influential ratepayers and citizens?—Certainly.

6118. To what cause do you attribute the existence of such a body to which the ratepayers subscribe so freely?—I think it is caused by a very laudable anxiety to improve the sanitary condition of the city, and so far as I am concerned, as a member of the Public Health Committee, I am most anxious that those gentlemen should co-operate with us, and any suggestions that they ever made, so far as I was personally able to achieve it, I have endeavoured to have carried out.

Sir *Arthur Guinness*—continued.

6119. Do you think that their existence is in consequence of any want of confidence in, and also want of information from, the corporation?—I think that in a great measure it has arisen from want of information on the part of the public with regard to the carriage of their duties by the corporation.

6120. And you would be in favour of affording every information to the public?—Yes, certainly; there is nothing to conceal; and, so far as I know, we have always endeavoured to give information.

6121. Are you aware that such information has not been generally afforded to the citizen's committee?—I am aware that on several occasions the Public Health Committee did not respond to inquiries, and one of the reasons that they did so was that the communications were not couched in that courteous style which is usual between public bodies, and that the requirements were demanded in a somewhat dictatorial way.

6122. Have you ever seen any of those dictatorial documents?—I did not myself think them dictatorial, but some persons did. I am always anxious personally to afford information to every gentleman who chooses to inquire.

6123. You did not yourself consider them in any way dictatorial?—I thought they might have been more courteous. If I had penned the communications, perhaps, I would have rounded the periods better, and made them more civil.

6124. Are you aware of the existence of such associations elsewhere?—I cannot say that I am.

6125. Did you ever hear of a ratepayers' association in England?—No; I may say that I was a member of the Sanitary Committee many years ago myself.

6126. Will you read the heading of that document (*handing a paper to the Witness*)?—"St. Mary Abbott's Ratepayers' Association. Fifth annual report presented by the committee at the general meeting, held at Onslow Hall, 25th February 1876."

6127. Who is the chairman of that?—Major General Sir H. Charles Daubeney, K.C.B.

6128. Will you look at the end, and see the subscriptions, showing that it is a voluntary society?—The balance sheet for 1875 shows subscriptions to the amount of 51 *l.* 16 *s.* 1 *d.*, and on the credit side disbursements to the amount of 51 *l.* 16 *s.* 1 *d.*

6129. Will you read the first two paragraphs, and see what the object of the association is?—"In presenting their fifth annual report, the committee wish to congratulate the members of the association on the continued success of their efforts in securing the election of their nominees as guardians and vestrymen during the past year. The guardians recommended by the committee were, as usual, elected by a very large majority. At the election of members for the vestry there was no contest, but all the gentlemen proposed by the committee were chosen. (2.) As regards the administration of the poor law, one of the greatest evils that had to be dealt with on the

Sir *Arthur Guinness*—continued.

the establishment of our association was the excessive amount of the out relief; this evil was not to be remedied in a day; it was only by a thorough investigation of the old cases, and a gradual weeding out of the most undeserving, as well as by a strict scrutiny of every new application, that any real good could be done. We think that the following statement will be deemed very satisfactory." Then it gives the cost of outdoor relief for the year ending Michaelmas 1870, 11,247 *l.* 4 *s.* 7 *d.*, and that it fell in 1875 to 5,868 *l.* 18 *s.* 8 *d.*

6130. Which this association attributed to their efforts?—Yes.

6131. Do you believe that the object of the members of the citizens' committee in Dublin is of a kindred kind to this?—Yes; and I think it a most laudable endeavour on their part; I am not aware that their suggestions have in any instance been thrown aside, or otherwise than attended to with promptness; at least that is my experience of Mr. Boyle and his officers.

6132. Then you are not aware that very many remonstrances which were sent on various subjects by the citizens' committee to the public health committee were marked "read," and no answer vouchsafed?—I am not aware that many were treated in that way.

6133. Are you aware that there was any attempt on the part of the citizens' committee to have a friendly interview with some members of the corporation to see what could be done, so far as regards the main drainage scheme?—Yes, and as I was most anxious to have been a party to that interview, I came up specially from circuit on purpose.

6134. Do you recollect that although an appointment was made with the Lord Mayor and other members, none of them attended to meet the citizens?—Yes, as I tell you, I came up specially, at very great inconvenience, from Belfast, where I was on circuit, to attend the meeting of the committee, but I was prevented by a letter which I received on my arrival in town, and to my very great regret, because I think a conference would have done a great deal of good.

6135. You think that the appointment ought to have been kept in common courtesy to the gentlemen who formed the deputation from the citizens' committee?—Yes, I do think that. I believe I explained before my regret that the appointment was not kept, and that in courtesy it ought to have been kept.

6136. Do you know what is the result of the investigations on the subject of Mr. Robinson's defalcations?—The corporation have engaged an independent auditor to investigate the accounts, and he is at present engaged in their examination, but roughly speaking, I believe the defalcations amount to something under 3,000 *l.*; 2,700 *l.* and odd, I believe it is, and that amount is secured to the corporation by a sum of 3,000 *l.* invested in Consols in the names of Alderman Campbell, ex-Alderman Ryan, and Mr. Robinson in the Bank of Ireland, which will be available for the repayment to the corporation account of the amount drawn from it. They also have a further guarantee of 3,000 *l.* from a guarantee society, so that the corporation funds will not in any way be put to loss.

6137. On the subject of gas; what is the present price of gas in Dublin; is it not very dear?—I forget what it is at the present moment; I

Sir *Arthur Guinness*—continued.

am aware that the citizens think that it might be had at a cheaper rate, and it will hereafter, I believe, be at a cheaper rate, because the Alliance Gas Company will be in a position to give it to the citizens on better terms than hitherto. They were in very great difficulties, but by efficient management they are extricating themselves from those difficulties, and hereafter I have no doubt that they will be able to give the citizens gas on better terms, both for public lighting and for their private consumption.

6138. When was the price raised to what it is now by lowering the standard of the gas?—That was consequent upon the Gas Bill of 1874, I think.

6139. Will you explain what the object of that Bill was?—The object of that Bill was to enable the gas company to reduce the standard of illuminating power.

6140. During the time that a contract was in existence?—Yes, during the time of the existence of the contract which, I think, will expire this year.

6141. Was not this the plea of the gas company, that unless the price was raised it would bring them to bankruptcy?—Yes; as I stated before, they were in very great difficulties, and both the labour market and the coal market were in an abnormal state.

6142. Previous to that the corporation wished to purchase the gas works?—Yes, they did so upon the recommendation of Messrs. Clemenshaw and Pritchard, and other gas engineers of great eminence, and upon the recommendation of Mr. Cotton their own gas engineer; and I stated in my examination on Tuesday that the recommendations of those gentlemen were founded upon great experience, and upon returns from various towns where the corporations had purchased the gas undertakings. The anticipations of those gentlemen have been fully realised; the gas company have not only regained a solvent position, but they have put all their debts in liquidation, and are in a most prosperous condition now, and are able to pay dividends to their shareholders.

6143. Are you aware that the report of Messrs. Clemenshaw at the time said that the gas ought not to be more than 3 *s.* 6 *d.*, even although the cost of coal was then much higher than it is at present?—I believe he stated so, and if you say so, I have no doubt of it.

6144. Now gas is at a considerably higher price than at that time, although coal is very much lower?—At that time the gas company's works were not at all in the efficient condition that they are in now; the gas mains were subject to leakages of an inordinate character, and the works were in such a condition that they could not obtain the same amount of cubic feet per ton of coal carbonised that they can now; I believe from 7,000 to 8,000 cubic feet only per ton, was at that time obtained from the coal carbonised, whereas now it is between 9,000 and 10,000 cubic feet, which makes a very great difference, and in addition they have as far as possible eliminated the leaks from the pipes.

6145. If the corporation had become the owners of the gas works at the time that they wished it, could they have gone to Parliament, and asked Parliament to allow them to raise the price to those with whom they had contracted, on the ground that they would be brought to bankruptcy;

Mr. *Norwood*, LL.D.

3d June 1876.

Mr. Norwood, LL.D.

30 June 1876.

Sir *Arthur Guinness*—continued.

bankruptcy; would they not have been told that they should raise the rates to meet that loss?—No; the corporation would have been in a better position than the gas company, for this reason: Mr. Cotton, who is now the secretary of the Alliance Gas Company, was at that time the gas inspector of the corporation, and he had made a contract for the supply of coal at an extremely favourable rate, contingent upon the corporation obtaining the sanction of Parliament to take over the gas undertaking; so favourable was it that it would have put the corporation in a much better position even than the gas company was under his management. I know it was his opinion that no such result as you anticipate would have arisen. I suppose that the corporation would have obtained from Parliament equal justice as the gas company did.

6146. When does the present contract expire?—I think it expires in this year.

6147. What do the corporation intend to do about the renewal or alteration of that contract?—They have received a tender from the gas company to supply the gas at 4 *s.* 3 *d.* per 1,000 feet.

Mr. *Collins.*

6148. What standard would that be?—I think that is 16-candle gas.

Sir *Arthur Guinness.*

6149. Are you sure it is 4 *s.* 3 *d.*?—I think it is 4 *s.* 3 *d.* I did not see the tender myself; I am not a member of No. 1 committee, and any information which I have been able to give you with regard to the transactions of 1872, 1873, and 1874, is from my knowledge of the application to Parliament for the Bills.

6150. Was the Waterworks Act in existence before the Pembroke Township Act was passed?—1861 was the date of the first Waterworks Act; my impression is that it was.

6151. Did the corporation, when the Pembroke Township Act was being passed, protect their rights of supplying the district with water under their Vartry Act, under which they had rights of supplying the township?—I scarcely understand the scope of your question. The Pembroke Local Act was the 26th and 27th of the Queen, c. 72, and the Dublin Waterworks Act was passed in 1861.

6152. You do not know whether the corporation used due diligence in maintaining and protecting their rights of supplying that district with water, which they had under the Waterworks Act?—I think that they did the best that they could, considering that they were opposed in the way that I have mentioned and as has been described by Mr. Stokes in his evidence.

6153. But you are of opinion that the townships should pay equally with the city for water, and for the maintenance of roads and bridges, are you not?—I think that the townships pay too low for water, and I should be very glad to see them pay much higher. I think they ought to do so, for they have no responsibility; and I think, for the reasons I have stated, that there being, as was expressed when the Metropolitan Board of Works Act was passed, a "common interest" amongst all the constituents and boards throughout the districts, they ought to have one general board of management.

6154. Do you consider that the bargains made with the townships were bad, so far as the city interests were concerned?—I think they were not so favourable as we might have got if we had not so skillful and vigorous opponents as Mr. Stokes. If he had not interfered Sir John Gray told me that they would have got 6 *d.* per 1,000 gallons from the townships. In the Act of 1874, the Provisional Order and the complementary Act, which was passed in the same year, we are entitled to charge 6 *d.* to extra municipal districts taking a supply of water.

6155. Mr. Stokes did not interfere, so far as Kingstown and Blackrock were concerned, did he?—No, he did not; but the supply to Pembroke, in a great measure, affected the market and arrangements made subsequently.

Mr. *Gibson.*

6156. You stated to the honourable Member for Youghal that the quorum of the corporation cannot be altered, and that it was fixed by a bye-law?—Yes; perhaps it is in the statute; I am not quite sure about that.

6157. I will draw your attention to the 92nd section of the statute, which states that the whole number of persons present at a meeting should not be less than one-third of the number of the whole council or board?—Yes, that is so.

6158. So that being in the Act of Parliament, it cannot be remedied without an Act?—That is so.

6159. Are you aware that that is fixed by the 92nd Section of the 3rd & 4th Victoria, c. 108?—Yes.

6160. The quorum of committees is regulated, I believe, by the 14th Section of the Dublin Improvement Act, 1849, which states that: "No business shall be transacted at any meeting of the committee, unless the quorum of members, if any, fixed by the council, and if no quorum be fixed, three members be present?—That is so.

6161. I believe that the corporation have never fixed any other number, and that the statutable number of 3 is what still obtains?—Yes, that is so.

6162. Then all your statements which you have made with reference to the proceedings upon changing bye-laws referred to bye-laws made under the Act of 1849?—Quite so.

6163. Are you of opinion, from the machinery that is pointed out for changing those bye-laws that are contained in that Act of 1849, it would be desirable to simplify the proceedings, and make the changing and adoption of bye-laws a little simpler?—I think so.

6164. You stated also, did you not, that the auditor had surcharged very few items of account?—Comparatively few.

6165. Is it not a fact consistent with that that several of the items brought before him may have been told to stand over?—Yes.

6166. Is it not a fact that a large number of accounts that have not been able to pass the auditor, although he has not surcharged them, remain as standing over accounts?—I am unaware of that if it be so, but I do not think it is so; I think he closes his account by his report each year; in some cases his decisions upon items disallowed were reversed upon appeal, either to the Local Government Board, or to the Courts.

6167. You stated also that you thought that many citizens disliked being on the burgess roll on account of the obligations it would entail of attending juries. Are you in favour of having a system in Dublin similar to the Central Criminal

Mr. Norwood, LL.D.

30 June 1876.

Mr. *Gibson*—continued.

Court system of London?—Yes, quite so; there is a single venue for the City of London and the county of Middlesex, and parts of Surrey and Kent, for all trials at the Central Criminal Court; and in Dublin, if that were so, it would save the summoning a great many juries, and would remove one cause why gentlemen do not wish to go upon the burgess roll for the city of Dublin.

Sir *Arthur Guinness.*

6168. Are you aware that the citizens have for many years expressed, at public meetings and in other ways, their wish that the corporation should apply for a Royal Commission with reference to the main drainage scheme?—Yes, certainly; I myself moved for a Royal Commission upon two occasions, and carried it in the town council; and we applied to Mr. Chichester Fortescue. In the first place we applied to my Lord Mayo, afterwards Governor General of India; and Lord Mayo said that in his opinion the corporation had obtained the advice of Mr., afterwards Sir Joseph, Bazalgette upon the subject of the main drainage of the district, and "that they had obtained the opinion of the highest authority in Europe upon that matter," and that if the Government were to issue a Royal Commission very probably they would issue it to that gentleman. Subsequently they applied, I think it was to the present Lord Carlingford (then Mr. Chichester Fortescue), and he expressed his willingness at an interview with the corporation to appoint a Royal Commission, but that the corporation should pay the costs of it. The expenses of the Vartry Commission were 1,950 *l.*; and the corporation did not see their way to spending 1,000 *l.* or 2,000 *l.* on that Commission; they thought they ought to have got the Commission free of cost. The other day a Committee of the whole House again recommended that a Commission should be granted by Her Majesty's Government to inquire into the whole thing and get us out of a dead lock. But they still ask that the executive should consider the propriety of granting that Commission, free of cost, to the citizens, and I hope they will do so.

6169. On that subject they decided, did they not, to do one day what they undid subsequently?—No. As I tell you, upon two occasions they passed resolutions of the council asking for a Commission during the time of the secretariat of Lord Mayo, and also during that of Mr. Chichester Fortescue.

6170. And they subsequently declined to accept a Commission?—They declined to accept a Commission upon the terms offered. At present, I believe, they are very willing to accept a Commission, but they do not see where the money is to come from to pay for it. I suggested that, as there was a main drainage rate, it might be considered to be a fair application of the money lying on deposit receipt now, but that we should get the sanction of the Legislature to expend the money in that way.

6171. Until they make up their minds upon that subject, matters remain as they are?—They have made up their minds unanimously, in a Committee of the whole House, to recommend the council to ask for a Royal Commission; and if Her Majesty's Government grant a Royal Commission, I trust it will be upon easy terms to the corporation, and that it may sit during the present summer, because unless something of that sort is done, it is almost hopeless to entertain any expectation of purifying the Liffey.

Sir *Arthur Guinness*—continued.

6172. Do you know when this application is to be made?—It has been on the paper for two or three weeks, and I suppose will be before the council on the first Monday in July.

Mr. *Collins.*

6173. You said, I think, that the first point of importance which would be necessary to carry out the improvements which you suggest would be a re-valuation?—I said that, as the basis of a sound constituency, I thought that a re-valuation was most desirable.

6174. That was the first point of importance to which you would direct the attention of the Committee?—Quite so, because I begin at the beginning, and as the franchise is based upon valuation, of course the valuation should be as perfect as possible, in order to produce a sound constituency.

6175. You said, did you not, that the chief difficulty respecting this re-valuation is that it would be unpopular lest it should have the effect of raising the general taxation?—Yes, for Imperial purposes, the income tax, and so on; and it also would have the effect of raising the taxation upon the citizens in cases where a maximum tax is imposed, because I need not tell you that all taxing bodies generally reach the maximum prescribed by Act of Parliament.

6176. Nevertheless, this re-valuation would have the effect of remedying the present inequalities which exist respecting the valuations generally?—Yes, it would have the effect of redressing the inequalities.

6177. You think that this re-valuation ought to extend to the surrounding townships, and that they ought to be embraced within it?—Yes, certainly.

6178. I believe that there exists no power at present to compel a re-valuation?—There is power under an Act of Parliament, the 15th & 16th Vict. c. 63, enabling the grand jury of a county, or county of a town, or county of a city, to apply to the Lord Lieutenant for what is called a primary valuation at the end of 14 years, and there is very considerable doubt as to whether the corporation of Dublin, under the Dublin Improvement Act, 1849, are the grand jury contemplated by the Act of the 15th & 16th Vict. c. 63.

6179. However, that power is inoperative, or rather it has never been acted upon?—It never has been acted upon.

6180. Can you make any suggestion with regard to a compulsory re-valuation?—I understand that Her Majesty's Government have in contemplation a General Valuation Act for Ireland, and if so, I suppose that that Act would provide for the valuation of the city of Dublin, as well as for the rest of Ireland.

6181. Might Dublin be brought under the operation of the general Act?—Certainly.

6182. It would not require a special Act for its special circumstances?—Certainly not; Parliament is omnipotent.

6183. Such valuation, I presume, ought to be periodical?—That was contemplated by the Act of the 15 & 16 Vict. c. 63, which prescribed periods of 14 years as being the proper time for what is called a general primary valuation. In the meantime, in the interval, of course, as buildings are

Mr. Norwood, LL.D.

30 June 1876.

Mr. *Collins*—continued.

are erected and buildings are improved, there is a gradual process of valuation going on; but unless the buildings be altered, the Commissioners of Valuation do not think themselves entitled to re-value or revise.

6184. Taking into consideration the circumstances of Dublin, do you think that an interval of 14 years would be a proper interval, or such an one as you would recommend?—I have never considered that point. I suppose it was very well considered when that Act was framed. The last primary valuation, as I have already stated, was in 1850, and there ought to have been a revision since. I think the time has come for a proper re-valuation.

6185. Respecting the franchise, is the present occupiers' qualification, that is of 4 *l.* rating, a satisfactory qualification in your estimation?—I would have much preferred that the original qualification as prescribed by 3 & 4 Vict. c. 108 (and which is that for all other municipal towns, except Dublin), should have been preserved; I think so far as I can express an opinion, and which is a very humble one, it is not a desirable thing that Dublin should be made an exception to the general municipalities throughout the country; as concerns qualification, I know that in Belfast the qualification under the 3 & 4 Vict. c. 108, produces an admirable constituency who return a town council second to none in the kingdom for efficiency and respectability; I think that if that result be produced by the Act of 3 & 4 Vict. c. 108, in a great town like Belfast, it might very well produce the same results in Dublin, with the improvements that I have suggested, namely, that owners should be empowered to vote, and the other improvements which I have indicated in the course of my examination.

6186. I think you suggested that the three years' occupancy was a counterpoise to this 4 *l.* rating qualification?—Yes, it was considered advisable, as I am informed, at that time; I did not take very much interest in the matter at that time.

6187. Would you recommend the abandonment of that three years' qualification, or its reduction to any extent?—If the parties in Dublin who were engaged in the passage of that Act, and the arrangements under it obtained the sanction of the Legislature after good consideration to that counterpoise, I think it ought to be preserved; I take it that there were good reasons for it, and I see no reason to disturb it, because I think it is important that you should guard against the nomadic population, and that a man who is not there more than seven or eight months is not so desirable a person as one who is longer.

6188. Do not you think that the effect of this three years' occupancy is that a great many persons who might well exercise the franchise are disqualified?—Unquestionably it reduces the number that otherwise could be and would be placed upon the burgess roll.

6189. Supposing that you altered this three years' qualification by reducing it, say to two years, and increased the valuation, how would that be likely to affect the municipal constituency in Dublin?—I think you would have a better constituency; it would be more numerous, and I use the word "better," in the sense of being of a more representative character.

6190. With regard to the qualification of owners of property, I think you say that you would give the same qualification to owners of property as exists at present under the Poor Law Act?—Yes; I think that the Poor Law Act works very well, and that all interests are fairly represented.

Mr. *Collins*—continued.

6191. Do you think that the same qualification would work equally well in municipal matters?—I see no reason to doubt it. I think the boards of guardians, those with whom I am acquainted, very fairly represent the interest of all parties connected with property as contributors to the rates.

6192. When you said that you would give the owners of property the same qualification, what did you mean by that?—The qualification of owners of property under the Poor Law is unlimited; I mean to say, upwards.

6193. You would not limit the qualification of owners of property in any way?—No.

6194. The simple fact of their being owners of property ought to entitle them to a vote?—Certainly.

6195. Respecting this franchise, the Committee has had many suggestions, some recommending the cumulative principle, others fancy franchises, and your recommendation is that of plurality?—Yes; I think that it is always well, as far as possible, to follow the lines laid down already, and the simpler you have matters connected with the franchise the better, and the fewer the changes consistent with a proper regard to reform the better.

6196. Do not you believe that the cumulative principle would have the effect of enabling the minority to be represented better than the plurality system?—Of course it would; and the opinion of several members of the corporation is in favour of the cumulative principle; but my own opinion is that it would be preferable to adopt the Poor Law system of plurality.

6197. You lean towards that opinion yourself?—Yes, quite so.

6198. With respect to residential requirements, you would extend the limit to beyond seven miles from Dublin, would you not?—Certainly; because of course the business and the social arrangements of the present day are far different from those of the period when the 3rd & 4th Vict. c. 108 was passed.

6199. Would you limit the distance at all in the case of Dublin?—My own opinion is that I would not limit the distance.

6200. You would not limit it in the case of Dublin, or in the case of any other towns?—I would rather not; but if the Legislature should determine upon a limit, I should say that 20 miles in Dublin and 20 miles in Belfast (and I speak of those towns because I know them best) would be a proper limit; seven miles is far too narrow a limit.

6201. But you would not restrict that limitation to Dublin and Belfast; do not you think that it would be likely to apply equally well to other towns in Ireland?—I dare say it would, but I do not speak from personal knowledge with regard to other towns, as I do from personal knowledge with regard to Dublin and Belfast.

6202. Taking into consideration the fact that the towns in Ireland generally speaking have a mixed population, partly urban and partly rural, would that influence your judgment in giving an opinion as to the extension of the distance

Mr. *Collins*—continued.

distance for a qualification?—I see no reason at the present day, considering the facilities for locomotion, and considering that all the great towns have railways radiating from them, why there should be a residential limit at all as there was in the olden times; and then my answer on that matter would apply, I have no doubt, equally well to Cork or Limerick, or Waterford or Londonderry, as it does to Belfast or Dublin.

6203. With regard to rating, you have given it as your opinion that it would facilitate matters very much if the principle of union rating were adopted instead of electoral division rating?—I spoke of that matter as concerns an injustice under which the city of Dublin suffers in consequence of its peculiar relations to the townships surrounding it; and I think that in those cases the union rating would be much fairer for the Dublin ratepayers, and not unfair to the township ratepayers, so far as the poor law taxes were concerned.

6204. Were there not considerable surcharges on the South Dublin Union recently?—There were. Since I have come to London I have seen the report of the public auditor upon that matter, in which surcharges of a considerable amount have been made upon some of the officials connected with the South Dublin Union.

6205. And were there scandals alleged respecting the fever sheds in the case of the South Dublin Union?—I do not know whether the term "scandal" could be exactly applied to it. There was a case in which some dealings in the purchase of fever sheds formed a subject of animadversion both at the Poor Law Board and in the public journals.

6206. No animadversion of that description was made to apply to the corporation in their dealings with such matters, under the public health arrangements?—No, certainly not. But you must not take me generally as stating that no animadversions were ever made upon the corporation, because that would not be the fact, because in many cases groundlessly, animadversions are made upon the corporation, upon their mode of transacting business and upon many of their actions.

6207. You state that in the case of the corporation, you do not believe that those animadversions are justified?—I do not.

6208. In the case of the South Dublin Union, have you formed an opinion as to whether those are justified?—I do not think they are justified, applied to the general body of the guardians of the South Union. The animadversions applied to the conduct of two or three of the board of guardians in the Union; but so far as the general body of the board of guardians were concerned, I do not think that they were obnoxious to the charges which were contained in those animadversions.

6209. You have had considerable experience, have you not, of the meetings of the guardians in the South Dublin Union?—Yes; I was for many years elected guardian of the South Dublin Union, and I am now an *ex officio* guardian of the North Dublin Union.

6210. Do they ever indulge in political discussions there?—There have been political discussions there, and I have also heard them sometimes at the North Dublin Union, but the majority of the guardians, I think, rather set themselves against such discussions.

Mr. *Collins*—continued.

Mr. *Norwood*, LL.D.

30 June 1876.

6211. Have you heard such political discussions at the meetings of the committees of the corporation?—No, none; they attend to their business in the committees.

6212. Then it is not fair or right to impute to them they do have those discussions?—It is not, and it is not right to say, as I see in one of the answers made by a gentleman before this Committee, that the corporation thought of nothing but politics at their committee meetings; they do not discuss politics at their committee meetings, for there is too much to be done; their work is extremely heavy, and requires all the attention that gentlemen can give to it for two or three hours in the day.

6213. Are there any of the members of the council of the corporation members also of the boards of the two unions?—I think there are some 20 or 30 members of council either *ex officio* or elected members of the boards of guardians of the North and South Dublin Unions; for instance, I am myself.

6214. Do they never carry their practice of political discussions at the boards of guardians into their meetings of the corporation?—Pardon me; I did not say that they have a practice of political discussions at the boards of guardians. I said that sometimes politics had been discussed at the boards of guardians, but not frequently, and that certainly members of the boards of guardians who are members of the corporation, do not discuss in their meetings of the corporation committees political affairs, or other affairs, except the business of each committee.

6215. In your judgment, you consider that they discharge their duties in both capacities well and effectively?—That is my experience.

6216. And that, in fact, there is no difference or change in the *personnel*, so far as their relations with the unions and with the meetings of the corporations are concerned, inasmuch as they are the same individuals, and any imputations that would apply in the one case, with regard to deficiencies of intelligence or inability, ought to apply in the other; you have not remarked any difference in that respect?—I do not see any difference in the mode of transacting their business by their going from the board of guardians to the City Hall, *cœlum non animum mutant qui trans mare currunt*. When they cross the river they do not change their disposition.

6217. I was greatly struck with a statement of one of the witnesses respecting the cabs for the removal of patients to the hospital; you state very distinctly that, as far as you know, there is an abundance of cabs for the removal of patients?—I think so, for all emergencies. I remember myself there was a member of my household attacked with small-pox, and I sent to the union for a cab, and it was at once furnished.

6218. After your attention has been directed to the subject from the evidence of witnesses here, do you think it would be necessary in any way, or desirable, to increase the existing number of cabs?—I think that in the event of any epidemic arising, the number of cabs would be increased to meet the emergency by the public health committee.

6219. Have you any idea what the present number is which is owned by the corporation?—There are two belonging to the corporation, and there are two, I think, at the North Dublin Union; there is one or two at the South Dublin Union,

Mr. Norwood, LL.D.

30 June 1876.

Mr. *Collins*—continued.

Union, and there is one at Cork-street for the peculiar service of that hospital.

6220. Those are ample, you think, for all emergencies at present?—Yes, at least for the present, and if happily we are spared from any epidemic, there will be no occasion to increase them for some time.

Mr. *Corry*.

6221. You have given the Committee very full information with reference to the Corporation of Dublin, and from your acquaintance with Belfast I would like to ask you one or two questions with reference to that borough. You stated that you were borough assessor there for a number of years?—Yes.

6222. Can you inform the Committee whether proper facilities are given for the burgesses to get upon the roll in Belfast?—During the time that I was borough assessor both the parties were extremely active (when I say parties I mean political parties) in serving notices of claims for putting burgesses on the roll, and they attended with great assiduity to the revision; and I think that the roll very fairly represents the ratepayers of that town. There are some 5,600 burgesses on an average on that roll.

6223. You are aware of the very rapid growth of the population of Belfast within the last 15 or 20 years?—Yes.

6224. And that a very large proportion of that population consists of the artisan and working classes?—Yes.

6225. And consequently that the house property which has been built in Belfast is very much for their accommodation?—Certainly; I have seen a Return which shows that during several years past from 1,200 to 1,500 houses have been erected annually within the borough of Belfast, and the majority of them are for the artisan class.

6226. I think you stated in answer to the honourable Member who has just been examining you, that you considered the present qualification in Belfast a very good one?—Yes, if I may judge of the result I think that the corporation of Belfast is as admirable a one as there is in the three kingdoms. I think that the gentlemen composing the town council of Belfast are not only energetic business men, but their social position is highly respectable.

6227. And in view of that case, looking to the probability of the deduction of the franchise, and the lowering of the class of property which has been erecting in Belfast for some time, what would you recommend as a counterpoise, so as to preserve the corporation in its present efficient state?—In Belfast where we have the experience of the qualification working well, I would leave it alone; *quieta non movere* is a very good motto; but I would give the owners of property in Belfast a control which they have not at present, as I have said on the poor law principle.

6228. But looking to the attempts that have been made, and will be made, towards a reduction of the franchise, not only as we may expect the present Parliamentary franchise, but, even going to the household franchise, do you think that any safeguards should be introduced to prevent the corporation getting into the hands of the owners of small house property?—With regard to the franchise in Belfast, which is practically an 8 *l.* one, although it is 10 *l.* in the Act of Parliament, still there being 2 *l.* allowed for landlords' repairs and insurance, I think 8 *l.* is quite low enough for a town like Belfast, and I would not wish to see the franchise reduced below that; I would rather make the general franchise throughout the whole country the same as it is under the 3 & 4 Vict. c. 108, and although I am very often in Belfast I have never heard any complaints about the franchise being objectionable.

Mr. *Corry*—continued.

6229. In the case of a reduction of the franchise, would you consider that an efficient way of meeting it would be by giving the plural vote?—Giving the plural vote, and giving the counterpoise which was given in Dublin when the franchise was reduced, that is to say, a longer residential occupation.

6230. From your experience of the Dublin Corporation and also of that of Belfast, would you be afraid that if the qualification of the franchise was reduced we might get into the same difficulty in Belfast as the Dublin Corporation has got into?—I think where experience has shown that the present qualification in Belfast produces such good results, it would be an experiment that I should not like to see tried to reduce the franchise there.

Mr. *Murphy*.

6231. In the course of your examination on the last day, you mentioned something about contrasting the sittings of the Recorder of Dublin with those of the Recorder of Belfast; what was it that you meant to convey by that?—The Recorder of Belfast sits, I think, eight times in the year, and he also sits at quarter sessions for the county four times, and the commercial men of Belfast have been greatly advantaged by the frequent sittings of that court. The Recorder in Dublin hitherto has only sat four times in the year, and the merchants and traders of Dublin are very anxious that arrangements should be made for the more frequent sittings of that court.

6232. What you mean by sittings of the Recorder four times a year in Dublin, and eight times a year in Belfast, is for civil business, is it not?—Yes, for civil business; I did not at all allude to criminal business. The corporation of course, in interfering in that matter, were merely concerned with the mercantile and trading interests of the borough.

6233. Is there any peculiar jurisdiction attached to the Court of Record in Dublin as arising out of ancient charters or otherwise?—The Recorder has criminal jurisdiction.

6234. I mean as to civil jurisdiction?—No; he is under the general law of the country regulating the chairmen of counties and assistant barristers. He is appointed Recorder under an ancient charter beyond all question.

6235. I want to know whether his jurisdiction under that ancient charter is that of a court of record?—It is a court of record.

6236. Can he try suits to any amount, or is he limited at all?—I think he is limited by the General Civil Bill Acts.

6237. I mean by the original charter?—I do not think he has unlimited jurisdiction.

6238. Are there any peculiar pleadings in the Court of Record of Dublin, or are they analogous to those in the superior courts?—No. The pleadings are all under the General Civil Bill Acts.

6239. Then

Mr. Norwood, LL.D.

30 June 1876.

Mr. *Murphy*—continued.

6239. Then I understand from you that the Recorder's Court in Dublin, so far as civil business is concerned, is analogous to the Civil Bill Courts?—Yes, quite so.

6240. Do you know whether there was any ancient jurisdiction in the Recorder's Court in Dublin to try records and to try suits between subject and subject?—None that I know of.

Mr. *Gibson*.

6241. You would not say that the old system might not be used, but that it has only fallen into disuetude?—That may be so, but I have never known any pleadings of any kind other than those in Civil Bill Courts.

6242. In many places, in Galway, and elsewhere, it has fallen into disuetude?—Yes, it may be. The honourable Member for Cork will not understand me as saying that it may not be so; but that the pleadings employed at the present day for the recovery of debts and other civil contracts in the Recorder's Court follow the precedents of those of the Civil Bill Courts throughout the country.

Mr. *Murphy*.

6243. The reason of my asking the question is this: in the Recorder's Court, under charter, the Recorder has power to try actions to any amount; the pleadings always have been similar to those of the superior courts of common law in this country; the old declaration, and plea, and rejoinder, and rebutter, and sur-rebutter, and those things were always practised in the Court of the Recorder in Cork; by the Common Law Procedure Act of England, all the pleadings in the Recorders' Courts in England were simplified, and made the same as the pleadings in the superior courts at common law in England; if such a court as that existed in Dublin with the Recorder presiding over it, do you or do you not consider that there would be any advantage?—I think that the present Recorder's Court is an admirable one; and all that the corporation want, and all that the interests of the mercantile community require in Dublin, is more frequent sittings.

6244. Then if the Recorder has not the power to try suits to any amount, if he is limited to the practice of civil bill proceedings, what use would that be?—The extent to which he can try cases at present, is quite sufficient for all the purposes of the trading community there.

6245. You are aware of course of the proposal which has been made to the Civil Bill Courts Amendment Bill which is going through the House, for the amalgamation of the chairmanship of the county of Dublin with the recordership of the city of Dublin?—Yes.

6246. Do you consider that an advantageous proposition?—I would rather have them distinct, for I am certain that if the sittings of the Recorder's Court in Dublin were more frequent, there would be a very large increase in the business of the court.

6247. Do you, at the same time, see any objection to the amalgamation of the chairmanship of the county of Dublin with the recordership of the city of Dublin, with a permanent judge to try all causes arising out of that amalgamated jurisdiction, and with more frequent sittings?—I think that a judge with that united jurisdiction would have a very serious amount of duty to discharge; and I think that it would be much better discharged as it is at present. I know that the feeling of the Bar would be against the amalgamation of those two jurisdictions.

6248. Why?—There are reasons peculiar to the Bar which I need not advert to more particularly, but they think that the system works very well at present; and I think that if the Recorder of Dublin sat as often as the Recorder of Belfast, the business would increase, and there would also be enough for one man to do; and there would also be enough for one man to do for the county, because in the county there ought also to be granted sittings in different parts of it. Many persons complain of having to come to Kilmainham from a great distance at the northern end of the county, whereas they think that more numerous districts should be assigned for the sittings of the court.

6249. Do not you think that all that could be remedied by the county and the city of Dublin being amalgamated if the recorder or the judge held more frequent sittings in the city, and went to the various quarter sessions or portions of the county of Dublin as well?—It is quite feasible, but I think it is more desirable to have a distinct judge for each jurisdiction.

6250. Are you not aware that in the city of Cork the recorder sits as a regular court of record, which is a court from week to week, in which the pleadings are just the same as are instituted in the superior courts, and that he sits once a month for criminal business regularly, so that the court goes on the entire year?—I have no doubt that the mercantile community in Cork feel the advantage of that, and in Dublin they would be very desirous of having as frequent sittings there; it has been a great advantage to Belfast, I know.

6251. The honourable and learned Member for the University spoke about the proceedings in the Recorder's Court falling into disuetude: that has occurred in Cork to a certain extent; for this reason, that whereas by the English Common Law Procedure Act provision was made for simplifying the pleadings in the Recorder's Courts in England, and that although in the Irish Common Law Procedure Act clauses were introduced analogous to those in the English Act, yet by some machinery or other, which I do not understand, those clauses were expressly struck out, and there is no power whatever of changing the old pleadings in the Recorder's Court in Cork, where they still remain in the old and cumbrous fashion in which they used to be formerly; I presume that I am not wrong in asking you the question as a lawyer, do you or do you not think that it would tend to the better administration of justice if the present simple pleadings were instituted in Cork instead of the old cumbrous ones?—I have not the smallest doubt upon the matter.

6252. You think that that is a subject well worthy the attention of the Legislature in any Irish Bill that is about to be passed, and that it would be a very happy result if it could be thus effected?—Certainly.

Mr. *Gibson*.

6253. I believe that the jurisdiction to which the honourable Member for Cork referred about the recorder

Mr. Norwood, LL.D.

30 June 1876.

Mr. *Gibson*—continued.

recorder is contained in the 168th Section of the 3 & 4 Vict. c. 108, and is as follows: "That the recorder of every borough continued or appointed under this Act shall hold once in every quarter of a year, or by adjournment, or otherwise, at such other and more frequent times as the said recorder, in his discretion, may think fit, or as the Lord Lieutenant shall, from time to time, think fit to direct, a Court of Quarter Sessions of the Peace, in and for such borough, of which Court the recorder of such borough shall sit as the sole judge;" that is the section with regard to cities or boroughs; and under the 181st Section, in the same Act of 1840, it saves the proceedings by attachment in the borough Courts of Record; are you aware, as a matter of fact, whether those proceedings by attachment do not at present exist in the Recorder's Court at Dublin; do you know whether that jurisdiction has been exercised by the recorder?—I am not aware.

6254. Further on it states: "Provided always, that in any borough in which by usage or charter the goods, monies, or credits of the defendant, may by process of foreign attachment be attached in the hands of a third person, such process by foreign attachment may, until Parliament shall otherwise provide, be proceeded upon in the Court of Record of such borough under this Act, with such rules of practice, and with the same powers and jurisdictions as belonged to the said court at the time of the passing of this Act," are you aware whether in Dublin this process by foreign attachment is exercised?—I believe not.

6255. You do not whether there is any special pleading on the subject?—I have never seen any other form of pleading in the Recorder's Court than the ones I have mentioned, namely, those in ordinary use in the Civil Bill Courts.

Mr. *Brooks*.

6256. You gave some evidence about the gas question, and you said, I think, that the corporation consented to an increase in the contract price?—A reduction in the illuminating power is virtually an increase in the price of gas.

6257. Was that done with the sanction of Parliament?—It was done with the sanction of Parliament.

6258. And it was the Act of Parliament, and not the act of the corporation?—It was the Act of the Legislature, of course.

6259. May I ask what you meant when you referred to the solvent condition of the gas company?—Perhaps it was an unfelicitous phrase; I meant that they were enabled to give dividends which they were not in previous years able to give, in consequence of the high price of coals, and other reasons, which have been remedied under the new management.

6260. You did not mean that the Committee should infer that the gas company were at any time in an insolvent condition?—No, not at all.

6261. With regard to the present carbonising powers of the gas company, do you know of your own knowledge that the effects are better now than they were then, or do you know it from having heard it?—I have heard it from what I conceive to be the best authority, that the improvements in their appliances, and in their arrangements for carbonising, are such that they

Mr. *Brooks*—continued.

are enabled to extract between 9,000 and 10,000 cubic feet of gas per ton from the coals, where formerly, under the less perfect arrangements, they were only able to extract between 7,000 and 8,000.

6262. Is your information derived from an official or authoritative source, or is it merely from general report?—I think I have read it in some of the reports of the gas company, but I have heard it also from some of the officials.

6263. With regard to the illuminating power, do you know what it is at the present time?—Sixteen-candle gas, I believe.

6264. Do you know, as a matter of fact, as one that is reported officially weekly, or periodically, that the gas obtained by the corporation is certified by the Local Government officer to be 17-candle gas, whereas the contract is for 16?—I believe the gas company, since the passing of that Act of Parliament, have maintained the illuminating power of the gas always a fraction above the statutable quality.

6265. Passing from the gas to the Royal Commission, what was the object of the Royal Commission; was it the recommendation of the citizen's committee that a Royal Commission should be appointed, in order to have some other scheme than that which had been approved of by Sir Joseph Bazalgette?—As I understand it, the citizen's committee were anxious to have a cheaper scheme, and one that they thought better for the purpose designed, namely, the purification of the River Liffey; I do not know which scheme they intended, but, certainly, if my opinion as to the scope of the Royal Commission were to have any weight, I should say that the Commissioners should be left perfectly unfettered to consider every scheme submitted to them, including Sir Joseph Bazalgette's.

6266. Was not the main drainage scheme the work of several years, and obtained at the expense of nearly 20,000 *l.*; and was it not approved of by the very highest authorities that were obtainable in the United Kingdom?—By the very highest authorities. The main drainage scheme formed the subject of consideration for many years of Mr. Neville; he elaborated it as far as he could, and then the corporation obtained the opinion of Sir Joseph Bazalgette, whom my Lord Mayo stated to be the highest authority on that branch of engineering in Europe. It was then submitted to Committees of the Houses of Lords and Commons, and before them were examined Mr. Bateman, Mr. Hemans, Sir Joseph Bazalgette, and two or three other engineers of the very highest eminence, all of whom stated that Sir Joseph Bazalgette's scheme was the very best calculated to serve the objects intended, namely, the purification of the Liffey, and the drainage of the whole district. I am aware that a great many persons think that it could be done in a much simpler fashion, but they are not aware of the difficulties attendant upon the drainage of a large area like that around the City of Dublin. A great portion of the city lies below high-water mark, and many of the schemes which are pronounced to be cheaper and more efficient do not provide for those low-lying districts, the ratepayers of which are entitled to have the sewage withdrawn from their basement stories, and to have the benefit of a general system of drainage. You cannot drain the City of Dublin without

providing

Mr. *Norwood*, LL.D.

30 June 1876.

Mr. *Brooks*—continued.

providing for a drainage area which comprehends within it the several townships.

Sir *Arthur Guinness*.

6267. You have not in any way asserted that the citizens' committee had any favourite scheme, or put forward any favourite scheme, to supersede that?—I never understood that they did; but they were of opinion that a cheaper scheme, and one as efficient, might be devised.

6268. Owing to the very much greater cost at which it appeared that this scheme could be carried out than was originally supposed?—But with regard to the cost of the main drainage scheme, permit me to observe that although the tenders were obtained for a very large amount, still, in consequence of the labour market and the cost of materials having receded to their normal condition, it is the opinion of Sir Joseph Bazalgette, and of Mr. Neville, that the scheme which they have prepared could, with certain modifications in the materials, be carried out for very much less than the lowest of the tenders which were sent in, and which the corporation declined to accept.

Mr. *Brooks*.

6269. If the request of the citizens' committee for a Royal Commission had been acceded to, would it not in point of fact have been, adopting the language of the honourable Member, to have undone in a day that which had been the work of many years, at a cost of several thousands of pounds, and undoing to-day what had been done yesterday?—It would have been returning to the starting point from which Sir Joseph Bazalgette started many years ago; Sir Joseph Bazalgette went over the whole district, and spent many many days considering the whole matter, and a Royal Commission could do nothing else.

Sir *Arthur Guinness*.

6270. Were you not practically brought to a stop in consequence of the immense increase upon the estimates?—Quite so; and the corporation would not be justified in carrying out a scheme which so far exceeds the statutable sum which they were enabled to borrow at that moment, namely, 350,000 *l.* But they now would be able to carry it out for a sum not very much in excess of that, at least, so I am informed. Of course I am merely relying upon the evidence of Sir Joseph Bazalgette, and other gentlemen.

Mr. *Brooks*.

6271. Do you continue to be of opinion that that is the very best scheme that can be adopted?—It is a subject which I have paid the closest attention to for upwards of 10 years. I have visited myself every city in Great Britain where main drainage was carried out some few years ago, and I do not believe that you can carry out the drainage of the city and the purification of the Liffey by any other means than that.

6272. Was there, on the part of the corporation, a most anxious desire to defer to and to carry out the wishes of the citizens?—Certainly.

6273. The honourable Member for Kinsale asked you some questions on the subject of re-valuation; may I ask you to carry your mind back to the condition of the corporation in 1849; can you say that the corporation was then at a very low ebb?—I can only speak by tradition, because I was not engaged in corporate affairs at that time, but I always understood so, and that a reformation became absolutely necessary.

6274. Will you inform the Committee how that was effected?—There was a general consent of all parties that a united effort should be made to return men of position to the corporation, and they sank party feelings, and united in returning to the corporation the best men, independent of party or politics.

6275. At that time do you think that we had a corporation composed of the first mercantile men, and of some of the most eminent of our citizens?—Sir Arthur Guinness's father was one of the leading members of it, and was the first Lord Mayor under the new system. Mr. George Roe, Mr. George Woods Mansell, Mr. Jameson, Alderman Campbell, Alderman Farrell, and gentlemen of position in commercial circles in Dublin were members of that corporation.

6276. I will ask you if the same means are not available to-day to the citizens of Dublin, to return to the corporation representatives of the same character, reputation, and intelligence?—The same means could be applied to-day, I have no doubt, if all parties united in a strenuous effort, as they did then, to restore the *personnel* of the corporation.

6277. Your evidence is, that the corporation does its business well, in the face of great difficulties?—Yes.

6278. And yet you advocate a change in the valuation?—I do.

6279. Would it not be better that the citizens who complain should sink their differences and unite for the common good, rather than obstruct the corporation who now devote so much time and labour to their corporate duties?—It would be a great deal better, but at the same time you must consider this, that where new owners are directly, and largely indirectly, taxed for city purposes, and practically have no control over the raising or the disbursement of those taxes, it is but their constitutional right that they should have that control, and you cannot give them that control without a change in the law.

6280. Do not you say that the same means exist to-day that existed in 1849, when we had a coalition of all parties, classes, and grades?—So far as those means are concerned they exist now as they existed then, but there are other matters now which require to be done which were not done then.

6281. Will you inform the Committee what are the changes which you would recommend?—I recommend a more equitable adjustment of the valuation. There are inequalities in the valuation existing at present which ought to be removed by a more equitable and even valuation.

6282. Would that be applicable to all the United Kingdom or only to the municipality of Dublin?—I confine my answer to the municipality of Dublin, because I am being questioned at the moment with regard to it; but I also take care to add that the valuation should include the townships and the neighbourhood.

6283. Why apply an exceptional mode of valuation to Dublin, and not to other towns in the kingdom?—I do not say that I would not apply it to other towns in the kingdom; I would do so, because I understood that the Government was about to bring in a General Valuation Act for the

Mr. Norwood, LL.D.

30 June 1876.

Mr. *Brooks*—continued.

the whole country, and I answered the honourable Member for Kinsale, that I thought it a most desirable thing.

6284. Then you do recommend a revision of the valuation for the kingdom?—Yes, certainly in justice to the inhabitants.

6285. And an enlargement of the boundaries, I think you said, you would recommend?—Yes, that is another point which I think would be most advantageous in the case of Dublin; of course I cannot speak with regard to the enlargement of the boundaries of other municipal towns, but I know that the borough boundary in Belfast was extended with great advantage to that town.

6286. Are there any other changes which you would recommend?—Yes, the conferring of the franchise upon owners and giving votes to ladies who largely contribute to the rates, and own considerable property in Dublin and the townships; the removal of the seven mile residental qualification would bring in a large number of respectable voters; and a proper adjustment of the venue would induce many respectable citizens to claim to be placed upon the burgess roll where they will not do so now in consequence of being compelled to serve both on county and city juries.

6287. Would you recommend a general election in Dublin as a means of enabling the various elements to coalesce, and so to have a reform in the constitution of the corporation?—I would rather that the constitution of the corporation were changed more gradually, for this reason: that if you had a general election, you might bring in a corporation so complety changed, that they will be very little acquainted with the work of the corporation, whereas, if you made the change more gradual, there at least would be some persons remaining in the corporation acquainted with the *modus operandi* and the carriage of its numerous departments.

6288. Much stress has been laid upon the number of persons, I think they amount to 13, in the corporation, who are licensed victuallers; would you recommend that persons engaged in that trade should be excluded from the management of local affairs?—I do not see any reason certainly, in the mode of transacting public business in the corporation by the members to whom you allude, that would lead me to conclude that they ought to be subjected to any such civil disability as that.

Mr. *Brooks*—continued.

6289. Do you think that the number is excessive, considering the manner in which trades are distributed in Dublin?—I have heard it objected to very strongly by a number of citizens, but some of the persons who are included in that trade are persons of the greatest advantage in the carriage of public business. There is one lately deceased, Alderman Redmond, than whom I never knew a better man of business or a more capable person in the discharge of public duty.

6290. Is their peculiar knowledge most useful in the administration of public affairs?—I cannot say that he had very peculiar knowledge, but he was a man of very large capacity and of very tolerant spirit.

6291. With regard to the animadversions upon the guardians of the South Dublin Union, there was one particular case, was there not, which was the subject of much comment?—Yes.

6292. Will you inform me if there has been any particular subject excepting the one that has been spoken of so often, namely, the refusal of the Public Health Committee to engage in controversial correspondence which has been made the subject of particular comment?—With regard to the animadversions upon the Corporation of Dublin, they are of a general kind. I observed throughout the evidence, that the gentlemen stated that they had their suspicions. I think that is not fair towards any public body. If you have any charge against a public body, make it specifically and the body can meet it; but to say you have suspicions of this and you have suspicions of that, is not fair either to individuals or to corporations.

6293. You are aware of the particular complaint that they have refused to engage in correspondence with the Sanitary Association, which is an irresponsible outside committee?—I have heard members of the Public Health Committee express themselves to that effect.

6294. There was some innuendo as to the absence of public clocks in Dublin; did you ever hear before the institution of this special committee, of the demand on the part of the citizens for public clocks?—No; I think there are a great number of public clocks throughout the city. The corporation took the trouble of placing their public clock in connection with the electrical arrangements of the Royal Dublin Society, in the same way that the Port and Docks Board placed their public clock in connection with the same electrical arrangements.

Tuesday, 4th July 1876.

MEMBERS PRESENT:

Sir Michael Hicks Beach.
Mr. Brooks.
Mr. Bruen.
Mr. Butt.
Mr. Collins.
Mr. J. P. Corry.
Mr. Kavanagh.
Sir Joseph M'Kenna.
Mr. Mulholland.
Dr. Ward.

SIR MICHAEL HICKS BEACH, BART., IN THE CHAIR.

Mr. EDMUND DWYER GRAY, called in; and Examined.

Mr. *Gray*.

4 July 1876.

Mr. *Butt*.

6295. I BELIEVE you are a Member of the Corporation of Dublin?—I am.

6296. How long have you been so?—Not very long; since the last election. As yet I am the junior member of the corporation.

6297. When was the last election?—In November last.

6298. I believe your father was for many years a very prominent and influential member of the corporation?—He was, and for some years I acted as his private secretary, and thereby came to have more knowledge of corporate matters from discussing them with him (and he was very much interested in them) than perhaps other members of my standing could possibly have.

6299. Have you since your election, yourself taken an active part in corporate affairs?—Yes, a very active part.

6300. Have you come here on any request from the corporation?—Yes, I have come here as a representative of the corporation, and as some misapprehension seems to exist in the minds of some of the Committee, I may as well explain how the gentlemen who represent the corporation here came to be appointed. The corporation were originally under the impression that this investigation would be purely one into the franchise and cognate subjects, and having but one opinion upon that subject as a body, and having already formally expressed it by a petition under their common seal, they nominated a sub-committee; they never nominated a deputation at all; but they nominated a sub-committee of gentlemen holding the same views to take charge of whatever evidence they desired to place before this Committee of the House. When subsequently they ascertained that the inquiry went into matters of administration, and more or less into the conduct of members of the council, they thought it would be only fair that both sides, Conservative and Liberal, should be invited to join in what they all regarded as a common defence, and therefore a Conservative was invited, and did come forward as one of the two representatives of the council. However, the opinion of the council as a body, of course,

Mr. *Butt*—continued.

is the same on the question of the franchise. Dr. Norwood came forward at the request of the council as the resolution put it, to "rebut the evidence given against the corporation."

6301. Do you mean to say that you and Dr. Norwood have come here in accordance with the resolution of the council?—In accordance with the formal resolution of the council.

6302. Have you that resolution with you?—The resolution of the council appointing Dr. Norwood and myself, was passed on the 17th of June: "That Councillors Norwood and Gray be requested to attend before the Parliamentary Committee to rebut the evidence placed before them against the corporation."

6303. Dr. Norwood belongs to the Conservative party in the city of Dublin, does he not?—Yes, he belongs to the Conservative party.

6304. He is a very active and much respected member of that party?—One of the most so.

6305. Has any resolution been since passed by the corporation with reference to the evidence to be given here?—Yes, a resolution was passed yesterday which I will read: "That this council protests against the introduction of any exceptional franchise for Dublin or for Ireland, and emphatically claims for the people of Dublin and of Ireland, the same municipal franchise as is accorded to the people of England. Councillors Norwood and Gray having by the following resolution of council, dated the 17th June 1876, been deputed to rebut the evidence against this council, given before the Select Committee of the House of Commons" (then the resolution is quoted): "That Councillor Gray be now requested to convey to the Select Committee of the House of Commons the views of the corporation on all questions affecting the municipal franchise, as expressed by this council."

6306. You have read, and I suppose carefully, the evidence taken here, which has been communicated to the corporation?—Yes, there was a sub-committee of six appointed for the purpose, and we have read the evidence carefully.

6307. Are there any inaccuracies in that evidence which you would desire on behalf of the corporation

Mr. Grey.

4 July 1876.

Mr. Butt—continued.

corporation to correct?—There are a great many inaccuracies, perhaps, not of very vital importance, but of importance to members of the council, which they desire to have corrected.

6308. Will you mention any points which you wish to correct?—It was suggested by, I think, Mr. M'Evoy, that the contribution of 500 *l.* to the French fund, which was mentioned here two or three times, was given by the Liberal section of the council, and that, in fact, it was a party vote.

6309. Will you state the facts correctly?—I produce the minute of the meeting, and I find that it was a unanimous vote, with the exception of one member, Mr. French, who voted against it, and that such prominent Conservatives as Councillor Sykes, Mr. Byrne, whom I may call the leaders of the Conservative party in the council, Mr. Casson, Mr. Dockrell, Mr. Alderman Jameson, Mr. Tickell, Alderman Purdon, and Councillor French, whose politics I really do not know, but at any rate the vote was unanimous, with the exception named, and a large number of Conservatives were there, and joined heartily in it.

Chairman.

6310. Was it ever alleged that it was a party vote; that it was a question of Liberal and Conservative?—It was alleged, as a matter of belief, by either Mr. M'Evoy or Mr. Pim. Unfortunately, I did not take down the number of the question, but I am quite positive that the witness expressed his belief, it was not an assertion, it was a belief expressed that it was a party vote.

6311. Is it Question 1696 that you refer to?—It may be that I am mistaken. However, as it was also alleged that that was one of the motives for getting the appointment of the Government Auditor delayed for a year, the corporation were anxious simply to place it on record that it was the unanimous vote of the council, with the exception named.

Mr. Butt.

6312. I believe we have it also in evidence that there had been a contribution made by the French in the time of the Irish famine?—Yes.

6313. If you will just tell me any point that you wish to correct, I will look at the evidence?—Dr. Norwood was under the impression that the council were deterred by a fear of unpopularity from recommending a re-valuation. I think the Committee are already in possession of the fact that the council have no power to demand a re-valuation; in fact I waited upon Mr. Ball Green in the Valuation Office, and asked him the question, and he told me that we had no power; but it was not a question of unpopularity which deterred the corporation from suggesting a re-valuation. Mr. Byrne gave a reason, which did not convince me, but which convinced the majority present. He said that it made no matter, as regards the local taxation, whether a man paid 2 *s.* in the pound on a valuation, one-half of the real value, or 1 *s.* in the pound on their rack rent, but that it would increase the Imperial taxation, and that is a matter to which I think we, in common with most local bodies, have not got any very special liking for. It was urged that it would increase the valuation for the purposes of the income tax, and that was our real reason for not bringing it forward.

6314. Is there anything else which you would wish to correct?—Some of those matters have already been dealt with; but I doubt if they have been brought before the Committee very clearly. It was suggested that the transfer of 18,000 *l.* in the waterworks account was smuggled by an Act of Parliament from the rates account to the loan fund account.

Mr. Butt—continued.

6315. Could you tell me what evidence you refer to?—That is Mr. Stokes's evidence. I merely desire to say that the whole matter was perfectly open; I am rather anxious about it, inasmuch as it would have been my father who smuggled the matter through if it were smuggled; the matter was done perfectly openly; there were three accounts running at the time, but there were a number of preliminary expenses, such as Parliamentary expenses, and others that were put to the debit of the rates account, inasmuch as no mony could be borrowed for those special purposes from the Public Works Loan Commissioners (they will only lend money for works to be executed; they will not even lend money for works that have been executed). When the whole of the funds were consolidated, these moneys, which were really expended on the capital account, were transferred to the capital account openly, and to the knowledge of every person; there was no smuggling in the matter, and it was considered to be a perfectly legitimate transaction.

6316. Do you recollect anything being said about a deputation to London on the subject of the agitation?—Yes; and Alderman Campbell, who was Lord Mayor at the time, is particularly anxious to place it on record that his expenses were not paid on that deputation, and none of the members' expenses were paid; in fact, we often have the privilege of going on deputations, but one of the chief privileges which we have is always to pay our own expenses. The officers' expenses of going in state to present a petition at the bar of the House, and who must accompany the Lord Mayor, were paid; but the members of a deputation never receive their expenses on such occasions.

6317. From what you know of the corporation, do you think that the appointments are influenced by sectarian feelings?—No, on the contrary, I think the appointments are particularly clear of anything of the sort. I have had a list made out of the Protestant officers holding high positions under the corporation, and I find that there are a large number; for instance, Mr. Neville, the city engineer; Mr. Grice, the assistant to the town clerk; two assistant engineers; the superintendent of the fire brigade; the supervisor of the waterworks; the medical officer of health and public analyst; the secretary to the public health committee; the assistant to the treasurer, whom we have now appointed treasurer; the inspector of weights and measures; and two supervisors of streets; those, amongst others, are Protestants; in fact the question of religion I do not think ever enters into the appointment of officers by the corporation.

6318. You yourself are a Protestant, are you not?—I myself am a Protestant.

6319. Something has been said in evidence, I think, with regard to the increase of salaries?—Yes. Dr. Norwood handed in a return on the last day, which shows all that, but it has not been

Mr. Grey.
4 July 1876.

Mr. Butt—continued.

been put into the evidence, and the corporation are rather anxious, if the Committee have no objection, that this return should be put in. It is desirable, because it analyses the increases, and shows in what they consist (*delivering in the same*).

6320. Can you state the circumstances under which the addition was made to the Lord Mayor's salary?—Yes, there were two reasons which caused that increase to be made. The secretary was heretofore paid by fees received at the Lord Mayor's Court, and it was suggested, and felt, that he, acting in a court of justice as a kind of registrar, or as an official of the court, it would be undesirable that he should continue to be paid by fees, or any portion of his salary by fees. That was one of the principal motives in giving the Lord Mayor an increase of salary, which actually goes to his secretary, of 260 guineas, or something of that kind.

6321. It is enough to say that the salary was given to him to enable him to let his secretary dispense with the fees?—Yes, and we are getting the fees.

6322. Can you tell me by whom that was done; who was Lord Mayor when that arrangement was made?—I forget at the moment.

6323. Has your attention been called to the allegation that the council wasted their time in political matters?—Yes, but that is not so. As a rule, when they have any political matter to discuss, which I may say is very seldom, they have a special meeting for the purpose when they would not meet at all otherwise, and therefore they do not waste the time of the council in political discussions. Of course, in the newspapers those matters are reported at great length, whereas the ordinary details of administrative work are not reported; and therefore the public may naturally assume that a large proportion of the whole time of the council is devoted to that which, as a matter of fact, is not so.

6324. Have you any return showing that?—Yes, I have a return, prepared by the assistant town clerk, of meetings at which political matters were discussed in the years 1873, 1874, and 1875. Of course, if an incidental question cropped up during an ordinary meeting of the council, there would not be notice of it. These are what are in the special notice paper. In 1874, January 26th, petition for Federal Local Government in Ireland; July 13, petition in favour of Municipal Privileges Bill. In 1875, March 12th, ditto, Local Government in Towns Bill, petition against, I presume. April 5th, ditto, Sale of Liquors on Sundays. This is signed by the assistant town clerk, and they are all the political meetings that he gives me for three years.

Chairman.

6325. May I ask if the Land Tenure (Ireland) Bill was considered by the corporation?—The Land Tenure Bill was considered on a letter which necessarily came before us.

Mr. Butt.

6326. But not as a special matter?—No, not as a special matter.

Chairman.

6327. Was there a resolution arrived at with regard to it?—Yes, to petition in its favour.

6328. May I ask on what ground the corporation of Dublin petitioned in favour of a Bill in relation to land?—They petitioned on the ground that they considered that the question affects the well-being and material prosperity of the entire country, and therefore it was a matter which legitimately came within the scope of their functions. Very probably it would reduce the rates, and undoubtedly it would add to the prosperity of the capital, and therefore it directly affects their interest.

6329. As a matter of general political interest to the country?—It might possibly be so. It was proposed to petition upon the ground that it affected materially the prosperity of the city.

Mr. Butt.

6330. Are you aware that the Corporation of London has always taken a very prominent and active part in every political question affecting the country?—Certainly, I was under the impression that most of the municipal corporations in England always did so. For instance, Birmingham, I think, has been very prominent. I think that the council are at liberty to deal with political matters.

Chairman.

6331. Do you know whether the Corporation of London took any part in petitioning for or against the Agricultural Holdings (England) Bill of last Session?—Really I do not know; but I take it that such a Bill as that would scarcely excite very much interest in any body.

Mr. Butt.

6332. Will you tell me this: it has been suggested, I think, that a 50 *l.* qualification by rating would be a good qualification for a town councillor; what is your opinion about that?—Yes, that has been suggested, and I find that it would disqualify a good many of the best of them. I have a return of the ratings of the members of the council, and I find, for instance, that it would have disqualified such men as the late Alderman Redmond, who possibly was one of the best men in the council, and I believe it would disqualify the leader of the Conservative party in the council, Mr. Byrne; I know that it would have disqualified Mr. McEvoy when he stood in 1868, and I think I have a memorandum of one or two that it would have disqualified; it would have disqualified Councillor Campell, and it would have disqualified the last witness that you had before you, Dr. Norwood.

6333. I believe he is the owner of very considerable property?—Yes, he is the owner of very considerable property, but it so happens that he is not rated in the city up to the sum named, and it would have disqualified him.

6334. Would you consider a 50 *l.* qualification too high?—I do not think that any such qualification really is necessary; it would be a hardship in exceptional cases; one man may be very good who is rated for 100 *l.*, while another man, who happens to be only rated for 10 *l.* within the city, may hold a large property within the suburbs worth hundreds. I do not think it would have any effect as regards improving the *personnel* of the corporation; I am quite certain of it.

Mr. Gray.

4 July 1876.

Mr. *Butt*—continued.

6335. It would narrow the range of selection?—Yes, it would narrow the range of selection, and would put out a few good men.

6336. Has your attention been called to a statement made by Mr. Stokes that the grand juries cess is levied for sewage works?—Yes, I have particularly inquired into that, and find that no such thing has ever been done, so far as I can ascertain, and if it were done, the auditor would disallow it.

6337. Have you seen any allegation that the gas in Dublin costs too much?—I have. One of the Members of the Committee asked some questions with reference to it, and I have endeavoured to ascertain the entire facts. The Committee will understand that we are in the midst now of a negotiation for the renewal of the contract, and we, some few days ago, issued a circular to the principal towns in England, asking them what each of the lamps cost per annum, and I have taken out every return that we have got up to this, and I find that Bath costs 3 *l.*; Bolton costs 1 *l.* 17 *s.* (that is an extraordinary thing, but they are very near the coal district, I presume); Blackburn, 2 *l.* 16 *s.* 3 *d.*; Coventry, 2 *l.* 10 *s.*; Dewsbury, 4 *l.* 3 *s.*; Fulham, 4 *l.* 15 *s.* to 5 *l.* 5 *s.* 8 *d.*; Leeds, 2 *l.* 18 *s.*; Liverpool, 3 *l.* 18 *s.* 10 *d.*; Southampton, 3 *l.* 17 *s.* I need not go through them all. London varies from 5 *l.* the highest, to 4 *l.* the lowest. Dublin at the present rate costs 2 *l.* 11 *s.* 3 *d.*, and even at the new rate of the proposed contract, which of course we have not accepted, and intend to fight against, it will come to about 3 *l.* 3 *s.*, so that therefore, even at what is considered an excessive rate under the contract, we should be paying much less per lamp on an average than other towns. In Blackburne, Bolton, and Coventry I now find that the low price is accounted for by the fact that the lamps are not lit continuously all the year from sunset to sunrise, as with us.

Sir *Joseph M'Kenna.*

6338. Have you any test with respect to the relative strength of the light in those towns and in Dublin?—No, I do not think I have, but I think that each lamp in Dublin gives at least as much light; anyhow, people say that they give at least as much light as each lamp in London.

6339. But you have not subjected that to any direct test?—No, I have not; I might explain that the Dublin lighting undoubtedly is not good, but it must be remembered that the streets of London have probably three lamps to our one; that is the point. The question is the cost per lamp; if we chose to increase the number of lamps we could increase the light.

6340. Does the defect of lighting the streets of Dublin proceed from the paucity of lamps and not from the quality of the gas?—Yes, quite so; we have fewer lamps; the lamps are too far apart.

Mr. *Collins.*

6341. You might ascertain by inquiry what the illuminating power of the street lamps of Dublin is in the public streets; we know, generally speaking, what it is throughout England; do you know the illuminating power?—I know the standard quality of the gas, of course, but I could not tell the actual consumption per lamp, or compare it with the actual consumption per lamp in English towns. (*Witness subsequently requested permission to state that the average consumption of gas in Dublin for each public lamp was four cubic feet per hour.*)

Mr. *Brooks.*

6342. Do you know the candle standard in Dublin?—It is nominally 16, but it is equal to 18, tested by the London standard burner.

6343. In fact, the gas company do supply it at 10 per cent. better than their contract?—I do not refer to that now.

6344. Is not that the return of the Government inspector?—Nominally the 16-candle gas of Dublin, as tested by such a burner as is used in London, the London Argand burner, would be equal to 18 candles; I also believe that it is slightly over the test which it must come up to; probably it equals about 19-candle gas tested by the London standard burner, which is the Argand.

Mr. *Butt.*

6345. Of course the gas company, by their own contract, are bound to submit to the Dublin test?—Yes, they are bound to submit to the Dublin test, which is an exceptional test.

6346. And that test would be equal to 18 of the London standard?—Yes.

6347. Do you wish to say anything about the sum of 500 *l.* that objection was made to before the auditor?—I had better explain to the Committee the exact circumstances of that matter. In 1873 the corporation promoted a Bill, which was thrown out on a technicality, from some of the notices not having been served. Of course the promotion of that Bill cost a considerable sum, and when they came to look into the matter they found that they had no power to pay the engineers or the others employed. In 1874 the gas company promoted a Bill, which was opposed both by the corporation and by the citizens' committee. Eventually a compromise was come to, and one element in the compromise was that the corporation should be paid a sum of 500 *l.*, and that the citizens' committee should also be paid the sum of 500 *l.* It was thoroughly understood, though of course it could not be embodied in that Act, that that 500 *l.* was to go towards paying the engineers and others their expenses. A question has now been raised about it; the corporation are very anxious to pay those gentlemen, but they have no funds to pay them with, and they consider that it would be a perfectly legitimate matter to use this 500 *l.* for the purpose for which it was in reality intended. They are trying in fact whether they can do that; they are not going to ask for the money from the gas company until they ascertain what they can do with it when they get it.

6348. In your opinion, is there a general feeling among the people of Dublin to demand a reform of the corporation?—No, I am quite certain there is not; there is that feeling amongst an influential section, who make themselves very conspicuous, who are constantly in the public prints, and who attract a great deal of attention, owing to their high position individually; but they are limited in point of numbers, and the matter is altogether, so far as I can judge, confined to them.

6349. So far as you can judge, would you say that the general feeling of the people of Dublin is in favour of a change in the corporate franchise

Mr. *Butt*—continued.

chise and corporate arrangements?—The general feeling of the popular party in Dublin is in favour of an assimilation of the franchise with that of England; they see no reason why a distinction, which is, so far as it goes, a stigma upon them, should be allowed to remain.

6350. I need scarcely ask you this, but do you think that there might be a possible improvement made in the *personnel* of the members of the corporation?—No doubt a considerable improvement, but I think I can assert, with tolerable safety, that the *personnel* of the Corporation of Dublin is at least equal to the *personnel* of similar bodies in other towns, English and Irish. No doubt it is capable of improvement; no doubt there are plenty of men who, if we could induce them to come in, we would be very glad to have in; for instance, Mr. Joseph Pim was pressed to come in, but he declined. Mr. Thomas Pim, also, was pressed to come in, and a deputation waited upon him, but he declined. We cannot force those gentlemen in, but they could come in if they liked, and we would be very glad to have them.

6351. Do you think that there is any elective body in the world which has elected the very best men that can possibly be found except, perhaps, the House of Commons?—Always, excepting the House of Commons, I do not. I think there is a fair proportion of good men in the council. Mr. Sullivan said that, perhaps, there were 10 or 12. I would put them at 25 or 30, and I think that is as large a proportion of really working men as will be found in any similar body. Some men go in, and do not attend after they are in.

6352. What is the number that is requisite to make a quorum?—The number, as fixed by Act of Parliament, is 20. That is our standing difficulty. The corporation are not here to deny that great improvements might not be effected, but they say that, if you relieve them of that shackle which ties them down, and prevents their being able to act, if you relieve them of that quorum difficulty, they will be able to do everything which is requisite themselves.

6353. What quorum would you suggest instead of 20?—The Poor Law Boards work very well with three or five, I am not sure which. I think that nine or 10 would be quite as good a quorum, and would ensure a better attendance of members than the present.

6354. Will you tell me how that would ensure better attendance?—It ensures good attendances at the Poor Law Boards, simply because, whenever there is anything of interest to any individuals, it may be dealt with, before they come, by a small quorum; they then attend promptly in order to secure their own voice in the matter. Under the present system, men rely on 20 members not being brought together for a long while, and they rely on a certain number of their own friends being amongst those 20, and, therefore, they are not so watchful as they would be with a smaller quorum.

6355. The corporation, I believe, themselves have been defeated in the assemblies of the council by persons opposing them leaving the house?—Constantly; that is on one side; I am not aware of the Liberals ever having adopted such tactics, but they have been adopted. Then I may mention there is one gentleman who has an idea

Mr. *Butt*—continued.

Mr. *Gray*.

4 July 1876.

that we can do nothing without having 20 members present; he almost lives in the Council Chamber, and he counts us out perpetually; one obstructive of that kind, with the tremendous power placed by Act of Parliament in the hands of a single member, owing to fixing the quorum at 20, obstructs the business fearfully, and involves double labour, on the men who want to work.

Sir Joseph M'Kenna.

6356. Is that Mr. French, to whom you are referring?—That is Mr. French; he takes his luncheon with him for fear that we should do any business when he went out to luncheon. If there are 19 members there he counts us out, and home we must go.

Mr. Brooks.

6357. Reading the minutes precedes all the other business in the corporation, does it not?—Yes, except counting the roll.

6358. Do you find that the members of the corporation defer, or propose to defer, their attendance on the corporation until the time occupied in reading the minutes has been past?—Very constantly, and therefore the house is not formed until very late, because the minutes cannot be read until a quorum is formed and the roll called.

6359. People defer their attendance until the minutes are read, in the hope that a quorum will be formed in their absence?—Quite so; in the hope that a quorum will be formed in their absence.

Mr. Butt.

6360. Have you turned your attention at all to this question, which incidentally I asked you before about, namely, the re-valuation of Dublin?—I think that re-valuation is essential in justice; I do not think that a re-valuation need involve necessarily an increased valuation, or a largely increased valution at any rate, but it need not necessarily involve an increase at all for the purposes of local taxation. It makes no real difference so long as the local bodies have sufficient taxing powers to meet their wants, what the poundage rate may be as compared with the valuation, but it makes all the difference in the world that the valuation shall bear a fair proportion all round to the letting value. That it does not do in Dublin; it is unequal as well as too low, and that is the worst point in it.

6361. With reference to this statement about the increase of taxation, have you turned your attention at all to it, to what it would be supposing there was a re-valuation all over Ireland, at the fair letting value of the land and houses?—I think what the increased taxation for Imperial purposes would be, would be a mere trifle, but still men are frightened at the sound of it, and it is used as an argument. Of course they do not take the trouble of analysing it, and seeing what it all means; it means levying 30,000 *l.* or 40,000 *l.* increase over the whole country.

6362. Supposing the income tax is 3 *d.* in the pound, and the valuation of Ireland to be increased by one-fourth, what addition would be put upon the Irish income tax?—The valuation at present is about 13 millions, take it at 12 millions, increase that by one-fourth, taking 6 *d.* in the pound, which is double the present amount, that would

Mr. *Gray*.

4 July 1876.

Mr. *Butt*—continued.

would add 18 million pence to the taxation of Ireland, or 75,000 *l.* exactly. I only put it at 3 *d.*, and I said it would be between 30,000 *l.* and 40,000 *l.*

6363. Are you aware that out of that 75,000 *l.* there would be a very large amount of deductions and remissions as being under the standard of the income tax?—Yes, I think the thing is a mere bugbear. I do not think it would be of any serious moment at all, one way or the other.

6364. Considering the advantage that there would be in having a general and true valuation of property all over Ireland, do you think that that additional increase of taxation over the country would countervail the advantage that would follow from a good and true valuation as regards the country generally?—That is rather a difficult question to answer. It would altogether, in my mind, depend upon the view that the landlords would take of it. I think myself it is always better to get the true facts; and I believe in a re-valuation, personally.

6365. Have you considered the question of the extension of the boundaries of Dublin?—Yes, I think that is essential, that it must be done some day, and the sooner it is done the better; Dublin has outgrown its limits. Every Member of the Committee knows how thoroughly portions of the suburbs are really portions of the city. The townships, knowing very well that some day or another they must be absorbed, are actuated by an intense feeling of jealousy against the corporation. Mr. Stokes very frankly acknowledged that. Apropos of that, I may mention, with reference to the introduction of the waterworks, a question was asked here the other day, Why we did not ourselves introduce the water into the townships. The Waterworks Act certainly gave us power to introduce the pipes and to sell water to individuals, but it gave us no rating power; we could only open the streets and sell it as a gas company would sell gas; and perhaps one man in a street would take the water from us; but the townships in consequence of this feeling of jealousy that I speak of, would undoubtedly, the very moment we attempted to do such a thing as that, have started a supply of their own in opposition, no matter what it might have cost, or how bad it might have been, and therefore we dare not attempt such a thing.

6366. Have you heard the evidence which has been given here with regard to protecting minorities in the representation in the corporation?—I have.

6367. Are you of opinion that there is any necessity for that?—Not in Dublin; the minorities are very well taken care of. There are a large number of Conservatives at this moment members of Liberal wards, and whenever they offer themselves for re-election no Liberal ever dreams of opposing them on account of their politics. I do not think that there has been a single instance of such a thing being done in Dublin. For instance, Alderman Jameson, who is a Conservative, is member for Arran Quay, which is a Liberal ward. Alderman Purdon, a Conservative, is member for the Rotunda Ward, the ward for which I also am a member; and I suppose we are pretty opposite to each other in most political matters. The present Lord Mayor is member for the Mansion House Ward, a Liberal ward. Councillor Tickell, of the North City Ward; Councillor Byrne, of the South City Ward, and Councillor Franklin, the member for Mountjoy Ward, all of which are Liberal wards, are Conservatives, and no person ever tried to interfere with them, or would interfere with them, and never touched them on account of their politics. There is nearly always a contest when first a man comes forward, but when he is in, if he does his business fairly, he is never interfered with by either side.

Chairman.

6368. May I ask whom you succeeded last November?—I succeeded Mr. Wallis.

6369. Had he been a member of the council for some time?—He had.

6370. Was there any difference between your political opinions and his?—Yes, he is a strong Conservative, and I am a strong Liberal.

6371. What was the reason why his case was an exception to the rule?—His case was not an exception to the rule. I canvassed against him simply because he did not attend the meetings of the council. I canvassed the Conservatives and Liberals throughout the ward on that ground, and on that ground alone. I said to every one of them that I would never dream of standing against Mr. Wallis if he attended the meetings of the council, and fairly did his business. That was the ground upon which I canvassed them, and that was the ground on which I was returned.

6372. Were there not one or two matters occurred which would lead one to suppose that the contest was a political contest?—It was made a good deal of in some of the journals; they sought to make it a political contest.

Mr. *Butt.*

6373. Were you aware that Mr. Wallis, upon one question at all events, agreed with the popular party that he was one of the earliest members of the Home Rule League?—Yes.

6374. And he continues so still?—Quite so; he can scarcely be put upon that ground as a Conservative, but, as a matter of fact, I canvassed against him solely on the ground that I mentioned. I would never dream of canvassing against him otherwise. There is one Conservative member, Alderman Purdon, who is in the same ward, but I believe he does attend to his business, and no one interferes with him.

6375. We have heard of Mr. Casson's rejection; do you know anything of that?—Yes. He was opposed on the same ground of non-attendance. It is self-evident that if a man does not take the trouble to attend the meetings of the council, he cannot possibly do the business for which he is returned.

6376. Have you heard of the proposition of the multiple vote; that is, give a person a vote in proportion to his rating?—Yes, I have.

6377. In your opinion, would that be acceptable to the great majority of the people of Dublin?—It would be viewed with the greatest disfavour. In the first place, I may say that the corporation have petitioned formally against it; but as regards outsiders, naturally they would simply regard it as a proposal to swamp the votes of the poor man by property votes. I think there is only one true way of estimating the result of such a system as that. We have it at work in Dublin with the Poor Law Boards, and the way to

Mr. *Butt*—continued.

Mr. *Gray.*

4 July 1876.

to see what its results would be, practically, is to see what its result has been there.

6378. Has the result been satisfactory, say in the South Dublin Union?—I think it has been most unsatisfactory. The Corporation of Dublin consists of a very large number of Catholics, in the proportion of 2 to 1, and they show an example which I think is an example that ought to be followed by the entire country, an example of toleration and consideration for their political opponents, and of equal distribution of patronage and of office in their gift. They appoint the Lord Mayor alternately from the minority and the majority. They appoint Protestant and Conservative officers with just as much freedom as though they belonged to the other side. In the South Dublin Union, where the members are elected under the multiple vote system, where the other party have a majority, they show the exactly opposite spirit, they have never appointed a Catholic chairman. The appointments of officers ever since they have been formed have been almost strictly sectarian. I think there are only two officers of the entire number (of course they must appoint a Catholic chaplain and a Catholic schoolmaster), but outside those necessarily religious appointments there are only two officers in the entire union whose salaries are over 100 *l.* a year who are Catholics, and those were appointed at a time when by accident the Liberals had a majority. There are a great number of small officials with 20 *l.*, 30 *l.*, 40 *l.*, or 50 *l.* a year who are Catholics, but that is the fact as regards the appointments to any offices worth having which are in their gift.

6379. Supposing the multiple vote to throw the election of the corporation into the hands of persons of property in Dublin, would it, in your opinion, promote sectarianism in the corporation?—I am quite convinced that it would have that result, for this reason. Our traditions are liberal. I do not mean liberal in the political sense, but truly liberal, and showing liberality in all our dealings. The bodies which now would be elected under a new system would start with new ideas, and I am afraid that they would be no improvement upon the old.

6380. Have you read the evidence of Mr. Sullivan, in which he proposed that new plan?—I have.

6381. That is what is called the plan of minority representation, following what has been done in some instances in the Parlimentary representation?—Yes, it is the three-cornered plan.

6382. In your opinion, could it be satisfactorily carried out in the city of Dublin?—I am quite certain that no possible system of exceptional legislation could be carried out without great dissatisfaction in Dublin, and great injury not merely to Dublin but to the entire country.

6383. What do you mean by exceptional legislation?—The introduction in Dublin of an exceptional franchise. If it were deemed desirable to introduce the three-cornered system universally over the three kingdoms, I take it that no great objection would be raised in Dublin to it; but, in my opinion, there is a very much better system, that is to say, the system of electing a certain proportion of the corporation by the votes of the entire city, which would insure your getting a better class of men, and no objection would be raised to it so long as it was a general proposal; but if one city or one country is singled out for exceptional treatment, that undoubtedly would create a great feeling, and a natural feeling, of dissatisfaction.

6384. I am rather asking you on the abstract merits of the three-cornered plan; if that is the notion which you urge, do you think that it could be satisfactorily carried out in Dublin?—I do not think it could. I think that its effect would be, as proposed by Mr. Sullivan, to place the minority in the position of the majority; to give them practically a preponderance of votes.

6385. Supposing that any representation of the minority was desirable generally, would you consider it more desirable to effect it by the cumulative vote, or by restricted voting?—The cumulative vote, I think, is only possible for large districts. I certainly think that the cumulative vote applied to the whole city would be an admirable system, but that is merely my individual opinion.

6386. Supposing that in addition to the four members returned from the wards, as they are at present, six members were to be returned by all the votes on the north side of the city, and nine on the south side, and those additional 15 to be elected by the cumulative vote, do you think that that would improve the corporation?—I doubt if the addition to the gross number would be any improvement; but I think that cumulative voting applied to the whole city, or to the two sides of it, would undoubtedly result in electing only first-class men, for the reason that it would never be worth the while of a man to canvas the whole city for a municipal election. Men would go forward simply on the weight of their names and their reputations, Liberal or Conservative, or whatever they might be, and it would destroy the preponderance of influence of a class in a small ward which, in Dublin, and every place else, is very strong, and often results in not sending in the best men.

6387. Do you think that a proposal of that kind would give dissatisfaction merely on the ground that it was different from the English arrangement?—Probably a proposal of that kind would not give so much dissatisfaction as the other, because I do not think it could have any political influence one way or the other which the multiple vote undoubtedly would have, but I think that the people of Dublin would be discontented with any exceptional legislation; they would regard it more or less as a stigma. The corporation certainly would. Their position is that they have done their business well in the face of great difficulties, and great opposition, and that nothing to their discredit has been proved against them, and that there are a very few bodies who would pass an ordeal of this kind as they have passed it, and they would feel as a stigma the introduction of any exceptional legislation, which would presuppose that there was something wrong in the present system.

Chairman.

6388. Was the Act of 1849, which specially applied to Dublin, and not to any other place, felt as a stigma at the time?—That I cannot say. I presume it was not.

6389. If that was not felt as a stigma then, I do not quite understand why an Act affecting Dublin

Mr. *Gray.*

4 July 1876.

Chairman—continued.

Dublin only should be felt as a stigma now?—The Act of 1849 was not preceded by a systematic attack outside on the administration of the corporation, and almost on their individual honour, and that certainly would have its effect.

Mr. *Butt.*

6390. Have you ever read the Parliamentary history of that Act; have you ever read the evidence that was taken before the Commission of Inquiry?—No, I have not read that evidence.

6391. Are you aware, without reading it, that the strongest possible objection was made to the unequal distribution of the wards in the corporation at that time?—I know there was a great piece of work made about that point. I never went into it personally.

6392. Did you know that there was one ward, containing 1,500 electors, and nearly one-fourth of the taxation of the city, and that that ward only returned the same number as another ward with 300 or 400 electors, and paying a very small proportion of the taxation?—Yes; I know that there were many great inequalities.

6393. And that was redressed by the Act of 1849, was it not?—Yes, I think so.

6394. And a new distribution of wards was made, which was supposed to be upon the principle of equality?—Equality of valuation, I think.

6395. And of population too?—I cannot speak to that.

6396. At the same time the franchise was supposed to be enlarged by assimilating it to the English franchise, which was a rating franchise, with 3 *l.* a year occupation?—Quite so. Now that you call my attention to it, I am not thoroughly conversant with the Act of 1849, but I am unaware that any exceptional franchise was introduced by that Act. I think it was more an assimilation to the English franchise; in fact, I am certain it was.

Chairman.

6397. Exceptional, as compared with all other Irish boroughs?—Yes, but it was an assimilation to the English franchise, and therefore it was rather an honour to Dublin than a stigma; picking out Dublin as the sole town in Ireland that should be assimilated.

6398. Then your view is, that giving the franchise to the owners of rateable property would be a stigma?—Not at all. My view is, that assimilating it to the English franchise would be a good thing, but selecting it for exceptional legislation would be the reverse.

Mr. *Butt.*

6399. Do not you think that persons might very fairly consider that if the Legislature trusted the whole of the inhabitants of Dublin with the franchise, it was a mark of confidence in their capacity?—Certainly.

6400. And do you think that if the Legislature thought proper to exclude a very large proportion of the inhabitants from the franchise, it might be considered the contrary?—Quite so. I think that that is the only interpretation that could be put upon it.

6401. Do not you think that all sensitive people, like the people of Dublin, might very fairly consider that if the power of electing the corporation was thrown into the hands of the

Mr. *Butt*—continued.

property classes, in a way that has never been attempted to be done in any corporation in England, they might also consider it a stigma upon the capacity of the great body of the people?—I do not see how they could avoid that suggestion.

6402. Especially if it was put upon the ground that, if the people had votes, they would tax property unfairly?—Quite so. It would intensify the feeling; in fact, that would be inevitable; they could not think anything else.

6403. Do you think that anything of that kind would provoke a great deal of discontent in Dublin?—Certainly; I am sure it would.

6404. I understand you to say that a mere cumulative vote would be preferable?—I am merely expressing my own individual opinion upon that.

6405. Have you at all considered the franchise given by the Towns Improvement Act?—Yes, that is a 50 *l.* ownership franchise.

6406. Apart from the objection of its being exceptional, and not so in England, do you think it would be an unpopular thing to do in Dublin?—I think it would. I do not think it would affect the franchise seriously, but I think it would be unpopular. There is less occasion, I think, for it now than there ever was in Dublin, for this reason, that under the old system the allegation in support of owners' votes was that the burden of taxation eventually falls upon them, whether it falls immediately or not. Under the old system, if we wanted to raise a loan, we issued perpetual debentures, and no doubt, when the leases fall out, the weight of the interest on those debentures fell upon the owners; but, under the present system, if we want a loan, we issue terminable annuities, some of them payable off in as short a time as 20 years, and none of them running for longer than 40 years; 35 is the average for the Water Works loan. The whole of the Water Works loan is to be paid off in 35 years. Leases in Dublin, I take it, would run for longer periods than 35 years, and, therefore, the occupier would alone be made liable for the entire weight of the whole thing, capital, interest, and everything else.

6407. Do you think that that proposal to admit 50 *l.* owners' votes, as exceptionally in the city of Dublin, would be unpopular?—Certainly.

6408. Have you considered at all the question of the mode of levying rates in Dublin?—I have; it is very unsatisfactory. We suffer a great deal of loss owing to fraudulent lessors, just as Mr. Taaffe explained at length. We suffer through the introduction of bills of sale which protect property, and we cannot levy. I myself know instances of men occupying very good positions, professional men occupying good houses; at least, I know of one instance of a man occupying a first-class house, and living in style, and he presents a bill of sale when the collector general goes to collect or to levy after obtaining a decree, and it cannot be done. I know of one case in which the rates are collected, or are in process of collection, from a man, for the simple reason that he occupies so good a house that his rates amount to over 40 *l.*, and we have put into operation the Bankruptcy Act, and thereby exercise a pressure which we could not otherwise use, so as to discredit the man, and rather than have that done

Mr. *Butt*—continued.

does he pays, but in respect of only 35 *l.* we are powerless.

6409. What remedy would you suggest for that with regard to the collection of the rates?—With regard to fraudulent lessors, I would give the power, as suggested by the collector general, to recover from the beneficial owner.

6410 When you say you would do this in the case of fraudulent lessors, could you do it without making it universal?—Of course you could not do it without making it universal.

6411. Would you think it desirable to make the city rates a charge on the property the same as the poor rate?—Yes, I would. Mr. Stokes, for instance, alleged, as showing the superiority of the mode of doing business in Rathmines over Dublin, that there were only, I think, 8 *l.* of rates uncollected in Rathmines, or something of that kind. But they have the power under their special Act which we want, or which the collector general wants, to enable him to collect the rates properly, that is to say, they have the power of dealing with the owners, and recovering from the property itself.

6412. Would you think it desirable that the rate should be put upon the same footing as the rent, and attach upon any property on the premises?—Certainly, I would consider that something of the kind ought to be done. The present system is a scandal, because there are some house jobbers who own 200 or 300 houses, and who never pay any rates. Something ought to be done to remedy that. I am scarcely capable of saying what the best mode of remedying it would be.

6413. But you think that something is wanted?—Something evidently is wanted.

6414. Have you considered at all the present mode of auditing the accounts?—I have, and it is unsatisfactory.

6415. In what respect?—The auditor surcharges of his own mere motion; and, even if he is proved to be wrong afterwards, the corporation have to pay the costs. I think that if the auditor were simply placed in the same position as a ratepayer is in law (though in practice he is not, for he does not examine the accounts with sufficient minuteness), that is to say, if he surcharge, and if the individuals who are surcharged do not pay it, the auditor, as a Government official, should make them pay, and make them pay in the same way as a ratepayer would, and run the risk; but if he is wrong let him pay the costs of his fault, and not throw them on the innocent.

Chairman.

6416. Out of what fund should he pay them, out of his own pocket?—No, I would not have him pay them out of his own pocket; but I certainly do not think they ought to be paid out of the corporate pocket.

6417. Out of Government money, would you say?—I think so.

6418. Why?—I certainly think it is very wrong that they should be paid out of the corporation money.

6419. But surely it is to the interest of the city, rather than of the Government, that the audit should be searching and thorough, and that the auditor should be encouraged rather than discouraged to surcharge where necessary?—Of

Chairman—continued.

course it is to the interest of the city; but still it undoubtedly is a hardship that when the auditor has been shown to be wrong the party who is in the right has to pay the expenses. *Mr. Gray.* 4 July 1876.

6420. Why should the expenses not be paid from the corporation funds?—There is this reason that I see against it, that I think it is an unusual thing for those who prove themselves to be in the right to be put to the expense of the costs.

Mr. *Butt.*

6421. Are you aware that at present, according to the law, any ratepayer may bring up any order of the corporation to the Court of Queen's Bench and have it quashed?—Yes, certainly.

6422. And if that order was illegally made, the costs would be paid by the persons who made it?—Certainly; but, on the contrary, if it were legally made, those who raised the point would run the risk.

6423. It is also a fact, is it not, that in the audit of the accounts the auditor does not merely check the payments so as to see that they were actually made, but he decides in the first instance upon the legality of each order?—He does, and sometimes he decides wrongly.

6424. If the corporation or any parties think he is wrong they may appeal, may they not, to the Local Government Board?—They may.

6425. Or they may appeal to the Court of Queen's Bench?—Yes.

6426. If they appealed to the Court of Queen's Bench, they would have the certainty of paying their own costs, if even they succeed?—Quite so.

6427. Do you know that in a great number of instances the Attorney General brings delinquencies as to corporate funds, as Attorney General, before the Courts by information in the Court of Chancery, where public funds are abused?—I am not aware that he does so.

6428 Do you think it would be possible to devise any means to prevent the inflicting of the hardship upon individuals that you point out; might there not be a case submitted to the Attorney General for him to judge whether it was a sufficient case for him to bring before the Court or not?—That might be a means; the operation is quite another thing.

6429. But you think there is a hardship in the mode of audit at present?—I think there is a hardship.

6430. You mean in leaving it to the decision of the auditors upon the pure question of law, which cannot be corrected except at the expense of the party against whom he erroneously decides?—That is the gist of the hardship that I see. I think undoubtedly it is a hardship. It may be difficult to find a remedy for it.

6431. He is, in fact, not a professional man?—He is not a lawyer, as a matter of fact.

6432. The cases are not argued before him by counsel?—No, I never heard of cases being argued before him by counsel.

6433. And yet he does, in fact, practically decide cases of great nicety and difficulty in point of law?—He does. Take, for instance, the case of that culvert under the Grattan Bridge; I think that was a very great hardship. Of course the surcharge, which was put on a few individuals, of 6,000 *l.* or 7,000 *l.*, in that case was only a technical

Mr. *Butt*—continued.

Mr. *Gray*.

4 July 1876.

technical one. The auditor has since announced his intention of not pressing the matter any further, inasmuch as the main drainage committee have passed a resolution that out of the first funds which they obtain on loan they will pay back that sum out of the loan fund, and credit the rates fund with it, which is a mere technical point altogether. But assuming that that enormous surcharge had been made, not upon professional men, but upon commercial men who were engaged in considerable commercial transactions, and whose credit at the moment did not stand at the very highest point, a surcharge of 6,000 *l.* or 7,000 *l.* suddenly made upon two or three individuals by the Government officer, might have resulted in their bankruptcy. It was on a purely technical point, and done purely for the good of the city.

6434. Did you ever hear anything of that kind occurring in the corporation of Belfast, where money was honestly expended, and the expenditure was for the good of the town, but there was an information filed, at the instance of the relator, by the Attorney General against the corporation?—I have heard of something of the kind, but I am not conversant with the details.

6435. Have you heard that one of the most respectable gentlemen in Belfast was arrested for 70,000 *l.*?—Yes.

6436. And an Act of Parliament was passed to relieve him and to relieve the corporation?—Yes, I think there was something of that kind.

Chairman.

6437. In that case of the culverts, did the corporation take any legal opinion as to whether the decision of the auditor was in accordance with the law or not?—I think the members of the committee did take a legal opinion, which was favourable to them; as well as I remember, Councillor Norwood was the chairman of that Committee, and I am under the impression that he gave you information upon that point; but whether it was legal or not, it was certainly done for the benefit of the citizens, and certainly did benefit them. The point was the merest technical one, and there was no idea of enforcing the payment, but it might have resulted in terrible hardship to some individuals who accidentally signed the cheque.

6438. It might have been on a technical point, and yet the decision of the auditor might have been strictly legal; such a decision, in fact, as the law bound him to give?—Quite so; I do not find fault with the auditor; I presume that he acted to the best of his ability; in fact, I think the auditor always acts with extreme fairness and extreme consideration, and the corporation have not the slightest fault to find with the public audit; indeed it is a great satisfaction to them to have it.

Mr. Butt.

6439. Do you know anything about any efforts that were made by the corporation or their officers, to put the Artisans Dwellings Act in force?—The corporation possibly did not take it up quite so soon as they might have done. I see that Birmingham has proceeded for a Provisional Order, and I presume that they will get an Act this Session. But we have taken steps to put the Act into operation, and although we are opposed by a section, and a section returned by some of the most aristocratic wards in the city, still I am in great hopes that we shall force it through in sufficient time to get an Act next Session. We certainly are not idle about it.

6440. Will not that Act involve additional taxation?—It will, and it must. That is the ground upon which it was opposed, that it must involve additional taxation.

6441. With regard to the wide streets, have you any power of levying any rate specially for wide streets?—No, we have no power. If we had we should constantly exercise it. The Wide Streets Commissioners had powers to make certain specified improvements, and power to levy rates to carry them out, but the time for doing that was limited, and they let the time lapse.

6442. Those powers were given by special Acts, were they not?—Yes.

6443. Had the Wide Street Board any general power of levying taxes for the improvement of Dublin?—No, they had no general power; and I would be very loth to grant to a body like the corporation general powers to interfere with property, and I very much doubt if Parliament would ever entertain such a proposition.

6444. You are aware that the Metropolitan Board of Works have the power of doing that?—They are a very special body constituted under very special circumstances.

6445. But the Corporation of Dublin have no power of that kind?—No, we have no such power. We have power to buy property but not to levy a rate for it, and not to take it compulsory.

6446. But you could buy it?—Yes, we could if we had the funds, but we have no means of raising funds for it; and, of course, we would pay three prices for it. There was a case in which I took some interest, the widening of Talbot-street; there is a little narrow gut there, and I was negotiating with the owner, on the part of No. 1 committee, to see if we could come to terms, but he is asking what I consider extravagant terms, and new houses will be built upon the spot, and the improvement never can be carried out. If we had power to make him submit to arbitration, we could take what we wanted.

6447. You say that you would object to compulsory powers of purchase in the corporation?—I would object to general compulsory powers, but I think there are necessary improvements in Dublin that are included in the schedule to some one or more of the old Acts that are very desirable, and it is quite possible that we might obtain a renewal of those Acts, and I think that those are included in them.

6448. Do not you think that that might be done by a Provisional Order?—Councillor Norwood has told you that Provisional Orders seem to be very difficult and troublesome things to obtain; I daresay it might be obtained by a Provisional Order.

6449. Supposing that there was a difficulty in obtaining a Provisional Order, legislation might make it easy if it is necessary?—Certainly; I only express a doubt that we can ever hope to get from Parliament general compulsory powers over

Mr. *Butt*—continued.

over the city for widening the streets; I do not think we can.

6450. A Provisional Order might give it to you in each case?—Yes, in each case if the machinery were a little simplified, and possibly that would do.

6451. Something has been said here about the credit of the corporation not being good; are you of that opinion?—I think we have a first-class credit. We can borrow at 4 per cent.; I believe the Metropolitan Board of Works can borrow a little cheaper, but there are very few corporations that can borrow at much less than 4 per cent.

6452. On what would you borrow at 4 per cent.?—We borrowed on the improvement rate some little time ago 50,000 *l.* at 4 per cent.

6453. Something has been said that the want of money by the corporation has obliged you to give a higher price for your contracts?—So it is said. Mr. Stokes, I think, said it was 30 per cent., and we brought the 30 per cent. down to 5 per cent., and I very much doubt even if it is as much as five. We do pay more for stone, and we pay more for gravel, but it is very hard to decide how much of the extra rate is due to the fact that we do not pay promptly in cash, and how much is due to the extra cost of carriage. The stone is more convenient for Rathmines, and is brought a less distance than to us. Undoubtedly there is something in the fact that we perhaps do not pay for two or three months, and that they pay immediately on delivery. We are pressed for funds; the improvement fund is very much pressed.

6454. The contractor who would expect from a body immediate payment, would of course be disposed to give better terms than if he had to wait two or three months?—Yes.

6455. Could it come to anything like the extent of 30 per cent.?—No; I think Mr. Neville put in a table showing that there was a penny per load, or something of that kind, difference.

6456. Did you hear anything said about the extravagant price for the forage of horses?—Yes.

6457. Do you know anything of that?—Yes, I have had a table prepared, and I think that we pay a very small price for forage. I know that we tried to reduce it some little time ago, but we found that the horses would not thrive on anything less. The cost of fodder for horses per week, including straw for bedding, averages 19 *s.* 3¾ *d.* That is taken from an official verified return, about which there can be no manner of doubt. This is a return which is verified by the public accountant (*delivering in the same*). The figures handed in by the city treasurer were the actual payments. Those payments might have been for a very different period; they might include back accounts, or they might not include accounts that were owing, and therefore they naturally never would correspond with the actual cost for the same period. He had no cognisance whatever of the cost of a horse; he only knew what sums he paid in cheques for a certain account, and they naturally would differ; it would have been an extraordinary coincidence if they were the same. As a matter of fact they are quite different years. I think he had no means of giving anything later than the year ending August 1875; this is the return for the year ending December 1875, and that of itself would make a difference, because the cost of forage went down in the meantime. But naturally the treasurer's return, which is the ordinary return of payments, and our analysis of the cost which we paid for the horses, would differ slightly. Over a series of years they would be the same, but over one year they would not be the same.

6458. How have you ascertained the cost of forage, fixing it at 19 *s.* 3¾ *d.*?—By our contracts. We make contracts for everything. We know the quantity that we use, and it makes no matter what time the accounts were paid. We have contracts for everything, and knowing our number of horses, we divide the one by the other.

6459. Have you a return which shows that?—Yes. Here is a summary of the horses, carts, and stable accounts (*producing the same*); it is from the verified analysis of the transactions of committee No. 1, and of the accounts of committee No 1. for the year ending December 1875; as it happens it was only finished and placed before the council, I think, after the treasurer's examination; but it had been prepared long before by Mr. Henry Brown, a public accountant, because the books fell into a little confusion, and when we changed the secretary, we got Mr. Brown to make up our books and to verify them and check them, and to sign them as being correct.

6460. Has this document in your hand been before the Committee yet?—I am not very certain; however, perhaps I had better put it in as a summary.

Mr. *Bruen*.

6461. Does this account include the cost of all the horses kept by the corporation?—I do not think it includes the fire-brigade horses; they go to the waterworks account; but it includes the great bulk of them. There are only four or five fire-brigade horses, and, except those, it includes them all.

Mr. *Kavanagh*.

6462. Is the price that you named, 19 *s.* 3¾ *d.*, the price per horse per week over the whole year?—Yes; this is an analysis prepared by the secretary to the committee, but it is taken from this summary (*delivering in the same*).

Mr. *Butt*.

6463. I see it is stated there that you have 18,205 horses; what is the meaning of that?—That is the day's work of the horses; the horse-power is perhaps what it should be put down as. Our horses, I may mention, work every day.

6464. Then this gives you, Mr. Brown's analysis of the accounts, the total cost of the forage; for instance, 3,779 *l.*, and you divide that amongst the horses that you have?—Yes.

6465. You make the average number of horses 75, and the forage and straw 19 *s.* 3¾ *d.*, the stable expenses 866 *l.* 5 *s.* 8 *d.*, and drivers' wages 17 *s.*?—Those, I presume, are the figures. This is all prepared by the secretary of No. 1 committee. I think the honourable Member for Youghal asked for that return, and it is prepared in the form he asked for.

6466. Are

Mr. Gray.

4 July 1876.

Mr. Kavanagh.

6466. Are the wages of the drivers included in this 19 *s.* 3¼ *d.*?—Certainly not; you will find on another page of the same return the wages of the drivers.

Mr. Butt.

6467. Will you read out the return?—First: The total cost per horse keep for a year, including drivers' wages and all charges whatsoever, 8,712 *l.* 8 *s.* 3 *d.* (2.) The total number of horses average for the year 75. (3.) The cost of fodder per horse per week, including straw for bedding, averages 19 *s.* 3¼ *d.* The honourable Member asked for a separate return for the fodder, but they come into one account with us, and we could not separate them. No. 4 was that, and it was included in No. 3. (5.) Veterinary charges, shoeing and all other stable expenses, but not including drivers' wages, but inclusive of rents, harness, repairs, gas, &c., 866 *l.* 5 *s.* 8 *d.*; and (6.) The number of drivers 75, and their wages per week per driver 17 *s.* 6 *d.*

Mr. Collins.

6468. What would be the average?—A little less than 1 *l.* a week for the entire number of horses. There happen to be two or three gentlemen on No. 1 committee who know a great deal about horses and their keep, and who have a large number of horses themselves, and they devote really a good deal of personal attention to this matter, and cut everything as fine as they possibly can consistently with having the work done.

Sir Joseph M'Kenna.

6469. Those are full prices, are they not?—Our horses are powerful horses, and they work seven days in the week; the scavenging and watering is carried on during the Sunday.

Mr. Butt.

6470. The fire brigade, I believe, is a very efficient one?—I believe it is one of the most efficient in the three kingdoms; we would be better, certainly, if we had a little more money for the fire brigade, and I think we must try and get it in some way or another. For instance, there is no fire-brigade station on the north side of the city, and there is none on the North Wall; we want them very badly.

Mr. Brooks.

6471. Is that the reason that they never have fires there?—We have been fortunate up to this, but we cannot count on an exemption.

6472. Do you wish to say anything about the sanitary association, as to any suggestions that they have made to the corporation; have they made any?—They have made a large number of suggestions, but I think that Mr. Boyle has shown that they are pretty well attended to; we find a difficulty in dealing with the sanitary association, for one reason: a number of gentlemen who are our own sanitary officers, paid by ourselves, come before us in one capacity one day, and on another day they come before us as an amateur association, and they write us letters which are not of a very complimentary character, and we find a difficulty certainly in treating them in their dual capacity with proper respect sometimes, and with proper rigour at other times as our own officers.

Chairman.

6473. In those accounts of No. 1 committee, which appear to relate to the year ending the 31st of December 1875, I see one rather curious item: Cleansing river Liffey, and labourers' two weeks wages, 14 *l.* 15 *s.* 9 *d.*; is that all that was spent during the year?—I cannot give you personal information as regards the sums that are spent, but I presume that it was an exceptional sum spent by No. 1 committee, and charged against the public health committee. It is the duty of the public health committee to deal with the matter, and they probably asked the loan of some scavengers, and we gave them to them for a week or two, or something of that kind. I know that they spent a good deal of money trying to cleanse the bed of the river unsuccessfully.

6474. Mr. Norwood, in his evidence at Question 6013, said as follows: "It has been a serious loss to us that Colonel Lake felt it to be his duty consistently with the discharge of other public departments connected with the police, to withdraw six constables from us, and the corporation would willingly pay the salaries of those constables if the department would only let us have them;" has the corporation ever passed any resolution to the effect that they would willingly pay the salaries of those constables?—I do not think that it has ever come before the corporation, but I know that the public health committee are very anxious about it, although I am not aware whether they have passed any resolution or not. I should think that they have communicated their views to the Government. I am not a member of the public health committee; but I know that they were very anxious, and felt it a serious loss losing those men.

6475. Since Dr. Norwood gave this evidence, I have communicated with Colonel Lake, and although I could not give any pledge upon the subject, I think I may say that the Government would very favourably consider such an application if it were made?—I am sure that the corporation will be delighted to hear it, and I am quite certain that they will with alacrity take what steps may be necessary to request Colonel Lake to do it.

Sir Joseph M'Kenna.

6476. Does the corporation exercise any authority in connection with the vehicles plying for hire in Dublin?—No, they have no authority whatever over them. I wish they had, because some of them are very discreditable to my mind.

6477. Do you not think it very desirable that the municipality should have charge of the business within the metropolis, and that the municipal body should also have authority over the car drivers and coach drivers within the municipal bounds?—I certainly do. I do not think that they possibly could be worse managed than they are at present. I think we should be able to manage them better. It appears to me that we get over a great many of the cast cabs from London that they will not permit to be used here any longer; at least I do not know where they get their shabby ones, if that is not it.

6478. You have no share in the revenue derived from the fines from them, I presume?—We have not; and we consider that a great hardship.

6479. Have you any idea what those fines

amount

Mr. Gray.

4 July 1876.

Sir *Joseph M'Kenna*—continued.

amount to in a year?—No, I do not know what they amount to.

6480. Would you think that any new plan for the government of the City of Dublin would be complete that did not include a provision for giving the corporation power over the drivers of vehicles, and the vehicles which are used for the carriage of persons and goods within the metropolis?—I think it is a most desirable thing that we should have such power, and I think the corporation is the proper body to exercise it, undoubtedly. There are a very great number of matters of detail that require change, and if, as I have said, we were once relieved from the quorum difficulty, which really impedes our action in everything, I think we would go forward; I am quite certain that we should go forward for a General Improvement Bill, such as we went for in 1849, and it is very probable that we would go for all those improvements in such a Bill, which would also involve, probably, a total change in the *personnel* of the corporation, by means of a general election.

Dr. *Ward*.

6481. Talking of the medical officers, do you think that the salaries at present paid to the sanitary medical officers of Dublin are sufficient to do the work efficiently?—Some time ago I looked into the amount of duty which those gentlemen perform; there are 14 of them; and I found that one of them had reported 350 cases in a year, and certainly I do not think that 25 *l.* is enough for that; I found that another had reported five, and that he got an average of 5 *l.* each for the cases that he reported, and I think that is too much; I think that we ought to have some means of seeing that those gentlemen do their duty, and I do not know that we have any means at present.

6482. But to do their work efficiently they should make a very much larger number of reports than that gentleman who sent in five, and they would have to give up a great deal of time to it; do you think that a professional man is well paid with 25 *l.* a year?—We would rather give them a better salary, and have more strict control and see that they did their duty better.

6483. You think that that would be for the good of the city?—I think it would if we had the means, as I say, of seeing that they did their duty.

6484. Have you read the evidence which Mr. Sullivan gave before this Committee?—I have.

6485. Do you agree with him that impecuniosity is one of the principal reasons for the defects in the Dublin corporation?—I do agree with him in that, certainly; many go into the corporation and do an enormous amount of work. The average attendances of the members are at least two per week all round, including sick and everything; but they can do nothing satisfactorily with their present want of means, and they get no thanks for their labour; but I do not agree with Mr. Sullivan in saying that taking the body as a whole, there is a lack of intelligence amongst them.

6486. Do you agree with him that the method of curing that is by a re-valuation?—Yes, I do. I think that would be a convenient means.

6487. Do you agree with this statement of Mr. Sullivan's: "I think there is a want upon the corporation of Dublin of men who could afford to defy what would be called unpopularity in firmly and courageously carrying out some necessary reforms"?—I do not.

Dr. *Ward*—continued.

6488. Is not that a reproach to which every elective assembly is open?—Yes, of course more or less we are amenable to the opinion of our constituents. But Mr. Sullivan instanced the Bill of 1867 as being a case in point. That was a general Bill for new markets, for abattoirs and for a great many things; and that Bill would have been carried through had our quorum been what it should have been. There were a few members who obstructed it, and a few fell off too, but the better men in the corporation supported it. Mr. William Lane Joynt was Lord Mayor at the time, and he would have carried it through, I am told, but for the quorum difficulty. We shall never carry any great improvement through without almost insuperable difficulty so long as we are hampered by that quorum nuisance.

6489 What quorum would you recommend?—I think nine has been talked of here I do not care very much about the exact number, but that would be a good working quorum.

6490. Taking that view of the case, you would not coincide with Mr. Sullivan in asking that there should be concessions given by the popular party?—No, I think it is an utterly demoralising principle to say that because there is a certain section outside, of men who do not agree with the majority in politics, and who, therefore, abstain from joining in the general work, concessions should be made to them when they can come in if they like, under the present system. There is no doubt whatever about it that any first-class merchant in Dublin, no matter what his politics, could enter the corporation whenever he liked, but if they will not, I should not go an inch towards giving them concessions, because respectable men can come in if they like.

6491. You think it would be retrograde legislation?—I think it would be so, and I think it would be demoralising.

6492. Are you in favour of enlarging the boundaries of the borough?—Yes.

6493. To what extent?—I think that what Mr. Sullivan suggested would be convenient; he took the Tolca and the River Dodder as being the new boundaries; but that, of course, would be a question for a Royal Commission if it were decided to be done.

6494. You agree with him, do you not, as to the necessity for abattoirs and a public market?—I do. Although a number of the slaughterhouses have been proved not to be that nuisance to health which it is supposed, I think they are very injurious in other ways; I think that they are injurious morally, and that they should be abolished. I may mention that an effort is being made now to introduce abattoirs, for there is a motion upon the paper about it, but I do not believe that we shall be able to carry it with the quorum difficulty that stares us in the face *àpropos* of everything.

6495. What have you to say to this statement of Mr. Sullivan's, in his answer to Question 4688: "I wish to impress the Committee with this fact, that the reforms which are needed in Dublin require a strong hand just now, and that the corporation itself can hardly be trusted to undertake them"?—That is what I deny completely; if we were relieved, as I have said, of the difficulty of the quorum, we would do everything

Mr. *Gray*.

4 July 1876.

Dr. *Ward*—continued.

everything else that is necessary ourselves; any reform which changed the *personnel* would probably effect the improvement in the council which is desired by a certain section. Just as in 1849, after a battle of a year or two, all sections of the citizens united in trying to put in the best men of all parties; so, too, it would be now if we went for a General Improvement Bill.

6496. Do you approve of the suggestion with regard to the franchise in Dublin by Mr. Sullivan, namely, what is called the three-cornered plan?—Theoretically and personally I have no objection to a minority vote; but in Dublin I am quite certain that it would not work well, because it would be felt as an additional effort to give more than their fair weight to a certain party; that is the objection to it in Dublin, that it would be felt that it was introduced solely from that motive.

6497. Do you think that the gas ought to be in the hands of the corporation?—Certainly; I do not mean to say at all that it would be an economical thing to purchase it now, but had we not been obstructed, and had we not been upset on a mere technical point in 1873, by gentlemen occupying a leading position, who should, I think, have known better and acted better, we would now have been in the possession of the gasworks, and be making a profit of 20,000 *l.* a year from them.

6498. May I ask you whether they are not the same set of gentlemen who generally obstruct the corporation?—Yes; you find them under different names; here one day and there the next; but if you follow them they are always the same.

6499. And they complain of the incapacity of the corporation after obstructing them?—Yes, after obstructing us and doing us that serious injury, they now complain.

6500. Do you think that the fire brigade in Dublin is equal to the city requirements?—No.

6501. Do you think it is at all like being adequate?—No, I am sure it is not. It is very efficient so far as it goes, but it is a great deal too small. We want two more stations at least, and we want a very important matter, namely, telegraphic communication between the various fire brigade stations and the central points in the city; that is a thing which we want very badly if we could only find the means of doing it.

6502. What does your present staff consist of?—I think there are about 18 men, and a superintendant and a sub-superintendant.

6503. Then how many would you recommend?—I would double that number. I may say that that is supported altogether out of what is known as the public water rate; there is no special rate levied for the fire brigade.

6504. Do you consider the salaries of the Dublin corporation officers too large or too small?—They are certainly not too large. I think they are too small. But with regard to the officers there are a great many details that we could be improved in. We are compelled by Act of Parliament to appoint many of our officers during good behaviour. If I had my way I would not appoint certain officers more than from year to year, so that if we found them inefficient, or if we found them incompetent, we could get rid of them. It is very hard when electing a man at first to ascertain his true quality. I would let him go if we found him inefficient. I think there is another matter which it is important to mention, and that is with reference to our committees. Under the Act of the 3 & 4 Vict., I think, but under one of our Acts, there are three standing committees fixed by the Act of Parliament. At the time that was very well, because there were only three committees, but now we have six committees, and the consequence is that men have to serve on two committees, and sometimes on three. I have an idea that 10 men on a committee can do the work very much better than 20, and I am sure that in the experience of most men who have to do with committees. I should like to have power to divide the work amongst six committees, 10 for each, instead of putting men on two or three committees. There are a great many things of that kind that we could improve largely had we the power, and were we not restricted in everything by the quorum difficulty.

Mr. *Kavanagh*.

6505. Is it a quorum that restricts you in those little minor details?—It is, because two or three obstructives with that large quorum can make it an almost interminable work to carry through any improvement.

6506. You mean by walking out, and leaving the quorum not made?—Quite so; or by staying in and watching till two or three men go out, and there are only perhaps 18 or 19 men in the room, and then forthwith counting the roll. I would put it to honourable Members how the business of the House of Commons would be done if it were necessary that 220 members should always be there when any thing was to be done, and when there were 219, somebody should send you home.

Mr. *J. P. Corry*.

6507. With reference to the franchise, you say that the Corporation of Dublin are of one opinion that the franchise should be assimilated to that in England?—Yes.

6508. That is to say, it should be a household franchise?—Yes, that is so.

6509. How does it happen, in your opinion, that the number of ratepayers are not larger on the burgess roll than they are just now?—The three years' limit of residence strikes a great number off. A man must reside for three years in the same house; that strikes a large number off, and some of them first-class men; then although we have a nominal household rating, as a matter of fact, no man who is rated at less than 4 *l.* is put on the rating books, therefore he does not get on the burgess roll; but the three years' limit is a great obstruction, and it is an obstruction to a good class of men very frequently.

6510. Is Dublin at present not exceptional in its franchise to any other borough in Ireland?—It is.

6511. How would you deal with a case of this kind where the number of ratepayers were in this proportion: where the number of ratepayers who pay 8 *l.* and under is 25,000, and the amount of taxation which is levied from them is 16,000 *l.*; but where the number of ratepayers paying 8 *l.* and upwards is 10,000, and the amount of taxation which they pay is upwards of 70,000;

Mr. *J. P. Corry*—continued.

Mr. *Grey.*

4 July 1876.

70,000; supposing that a reduction of the franchise took place in that borough, how would you protect the 10,000 against the 25,000?—I think that the 10,000, if they took any practical interest in municipal affairs, would always be thoroughly competent to protect themselves. There is a legitimate influence attaching to men of property and position, and I think the 25,000 poor men would readily elect a sufficient number out of the 10,000 rich men to represent them. That, I consider, is the legitimate influence of property which can never be destroyed, except by the individual holders themselves, by their neglect, or something of that kind. But certainly I do think it is totally contrary to the whole course of modern legislation to say, that because a man pays a larger proportion individually of taxes, you would give him a larger number of votes, or any preponderating influence proportionate to the amount of taxation which he pays.

6512. What I want to point out to you is this: that the property valued at 8 *l.* and upwards, would be entirely swamped by the number of those who pay a smaller amount of taxation, and that the chances are that the entire representation on the town council might get into the hands of the people paying the smaller amount of taxation?—The only point on which I differ from you is in saying that it would be swamped; theoretically it might be swamped, I grant; and it would be swamped if the rich class that you refer to totally abstained from taking any interest in the matter, if they altogether held aloof; but if they took any interest in the matter, if they desired election, or if they desired to influence the election, their personal influence would prevent their being swamped. In fact, taking household suffrage for the Parliamentary elections, that has not swamped the House of Commons with men selected from that lower stratum that was admitted under the household suffrage.

6513. Do you not think that there is a considerable difference between the Parliamentary franchise, where they cannot and the municipal franchise where it is possible that a large number of ratepayers who pay a small amount of taxation and who would possibly get a preponderance upon the corporation, were expending the ratepayers' money?—One of the great functions of Parliament, after all, is the spending of taxes, and they are elected by men who pay the least taxes, as a matter of fact. I grant you, theoretically, the rich minority might be swamped by the poor majority, but I deny as a matter of practice that such would be the result. At present every man in Dublin who is rated at 4 *l.* has a vote, but they do not return men who are simply rated at 4 *l.* I have a return here which shows that the average rating of the members of the corporation is 167 *l.* They are very wealthy men, many of them. The same argument would, in a modified form, hold at this moment, but it does not operate as a matter of practice; our difficulty is to get the wealthy classes to take an interest.

6514. Is that return in evidence?—No, I will give this return in. If it is looked over it will be found that of the burgesses of Dublin at present going down to the 4 *l.* franchise, the majority of them must be poor men, but they do not for that reason select poor representatives. Nor would they do it under an assimilation to the English system. That is at least my view.

6515. Then you would give no protection to the large ratepayer against the small ratepayer?—I think there is abundant protection in his personal character and influence if he desires to exercise it. I would give him no exceptional privileges, which I think would probably result to his own injury, and undoubtedly would result to the injury to the community.

6516. You think that the system which is adopted in the poor law franchise is not a desirable one to be extended?—I think it is a very undesirable one, and I think that the best evidence of that is not theory at all, but practice. We have it at work in Dublin at this moment; we know how it operates, and certainly the experience that we have had of it does not tend to make us desirous of its extension.

6517. Do you think that it operates in the same way all over Ireland and England?—I do not know about England, but I certainly think, in fact I am quite convinced, that the boards of guardians elected under the multiple system in Ireland are not equal to, or, at any rate, not better than the members of municipal councils elected under the single vote system. I am quite certain of that.

6518. Are you aware that in the townships the qualification is very much higher for the members of the town commissioners than for the poor law guardians?—Yes; but I am not talking about townships, I am talking about municipalities; but I prefer very much dealing with something that I have more of a personal knowledge of. I say that we have a sample of the multiple vote system in Dublin, and it is enough to discourage us from desiring its extension. I will take the port and docks board, which was mentioned here as a body whose example we should follow. The port and docks board undoubtedly is composed of individuals of the highest respectability, and those who are elected are elected under the multiple vote system; I do not think that the port and docks board is a criterion, in the first place, because it is really a trading body looking after trade interests. But when it comes to deal with the interests of the public, I do not think that it does look after them as well as we do. It shows a spirit of exclusiveness and a spirit of illiberality in all its dealings which is the bane of Ireland, and which we ought to try to do away with, instead of increasing it.

6519. Following up that idea of yours, that the port and docks board is elected as a trade body to look after trade interests, do you not think that the large owners of property would also protect themselves in looking after property if they had multiple votes in municipalities?—I do think it is a portion of the duty of municipalities to look after the interests of property; but they have very much wider and larger duties than that. It is their duty to look after the interests of the poorer classes and the classes who are not represented at all. No trades body, I consider, have this responsible duty. It is simply the interests of their own individual trade that they look to, and in benefiting that, they benefit the city, doubtless; but they look to that first. Their duty commences and ends there; but our duty does not commence and end in looking after the interests merely of the ratepayers;

Mr. Gray.

4 July 1876.

Mr. J. P. Corry—continued.

payers; there are 5,000 or 6,000 ratepayers who are voters in Dublin, but we have to look after the interests of 300,000 or 400,000 individuals. I think that the functions are totally different.

6520. Are you aware of any instances in which the port and docks board have neglected their duty in any way?—I am aware of an instance in which I think there is great neglect. Constantly sailors are drowned along the quays; inquests have been held, and verdicts have been returned that they are drowned in consequence of the unprotected state of the quays. A case came before my own knowledge about two months ago, in which a drunken sailor walked over the quay and was drowned. The captain of his ship testified that Dublin was the most unprotected port he had ever been at, and the coroner's jury returned a verdict that he died in consequence of the unprotected state of the quay walls. Thereupon we got a letter written to the port and docks board, asking them whether they would protect them; but I do not think we have got an answer, and I do not see any prospect of their doing it, because they have been asked again and again to do it. Drunken sailors are cheap, I presume; and they say they have no money for the purpose. That, I think, is a thing that a body like the corporation would not do and could not do.

6521. I have no doubt you have seen the River Thames here; what protection is there to prevent people from falling in?—In all the public portions of it there is a wall; there is none in Dublin at the part I speak of.

6522. Where the ships are lying is there a wall?—Where the ships are lying I think they are shut in at night, more or less; in the docks the gates are shut, at any rate. It is scarcely a public thoroughfare along the docks.

6523. Along the river quays in Belfast we have no protection at all?—Does the honourable Member mean to say that they have no chains and no watchmen?

6524. We have watchmen?—But in Dublin we have no watchmen. I do not suggest that a wall should be built; I suggest that, having the sworn evidence of this captain, who said that he had been in every seaport in the kingdom, and he had never met with one so unprotected as Dublin, something should be done. Chains might be put up, or watchmen employed by the port and docks board.

Dr. *Ward.*

6525. That was not the only case in which the coroner's jury have given such a verdict?—No; there are a few of them drowned every year.

Mr. *J. P. Corry.*

6526. That is the only instance where you think the port and docks board neglect their duty?—I make no accusation of general neglect of duty against the port and docks board; I think that they look after their special duties uncommonly well; but I very much doubt whether they would look after general duties, duties to the whole body of citizens as contra-distinguished from special trade interests. I do not think they are constituted for that purpose, and I do not think they do it either.

6527. I suppose I may gather from your evidence that if the municipal franchise in Dublin and all over Ireland were reduced to what it is in England, the character of the corporation would be improved instead of being deteriorated?—I think it would be improved. I think that widening the franchise would improve the *personnel;* it would probably put in a better class of men. I think that a narrow franchise, consisting of the lower class of *bourgeoisie,* is not a desirable franchise; and I think it is always better to depend upon a popular franchise; I think it generally returns better men.

6528. I gather from the whole tenor of your evidence that you think that the charges which have been made against the Dublin corporation from time to time have been totally unfounded?—So many charges have been made, and are made so constantly, that I do not know that I have read them all; but as a member of the council who has no personal interest to serve, and who personally is not connected with any of the things which have been attacked, I believe the attacks to be unfounded; I believe that the persons who have made them have not taken the trouble to make themselves acquainted with the facts; that they have been to a considerable extent influenced, I do not say by personal motives, but I think blinded by party feeling. They oppose everything that we propose.

6529. Do you mean to say that the opposition arises entirely from one political party?—Yes, there can be no doubt about it; it is purely political. Take the opposition to the Vartry Waterworks which was carried on for years; they eventually agreed to submit everything to a Royal Commission, and to abide by the result; but after the result was come to and the corporation proceeded under the verdict of the Royal Commission, the opposition was as fierce as ever, and that was a purely political opposition. I have in my bag a report written by my late father, in which he describes how step by step they fought this improvement, and that really one would have imagined that it was a new battle of the Boyne; religious and political animosities were introduced into it, when it was a simple question of where they could get the best water. That is a sample of the entire thing that is carried on in Dublin; and I believe that the result of this investigation showing to the entire of the citizens that the charges which have been so frequently circulated against the council are without foundation, will dispel a great deal of the prejudice which has been got up against the corporation, and will place us in a very much better position, and enable us to do a great deal more good than we could have done before, hampered as we were with suspicions and charges which we never could get in such a form as to be able to deal with them and crush them.

6530. Are the Committee to gather from your evidence that the association called the sanitary association is a purely political one?—I do not go so far as that at all; I think it has a political tinge; I think if you take and examine its *personnel,* you will find that to be so; but I do not go so far as that; I think that they do not do their business in the way they should do it. The honourable Baronet, the Member for Dublin, instanced a case in London, and he quoted the report of the St. Mary Abbots' Association, but the way in which they went to work was a reasonable way; they selected certain candidates for

Mr. *J. P. Corry*—continued.

for the vestry, and worked for those candidates, and pushed forward their claims and brought them in, and got them to carry out the sanitary improvements that were required. The Dublin Sanitary Association never does anything like that; they write letters to the newspapers, and bring out reports; they write sharp letters to us, which elicit possibly sharp replies or silence, but I never heard of their going to try to influence an election in a ward by putting in a good man instead of a bad man; if they did something practical instead of mere complaints, I think they would do more good; I do not at all suggest that they are not actuated by the best motives; I have endeavoured to co-operate personally with them as far as I possibly could where I thought they were right.

6531. Take the gentlemen who compose the citizens' committee with reference to the sewage scheme, do you consider that they are influenced by political motives?—To accuse men of being influenced altogether by political motives is scarcely fair; I do not think they are, but I think they are prejudiced by political feeling. I have no doubt that they do not imagine that they are influenced by political motives, but ever since the 1839 corporation was returned with a majority of Liberals, and ever since then it has been held by Liberals, it has been systematically attacked by the Conservative party and by the Conservative press in Dublin. I do not blame them for it; it is a mere matter of fact that every person in Dublin knows perfectly well.

6532. Do you think that an idea such as you express is in the minds of the corporation when they receive letters from such an association as the sanitary association, and that it leads them not to give that deference and respect to them that they otherwise would do?—The corporation as a body never receive representations from the sanitary association; it is the public health committee. When once we get into committee, we always forbid politics to be discussed, and I will say, whilst upon that point, that no communication whatever from the sanitary association was ever neglected. The public health committee considered that certain letters of the sanitary association were not written in that courteous manner in which they should be written, and they also considered that many of them were dictated by their own sanitary officers, acting in another capacity as amateur members of the sanitary association. Those two motives certainly have actuated them to a very considerable extent in ignoring or declining to reply to their communications and to get into a wordy war with the sanitary association, but they do the work, and there never was a single communication from the sanitary association, as was proved by Mr. Boyle, that was not attended to.

6533. Could you give the Committee any instance in which the sanitary association has not put forward a candidate, because the test was a political one in the ward?—They never put forward a candidate at all; they never devote themselves to that; that, I think would be a good practical purpose for them.

6534. Then I gather that the contests are not political in the different wards?—Yes; they are to a considerable extent political, as in all municipalities, but a good Tory, even in a Liberal ward, I take it, would beat a bad Liberal, and *vice versâ*.

Mr. *J. P. Corry*—continued.

6535. Who is the president of the sanitary association in Dublin?—I think Dr. Churchill either is or was the president.

6536. Is it not the late Member for Dublin?—He may be the present president; I daresay he is.

6537. I see Mr Pim is president?—I was under the impression that Dr. Churchill had been.

6538. Of course Mr. Pim is not a Conservative?—I do not know really what you would define Mr. Pim's politics to be.

6539. You would rather refer that question to himself; possibly he would be able to give it more satisfactorily?—Yes, I think so.

Mr. *Kavanagh.*

6540. Did not Mr. Pim sit on the Liberal side of the House?—He did.

6541. So far as that goes, has be made any declaration of his politics?—So far as that goes, yes; but I think Mr. Pim might now be defined as what you would call a moderate Conservative.

Mr. *Bruce.*

6542. With regard to the sanitary association, I think you have just stated to the Committee that one of the reasons why the public health committee of the corporation did not attend to their letters was because they thought they had been written by their own officers?—I never stated that they did not attend to them, but that they did not answer them. I am not a member of the committee, but I believe it was under the impression with regard to the sanitary association, that to a certain extent, the active members of it were composed of their own sanitary medical officers acting as amateurs, and dealing, therefore, with the corporation in a manner, and adopting a tone, which they would not adopt in their other capacity as paid officers of the council.

6543. Do you know how many of those paid officers are members of the sanitary association?—Dr. Charles Moore is a member. You will understand me distinctly as not suggesting that those gentlemen really have been responsible for any individual letters. In fact, I do not know a letter that the public health committee complain of; but they say there is a tone running through them which is offensive. Dr. Charles Moore is a paid sanitary officer of the corporation, and he is also a member and an active member, I think, of the sanitary association. Dr. Speedy is the same, Dr. Purcell is the same, Dr. Kenny the same, Dr. Peill the same, and Dr. Dudley White the same. That is one-half, say, of our sanitary medical officers; Dr. Grimshaw is not one.

6544. You say there are six of the sanitary committee who are officers under the Dublin Corporation?—Yes, that are paid by the Dublin Corporation.

6545. And that one of the reasons why the representations of the sanitary association were not acknowledged, was that it was considered that the letters were written by those officers?—I daresay it was; I should think so. When I say written by those officers, I scarcely mean to convey that, but that they had something to do with

Mr. *Grey.*

4 July 1876.

Mr. *Gray*.

4 July 1876.

Mr. *Bruce*—continued.

with them, that they were acting in a double capacity, and that it would be better for them to come to our officers and make their reports to us, than go to the sanitary association and get formal letters written to be published in the newspapers, and if we did not give a proper reply to them, an attack to be founded upon them.

6546. Is this merely suspicion, or have you any grounds for forming that opinion?—I am very sorry that Councillor Norwood was not asked that question, because I am not a member of the committee, and I do not know whether there were any grounds, or what they were, but when you find gentlemen acting as members of the association, and when you find them in a double capacity, the assumption would be a natural one.

6547. Do you say that it would be a natural assumption, and a right assumption on the part of the public health committee, that those letters which they objected to were written by their own officers?—I think it would be. If I were on the committee I would have assumed that.

6548. It is upon that assumption that you make that statement to the Committee?—Yes, quite so; not upon any absolute ground. I am not a member of the committee, as I mentioned. I am a member of No. 1 committee, and I am very anxious to get upon the public health committee, but I have not yet succeeded.

6549. Are the expenses of the fire brigade at present a part of the expenses of the sanitary administration of the city?—No, it is paid out of the public water rate, and it is under the water works committee.

6550. Can you tell me whether the cost of the fire brigade is equal to the cost of the sanitary administration of the city?—I know that the cost of the sanitary administration of the city is not much; we have never levied a rate yet; I am inclined to think they are about the same, speaking roughly, I cannot speak from absolute knowledge, but my impression is that they are about the same. I think from about 2,000 *l.* to 3,000 *l.* is expended on each.

6551. What is your opinion of the sanitary condition of Dublin?—My opinion of the sanitary condition of Dublin is that it requires great improvement, but I must qualify that by saying that, from what I have been able to learn, it is not so very much worse than the sanitary condition of many other towns, but that it is undoubtedly very bad, and that we want great improvement, there can be no mistake whatever about.

6552. I think that the leading journal in Dublin, with which you are so intimately connected, at one time sent a sanitary commissioner to inquire into the sanitary condition of Dublin?—It did.

6553. And that he reported, did he not?—Yes, he reported.

6554. Were his reports favourable or unfavourable?—They were very unfavourable. Will you pardon me for explaining that I have no doubt for a moment that those reports were absolutely accurate, so far as that gentleman's knowledge went; I do not mention his name, although I have great personal respect for the gentleman, but I may explain that he is a member of the sanitary association, and possibly he might have taken, therefore a little more gloomy

Mr. *Bruce*—continued.

view of the conduct of the council than he otherwise would.

6555. But still you think that perfect reliance is to be placed upon his reports?—I place perfect reliance upon them; I never checked them in any way; I said, "Write those reports; I rely upon you to make them accurate."

6556. In the "Freeman's Journal" were there not some very severe strictures in connection with this state of things, passed upon the management of the corporation?—Undoubtedly, based upon those reports obtained as I tell you.

6557. But still the reports, in your opinion, were quite accurate?—I had no means of judging of that further than by the character which the gentleman has. He is a gentleman of high character.

6558. Do you think that the deduction which was made from those reports, and which called forth those severe strictures, was a just and fair deduction?—I have no doubt that the deductions were pretty fair. You will understand that in newspaper writing you must put it in pretty strong terms to have effect. I daresay that quite as sensational reports could have been written of other places. They were written under the circumstances I mentioned.

6559. At the time it was supposed that the corporation had really done little or nothing to improve the sanitary condition of Dublin?—I think that was supposed, but I think the generality of the public have very little knowledge of the real work done by the corporation, and therefore it is that I say that we anticipate the greatest possible good from the result of the investigations of this committee.

6560. Perhaps you will allow me, in reference to this matter, to read to you a short extract of what appears in the "Freeman's Journal" of the 24th September 1873, in one of the leading articles; that was just about the time, I think, when your commissioner was making his report.

6561. It says: "In consequence of information received within the last few days, we visited a certain house in Meath-street well known to the sanitary authorities in Dublin and to the magistrates." It then goes on to describe the state of the house, and then it says: "The yard which encroaches upon what was originally the back part of the house, is in a shocking state; its surface is nearly quite covered with manure, and a reeking pool of filthy fluid lies over its lowest portion. There are pigstyes and pigs, while there is a complete absence of any sanitary accommodation whatever; the place is a nuisance in every sense of the word. We believe that the owner has been repeatedly summoned, and that on one occasion Dr. Mapother inspected the place in person, and of course condemned it; but the law has been of no avail to abate the nuisance, and the fact remains. One of the worst nuisances in all Dublin has again and again been reported upon, and still flourishes as foul as ever." Is not that a very severe comment upon the sanitary management of the corporation of Dublin?—That is a very severe comment upon the law; we say that where a summons has been taken out you ought to blame the dilatory operations which must be gone through under the present sanitary laws which Mr. Boyle explained; it takes an enormous time now to touch the most apparent nuisance; I know nothing about that case,

Mr. Gray. 4 July 1876.

Mr. Bruce—continued.

case, but I assume that the public health committee did its best in summoning the man, and what more could it do.

6562. Then the interpretation to be put upon this state of Dublin is that the law is insufficient?—I think so in that case. We ought to do more sanitary work, and I think we have been deterred too much by our anxiety not to put on rates, and certainly if I had my way, I would put on immediately a sanitary rate, and I would do more sanitary work and do more radical work about it, but then the ratepayers have a curious objection to being taxed.

6563. You think that this indisposition on the part of the corporation to interfere is partly owing to their knowledge that the rates necessarily would be increased?—Just in the same way as Parliament hesitates very much about increasing the income tax a penny.

6564. Still the fact remains?—Yes; I think on the part of the corporation there is too much disinclination to levy additional rates, which they have power to do. They have power under the Sanitary Acts; but it is in a very complex, roundabout way that they can levy a rate. I would like to see them given power to levy a special direct sanitary rate for sanitary purposes; they have no such power at present to levy a special rate or keep a special sanitary account.

6565. Do you think that this fear on the part of the corporation of incurring unpopularity by levying rates for those necessary sanitary expenses is at all due to particular members of the corporation being influenced by the constituencies which they represent?—I do not know; I can only give you information on such subjects by dealing with special cases. When they tried to put the Artizans' Dwellings Act into force there was an objection to the expense by the leader of the Conservative party which stopped us for a long while; he is also really the managing man of the public health committee.

6566. Will you give us his name?—Mr. Byrne. I think there is a disinclination to have a rate levied, but I think we shall have to levy a special rate for sanitary works.

6567. Was Mr. Byrne the only person who objected?—He was the gentleman, undoubtedly, who objected and stopped us going on with the Artizans' Dwellings Act as fast as I was anxious to have done, and I think I can say, without accusing or misrepresenting him, that in the public health committee he has always, so far, strenuously opposed a sanitary rate. Now the fact is, that the borough fund is overdrawn, and we must impose a sanitary rate.

6568. I suppose that Mr. Byrne would not himself have stopped it if the majority of the corporation had been in favour of introducing that Act?—Mr. Byrne is a very able and a very active member of the corporation, and he has an enormous amount of personal influence, especially in the public health committee, and I think practically he could stop anything that he desired to stop on that committee. He is a gentleman who devotes an enormous amount of his time and an enormous amount of labour to corporate affairs, and the influence which he possesses is a very considerable and a perfectly legitimate one, it is simply due to the work which he does, and to the knowledge which he possesses.

6569. And also, I suppose, to his being supported in his views by the majority of the corporation or of the committee on which he acts?—Certainly.

6570. I think you have said before that the majority of the corporation are Liberals?—They are. I think it shows their liberality that in a great many matters they are practically guided by Mr. Byrne, who is a Conservative.

6571. In opposing those necessary sanitary regulations, do you mean?—I do not think that those sanitary regulations ever came before the corporation as a body. It is the duty of the committee to take the initiative in such matters. I do not think that the public health committee have ever before formally proposed to levy a sanitary rate, or a borough rate for sanitary purposes, but I believe they are about to do it now.

6572. It must be initiated, you think, in the committee?—Ordinarily, in such matters, the initiative is in the Committee, or it might have its initiative in the council; any member can propose anything he likes, but the ordinary course is for the committee having charge of the expenditure to suggest the proper means for dealing with it.

6573. I think you mentioned something about Mr. Pim having been invited to become a candidate for the representation of a Liberal ward?—Yes, and not for the first time. I, myself, in September 1873, had been speaking to my father about the desirability of trying to get some of those gentlemen who were so active in finding out faults, to come in and do their share of the work, and I instanced Mr. Pim. He asked me to speak to him, and it so happened that the next day I met him, and I asked him why he would not go in. I told him that I had no influence in the matter, but I told him, on behalf of my father, who had a great deal of influence with the Liberal party of Dublin, that the Liberals would put him in if the Conservatives would not, if he would stand, but he refused.

Mr. Brooks.

6574 Which of the Messrs. Pim do you refer to?—I refer to Mr. Joseph Pim. Mr. Thomas Pim, his brother, who was an active opponent in the gas case, was invited by a deputation, or by some gentlemen, a few days ago, to stand for the Mansion House ward, but he refused. Mr. Joseph Pim was then invited, and he refused, and Mr. Joseph Pim gave as a reason that he was only a burgess by courtesy, that is to say, if he had been opposed at the revision court, his name might have been struck off, but his name being on he might have been perfectly certain that no person would have struck it off. I pressed him very strongly, and showed him that it would be a most desirable thing if men of his position would enter the corporation, as I hoped it would lead to two or three men like him coming in.

6575. Did he agree with your idea that it was absolutely his duty to come in, if he could come in, instead of merely criticising outside?—He does not take that view of it.

Mr. Bruce.

6576. You wish to inform the Committee that Mr. Joseph Pim has been more than once pressed by the Liberal party to allow himself to be put in nomination?—Yes.

Mr. Gray.

4 July 1876.

Mr. *Brien*—continued.

6577. Would you believe Mr. Joseph Pim himself if he were to tell you that that was not so?—I should believe that he had forgotten the circumstances, but that if I brought them to his memory he would remember them at once, because I could tell him where I met him, and all about the conversation.

6578. I find in the "Freeman's Journal" a report of a meeting in Dublin, on the 20th of June last, in which Mr. Joseph Pim is reported to have said, "He was not aware of any member of the Executive Sanitary Association having been asked to become a member of the corporation and having refused. As a matter of fact he had never been asked to become a member of the corporation." "In fact, he was informed on Saturday by a lawyer that he was disqualified. As a matter of fact he was a burgess by the courtesy of Mr. Dennehy. He was objected to by the representatives of the great Liberal party in the Royal Exchange Ward, and these were the gentlemen who, he was told, were most anxious to return him as a member for the Royal Exchange Ward if he would come forward. He did not believe it was the business of the corporation to indulge in political matters, and he would never enter it as a political partisan." That was a report of the speech made on the 20th June, and I imagine it is a true and verbatim report, because it appears in the "Freeman." I think that is evidence on the part of Mr. Pim which rather contradicts the idea which you have put before the Committee?—Quite so. I think that this is due to a lapse of memory on the part of Mr. Joseph Pim, or to the fact that possibly he assumed that my merely speaking in my father's name and my own was not a proposal from the Liberal party, that it was only from us individually. He may have taken that view, but I think myself that the fact is that he forgets the circumstance. I remember it perfectly. I met him in Dame-street and stopped him, and I spoke to him upon it, and he said that there would be no good, in any case, in a single man going in; that a single man could do no good, and even if he went in, if he did not vote for every political crotchet of whichever party put him in, they would put him out at the next election. I tried to impress upon him that he was wrong in both his views. I am quite certain that if I met Mr. Pim and reminded him of these facts, he would say that he had forgotten the circumstances; also, he was pressed the other day and refused.

6579. Are you satisfied of the identity of the gentleman that you are speaking of?—Quite so; I do know that he was pressed the other day, and he refused practically on the same grounds. I do not speak of my experience as a member of the council, but I have a knowledge of these matters, for years having to look at such things; and I do not believe that a Conservative within the last 10 years at any rate ever was turned out of the council on account of his political opinions, or for the matter of that, a Liberal either. I do not think that either of them would be, so long as they did their business fairly. If a man does not attend then he is attacked, whether he is a Conservative or a Liberal, and if Mr. Pim had once gone in he never would have been put out so long as he desired to stay in.

6580. But there have been within the last 10 years Conservatives who have been unseated?—

Mr. *Brien*—continued.

Of course there have. The late Lord Mayor, Alderman Durdin, was unseated.

6581. It has been always owing to some personal fault?—Some personal objection.

6582. In fact the Liberal party in Dublin act completely up to their name?—I think you would search the United Kingdom in vain to find a body having such a preponderating power as the Liberal party in Dublin which exercises it with such moderation, and that is a matter of simple proof, and not of opinion.

6583. At all events they do not exercise that preponderating power in a way which will give their opponents a voice which can be exercised with any degree of influence in the corporation; they take care to keep them in a minority?—They keep them in proportion to the ratepayers; but I have to point to the way in which they exercise that power in electing the Lord Mayor from the minority every alternate year, a thing which I do not think is done in any other town in the United Kingdom. I do not know whether it is done in Belfast, but I am not aware of it if it is.

6584. I think you began your examination with informing us that the corporation of Dublin have sent you here in some measure to contradict the evidence given by the other nominee of the corporation who attended on the former day, namely, Dr. Norwood?—As to Dr. Norwood and myself, a sub-committee of six were first appointed to deal with this matter, the assumption of the council then being that it was a pure question of franchise; but when it was found that it also involved questions of administration in the council, it was felt that both sides should be represented as regards that aspect of the inquiry, and, therefore, Dr. Norwood and myself were nominated. The council, however, never having wavered in its views as to the question of franchise, desired that there should be no ambiguity whatsoever as to its opinions upon that point. Dr. Norwood comes forward as a representative member of the council to deal with the questions of administration which had been mentioned before the committee, and he gave very fairly his opinions, as an individual, with reference to the franchise.

6585. At all events that resolution which was passed by the corporation to which you have referred I think seems to imply that you were sent here to contradict certain evidence that Dr. Norwood has given?—Not to contradict it, but to explain that it is not the opinion of the council. It would be absurd for the council to have any such opinion; they having already petitioned in very strong terms against the Bill which has been introduced, I think, by yourself and other honourable Members.

6586. Was it a meeting summoned specially to pass that resolution?—It was.

6587. With what notice?—With the usual notice.

6588. What is the usual notice?—I think it is three or four clear days; in fact it was summoned immediately Dr. Norwood's evidence was read in Dublin; there is no doubt about that, because it was felt that possibly there might be a certain amount of ambiguity about his evidence.

6589. Are those the circumstances that the evidence was read, the matter was talked over, and you were authorised to say that you do not agree?

Mr. *Bruen*—continued.

agree?—No, I was authorised simply to express to the Committee the views already come to by the council.

6590. Was the resolution passed unanimously at that meeting?—No; it was passed by a very large majority.

6591. There was a quorum then?—There was a quorum then. Yesterday we had to elect the Lord Mayor, and generally we form a quorum for that purpose.

6592. It is the practice, you have informed us, that special meetings of the corporation should be summoned to discuss political matters?—Whenever they have to be discussed. I think there were only three or four within the last three years.

6593. But you cannot say at how many ordinary meetings of the corporation political matters have been discussed during that time?—I cannot, but they are very few; it is very difficult to define political matters. With reference to this Committee, it was purely a question of the gentlemen who should be sent forward to give evidence here that was discussed; but again those Bills which had been introduced were discussed, and they may be called political matters. We consider that they affect our interests, whether adversely or favourably, and we are bound to take some notice of them. I suppose they may be called political discussions, but they are forced upon us.

6594. Do you think it is at all owing to the fact of political considerations being introduced into the ordinary meetings of the corporation that so often a quorum does not attend, or that a quorum having been formed, a sufficient number leave the room to prevent the meeting being legally continued?—You must understand that I, of course, speak as a very strong party man. Sometimes a meeting of the council is dissolved if a political matter comes on. If the Conservative section see themselves in a minority of the members present, they sometimes adopt the *ruse* of walking out in a body to dissolve the meeting; but they never adopt that *ruse* if they have a working majority on that day to carry their point.

6595. Has that ever happened?—Yes, I think so.

6596. Can you point out, or can you tell the Committee of any occasion on which it happened?—I cannot specifically, but undoubtedly it has happened sometimes. I do not mean to say on any question of large political importance, when a special meeting or anything of that kind had been summoned. Of course the majority take care to have their views carried.

6597. Do you remember, in fact, an occasion whenever it occurred that you can point out in which there has been a Conservative majority?—Not that I can point out. My personal recollection does not extend very far back; it is a general one.

6598. Your contention is that the Conservatives, whenever they have a chance, when political questions are discussed, walk out, and so produce the state of non-quorum; but that if, on the other hand, they happen to be in the majority, the Liberals never do the same thing?—I have never known the Liberals do anything of the kind, and I do not say that the Conservatives always do; but sometimes they do it. As

Mr. *Bruen*—continued.

for political discussions in the corporation, I think the business of municipal representatives, or their rights, at any rate, extend something further than the mere discussion of scavenging and such works, and that they are perfectly within their right of action in discussing political matters, and I think it would be a misfortune to the country if they were precluded from doing it.

6599. Your opinion is that a change in the rule requiring a large quorum would produce all that is necessary for the corporation to become a thoroughly efficient body?—My opinion is that it would give us power to carry out the necessary reforms ourselves. We want a general Improvement Bill in Dublin, no doubt, and if we were to go forward for it, I believe we would carry it soon were we freed from that restriction.

6600. Can you explain to the Committee how that would come about?—A few men, or one, two, or three men, have it now in their power so to hamper the action of the council on any matter, that it tires people out so that they cannot carry things through, except they have herculean power. My father, for instance, took seven or eight years to carry the water works through, a thing that might have been done in a year but for those difficulties.

6601. Will you explain how those two or three men have that power?—They have that power, simply because you cannot secure a ceaseless attendance of twenty members during the whole of a long day's discussion.

6602. You cannot secure a ceaseless attendance of twenty members, out of a total of sixty, I think, to discuss those very important sanitary matters with regard to Dublin?—If they could be discussed and settled in a day, or if they could be discussed and settled in two or three days, we would; but the forms of the House admit of obstructions being raised on every petty point of progress in a change of this kind, and men are wearied out by the constant abuse of those forms. Every change is rendered a matter of terrible difficulty, and except a few men of great power of perseverance and great power of lungs, go to work and determine to carry the thing through, it is very difficult to carry any matter through, especially if there is an outside opposition to back up the opposition of a few members inside. I may say as regards the matter of the quorum, that many of the Conservative members of the Council are quite as anxious to see a change as the Liberals.

6603. Does not it come to this, that the ordinary privileges of a minority, which the minority in the Dublin Town Council possess, not in a greater degree than in other bodies, seem to you to stand in the way of the carrying out of this great object?—Not at all; it is not a question of the exercise of the privileges of the minority, it is a question of the exercise of the power of obstruction by individuals. The Conservative party, as I told you, are most anxious, as a party in the council, to see this change carried. In fact, there is only one gentleman in the entire council who is against it, and all his occupation would be gone if there were this change made. It is simply a question of protecting the majority of 59 against the tyranny of the minority of one.

6604. Would not a much shorter way be to bring in a Bill to abolish Councillor French?—It

Mr. *Gray*.

4 July 1876.

Mr. Gray.

4 July 1876.

Mr. *Brun*—continued.

It would; if we could do something of that kind it would be most useful.

Mr. *Kavanagh.*

6605. Is Councillor French a Conservative?—I really do not know; I do not think he has any special politics; he is a nondescript, I might say.

6606. Are his politics as undeclared as Mr. Pim's?—I do not think he ever went so far as Mr. Pim; his politics are to oppose anything which involves any change in the existing state of things.

Mr. *Brun.*

6607. I am very sorry to press this point so minutely, but does this minority of one or whatever the number may be, carry these obstructions in any way beyond the ordinary rights and privileges which a small number of members in every deliberative body have?—I would be very sorry that you should be under the impression that there is an obstructing minority of three or four on ordinary occasions; there is simply an obstructing minority of one. I do not know any other member of the Council, Conservative or Liberal, who obstructs for obstruction's sake. We would not at all desire to do anything which would weaken the power of the minority in the due exercise of their rights; we would desire to see a reform of what hampers our action in an unreasonable degree, and it applied to any other body that I know, would prevent their being able to act at all. Take for instance, the House of Commons; suppose you could do nothing except there were 220 Members always present, how much business would be done during the Session. It is not a question of party, it is a question of putting aside Mr. French. We cannot have Mr. French for ever with us, although I hope we shall have him for a long time, because I do not wish him ill; but it is simply an unworkable arrangement, insisting on such a quorum; and experience has proved it to be quite unnecessary; the Poor Law Boards could not do their work with such a quorum.

6608. You seem to anticipate too that a change in the number of the quorum would produce a change in the *personnel* of the members of the corporation?—Indirectly; the whole of the council acknowledge and feel that a great improvement is necessary; and there are many of them who do not deny that an improvement in the *personnel* is desirable; but they all acknowledge that an improvement is necessary in other respects. For instance, that we must have an increase of revenue, get it from what source we may, for the purpose of scavenging, and that we should have a building Act, and increased powers for abattoirs, and for various improvements that are rendered necessary since the last General Improvement Act was carried, a quarter of a century ago. I believe that if these improvements were proposed to be carried out, what would occur during the progress of carrying them out would be that the best men of the two parties, who are at present opposed, to a considerable extent, would coalesce, to carry them out; and then a new corporation would be elected, consisting of the best men of the old corporation and the best men of the opposition. That was the result in 1851, and there is no reason why a similar result should not occur in 1876; and it would occur, I feel confident. That was the way in which the corporation of 1851, which was constantly praised for consisting of such good men, and which did, as a matter of fact, consist of first-class men, was constituted. There is nothing to prevent our doing the same again, and we hope to do it.

6609. The general result, then, of this particular part of your evidence is that the opportunity of the corporation for effecting these general improvements is denied to them by the fact of this large quorum, and that this law, requiring a large quorum, is made unworkable by Councillor French?—That is, frankly, my opinion.

6610. We may narrow it down to one very small point, then?—No, because you cannot tell when such a power may be exercised by any other individual.

6611. I want to ask you one question with regard to the re-valuation. You said, I think, that a re-valuation did not necessarily involve an increased valuation?—No, it need not necessarily; it would, I think, but it need not.

6612 Do not you think that it would inevitably lead to an increased valuation?—It would altogether depend upon the rules which were laid down for the guidance of the valuators. They might be told to take a standard of 25 per cent. under the rack rent, or whatever it might be, or they might be told to take the existing standard only to equalise it; it would altogether depend upon circumstances.

6613. In your opinion, is there the remotest chance of a new valuation not leading to increased valuation?—There has been so much talk about the increased valuation, and the necessity of it, and I believe myself in the necessity of it, that I apprehend that probably it would lead to an increased valuation, but, as I said, not necessarily so.

6614. Your own opinion has been stated with regard to the cumulative vote, that, individually, you are rather in favour of that as an abstract idea?—As an abstract idea purely, individually, and applied generally; the cumulative vote for a certain section. I would not like to see the wards unrepresented, but I would like to see the experiment tried of having a certain number elected by the whole city, and I think you would get better men.

6615. That is very much in accordance with the opinion expressed here by Dr. Hancock on that particular point, is it not?—He had three or four separate franchises. I think his plan was too complex.

6616. He expressed an opinion with regard to the cumulative vote being applied to the election of a certain number of members of the corporation from the whole city?—Yes; I daresay that it was reading his evidence that made me think of it, but he also suggested that a certain section should be elected by owners alone. I think that would be pernicious, and would give rise to a kind of contest very much worse than political contests, namely, class contests.

6617. With regard to your individual opinion of the cumulative vote, I apprehend that you are not quite in accord with the corporation in that matter?—They have never expressed any opinion upon it, and I desire expressly to guard myself in expressing my own opinion; the question was asked me, and I gave my opinion purely as an individual

Mr. *Gray.*

4 July 1876.

Mr. *Bruen*—continued.

individual. The matter has never come before the corporation.

6618. You object, do you not, to the admission of property owners to the franchise?—I do, except they are occupiers.

6619. Is that on the ground that at present the occupiers pay all the taxes?—I did not go so far as that. I said that there is less reason now in my opinion than there ever was for the introduction of a franchise of that class. As a matter of fact a very large number of the owners in Dublin are also occupiers.

6620. Take the case of an owner, who is not an occupier, if a portion of the tax was levied upon him directly, do you think that it would be fair to give him a vote?—I think that as a means of admission of a greater number of voters it would have little effect. I think possibly there might be some injustice where owners had leased their property on certain terms until the time that the lease expired, but for those who bought after those leases expired it would work then just the same as before, and they would get an increased rent.

6621. I am asking your opinion whether if taxes were levied directly upon the owners of property it would then be right to give them votes?—If they paid the rates I would give them a vote.

6622. I think you have already said that you would make some change in the collection of rates, so as to make them leviable from the owners of property in case the occupiers do not pay?—That was the plan suggested by Mr. Taaffe, and so far as I see it would be a desirable plan; in fact, that is the only means that I can see out of the present difficulty.

6623. In that case, if that change were effected, and those rates were levied from the owners of property directly, do you think it would be fair to exclude them from the franchise?—I do not think the rates in that case would be levied as a matter of fact in Dublin from the owners of property; it would simply put an end to the system of petty tricks which are at present practised.

6624. But supposing that they were, will you assume that?—Supposing that they were, I can only say that I should look carefully to see whether they paid the rates; but I doubt if that would hold good, for a man might pay the rates once in 10 or 20 years owing to his having selected a bad tenant, and I think that would be a doubtful class of man to give a vote to. Personally, my principal objection to giving owners votes is that I do not see that they have a sufficiently direct interest.

6625. Their direct interest being their joining in bearing the burthen of the rates?—Quite so.

6626. If they had a direct interest, you think it would be fair to give them a share in the distribution of those rates?—If they had really a direct interest, not merely a nominal one.

6627. That is to say, a direct interest in the payment of the rates?—It would depend upon whether it would really give them a direct interest or not. I think that after the lapse of a certain period they would simply have so much added to their rent; but if you were to so change matters as to make the owner pay half the rates I would give him a vote.

Mr. *Kavanagh.*

6628. About the forage of horses, you say that the cost is 19 *s.* 3¾ *d.* per horse per week, independently of carter's wages and stables, or anything of that sort?—I think that is for forage and bedding.

6629. Are you aware what the price of hay is in Dublin?—I cannot say that I am; I really know very little about those matters.

6630. Do you know anything near it; is it 10 *l.* a ton?—I do not think it is as much as that, but I must confess that if I gave you any information upon those points it would be merely a guess. I am a member of No. 1 committee, which has charge of those matters, but as a matter of fact we leave that practically to the working of a sub-committee, consisting of men who from their own business know most about it. Mr. Neville gave you those prices.

6631. At all events, you are aware that hay is dearer in London than it is in Dublin?—I think it is.

6632. Would you be surprised if you heard that you can feed a horse in London for the three months of the season for 18 *s.* a week?—That would altogether depend upon what kind of horse it was; our horses are very strong; I would like to ascertain before answering that what kind of horse it was; for instance, is it a Clydesdale, or is it a big dray horse, or a light horse doing light work? it would all depend upon that.

6633. A horse hard worked requiring the best food; hay, oats, and the ordinary cavalry allowance?—Does that mean the best as regards quality; I am under the impression that that class of work we do economically.

6634. Are you under the impression that 1 *s.* a week more in Dublin for a whole year is cheaper than a contract at 1 *s.* less in the height of the season in London?—I should be misleading the Committee if I instituted a comparison which I do not understand; I know that our horses have a great deal of work to do; they work seven days in the week, and I know that everything connected with them is looked after by one or two members of the committee, who have a technical knowledge of the matter, who have horses of their own, and I know that great attention is paid to them, and I believe that we do the work as economically as we possibly can; I know that we attempted to reduce the quantity of forage per horse, and we found that the work was reduced too, because they could not do it on a less allowance.

Mr. *Butt.*

6635. Do you work the horses on Sunday?—Yes.

Mr. *Kavanagh.*

6636. In Rathmines they do not work them on Sundays?—In Rathmines I do not think they work them on Sundays.

Mr. *Butt.*

6637. What do your horses do on Sunday?—The scavenging early in the morning and the watering.

Mr. *Kavanagh.*

6638. In the beginning of your examination you said that the corporation had only one idea as to the franchise, and that that idea was that the franchise should be the same as in England?—I did not say that they were unanimous, but I said

Mr. *Gray.*

4 July 1876.

Mr. *Kavanagh*—continued.

I said that as a body they had but one opinion; you very seldom get a body of 60 men to be unanimous, but as a body they can only pronounce the opinion of the majority; I know that there is a section of the minority who are in favour of the multiple vote, but the opinion of the corporate body must be the opinion entertained and expressed by the majority.

6639. The opinion of the majority is that the franchise should be the same as in England?—Yes.

6640. Then the franchise being the same as in England means really simply lowering it?—It means lowering it.

6641. And extending it in no other direction?—If it is supposed that the franchise will be lowered, and assuming that in subsequent legislation you bring in a measure to change the franchise throughout the kingdom, no objection would be raised by the Corporation of Dublin, even though the franchise were perhaps raised; what they do object to is exceptional legislation in their regard, or in regard even of all Ireland.

6642. My question was, whether in extending the franchise and assimilating it to England, it would not be lowering it?—No doubt.

6643. That is what the majority of the corporation in Dublin are in favour of, is it?—They are, but on the principle of equalisation, without going into the question of lowering or increasing so much.

6644. Then I understand from your guarded answer, that you are not so very clear in your own mind that this lowering of the franchise would tend to improve the *personnel* of the corporation?—I am perfectly clear about that; as I have said to the honourable Member for Belfast, I have no doubt that widening the franchise would really improve the *personnel* of the corporation.

6645. Do you think that simply lowering the franchise would improve the *personnel* of the council or the corporation?—I think it would. As I said, it is always better to depend upon a broad and popular basis. Of course you will understand that I speak from very decided views.

6646. Have you any faith in education being of any advantage to a man?—Yes, I have.

6647. And is it not the fact that there is a great difference in intelligence and education in different classes; I mean that there is a class of persons many of whom do not know how to read and write, and there are others as well educated, such as yourself?—Quite so.

6648. But still you think that the opinion of a man who can neither read nor write is quite as much to be depended upon as your own?—I think that people may always be relied upon to do far better for themselves than a section of them, and I think that that question was abundantly threshed out, and was proved to be true by the introduction of household suffrage for the Parliamentary franchise, which many persons said would be the ruin of the country until it was done.

6649. I think my question was very plain; do you think a person who cannot read and write is as capable of forming an opinion upon different matters as a man who has received a good education?—No, I do not.

6650. Still you think that extending the franchise entirely to the lower classes is the most hopeful way of improving the *personnel* of the body whom they would elect?—I do; I think that the only reform which can result in good, is the equalisation and the consequent reduction of the franchise. I think that a small restricted constituency, no matter how composed, even if composed of the best educated men in the whole country, is an undesirable constituency to elect representatives. Although it may have intelligence, I doubt if it always elects better men; in fact, I am sure it does not elect better men than a wider constituency, because they are more influenced by personal motives.

6651. May I ask what you mean by a restricted constituency?—The present constituency is very restricted, and a new constituency giving to individuals the votes of five or six would be practically an additional restriction of the constituency.

6652. Although you lowered the franchise to the lowest possible qualification?—It would require an arithmetical calculation to answer that, but I believe it would; I am sure it would be an additional restriction.

6653. Your opinion is that it would be a restriction?—I think it would be practically a restriction. If you give one man six votes you neutralise the votes of five other men who may vote against him.

6654. Why do you think the present system restrictive?—Because there are only 5,000 and odd burgesses in Dublin.

6655. It is not because it shuts out one class of persons altogether from the franchise that you call it restricted?—It shuts out a certain section of payers of rates, the poorer householders.

6656. I am not alluding to the poorer householders, but to the rich class, the owners of property?—I do not think it shuts out any except those who are not in the habit of residing in the one house for three years.

6657. Of course they have not votes under the present franchise?—No, of course they have not votes.

6658. Are not they worthy of being designated as a class?—Certainly.

6659. They are shut out, are they not?—Yes, they are shut out.

6660. Therefore it is restrictive above as well as below?—It is restrictive below as well as above, but the exclusion of non-resident owners is not a restriction of the franchise for the citizens.

6661. But it is restrictive to those who have considerable interest in it, is it not?—If they are non-resident, or such owners as are purely owners and not occupiers, they are restricted.

6662. You do not deny that they have a very large interest in their property?—I do not deny that they have a very large interest in their property.

6663. Would it not be the fact that if the corporation had borrowed a large sum of money for a certain object, and that sum was mortgaged upon the rates for a long time, the owners of property would really have more interest in the way that the principal is spent, which they have to repay virtually, than the occupiers who are only there for a year or two?—That was exactly the point which I explained a few minutes ago. Take the average of the leases in the city first, and ascertain their length, and they would at least average all round between 30 and 40 years; the

leases

Mr. Gray.

4 July 1876.

Mr. Kavanagh—continued.

loans now under our new system of payments are paid back, principal and interest, and all in that period, and the whole burthen falls on the occupier. In ancient days if we wanted a loan, we borrowed it without the intention of ever repaying it; it was a perpetual debt the same as the National Debt, and then, undoubtedly, the burthen did fall upon the owners; I do not think that the burthen of these short loans is felt nearly so much now.

6664. Then am I to understand from you that there is no such thing as an old debt existing in Dublin now?—Yes, there is an old debt.

6665. Then probably the repayment of it does affect in some degree the interest of the owners?—Yes; but that matter has long since been regulated in the rent. As I understood your question, I took it as a matter only applying to the new loans; the other matter, I take it, is a standing debt, and has long since regulated itself in the purchase money and rent.

6666. I understand you to say that the old loan regulated itself, the effect of which regulation would be, if I take you up rightly, to do away with the landlord's interest in it?—I understood your question to apply to new loans. The old loans, I presume, do fall, not on the occupier, but they do not appear to fall upon the owners, because the interest on them is paid out of the borough rate which is city property, and not out of the rates. There is not a halfpenny of the old loan owing by the Dublin corporation which is paid by the rates.

6667. Then not a halfpenny of the old loan falls on anybody, either the owner or the occupier?—Neither the owner nor the occupier, that I know of. It is all paid by the borough rate.

6668. What I take to be the gist of your answer is this,—that no matter how high the rates are on a place it does not affect the actual value of that place at all?—That could scarcely be said. I was talking of the votes of leaseholders and owners; it can be very fairly argued, and it is a fact that the incidence of taxation is shared far more equally than would appear at first sight. As regards the person who immediately pays the rate, of course the higher the rates on the property the less rent *cæteris paribus*. That is a self-evident matter; there is no doubt about it.

6669. I am not the owner of town property, and therefore I do not profess to know anything about it, but should I be wrong in supposing that a landlord's rent is lessened by the excessive rates on a house?—I am not a landlord, but I imagine his rent would be lessened.

6670. Possibly he might then feel some interest in those rates?—He might, but the question is whether it is sufficiently direct and immediate to justify his getting the franchise.

6671. Is it not generally supposed that the interest that touches the pocket is very direct?—Yes, but a man who buys a glass of whisky does not realise that he is paying three-fourths of the price as a tax. The indirect incidence of a tax is not realised in the same way that a direct tax is. That it does indirectly fall as an economical theory upon the back of the owner to some extent, there is no doubt whatever about.

Mr. Bruen.

6672. You said just now that in consequence of all the interest on the old permanent debt of Dublin being paid out of the proceeds of the town property, therefore the owners of property in Dublin were not directly affected by it at all?—I said they paid no rates for it. Of course if the interest were not paid out of the borough fund the borough fund would go to some other purpose in relief of the rates. It is merely that they do not feel it directly; that it does affect them is self-evident.

6673. They really do feel it then?—I do not know that they feel it. It is there, and the question is whether they do really feel it and recognise it or not. I do not think they do.

Mr. Mulholland.

6674. It is really only a question of book-keeping, is it?—Certainly: the question of the eventual incidence of taxation is a very complex one.

6675. It is a question of putting the total income on one side, and putting the total expenditure on the other?—Yes.

Mr. Kavanagh.

6676. You were asked about the political discussions at the corporation, and I think you gave in a Return upon the subject?—I gave in a Return, which was prepared by the assistant town clerk, but the Right Honourable Chairman asked me with reference to a little discussion; incidental matters, no doubt, arise over and above those.

6677. That little discussion was quite an incidental thing; it was not political at all?—I did not say so.

6678. It was not an important thing, but it casually cropped up?—It cropped up over a letter from the secretary of the Central Tenants Association.

6679. I think you said that it was on your own motion that a petition in favour of it was adopted?—It was.

6680. You stated a minute ago that the majority of the corporation were Liberals?—Certainly.

6681. Was any opposition made to it?—There was, certainly.

6682. Was there a division, or anything of that sort?—Yes, there was a division.

6683. And the fact was, of course, that the petition was carried?—The petition was carried.

6684. I think you were the mover in that, if I understand rightly?—No, I was not; it came before me the day it came on. I was asked to propose the petition, and I felt great pride in doing so.

6685. I understood you, that you were the mover of it?—Yes, I was the mover of it in the council; I proposed the petition.

6686. And I think you said that you were not a landlord?—No, I do not hold land.

6687. It could not possibly be thought to be a case of liberality with other people's property?—I do not see that. If men were to be shut out from dealing with any interests except their own I am afraid that a very narrow spirit would prevail, and not at all a desirable one.

6688. Are the majority of the corporation landlords,

Mr. *Grey.*

4 July 1876.

Mr. *Kavanagh*—continued.

landlords, or not?—The proposal was seconded by a large landed proprietor.

6689. One of the reasons that you gave for not wishing to give the owners of property votes was, that you thought that the legitimate influence of property was quite enough influence for the owners to have?—The only influence that I think they should have.

6690. You considered that that was evident, and you instanced the Parliamentary representation?—I do not know; I daresay I did.

6691. If you were to go through the list of Irish Members that are at present sitting in this House, do you think that upon careful consideration you could say that property had its real influence?—I must enter into particulars. I think that if the landlords of Ireland identified themselves with the aspirations and wishes of the people they would find very little difficulty in using their legitimate influence to an extent probably superseding all other influences, because the Irish are a very peculiar people in that way; they have the greatest respect for land and for the possession of property.

6692. We are not dealing with an hypothesis, but we are dealing with facts, and I merely ask you is it not the fact. I do not say that so-and-so might happen, but is it the fact now?—There are a good many landed proprietors in the House from Ireland.

6693. Are you prepared to say that the majority of the Irish Members of the House are the representatives of landed property?—No; I have never analysed them, but I take it that proportionately to the state of the population and other tests they are tolerably adequately represented. The question was asked me *à propos* of a proportion of a given number, 25,000 in one class, to the number of 10,000 in another. I think that the proportion of the landed proprietors in the House at this moment shows conclusively that their mere number has had a far greater influence than the proportion of that number to the general population, that is to say, they exercise that legitimate influence of which I speak.

6694. To go back to municipal affairs purely, I think you were asked about the elections to the corporation, and you said that you believed that any first-rate merchant could enter the corporation if he chose?—I do think so.

6695. I am utterly ignorant of the matter, but who is Mr. Wallis?—Mr. Wallis is a currier; he is in the same class of business as Fishbourne, and Chaplin and Horne. He is a man of very good position.

6696. He is not what you call a first-class merchant?—No, he is not a merchant at all.

6697. He is not one of those whom you designate as one who could enter the corporation if he liked?—I think that his position would not justify him in assuming that he could walk in, for undoubtedly he fought his way in, but being in he never would have been disturbed if he had thought fit to attend the meetings fairly. But he is not one of the class of men that I spoke of as being men of leading position, although he is a man in a very good position.

6698. But he does not possess the confidence of the ratepayers?—So the election proved.

6699. So you managed to prove for him?—So I managed to prove for him. The ward which I represent is one of the highest class wards in the city; the popular element is not represented in the ward at all scarcely. They are squares occupied by barristers and lawyers, and that class of men; for instance, Mountjoy-square is in it, and Gardiner-street and Upper George's-street, and that class of streets, so that the more popular element had little to do with my return.

Mr. *Mulholland.*

6700. Are you quite sure that you are right in saying that the greater number of houses are let on leases of from 30 to 40 years in Dublin?—I am not quite sure, but no man would take business premises on a less lease than that, as a rule, and no man occupying a good private house would care to take it and expend money upon it except on a lease.

6701. Are not the great majority of houses, inhabited by those who are comparatively in the lower classes, let from year to year; there are no leases, so far as I know, in other towns used for such class of houses inhabited by operatives?—No, not those inhabited by that class.

6702. Under the system of representation which you suggest, it would not be the leaseholders of mercantile establishments or large houses who would form the majority of the electors; it would be the operative classes and those inhabiting houses from year to year?—The majority of the occupiers I should think would be so, but I question if a large majority of the voters would; there are a very large number of small shopkeepers, the operative class, as you understand, occupy tenement houses; the greater proportion of them do not occupy a house at all; they merely occupy rooms, and they form a very large proportion.

6703. Still my experience in Belfast is that the class of operatives will out-number in the proportion of three or four to one all the classes above them, and of course if it came to voting any great expenditure they would be able to carry it all their own way, and the counterbalancing consideration that you suggested that the money was borrowed on terminable annuities corresponding with the length of the lease would not enter into the question; in such a case as that the owners of property would require to be represented, would they not, to protect their own interests?—In the first place in Belfast there is a very large class of operative artizans, very much larger than in Dublin, who occupy small houses which we have not got in Dublin, and therefore the population of Belfast cannot be taken as a criterion for Dublin, because the class who would rent houses in Belfast live in rooms in Dublin; but, of course, as regards those who do live in houses from year to year, what you say would be quite accurate; but those are really the class of men, I take it, who most object to any increased rate of taxation, because the tax falls directly on themselves, and they may have died before they get a reduction of rent in consequence; but instead of their being a class from whom owners would require defence, as I take it, they are the very class which it is most difficult to reconcile to increased taxation. As a class, the class of small shopkeepers are the most difficult of all to reconcile to any increase of taxation. I think that the small shopkeeping class is the worst in that respect.

6704. The proportion may vary in Dublin to

Mr. *Mulholland*—continued.

to what you find to be the case in Belfast, but I should think you would find that the houses that I speak of would very much out-number the others?—Probably that would be so.

6705. I admit that your argument would be quite fair if all the house property was held on tenures corresponding with the length of term for which terminable annuities were borrowed?—I did not mean to convey that that was all, but that there was a large number of houses representing a large proportion of the entire property so held. I do not know how the balance of value would be; I take it that it would rather tend towards my view, but it is a question that I cannot answer how much might fall one way or the other.

6706. When houses are held from year to year it is an undisputed axiom of political economy that the rates do really fall upon the landlord, and that the rent is regulated by them; in such a case as that, would not it be fair that the owners of property should be represented?—I doubt it.

Chairman.

6707. Will you just look at this book (*handing a book to the Witness*); it is an almanac containing certain facts with regard to the Corporation of Dublin for the year ending November 1875?—Quite so.

6708. I see that in one year there were 46 meetings of the council?—Yes.

6709. Out of those 46 meetings, how many did Councillor Wallis attend?—He attended 21 times.

6710. Excluding two members of the council, the late Sir John Gray and Mr. Brooks, the honourable Member for Dublin, who, of course, has occupations here, how many members do you find out of the 60 members of the Dublin Town Council who attended less than Councillor Wallis?—I find 37, including those two, or 35 not including them, who attended a greater number of terms than Councillor Wallis, but you must remember that the year in which a man goes out of office is a bad criterion. There is generally a better attendance that year than any other year; but, as a matter of fact, there is more than a majority of the council who beat Mr. Wallis.

6711. Are you aware what Mr. Wallis's attendance at committees was?—No, not at this moment; but I know that, on looking the matter up at the time, I found that his attendance was very, very slight. In fact, it so happened that I met Mr. Wallis one day in my candidature—he and I know each other pretty well—and he said: "What is the meaning of your coming to oppose me; cannot you go somewhere else." And I said, "I would not oppose you if you would attend." He then said, "I do not think it is fair;" but he did not at all deny the fact. In point of fact I would be very happy to prepare a return for three years, which I think a fair criterion; you ought not to take the year before a man goes out, because, perhaps, the man is rather more attentive than the year he comes in.

6712. At any rate there were a good many members who attended less than Mr. Wallis, and yet were fortunate enough to be re-elected?—There were 35, and allowing for the two whom you mentioned, there were 37 who attended more than he, and that is a large proportion.

Mr. Butt.

6713. Whether or not, do you think that it was the belief that he had not attended regularly that influenced the election?—I know I canvassed on that ground. I daresay that both considerations influenced the electors. I think the fact of my being the son of a man who had worked very hard in municipal affairs was really what influenced the election to the greatest extent. I think that it was my being my father's son that influenced the election, but I know that I would not have opposed Mr. Wallis had he been a fair attendant.

Mr. *Butt*—continued.

Mr. Gray.

4 July 1876.

6714. Would any one else have defeated him?—I was told that any person would have defeated him, but I do not think that any person except myself, and I do not think that I, except under the exceptional circumstances which I have mentioned, would have defeated him by two to one, as I did.

6715. Have you studied political economy at all?—Every person professes to have a smattering of political economy.

6716. It is not conceded, is it, that the whole tax falls upon the landlord?—No.

6717. I believe that the opinion of the most eminent writers on political economy is that it partially falls upon the landlord, and partially on the occupier?—Yes.

6718. I think what you intended to say was this: that if a house was let on lease for 40 years, and a loan was effected by the corporation, to be paid out of the rates, which would be entirely paid off within 40 years, it would fall entirely on the lessee?—That is exactly what I meant to convey.

6719. Of course if the lessee had again let it to the occupier, the next year it would fall upon him, and he would be then, for that purpose, the landlord?—Certainly.

6720. As to the quorum, I did not understand you to say that it was upon political questions that the House was counted out?—The House is constantly counted out, not at all upon political questions, but on general questions. For instance, a good deal was made of the fact that when I introduced a resolution to put the Artizans' and Labourers' Dwellings Act into force the House was counted out; but we have got to regard the House being counted out as workmen regard being counted out at five o'clock. It was counted out at a quarter to six that day; but, as a matter of fact, it is generally counted out, not on political matters at all, but whenever there is a chance.

6721. From your experience in the corporation, do you think that useful measures have been stopped by the exercise of the power of counting out?—They have been constantly impeded. In fact, Mr. Sullivan testified to the same thing, that there is too much power given to obstruct purely for obstruction's sake.

6722. That is, that the quorum is much too large?—Yes, the quorum is much too large.

Mr. Brooks.

6723. Concerning the *personnel* of the corporation, do you think that if the present disability of the corporation to elect sheriffs was removed, and that that duty was thrown upon them as it is upon the English corporations, and the stigma thereby removed, that a better class of men would present themselves to the corporation?—I do. I anticipate a good deal of benefit in that respect from conferring that right upon the corporation,

Mr. *Gray.*

4 July 1876.

Mr. *Brooks*—continued.

corporation, if it be given to them. I think myself (of course I am now only speaking individually) that if we were to get such a right as that, the proper thing eventually would be to make the Lord Mayor of one year the sheriff of the next That would secure that it would be given to Conservatives and Liberals alternately, and not, as at present, the nomination nearly altogether being from one side. The office having been occupied by men of very high position in Dublin, is an object of considerable ambition to city men, and no doubt it would induce men to come into the council simply with the view of getting appointed high sheriff afterwards. I anticipate a good deal of benefit from a change in the direction that I indicate, as it will give men an ambition to come in. I think it would be an advisable plan to make the Lord Mayor one year sheriff of the next, because that would put an end to all discussion about who is to be the sheriff. The Lord Mayor at present has the privilege of paying a very large sum out of his own pocket, and it might be a little compensation to him to give him that honour the succeeding year, which is not a very expensive one. Of course I cannot assume to know what the council may do if they do get the power, but that is my impression of what it will come to.

6724. Do you think that if the proposal to remove the existing power from the board of superintendence is carried out in the opinion of the present board of superintendence and the corporation, a stigma would be thrown upon them?—The position of the board of superintendence of Dublin is peculiar and very exceptional; we have not the appointment of our own officers as every other board of superintendence in the United Kingdom has, and therefore, we would feel in Dublin the relief from local taxation, and we would not feel the disagreeableness of having our patronage taken away from us. We would feel that as much as other powers would; but there is a feeling, I do not know whether it is in the corporation, but there is a feeling in Dublin to a considerable extent that the centralising effect of the Bill would be injurious, and there is a section of the people at any rate who would rather continue to bear the local burthens and to have the local control than to transfer the burthens and the control both to the Imperial Government.

6725. If the power or the duty which is now upon the corporation to elect boards of superintendence be superseded, would not a source of attraction to men to go into the corporation cease?—Yes, to a certain extent it is a weakening of course of local authority; and I should say that a certain attraction to men to go in would be removed. But the attraction is not so large in Dublin as in many other towns, for the simple reason that they have removed our patronage long ago. Dublin stands exceptional in that respect. I do not think that there is any other town that stands exactly in the same position as regards that matter as Dublin.

Mr. *J. P. Corry.*

6726. Would you be surprised to hear that the corporation of Belfast has no voice whatever in the Board of Superintendence of Prisons, although they contribute 90 per cent. of the rates?—That is true. Your police were taken away too.

Mr. *Brooks.*

6727. Do you know if the corporation of Belfast had the duties thrown upon them of electing certain sitting magistrates from their own body?—I do not know that it is so; I know very little about Belfast

6728 Mention was made that a Conservative alderman, Alderman Dudin, was superseded in Dublin; can you say by whom he was replaced?—He was superseded by Alderman Harris, who went in as a neutral.

6729. Does he not sit on the Conservative side of the house?—Yes, he went in as a neutral, but he practically is a Conservative; but he takes a very little part. I do not know what he is, but he went in as a neutral.

6730. He is of the Jewish persuasion, I think?—Yes, he is.

6731. With regard to the fear of unpopularity which is said would attach to the members of the corporation who would seek to impose a sanitary rate, is it not the fact that the ratepayers of Dublin are exceptionally poor and are exceptionally heavily taxed already?—In the first place I do not consider that it is the fear of unpopularity; I am afraid I misconveyed my meaning; it is their dislike to impose taxation, far more than their fear that a penny or a twopenny rate would affect their seats. Because, although the inhabitants of Dublin are poor compared to those of other towns, I do not think they are exceptionally heavily taxed. They imagine they are because of the lowness of the valuation.

6732 I mean, not in proportion to the taxation of other towns, but in proportion to the means of the poorer ratepayers?—They are heavily taxed no doubt.

6733. And the burthen is exceptionally heavy?—I cannot say that, because I do not know it, but it is very heavy, but they are able to bear more taxation for useful purposes, and I would put more on them for useful purposes without any hesitation, and I do not think that I would imperil my seat by it.

6734. May the alleged inattention of the Public Health Committee to the letters of the Sanitary Association be attributed more to the groundlessness of the charges than to the fact that those charges came from their own officers?—I suppose it may; it was the habit of the Public Health Committee, as I understand, at first to acknowledge and reply to every letter; it may be that their not doing so led to its being attributed to many causes, and it may be attributed to many in addition to those which I suggested; it may be attributed to the fact that the work of the public health committee and the work of its executive officers has largely increased, and I daresay they have less time to write mere formal letters than they had formerly. I daresay it may be attributed to that.

6735. If I remember rightly, you were asked if the silence of the Public Health Committee to the complaints of the sanitary association was not due to the fact that the complainants were officers of the corporation?—Yes, I was asked that.

6736. Was it not rather due to the groundlessness of the complaints than to the fact of their being officers of the corporation?—I cannot answer that; some complaints were groundless and some were not; if it were due altogether to groundless complaints the latter would not be answered,

Mr. *Brooks*—continued.

answered, while any reports on good grounds would be answered, and as a matter of fact they were all attended to, but none were answered for the last few months.

6737. Is there any class of persons resident in Dublin who, as a class, are excluded from the franchise?—There are large classes; no ratepayers are excluded, but if I understand you to ask me whether any class are excluded from entering the council, there are a vast number. There are certain classes who exclude themselves to a considerable extent.

6738. Property owners who reside in Dublin are not excluded, are they?—Property owners who reside in Dublin are not excluded.

Mr. *Brun*.

6739. With regard to what you said about the South Dublin Union; you said that the experience which you had had of the management of affairs by a body elected by the multiple vote was not favourable; can you give to the Committee any justification for that opinion, with reference to anything that you found fault with in the South Dublin Union?—I said that the Local Government Board held an inquiry into the way in which they did their business the other day, and surcharged them with 2,000 *l.* and odd for deficiencies of various kinds; it is a very sweeping report, making all kinds of accusations of neglect of duty; not anything worse than mere neglect, but very strong accusations of neglect on the whole body of guardians who neglected their business; they should have taken stock themselves every half year, but they never did it at all, and they let everything get into frightful confusion. They have since held a meeting, and I understand that they passed a vote not to punish the master.

Mr. *Butt*.

6740. Was not that on the ground that they were all as guilty as he was?—I believe that was so practically.

Mr. *Brwen*.

6741. You spoke of the South Dublin Union as being an evidence that the conduct of affairs was not liberal by them, and that nearly all the officers were Protestants?—Yes, except those necessarily Catholic.

6742. You assume further that religion is made a ground of preference in this case?—Religion and politics.

6743. What ground have you for that assumption?—No more than the self-evident fact that there is always a contest for appointments.

6744. Who is the vice chairman of that board?—The vice-chairman is Sir James Mackey, who is a Catholic, but they have never appointed a Catholic chairman.

6745, It is a general rule all through Ireland, is it not, in almost all cases where there is a division of opinion, that the chairman and vice chairman are appointed from different parties?—That may be so.

6746. Is not that the case in the South Dublin Board?—I think it is only some five or six years ago that they went so far as to appoint a Catholic vice-chairman.

6747. Supposing that in the South Dublin Union Board or the North Dublin Union Board there are a majority of Liberals, they do not carry out that rule, because their vice-chairman, I think, is a Conservative and a Protestant?—The rule has been general with reference to the county to select men of the highest social position. The North Dublin Union is Liberal, but the chairman, Mr. M'Farlane, is a Protestant.

6748. Even supposing that the South Dublin Board had not performed its duties sufficiently, do you think that that single instance is sufficient to condemn a system which has given great satisfaction throughout Ireland, a system under which the poor law guardians are elected, and the local government in that particular case is carried on?—I think, whether it is sufficient to condemn the system or not, I would not venture a sweeping condemnation of any system on a single instance, but I think it is a good criterion of what would occur in the same locality. It must be remembered that if the poor law system is accepted and generally adopted throughout Ireland (I take your assurance upon that point, I am not aware of it myself), it was a totally new system; but supposing the franchise under the poor law system had been simply to occupiers, and that there had been a chance of the multiple vote being introduced, I am quite certain that it would not have been received with satisfaction.

Mr. *Kavanagh*.

6749. With regard to those Protestant officers who were elected by the South Dublin Union, do you say that they are unfit for the position?—No, indeed I do not; certainly not.

6750. Did you say that the Roman Catholic candidates who stood against them were more fit?—I did not enter into that.

6751. Then it is merely an assumption of your own, that it was religion that influenced the Board?—It is a certainty; it is a matter of notoriety.

6752. How can it be a certainty?—I assert certainly that if I had an opportunity of analysing the former candidates, I could show that the other candidates were at least equal to them. I would not like to throw any aspersions upon them, but when you find a body always appointing men of a certain creed, I think that the assumption becomes a certainty; it is like the doctrine of chances, it becomes a certainty after a certain time.

6753. Then it is an assumption, and not a certainty?—I think it becomes, for all practical purposes, a certainty.

6754. You could not take your oath of it if you were sworn before a jury?—I could take my oath of my conviction.

Mr. *Butt*.

6755. Did you hear the evidence of Mr. Stokes, who is a member of the South Dublin Union?—I did.

6756. At Question 2961, he was asked, "But in fact, in the South Dublin Union do not you think that the offices in the workhouse are so far to a great extent exclusively given to one religion;" to which he replied, "I do; but I may add to that that the South Union is or has been lately in the hands, and almost entirely governed by a clique of the corporation. (*Q.*) It being all Conservative? (*A.*) Mostly Conservative. (*Q.*)

Mr. *Gray*.

4 July 1876.

Mr. *Gray.*

4 July 1876.

Mr. *Butt*—continued.

(*Q.*) Is it a Conservative clique that governs it? (*A.*) They all stick together there, but the majority are Conservatives." He was also asked, "Have you found the mode of election in the South Union very effective in excluding religious and political consideration;" and he replied, "No, I do not think it has?—Whatever effect it may be thought that the multiple vote would have in changing the *personnel*, it certainly cannot be anticipated to have an influence at all as regards political discussion.

Dr. *Ward.*

6757. Do not you know as a matter of fact with regard to the dispensary medical officers that the appointments made by the South Dublin Union have been invariably to Protestants?—Almost invariably, I believe.

6758. Although the greatest number of their patients has always been Catholic?—Always.

6759. And although the mass of ratepayers in the district are Catholics, or at least the people who have to be attended by the dispensary doctors?—Quite so.

Dr. *Ward*—continued.

6760. Do you believe that there is a very strong feeling with regard to that?—Yes.

6761. I suppose there is no doubt that there was that feeling animating the South Dublin Union in the election this week?—I do not think there is the slightest doubt about it. There is another important matter; they take care to keep their rate collectors Protestant.

Mr. *Corry.*

6762. Do you know at all the number of officials belonging to the South Dublin Union?—There are a very large number; I spoke of officials having salaries of over 100 *l.* a year; there are a very large number of officials at small salaries who are Catholics.

Mr. *Kavanagh.*

6763. It is at the rate of a hundred a year that the religion comes in?—About that; it does not come in anywhere under that.

Friday, 7th July 1876.

MEMBERS PRESENT:

Mr. Assheton.
Sir Michael Hicks Beach.
Mr. Brooks.
Mr. Bruen.
Mr. Butt.
Mr. Collins.
Mr. J. P. Corry.
Mr. Gibson.
Sir Arthur Guinness.
Mr. Kavanagh.
Mr. Charles Lewis.
Sir Joseph M'Kenna.
Mr. Mulholland.
Mr. O'Shaughnessy.
Dr. Ward.

SIR MICHAEL HICKS BEACH, BART., IN THE CHAIR.

Mr. JOHN BALL GREENE, called in; and Examined.

Mr. *J. B. Greene.*

7 July 1876.

Chairman.

6764. WHAT is your position?—I am Commissioner of Valuation for Ireland.

6765. How long have you been so?—Since October 1868.

6766. Are you of opinion that a new valuation for Ireland is desirable?—Yes, I am.

6767. For what reason?—Because the different classes of property have become very unequal, and, therefore, the taxation for the purpose of which it is intended bears unduly on one class more than on another.

6768. When was the present valuation made?—For some counties it was completed, and has come into operation for about 25 years. A good many counties in the south-west of Ireland have been completed for 25 years, and in others from 18 to 20. Of course the valuation commenced prior to that time, because it takes some time to value each county, so that from the commencement I suppose it has averaged 27 or 28 years.

6769. What are the provisions in the Valuation Acts for a re-valuation?—There is one section, the 34th, of 15 & 16 Vict. c. 63, which authorises the grand jury of any county to apply to the Lord Lieutenant to cause a re-valuation to be made, provided the previous valuation has been made for 14 years. That provision extends to a county, or poor law union, or a barony.

6770. That provision relates to a new valuation altogether, does it not?—Yes, a new valuation.

6771. Have there been any applications of that kind?—There has been but one that I can recollect, and that is in the county of Antrim. They were anxious to have a re-valuation of the borough of Belfast, and the grand jury of Antrim applied to the Lord Lieutenant, but the grand jury of the county Down did not apply, there being a portion of the borough extending into that county, and it was considered that there was no authority to proceed with the valuation.

6772. Could a grand jury, under that section, apply for and obtain a valuation of part only of their county?—The grand jury could apply for a poor law union or a barony, but even had the grand jury of Down applied as well, as they wished to confine it to the borough, there is no provision for valuing a borough separately.

Chairman—continued.

6773. So that that application was not complied with?—No, it was not complied with.

6774. Have the corporation of Dublin ever made an application for a re-valuation?—I do not think they have made it officially. They have been anxious about it, and spoke to me on various occasions, and I showed them the difficulty in the way of it.

6775. What is the difficulty about the law?—The same difficulty, that there is no power under that section of the Act. They must apply for either a county or barony or a poor law union, and they should apply for the whole union.

6776. Would there be anything to prevent the corporation of Dublin, as the grand jury of the county of the city of Dublin, applying for and obtaining a re-valuation of the whole of the county of the city of Dublin?—That has not occurred to me, probably it would come under the county of the city. The grand jury of Dublin, I should think, could do it.

6777. The grand jury could do it, if I understand you, but not the corporation?—Not the corporation.

6778. Besides that provision for a new valuation altogether, are there not some provisions in the Act for an annual revision of the valuation?—Yes, under the 17 Vict. there is provision for an annual revision, and the machinery is this, that any collector of poor rates in any union, in going through his district to collect the rates, if he sees any case requiring revision, or new buildings, or anything of that sort, he takes a note of them, and on the 15th of November in each year he sends it to the board of guardians, and the guardians transmit it to me on the 27th of November, stating to me that the changes ought to be attended to. That is the machinery, and any ratepayer may also send in a list.

6779. Do those provisions secure, in your opinion, a satisfactory annual revision of the valuation?

Mr. *J. B. Greene.*

7 July 1876.

Chairman—continued.

valuation?—Yes, so far as the actual annual revision goes; I believe there has been no dissatisfaction expressed with all the changes that are carried out, or at least the majority of them.

6780. But is there not some provision in the law which limits the effect of that annual revision very considerably?—Yes. According to the Act we have no power, in the first place, to alter the valuation of any land. We may re-distribute it. For instance, if a town land is valued at 300 *l.*, and there are 30 tenants on it, 25 of them leave, we then distribute the 300 *l.* over the five remaining tenants, and we correct the map to correspond.

6781. Then the revision, in fact, is only a redistribution for fixed limit of value?—Precisely so.

6782. You cannot increase the total limit?—No, we cannot increase the total limit.

Mr. Bruen.

6783. Is that limitation confined to the town lands, or what is the area which is fixed?—The town land.

Chairman.

6784. Returning to the question of a new valuation, what have you to say as to the basis upon which the existing valuation is framed?—The basis of the existing valuation was made upon the scale of agricultural prices ascertained, I think, in about the years 1849 and 1850. I think they were based upon the prices then prevailing of the several articles of produce mentioned in the Act, which do not represent the present prices at all by any means.

6785. Will you tell us what those articles are, and what prices were attached to them?—In the Act of 1852, the prices, I think, were made on the basis of the three years previous to that. Wheat was 7 *s.* 6 *d.* per cwt.; oats, 4 *s.* 10 *d.*; barley, 5 *s.* 6 *d.*; butter, 65 *s.* 4 *d.*; beef, 35 *s.* 6 *d.*; mutton, 41 *s.*; pork, 32 *s.*; and flax, 49 *s.*

6786. Have you obtained a return for the year 1873, which will enable you to compare those figures with the prices of 1873?—Yes; there was a Return presented to the House of Lords in July 1873, and that Return was compiled from information obtained throughout the 13 or 14 market towns that were mentioned in the order; and the average prices in 1873 were, wheat, 12 *s.*; oats, 6 *s.* 10 *d.*; barley, 8 *s.* 6 *d.*; butter, 110 *s.*; beef, 70 *s.*; mutton, 74 *s.*; pork, 50 *s.*; and flax, 66 *s.* 7 *d.*

6787. So that I understand, from what you have stated, that in any new valuation it would be necessary to alter the basis now fixed by law for the valuation?—Certainly. Assuming that the grand jury of a county do apply, under that 34th Section, to have a valuation, I do not think there would be a change in it, because that 34th Section says that you are to make it upon the same scale of prices; and therefore if the original valuation was accurately made, the re-valuation on that scale ought to be the same, except where there had been great improvements.

6788. Can you give the Committee any idea, roughly speaking, judging from the scale of prices which you have given us, what per-centage of increase there would be in a new valuation?—It would vary in certain counties, the prices have become so altered for butter and grass land, and have gone up so very high, that the counties where

Chairman—continued.

that class of land prevails would be raised from 50 to 60 per cent., whereas in tillage grounds I do not suppose it would be 25 per cent.

6789. Are there any other points, besides the increase of prices, since the original valuation, which would lead you to consider that a fresh valuation would be higher than the present one?—I do not think that the question of taxation would materially affect it. Taxation was much higher then, and of course we were bound to consider it; but it would have some influence.

6790. I suppose the opening of railways has made a difference?—Yes, no doubt there has been a very considerable improvement caused in certain districts by the construction of railways and the equalisation of market prices. In remote districts, where oats and this class of cereal produce used to be raised, the prices were very much lower than in towns on the eastern coast, but railways have opened up the markets on the eastern side.

6791. Where any land has been reclaimed or improved by drainage, have you power to value improvements of that kind?—There is great doubt about it. There is a clause which says that land may be valued at the expiration of seven years from the completion of the improvements; but we find that we have no power to do it. It was not sufficiently defined.

6792. What prevents you?—It is the construction of the Act. The 15 & 16 Vict., c. 63, s. 14, says: "No hereditament or tenement shall be liable to be rated in respect of any increase in the value thereof arising from any drainage, reclamation, or embankment from the sea, or any lake or river, or any erection of farm, outhouse, or office, buildings, or any permanent agricultural improvement as specified under the provisions of an Act passed in the Session of Parliament, held in the 10th and 11th years of the reign of Her present Majesty, c. 32, s. 4, made or executed thereon within seven years next before the making of such valuation or revision." A construction has been put upon that, that with respect to rating, there is no power to introduce into the valuation, lands reclaimed. It is not sufficiently defined that, at the expiration of seven years, such land as is described should be valued for rating purposes.

6793. Has the question of exemption of property from taxation also arisen?—Yes; it has been a very serious question for a long time, and there has been a good deal of discussion about it, and some few years ago a deputation waited upon Lord Hartington on the subject, in Dublin Castle, at which I was present. Sir Dominic Corrigan, I think, was in Parliament at the time, and he and several Irish Members waited on Lord Hartington, to ask him to introduce a measure to abolish exemptions altogether, as they considered that they were unjust and unfair. There was a measure prepared but it was not carried.

6794. What are the exemptions now?—The total of the exemptions in Ireland amount to 501,000 *l.* in annual value.

6795. Will you tell us what they are?—Churches and chapels of all denominations, 120,000 *l.*; schools of all denominations, including Christian Brothers, convent schools, national schools, and endowed schools, 52,000 *l.*; county buildings, court houses, jails, bridewells, county hospitals, infirmaries, lunatic asylums, tolls

Mr. J. B. Greene. 7 July 1876.

Chairman—continued.

tolls and market houses, 60,000 *l.* Then there is property that has been recently rated, that is Government property, amounting to 104,000 *l.* I may say that that should be struck out, for the Government now contribute to the rates on that valuation. Then there are charitable institutions, workhouses, dispensaries, hospitals, orphanages, asylums for the blind, old, and destitute, and magdalen asylums, &c., 65,000 *l.* Then there is municipal property, docks, wharfs, tolls, bridges, harbour dues, town halls, &c., 100,000 *l.*, making a total of 501,000 *l.*, from which the Government property, I think, should be deducted

6796 Has there not been some litigation on that last head?—There has been very considerable litigation on that last head. We have been endeavouring to rate the port and docks of Dublin, which appear to be similar to the Mersey Docks, and are held in a similar way. It is at present in the superior courts. There has been no final decision yet.

6797. What is the contention of those who claim to be exempted?—They claim that it is public property. I am of opinion that it is not public property in the sense in which we look upon it.

6798. Did you say that, in your own opinion, that property was in the same position as the Mersey Dock property at Liverpool—Yes.

6799. Are the Mersey Docks now liable to rates?—Yes; they pay something like 40,000 *l.* a year; we thought that it was somewhat similar to the Vartry Waterworks, which are in the hands of the corporation of Dublin, and now rated.

6800. What effect has this present low valuation upon any calculations with reference to local taxation in Ireland?—As regards two of the principal items, there is the grand jury cess which is 1,200,000 *l.* a year, and, I suppose, the poor rate is something like 800,000 *l.* a year now. A low valuation makes the poundage rate very much higher. The average county cess on the present valuation is about 1 *s.* 9 *d.*; under a new valuation it would be about 1 *s.* 5 *d.* The poor rate from 1 *s.* 3 *d.* would be reduced to 10 *d.* in the pound. Of course, it would practically come to the same thing.

Sir *Joseph M'Kenna.*

6801. Except for removing inequalities as between one holder and another?—Yes.

Chairman.

6802. What would you recommend as the basis of a new valuation?—I would recommend the rent; I would adopt the English Act, which states that "Every valuation should be made upon an estimate of the nett annual value of the hereditaments, that is to say, the rent for which one year with another each hereditament might in its then actual state be reasonably expected to let from year to year, the tenant paying all usual tenants' rates and taxes, but deducting the probable average annual cost of the landlord's repairs, insurance, and other expenses (if any) necessary to maintain the tenement in a state to command such rent." I think that would be a fair and just means of ascertaining the proper valuation as the basis for taxation, both local and general.

6803. Would not that be the adoption of quite

Chairman—continued.

a new principle in the Irish valuation system?—No, it would not.

6804. The existing valuation is calculated not on the rent but on a scale of prices, is it not?—Yes; but if you made a valuation now it should be based upon the existing scale of prices, because the rent that a man gives must be also based on the present prices You must have a basis, and prices must be the basis in that very section which I have just read.

6805 Are you acquainted with the Acts under which the valuation is conducted in England by the assessment committees of the Poor Law Board?—Not remarkably well; I know a little about them.

6806. Is there any scale of prices fixed in those Acts?—No, there is not. The words in this section are copied from the English Act. I do not think it would be necessary.

6807. Would you not require a schedule of prices?—I do not think it is necessary, because if we sent a valuer down to value now, he would have to take into account the present price of produce before he could value, and then he could easily carry his scales of value from class to class.

6808. Besides the alterations in the law relating to valuation which you suggest, have you experienced any difficulty from the number of the Acts?—Yes, there is great confusion.

6809. You would suggest, perhaps, that they should be codified?—Yes, I think it is absolutely necessary, the law is very unsettled in consequence of so many amendments to the general Act.

6810. Have any attempts been made in the last 12 or 13 years by the different governments to legislate on this matter?—Yes, in 1865 Sir Richard Griffith, the then commissioner, was directed to prepare a Bill, which was introduced by the then Secretary, Mr. Chichester Fortescue, Mr. Cardwell, and the then Attorney General for Ireland. I believe it was read a second time and withdrawn for want of time. Then, again in 1872 there was a Bill prepared, and there was another prepared in 1873, and that was also read a second time, but withdrawn in Committee by Mr. Gladstone.

6811. The Committee have had a good deal of evidence about the condition of the valuation of the City of Dublin; have you made any calculations as to how far the existing valuation represents the real value of property there?—I have a calculation upon the subject. The valuation of the city at present is 620,534 *l.* If there were a new valuation, it would be increased to 781,000 *l.*

6812. If such an increase were made, what difference would be effected in the poundage rate?—The poundage rate would be reduced, I suppose, from, as at present, about 8 *s.* 4 *d.* to about 6 *s.* 4 *d.*

6813. Is there any other point occurs to you to mention to the Committee?—Nothing more than that I consider the valuation has become so irrelative, owing to the alteration in the prices of produce, that a re-valuation is necessary for a more equitable adjustment of taxation. I think it bears unduly, at present, on one party more than on another.

6814. On which party?—The party whose lands are not valued sufficiently high; for instance, grass lands are absurdly low, and the poorer class of farmers who live in tillage districts are paying on a valuation much nearer the truth, therefore they are paying an unjust proportion. It

Mr. J. B. Greene.

7 July 1876.

Chairman—continued.

It is entirely upon the ground of a better and more equitable adjustment of taxation that it is necessary.

Mr. *Butt.*

6815. Am I right in saying that the counties in Ireland have now been valued under three different Acts?—No.

6816. Are you acquainted with the Act of the 6 & 7 Will. 4, c. 84?—Yes, although I was not employed under it, but still I know it.

6817. Was not that the first Act under which any valuation was made?—Yes, but you will recollect there was only a portion of Ireland valued under it.

6818. But there was a valuation made in some counties in Ireland, under that Act of the 6 & 7 Will. 4, c. 84?—Yes.

6819. I think that was the first Act under which there was a valuation?—Yes, it was.

6820. Am I right in saying, that there had been a previous Act, providing for a valuation that came into force when the Ordnance survey was completed, but when the Ordnance survey was completed, the Act of the 6 & 7 Will. 4 was substituted for the previous Act?—Yes.

6821. Therefore we may take the 6 & 7 Will. 4 as the first operative Act in valuation?—Yes, just so.

6822. The next Act was passed in 1846, the 9 & 10 Vict. c. 110, "An Act to amend the law relating to the valuation of rateable property in Ireland"?—Yes.

6823. Let me ask your attention to the preamble, and the first section of that Act?—The preamble is, "Whereas it is expedient to amend the laws now in force for the valuation of lands and tenements in the several baronies, parishes, and other divisions of counties in Ireland: Be it therefore enacted by the Queen's most excellent Majesty, by and with the advice and consent of the Lords Spiritual and Temporal and Commons in the present Parliament assembled, and by the authority of the same. That so much of an Act passed in the Session of Parliament, held in the 6th and 7th years of the reign of his late Majesty King William the Fourth, entituled, 'An Act to consolidate and amend the several Acts, for the uniform valuation of lands and tenements in Ireland, and to incorporate certain detached portions of counties and baronies, with those counties and baronies respectively whereunto the same may adjoin, or wherein the same are locally situate as relates to the valuation of any county of a city or county of a town which shall hereafter be valued under the provisions of this Act, and to the apportionment of county or grand jury cess therein,' shall be repealed."

6824. As you see, that Act only repeals the previous Act as to counties that were not already valued?—Just so.

6825. Therefore the provisions of the previous Act remained as to counties already valued?—Yes.

6826. Will you read the next section?—"Be it enacted that, from and after the passing of this Act, the provisions of this Act shall and may be applied in the following counties and counties of cities (that is to say) the counties of Dublin, Tipperary, Waterford, Limerick, Cork, and

Mr. *Butt*—continued.

Kerry, and the counties of the cities of Waterford, Limerick, Cork, and Kilkenny."

6827. Are you able to tell me whether in 1846 the valuation of all Ireland, except the counties named in that second section had not been completed?—No, certainly they had not.

6828. Can you tell me how much was done under the previous Act in the 10 years between 1836 and 1846?—I think the valuation must have been made in 10 years, for I think all Ireland, except those counties, was valued under it, except the province of Munster.

6829. Was all Ireland, do you think, except those counties, valued in 1846?—It was valued in town lands in gross, not in tenements. There was no tenement valuation. There were no poor rates at that time, and the tenement valuation was not necessary; it was valued in town lands for the levying of grand jury cess only.

6830 Then the first tenement valuation was under the 9th and 10th of Victoria?—Yes.

6831. That was again amended by a statute passed six years afterwards in 1852?—Yes.

6832. Will you look at the 9th section of the 9 & 10 Vict., c. 110, that is the tenement valuation, and read it to the Committee?—"And be it enacted, that in every valuation hereafter to be made under the provisions of this Act, the Commissioner of Valuation shall cause to be valued every tenement which is a rateable hereditament under the provisions of an Act passed in the Session of Parliament held in the first and second years of the reign of Her present Majesty Queen Victoria, entituled, 'An Act for the more effectual Relief of the Destitute Poor in Ireland,' and shall also cause every such tenement to be separately valued by the valuator, and the valuation thereof shall be made upon an estimate of the net annual value (that is to say) of the rent for which, one year with another, the same might, in its actual state, be reasonably expected to let from year to year, the probable annual average cost of the repairs, insurances, and other expenses (if any) necessary to maintain the hereditament in its actual state, and all rates, taxes, and public charges (if any), except tithe rentcharge, being paid by the tenant."

6833. Do you see that that 9th Section of the Act of 1846 directs every tenement to be valued "upon an estimate of the net annual value (that is to say) of the rent for which, one year with another, the same might in its actual state be reasonably expected to let from year to year, the probable annual average cost of the repairs, insurance, and other expenses, if any, necessary to maintain the hereditament in its actual state, and all rates, taxes, and public charges (if any), except tithe rentcharge, being paid by the tenant;" is that provision now acted upon at all?—No, that has been repealed.

6834. When was it repealed?—It was repealed by the Act of 1852; and all the valuations that were made under that Act were to be reduced to the standard of this one before they were issued for any public service.

6835. Is that the 11th Section of the Act of 1852?—If you will take the Act of 1852, the 2nd Section, you will see that it is so.

6836. Does not the 1st Section provide this: "That the tenement valuation for poor-law purposes so made and completed in or for any county or barony, county of a city, or county of a town, under the provisions of the said Act shall, anything

Mr. *J. B. Greene.*

7 July 1876.

Mr. *Butt*—continued.

anything in the said Act to the contrary notwithstanding, be in force and be used as well for the purposes of all county assessments or grand jury rates, or city, town, or parish rates, or for the purpose of poor-law assessments or rates, but, subject nevertheless to such correction and revision as by this Act is hereinafter provided?"—Yes, that is so.

6837. Then the 11th Section says: "In every valuation hereafter to be made or to be carried on, or completed under the provisions of this Act, the Commissioner of Valuation shall cause every tenement or rateable hereditament hereinafter specified to be separately valued, and such valuation in regard to the land shall be made upon an estimate of the net annual value thereof with reference to the average prices of the several articles of agricultural produce hereinafter specified, all peculiar local circumstances in each case being taken into consideration, and all rates, taxes, and public charges, if any (except tithe rentcharge), being paid by the tenant (that is to say)." Then it repeats the articles of produce mentioned in the Act of 1836, but diminishing their price?—Yes, but if you look at the 2nd Section of the Tenement Valuation Act you will see that it is directed that any baronies or portions of a county that were valued under the 9 & 10 Vict. were to be brought to the standard of this Act.

6838. That only referred to where it was only partially made, but was not completed?—Yes; but there was not a single county in Ireland, or a portion of a county, completed under 9 & 10 Vict.

6839. Then, in point of fact, that which I read to you of the valuation, according to the net value, becomes completely a dead letter?—Yes.

6840. And you now value solely according to agricultural prices?—Yes, that is the fact.

6841. Is there any difference in the standard of value upon which the present valuation was made in different parts of Ireland?—No.

6842. Are there none made under the old Act?—None whatever.

6843. Are all of them reduced to the one standard?—Yes.

6844. What is the case with regard to houses?—In the 11th section you will see it says, as to buildings, "And such valuation shall be made upon an estimate of the rent one year with another."

6845. So that the valuation of houses was fixed upon the rent?—Yes.

6846. And of the land upon a calculation of prices?—Yes.

6847. What difference is there in the rate between what is fixed on a calculation of prices and what is fixed on the rent; would you make any difference whether the land was valued under the Act of 1846 or under this Act of 1852?—If the prices in 1846 were the same as the prices under the Act of 1852, the valuation ought to be very nearly the same.

6848. No matter whether it was nominally based upon the rent or upon the prices of produce?—No.

6849. In the case of towns, where the valuation was fixed upon the rent, take the city of Dublin for example (of which we have had a good deal of evidence), has the rent of houses increased in the city of Dublin since the valuation was made?—Very considerably.

Mr. *Butt*—continued.

6850. Supposing there are improvements made in a house, you may be called upon at once to re-value it, may you not?—We may; that is the fact.

6851. Then the seven years' limit does not apply to houses in case of improvements?—No.

6852. So that you may at once be called upon to value a house for an improvement made in it?—Certainly.

6853. Supposing you were called upon to value a house for improvements made, how would you value it?—That is a very important question, and I suppose the better plan would be to tell you the principle which we have gone upon, which is this: when we value a new house, for instance, we do not value it up to the rent, for this reason, that we constantly have a house adjoining it that was valued, originally, say at 50 *l.*; the rent of the new house being, we will say, 100 *l.*, and we have therefore tried to make it tolerably relative by not going as high as we might do, as we are afraid that we might be acting unjustly by putting a greater amount of taxation upon the man who built the new house, so that we do not adhere strictly to the Act of Parliament in valuing new houses, up to the very last shilling.

6854. That would be because the adjoining houses had been valued at a lower scale?—Yes.

6855. But, still, were the new houses valued on a higher scale than the old ones?—Somewhat on a higher scale; generally speaking we went higher.

6856. But not to the full extent to which you might have rated them, or to which the last Act would have obliged you to carry it?—Quite so.

6857. Would the same thing apply to a person improving his house of business, that is to say, would he be valued on a higher scale than if he left his house alone?—Yes.

6858. So that the improvement would make the scale of his taxation higher?—Yes. The great improvement in Dublin, Belfast, Londonderry, Cork, and other towns shows the necessity for some revision of the valuation.

6859. That applies peculiarly to cities?—Yes.

6860. Why do you say grass lands are valued lower in proportion to their value than tillage lands?—For this reason, the difference in the price of the produce. For instance, take butter; butter is 65 *s.*, in the old Act it is 110 *s.*, the average of all the butter markets in Ireland now, whereas if you take wheat and oats you will find that the difference in the price is not nearly so great.

6861. In the Act of 1852 wheat is valued at 7 *s.* 6 *d.* a cwt., what is it now?—It is 12 *s.*

6862. Oats I see are 4 *s.* 10 *d.*, what are they now?—Six shillings and tenpence.

6863. Wheat land has risen more in value than oat land, has it not?—Yes.

6864. Barley I see was at the general average price of 5 *s.* 6 *d.*, what is it now?—Eight shillings and sixpence.

6865. Flax was 49 *s.*, what is it now?—Flax is 66 *s.* now.

6866. Butter at that time was 65 *s.* 4 *d.*, what is it now?—Butter is 110 *s.* now.

6867. Then the lands producing butter are far more below their present value than either wheat, oat, or barley lands are?—Yes, you will see that beef is doubled. It was 35 *s.* 6 *d.*, and it is 70 *s.* now.

Mr. *J. B. Greene.*

7 July 1876.

Mr. *Butt*—continued.

now. Mutton was 41 *s.*, now it is 74 *s.*, and you will see that pork was 32 *s.*, and is now 50 *s.*

6868. Then it appears to be plain under the present valuation of Ireland, the great grazing farms do not pay their fair proportion of the taxation of the country?—They do not.

6869. And that to a very considerable extent?—Yes, to a very considerable extent.

Sir *Joseph M'Kenna.*

6870. Are you familiar with the instructions which were issued to the valuers in 1852, at the time that Sir Richard Griffiths' valuation was about being made?—Yes.

6871. There were other ingredients in the computation of value besides the prices of produce, were there not?—There were local circumstances, for instance.

6872. One of which was the chemical or geological nature of the land?—Yes, the nature of the soil, and the capabilities of produce.

6873. And the relative proximity to towns?—Yes, and their altitude and aspect.

6874. There was no ingredient for computation prescribed to the valuers with respect to the wages of agricultural labourers?—Nothing, I think, in the instructions; but a valuer could not properly value without taking labour into account. It would be impossible for him to fix the value without.

6875. I am now taking it so far as the fixed basis for the computation of the value of particular lands was concerned; there was nothing in the basis laid down for computation of the value of the land, said about the prices of agricultural labour?—No, there was not.

6876. Am I then right in saying that although the prices of agricultural produce, which is largely the result of the employment of labour, may have increased in the proportion, say, of 20 per cent. in value, if the wages of labour in that particular district where the produce was raised increased in an equal or a greater proportion; there would be no ground to assert positively beforehand, without examination of the particular case, that the value of tillage land must necessarily have increased because the value of the produce has increased?—No; if the labour was not taken into account at the time the valuation was made, and the labour has increased 20 or 25 per cent. over what it was at that time, and it be taken into account now, the valuation, of course, should be somewhat less; but I must explain that it would be quite impossible to have made a valuation at that time without taking labour into account, no matter whether it was specified or not.

6877. I quite agree, that is to say I agree, that the condition of the then current prices and wages of labour, although not an ingredient specified to the valuators, must have been taken into consideration when a scale was fixed for the valuators to guide them in arriving at the actual value to be applied to each particular tenement?—Quite so.

6878. The lands which would have most increased in value owing to the increase of the prices of produce would be necessarily those, if they increased at all, in which the minimum of labour had to be applied; for example, say that the price of barley, which is largely the result of the employment of wages of labour, has increased 30 per cent., yet if the wages of labour in the

Sir *Joseph M'Kenna*—continued.

same period had increased 50 per cent. it might not be so profitable to grow barley now at the increased price of 30 per cent. as it formerly was when the wages were at a low price?—It might not; but we must take into consideration that the price of wages has been modified a good deal by the introduction of machinery and improved implements, and all that which to a certain extent must save and does save labour.

6879. I am endeavouring to get your evidence specifying upon what grounds we ought to arrive at a computation of values; and we wish to know if (as a matter of course) the increased values of produce which least depend upon manual labour will not indicate a greater proportionate increase of the value of land than the increase of produce, which, like all tillage produce, is necessarily largely the result of the employment of labour?—Unquestionably.

6880. And, therefore, that although the price of butter, and of beef, and of mutton may have increased 100 per cent., may have doubled in point of price, and although the prices of corn, wheat, barley, and oats may have increased 50 per cent., the increase of the value of the land which produces the butter, the beef, and the mutton (on account of there being a minimum application of labour to those areas), is likely to be a much greater relative increase as compared with the increase in the value of tillage lands, than the proportion of 100 to 50?—Of course, in all pastoral districts the labour is comparatively small as compared with tillage districts. Take Kilkenny, for instance, where it is mostly tillage; there is a much greater amount of labour there, and therefore it would go to diminish the value of a tillage district as compared with a pastoral district.

6881. May I take this as the result of the answers that you have already given to me, that whilst the increase of the value of tillage produce does not necessarily denote the increase of the value of land, unless a computation of labour at the same time is taken into account, the increase of the value of beef and of mutton, and of butter does almost of necessity denote a largely increased value in the case of pastoral lands?—Certainly.

Mr. *O'Shaughnessy.*

6882. In towns, like Limerick and Cork, are re-valuations for poor law purposes of frequent occurrence?—There are no re-valuations. The Government valuation is the poor law valuation. Unless there is a new house built, or an improvement made, there can be no re-valuation. Annually we revise and correct the valuation.

6883. But that is not a re-valuation?—No.

6884. What does the revising and correcting consist of?—For instance, as this valuation is used for all purposes, for Parliamentary representatives, and the municipal franchise, we correct the names of the owners and occupiers of property, and if there are sub-divisions of property, and a man lets off a stable on it, he would be deprived of his franchise unless there was a separate valuation made of it; and the books are corrected annually and sent down for the purpose.

6885. On those occasions is there no re-valuation except where a sub-division makes it necessary?—There is no re-valuation, only in the case of a new house or the improvement of a house.

6886. Is

Mr. *J. S. Greene.*

7 July 1876.

Mr. *O'Shaughnessy*—continued.

6886. Is the expense of correction or revision of the valuation borne by the occupier?—No, the Government pay the greater proportion of the cost, and the balance, which is something between 7,000 *l.* and 8,000 *l.* a year all over Ireland, is paid out of the county rate.

6887. By the occupier?—Yes.

6888. Therefore it does fall upon the occupier?—Yes.

6889. Would it strike you that it would be a more equitable arrangement that it should be borne like the poor rate, partially by the owner and partially by the occupier?—The thing is so trifling, that really I did not think about it. When the work is done, the occupation franchise is based upon it. The occupier, I daresay, has as great an interest in having it corrected as the owner, because if it is not corrected, he will have to pay probably excessive taxation; for instance, if he lets off a portion of his premises. There are 150,000 alterations made every year, but the thing is so small when it only comes to about 7,000 *l.*, and you spread it over the rateable value of all Ireland, it is hardly worth consideration. I never considered the question.

6890. Have you any idea whether in a town like Limerick their share of the annual expense would be covered by 100 *l.*?—Taking Limerick, it would be 40 *l.* a year levied off the entire city of Limerick.

Mr. *Collins.*

6891. You would by all means recommend a re-valuation of Ireland for the purpose of remedying the present inequalities?—Yes.

6892. And you would also recommend that the English system of taking the rent which the tenant paid as the basis, instead of the present produce basis of valuation?—I would.

6893. With respect to exemptions, they amount, I find, to 501,000 *l.* a year, inclusive of the 104,000 *l.* for Government buildings?—Yes.

6894. Have you formed any opinion with respect to those exemptions, whether they ought to be introduced into a system of valuation, or whether you would continue them under any form?—Of course it is a question which, perhaps, does not come within my province as to the policy of the thing or not; but I would be inclined to do away with all exemptions except places of public worship.

Mr. *J. P. Corry.*

6895. You have given the Committee evidence with reference to what difference there would be in the valuation of Dublin, supposing a re-valuation were to take place; could you give the Committee an idea of what the difference would be in Belfast?—Yes. The present valuation of Belfast is, in round numbers, 490,000 *l.*; and under a new valuation it would be raised to 612,000 *l.*

6896. The proportion then would be greater than in Dublin apparently?—Yes, somewhat greater.

6897. How do you account for the difference of increase?—In this way, that the north side of Dublin has not kept pace with the south side, and therefore the north side of Dublin will not be largely increased. The property on the north side of Dublin, taken on the whole, has not increased to the same extent as the south side, and that reduces the average.

Mr. *J. P. Corry*—continued.

6898. Could you give the Committee any idea of what the reduction in the taxation would be on the poundage rate?—It would reduce it from 6 *s.* 8 *d.* to about 5 *s.* 4 *d.*

6899. Can you give the Committee any information as to the difference in the valuation of property in Belfast?—The difference in the valuation of Belfast is this: Belfast has grown so rapidly. In 1864 the population was about 120,000, and considering that the population has increased to 190,000, the valuation of commercial property has increased immensely in Belfast; so that the new houses that are improved for commercial purposes are valued, as in Dublin, higher in proportion to the old houses which are not repaired; and the rents of which have gone up in the same proportion.

6900. Are you aware of the difference of opinion that exists between the Belfast Corporation and the Harbour Board with reference to the valuation of the dock property?—Yes, that has been under contention for some time.

6901. Are you aware how it has been settled?—I was not aware that it was settled.

6902. It has been settled, and the dock property is now liable to taxation to the corporation; on what principle do you value dock property?—The same as a house: it is valued at the rent, or the same as a railway; we value a railway at the rent that a tenant would give for it.

6903. How do you arrive at the rent of a dock?—You cannot value a dock by going and looking at it in the way you value land or a house, but we ascertain the gross receipts from the authorities, and from that we deduct the expenses, and there is a further reduction for maintenance and renewal and other things, which reduces it to the net annual value.

6904. Then your opinion I gather is, that a revision of all Ireland should take place, and not of any particular part of it?—Yes, that is my opinion.

6905. Are you aware that the Corporation of Belfast are very anxious for a re-valuation of the borough?—Yes, I am.

6906. Are you aware that the borough of Belfast has a very extended area?—Yes, there are 6,805 acres within the area of the borough.

6907. Could you mention to the Committee the extent of the area of Dublin?—It is only 3,807 acres.

6908. So that the area of Belfast is nearly double the area of Dublin?—Yes.

Mr. *Bruen.*

6909. When you say that you make deductions in estimating the rental of a dock, what are the deductions which you make?—The deductions for renewals, and also there are deductions for the annual repairs of the dock. Assuming that at the end of 50 or 60 years it would be necessary to rebuild it, we allow a sum that will rebuild it at the expiration of 50 years, or whatever length of life we give to the docks or any other class of property.

6910. That is a sort of sinking fund for renewal, is it not?—Yes.

6911. Are there any other deductions in the way of expense?—There are the actual outgoing expenses to maintain the property to earn the tolls, then there is the renewal and the repair. Those

Mr. J. B. Greene.

7 July 1876.

Mr. *Bruen*—continued.

Those are the only things that are deducted upon that class of property

6912. Does the labour incurred in unloading the vessels, and which may be partly borne by the Dock Commissioners, come into your calculation?—All the labour that is charged against the Commissioners who receive tolls is charged and none other.

6913. Do you get from the Dock Commissioners returns of that labour?—Yes.

6914. So that the estimate of the rental which you make is based upon information which you receive from the owners of the docks?—Yes, for instance, the Dublin port and docks were formerly rated, and we had some criterion to guide us. Messrs. Scovell, as long as they rented the port and docks and Custom House stores of Dublin, were rated, but when they came into the hands of the Port and Docks Corporation they said that the property was public, and that is what has caused a reconsideration. So long as it was in the hands of an occupier, who rented it, it was rated.

6915. Then the change of the tenure was held to create a change in the nature of the property?—Yes.

6916. You have told the Committee the total valuation of Dublin and of Belfast, and what the valuation would be under the proposed new valuation, but I do not think you have given the Committee the result for the whole of Ireland; what is the present valuation for the whole of Ireland?—The present valuation for the whole of Ireland is within a few pounds of 13,500,000 *l.* It is rather a curious thing that Ireland and Lancashire are valued at exactly the same amount. The rateable value of Lancashire is 13,500,000 *l.*, and the rateable value of Ireland is 13,500,000 *l.*

6917. What is your estimate of the new valuation?—Practically, it is 18 000,000 *l.*

Sir *Joseph M'Kenna.*

6918. What do you think the new valuation of Lancashire would amount to?—They carry on the valuation from year to year there.

6919. But there is no mode of ascertaining the rack rent value of large factories, is there?—Yes, there is; they are valued the same as other places.

Mr. *Bruen.*

6920. So that, in fact, it would be an increase of one-third upon the present valuation?—Yes.

6921. And in some places, I think you told the Committee, that the increase would be greater than that; it would be from 50 to 60 per cent.?—Yes, that is in some particular places; but the average for all Ireland is about one-third.

6922. In these particular places, where the increase would amount to 50 per cent. and I suppose that as over the whole of Ireland it would amount to one-third, there would be a very considerable portion in which it would amount to 50 per cent.?—Yes.

6923. Under those circumstances, a person who now has property of 30 *l.* valuation, would, under the new valuation, be rated at 40 *l.*, would he not?—Yes.

6924. I suppose you are aware of a new Jury Bill having just been passed through the Houses of Parliament, by which the qualification for jurors was raised from a 30 *l.* to a 40 *l.* valuation?—Yes.

Mr. *Bruen*—continued.

6925. Under the new valuation, persons who are now valued at 30 *l.* would again become eligible for the jury list?—Yes.

6926. Then, in fact, your new valuation would amount to a repeal of the new Jury Act?—No. The only effect would be to bring in a greater number upon the jury list; that is all.

6927. That would put those upon the jury list who are now disqualified by reason of their valuation being too low?—Yes, it would add to their number.

6928. Have you had any complaints of your valuation as to its acting unevenly and unfairly?—I am sorry to say that we have.

6929. By whom have those complaints been made chiefly?—By the ratepayers; they often say that the man next door has got a house three times as good, and he pays three times, or twice as much rent as I do, and I am paying as much taxes as he is.

6930. The complainers wish to have their neighbours higher rated?—Yes.

6931. Have those complaints been very general?—I really cannot say that they have been very general, but they have been general enough to lead me to know that such inequalities exist.

6932. There is no means of remedying it on a large scale, but you can remedy it, can you not, within the limits of town lands?—No.

6933. Can you not readjust the valuation within a town land?—No, if the valuation that is placed on any townland is 300 *l.*, it must remain 300 *l.* in that town land. We can only applot it differently, it must be the same amount.

6934. Supposing that in a town land valued at 300 *l.* there were two farms, one a tillage farm and the other a grass farm, have you not power, under the Act, to value the grass farm higher, and the tillage farm lower, provided you keep the totals the same?—No, because we go to the valuer's notes that he made at the time of the original valuation, and if he valued the grass land higher we should adhere to it, in regulating the value of the land taken from one man and given to another.

6935. How is the work done by your men in the field, do they themselves make an estimate of the value, or do they make their reports, and are the field books sent up to your office, and the estimates made there?—If there is any difficulty in applotting in the country, they send up and get back a copy of the original valuator's notes, showing the proportion, if there has been what we call striping, or any great sub-division, but they do not do so in every case; we allow the valuer to exercise his own judgment in ordinary cases.

6936. I suppose I am right in concluding that the greatest part of the valuation which is done in Ireland is entrusted to men who go about and perambulate the country, and they, in fact, are the persons who do it?—They do the field portion of it, and the office work is done in town.

6937. What is the office portion?—The office portion is when the valuator sends up his books. Having revised a town land and found several changes, when his books come to the office they are examined, and if there is a discrepancy it is corrected in the office and returned to him; but he is required, in all cases where there is a serious change, to send his book to the office to be examined with the original field-book, after which

Mr. *Bruen*—continued.

which new or corrected lists are issued from the office.

6938. Does the original field-book give you the different qualities of the soil?—It does.

6939. Divided into minute portions?—No, it will give the valuation, say of land at 20 *s*., and land at 15 *s*., and land at 12 *s*., and bog land, and so on.

6940. Those are marked on the map, are they not?—Yes.

6941. In the proposed new valuation would very much the same system be pursued?—I think I would make some modification in the system; the existing books for a new valuation have the names of the owners and occupiers, and the areas; and if we were going to make a re-valuation now, I would put those books into the valuer's hands, and I would make him specify the number of acres of different qualities in each man's farm, and carry out the valuation. I think that would be the most practical way of doing it.

6942. I believe there are in your office instructions issued to the valuers to guide them in their work?—There were in 1852.

6943. And are those acted upon still, so far as they can be acted on?—The instructions then were chiefly for the purpose of making a valuation; there is not much as regards the revision, I think.

6944. But as regards the making of a new valuation, would those instructions now be applicable?—There certainly would have to be an issue of revised instructions.

6945. I understand you to say that you do not approve of putting a scale of agricultural prices into the new Act as the basis of your valuation?—I think it is immaterial. Prices must be taken into account in making a new valuation. When once a valuer has laid down a standard calculated upon the present prices as to the different qualities of land, he can carry this standard in his mind from farm to farm. It is not necessary to have a scale of prices in the Act.

6946. If it is necessary to the re-valuation, why should it be immaterial to have it in the Act?—It is necessary to the valuation; all rent must be based on a scale of prices, because, whether it is in the Act or not, we should follow a scale of prices.

6947. If you do follow it, why should not you put it into the Act?—I would put it in as a schedule to it.

6948. Still it would be within the four corners of the Act, although not perhaps in a clause?—Yes.

6949. I find in your instructions that were issued in 1853, one of them to this effect: "In fixing the value of the land, the valuator is to act as if he were employed by a liberal landlord to value land for letting to a respectable tenant at the then average price for agricultural produce." Would you consider that a fair instruction for your valuators, now, for a new valuation?—Yes, I would.

6950. The instruction goes on to say: "This valuation will be afterwards corrected and reduced to the scale of prices for agricultural produce prescribed by the Act; by comparing current prices with those mentioned in the Act which, as already stated, are 2 *s*. 6 *d*. in the pound lower than the average prices of agricultural produce throughout Ireland previous to the commencement of the valuation." Were those prices that you read out to the Committee just now actually 2 *s*. 6 *d*. in the pound lower than the average prices?—No, they were not; they were the actual average prices.

Mr. *J. B. Greene.*

7 July 1876.

Mr. *Bruen*—continued.

6951. Let me read the words to you again: "By comparing current prices with those mentioned in the Act, which, as already stated, are 2 *s*. 6 *d*. in the pound lower than the average prices of agricultural produce throughout Ireland." Does not this instruction seem to say that they are to be lower?—You are quite correct. I was referring to the prices that have been recently taken.

6952. Those prices in the clause of the Act of 1852 are, in fact, 2 *s*. 6 *d* in the pound lower than the actual prices?—Yes.

6953. And those prices which you have read out to the Committee have not had that reduction made to them which are mentioned in the Act of 1873?—No, they have not.

6954. And those prices of 1873, I think you said, were laid before the House of Lords?—Yes.

6955. Were they the result of an average of years, or were they only for one year?—I think they were only for one year; for the year ending the 30th of April 1873.

6956. I suppose that such a scale of prices as could be brought into an Act, or the schedule of an Act, would be liable to reduction by 2 *s*. 6 *d*. in the pound, in the same manner as in the former Act?—I would not recommend that; I do not see why it should. I would have the actual prices in it.

6957. I am not quite sure whether I entirely understand you with regard to the basis of valuation; you say that the basis of valuation must be the scale of prices of agricultural produce; would that be altogether the consideration that the valuator was to have in his mind; would he not have recourse to any information as to what the actual rent was?—I should say that the valuer would, very probably; if he observed what he considered a rent that bore out the scale of prices he would, in the valuation of similar land, bear that in mind.

6958. Do you think there is much discrepancy between a valuation based upon those agricultural prices and the actual rent of the land?—That depends upon the period at which the letting will take place. For instance, I am sure in the lettings at the present day there would be a very considerable increase over the rents of 1852.

6959. I am not speaking of the scale of prices of the Act of 1852, but of the scale of prices which you read out to the Committee of 1873; do you think that there is any considerable discrepancy between a valuation based upon those prices, and the usual rent of land?—I cannot answer that question generally. If I knew of any particular case I would endeavour to answer it.

6960. Are you of opinion that the valuation should very closely approach the rent?—I think it ought to be the rent.

6961. Do you mean to say that you think that there ought to be valued rents throughout the whole of Ireland?—No, I do not. I go in for a valuation for purely fiscal purposes; but I think that to arrive at it equitably it ought to be the rent.

6962. Do you think there is any possible means of arriving at an equitable rent; could it be the rent which by fair competition the land would fetch

Mr. J. B. Greene.

7 July 1876.

Mr. *Bruen*—continued.

fetch in the open market?—I think in Ireland that is not altogether a true test.

6963. In what way is it not a true test?—There is too great a competition for land.

6964. Do you think that the people actually lose by the land that they take?—I do not know. I cannot answer the question whether they lose or not, but there is considerable competition to get possession of land.

6965. Would not the inference be that if the competition isso great, and the rent so high, the men who take it at so high a rent would lose by it?—I do not think that in Ireland the farmers go in as they do in Scotland to get a certain percentage on their capital and labour; but I think they go in to make a living in the best way they can.

6966. Do you suppose that they do not make a living; do you think that in general the lettings which are made enable a farmer to live on his land?—I do not think that the farmers live as well in Ireland as they live in England or Scotland.

6967. What was the cost of the townland valuation which, I think, was made for only a part of Ireland?—It was made for all except the province of Munster, I do not recollect now what the cost was.

6968. Could you say what the cost of the tenement valuation was?—I cannot. There is a Parliamentary Paper showing that, which I have not got.

6969. Have you made any estimate of what the expense of a revision of the valuation would be now?—Not recently.

6970. You could not give the Committee any idea of what would be the cost of a revision under the new Act?—No, it would be comparatively small from the reasons which I have stated with regard to the most expensive portion of the work being already done.

6971. Would it necessitate a large increase in the staff in your office?—It would.

6972. And how long do you compute that it would take?—About five years.

6973. Can you say about what increase it would necessitate; would it double your staff?—It would only necessitate an increase in the class of valuers, but I have not gone into that question very closely. In the Bill which was introduced by Mr. Gladstone in 1873, there was a clause authorising the Treasury to appoint whatever additional assistants became necessary.

6974. Would you recommend in the new Act any alteration in the existing Acts as to future revisions, and as to the power of applying for them, or the power of the Government to make them without application?—I certainly think if there is a re-valuation completed now within five years, it ought not to be disturbed say for 15 or 20 years.

6975. When that period had elapsed, should you give an absolute power to the Government to institute a new valuation?—Certainly.

6976. Without recourse to any local authority, or any local consent?—No; there is a clause in the Act authorising applications by the grand juries of corporate towns at an earlier period, within seven years if necessary.

6977. But excepting on such an occasion, you would prohibit a new valuation for 15 or 20 years?—I would.

6978. In all probability the amount of local

Mr. *Bruen*—continued.

taxation which is raised now would not be very materially affected, would it, by a new valuation?—No, it would be more equally distributed, that is all.

6979. Do you anticipate that a very large increase of taxation would result from the fact that the present limits which are imposed upon many local Government bodies would be enlarged by raising the valuation?—I do not know about that.

6980. With regard to the Imperial taxation, it would increase that one-third, you think?—If the honourable Member is speaking of the income tax now, under Schedules A. and B. at 3*d.* in the pound, it would be an increase of about 50,000*l.* a year all over Ireland.

6981. The principal change I understand you to say, would be in the south and west of Ireland, not in the north?—In the north of Ireland the increase would not be so great; the valuation was made much more recently there.

6982. But was not the valuation then made upon the same basis of prices as elsewhere?—Yes, with the addition of flax.

6983. In round numbers you say; what should you say would be the difference between the proposed new valuation and the present one in the province of Ulster?—The present valuation of Ulster is 4,223,271 *l.*, and the new valuation would be 4,927,000 *l.*

6984. It would leave the proportion of increase in the south and west of Ireland very much higher?—Yes.

6985. Have you great confidence in the capacity of your valuators to perform these new valuations?—There are some very good valuators, but unfortunately some are becoming aged. We should have to import a good many additional hands into it.

6986. It is a very important office, is it not, requiring the greatest integrity; what qualifications do you specially require?—We require a man having a very good knowledge, or a fair knowledge, of agriculture and farming, and who has had experience in agricultural pursuits.

6987. Would you require any knowledge of chemistry?—I do not know whether that might be necessary, practically. I would not care very much about going into that, because I know that in a public valuation, if we attempted such details it would only break down. It may be necessary to have some general knowledge as regards the value of soils, but as for a knowledge of chemistry generally, I do not see that it is necessary.

6988. Should they not have a knowledge of agricultural chemistry?—Yes.

Mr. *Mulholland.*

6989. What valuation is this to which you refer in Ulster, as amounting to 4,223,271 *l.*?—The present tenement valuation which is in force, the Government valuation, which has been many years in operation, and is used for all purposes, public and local.

6990. What is the 4,927,000 *l.*?—That is only assuming that a re-valuation of Ulster was made, there would probably be that increase.

6991. What is the basis of that calculation?—The knowledge that I possess, as to the present valuation being so much below the existing scale of prices upon which a new valuation would be based.

6992. You merely add a certain per-centage to

Mr. *Mulholland*—continued.

to the old valuation?—To the valuation of each county, and it brings out that result.

6993. Were the prices in 1852 different from those of Ulster, except for the small discrepancy that you have alluded to; they were the same basis of prices, were they not?—Yes.

6994. How do you account for it that you could raise the valuation there now 16 per cent.?—Because the valuation is higher although based upon the scale of prices of the valuation of Ulster. First of all it was made more recently, and it was the last part of Ireland that was valued, and the taxes were not so high as in other parts that were valued during the famine time; and in the next place, there is a greater quantity of produce per acre taken out of the soil of Ulster than there is out of the soil of Munster, and therefore the produce is greater.

6995. But would not that apply to the new valuation as well as to the former one?—No, because I suppose the increase of produce has not been in the same ratio.

6996. That would be no reason for having a smaller per-centage additional to a new valuation in Ulster than in the other provinces; the Ulster lands return a larger amount of produce?—Yes, it would. If you get out of an acre of ground 20 barrels of wheat, owing to industry and an improved system, you calculate on the price of the produce of 20 barrels of wheat at 25 *s.* a barrel, whereas if you go down into Roscommon there you will only get 12 or 14 barrels, and, therefore, the value per acre must be lower than the value per acre in Ulster, although both may be based upon the same scale of prices.

6997. But that consideration would be a constant quantity for the valuations, both in 1851 and 1873, and the per-centage of change in price would be the only fluctuation?—I daresay it is so.

6998. Do you believe that there are many irregularities or discrepancies in any county at present between one district of a county and another, that the line you would draw, and that the present valuation is in any case more lightly or more lowly put than another?—Yes, I do.

6999. Do you think that that can be avoided in a new valuation?—Certainly.

7000. How did it arise?—It arose in this way. For instance, if you were to go to a portion of the county of Meath, you would find now that there is a large tract of what they call fattening land. Take another portion of it down about Skreen, or in that direction, and you will find it all tillage land.

7001. Then the discrepancies have arisen from change of condition since, but at the time the valuation was a fair one over the district?—Yes.

7002. You do not anticipate that there will be any difficulty in getting a sufficient number of qualified assistants, to have a fair and uniform valuation over the whole of Ireland now?—I do not.

Mr. *Kavanagh.*

7003. You said, in answer to the honourable Member for Youghal, did not you, that you thought it was right to take into account the rate of wages in valuing tillage land?—I said that it must be taken into account.

7004. Then, in the event of the tremendous increase there has been in wages within the last 10 or 12 years, you would consider that as reducing

Mr. *Kavanagh*—continued.

the value of tillage land?—If there was a re-valuation made now, the increased wages given would be taken into account.

7005. In the matter of grazing land, if there was any prevalence of disease amongst cattle, would you take that into consideration?—No, I would not take that as an element of valuation.

7006. Supposing it was proved that there was a regular prevalence of disease, to a much greater extent than there was when the last valuation was made, you would not think that that told upon the value of grazing land at all?—I would not. In the valuing of railways we never take into account the amount of compensation paid for accidents on the railway.

7007. You think that that would be a foreign element altogether?—Yes.

Mr. *Mulholland.*

7008. Do not you think that the consideration of rent by the valuator is likely to mislead; because if the rents in the country are being periodically revised, say, every 30 years, some estates would have been just revised, and others would be about to be revised, so that there would be always an irregularity in the rent?—It would be their duty, in a re-valuation, to compare the rents, and put them down in the books, though not to be guided by them in making the valuation.

Mr. *Butt.*

7009. Supposing there was an estate let at a very exorbitant rent, and another let at a fair, moderate rent, you would not, I presume, put a higher value on the estate which was let exorbitantly?—Certainly not.

Mr. *Kavanagh.*

7010. You would not consider the rent only?—No.

Mr. *Collins.*

7011. About what is the remuneration of the valuators?—About 460 *l.* a year, and expenses.

7012. Are they paid their travelling expenses and maintenance?—Yes, they are.

7013. How many are there at present?—There are about 32, I think.

7014. You would exempt simply the churches and places of worship, in the case of re-valuation?—Yes.

7015. Why not equally exempt such establishments as almshouses or public hospitals; why do you make an exception simply in favour of churches and chapels?—I think the exemption of those classes of property is more or less an endowment of them.

7016. But almshouses would be also endowed institutions, would they not?—Yes. It appears to me that at the meeting which I have described of the deputation that waited upon Lord Hartington, hospitals were specially stated. Sir Dominic Corrigan said that, in his opinion, hospitals should not be exempted. I was inclined to think that hospitals, and that class of property, should be exempted as charities.

7017. Then your judgment is influenced more by the opinions of the deputation to which you have referred than by any other circumstance?—Yes, certainly.

7018. In your own judgment those establishments, such as almshouses and public hospitals, ought to be exempt equally with churches of various

Mr. *J. B. Greene.*

7 July 1876.

Mr. J. B. Greene.

7 July 1876.

Mr. *Collins*—continued.

various denominations?—I think they should; I am not sure whether they are in the draft Bill which I prepared. I think that in the Bill of 1873 hospitals, almshouses, and this class of property were included.

7019. Might the Committee take it as your own recommendation, that churches and chapels of various denominations should be exempt, and that you would equally include almshouses and public hospitals?—Yes, I think that that class clearly comes within the purview of charitable institutions, and I would add them to the others.

Mr. *Brooks*.

7020. In the valuation of land we will take the case of adjoining lands, one in the hands of an improving proprietor or occupier, and the other in the hands of a negligent proprietor or occupier, excluding buildings and drainage, and other permanent improvements, and taking into consideration only the condition of the lands, do you raise your valuation of the land which is in good condition, above that of the land which is in other respects alike in aspect and soil, but negligently maintained?—We do; we value the thing as we find it. At the time that the valuator goes on the ground, his instructions are to value it then and there; of course, if we find the land very highly improved, and the next neighbour has neglected his land very much, the neglected land is valued lower, no doubt.

7021. Then, that penalises the improving proprietor to the extent that it diminishes the valuation of the negligent proprietor or occupier?—To some extent that may be so, but we cannot value good land the same as neglected. I do not see how it could be carried out differently; I should probably explain that in all the Acts, and in the draft Act prepared for the drainage, and reclamation and improvement, the increased value is not to be assessed for seven years, but merely the common question of high manuring, or high farming, or that class of things makes no difference; but where a man is expending money on drainage or reclamation, or a permanent class of improvements, then he is not to be rated on the increased value for seven years, so that in that way he escapes to a certain extent.

Dr. *Ward*.

7022. You said that Sir Dominic Corrigan objected to the exemption of hospitals; on what ground did he object?—The deputation wished a Bill brought in, and I believe there was a similar Bill introduced for Scotland, to abolish exemptions from rating altogether. This deputation waited upon Lord Hartington, and asked him to introduce a measure to do away with the exemptions altogether, as they thought it was an unjust principle. I would not carry it out to that extent.

7023. You would allow exemptions on churches, chapels, and hospitals; would you allow charity schools to be exempted?—They are exempted at present, and I would allow the exemptions to continue; in fact, there are not very many of them, so that the exemptions would be very immaterial in amount.

Dr. *Ward*—continued.

7024. You would embrace in the exemptions such things as industrial schools?—Yes, I would carry out the law as it is at present.

Mr. *Bruen*.

7025. With regard to the valuation of town parks (you know the class of land to which I allude), should you go upon the agricultural value of the land in making your new valuation?—Certainly, including local circumstances. The agricultural value, of course, would be enhanced by its contiguity to the town, and the facility for procuring manure, and other causes. Town parks near a small town would not be so valuable as town parks near a city; it depends upon the population a good deal.

Mr. *Kavanagh*.

7026. With reference to town versus country, do you think that towns are higher valued or lower valued in proportion?—They are a little higher valued; all towns are.

7027. You consider that in any new valuation the main increase would be upon the rural districts?—There would be an increase in the principal towns; some small country towns I do not think would be very much affected.

7028. The increase on the towns would not be in the same proportion as it would be on the country?—No, it would not.

Mr. *Butt*.

7029. How do you value market gardens?—They are valued as town parks.

7030. They are not valued as such?—No.

7031. A valuation based upon the price of agricultural produce would not touch them?—No.

7032. Is not the increase in the value of market gardens owing to the extra labour expended on them?—Yes, a good deal of it is.

Mr. *Brooks*.

7033. They are more highly manured, are they not?—Yes.

Mr. *Butt*.

7034. Would not a piece of ground near Dublin, capable of being a market garden, let beyond its value if it was to be grown in oats or wheat?—It would not.

7035. A piece of ground near Dublin capable of being used as a market garden would let far higher, would it not, than if it was let under covenant, for instance, only to grow wheat?—Not capable, but worked as a market garden; I doubt very much whether there would be any difference in the value; owing to the enormous amount of manure that is used, and the carting of it, and the excess of labour, I think probably it would not fetch much more than what we call accommodation land, let for town parks or for grazing.

7036. Supposing a man took a field and made a market garden of it, you would not ask a higher rent for it than for the adjoining field, merely because of the use that he was going to put it to?—No.

LIST OF APPENDIX.

Appendix, No. 8.

Appendix, No. 9.

Appendix, No. 10.

APPENDIX.

Appendix, No. 1.

PAPER handed in by Dr. *Neilson Hancock*.

RETURN as to Towns, showing Number of Authorities which the Towns are under, and which exercised powers entrusted to any Town Authority.

Appendix, No. 1.

	Number.
(A.)—Towns with Four Authorities within Town Boundary - - - -	3
(B.)—Towns with Three Authorities within Town Boundary - - -	77
(C.)—Towns with Two Authorities within Town Boundary - - - -	21
(D.)—Towns under a Single Authority within the Town Boundary - -	10
	111

1 May 1876. *W. Neilson Hancock.*

(A.) *Towns with Four Authorities within Town Boundary.*

Lisburn.—Town Commissioners, Court Leet of Manor of Kilultagh, County of Antrim Grand Jury, and County of Down Grand Jury.

Ballina.—Town Commissioners, Board of Guardians, County of Mayo Grand Jury, and County of Sligo Grand Jury.

Ballinasloe.—Town Commissioners, Board of Guardians, County of Galway Grand Jury, and County of Roscommon Grand Jury.

(B.) *Towns with Three Authorities within Town Boundary.*

Carrickfergus.—Municipal Commissioners, Board of Guardians, and County of the Town of Carrickfergus Grand Jury.

Carlow.—Town Commissioners, County of Carlow Grand Jury, and Queen's County Grand Jury.

Carrick-on-Suir.—Town Commissioners, County of Tipperary Grand Jury, and County of Waterford Grand Jury.

New Ross.—Town Commissioners, County of Wexford Grand Jury, and County of Kilkenny Grand Jury.

Athlone.—Town Commissioners, County of Westmeath Grand Jury, and County of Roscommon Grand Jury.

Clonmel.—Town Council, County of Tipperary Grand Jury, and County of Waterford Grand Jury.

Coleraine.—Town Commissioners, County of Londonderry Grand Jury, and the Society of the Governor and Assistants of London of the New Plantation in Ulster.

Tipperary.
Mallow.
Dungannon.
Omagh.
Monaghan.
Downpatrick.
Wicklow.
Fethard.
} Lighting and Cleansing Commissioners, Board of Guardians, and Grand Jury of County at large in which situate.

Appendix, No. 1.

(B.) *Towns with Three Authorities within Town Boundary*—continued.

Nenagh. Banbridge. Enniscorthy. Killarney. Tullamore. Mullingar. Thurles. Parsonstown. Cashel. Athy. Westport. Longford. Tuam. Strabane. Navan. Skibbereen. Naas. Middleton. Holywood. Castlebar. Clonakilty. Cookstown. Templemore. Cavan. Boyle. Mountmellick. Larne. Newbridge. Loughrea. Ardee.	Ballyshannon. Kells. Ballymoney. Newtown Limavady. Maryborough. Gilford. Gorey. Bangor. Rathkeale. Dromore. Callan. Roscommon. Balbriggan. Bagnalstown. Killiney and Ballybrack. Trim. Clones. Letterkenny. Antrim. Carrickmacross. Lismore. Cootehill. Keady. Castleblayney. Belturbet. Ballybay. Aughnacloy. Tandragee.	Town Commissioners, Board of Guardians, and Grand Jury of County at large in which Towns situate.
Blackrock. Kingstown. Pembroke. Bray.		Township Commissioners, Town Council of Dublin, and Grand Jury of County of Dublin.

(C.) *Towns with Two Authorities within the Town Boundaries.*

Londonderry.—Town Council and Society of the Governor and Assistants of London of the New Plantation of Ulster.
Belfast.—Town Council and Water Commissioners.
Waterford.—Town Council and County of City Grand Jury.
Kilkenny.—Town Council and County of City Grand Jury.
Drogheda.—Town Council and County of the Town Grand Jury.
Galway.—Town Improvement Commissioners and County of the Town Grand Jury.

Tralee. Armagh. Bandon. Youghal.	Lighting and Cleansing Commissioners and Grand Jury of County at large in which Town situate.
Dundalk. Lurgan. Newtownards. Ballymena. Fermoy. Portadown. Ennis. Kinsale.	Town Commissioners and Grand Jury of County at large in which Town situate.
Clontarf. Dalkey. New Kilmainham.	The Township Commissioners and the Grand Jury of the County of Dublin.

(D.) *Towns with a Single Authority within the Municipal Boundary.*

Dublin. Cork. Limerick. Sligo. Wexford.	The Town Council.

Rathmines and Rathgar.—The Town Improvement Commissioners.
Newry.—The Town Commissioners incorporated by Special Act.
Enniskillen.—The Commissioners of the Borough.
Queenstown.—The Town Commissioners.
Dungarvan.—The Town Commissioners.

1 May 1876. *W. Neilson Hancock.*

Appendix, No. 2.

PAPER handed in by Dr. *Hancock*, 5 May 1876.

TABLE showing DUPLICATE or CUMULATIVE PROVISIONS conferring Executory Powers on Town Authorities in *Ireland* in 1873.*

<table>
<tr><th>Description of Executory Power.</th><th>Lighting and Cleansing Commissioners.</th><th>Town Councils.</th><th>Towns Improvement Commissioners.</th><th>Municipal Commissioners.</th></tr>
<tr><td rowspan="2">Sewers, Drainage of Houses, and Sewage Disposal.</td><td>Lighting and Cleansing Act, 1829.</td><td>6 Towns Local Acts.
4 Towns Improvement Act, 1854.
1 None.</td><td>Towns Improvement Act, 1854, secs. 32 35.
Ditto Clauses Act, 1847, secs. 22 to 50.</td><td>None.</td></tr>
<tr><td colspan="4">Sewage Utilisation Act, 1865; entire Act.
Public Health Act, secs. 45, 46, 68, 74.
Local Government Act, 1858; secs. 4, 5, 6.
Sanitary Act, 1866, secs. 4, 6, 9, 10, 49.</td></tr>
<tr><td rowspan="2">Water Supply.</td><td>Lighting and Cleansing Act, 1829.</td><td>6 Towns Local Acts.
4 Towns T. Improvement Act, 1854.
1 None.</td><td>Towns Improvement Act, secs. 52, 54.
Towns Clauses Act, sec. 124.</td><td>None.</td></tr>
<tr><td colspan="4">Sanitary Acts, 1866; secs. 11, 12, 18, 50.
Public Health Act, 1848; secs. 75 to 80.
Local Government Act, 1858; secs. 51 to 53.
Ditto - ditto - 1861; sec. 21.</td></tr>
<tr><td rowspan="2">Nuisance Removal and Prevention.</td><td>Lighting and Cleansing Act.</td><td>6 Towns Local Acts.
4 Towns T. Improvement Act, 1854.
1 None.</td><td>Town Improvement Act, secs. 70 to 73.
Towns Improvement Clauses Act, secs. 90 to 108, 125, 127.</td><td>None.</td></tr>
<tr><td colspan="4">Sanitary Act, 1866; 15 to 20, 54.
Nuisance Removal Act, 1855.
Ditto - ditto - 1860.
Sanitary Act Amendment Act.
Nuisance Removal Act Amendment Act.</td></tr>
<tr><td rowspan="2">Regulations for Lodging-houses, Bakehouses, and Workshops.</td><td>—</td><td>6 Towns Local Acts.
4 Towns T. Improvement Act.
1 None.</td><td>Towns Improvement Act, 1854; secs. 45, 46.
Towns Clauses Act, secs. 117, 118.</td><td>—</td></tr>
<tr><td colspan="4">Common Lodging-house Acts of 1851, 1853, and 1860.
Sanitary Act, 1866; secs. 35, 30, 32, and 41.
Bakehouse Regulations Act, 1863.
Workshop Regulations Act, 1867.</td></tr>
<tr><td rowspan="2">Cellar Dwellings.</td><td>—</td><td>—</td><td>Towns Improvement Act.
Towns Clauses Act, secs. 113 to 115.</td><td>—</td></tr>
<tr><td colspan="4">Public Health Act, 1848; sec. 67.</td></tr>
<tr><td rowspan="2">Regulation of Sale of Food.</td><td>—</td><td>6 Towns Local Acts.
4 Towns T. Improvement Act.
1 Town none.
Adulteration Act, 1860.</td><td>Towns Improvement Act, secs. 48, 50.</td><td>—</td></tr>
<tr><td colspan="4">Nuisance Removal Act, 1855.
Ditto - ditto - Amendment Act, 1863.</td></tr>
<tr><td rowspan="2">Powers of entry to do Works.</td><td>—</td><td>6 Towns Local Acts.
4 Towns T. Improvement Act.
1 Town none.</td><td>Town Improvement Act, Sec. 5.
Ditto - ditto - Clauses Act, secs. 144, 148.</td><td>—</td></tr>
<tr><td colspan="4">Public Health Act, 1848; sec. 143.
Nuisance Removal Act, 1855; sec. 11.
Sanitary Act, 1866; sec. 91.</td></tr>
<tr><td rowspan="2">Arbitration.</td><td>—</td><td>—</td><td>Towns Improvement Act, 1854.
Local Clauses Act, 1845; secs. 26, 27.</td><td></td></tr>
<tr><td colspan="4">Public Health Act, 1847; secs. 123 to 126.</td></tr>
</table>

* From Report of William Mulholland, Esq., to Statistical and Social Inquiry Society of Ireland, with one correction in Town Councils.

Appendix, No. 3.

PAPER handed in by Dr. *Hancock*.

RETURN showing the Result in *Belfast* and *Dublin* of Plans of constituting Town Authorities on the following Basis :—

1. One half the governing body to be lessors' and owners' representatives, and one half to be inhabitants' and occupiers' representatives.

2. Lessors' representatives to be chosen thus :—

(*a.*) The lessors' *ward* representative to be lessor or owner of highest value in ward, if a J. P., or naming son or agent (if J. P.), or if a company, naming a director, or if a department of government, naming a civil servant.

(*b.*) Rest of lessors' representatives to be *town* representatives, to be elected by lessors and owners of whole town, with one right of voting for each 10 *l.* of valuation, to vote for all lessors' town representatives, and with power to accumulate their votes on one or more candidates.

3. Inhabitants' representatives to be chosen thus :—

(*a.*) The inhabitants' *ward* representative to be elected by inhabitants, heads of families in each ward (only one to vote for each two families if more than one in a house), and by occupiers of offices, warehouses, counting-houses, and shops, though resident out of borough, if heads of families.

(*b.*) Rest of inhabitants' representatives to be *town* representatives, and be selected by inhabitants and occupiers of whole town, with a right of voting for all the inhabitants' *town* representatives, and with power to accumulate their votes on one or more candidates.

BELFAST.

Lessors' *ward* representatives, *ex officio* - - - - - - - 5
Lessors' *town* representatives - - - - - - - - - 15

Estimated number of lessors' and owners' rights of voting, allowing one right to vote for each 10 *l.* of valuation (exclusive of value held by *ex-officio* owners, lessors directly represented, assumed, in the absence of statistics for this calculation, to be one-fourth of the whole) - - - - - - - 30,443
Number of such 10 *l.* rights of voting that could, by accumulation, be certain to return one candidate. Any number above 1-16th, or 6¼ per cent. - - 1,903
Annual value, the lessors or owners of which could, by accumulating their votes, be certain to return one candidate at election of lessors' *town* representatives £. 21,141

Inhabitants' *Ward* Representatives, one for each *ward* - - - - 5

WARD.	Estimated New Constituency of Inhabitants and Occupiers.
Cromac - - - - - - - - - -	8,156
Dock - - - - - - - - - -	5,139
St. Anne's - - - - - - - - - -	9,061
St. George's - - - - - - - - - -	6,840
Smithfield - - - - - - - - - -	6,098
TOTAL - - -	35,294

Inhabitants' *town* representatives - - - - - - - - 15

Total of new constituency of inhabitants and occupiers - - - -	35,294
Present constituency - - - - - - - - - -	5,214
Increase - - -	30,080

Number of inhabitants and occupiers who could, by accumulating their votes, be certain to return one candidate at election of inhabitants' *town* representatives. Any number above 1-16th, or 6¼ per cent. - - - - 2,206

DUBLIN.

Lessors' *ward* representatives, *ex officio* - - - - -	15
Lessors' *town* representatives - - - - - - -	15

Estimated number of lessors and owners' rights of voting, allowing one right of voting for each 10 *l.* of valuation (exclusive of value held by *ex-officio* owners or lessors directly represented, assumed in absence of statistics for this calculation to be one-half of the whole) - - - - - - - 31,950

Number of such 10 *l.* rights of voting that could, by accumulation, be certain to return one candidate. Any number above 1-16th or 6¼ per cent - - - 1,998

Annual value the lessors or owners of which could, by accumulating their votes, be certain to return one candidate at election of lessors' *town* representatives £. 32,167

Inhabitants' *Ward* Representatives, one for each *ward* - - 15

WARDS.	Estimated New Constituency of Inhabitants and Occupiers.	WARDS.	Estimated New Constituency of Inhabitants and Occupiers.
Arran Quay - - -	3,762	Royal Exchange - -	1,929
Inns Quay - - -	3,600	South City - - -	1,480
Mountjoy - - -	3,850	South Dock - - -	2,311
North City - - -	2,186	Trinity - - - -	2,416
North Dock - - -	3,905	Usher's Quay - - -	2,973
Rotunda - - - -	1,761	Ward Quay - - -	3,552
Fitzwilliam - - -	1,068		
Mansion House - -	1,986	TOTAL - - -	40,278
Merchants' Quay - -	3,486		

Inhabitants' *town* representatives - - - - - - 15

Total of new constituency of inhabitants and occupiers - - - -	40,278
Present constituency - - - - - - - - - -	5,599
Increase - - - - - - - - - -	34,679

Number of inhabitants and occupiers that could by accumulating their votes be certain to return one candidate at election of inhabitants' *town* representatives. Any number above 1-16th, or 6¼ per cent. - - - - - 2,518

11 May 1876.

W. Neilson Hancock.

PAPERS delivered in by Mr *Henry*

TABLE, No [illegible]

	1845.	1846.	1847	1848	1849	1850.
	£ s d	£ s d	£ s d	£ s d	£ s d	£ s d
Paving Tax	[illegible] 1 5	[illegible] 15 6	[illegible] 1 8	[illegible]	[illegible]	[illegible] 10 5
Watering Tax	[illegible] 15 4	[illegible] 3 9	[illegible]	[illegible]	2,344 – 9	[illegible]
Miscellaneous Receipts	[illegible] 17 6	46 19 4	45 [illegible] –	[illegible]	[illegible]	[illegible]
Borrowed from Corporation	[illegible] 1 8	341 [illegible]	[illegible] 1 8	–	341 [illegible]	—
Scavenging and sold	734 6 9	[illegible]	[illegible]	[illegible] – 6	[illegible]	[illegible] 7 9
*Amount received for private works	[illegible]	[illegible] 14 –	[illegible]	[illegible]	[illegible]	[illegible]
	[illegible]	[illegible]	[illegible]	[illegible]	[illegible]	[illegible]
Deduct amount paid to [illegible]	[illegible]	[illegible]	[illegible]	[illegible]	[illegible]	[illegible]
	[illegible]	[illegible]	[illegible]	[illegible]	[illegible]	[illegible]
Deduct poundage for collection	[illegible]	[illegible]	[illegible]	[illegible]	[illegible]	[illegible]
Amount at disposal of Paving Commissioners for lighting, cleansing, repairs, and watering [illegible]	[illegible]	[illegible]	[illegible]	[illegible]	[illegible]	[illegible]

[illegible]	1851	1852	1853	1854	[illegible]
	£ s d	£ s d	£ s d	£ s d	
Cash Balance handed over by Paving Commissioners to Corporation, [illegible] January 1851	[illegible]	—	—	—	[illegible]
Ditto, by Wide Street Commissioners	[illegible]	—	—	—	[illegible]
Amount of [illegible] due to Wide Street Commissioners and collected by Collector General	[illegible]	—	—	—	[illegible]
Improvement Rate [illegible]	[illegible]	[illegible]	[illegible]	[illegible]	[illegible]
Wide Street [illegible] available [illegible]	[illegible]	[illegible]	[illegible]	[illegible]	[illegible]
Scavenging and sold	[illegible]	[illegible]	[illegible]	[illegible]	[illegible]
Amount received for the execution of private works [illegible]	[illegible]	[illegible]	[illegible]	[illegible]	[illegible]
	[illegible]	[illegible]	[illegible]	[illegible]	[illegible]
EXTRAORDINARY EXPENDITURE.					
Amount paid for Parliamentary [illegible]	[illegible]	[illegible]	[illegible]	—	[illegible]
	[illegible]	[illegible]	[illegible]	[illegible]	[illegible]
Sums chargeable on Improvement Rate [illegible]	[illegible]	[illegible]	[illegible]	[illegible]	[illegible]
Amount at disposal of Committee, [illegible], for lighting, cleansing, repairs and watering of streets	[illegible]	[illegible]	[illegible]	[illegible]	[illegible]

* A considerable portion of [illegible] was paid Commissioners for [illegible] works.
† This year there was [illegible] received as the purchase money of the old Paving Board House in [illegible]-street, also [illegible], the purchase money of [illegible] belonging to Wide Street Estate sold [illegible], for Trinity Church, which was paid to [illegible] Wide Street [illegible], but is not included in this sum

Appendix, No. 4.

PAPER delivered in by Mr Henry

TABLE, No. 4.

[illegible] of the Improvement Rate during the Years from 18[illegible] to 18[illegible] inclusive, and the Sum which remains, after deducting the Charges set forth in Table No. [illegible], applicable and at the disposal of Committee No. 1 for the Lighting, Cleansing, Repair and Maintenance of the Streets, &c.

	1855	1856.	1857	1858	1859	1860	1861	1862	1863	1864.	1865	1866	1867.	1868
	£ s d	£ s d	£ s d	£ s d	£ s d	£ s d	£ s d	£ s d	£ s d	£ s d	£ s d	£ s d	£ s d	£ s d
1	—	—	—	—	—	—	—	—	—	—	—	—	—	—
2	—	—	—	—	—	—	—	—	—	—	—	—	—	—
3	—	—	—	—	—	—	—	—	—	—	—	—	—	—
4	[illegible]	[illegible]	[illegible]	[illegible]	[illegible]	[illegible]	[illegible]	[illegible]	[illegible]	[illegible]	[illegible]	[illegible]	[illegible]	[illegible]
5	[illegible]	[illegible]	[illegible]	[illegible]	[illegible]	[illegible]	[illegible]	[illegible]	[illegible]	[illegible]	[illegible]	[illegible]	[illegible]	[illegible]
6	[illegible]	[illegible]	[illegible]	[illegible]	[illegible] to 20th April	. . .	. . .	. . .	. . .	. . .	. . .	. . .	-	111 10 -
7	[illegible]	[illegible]	[illegible]	[illegible]	[illegible]	[illegible]	[illegible]	[illegible]	[illegible]	[illegible]	[illegible]	[illegible]	[illegible]	[illegible]
8	[illegible]	[illegible]	[illegible]	[illegible]	[illegible]	[illegible]	[illegible]	[illegible]	[illegible]	[illegible]	[illegible]	[illegible]	[illegible]	[illegible]
9	—	—	—	—	—	—	—	—	—	—	—	—	—	—
10	[illegible]	[illegible]	[illegible]	[illegible]	[illegible]	[illegible]	[illegible]	[illegible]	[illegible]	[illegible]	[illegible]	[illegible]	[illegible]	[illegible]
11	[illegible]	[illegible]	[illegible]	[illegible]	[illegible]	[illegible]	[illegible]	[illegible]	[illegible]	[illegible]	[illegible]	[illegible]	[illegible]	[illegible]
12	[illegible]	[illegible]	[illegible]	[illegible]	[illegible]	[illegible]	[illegible]	[illegible]	[illegible]	[illegible]	[illegible]	[illegible]	[illegible]	[illegible]

Appendix, No. 5.

Appendix, No. 5.

IRISH REFORM ACT, 1868.

CASE on behalf of the Collector General of Rates, and OPINION of the Right Honourable *R. A. Warren* thereon.

CASE.

COUNSEL's attention is requested to the Collection of Rates Act (12 & 13 Vict. c. 91), and to the Representation of the People (Ireland) Act, 1868 (31 & 32 Vict. c. 49).

It is enacted by the 63rd section of the former Act, that owners of all rateable property, of which the full net annual value does not exceed 8 *l.*, or which are let to weekly or monthly tenants, or in separate apartments, shall be rated to and pay the rates thereby directed to be made instead of the occupiers thereof.

The 66th section enacts that occupiers of any rateable property may demand to be assessed therefor, and to pay the rates in respect thereof, and that the Collector General shall assess every such occupier so long as he duly pays said rates, anything thereinbefore contained notwithstanding.

Provision is made by the 75th & 76th sections for recovery of rates due by an owner, and three months in arrear, from the occupier (not exceeding the amount of the occupier's rent), in like manner as rates may be recovered from the occupiers of any property liable to be rated.

By the 31 & 32 Vict. c. 49, the 63rd section of the Collection of Rates Act is repealed, "so far as regards poor rate," in respect of lands, tenements, and hereditaments, of which the net annual value shall be more than 4 *l.*; and it is directed that whenever the net annual value of the whole of the rateable hereditaments in any electoral division, situate wholly or in part in the borough of Dublin, occupied by any person or persons as tenant from year to year, or under lease or agreement made after 24th August 1846, shall not exceed 4 *l.*, the poor rate in respect of such hereditament shall be made on the immediate lessor or lessors of such person or persons.

The Collector General is desirous of being advised as to what alterations he is to make in the rating of premises where the net annual value shall exceed 4 *l.*, and shall not exceed 8 *l.*, or where either within those limits, or exceeding 8 *l.* in valuation, the rated premises are let to weekly or monthly tenants, or in separate apartments.

Hitherto the owner has been rated for all such premises; and it would seem for the future the owner should be rated in respect of all rates where the annual value of the rateable premises does not exceed 4 *l.*, and that where the annual valuation exceeds 4 *l.*, and does not exceed 8 *l.*, or where (independently of value) the premises are let to weekly or monthly tenants, or in separate apartments, the owners should be rated in respect of all rates, except poor rate, in respect of which the occupier should be rated.

One of the rate books for the years 1867 and 1868 is sent herewith, in order that counsel may see how the assessments have been hitherto made.

> Counsel will please say whether the effect of the alterations made in the law by the 31 & 32 Vict. c. 49, is correctly stated above, and if not, what is the effect of such alterations, and prepare a form of the new ratings; and say whether in cases where the occupier is to be rated as regards poor rate, and the owner as regards other rates, it will be sufficient to rate the owner and occupier together (giving the occupier's name and the owner's, when the latter is known) for the entire rates, distributing the payment of the rates between the owner and occupier according to their respective liabilities; or must it be shown in separate figures the amounts payable by the owner and by the occupier respectively? If the former will be sufficient, it will save a great number of calculations, and a corresponding quantity of time and trouble in the making up of the rate books.

It will be seen that the 63rd section of the Rates Act is repealed by the 31 & 32 Vict. c. 49, so far as regards the rating, &c., for poor rate, in cases where the annual value of the rateable premises shall exceed 4 *l.*; and the occupiers in all such cases are required to be rated for poor rate without excepting cases where the premises are let, wholly or in part, in separate apartments.

> Who is the proper person to be rated for the future for the poor rate, where the annual value shall exceed 4 *l.*, where the premises are let, wholly or in part, in separate apartments; and is it from the owner of such premises, or from the occupiers, that poor rate should be recovered; and if from the occupiers, must not the Valuation Department furnish the Collector General with a separate valuation for each separate apartment?

Sections

Sections 21, 22, and 23, of the Irish Reform Act, impose certain duties on the Collector General. Appendix, No. 5.

Counsel is requested to advise the Collector General generally as to the alterations of rating rendered necessary to be made by said statute of the 31 & 32 Vict. c. 49, and what changes are thereby made in the liability to the payment of rates collectible by the Collector General, or in the mode of enforcing payment of such rates.

Counsel's general advice for the guidance of the Collector General is requested.

OPINION.

The question involved in this Case is one of extreme difficulty; but, after the best consideration in my power, I have arrived at the conclusion that the 63rd section, 12 & 13 Vict. c. 91, is not repealed as to rateable property let to weekly or monthly tenants, or in separate apartments. The collection of annual rates from weekly or monthly tenants presents an absurdity, and certainly was not intended by the Legislature. I concur in Mr. Serjeant Barry's opinion on all the points of the Case, and strongly recommend the proceedings to enforce rates in respect of weekly or monthly holdings, or separate apartments, should be taken by summons, and not by distress.

(signed) *Rob. A. Warren.*

Fitzwilliam-square, 11 November 1868.

IRISH REFORM ACT, 1868.

CASE on behalf of the Collector General of Rates, and Opinion of Mr. Serjeant *Barry*, M.P., thereon.

CASE.

Counsel's attention is requested to the Collection of Rates Act (12 & 13 Vict. c. 91), and to the Representation of the People (Ireland) Act, 1868 (31 & 32 Vict. c. 49).

It is enacted by the 63rd section of the former Act, that owners of all rateable property, of which the full net annual value does not exceed 8 *l.*, or which are let to weekly or monthly tenants, or in separate apartments, shall be rated to and pay the rates thereby directed to be made instead of the occupiers thereof.

The 66th section enacts that occupiers of any rateable property may demand to be assessed therefor, and to pay the rates in respect thereof; and that the Collector General shall assess every such occupier so long as he duly pays said rates, anything thereinbefore contained notwithstanding.

Provision is made by the 75th and 76th sections for recovery of rates due by an owner, and three months in arrear, from the occupier (not exceeding the amount of the occupier's rent), in like manner as rates may be recovered from the occupier of any property liable to be rated.

By the 31 & 32 Vict. c. 49, the 63rd section of the Collection of Rates Act is repealed, "so far as regards poor rate," in respect of lands, tenements, and hereditaments, of which the net annual value shall be more than 4 *l.*; and it is directed that whenever the net annual value of the whole of the rateable hereditaments in any electoral division, situate wholly or in part in the borough of Dublin, occupied by any person or persons as tenant from year to year, or under lease or agreement made after 24th August 1843, shall not exceed 4 *l.*, the poor rate in respect of such hereditament shall be made on the immediate lessor or lessors of such person or persons.

The Collector General is desirous of being advised as to what alterations he is to make in the rating of premises where the net annual value shall exceed 4 *l.*, and shall not exceed 8 *l.*, or where either within those limits or exceeding 8 *l.*, in valuation, the rated premises are let to weekly or monthly tenants, or in separate apartments.

Hitherto the owner has been rated for all such premises; and it would seem for the future the owner should be rated in respect of all rates where the annual value of the rateable premises does not exceed 4 *l.*, and that where the annual valuation exceeds 4 *l.*, and does not exceed 8 *l.*, or where (independently of value) the premises are let to weekly or monthly tenants, or in separate apartments, the owners should be rated in respect of all rates, except poor rate, in respect of which the occupier should be rated.

One of the rate books for the years 1867 and 1868 is sent herewith, in order that counsel may see how the assessments have been hitherto made.

Counsel will please say whether the effect of the alterations made in the law by the 31 & 32 Vict. c. 49, is correctly stated above, and if not, what is the effect of such alterations, and prepare a form of the new ratings; and say whether in cases where the occupier is to be rated as regards poor rate, and the owner as regards other rates, it

Appendix, No. 6.

it will be sufficient to rate the owner and occupier together (giving the occupier's name and the owner's, when the latter is known) for the entire rates, distributing the payment of the rates between the owner and occupiers according to their respective liabilities; or must it be shown in separate figures the amounts payable by the owner and by the occupier respectively? If the former will be sufficient, it will save a great number of calculations, and a corresponding quantity of time and trouble in the making up of the rate books.

It will be seen that the 63rd section of the Rates Act is repealed by the 31 & 32 Vict. c. 49, so far as regards the rating, &c., for poor rate, in cases where the annual value of the rateable premises shall exceed 4 *l.*; and the occupiers in all such cases are required to be rated for poor rate without excepting cases where the premises are let, wholly or in part, in separate apartments.

Who is the proper person to be rated for the future for the poor rate, where the annual value shall exceed 4 *l.*, where the premises are let, wholly or in part, in separate apartments; and is it from the owner of such premises, or from the occupiers, that poor rate should be recovered; and if from the occupiers, must not the Valuation Department furnish the Collector General with a separate valuation for each separate apartment?

Sections 21, 22, and 23, of the Irish Reform Act, impose certain duties on the Collector General.

Counsel is requested to advise the Collector General generally as to the alterations of rating rendered necessary to be made by said statute of 31 & 32 Vict. c. 49, and what changes are thereby made in the liability to the payment of rates collectible by the Collector General, or in the mode of enforcing payment of such rates.

Counsel's general advice for the guidance of the Collector General is requested.

COUNSEL'S OPINION.

I am clearly of opinion that, in the Irish Reform Act of last Session, the Legislature had no intention of in any way altering the rating of premises let in separate apartments, or to weekly or monthly tenants. The general language of the Repealing Clause in the 19th section creates a difficulty, but I will advise the Collector General to assess such premises, or the owner, exactly as before.

As regards premises value over 4 *l.* (not let in separate apartments, or to weekly or monthly tenants), where the occupier under the Reform Act is liable to poor rate, and the owner remains liable to the other taxes, I think the amount of poor rate should be brought out against the occupier in a distinct rating. The precise mode of doing this is rather matter for the technical experience of the officials than for counsel. It seems to me that the simplest mode of doing it is to have, instead of as at present, one column headed "assessments," to have two columns as follows:—

Assessments (not including Poor Rate when it is Payable by Occupier, the Owner or Lessor being liable to the other Assessments).	Poor Rate when Payable by Occupier, the other Assessments being Payable by Owner or Lessor.
£. s. d.	£. s. d.

The above seems to me a simple form, and more in accordance with the present system than either of the forms sent to me; but as I have said, it is a matter on which the experienced officials are more competent to decide than I am.

5 November 1868. (signed) *C. R. Barry.*

Appendix, No. 6.

PAPER handed in by Mr *Henry*, and referred to in his Evidence, Q. 1466.

RETURN of Number of Meetings of the Town Council of *Dublin*, with Hours for which they were Summoned, and Hour of forming Quorum, &c., for the Years 1873, 1874, and 1875.

1873.

Number of Meetings summoned - 48

No.		o'clock.	No.		o'clock.
[illegible]	Summoned for	[illegible]	[illegible]	Quorum formed at	[illegible]
[illegible]	" "	[illegible]	[illegible]	"	[illegible]
[illegible]	" "	[illegible]	[illegible]	"	[illegible]
[illegible]	Summoned for	[illegible]	[illegible]	"	[illegible]
[illegible]	Summoned for	[illegible]	[illegible]	"	[illegible]
7	No meetings		7	No quorum formed.	
48			48		

There were four counts out in the year during transaction of business.

* Election of Secretary Waterworks Company, 7 July; Gas Inspector 1 December; summoned for 1 o'clock, quorum 1.15.

† Election of Superintendent Cattle Market, [illegible] February; Treasurer, 3 June; summoned for 1 o'clock, quorum 1.25.

1874.

Number of Meetings summoned - 50

No.		o'clock.	No.		o'clock.
[illegible]	Summoned for	[illegible]	[illegible]	Quorum formed at	[illegible]
[illegible]	" "	[illegible]	[illegible]	"	[illegible]
[illegible]	Summoned for	[illegible]	[illegible]	"	[illegible]
[illegible]	" "	[illegible]	[illegible]	"	[illegible]
[illegible]	Summoned for	[illegible]	[illegible]	"	[illegible]
[illegible]	Summoned for	[illegible]	[illegible]	"	[illegible]
[illegible]	" "	[illegible]	[illegible]	"	[illegible]
[illegible]	No meetings		[illegible]	No quorum	
50			[illegible]		

There were seven counts out in the year during transaction of business.

* Election of [illegible], [illegible] November; summoned for 11.45; quorum 12.14.

† Election of law agent, [illegible] October; summoned for 1 o'clock, quorum 1.20.

1875.

Number of Meetings summoned - [illegible]

No.		o'clock.	No.		o'clock.
[illegible]	Summoned for	[illegible]	[illegible]	Quorum formed at	[illegible]
[illegible]	Summoned for	[illegible]	[illegible]	"	[illegible]
[illegible]	" "	[illegible]	[illegible]	"	[illegible]
[illegible]	" "	[illegible]	[illegible]	"	[illegible]
[illegible]	Summoned for	[illegible]	[illegible]	"	[illegible]
[illegible]	Summoned for	[illegible]	[illegible]	"	[illegible]
[illegible]	No meetings		[illegible]	No quorum	
[illegible]			[illegible]		

There were seven counts out in the year during transaction of business.

Appendix, No. 7.

PAPER handed in by Mr. *J. A. Curran.*

SCHEDULE showing the Number of NAMES on the BURGESS LIST, as furnished by the TOWN CLERK of the BOROUGH of DUBLIN for the LAST REVISION (1875); the Number of OBJECTIONS served, and the Result in the formation of the BURGESS ROLL for the Year 1875-76.

Total Number of Objections served -	–	1,979
Deduct Number of Objections served on Parties whose Names would also have been struck out as Double Entries -	450	
Deduct Number of Objections dealt with in consequence of the appearance of the Parties objected to, or of the proof or failure in proof of Objections to Parties whose Names had been on the Burgess Roll of the preceding Year:		
Admitted - - - 520		
Struck out - - - 50		
	570	
		1,020
The remainder will be the Number of Names struck out in consequence of Non-attendance of Parties to sustain their cases having been put on proof thereof by reason of the service of Objections - - - - - -	–	959

Total Number on Burgess List - -	–	7,813*
Deduct Number of Double Entries:		
Objected to - - - - -	450	
Not Objected to - - -	1,199	
TOTAL Number of Double Entries -	1,649	
Deduct Number (not Double Entries) struck out in consequence of service of Objections:		
For failure to prove case - 50		
For failure to appear - 953		
	1,003	
		2,652
		5,161
Add Number admitted on Claim Lists -	–	178
NUMBER on Burgess Roll - - - -	–	5,339

From the above it will be seen that the Number on the Burgess List for this Year (1875-76) was 7,813; that the Number on the Burgess Roll for the same year, after revision, is 5,339; and that 953 of those who were returned by the Town Clerk as qualified, were deprived of the Franchise by mere proof of the service of an objection. This will be found an average year.

* This is the item required by the Chief Secretary.

John Ady Curran,
Revising Assessor, Borough of Dublin.

Appendix, No. 8.

PAPERS handed in by Mr. *James Boyle*, 20 June 1876.

PUBLIC HEALTH COMMITTEE.

RETURN of SANITARY OPERATIONS, from the Application of the Sanitary Acts to Dublin, on 22nd August 1866, to 1st January 1876.

Sewers and house drains constructed	Enforced	8,006
Ditto - - - repaired and cleansed	"	8,890
Privies and water closets constructed	"	2,706
Ditto - - - repaired	"	12,250
Ashpits constructed	"	2,302
Privies and ashpits, cleansings of	"	60,040
Dwellings, repairs and cleansings	"	60,705
Dwellings condemned and closed, being unfit for human habitation		646
Dwellings reported to the city engineer as being dangerous		437
Cellar dwellings condemned and closed		207
Yards and external premises, cleansings of,	Enforced	24,529
Lanes and alleys, cleansings of, by private parties	"	2,000
Accumulations of manure removed	"	7,713
Swine removed from dwellings	"	2,085
Other animals removed from dwellings	"	700
Swine removed from yards where kept offensively	"	7,403
Nuisances from smoke abated		36
Ditto - chandleries		0
Ditto - bone yards		7
Ditto - glue and size manufactories		8
Ditto - chemical works		13
Ditto - manure works		8
Ditto - other manufactories		16
Miscellaneous nuisances abated		1,404
Inspections of tenement houses		348,001
Ditto - tenement rooms		707,249
Ditto - nightly lodging-houses		33,007
Ditto - bakeries		13,409
Ditto - slaughter-houses		23,363
Ditto - dairy yards		4,170
Certificates of destitution to entitle to gratuitous interment		1,109
Water supplied to tenement houses	Enforced	1,343
Sanitary defects discovered		106,200
Sanitary defects remedied		186,110
Infected dwellings inspected and cleansed	Enforced	6,776
Ditto - chemically disinfected	"	2,105
Reports received from medical sanitary officers		1,021
Detections of unsound meat		1,088
Ditto - - ditto fish		91
Ditto - - ditto fruit		38
Ditto - - ditto vegetables		30
Ditto - adulterated milk		727
Ditto - - ditto butter		1
Ditto - - ditto coffee		40
Ditto - - ditto mustard		30
Ditto - - ditto tea		2

	No.		Tns.	cts.	qrs.	lbs.
Confiscations of diseased meat	3,855	Weight	896	11	0	10
Ditto - ditto fish	109	"	19	6	1	23
Ditto - ditto fruit	43	"	10	1	1	4
Ditto - ditto vegetables	89	"	5	0	7	1
Ditto - ditto tea	2	"	6	2	1	16
Ditto - ditto flour	2	"	0	19	1	14
Ditto - ditto bread	8	"	4	13	1	6
Ditto - ditto butter	1	"	6	1	1	16

Convictions for possession or sale of unsound meat	80
Ditto - ditto - ditto - fish	12
Ditto - ditto - ditto - fruit	6
Ditto - ditto - ditto - vegetables	3
Ditto - ditto - ditto - mustard	2
Ditto - ditto - ditto - confectionary	11
Convictions for sale, or possession for sale, of adulterated milk	220
Ditto - for sale, or possession for sale, of adulterated coffee	19
Ditto - for sale, or possession for sale, of adulterated mustard	11
Ditto - for nuisances from smoke	0
Ditto - - ditto - manufactories	10
Ditto - - ditto - manure works	3
Ditto - nightly lodging keepers for breaches of bye-laws	45
Ditto - butchers for - ditto - ditto	74
Ditto - bakers for - ditto - ditto	23
Ditto - for slaughtering in unlicensed premises	75
Ditto - of dairy yard owners for filthy premises	197
Convictions for ordinary sanitary offences	23,749
Notices served	69,580
Summonses served	26,009
Total number of convictions	26,435
*Cases dismissed	189

	£.	s.	d.
Penalties imposed	3,004	-	-
Costs imposed	321	-	-
Total Imposed - - - £.	3,435	-	-
Penalties levied	2,874	-	-
Costs levied	521	-	-
Total Levied - - - £.	3,395	-	-

Number of persons imprisoned for sale, or possession for sale, of unsound meat, &c.	27
Number of persons imprisoned for ordinary sanitary offences	15
Disinfecting chamber used by persons	1,941
Number of articles disinfected	64,078
Number of registered nightly lodgings	116
Ditto - ditto - slaughter houses	123
Ditto - ditto - ditto - in use (average)	83
Number of patients conveyed to hospitals by corporation cabs	2,200
Number of journeys of corporation van in conveying articles to and from the disinfecting chamber	2,106

—	General Mortality.	Total Deaths from Zymotics.	Deaths from Fevers.
1875	8,483	1,298	247
1874	8,190	1,916	352
1873	8,212	1,378	274
1872	8,073	2,523	321
1871	8,144	1,726	398
1870	7,728	1,679	371
1869	7,075	1,556	296
1868	8,004	1,962	313
1867	8,607	1,909	339
1866	9,034	2,881	537
1865	8,161	1,009	526

Total disbursements - - - - - £. 21,646. 4. 8.

* Only four cases were dismissed on the merits. The other cases, chiefly prosecutions for adulterations of food, were dismissed on legal technicalities.

City Hall, Dublin, March 1876.

James Boyle, C.E.
Secretary.

Read, Approved, Report to Council, this 9th June 1876.
J. Byrne, Chairman.

DUBLIN URBAN SANITARY AUTHORITY.

Sanitary Staff.

Secretary and Executive Officer, City Hall:

James Boyle, C.E. - - - - - - - City Hall,
9, Brookfield-terrace, Donnybrook.

Consulting Sanitary Officer:

Edward Dillon Mapother, M.D. - - - - - 16, Merrion-square, North.

Medical Officer of Health and City Analyst:

Charles Alexander Cameron, M.D. - - - - 15, Pembroke-road.

Medical Officers of Dispensaries, being Sanitary Officers:

No.	Dispensaries.	Situation.	Name of Officers.	Address.
1	North City	10, Summer-hill -	J. R. Ferguson, M.D. - John P. Nowlan, M.D. -	20, Upper Sherrard-street. 46, Talbot street.
2	- ditto -	20, Coleraine-street	Richard F. Wilson, M.D. Joseph E. Kenny, M.D. -	34, North Frederick-street. 71, Lower Gardiner-street.
3	- ditto -	32, Blackhall-street	Albert O. Speedy, M.D. - Wm. Dudley White, M.D.	28, North Frederick street. 58, Blessington-street.
1	South City	91, Meath street -	H. G. Crolly, M.D. - Thomas Purcell, M.D. -	27, Harcourt street. 71, Harcourt-street.
2	- ditto -	53, High-street -	John Ryan, M.D. - - D. T. T. Macneill, M.D. -	118, Francis-street. 1, Harrington terrace.
3	- ditto -	16, Peter-street -	Charles F. Moore, M.D. - John Shortt, M.D. - -	10, Upper Merrion-street. 8, Harrington-street.
4	- ditto -	Grand Canal-street	Hamilton Labatt, M.D. - John A. Byrne, M.D. -	1, Upper Fitzwilliam-street. 37, Westland row.

SANITARY POLICE.

Sanitary Inspectors:

Acting Inspector James Halligan - - - - - - 20, Upper Dorset-street.
Serjeant Joseph Berry - - - - - - - - 31, Granville-street.

Sanitary Serjeants:

			Station.
Serjeant Timothy Fay	- - - -	15 A -	Kevin-street Barracks.
Ditto Patrick Reddy	- - - -	2 B -	Lower Castle-yard ditto.
Ditto John Dagg -	- - - -	6 D -	Bridewell-lane.
Ditto Paul Lyons -	- - - -	17 D -	Green-street.
Acting Serjeant James Kavanagh	- -	164 A -	Newmarket.
Ditto - Robert M'Camish	- -	87 A -	Kilmainham.
Ditto - Michael Neill -	- -	30 B -	Lad-lane.
Ditto - Thomas Balmer	- -	47 C -	Sackville-place.
Ditto - Thomas Hoynes	- -	28 D -	Summer-hill.

Police employed in Detection of Unsound Meat and Food, &c.

Acting Serjeant Charles Cockerry	- -	60 C -	Sackville-place.
Ditto - John Toole	- -	31 B -	College-street.
Constable Matthew Carroll	- -	167 D -	Bridewell-lane.
Ditto William Mallin	- -	129 A -	Kevin-street.

Clerk:

Mr. Robert Alcock - - - - - - City Hall.

Disinfecting Chamber - - - - - Corporation Depôt, Marrowbone-lane.

Mortuary House and Coroner's Court - 2, Marlborough-street.

Hospital Cabs, Vans, &c.—Application at City Hall, Mr. W. Flynn, 13, Bass-place, or at No. 17, M'Guinness'-place.

Appendix, No. 9.

PAPERS handed in by Mr. *Boyle.*

CORPORATION OF DUBLIN.—PUBLIC HEALTH COMMITTEE.

Appendix, No. 9.

LIST OF SANITARY STAFF.

	£.	s.	d.
Secretary, Engineer, and Executive Sanitary Officer - -	300	-	-
Consulting Sanitary Officer - - - - - - - - -	300	-	-
Medical Officer of Health and City Analyst - - - - -	300	-	-
*14 Medical Sanitary Officers, at 25 *l.* per annum - - -	350	-	-
2 Sanitary Inspectors, at 160 *l.* - - - - - - - -	320	-	-
4 Sanitary Serjeants Inspectors of Nuisances, at 94 *l.* - -	376	-	-
3 Acting Serjeants, at 89 *l.* 4 *s.* - - - - - - -	267	12	-
4 Inspectors of Meat, Milk, Fish, &c. - - - - - - -	176	-	-
Office Clerk - - - - - - - - - - -	52	-	-
Keeper of Disinfecting Chamber - - - - - - - -	39	-	-
Disinfection of Dwellings - - - - - - - - -	65	-	-
Messenger to City Analyst - - - - - - - - -	19	10	-
TOTAL - - - - £.	2,565	2	-

* The salaries of the medical sanitary officers are defrayed by the guardians from the poor rates.

8 June 1878. *James Boyle*, Secretary.

CORPORATION OF DUBLIN.—PUBLIC HEALTH COMMITTEE.

DR. GRIMSHAW'S LISTS of HOUSES (referred to by him in Reply to Questions 3929–3934. 3936. 3948–3950).

ABSTRACT of Proceedings by the Public Health Committee in relation to these Houses since 1871.

Total number of Houses referred to in Lists - - - - -	115
Summonses issued against Owners - - - - - - -	211
Number of Owners fined - - - - - - - - -	26
Amount of Penalties imposed and levied - - - - - -	25 *l.* 5 *s.*
Number of Owners imprisoned - - - - - - -	2
Ditto - Dwellings closed - - - - - - - -	4
Ditto - - ditto - taken down - - - - - - -	4
Ditto - - ditto - partly unoccupied - - - - - -	2

Condition of Dwellings on 8th June 1878.

Good - - - - - - - - - - - - -	60
Fair - - - - - - - - - - - - - -	39
Bad (one ordered to be closed; others proceeded against) -	6

8 June 1878. *James Boyle.*

Details, in all instances, annexed.

J. Boyle, O.B., Secretary.

8 June 1878.

Appendix, No. 9.

Corporation of Dublin.—Public Health Committee.

"Fever Dens."

(Questions 3929. 3934–36. 3948–50—In re Dr. *Grimshaw's* two printed Lists).

Extracted from the Official Reports of the Medical Sanitary Officers, on the South side of the City, to 1st May 1876.

The object of this Return is to show that inasmuch as but three of the houses noted in Dr. Grimshaw's lists are included in this Return, they have ceased to be "Fever Dens;" these three houses are marked thus.*

Dr. Purcell.

61, Coombe - - -	1	Measles.
23, Engine-alley - -	1	"
8, Meath Market -	1	Fever.
9, South Earl-street -	1	Scarlatina.
61, Meath-street - -	1	Fever.
29, Stanbary-lane - -	1	Scarlatina.
*72, Coombe - - -	1	Fever.
35, Thomas-court - -	1	Scarlatina.
10, Newport-street -	1	"
123, Thomas-street - -	1	Measles.
9, Parke-street - -	1	Scarlatina.
5, Cork-street - -	1	"
112, Francis-street - -	1	"
8, Parke-street - -	1	Measles.
17, Pimlico - - -	1	Fever.
8, Pimlico - - -	1	"
26, Thomas-street - -	1	"
4, Wormwood Gate -	1	"
18, John-street - -	1	Scarlatina.
100, Francis-street - -	1	"
80, Meath-street - -	1	Fever.
118, Cork-street - -	1	Scarlatina.
98, Thomas street - -	1	"
9, Basin-lane - -	1	"
116, Thomas-street - -	1	"
1, Poole-street - -	1	"
22, Cork-street - -	1	"
31, Chamber-street -	1	"
*18, Ardee-street - -	1	"
77, Cork street - -	1	Fever.
26, Earl-street - -	1	Scarlatina.
23, Earl-street - -	1	"
24, Earl-street - -	2	Fever.
13, Earl-street - -	2	Scarlatina.
119, Cork-street - -	2	"
Commons-court -	2	"
16, Braithwaite-street -	1	Diarrhœa.
2, Catherine-street -	1	Fever.
6, Ramsford-street -	1	Scarlatina.
1, Morrey Villa - -	1	"
17, Newport-street -	1	"
41, Chamber-street -	1	Measles.

38 Houses reported once.
4 Houses reported twice.

Total - 42 Houses.

Dr. Crolly.

5, Lambe's-court - -	1	Fever.
184, Thomas-street - -	1	Scarlatina.
19, Bow-lane - -	1	Fever.
36, James's-street - -	1	"
18, Bow-lane - -	1	"
48, Watling-street - -	1	"
153, James's street - -	1	Scarlatina.
23, Bow-lane - -	1	Fever.

Dr. Crolly—*continued.*

52, James's-street - -	1	Scarlatina.
179, James's-street - -	1	Fever.
51, Marrowbone-lane -	1	"
1, Island-bridge - -	1	"
21, Dolphin's-barn -	1	Scarlatina.
34, Coombe - - -	1	"
7, Irwin-street - -	1	Diphtheria.
39, James's-street - -	1	Scarlatina.
38, James's-street - -	1	"
1, Bow-lane - -	1	Fever.
76, Cork-street - -	1	Scarlatina.
8, Mount Brown - -	1	"
16, Irwin-street - -	1	Fever.
10, Middle Basin-lane -	1	Scarlatina.
20, James-street - -	1	"
2, Connor's-cottages -	1	"
6, Grand Canal harbour	1	"
1, Irwin-street - -	1	Fever.
1, Reilly's-avenue -	1	Scarlatina.
10, Upper Basin-lane -	1	"
5, Nash's-court - -	1	"
16, Bow-bridge - -	1	"
47, Dolphin's Barn-lane	1	Fever.
44, Watling street - -	1	Scarlatina.
12, Upper Basin-lane -	1	"
11, Upper Basin-lane -	1	"
15, Bow-bridge - -	1	"
50, Bow-lane - -	1	Diarrhœa.
61, Old Kilmainham -	2	Fever.
41, James-street - -	4	"
47, James's-street - -	2	"

36 Houses reported once.
2 Houses reported twice.
1 House reported four times.

Total - 30 Houses.

Dr. Moore.

14, Peter-street - -	1	Fever.
79, Bride-street - -	1	"
8, Peter's-row - -	1	Measles.
7, Peter's-row - -	1	"
61, Bride-street - -	1	"
28, Golden-lane - -	1	"
9, Great Longford-street	1	"
22, South King-street -	1	Fever.
26, Whitefriar-street -	1	Scarlatina.
44, Bride-street - -	1	Fever.
8, Ardee-row - -	1	"
7, Leinster-row - -		—
24, Newmarket - -	1	Fever.
5, Great Longford-street	1	"
1, Grace's-court - -	1	Measles.
80, Bishop-street - -	1	Scarlatina.
9, Whitefriar-street -	1	Fever.
4, Peter-street - -	1	"

Appendix, No 9.

Corporation of Dublin.—Public Health Committee.—"Fever Dens," &c.—*continued.*

Dr. Moore—*continued.*

Widow's house, 10, Longford-street.	1 Fever.
61, New-street - -	1 Diarrhœa.
3, Great Longford-street	1 Fever.
49, New-street - -	1 Scarlatina.
28, Golden-lane - -	1 Measles.
71, New-street - -	1 "
50, Bride-street - -	1 Diarrhœa.
4, Great Longford street	1 Scarlatina.
2, Tarns-court - -	1 Measles.
21, Aungier-street -	1 Scarlatina.
*73, Coomber - -	1 Measles.
2, Goodman's-lane -	1 Fever.
49, Patrick-street - -	1 Scarlatina.
40, New-row, South -	1 "
10, Aungier-street -	1 "
9, Golden-lane - -	1 "
6, Longford-street -	1 Diarrhœa.
7, Lower Mercer-street	2 Diphtheria and scarlatina.
63, Aungier-street -	1 Scarlatina.
7, Great Longford-street	1 "
69, New-street - -	1 Fever.
24, Stephen street - -	1 Measles.
*16, Golden-lane - -	1 "
41, Bride-street - -	1 "
62, Aungier street -	1 Scarlatina.

41 Houses reported once.
2 Houses reported twice.

Total - 43 Houses.

Dr. Byrne.

28, Townsend-street -	1 Scarlatina.
6, Tennis-court - -	1 Fever.
7, Tennis-court - -	1 "
11, Moss-street - -	2 "
22, George's Quay -	1 Diarrhœa.
5, Sandwith-street -	1 "
2, Lemon-street - -	1 Fever.
5, Lemon-street - -	1 "
19, Cumberland-street (Rere).	1 Diphtheria.
47, Townsend-street -	3 Fever.
60, Townsend-street -	1 "
11, Shoe-lane - -	1 "
150, Townsend-street -	1 Diphtheria.

11 Houses reported once.
1 House reported twice.
1 House three times.

Total - 13 Houses.

Dr. Labatte.

7, Cumberland-street -	1 Scarlatina.
28, Queen's-square -	1 Fever.
15, Merrion Market -	1 "
35, Sandwith-place -	1 "
6, Hanover Quay -	1 Scarlatina.
1, Grattan-court - -	1 Fever.
4, Boyne-lane - -	1 Scarlatina.
7, Boyne-street - -	1 "

8 Houses reported once.

Dr. Peele.

14, Drury-lane - -	1 Fever.
20, Anglesea - -	2 Scarlatina.
5, Bedford-row - -	1 Fever.
7, Chancery-lane -	1 Scarlatina.

3 Houses reported once.
1 House reported twice.

Total - 4 Houses.

Dr. Ryan.

9, Bride's-alley - -	1 Fever.
28, Francis-street - -	1 "
Derby-square - -	1 "

3 Houses reported once.

Dr. Smyth.

48, Lower Clanbrassil-street.	1 Fever.
42, Cuffe-street - -	1 "
7, Cuffe-street - -	1 Scarlatina.
18, Cuffe-lane - -	1 Fever.
2, Lamille's-lane - -	1 Scarlatina.

5 Houses reported once.

145 once, and
12 twice, and more.

Total - - 157

3 June 1876.

James Boyle, C.E., Secretary.

Appendix, No. 10.

PAPER handed in by Mr. *Gray*.

COMPARATIVE STATEMENT showing the SALARIES paid by the CORPORATION of DUBLIN to their OFFICERS in the Years 1863–64 and 1875–76, with Analysis.

OFFICE.	SALARIES.		ANALYSIS OF SALARIES.				OBSERVATIONS.
	1863–64.	1875–76.	1st. Simple Increase.	2nd. For New Duties.	3rd. New Appointments.	Decrease.	
	£.	£. s.	£. s.	£.	£.	£.	
The Lord Mayor - - - - - -	3,000	3,262 10	262 10	-	-	-	To enable the Lord Mayor to pay salary to his secretary, in lieu of now fees now paid into borough fund.
Town Clerk - - - - - - -	600	800 –	200 –	-	-	-	
Assistant to Town Clerk - - -	300	350 –	50 –	-	-	-	
Office Assistant to Town Clerk - -	- -	225 –	- -	-	225	-	New appointment.
City Treasurer and Chief Clerk, two offices recently existing, now consolidated - - - - - - -	710	360 –	- -	-	-	350	Treasurer's cash responsibility reduced to a minimum by Act of Council of 13th June 1876, and salary reduced by 350 *l.*
City Accountant - - - - - -	500	550 –	50 –	–	-	–	Ex-accountant had 550 *l.* at date of retirement.
City Engineer - - - - - -	500	750 –	100 –	150	-	–	Enlarged responsibility connected with waterworks, and salary in connection with main drainage continued.
Law and Land Agent - - - - -	250	500 –	100 –	150	-	-	New duties as land agent.
Law Agent (Mr. M'Sheehy), and for his Clerk 150 *l.* - - - - - -	250	950 –	- -	700	-	-	Of this sum Mr. M'Sheehy's clerk gets 150 *l.* The late Mr. Smyth was paid a large sum annually for Parliamentary and other costs as between solicitor and client, but the 950 *l.* in column covers salary, Parliamentary costs, &c., and in fact the result is a saving to the corporation.
Two Water Bailiffs - - - - -	400	400 –	—	-	-	-	
City Marshal - - - - - -	350	300 –	- -	-	-	50	Salary in lieu of fees of larger amount.
Sword Bearer - - - - - -	250	250 –	—	-	-	–	
Mace Bearer and Officer of Commons -	150	200 –	50 –	–	-	-	
High Constable and Billet Master - -	100	100 –	—	-	-	-	
Secretary to Water Works and Committee No. 2 - - - - - -	300	300 –	—	-	-	-	
Assistant Secretary to Water Works and Committee No. 2 - - - - -	120	- -	- -	-	-	120	Extinct office in 1875.
Engineer's Assistant, in room of late Supervisor - - - - - -	300	200 –	- -	-	-	100	This salary is 100 *l.* under former figure.
Superintendent of Fire Brigade - -	200	400 –	200 –	-	-	-	
Lieutenant of ditto - - -	- -	100 –	- -	-	100	-	New appointment, and paid 52 *l.* in weekly wages, as storekeeper to No. 1 Committee, not in column.
Superintendent of New Cattle Market, and Collector of Tolls - - -	100	100 –	—	-	-	-	
Assistant to the City Accountant - -	75	120 –	45 –	-	-	-	
Secretary to No. 1 Committee - -	300	300 –	—	-	-	-	
First Clerk in Office of Secretary - -	120	150 –	30 –	-	-	–	
Second ditto - ditto - - -	80	65 –	- -	-	-	15	This salary reduced on new appointment.
Book-keeper in - ditto - - -	150	100 –	- -	-	-	50	This also reduced on new appointment.

COMPARATIVE STATEMENT showing the Salaries paid by the Corporation of Dublin to their Officers, &c.—*continued*.

OFFICE.	SALARIES. 1863-64.	SALARIES. 1875-76.	ANALYSIS OF SALARIES. 1st. Simple Increase.	2nd. For New Duties.	3rd. New Appointments.	Decrease.	OBSERVATIONS.
	£.	£. s.	£. s.	£.	£.	£.	
Two Assistant Supervisors of Paving in Office of Secretary, present representative of the two receives 125*l*.	240	125 –	–	–	–	175	These also reduced on new appointments.
Two Inspectors of Streets	229	330 –	101 –	–	–	–	
Inspector of Sewers	–	100 –	–	–	100	–	New appointment.
Assistant Surveyor in Engineer's Department	150	175 –	25 –	–	–	–	
Inspector of Lamps and Tester of Gas Meters	265	300 –	35 –	–	–	–	
Executive Sanitary Officer	–	300 –	–	–	300	–	Appointed under Public Health, 1874.
City Analyst, Medical Officer of Health, 200*l*.; City Analyst, 100*l*.	100	300 –	–	–	200	–	
Consulting Sanitary Officer	–	200 –	–	–	200	–	
Inspector of Petroleum Licences	–	10 –	–	–	10	–	Appointed at 200*l*. under Public Health Act, 1874.
Keeper of Morgue	–	30 –	–	–	30	–	
Keeper of Disinfecting Chamber	–	30 –	–	–	30	–	
Two Inspectors of Weights and Measures, and of Diseased Meat	190	232 –	42 –	–	–	–	Increase for new duties under Public Health Act, 1874.
Inspector of Nuisances	75	52 –	–	–	–	23	
Clerk to Sanitary Office	100	52 –	–	–	–	48	Reduced on new appointment.
Inspector of Hay and Straw Market	75	100 –	25 –	–	–	–	Reduced on new appointment, under Public Health Act, 1874.
Assistant to City Engineer, Water Works, Country Department	–	350 –	–	–	350	–	
Assistant to City Engineer, City Department	–	250 –	–	–	250	–	
Inspector of Water Taps	–	128 –	–	–	128	–	New appointments under Waterworks Acts.
Telegraph Clerk in Office of Engineer	–	117 –	–	–	117	–	
Clerk in ditto	–	104 –	–	–	104	–	
Clerk in ditto	–	104 –	–	–	104	–	
Pay Clerk in Treasurer's Office, for No. 1 Committee	30	95 –	65 –	–	–	–	
Clerk of Licences in Treasurer's Office	–	104 –	–	–	104	–	Appointed in 1866.
Pay Clerk in Treasurer's Office for Water Works Committee	–	91 –	–	–	91	–	Appointed in 1874.
General Clerk of Works	–	100 –	–	–	100	–	He receives 52*l*. for work [at Cattle Market.
Estimates for Fees heretofore received by Lord Mayor's Secretary	–	–	–	–	–	40	The fees exceed this estimate.
Salaries at Foot Note	1,744	1,744 –	–	–	–	–	
TOTAL - - - £.	10,998	15,250 –	1,380 10	1,060	2,836	366	
Deduct for Decreased Salaries	–	–	920 –				
Net actual Increase, irrespective of New Duties	–	–	460 10				

Per-centage of Increase in 12 years, irrespective of new duties, 3·2 per cent.

Note.—The Recorder, the Clerk of the Peace and his assistants, and officers of the Sessions Court, are paid salaries by the Corporation, but are neither appointed by, nor are they officers of, the Corporation.

	£. s. d.
The Recorder's Salary	369 4 5
Clerk of Peace	975 – –
Sessions Court Officers	400 – –
£.	1,744 4 5

25 June 1876.

John Curtis, City Treasurer.

ANALYSIS OF INDEX.

LIST of the PRINCIPAL HEADINGS in the following INDEX, with the Pages at which they may be found.

INDEX.

[*N.B.*—In this Index the Figures following the Names of the Witnesses, and those in the Analysis of Evidence, refer to the Questions in the Evidence; and the Figures following *App.* to the Pages in the Appendix.]

A.

ABATTOIRS (DUBLIN). Comment upon the neglect of the Corporation of Dublin to provide abattoirs, there being much abuse in the matter of slaughter-houses, *Pim* 2458-2462—— Power of the corporation to construct abattoirs, though none have yet been provided, *Grimshaw* 3959-3961.

Promotion by witness of an Abattoir Bill, when he was in the corporation, whereby he rendered himself obnoxious to nearly all the butchers, *Sullivan* 4688——Necessary withdrawal of a Building Bill promoted by the corporation in 1867, on account of the agitation raised against the provisions for the construction of abattoirs, *Neville* 5433.

Necessity for abattoirs and a public market, *Gray* 6494——Effort now being made in the corporation to introduce abattoirs, *ib.*——Want of increased powers on the subject, *ib.* 6608.

Accounts (*Corporation of Dublin*). Practice as to lodging the amounts collected from the several rates to separate accounts in the Bank of Ireland, *Taafe* 489, 490. 521-525—— Separate accounts at the Bank to which the proceeds of the different rates are paid, *Henry* 1146-1149—— Separation of accounts at the suggestion of the auditor, *ib.* 1328-1331——Objectionable practice of paying one account by transfer from another, *M'Evoy* 2070-2072.

Explanation on the subject of the accounts kept at the Bank of Ireland of the funds of the corporation, *Robinson* 2640 *et seq.*——Particulars relative to certain transfers and repayments between one fund and another; sanction by the auditor in these cases, *ib.* 3397-3403——The corporation has accounts for only seven separate funds at the Bank of Ireland, *ib.* 3475.

Explanation that the payments which go to the credit of the personal account of the treasurer are not more than about 2,000 *l.* a year; character of the payments made to the credit of this account, and practice as to their subsequent transfer, *Robinson* 3475-3485.

Grounds for the conclusion that misapplication is involved in the practice of drawing indiscriminately upon the different funds lodged in the Bank of Ireland; repeated suggestions made by witness in his reports for keeping the several funds and the accounts thereof entirely separate, *Finlay* 4299-4309. 4440-4446.

Necessity of some further check upon the returns sent in to the corporation by the different accounting officers; suggestions to this effect, *Finlay* 4315-4318——Proposal that all the accounts of the several committees of the corporation be transferred to the city accountant, who should conduct a strict examination into all receipts and payments, *ib.* 4316, 4317——Great improvement effected in the accounts of No. 1 committee of the corporation, *ib.* 4317.

Importance of separate accounts of the corporation funds in the Bank of Ireland, though witness does not ask for power in the auditor to compel their being kept, *Finlay* 4480-4485. 4488——Banking arrangement by which the illegality of drawing upon one fund for the purposes of another might be obviated, *ib.* 4570, 4571.

Concurrence in the view that amendment is required as regards the mode of keeping the accounts in the Bank of Ireland, the separate funds not being separately dealt with, *Sullivan* 4710-4718.

Accounts (*Corporation of Dublin*)—continued.

Suggestion on the part of the corporation that the accounts in all the departments should be closed on the 31st of December, *Norwood* 5953——Very good management of the accountant's department, whilst the accounts generally are very carefully kept, *ib.* 6630.

See also Audit.

Accounts (*Generally.*) Satisfaction expressed with the present accounts of towns in witness' district under the Act of 1854; readiness shown by the local authorities to adopt the improvements suggested by witness, *Finlay* 4373. 4496. 4574.

Act 9 *Geo.* 4, *c.* 82 (1828). Four towns with urban sanitary authorities under the Act 9 Geo. 4 (1828), *Hancock* 2——Several respects in which the Act of 1828 (9 Geo. 4) was recognised by the Act of 1840; partial adoption of the former Act as to the mode of election, *ib.* 19——Adoption of the Act of 1828 by sixty-six towns, only twelve of these being still under the Act; particulars hereon as to the deficiencies of this Act in comparison with the Act of 1854, *ib.* 24–29——Want of a complete repeal of the Act of 1828, *ib.* 88.

Examination relative to some twelve towns having commissions under the Act 9 Geo. 4, c. 82; co-existence of commissioners, and of a corporation in the case of Clonmel, *Hancock* 663–706.

Act 3 & 4 *Vict.* c. 108 (1840). Full powers of town councils under the Municipal Reform Act of 1840, as to the management of corporate property and the appointment of officers, *Hancock* 38, 39——Statement of the qualifications of town councillors and aldermen in the ten large towns that have got charters under the Act of 1840; defect in the Act on this score, *ib.* 122, 123.

Further statement as to the number of corporations dealt with by the General Municipal Reform Act for Ireland, and as to the proportion of these with self-elective and irresponsible governing bodies, *Hancock* 573–582. 588——Enumeration of ten towns which got new corporations without new charters; nominal retention of their former powers by these towns after the application of the Act of 1840, *ib.* 583–588. 602–628——Mention of the several counties of cities among the ten corporations that did not get new charters under the Municipal Reform Act, *ib.* 593–598.

Reference to the general report of the Municipal Commissioners in 1835, as setting forth the principal objects to be dealt with by the Act of 1840, in the reform of the corporations, *Hancock* 600, 603——Belief further expressed as to very little power having been reserved to the corporations under the Act of 1840, *ib.* 783, 784.

Act 12 & 13 *Vict.* (1849). Explanations in connection with the provisions of the Municipal Corporations Amendment Act of 1849 for the regulation of the municipal franchise in Dublin, *Hancock* 129–151. 632, 633——Belief as to all parties in Dublin having assented to the Act of 1849, and to the assimilation of the franchise to that in England, *ib.* 634–643. 785, 786——Important change made in the municipal franchise by the Act of 1849, so that the constituency was entirely altered, *Henry* 1092–1098.

Statement as to the Act of 1849 having assimilated the franchise in Dublin to that in England, so that it was not felt as a stigma by the public, *Gray* 6388–6399.

Act 17 & 18 *Vict.* c. 103 (1854). Sixteen towns under urban sanitary authorities under the Towns Improvement Act of 1854, *Hancock* 2——Total of seventy-six towns under the Act of 1854; enumeration of sixty of these with a population under 6,000 and above 1,500, *ib.* 30–33——Partial extent to which several towns have adopted the Act of 1854, whilst local Acts have been already necessitated, independently of the former, *ib.* 34–37. 40–42. 56.

Conclusion as to the expediency of an amendment of the Act of 1854, concurrently with a repeal of the local Acts since passed in order to supply the deficiencies of the former, *Hancock* 86, 87. 90, 91.

Explanation as to the provisions of the Towns Improvement Act of 1854, in regard to the qualifications for the municipal franchise, *Hancock* 707–726——Execution of the Act of 1854 by Commissioners appointed under it; facility to corporations (with some exceptions) in getting the powers of the Act, *ib.* 727–736——Four distinct franchises under the Act, *ib.* 771–774.

Suggestion that as to the numerous small towns under the Act of 1854, the Act shall be deemed to be a local Act for the purpose of the provisions of the Acts 34 & 35 Vict. and 37 & 38 Vict., *Curran* 2217–2224.

Admiralty Jurisdiction. Repeal by the Municipal Reform Act of 1840 of Admiralty jurisdiction formerly possessed by some corporations, *Hancock* 608, 609. 742–745.

Alienations of Corporate Property. Several instances, as at Athy, of old corporations having had property of which there is now no trace; comment upon the transfer of this property, as at Naas, *Finlay* 4358–4368. 4467–4469——Comments upon the extensive alienations of corporate property in the last century, *Sullivan* 4672–4676.

All Hallows College (Dublin City Estates). Explanation relative to the re-letting of All Hallows College on the Clonturk estate, to the late Rev. J. Hand in 1852, on lease for 1,000 years at a renewed rent of 137 *l.* 11 *s.* or 10 *l.* an Irish acre; consent of the Treasury in this case, *Morgan* 3546–3560. 3812–3826.

Amount of Local Taxation. Statement of the amount of local taxation in towns and counties respectively, in 1871; that is, exclusive of poor rate, *Hancock* 112–115 —— Average of 3 *s.* 2 *d.* for all Ireland, *ib.* 113. ——*See* also *Rates.*

Anti-Political Ratepayers' Association (Dublin). Opposition unfairly met with by the corporation from the Anti-Political Ratepayers' Association in applying the sanitary laws to tenement house property, *Sullivan* 4681. 4852–4863.

Appointment of Officers. Powers of the Corporation of Dublin under the 93rd and 94th sections of the Act of 1840, as to the appointment of officers, *Hancock* 756–758 —— Necessary sanction of the Lord Lieutenant before the appointment of any new officers by the corporation; sanction also as regards the salary on appointment, *Henry* 1396–1402.

Strong objections to the present practice of appointment and dismissal of municipal officers, *M'Evoy* 1736–1739 —— Great improvement if these appointments were subject to a competitive or qualifying examination, *ib.* 1736–1739. 1743 —— Importance of inquiry by the Local Government Board in cases of misconduct, and of a power of dismissal, *ib.* 1736. 1739–1742. 1744 —— Patronage exercised in municipal appointments in Dublin, there being no examination and no security for competency; frequent appointment of relations of aldermen or town councillors, *ib.* 1737, 1738.

Examination in support of the statement that officers of the corporation had been appointed through relationship with members of the corporation or through other interest, *M'Evoy* 1911–1953 —— Belief that generally the officers of the corporation take no part in politics, *ib.* 1962–1965.

Several instances of superior officers in Dublin who are Protestants and Conservatives, *Sullivan* 4766 —— Entire inaccuracy of the charge that appointments were made by the corporation on political or religious grounds; several superior officers (including witness) who are Conservatives and Protestants, *Boyle* 5260–5262 —— Witness and several other officers of the corporation are Protestants, *Neville* 5521, 5522.

Obstacles to a competitive or qualifying examination of the corporation officers; good officers now obtained, *Norwood* 6003 —— Erroneous character of most of the imputations as to nepotism in the appointment of officers; instances of this, *ib.* 6009, 6010 —— Denial that the corporation appointments are influenced by sectarian feelings; large number of Protestant officers holding high positions, *Gray* 6317, 6318. 6378 —— Improvement if the officers could be appointed only from year to year, *ib.* 6504.

See also *City Marshal. City Treasurer. Engineer and Surveyor. South Dublin Union. Town Clerk.*

Area of Dublin (Municipal Boundaries):

1. *Suggestions for an Extension of the Municipal Area, so as to include Rathmines and other adjacent Townships.*
2. *Objections to the proposed Extension.*
3. *Fiscal Effect of Extension from the Circular Road to the Canal.*
4. *Suggested Re-constitution of the Corporation, the Area being enlarged.*

1. *Suggestions for an Extension of the Municipal Area, so as to include Rathmines and other adjacent Townships:*

Expediency of an extension of the municipal boundaries, there having been no increase since 1849, and many buildings being erected outside the boundaries, so as to escape the city rates, *Henry* 1210–1212. 1539–1553. 1610 —— Expediency of Rathmines being included in the municipal area, and being taxed for the city roads, *ib.* 1213–1227. 1539–1542.

Conclusion as to the necessity of an enlargement of the municipal area; suggestions a to the boundary which might be adopted, *Sullivan* 4682. 4693–4695. 4720 —— Belief that by an extension of the municipal boundary, and a re-adjustment of the valuation, sufficient funds would be obtained for an efficient administration, *ib.* 4794. 4795. 4802, 4804–4810 —— Absence of any good claim in the townships round Dublin to continue outside the municipal area, *ib.* 4871–4873.

Grounds for the conclusion that Rathmines and other townships should contribute to the paving and maintenance of the city streets, the municipal area being extended for this and other purposes, *Neville* 5535, 5536 —— Impression that the extended area proposed by witness would double the present area, though the rates would not be nearly doubled, *ib.* 5586–5589 —— Fairness in the townships being joined to the city for poor-rate purposes, *ib.* 5590, 5591 —— Expediency of the townships contributing equally with the city to the repair of the roads and bridges, and to the main drainage, though this principle has

Area of Dublin (Municipal Boundaries)—continued.

1. *Suggestions for an Extension of the Municipal Area, &c.*—continued.

for certain reasons been departed from as regards water supply and drainage, *Neville* 5717–5720. 5738–5740.

Advocacy of an extension of the municipal boundary, so as to embrace Rathmines, Pembroke, and other townships having a community of interest with the city in many fiscal matters, *Norwood* 5905–5909. 6285——Injustice in these townships not being united with the city for poor rate and other burdens, *ib.* 5909, 5910.

Concurrence in the view as to the necessity of an extension of the boundaries of Dublin, so as to embrace the adjacent townships, *Grey* 6365. 6492, 6493——Intense feeling of jealousy on the part of the townships towards the corporation, *ib.* 6365.

2. *Objections to the proposed Extension:*

Difficulty in extending the area of the municipal borough on account of the lighter taxation in the outlying districts, *Pim* 2431——Regret that the outlying townships have been allowed to become separate governments, *ib.*——Opinion that the outside inhabitants have acquired a vested interest in a low rate of taxation which cannot now be fairly interfered with, *ib.*

Decided objections to proposals for annexing Rathmines township to the city; large proportion of ratepayers in the former not interested in the trade of the city, *Stokes* 2924–2926 3366——Grounds for the conclusion that an extension of the city area so as to include Rathmines would not benefit the citizens, whilst it would be injurious to the township, *ib.* 3366.

3. *Fiscal Effect of Extension from the Circular Road to the Canal:*

Very unwise act of the corporation in annexing the unremunerative district between the Circular Road and the Canal, including Mud Island; heavy charge involved, *Stokes* 2931–2933. 3360–3365.

Inaccuracy of the statement by Mr. Stokes that the extension of the city area in 1850 had proved a great loss to the corporation; gradual increase in the rateable value of the district taken in, *Neville* 5457. 5458.

4. *Suggested Re-constitution of the Corporation, the Area being enlarged:*

Proposal that there still be but sixty representatives, the municipal area being extended; this would take one representative from each of the present wards, *Sullivan* 4691——Scheme for the relative representation of the townships and the city if there be but one municipal body; total of about ninety members, *Norwood* 5911, 5912.

Artizans' Dwellings Act. Circumstance of the Corporation of Dublin not having yet applied the Artizans' Dwellings Act of 1875, *Pim* 2432, 2433. 2446–2450——Views of the medical sanitary officers as to the necessity of applying the Artizans' Dwellings Act, *Grimshaw* 4034——Approval of an application of the Act to Dublin, *Sullivan* 4849.

Considerable expense involved in putting the Artizans' Dwellings Act into operation, *Norwood* 6022——Steps being taken to put the Act in force; opposition made on account of the expense involved, *Grey* 6439, 6440——Successful opposition made by Mr. Byrne (the leader of the Conservative party in the corporation) to the expense of applying the Act, *ib.* 6565–6570.

Ash-pits and Privies (Domestic Scavenging). See *Sanitary Administration*, 1.

Asphalte Pavements (Dublin). Limited extent to which streets have been asphalted; the Limmer asphalte has answered the best, *Neville* 5630–5633.

Assessors (Revision of Burgess Roll). Defence of the system of popular election of the assessors in Dublin; improvement if the election were triennial, *Curran* 2183–2189——Expediency of one or both assessors being necessarily barristers, *ib.* 2191, 2192——Rate of payment of the assessors, and time occupied in revision, 2193–2196.

Objection to the assessors being subject to annual popular election, *Norwood* 6097.

See also Revision of Burgess Roll.

Athy. Disappearance of some property formerly owned by the old corporation of Athy; that is, unless certain tolls be identical with this property, *Finlay* 4359–4361. 4612–4615——Doubt as to the expenditure of Athy being excessive as compared with that of Carlow and other towns, *ib.* 4616–4620——They appear to do matters very well in Athy, *ib.* 4616.

Report, 1878—*continued.*

AUDIT:

1. *As to the Operation generally of the Government Audit of Municipal Accounts.*
2. *Exemption of some Towns from Public Audit; Inexpediency thereof.*
3. *Dublin Corporation Accounts.*
4. *System of Appeal from the Auditor's Decisions, and Practice as to Costs; Suggestions hereon.*

1. *As to the Operation generally of the Government Audit of Municipal Accounts:*

Arrangement as to the audit of accounts under the Local Government Act of 1871; objection to which open, though the system is in the main an admirable one, *Hancock* 116-118——Expediency of every town or governing body being subject to an adequate public audit; suggestion as to their having protection through the Court of Queens Bench or Local Government Board, in the matter of doubtful expenditure, *ib.* 116-118. 796-800——Stringent operation of the present system of audit further adverted to; exceptions from the Act of 1871 in the case of Kilkenny, Cork, and Waterford, *ib.* 956-961. 1047-1061. 1066-1068.

Satisfactory working of the Local Government audit in Kingstown, *M'Evoy* 1730, 1731——Power of the auditor of the Local Government Board to decide important questions as to the legality of payments, *ib.* 1865-1869.

Varying charges of the auditor; discrepancy on this subject, it being desirable that the Treasury should bear all the cost, *Finlay* 4421-4426. 4475——Voluntary adoption of the audit provisions by Kingstown, Blackrock, and Dalkey; irregularities reported by witness in each of these townships, *ib.* 4489-4494——Statement to the effect that the auditor has already sufficient means of ascertaining what items should be received by any corporate authority, *ib.* 4538-4552——Course adopted by the auditor when illegal payments ordered to be reinstated are not reinstated by the next audit, *ib.* 4553-4555.

Provision in the Act of 1871 as to the accounts of each town being audited "once a year," *Finlay* 4556, 4557——Invariable practice of witness to require vouchers for all payments, *ib.* 4567-4569——Explanation that witness' inquiry does not extend to the question of insufficient payment of rent as compared with the valuation, *ib.* 4583-4590——Extent to which witness' reports to the Local Government Board are made public in the localities; expediency of the reports being accessible to the ratepayers, *ib.* 4644-4649.

2. *Exemption of some Towns from Public Audit; Inexpediency thereof:*

Advantage of all boards throughout Ireland having independent auditors, *Hancock* 116. 796-800; *Norwood* 5994-5996——Difficulty of legislation which led to the exemption of certain places in Ireland from the audit of the Local Government Board, *Finlay* 4419——Witness sees no good ground for the exemption of any place, *ib.* 4420.

3. *Dublin Corporation Accounts:*

Check through the auditor upon the allocation of the rates, *Taafe* 521-523——Approval of a Government auditor rather than of an elected one, *Henry* 1523, 1524.

Urgent need felt for a Government audit of the city accounts, though in England the local corporations audit their own accounts, *M'Evoy* 1695——Limited powers of the former elected auditors as to checking illegal expenditure; power of appeal in the ratepayers, *ib.* 1856-1864——Statement to the effect that the corporation did not apply for, and were not favourable to, the appointment of a public auditor, *ib.* 1981-1988. 2086——The application for the auditor was postponed, lest he should disallow the contribution to the French fund, *ib.* 2086.

Approval of independent public auditors for large corporations, like Dublin, though inconvenience sometimes arises on legal points, *Stokes* 3114-3131.

Public audit first applied to the corporation accounts for the year ending 31st August 1872, *Robinson* 3440——Steps taken by the corporation which led to the appointment of a Government auditor, *ib.* 3441——The audit occupies about three months in each year, *ib.* 3442——Explanations in detail relative to the disallowances and surcharges by the auditor in each year since 1871-72, *ib.* 3443-3457. 3463——Opinion that the present system of audit is a very satisfactory one, and that the auditor is a most able and careful official, *ib.* 3458.

Extent of witness' district as an auditor of the Local Government Board; this includes the city of Dublin, the accounts of which he has audited since 1871, *Finlay* 4262-4266——Explanation of the system adopted by witness in his examination of receipts and payments respectively, his function being to see that there is no omission of receipts, and to disallow all payments that are not legal, *ib.* 4267——Ready facilities afforded to witness on all occasions by the corporation, *ib.* 4447, 4448.

Very public character of witness' audits in the city of Dublin, *Finlay* 4651-4653——The

Report, 1876—*continued.*

AUDIT—continued.

3. *Dublin Corporation Accounts*—continued.

The audit room is open to the general public, and to the representatives of the press, *Finlay* 4652.

Statement as regards the audit, to the effect that the proposition for the appointment of a Government auditor emanated from the town council, *Norwood* 5988–5990——Reason why the change in the audit system was postponed; denial that the postponement had any connection with the donation to the French Relief Fund, *ib.* 5990.

Exceedingly small surcharges by the auditor, these being on technical points, *Norwood* 6087, 6088——Doubt as to the auditor having left many items to stand over in addition to the actual surcharges, *ib.* 6164–6166——Extreme fairness of the auditor, the audit being on the whole a great satisfaction to the corporation, *Gray* 6438.

4. *System of Appeal from the Auditor's Decisions, and Practice as to Costs; Suggestions hereon:*

Exceptions taken to the practice of the Government auditor in giving legal decisions, whilst if these are overruled on appeal, the costs fall on the corporation; amendment required in this respect, *Henry* 1511–1522. 1643. 1644——Disapproval of the present system of appeal from the auditor's decision; suggested appeal to a court of law, *M'Evoy* 1710. 1712, 1713.

Expediency of the costs on appeal from the auditor falling on the corporate authority, and not on the Local Government Board, *Finlay* 4470–4474——Very few appeals from witness' disallowances to the Court of Queen's Bench, *ib.* 4524, 4525——Frequent appeals from witness' decisions to the Local Government Board, these not necessarily involving any expense, *ib.* 4526–4531——Question considered as to the expediency of facilities for obtaining the opinion of a court of law before any doubtful expenditure is incurred, *ib.* 4532–4535.

Suggestion by No. 3 committee of the corporation, for an amended procedure in regard to surcharges, and the question of legality of any payment, *Norwood* 5953–5962——Expediency of appeals to a court of law from the decisions of the auditor, *ib.* 5991–5993——Approval of a suggestion that a legal decision be obtained before any doubtful expenditure is incurred, *ib.* 5992.

Hardship in those who are surcharged by the auditor being liable for costs in the event of successful appeals from the auditor's decisions; amendment desirable, *Norwood* 5993; *Gray* 6414–6438.

See also *Accounts.* *Collection of Rates*, 4. 6. *Rathmines*, 5.

B.

Bagnalstown. Information relative to certain disallowances by witness in his last audit of the Bagnalstown accounts, *Finlay* 4372.

Bagotrath Estate (*Corporation of Dublin*). Statement as to the claim of the corporation to the Bagotrath property, which is now held by Lord Pembroke, and is exceedingly valuable; expediency of this claim being re-urged, *Morgan* 3661–3664. 3683–3691——This property would fetch more than 10,000 *l.* a year if it were let at the present time, *ib.* 3662.

BALDOYLE PROPERTY (*CORPORATION OF DUBLIN*):

Failure of the corporation to make the most of the Baldoyle property, *M'Evoy* 2089–2091. 2094.

Information relative to this property, the rental being about 1,200 *l.* a year, *Robinson* 2474–2479. 2483–2492——Stipulations in a certain bye-law as to the re-letting or sale of any of the properties being by public auction; departure from this regulation in the case of the Baldoyle property, the rent having been subsequently reduced, *ib.* 2504. 2529–2535.

Explanation in connection with a bye-law made in 1871 relative to the letting by auction of the corporation lands; special Act in 1864 for reducing the rents previously obtained by public auction for the Baldoyle land, *Henry* 2537–2547.

Area of 621 acres comprised in the Baldoyle property; this property was re-let to sixteen tenants in 1855 on leases for thirty-one years, *Morgan* 3621, 3622——Considerable advance in 1855 upon the former rents; unduly high rents obtained owing to the competition by public auction, so that it became necessary to apply to Parliament for power to reduce the rents, *ib.* 3623–3654——Particulars relative to certain of the lettings in 1855, the rent as compared with the valuation, and the subsequent reductions allowed, *ib.* 3627–3658. 3720–3775. 3827–3838.

Baldoyle Property (Corporation of Dublin)—continued.

Transfer of Mr. Darley's holding at Baldoyle to Mr. Van den Eynde; reduction allowed in this case, *Morgan* 3635. 3648-3651. 3740, 3741. 3770, 3771. 3834-3837 ——Explanation in regard to the land leased to Lord Annaly having been sublet by him to Mr. Lane Joynt and two other persons, and as to the reduction of rent allowed in this case, *ib.* 3636-3647. 3729-3738. 3772-3775. 3874-3876——Covenant in the leases that the holdings are not to be sublet without consent of the corporation, *ib.* 3655——Information relative to the tenure of the town parks at Baldoyle, these lands being worth about 4 *l.* an Irish acre, *ib.* 3656-3658. 3827-3833.

Summary of the proceedings in connection with the Corporation Bill of 1864, in reference to the reduction of the Baldoyle rents; several amendments adopted during the progress of the Bill through Parliament, *Morgan* 3692-3719——Explanation in connection with the clause in the Bill of 1864 relative to Mr. Crampton's lease, and the reduction to be made in his rent in consideration of a large expenditure by him in building; relative rent and valuation in this case, *ib.* 3705-3719. 3743-3751. 3761, 3762.

Further statement of the circumstances under which the Baldoyle holdings were re-let by public auction in 1855, witness submitting that the rents obtained were excessive, *Morgan* 3752-3769——Explanation as to James Duffy, one of the tenants, not having claimed any reduction, though his rent is more than 4 *l.* an acre, *ib.* 3762-3768.

Duties discharged by the city treasurer in the collection of the Baldoyle rents, the recovering of arrears, &c.; allowance of ten per cent. to Mr. Patrick Butterly for collection of the small weekly rents, *Morgan* 3778-3780. 3795-3800——Great want of some new cottages; enhanced value of the holdings thereby, *ib.* 3794. 3804, 3805. 3854, 3855. 3867——Explanation relative to some arrears in the collection of the weekly rents; wretched character of this property, *ib.* 3801-3804. 3806. 3855. 3865-3867.

Exceptional instance of a very low rent at Baldoyle in the case of Patrick Butterly, *Morgan* 3809-3833——Retrospective operation of the Act of 1864 relative to the rents, *ib.* 3838-3841.

Very poor character of the Baldoyle property; great difficulty in collecting the rents, *Finlay* 4282, 4283. 4289. 4432-4435——Suggestion made by witness that the irrecoverable arrears should be ascertained and written off, *ib.* 4288——Circumstance of its having been proposed to sell the Baldoyle property, *ib.* 4290-4293.

Ballast Board (Dublin). Division of the former Ballast Board into the Port and Docks Board, and the Irish Lights Board, *Henry* 1179-1185.

Ballina. Comment upon the case of Ballina, the local authority not having succeeded in obtaining a Provisional Order or a Local Act, *Hancock* 44-47——Explanation that the board of guardians are the town authority for sanitary purposes, *ib.* 997-1000. 1009-1014——Further reference to the veto exercised by the grand jury in the case of Ballina, *ib.* 1039-1041.

Ballycoolane Estate (Corporation of Dublin). Details relative to the area, valuation, rental, &c., of the Ballycoolane Estate; large increase of revenue to be derived in 1880, when many of the leases fall in, *Morgan* 3520-3535.

Bankruptcy Disqualification (Corporation of Dublin). Amendment suggested in the bankruptcy disqualification, *M'Evoy* 1682.

Belfast. Important effect of the Municipal Reform Act as regards Belfast, both with respect to the municipal and Parliamentary franchise, *Hancock* 589-592——Twofold size of the municipal area of Belfast as compared with Dublin, *Sullivan* 4830, 4831.

Satisfactory working of the burgess qualification in Belfast, *Norwood* 6185——Information relative to the burgess roll, witness objecting to any reduction of the qualification, which is practically an 8 *l.* one, and works very well, *ib.* 6221-6230.

Explanation as to the failure of an application for a new valuation of Belfast, *Greene* 6771, 6772——Effect of a new valuation to raise the amount from 490,000 *l.* to 612,000 *l.*, and to reduce the poundage rate from 6 *s.* 8 *d.* to about 5 *s.* 4 *d.*, *ib.* 6895-6899——Anxiety of the corporation of Belfast for a re-valuation of the borough, *ib.* 6905-6908.

Return submitted by Dr. Hancock, showing the result as regards Belfast of a plan for constituting the town authority on a certain basis, involving cumulative voting, *App.* 402, 403.

Bills in Parliament. Large sums spent by the corporation of Dublin between 1864 and 1872, in promoting and in opposing Private Bills, *Henry* 1305——Excessive expenditure incurred in promoting and opposing Private Bills, the check of the auditor being very useful in this respect, *M'Evoy* 1695-1709. 1998-2005——Heavy costs incurred in connection with an Improvement Bill for Kingstown, *ib.* 1899-1902.

Statement as to a large sum (amounting to many thousands) being due by the corporation of Dublin for notices of Bills and for costs of counsel, agents, and others, in connection

Bills in Parliament—continued.

nection with gas and other Bills; non-payment of these expenses through fear of disallowance by the auditor, *Finlay* 4404–4412 —— Belief that there is no personal liability in the members of the town council for costs in respect of abortive Bills, *ib.* 4450, 4451. 4572. 4579–4582.

Explanation and defence of the action of the corporation of Dublin, and of the expense incurred in promoting and opposing Private Bills, *Neville* 5406–5468; *Norwood* 5997–5999——Immense expense incurred by Kingstown and adjacent townships, *Norwood* 5999.

See also Bray and Ennisherry Railway Bill. Gas Bills, &c. Provisional Orders.

Blackrock. Particulars as to some disallowances at different audits in the case of Blackrock, and as to the result of appeals from witness' decisions, *Finlay* 4372.

Boards of Guardians. Explanation as to the boards of guardians in Dublin not having sanitary authority in the city, *Grimshaw* 4209–4212.

Reference to boards of guardians, elected under the multiple system, as not equal to municipal bodies, *Gray* 6516, 6517——*See* also *South Dublin Union.*

Boards of Superintendence. Exceptional position of the Boards of Superintendence in Dublin in not having the power of appointing its own officers, *Gray* 6724——Slight effect as regards the corporation by withdrawing the power of election of boards of superintendence, *ib.* 6724, 6725.

Borough Estates (Dublin). See *City Estates (Dublin).*

Borough Fund (Dublin). Statement of the receipts and expenditure on account of the borough fund in the several years 1861–65, and in the past year, *Robinson* 2834–2845 ——Total receipts to the amount of 37,411 *l.* last year, whilst the expenditure was 39,962 *l.*, *ib.* 2837, 2838, 2841——Salaries charged against the borough fund to the amount of 6,345 *l.* *ib.* 2838. 2845.

Borough Rate (Dublin). Power of the corporation to levy a borough rate of 3 *d.*; belief that this power has only twice been exercised, *Henry* 1277–1282——Explanation that the borough rate could not be applied in aid of the improvement rate, *ib.* 1531, 1532. 1608 ——Power of levying a borough rate of 3 *d.* in the pound; belief as to this power having never been exercised, *Neville* 5548–5550.

Borrowing Powers. Exceedingly defective provisions with regard to borrowing powers of towns in Ireland, as under the Act of 1847 and other Acts; illustration in the case of Newry, *Hancock* 59–67.

Want of further borrowing powers by the corporation of Dublin for the construction of new markets and abattoirs, and for other purposes, *Neville* 5442, 5443——Suggestions by committee No. 1 of the corporation for increased borrowing facilities, *Norwood* 5943.

See also Debt, &c.

Boundaries of Dublin. See *Area of Dublin.*

Boyle, James. (Analysis of his Evidence.)—Considerable experience of witness as a civil engineer; he is now secretary and engineer to the Public Health Committee of the corporation of Dublin, and acts also as sanitary officer under the Local Government Board, 4898–4901——Denial that there is excessive mortality from zymotic diseases in Dublin, as stated by Dr. Grimshaw; steady decrease since 1866; 4902–4904. 5233–5237——Explanation that Dublin was not exceptional in having a high death rate in the year 1874; 4905.

Enumeration of the sanitary officers of different kinds in Dublin, 4906, 4907——Constitution of the Public Health Committee; total of thirty members, 4908——Return adverted to as showing the large number of houses which have been improved in sanitary respects, or have been closed, since the appointment of the public health committee, 4909——Total of 24,000 houses in Dublin, of which 9,700 are tenement houses, 4910.

Information relative to the action taken as regards 115 houses reported by Dr. Grimshaw in 1872, and designated by him as fever dens; effectual remedies applied, whilst since 1874 only three cases of fever have been reported from these houses, 4911–4923 ——Effectual precautions taken in disinfecting houses where epidemics have broken out; also in disinfecting clothes and bedding, 4919. 4920. 4942–4949——Difficulty experienced in inducing persons to go to the hospitals, 4920–4922——Invariable report of infectious cases to witness by the sanitary police or other officers, 4923——Prompt steps taken in 1872 for remedying the bad condition of a house in Chancery-lane, 4924, 4925.

Exceeding

Boyle, James. (Analysis of his Evidence)—*continued.*

Exceeding efficiency of the sanitary police staff; stimulants to zeal on their part, 4926–4928. 5191–5197. 5250–5252——Penalties to the amount of 3,004 *l.* imposed through the action of the Public Health Committee; several instances of imprisonment, 4929——Readiness shown by the magistrates to aid the action of the committee, 4930——Way in which action is taken in each case reported to witness by the medical sanitary officers, 4931——Efficient services rendered by the consulting sanitary officer, his recommendations being invariably carried out, 4932–4934.

Provision by the Public Health Committee of two cabs for the removal of the sick to the hospitals, there being also an arrangement for the use of the cabs of the North and South Dublin Unions, 4935——Examination to the effect that sufficient facilities are provided for the removal of the sick and of epidemic cases, 4935–4941. 5107–5121——Duty of the Local Government Board and of the unions, since 1874, to take steps for preventing the spread of epidemics; assistance to be rendered by the corporation, 4950–4952. 5222–5224.

Particulars relative to the scavenging depôts of the corporation; great improvement in their condition, so that they are now innoxious, 4953–4958——Obstacles to a removal of the depôts outside the city, 4959——Explanation as to the street sweepings, &c., not bringing in some revenue, 4959, 4960——Strict supervision over the private manure depôts, four in number; satisfactory condition of these at the present time, 4961–4964——Salutary effect of the action of the Public Health Committee in the matter of domestic scavenging, 4965–4967.

Due attention paid by the Public Health Committee to complaints from the Sanitary Association; particulars hereon, 4968–4986——Information relative to a complaint about the condition of a house in Ardee-street; result of a special inquiry that this house was in a satisfactory state, 4982–4986. 5287–5290——Reference to certain correspondence with the Local Government Board as showing that the Board did not deem it necessary to require the corporation to undertake the cleansing of ashpits, &c., in all cases, 4987–4990——Satisfaction expressed by the late inspector of the Board with the state of the manure depôts, 4990,* 4991.

Evidence in detail relative to the condition of the dairy-yards, the action taken by witness with a view to their better regulation, and the difficulty of enforcing improvement on account of deficient legislation, 4992–5013——Report by witness in July 1875, showing the condition of these yards, and the amendment required as regards increase of cubic space, &c., 4993–4996. 5011, 5012——Instance of successful proceedings before a magistrate with a view to a large reduction in the number of cattle in one of these yards, 4998–5004. 5045, 5046.

Increased sanitary staff required for preventing the sale of unsound meat, 5014, 5015——Insufficient means at the disposal of the Public Health Committee out of the borough fund, so that the staff cannot be increased, 5016–5023——Total expenditure of 2,548 *l.* by the committee, 5024——Inaccuracy of any statement as to persons dwelling over slaughter-houses, 5025–5027——Report made by witness offering sundry suggestions for the amendment of the Sanitary Act, 5028–5033——Importance of simplifying the procedings for the abatement of nuisance; great number of forms now necessary, and undue delay in consequence, 5030–5033. 5274–5278.

Further considerations as to the difficulty in taking action before the magistrates against the dairy yards, and as to the remedy required in the matter of cubic space, 5034–5046——Ample powers of the Public Health Committee for preventing accumulations of manure, 5047.

Particulars with further reference to the action of the corporation as regards the cleansing of ashpits, &c., and the supervision exercised; proceedings taken, when necessary, in order to compel the owners not to neglect this duty, 5048–5058. 5103–5106. 5172–5174. 5198–5221. 5291–5293——Explanation more especially as to the corporation not undertaking to do the domestic scavenging in the tenement houses, and as to the rates charged by private persons for this work, 5051–5054. 5198–5221. 5342–5345.

Sufficiency of a staff of fifteen sanitary police officers, there being now but nine; assistance rendered by the police force generally, 5058–5062. 5066, 5067. 5169–5171——Great opposition by the ratepayers if it be attempted to levy a rate in aid for sanitary purposes; opinion that it is preferable to levy a distinct sanitary rate, though this would be attended with much difficulty, 5063–5065. 5070. 5270–5272. 5331–5335——Estimate of 3,100 *l.* a year as sufficient for the sanitary department; expenditure of 4,100 *l.* in 1874 for exceptional causes, 5068, 5069. 5225–5228. 5238–5241. 5267–5269. 5304–5306. 5336–5341.

Various duties discharged by witness without finding himself unequal to the work, 5071–5073——Representation of witness, when absent from the sanitary office, by a clerk, who has but a small salary, 5074–5078——Zealous and excellent discharge of their duties by the members of the Public Health Committee, 5079. 5080——Explanation

Boyle, James. (Analysis of his Evidence)—*continued.*

nation as to the committee having sometimes declined to notice complaints by the sanitary association, as in the matter of slaughter-houses, 5081–5090.

Reference to the manure manufactories in the city as not now constituting any nuisances, 5091–5097——Small amount of the average fine upon each person convicted under the Sanitary Act, 5098–5102. 5229–5232——Insufficiency of staff, but for which certain provisions as to the cleaning of ashpits, &c., in the case of tenement houses, would be more stringently enforced, 5103–5106——Circumstances under which a former member of the Public Health Committee (Mr. McGrath) was summoned by witness and compelled to abate a nuisance on some tenement premises, 5122–5125——Conviction obtained also against Mr. McAnaspie in respect of a nuisance from a manure heap, 5126–5130.

Computation of the number of nuisances by the number of houses in which they arise, 5131–5134. 5172–5174——Circumstance of the corporation not having erected any public clocks; doubt as to there being any demand for them, 5135, 5136. 5330——Statement in defence of the action of the corporation in not providing public privies, save in one or two places; intolerable nuisance experienced, 5137–5168. 5328, 5329.

Annual reports published by the Public Health Committee since its establishment, showing the number of prosecutions, &c., in each year, 5175–5181——Considerable increase of prosecutions in the last two years, though the number of sanitary police serjeants has been reduced from fifteen to nine, and their districts enlarged, 5182–5190——Contribution of 1,100 *l.* in 1874 towards a floating hospital, 5239——Careful attention paid to all complaints of sanitary defects which come before witness, 5242, 5243——Inaccuracy of a statement that the inspector of the Local Government Board does not properly investigate cases, 5245–5249.

Exceptions further taken to the evidence of Dr. Grimshaw as to the disinfection of houses being imperfect, 5253–5257——Ample supply of medical sanitary officers, 5258, 5259——Entire inaccuracy of the charge that appointments were made by the corporation on political and religious grounds; several superior officers (including witness) who are Conservatives and Protestants, 5260–5262.

Further statement that the sanitary arrangements would be quite satisfactory if there were fifteen sanitary police officers, and if the expenditure were 3,100 *l.* a year, 5264–5269——Larger staff required for cleansing arrangements, 5273——Concurrence with Mr. Pim as to the injurious effect of slaughter-houses surrounded by the dwellings of the lower classes, 5279–5288.

Admission that the sanitary condition of Dublin is not so good as it ought to be, though it is not so bad as was described by Dr. Grimshaw, 5294–5308. 5346——Further statement purporting to refute Dr. Grimshaw's evidence as to numerous tenement houses being in a disgraceful and unimproved condition, 5296. 5313–5317——Preventive rather than remedial measures required in the case of a large number of very old houses, 5302–5307——Further contradiction also of Dr. Grimshaw's evidence on the subject of the death-rate, 5309–5312.

Explanation on the subject of the provision of the floating hospital, and of the expense involved as compared with the benefits to be derived; hitherto it has had but one patient, 5318–5323. 5347–5358——Long hours devoted daily by witness to the discharge of his duties, 5324——Discourteous character of some representations by the sanitary association which were not attended to by the Public Health Committee, 5325–5327.

Boyle, Mr. Strong testimony to the efficiency of Mr. Boyle in his capacity as secretary of the Public Health Committee, *Sullivan* 4706.

Bray. Explanation in connection with disallowances by witness in 1873 to the amount of 33 *l.* in the case of Bray, *Finlay* 4374–4379——Grounds for witness' dissatisfaction with the collection of the rates in Bray, *ib.* 4374. 4379. 4383.

Bray and Enniskerry Railway Bill. Grounds for objecting to an expenditure of 65 *l.* in opposing the Bray and Enniskerry Railway Bill, *M'Evoy* 1695, 1696. 1698–1708. 1998–2000——Reference to the opposition to the Bray and Enniskerry Railway Bill, on having been made in order to obtain protection for the water mains, *Robinson* 2826, 2827——Good reason for the opposition to the Bray and Enniskerry Railway Bill, *Neville* 5467, 5468.

Bridge Rate (Bridges and Quay Walls). Explanation in connection with the bridge rate in Dublin, its amount, and mode of application, *Moylan & Taafe* 254–262——Levy of the bridge rate at 2 *d.* in the pound for three years, for the building of Grattan Bridge, *Taafe* 483–486——Statement as to the amount realised by the bridge rate, and as to its being collected from the entire metropolitan police district, *Taafe & Moylan* 492–496. 498. 570.

Explanations in connection with the provisions of the Act 17 & 18 Vict. c. 22, whereby the taxation for bridges and quay walls is levied over the metropolitan police district; extensive area of this district, *Henry* 1151–1172——Functions of the Dublin Port

Report, 1876—*continued*

Bridge Rate (Bridges and Quay Walls)—continued,

Port and Docks Board in the origination of bridges and quay walls, *Henry* 1158-1161——Necessary approval by the corporation of the plans and estimates of the Port and Docks Board for bridges and quay walls; expediency of this check in the corporation as being the taxing body, *ib.* 1554-1558. 1566-1576.

Building Act (Dublin). Views of the medical sanitary officers as to the want of a new Building Act, *Grimshaw* 4034——Urgent want of a Building Act for Dublin on sanitary grounds; failure of attempts in 1867 to obtain an Act, *Sullivan* 4686-4688. 4721.

Further statement as to the corporation having promoted a Building Bill, but having failed to carry it, *Sullivan* 4754-4756. 4811-4813——Circumstance of the Building Bill having been modelled on the Belfast Building Act, *ib.* 4830.

Great want of a Building Act in Dublin, *Neville* 5431*-5434——Steps being taken to promote a Building Bill next Session; cause of failure of a Bill promoted in 1867, *ib.* 5432-5434.

Amendment suggested by No. 1 Committee as regards the powers of the corporation in respect of new buildings; reference hereon to the excellent Building Act obtained by Belfast, *Norwood* 5936. 5944-5946.

See also Dilapidated and Dangerous Structures.

Burgess Roll (Dublin). See *Assessors. Franchise. Revision of Burgess Roll.*

Burial Rate (Dublin). Small amount of the burial rate, this being expended by the corporation, *Moylan* 247-251——The burial rate is expended by the Public Health Committee of the corporation, *ib.* 253.

Byrne, Mr. Great ability and efficiency of Mr. John Byrne as one of the Public Health Committee, *Boyle* 4985.

C.

Cab and Car Drivers (Dublin). Expediency of the corporation being entrusted with authority over the cab and car drivers, *Gray* 6476, 6477. 6480——Hardship in the corporation not receiving any portion of the fines from cabmen, *ib.* 6478, 6479.

Carlow. Very unsatisfactory collection of rates in Carlow by the late collector; improved arrangements now in force, *Finlay* 4607-4611.

Carriage Tax (Dublin). Belief as to there being a hackney carriage-tax in Dublin, *Taafe* 379, 380——Claim of the corporation to the carriage rents or licenses, *Sullivan* 4802, 4803——Suggestion by No. 1 Committee that the receipts from hackney carriage licenses should go towards the repair and maintenance of the thoroughfares, *Norwood* 5936.

Carrickfergus. Exceptional position of the town of Carrickfergus, the board of guardians being still the local sanitary authority, *Hancock* 15-18——Absurdity of the exceptional position of Carrickfergus, *ib.* 89——Reference to the county of the town of Carrickfergus as not having got a new corporation under the Act of 1840, *ib.* 597. 598. 601.

Casson, Mr. Statement as to Mr. Casson, an old member of the corporation of Dublin, having lost his election on political grounds; previous attendances of Mr. Casson adverted to hereon, *Stokes* 2186. 3334-3346.

Rejection of Mr. Casson on the ground of non-attendance, irrespectively of politics, *Gray* 6375.

Cattle (Driving through the Streets). Amended regulations now in force as to driving cattle through the streets, *Norwood* 5950.

Cattle Market (Dublin). Very good cattle market constructed some years ago, *Pim* 2465 2466——Total of 24,450 *l.* borrowed from time to time since 1840, for cattle market purposes, none of which has been paid off, *Robinson* 2637-2644——Explanation as to the surplus of annual receipts over expenditure in respect of the cattle market not having been devoted to the reduction of the capital debt; particulars hereon relative to the separate accounts now kept of the receipt and expenditure of the different departments of the corporation, *ib.* 2640-2686.

Success of the new cattle market, built at a cost of about 25,000 *l.*, *Neville* 5443. 5460——Reasons for the opposition of the corporation to the Bill for a cattle market on the North Wall; cost incurred in opposition, *ib.* 5645-5649——Promotion by the corporation (in conjunction with the sales masters) of the new market in Prussia-street, which has been a great success; enforced delay through want of funds, *ib.* 5647. 5650-5654.

Charities. Transfer by the Municipal Reform Act of 1840 of the administration of charities from the corporations to trustees, *Hancock* 626, 627.

Charter Justices. Statement as to several corporations having formerly had the exclusive power of appointing charter justices within their jurisdiction, this power having been taken away by the Act of 1840, or by concurrent legislation, *Hancock* 603–607.. 614. 738–741.

City Estates (Dublin):

1. *Summary of the Estates and Properties of the Corporation.*
2. *Management; System of Leases, &c.*
3. *Rental.*
4. *Collection and Arrears.*
5. *Sales, and Question of further Sales.*

1. *Summary of the Estates and Properties of the Corporation*:

Property of the corporation at Marino and other places outside the city boundary, as well as at Baldoyle and Cooleck, *Robinson* 2559–2575.

Enumeration of the different estates and lands owned by the corporation outside the municipal limits, *Morgan* 3497–3502——The several properties on the north side of the city are those of Ballycoolane, Clonturk, Donnycarney, Grange, and Baldoyle, *ib.* 3497——These were part of the lands of the suppressed monastery of All Hallows, *ib.* 3498, 3499——On the south side there are estates at Colganstown and Ringwood, *ib.* 3500——There is also the valuable property of Baggotrath, *ib.* 3501, 3502.

2. *Management, System of Leases, &c.*:

Practice as to new leases and as to obtaining Treasury sanction, *M'Evoy* 2060, 2061. 2091, 2092——Explanation that witness' department does not deal with the question of rental, or the mode of letting, upon which points the land and law agent is the proper authority, *Robinson* 2499–2503. 2551–2558. 2583, 2584.

Application recently made to the Treasury to appoint a valuator, in order to fix the value of several properties nearly out of lease, instead of their being put up to public auction, *Morgan* 3672, 3673——Lease for thirty-one years granted in the case of tenements, and for seventy-five years in the case of rebuilding, *ib.* 3674.

Very limited extent, if any, to which witness exercises the functions of land agent in connection with the corporation estates; he neither receives nor collects the Baldoyle rents, and is not placed in a position to carry out any efficient inspection of the property, *Morgan* 3778–3791——Very imperfect inspection of the property by the corporation personally, *ib.* 3792–3794——Several instances of very poor or old property in Dublin let at low rents in reference to the valuation; absence of competition in some cases when the rents are low, *ib.* 3842–3852.

Absence of stringent covenants in the old leases as to repairs and maintenance, *Morgan* 3853. 3856——Want of more efficient inspection of the city property generally; obstacle to this being undertaken by witness or by the city architect, *ib.* 3856–3859.

Comments upon the extensive alienations of corporate property in the last century, *Sullivan* 4672–4676——Very valuable property obtained by Trinity College from the corporation gratuitously, *ib.* 4672.

Suggestion by Committee No. 3 for a power to grant building leases for a term of 150 years, *Norwood* 5951.

3. *Rental*:

Comment upon the small increase in the rental from the borough estates, *M'Evoy* 2058, 2059. 2089——Prospect of a large increase from some of the property in Dublin, *ib.* 2093.

Statement of the rental of the city estates in 1850–51, 1870–71, and 1874–75; gross rental of 18,700 *l.* in the latter year, the property consisting chiefly of houses, *Robinson* 2470–2475——Information also relative to some property near Cooleck, the present rent being about 500 *l.* a year, *ib.* 2480–2482. 2493–2507——Circumstance of the rental account including not only house and ground-rents, but an old grant from Government since the time of Charles the Second, *ib.* 2548–2550.

Summary of the ancient revenues of the corporation as acquired under Royal Charter; various holdings comprised, and amount derived in each case, *Morgan* 3503–3505——Produce of about 18,000 *l.* a year by the landed estates after various deductions, but without allowing for poor rate and income tax, *ib.* 3506–3515——Information relative to Lord Charlemont's tenure of the property at Marino, and the rent paid in proportion to the valuation, *ib.* 3603–3608——Increase of about 1,000 *l.* a year in the rental from the estates since 1867, *ib.* 3669–3671.

Concurrence in the statements in a certain report by Mr. Morgan upon the subject of the corporation property and rental, *Sullivan* 4676–4680.

4. *Collection*

CITY ESTATES (DUBLIN)—continued.

4. *Collection and Arrears:*

Statement as to the amount of the gross and net rental respectively, and the amount of arrears at different periods, *Robinson* 2508–2528——Very fair collection of the corporation rents, save in the case of Baldoyle; diminishing amount of the arrears generally, *Finlay* 4282–4286. 4427, 4428——Check suggested by witness for testing the accuracy of the outstanding arrears of rent due to the corporation, *ib.* 4428.

Explanations submitted in reference to the arrears in the collection of the city rents; report by the city treasurer on this subject several years ago, and statement thereon by No. 3 Committee, to the effect that the losses have been exceedingly small, *Norwood* 5983.

5. *Sales, and Questions of further Sales:*

Advantage if some of the estates were sold in order to pay off the debenture debt, *M'Evoy* 2062, 2063——Information relative to certain sales of corporation property, the proceeds having been invested in the purchase of city debentures, *Morgan* 3675–3682——Calculation by witness that the corporation would save over 1,000 *l.* a year by selling property at Baldoyle and elsewhere, and by paying off their debenture debt, *ib.* 3860–3864.

See also All Hallows College. Bagotrath Estate. Baldoyle Property. Ballycoolane Estate. Clonturk Property. Colganston Property. Custom House. North Liffey Strand. Oxmantown Property. Ringwood Property. Trinity College (Dublin).

City Marshal (Dublin). Salary paid to the marshal of Dublin by the corporation, out of the fees received by him as registrar of pawnbrokers, *Henry* 1479–1484——Statement as to the late and present city marshal having been relatives of lord mayors, *M'Evoy* 1912–1919——Litigation pending upon the question of fees in the office of the city marshal, *Robinson* 3454–3456.

Proposed abolition of the office of city marshal, *Sullivan* 4831——The office is a perfectly needless one, *ib.*——Instance in the case of the city marshal of the economy effected by the corporation in reduction of salaries, *ib.* 4832.

Explanation that certain defalcations in the marshal's office were caused by the subordinates, not by the late marshal, *Norwood* 6095, 6096.

City Treasurer (Dublin). Satisfactory precautions as to the security given by the city treasurer, *Finlay* 4429, 4430——Examination as regards the office of city treasurer, to the effect that it is hardly feasible to dispense with this officer by the appointment of a banker as treasurer, as in smaller corporations, *ib.* 4497–4511. 4575–4577.

See also Accounts. Robinson, Mr.

Clerk of the Peace (Dublin). Reference to the salary and fees of the clerk of the peace as each amounting to about 800 *l.* a year, *Henry* 1477, 1478.

Clocks (Dublin). Non-erection of any public clocks by the corporation, *Henry* 1460——Doubt as their being any demand for public clocks, *Boyle* 5135, 5136. 5330——Sufficiency of the supply of public clocks throughout the city, *Norwood* 6294.

Clonturk Property (Corporation of Dublin). Particulars in connection with the Clonturk property, which comprises 386 acres; circumstances under which certain leases have been granted and renewed, the result being that the present rents are far below the value, *Morgan* 3636 *et seq.*

Particulars as to the circumstances under which a new lease was granted to Thomas Doolan in 1854, for sixty-six years, in respect of some property at Clonturk previously under lease to Mr. Duval; rental of 70 *l.* in this case, Mr. Dooley having since sold his interest under the lease for 3,000 *l.*; *Morgan* 3561–3581.

Details in connection with land and premises at Clonturk leased to Blaney Mitchell in 1852, for thirty-one years, at a rental of 40 *l.* 16 *s.* 6 *d.*; relation between this rent and the valuation of the property, *Morgan* 3582–3602. 3809–3812.

Cole Alley (Dublin). Very poor character of the houses in Cole Alley, their contribution to the rates being exceedingly small; expediency of a limitation of the franchise in this case, *M'Evoy* 1662–1668. 1762–1767. 1954–1961.

Colganston Property (Corporation of Dublin). Area of about 200 acres comprised in the Colganston property; steps being taken for re-letting this land, *Morgan* 3659, 3660.

Collection of Rates:

1. *Collecting Staff in Dublin; Functions of the Collector General.*
2. *Cost of Collection in Dublin.*
3. *Loss in Collection; Evasion on different Grounds, and Remedies suggested.*
4. *Audit in Dublin.*
5. *Question of dispensing with the Collector General's Department.*
6. *Collection and Audit generally.*

1. *Collecting Staff in Dublin; Functions of the Collector General:*

Functions of witness as Collector General of Rates in Dublin, under the Act 12 & 13 Vict. c. 91, s. 63, *Moylan* 231-233. 236——Staff of ten collectors under witness, *ib.* 234——Consolidated system of collection under the Act 12 & 13 Vict., there having been several collectors previously for the different authorities, *ib.* 238, 239.

Power of the Lord Lieutenant to call the Collector General to account, *M'Evoy* 1850, 1851——Instances of complaints by boards of guardians against the system of collection, the Collector General being, however, totally independent of all the local bodies, *ib.* 1852-1855. 2006-2008.

2. *Cost of Collection in Dublin:*

Limit of the cost of collection of the rates in Dublin to two and a-half per cent., the actual cost for the last five years or so having been always under this limit; much greater cost in previous years, *Taafe & Moylan* 510-515.

Great increase in the cost of the Collector General's office, only half the charge being for the collector's salary, *M'Evoy* 1734——Conclusion that a cost of 6 *d.* in the pound for collection of the rates is very excessive, *ib.* 2020-2022.

Particulars as to the causes of the increased charge for the Collector General's department; this is mainly due to the increase of poundage, and not of salaries, *Norwood* 6100.

3. *Loss in Collection; Evasion on different Grounds, and Remedies suggested:*

Annual loss of about eight per cent. of the amount levied, about half this loss being due to the operation of bills of sale, and the system of tenement houses, *Taafe & Moylan* 284-298——Difficulty as to collection in the case only of the low class of property, *Taafe* 322-324.

Further particulars relative to the extensive evasion of rates in the case of tenement houses; that is, through the system of sham immediate lessors, *Taafe* 354-365. 473. 491, 492——Further reference also to the effect of bills of sale in preventing recovery of rates, *ib.* 366-369——Means suggested for remedying the abuse in respect of recovery from immediate lessors, by rendering liable the person in beneficial receipt of the rack rents; consideration of objections thereto, *ib.* 370, 371. 409-415. 420-434.

Considerable number of fraudulent immediate lessors, *Taafe & Moylan* 416-419——Information obtained through the collectors, as well as directly by witness, as to the terms of letting between the head landlord and the immediate lessor, and as to the tenancies being weekly or monthly, *Taafe* 420-432. 451-461——Indirect effect, as regards increase of the franchise, of the proposal for remedying the evasion on the part of immediate lessors, *ib.* 467, 468. 547-550.

Comments made by witness (through the press) upon the very unsatisfactory character of the Collector General's report, and upon the laxity in collection of the rates; statement also in letter from Master Fitzgibbon, as to the excessive arrears, and the undue loss in collection, *M'Evoy* 1716-1729.

Further comment upon the Collector General's report, though some errors in printing may explain away some of witness' objections, *M'Evoy* 2011-2016——Bad collection of the rates in Dublin; unduly large per-centage lost, *Stokes* 2906. 2908, 2909.

Importance of some means of reducing the loss of rates in collection, *Neville* 5459——Success of the present system of collection; moderate amount of arrears, considering the poverty of many of the ratepayers, *Norwood* 5923, 5924——Great loss in collection, owing to the action of fraudulent lessors, and the system of bills of sale, *Gray* 6408. 6412——Importance of a power of recovering from the beneficial owner, the rates being a charge on the property itself, *ib.* 6409-6413.

Case on behalf of the Collector General of rates, and opinions of the Right Hon. R. A. Warren and Mr. Serjeant Barry thereon, in November 1868, *App.* 406-408.

4. *Audit in Dublin:*

Reference to a letter from Master Fitzgibbon, auditor of the Collector General's accounts, in which complaint is made as to the inefficiency of the audit, *M'Evoy* 1714-1718. 1729——Statement as to Master Fitzgibbon having contended that his functions as auditor entitled him to see that the rates were properly collected, *ib.* 1839-1849——Importance of

COLLECTION OF RATES—continued.

3. *Audit in Dublin*—continued.

of a strict audit of the Collector General's accounts as a means of reducing the arrears, *M'Evoy* 2055–2057.

Due payment to the bank of the amount of rates collected, *Finlay* 4318–4320—— Advantage if the accounts of the Collector General were subjected to the same audit as the corporation accounts, *ib.* 4578—— Prospective abolition of the office of Receiver Master in Chancery, by whom the accounts are now audited, *ib.*

Explanation that the Collector General's accounts in Dublin have always been audited by the Receiver Master of the Court of Chancery, *Finlay* 4650.

5. *Question of dispensing with the Collector General's Department:*

Conclusion as to the expediency of the several representative bodies being responsible for the collection of their own rates, *M'Evoy* 1729. 1732–1734—— Way in which the Collector General's staff might be distributed, if the office were not retained as a separate department, *ib.* 2023.

Objection to the collection of rates being transferred to the different boards by whom they are levied, *Norwood* 5923.

6. *Collection and Audit generally:*

Audit by witness of the collection of rates, save in Dublin; he is satisfied with the collection generally, *Finlay* 4380–4382—— Doubt as to the expediency of further powers in witness in cases where the collection of rates is excessively in arrear; sufficiency of representations to the town commissioners, *ib.* 4519–4523.

See also Accounts.

Collection of Rents. See *Baldoyle Property. City Estates.*

Commercial Buildings (Dublin). Statement as to Commercial Buildings in Dublin being rated to only one person, and conferring only one vote, *M'Evoy* 1683–1685. 1749–1753. 2024, 2025—— Explanation as to witness being the only burgess in respect of Commercial Buildings; his object in retaining his name on the burgess list, *Stokes* 2983–2991. 3087–3089.

Commissioners. Eleven towns governed by commissioners under local or special Acts, *Hancock* 1—— Suggestion that the system of municipal commissioners be abolished, *ib.* 89.

Committees (Corporation of Dublin). See *Corporation of Dublin*, 8. 9. 14.

Cork. Illustration in the case of Cork of the want of facilities for local improvements by means of provisional orders instead of by special Act, *Hancock* 70–75.

Advantage if simple pleadings were adopted in the Recorder's Court in Cork, *Norwood* 6251, 6252.

CORPORATION OF DUBLIN:

1. *Functions of the Corporation.*
2. *Constitution of the Corporation; Complaints on this Score.*
3. *Political Influence at Elections.*
4. *Question of a 50 l. Qualification.*
5. *Question of Property Representation.*
6. *Suggestions for an amended System of Election.*
7. *Political Discussions in the Corporation.*
8. *Working of the Corporation by means of Committees.*
9. *Improvement if there were Six instead of Three Committees.*
10. *Financial Administration.*
11. *Great Obstruction through the necessity of a Quorum of Twenty Members; reduced Quorum suggested.*
12. *Obstruction to Suspension of Bye-laws.*
13. *Difficulties attributable to want of Funds.*
14. *Resolutions Explanatory of the Views of the Corporation and of its Committees as to the various Improvements required.*
15. *Representation of the Corporation before the present Committee.*

1. *Functions of the Corporation:*

Great change made in the local management of Dublin between 1841 and 1849; transfer to the Corporation of the powers of the former Paving Board and Wide Streets Board, and of the fiscal powers of the grand jury, &c., *Henry* 1075–1090. 1104–1112——

CORPORATION OF DUBLIN—continued.

1. *Functions of the Corporation*—continued.

Powers of the corporation under the Act of 1849 to levy a sewer rate and to make sewers, *Henry* 1106–1109—— Increased sanitary duties vested in the corporation since the Act of 1849; local Acts also for a better water supply, *ib.* 1112–1115.

Approval of the corporation having control not only of the gas supply but of public markets, abattoirs, and several other improvements; that is, if there are funds for the purpose, and if the constitution of the corporation be improved, *Sullivan* 4747–4749. 4895, 4896—— Main duty of the corporation to see to the expenditure of the rates and the sanitary condition of the city, *ib.* 4760–4762.

2. *Constitution of the Corporation; Complaints on this Score:*

Opinion that the inhabitants generally are fairly represented in the municipal council, *Henry* 1609, 1610.

Exclusion of the upper and middle classes from their fair share in the municipal administration under the present system, *M'Evoy* 1657, 1658. 1903–1910——Advantage if the same person were not eligible for election to several different boards or local bodies, *ib.* 1662. 2048–2051——Belief that the present corporation is powerless alike for good or evil, *ib.* 1693. 1903.

Witness considers that throughout Ireland, and especially in Dublin, municipal government is in an unsatisfactory condition, *Pim* 2297 *et seq.*—— Gradual deterioration in the character of the town council of Dublin, many of the largest ratepayers being anxious for some change, *ib.* 2299–2302—— Twofold reason why the leading mercantile men abstain from municipal administration, *ib.* 2301, 2302. 2416–2418.

Explanation that witness makes no objection as to the social position of the members of the corporation of Dublin, though he repeats that many of the leading men are deterred from entering the corporation by the necessity of their acting as political partisans, *Pim* 2352–2368. 2383–2385——Few men of high mercantile position in the corporation out of those who were members in 1851, *ib.* 2353–2355. 2351, 2361.

Gradual deterioration in the constitution of the corporation of Dublin since it was reformed in 1850; very inadequate representation of all the better and wealthier class of ratepayers, *Stokes* 2887–2889. 2943–2945——Undue representation of the publican interest in the corporation, there being some fifteen publicans in the council; examination as to witness' grounds for this statement, *ib.* 2890, 2891. 3019–3041. 3067–3077 —— Statement as to Mr. Sullivan having been expelled from the corporation through the interest of the publicans, *ib.* 2891—— Nothing would induce witness to enter the corporation, though personally the members have always treated him with every courtesy, *ib.* 2936–2942. 3081—— Recent instance of the reluctance of respectable citizens to join the corporation, *ib.* 2942——Very few of the leading merchants who are members of the corporation, *ib.* 3079–3081.

Zeal and integrity with which the duties of the corporation were discharged within witness' experience, though there is doubtless some need of reformation in the constitution and working of the council, *Sullivan* 4660. 4663, 4664——Defeat of witness when seeking re-election in 1870 or 1871, since which period he has not been in the council, *ib.* 4661, 4802——Effect of the want of funds in deterring many men of position and capacity from entering the corporation or remaining in it, *ib.* 4666, 4667. 4793.

Prejudicial effect of the influential antagonism to the reformed corporation on political grounds; that is, up to the year 1851, *Sullivan* 4668——Objection by leading merchants to join the corporation, as involving too much demand on their time, *ib.* 4686—— Antagonism of various interests which prevented witness' re-election, he having promoted several obnoxious reforms, *ib.* 4688.

Less efficiency doubtless of some members of the corporation than of others, this being the case in all public bodies, *Norwood* 5885——Reluctance of leading merchants to join the corporation on account of the work involved, and the demands upon their time, *ib.* 5913, 5914——Explanation that the majority of the members of the corporation are very large ratepayers, *ib.* 6041.

Numerous engagements of many of the leading merchants, so that they could not spare time to serve in the town council, *Norwood* 6042, 6043——Several instances of leading merchants who do serve on the corporation, *ib.* 6044——Inexpediency of any restriction upon the number of members engaged in trade or as licensed victuallers; great efficiency of the late Alderman Redmond adverted to hereon, *ib.* 6288–6290.

Room for much improvement in the *personnel* of the corporation, though this may equally be said of all elected bodies, *Gray* 6350, 6351——Refusal by Mr. Joseph Pim and Mr. Thomas Pim to enter the corporation, though pressed to do so, *ib.* 6350—— Fair proportion of good men in the council, *ib.* 6351.

Admission as to members being more or less amenable to the opinion of their constituents,

CORPORATION OF DUBLIN—continued.

2. *Constitution of the Corporation; Complaints on this Score*—continued.

stituents, *Gray* 6487, 6488 —— Political feeling by which the opposition to the corporation and the charges against its members are more or less influenced, *ib.* 6528–6531 —— Grounds for the statement that Mr. Joseph Pim (as well as Mr. Thomas Pim) had been invited to join the corporation but had declined, *ib.* 6573–6579.

3. *Political Influence at Elections:*

Instances of Liberal wards selecting Conservative representatives; these are, however, exceptions to the rule, *Henry* 1239–1246. 1303–1309. 1559, 1560. 1577, 1578 —— Conduct of the elections for the corporation on political grounds, with very few exceptions, *Stokes* 2892, 2893. 3185–3187.

Exceptional liberality evinced by the reformed corporation in its tolerance of minority dissent, as in appointing to the office of lord mayor, &c., irrespectively of political considerations, *Sullivan* 4671. 4766–4771 —— At present about two-thirds of the corporation are Liberals and one-third Conservatives, *ib.* 4682.

Election of witness apart from political grounds; admission, however, that the election of many members is due to political influence, *Norwood* 6045–6048 —— Several instances of Liberal wards returning Conservative members, politics not being a ground of opposition, *Gray* 6366, 6367. 6374. 6534 —— Liberality in political matters in Dublin, as shown by the return of Conservatives for Liberal wards, *ib.* 6579–6583.

4. *Question of a 50 l. Qualification:*

Suggested increase of the qualification for members of the corporation; opinion favourable to the adoption of the special jurors' qualification, which is 50 *l.* in Dublin, *M'Evoy* 1682. 1833–1838.

Grounds for the conclusion that a 60 *l.* rating as qualification for the town council is much too high, *Curran* 2163–2173. 2243–2250 —— Question as to this rating disqualifying Mr. M'Evoy, *ib.* 2164–2166. 2243–2250 —— It would exclude Mr. Norwood, *ib.* 2169–2173 —— Objections to a 50 *l.* qualification for town councillors, disqualification thereby of many very efficient members, *Gray* 6332–6335.

5. *Question of Property Representation:*

Argument as to the expediency of a direct representation of the large rated proprietors in the management of the rates; reference especially to Government buildings, breweries, banks, colleges and other large institutions, *M'Evoy* 1661, 1662 —— Expediency of the property qualification for the corporation being in respect of property in exclusive possession; this would disqualify hotel keepers and tavern proprietors, *ib.* 1682.

Want of men in the corporation who could afford to defy unpopularity, and would persist in carrying out necessary reforms, *Sullivan* 4631 —— Approval of some concessions by the popular party, so as to bring into the corporation the co-operation of a larger number of influential citizens, *ib.* 4681, 4682. 4776. 4784 —— Failure of some efforts of Mr. Maclean (the highly efficient chairman of the Public Health Committee) and of witness to induce influential men to enter the corporation, political considerations being waived, *ib.* 4665.

Explanation with further reference to witness' former experience as a member of the corporation, and his reason for proposing some concession to property owners in the case of Dublin, *Sullivan* 4822–4828. 4835–4842.

Approval of some change in the constitution of the corporation, in deference to public opinion on the subject, *Norwood* 5883–5885. 5980–5982 —— Confidence in the corporation if property were more directly represented, and if the leading citizens were induced to take part in its affairs, *ib.* 5981–5983.

Non-exclusion from the corporation of property owners who reside in Dublin, *Gray* 6737, 6738.

6. *Suggestions for an amended System of Election:*

Conclusion that one-third is too large a proportion of the corporation to be in peril of their seats every year; obstacle to any useful reforms on account of the liability of independent members to lose their seats, *Sullivan* 4688, 4689 —— Suggestion that in five wards in the city three members might be elected simultaneously, *ib.* 4690–4692.

Improvement if town councillors were elected for five instead of three years, *Norwood* 5921, 5922 —— Objection to a general election, instead of a gradual change in the constitution of the corporation, *ib.* 6287.

7. *Political Discussions in the Corporation:*

Objection by the leading merchants to enter the corporation on account partly of the political discussions which arise, *M'Evoy* 2009, 2010 —— Waste of much time in political discussions at the meetings of the council; strong disapproval of this practice, its effect

CORPORATION OF DUBLIN—continued.

7. *Political Discussion in the Corporation*—continued.

effect being moreover to prevent many men of position from joining the corporation, *Pim* 2300–2303. 2361–2366. 2383–2396.

Grounds for the conclusion that in some respects political discussion in the corporation of Dublin has been productive of much public good, *Sullivan* 4757–4759.

Reference to the political discussions in the corporation (in which witness never takes part) as not interfering with the transaction of business, which really takes place in the committees, *Norwood* 6039–6041——Denial that politics are discussed at the committee meetings of the corporation, *ib.* 6081–6086. 6211, 6212——Entire absence of political discussions in the main drainage committee, of which committee Mr. Stokes is a very efficient member, 6081–6086.

Exceptional instances of political meetings of the council; official return to this effect, *Gray* 6323, 6324——Further statement explanatory of the extent to which political discussions take place in the corporation, *ib.* 6592–6598. 6676–6688.

8. *Working of the Corporation by means of Committees:*

System of committees by which the corporation acts in the management of the expenditure; control of the paving, lighting, and cleansing by No. 1 Committee, *Henry* 1315–1322——Frequent instances of great delay before reports of committees are acted upon by the council, *Stokes* 3194.

Grounds for objecting to the transaction of corporation business by Committees of the Whole House, *Sullivan* 4877, 4878——Private character of the meetings of the several committees, the business being excellently conducted, *ib.* 4881–4884.

Transaction of the real business of the corporation in its committees, these working earnestly in the interests of the ratepayers, *Norwood* 5884——Excellent attendance at the committee meetings, *ib.* 6031.

9. *Improvement if there were Six instead of Three Committees:*

Advantage if there were power to have six committees with only ten members on each *Gray* 6504.

10. *Financial Administration:*

Explanation as regards certain instances of objectionable expenditure, that witness would not question these items if the corporation were a properly elected body, *M'Evoy* 1874–1883——Very general feeling that the financial affairs of the corporation are not well managed, *Pim* 2300. 2415——People very often talk of jobbery, and there is a good deal of feeling of suspicion as to the way in which things are done, *ib.* 2300.

Opposition frequently offered by large ratepayers, at considerable expense, to financial schemes of the corporation, the constitution of that body not entitling it to confidence and respect, *Pim* 2320, 2422–2428——Further statement as to the local complaints frequently made in regard to the financial administration; want of economy on the one hand, whilst on the other there is much neglect in the matter of improvements, *ib.* 2369–2376. 2405——Witness does not say there is any malversation of funds, *ib.* 2376. 2405.

Judgments debts against the corporation to the amount of about 2,800 *l.* in 1849, for which a receiver was put over the city estates, *Robinson* 2611–2612.

Explanation as to witness having lent 36,000 *l.* to the corporation at five per cent. interest, with a commission of two per cent; considerable profit made by him on this transaction, *Stokes* 3180–3182. 3204–3218. 3373. 3377. 3378——Frequent loans made to the corporation by Mr. Jameson, *ib.* 3183——Urgent need of the corporation some years ago, when they borrowed 5,000 *l.* from their newly-appointed treasurer, *ib.* 3184——Particulars relative to the issue of debentures by the corporation, and the low price obtained as compared with the rate of interest, *ib.* 3200, 3201. 3204–3218. 3228, 3229. 3232–3240. 3377–3389.

Disposition of the corporation in the direction of parsimony rather than of extravagance, *Norwood* 6046——Denial that any jobbery has taken place, *ib.* 6049——Careful scrutiny by the corporation in all matters of expenditure, *ib.* 6052. 6054.

Animadversions made upon the corporation upon certain subjects, but without foundation, *Norwood* 6206, 6207. 6291–6294——Comment upon the vague and general character of some insinuations against the corporation, *ib.* 6292.

Excellent credit of the corporation, money being borrowed at four per cent., *Gray* 6451, 6452.

11. *Great Obstruction through the necessity of a Quorum of Twenty Members; reduced Quorum suggested:*

Very irregular attendance at the meetings of the town council; frequent difficulty in obtaining

Report, 1876—*continued*.

CORPORATION OF DUBLIN—continued.

11. *Great Obstruction through the Necessity of a Quorum, &c.*—continued.

obtaining a quorum, so that there is much waste of time, *Pim* 2300. 2302. 2383——Frequent waste of time in waiting till a quorum is formed; instance of this, *ib.* 2383. 2386, 2387. 2419.

Recommended reduction of the quorum of the corporation from twenty to seven or ten members, *Stokes* 3137-3143——Great obstruction to business in the corporation by the necessity of a quorum of twenty members; sufficiency of a quorum of thirteen, *Sullivan* 4812-4814.

Great improvement if the quorum for corporation meetings were reduced from twenty to nine; *Norwood* 6033-6036. 6050. 6106——Difficulties in the way of an alteration of the bye-law, or rather of the provision in the Act, by which the quorum of members is fixed at twenty; facility desirable as regards the alteration of bye-laws under the Act of 1849; *ib.* 6103-6105. 6156-6163——Conclusion further expressed in favour of a reduction of the quorum to nine or to seven, *ib.* 6106-6113.

Great obstruction to business and great waste of time by the necessity of a quorum of twenty members; expediency of the number being reduced to nine or ten, *Gray* 6352-6359. 6488, 6489. 6494-6500——Very prejudicial operation of the quorum regulation in preventing the consideration of improvements, *ib.* 6480. 6488. 6494, 6495. 6504-6506——Competency of the present corporation to carry out the required improvements generally, if relieved from the quorum difficulty, *ib.* 6494, 6495.

Comment upon the course sometimes adopted by the Conservative members in leaving meetings when they are in a minority, so that business cannot be transacted through a want of a quorum; the Liberals never adopt these tactics, *Gray* 6594-6598——Witness repeats that constant obstructions arise under the quorum difficulty, and that with a smaller quorum the necessary reforms could be carried out by the corporation, *ib.* 6599-6610. 6720-6722——Facility expected in carrying a new Improvement Bill but for the quorum difficulty, *ib.* 6608.

Return of the number of meetings of the town council of Dublin, with hours for which they were summoned, and hour for forming quorum, &c., for the years 1873, 1874, and 1875; *App.* 409.

12. *Obstruction to Suspension of Bye-laws:*

Instances of obstruction of business at the public sittings of the corporation through one member objecting to suspend the bye-laws, *Sullivan* 4878-4880.

13. *Difficulties attributable to want of Funds:*

State of chronic impecuniosity to which the inefficient management of the city of Dublin is mainly owing, *Sullivan* 4665-4668. 4719——Removal of all causes of complaint against the corporation if the funds at their disposal were sufficient, *Norwood* 6114, 6115——Improving resources of the corporation whilst the expenses of street repairs will be much diminished, *ib.* 6115——Concurrence with Mr. Sullivan that impecuniosity is the main cause of the defects in the working of the corporation, *Gray* 6485, 6486.

14. *Resolutions explanatory of the Views of the Corporation and of its Committees as to the various Improvements required:*

Witness submits sundry resolutions and suggestions in detail, as prepared by the different committees of the corporation; evidence in elucidation of the various amendments proposed, *Norwood* 5934-5976——All the suggestions drawn up by the several committees have been adopted by the corporation, *ib.* 5935. 5985, 5986.

15. *Representation of the Corporation before the present Committee:*

Justification of the course pursued by the corporation in their selection of representatives before the present committee, *Sullivan* 4763-4765. 4891-4893——Suggestion that Mr. Byrne or Mr. Norwood, who are strong Conservatives and most efficient members, be summoned by the Committee to give evidence, *ib.* 4892.

Witness has been deputed to represent the corporation, but explains that on certain points he expresses his individual opinions, and not those of the council, *Norwood* 5880.

Explanation of the circumstances under which Mr. Norwood and witness (the one a Conservative, the other a Liberal) have been deputed to represent the corporation, and to rebut the evidence given before the Committee on certain points, *Gray* 6300-6307.

See also the Headings generally throughout the Index.

County Surveyors. Circumstance of there being an examination for county surveyorships, *M'Evoy* 1738. 1747, 1748.

Cumulative Voting. Details of witness' plan for the election of the representatives of the occupiers; advantage by applying the cumulative principle, *Hancock* 154-156. 163——

Cumulative Voting—continued.

Way in which the cumulative principle as applied to the election of both owners and occupiers, would solve the religious difficulty as regards local representation and taxation, *Hancock* 156. 165–169.

Explanation that witness does not propose any multiple voting among occupiers, though each occupier should have cumulative votes for the number of candidates; way in which this principle would operate in Dublin, *Hancock* 170–177——Strong approval of cumulative voting, *M'Evoy* 2029, 2030.

Grounds for objecting to the cumulative system of voting in municipal elections, though it has been found successful at School Board elections, *Pim* 2308–2310——Way in which cumulative voting would be used by Protestants and Roman Catholics respectively, in order to secure the election of men holding their respective religious opinions; great evil thereof, *ib.* 2309, 2310.

Proposal for the adoption of cumulative voting, so that the minority in any ward may be able to return a member; concession thereby to the Conservatives, *Sullivan* 4682. 4696, 4697.

Great disfavour with which multiple voting, or the representation of minorities, would be regarded in Dublin; strong feeling of dissatisfaction if it be attempted to apply any exceptional legislation, such as the three-cornered system, *Gray* 6376–6403. 6496——Advantage of cumulative voting over the whole city for the election of a limited number of members; first-class men likely to be returned, *ib.* 6383. 6385–6387. 6404.

Explanation that in approving of the election of a limited number of councillors by cumulation voting over the whole city, witness does not profess to represent the views of the corporation, *Gray* 6614–6617.

Return, submitted by Dr. Hancock, showing the result of a plan for constituting the town authority on a certain basis involving cumulative voting, *App.* 403.

Curran, John Adye. (Analysis of his Evidence.)—Experience of witness since 1868 as one of the assessors at the revision of the burgess roll for Dublin, 2105–2110——Large number of burgesses, properly qualified, who are annually struck off the list through the wholesale service of objections, 2111–2117. 2179–2182——Necessity of persons who are on the list for the first time attending in proof of their claim if objected to; different practice as to onus of proof when a person has once got on the list, 2111–2113. 2197–2199——Service of 1,979 objections last year, about 1,000 names having been struck off through no appearance having been put in, 2114, 2115.

Statement to the effect that until 1874 all occupiers at or under 8 *l.* were struck off the burgess roll, they not having been on the rate book under the Collection of Rates Act, 2118–2124——Effect also of this Act in excluding weekly and monthly tenants from the municipal franchise, 2122–2126——Conclusion arrived at by witness, and acted upon in 1874, that under the Representation of the People Act of 1868, all persons liable to be rated between 4 *l.* and 8 *l.* were qualified for the burgess roll, 2127–2130. 2202–2206——Difference of opinion between witness and Mr. Hyndham (his co-assessor) on the foregoing point; decision of the Lord Mayor in favour of witness' view, 2131–2133.

Conclusion also arrived at by witness in 1874 as to the admission of weekly and monthly tenants; statement hereon as to the Collector General refusing to rate these persons, 2133–2145. 2207–2209——Circumstance of the Collector General's opinion having been supported by that of Judge Barry and of Judge Warren, 2137. 2251, 2252——Comment upon the obligation as to a continuous residence of two years and eight months as a condition of admission to the burgess roll; exceptional position of Dublin in this respect, 2146–2151. 2256.

Hardship in persons frequently losing the franchise for a short break of residence over a period of two years and eight months; liberal interpretation of the law by witness on this point, 2148–2162. 2174–2176. 2210–2213. 2230, 2231. 2250–2267——Refusal of witness in the case of Mr. Fry to strike that gentleman off the list because of a few days' break of residence; judgment of the Court of Queen's Bench in favour of witness' decision, 2151–2162. 2212–2216. 2268.

Grounds for the conclusion that a 50 *l.* rating as qualification for the town council is much too high, 2163–2173. 2243–2250——Opinion that if the law were properly amended, and if wholesale objections were stopped, there would be nearly 15,000 instead of about 5,000 names on the burgess roll for Dublin, 2177–2182. 2253–2258.

Defence of the system of popular election of the assessors: improvement if the election were triennial, 2183–2189——Practice of the Lord Mayor usually to decide in favour of enfranchisement, in the event of a difference between the two assessors, 2190, 2191. 2282, 2283——Expediency of one or both assessors being necessarily barristers, 2191, 2192——Rate of payment of the revising barristers, the revision extending from the 20th October to the 10th November, 2193–2196——Assistance rendered by both political parties in striking off names, but not in putting them on, 2200, 2201.

Suggestion

Curran, John Adye. (Analysis of his Evidence)—*continued.*

Suggestion that as to the numerous small towns under the Act of 1854, the Act shall be deemed to be a local Act for the purpose of the provisions of the Acts 34 & 35 Vict. and 37 & 38 Vict., 2217–2224——Amendments suggested as to the power of the police to prosecute for drunkenness in towns under the Act of 1854; alteration required as to the disposal of the fines in such cases, 2225–2229.

Examination upon the question as to the accuracy of witness' statement that the Collector General of rates did not put on his list any weekly or monthly tenants; doubt as to his refusing to rate those who tender their rates, 2232–2238. 2249–2281——Explanation as to witness not having admitted till 1874 the claim of weekly or monthly tenants, though the claim rested on the Act of 1868; 2239–2242.

Exclusive effect of the provision as to residence within seven miles of Dublin; suggested extension to twelve miles, so that Bray and other places may be included, 2284–2287——Ambiguity of the present law in Ireland as to the qualification of persons who claim by descent or marriage; suggestion as to the amendment desirable, 2288, 2289——Grounds for the suggestion that the mode of service of objections be by post at the residence, 2289.

Frequent disfranchisement of occupiers in consequence of the non-payment of taxes by the landlord, 2289——Amendments proposed in connection with the payment of taxes in order to facilitate the enfranchisement of claimants; facility at the same time to the collection of taxes, 2289–2290——Sufficiency of the payment of taxes at the time of voting in some of the townships around Dublin, 2293, 2294.

Custom House (Dublin). Unexpired lease from the corporation of nearly 100 years in the case of the Custom House, *Morgan* 3665.

D.

Dairy Yards (Dublin). Extremely filthy state of the dairy yards; great nuisance from the large accumulations of manure, *Grimshaw* 3962——Powers of the corporation for dealing with the dairy yards, *ib.* 3963.

Evidence in detail relative to the condition of the dairy yards, the action taken by witness with a view to their better regulation, the difficulty of enforcing improvement on account of deficient legislation, *Boyle* 4992–5013——Report by witness in July 1875, showing the condition of these yards, and the amendments required as regards increase of cubic space, &c., *ib.* 4993–4996. 5011, 5012——Undue amount of pleuro-pneumonia on account of the insufficiency of cubic space, *ib.* 4997——Instance of successful proceedings before a magistrate with a view to a large reduction in the number of cattle in one of these yards, *ib.* 4998–5004. 5045, 5046.

Further considerations as to the difficulty in taking action before the magistrates against the dairy yards, and as to the remedy required in the matter of cubic space, *Boyle* 5034–5046.

Dalkey. Details relative to the great irregularity and abuse which formerly prevailed in the collection of rates in Dalkey, the collector having committed frauds, and the accounts having been in the greatest confusion; extracts from witness' reports in full explanation of these irregularities, *Finlay* 4383–4388. 4392——Unaccountable delay in completing the proceedings taken against the collector, *ib.* 4384–4387. 4391——Adoption of witness' suggestions by the Dalkey Commissioners, everything now going on in a satisfactory manner, *ib.* 4388.

Dangerous Structures. See *Dilapidated and Dangerous Structures.*

Debenture Stock. Advocacy of similar facilities in the corporation of Dublin for raising loans by the issue of debenture stock, as in the case of the Metropolitan Board of Works, *Hancock* 59. 64–66. 82.

Debt (Corporation of Dublin). Total of 292,723 *l.* as the debt of the corporation in 1850, *Robinson* 2623–2626——Information relative to the debenture debt; reduction effected at the rate of 500 *l.* a year, *ib.* 2627–2636——Total of 834,329 *l.* as the debt of the corporation at the present time, *ib.* 2709——Sale of two houses in College Green for 13,000 *l.*, which has been applied in the extinction of debentures, *ib.* 2715–2710.

Comment upon the course pursued by the old corporation in largely borrowing on debenture instead of in raising taxes for current expenditure, *Sullivan* 4658. 4709——Debt of about 230,000 *l.* left by the old corporation, who appear to have never levied a tax while they could borrow, *ib.* 4707–4709——Numerous improvements which devolved upon the new corporation, besides which they had to pay interest on the debt, *ib.* 4707, 4708.

Debt (Corporation of Dublin)—continued.

Further statement in connection with the large debt and the bad credit inherited by the new from the old corporation; effect as regards the price at which money was raised on debentures, *Sullivan* 4787–4792.

Suggestion by the Committee of the Whole House relative to a consolidation of the various loans of the corporation, *Norwood* 5969.

See also Corporation of Dublin, 10. *Water Supply,* 1.

Deputations (Corporation of Dublin). Explanation that when members of the corporation go on deputations to London, their expenses are paid by themselves, *Gray* 6316.

Dilapidated and Dangerous Structures. Large number of empty houses and of houses out of repair in Ireland owing to their being no provision by law as to repairs where there is a bad title; remedy of this evil by extending to Ireland a Scotch Act of the year 1863, still in effective operation, *Hancock* 787–795——Provisions of the foregoing Act as to the repair of ruinous houses by the local authorities, *ib.* 788——Steps taken by Belfast in favour of the adoption of the Scotch Act, *ib.* 788, 789.

Statement of witness' powers from the corporation of Dublin for preventing accidents from dilapidated houses; particulars as to the action taken in these cases, *Neville* 5426. 5434——Explanations relative to the fall of two houses in George-street near Messrs. Pim's, and of a house in Sackville-street; belief that these were not reported to witness before they fell, *ib.* 5427–5431. 5597–5600.

Numerous cases of ruinous or unhealthy houses reported by the police and by the sanitary serjeants of the force; inadequacy of the inspection now applied as regards dangerous structures, *Neville* 5770–5781——Recent fall of some houses, a new Building Act being greatly required, so that there may be a proper check upon the plans and mode of construction, *ib.* 5777–5781.

Proposal by No. 1 Committee of the corporation of Dublin for extending to Ireland the Scotch law as to ruined houses; good grounds for such extension, *Norwood* 5936–5942.

Disinfection. Defective arrangements in Dublin for preventing the spread of contagion, and for conveying clothing to and from the disinfecting place, *Grimshaw* 3964. 3969, 3970——Useless process adopted in the disinfection of houses, *ib.* 3984, 3985.

Effectual precautions taken under witness in disinfecting houses where epidemics have broken out; also in disinfecting clothes and bedding, *Boyle* 4919, 4920. 4922–4949——Exceptions further taken to the evidence of Dr. Grimshaw as to the disinfection of houses being imperfect, *ib.* 5253–5257.

Division of Rates. See *Owners,* 1.

Docks. Claim to rate the port and docks of Dublin; liability of the Mersey docks, *Greene* 6796–6799——Explanation of the principle in the valuation of dock property, as in Belfast and Dublin; deductions allowed for renewals and repairs, *ib.* 6900–6903. 6909–6915.

Domestic Scavenging (Dublin). See *Sanitary Administration.*

Drunkenness. Amendment suggested as to the power of the police to prosecute for drunkenness in towns under the Act of 1854; alteration required as to the disposal of the fines in such cases, *Curran* 2225–2229.

Dublin. See *the Headings generally throughout the Index.*

Dwellings of the Lower Classes (Dublin). See *Artizans' Dwellings Act.* *Building Act.* *Sanitary Administration,* 1. *Slaughter-houses.*

E.

Election of Town Councillors. Opinion favourable to three years' election, save in the case of *ex-officio* men, who should sit permanently, *Hancock* 190–194.

See also Corporation of Dublin. *Franchise.* *Wards.*

Engineer and Surveyor (City of Dublin). Salary of 750 *l.* a year now received by witness; much larger salaries of similar officers in other constituencies, *Neville* 5516–5520——Information as to the staff of witness' office, and as to the salaries, *ib.* 5799–5801——Increase of witness' salary from time to time as new duties have been entrusted to him, *ib.* 5802–5807——Arrangement as to witness' whole time being given to the corporation, whilst he receives no commission on any works in addition to his salary, *ib.* 5804–5812.

Enniscorthy. Very small expenditure of the town commissioners of Enniscorthy; prompt correction of an irregularity pointed out by witness, *Finlay* 4595–4597.

Report, 1876—*continued.*

Epidemics (Dublin). See *Disinfection. Sanitary Administration.*

Ex-Officio Members (Town Councils). Suggestions for the election of some owners as *ex-officio* members of local boards; these should be magistrates, *Hancock* 159 *et seq.*——Statement to its being proposed by witness to empower *ex-officio* members to nominate substitutes on certain conditions, *ib.* 162. 178–183——Advantage of the *ex-officio* element to a certain extent, *ib.* 162. 189.

Exemption from Rates. In Rathmines township (Dublin) unoccupied houses are not exempt; injustice of any such exemption, *Stokes* 2910.

Action taken some years since in order to abolish all exemptions from taxation; approval, however, of hospitals, churches, &c., being still exempt, *Greene* 6793. 6893, 6894. 7014–7019. 7022–7024——Total of 501,000 *l.* in annual value represented by the exemptions in Ireland; recent rating of Government property comprising 104,000 *l.* of this amount, *ib.* 6794, 6795.

F.

Fairs and Markets. Very limited extent to which town authorities have control over fairs and markets; very unsatisfactory position of this matter at the present time, *Hancock* 56–59.——*See also Cattle Market, Dublin.*

Female Franchise. Expediency of a female franchise for municipal purposes, ladies largely contributing to the rates, *M'Evoy* 1681; *Norwood* 5901. 6186.

Finlay, George William. (Analysis of his Evidence.)—Extent of witness' district as an auditor of the Local Government Board; this includes the city of Dublin, the accounts of which he has audited since 1871; 4260–4266——Explanation of the system adopted by witness in his examination of receipts and payments respectively, his function being to see that there is no omission of receipts, and to disallow all payments that are not legal, 4267.

Discovery by witness in his audit of the city of Dublin accounts for 1872, that certain market tolls had not been duly accounted for by the superintendent of the market; regulation adopted, at witness' suggestion, for preventing similar defalcations in future, 4268–4272——Failure of duty in the foregoing matter on the part of Mr. Robinson, secretary to No. 2 Committee of the corporation, 4271. 4273.

Statement as to the present town clerk (Mr. Henry) having never accounted to the corporation for certain fees received by him; witness has constantly called attention to this omission, but the corporation are satisfied with the reasons given by Mr. Henry for retaining the fees, 4274–4281.

Very fair collection of the corporation rents, save in the case of Baldoyle; diminishing amount of the arrears generally, 4282–4286. 4427, 4428——Very poor character of the Baldoyle property; great difficulty in collecting the rents, 4282, 4283. 4289. 4432–4435——Suggestion made by witness that the Baldoyle irrecoverable arrears should be ascertained and written off, 4288——Circumstance of its having been proposed to sell the Baldoyle property, 4290–4293.

Grounds for a suggestion made by witness that there should be more publicity in the sale of old stores, 4294——Statement as to the corporation omitting to apply to the gas company for a sum of 500 *l.*, which the latter are prepared to hand over in payment of some costs previously incurred by the corporation in promoting Gas Bills, 4294–4296. 4579, 4580——Comment upon the increase of the Lord Mayor's salary in consideration of his paying the salary of his secretary, and of the latter handing over his fees to the corporation; small amount handed over as compared with the extra payment to the Lord Mayor, 4297, 4298. 4436–4439.

Grounds for the conclusion that misapplication is involved in the practice of drawing indiscriminately upon the different funds lodged in the Bank of Ireland; repeated suggestions made by witness in his reports for keeping the several funds and the accounts thereof entirely separated, 4299–4309. 4440–4446——Omission on the part of the corporation in not obtaining a bond or security from their former market superintendent; defalcation and loss in this case, 4310–4312——Belief that there is now no neglect in taking proper security for their officers, 4313, 4314. 4431.

Necessity of some further check upon the returns sent in to the corporation by the different accounting officers; suggestions to this effect, 4315–4318——Proposal that all the accounts of the several committees of the corporation be transferred to the city accountant, who should conduct a strict examination into all receipts and payments, 4316. 4317——Great improvement effected in the accounts of No. 1 Committee, 4317——Due payment to the bank of the amount of rates collected, 4318–4320.

Details in connection with witness' audit of the accounts of the Town Commissioners of

Finlay, George William. (Analysis of his Evidence)—*continued.*

of Wicklow, under the Act 9 Geo. 4; objections raised by him on various points, 4321–4332——Improvement made in the mode of accounting for the rents in Wicklow, and in the accounts generally, witness being satisfied with the present system, 4323. 4327. 4328. 4337. 4338——Good rental of the Commissioners, who make no rates; heavy charge on the other hand for interest on debt, 4324–4326——Comments upon the action of the Commissioners in dealing with the corporate property, on expiration of the leases; obstacle to any satisfactory remedy in the ratepayers, 4328–4336. 4449. 4486, 4487.

Grounds for the complaints made by witness in his report in 1873, upon the manner in which the Town Commissioners of Trim deal with their landed property; belief that no action has been taken upon this report, 4339–4348——Particulars as to several disallowances by witness in his audit of the Trim accounts, and as to the litigation and costs incurred in connection therewith, 4349–4357.

Several instances, as at Athy, of old corporations having had property of which there is now no trace; comment upon the transfer of this property, as at Naas, 4358–4368. 4467–4469——Approval of the limit of the rates by the Act of 1854; several towns below the limit, though the majority may be up to it, 4369–4371. 4661–4666——Information relative to certain disallowances by witness in his last audit of the Bagnalstown accounts, 4372——Particulars as to some disallowances at different audits in the case of Blackrock, and as to the result of appeals from witness' decisions, *ib.*

Satisfaction expressed with the present accounts of towns in witness' district under the Act of 1854; readiness shown by the local authorities to adopt the improvements suggested by witness, 4373. 4496. 4574——Explanation in connection with disallowances by witness in 1873 to the amount of 337 *l.* in the case of Bray, 4374–4379——Grounds for witness' dissatisfaction with the collection of the rates in Bray, 4374. 4379. 4383——Audit by witness of the collection of rates, save in Dublin; he is satisfied with the collection generally, 4380–4382.

Details relative to the great irregularity and abuse which formerly prevailed in the collection of rates in Dalkey, the collector having committed frauds, and the accounts having been in the greatest confusion; extracts from witness' reports in full explanation of these irregularities, 4383–4388. 4392——Unaccountable delay in completing the proceedings taken against the collector, 4384–4387. 4392——Adoption of witness' suggestions by the Dalkey Commissioners, everything now going on in a satisfactory manner, 4388.

Exemption of Rathmines from witness' audit, as being under a special Act, 4389, 4390. 4454–4456——Explanations relative to several disallowances by witness in the case of Kingstown, 4393, 4394. 4402——Exceptions taken to a double payment by the Kingstown Commissioners to their former secretary, 4394——Comments made by witness in his report upon the conduct of one of the Commissioners in reference to an arrear of rates upon a house purchased by him; complaint made by the Commissioners to the Local Government Board relative to this report, the board however not objecting to it, 4394–4401.

Confirmation, on appeal, of witness' disallowance of the expense incurred for advertisements and costs in connection with an abortive Bill which the Town Commissioners of Kingstown had promoted, 4402. 4476, 4477. 4573——Statement as to a large sum (amounting to many thousands) being due by the Corporation of Dublin for notices of Bills and for costs of counsel, agents, and others in connection with Gas and other Bills; non-payment of these expenses through fear of disallowance by the auditor, 4404–4412.

Evidence as to the grounds upon which witness recommended that the Corporation of Dublin should claim the refund of certain fees received by Mr. Henry, as town clerk, and by Mr. Hayes, as city marshal; result of the legal proceedings in each case, 4413–4418.

Difficulty of legislation which led to the exemption of certain places in Ireland from the audit of the Local Government Board, 4419——Witness sees no good ground for the exemption of any place, 4420——Varying charges of the auditor; discrepancy on this subject, it being desirable that the Treasury should bear all the cost, 4421–4426. 4475.

Check suggested by witness for testing the accuracy of the outstanding arrears of rent due to the Dublin Corporation, 4428——Satisfactory precautions as to the security given by the treasurer in Dublin, 4429, 4430——Ready facilities afforded to the auditor on all occasions by the corporation, 4447, 4448——Belief that there is no personal liability in the members of the town council for costs in respect of abortive Bills, 4450, 4451. 4572. 4579–4582.

Conclusion that Rathmines township should be brought under Government audit, and that the ground of objection raised by Mr. Stokes is rather a reason for a public audit, 4457–4460. 4654–4656——Expediency of the costs on appeal from the auditor falling on the corporate authority, and not on the Local Government Board, 4470–4474——Importance of separate accounts of the corporation funds in the Bank of Ireland, though witness does not ask for power in the auditor to compel their being kept, 4480–4485. 4488–

Finlay, George William. (Analysis of his Evidence)—*continued.*

4488——Voluntary adoption of the audit provisions by Kingstown, Blackrock, and Dalkey; irregularities reported by witness in each of these townships, 4489-4494.

Examination, as regards the office of city treasurer in Dublin, to the effect that it is hardly feasible to dispense with this officer by the appointment of a banker as treasurer, as in smaller corporations, 4497-4511. 4575-4577——Concurrence in a suggestion that towns under the Act of 1854 be regarded as under a special Act, in order that they may have facilities in obtaining Provisional Orders, 4512-4518——Doubt as to the expediency of further powers in witness in cases where the collection of rates is excessively in arrear; sufficiency of representations to the Town Commissioners, 4519-4523.

Very few appeals from witness' disallowances to the Court of Queen's Bench, 4524, 4525——Frequent appeals from witness' decisions to the Local Government Board, these not necessarily involving any expense, 4526-4531——Question considered as to the expediency of facilities for obtaining the opinion of a court of law before any doubtful expenditure is incurred, 4532-4536——Instance of unauthorised expenditure incurred in the printing of summonses to the jurors in Dublin, 4535-4537.

Statement to the effect that the auditor has already sufficient means of ascertaining what items should be received by any corporate authority, 4538-4552——Course adopted by the auditor when illegal payments ordered to be reinstated are not reinstated by the next audit, 4553-4555——Provision in the Act of 1871 as to the accounts of each town being audited "once a year," 4556, 4557.

Absence of power to punish for misapplication of funds, save by legal proceedings on the part of burgesses or ratepayers, 4558-4566——Invariable practice of witness to require vouchers for all payments, 4567-4569——Banking arrangement by which the illegality of drawing upon one fund for the purposes of another might be obviated, 4570, 4571——Advantage if the accounts of the collector of rates in Dublin were subject to the same audit as the corporation accounts, 4578.

Explanation that witness' inquiry does not extend to the question of insufficient payment of rent as compared with the valuation, 4583-4590——Objection made by witness, but without effect, to payments in Dublin in advance of officers' salaries, 4591-4594——Very small expenditure of the Town Commissioners of Enniscorthy; prompt correction of an irregularity pointed out by witness, 4595-4597.

Debt in the case of Wexford; satisfactory management of the corporate property, 4598-4601——Complaint recently made to witness as to an alleged illegal expenditure in Wexford, 4602——Important effect of the rents in Wexford in lightening the rates, 4603-4606——Very unsatisfactory collection of rates in Carlow by the late collector; improved arrangements now in force, 4607-4611——Question further considered as to the disappearance of a small property belonging to the old corporation of Athy, 4612-4615——Doubt as to the expenditure of Athy being excessive as compared with that of Carlow and other towns, 4616-4620.

Very unsatisfactory state of things in Wicklow, the town improvements not being commensurate with the expenditure, 4621-4625——Inability of the Wicklow Harbour Commissioners to contribute anything towards the interest or principal of the loan from the Town Commissioners, 4626-4629——Careful administration in Tullamore, 4630, 4631——Satisfactory management also in Naas, Gorey, and Mountmellick, 4632-4633——Irregularities of expenditure and account in the case of Maryborough, 4634-4637——Data upon which witness concluded that the receipts from the corporation lands at Trim were insufficient, 4638-4641.

Extent to which witness' reports to the Local Government Board are made public in the localities; expediency of the reports being accessible to the ratepayers, 4644-4649——Explanation that the Collector General's accounts in Dublin have always been audited by the Receiver Master of the Court of Chancery, 4650——Very public character of witness' audits in the city of Dublin, 4651-4653.

Fire Brigade (Dublin). Efficiency of the management of the fire brigade, *Pim* 2393-2395——Testimony to the efficiency of Captain Ingram, chief of the brigade, *Sullivan* 4760——Support of the fire brigade by a charge of 1½*d.* in the pound deducted from the water rate, *Neville* 5545, 5546; *Gray* 6549.

Efficiency of the fire brigade so far as it goes, though some more stations are wanted, and the staff should be doubled, *Gray* 6470, 6471. 6500-6503——Want also of telegraphic communication between the various stations and the central points in the city, *ib.* 6501——About equal charge for the fire brigade and for sanitary administration, *ib.* 6550.

Floating Hospital (Dublin). Contribution of 1,100 *l.* in 1874 towards a floating hospital, *Boyle* 5239——Explanation on the subject of the provision of the floating hospital, and of the expense involved as compared with the benefits to be derived; hitherto it has had but one patient, *ib.* 5318-5323. 5347-5358.

Forage (Dublin). Charge of 4,051 *l.* incurred by the Corporation of Dublin in one year for forage, there being eighty horses, *Robinson* 2725. 2765–2768——Apparently excessive cost of forage for the horses of the corporation, *Stokes* 3278–3290.

Information relative to the cost of forage, &c., for the corporation horses; total cost of about 7 *s.* 6 *d.* a day for each horse and driver, *Neville* 5499–5514——Details submitted in support of the conclusion that the cost of forage is very low, the total cost per horse, including straw for bedding, averaging 19 *s.* 3½ *d.* per week, *Gray* 6456–6469——Considerations as to the comparative price of horse-keep in London and in Dublin, with reference to the cost of forage for the corporation horses; circumstance of the latter working seven days in the week, *ib.* 6628–6637.

FRANCHISE:

1. *Qualification for the Municipal Franchise in Dublin, as regards Payment of Rates.*
2. *Qualification as regards continuous Residence; Suggestions on this Subject.*
3. *Qualification as to Residence within Seven Miles of Dublin; Extension suggested.*
4. *Extent of the Burgess Roll.*
5. *System of Claims and Objections; numerous Claims and Objections by Political Agents.*
6. *Suggested Service of Objections by Post.*
7. *Evidence favourable to a Property Qualification, and to the Admission of Owners to the Franchise.*
8. *Evidence adverse to the foregoing Conclusions.*
9. *Suggested Exclusion of Occupiers of Houses under 4 l. Rateable Value.*
10. *Proposed Enfranchisement of Female Occupiers.*
11. *Question of a Non-Residential Occupancy Franchise.*
12. *Facility suggested in connection with the period of Payment of Taxes.*
13. *Suggested Enfranchisement of Occupiers of Offices.*
14. *Amendment proposed as regards Claims by Descent or Marriage.*
15. *Question of a Reduction of the Municipal Franchise.*
16. *Other Details and Suggestions on various Points.*

1. *Qualification for the Municipal Franchise in Dublin, as regards Payment of Rates:*

Particulars relative to the qualification of electors in Dublin, under the Dublin Municipal Amendment Act of 1849, payment of five rates being necessary; statement hereon as to the landlord paying all the local rates and taxes up to 8 *l.*, *Hancock* 129–151. 632, 633.

Further information relative to the qualification of a burgess in Dublin, and the restriction as to rating; respects in which there is a different provision for the municipal rates and for the Parliamentary rates, *Hancock* 201–229.

Necessity of those who are on the rate-book paying the rates before they can claim the franchise, *Taafe* 470–472——Explanation that all yearly tenants, not under 4 *l.*, are rated preliminary to payment, and that the rate-book takes no notice of those under 4 *l.*, *ib.* 470, 471. 531–541. 557. 562–565.

Important change in the qualifications for the franchise, under the Act of 1849, *Henry* 1092–1098——Explanation as to the several rates which must be paid as a qualification for the franchise; collection of these rates and the poor rate at the same time, *ib.* 1257–1261. 1290–1295. 1371–1373.

Instances of disqualification, owing to there being no notice of the necessity of payment, as in the case of the Parliamentary franchise, *Henry* 1262–1267. 1290–1297——Disqualification through the payment of rates by the landlord without the occupier's name going on the rate-book, *ib.* 1268–1272——Frequent complaint made as to the landlords not paying the tenants' taxes by the proper time, *ib.* 1273. 1353.

Particulars as to the course pursued by witness, as town clerk, in forming the municipal register or burgess list; every name in the Collector General's books, whatever the rating, appears on the list, *Henry* 1283–1289. 1348, 1349——Witness has had no complaints from occupiers that their names have not been in the rate-book; he cannot say whether they are omitted or not, *ib.* 1613–1615. 1648–1652.

Conclusion arrived at by witness, and acted upon in 1874, that under the Representation of the People Act of 1868 all persons liable to be rated between 4 *l.* and 8 *l.* were qualified for the burgess roll, *Curran* 2127–2130. 2202–2206——Difference of opinion between witness and Mr. Hyndham (his co-assessor) on the foregoing point; decision of the Lord Mayor in favour of witness' view, *ib.* 2131–2133——Frequent disfranchisement of occupiers in consequence of the non-payment of taxes by the landlord, *ib.* 2989.

Exclusion from the burgess roll of all those rated at less than 4 *l.*, *Gray* 6509. 6513.

2. *Qualification*

FRANCHISE—continued.

2. *Qualification as regards continuous Residence; Suggestions on this Subject:*

Important limitation to the municipal franchise by the necessity of a continued occupation of two years and eight months, *Henry* 1247–1256. 1299. 1350–1352. 1363–1365. 1811——Suggestion as regards continued occupation, that a break of residence for a month or so might be allowed without causing disqualification, *ib.* 1298–1302——Probability of the roll being nearly doubled if the occupation were reduced to one year, *ib.* 1352. 1504——Suggestion that the residential period be reduced to twelve months, *M'Evoy* 1735.

Comment upon the obligation as to a continuous residence of two years and eight months as a condition of admission to the burgess roll; exceptional position of Dublin in this respect, *Curran* 2146–2151——Hardship to persons frequently losing the franchise for a short break of residence over a period of two years and eight months; liberal interpretation of the law by witness on this point, *ib.* 2148–2162. 2174–2176. 2210–2213. 2230, 2231. 2259–2267.

Reduction suggested in the term of residence as to qualification for the franchise in Dublin, *Pim* 2343——Effect of the residential term of three years in striking many names off the burgess list, *Gray* 6509.

Satisfaction expressed with the residential term of three years, *Norwood* 5916——Doubt as to the expediency of reducing the residential term of three years, unless the rating be raised, *ib.* 6186–6189. 6219.

3. *Qualification as to Residence within Seven Miles of Dublin; Extension suggested:*

Approval of an extension of the seven-mile limit; small increase of burgesses by extending the limit to twelve miles, *Henry* 1366–1370. 1505——Advantage of extending the residential limit for the municipal franchise to fifteen miles round Dublin, *M'Evoy* 1821——Exclusive effect of the provision as to residence within seven miles of Dublin; suggested extension to twelve miles, so that Bray and other places may be included, *Curran* 2284–2287.

Decided objection to the restriction as to residence within seven miles of Dublin; large extension required, *Pim* 2344——If there be any limit, it should not be less than twenty miles, *ib.*——Disapproval of the seven-mile residential limit; sufficiency of a twenty-mile limit, *Norwood* 5902–5904——Opinion favourable to an entire removal of the residential limit as regards Dublin, and other towns, *ib.* 6198–6202. 6286.

4. *Extent of the Burgess Roll:*

Small increase of the burgess roll since 1843, *Henry* 1274——In 1843 there were 4,445 burgesses, the present number being 5,339, *ib.* 1274, 1275——Conclusion as to the unduly small number on the burgess roll in proportion to the population, *ib.* 1500–1503.

Opinion that if the law were properly amended, and if wholesale objections were stopped, there would be nearly 15,000, instead of about 5,000, names on the burgess roll for Dublin, *Curran* 2177–2182. 2253–2258.

Abstention of the mercantile classes from interference in municipal affairs under the present system of election; circumstances of many of the large ratepayers not being on the burgess roll, *Pim* 2377–2382——Large number of those on the burgess roll who do not vote at elections, *ib.* 2429, 2430.

Total of 7,854 names on the burgess list; deductions to which subject before the franchise is conferred, *Henry* 1467, 1468.

Return showing the number of names on the burgess list for the last revision (1875), the number of objections served, and the result in the formation of the burgess roll for the year 1875–76, *App.* 410.

5. *System of Claims and Objections; numerous Claims and Objections by Political Agents:*

Statement as to the political or registration agents serving numerous claims to be rated, and tendering at the same time a portion of the poor-rate, though the money is never paid; belief that these claims are admitted by the revising barrister, *Taaffe* 325–331. 372–377. 462–466——Practice as to appearance in support of their claims in the case of persons objected to as regards the Parliamentary and municipal franchise respectively, *ib.* 402–405——Numerous claims by registration agents, some being served in duplicate, each claim being investigated by the collector, *ib.* 474–482. 551–554.

Requirement as to claims and objections being lodged on the 1st October, and published between the 1st and 11th October, *Henry* 1085——Question considered whether there

FRANCHISE—continued.

5. *System of Claims and Objections, &c.*—continued.

there is not every facility to claims under the present system, *Henry* 1374–1378. 1389–1392.

Large number of burgesses, properly qualified, who are annually struck off the list through the wholesale service of objections, *Curran* 2111–2117. 2179–2182. 2253–2258 ——Service of 1,979 objections last year, about 1,000 names having been struck off through no appearance having been put in, *ib.* 2114, 2115——Assistance rendered by both political parties in striking off names, but not in putting them on, *ib.* 2200, 2201 ——Undue restriction of the burgess roll on account of the obstructions by political agents, *Sullivan* 4835.

6. *Suggested Service of Objections by Post:*

Grounds for the suggestion that the mode of service of objections be by post at the residence, *Curran* 2289.

7. *Evidence favourable to a Property Qualification, and to the Admission of Owners to the Franchise:*

Concurrence of evidence favourable to the admission of owners to the municipal franchise, *Hancock* 153. 160–162. 184–188. 938–945; *Pim* 2315 *et seq.*; *Grimshaw* 4246–4248——Expediency of a real representation of property rather than a limit of rating, *Hancock* 912–914. 938–951.

Numerous large buildings and institutions in Dublin which are heavily rated, but are unrepresented in the expenditure of the money, *M'Evoy* 1661——Several charges which are or may be put upon the property in Dublin, it being only fair that there should be a property franchise, *ib.* 1677——Conclusion that, instead of the immediate lessor, every person possessing a beneficial interest of 50 *l.* and upwards in house property should have a vote, *ib.*

Conclusion as to the expediency of a better representation of property in the city elections; advantage of plural voting, and of a property qualification, *Stokes* 2943–2947. 3149–3153. 3179——Suggestion that there be a property qualification of 200 *l.* a year, *ib.* 2943. 3149–3153.

Several respects in which the franchise might be developed by way of concession by the popular party, *Sullivan* 4682——Suggestion that property owners, non-resident in the city, be allowed to vote, there being a qualification of 50 *l.* a year, *ib.* 4682. 4776. 4815–4821.

Importance attached to the municipal enfranchisement of owners of property, as under the Poor Law Act; representations in detail in support of this change, *Norwood* 5895–5898. 5915. 5981. 6190–6194. 6279. 6286.

8. *Evidence adverse to the foregoing Conclusions:*

Argument in detail in opposition to the proposed enfranchisement of owners, *Grey* 6405–6407. 6511–6513. 6616–6627. 6689–6693——Further and strong objection to any concessions by the popular party in order to promote the election of property representations, *ib.* 6490, 6491——Argument that in practice the rich ratepayers are not swamped in the representation by the poor and more numerous ratepayers, and that it is altogether impolitic to give a plurality of votes in proportion to the amount of taxation, *ib.* 6510–6518.

Explanation that Dr. Norwood's evidence on the franchise question does not represent the views of the council, a large majority being opposed to the alterations advocated by him, *Grey* 6584–6591——Way in which a property qualification and multiple voting would be an additional restriction upon the present restricted constituency, *ib.* 6650–6653.

9. *Suggested Exclusion of Occupiers of Houses under 4 l. Rateable Value:*

Grounds for the conclusion that all occupiers should have a vote, save the occupiers of small houses unfit for habitation, or of houses under 4 *l.* rateable value, *M'Evoy* 1662–1674. 1762–1790——Prospect of all houses in Ireland being raised to the 4 *l.* limit under a reformed local administration, *ib.* 1674. 1770.

Consideration of objections to the proposal that occupiers of houses in large towns generally under 4 *l.* rateable value should not exercise the franchise in municipal or sanitary matters, *M'Evoy* 1771–1789.

Examination in further support of excluding from the franchise occupiers of small houses under 4 *l.* value in large towns generally, but not in small towns, *M'Evoy* 2031–2047.

10. *Proposed*

FRANCHISE—continued.

10. *Proposed Enfranchisement of Female Occupiers:*

Large amount of valuable property in the occupation of females, it being expedient that these should possess the municipal franchise as in England, *M'Evoy* 1681; *Norwood* 5901. 6286.

11. *Question of a Non-Residential Occupancy Franchise:*

Evidence in favour of a non-residential occupancy franchise, the qualification to be fixed at a much higher amount than that for residential occupiers, *M'Evoy* 1677. 1814–1820. 1822.

12. *Facility suggested in connection with the period of Payment of Taxes.*

Increased admission to the roll if the period for payment of taxes were extended close up to the day of voting, *Henry* 1506–1508——Amendments proposed in connection with the payment of taxes in order to facilitate the enfranchisement of claimants; facility at the same time to the collection of taxes, *Curran* 2289–2293——Sufficiency of the payment of taxes at the time of voting in some of the townships around Dublin, *ib.* 2293, 2294.

13. *Suggested Enfranchisement of Occupiers of Offices:*

Numerous instances in Dublin of persons occupying separate offices who are not separately rated, amendment being much required by the enfranchisement of these persons, *M'Evoy* 1686–1692. 1791–1802. 1989, 1990.

14. *Amendment proposed as regards Claims by Descent or Marriage:*

Ambiguity of the present law in Ireland as to the qualification of persons who claim by descent or marriage; suggestion as to the amendment desirable, *Curran* 2288, 2289.

15. *Question of a Reduction of the Municipal Franchise:*

Conclusion that the present limit of the occupiers' franchise should be greatly lowered in order that all classes may have a voice in the representation, *Hancock* 163–165. 188.

Decided objection to the proposal for assimilating the Irish franchise to the English franchise; this change would only intensify existing evils, *Pim* 2304–2307——Calculations to the effect that a mere reduction of the franchise to the English level without any compensating arrangements would place the control of the representation and of the taxation in the hands of those least capable of exercising such control, *ib.* 2305–2307. 2315——Doubt as to the expediency of admitting tenement lodgers to the municipal franchise, *ib.* 2338–2340.

Expediency of the basis of the franchise being widened concurrently with some concession to property owners; this latter concession should apply to other places as well as Dublin if the circumstances are the same, *Sullivan* 4682. 4815–4821. 4836–4842. 4864–4870.

Approval of a higher qualification than a 4 *l.* rating for the municipal franchise, *Norwood* 5915. 5920. 6185. 6189.

Popular feeling in Dublin in favour of an assimilation of the franchise to that in England, *Gray* 6349——Expected improvement in the *personnel* of the corporation if the basis of the franchise were widened as in England, *ib.* 6507, 6508. 6527. 6640–6650——Opinion of the majority of the corporation that the franchise should be assimilated to the English franchise; this would doubtless be to lower it, *ib.* 6638–6643.

16. *Other Details and Suggestions on various Points:*

Statement of the qualifications of electors under the Acts of 1898 and 1854, and under the Act of 1840; amendment in 1871 whereby the payment of the town rate is sufficient, *Hancock* 127, 128—— Explanation as regards the franchise established by the Municipal Corporations Act that the 10 *l.* valuation is considered equivalent to about 8 *l.* 10 *s.* poor-law rating, *ib.* 629–631——Four distinct franchises in corporate towns in Ireland under the Act of 1854, there being also special modifications under other Acts, *ib.* 771–775.

Several amendments suggested in the qualification of municipal electors, witness not proposing to make the rating to the poor law a qualification, *Hancock* 921–924. 927——Suggestion that the receipt of relief within seven years be a disqualification, *ib.* 922–924——Suggested disqualification for conviction of felony or repeated conviction for minor offences, *ib.*

Necessity of some change in the municipal franchise of Dublin, whereby the representation will be adjusted with more fairness in proportion to the incidence of taxation, *Pim* 2302

Report, 1876—*continued.*

FRANCHISE—continued.

16. *Other Details and Suggestions on various Points*—continued.

2302 *et seq.*——Importance in the first instance of a satisfactory electoral body rather than of a high rating qualification in the elected, *Pim* 2406.

Summary of the measures desirable for the improvement of the burgess roll in Dublin; that is, in the direction of a better representation of large ratepayers and of owners, *Norwood* 5895 *et seq.*; 6286——Approval generally of the present occupation franchise, *ib.* 5915. 5920——Expediency of the same franchise throughout the whole district, if the townships be added to the city, *ib.* 5917–5920.

See also Belfast. Corporation of Dublin. Cumulative Voting. Household Suffrage. Owners. Plural Voting. Revision of Burgess Roll. Valuation, L, 3. *Wards. Weekly and Monthly Tenants.*

Freemen. Impression as to the freemen in Dublin taking some part in the municipal government, *Hancock* 660–662. 737——Certain number of honorary freemen in Dublin before the Act of 1840; there are not any now, *ib.* 752–755.

French, Mr. Constant obstructiveness of Mr. French as member of the Dublin Town Council, *Gray* 6355, 6356. 6603–6607.

French Relief Fund. Exceptions taken to the contribution of 500 *l.* by the Corporation of Dublin out of the city funds to the French Relief Fund during the war, *M'Evoy* 1696. 1874, 1875. 1991–1997——Comment upon the donation of 500 *l.* from the corporation to the French Relief Fund as an instance of misplaced liberality; neglect at the same time of sanitary arrangements, *Pim* 2434–2445.

Reference to the contribution of 500 *l.* by the corporation to the French Relief Fund as having been voted alike by Conservative and Liberal members, *Gray* 6308–6312.

See also Audit, 3.

Fry, Mr. Refusal of witness in the case of Mr. Fry to strike that gentleman off the burgess list for Dublin, because of a few days' break of residence; judgment of the Court of Queen's Bench in favour of witness' decision, *Curran* 2151–2162. 2212–2216. 2268.

G.

Galway. Special legislation as regards Galway, both in the Act of 1840 and in subsequent local Acts, *Hancock* 598–601——Details relative to the local government and taxation of Galway under different special Acts and Provisional Orders; anomalous position of this town in several respects, *ib.* 801–863.

Circumstance of the qualification of a voter for commissioners being twice as high in Galway as in other towns; assimilation desirable, *Hancock* 808–810. 817–821. 863——Long existence of the toll thorough and other tolls in Galway; these were condemned by Commissions in 1835 and 1853, and should be abolished, *ib.* 811–813. 822. 833–835. 856–862. 873–875——Equal division of rates between owner and occupier in Galway, *ib.* 825.

Gas Bills and Gas Supply (Dublin). Payment of 6,970 *l.* for public lighting including certain salaries, *Robinson* 2790–2793.

Statement as to the corporation omitting to apply to the gas company for a sum of 500 *l.*, which the latter are prepared to hand over in payment of some costs occurred by the corporation in promoting Gas Bills, *Finlay* 4294–4296. 4579, 4580.

Belief that if the corporation had not been obstructed in their attempt to acquire the gas works the ratepayers would have largely benefited, *Sullivan* 4745–4747. 4894–4897.

Calculation that the cost of lighting is now much less per lamp than under the Paving Board, *Neville* 5411–5417——Failure of objections raised by Mr. M'Evoy before the auditor relative to certain expenditure for gas, *ib.* 5568–5574.

Comment upon the opposition to the proposed transfer of the works of the Alliance Gas Company to the corporation, *Norwood* 5979——Information relative to the gas supply, and the reasons for the increase of price; prospect of reduction, the gas company having now surmounted the difficulties under which it formerly laboured, *ib.* 6137–6149. 6256–6264——Belief that a tender has recently been received by the corporation for the supply of 16-candle gas at 4 *s.* 3 *d.* per 1,000 feet, *ib.* 6147–6149.

Statement

Report, 1876—*continued.*

Gas Bills and Gas Supply (Dublin)—continued.

Statement as regards the public gas supply, that the price is moderate as compared with other large towns and that the quality is satisfactory, *Gray* 6337-6346 —— Average consumption of each public lamp at the rate of four cubic feet per hour, *ib.* 6341 —— Explanation in connection with a proposed payment of 500 *l.* for the services of engineers upon a Gas Bill promoted by the corporation in 1873, *ib.* 6347 —— Profitable possession of the gas works by the corporation but for the opposition of some of its constant opponents, *ib.* 6497-6499.

Gorey. Satisfactory local management in Gorey, *Finlay* 4633.

Government Loans. Suggestion in regard to Government lending money to the corporation of Dublin on easy terms for the execution of necessary works, *Sullivan* 4794-4801.

Government Property. Approval of Government property being represented, if it be rated, *Hancock* 935-937. 950, 951 —— Payment of rates by Government, in 1875, in respect of its property in Dublin, *Henry* 1335 —— Suggestion that in Dublin there should be a direct representation of Government property, as contributing very largely to the rates, *M'Evoy* 1661.

Grand Juries. Statement to the effect that in Dublin, and other places which are counties of cities, the fiscal power of the grand juries has been transferred to the corporations, *Hancock* 646-657.

Evidence in support of the opinion that the powers of grand juries, within the urban districts, should, in certain cases, be transferred to the urban authority; contemplated inquiry before the Local Government Board previously to re-adjustment in this respect, *Hancock* 877-890. 962 *et seq.*

Grand Jury Cess (Dublin). There is no limit to the grand jury cess in Dublin, *Moylan* 943 —— Several purposes, as provided by presentment, for which the grand jury rate in Dublin is levied, *Henry* 1141-1145 —— Reference to the grand jury cess as being a yearly presentment for prisons, &c., and for the payment of instalments to Government, *ib.* 1605-1606.

Total of 55,781 *l.* 10 *s.* 4 *d.* as the proceeds of the grand jury cess in the year ending 31st August 1875, *O'Donnell* 3405, 3406 —— Purposes for which the grand jury cess is levied, and authorities by whom expended, *Neville* 5551. 5554-5558 —— Inaccuracy of a statement that the grand jury cess has been levied for sewage works, *Gray* 6336.

Grattan Bridge (Dublin). Difficulty raised by the auditor about an expenditure of 6,700 *l.* out of the main drainage rate in connection with Grattan Bridge, *Henry* 1324-1327. 1511, 1512. 1624-1626.

Objection raised by witness as regards an expenditure of about 7,000 *l.* in connection with Essex Bridge; this question has been decided against the corporation by the auditor, *M'Evoy* 1870-1873.

Legal grounds upon which the auditor surcharged an excess of expenditure of 6,708 *l.* in respect of Grattan Bridge, *Neville* 5496-5498.

Extended area, comprising the several townships, over which the rate for re-building Grattan Bridge was levied; objection raised, without effect, by the Rathmines Commissioners, *Neville* 5530-5534 —— Instance of hardship in the case of the expenditure for Grattan Bridge; surcharge on a mere technical point, *Gray* 6433. 6437.

Gray, Edmund Dwyer. (Analysis of his Evidence.)—Active part taken by witness as a member of the Corporation of Dublin since November last, 6295-6299 —— Explanation of the circumstances under which Mr. Norwood and witness (the one a Conservative, the other a Liberal) have been deputed to represent the corporation and to rebut the evidence given before the Committee, 6300-6307 —— Resolution of the council by which witness was authorised to speak on the question of the franchise, 6305.

Reference to the contribution of 500 *l.* by the corporation to the French Relief Fund as having been voted alike by Conservative and Liberal members, 6308-6312 —— Reluctance of the corporation to promote an increased valuation of Dublin as increasing the liability to the income tax, 6313 —— Absence of power in the town council to demand a re-valuation, *ib.* —— Perfectly open manner in which an item of about 18,000 *l.* was transferred, and properly so, from the waterworks rates account to the capital account; there was no "smuggling" in the matter, 6314, 6315 —— Explanation that when members of the corporation go on deputations to London their expenses are paid by themselves, 6316.

Denial that the corporation appointments are influenced by sectarian feelings; large number of Protestant officers holding high positions, 6317, 6318 —— Return handed in explanatory

Gray, Edmund Dwyer. (Analysis of his Evidence)—*continued.*

explanatory of the increase of salaries, 6319——Increase of the Lord Mayor's salary in order that he might pay his secretary, instead of the latter being paid by fees, 6320–6322——Exceptional instances of political meetings of the council; official return to this effect, 6323, 6324——Statement in justification of the action of the council in petitioning in favour of the Land Tenure (Ireland) Bill, 6325–6331. 6676–6688.

Grounds for objecting to a 50 *l.* qualification for town councillors; disqualification thereby of many very efficient members, 6332–6335——Inaccuracy of a statement that the grand jury cess has been levied for sewage works, 6336——Statement as regards the public gas supply, that the price is moderate as compared with other large towns, and that the quality is satisfactory, 6337–6346——Average consumption of each public lamp at the rate of four cubic feet per hour, 6341——Explanation in connection with a proposed payment of 500 *l.* for the services of engineers upon a Gas Bill promoted by the corporation in 1873; 6347.

Denial that there is any strong and general feeling among the people of Dublin in favour of a reform of the corporation, though a reform is demanded by a small but influential section, 6348——Popular feeling in favour of an assimilation of the franchise to that in England, 6349——Room for much improvement in the *personnel* of the corporation, though this may be equally said of all elected bodies, 6350, 6351——Refusal by Mr. Joseph Pim and Mr. Thomas Pim to enter the corporation, though pressed to do so, 6350——Fair proportion of good men in the council, 6351——Great obstruction to business and great waste of time by the necessity of a quorum of twenty members; expediency of the number being reduced to nine or ten, 6352–6359. 6488, 6489. 6494. 6504–6506——Constant obstructiveness of Mr. French, a member of the town council, 6355, 6356. 6603–6607.

Conclusion that a re-valuation of Dublin is essential in practice, with a view more especially to the correction of inequalities, 6360——Very trifling effect of a re-valuation of Ireland as regards the increased liability for Imperial taxation, 6361–6364——Necessity of an extension of the boundaries of Dublin so as to embrace the adjacent townships, 6365. 6492, 6493——Reason for the non-introduction of water-pipes by the corporation into the townships, 6365——Intense feeling of jealousy on the part of the townships towards the corporation, *ib.*

Several instances of Liberal wards returning Conservative members, politics not being a ground of opposition, 6366, 6367. 6374. 6534——Election of witness in lieu of Mr. Wallis, because the latter did not attend the meetings of the council, and not on political grounds, 6368–6374——Rejection also of Mr. Casson on the ground of non-attendance, irrespectively of politics, 6375.

Great disfavour with which multiple voting, or the representation of minorities, would be regarded in Dublin; strong feeling of dissatisfaction if it be attempted to apply any exceptional legislation, such as the three-cornered system, 6376–6403. 6496——Very unsatisfactory results of the direct representation of property in the board of the South Dublin Union; strictly sectarian character of the appointments by the board, 6377, 6378——Entire absence of sectarian spirit in the appointments by the corporation, 6378.

Advantage of cumulative voting over the whole city for the election of a limited number of members; first-class men likely to be returned, 6383. 6385–6387. 6404——Strong objection to multiple voting in Dublin, as being more or less a stigma, 6387. 6400–6403——Statement as to the Act of 1849 having assimilated the franchise in Dublin to that in England, so that it was not felt as a stigma, 6388–6399——Decided unpopularity in Dublin of a 50 *l.* ownership franchise, 6405–6407.

Great loss in the collection of rates, owing to the action of fraudulent lessors and the system of bills of sale, 6408. 6415——Importance of a power of recovering from the beneficial owner, the rates being a charge on the property itself, 6409–6413——Hardship on those who are surcharged by the auditor being liable for costs in the event of successful appeals from the auditor's decisions; amendment desirable, 6414–6438——Instance of hardship in the case of the Grattan Bridge surcharge, on a mere technical point, 6432. 6437——Extreme fairness of the auditor, the audit being on the whole a great satisfaction to the corporation, 6438.

Steps being taken to put the Artizans Dwellings Act in force; opposition made on account of the expense involved, 6439, 6440——Absence of power to levy a rate for widening the streets, 6441, 6442——Objections to a power in the corporation of taking property compulsorily for street improvements, 6443–6449——Approval of Provisional Orders, if they can be readily obtained, as a means of securing possession of property required for improvements, 6448–6450.

Excellent credit of the corporation, money being borrowed at 4 per cent., 6451, 6452——Very small increase in the cost of materials, owing to cash not being paid, 6453–6455——Details submitted in support of the conclusion that the cost of forage is very low, the total cost per horse, including straw for bedding, averaging 19 *s.* 3½ *d.* per week, 6456–

Gray, Edmund Dwyer. (Analysis of his Evidence)—*continued.*

6456-6469——Efficiency of the fire brigade, so far as it goes, though some more stations are wanted, and the staff should be doubled, 6470, 6471. 6500-6503.

Due attention paid by the corporation to the representations made by the sanitary association, 6472. 6532——Difficulty as regards communication with the association by reason of some of its members being paid officers of the corporation, 6472. 6532. 6542-6548——Explanation of a small item of expenditure, by No. 1 Committee of the corporation, upon the cleansing of the Liffey, 6473——Anxiety of the public health committee to obtain the services of some constables, whose salaries they would willingly pay, 6474, 6475.

Expediency of the corporation being entrusted with authority over the cab and car drivers, 6476, 6477. 6480——Hardship in the corporation not receiving any portion of the fines from cabmen, 6478, 6479——Very prejudicial operation of the quorum regulation in preventing the consideration of improvements, 6480. 6488. 6494-6495. 6504-6506——Want of better control of the medical sanitary officers, their salaries being at the same time raised, 6481-6483.

Concurrence with Mr. Sullivan that impecuniosity is the main cause of the defects in the working of the corporation, 6485, 6486——Approval of a re-valuation, as a means of improving the *personnel* of the corporation, 6487——Admission as to the members being more or less amenable to the opinion of their constituents, 6487, 6488——Further and strong objection to any concessions by the popular party in order to promote the election of property representatives, 6490, 6491.

Necessity for abattoirs and a public market, 6494——Demoralising effect of the slaughter-houses, *ib.*——Effort being made in the corporation to introduce abattoirs, *ib.* ——Competency of the present corporation to carry out the required improvements generally, if relieved from the quorum difficulty, 6494, 6495——Profitable possession of the gas works by the corporation, but for the opposition of some of its constant opponents, 6497-6499.

Reference to the salaries as being too small rather than too large, 6503——Improvement if the officers could be appointed only from year to year, *ib.*——Advantage also if there were power to have six committees with only ten members on each, *ib.*

Further approval of a household franchise in Dublin as in England; improvement of the corporation thereby, 6507, 6508. 6527——Effect of the residential term of three years in striking many names off the burgess list, 6509——Exclusion from the roll of all those rated at less than 4 *l.*, 6509. 6513——Argument that in practice the rich ratepayers are not swamped in the representation by the poor and more numerous ratepayers, and that it is altogether impolitic to give a plurality of votes in proportion to the amount of taxation, 6510-6518——Legitimate influence of owners of property under the present franchise; reference hereon to this influence in Parliamentary representation, 6511-6513. 6689-6693.

Further reference to boards of guardians, elected under the multiple system, as not equal to municipal bodies, 6516, 6517——Respects in which the Port and Docks Board, elected by multiple votes, is much less efficient than the corporation, as regards its care of the public interests; unprotected and dangerous state of the quays adverted to hereon, 6518-6526——Expected improvement in the *personnel* of the corporation if the basis of the franchise were widened, as in England, 6527. 6640-6650.

Political feeling by which the opposition to the corporation and the charges against its members are more or less influenced, 6528-6531——Political character of the opposition to the Vartry Waterworks, 6529——Respects in which the Sanitary Association has a political tinge, 6530. 6535-6541——Explanation as to letters or complaints from the association not being always noticed by the corporation, 6530. 6532. 6542-6548.

Payment of the fire brigade expenses out of the water rate, 6549——About equal charge for the fire brigade and for sanitary administration, 6550——Admission that the sanitary condition of Dublin is very bad; reliable character of some special reports on the subject in the "Freeman's Journal," 6551-6581——Insufficiency of the law, to which, rather than to default of the corporation, the want of improved sanitary arrangements is chiefly attributable, 6559-6564.

Undue disinclination in the corporation to levy additional taxation, 6562-6572——Expediency of power to levy a special sanitary rate; initiative with the public health committee in the matter, 6562. 6564. 6571, 6572——Successful opposition made by Mr. Byrne (the leader of the Conservative party in the corporation) to the expense of applying the Artisans Dwellings Act, 6565-6570.

Grounds for the statement that Mr. Joseph Pim (as well as Mr. Thomas Pim) had been invited to join the corporation but had declined, 6573-6579——Liberality in political matters in Dublin, as shown by the return of Conservatives for Liberal wards, 6579-6583——Explanation that Dr. Norwood's evidence on the franchise question does not represent the views of the council, a large majority being opposed to the alterations advocated by him, 6584-6591.

Gray, Edmund Dwyer. (Analysis of his Evidence)—*continued.*

Further statement explanatory of the extent to which political discussions take place in the corporation, 6592–6598. 6676–6688——Comment upon the course sometimes adopted by the Conservative members in leaving meetings, when they are in a minority, so that business cannot be transacted through want of a quorum; the Liberals never adopt these tactics, 6594–6598——Witness repeats that constant obstructions arise under the quorum difficulty, and that with a smaller quorum the necessary reforms could be carried out by the corporation, 6599–6610. 6720–6722——Repeated obstruction by Councillor French for obstruction's sake, 6603–6607.

Facility expected in carrying a new Improvement Bill, but for the quorum difficulty, 6608——Probability of a re-valuation involving an increased valuation, 6611–6613——Explanation that in approving of the election of a limited number of councillors by cumulative voting over the whole city, witness does not profess to represent the views of the corporation, 6614–6617.

Argument in further opposition to the admission of property owners to the franchise, except they are also occupiers; approval, however, of the owner being enfranchised if he directly pays half the rates, 6616. 6618–6627——Considerations as to the comparative price of horse-keep in London and in Dublin, with reference to the cost of forage for the corporation horses; circumstance of the latter working seven days in the week, 6628–6637.

Opinion of the majority of the corporation that the franchise should be assimilated to the English franchise; this would doubtless be to lower it, 6638–6643——Way in which a property qualification and multiple voting would be an additional restriction upon the present restricted constituency, 6650–6653——Restriction at present by the exclusion not only of the small ratepayers, but of owners of property, 6654–6661.

Examination upon the question whether owners are not under certain circumstances as much interested as occupiers in the incidence and in the expenditure of the rates; doubt, however, as to the expediency of any representation of owners, 6662–6675. 6700–6706. 6715–6719——Further explanation of the circumstances under which Mr. Wallis was rejected by the ratepayers in favour of witness; reference more especially to the attendances of Mr. Wallis, 6694–6699. 6707–6714.

Benefit anticipated from empowering the corporation to elect sheriffs; advantage also if the lord mayor of one year were the sheriff of the next, 6723——Exceptional position of the board of superintendence in Dublin in not having the power of appointing its own officers, 6724——Slight effect as regards the corporation by withdrawing the power of election of boards of superintendence, 6724, 6725.

Heavy taxation of the ratepayers of Dublin, though witness would not hesitate to tax them additionally for useful purposes, 6731–6733——Reasons further assigned for the omission to answer some of the complaints submitted to the public health committee by the sanitary association, 6734–6736——Non-exclusion from the corporation of property owners who reside in Dublin, 6737, 6738.

Great neglect in the administration of the South Dublin Union, as shown by the heavy surcharges, 6739, 6740——Evidence in further support of the conclusion that religion and politics influence the appointments in the union, all the highly salaried officers being Protestants, whilst the subordinate offices are given to Roman Catholics, 6741–6763.

Greene, John Ball. (Analysis of his Evidence).—Is Commissioner of Valuation for Ireland, 6764, 6765——Considers that a new valuation of Ireland is desirable for the purpose of remedying existing inequalities, 6766, 6767. 6813, 6814. 6891——Different dates at which the present valuation was completed in different counties, 6768——Provision in the Valuation Act on the subject of re-valuation of any county, poor law union, or barony; absence of power to demand a new valuation of any borough, such as Dublin or Belfast, 6769–6775——Probable power of the grand jury of the county of the city of Dublin to call for a new valuation of the county of the city, 6776, 6777.

Provision for an annual revision, as in the case of new buildings; satisfaction generally given 6778, 6779——Condition in the annual re-valuation of town land that the total limit cannot be increased, though the amount may be re-distributed, 6780–6783. 6932–6934——Scale of agricultural prices in 1849 and 1850 upon which the present valuation was based; great increase of prices since that period, the value of land having largely increased, 6784–6790. 6860–6869——Much greater inequality of valuation in the case of grass lands than of tillage lands, 6788. 6813, 6814. 6860–6869.

Doubt as to there being legal power to value land reclaimed or improved by drainage, 6791, 6792——Action taken some years since in order to abolish all exemptions from taxation; approval, however, of hospitals, churches, &c., being still exempt, 6793. 6893, 6894. 7014–7019. 7022–7024——Total of 501,000 *l.* in annual value represented by the exemptions; recent rating of Government property, comprising 104,000 *l.* of this amount, 6794, 6795——Claim to rate the port and docks of Dublin; liability of the Mersey Docks, 6796–6799.

Effect

Greene, John Ball. (Analysis of his Evidence)—*continued.*

Effect of the present low valuation in largely increasing the amount in the pound of the county cess and of the poor rate, 6800, 6801——Grounds for the conclusion that the rent should be the basis of a new valuation, as in England, 6802–6807. 6892——Necessity of a codification of the several Valuation Acts and Amendment Acts, 6808–6810——Effect of a new valuation of Dublin to increase the amount from 620,534 *l.* to 781,000 *l.*, and to decrease the poundage rate from about 8 *s.* 4 *d.* to about 6 *s.* 4 *d.*, 6811, 6812.

Consideration of the several Acts or Amendment Acts under which the valuation of Ireland has been carried out, the system of valuation according to the net value having become a dead letter, and the sole basis being now that of agricultural prices, 6815–6848——Provision as to the valuation of houses being made upon an estimate of the rent one year with another, 6844, 6845——Great increase in the rent of houses in Dublin since the valuation was made, 6849——Liability of witness' department to be called upon to value at once improvements to houses, 6850–6852——Explanation as to improvements or new houses not being valued up to the full extent, 6853–6859.

Reference to the increased price of labour in modifying the effect of the increased price of wheat, barley, &c., as regards the value of tillage lands; this does not equally apply to the case of pasture lands, 6870–6881——Statement as to there being no re-valuation annually, but a revision and correction of the old valuation; that is, unless in the case of a new house or the improvement of a house, 6882–6885——Payment of portion of the cost of valuation out of the county rate; very small amount of this payment in reference to the rateable value of the country, 6886–6890.

Effect of a new valuation of Belfast to raise the amount from 490,000 *l.* to 612,000 *l.*, and to reduce the poundage rate from 6 *s.* 8 *d.* to about 5 *s.* 4 *d.*, 6895–6899——Explanation of the principle in the valuation of dock property, as in Belfast and Dublin; deductions allowed for renewals and repairs, 6900–6903. 6909–6915——Expediency of a re-valuation embracing all Ireland, 6904——Anxiety of the corporation of Belfast for a re-valuation of the borough; very large area within the borough, 6905–6908.

Estimate of 18,000,000 *l.* as the amount of a new valuation of Ireland, the present valuation being 13,500,000 *l.* (the same as that of Lancashire), 6916–6920——Increase from 50 to 60 per cent. in some places, the average being about 33 per cent., 6920–6923——Effect of an increased valuation in adding to the number of ratepayers on the jury list, 6924–6927——Complaints made by ratepayers as to the inequality and injustice of the present valuation, 6928–6931.

Information as to the way in which the work is done by the valuators in the country and by the office staff, respectively, 6935–6940——Importance of revised instructions to the valuators, and of a modification of details, if a new valuation be decided upon, 6941–6944——Necessity of prices being still taken into account in making a new valuation; there might be a scale of actual prices in a schedule to the Act, 6945–6959.

Opinion that the valuation should be the rent; difficulty in arriving at the rent by the price obtained after competition, 6960–6966——Comparatively small expense of a general revision; increased staff of valuers required, the work occupying about five years, 6967–6973——Inexpediency of disturbing a new valuation for fifteen or twenty years, 6974–6977.

More equal distribution of local taxation by a new valuation, 6978, 6979——Calculation as to the increase of imperial taxation that would accrue from a new valuation, 6980——Estimated increase from 4,223,871 *l.* to 4,927,000 *l.* in the valuation of Ulster; data for this calculation, 6981–6984. 6989–6997——Suggestions as to the qualifications desirable in valuators; facility of obtaining competent men, 6985–6988. 7002.

Instances of discrepancy between one district of a county and another, owing to changes in the cultivation and condition of the land, 6998–7001——Necessity in valuing tillage land of taking the rate of wages into account, whilst in the case of grazing land, cattle disease should not be taken into consideration, 7003–7007——Explanation that the valuation should not be based only on the actual rent, 7008–7010——Total of about thirty-two valuators, who are paid about 460 *l.* a year, and expenses, 7011–7013.

Instructions to the valuators to value lands as they find them, according to their condition, neglected land being valued lower than land in good condition, 7020, 7021——Higher value placed upon town parks near a large town than near a small one, 7025——Greater increase by re-valuation in the case of large towns than of small ones, 7026–7028——Explanation in regard to market gardens being valued as town parks, 7029–7036.

Grice, George. Testimony to the efficiency of Mr. Grice, who is chief assistant in the town clerk's office in Dublin and is a strong Conservative, *Sullivan* 4766.

Grimshaw, Thomas Wrigley, M.D. (Analysis of his Evidence.)—Professional position and extensive experience of witness in Dublin; several hospitals with which he is officially connected, 3881–3884——Active part taken by witness as a member of the Dublin Sanitary

Grimshaw, Thomas Wrigley, M.D. (Analysis of his Evidence)—*continued.*

Sanitary Association; particulars as to the constitution, objects, and operation of the association, 3885–3893——Several occasions upon which witness has been examined as an expert in sanitary matters, 3894.

Very unfavourable opinion formed by witness as to the health of Dublin in comparison with that of other towns similarly situated; statistics of mortality in support of this conclusion, 3895–3903——Favourable character, on the whole, of the natural situation of Dublin, 3904——Belief that the high mortality depends on the want of ordinary sanitary precautions, 3905.

Information as to the sanitary staff, and as to the constitution of the Public Health Committee of the Corporation, which was first appointed in 1866; 3906–3909——Opinion that the committee does not discharge its duties satisfactorily, 3911——Frequent and strong complaints in the public press relative to the sanitary management of the city, 3912–3914. 3988——Extremely filthy state of the liberties of Dublin; practice of the poorer classes to throw filth into the street, as they have no means of removing it from their houses, 3915–3918.

Great want of a system of domestic scavenging, the corporation being much to blame in the matter; explanation hereon as to the Local Government Board not having issued an order on the subject, 3918–3923——Exceedingly noxious state of the corporation scavenging depôts, as well as of the private depôts; difficulty in interfering with the latter so long as the former are allowed to continue so offensive, 3924–3928. 4219–4225.

Great number of tenement houses visited by witness and found in a most filthy and disgraceful condition, 3929–3942——Plentiful supply of fever patients for the hospitals from these houses, many of which are quite unfit for human habitation, 3929. 3931. 3933. 4236, 4237——Absence of any practical improvement in many of these wretched tenements since witness first reported upon them in 1871; 3929. 3934–3937. 4192——Instances of glaring nuisances from ash-pits, &c., which the Public Health Committee refused to consider a cause of complaint when reported by the Sanitary Association, 3939–3942. 4033.

Want of an increased staff of sanitary inspectors; large amount of their time occupied in the service of notices, 3943–3947——Prejudicial effect of the present requirements as to notices, and of the practice as to fines and imprisonment; immunity from punishment in the great majority of cases, 3944–3952——Remedy obtained in some cases by persistent action on the part of the Sanitary Association, 3953.

Great abuse in the licensing of slaughter-houses, whilst some of them are in a very filthy and noxious condition, 3954–3958——Power of the corporation to construct abattoirs, though none have yet been provided, 3959–3961——Extremely filthy state of the dairy yards; great nuisance from the large accumulations of manure, 3962——Powers of the corporation for dealing with the dairy yards, 3963.

Defective arrangements for preventing the spread of contagion, and for conveying clothing to and from the disinfecting place, 3964. 3969–3978——Exceedingly imperfect provision for the conveyance of patients to the hospitals, the corporation having only one old cab, whilst the horse is hired, and is not kept in the same place as the cab, 3964–3969. 3979–3983——Provision of some cabs by the North and South Dublin Unions for the removal of patients, 3966——Instances of persons, attacked with scarlatina and with small-pox, being removed to the hospitals in the public cabs, 3979. 3983. 4089–4097—— Useless process adopted in the disinfection of houses, 3984, 3985.

Opinion that the members of the Public Health Committee have not the proper mental capacity for sanitary duties; examination hereon to the effect that witness makes no charge of general incapacity against individuals, 3986, 3987. 4054. 4155–4176.* 4203–4206——Active part taken by Mr. Gray of the "Freeman's Journal," in moving the corporation to adopt better sanitary arrangements, 3988. 4238——Want of an efficient medical superintendent, with adequate powers, at the head of the sanitary staff; statement as to neither Dr. Mapother nor Mr. Boyle now holding this position, 3984–4012.

Explanation relative to the duties of Dr. Mapother, as consulting sanitary officer, his salary being 300 *l.* a year; he is perfectly qualified for the general superintendence of the department, 3990–3992. 3997–4001. 4011–4013——Expediency of the superintendence being vested in a medical man, Mr. Boyle not being qualified, 4001*–4011——Very inadequate payment of the medical sanitary officers, fourteen in number; statement hereon as to their salaries being only 25 *l.* a year. 4014–4032.

Attendance of eleven medical sanitary officers at a meeting called to consider the causes of the high mortality; resolutions agreed to by nine of these as to the improvements urgently required in sanitary matters, 4034–4037——Comment upon the course pursued by the Public Health Committee as regards the publication of the report of the foregoing meeting, 4037–4047.

Average of about 2,000 *l.* a year expended for sanitary purposes, and charged upon the borough fund, 4048. 4102–4106. 4202——Full power of the corporation to levy rates for sanitary

Grimshaw, Thomas Wrigley, M.D. (Analysis of his Evidence)—*continued.*
sanitary improvements; comment upon their omission in this respect, 4049-4053. 4109-4110——Illustrations of the unsatisfactory way in which some of the inspectors under the Local Government Board conduct inquiries when nuisances are brought to their notice, 4056-4058. 4114-4125.

Examination to the effect that the cabs at the unions are not kept there for the use of the general public, witness further contending that there has been great neglect in the corporation on this subject, 4060-4097. 4126-4128.

Further advocacy of the appointment of a well-paid medical superintendent in charge of the sanitary department; suggestion made by Mr. Gray on this point, 4099-4101. 4111-4113. 4193, 4194. 4231-4233——Conclusion that the excess of mortality in Dublin as compared with other towns is not accounted for by the extensive resort of country patients to hospitals in the former town, 4129-4133.

Examination relative to correspondence in 1875 between the Sanitary Association and the Local Government Board upon the subject of the sanitary arrangements, and the question of the board issuing an order for Dublin under the 39th section of the Public Health Act of 1874; 4134-4144——Charge on the part of the association, in letter of 18th February, and in memorial of 11th May 1875, that the corporation had failed to make due provision for the removal of house refuse and the cleansing of ash pits, cesspools, &c., 4137-4144——Explanation offered by the corporation (Public Health Committee) on the forgoing subject, in letter of 19th March 1875; 4140.

Very influential character of the names attached to the memorial of the association, sent to the Local Government Board in May 1875; remedial measures strongly urged therein, 4144-4147——Large expense involved in the proposed improvements, 4148, 4149.

Active part taken by the Sanitary Association since its appointment, with a view to an improved system in the townships as well as in Dublin, 4150-4152——Duties of the Public Health Committee in reference to the analysis of food and the inspection of meat; impression that the latter work is very well done, 4177-4179. 4184, 4185——Duties of the sanitary serjeants, nine in number; they are a good class of men, but the number is insufficient, 4180-4183——Satisfactory discharge of their duties by the medical sanitary officers, as a body, 4186-4191.

Exceedingly small improvement which appears to have resulted from the labours of the sanitary officers, whose reports are often left unattended, 4190-4196——Further reference to the want of an increased staff as a great cause of the continued existence of nuisances, 4194-4198——Steps taken in the removal of pigs from houses, though not always with success, 4198-4201.

General character of the supervision exercised over the Public Health Committee by the Local Government Board, 4207, 4208——Explanation as to the boards of guardians not having sanitary authority in the city, 4209-4212——Statement to the effect that there seems to be no arrangement, as in Leeds and London, for the prompt inspection of localities where epidemics break out, with a view to preventing the spread of disease, 4213-4218——Instances of salutary punishment of cabmen for carrying fever patients, 4229, 4230.

Further statement in disapproval, to some extent, of the action of the Local Government Board through its inspectors, 4234, 4235——Importance of clearing away a large number of dwellings unfit for habitation; prominent part taken in this matter by Mr. Gray, as one of the corporation, 4236-4238——General opinion in Dublin (in which witness concurs) that much more might be done than is done with the present amount of expenditure, though an increase is doubtless necessary for sanitary purposes, 4239-4241——Practice as to the sale of the ash-pits' contents; considerable value of the refuse, 4242-4245.

Decided opinion that owners should have a voice in the municipal administration, 4246-4248——Very injurious effect of the present state of the Liffey upon the health of Dublin, 4249-4252——Information relative to the appointment and action of the Citizens' Main Drainage Committee; conclusion as to certain resolutions adopted by the committee having shown a want of confidence in the corporation, 4253-4261.

H.

Hancock, William Neilson, LL.D. (Analysis of his Evidence.)—Official employment of witness on several occasions to report upon the question of local government and municipal taxation in Ireland; reference to the different reports made by him, 1.

Distinction drawn by the Public Health Act of 1874, whereby in every town having more than 6,000 inhabitants the town authorities are declared to be the urban sanitary authority, 2——Four towns with urban sanitary authorities under the Act 9 Geo. 4 (1828),

Hancock, William Neilson, LL.D. (Analysis of his Evidence)—*continued.*

(1828), *ib.*——Sixteen such towns under the Towns Improvement Act of 1854 *ib.*——Eleven towns under town councils, five being under the Act of 1854, and six under local Acts, 2. 20——Eleven towns governed by commissioners under local or special Acts, 2.

Several Irish Acts of the last century, founded on the vestry system of management; unpopularity of these vestries at the time of the Act of 1828; 3, 4——Decaying condition for many years previously to the Act of 1840 of the old corporations in existence at the time of the Union; final abolition of these bodies in 1840; 4–15——Exceptional position of the town of Carrickfergus, the board of guardians being still the local sanitary authority, 15–18.

Several respects in which the Act of 1828 was recognised by the Act of 1840; partial adoption of the former Act as to the mode of election, 19——Explanation as to witness having advised the town of Lurgan not to apply for a charter, this town still being under the Act of 1854; 21–23——Adoption of the Act of 1828 by sixty-six towns, only twelve of these being still under the Act; particulars hereon as to the deficiencies of this Act in comparison with the Act of 1854; 24–29——Local Acts obtained by Kingstown, Belfast, Dublin, and other places, instead of remaining under the Act of 1828; 26.

Total of seventy-six towns under the Act of 1854; enumeration of sixty of these with a population under 6,000 and above 1,500; 30–33——Partial extent to which several towns have adopted the Act of 1854, whilst local Acts have been largely necessitated, independently of the former; 34–37. 40–42. 56——Full powers of town councils under the Act of 1840 as to the management of corporate property, and the appointment of officers, 38, 39.

Several instances of towns having obtained local Acts by reason of the divided authority over the streets; particulars hereon, 41, 42. 48–55——Obstacles to the obtaining of Provisional Orders under the Local Government Act of 1871; veto imposed by the grand jury in several instances, 42–44. 52——Comment upon the case of Ballina, the local authority not having succeeded in obtaining a Provisional Order or a local Act, 44–47.

Very limited extent to which town authorities have control over fairs and markets; very unsatisfactory position of the matter at the present time, 56–50——Exceedingly defective provisions with regard to borrowing powers of towns in Ireland, as under the Act of 1847 and other Acts; illustration in the case of Newry, 59–67——Advocacy of similar facilities for raising loans by the issue of debenture stock, as in the case of the Metropolitan Board of Works, 59. 64–66. 82.

Great cost of some local Acts as compared with the cost of Provisional Orders, 66. 68–70——Suggestions for facilitating the obtaining of Provisional Orders, and for otherwise dispensing with the necessity of costly local Acts, 70. 76–82——Illustration in the case of Cork of the want of facilities for local improvements by means of Provisional Orders instead of by special Act, 70–75——Proposal with a view to the Local Government Board passing general enactments of which the smaller towns may avail themselves, 79–82.

Great inconvenience as regards sanitary powers resting mainly on an extension of the English law to Ireland in 1866; 83——Grounds for the conclusion that the English Sanitary Code of 1875 might be extended to Ireland in about ten clauses, with very beneficial results, 83, 84——Expediency of an amendment of the Act of 1854, concurrently with a repeal of the local Acts since passed in order to supply the deficiencies of the former, 86, 87. 90, 91——Want of a complete repeal of the Act of 1828; 88——Suggestion also that the system of municipal commissioners be abolished, 89——Absurdity of the exceptional position of Carrickfergus, *ib.*

Information relative to the powers of taxation of town authorities under the Acts of 1828 and 1854, and the limits with reference to the rating, 92–97——Series of limits in all the local Acts, 98——Provisions in the Borough Rate Act (3 & 4 Vict. c. 109) as to the maximum rate of assessment, &c., 99——Departure from the limit of rating, when charges under the Sanitary Act are put upon the borough fund, 99, 100——Circumstance of Waterford not having powers of rating, 101–103.

Limit of 2 s. in the 1 *l.* as the amount of the improvement rate in Dublin under the Act of 1849; application of this rate to the payment of interest on debt and to other charges, 104–110——Grounds for the conclusion that the limits placed upon the rating powers of town authorities are very unwise, and cause much complication, 111——Statement of the amount of local taxation in towns and counties, respectively; that is, exclusive of poor rate, 112–115——Arrangement as to audit of accounts under the Local Government Act of 1871; objection to which open, though the system is in the main an admirable one, 116–118.

Qualifications of commissioners or town councillors as to rating, residence, &c., under the Acts of 1828 and 1854, respectively, 119–121——Introduction by the Act of 1854 of a new class, that of lessors residing within five miles; defect on account of the restriction as to residence, 119–121——Statement of the qualifications of town councillors and aldermen

Hancock, William Neilson, LL.D. (Analysis of his Evidence.)—*continued*.

aldermen in the ten large towns that have got charters under the Municipal Act of 1840; defect in the Act on this score, 122, 123——Inexpediency of the seven miles limit in the case of Dublin, and of the residence limit in other towns, 124, 125——Varying qualifications in different towns as regards resident and non-resident local authorities, 126.

Statement of the qualifications of electors under the Acts of 1828 and 1854, and under the Act of 1840; amendment in 1871, whereby the payment of the town rate is sufficient, 127, 128——Particulars relative to the qualification of electors in Dublin under the Dublin Municipal Amendment Act of 1849, payment of five rates being necessary; statement hereon as to the landlord paying all the local rates and taxes up to 8 *l.*; 129–151——Deduction allowed to the owner on payment of the occupier's rates in Belfast, Sligo, and Dublin, 150, 151.

Great importance attached to an equal division of town taxation between owners and occupiers, 152——Division of the poor rate between the owner and the occupier; division also in the case of certain grand jury cess contracts, *ib.*——Proposal that, the rates being divided, half the local board for each town be elected by the owners, and half by the occupiers; beneficial results anticipated, 153. 160–162. 184–188——Details of witness' plan for the election of the representatives of the occupiers; advantage by applying the cumulative principle, 154–156. 163.

Suggestions also for the election of owners, some members being *ex officio* in respect of property, and some being chosen on the cumulative principle, 156 *et seq.*——Proposed condition that owners who are *ex officio* members must be magistrates, 156. 181——Way in which the cumulative principle as applied to the election of both owners and occupiers would solve the religious difficulty as regards local representation and taxation, 156. 165–169.

Statement to its being proposed by witness to empower *ex officio* members to nominate substitutes, on certain conditions, 162. 178–183——Advantage of the *ex officio* element to a certain extent, 162. 189——Conclusion that the present limit of the occupiers' franchise should be greatly lowered, in order that all classes may have a voice in the representation, 163–165. 188——Advantage of the School Board principle of election as regards occupiers, 168–171.

Explanation that witness does not propose any multiple voting among occupiers, though each occupier should have cumulative votes for the number of candidates; way in which this principle would operate in Dublin, 170–177——Result of witness' scheme if put in operation in the principal towns; number of representatives of different classes, there being, on the whole, an equal number of owners and occupiers in each case, 184–187.

Objection to an entire discontinuance of the ward system of election in large towns, 189——Opinion favourable to three years' election, save in the case of *ex officio* men who should sit permanently, 190–194——Impression as to the aldermen in Dublin going out every three years, 194. 198–200——Information relative to the qualification of a burgess in Dublin, and the restriction as to rating; respects in which there is a different provision for the municipal rates, and for the parliamentary rates, 201–229.

[Second Examination.] Return, delivered in (*App.* 399, 400), showing the number of different authorities of the various towns, 230.

[Third Examination.] Further statement as to the number of corporations dealt with by the General Municipal Reform Act for Ireland, and as to the proportion of these with self-elective and irresponsible governing bodies, 573–582. 588——Enumeration of ten towns which got new corporations without new charters; nominal retention of their former powers by these towns after the application of the Municipal Reform Act, 583–588. 602–628——Important effect of the Act as regards Belfast, both with respect to the municipal and Parliamentary franchise, 589–592.

Mention of the several counties of cities among the ten corporations that did not get new charters under the Municipal Reform Act, 593–593——Anomaly in the case of Londonderry, which was not strictly a county of a city, 594–596——Reference to the county of the town of Carrickfergus, as not having got a new corporation under the Act of 1840; 597, 598. 601——Special legislation as regards Galway, both in the Act of 1840 and in subsequent local Acts, 598–601.

Reference to the General Report of the Municipal Commissioners in 1835, as setting forth the principal objects to be dealt with by the Act of 1840 in the reform of the corporations, 602, 603——Statement as to several corporations having formerly had the exclusive power of appointing charter justices within their jurisdiction, this power having been taken away by the Act of 1840, or by concurrent legislation, 603–607. 614. 738–741——Repeal, by the Act of 1840, of Admiralty jurisdiction formerly possessed by some corporations, 608, 609. 742–745.

Provisions in the Municipal Reform Act relative to the transfer from certain corporations to the Crown of the appointment of sheriff and clerk of the peace, 609. 612, 613——Special powers still possessed by the Corporation of Dublin for regulating the trade of

Hancock, William Neilson, LL.D. (Analysis of his Evidence.)—*continued*.

of pawnbroking, 610, 611——Powers still retained by the corporations in regard to regulating markets and levying tolls, 615–623——Transfer, by the Act of 1840, of the administration of charities from the corporations to trustees, 626, 627.

Explanation as regards the franchise established by the Municipal Corporations Act that the 10 *l.* valuation is considered equivalent to about 8 *l.* 10 *s.* poor-law rating, 629–631——Provisions of the Municipal Corporations Amendment Act of 1849 for the regulation of the municipal franchise in Dublin, 632, 633——Belief as to all parties in Dublin having assented to the Act of 1849, and to the assimilation of the franchise to that in England, 634–643. 785, 786——Reference to the Dublin Improvement Act of 1849, as regards the powers given thereby to the corporation in the matter of paving, lighting, &c., 644, 645. 658, 659.

Statement to the effect that in Dublin and other places which are counties of cities, the fiscal power of the grand juries has been transferred to the corporations, 646–657——Impression as to the freemen in Dublin taking part in the municipal government, 660–662. 737——Examination relative to some twelve towns having commissioners under the Act 9 Geo. 4, c. 82; co-existence of commissioners and of a corporation in the case of Clonmel, 663–706——Explanation as to the provisions of the Towns Improvement Act of 1854, in regard to the qualifications for the municipal franchise, 707–726——Execution of the Act of 1854 by commissioners appointed under it; facility to corporations (with some exceptions) in getting the powers of the Act, 727–736.

Very large number of writs issued by the sheriff of the City of Dublin, 746–751——Certain number of honorary freemen in Dublin before the Act of 1840; there are not any now, 752–755——Powers of the corporation of Dublin under the 93rd and 94th Sections of the Act of 1840 as to the appointment of officers, 756–758.

Revision of the burgess roll by two assessors appointed by popular election; casting vote of the lord mayor when there is a difference between the assessors, 759–764——Abuse to which this system of revision is liable, though in practice none may have occurred; reference hereon to the satisfactory character of the Parliamentary revision, 761–767——Special privileges of the corporation of Dublin in regard to the pawnbroking trade in Ireland generally; amendment desirable, 768–770.

Four distinct franchises in corporate towns in Ireland under the Act of 1854, there being also special modifications under other Acts, 771–775——Great number of local Acts, there being also numerous general Acts relating to sewers, water supply, the removal of nuisances, &c.; duplicate or cumulative provisions thus requiring simplification, 776–781——Opportunity for sweeping away duplicate powers at the time of the passing of the Sanitary Act of 1866; 781, 782——Belief further expressed as to very little power having been reserved to the corporations under the Act of 1840; 783, 784.

Large number of empty houses and of houses out of repair in Ireland, owing to there being no provision by law as to repairs where there is a bad title; remedy of this evil by extending to Ireland a Scotch Act of year 1663, still in effective operation, 787–795——Provisions of the foregoing Act as to the repair of ruinous houses by the local authorities, 788——Steps taken by Belfast in favour of the adoption of the Scotch Act, 788, 789——Expediency of every town or governing body being subject to an adequate public audit; suggestion as to their having protection through the Court of Queen's Bench or Local Government Board, 796–800.

Details relative to the local government and taxation of Galway under different special Acts and provisional orders; anomalous position of this town in several respects, 801–863——Circumstance of the qualification of a voter for commissioners being twice as high in Galway as in other towns; assimulation desirable, 808–810. 817–821. 863——Long existence of the toll thorough and other tolls in Galway; these were condemned by commissions in 1835 and 1853, and should be abolished, 811–813. 822. 833–835. 856–861. 873–875——Equal division of rates between owner and occupier in Galway, 845.

System of nomination and appointment of the sheriffs in the City of Dublin; relative proportion of Protestants and Roman Catholics appointed, 864–872——Evidence in further support of the opinion that the powers of grand juries within the urban districts should in certain cases be transferred to the urban authority; contemplated inquiry before the Local Government Board, previously to readjustment in this respect, 877–890——Recent instance at Lisburn of the hardship through the grand jury objecting to an outlay for flagging the footways, 881–886——Bad state of one of the roads out of Dublin, as not being in charge of the township authorities, 886.

Consideration of objections to witness' proposal that the Local Government Board should obtain power for extending to small towns the provisions of Acts already sanctioned for large towns; check through the Board upon undue interference with private rights, 891–904——Approval of an assimilation of the different systems of town government being extended so as to embrace all towns down to those with 1,500 inhabitants, 905–910——High rates in small towns owing to the absence of union rating, 910, 911——Expediency of a real representation of property rather than a limit of rating, 912–914.

Explanation

Hancock William Neilson, LL.D. (Analysis of his Evidence.)—*continued.*

Explanation that witness proposes to retain to a certain extent the ward system of election in large towns, merely as being an existing institution, 915-920——Several amendments suggested in the qualification of municipal electors, witness not proposing to make the rating to the poor-law a qualification, 921-924. 927——Strong approval of the recommendations of the Select Committee on Local Taxation in 1870 for a division of rates between owners and occupiers, existing contracts being respected, 925-929.

Illustration in the case of the Dublin Port and Docks Board of the satisfactory result of the representation of different interests, 931-934 —Approval of Government property being represented if it be rated, 935-937. 950, 951——Several precedents and high authorities further cited in support of the municipal franchise being conferred on owners as well as well as occupiers, there being a division of rates between the two, 938-945.

Further advocacy of a full representation of property by means of plural voting, 946-951——Explanation as regards the fund for cleansing the streets in Dublin, that the Paving Board and the Wide Streets Board were not transferred until 1849; 952-955 —— Stringent operation of the present system of audit further adverted to; exceptions from the Act of 1871 in the case of Kilkenny, Cork, and Waterford, 956-961. 1047-1061. 1066-1068.

Examination in detail in further support of increased facilities in towns for separating themselves from counties in reference to expenditure of local rates in street improvements and sanitary matters generally, 962 *et seq.*——Statement as to the authority of the court-leet in Lisburn extending beyond the area of the town authority, 976, 977. 994-996——Exceptions taken to the local authority being entrusted generally with the control of the police, or to the stipendiary magistrates having anything to do with the rating, 984-993.

Illustrations of the inconvenience in sanitary matters by the overlapping of areas, and by the existence of several authorities in the same area, 994-1014——Explanation as regards Ballina, that the board of guardians are the town authority for sanitary purposes, 997-1000. 1009-1014——Objection further made to the present veto in the grand jury as regards towns obtaining provisional orders through the Local Government Board, 1015-1041——Circumstance of the city magistrates of Dublin not exercising any criminal powers nor sitting in the police courts, 1062-1065.

Health of Dublin. Very unfavourable opinion formed by witness as to the health of Dublin in comparison with that of other towns similarly situated; statistics of mortality in support of this conclusion, the death-rate having been very high in 1874, *Grimshaw* 3895-3903——High zymotic death-rate as compared with London, *ib.* 3900——Favourable character on the whole of the natural situation of Dublin, *ib.* 3904——Belief that the high mortality depends on the want of ordinary sanitary precautions, *ib.* 3905——

Conclusion that the excess of mortality in Dublin, as compared with other towns, is not accounted for by the extensive resort of country patients to hospitals in the former town, *Grimshaw* 4126-4133.

Denial that there is excessive mortality from zymotic diseases in Dublin, as stated by Dr. Grimshaw; steady decrease since 1866, *Boyle* 4902-4904. 5233-5237——Explanation that Dublin was not exceptional in having a high death-rate in the year 1874, *ib.* 4905.

Further contradiction of Dr. Grimshaw's evidence on the subject of the death-rate, *Boyle* 5309-5312.

See also Dairy Yards. Disinfection. Sanitary Administration. Slaughter Houses.

Henry, William Joseph. (Analysis of his Evidence.)—Has been town clerk of Dublin since 1864; makes out the burgess-roll and the Parliamentary-roll, 1069-1075——Great change made in the local management of Dublin between 1841 and 1849; transfer to the corporation of the powers of the former Paving Board and Wide Streets Board, and of the fiscal powers of the grand jury, &c., 1075-1090. 1104-1112——Re-arrangement of the area of the wards, with reference to population, by the Municipal Corporations Amendment Act; great inequalities previously, 1091. 1099-1103——Important change made in the municipal franchise by the Act of 1849, so that the constituency was entirely altered, 1092-1098.

Powers of the corporation under the Act of 1849 to levy a sewer-rate and to make sewers, 1106-1109——Increased sanitary duties vested in the corporation since the Act of 1849; local Acts also for a better water supply, 1112-1115——Provisions in the Act of 1849 authorising the levy of an improvement rate up to 2 s. in the pound, and setting forth the purposes to which to be applied; debts to be paid off out of the rate, as due by the Wide Streets Commissioners and the Paving Board, 1116-1139.

Separate provisions as to the sewer-rate, which has its own liabilities, 1140——Several purposes, as provided by presentment, for which the grand jury rate in Dublin is levied, 1141-1145——Separate accounts at the Bank of Ireland to which the proceeds of the different rates are paid, 1146-1149——Explanations in connection with the provisions of the

Report, 1876—continued.

Henry, William Joseph. (Analysis of his Evidence.)—*continued.*

the Act 17 & 18 Vict. c. 22, whereby the taxation for bridges and quay-walls is levied over the metropolitan police district; extensive area of this district, 1151–1178.

Functions of the Port and Docks Board in the origination of bridges and quay walls, 1156–1161——Division of the former Ballast Board into the Port and Docks Board and the Irish Lights Board, 1179–1185——Particulars relative to the constitution of the Port and Docks Board, and the qualifications of the electing body, as under the Act 30 & 31 Vict. c. 81; witness has never heard a complaint against the working of the Board, 1186–1192. 1485.

Insufficiency of the improvement rate of 2*s.*, the demands upon it having greatly increased since 1849, on account of the building of new streets, and the advance in the price of labour and materials, 1193–1209——Inferior class of the new houses, so that the rates therefrom do not cover the increased cost for paving, &c., 1198–1202. 1533–1538——Opinion as to the insufficiency of the municipal area, 1210–1212——Expediency of Rathmines being included in the municipal area, and being taxed for the city wards, 1213–1227. 1539–1542.

Alternate selection of Protestant and Roman Catholic lord mayors since 1849; 1228–1238. 1579–1583. 1631–1642——Instances of Liberal wards selecting Conservative representatives; these are, however, exceptions to the rule, 1239–1246. 1303–1309. 1559, 1560. 1577, 1578.

Important limitation to the municipal franchise, by the necessity of a continued occupation of two years and eight months, 1247–1256. 1299. 1350–1352——Explanation as to the several rates which must be paid as a qualification for the franchise; collection of these rates and the poor rate, at the same time, 1257–1261. 1290–1295. 1371–1373——Instances of disqualification owing to there being no notice of the necessity of payment, as in the case of the Parliamentary franchise, 1260–1267. 1290–1297——Disqualification through the payment of rates by the landlord without the occupier's name going on the rate-book, 1268–1272——Frequent complaint made as to the landlords not paying the tenants' taxes by the proper time, 1273. 1353.

Small increase of the burgess roll since 1843; 1274——Power of the corporation to levy a borough rate of 3 *d.*; belief that this power has only twice been exercised, 1277–1282——Particulars as to the course pursued by witness, as town clerk, in forming the municipal register or burgess list; every name in the collector general's books, whatever the rating, appears on the list, 1283–1289. 1348–1349——Requirement as to claims and objections being lodged on the 1st October, and published between the 1st and 11th October, 1285.

Suggestion as regards continued occupation, that a break of residence for a month or so might be allowed without causing disqualification, 1298–1302——Constitution of the Irish Lights Board, the members being self-elective, 1310——Practice as to the preparation of estimates for the different services to be charged against the improvement rate, 1312–1315——System of committees by which the corporation acts in the management of the expenditure; control of the paving, lighting, and cleansing by No. 1 Committee, 1316–1322.

Audit of the corporation accounts by an officer of the Local Government Board, 1323——Difficulty raised by the auditor about an expenditure of 6,700 *l.* out of the main drainage rate in connection with Grattan Bridge, 1324–1327. 1511, 1512. 1624–1626——Separation of accounts at the suggestion of the auditor, 1328–1331.

Total of 596,099 *l.* as the valuation of Dublin in 1875; doubt, however, as to Government property being included, 1332–1334——Payment of rates by Government in 1875; 1335——Statement to the effect, that the valuation has much decreased since 1849; causes of this, 1337–1340. 1354–1361——Insufficiency and inequality of the valuation at the present time, 1341–1347.

Operation of the residential qualification of two years and eight months as a check upon a very extended franchise, 1350–1352. 1363–1365——Probability of the roll being nearly doubled if the occupation were reduced to one year, 1352–1504——Approval of an extension of the seven mile limit; small increase of burgesses by extending the limit to twelve miles, 1366–1370. 1505——Question considered whether there is not every facility to claims under the present system, 1374–1378. 1383–1392——Power of compounding with landlords for payment of rates, though it has never been exercised, 1379–1382.

Large sums spent by the corporation between 1864 and 1872, in promoting and in opposing Private Bills, 1395——Necessary sanction of the Lord Lieutenant before the appointment of any new officers by the corporation; sanction also as regards the salary on appointment, 1396–1402——Power and practice of the corporation to increase the salaries from time to time, 1403–1406. 1418——Increase of witness' salary from 400 *l.* to 600 *l.* a year, over a period of thirteen years; smallness of his remuneration as compared with that of town clerks in England, 1407–1417. 1420, 1421. 1432. 1525–1527.

Increase

Henry, William Joseph. (Analysis of his Evidence.)—*continued.*

Increase of the Lord Mayor's salary by 200 guineas, so that he may have a secretary, 1419——Appointment of the secretaries of the different committees by the council, the salaries being limited to 400 *l.* a year; this limit does not apply to Mr. Boyle, secretary of the Public Health Committee, 1422–1431. 1561, 1562——Supervision exercised over the officers by the council and the committees, 1434–1436. 1494–1499. 1645.

Approval of a limit to the improvement rate, though the 2 *s.* limit should be extended, 1437–1447——Full limit reached by all the rates, 1441–1446——Very recent action of the corporation in the direction of providing dwellings for the working classes, 1448–1459——Non-erection of any public clocks by the corporation, 1460——Impression as to the power having been exercised by the corporation of removing ashes and night soil from the houses, 1461–1464——Information to be supplied as to the meetings of the council, and the attendance of members, twenty being a quorum, 1465–1467.

Explanation on the subject of the fees paid to the high sheriff of Dublin by the corporation; the money really goes to the sub sheriff, 1468–1476——Reference to the salary and fees of the clerk of the peace, as each amounting to about 800 *l.* a year, 1477, 1478——Salary paid to the Marshal of Dublin by the corporation, out of the fees received by him, as registrar of pawnbrokers, 1479–1484——Further reference to the limited salary of witness, all his time being devoted to his office, 1486–1493.

Conclusion as to the unduly small number on the burgess roll in proportion to the population, 1500–1503——Increased admission to the roll if the period for payment of taxes were extended close up to the day of voting, 1506–1508——Opinion that the inhabitants generally are fairly represented on the municipal council, 1509, 1510.

Exceptions taken to the practice of the Government auditor in giving legal decisions, whilst, if these are overruled on appeal, the costs fall on the corporation; amendment required in this respect, 1511–1522. 1643, 1644——Approval, however, of a Government auditor rather than of an elected one, 1523, 1524——Power of the corporation to superannuate its officers up to two-thirds of their salaries, 1528–1530.

Explanation that the borough rate could not be applied in aid of the improvement rate, 1531, 1532. 1608——Expediency of an extension of the municipal boundaries, there having been no increase since 1849, and many buildings being erected outside the boundaries, so as to escape the city rates, 1539–1553. 1610——Necessary approval by the corporation of the plans and estimates of the Port and Docks Board, for bridges and quay walls; expediency of this check in the corporation as being the taxing body, 1554–1558. 1566–1576——Jurisdiction of the Irish Lights Board all round Ireland, 1563, 1564.

Admission as to there still being much inequality between some of the wards as regards their relative valuation and representation, 1586–1595. 1627–1630——Circumstance of fresh debts having accumulated against the improvement rate since the old debts were paid off, 1596–1600——Belief that there are no debts on the sewers rate, 1601——Reference to the grand jury cess, as being a yearly presentment for prisons, &c., and for the repayment of instalments to Government, 1602–1606——Income from the corporate property adverted to as not being applicable in aid of the improvement rate, 1607–1609.

Further reference to the disfranchising effect of breaks of residence, 1611——Instance of the sewers rate not having been up to the maximum, 1612——Witness has had no complaints from occupiers that their names have not been in the rate book; he cannot say whether they are omitted or not, 1613–1616. 1648–1652.

Authority in the Dublin Improvement Act of 1849, for the appointment of salaried secretaries of committees, 1616–1620——Provisions of the Act 1 & 2 Geo. 4, c. 77, as to the payment of fees to sheriffs, under sheriffs and other officers, 1621–1623.

[Second Examination.] Total of 7,854 names on the burgess list; deductions to which subject before the franchise is conferred, 2467, 2468.

Explanation in connection with a bye-law made in 1871, relative to the letting by auction of the corporation lands; special Act in 1864, for reducing the rents previously obtained by public auction for the Baldoyle lands, 2537–2547.

Household Suffrage. Conclusion that, with the safeguards proposed by witness, the municipal franchise in Ireland should be reduced to household suffrage, *Pim* 2337, 2338——Approval of a household franchise in Dublin as in England; improvement of the corporation thereby, *Gray* 6507, 6508. 6527. 6640–6650.

Improvement Rate (Dublin):

Limit of 2 *s.* in the 1 *l.* as the amount of the improvement rate in Dublin under the Act of 1849; application of this rate to the payment of interest on debt, and to other charges, *Hancock* 104–110——Further reference to the Improvement Act of 1849 as regards the powers given thereby to the corporation in the matter of paving, lighting &c., *ib.* 644, 645. 658, 659.

Provisions in the Act of 1849 authorising the levy of an improvement rate up to 2 *s.* in the 1 *l.*, and setting forth the purposes to which to be applied; debts to be paid off out of the rate, as due by the Wide Streets Commissioners and the Paving Board, *Henry* 1116–1139——Insufficiency of the rate, the demands upon it having greatly increased since 1849 on account of the building of new streets, and the advance in the price of labour and materials, *ib.* 1193–1209——Inferior class of the new houses, so that the rates therefrom do not cover the increased cost for paving, &c., 1198–1202. 1533–1538——Practice as to the preparation of estimates for the different services to be charged against the rate, *ib.* 1312–1315

Approval of a limit to the improvement rate, though the 2 *s.* limit should be extended, *Henry* 1437–1447——Circumstance of fresh debts having accumulated against the rate since the old debts were paid off, *ib.* 1596–1600——Income from the corporate property adverted to as not being applicable in aid of the improvement rate, *ib.* 1607–1609.

Statement as to the improvement rate fund being much in debt, *M'Evoy*, 2067–2069——Doubt whether any reduction can be made in the rate, *Pim* 2398.

Loan of 50,000 *l.* being raised under the Improvement Act of 1849 for street improvements, *Robinson* 2712–2715——Receipt of 52,909 *l.* from the improvement rate of 2 *s.* in the 1 *l.* in the year ending 31st August 1875; particulars as to the items of expenditure charged against the rate, *ib.* 2721–2731——Limited extent to which any payment of interest as repayment of debt is charged against the rate, *ib.* 2722–2725. 2749–2763.

Entire dissent from a statement that the insufficiency of the Dublin improvement rate is due to the construction of new streets of a low class, *Stokes* 3173–3175. 3241–3244.

Effect of the unduly low valuation in rendering the improvement rate of 2 *s.* in the 1 *l.* altogether inadequate to meet the demands upon it, *Sullivan* 4672. 4682——Operation of the Dublin Improvement Act since 1st January 1851, it having been passed in 1849, *Neville* 5362.

Statement on the question of a transfer of 2,482 *l.* 12 *s.* 8 *d.* from the north and south sewers rate being included in the improvement rate of 52,909 *l.*, *Robinson* 2727–2739

Explanation that a transfer of 2,482 *l.* 12 *s.* 8 *d.* from the sewers' rate to the credit of the improvement fund was made in order to recoup a previous advance from the latter fund, *O'Donnell* 2741–2746. 3400; *Norwood* 6091——The above item is in addition to the amount of 52,909 *l.* realised by the improvement rate in the year 1874–75, *O'Donnell* 2747, 2748.

Transfer or loan of 2,800 *l.* from the sewer rate to the improvement rate; irregularity of this transaction, *Stokes* 3192, 3193.

Return showing the amount received and placed at the credit of the improvement rate during the years 1851–68, and the sum which remained applicable after deducting certain charges for the lighting, cleansing, repair, and maintenance of the streets, *App.* 404, 405.

Industrial Dwellings Company. Explanation in connection with the ill success of the Industrial Dwellings Company in Dublin; private enterprise in this direction, *M'Evoy* 1973–1980. 2081–2085.

Irish Lights Board. Constitution of the Irish Lights Board, the members being self-elected, *Henry* 1310——Jurisdiction of the Board all round Ireland, *ib.* 1563, 1564.

J.

Jury Lists. Effect of an increased valuation in adding to the number of ratepayers on the jury lists, *Greene* 6924–6927.

K.

Kingstown. Explanations relative to several disallowances by witness in the case of Kingstown, *Finlay* 4393, 4394. 4402——Exceptions taken to a double payment by the Kingstown Commissioners to their former secretary, *ib.* 4394.

Kingstown—continued.

Comments made by witness in his report upon the conduct of one of the commissioners in reference to an arrear of rates upon a house purchased by him; complaint made by the commissioners to the Local Government Board relative to this report, the Board, however, not objecting to it, *Finlay* 4394–4401.

Confirmation, on appeal, of witness' disallowance of the expense incurred for advertisements and costs in connection with an abortive Bill which the Town Commissioners of Kingstown had promoted, *Finlay* 4402. 4476, 4477. 4573.

L

Labourers (*Dublin*). Want of a more efficient superintendence of workmen by the Dublin Corporation, *M'Evoy* 2073——Better labourers under the Rathmines Commissioners than under the Corporation of Dublin, *Stokes* 2904, 2905.

Land Tenure (*Ireland*) *Bill*. Statement in justification of the action of the Dublin Town Council in petitioning in favour of the Land Tenure (Ireland) Bill, *Gray* 6325–6331. 6676–6688.

Lawler, Mr. Statement as to Mr. Lawler, secretary of the Waterworks Committee (Dublin), being brother of a late town councillor, *M'Evoy* 1920–1930.

Legislation. Suggestions for an amendment of the Towns Improvement Act, concurrently with a repeal of the Local Acts since passed in order to supply the deficiencies of the former, *Hancock* 86, 87. 90, 91——Great number of Local Acts for different towns in Ireland, there being also numerous General Acts relating to sewers, water supply, the removal of nuisances, &c.; duplicate or cumulative provisions thus requiring simplification, *ib.* 776–781——Opportunity for sweeping away duplicate powers at the time of the passing of the Sanitary Act of 1866, *ib.* 781, 782——Approval of an assimilation of the different systems of town government being extended so as to embrace all towns down to those with 1,500 inhabitants, *Hancock* 905–910.

Table, submitted by Dr. Hancock, showing duplicate or cumulative provisions conferring executory powers on town authorities, *App.* 401.

See also Act 9 *Geo.* 4, *c.* 82. *Act* 3 & 4 *Vict.*, c. 108. *Act* 12 & 13 *Vict.* (1849). *Act* 17 & 18 *Vict.*, c. 103. *Local Acts.* *Provisional Orders.*

Licensed Work (*Dublin*). Explanation of the practice in executing and charging for paving or other licensed work done by the corporation for private individuals; belief that the full cost is always charged, *Neville* 5613–5619.

Liffey, The. Opinion that something should be done towards improving the condition of the river, before adopting a costly main drainage scheme, *Pim* 2399, 2400——Very injurious effect of the present state of the Liffey upon the health of Dublin, *Grimshaw* 4249–4252.

Explanation of a small item of expenditure by No. 1 Committee of the corporation upon the cleansing of the Liffey, *Gray* 6473.

See also Main Drainage.

Lighting of Dublin. See *Gas Bills and Gas Supply.*

Lisburn. Recent instance at Lisburn of the hardship through the grand jury objecting to an outlay for flagging the footways, *Hancock*, 881–886 — Statement as to the authority of the court-leet in Lisburn extending beyond the area of the town authority, *ib.* 976, 977. 994–996.

Local Acts. Local Acts obtained by Kingstown, Belfast, Dublin, and other places, instead of remaining under the Act of 1828, *Hancock* 26——Suggested repeal of the various Local Acts since the Town Improvement Act of 1854, this Act being at the same time amended, *ib.* 86, 87. 90, 91.

Local Government Board. Proposal with a view to the Local Government Board passing general enactments, of which the smaller towns may avail themselves, *Hancock* 79–82——Consideration of objections to witness' proposal that the Local Government Board should obtain power for extending to small towns the provisions of Acts already sanctioned for large towns; check through the Board upon undue interference with private rights, *ib.* 891–904.

Advantage if the Local Government Board were strengthened in Dublin, so that it might advise and instruct the local authorities upon all difficult questions, *M'Evoy* 1711–1713.

Illustrations of the unsatisfactory way in which some of the inspectors, under the Local Government

Local Government Board—continued.

Government Board in Dublin, conduct inquiries when nuisances are brought to their notice, *Grimshaw* 4056-4058. 4114-4125. 4234. 4235——General character of the supervision exercised over the Public Health Committee by the Local Government Board, *ib.* 4207, 4208.

Inaccuracy of a statement that the inspector of the Local Government Board does not properly investigate cases, *Boyle* 5245-5249.

See also Audit. Sanitary Administration, I. 2.

Local Inquiry. Conclusion of the Committee that a material portion of their inquiry could be more advantageously and conveniently conducted by means of a local investigation, *Rep.* iii.——Suggestions as to the scope of the proposed inquiry, *ib.*

Londonderry. Anomaly as regards the effect of the Municipal Reform Act in the case of Londonderry, which was not strictly a county of a city, *Hancock* 594-596.

Lord Mayors (Dublin). Alternate selection of Protestant and Roman Catholic lord mayors since 1849, *Henry* 1228-1238. 1579-1583. 1631-1642——Increase of the lord mayor's salary by 200 guineas, in order that he may have a secretary, *ib.* 1419.

Comment upon the increase of the lord mayor's salary in consideration of his paying the salary of his secretary, and of the latter handing over his fees to the corporation; small amount handed over as compared with the extra payment to the lord mayor, *Finlay* 4297, 4298. 4436-4439.

The salary of the lord mayor is too low, *Sullivan* 4750——Illustration in the election of lord mayors, of the liberal action of the corporation, irrespectively of politics, *ib.* 4766-4769.

Increase of the lord mayor's salary in order that he might pay his secretary instead of the latter being paid by fees, *Gray* 6320-6322——Special liberality evinced in the alternate selection of the lord mayor from the minority in the council, *ib.* 6378.

Lord Mayor's Court. Amendment proposed by No. 3 Committee in the jurisdiction and procedure of the lord mayor's court, *Norwood* 5951.

Lunatic Asylums (Dublin). Details relative to the expenditure charged upon the grand jury cess on account of lunatic asylums and the causes of the increased payments in 1874-75; *O'Donnell* 3418-3426——*See* also *Richmond District Lunatic Asylum.*

Lurgan. Explanation as to witness having advised the town of Lurgan not to apply for a charter, this town still being under the Act of 1854, *Hancock* 21-23.

M.

M'Anaspie, Mr. (Dublin Corporation). Conviction obtained against Mr. McAnaspie in respect of a nuisance from a manure heap, *Boyle* 5126-5130.

McCann, Mr. Charge of misappropriation consequent upon the audit of the accounts for 1871-72, in the case of Mr. McCann, collector of the cattle market; report of the auditor, containing strong comments upon this case, *Robinson* 3447-3450. 3463.

Discovery by witness in his audit of the City of Dublin accounts for 1872, that certain market tolls had not been duly accounted for by the superintendent of the market; regulation adopted, at witness' suggestion, for preventing similar defalcations in future, *Finlay* 4268-4272——Failure of duty in the foregoing matter on the part of Mr. Robinson, secretary to No. 2 Committee of the corporation, *ib.* 4271. 4273.

M'Evoy, John. (Analysis of his Evidence.)—Considerable interest taken by witness, who is a merchant in Dublin, in the municipal government of that city and of Kingstown, 1653-1656——Exclusion of the upper and middle classes from their fair share in the municipal administration under the present system, 1657, 1658——Argument as to the expediency of a direct representation of the large rated proprietors in the management of the rates; reference especially to Government buildings, breweries, banks, colleges, and other large institutions, 1661, 1662.

Suggestion that in Dublin there should be a direct representation of Government, as contributing very largely to the rates, 1661——Numerous large buildings and institutions in Dublin which are heavily rated, but are unrepresented in the expenditure of the money, 1661——Proposition for a re-arrangement of the wards in Dublin, with a view to a fair representation of property of large rateable value, 1662.

Grounds for the conclusion that all occupiers should have a vote, save the occupiers of small houses unfit for habitation, or of houses under 4 *l.* rateable value, 1662-1674. 1762-1790——Very poor character of the houses in Cole-alley, their contribution to the rates being exceedingly small; expediency of a limitation of the franchise in this case, 1662-1668. 1762-1767——Prospect of all houses in Ireland being raised to the 4 *l.* limit under a reformed local administration, 1674. 1770.

M'Evoy, John. (Analysis of his Evidence)—*continued*.

Difficulty of the question whether it is the owner or occupier who really pays the rates when the former is not directly rated, 1675–1677——Several charges which are or may be put upon the property in Dublin, it being only fair that there should be a property franchise, 1677——Conclusion that instead of the immediate lessor, every person possessing a beneficial interest of 50 *l.* and upwards in house property should have a vote, *ib.*

Evidence in favour of a non-residential occupancy franchise, the qualification to be fixed at a much higher amount than that for residential occupiers, 1677. 1814–1820. 1822——Illustration in the case of the Royal Exchange ward of the unduly large representation of small ratepayers not friendly to sanitary improvement, 1678–1681——Large amount of valuable property in the occupation of females, it being expedient that these should possess the municipal franchise, as in England, 1681

Suggested increase of the qualification for members of the corporation; opinion favourable to the adoption of the special juror's qualification, which is 50 *l.* in Dublin, 1682. 1823–1838——Expediency of the property qualification for the corporation being out of property in exclusive possession; this would disqualify hotel keepers and tavern proprietors, 1682——Amendment suggested in the bankruptcy disqualification, *ib.*——Advantage if the same person were not eligible for election to several different boards or local bodies, *ib.*

Exceptions taken to the working of the system of Government valuation in Ireland, as compared with the local valuations in England; disfranchising effect in Ireland in the case of large buildings let out in offices, 1682–1692. 1749–1757. 1791–1802——Statement as to Commercial Buildings in Dublin being rated to only one person and conferring only one vote, 1683–1685. 1749–1753. 2024, 2025——Numerous instances in Dublin of persons occupying separate offices who are not separately rated, amendment being much required by the enfranchisement of these persons, 1686–1692. 1791–1802.

Entire want of public confidence in the corporation of Dublin as at present constituted, 1693——Comment upon the circumstance of a Market Bill being promoted by some private individuals instead of by the corporation, 1693–1695——Urgent need felt for a Government audit of the city accounts, though in England the local corporations audit their own accounts, 1696——Excessive expenditure incurred in promoting and opposing Private Bills, the check of the auditor being very useful in this respect, 1695–1709. 1998–2005——Grounds for objecting to an expenditure of 68 *l.* in opposing the Bray and Enniskerry Railway Bill, 1695, 1696. 1698–1708. 1998–2000——Exceptions taken to the contribution of 500 *l.* out of the city funds to the French relief fund during the war, 1696. 1874, 1875. 1991–1997.

Disapproval of the present system of appeal from the auditor's decision; suggested appeal to a court of law, 1710. 1712, 1713——Advantage if the Local Government Board were strengthened in Dublin so that it might advise and instruct the local authorities upon all difficult questions, 1711–1713.

Reference to a letter from Master Fitzgibbon, auditor of the Collector General's Accounts, in which complaint is made as to the inefficiency of the audit, 1714–1718. 1729——Comments made by witness (through the press) upon the very unsatisfactory character of the Collector General's report, and upon the laxity in collection of the rates; statement also in Master Fitzgibbon's letter as to the excessive arrears and the undue loss in collection, 1716–1729——Conclusion as to the expediency of the several representative bodies being responsible for the collection of their own rates, 1729. 1732–1734——Great increase in the cost of the Collector General's office, only half the charge being for the collectors' salaries, 1734.

Grounds for the conclusion that it would be a great improvement if the burgess list were revised by the revising barrister for Parliamentary purposes, 1735——Suggestion also that the residential period be reduced to twelvemonths, *ib.*

Strong objections to the present practice of appointment and dismissal of municipal officers, 1736–1739——Great improvement if these appointments were subject to a competitive or qualifying examination, 1736–1739. 1743——Advantage if the salary were fixed at a certain sum, increasing by yearly increments, 1736.

Importance of inquiry by the Local Government Board in cases of misconduct, and of a power of dismissal, 1738. 1739–1742. 1744——Patronage exercised in municipal appointments in Dublin, there being no examination, and no security for competency; frequent appointment of relations of aldermen or town councillors, 1737, 1738——Circumstance of there being an examination for county surveyorships, 1738. 1747, 1748.

Expediency of a complete re-valuation, the present valuation being very low and unequal, 1754–1781——Effect of the present system in discouraging building improvements, 1755–1757——Consideration of objections to the proposal that occupiers of houses in large towns generally under 4 *l.* rateable value, should not exercise the franchise in municipal or sanitary matters, 1771–1789.

Particulars as to the circumstances under which the arrangement for a re-distribution of the Dublin wards was agreed to in 1849; eventual adoption of the English principle,

MEvoy, John. (Analysis of his Evidence)—*continued*.

1803–1812——Heavy costs charged upon the rates in respect of the three Bills which had been promoted relative to the re-arrangement of the wards, 1812, 1813.

Advantage of extending the residential limit for the municipal franchise to fifteen miles round Dublin, 1841——Statement as to Master Fitzgibbon having contended that his functions as auditor entitled him to see that the rates were properly collected, 1839–1849——Power of the Lord Lieutenant to call the Collector General to account, 1850, 1851——Instances of complaints by boards of guardians against the system of collection, the Collector General being, however, totally independent of all the local bodies 1852–1855. 2006–2008.

Limited powers of the former elected auditors as to checking illegal expenditure; power of appeal in the ratepayers, 1856–1864——Power of the auditor of the Local Government Board to decide important questions as to the legality of payments, 1865–1869——Objection raised by witness as regards an expenditure of 7,000 *l.* in connection with Essex Bridge; this question has been decided against the corporation by the auditor, 1870–1873.

Explanation as regards certain instances of objectionable expenditure, that witness would not question these items if the corporation were a properly elected body, 1874–1883——Consideration of the character of the opposition to the Vartry water scheme; witness not concurring in the view that the great majority of the upper classes were vehement opponents, 1884–1894. 2052.

Circumstances of witness not being now chairman of the Kingstown Commissioners, 1895–1898—— Heavy costs incurred in connection with an Improvement Bill for Kingstown, 1899–1902——Further reference to the very defective constitution of the corporation; very few of the leading merchants of the city in the council, 1903–1910.

Examination in support of the statement that officers of the corporation had been appointed through relationship with members of the corporation or through other interest, 1911–1953——Very poor character of the houses in Cole-alley further adverted to, 1954–1961——Belief that generally the officers of the corporation take no part in politics, 1962–1965.

Explanation in connection with the ill success of the Industrial Dwellings Company in Dublin, 1966–1972——Great want of public retail markets; private enterprise in this direction, 1973–1980. 2081–2085——Statement to the effect that the corporation did not apply for, and were not favourable to the appointment of a public auditor, 1981–1988. 2086——Further statement as to the expediency of the occupiers of offices being rated separately, 1989, 1990——Objection by the leading merchants to enter the corporation on account partly of the political discussions which arise, 2009, 2010.

Further comment upon the Collector General's Report, though some errors in printing may explain away some of witness' objections, 2011–2016——Erroneous impression of witness in supposing that salaries of corporation officers could not be increased without consent of the Lord Lieutenant, 2017–2019. 2026, 2027——Conclusion that a cost of 6 *d.* in the pound for collection of the rates is very excessive, 2020–2022——Way in which the Collector General's staff might be distributed if the office were not retained as a separate department, 2023.

Strong approval of cumulative voting, 2029, 2030——Examination in further support of excluding from the franchise occupiers of small houses under 4 *l.* value in large towns generally, but not in small towns, 2031–2047——Further opinion in favour of disallowing election for several boards, 2048–2051——Twofold cost of the Vartry scheme beyond the estimates, 2053, 2054.

Importance of a strict audit of the Collector General's accounts as a means of reducing the arrears, 2055–2057——Comment upon the small increase in the rental from the borough estates, 2058, 2059. 2089——Practice as to new leases and as to obtaining Treasury sanction, 2060, 2061. 2091, 2092——Advantage if some of the estates were sold in order to pay off the debenture debt, 2062, 2063.

General feeling in Dublin that the corporation has neglected its duties in sanitary matters; instances of omission in this respect, 2064–2066——Statement as to the Improvement Rate Fund being much in debt, 2067–2069——Objectionable practice of paying one account by transfer from another, 2070–2072——Large increase of salaries between 1863 and 1876, the staff of officers being now too large, 2073——Want of a more efficient superintendence of workmen, *ib.*——Unduly heavy burden on the rates in respect of pensions; grounds for this statement, 2073–2077. 2095–2104.

Circumstance of the corporation not having utilised the powers which they have inherited from the Wide Streets Commissioners, 2078–2080——Expediency of a revaluation extending to all Ireland, 2087, 2088——Failure of the corporation to make the most of the Baldoyle property, 2089–2091. 2094——Prospect of a large increase from some of the corporation property in Dublin, 2093.

Report, 1876—*continued.*

M'Evoy, Mr. Constant opposition on the part of Mr. M'Evoy to the various improvemen schemes of the corporation, *Neville* 5827–5830.

M'Grath, Mr. (*Dublin Corporation*). Circumstances under which a former member of the Public Health Committee (Mr. M'Grath) was summoned by witness and compelled to abate a nuisance at some tenement premises, *Boyle* 5122–5125.

Magistrates. Statement as to the city magistrates of Dublin not exercising any criminal powers, nor sitting in the public courts, *Hancock* 1062–1065.

MAIN DRAINAGE (DUBLIN):

Explanation in reference to the main drainage scheme, and the cause of its breakdown; great cost involved in the plan over and above the estimates, *Stokes* 3245–3249. 3367–3372——Information relative to the appointment and action of the Citizens' Main Drainage Committee; conclusion as to certain resolutions adopted by the committee having shown a want of confidence in the corporation, *Grimshaw* 4253–4261.

Comment upon the opposition experienced by the corporation in reference to the main drainage scheme, for the cleansing of the Liffey; examination hereon, *Sullivan* 4681. 4727–4744——Disapproval of the hesitation shown in carrying out Mr. Bazalgette's scheme, notwithstanding that the cost will be enormously in excess of the Parliamentary Estimate, *ib.* 4736. 4739–4744——Necessary character of a large portion of the increased cost of the scheme beyond the original estimates; that is, on account of the large advance of materials, *ib.* 4835–4890.

Depreciation of any abandonment of the main drainage scheme as sanctioned by Parliament after great labour and expense had been incurred, *Neville* 5490——Causes of the great excess of the tenders for the works beyond the Parliamentary Estimates which were made in 1870, *ib.* 5491–5494——Conclusion that the scheme may now be carried out for about 430,000 *l.*, *ib.* 5493.

Evidence showing that there was no engineering difficulty in carrying out the scheme, and no error whatever in the levels, *Neville* 5495——Date upon which the tenders reserved for the works were estimated; reduced prices on which new tenders would be based, *ib.* 5575–5580.

Examination relative to the progress made by the corporation with the main drainage scheme since its inception and as to the causes which prevented the receipt of tenders till the year 1873, the Act having been obtained in 1871, *Neville* 5655–5672. 5844–5847——Agitation in 1874 against the scheme; eventual determination to ask for a Royal Commission on the subject, *ib.* 5673–5681.

Consent of Government to increased borrowing powers in the corporation on condition of their obtaining a Bill for carrying out the works; cause of the failure of the Bill promoted for this purpose in 1875, *Neville* 5682–5694——Hitch at present through the Public Works Loans Commissioners considering the security insufficient, *ib.* 5838–5843.

Resolution adopted by a Committee of the whole house, asking for the appointment of a Royal Commission upon the main drainage of Dublin and its vicinity, *Norwood* 5876——Explanation of the steps taken by the corporation at different times upon the question of obtaining a Royal Commission relative to the main drainage; further application about to be made for a commission, *ib.* 6168–6172.

Evidence strongly in favour of the scheme as approved by Sir Joseph Bazalgette and other high authorities, rather than of any other scheme which has been proposed for the drainage of the city and the purification of the Liffey, *Norwood* 6265–6272——Reduced cost at which the approved scheme may now be carried out, *ib.* 6268. 6270——Prejudicial effect if the request of the Citizens' Committee for a Royal Commission on the main drainage had been acceded to, *ib.* 6269.

See also Liffey, The.

Main Drainage Rate. Belief that there is no limit as regards the main drainage rate, *Meylan* 265. 266——Levy of the main drainage rate for two years at 4 *d.* in the pound, and for two other years at 2 *d.* in the pound, *Taafe* 487–489.

Mansion House (*Dublin*). Varying annual charge for repairs at the Mansion House, and for furniture, &c., *Robinson* 3392–3394.

Manure Manufacturers (*Dublin*). Reference to the manure manufactories in the city as not now constituting any nuisances, *Boyle* 5091–5097.

See also Sanitary Administration, I. 8.

Marine Store Dealers (*Dublin*). Steps taken by witness, when in the Dublin Corporation, with a view to enforcing the law as to the registration of marine store dealers, *Sullivan* 4688.

Markets. Powers still retained by the corporations generally in regard to regulating markets and levying tolls, *Hancock* 615–623.

Comment upon the circumstance of a Market Bill for Dublin being promoted by some private individuals instead of by the corporation, *M'Evoy* 1693–1695——Explanations relative to certain suggestions by No. 2 Committee of the corporation, as embodied in a Bill in 1868, for improved market regulations, &c., *Norwood* 5947–5949.

See also *Cattle Market.*

MATERIALS (DUBLIN STREETS):

1. *Price.*
2. *Quality.*

1. *Price :*

Much higher prices paid in the city than in Rathmines for materials, the corporation taking credit and the commissioners paying cash, *Stokes* 2899–2903. 3008–3013. 3223, 3224. 3278–3290——Decided economy in the purchase of materials if the corporation had put themselves in funds by means of a loan, *ib.* 3013–3018. 3225–3229.

Particulars relative to the great increase since 1851 in the price of street materials and of wages, *Neville* 5390–5404. 5435——Advantage of increased borrowing powers so that materials may be purchased at cash prices; saving to be effected thereby, *ib.* 5443–5456——Small increase of the corporation prices beyond those of the Rathmines commissioners, *ib.* 5444. 5454——Every effort is now made by the corporation to contract for materials at the cheapest rate, *ib.* 5455, 5456.

Particulars relative to the quality and cost of the stone used for repairing the streets; reasons for the price being higher than that paid by the Rathmines commissioners, *Neville* 5621–5629——Explanation as to the lower price paid in Rathmines than in the city for gravel, *ib.* 5634–5637.

Further information relative to the price and quality of bricks and stone as now purchased by the corporation; great advance in prices, *Neville* 5761–5769——Very small increase in the cost of materials owing to cash not being paid, *Gray* 6453–6455.

2. *Quality :*

Explanation as regards the scavenging and cleansing of the city that the bad condition of Dublin in this repect is mainly owing to the very inferior quality of the stone used for the streets, *Sullivan* 4668. 4670——Undue cost of stone from Wales, though far superior to the Dublin stone, *ib.* 4668–4670.

Special circumstances which enhance the difficulty of scavenging in Dublin, *Neville* 5559, 5560——Inferior character of the material available for macadamising, *ib.* 5561–5563——The Bonabreena stone is very hard and does not bind well, *ib.* 5621, 5622. 5822–5824.

Further reference to the unsuitable quality of some of the stone used for macadamising the streets, *Neville* 5821–5824.

Maryborough. Irregularities of expenditure and account in the case of Maryborough, *Finlay* 4634–4637.

Meat, Inspection of (Dublin). Duties of the Public Health Committee in reference to the analysis of food and the inspection of meat; impression that the latter work is very well done, *Grimshaw* 4177–4179. 4184, 4185——Several imprisonments for the sale or possession of unsound meat, *Boyle* 4929——Increased sanitary staff required for preventing the sale of unsound meat, *ib.* 5014, 5015.

Medical Sanitary Staff. See *Sanitary Administration,* I. 4. 12.

Misapplication of Funds. Absence of power to punish for misapplication of municipal funds, save by legal proceedings on the part of the burgesses or ratepayers, *Finlay* 4558–4566.——*See* also *Accounts. Audit.*

Morgan, Francis. (Analysis of his Evidence.)—Experience of witness for thirty-three years as law and land agent for the Corporation of Dublin, 3494–3496——Enumeration of the different estates and lands owned by the corporation outside the municipal limits, 3497–3502——Summary of the ancient revenues of the corporation as acquired under Royal Charter; various holdings comprised and amount derived in each case, 3503–3505——Produce of about 18,000 *l.* a year by the landed estates, after various deductions, but without allowing for poor rate and income tax, 3506–3515——Inability of witness to explain the deduction under the head of Pell's Poundage, 3516–3519.

Details relative to the area, valuation, rental, &c., of the Ballycoolane estate; large increase of revenue to be derived in 1880 when many of the leases fall in, 3520–3535——Particulars in connection with the Clontarf property, which comprises 386 acres; circumstances under which certain leases have been granted and renewed, the result being that the present rents are far below the value, 3536 *et seq.*

Explanation

Morgan, Francis. (Analysis of his Evidence)—*continued.*

Explanation relative to the re-letting of All Hallowes College, on the Clonturk Estate, to the late Rev. J. Hand in 1852, on lease for 1,000 years at a renewed rent of 10 *l.* an acre; consent of the Treasury in this case, 3546-3560. 3812-3826——Particulars as to the circumstances under which a new lease was granted to Thomas Doolan in 1854, for sixty-six years, in respect of some property at Clonturk previously under lease to Mr. Duval; rental of 70 *l.* in this case, Mr. Dooley having since sold his interest under the lease for 3,000 *l.*; 3561-3581.

Details in connection with land and premises at Clonturk leased to Blaney Mitchell in 1862 for thirty-one years at a rental of 40 *l.* 16 *s.* 6 *d.*; relation between this rent and the valuation of the property, 3582-3602. 3809-3812——Information relative to Lord Charlemont's tenure of the property at Marino, and the rent paid in proportion to the valuation, 3603-3608——Area of fifty-five acres comprised in some wet lots, called North Liffey Strand, which were sold by the corporation in 1717, but have never been enclosed or utilised; expediency of the corporation re-entering into possession of this land, 3607-3620.

Area of 621 acres comprised in the Baldoyle property; this property was re-let to sixteen tenants in 1855 on leases for thirty-one years, 3621, 3622——Considerable advance in 1855 upon the former rents; unduly high rents obtained owing to the competition by public auction, so that it became necessary to apply to Parliament for power to reduce the rents, 3623-3654——Particulars relative to certain of the Baldoyle lettings in 1856, the rent as compared with the valuation, and the subsequent reductions allowed, 3627-3638. 3720-3775. 3827-3838.

Transfer of Mr. Darley's holding at Baldoyle to Mr. Van den Eynde; reduction allowed in this case, 3635. 3648-3651. 3740, 3741. 3770, 3771. 3834-3837——Explanation in regard to the land leased to Lord Annaly at Baldoyle having been sublet by him to Mr. Lane Joynt and two other persons, and as to the reduction of rent allowed in this case, 3636-3647. 3729-3738. 3772-3775. 3874-3876——Covenant in the Baldoyle leases that the holdings are not to be sublet without consent of the corporation, 3655——Information relative to the tenure of the town parks at Baldoyle, these lands being worth about 4 *l.* an Irish acre, 3656-3658. 3827-3833.

Area of about 200 acres comprised in the Colganston property; steps being taken for re-letting this land, 3659. 3660——Good condition of the Ringwood property, 3660——Statement as to the claim of the corporation to the Bagotrath property, which is now held by Lord Pembroke, and is exceedingly valuable; expediency of this claim being re-urged, 3661-3664. 3683-3691——Unexpired lease of nearly 100 years in the case of the Custom House, 3665——Rental of only 36 *l.* 4 *s.* 7 *d.* now produced by the Oxmantown property, whereas on expiration of the lease in 1881 about 4,000 *l.* a year will be obtained, 3665-3668. 3869-3873.

Increase of about 1,000 *l.* a year in the rental from the estates since 1867, 3669-3671——Application recently made to the Treasury to appoint a valuator in order to fix the value of several properties nearly out of lease, instead of their being put up to public auction, 3672, 3673——Lease for thirty-one years granted in the case of tenements, and for seventy-five years in the case of re-building, 3674——Information relative to certain sales of corporation property, the proceeds having been invested in the purchase of city debentures, 3675-3682.

Summary of the proceedings in connection with the Corporation Bill of 1864 in reference to the reduction of the Baldoyle rents; several amendments adopted during the progress of the Bill through Parliament, 3692-3719——Explanation in connection with the clause in the Bill of 1864 relative to Mr. Crampton's lease, and the reduction to be made in his rent in consideration of a large expenditure by him in building; relative rent and valuation in this case, 3705-3729. 3743-3761. 3761, 3762.

Further statement of the circumstances under which the Baldoyle holdings were re-let by public auction in 1855, witness submitting that the rents obtained were excessive, 3762-3769——Explanation as to James Duffy, one of the Baldoyle tenants, not having claimed any reduction, though his rent is more than 4 *l.* an acre, 3762-3768.

Very limited extent, if any, to which witness exercises the functions of land agent in connection with the corporation estates; be neither receives nor collects the Baldoyle rents, and is not placed in a position to carry out any efficient inspection of the property, 3778-3791——Duties discharged by the city treasurer in the collection of the Baldoyle rents, the recovery of arrears, &c.; allowance of ten per cent. to Mr. Patrick Butterly for collection of the small weekly rents, 3778-3780. 3795-3800——Very imperfect inspection of the property by the corporation personally, 3792-3794.

Great want of some new cottages at Baldoyle; enhanced value of the holdings thereby, 3794. 3804, 3805. 3854, 3855. 3867——Explanation relative to some arrears in the collection of the weekly rents at Baldoyle; wretched character of this property, 3801-3804. 3806. 3855. 3865-3867——Exceptional instance of a very low rent at Baldoyle in the case of Patrick Butterly, 3829-3833——Retrospective operation of the Act of 1864, relative to the Baldoyle rents, 3838-3841.

Several

Morgan, Francis. (Analysis of his Evidence)—*continued.*

Several instances of very poor or old property in Dublin let at low rents in reference to the valuation; absence of competition in some cases where the rents are low, 3842-3852——Absence of stringent covenants in the old leases as to repairs and maintenance, 3853. 3856——Want of more efficient inspection of the city property generally; obstacle to this being undertaken by witness or by the city architect, 3856-3859.

Calculation by witness that the corporation would save over 1,000 *l.* a year by selling property at Baldoyle and elsewhere, and by paying off their debenture debt, 3860-3864.

Mountjoy-square Sewer. Complaint made by Mr. Dennehy as to the state of the Mountjoy-square sewer; necessary delay in applying a remedy, *Neville* 5741-5744.

Mountmellick. Satisfactory local management in Mountmellick, *Finlay* 4634.

Moylan, Denis, and M. P. V. Taafe. (Analysis of their Evidence.)—(*Mr. Moylan.*) Functions of witness as Collector General of Rates in Dublin under the Act 12 & 13 Vict. c. 91, s. 63; 231-233. 236——Staff of ten collectors under witness, 234——Summary of the various rates collected, and of the amount in each case, 237. 240-247——Consolidated system of collection under the Act 12 & 13 Vict., there having been several collectors previously for the different authorities, 238, 239.

Limitation of the improvement rate of the corporation to 2 *s.* in the pound, 240-242——There is no limit to the grand jury cess, 243——The water rate for domestic purposes is fixed at 1 *s.* in the pound, the public rate being 3 *d.*, 244-246——Small amount of the burial rate, this being expended by the corporation, 247-251.

(*Mr. Taafe.*) Witness is chief clerk in the Collector General's office, 252——He explains that the burial rate is expended by the Public Health Committee of the corporation, 253.

(*Mr. Moylan* and *Mr. Taafe.*) Explanation in connection with the bridge rate; its amount and mode of application, 254-262——Small amount and temporary character of the vestry cess, 263. 264——Varying amount raised annually by the different rates; total of 213,000 *l.* in 1870, and of 276,000 *l.* in 1874; 265-268. 275-281. 287——(*Mr. Taafe.*) Amount of each rate in the years 1870 and 1871, respectively, 270-274. 378.

(*Mr. Taafe* and *Mr. Moylan.*) Annual loss of about eight per cent. of the amount levied, about half this loss being due to the operation of bills of sale and the system of tenement houses, 284-298——(*Mr. Taafe.*) Liability of the occupier for the rate, if the premises are valued over 8 *l.*, and if he is a yearly tenant, 299——Liability of the owner where the premises are over 4 *l.* and under 8 *l.* in value; practice, however, of rating the occupier as well as the owner in these cases, if the former be a yearly tenant, 300-316. 332-339.

Explanation as to occupiers who are weekly or monthly tenants not being entered in the rate-book; authority of Judge Barry for this course, 317-321. 332-339——Difficulty as to collection in the case only of the low class of property, 322-324——Statement as to political or registration agents serving numerous claims to be rated, and tendering at the same time a portion of the poor rate, though the money is never paid; belief that these claims are admitted by the revising barrister, 325-331. 372-377. 462-466.

Considerable number of weekly or monthly tenants excluded from the rate book and from the Parliamentary roll; duty of the collectors to supply information as to such tenants, 339-353.

Further particulars relative to the extensive evasion of rates in the case of tenement houses; that is, through the system of sham immediate lessors, 354-365. 473. 491, 492——Further reference also to the effect of bills of sale in preventing recovery of rates, 366-369——Means suggested for remedying the abuse in respect of recovery from immediate lessors, by rendering liable the person in beneficial receipt of the rack rent; consideration of objections thereto, 370, 371. 409-415. 420-434——Belief as to there being a hackney carriage tax in Dublin, 379, 380——Doubt as to a rate being levied for the purposes of science and art, or for a free library and museum, 381-383.

(*Mr. Taafe* and *Mr. Moylan.*) Refusal to rate a weekly or monthly tenant, even though he may tender the rate; that is, upon the authority of Judge Barry and Judge Warren, 384-401. 406-408——Statement to the effect that the legal opinion in the foregoing matter can be produced to the Committee, 395-401——(*Mr. Taafe.*) Practice as to appearance in support of their claims in the case of persons objected to as regards the Parliamentary and municipal franchise, respectively, 402-405.

(*Mr. Taafe* and *Mr. Moylan.*) Considerable number of fraudulent immediate lessors, 416-419——(*Mr. Taafe.*) Information obtained through the collectors, as well as directly by witness, as to the terms of letting between the head landlord and the immediate lessor, and as to the tenancies being weekly or monthly, 420-432. 451-461——Statement as to the impracticability of witness' department getting into possession of tenement houses and

Moylan, Denis, and M. P. V. Taafe. (Analysis of their Evidence)—*continued.*

and receiving the weekly or monthly rents; failure of steps taken in this direction, 435–450.

Indirect effect, as regards increase of the franchise, of the proposal for remedying the evasion on the part of immediate lessors, 467, 468. 547–550——Absence of power under the collection of Rates Act to compound with the owners in the case of weekly tenants, 469——Explanation that all yearly tenants not under 4 *l.* are rated, preliminary to payment, 470, 471. 531–541. 557. 562–565——Necessity of those who are on the rate book paying the rates before they can claim the franchise, 470–473——Numerous claims by registration agents, some being served in duplicate, each claim being investigated by the collector, 474–482. 551–554.

Levy of the bridge rate, at 2 *d.* in the pound, for three years, for the building of Grattan Bridge, 483–486——Levy of the main drainage rate for two years at 4 *d.* in the pound, and for two other years at 2 *d.* in the pound, 487–489——Practice as to lodging the amounts collected to separate accounts in the bank, 489, 490. 521–525——(Mr. *Taafe* and Mr. *Moylan.*) Statement as to the amount realised by the bridge rate, and as to its being collected from the entire metropolitan police district, 492–496. 498. 570——Provision in the Collection of Rates Act for the collection of the police tax outside as well as within the municipal area, 497. 569.

Power to be given to the owner to recover from the tenant under the proposal for rendering the former liable to payment on default of the latter, 499–501——(Mr. *Taafe.*) Conclusion as to its being useless merely to give power to the occupier to recover from the owner, 502–505——Maximum at which several rates have been levied since 1870, whilst the grand jury cess and poor rate have been increased, 506–509. 519, 520. 566.

(Mr. *Taafe* and Mr. *Moylan*). Limit of the cost of collection of the rates to two and a-half per cent., the actual cost for the last five years or so having been always under this limit; much greater cost in previous years, 510–515——(Mr. *Moylan*). Recovery of a large sum from the corporation for water mains; also of a large sum from the Docks Board, 516–518——(Mr. *Taafe.*) Check through the auditor upon the allocation of the rates, 521–523.

Difficulty in some cases of ascertaining the owner's name, the word "owner" being entered temporarily in the rate book, 526–528——Practice of striking out the names of occupiers in arrear of poor rates, with reference to the Parliamentary franchise, 529, 530——Further statement as to weekly or monthly tenants tendering payment of the poor rate being placed on the rate book; that is, if they occupy the whole house, 531–546.

Separate estimates made for the north sewer rate and the south sewer rate, 558, 559——Explanation that the rate book takes no notice of the occupiers of premises under 4 *l.*, 562–565——Limited extent to which the increased amount collected is due to increased valuation, 566–568.

Municipal Area (Dublin). See *Area of Dublin.*

Municipal Council. See *Corporation of Dublin.*

Municipal Franchise. See *Franchise.*

N.

Naas. Comment upon the transfer of the property of the old corporation of Naas to the Protestant Orphan Society of Kildare, *Finlay* 4361, 4362. 4467–4469——Satisfactory local management in Naas, *ib.* 4632.

Neville, Park. (Analysis of his Evidence.)—Is Engineer and Surveyor to the City of Dublin, having held the appointment since 1851; 5359–5361——Operation of the Dublin Improvement Act since 1st January 1851, it having been passed in 1849; 5362——Retention by the corporation in 1851 of many of the officers previously employed by the Paving Board, the Wide Streets Board, and the term grand jury; charge incurred for compensation in respect of those officers whose services were dispensed with, 5363–5368——Limited powers of the Wide Streets Board as to levying rates and carrying out improvements, 5369——Power of the corporation to levy an improvement rate of 2 *s.* and a sewer rate of 4 *d.*, 5370.

Small staff employed by the corporation of Dublin as compared with other large municipalities, 5371——Total increase of salaries to the amount of 3,619 *l.* since 1851; that is, including several additional appointments, 5372, 5373——Expenditure of about 11,000 *l.* a year by the former Paving Board on the scavenging and watering of eighty-eight miles of streets, whilst the corporation spend 16,716 *l.* on 110 miles, 5374–5384. 5407——Fluctuation in the valuation and in the annual sum available for the paving, &c., of the streets under the Paving Board and under the corporation, 5385–5389.

Particulars

Neville, Park. (Analysis of his Evidence)—*continued.*

Particulars relative to the great increase since 1851 in the price of street materials and of wages, 5390–5407. 5435——Calculation that in proportion to the expenditure by the Paving Board on watering and scavenging, the expenditure by the corporation should be very much greater than it is, making allowance for the increased price of materials and labour and the increased mileage, 5407–5411——Calculation also that the cost of lighting is now much less per lamp than under the Paving Board, 5411–5417.

Large expenditure by the corporation on new pavements, the money having been raised under a certain clause in the Ballast Board Act of 1792, copied into the Port and Docks Act of 1869; 5418, 5419——Conclusion that the foregoing clause was not smuggled into the Act of 1869 by the corporation, 5419–5421. 5592–5596——Great improvements made by the corporation in the sewers out of the sewer rate of 4 *d.*; large outlay involved, 5422, 5423——Limited extent to which the corporation have been able to widen streets, 5425.

Statement of witness' powers from the corporation for preventing accidents from dilapidated houses; particulars as to the action taken in these cases, 5426. 5434——Explanations relative to the fall of two houses in George-street, near Messrs. Pims', and of a house in Sackville-street; belief that these were not reported to witness before they fell, 5427–5431. 5597–5600——Great want of a Building Act in Dublin, 5431*–5434——Steps being taken to promote a Building Bill next Session; cause of failure of a Bill promoted in 1867; 5432–5434.

Entire insufficiency of the funds at the disposal of the corporation for the proper maintenance of the streets, 5435–5438——Conclusion that the valuation is much too low and is very unequal; authority of Mr. Ball Greene to this effect, 5435. 5439–5441——Want of further borrowing powers for the construction of new markets and abattoirs, and for other purposes, 5442, 5443——Success of the new cattle market, built at a cost of about 25,000 *l.*, 5443. 5460.

Advantage of increased borrowing powers, so that materials may be purchased at cash prices; saving to be effected thereby, 5443–5456——Small increase of the corporation price beyond those of the Rathmines Commissioners, 5444. 5454——Every effort is now made by the corporation to contract for materials at the cheapest rate, 5455, 5456.

Inaccuracy of a statement by Mr. Stokes that the extension of the city area in 1850 had proved a great loss to the corporation; gradual increase in the rateable value of the district taken in, 5457. 5458——Importance of some means of reducing the loss of rates in collection, 5459——Obstacles to a system of domestic and street scavenging in Dublin, as in large towns in England, 5461–5465.

Defence of the course pursued by the corporation, and of the expenditure incurred in promoting and opposing Bills in Parliament, 5466–5468——Good reason for the opposition to the Bray and Enniskerry Railway Bill, 5467, 5468——Good ground also for the opposition to the Stephen's Green Bill of 1866; 5468.

Very heavy expenditure in promoting the Bills of 1860 and 1861 for an improved water supply; comment more especially upon the opposition to the Vartry Waterworks Bill, 5468–5472——Total of 541,400 *l.* as the cost of the Vartry works; several causes of the large excess of the original estimate, 5469——Inadequacy of the Coyford or the Ballysmutten scheme for the supply of the outlying townships, 5473. 5475——Abundant supply from the Vartry for all purposes, 5473–5475. 5488; 5489.

Objectionable quality of the supply from the Grand Canal for Rathmines township; very bad pressure in reference to fires, 5476–5487——Income of about 4,800 *l.* a year derived from the supply to the out townships; further receipt of 2,000 *l.* a year expected for extra supply, 5488——Facility for greatly increasing the supply from the Vartry, *ib.*——Present supply of between 14,000,000 and 15,000,000 gallons daily, 5489.

Depreciation of any abandonment of the main drainage scheme, as sanctioned by Parliament after great labour and expense had been incurred, 5490——Causes of the great excess of the tenders for the works beyond the Parliamentary estimates which were made in 1870; 5491–5494——Conclusion that the scheme may now be carried out for about 430,000 *l.*; 5492, 5493——Evidence showing that there was no engineering difficulty in carrying out the scheme and no error whatever in the levels, 5495.

Legal grounds upon which the auditor surcharged an excess expenditure of 6,708 *l.* in respect of Grattan Bridge, 5496–5498——Information relative to the cost of forage, &c., for the corporation horses; total cost of about 7 *s.* 6 *d.* a day for each horse and driver, 5499–5514——Amalgamation in August 1871 of the separate accounts of the waterworks rate fund and loan fund, 5515——Salary of 750 *l.* a year now received by witness; much larger salaries of similar officers in other constituencies, 5516–5520——Witness and several other officers of the corporation are Protestants, 5521–5522.

Explanation that re-valuation of premises rests entirely with the Valuation Office and not with the corporation, 5523–5529——Much higher scale now adopted for new buildings

Neville, Park. (Analysis of his Evidence)—*continued*.

ings than that applied thirty years ago; doubt as to rebuilding being actually stopped by the higher scale, 5529. 5581-5585.

Extended area, comprising the several townships, over which the rate for re-building Grattan Bridge was levied; objection raised, without effect, by the Rathmines Commissioners, 5530-5534——Grounds for the conclusion that Rathmines and other townships should contribute to the paving and maintenance of the city streets, the municipal area being extended for this and other purposes, 5535. 5536.

Maximum reached by nearly all the rates since 1870; 5537. 5550-5553——Explanation as to the corporation having to pay a very heavy rate on their own water mains, 5537-5544——Support of the fire brigade by a charge of 1½ *d.* in the pound deducted from the water rate, 5545. 5546——Distinct character of the sewer rate, which has never been applied for grand jury purposes, 5547——Power of levying a borough rate up to 3 *d.* in the pound, this power having never been exercised, 5548-5550——Purposes for which the grand jury cess is levied, and authorities by whom expended, 5551. 5554-5558.

Special circumstances which enhance the difficulty of scavenging in Dublin, 5559, 5560——Inferior character of the material available for macadamising, 5561-5563——Partial extent to which the corporation are liable for the repair of Rock-road, 5564-5566——Charge of the Port and Docks Board over the repair of the port and of the quay walls and bridges, 5567——Failure of objections raised by Mr. M'Evoy before the auditor relative to certain expenditure for gas, 5568-5574.

Data upon which the tenders received for the main drainage works were estimated; reduced prices upon which new tenders would be based, 5575-5580——Impression that the extended area proposed by witness would double the present area, though the rates would not be nearly doubled, 5586-5589——Fairness in the townships being joined to the city for poor rate purposes, 5590, 5591——Explanations in reference to several items of cost involved in the Vartry Works, the total cost having been 541,400 *l.*; 5601-5611,

[Second examination]. Belief as to all the powers of the Wide-street Commissioners (except the rating power) having been transferred to the corporation, 5612——Explanation of the practice in executing and charging for paving or other licensed work done by the corporation for private individuals; belief that the full cost is always charged, 5613-5619——Bad state of several of the streets, as not having been paved for about eighteen years, 5620.

Particulars relative to the quality and cost of the stone used for repairing the streets; reason for the price being higher than that paid by the Rathmines Commissioners, 5621-5629——Limited extent to which streets have been asphalted; the Limmer asphalte has answered the best, 5630-5633——Explanation as to the lower price paid in Rathmines than in the city for gravel, 5634-5637——Advantages of a proposal supported by witness in 1869 for removing the scavenging soil in barges; larger outlay now required for barges, &c. than in 1869; 5638-5644.

Reasons for the opposition of the corporation to the Bill for a cattle market on the North Wall; cost incurred in opposition, 5645-5649——Promotion by the corporation in conjunction with the sales' masters, of the new market in Prussia-street, which has been a great success; enforced delay through want of funds, 5647. 5650-5654.

Examination relative to the progress made by the corporation with the main drainage scheme since its inception, and the causes which prevented the receipt of tenders till the year 1873, the Act having been obtained in 1871; 5655-5672. 5844-5847——Agitation in 1874 against the main drainage scheme; eventual determination to ask for a Royal Commission on the subject, 5673-5681——Consent of Government to increased borrowing powers in the corporation on condition of their obtaining a Bill for carrying out the works; cause of the failure of the Bill promoted for this purpose in 1875; 5682-5694.

Explanation as to witness having stated in 1859 that the waters of the canal were of good wholesome quality, 5695-5698——Strong opposition made to the Coyford scheme, as first recommended by Mr. Hawkesley and witness, 5699, 5700——Borrowing power of 75,000 *l.* given in the Vartry Act conditional upon the supply of the townships, 5701-5709.

Examination as to the reasons for the cheaper supply of water to Pembroke and the other townships than to the city; compromise in the former case, there being moreover a profit on the supply, 5701-5740. 5831-5834——Expediency of the townships contributing equally with the city to the repair of the roads and bridges and to the main drainage, though this principle has for certain reasons been departed from as regards water supply and drainage, 5717-5720. 5738-5740——Basis of supply for manufacturing purposes, 5725-5728. 5831.

Complaint made by Mr. Denneby as to the state of the Mountjoy-square sewer; necessary

Neville, Park. (Analysis of his Evidence)—*continued.*

necessary delay in applying a remedy, 5741–5744——Statement as regards some actions brought successfully against the corporation on account of flooding from the sewers, that this does not prove any defective construction, 5745–5749.

Further information relative to the price and quality of bricks and stone as now purchased by the corporation; great advance in prices, 5751–5759——Saving expected from the use, by the contractors, of machinery for breaking stone for the streets; objection to the corporation having machinery for the purpose, 5760–5763——Doubt further expressed as to its being legally in the power of the corporation to procure a complete re-valuation, 5764–5769.

Numerous cases of ruinous or unhealthy houses reported by the police, and by the sanitary serjeants of the force; inadequacy of the inspection now applied as regards dangerous structures, 5770–5781——Recent fall of some houses, a new Building Act being greatly required, so that there may be a proper check upon the plans and mode of construction, 5777–5781.

Statement strongly in favour of Stephen's Green being opened to the public, 5782–5784. 5848–5851. 5860——Examination to the effect that in 1866 the corporation opposed the opening of Stephen's Green as involving the loss of a rent of 300 *l.* a year, and have since opposed unless the management be transferred to them; question at issue whether the corporation or the Board of Works should be intrusted with the care of the Green, 5785–5798. 5813–5821. 5835–5837. 5852–5874.

Information as to the staff of witness' office and as to the salaries, 5799–5801——Increase of witness' salary from time to time as new duties have been entrusted to him, 5802–5807——Arrangement as to witness' whole time being given to the corporation, whilst he receives no commission on any works in addition to his salary, 5804–5812.

Further reference to the unsuitable quality of some of the stone used for macadamising the streets, 5822–5824——Removal of a great deal of the scavenging materials without charge to the corporation, the cost of barges, &c., having hitherto been saved, 5825, 5826——Constant opposition on the part of Mr. M'Evoy to the various schemes of the corporation, 5827–5830——Limited supply of water per head in the townships but not in Dublin, 5832–5834——Hitch at present in the main drainage scheme, through the Public Works Loan Commissioners considering the security insufficient, 5838–5843.

North Liffey Strand (*Dublin City Estates*). Area of fifty-five acres comprised in some wet lots, called North Liffey Strand, which were sold by the corporation in 1717, but have never been inclosed or utilised; expediency of the corporation re-entering into possession of this land, *Morgan* 3607–3620.

North Wall and City Quays (*Dublin*). Amount received from the grand jury account in respect of the repairing and paving of the roadway of North Wall and the City Quays, *Robinson* 2796–2799——Information on the subject of the presentment made by the grand jury in respect of paving and repairing the roads at the North and South Quays, *ib.* 2800–2810. 2812.

Irregular course pursued by the corporation in regard to levying out of the grand jury rate the sum required for repairs to the North Wall, whilst a portion of the improvement rate had been lent for sewer purposes; decisions of the judges adverse to the corporation, *Stokes* 3188–3191. 3291–3300——The clause in the Port and Docks Act of 1869, under which a rate is levied for paving, was smuggled into the Act by the corporation, *ib.* 3188–3191.

Explanation as to the repair of the quay roads being defrayed by grand jury presentments under the Dublin Port and Docks Act, *O'Donnell* 3427, 3428——Conclusion that the clause in question was not smuggled into the Act of 1869 by the corporation, *Neville* 5419–5421. 5502–5506.

Norwood, John, LL.D. (Analysis of his Evidence.)—Experience of witness as a member of the Town Council of Dublin, and of several committees of the council; also as a guardian of the North and South Dublin Unions, and as member of other public boards, 5875–5879——He has been deputed by the corporation to give evidence before the Committee, 5880.

Approval of some change in the constitution of the corporation, in deference to public opinion on the subject, 5883–5885. 5980–5982——Mis-statement and mis-conception on which the adverse public opinion which prevails is largely founded, 5884, 5885——Transaction of the real business of the corporation in its committees, these working earnestly in the interests of the ratepayers, 5884——Less efficiency, doubtless, of some members of the corporation than of others, this being the case in all public bodies, 5885.

Expediency of a re-valuation of the city as the foundation of a sound constituency; prejudicial effects of the present unequal system, 5886, 5887——Resolution recently passed

Norwood, John, LL.D. (Analysis of his Evidence)—*continued.*

passed by the corporation, through a committee, in favour of a new valuation, embracing not only the city, but the townships and the county, 5887, 5888——Grounds for the conclusion that the corporation have not the legal power to call for a re-valuation, this power being in fact still vested in the grand jury of the county of the city, 5889-5894.

Evidence in favour of owners of property being admitted to the municipal franchise; beneficial results anticipated, 5895-5898. 5915. 5981——Approval of a system of plural voting upon the poor law principle, 5899, 5900. 5915——Expediency of a female franchise for municipal purposes, 5901——Disapproval of the seven-mile residential limit; sufficiency of a twenty-mile limit for Dublin, 5902-5904.

Advocacy of an extension of the municipal boundary so as to embrace Rathmines, Pembroke, and other townships having a community of interest with the city in many fiscal matters, 5905-5909——Injustice in these townships not being united with the city for poor-rate and other burdens, 5909, 5910——Suggestions as to the relative representation of the townships and the city, if there be but one municipal body; total of about ninety members, 5911, 5912.

Reluctance of leading merchants to join the corporation on account of the work involved, and the demands upon their time, 5913. 5914——Approval of the present occupation franchise, 5915. 5920——Satisfaction expressed also with the residential term of three years, 5916——Expediency of the same franchise throughout the whole district if the townships be added to the city, 5917-5920——Improvement if town councillors were elected for five instead of three years, 5921, 5922.

Objection to the collection of rates being transferred to the different boards by whom they are levied, 5923——Success of the present system of collection; moderate amount of arrears, considering the poverty of many of the ratepayers, 5923, 5924.

Explanatory statement showing the defects of the present system of Private Bill legislation as affecting Dublin, and the difficulties and expense involved under the present working of the Provisional Order system, 5925-5933.

Witness submits sundry resolutions and suggestions in detail, as prepared by the different committees of the corporation; evidence in elucidation of the various amendments proposed, 5934-5976——The majority of these suggestions, if not all, have been approved by the corporation, 5935.

Representations in detail on the part of Committee No. 1 as to the want of increased powers and augmented revenue in connection with paving, cleansing, lighting, &c., 5936——Suggestions by this Committee that the receipts from hackney carriage licenses should go towards the repair and maintenance of the thoroughfares, *ib.*——Amendment suggested by the Committee as regards the powers of the Corporation in respect of new buildings; reference hereon to the excellent Building Act obtained by Belfast, 5936. 5944-5946.

Proposal by No. 1 Committee for extending to Ireland the Scotch law as to ruined houses; good grounds for such extension, 5936-5942——Enlarged powers also required as regards the widening of streets and the removal of obstructions, 5937-5942——Suggestions also by Committee No. 1 for increased borrowing facilities, 5943.

Explanations relative to certain suggestions by No. 2 Committee of the Corporation, as embodied in a Bill in 1868 for improved market regulations, &c., 5947-5949——Amended regulations now in force as to driving cattle through the streets, 5950.

Suggestion by Committee No. 3 for a power to grant building leases for a term of 150 years, 5951——Amendment proposed by this committee in the jurisdiction and procedure of the Lord Mayor's Court, *ib.*——Reasons urged by this committee for transferring the repair of Rock-road to the townships of Pembroke and Blackrock, *ib.*——Representations by the committee as to the increased powers required from Parliament in order to carry out certain sanitary and street improvements; proposal for a distinct rate for sanitary purposes, 5951-5953.

Explanations in connexion with sundry other suggestions by Committee No. 3, in reference to fines and penalties, the sale of coals, the fees of the city marshal and other officers, 5959-5962——Suggestion by the committee for an amended procedure in regard to surcharges and the question of legality of any payment, *ib.*

Particulars relative to the suggestions by No. 3 Committee for enabling the corporation to check the accounts and expenditure of the Richmond District Lunatic Asylum; little, if any, control at present, 5953-5960——Immense increase in the annual expenditure of the asylum, 5954——Complaint made in the town council that unduly expensive buildings had been erected by the asylum authorities, 5955——Proposal also by Committee No. 3 that there be more frequent sittings of the Recorder's Court, as in Belfast, 5960.

Recommendations handed in on the part of the Public Health Committee, 5963——Authority given to witness to represent the Waterworks Committee in reference to the grievance arising out of the rating of the mains and other works for poor-rate purposes; unfair burden in this respect, 5964-5968——Suggestion by the committee of the whole House relative to a consolidation of the various loans of the corporation, 5969.

Norwood, John, LL.D. (Analysis of his Evidence)—*continued.*

Explanations in connexion with certain recommendations by the Board of Superintendence of City Prisons relative to the appointment and dismissal and the salaries of prison officers, 5969–5975——Amended legislation proposed in order to give effect to the suggestions of the Board of Superintendence on various points, 5975——Resolution adopted by a Committee of the whole House asking for the appointment of a Royal Commission upon the main drainage of Dublin and its vicinity, 5976.

Serious obstacles to the successful promotion of a Private Bill by the corporation, in order to give effect to many of the foregoing suggestions, as made by its committees; local opposition apprehended, there being a great want of confidence in the corporation, 5977–5981——Comment upon the opposition to the proposed transfer of the works of the Alliance Gas Company to the corporation, 5979——Confidence in the corporation if property were more directly represented, and if the leading citizens were induced to take part in its affairs, 5981–5983.

Explanations submitted in reference to the arrears in the collection of the city rents; report by the city treasurer on this subject several years ago, and statement thereon by No. 3 Committee to the effect that the losses have been exceedingly small, 5983.

[Second Examination.]—Further reference to the large expenditure upon the Richmond Asylum buildings, 5984——Large increase in the number of patients in the asylum, so that the cost of maintenance has necessarily increased, 5984, 5985——Explanation that all the suggestions drawn up by the several committees have been adopted by the corporation, 5985, 5986.

Statement, as regards the audit, to the effect that the proposition for the appointment of a Government auditor emanated from the town council, 5989–5990——Reason why the change in the audit system was postponed; denial that the postponement had any connection with the donation to the French Relief Fund, 5990.

Expediency of appeals to a court of law from the decisions of the auditor, 5991–5993 Approval of a suggestion that a legal decision be obtained before any doubtful expenditure is incurred, 5992——Hardship in the costs falling on the corporation when successful in appeals, 5993——Advantage of all boards throughout Ireland having independent auditors, 5994–5996.

Explanation and defence of the action of the corporation, and of the expense incurred, in promoting and opposing private Bills, 5997–5999——Grounds for the conclusion that the Parliamentary revising barrister should revise also the municipal lists and the jurors' lists, 6000–6002, 6097, 6098——Obstacles to a competitive or qualifying examination of the corporation officers; good officers now obtained, 6003——Small increase of salaries, save in respect of new offices; very moderate salaries generally, 6004, 6006–6008, 6040——Moderate character of the superannuations; careful checks applied, 6005, 6040——Economy as to salaries in the appointment of secretaries to the standing committees, 6008.

Erroneous character of most of the imputations as to nepotism in the appointment of officers; instances of this, 6009, 6010——Causes of the great fluctuation in the fees received from pawnbrokers, 6011——Steps taken with a view to obtaining from the townships their proper quota for excess of water supply, 6012.

Prompt attention given by the Public Health Committee in sanitary matters; certain amendments are, however, much required in the sanitary laws, 6013–6017——Advantages anticipated from the appointment of a sanitary magistrate for the metropolitan district, 6018–6020——Objection to the removal of nuisances from dwellings at the expense of the ratepayers, this work being fairly attended to at present, 6021——Considerable expense involved in putting the Artisans' Dwellings Act into operation, 6022——Suggestion made by witness several years ago for the construction of a wide street in St. Michan's parish, 6023, 6024.

Inaccuracy of a statement as to the corporation having too large a staff of officers, 6025, 6026——Very good management of the accountant's department, whilst the accounts generally are very carefully kept, 6030——Excellent attendance at the committee meetings, 6031——Great improvement if the quorum for corporation meetings were reduced from twenty to nine, 6033–6036, 6050, 6106——Reference to the political discussions in the corporation (in which witness never takes part) as not interfering with the transaction of business which really takes place in the committees, 6039–6041.

Disposition of the corporation in the direction of parsimony rather than of extravagance, 6040—Explanation that the majority of the members of the corporation are very large ratepayers, 6041——Numerous engagements of many of the leading merchants in Dublin so that they could not spare time to serve in the town council, 6042, 6043——Several instances of leading merchants who do serve on the corporation, 6044——Election of witness apart from political grounds; admission, however, that the election of many members is due to political influence, 6045–6048——Denial that any jobbery has taken place, 6049.

Satisfactory discharge of business by the Port and Docks Board, the quorum of members being five, 6050–6052——Careful scrutiny by the corporation in all matters of expenditure,

Norwood, John, LL.D. (Analysis of his Evidence)—*continued.*

expenditure, 6053. 6054——Excellent discharge of their duties by the constabulary generally, as well as by those in connection with the public health committee, 6055, 6056.

Decided improvement in the sanitory condition of Dublin owing to the action of the public heath committee; numerous instances of enforcement of fines, 6057-6067——Weekly inspection of the slaughter-houses, 6062——Constant inspection by Dr. Mapother, who is a most valuable officer, 6063——Fair salaries paid to the medical sanitary officers, 6064——Periodical reports published by the public health committee, 6065——Explanation as to the supply of cabs at the unions for the removal of patients to the fever and other hospitals, 6069, 6070. 6217-6220——Satisfactory constitution of the public health committee, 6071-6073.

Explanation as to the low rate at which the corporation were constrained to supply water to Pembroke and other townships; competition of Rathmines in the matter, 6074-6076——Better quality of the water in Rathmines, and reduced cost, if supplied from the Vartry: advantage also by the greater pressure, 6077-6080——Entire absence of political discussions in the main drainage committee, of which committee Mr. Stokes is a very efficient member, 6081-6086——Exceedingly small surcharges by the auditor, these being on technical points, 6087, 6088.

Less unwillingness of ratepayers to be placed on the burgess roll if they were not thereby subjected to serve on both county and city juries; advantage if there were a single venue for the city and county, 6089. 6167. 6286——Reference to a certain transfer from the sewer fund to the improvement fund as a mere question of account, 6091——Increase of the waterworks estimate owing mainly to the additional works constructed, 6092——Intention from the first to have filter beds 6093——Provision in the Pembroke Township Act as to the contribution by the corporation towards the repair of the Rock-road, 6094.

Explanation that certain defalcations in the marshal's office were caused by the subordinates, not by the late marshal, 6095, 6096——Extension desirable as regards the time for completing the revision of the burgess list, 6099. 6101——Particulars as to the causes of the increased change for the Collector General's department; this is mainly due to the increase of poundage, and not of salaries, 6100——Opinion that it is not legal to put weekly and monthly tenants on the burgess roll, 6102.

Difficulties in the way of an alteration of the bye-law, or rather of the provision in the Act, by which the quorum of members is fixed at twenty; facility desirable as regards the alteration of bye-laws under the Act of 1849; 6103-6105. 6156-6163——Conclusion further expressed in favour of a reduction of the quorum to nine, or to seven, 6106-6113——Removal of all causes of complaint against the corporation if the funds at their disposal were sufficient, 6114, 6115——Improving resources of the corporation, whilst the expenses of street repairs will be much diminished, 6115.

Examination as to the constitution and action of the citizens' committee on sanitary matters, and as to the treatment of the committee and its representations by the public health committee, 6116-6135. 6291-6293——Explanation that the corporation funds will not suffer by the defalcations of Mr. Robinson, 6136.

Information relative to the gas supply and the reasons for the increase of price; prospect of reduction, the gas company having now surmounted the difficulties under which it formerly laboured, 6137-6149. 6256-6264——Probability that the corporation would have obtained better rates for the water supply in Pembroke and other townships but for the opposition by Mr. Stokes, 6150-6155——Doubt as to the auditor having left many items to stand over in addition to the actual surcharges, 6164-6166.

Explanation of the steps taken by the corporation at different times upon the question of obtaining a Royal Commission relative to the main drainage; further application about to be made for a commission, 6168-6172——Further evidence in favour of a general revaluation; advantage of this being compulsory for all Ireland, and of a periodical revision subsequently, 6173-6184.

Approval of a higher qualification than a 4 *l.* rating for the municipal franchise, 6185. 6189——Satisfactory working of the qualification in Belfast, 6185——Doubt as to the expediency of reducing the residential term of three years, unless the rating be raised, 6186-6189. 6229——Importance further attached to the municipal enfranchisement of owners of property, as under the Poor Law Act, 6190-6194.

Further approval of the system of plural voting, as under the poor law, rather than of the cumulative principle, 6195-6197——Opinion favourable to an entire removal of the residential limit as regards Dublin and other towns, 6198-6202. 6286——Fairness of union rating, so as to embrace the townships with the city for poor law purposes, 6203.

Considerable surcharges made by the auditor upon some of the officials of the South Dublin Union, 6204——Statement to the effect that the guardians of the union, as a body, are not open to certain animadversions passed upon the board; instances of political discussions at the board; 6205. 6208-6216——Animadversions made also upon the corporation,

Norwood, John, LL.D. (Analysis of his Evidence).—*continued.*

poration, upon certain subjects, but without foundation, 6206, 6207. 6291–6294——Denial that politics are discussed at the committee meetings of the corporation, 6211, 6212.

Information relative to the burgess roll in Belfast, witness objecting to any reduction of the qualification, which is practically an 8 *l.* one, and works very well, 6221–6230——Further reference to and disapproval of the less frequent sittings of the recorder's court in Dublin than in Belfast, 6231, 6232. 6243. 6250——Considerations as to the jurisdiction exercised by the recorder of Dublin, and as to the form of pleading in the court, 6233–6244. 6253–6255——Objection to an amalgamation of the recordership of the city with the chairmanship of the county, 6245–6249——Advantage if simple pleadings were adopted in the recorder's court in Cork, 6251, 6252.

Evidence strongly in favour of the main drainage scheme, as approved by Sir Joseph Bazalgette and other high authorities, rather than of any other scheme which has been proposed for the drainage of the city and the purification of the Liffey, 6265–6272——Reduced cost at which the approved scheme may now be carried out, 6268. 6270——Prejudicial effect if the request of the citizens' committee for a Royal Commission on the main drainage had been acceded to, 6269.

Obstacles on account of the unequal valuation and other causes to the formation of a corporation similarly constituted to that of 1849; 6273–6281——Expediency of owners, as being largely taxed, having control over the disbursement of the rates, 6279. 6286——Further advocacy of a re-valuation which shall embrace not only Dublin and the adjacent townships, but all Ireland, 6281–6284——Want of an enlargement of the city boundaries further adverted to, 6285.

Summary of other measures desirable for the improvement of the burgess roll, 6286——Objection to a general election, instead of a gradual change in the constitution of the corporation, 6287——Inexpediency of any restriction upon the number of members engaged in trade or as licensed victuallers: great efficiency of the late Alderman Reynolds adverted to hereon, 6288–6290——Comment upon the vague and general character of some insinuations against the corporation, 6292——Sufficiency of the supply of public clocks throughout the city, 6294.

Number of Town Authorities. Return showing the several towns with four authorities within town boundary, these being Lisburn, Ballina, and Ballinasloe, *App.* 399——Total of seventy-seven towns with three authorities within town boundary: names of these towns, *ib.* 399, 400——Names of twenty-one towns with two authorities within town boundary, *ib.* 400——Names of ten towns under a single authority within the town boundary, *ib.*

O.

Occupiers. See *Franchise.* *Owners,* 1. *Rates.* *Weekly and Monthly Tenants.*

O'Donnell, Thomas. (Analysis of his Evidence.)—Is City Accountant of Dublin, 2740——Explanation that a transfer of 2,482 *l.* 12 *s.* 8 *d.* from the sewers' rate to the credit of the improvement fund was made in order to recoup a previous advance from the latter fund, 2741–2746——The above item is in addition to the amount of 52,909 *l.* realised by the improvement rate in the year 1874–75; 2747, 2748.

Information on the subject of the presentment made by the grand jury in respect of paving and repairing the roads at the north and south quays, 2800–2810. 2812——Statement of the salaries of different officers of the corporation, as charged against the borough fund, amounting to 6,345 *l.* in the year 1874–75; 2847–2852.

[Second Examination.]—Further explanation relative to a certain payment by way of adjustment between the improvement rate and sewer rate, 3400——Total of 55,781 *l.* 10 *s.* 4 *d.* as the proceeds of the grand jury cess in the year ending 31st August 1875; 3405, 3406——Large increase between 1870 and 1875 in the payment out of the grand jury cess for reformatory and industrial schools, 3407, 3408——Particulars relative to the expenditure out of the grand jury cess in respect of prisons, and the causes of the large increase since 1870; 3409–3417.

Details relative to the expenditure charged upon the grand jury cess on account of lunatic asylums, and the causes of the increased payments in 1874–75; 3418–3426——Explanation as to the repair of the quay roads being defrayed by grand jury presentments, under the Dublin Port and Docks Act, 3427, 3428——Several items comprised in the quarter sessions account; that is, for expenses in connexion with the Recorder's Court and the Sessions Court in Green-street, 3429.

Considerable payments for salaries and wages of persons not directly employed by the corporation, as in the case of prison officers, 3430–3435——Presentment of about 284 *l.* a year for the repair of Rock-road; responsibility of the grand jury of the county, and not of the corporation, for the condition of this road, 3436–3439.

Checks applied as to the number of boys in industrial and reformatory schools in respect

Report, 1876—*continued.*

O'Donnell, Thomas. (Analysis of his Evidence)—*continued.*
respect of whom payments are made out of the grand jury cess, 3472–3474——Practice as to the payment to, and transfer from, the personal account of the treasurer of the amount for the maintenance of prisoners, 3481.

[Third Examination.]—Ancient custom under which the Paymaster General retains a per-centage of the Royal Grants in the shape of Pell's poundage, 3877–3880.

Old Stores. Grounds for a suggestion made by witness that there should be more publicity in the sale of old stores by the corporation of Dublin, *Finlay* 4294.

OWNERS:

1. *Question of a Division of Rates between Owners and Occupiers.*
2. *Question of Municipal Enfranchisement of Owners, and of their direct Representation on Town Councils.*

1. *Question of a Division of Rates between Owners and Occupiers:*

Great importance attached to an equal division of town taxation between owners and occupiers, *Hancock* 152; *Pim* 2315–2336——Division of the poor-rate between the owner and the occupier; division also in the case of certain grand jury cess contracts, *Hancock* 152——Strong approval of the recommendations of the Select Committee on Local Taxation in 1870 for a division of rates between owners and occupiers, existing contracts being respected, *ib.* 925–929.

Expediency of owners being directly liable for half the rates, concurrently with their possessing half the representation, *Pim* 2321–2324.

Evidence adverse to a division of rates between owners and occupiers, *Stokes* 2945, 2946. 3154–3161. 3250–3277.

2. *Question of Municipal Enfranchisement of Owners, and of their direct Representation on Town Councils:*

Proposal that the rates being divided, half the local board for each town be elected by the owners and half by the occupiers; beneficial results anticipated, *Hancock* 153. 160–162. 184–188——Suggestions for the election of owners, some members being *ex-officio* in respect of property, and some being chosen on the cumulative principle, *ib.* 156 *et seq.*; 912–914. 946–951——Proposed condition that owners who are *ex-officio* members must be magistrates, *ib.* 156. 181——Result of witness's scheme, if put in operation in the principal towns; number of representatives of different classes, there being on the whole an equal number of owners and occupiers in each case, *ib.* 184–187.

Several precedents and high authorities cited in support of the municipal franchise being conferred on owners as well as occupiers, there being a division of rates between the two, *Hancock* 938–945.

Argument in strong support of an equal division of taxation and representation between owners and occupiers, *Pim* 2315–2336——Several precedents in England and Scotland for giving votes to owners in municipal elections, *ib.* 2316, 2317——Grounds for concluding that it is a positive injustice to owners in Irish municipal boroughs to exclude them from the municipal franchise, and that such exclusion is exceedingly injurious to the interests of the towns, *ib.* 2317–2320.

Conclusion that municipal boards composed equally of owners and occupiers would work smoothly, *Pim* 2325–2336——Mixed constitution of the Scotch county boards with satisfactory results; reference also to boards of guardians in Ireland as being mixed boards, comprising owners and occupiers, *ib.* 2325–2329.

Opinion that owners, as not directly paying rates, should not take part in the elections; objections also to a direct representation of the former, *Stokes* 2945, 2946. 3154–3161. 3250–3277.

Decided opinion that owners should have a voice in the municipal administration, *Grimshaw* 4246–4248.

Suggested qualification of 50 *l.* a year in the case of non-resident owners, direct payment of taxes being dispensed with as a qualification, *Sullivan* 4682. 4698. 4776. 4815–4821——Great evil in owners of property not being better represented in the Dublin municipal council, *ib.* 4723. 4772.

Examination adverse to the proposition that owners, as in Scotland, should be liable for half the rates, and should share the municipal representation with the occupiers; approval however of some concessions in order to induce owners to enter the corporation, *Sullivan* 4772–4786.

Evidence in favour of owners of property being admitted to the municipal franchise; beneficial results anticipated, *Norwood* 5895–5898. 5915. 5981. 6190–6194——Expediency of owners, as being largely taxed, having control over the disbursement of the rates, *ib.* 6279. 6286.

Decided unpopularity in Dublin of a 50 *l.* ownership franchise, *Gray* 6405–6407——Legitimate

OWNERS—continued.

2. *Question of Municipal Enfranchisement of Owners, &c.*—continued.

Legitimate influence of owners of property under the present franchise; reference hereon to this influence in Parliamentary representation, *Gray* 6511–6513. 6689–6693.

Argument in further opposition to the admission of property owners to the franchise, except they are also occupiers; approval however of the owner being enfranchised if he directly pays half the rates, *Gray* 6616. 6618–6627——Restriction at present by the exclusion not only of the small ratepayers but of owners of property, *ib.* 6654–6661.

Examination upon the question whether owners are not, under certain circumstances, as much interested as occupiers in the incidence and in the expenditure of the rates; doubt however as to the expendiency of any representation of owners, *Gray* 6662–6673. 6700–6706. 6715–6719.

See also Corporation of Dublin, 5. *Franchise*, 7, 8. *Rates*, 3.

Oxmantown Property (*City of Dublin*). Rental of only 36 *l.* 4 *s.* 7 *d.* now produced by the Oxmantown property, whereas on expiration of the lease in 1881 about 4,000 *l.* a year will be obtained, *Morgan* 3665-3665. 3869–3873.

P.

Parliamentary Franchise. Practice of striking out the names of occupiers in arrear of poor rates, with reference to the Parliamentary franchise in Dublin, *Taafe* 529, 530.

Paving, Lighting, &c. (*Dublin*). See *Asphalte Pavements.* *Improvement Rate. Materials.* *Sanitary Administration*, I. *Streets* (*Paving, &c.*)

Pawnbrokers. Special powers still possessed by the Corporation of Dublin for regulating the trade of pawnbroking; amendment desirable, *Hancock* 610, 611. 768–770——Particulars as to the receipts of the Dublin Corporation from fees paid by pawnbrokers in Ireland on licenses, &c.; considerable decrease in this item, *Robinson* 2590–2609——Opinion that the Corporation should give up the receipts from pawnbrokers' licenses issued all over Ireland, receiving on the other hand the carriage licenses, *Sullivan* 4802——Causes of the great fluctuation in the fees received from pawnbrokers, *Norwood* 6011.

Pell's Poundage. Ancient custom under which the Paymaster General in Dublin retains a per-centage of the Royal grants in the shape of Pell's Poundage, *O'Donnell* 3877–3880——Inability of witness to explain the deduction under the head of Pell's Poundage, *Morgan* 3516–3519.

Pensions (*City of Dublin*). Power of the corporation to superannuate its officers up to two-thirds of their salaries, *Henry* 1528–1530——Unduly heavy burden on the rates in respect of pensions; grounds for this statement, *M'Evoy* 2073–2077. 2095–2104——Particulars relative to the charges on account of compensations or pensions, these being on the decrease, *Robinson* 2780–2789——Moderate character of the superannuations; careful checks applied, *Norwood* 6005. 6040.

Pim, Joseph T. (Analysis of his Evidence.)—Is a member of the firm of Pim Brothers & Co; has devoted much attention to the question of municipal arrangements in Dublin, 2295, 2296——Considers that throughout Ireland, and especially in Dublin, municipal government is in an unsatisfactory condition, 2297 *et seq.*

Gradual deterioration in the character of the town council of Dublin, many of the largest ratepayers being anxious for some change, 2299–2302——General feeling in the city that the streets are badly kept, and that the back streets are especially neglected, 2300. 2370——Insufficient care given to sanitary matters, *ib.*——Unhealthy and unsafe character of a considerable number of the dwellings of the lower classes *ib.*——Very general feeling that the financial affairs of the corporation are not well managed, jobbery being often talked of by the people, 2300. 2415.

Very irregular attendance at the meetings of the town council; frequent difficulty in obtaining a quorum, so that there is much waste of time, 2300. 2302. 2383——Waste of much time also in political discussions at the meetings of the council; strong disapproval of this practice, its effect being moreover to prevent many men of position from joining the corporation, 2300–2303. 2361–2366. 2383. 2396——Twofold reason why the leading mercantile men abstain from municipal administration, 2301, 2302. 2416–2418.

Conclusion as to the necessity of some change in the municipal franchise, whereby the representation will be adjusted with more fairness in proportion to the incidence of taxation, 2302——Decided objection to the proposal for assimilating the Irish franchise to the English franchise; this change would only intensify existing evils, 2304–2307——Calculations to the effect that a mere reduction of the franchise to the English level,

without

Pim, Joseph T. (Analysis of his Evidence)—*continued*.

without any compensating arrangements, would place the control of the representation and of the taxation in the hands of those least capable of exercising such control, 2305–2307. 2315.

Grounds for objecting to the cumulative system of voting in municipal elections, though it has been found successful at school board elections, 2308–2310——Way in which cumulative voting would be used by Protestants and Roman Catholics, respectively, in order to secure the election of men holding their respective religious opinions; great evil thereof, 2309, 2310.

Advocacy of the system of plural voting with a view to a better representation of the large ratepayers, 2311, 2312——Several considerations by which large ratepayers, having plural votes, would be induced to make good choice of representatives, *ib.* ——Effect of plural votes to increase the voting power in Roman Catholics and to soften the conflict between religious parties, 2311–2314.

Argument in strong support of an equal division of taxation and representation between owners and occupiers, 2315–2336——Several precedents in England and Scotland for giving votes to owners in municipal elections, 2316, 2317——Grounds for concluding that it is a positive injustice to owners in Irish municipal boroughs to exclude them from the municipal franchise, and that such exclusion is exceedingly injurious to the interests of the towns, 2317–2320.

Prejudicial effect in Dublin of the heavy taxation within the area of the city as compared with lighter taxation outside; great check thereby to commercial enterprise, and great injury to house property, 2318, 2319——Opposition frequently offered by large ratepayers, at considerable expense, to financial schemes of the corporation, the constitution of that body not entitling it to confidence and respect, 2320. 2422–2428——Expediency of owners being directly liable for half the rates concurrently with their possessing half the representation, 2321–2324.

Grounds for concluding that municipal boards, composed equally of owners and occupiers would work smoothly, 2325–2336——Mixed constitution of the Scotch County Boards, with satisfactory results; reference also to boards of guardians in Ireland as being mixed boards, 2325–2329——Smooth and efficient working of the Port and Docks of Dublin, though its constitution is of a very mixed character, 2330–2336.

Conclusion that, with the safeguards proposed by witness, the municipal franchise in Ireland should be reduced to household suffrage, 2337, 2338——Doubt as to the expediency of admitting tenement lodgers to the municipal franchise, 2339–2340——Suggested adoption of the poor law system as regards plurality of votes, 2341——Opinion that if the corporation of Dublin be so constituted that those who pay the taxes are fairly represented, the limitation of taxation power should be removed, 2342.

Reduction suggested in the term of residence as a qualification for the franchise in Dublin, 2343——Decided objection to the restriction as to residence within seven miles of Dublin; large extension required, 2343——Disapproval of the system of revision of the burgess list; improvement if it were conducted in the same way as the Parliamentary revision, 2345——Respects in which the present system of valuation in Dublin is very unequal and unsatisfactory; want of a re-valuation not only for Dublin but for all Ireland, 2346–2351.

Explanation that witness makes no objection as to the social position of the members of the Corporation of Dublin, though he repeats that many of the leading men are deterred from entering the corporation by the necessity of their acting as political partisans, 2352–2368. 2383–2385——Few men of high mercantile position in the corporation out of those who were members in 1851; 2353–2355. 2361, 2362.

Further statement as to the loud complaints frequently made in regard to the financial administration; want of economy on the one hand, whilst on the other there is much neglect in the matter of improvements, 2369–2376. 2405——Statement in further reference to the abstention of the mercantile classes from interference in municipal affairs under the present system of election; circumstance of many of the large ratepayers not being on the burgess roll, 2377–2382——Witness repeats that those who pay heavy taxes should have a much stronger voice in the representation, 2376. 2397.

Frequent waste of time in waiting till a quorum is formed; instance of this, 2383. 2386, 2387. 2419——Statement as to there never being any difficulty about a quorum in the case of the Port and Docks Board, 2388–2392. 2420.——Efficiency of the management of the fire brigade, 2393–2395.

Exceptionally high rate of local taxation in Dublin, 2397——Doubt whether any reduction can be made in the improvement rate of 2 s., 2398——Opinion that something should be done towards improving the condition of the river before adopting a costly main drainage scheme, 2399. 2400——Improbability of a reduction of taxation by electing the corporation on the system of plural votes; opinion that more value would be obtained for the money spent, 2401–2405.

Pim, Joseph T. (Analysis of his Evidence)—*continued*.

Importance in the first instance of a satisfactory electoral body, rather than of a high rating qualification in the elected, 2406——Further statement as to the inadequate powers exercised by the corporation in reference to dilapidated and dangerous structures; instance of this, 2407–2414.

Large number of those on the burgess roll who do not vote at elections, 2429, 2430——Difficulty in extending the area of the municipal borough, on account of the higher taxation in the outlying districts, 2431——Circumstance of the corporation not having yet applied the Artisans' Dwellings Act, 2432, 2433. 2448–2450——Comment upon the donation of 500 *l.* from the corporation to the French Relief Fund as an instance of misplaced liberality; neglect at the same time of sanitary arrangements, 2434–2445——Important improvement expected as regards sanitary expenditure by amending the franchise as approved by witness, 2437–2439.

Exceptions taken to the refusal by the corporation of Sir Arthur Guinness' offer to contribute 5,000 *l.* towards the opening of Stephen's Green, 2451–2456——Source whence the corporation might obtain funds for improving the sanitary condition of the city, 2457, 2458——Comment upon the great abuse in the matter of slaughter-houses, and upon the neglect of the corporation to provide abattoirs, 2458–2462——Belief as to the corporation not having applied to the Local Government Board for powers to execute works by means of Provisional Orders, 2463, 2464——Very good cattle market constructed some years ago, 2465, 2466.

Plural Voting (*Municipal Elections*). Advocacy of a full representation of property by means of plural voting, *Hancock*, 156 *et seq.* 912–914. 938–951——Expediency of a system of plural voting, with a view to a better representation of the large ratepayers in Dublin, *Pim* 2311, 2312——Several considerations by which large ratepayers having plural votes would be induced to make good choice of representatives, *ib.*——Effect of plural votes to increase the voting power in Roman Catholics, and to soften the conflict between religious parties, *ib.* 2311–2314.

Suggested adoption of the poor law system as regards plurality of votes in Dublin, *Pim* 2341——Witness repeats that those who pay heavy taxes should have a much stronger voice in the representation, 2378. 2397——Improbability of a reduction of taxation by electing the corporation on a system of plural votes; opinion that more value would be obtained from the money spent, *ib.* 2401–2405.

Approval of the system of plural voting, as under the poor law, rather than of the cumulative principle, *Norwood* 5899, 5900. 5915. 6195–6197.

Decided objection to a plurality of votes at municipal elections in Dublin, *Sullivan* 4899——Strong objection to multiple voting in Dublin, as being more or less a stigma, *Gray* 6387. 6400–6403. 6650–6653.

Police. Provision in the Collection of Rates Act for the collection of the police tax in Dublin outside, as well as within the municipal area, *Taaffe and Moylan* 497. 569.

Exceptions taken to the local authority being entrusted generally with the control of the police as to the stipendiary magistrates having anything to do with the rating, *Hancock* 984–993.

Excellent discharge of their duties by the Dublin constabulary generally, as well as by those in connection with the Public Health Committee, *Norwood* 6055, 6056.

Political Discussions. See *Corporation of Dublin*, 7. *Land Tenure (Land) Bill.*

Political Influence. See *Appointment of Officers.* *Corporation of Dublin*, 2. *Franchise*, 5. *Lord Mayors.*

Poor Rate (*City of Dublin*). Decreasing poor-rate in the city, and increasing rate in Rathmines, owing to union rating, *Stokes* 3063.

Authority given to witness to represent the Waterworks Committee in reference to the grievance arising out of the rating of the mains and other works for poor-rate purposes; unfair burden in this respect, *Norwood* 5964–5968——Fairness of union rating, so as to embrace the townships with the city for poor law purposes, *ib.* 6903.

See also Franchise. Rates. Water Mains.

Port and Docks Board (*Dublin*). Illustration, in the case of the Dublin Port and Docks Board, of the satisfactory result of the representation of different interests, *Hancock* 931–934——Particulars relative to the constitution of the Port and Docks Board, and the qualifications of the electing body, as under the Act 30 & 31 Vict. c. 81; witness has heard no complaint against the working of the board, *Henry* 1186–1192. 1485——The leading merchants of Dublin are on the board, *ib.* 1485.

Smooth and efficient working of the Port and Docks Board, though its constitution is of a very mixed character, *Pim* 2330–2336——Statement as to there never being any difficulty about a quorum in the case of the Port and Docks Board, *ib.* 2388–2392. 2420

——General

Port and Docks Board (*Dublin*)—continued.

——General confidence enjoyed by the board, *Stokes* 3202, 3203——Charge of the board over the repair of the Port, and of the quay walls and bridges, *Neville* 5567.

Higher relative salaries in the Port and Docks Board than in the corporation, *Norwood* 6007——Satisfactory discharge of business by the board, the quorum of members being five, *ib.* 6050–6052.

Respects in which the Port and Dock Board, elected by multiple votes, is much less efficient than the corporation, as regards its care of the public interests; unprotected and dangerous state of the quays adverted to hereon, *Gray* 6518–6526.

See also North Wall and City Quays.

Prisons (*Dublin*). Particulars relative to the expenditure out of the grand jury cess in respect of prisons, and the causes of the large increase since 1870, *O'Donnell* 3409–3417——Practice as to the payment to and transfer from the persons' account of the treasurer of the amount for the maintenance of prisoners, *ib.* 3481.

Explanations in connection with certain recommendations by the Board of Superintendence of City Prisons, relative to the appointment and dismissal, and the salaries of prison officers, *Norwood* 5969–5975——Amended legislation proposed in order to give effect to the suggestions of the Board of Superintendence on various points, *ib.* 5975.

Private Bills. See *Bills in Parliament.* *Provisional Orders.*

Property Qualification. See *Cumulative Voting.* *Franchise*, 7, 8. *Owners.* *Plural Voting.*

Provisional Orders. Obstacles to the obtaining of Provisional Orders under the Local Government Act of 1871; veto imposed by the grand jury in several instances, *Hancock* 42–44. 52——Great cost of some Local Acts as compared with the cost of Provisional Orders, *ib.* 66. 68–70——Suggestions for facilitating the obtaining of Provisional Orders, and for otherwise dispensing with the necessity of costly Local Acts, *ib.* 70. 76–82.

Objection further made to the present veto in the grand jury as regards towns obtaining Provisional Orders through the Local Government Board, *Hancock* 1015–1041.

Belief as to the corporation of Dublin not having applied to the Local Government Board for powers to execute works by means of Provisional Orders, *Pim* 2463, 2464.

Concurrence in a suggestion that towns under the Act of 1854 be regarded as under a special Act in order that they may have facilities in obtaining Provisional Orders, *Finlay* 4512–4518.

Explanatory statement showing the defects of the present system of Private Bill legislation, as affecting Dublin, and the difficulties and expense involved under the present working of the Provisional Order system, *Norwood* 5925–5933.

Approval of Provisional Orders, if they can be readily obtained, as a means of securing possession of property required for improvements, *Gray* 6448–6450.

Public Health Committee (*Corporation of Dublin.*) See *Sanitary Administration*, I.

Public, The (*City of Dublin.*) Entire want of public confidence in the corporation of Dublin as at present constituted, *M'Evoy* 1693——Want of confidence in the financial administration of the corporation, *Pim* 2300. 2320. 2366–2376. 2415. 2422–2428.

Mischievous misleading of the public mind by the statements put forward by different amateur societies, who are not always conversant with the correct facts, *Sullivan* 4681——Opinion that the required reforms in sanitary and other matters can only be carried out by a Public Bill; inability of the corporation to pass a Bill for the purpose, *ib.* 4688. 4719–4722.

Mis-statements and mis-conception on which the adverse public opinion which prevails is largely founded, *Norwood* 5884, 5885——Serious obstacles to the successful promotion of a Private Bill by the corporation in order to give effect to various suggestions, as made by its committee; local opposition apprehended, there being a great want of confidence in the corporation, *ib.* 5977–5981.

Denial that there is any strong and general feeling among the people of Dublin in favour of a reform of the corporation, though a reform is demanded by a small, but influential section, *Gray* 6348——The generality of the public have very little knowledge of the real work done by the corporation, *ib.* 6559.——*See also Corporation of Dublin*, 2.

Q.

Quarter Sessions (*Dublin.*). Several items comprised in the Quarter Sessions Account, for expenses in connection with the Recorder's Court and the Sessions Court, in Green-street, *O'Donnell* 3419.

Quay Walls (*Dublin.*) See *North Wall and City Quays.*

Quorum (*Corporation of Dublin.*) See *Corporation of Dublin*, 11.

R.

RATES:

1. *Limits as to Rating in Towns generally.*
2. *Amount of the Rates in Dublin; comparison with other Places.*
3. *Liability for Payment of Rates.*

1. *Limits as to Rating in Towns generally:*

Information relative to the powers of taxation of town authorities under the Acts of 1828 and 1854, and the limits with reference to the rating, *Hancock* 92–97——Series of limits as to rating in all the Local Acts, *ib.* 98——Provisions in the Borough Rate Act (3 & 4 Vict. c. 109), as to the maximum rate of assessment, &c., *ib.* 99——Departure from the limit of rating when charges under the Sanitary Act are put upon the borough fund, *ib.* 99, 100.

Grounds for the conclusion that the limits placed upon the rating powers of town authorities are very unwise, and cause much complication, *Hancock* 111.

Approval of the limit of the rates by the Act of 1854; several towns below the limit, though the majority may be up to it, *Finlay* 4369–4371. 4661–4666.

2. *Amount of the Rates in Dublin; comparison with other Places:*

Statement showing the amount of rates in Dublin, and in various other towns throughout Ireland, *Hancock* 112–116.

Summary of the various rates collected, and of the amount in each case, *Moylan* 237. 240–247——Varying amount raised annually by the deficient rates; total of 213,000 *l.* in 1870, and of 276,000 *l.* in 1874, *Moylan and Taafe* 265–268 287. 275–281——Amount of each rate in the years 1870 and 1871, respectively, *ib.* 270–274. 378.

Maximum at which several rates have been levied 1870, whilst the grand jury cess and poor rate have been increased, *Taafe* 506–509. 519. 520. 566——Limited extent to which the increased amount of rates collected is due to increased valuation, *ib.* 566–568.

Increase of building outside rather than inside the municipal area, so that the rates have not greatly increased, *Henry* 1340. 1358–1361——Full limit reached by all the rates, *ib.* 1441–1446.

Prejudicial effect in Dublin of the heavy taxation within the area of the city as compared with the lighter taxation outside; great check thereby to commercial enterprise, and great injury to house property, *Pim* 2318, 2319——Opinion that if the corporation of Dublin be so constituted that those who pay the taxes are fairly represented the limitation of taxing power should be removed, *ib.* 2342——Exceptionally high rate of local taxation in Dublin, *ib.* 2397.

Rates of 5 *s.* 7 *d.* in Dublin as compared with 2 *s.* in Rathmines, *Stokes* 2882——Examination to the effect that in view of the very low valuation in Dublin the difference between the rates in the city and in Rathmines is not so great as it appears, *ib.* 3042–3059.

Further information as to the relative amount of rating in the case of the Rathmines commissioners and of the corporation; examination hereon showing that witness has been misinformed, *Stokes* 3165–3169. 3301–3333.

Undeserved unpopularity of the reformed corporation through having greatly increased the taxation, whereas this was unavoidable, *Sullivan* 4668. 4707, 4708——Fallacy of the notion that the municipal taxation of Dublin is excessively high as compared with that of other large towns; grounds for the opposite conclusion, *ib.* 4672.

Power of the corporation to levy an improvement rate of 2 *s.* and a sewer rate of 4 *d.*, *Neville* 5370——Maximum reached by nearly all the rates since 1870, *ib.* 5537. 5550–5553.

Undue disinclination in the corporation to levy additional taxation, *Gray* 6560–6572——Heavy taxation of the ratepayers of Dublin, though witness would not hesitate to tax them additionally for useful purposes, *ib.* 6731–6733.

3. *Liability for Payment of Rates:*

Deduction allowed the owner on payment of the occupiers' rates in Belfast, Sligo, and Dublin, *Hancock* 150, 151.

Liability of the occupier in Dublin for the rate, if the premises are valued over 8 *l.*, and if he is a yearly tenant, *Taafe* 299——Liability of the owner where the premises are over 4 *l.* and under 8 *l.* in value; practice, however, of rating the occupier as well as the owner in these cases, if the former be a yearly tenant, *ib.* 300–316. 322–339.

Explanation that the rate book takes no notice of the occupiers of premises under 4 *l.*, whilst all yearly tenants over 4 *l.* are rated, *Taafe* 470, 471. 531–541. 562–565——Power to be given to the owner to recover from the tenant under the proposal for rendering the former

Report, 1876—*continued.*

RATES—continued.

3. *Liability for Payment of Rates*—continued.

former liable to payment in default of the latter, *Taafe and Moylan* 499–501——Conclusion as to its being useless merely to give power to the occupier to recover from the owner, *Taafe* 502–505——Difficulty in some cases of ascertaining the owner's name, the word "owner" being entered temporarily in the rate book, *ib* 526–528.

Power of compounding with landlords for payment of rates, though it has never been exercised in Dublin, *Henry* 1379–1382——Difficulty of the question whether it is the owner or occupier who really pays the rates when the former is not directly rated, *M'Evoy* 1675–1677.

See also Accounts. Area of Dublin. Borough Fund. Borough Rate. Bridge Rate. Burial Rate. Carriage Tax. Collection of Rates. Corporation of Dublin, 10. 13. *Franchise. Government Property. Grand Jury Cess. Improvement Rate. Main Drainage Rate. Owners. Poor Rate. Rathmines, &c.*, 3. *Sanitary Administration*, I. 10. *Sewers and Sewer Rate. Streets, &c. Valuation*, 1. *Water Supply*, 2.

RATHMINES AND RATHGAR TOWNSHIP (DUBLIN):

1. *Population and Valuation of the Township.*
2. *Constitution and Action of the Rathmines Commissioners.*
3. *Rates in the Township as compared with the City Rates.*
4. *Collection of Rates.*
5. *Audit.*
6. *Other Details generally.*

1. *Population and Valuation of the Township:*

Population of about 22,000 in the township, the valuation being about 92,000 *l.* *Stokes* 2857, 2858——Very large increase in the valuation of the township since 1850, *ib.* 2927——Low valuation in Rathmines though much higher than in the city, *ib.* 2974. 3043–3049.

2. *Constitution and Action of the Rathmines Commissioners:*

Special Act in 1847, under which the commissioners are constituted, the numbers being twenty-one, and the qualification being a rating of 30 *l.* for residents, *Stokes* 2859–2861——Election of the commissioners in Rathmines without any reference to politics; the great majority of members being, however, Conservatives, *ib.* 2894–2898. 2948–2955——Practice of the commissioners to elect Roman Catholics whenever a vacancy occurs; the great majority of the ratepayers are, however, Protestants and Conservatives, *ib.* 2894, 2895. 2950–2954——Very rare complaints in the township as to the administration by the commissioners, *ib.* 3066.

Denial that the commissioners, as such, ever take any part in politics; facility to the conduct of business by abstaining from political discussions, *Stokes* 3082–3086. 3144–3148——Punctual attendance at the meetings of the commissioners, a quorum of five members being always present, *ib.* 3132–3136——Exceptional instance of complaint by the Sanitary Committee of Dublin with respect to Rathmines, *ib.* 3176–3178.

3. *Rates in the Township as compared with the City Rates:*

Present rate in the township of 2 *d.* in the pound, this amount having never been exceeded; this includes paving and lighting, water, grand jury cess, and sewerage. *Stokes* 2863–2868. 2875–2878——Rates to the amount of 2 *d.* in the pound as compared with 5 *s.* 7 *d.* in Dublin; examination as to the accuracy of this calculation, *ib.* 2882. 3042–3059. 3165–3169. 3301–3333——Police tax of 8 *d.* in the township, being the same as in the city, *ib.* 2883——Poor rate of 1 *s.* 2 *d.*, as compared with 1 *s.* 10 *d.* in the city; very few paupers in the township, *ib.* 2884–2886. 2992–2997——Inducement to persons to leave the city for Rathmines on account of the lower taxes, *ib.* 3060–3065.

4. *Collection of Rates:*

Exceedingly close collection of the rates in Rathmines and Rathgar; explanation hereon as to the precautions taken so as to secure full recovery, *Stokes* 2910–2923.

5. *Audit:*

Explanation and defence of the system of election by the ratepayers of two auditors for Rathmines township; objection to a public audit as adding to the expense, and as necessitating too strict a compliance with legal forms, *Stokes* 3105–3131.

Exemption of Rathmines from witness' audit, as being under a special Act, *Finlay* 4389, 4390. 4454–4456——Conclusion that Rathmines should be brought under Government audit, and that the ground of objection raised by Mr. Stokes is rather a reason for a public audit, *ib.* 4457. 4460. 4654–4656.

Rathmines and Rathgar Township (Dublin)—continued.

6. *Other Details generally :*

The qualification of electors is 10 *l.* occupation, there being no owners' qualifications, *Stokes* 2862——Independent water supply of the township, the rate being now 4 *d.*; debt of 22,000 *l.* due on account of the works, *ib.* 2867–2871——Out of the original cost a sum of 6,000 *l.* or 7,000 *l.* has been repaid, *ib.* 2870, 2871——Lower rate of interest paid for the water loans than is paid by the Corporation of Dublin on their loans, *ib.* 2872, 2873.

Power of the commissioners as to maintenance of the roads, *Stokes* 2874——Payment made to the grand jury in respect of gaols and lunatic asylums, *ib.* 2875——Contribution also towards the bridges and quay walls in the city, *ib.* 2876, 2877——There is no debt save for waterworks, *ib.* 2879.

Excellent system of sewers in the townships, *Stokes* 2880, 2881——Total of 3,300 ratepayers, of whom 788 are females; the latter do not vote at elections, *ib.* 2928–2930——Relative requirements of Rathmines and of the city in the matter of gas lights and water pipes, *ib.* 2970–2973——Low rate of mortality, *ib.* 3162–3164.

See also Area of Dublin, 1. *Water Supply*, 4.

Re-appointment of Committee. Recommendation that the Committee be re-appointed in the next Session, a local inquiry being in the meanwhile carried out, *Rep.* iii.

Recorder of Dublin. Annual payment of 366 *l.* 3 *s.* to the Recorder out of the borough fund, *Robinson* 3337——Explanation that the only payment by the corporation to the Recorder is that from the borough fund, *ib.* 3490–3493.

Proposal by committee No. 3 of the corporation that there be more frequent sittings of the Recorder's Court, as in Belfast, *Norwood* 5960.

Further reference to and disapproval of the less frequent sittings of the Recorder's Court in Dublin than in Belfast, *Norwood* 6231, 6232. 6243. 6250——Considerations as to the jurisdiction exercised by the Recorder of Dublin, and as to the form of pleading in the Court, *ib.* 6233–6244. 6253–6255——Objection to an amalgamation of the recordership of the city with the chairmanship of the county *ib.* 6245–6249.

Redmond, Alderman (Corporation of Dublin). Strong testimony to the efficiency of Alderman Redmond, *Stokes* 3021–3023.

Reformatory and Industrial Schools (Dublin). Large increase between 1870 and 1875 in the payment out of the grand jury cess for reformatory and industrial schools, *O'Donnell* 3407, 3408——Checks applied as to the number of boys in industrial and reformatory schools in respect of whom payments are made out of the grand jury cess, *ib.* 3472–3474.

Rental of Estates. See City Estates.

Residence Qualification. Introduction by the Act of 1854 of a new class of electors, that of lessors residing within five miles; defect on account of the restriction as to residence, *Hancock* 119. 121——Inexpediency of the seven miles limit in the case of Dublin, and of the residence limit in other towns, *ib.* 124, 125——Varying qualifications in different towns as regards resident and non-resident local authorities, *ib.* 126.

See also Franchise, 2, 3.

Revision of Burgess Roll (Dublin). Revision of the burgess roll by two assessors appointed by popular election; casting vote of the Lord Mayor when there is a difference between the assessors, *Hancock* 759–764——Abuse to which the system of revision is liable, though in practice none may have occurred; reference hereon to the satisfactory character of the Parliamentary revision, *ib.* 761–767.

Grounds for the conclusion that it would be a great improvement if the burgess list were revised by the revising barrister for Parliamentary purposes, *M'Evoy* 1735; *Pim* 2345.

Necessity of persons who are on the list for the first time attending in proof of their claim if objected to; different practice as to onus of proof when a person has once got on the list, *Curran* 2111–2113. 2197–2199——Statement to the effect that until 1874 all occupiers at or under 8 *l.* were struck off the burgess roll, they not having been on the rate book under the Collection of Rates Act, *ib.* 2118–2124——Practice of the Lord Mayor usually to decide in favour of enfranchisement, in the event of a difference between the two assessors, *ib.* 2190, 2191. 2282, 2283——Rate of payment of the revising barristers, the revision extending from the 20th October to the 10th November, *ib.* 2193–2196.

Several items comprised in a charge of 483 *l.* 11 *s.* 5 *d.* in connection with the burgess list, and its revision in 1874–75, *Robinson* 3395–3397.

Conclusion that the Parliamentary revising barrister should revise also the municipal lists

Revision of Burgess Roll (Dublin)—continued.

lists and the jurors' list, *Norwood* 6000–6002. 6097, 6098——Extension desirable as regards the time for completing the revision of the burgess list, *ib.* 6099. 6101.

See also Assessors. Franchise, 5.

Richmond District Lunatic Asylum. Particulars relative to the suggestions of No. 3 committee for enabling the corporation to check the accounts and expenditure of the Richmond District Lunatic Asylum; little if any control at present, *Norwood* 5953–5959——Immense increase in the annual expenditure of the asylum, *ib.* 5954——Complaint made in the town council that unduly expensive buildings had been erected by the asylum authorities, *ib.* 5956.

Further reference to the large expenditure upon the Richmond Asylum buildings, *Norwood* 5984——Large increase in the number of patients in the asylum, so that the cost of maintenance has necessarily increased, *ib.* 5984, 5985.

Ringwood Property (City of Dublin). Good condition of the Ringwood property of the Corporation of Dublin, *Morgan* 3660.

Robinson, Nugent. (Analysis of his Evidence.)—Is City Treasurer of Dublin, 2469——Statement of the rental of the city estates in 1850–51, 1870–71, and 1874–75; gross rental of 18,700 *l.* in the latter year, the property consisting chiefly of houses, 2470–2475——Information relative to the Baldoyle property of the corporation, the rental being about 1,200 *l.* a year, 2474–2479. 2483–2492——Information also relative to some property near Coolock, the present rent being about 500 *l.* a year, 2480–2482. 2493–2507.

Explanation that witness' department does not deal with the question of rental or the mode of letting, upon which points the land and law agent is the proper authority, 2499–2503. 2551–2558. 2583, 2584——Stipulations in a certain bye-law as to the re-letting or sale of any of the properties being by public auction; departure from this regulation in the case of the Baldoyle property, the rent having been subsequently reduced, 2504. 2529–2535.

Statement as to the amount of the gross and net rental respectively, and the amount of arrears at different periods, 2508–2528——Circumstance of the rental account including not only house and ground rents, but an old grant from Government since the time of Charles the Second, 2548–2550——Inability of witness to supply details as to the corporation property, this department of his office being in immediate charge of his chief assistant, 2551–2558. 2576.

Property of the corporation at Marino and other places outside the city boundary as well as at Baldoyle and Coolock, 2559–2575——Explanation relative to the "shippage and anchorage" and other dues paid to the corporation by vessels entering the harbour; decreased receipts from this source, 2577–2589——Particulars relative to the receipts of the corporation from fees paid by pawnbrokers in Ireland on licenses, &c.; considerable decrease in this item, 2590–2609.

Re-payment of two debts amounting to nearly 40,000 *l.* due by the Commissioners of Wide Streets to the Treasury at the time of the Act of 1849; 2610, 2611. 2710, 2711——Judgment debts to the amount of about 2,800 *l.* in 1849, for which a receiver was put over the city estates, 2611–2622——Total of 292,723 *l.* as the debt of the corporation in 1850; 2623–2626——Information relative to the debenture debt; reduction effected at the rate of 500 *l.* a year, 2627–2636.

Total of 24,450 *l.* borrowed from time to time since 1849 for cattle market purposes, none of which has been paid off, 2637–2644——Explanation as to the surplus of annual receipts over expenditure in respect of the cattle market not having been devoted to the reduction of the capital debt; particulars hereon relative to the separate accounts now kept of the receipt and expenditure of the different departments of the corporation, 2640–2686.

Particulars relative to the large debt of the corporation on account of waterworks, the amounts borrowed from different sources, and the reduction being effected, 2687–2708. 2715——Total of 834,329 *l.* as the debt of the corporation at the present time, 2709——Loan of 50,000 *l.* being raised under the Improvement Act of 1849 for street improvements, 2712–2715——Sale of two houses in College Green for 13,000 *l.*, which has been applied in the extinction of debentures, 2715–2720.

Receipt of 52,909 *l.* from the improvement rate of 2 *s.* in the pound in the year ending 31st August 1875; particulars as to the items of expenditure charged against the rate, 2721–2731——Limited extent to which any payment of interest or repayment of debt is charged against the improvement rate, 2722–2726. 2749–2763——Statement on the question of a transfer of 2,482 *l.* 12 *s.* 8 *d.* from the north and south sewers rate being included in the improvement rate of 52,909 *l.*, 2727–2739.

Large amount of the improvement rate spent in paving, macadamising, and scavenging, 2765–

Report, 1876—*continued.*

Robinson, Nugent. (Analysis of his Evidence)—*continued.*

2756–2758. 2764——Large expenditure also on the horse account; reference to the secretary of No. 1 committee of the corporation for explanation on this point, 2765–2775——Statement of the salaries charged against the improvement rate, amounting to 2,266 *l.*, 2776–2779——Particulars relative to the charges on account of compensations or pensions, these being on the decrease, 2780–2789.

Payment of 6,970 *l.* for public lighting, including certain salaries, 2790–2793——Amount received from the grand jury account in respect of the repairing and paving of the roadway of North Wall and the city quays, 2796–2799——Details of the annual receipts and expenditure on account of the water supply; large sum paid for interest and for reduction of debt, 2813–2825——Reference to the opposition to the Bray and Enniskerry Railway Bill as having been made in order to obtain protection for the water mains, 2826, 2827.

Large increase in the public health charges, these being defrayed out of the borough fund; various heads of expenditure, 2828–2833——Statement of the receipts and expenditure on account of the borough fund in the several years 1861–65, and in the past year, 2834–2845——Total receipts to the amount of 37,411 *l.* last year, whilst the expenditure was 39,962 *l.*, 2837, 2838. 2841——Salaries charged against the borough fund to the amount of 6,545 *l.*, 2838. 2845——Charge of 960 *l.* for water bailiffs under the head of shippage and anchorage; duties of these officers, 2838–2841. 2845–2847.

[Second Examination.] Details of the annual expenditure out of the borough fund and other funds on account of the salaries of the several officers of the corporation, 3387–3391——Varying annual charge for repairs at the Mansion House, and for furniture, &c., 3392–3394——Several items comprised in a charge of 483 *l.* 11 *s.* 5 *d.* in connection with the burgess list and its revision in 1874–75; 3395–3397——Explanation in reference to certain transfers and repayments between one fund and another; sanction by the auditor in these cases, 3397–3403.

Public audit first applied to the corporation accounts for the year ending 31st August 1872; 3440——Steps taken by the corporation which led to the appointment of a Government auditor, 3441——The audit occupies about three months in each year, 3442——Explanations in detail relative to the disallowances and surcharges by the auditor in each year since 1871–72; 3443–3457. 3463.

Litigation pending upon the question of fees in the office of the city marshal, 3454–3456——Opinion that the present system of audit is a very satisfactory one, and that the auditor is a most able and careful official, 3458——Explanation relative to an advance in April 1873 in respect of the salary of Mr. Cotton, formerly gas inspector, 3464–3471.

Statement that the corporation has accounts for only seven separate funds at the Bank of Ireland, 3475——Explanation that the payments which go to the credit of the personal account of the treasurer are not more than about 2,000 *l.* a year; character of the payments made to the credit of the account, and practice as to their subsequent transfer, 3475–3483.

Maximum reached by the water rate, both for public and domestic purposes, 3487, 3488——Explanation that the only payment by the corporation to the recorder is that from the borough fund, 3490–3493.

Robinson, Mr. Explanation that the corporation funds will not suffer by the defalcations of Mr. Robinson, *Norwood* 6136.

Rock-Road. Bad state of one of the roads out of Dublin as not being in charge of the township authorities, *Hancock* 886——Presentment of about 284 *l.* a year for the repair of Rock-road; responsibility of the grand jury of the county, and not of the corporation, for the condition of this road, *O'Donnell* 3436–3439——Partial extent to which the corporation are liable for the repair of Rock-road, *Neville* 5564–5566.

Reasons urged by No. 3. committee for transferring the repair of Rock-road to the townships of Pembroke and Blackrock, *Norwood* 5951——Provision in the Pembroke Township Act as to the contribution by the corporation towards the repair of the Rock-road, *ib.* 6094.

Royal Exchange Ward (Dublin). Illustration in the case of the Royal Exchange Ward of the unduly large representation of small ratepayers not friendly to sanitary improvement, *M'Evoy* 1678–1681.

S.

SALARIES (CITY OF DUBLIN):

Power and practice of the corporation to increase the salaries from time to time, *Henry* 1403–1406. 1418——Advantage if the salary were fixed at a certain sum, increasing by yearly increments, *M'Evoy* 1736——Erroneous impression of witness in supposing that salaries of corporation officers could not be increased without consent of the Lord Lieutenant, *M'Evoy* 2017–2019. 2026, 2027——Large increase of salaries between 1863 and 1875, the staff of officers being now too large, *ib.* 2073.

Statement of the salaries of different officers of the corporation as charged against the borough fund, amounting to 6,345 *l.* in the year 1874–75; *O'Donnell* 2847–2852——Considerable payments for salaries and wages of persons not directly employed by the corporation, as in the case of prison officers, *ib.* 3430–3435.

Details of the annual expenditure out of the borough fund and other funds on account of the salaries of the several officers of the corporation, *Robinson* 3387–3391——Explanation relative to an advance in April 1873 in respect of the salary of Mr. Cotton, formerly gas inspector, *ib.* 3464–3471.

Objection made by witness, but without effect, to payments in Dublin in advance of officers' salaries, *Finlay* 4591–4594.

Economy introduced by the reformed corporation whenever vacancies occurred in any of the old offices, *Sullivan* 4718. 4750. 4832——Defence of the additions made to officers' salaries in face of the insufficient resources of the corporation; unduly low salaries at present, *ib.* 4749, 4750——Approval of the policy of reduced salaries on first appointment, rising to a maximum according to service, *ib.* 4832–4834——Total increase of salaries to the amount of 3,619 *l.* since 1851; that is, including several additional appointments, *Neville* 5372, 5373.

Small increase of salaries, save in respect of new officers; very moderate salaries generally, *Norwood* 6004. 6006–6008. 6040——Reference to the salaries as being too small rather than too large, *Gray* 6504.

Comparative statement showing the salaries paid by the Corporation of Dublin to their officers in the years 1863–64 and 1875–76, together with extent and causes of increase or decrease in each case, *App.* 416, 417.

See also *City Marshal. Engineer and Surveyor. Lord Mayors. Pensions. Sanitary Administration,* I. 12–14. *Secretaries (Committees, &c.). Town Clerk.*

SANITARY ADMINISTRATION:

I. *Dublin:*

1. Complaints generally as to the Defective Action of the Corporation, and of the Public Health Committee.
2. Explanations generally on the Part of the Corporation, and of the Committee; Amendments suggested in the Sanitary Act.
3. Correspondence between the Sanitary Association, Local Government Board, and Public Health Committee.
4. Resolutions adopted at a Meeting of the Medical Sanitary Officers.
5. Domestic and Street Scavenging.
6. Tenement Houses and Dwellings of the Lower Classes.
7. Conveyance of Patients to the Hospitals.
8. Scavenging Depôts and Private Manure Depôts.
9. Limited Provision of Public Privies.
10. Expenditure by the Public Health Committee; Want of increased Funds.
11. Constitution of the Committee; Services rendered by the Secretary.
12. Staff of Medical Sanitary Officers; Salaries paid.
13. Duties and Salary of the Consulting Sanitary Officer.
14. Sanitary Police and Staff generally; Increase required.
15. Suggested Appointment of a Medical Superintendent.
16. Advantage of a Sanitary Magistrate.
17. Constitution and Action of the Dublin Sanitary Association; Way in which its Representations are received by the Public Health Committee.

II. *Jurisdiction and Authorities in Towns generally.*

I. *Dublin:*

1. Complaints generally as to the Defective Action of the Corporation, and of the Public Health Committee:

General feeling in Dublin that the corporation has neglected its duties in sanitary matters; instances of omission in this respect, *M'Evoy* 2064–2066——Insufficient care given

SANITARY ADMINISTRATION—continued.

.1 *Dublin*—continued.

1. Complaints generally as to the Defective Action, &c.—*continued.*

given to sanitary matters, *Pim* 2300. 2370——Important improvement expected as regards sanitary expenditure by amending the franchise, as proposed by witness, *ib.* 2437–2439.

Opinion that the Public Health Committee does not discharge its duties satisfactorily, *Grimshaw* 3911——Frequent and strong complaints in the public press relative to the sanitary management of the city, *ib.* 3912–3914. 3988.

Prejudicial effect of the present requirements as to notices, and of the practice as to fines and imprisonment; immunity from punishment in the great majority of cases, *Grimshaw* 3944–3952——Active part taken by Mr. Gray, of the "Freeman's Journal," in moving the corporation to adopt better sanitary arrangements, *ib.* 3988. 4238.

Exceedingly small improvement, which appears to have resulted from the labours of the sanitary officers, whose reports are often left unattended, *Grimshaw* 4190–4196——Statement to the effect that there seems to be no arrangement, as in Leeds and London, for the prompt inspection of localities where epidemics break out, with a view to preventing the spread of disease, *ib.* 4213–4218.

2. Explanations generally on the Part of the Corporation and of the Committee; Amendments suggested in the Sanitary Act:

Invariable report of infectious cases to witness by the sanitary police or other officers, *Boyle* 4923——Penalties to the amount of 3,004 *l.* imposed through the action of the Public Health Committee; several instances of imprisonment, *ib.* 4929——Readiness shown by the magistrates to aid the action of the committee, *ib.* 4930——Way in which action is taken in each case reported to witness by the medical sanitary officers, *ib.* 4931.

Duty of the Local Government Board and of the unions, since 1874, to take steps for preventing the spread of epidemics; assistance to be rendered by the corporation, *Boyle* 4950–4952. 5222–5224.

Report made by witness offering sundry suggestions for the amendment of the Sanitary Act, *Boyle* 5028–5033——Importance of simplifying the proceedings for the abatement of nuisances; great number of forms now necessary, and undue delay in consequence, *ib.* 5030–5033. 5274–5278——Small amount of the average fine upon each person convicted under the Sanitary Act, *ib.* 5098–5102. 5229–5232——Computation of the number of nuisances by the number of houses in which they arise, *ib.* 5131–5134. 5172–5174.

Annual reports published by the Public Health Committee since its establishment, showing the number of prosecutions, &c. in each year, *Boyle* 5175–5181——Considerable increase of prosecutions in the last two years, though the number of sanitary police serjeants has been reduced from fifteen to nine, and their districts enlarged, *ib.* 5182–5190——Careful attention paid to all complaints of sanitary defects which come before witness, *ib.* 5242, 5243.

Admission that the sanitary condition of Dublin is not so good as it ought to be, though it is not so bad as was described by Dr. Grimshaw, *Boyle* 5294–5308. 5346.

Recommendations handed in on the part of the Public Health Committee, *Norwood* 5963——Prompt attention given by the committee to sanitary matters; certain amendments are, however, much required in the sanitary laws, *ib.* 6013–6017——Decided improvement in the sanitary condition of Dublin, owing to the action of the committee; numerous instances of enforcement of fines, *ib.* 6057–6067——Periodical reports published by the committee, *ib.* 6065.

Admission that the sanitary condition of Dublin is very bad; reliable character of some special reports on the subject in the "Freeman's Journal," *Gray* 6551–6561——Insufficiency of the law, to which rather than to default of the corporation the want of improved sanitary arrangements is chiefly attributable, *ib.* 6559–6564.

Return of sanitary operations, since the application of the Sanitary Acts to Dublin, from 22nd August 1866 to 1st January 1876, *App.* 411.

3. Correspondence between the Sanitary Association, Local Government Board, and Public Health Committee:

Examination relative to correspondence in 1875 between the Sanitary Association and the Local Government Board, upon the subject of the sanitary arrangements, and the question of the Board issuing an order for Dublin under the 39th section of the Public Health Act of 1874, *Grimshaw* 4134–4144.

Charge on the part of the association in letter of 18th February, and in memorial of 11th May 1875, that the corporation had failed to make due provision for the removal of

SANITARY ADMINISTRATION—continued.

I. *Dublin*—continued.

3. Correspondence between the Sanitary Association, &c.—*continued.*

of house refuse, and the cleansing of ash-pits, cesspools, &c., *Grimshaw* 4137. 4144——Explanation offered by the corporation (Public Health Committee) on the foregoing subject, in letter of 12th March 1875, *ib.* 4140.

Very influential character of the names attached to the memorial of the association sent to the Local Government Board in May 1875; remedial measures strongly urged therein, *Grimshaw* 4144–4147.

4. Resolutions adopted at a Meeting of the Medical Sanitary Officers:

Attendance of eleven medical sanitary officers at a meeting called to consider the causes of the high mortality; resolutions agreed to by nine of these as to the improvements urgently required in sanitary matters, *Grimshaw* 4034–4037——Comment upon the course pursued by the Public Health Committee as regards the publication of the report of the foregoing meeting, *ib.* 4037–4047.

5. Domestic and Street Scavenging:

Impression as to the power having been exercised of removing ashes and night soil from the houses, *Henry* 1461–1464.

Great want of a system of domestic scavenging, the corporation being much to blame in the matter; explanation hereon as to the Local Government Board not having issued an order on the subject, *Grimshaw* 3915–3923——Extremely filthy state of the liberties of Dublin; practice of the poorer classes to throw filth into the street, as they have no means of removing it from their homes, *ib.* 3915–3918.

Instances of glaring nuisances from ash-pits, &c., which the Public Health Committee refused to consider a cause of complaint when reported by the sanitary association, *Grimshaw* 3939–3942. 4038——Practice as to the sale of the ash-pits contents; considerable value of the refuse, *ib.* 4242–4245.

Explanation as to the street sweepings, &c. not bringing in some revenue, *Boyle* 4959, 4960——Salutary effect of the action of the Public Health Committee in the matter of domestic scavenging, *ib.* 4965–4967——Reference to certain correspondence with the Local Government Board as showing that the Board did not deem it necessary to require the corporation to undertake the cleansing of ash-pits, &c. in all cases, *ib.* 4987–4990.

Particulars with further reference to the action of the corporation as regards the cleansing of ash-pits, &c., and the supervision exercised; proceedings taken, when necessary, in order to compel the owners not to neglect this duty, *Boyle* 5048–5058. 5103–5106. 5172–5174. 5198–5221. 5291–5293——Explanation more especially as to the corporation not undertaking to do the domestic scavenging in the tenement houses, and as to the rates charged by private persons for this work, *ib.* 5051–5054. 5198–5221. 5342–5345——Insufficiency of staff, but for which certain provisions as to the clearing of ash-pits, &c. in the case of tenement houses, would be more stringently enforced, *ib.* 5103–5106.

Obstacles to a system of domestic and street scavenging in Dublin as in large towns in England, *Neville* 5461–5465.

Advantages of a proposal supported by witness in 1869 for removing the scavenging soil in barges; larger outlay now required for barges, &c. than in 1869, *Neville* 5638–5644——Removal of a great deal of the scavenging materials without charge to the corporation, the cost of barges, &c. having hitherto been served, *ib.* 5825, 5826.

Objection to the removal of nuisances from dwellings at the expense of the ratepayers, this work being fairly attended to at present, *Norwood* 6021.

6. Tenement Houses and Dwellings of the Lower Classes:

Very recent action of the corporation in the direction of providing dwellings for the working classes, *Henry* 1448–1459——Unhealthy and unsafe character of a considerable number of the dwellings of the lower classes, *Pim* 2300. 2370. 2407–2414.

Great number of tenement houses visited by witness and found in a most filthy and disgraceful condition, *Grimshaw* 3929–3942——Plentiful supply of fever patients for the hospitals from these houses, many of which are quite unfit for human habitation, *ib.* 3929. 3931. 3933. 4236, 4237——Absence of any practical improvement in many of these wretched tenements since witness first reported upon them in 1871, *ib.* 3929. 3934–3937. 4192——Frightful condition of the ash-pits and privies attached to the tenement houses, *ib.* 3929. 3939, 3940——Steps taken in the removal of pigs from houses in Dublin, though not always with success, *ib.* 4198–4201.

Importance of clearing away a large number of dwellings unfit for habitation; prominent part taken in this matter by Mr. Gray as one of the corporation, *Grimshaw* 4236–4238.

SANITARY ADMINISTRATION—continued.

I. *Dublin*—continued.

6. Tenement Houses and Dwellings of the Lower Classes—*continued.*

Explanation relative to the difficulties experienced in enforcing the Sanitary Act, more especially through the antagonism of the tenement house owners, *Sullivan* 4681. 4852–4863.

Return adverted to as showing the large number of houses which have been improved in sanitary respects or have been closed since the appointment of the Public Health Committee, *Boyle* 4909——Total of 24,000 houses in Dublin, of which 9,700 are tenement houses, *ib.* 4910——Information relative to the action taken as regards 115 houses reported by Dr. Grimshaw in 1872, and designated by him as fever dens; effectual remedies applied, whilst since 1871 only three cases of fever have been reported from these houses, *ib.* 4911–4923——Prompt steps taken in 1872 for remedying the bad condition of a house in Chancery-lane, *ib.* 4924, 4925——Information relative to a complaint about the condition of a house in Ardee-street; result of special inquiry that this house was in a satisfactory state, *ib.* 4982–4986. 5287–5290.

Further statement purporting to refute Dr. Grimshaw's evidence as to numerous tenement houses being in a disgraceful and unimproved condition, *Boyle* 5296. 5313–5317——Preventive rather than remedial measures required in the case of a large number of very old houses, *ib.* 5302–5307.

Many of the tenement houses are in a most dilapidated and filthy state, *Neville* 5434.

Abstract of proceedings by the Public Health Committee since 1871, in relation to 115 houses in Dr. Grimshaw's lists; condition of the dwellings on 8th June 1876, *App.* 413.

Return showing the locality of various houses, and the cases of fever, &c. in each house; result shown that save in three instances these houses have now ceased to be "fever dens," *App.* 414, 415.

7. Conveyance of Patients to the Hospital:

Exceedingly imperfect provision for the conveyance of patients to the hospitals, the corporation having only one old cab, whilst the horse is hired and is not kept in the same place as the cab, *Grimshaw* 3964–3969. 3979–3983——Provision of some cabs by the North and South Dublin unions for the removal of patients, *ib.* 3966——Instances of persons attacked with scarlatina and with small-pox being removed to the hospitals in the public cabs, *ib.* 3979. 3983. 4089–4097.

Examination to the effect that the cabs at the unions are not kept there for the use of the general public, witness further contending that there has been great neglect in the corporation on this subject, *Grimshaw* 4060–4097. 4226–4228——Instances of salutary punishment of cabmen for conveying fever patients, *ib.* 4229, 4230.

Difficulty experienced in inducing persons to go to the hospitals, *Boyle* 4920–4922——Examination to the effect that sufficient facilities are provided for the removal of the sick and of epidemic cases, *ib.* 4935–4941. 5107–5121——Provision by the committee of two cabs for the removal of the sick to the hospitals, there being also an arrangement for the use of the cabs of the North and South Dublin unions, *ib.*

Explanation as to the supply of cabs at the unions for the removal of patients to the fever and other hospitals, *Norwood* 6069, 6070. 6117–6120.

8. Scavenging Depôts and Private Manure Depôts:

Exceedingly noxious state of the corporation scavenging depôts as well as of the private depôts; difficulty in interfering with the latter so long as the former are allowed to continue so offensive, *Grimshaw* 3924–3928. 4219–4225.

Particulars relative to the scavenging depôts of the corporation; great improvement in their condition, so that they are now innoxious, *Boyle* 4953–4958——Obstacles to a removal of the depôts outside the city, *ib.* 4959.

Street supervision over the private manure depôts, four in number; satisfactory condition of these at the present time, *Boyle* 4961–4964——Satisfaction expressed by the late inspector of the Local Government Board with the state of the manure depôts, *ib.* 4990, 4991——Ample powers of the Public Health Committee for preventing accumulations of manure, *ib.* 5047.

9. Limited Provision of Public Privies:

Statement in defence of the action of the corporation in not providing public privies save in one or two instances; intolerable nuisance experienced from these places, *Boyle* 5137–5168. 5328, 5329.

10. Expenditure by the Public Health Committee; Want of increased Funds:

Sources whence the corporation might obtain funds for improving the sanitary condition of the city, *Pim* 2457, 2458——Large increase in the public health charges, these being

SANITARY ADMINISTRATION—continued.

I. *Dublin*—continued.

10. Expenditure by the Public Health Committee, &c.—*continued.*

being defrayed out of the borough fund; various heads of expenditure, *Robinson* 2828–2833.

Average of about 2,000 *l.* a year expended for sanitary purposes, and charged upon the borough fund, *Grimshaw* 4048. 4102–4106. 4202——Full power of the corporation to levy a rate for sanitary improvements; comment upon their omission in this respect, *ib.* 4049–4055. 4102–4110——Large expense doubtless involved in the improvements proposed by witness, *ib.* 4148, 4149.

General opinion in Dublin (in which witness concurs) that much more might be done than is done with the present amount of expenditure, though an increase is doubtless necessary for sanitary purposes, *Grimshaw* 4239–4241.

Total expenditure of 21,540 *l.* by the committee since its establishment, *Boyle* 5124——Great opposition by the ratepayers if it be attempted to levy a rate-in-aid for sanitary purposes; opinion that it is preferable to levy a distinct sanitary rate, though this would be attended with much difficulty, *ib.* 5063–5065. 5070. 5270–5272. 5331–5335——Estimate of 3,100 *l.* a year as sufficient for the sanitary department; expenditure of 4,100 *l.* in 1874, for exceptional causes, *ib.* 5068, 5069. 5225–5228. 5238–5241. 5267–5269. 5304–5306. 5336–5341.

Further statement that the sanitary arrangements would be quite satisfactory if there were fifteen sanitary police officers, and if the expenditure were 3,100 *l.* a year, *Boyle* 5264–5269.

Representations by No. 3 committee of the corporation as to the increased powers required from Parliament in order to carry out certain sanitary and street improvements; proposal for a distinct rate for sanitary purposes, *Norwood* 5951–5953——Expediency of power to levy a special sanitary rate; initiative with the Public Health Committee in the matter, *Gray* 6562. 6564. 6571, 6572.

11. Constitution of the Committee; Services rendered by the Secretary:

Information as to the constitution of the Public Health Committee of the corporation which was first appointed in 1866, *Grimshaw* 3908–3909——Opinion that the members of the committee have not the proper mental capacity for sanitary duties; examination hereon to the effect that witness makes no charge of general incapacity against individuals, *ib.* 3986, 3987. 4054. 4155–4176. 4203–4206.

Testimony to the efficiency of the Public Health Committee; defects of legislation rather than of the committee to which the non-correction of sanitary abuses is owing, *Sullivan* 4703–4706——Exceeding efficiency of the secretary of the committee, *ib.* 4706——Opinion as to the satisfactory constitution of the committee, *Norwood* 6071–6073.

Particulars as to the constitution of the Public Health Committee; total of thirty members, *Boyle* 4908——Various duties discharged by witness without finding himself unequal to the work, *ib.* 5071–5073——Representation of witness, when absent from the Sanitary office, by a clerk who has but a small salary, *ib.* 5074–5078——Zealous and excellent discharge of their duties by the members of the committee, *ib.* 5079, 5080——Long hours devoted daily by witness to the discharge of his duties, *ib.* 5324.

12. Staff of Medical Sanitary Officers; Salaries paid:

Very inadequate payment of the medical sanitary officers, fourteen in number; statement hereon as to their salaries being only 25 *l.* a year, *Grimshaw* 4014–4032——Satisfactory discharge of their duties by the medical sanitary officers, as a body, *ib.* 4186–4191.

Ample supply of medical sanitary officers, *Boyle* 5258, 5259——Fair salaries paid to the medical sanitary officers, *Norwood* 6064——Want of better control of the medical sanitary officers, their salaries being at the same time raised, *Gray* 6481–6483——Instance of one officer having reported 350 cases for his salary of 25 *l.* a year, whilst another reported only five, *ib.* 6481.

13. Duties and Salary of the Consulting Sanitary Officer:

Explanation relative to the duties of Dr. Mapother, as consulting sanitary officer, his salary being 300 *l.* a year; he is perfectly qualified for the general superintendence of the department, *Grimshaw* 3990–3992. 3997–4001. 4011–4013.

Efficient services rendered by the consulting sanitary officer, his recommendations being invariably carried out, *Boyle* 4932–4934——Constant inspection by Dr. Mapother, who is a most valuable officer, *Norwood* 6063.

14. Sanitary Police and Staff generally; Increase required:

Want of an increased staff of sanitary inspectors; large amount of their time occupied in

SANITARY ADMINISTRATION—continued.

I. *Dublin*—continued.

13. Sanitary Police and Staff generally; Increase required—*continued.*

in the service of notices, *Grimshaw* 3943-3947—— Duties of the sanitary serjeants, nine in number; they are a good class of men, but their number is insufficient, *ib.* 4180-4189 ——Further reference to the want of an increased staff as a great cause of the continued existence of nuisances, *ib.* 4194-4198.

Enumeration of the sanitary officers of different kinds in Dublin, *Boyle* 4906, 4907—— Exceeding efficiency of the sanitary police staff; stimulants to zeal on their part, *ib.* 4926-4928. 5191-5197. 5256, 5257——Report by the sanitary police to the Commissioners of Police as well as to the Public Health Committee, *ib.* 4926. 5250-5252.

Insufficient means at the disposal of the Public Health Committee out of the borough fund, so that the staff cannot be increased, *Boyle* 5016-5023——Sufficiency of a staff of fifteen sanitary police offices, there being now but nine; assistance rendered by the police force generally, *ib.* 5058-5062. 5066, 5067. 5169-5171.

Anxiety of the Public Health Committee to obtain the services of some constables whose salaries they would willingly pay, *Gray* 6474, 6475.

Particulars as to the sanitary staff, including the sanitary police, *App.* 412.

Return showing the salaries of the several grades of sanitary officers, *App.* 413.

14. Suggested Appointment of a Medical Superintendent:

Want of an efficient medical superintendent with adequate powers at the head of the sanitary staff; statement as to neither Dr. Mapother nor Dr. Boyle now holding this position, *Grimshaw* 3983-4012——Expediency of the superintendence being vested in a medical man, Mr. Boyle not being qualified, *ib.* 4001*-4011.

Further advocacy of the appointment of a well-paid medical superintendent in charge of the sanitary department; suggestion made by Mr. Gray on this point, *Grimshaw* 4099-4101. 4111-4113. 4193. 4194. 4231-4233.

16. Advantage of a Sanitary Magistrate:

Advantages anticipated from the appointment of a sanitary magistrate for the metropolitan district, *Norwood* 6016-6020.

17. Constitution and Action of the Dublin Sanitary Association; Way in which its Representations are received by the Public Health Committee:

Active part taken by witness as a member of the Dublin Sanitary Association; particulars as to the constitution, objects, and operation of the association, *Grimshaw* 3885-3893——Remedy obtained in some cases by persistent action on the part of the Sanitary Association, *ib.* 3953——Active part taken by the Association since its appointment with a view to an improved system in the townships as well as in Dublin, *ib.* 4150-4152.

Doubt as to the amateur associations of citizens having been refused information when properly applied for, *Sullivan* 4724-4726.

Due attention paid by the Public Health Committee to complaints from the Sanitary Association; particulars hereon, *Boyle* 4968-4986——Explanation as to the committee having sometimes declined to notice complaints by the Association, as in the matter of slaughter-houses, *ib.* 5081-5090——Discourteous character of some representations by the Association which were not attended to by the Public Health Committee, *ib.* 5325-5327.

Examination as to the constitution and action of the citizens' committee on sanitary matters, and as to the treatment of the committee and its representations by the Public Health Committee, *Norwood* 6116-6135. 6291-6293.

Due attention paid by the corporation to the representations made by the Sanitary Association, *Gray* 6472. 6532——Difficulty as regards communication with the association by reason of some of its members being paid officers of the corporation, *ib.* 6472. 6532. 6542-6548——Respects in which the association has a political tinge, *ib.* 6530. 6535-6541——Explanation as to letters or complaints from the association not being always noticed by the corporation, *ib.* 6530. 6532. 6542-6548.

Reasons further assigned for the omission to answer some of the complaints submitted to the Public Health Committee by the Sanitary Association, *Gray* 6734-6736.

II. *Jurisdiction and Authorities in Towns generally:*

Distinction drawn by the Public Health Act of 1874, whereby in every town having more than 6,000 inhabitants the town authorities are declared to be the urban sanitary authority, *Hancock* 2——Four towns with urban sanitary authorities under the Act 9 Geo. 4 (1828), *ib.*——Sixteen such towns under the Towns Improvement Act of 1854, *ib.*

Great

Report, 1876—*continued.*

SANITARY ADMINISTRATION—continued.

II. *Jurisdiction and Authorities in Towns generally*—continued.

Great inconvenience as regards sanitary powers resting mainly on an extension of the English law to Ireland in 1866, *Hancock* 83——Grounds for the conclusion that the English Sanitary Code of 1875 might be extended to Ireland in about ten clauses with very beneficial results, *ib.* 83, 84.

Illustrations of the inconvenience in sanitary matters by the overlapping of areas, and by the existence of several authorities in the same area, *Hancock* 994–1014.

Return of the different towns with one or more authorities within the town boundary, *App.* 399, 400.

See also Abattoirs. Artisans' Dwellings Act. Building Act. Dairy Yards. Disinfection. Floating Hospital. Health of Dublin. Liffey, The. Local Government Board. Main Drainage. Manure Manufactories. Meat, Inspection of. Slaughter-houses. Streets (Paving, &c.).

Scavenging (Dublin). See *Materials (Dublin Streets). Sanitary Administration*, I, 5. 8. *Streets (Paving, Scavenging, &c.).*

School Boards. Advantage of the school board principle of election as regards occupiers, *Hancock* 168–171.

Secretaries (Committees of the Corporation of Dublin). Appointment of the secretaries of the different committees by the council, the salaries being limited to 400 *l.* a year; this limit does not apply to Mr. Boyle, secretary of the Public Health Committee, *Henry* 1422–1431. 1561, 1562——Authority in the Dublin Improvement Act of 1849 for the appointment of salaried secretaries of committees, *ib.* 1616–1620——Economy as to salaries in the appointment of secretaries to the standing committees, *Norwood* 6308.

Security (Municipal Officers). Omission on the part of the Corporation of Dublin in not obtaining a bond or security for each of their officers, *Finlay* 4313. 4314. 4431.

Sewers and Sewer Rate (Dublin). Separate estimates made for the north sewer rate and the south sewer rate, *Taafe* 558, 559——Powers of the corporation under the Act of 1849 to levy a sewer rate and to make sewers, *Henry* 1106–1109——Separate provisions as to the sewer rate, which has its own liabilities, *ib.* 1140——Belief that there are no debts on the sewer rate, *ib.* 1601——Instance of the sewer rate not having been up to the maximum, *ib.* 1612.

Great improvements made by the corporation in the sewers out of the sewer rate of 4 *d.*; large outlay involved, *Neville* 5422, 5423——Distinct character of the sewer rate, which has never been applied for grand jury purposes, *ib.* 5547.

Statement as regards some actions brought successfully against the corporation on account of flooding from the sewers, that this does not prove any defective construction, *Neville* 5745–5749.

See also Mountjoy Square Sewer.

Sheriffs. Provisions in the Municipal Reform Act relative to the transfer from certain corporations to the Crown of the appointment of sheriff and clerk of the peace, *Hancock* 609. 612, 613——Very large number of writs issued by the sheriff of the city of Dublin, *ib.* 746–751.

System of nomination and appointment of the sheriffs in the city of Dublin; relative proportion of Protestants and Roman Catholics appointed, *Hancock* 864–872.

Explanation on the subject of the fees paid to the high sheriff of Dublin by the corporation; the money really goes to the sub-sheriff, *Henry* 1468–1476——Provisions of the Act 1 & 2 Geo. 4. c. 77, as to the payment of fees to sheriffs, under-sheriffs, and other officers, *ib.* 1621–1623.

Benefit anticipated from empowering the corporation to elect sheriffs; advantage also if the Lord Mayor of one year were the sheriff of the next, *Gray* 6723.

Shippage and Anchorage Dues (Port of Dublin). Explanation relative to the "shippage and anchorage" and other dues paid to the corporation by vessels entering the harbour; decreased receipts from this source, *Robinson* 2577–2589——Charge of 900 *l.* for water bailiffs under the head of shippage and anchorage; duties of these officers, *ib.* 2838–2841. 2845–2847.

Slaughter-houses (Dublin). Comment upon the great abuse in the matter of slaughter-houses, these being generally surrounded by the dwellings of the poorer classes, *Pim* 2455–2469——Great abuse in the licensing of slaughter-houses, whilst some of them are in a very filthy and noxious condition, *Grimshaw* 3954–3958.

Inaccuracy of any statement as to persons dwelling over slaughter-houses, *Boyle* 5025–5027——Concurrence with Mr. Pim as to the injurious effect of slaughter-houses surrounded by the dwellings of the lower classes, *ib.* 5279–5286.

Slaughter-houses (Dublin)—continued.

Weekly inspection of the slaughter-houses, *Norwood* 6081——Demoralising effect of the slaughter-houses, *Gray* 6494.

See also Abattoirs.

South Dublin Union. Examination upon the question whether the administration of the South Dublin Union has not been very defective, the guardians being mostly Conservatives, *Stokes* 2955–2969.

Considerable surcharges made by the auditor upon some of the officials of the South Dublin Union, *Norwood* 6204——Statement to the effect that the guardians of the union, as a body, are not open to certain animadversions passed upon the Board; instances of political discussions at the Board, *ib.* 6205. 6208–6218.

Very unsatisfactory results of the direct representation of property in the Board of the South Dublin Union; strictly sectarian character of the appointments by the Board, *Gray* 6377, 6378——Great neglect in the administration of the South Dublin Union, as shown by the heavy surcharges, *ib.* 6739, 6740.

Evidence in further support of the conclusion that religion and politics influence the appointments in the union, all the highly-salaried officers being Protestants, whilst the subordinate offices are given to Roman Catholics, *Gray* 6741–6763.

Staff (Corporation of Dublin). Supervision exercised over the officers by the council and the committees, *Henry* 1434–1436. 1494–1499. 1645——Retention by the corporation in 1851 of many of the officers previously employed by the Paving Board, the Wide Streets Board, and the Term Grand Jury; charge incurred for compensation in respect of those officers whose services were dispensed with, *Neville* 5363–5368——Small staff employed by the corporation of Dublin as compared with other large municipalities, *ib.* 5371——Inaccuracy of a statement as to the corporation being too large a staff of officers, *Norwood* 6025, 6026.

See also Appointment of Officers. Pensions. Salaries.

Stephen's Green. Objection to the large expenditure incurred in opposing the Stephen's Green Bill, *M'Evoy* 1708——Exceptions taken to the refusal by the corporation of Sir Arthur Guinness' offer to contribute 5,000 *l.* towards the opening of St. Stephen's Green, *Pim* 2451–2456.

Good ground for the opposition to the Stephen's Green Bill of 1866, *Neville* 5468——Statement strongly in favour of Stephen's Green being opened to the public, *ib.* 5782–5784. 5848–5851. 5860.

Examination to the effect that in 1866 the corporation opposed the opening of Stephen's Green as involving the loss of a rent of 300 *l.* a year, and have since opposed, unless the management be transferred to them; question at issue whether the corporation or the Board of Works should be entrusted with the care of the Green, *Neville* 5785–5798. 5813–5821. 5835–5837. 5852–5874.

Conditional offer of 7,000 *l.* by Sir Arthur Guinness for the improvement of the Green; offer also of 600 *l.* a year by Government, *Neville* 5853–5856——Explanation as to these offers having fallen through, *ib.* 5857–5866.

Stokes, Frederick. (Analysis of his Evidence.)—Long experience of witness as Chairman of the Township Commissioners of Rathmines and Rathgar, 2855——Population of about 22,000 in the township, the valuation being about 93,000 *l.*, 2857, 2858——Special Act in 1847, under which the commissioners are constituted, the number being twenty-one, and the qualification being a rating of 30 *l.* for residents, 2859–2861——The qualification of electors is 10 *l.* occupation, there being no owner's qualification, 2862.

Present rate in the township of 2 *s.* in the pound, this amount having never been exceeded; this includes paving and lighting, water, grand jury cess, and sewerage, 2863–2868. 2875–2878——Independent water supply of the township, the rate being now 4 *d.*; debt of 22,000 *l.* due on account of the works, 2867–2871——Lower rate of interest paid for the water loans than is paid by the corporation of Dublin on their loans, 2872, 2873——Power of the commissioners as to maintenance of the roads, 2874——Payment made to the grand jury in respect of gaols and lunatic asylums, 2875——Contribution also towards the bridges and quay walls in the city, 2876, 2877.

Excellent system of sewers in the township, 2880, 2881——Rates of 5 *s.* 7 *d.* in Dublin as compared with 2 *s.* in Rathmines, 2882——Police tax of 8 *d.* in the township, being the same as in the city, 2883——Poor rate of 1 *s.* 2 *d.* as compared with 1 *s.* 10 *d.* in the city; very few paupers in the township, 2884–2889. 2992–2997.

Gradual deterioration in the constitution of the corporation of Dublin since it was reformed in 1850; very inadequate representation of the better and wealthier class of ratepayers, 2887–2889. 2943–2945——Undue representation of the publican interest in the corporation,

Stokes, Frederick. (Analysis of his Evidence)—*continued.*

corporation, there being some fifteen publicans in the council; examination as to witness' grounds for this statement, 2890. 2891. 3019–3041. 3067–3077.

Conduct of the elections for the corporation on political grounds, with very few exceptions, 2892, 2893. 3185–3187——Election of the commissioners in Rathmines without any reference to politics, the great majority of members being, however, Conservatives, 2894–2898. 2948–2956——Much higher prices paid in the city than in Rathmines for materials, the corporation taking credit, and the commissioners paying cash, 2899–2903. 3008–3013. 3223. 3224. 3278–3290——Better labourers under the commissioners than under the corporation, 2904, 2905.

Statement as to the valuation of the city being shamefully low and exceedingly unequal; examination as to the grounds for this conclusion, 2906, 2907. 2975–2982——Bad collection of the rates in Dublin; unduly large per-centage lost, 2906. 2908, 2909——Exceedingly close collection of the rates in Rathmines and Rathgar; explanation hereon as to the precautions taken so as to secure full recovery, 2910–2923.

Decided objection to proposals for annexing the township to the city; large proportion of ratepayers in the former not interested in the trade of the city, 2924–2926. 3366——Very large increase in the valuation of the township since 1850; 2927——Total of 3,300 ratepayers, of whom 788 are females: the latter do not vote at elections, 2928–2930——Very unwise act of the corporation in annexing the unremunerative district between the Circular-road and the Canal, including Mud Island; heavy charge involved, 2931–2933. 3360–3365.

Good work performed by the old paving board in Dublin, whilst the rate for the roads, &c. was much lower than at present, 2934–2937——Nothing would induce witness to enter the corporation, though personally the members have always treated him with every courtesy, 2938–2942. 3081——Recent instance of the reluctance of respectable citizens to join the corporation, 2942.

Conclusion as to the expediency of a better representation of property in the city elections; advantage of plural voting and of a property qualification, 2943–2947. 3149–3153. 3179——Opinion that owners, as not directly paying rates, should not take part in the elections; objections also to a division of rates between owners and occupiers, and to a direct representation of the former, 2945, 2946. 3154–3161. 3250–3277.

Examination upon the question whether the administration of the South Dublin Union has not been very defective, the guardians being mostly Conservatives, 2955–2969——Relative requirements of Rathmines and of the city in the matter of gas lights and water pipes, 2970–2973——Low valuation in Rathmines though much higher than in the city, 2974. 3043–3049——Explanation as to witness being the only burgess in respect of Commercial Buildings; his object in retaining his name on the burgess list, 2983–2991. 3087–3089.

Comment upon the omission of the corporation to provide for a complete re-valuation of the city, in lieu of the partial and unequal system now in operation, 2998–3007. 3090, 3091——Decided economy in the purchase of materials if the corporation had put themselves in funds by means of a loan, 3013–3018. 3225–3229——Examination to the effect that in view of the very low valuation in Dublin, the difference between the rates in the city and in Rathmines is not so great as it appears, 3042–3059.

Inducement to persons to leave the city for Rathmines on account of the lower taxes, 3060–3065——Decreasing poor rate in the city and increasing rate in Rathmines, owing to union rating, 3063——Very rare complaints in the township as to the administration by the commissioners, 3066——Very few of the leading merchants who are members of the corporation, 3079–3081——Denial that the commissioners, as such, ever take any part in politics; facility to the conduct of business by abstaining from political discussions, 3082–3086. 3144–3148.

Different standards of valuation adopted in Dublin previously to 1850 and in that year; much higher standard at the present time, 3090–3104——Explanation and defence of the system of election by the ratepayers of two auditors for Rathmines township, 3105–3131——Approval, however, of independent public auditors for large corporations like Dublin, though inconvenience sometimes arises on legal points, 3114–3131.

Punctual attendance at the meetings of the Rathmines Commissioners, a quorum of five members being always present, 3132–3136——Recommended reduction of the quorum of the corporation from twenty to seven or ten members, 3137–3143——Low rate of mortality in Rathmines, 3162–3164——Information as to the relative amount of rating in the case of the commissioners and of the corporation; examination hereon showing that witness has been misinformed as to the rating of some members of the corporation, 3165–3169. 3301–3333.

Entire dissent from a statement that the insufficiency of the Dublin improvement rate is due to the construction of new streets of a low class, 3173–3175. 3241–3244——Exceptional instance of complaint by the sanitary committee of Dublin with respect to Rathmines, 3176–3178——Explanation as to witness having lent 35,000 *l.* to the corporation

Stokes, Frederick. (Analysis of his Evidence)—*continued.*

portion at five per cent. interest, with a commission of two per cent.; considerable profit made by him on this transaction, 3180–3182. 3204–3218. 3373–3377, 3378——Frequent loans made to the corporation by Mr. Jameson, 3183——Urgent need of the corporation some years ago when they borrowed 5,000 *l.* from their newly appointed treasurer, 3184.

Statement as to Mr. Casson, an old member of the corporation, having lost his election on political grounds; previous attendances of Mr. Casson adverted to hereon, 3186. 3334–3346——Irregular course pursued by the corporation in regard to levying out of the grand jury rate the sum required for repairs to the North Wall, whilst a portion of the improvement rate had been lent for sewer purposes; decisions of the judges adverse to the corporation, 3188–3191. 3291–3300——Instance of a transfer or loan of 2,800 *l.* from the sewer rate to the improvement rate; irregularity of this transaction, 3192, 3193.

Frequent instances of great delay before reports of committees are voted upon by the council, 3194——Circumstance of the Vartry waterworks having cost about twice the original estimate, 3195, 3196——Opposition made by witness to the Vartry scheme; belief that the Coy Ford or Ballysmuttan scheme could have been carried out at half the cost, 3197, 3198. 3347——Good quality of the Vartry supply, 3198, 3199.

Particulars relative to the issue of debentures by the corporation, and the low price obtained as compared with the rate of interest, 3200, 3201. 3204–3218. 3228, 3229. 3232–3240. 3377–3380——General confidence enjoyed by the Port and Docks Board, 3202, 3203——Expediency of a compulsory re-valuation, 3219–3222——Explanations in reference to the main drainage scheme, and the cause of its break-down; great cost involved in the plan over and above the estimates, 3245–3249. 3367–3372.

Apparently excessive cost of forage for the horses of the corporation, 3278–3290——Question considered whether the outlying townships could have been as well served with water under the Coy Ford scheme as the Vartry scheme, 3348–3354——Exceptions taken as regards the water rate charged by the corporation, 3354–3359——Grounds for the conclusion that an extension of the city area so as to include Rathmines, would not benefit the citizens, whilst it would be injurious to the township, 3366.

Power under the Waterworks Act of raising money on security of taxation over and above the maximum water rate, 3373–3376——Comment upon the course pursued in liquidating out of capital a deficiency of 19,000 *l.* incurred during the earlier years of the new water supply, through the inadequacy of the rate, 3381–3386.

Streets (Paving, Scavenging, &c.) and Street Improvements:

1. *As to the Paving and Scavenging of Streets in Dublin, and the Want of increased Funds for the Purpose.*
2. *As to the Improvement and Widening of Streets in Dublin, and the Powers available in respect thereof.*
3. *As to the Authority in Towns generally for effecting Street Improvements.*

1. *As to the Paving and Scavenging of Streets in Dublin, and the Want of increased Funds for the Purpose:*

Explanation as regards the fund for cleansing the streets in Dublin that the paving board and the wide streets board were not transferred until 1849, *Hancock* 952–955.

General feeling in the city that the streets are badly kept, and that the back streets are especially neglected, *Pim* 2300. 2370——Good work performed by the old paving board in Dublin, whilst the rate for the roads, &c. was much lower than at present, *Stokes* 2934–2937.

Unsatisfactory supervision of the streets if the borough engineer should be occupied upon the main drainage, *Sullivan* 4751–4753——Larger staff required for cleansing arrangements, *Boyle* 5273.

Expenditure of about 11,000 *l.* a year by the former paving board on the scavenging and watering of eighty-eight miles of streets, whilst the corporation spend 15,716 *l.* on 110 miles, *Neville* 5374–5383. 5407——Fluctuation in the valuation and in the annual sum available for the paving, &c. of the streets under the paving board and under the corporation, *ib.* 5385–5389.

Calculation that in proportion to the expenditure by the paving board on watering and scavenging, the expenditure by the corporation should be very much greater than it is, making allowance for the increased price of materials and labour, and the increased mileage, *Neville* 5407–5411——Large expenditure by the corporation on new pavements, the money having been raised under a certain clause in the Ballast Board Act of 1792, copied into the Port and Docks Act of 1869, *ib.* 5418, 5419.

Entire insufficiency of the funds at the disposal of the corporation for the proper maintenance of the streets, *Neville* 5435–5438——Bad state of several of the streets as not having been paved for about eighteen years, *ib.* 5620——Saving expected from the use by the

STREETS (PAVING, SCAVENGING, &c.) AND STREET IMPROVEMENTS—continued.

1. *As to the Paving and Scavenging of Streets in Dublin, &c.*—continued.

the contractors of machinery for breaking stone for the streets; objection to the corporation buying machinery for the purpose, *Neville* 5760-5763.

Representations in detail on the part of committee No. 1 as to the want of increased powers and augmented revenue in connection with paving, cleansing, lighting, &c., *Norwood* 5936——Necessity of an increase of revenue for the purpose of scavenging, *Gray* 6608.

Return showing the amount received by the late paving board commissioners during the years 1845-50, which was applicable for the lighting, cleansing, repair, and maintenance of the streets, *App.* 454.

2. *As to the Improvement and Widening of Streets in Dublin, and the Powers available in respect thereof:*

Circumstance of the corporation not having utilised the powers which they have inherited from the Wide Streets Commissioners, *M'Evoy* 2078-2080——Entire inadequacy of the powers of the corporation for clearing away ruinous property and effecting street improvements, the powers of the Wide Street Commissioners not having been fully transferred to the corporation, *Sullivan* 4682-4684.

Limited extent to which the corporation have been able to widen streets, *Neville* 5425——Belief as to all the powers of the Wide Street Commissioners (except the rating power) having been transferred to the corporation, *ib.* 5612.

Enlarged powers required as regards the widening of streets and the removal of obstructions, *Norwood* 5937-5942——Suggestion made by witness several years ago for the construction of a wide street in St. Michan's parish, *ib.* 6023, 6024.

Absence of power to levy a rate for widening the streets, *Gray* 6441, 6442——Objections to a power in the corporation of taking property compulsorily for street improvements, *ib.* 6443-6449.

3. *As to the Authority in Towns generally for effecting Street Improvements:*

Several instances of towns having obtained local Acts by reason of the divided authority over the streets; particulars hereon, *Hancock* 41, 42. 48-65.

Examination in detail in support of increased facilities in towns for separating themselves from counties in reference to expenditure of local rates in street improvements and sanitary matters generally, *Hancock* 877-890. 962 *et seq.*

See also *Asphalte Pavements.* *Building Act.* *Improvement Rate.* *Materials.* *North Wall and City Quays.* *Rock-road.* *Sanitary Administration*, 1.

Sullivan, Alexander M. (*Member of the House*). (Analysis of his Evidence.)—Experience of witness for several years as a member of the Municipal Corporation of Dublin; he acted upon nearly all the committees, 4657-4659——Zeal and integrity with which the duties of the corporation were discharged, though there is doubtless some need of reformation in the constitution and working of the council, 4660. 4663. 4664——Defeat of witness when seeking re-election in 1870 or 1871, since which period he has not been in the council, 4661, 4662.

State of chronic impecuniosity to which the inefficient management of the city of Dublin is mainly owing, 4665-4668. 4719——Effect of the want of funds in deterring many men of position and capacity from entering the corporation or remaining in it, 4666, 4667. 4793——Comment upon the course pursued by the old corporation in largely borrowing on debenture instead of in raising taxes for current expenditure, 4668. 4709——Undeserved unpopularity of the reformed corporation through having greatly increased the taxation, whereas this was unavoidable, 4668. 4707, 4708.

Prejudicial effect of the influential antagonism to the reformed corporation on political grounds; that is, up to the year 1851; 4668——Explanation as regards the scavenging and cleansing of the city that the bad condition of Dublin in this respect is mainly owing to the very inferior quality of the stone used for the streets, 4668. 4670——Undue cost of stone from Wales, though far superior to the Dublin stone, 4668-4670.

Exceptional liberality evinced by the reformed corporation in its tolerance of minority dissent, as in appointing to the office of Lord Mayor, &c., irrespectively of political considerations, 4671. 4766-4771——Fallacy of the notion that the municipal taxation of Dublin is excessively high as compared with that of other large towns; grounds for this conclusion, 4762——Effect of the unduly low valuation in rendering the improvement rate of 2 *d.* in the pound altogether inadequate to meet the demands upon it, 4672. 4682.

Comments upon the extensive alienations of corporate property in the last century, 4672-4676——Very valuable property obtained by Trinity College from the corporation, gratuitously, 4672——Concurrence in the statements in a certain report by Mr. Morgan upon the subject of the corporation property and rental, 4676-4680.

Sullivan, Alexander M. (*Member of the House*). (Analysis of his Evidence)—*continued.*

Opposition unfairly met with by the corporation from the Anti-political Ratepayers' Association in applying the sanitary laws to tenement house property, 4681——Mischievous misleading of the public mind by the statements put forward by different amateur societies, who are not always conversant with the correct facts, *ib.*——Comment upon the opposition experienced by the corporation in reference to the main drainage scheme for the cleansing of the Liffey, *ib.*

Want of men in the corporation who could afford to defy unpopularity, and would persist in carrying out necessary reforms, 4681——Approval of some concessions by the popular party, so as to bring into the corporation the co-operation of a large number of influential citizens, 4681, 4682. 4776-4784——Several respects in which the franchise might be developed, by way of concession by the popular party, 4682.

Suggestion that property owners non-resident in the city be allowed to vote, 4682. 4776——Proposal for the adoption of cumulative voting, so that the minority in any ward may be able to return a member; concession thereby to the Conservatives, 4682. 4696, 4697——Conclusion as to the necessity of an enlargement of the municipal area; suggestions as to the boundary which might be adopted, 4682. 4693-4695. 4720.

Want of an adjustment of the existing valuation; a fair valuation would increase the corporate funds by from 10,000 *l.* to 15,000 *l.* a year, 4682. 4804, 4805——Entire inadequacy of the powers of the corporation for clearing away ruinous property and effecting street improvements, the powers of the Wide Street Commissioners not having been fully transferred to the corporation, 4682-4684——Failure of some efforts by Mr. Maclean (the highly efficient chairman of the Public Health Committee), and of witness to induce influential men to enter the corporation, political considerations being waived, 4685——Objections by leading merchants to join the corporation as involving too much demand on their time, 4686.

Urgent want of a Building Act for Dublin, on sanitary grounds; failure of attempts in 1867 to obtain an Act, 4685-4688. 4721——Conclusion that one-third is too large a proportion of the corporation to be in peril of their seats every year; obstacle to any useful reforms on account of the liability of independent members to lose their seats, 4688, 4689——Antagonism of various interests which prevented witness' re-election, he having promoted several obnoxious reforms, 4688——Opinion that the required reforms in sanitary and other matters can only be carried out by a public Bill; inability of the corporation to pass a Bill for the purpose, 4688. 4719-4722.

Suggestion that in five wards in the city three members might be elected simultaneously, 4690-4692——Too many representatives at present for each ward, 4690, 4691——Proposal that there still be but sixty representatives, the municipal area being extended, 4691——Suggested qualification of 50 *l.* a year in the case of non-resident owners, direct payment of taxes being dispensed with as a qualification, 4698. 4815-4821——Decided objection to a plurality of votes, 4699.

Further evidence as to the want of a compulsory re-valuation of Dublin, or of a re-adjustment, and as to the inability of the corporation to obtain it; great opposition apprehended on the part of the ratepayers, 4700-4703. 4720. 4804-4810——Testimony to the efficiency of the Public Health Committee of the corporation, and of its secretary, Mr. Boyle; defects of legislation rather than of the committee to which the non-correction of sanitary abuses is owing, 4703-4706.

Debt of about 230,000 *l.* left by the old corporation, who appear to have never levied a tax while they could borrow, 4707-4709——Numerous improvements which devolved upon the new corporation, besides which they had to pay interest on the debt, 4707. 4708——Concurrence in the view that amendment is required as regards the mode of keeping the accounts in the Bank of Ireland, the separate funds not being separately dealt with, 4710-4718——Economy introduced by the reformed corporation whenever vacancies occurred in any of the old offices, 4718. 4750. 4832.

Great evil in owners of property not being better represented in the municipal council, 4723. 4772——Doubt as to the amateur associations of citizens having been refused information when properly applied for, 4724-4726——Examination with further reference to the action respectively of the citizens' committee and of the corporation as regards the main drainage scheme, 4727-4744——Disapproval of the hesitation shown in carrying out Mr. Bazalgette's scheme, notwithstanding that the cost will be enormously in excess of the Parliamentary Estimate, 4736. 4739-4744.

Belief that if the corporation had not been obstructed in their attempt to acquire the gas works the ratepayers would have largely benefited, 4745-4477. 4894-4897——Approval of the corporation having control not only of the gas supply, but of public markets, abattoirs, and several other improvements; that is, if there are funds for the purpose, and if the constitution of the corporation be improved, 4747-4749. 4895. 4896.

Defence of the additions made to officers' salaries in face of the insufficient resources of the corporation; unduly low salaries at present, 4749. 4750——Unsatisfactory supervision

Report, 1876—*continued.*

Sullivan, Alexander M. (*Member of the House*). (Analysis of his Evidence)—*continued.*

vision of the streets if the borough engineer should be occupied upon the main drainage 4751–4753——Further statement as to the corporation having promoted a Building Bill, but having failed to carry it, 4754–4756. 4811–4813.

Grounds for the conclusion that in some respects political discussion in the Corporation of Dublin has been productive of much public good, 4757–4759——Main duty doubtless of the corporation to see to the expenditure of the rates and the sanitary condition of the city, 4760–4762——Justification of the course pursued by the corporation in their selection of representatives before the present committee, 4763–4765——Instances of the liberality of the corporation in making appointments irrespectively of politics, 4766——Illustration of the foregoing principle in the election of Lord Mayors, 4766–4769.

Examination adverse to the proposition that owners, as in Scotland, should be liable for half the rates, and should share the municipal representation with the occupiers; approval however, of some concession, in order to induce owners to enter the corporation, 4772–4786——Comment upon the course pursued by certain leading men in opposing the Vartry Water scheme, 4786.

Further statement in connection with the large debt and the bad credit inherited by the new from the old corporation; effect as regards the price at which money was raised on debenture, 4787–4792——Belief that by an extension of the municipal boundary, and a re-adjustment of the valuation, sufficient funds would be obtained for an efficient administration, 4794, 4795. 4802. 4804–4810——Suggestion in regard to Government lending money to the corporation on easy terms for the execution of necessary works, 4794–4801.

Claim of the corporation to the carriage rents or licenses, 4802, 4803——Opinion that on the other hand the corporation should give up the receipts from pawnbrokers' licenses issued all over Ireland, 4802——Proposed abolition of the office of city marshal, *ib.*——Great obstruction to business in the corporation by the necessity of a quorum of twenty members; sufficiency of a quorum of thirteen, 4812–4814.

Explanation with further reference to witness' former experience as a member of the corporation, and his reason for proposing some concession to property owners in the case of Dublin, 4822–4828. 4835–4842——Approval of applying to Dublin the Artizans' Dwellings Act of 1875, 4829——Circumstances of the Building Bill having been modelled on the Belfast Building Act, 4830——Twofold size of the municipal area of Belfast as compared with Dublin, 4830, 4831——Approval of the policy of reduced salaries on first appointment, rising to a maximum according to service, 4832–4834.

Undue restriction of the burgess roll on account of the obstructions by political agents, 4835——Expediency of the basis of the franchise being widened concurrently with some concession to property owners: this latter concession should apply to other places as well as Dublin if the circumstances are the same, 4836–4842. 4864–4870——Special reasons which apply in the case of Dublin in favour of a re-adjustment of the valuation, the inequalities being very great, 4843–4851.

Further explanation relative to the difficulties experienced in enforcing the Sanitary Act, more especially through the antagonism of the tenement house owners, 4852–4863——Absence of any good claim in the townships round Dublin to continue outside the municipal area, 4871–4873——Reason for re-valuation generally where the values of properties have changed, 4874–4876.

Grounds for objecting to the transaction of corporation business by Committees of the whole House, 4877, 4878——Instances of obstruction of business at the public sittings of the corporation through one member objecting to suspend the bye-laws, 4878–4880——Private character of the meetings of the several committees, the business being excellently conducted, 4881–4884.

Necessary character of a large portion of the increased cost of the main drainage scheme beyond the original estimates; that is, on account of the large advance in the price of materials, 4885–4890——Further explanation in defence of the action of the corporation as regards members being deputed to represent them before the present Committee, 4891–4893——Suggestion that Mr. Byrne or Mr. Norwood, who are strong Conservatives and most efficient members, be summoned by the Committee to give evidence, 4892.

Summonses to Jurors. Instance of unauthorised expenditure incurred in the printing of summonses to the jurors in Dublin, *Finlay* 4535–4537.

T.

Taafe, M. P. V. See *Moylan, Denis, &c.*

Tenement Houses (Dublin). See *Rates.* *Sanitary Administration*, I. 6.

Town Clerk (Dublin). Increase of witness' salary from 400 *l.* to 600 *l.* a year over a period of thirteen years; smallness of his remuneration as compared with that of town clerks in England, *Henry* 1407–1417. 1420, 1421. 1432. 1525–1527——Further reference to the limited salary of witness, all his time being devoted to his office, *ib.* 1486–1493.

Statement as to the town clerk having never accounted to the corporation for certain fees received by him; witness has constantly called attention to this omission, but the corporation are satisfied with the reasons given by Mr. Henry for retaining the fees, *Finlay* 4274–4281.

Evidence as to the grounds upon which witness recommended that the Corporation of Dublin should claim the refund of certain fees received by Mr. Henry as town clerk, and by Mr. Hayes as city marshal; result of the legal proceedings in each case, *Finlay* 4413–4418.

Shamefully low salary of the town clerk, *Sullivan* 4750.

Town Councils. Eleven towns in Ireland under town councils, five being under the Towns Improvement Act of 1854 and six under local Acts, *Hancock* 2–20.

See also Corporation of Dublin.

Towns Improvement Act. See *Act* 17 *&* 18 *Vict. c.* 103 (1854).

Townships (Dublin). See *Area of Dublin.* *Rathmines and Rathgar Township Water Supply.*

Tramways (Dublin). Considerable relief being obtained through the Tramway Company as regards the maintenance of the streets, *Norwood* 6115.

Trim (Meath). Grounds for the complaints made by witness in his report in 1873 upon the manner in which the Town Commissioners of Trim deal with their landed property; belief that no action has been taken upon his report, *Finlay* 4339–4348——Particulars as to several disallowances by witness in his audit of the Trim accounts, and as to the litigation and costs incurred in connection therewith, *ib.* 4349–4357——Data upon which witness concluded that the receipts from the corporation lands were insufficient, *ib.* 4638–4641.

Trinity College (Dublin). Very valuable property obtained by Trinity College from the corporation gratuitously, *Sullivan* 4670. 4682.

Proposal on the part of the corporation that Trinity College and similar institutions be required to pay grand jury and other rates, *Norwood* 5953.

Trinity Ward (Dublin). Not a single burgess is on the roll for Trinity ward in which Trinity College stands, *M'Evoy* 1661.

Tullamore. Careful administration in Tullamore, *Finlay* 4630, 4631.

U.

Ulster. Estimated increase from 4,223,271 *l.* to 4,927,000 *l.* in the valuation of Ulster by a re-valuation; data for this calculation, *Greene* 6981–6984. 6989–6997.

Union Rating. High rates in small towns owing to the absence of union rating, *Hancock* 910, 911.——*See also Poor Rate.*

V.

VALUATION:

I. *Dublin*:

1. Unduly low and very unequal Valuation now in force; urgent Want of a Re-valuation:

Total of 596,099 *l.* as the valuation of Dublin in 1875; doubt, however, as to Government property being included, *Henry* 1322–1324——Statement to the effect that the valuation has much decreased since 1849; causes thereof, *ib.* 1337–1340. 1354–1361——Insufficiency and inequality of the valuation at the present time, *ib.* 1341–1347——It is nearly twenty-five per cent. under the proper amount, *ib.* 1343.

Expediency of a complete re-valuation, the present valuation being very low and unequal, *M'Evoy* 1754–1761——Respects in which the present system of valuation in Dublin is very unequal and unsatisfactory; want of a re-valuation not only for Dublin but for all Ireland, *Pim* 2346–2351; *Norwood* 6173–6184. 6281–6284.

Statement as to the valuation of the city being shamefully low and exceedingly unequal; examination as to the grounds for this conclusion, *Stokes* 2906, 2907. 2975–2981——In many cases the valuation is not one-half, and in some cases not one-third of what it should be, *ib.* 2907——Particular instances of great inequality, *ib.* 2976–2981——Different standards of valuation adopted in Dublin previously to 1850 and in that year; much higher standard at the present time, *ib.* 3090–3104——Expediency of a compulsory re-valuation, *ib.* 3219–3222.

Glaring inequalities now existing, *Sullivan* 4682——Special reasons which apply in the case of Dublin in favour of a re-adjustment of the valuation, the inequalities being very great, *ib.* 4700–4703. 4804–4810. 4843–4851.

Conclusion that the valuation is much too low, and is very inadequate; authority of Mr. Ball Greene to this effect, *Neville* 5435. 5439–5441——A re-valuation of Dublin is essential in justice, with a view more especially to the correction of inequalities, *Gray* 6360——Probability of a re-valuation involving an increased valuation on the whole, *ib.* 6611–6613.

Great increase in the rent of houses in Dublin since the valuation was made, *Greene* 6849.

2. Increase by Re-Valuation; Effect as regards the Amount of Rates:

The valuation might be raised from 596,000 *l.* to 800,000 *l.*, and still be low, *Stokes* 2982. 3048, 3049——Conclusion that a fair valuation would increase the corporate funds by from 10,000 *l.* to 15,000 *l.* a year, *Sullivan* 4682. 4804, 4805.

Effect of a new valuation of Dublin to increase the amount from 620,534 *l.* to about 781,000 *l.*, and to decrease the poundage rate from about 8 *s.* 4 *d.* to about 6 *s.* 4 *d.*, *Greene* 6811, 6812.

VALUATION—continued.

I. *Dublin*—continued.

3. Effect of the Valuation as regards the Franchise, and the Constitution of the Corporation:

Exceptions taken to the working of the system of Government valuation in Ireland, as compared with the local valuations in England; disfranchising effect in Dublin in the case of large buildings let out in offices, *M'Evoy* 1682–1692. 1749–1757. 1791–1802 ——Expediency of a re-valuation of the city as the foundation of a sound constituency; prejudicial effects of the present unequal system, *Norwood* 5886, 5887——Obstacles on account of the unequal valuation, and other causes, to the formation of a corporation similarly constituted to that of 1849, *ib.* 6273–6281——Approval of a re-valuation as a means of improving the *personnel* of the corporation, *Gray* 6487.

4. Effect as regards Building Improvements:

Prejudicial effect of the present valuation system in discouraging building improvements, *M'Evoy* 1755–1757——Much higher scale now adopted for new buildings than that applied thirty years ago; doubt as to re-building being actually stopped by the higher scale, *Neville* 5529. 5581–5585.

5. Authority for a Re-valuation; Power of the Corporation of Dublin in the Matter:

Comment upon the omission of the corporation to provide for a complete re-valuation of the city, in lieu of the partial and unequal system now in operation, *Stokes* 2998–3007. 3090, 3091.

Evidence as to the want of a compulsory re-valuation of Dublin, or of a re-adjustment, and as to the inability of the corporation to obtain it; great opposition apprehended on the part of the ratepayers, *Sullivan* 4700–4703. 4720. 4804–4810——Explanation that a re-valuation of premises rests entirely with the Valuation Office, and not with the corporation, *Neville* 5523–5529——Doubt further expressed as to its being legally in the power of the corporation to procure a complete re-valuation, *ib.* 5764–5769.

Resolution recently passed by the corporation, through a committee, in favour of a new valuation, embracing not only the city, but the townships and the county, *Norwood* 5887, 5888——Grounds for the conclusion that the corporation have not the legal power to call for a re-valuation, this power being in fact still vested in the grand jury of the county of the city, *ib.* 5889–5894.

Reluctance of the corporation to promote an increased valuation of Dublin as increasing the liability to the income tax, *Gray* 6313—— Absence of power in the town council to demand a re-valuation, *ib.*

Provision in the Valuation Act on the subject of re-valuation of any county, poor law union, or barony; absence of power to demand a new valuation of any borough, such as Dublin or Belfast, *Greene* 6769–6775——Probable power of the grand jury of the county of the city of Dublin to call for a new valuation of the county of the city, *ib.* 6776, 6777.

II. *Ireland, Generally:*

1. Scale of Prices upon which the Valuation is based; amended Basis required for a New Valuation:

Scale of agricultural prices in 1849 and 1850 upon which the present valuation was based; great increase of prices since that period, the value of land having largely increased, *Greene* 6784–6790. 6860–6869——Grounds for the conclusion that the rent should be the basis of a new valuation, as in England, *ib.* 6802–6807. 6892.

Consideration of the several Acts, or Amendment Acts, under which the valuation of Ireland has been carried out; the system of valuation according to the net value having become a dead letter, and the sole basis being now that of agricultural prices, *Greene* 6815–6848.

Necessity of prices being still taken into account in making a new valuation; there might be a scale of actual prices in a schedule to the Act, *Greene* 6945–6959——Further expression of the opinion that the valuation should be the rent; difficulty in arriving at the rent by the price obtained after competition, *ib.* 6960–6966——Explanation that the valuation should not be based only on the actual rent, *ib.* 7008–7010.

2. Time occupied in the Valuation, and Cost incurred:

Different dates at which the valuation was completed in different counties, *Greene* 6768——Payment of portion of the cost of valuation out of the county rate; very small amount of this payment in reference to the rateable value of the country, *ib.* 6886–6890.

3. Staff

VALUATION—continued.

II. *Ireland, Generally*—continued.

3. Staff of Valuators, and Mode of Operation:

Information as to the way in which the work is done by the valuators in the country and by the office staff respectively, *Greene* 6935–6940——Importance of revised instructions to the valuators, and of a modification of details, if a new valuation be decided upon, *ib.* 6941–6944——Suggestions as to the qualifications desirable in valuators; facility of obtaining competent men, *ib.* 6985–6988. 7002——Total of about thirty-two valuators who are paid about 160 *l.* a year and expenses, *ib.* 7011–7013.

4. Practice in the Valuation of different Qualities of Land:

Condition in the annual re-valuation of townland, that the total limit cannot be increased, though the amount may be re-distributed, *Greene* 6780–6783. 6932–6934——Much greater inequality of valuation in the case of grass lands than of tillage lands, *ib.* 6788. 6813, 6814. 6860–6869——Doubt as to there being legal power to value land reclaimed or improved by drainage, *ib.* 6791, 6792.

Reference to the increased price of labour in modifying the effect of the increased price of wheat, barley, &c., as regards the value of the tillage lands; this does not equally apply to the case of pasture lands, *Greene* 6870–6881——Necessity in valuing tillage land of taking the rate of wages into account, whilst in the case of grazing land cattle disease should not be taken into consideration, *ib.* 7003–7007.

Instructions to the valuators to value lands as they find them according to their condition, neglected lands being valued lower than land in good condition, *Greene* 7020, 7021——Higher value placed upon town parks, near a large town, than near a small one, *ib.* 7025——Explanation in regard to market gardens being valued as town parks, *ib.* 7029–7036.

5. Houses and New Buildings:

Provision for an annual revision as in the case of new buildings; satisfaction generally given, *Greene* 6778, 6779——Provision as to the valuation of houses being made upon an estimate of the rent one year with another, *ib.* 6844, 6845——Liability of witness' department to be called upon to value at once improvements to houses, *ib.* 6850–6852.

Explanation as to improvements or new houses not being valued up to full extent, *Greene* 6853–6859——Statement as to there being no re-valuation annually, but a revision and correction of the old valuation; that is, unless in the case of a new house or the improvement of a house, *ib.* 6882–6885.

6. Conclusions as to the Expediency of a General Re-valuation:

Expediency of a re-valuation extending to all Ireland, *M'Evoy* 2087, 2088——Advocacy of a re-valuation which shall embrace not only Dublin and the adjacent townships, but all Ireland, *Pim* 2346–2351; *Norwood* 6173–6184. 6281–6284——Further evidence in favour of a general re-valuation; advantage of this being compulsory for all Ireland, and of a periodical revision subsequently, *Norwood* 6173–6184——Reason for re-valuation generally where the values of properties have charged, *Sullivan* 4874–4876.

Opinion that a new valuation of Ireland is desirable for the purpose of remedying existing inequalities, *Greene* 6766, 6767. 6813, 6814. 6891. 6904——Complaints made by ratepayers as to the inequality and injustice of the present valuation, *ib.* 6928–6931——Instances of discrepancy between one district of a county and another, owing to changes in the cultivation and condition of the land, *ib.* 6998–7001——Greater increase by re-valuation in the case of large towns than of small ones, *ib.* 7026–7028.

7. Increase by a New Valuation:

Estimate of 18,000,000 *l.* as the amount of a new valuation of Ireland, the present valuation being 13,500,000 *l.* (the same as that of Lancashire), *Greene* 6916–6920——Increase from fifty to sixty per cent. in some places, the average being about thirty-three per cent., *ib.* 6920–6923.

8. Cost of a General Revision, and Time required:

Comparatively small expense of a general revision; increased staff of valuers required, the work occupying about five years, *Greene* 6967–6973.

9. Effect of a Re-valuation as regards Local and Imperial Taxation, respectively:

Very trifling effect of a re-valuation of Ireland as regards the increased liability for Imperial taxation, *Grey* 6361–6364.

Effect of the present low valuation in largely increasing the amount in the pound of the county cess and of the poor rate, *Greene* 6800, 6801——More equal distribution of local taxation by a new valuation, *ib.* 6978, 6979——Calculation as to the increase of Imperial taxation that would accrue from a new valuation, *ib.* 6980.

VALUATION—continued.

II. *Ireland, Generally*—continued.

10. Duration proposed for a New Valuation:

Inexpediency of disturbing a new valuation for fifteen or twenty years, *Greene* 6974–6977.

11. Suggested Codification of Valuation Acts:

Necessity of a codification of the several Valuation Acts and Amendment Acts, *Greene* 6808–6810.

See also Belfast. Ulster.

Vartry Water Works. See *Water Supply.*

Venue (Juries). Less unwillingness of ratepayers to be placed on the burgess roll if they were not thereby subjected to serve on both county and city juries; advantage if there were a single venue for the city and county, *Norwood* 6089. 6167. 6288.

Vestries. Several Irish Acts of the last century founded on the vestry system of management; unpopularity of these vestries at the time of the Act of 1828, *Hancock*, 3, 4——Decaying condition for many years previously to the Act of 1840 of the old corporations in existence at the time of the union; final abolition of these bodies in 1840, *ib.* 4–15.

Vestry Cess (Dublin). Small amount and temporary character of the vestry cess, *Moylan and Taafe* 263, 264.

W.

Wallis, Mr. (Corporation of Dublin). Election of witness in lieu of Mr. Wallis, because the latter did not attend the meetings of the council, and not on political grounds, *Gray* 6368–6374.

Further explanation of the circumstances under which Mr. Wallis was rejected by the ratepayers in favour of witness; reference more especially to the attendances of Mr. Wallis, *Grey* 6694–6699. 6707–6714.

Wards (Election of Town Councillors). Objection to an entire discontinuance of the ward system of election in large towns, *Hancock* 189——Explanation that witness proposes to retain to a certain extent the ward system of election in large towns, merely as being an existing institution, *ib.* 915–920.

Re-arrangement of the area of the Dublin wards with reference to population by the Municipal Corporations Amendment Act; great inequalities previously, *Henry* 1091. 1099–1103——Admission as to there still being much inequality between some of the wards as regards their relative valuation and representation, *ib.* 1586–1595. 1627–1630.

Proposition for a re-arrangement of the wards in Dublin, with a view to a fair representation of property of large rateable value, *M'Evoy* 1662——Particulars as to the circumstances under which the arrangement for a re-distribution of the Dublin wards was agreed to in 1849; eventual adoption of the English principle, *ib.* 1803–1812——Heavy costs charged upon the rates in respect of the three Bills which had been promoted relative to the re-arrangement of the wards, *ib.* 1812, 1813.

Too many representatives at present for each ward in Dublin, *Sullivan* 4690, 4691.

Water Bailiffs (Dublin). See *Shippage and Anchorage Dues.*

Water Mains (Poor Rates). Recovery of a large sum from the Corporation of Dublin for water mains, *Moylan* 516–518——Explanation as to the corporation having to pay a very heavy rate on their own water mains, *Neville* 5537–5544.

WATER SUPPLY (DUBLIN):

1. *Vartry Scheme; Opposition experienced, and Cost and Character of the Supply.*
2. *Water Rate in Dublin.*
3. *Supply to the Townships, and Rates charged.*
4. *Character of the Rathmines Supply from the Canal.*
5. *Coy Ford and Ballysmuttan Schemes.*
6. *Transfer of a large Item from Waterworks Capital Account.*
7. *Increase of Work in connection with the Water Supply.*

1. *Vartry Scheme; Opposition experienced, and Cost and Character of the Supply:*

Consideration of the character of the opposition to the Vartry Water scheme, witness not concurring in the view that the great majority of the upper classes were vehement opponents

WATER SUPPLY (DUBLIN)—continued.

1. *Vartry Scheme: Opposition experienced, &c.*—continued.

opponents, *M'Evoy* 1884–1894. 2052——Witness supported the Vartry project, the result having been most beneficial, *ib.* 1885, 1886——Two-fold cost of the Vartry scheme beyond the estimates, *ib.* 2053, 2054.

Particulars relative to the large debt of the corporation on account of waterworks, the amounts borrowed from different sources, and the reduction being effected, *Robinson* 2687–2708. 2715——Loan of 382,000 *l.* obtained from the Public Works Loan Commissioners; reduction being effected, *ib.* 2687–2690——Considerable amounts borrowed also from other sources, *ib.* 2690–2706——Details of the annual receipts and expenditure on account of the water supply; large sum paid for interest and for reduction of debt, *ib.* 2813–2825.

Circumstance of the Vartry Waterworks having cost about twice the original estimate, *Stokes* 3195, 3196——The real cost was between 600,000 *l.* and 700,000 *l.*, *ib.* 3196——Opposition made by witness to the Vartry scheme; belief that the Coy Ford or Ballysmuttan scheme could have been carried out at half the cost, *ib.* 3197, 3198. 3347——Good quality of the Vartry supply, *ib.* 3198, 3199——Comment upon the course pursued by certain leading men in opposing the Vartry Water scheme, *Sullivan* 4786——Very heavy expenditure in promoting the Bills of 1860 and 1861 for an improved water supply; comment more especially upon the opposition to the Vartry Waterworks Bill, *Neville* 5468–5472.

Total of 541,400 *l.* as the cost of the Vartry works; several causes of the large excess of the original estimate, *Neville* 5469——Abundant supply from the Vartry for all purposes, *ib.* 5473–5475. 5488, 5489——Facility for greatly increasing the supply, *ib.* 5488——Present supply of between fourteen and fifteen million gallons daily, *ib.* 5489——Explanations in reference to several items of cost involved in the Vartry works, the total cost having been 541,400 *l.*, *ib.* 6601–5811.

Increase of the waterworks estimate owing mainly to the additional works constructed, *Norwood* 6092——Intention from the first to have filter beds, *ib.* 6093——Political character of the opposition to the Vartry scheme, *Gray* 6529.

2. *Water Rate in Dublin:*

The water rate for domestic purposes as fixed at 1 *s.* in the pound, the public rate being 3 *d.*, *Moylan* 244–246——Large increase in the receipts since 1874, *Robinson* 2815–2817——Maximum reached by the water rate, both for public and domestic purposes, *ib.* 3487, 3488.

Exceptions taken as regards the water rate charged by the corporation, *Stokes* 3354–3359——Power under the Waterworks Act of raising money on account of taxation over and above the maximum water rate, *ib.* 3373–3376.

3. *Supply to the Townships, and Rates charged:*

Income of about 4,800 *l.* a year derived from the supply to the out townships; further receipt of 2,000 *l.* a year expected for extra supply, *Neville* 5488——Examination as to the reasons for the cheaper supply of water to Pembroke and the other townships than to the city; compromise in the former case, there being moreover a profit on the supply, *ib.* 5701–5740. 5831–5834——Borrowing power of 75,000 *l.* given in the Vartry Act, conditional upon the supply of the townships, *ib.* 5701–5709——Limited supply of water per head in the townships, but not in Dublin, *ib.* 5832–5834.

Steps taken with a view to obtaining from the townships their proper quota for excess of water supply, *Norwood* 6012——Explanation as to the low rate at which the corporation were constrained to supply water to Pembroke and other townships; competition of Rathmines in the matter, *ib.* 6074–6076——Probability that the corporation would have obtained better rates for the water supply in Pembroke and other townships, but for the opposition by Mr. Stokes, *ib.* 6150–6155.

Reason for the non-introduction of water pipes by the corporation into the townships, *Gray* 6365.

4. *Character of the Rathmines Supply from the Canal:*

Objectionable quality of the supply from the Grand Canal for Rathmines township; very bad pressure in reference to fires, *Neville* 5476–5487——Explanation as to witness having stated in 1859 that the waters of the canal were of good wholesome quality, *ib.* 5695–5698——Better quality of the water in Rathmines, and reduced cost if supplied from the Vartry; advantage also by the greater pressure, *Norwood* 6077–6080.

5. *Coy Ford and Ballysmuttan Schemes:*

Much less cost of the Coy Ford and Ballysmuttan schemes than of the Vartry scheme, *Stokes*

WATER SUPPLY (DUBLIN)—continued.

5. *Coy Ford and Ballysmuttan Schemes*—continued.

Stokes 3197, 3198. 3347——Question considered whether the outlying townships could have been as well served with water under the Coy Ford scheme as the Vartry scheme, *ib.* 3348–3354.

Inadequacy of the Coy Ford or the Ballysmuttan scheme for the supply of the outlying townships, *Neville* 5473. 5475——Strong opposition made to the Coy Ford scheme first recommended by Mr. Hawkesley and witness, *ib.* 5699, 5700.

6. *Transfer of a large Item from Waterworks Capital Account*:

Comment upon the course pursued in liquidating out of capital a deficiency of 19,000 *l.* incurred during the earlier years of the new water supply through the inadequacy of the rate, *Stokes* 3351–3386.

Amalgamation in August 1871 of the separate accounts of the Waterworks Rate Fund and Loan Fund, *Neville* 5115——Perfectly open manner in which an item of about 18,000 *l.* was transferred, and properly so, from the waterworks capital account; there was no "smuggling" in the matter, *Gray* 6314, 6315.

7. *Increase of Work in connection with the Water Supply*:

Great addition to the work of the corporation in connection with the water supply, *Norwood* 5914.

See also Rathmines, &c., 6.

Waterford. Circumstance of Waterford not having powers of rating, *Hancock* 101–103.

Weekly and Monthly Tenants (Municipal Franchise). Explanation as to occupiers in Dublin who are weekly or monthly tenants not being entered in the rate book; authority of Judge Barry for this course, *Taafe* 317–321. 332–339——Considerable number of weekly or monthly tenants excluded from the rate book and from the Parliamentary roll; duty of the collectors to supply information as to such tenants, *ib.* 339–353.

Refusal to rate a weekly or monthly tenant, even though he may tender the rate; that is, upon the authority of Judge Barry and Judge Warren, *Taafe and Moylan* 314–401. 406–408——Statement to the effect that the legal opinion in the foregoing matter can be produced to the committee, *ib.* 396–401.

Impracticability of witness' department getting into possession of tenement houses and receiving the weekly or monthly rents; failure of steps taken in this direction, *Taafe* 435–450——Absence of power under the Collection of Rates Act to compound with the owners in the case of weekly tenants, *ib.* 469——Further statement as to weekly or monthly tenants tendering payment of the poor rate being placed on the rate book; that is, if they occupy the whole house, *ib.* 531–546.

Effect of the Collection of Rates Act in excluding weekly and monthly tenants from the municipal franchise, *Curran* 2122–2126——Conclusion arrived at by witness in 1874 as to the admission of weekly and monthly tenants; statement hereon as to the Collector General refusing to rate these persons, *ib.* 2133–2145. 2207–2209——Circumstance of the Collector General's opinion having been supported by that of Judge Barry and of Judge Warren, *ib.* 2137. 2251. 2252.

Examination upon the question as to the accuracy of witness' statement that the Collector General of rates did not put on his list any weekly or monthly tenants; doubt as to his refusing to rate those who tender their rates, *Curran* 2232–2238, 2269–2281——Explanation as to witness not having admitted till 1874 the claims of weekly or monthly tenants, though the claim rested on the Act of 1868, *ib.* 2239–2242.

Opinion that it is not legal to put weekly and monthly tenants on the burgess roll, *Norwood* 6103.

Wexford. Debt in the case of Wexford; satisfactory management of the corporate property, *Finlay* 4598–4601——Complaint recently made to witness as to an alleged illegal expenditure in Wexford, *ib.* 4602——Important effect of the rents in Wexford in lightening the rates, *ib.* 4603–4606.

Wicklow. Details in connection with witness' audit of the accounts of the town commissions of Wicklow under the Act 9 Geo. 4; objections raised by him on various points, *Finlay* 4321–4338——Improvement made in the mode of accounting for the rents in Wicklow and in the accounts generally, witness being satisfied with the present system, *ib.* 4323. 4327, 4328. 4337, 4338——Good rental of the commissioners, who make no rates; heavy charge on the other hand for interest on debt, *ib.* 4324–4326.

Report, 1876—*continued.*

Wicklow—continued.

Comments upon the action of the commissioners in dealing with the corporate property on expiration of the leases; obstacle to any satisfactory remedy in the ratepayers, *Finlay* 4328–4336. 4449. 4486, 4487——Very unsatisfactory state of things in Wicklow, the town improvements not being commensurate with the expenditure, *ib.* 4621–4625——Inability of the Wicklow Harbour Commissioners to contribute anything towards the interest or principal of the loans from the town commissioners, *ib.* 4626–4629.

Wide Streets Commissioners (Dublin). Repayment by the corporation of two debts amounting to nearly 40,000 *l.* due by the Commissioners of Wide Streets to the Treasury at the time of the Act of 1849, *Robinson* 2610, 2611, 2710, 2711——Limited powers of the Wide Streets Board as to levying rates and carrying out improvements, *Neville* 5369.

See also *Streets (Paving, &c.)*

www.ingramcontent.com/pod-product-compliance
Lightning Source LLC
Chambersburg PA
CBHW051156300426
44116CB00006B/331
9783741105234